PUBLIC PAPERS OF THE PRESIDENTS
OF THE
UNITED STATES

PUBLIC PAPERS OF THE PRESIDENTS
OF THE
UNITED STATES

George W. Bush

2004

(IN THREE BOOKS)

BOOK III—OCTOBER 1 TO DECEMBER 31, 2004

UNITED STATES GOVERNMENT PRINTING OFFICE
WASHINGTON : 2007

Published by the
Office of the Federal Register
National Archives and Records Administration

For sale by the Superintendent of Documents, U.S. Government Printing Office
• Internet: bookstore.gpo.gov • Phone: (202) 512–1800 • Fax: (202) 512–2250
• Mail: Stop SSOP, Washington, DC 20401

Foreword

This volume collects my speeches and papers from the second half of 2004.

During these 6 months from July to December, I outlined my vision for the future of our Nation, and I advocated Government policies that put trust and power into the hands of the people. In September, at my nominating convention, I presented a clear plan to build a safer world, and a more hopeful America. I spoke of our Nation's need to build an ownership society where every citizen has a stake in America and all have an opportunity to succeed. I described the need to simplify the tax code; improve education and worker training; build opportunity zones in areas without hope; make health care more affordable; and reform Social Security to provide voluntary personal-retirement accounts for all Americans.

During this period, the American economy continued to expand and grow. Thanks to the ingenuity and entrepreneurship of the American people and the tax cuts of 2001, 2002, and 2003, our Nation added new jobs, built new businesses, and led the world in innovation and achievement. In the second half of 2004, the American economy gained strength—creating almost 1 million new jobs. To sustain this impressive economic growth, in October I signed a tax relief bill that helped millions of families by extending the child tax credit and marriage-penalty relief, and helped prevent middle-class families across America from being hit with the Alternative Minimum Tax. In addition, in December, my Administration hosted an important conference at the White House on America's economic future. We heard from business owners, workers, economists, and many other Americans who saw hopeful signs of growth throughout our country. We also discussed some of the fundamental challenges facing our economy—from frivolous lawsuits and burdensome regulations to the need for vital reforms in education, health care, entitlements, and the tax code.

To address these and many other issues in my second term, I built another outstanding Cabinet. In November, I named Alberto Gonzales to serve as Attorney General; Condoleezza Rice to serve as Secretary of State; Margaret Spellings to serve as Secretary of Education; and Carlos Guttierez to serve as Secretary of Commerce. In December, I named Mike Leavitt as Secretary of Health and Human Services; Samuel Bodman as Secretary of Energy; Jim Nicholson as Secretary of Veterans Affairs; and Mike Johanns as Secretary of Agriculture.

The second half of 2004 was also a time when we showed the compassionate heart and giving spirit that have made America a great Nation. In July, America commemorated the 40th anniversary of the Civil Rights Act—a day when justice and equality triumphed over discrimination and indignity. Later that same month, I announced my initiatives to combat human trafficking. By working to provide prosecutors with new law enforcement tools and give outreach programs more help to support victims of trafficking, we took a stand for the value and dignity of every human life. In December, our Nation answered the call from our brothers and sisters in need half a world a way. America provided more than $850 million in humanitarian relief and reconstruction aid to help the people of South Asia whose lives and homes were devastated by the massive Bay of Bengal earthquake and tsunami.

As we worked to fulfill America's highest ideals of compassion and justice, we also continued to strengthen our Nation's ability to defend those ideals at home and abroad. In July, I signed the Project Bioshield Act. The Act was designed to help purchase, develop, and deploy cutting-edge defenses against catastrophic attack. Later that same month, I addressed the 9-11 Commission's recommendations. I discussed how my Administration's actions were consistent with the Commission's recommendations in detecting and disrupting terrorist cells; building a democratic Afghanistan; and improving our intelligence operations. In December, I signed the Intelligence Reform and Terrorism Prevention Act—the most significant reform of our Nation's intelligence capabilities since President Harry S. Truman signed the National Security Act of 1947. The intelligence reforms of 2004 created the position of Director of National Intelligence; made it easier for law enforcement to share information about terrorists; and were designed to make all our intelligence efforts better coordinated, more efficient, and more effective.

Throughout the second half of 2004, thanks to our men and women in uniform and our international allies, we advanced the cause of freedom around the world, and the people of Afghanistan and Iraq continued to advance down the path of democracy and self-determination. On October 9, the people of Afghanistan held their first presidential election under their new constitution with more than 8 million Afghans going to the polls. On December 7, Hamid Karzai was inaugurated as Afghanistan's democratically elected president. In August, after the Coalition transfer of power, Iraqis selected a national assembly to act as a parliament until the elections of January 2005. In the months that followed, election rules were published, voters were registered, and candidates came forward to be elected to a transition government that would represent all the Iraqi people.

In the midst of all these historic steps on the road to freedom and peace, the world was reminded of the ruthless nature of our terrorist enemies. In Iraq, terrorists and insurgents continued to unleash savage attacks on those working to build a free and democratic Iraq. In late October of 2004, Al-Qaida released a tape from Osama Bin Laden that made further threats against America. I was very clear in my response: "Americans will not be intimidated or influenced by an enemy of our country." On October 31st, I told my fellow Americans: "Since that terrible morning of September the 11th, 2001, we fought the terrorists across the Earth—not for pride, not for power, but because the lives of our citizens are at stake. Our strategy is clear. We've strengthened protections for the homeland. We're reforming and strengthening our intelligence services. We're transforming our military . . . We are fighting the terrorists abroad so we do not have to face them here at home. We are determined, we are relentless, and we are succeeding."

Preface

This book contains the papers and speeches of the 43d President of the United States that were issued by the Office of the Press Secretary during the period October 1–December 31, 2004. The material has been compiled and published by the Office of the Federal Register, National Archives and Records Administration.

The material is presented in chronological order, and the dates shown in the headings are the dates of the documents or events. In instances when the release date differs from the date of the document itself, that fact is shown in the textnote. Every effort has been made to ensure accuracy: Remarks are checked against a tape recording, and signed documents are checked against the original. Textnotes and cross references have been provided by the editors for purposes of identification or clarity. At the request of the Office of the Press Secretary, the Bush property known as Prairie Chapel Ranch in Crawford, Texas, is referred to simply as the Bush Ranch. Speeches were delivered in Washington, DC, unless indicated. The times noted are local times. All materials that are printed full-text in the book have been indexed in the subject and name indexes, and listed in the document categories list.

The Public Papers of the Presidents series was begun in 1957 in response to a recommendation of the National Historical Publications Commission. An extensive compilation of messages and papers of the Presidents covering the period 1789 to 1897 was assembled by James D. Richardson and published under congressional authority between 1896 and 1899. Since then, various private compilations have been issued, but there was no uniform publication comparable to the Congressional Record or the United States Supreme Court Reports. Many Presidential papers could be found only in the form of mimeographed White House releases or as reported in the press. The Commission therefore recommended the establishment of an official series in which Presidential writings, addresses, and remarks of a public nature could be made available.

The Commission's recommendation was incorporated in regulations of the Administrative Committee of the Federal Register, issued under section 6 of the Federal Register Act (44 U.S.C. 1506), which may be found in title 1, part 10, of the Code of Federal Regulations.

A companion publication to the Public Papers series, the Weekly Compilation of Presidential Documents, was begun in 1965 to provide a broader range of Presidential materials on a more timely basis to meet the needs of the contemporary reader. Beginning with the administration of Jimmy Carter, the Public Papers series expanded its coverage to include additional material as printed in the Weekly Compilation. That coverage provides a listing of the President's daily schedule and meetings, when announced, and other items of general interest issued by the Office of the Press Secretary. Also included are lists of the President's nominations submitted to the Senate, materials released by the Office of the Press Secretary that are not printed full-text in the book, and proclamations, Executive orders, and other Presidential documents released by the Office of the Press Secretary and published in the *Federal Register*. This information appears in the appendixes at the end of the book.

Volumes covering the administrations of Presidents Herbert Hoover, Harry S. Truman, Dwight D. Eisenhower, John F. Kennedy, Lyndon B. Johnson, Richard Nixon, Gerald R. Ford, Jimmy Carter, Ronald Reagan, George Bush, and William J. Clinton are also included in the Public Papers series.

The Public Papers of the Presidents publication program is under the direction of Frances D. McDonald, Managing Editor, Office of the Federal Register. The series is produced by the Presidential and Legislative Publications Unit, Gwendolyn J. Henderson, Chief. The Chief Editor of this book was Stacey A. Mulligan, assisted by William K. Banks, Loretta F. Cochran, Kathleen M. Fargey, Michael J. Forcina, Stephen J. Frattini, Alison M. Gavin, Diane Hiltabidle, Alfred Jones, Ashley Merusi, Matthew R. Regan, and Michael J. Sullivan.

The frontispiece and photographs used in the portfolio were supplied by the White House Photo Office. The typography and design of the book were developed by the Government Printing Office under the direction of William H. Turri, Acting Public Printer.

Raymond A. Mosley
Director of the Federal Register

Allen Weinstein
Archivist of the United States

Contents

Cabinet

Secretary of State .... Colin L. Powell

Secretary of the Treasury .... John Snow

Secretary of Defense .... Donald H. Rumsfeld

Attorney General .... John Ashcroft

Secretary of the Interior .... Gale A. Norton

Secretary of Agriculture .... Ann M. Veneman

Secretary of Commerce .... Donald L. Evans

Secretary of Labor .... Elaine L. Chao

Secretary of Health and Human
Services .... Tommy G. Thompson

Secretary of Housing and Urban
Development .... Alphonso R. Jackson

Secretary of Transportation .... Norman Y. Mineta

Secretary of Energy .... Spencer Abraham

Secretary of Education .... Roderick R. Paige

Secretary of Veterans Affairs .... Anthony J. Principi

Secretary of Homeland Security .... Tom Ridge

Chief of Staff .... Andrew H. Card, Jr.

Administrator of the Environmental
Protection Agency .... Michael O. Leavitt

United States Trade Representative .... Robert B. Zoellick

Director of the Office of Management
and Budget .... Joshua B. Bolten

Director of National Drug Control
Policy .... John P. Walters

Administration of George W. Bush

2004

Remarks in Allentown, Pennsylvania
October 1, 2004

The President. Thank you all. Thank you all for coming. It is great——

Audience members. Four more years! Four more years! Four more years!

The President. Thank you all for coming. It's—what a beautiful day to be here in the Lehigh Valley. It's great to be back in Allentown. It's a wonderful place to come after a debate.

I'm so honored John McCain is traveling with me today. I'm proud of his friendship. I appreciate his leadership. I appreciate his courage, and I'm really grateful he's for me for President.

We had a great debate last night. It highlighted some of the fundamental differences between my opponent and me, differences I believe are crucial for our national security. It's a big difference when it comes to supporting our troops. When America puts our troops in harm's way, I believe they deserve the best training, the best equipment, and the wholehearted support of our Government.

My opponent last night said our troops deserve better. They certainly deserve better than they got from Senator Kerry when he voted to send them to war and then voted against funding our troops in combat.

Audience members. Boo-o-o!

The President. You may remember his famous quote about the supplemental funding that I sent up to Congress. He said, "I actually did vote for the $87 billion, right before I voted against it." [*Laughter*] I understand.

Last night——

Audience members. Flip-flop! Flip-flop! Flip-flop!

The President. Last night, he said he made a mistake in how he talked about that vote, but the mistake wasn't what Senator Kerry said. The mistake was what Senator Kerry did.

He voted against supplying our troops after voting for putting them in harm's way. He then went on to say—after saying the 87 billion line, they kept pressing him. He said he was proud of his vote. And finally, he said, "The whole thing was a complicated matter." Then he had a new wrinkle, a new explanation. During an interview this week, he described it as a protest vote.

Audience members. Boo-o-o!

The President. When we put American troops in harm's way, they certainly deserve better than to have a candidate for President use them as a protest.

Last night, Senator Kerry only continued his pattern of confusing contradictions. After voting for the war, after saying my decision to remove Saddam Hussein from power was the right decision, he now says it was all a mistake.

Audience members. Boo-o-o!

The President. But I asked a logical question, does that mean our troops our dying for a mistake?

Audience members. No-o-o!

The President. That's what he said, "No." You can't have it both ways. You can't say it's a mistake and not a mistake. You can't be for getting rid of Saddam Hussein when things look good and against it when times are hard. You can't claim terrorists are pouring across the border into Iraq yet, at the same time, try to claim that Iraq is somehow a diversion for war against terrorism. The President cannot keep changing his mind. The President must speak clearly, and the President must mean what he says.

Audience members. Four more years! Four more years! Four more years!

The President. A crucial difference between my opponent and me is the most important question for voters this election: Who can lead this war against terror to victory? Which candidate can best protect America's families and our national security? And here my opponent has a fundamental misunderstanding of the nature of the war against terror, and he has no plan to win in Iraq. The cornerstone of Senator Kerry's plan for Iraq is that he would convene a summit.

Audience members. Boo-o-o!

The President. I've been to a lot of summits. [*Laughter*] I've never seen a meeting that would depose a tyrant or bring a terrorist to justice. Senator Kerry claims that he can work with our allies, yet he said those who are standing with us are not a part of a genuine coalition.

Audience members. Boo-o-o!

The President. He earlier called them "a coalition of the coerced and the bribed," dismissed their sacrifices as window dressing. You cannot lead by pushing away the allies who are already with us or expect any support for a cause you've called a "mistake" or a "grand diversion" or "the wrong war at the wrong place at the wrong time." The way to lead this coalition is not be disdainful or dismissive. The way to lead this coalition to victory is to be clear in our thinking, grateful for the sacrifices, and resolute in our determination to defeat the enemy.

One other point I want to make about the debate last night. Senator Kerry last night said that America has to pass some sort of "global test"——

Audience members. Boo-o-o!

The President. ——before we can use American troops to defend ourselves. He wants our national security decisions subject to the approval of a foreign government.

Audience members. Boo-o-o!

The President. Listen, I'll continue to work with our allies and the international community, but I will never submit America's national security to an international test. The use of troops to defend America must never be subject to a veto by countries like France. The President's job is not to take an international poll. The President's job is to defend America.

I'm grateful you all are here today, because I'm here to ask for your vote. That's what I'm doing. Not only am I here to ask for your vote; I'm here to ask for your help. Listen, I know a lot of people worked hard to put this great crowd together, and I thank you for working hard to do so. I know there's a lot of people working hard to register people to vote, and I want to thank you for doing that too.

And as you register people to vote, make sure you don't overlook discerning Democrats like Zell Miller. And after you get them registered to vote, I encourage you to turn out that vote. Get them headed to the polls. And remind them if they want a safer America, a stronger America, a better America, to put me and Dick Cheney back in office.

Audience members. Four more years! Four more years! Four more years!

The President. Listen, I like traveling with John McCain a lot. My only regret is that Laura is not here instead of him. [*Laughter*] I kissed her goodbye this morning in Miami, and she said, tell everybody hello in the Lehigh Valley. She was a public school librarian, and when I asked her to marry me, she said, "Fine, I'll marry you, just so long as I never have to give a political speech." [*Laughter*] I said, "You've got a deal." [*Laughter*] Fortunately, she didn't hold me to the promise. She's my best advocate. She's a great First Lady.

Audience members. Laura! Laura! Laura!

The President. Listen, I agree with you. I'm going to give you some reasons to put me back in, but perhaps the most important one is so that Laura will be First Lady for 4 more years.

I'm proud of my runningmate. I'm running with a good man in Dick Cheney. He doesn't have the waviest hair in the race. I didn't pick him for his hair. I picked him because of his judgment, his experience. I picked him because he can get the job done for the American people.

I'm proud of the—Tom Ridge. He's done a fabulous job. I want to thank you for preparing him for an incredibly important assignment that he's doing.

I know Arlen Specter is here. I want to—I urge you to put Arlen back in the United States Senate. I want to thank Congressman Pat Toomey. He's a classy guy. He really is. I'm honored to call him friend.

I urge you to put Charlie Dent in the United States Congress. I want to thank all the candidates who are here. I want to thank the local officials who are here. I want to thank the Wil Gravatt Band, who is here. I want to thank the high school band that is here. But most of all, thank you all for coming. It's great to be with so many people.

I'm really looking forward to this campaign. I'm going to tell the people what—where I stand, what I believe, and where I'll lead this Nation for the next 4 years.

I believe every child can learn and every school must teach. I went to Washington to challenge the soft bigotry of low expectations. I believe we've got to raise the bar. I believe we must measure early to solve problems before it's too late. I know we've got to trust the local people to make the right decisions for your schools. We're making progress in America. We're closing the achievement gap, and we're not going to turn back to the old days.

I believe we have a moral responsibility to honor our seniors with good health care. Medicare was not modernizing the way medicine was. See, I think the seniors got to have the best when it comes to health care. We used to pay—we'd pay $100,000 when it comes to heart surgery but not one dime for prescription drugs to prevent the heart surgery from being needed in the first place. That didn't make any sense for our seniors. It didn't make any sense for the taxpayers. We're modernizing Medicare for seniors to get prescription drug coverage in 2006, and we're not going to turn back.

I believe in the energy, innovation, and the entrepreneurial spirit of our workers and small-business owners and farmers and ranchers. That's why we unleashed that energy with the largest tax relief in a generation.

When you're out gathering up the vote, remind people what this economy has been through. The stock market started going down about 5 or 6 months before Dick Cheney and I showed up in Washington. Then we had a recession. Then we had some corporate scandals. By the way, we passed new laws. It's abundantly clear to people of this country we're not going to tolerate dishonesty in the boardrooms of this country. And then we got attacked, and that attack hurt our economy.

But this economy is strong, and it's getting stronger, growing at rates as fast as any in nearly 20 years. It's strong because our spirit is strong, and it's strong because of well-timed tax cuts.

We've added about 1.7 million new jobs since last summer. The national unemployment rate is 5.4 percent. That is lower than the average rate of the 1970s, 1980s, and 1990s. The unemployment rate here in Pennsylvania is 5.6 percent. So long as anybody is looking for a job, we'll continue to expand with pro-growth, pro-small-business, pro-entrepreneur economic policies.

I believe the most solemn duty of the American President is to protect the American people. If America shows uncertainty and weakness in this decade, the world will drift toward tragedy. This is not going to happen on my watch.

Audience members. Four more years! Four more years! Four more years!

The President. I am running for President with a clear and positive plan to build a safer world and a more hopeful America.

I'm running with a compassionate conservative philosophy that Government should help people improve their lives, not try to run their lives. I believe this Nation wants steady, consistent, principled leadership, and that is why, with your help, we'll carry Pennsylvania and win a great victory in November.

The world in which we live is changing, and I understand that. Think about the workplace a couple of decades ago. A person would generally have one job, one career, one pension plan, one health care plan, and that person was usually a male. Today, the workforce has changed a lot. People change careers. They change jobs. Women are working inside the house and outside the house. It's a changing world we live in, and yet, the fundamental institutions of our Government, the fundamental systems, the Tax Code, health coverage, pension plans, worker training, were created for the world of yesterday, not tomorrow. In a new term, we'll transform these systems so that all citizens are equipped, prepared, and thus truly free to make your own choices so you can pursue the great dreams of America.

A hopeful society is one in which this economy continues to grow. To create more jobs in America, America must be the best place in the world to do business. If you want jobs here, this has got to be the best place in the world for people to employ people. That means less regulations on our small businesses. That means legal reform so frivolous lawsuits don't make it hard for expanding the job base.

In order to keep jobs here, Congress needs to pass my energy plan that encourages conservation, spends money on research so we can better use renewable sources of energy, promotes clean coal technology, uses technology to explore for natural gas in environmentally friendly ways. We want jobs here; this country must become less dependent on foreign sources of energy.

To keep jobs here, we've got to reject economic isolationism and open up markets for U.S. products. We've opened up our markets, and it's good for you. The more products you have to choose from, the more likely it is you're going to get what you want at a better price or a higher quality. That's how the marketplace works. So I'm saying to places like China, "You treat us the way we treat you." See, we can compete with anybody, anytime, anywhere if the rules are fair.

Finally, to make sure we got jobs here and this economy stays strong, we've got to be wise about how we spend your money in Washington and we've got to keep your taxes low. Taxes are an issue in this campaign. I'm running against a fellow who has promised at least $2.2 trillion in new spending——

Audience members. Boo-o-o!

The President. ——so far. [*Laughter*] Just getting into October. [*Laughter*] Two-point-two trillion is a lot, even for a Senator from Massachusetts. [*Laughter*] So they said, "How are you going to pay for it?" He said, "That's easy. We'll just tax the rich." Yes, we've heard that before, haven't we? [*Laughter*] You can't raise enough money by taxing the rich to pay for $2.2 trillion of new spending. There's a tax gap. Guess who fills the tax gap?

Audience members. [*Inaudible*]

The President. Yes. You've heard "tax the rich" before, but the rich hire lawyers and accountants for a reason—to stick you with the bill. The good news is, we're not going to let him tax you because we're going to win in November.

When it comes to taxes, we've got to do something about the Tax Code. It's a complicated mess, full of special interest loopholes. In a new term, I'll bring Republicans and Democrats together to make this Tax Code more fair for you. We'll make sure our workers have the skills they need. We'll make sure these training programs work and make sure they've got the opportunity to go to community colleges to be able to match their desire to work with the skills necessary to fill the jobs of the 21st century.

I'll tell you what also I understand in a changing world, most new jobs are filled by people with at least 2 years of college, yet, that's why I'm for—yet, only one in four of our students gets there. That's why I'm for early intervention programs in our high schools to help our at-risk kids. That's why I'm for emphasizing math and science in the classrooms. That's why, over time, we should require a rigorous examination before graduation. By raising performance in our high schools and by expanding Pell grants for low- and middle-income families, we will help more Americans start their career with a college diploma.

In a time of change, we've got to do something about the health care system. The costs are rising rapidly. They burden our economy, and too many people are uninsured. I have a commonsense, practical plan to make high quality health care more available and more affordable. And we have a difference in this campaign when it comes to health care. If you listen carefully to what my opponent proposes, he wants Government to dictate. He wants Government to tell you how to purchase your health care. He wants the Federal Government to run health care. I want you to decide. I want you to be the decisionmaker when it comes to health care.

More than half of Americans who are currently uninsured work for small businesses. Small businesses are having trouble affording health care. We've got to change the law to allow small businesses to join together so they can purchase insurance at the same discounts big businesses get to do.

We'll expand tax-free health savings accounts. We'll give small businesses tax credits to pay into health savings accounts for their employees. We want more workers to have their own health accounts so they can base medical decisions on advice from their doctor, not in negotiations with an HMO. It makes sense for people to own their own health account. If you're changing jobs or careers, you want to be able to carry your health account with you. You want to be able to manage it yourself.

Listen, I understand we need to take care of the poor and the indigent in this country, and we will by expanding community health centers to every poor county in America.

But let me tell you what else we need to do to make sure health care is available and affordable. We need to do something about these frivolous lawsuits that are running good docs out of business. You cannot be pro-doctor, pro-patient, and pro-trial-lawyer at the same time. You have to choose. My opponent made his choice, and he put a trial lawyer on the ticket.

Audience members. Boo-o-o!

The President. I made my choice. I'm for medical liability reform—now. In all we do to make sure we reform health care, I will make sure that the medical decisions are made by patients and doctors, not by bureaucrats in Washington, DC.

We'll continue to promote an ownership society in America—in changing times, provide stability in somebody's life if they own their own home. Homeownership rates are at an alltime high in America. Over the next 4 years, we'll continue to expand ownership—homeownership to every corner of America. I want more and more people opening the door where they live saying, "Welcome to my house. Welcome to my piece of property."

Let me talk about Social Security right quick. You remember what happened in the campaign in 2000. They said, "If George W. gets elected, they're going to take away the checks of the seniors on Social Security." You remember that, don't you? Yes, it didn't happen. So when they try and say it again in 2004, don't believe them. You'll get your checks. If you're a baby boomer like me, we're okay; we'll get our checks.

But we need to worry about our children or grandchildren when it comes to Social Security. I believe younger workers ought to be able to take some of their own tax money and set up a personal savings account to make sure Social Security fulfills its promise, a personal savings account they call their own, a personal savings account that Government cannot take away.

In this world of change, some things do not change, the values we try to live by, courage and compassion, reverence and integrity. In times of change, we'll support the institutions that give our lives direction and purpose, our families, our schools, our religious congregations. We stand for a culture of life in which every person counts and every being matters. We stand for marriage and family, which are the foundations of our society. We stand for the appointment of Federal judges who know the difference between personal opinion and the strict interpretation of the law.

This election will also determine how America responds to the continuing danger of terrorism. Since that terrible morning of September the 11th, 2001, we have fought the terrorists across the Earth, not for pride, not for power, but because the lives of our citizens are at stake. Our strategy is clear. We're defending the homeland. We're transforming our volunteer army. We will keep it an All-Volunteer Army. We're reforming and strengthening our intelligence services. We're staying on the offensive. We'll strike the terrorists abroad so we do not have to face them here at home. We will work to advance liberty in the broader Middle East and around the world, and we will prevail.

Our strategy is succeeding. Think about this: Four years ago, Afghanistan was the home base of Al Qaida; Pakistan was a transit point for terrorist groups; Saudi Arabia was fertile ground for terrorist fundraising; Libya was secretly pursuing nuclear weapons; Iraq was a gathering threat; and Al Qaida was largely unchallenged as it planned attacks.

Because America led, Afghanistan is free and is fighting terror; Pakistan is capturing terrorist leaders; Saudi Arabia is making raids and arrests; Libya is dismantling its weapons programs; the army of a free Iraq is fighting for freedom; and more than three-quarters of Al Qaida's key members have been brought to justice.

This progress involved careful diplomacy, clear moral purpose, and some tough decisions. And the toughest came on Iraq. We knew Saddam Hussein's record of aggression. We knew his support for terror. Remember, Saddam harbored Abu Nidal, the leader of a terrorist organization that carried out attacks in Europe and Asia. We knew he harbored Abu Abbas, who took refuge in Baghdad after he killed an American, Leon Klinghoffer, because he was Jewish. We knew Zarqawi was in and out of Baghdad. We knew Saddam Hussein's long history of pursuing and even using weapons of mass destruction. He was a threat.

Audience members. Yes!

The President. And we understand that after September the 11th, we must take threats seriously before they fully materialize. That's a lesson we must never forget. I'll never forget it. I went to the Congress. Members of both political parties, including my opponent, looked at the same intelligence I looked at and came to the same conclusion as my administration came to, that Saddam Hussein was a threat. They authorized the use of force.

Before the Commander in Chief ever commits troops into harm's way, we must try everything possible to deal with threats—everything possible. So I went to the United Nations in the hopes that diplomacy would work. I hoped that Saddam Hussein would listen to the demands of the free world. The United Nations debated the issue. They voted 15 to nothing to say to Saddam Hussein, "Disclose, disarm, or face serious consequences." I believe when an international body speaks, it must mean what it says in order to keep this world peaceful. When you say something, you better mean it.

But Saddam Hussein didn't believe the United Nations. After all, he'd ignored 16 other resolutions. Last night, my opponent said something about, "Well, maybe another resolution would have helped." I just don't think it's realistic. As a matter of fact, the U.N. sent inspectors into Iraq, and as David Kay's report showed, Saddam Hussein was systematically deceiving the inspectors. Somehow thinking inspectors would have caused Saddam Hussein to change is not very clear thinking.

And so at this point in time, I realized diplomacy wasn't working. And so I had a choice to make: Do I take the word of a madman and forget the lessons of September the 11th, or take action to defend this country? Given that choice, I will defend America every time.

We didn't find the stockpiles everybody thought was there. But knowing what I know today, I would have taken the same action. And the reason why is because Saddam Hussein had the capability of making weapons of mass destruction. And had the world turned its head, he would have made those weapons. Had we hoped that a resolution would have worked, he would have been able to realize his dreams. He could have passed that capability or those weapons on to terrorists that hate us. After September the 11th, that was a chance we could not afford to take. The world is better off with Saddam Hussein sitting in a prison cell.

By protecting ourselves, 50 million people now live in freedom in Afghanistan and Iraq. And that's in our national interest. Just think about what's happened in Afghanistan. It used to be run by this barbaric group called the Taliban. Many young girls were not allowed even to go to school. Their mothers were taken in the public square and whipped because they refused to toe the line of their dark ideology of hatred. Because we acted, 10 million citizens, 41 percent of whom are women, have

registered to vote in the upcoming Presidential election. In 3 short years, those people have gone from darkness to light because of liberty. And now Afghanistan is an ally in the war on terror, and they serve as a bright example for others who wonder whether or not they can live in a free society.

In Iraq, it's hard work. You know it's hard work, and so do I. But Iraq now has a strong Prime Minister, a National Council, and national elections are scheduled for January. We'll succeed in Iraq if we don't send the wrong messages. We'll succeed in Iraq because we've got a plan. And here's the plan. We'll train Iraqis so they can do the hard work in defending themselves; 100,000 troops are trained today, 125,000 by the end of the year. We'll continue to work with them, to give them the equipment, the training they need to defend themselves against the attacks of these terrorists. We'll help them to get the stability, help them on the road to democracy. And then our troops will come home with the honor they have earned.

We've got a great United States military, and I want to thank the veterans who are here today for having set such a great example for those who wear the uniform.

I believe in the transformational power of liberty. I've talked to Prime Minister Koizumi quite a bit since I've been your President. He's the Prime Minister of Japan. I like to tell this story because I want people to understand exactly what I mean by the transformational power of liberty. It's generally a little longer word than I use—[*laughter*]—transformational. [*Laughter*]

Prime Minister Koizumi is the head of a country that was our sworn enemy some 60 years ago. Think about that. My dad fought against the Japanese. John's dad, grandfather, many of your dads and grandfathers did the same thing. Japan was the sworn enemy of America. Harry Truman, after World War II, believed that liberty could transform an enemy into an ally. So after we won that war, despite skepticism of some, he worked to help Japan become a democracy. And as a result of the belief that liberty can change societies, today, I sit down at the table, talking about the peace we all long for, with the head of Japan. Someday, when we succeed in Iraq, an American President will be sitting down with a duly elected leader of Iraq talking about the peace, and the world our children and grandchildren will grow up in will be better for it.

I believe people long to live in a free society. I believe women in the greater Middle East long to live in freedom. I believe that if given the chance, the people of that troubled part of the world will embrace the most honorable form of Government ever devised by man. I believe all these things because freedom is not America's gift to the world; freedom is the Almighty God's gift to each man and woman in this world.

This young century will be liberty's century. By promoting freedom at home and abroad, we will build a safer world and a more hopeful America. By reforming our systems of Government, we'll help more Americans realize their dreams. We'll spread ownership and opportunity to every corner of this country. We'll pass the enduring values of our country to a new generation. We will continue to make the world more peaceful and more free.

For all Americans, these years in our history will always stand apart. There are quiet times in the life of our Nation when little is expected of its leaders. This isn't one of those times. This is a time when we need firm resolve, clear vision, and a deep faith in the values that makes this a great nation.

None of us will ever forget that week when one era ended and another began. On September the 14th, 2001, I stood in the ruins of the Twin Towers. It's a day that I'll never forget. There were workers in hardhats yelling at me at the top of their lungs, "Whatever it takes." I remember trying to console people as best I could, and a guy grabbed me by the arm, and he said, "Do not let me down." Every day since that day, I wake up trying to figure out how better to protect our country. I will never relent in defending America, whatever it takes.

Four years ago, as I traveled your great State asking for the vote, I made a pledge that if you gave me a chance to serve, I would uphold the dignity and the honor of the office to which I had been elected. With your help, with your hard work, I will do so for 4 more years.

Thanks for coming. God bless. I appreciate you all. Thank you all.

NOTE: The President spoke at 11:33 a.m. at Lehigh Parkway. In his remarks, he referred to Senator Zell Miller of Georgia, who made the keynote address at the 2004 Republican National Convention; Charles W. Dent, candidate for Congress in Pennsylvania's 15th Congressional District; senior Al Qaida associate Abu Musab Al Zarqawi; David Kay, former CIA Special Advisor for Strategy Regarding Iraqi Weapons of Mass Destruction Programs; Prime Minister Ayad Allawi of the Iraqi Interim Government; and Prime Minister Junichiro Koizumi of Japan.

Remarks in Manchester, New Hampshire
October 1, 2004

The President. Thanks for coming. I appreciate you all coming. Thanks. It's great to be back in the great State of New Hampshire.

So guess what happened? We pulled up in our entourage, and I opened the door. I come bounding in the tent, and Mother's there checking up on me. They said—you know, sometimes they say I get a little too blunt, reminds me of the time a woman in Texas said, "Well, you got your daddy's eyes and your mother's mouth." [*Laughter*] I love you, Mom. Thanks for coming.

I'm keeping really good company up here on the stage. First, I'm proud to be standing with your great United States Senator, Judd Gregg. He's as solid as the granite in this State. I know you're going to send him back for 6 more years.

And I'm proud to be in New Hampshire with John McCain. What a fine American he is and a good friend. He told me a little something about New Hampshire politics—in case you forgot. [*Laughter*] I didn't. I picked up on the lessons and carried the State of New Hampshire in 2000, and with your help, we'll carry it again in 2004.

We had a great debate last night. It highlighted some fundamental differences between my opponent and me, differences I believe are crucial to our Nation's national security. First of all, there's a big difference when it comes to supporting our troops in harm's way. When America puts our troops in combat, I believe they deserve the best training, the best equipment, the full support of our Government. Last night my opponent said our troops deserve better. They certainly deserve better than they got from Senator Kerry when he voted to send them to war, then voting—voted against funding our troops in combat.

Audience members. Boo-o-o!

The President. You may remember his quote when they asked him about his vote. He said, "Well, I actually did vote for the $87 billion, right before I voted against it." [*Laughter*] Not a lot of people in New Hampshire talk that way. Last night he said he had made a mistake in how he talked about that vote. I don't know if you remember that part of the debate or not.

I certainly do. But the mistake wasn't what Senator Kerry said. The mistake was what Senator Kerry did.

During the course of this campaign, they kept asking him to explain the vote. He said the famous quote. Then he went on and said he was proud of his vote. He said, "The whole thing was a complicated matter." And earlier this week he gave yet another explanation of his vote. He said, "Well, it was a protest vote." [*Laughter*] Exactly what he said, "protest vote."

Audience members. Boo-o-o!

The President. When we put American troops in harm's way, they certainly deserve better than to have a candidate for President use them as a protest.

Last night was very revealing. He continued his pattern of confusing contradictions. After voting for the war, after saying my decision to remove Saddam Hussein from power was the right decision, he now said it was all a mistake. But asked a logical question, "Does that mean our troops are dying for a mistake?" He said, "No." You can't have it both ways. You can't say it's a mistake and not a mistake. You can't be for getting rid of Saddam Hussein when things look good and against it when times are difficult. You can't claim terrorists are pouring across the border into Iraq yet, at the same time, try to claim that Iraq is somehow a diversion from the war on terror. The American President must speak clearly, and when he speaks, must mean what he says.

The crucial difference between my opponent and me is the most important question for voters in this election, and that is: Who can lead this war against terror to victory? And here my opponent has a fundamental misunderstanding of the nature of this war against terror, and he has no plan to win in Iraq. The cornerstone of Senator Kerry's plan for Iraq is to convene a summit. That's what he said. Now, look, I've been to a lot of summits. [*Laughter*] Since I've been your President, I've been honored to be at summits throughout the world. I've never been to a meeting that has deposed a tyrant or brought a terrorist to justice. The way to defeat the terrorists is to stay on the offense and bring them to justice.

My opponent last night claims he can work with our allies. Yet he said those who are standing with us are not a part of a genuine coalition.

Audience members. Boo-o-o!

The President. He earlier called them a "coalition of the coerced and bribed" and dismissed their sacrifices as "window dressings."

Audience members. Boo-o-o!

The President. See, you cannot lead by pushing away the allies who are already with us, who are sacrificing along with our soldiers. You can't expect any support for a cause you have called a "mistake," a "grand diversion," or "the wrong war at the wrong time." As I said last night, I've been meeting with these leaders around the world. Imagine walking into a room, and say, "Get your sons to sacrifice and your daughters to sacrifice for the wrong war at the wrong place at the wrong time." Imagine. [*Laughter*] The way to lead this coalition is not to be disdainful or dismissive. The way to lead this coalition to victory is to be clear about our thinking, grateful for their sacrifices, and resolute in our determination to achieve victory.

Let me say one other thing, one more thing I want to share with you about last night's debate. Perhaps it was the most disturbing aspect of the debate. Senator Kerry said that America has to pass some sort of "global test"——

Audience members. Boo-o-o!

The President. ——before we can use our troops to defend ourselves. Think about that. He wants our national security decisions subject to the approval of a foreign government.

Audience members. Boo-o-o!

The President. Listen, I'll continue to work with our allies. I'll work with the international community, but I will never submit America's national security to an international test. The President's job is not to take an international poll. The President's job is to defend the United States of America.

Audience members. U.S.A.! U.S.A.! U.S.A.!

The President. I've come for more reasons than just to talk about last night's debate and to see my mother. [*Laughter*] I have come back to New Hampshire to ask for your vote, and I am here to ask for your help. I ask you to register your friends and neighbors. I ask you, then, to head them to the polls come the voting time. And as you do so, remind them if they want a safer America, a stronger America, and a better America, to put me and Dick Cheney back in office.

I'm glad my mother is here, but I really wish Laura were here. What a great First Lady. You know, when I asked her to marry me, she said, "Fine, just so long as I never have to give a political speech." [*Laughter*] I said, "Okay, you'll never have to give one." [*Laughter*] Fortunately, she didn't hold me to that promise. In New York, at our convention, America got to see a compassionate, strong, fine First Lady in Laura Bush.

And I'm proud—I'm proud I'm running with Dick Cheney. He's a fine man. I concede, he doesn't have the waviest hair in the race. [*Laughter*] I didn't pick him because of his hair. I picked him because of his experience, his judgment, and because he can get the job done for the American people.

I want to sing the praises of your other United States Senator, John Sununu. You've got two really fine Senators in Judd and John, and I'm proud to work with them. They're kind of independent sometimes—[*laughter*]—just like the people of New Hampshire.

I appreciate your Governor, Craig Benson. I hope you put him back into office. Thanks for coming, Craig. I appreciate you being here, Craig. I'm proud of Congressman Jeb Bradley's work in the United States Congress, a fine Member of the House of Representatives. I want to thank Ted Gatsas and his wife, Cassandra. I want to thank Brian Golden, who's a Democrats for Bush member from Massachusetts. I am honored you're here, Brian. Thank you for coming.

I want to thank all the other State and local officials. But most importantly, I want to thank the grassroots activists and those who are doing the hard work, getting ready to turn out the vote come November.

I appreciate the Oak Ridge Boys who are here with us today. I'm proud to call them friends. And I want to thank Kaleigh Cronin, the student from Manchester Central High, who performed the National Anthem. I want to thank Manchester Central High School Band for being here today. I'll try to keep my speech short so you can get home and do your homework. [*Laughter*]

Listen, I'm looking forward to this campaign. I like coming here to New Hampshire, and I'm coming back. I want to tell the people where I stand, what I believe, and where I'll lead this country for the next 4 years.

I believe every child can learn and every school must teach. That's what I believe. I went to Washington to challenge the soft bigotry of low expectations. I didn't like the practice of having such low expectations that we would shuffle some children through the schools, grade after grade, year after year, without teaching them the basics. I know we can do better in America. So we changed the law to measure early, so we can solve problems. We believe in local control of schools. We're closing the achievement gap in America, and we're not going to go back to the old days of failed policy.

I believe we have a moral responsibility to honor our seniors with good health care. See, I went to Washington to fix problems. I saw a problem in Medicare. For example,

Medicare would pay nearly $100,000 for heart surgery but not one dime for the prescription drugs that might prevent the heart surgery from being needed in the first place. That wasn't fair to our seniors, and it wasn't fair to the taxpayers. We worked with Republicans and Democrats to modernize Medicare. Seniors will get prescription drug coverage in 2006, and we're not going back to the old days.

I believe in the energy and innovation and the spirit of America's workers, small-business owners, and farmers and ranchers. That's why we unleashed that energy with the largest tax relief in a generation.

I want you to remind your friends and neighbors what this economy has been through. The stock market was heading down before Dick Cheney and I showed up in Washington. Then we had a recession just as soon as we showed up. And then we had some corporate scandals, which affected our economy. We passed tough laws. We've made it abundantly clear we will not tolerate dishonesty in the boardrooms of America. And then the attacks came, of September the 11th, and that affected our economy.

But because we acted, our economy is growing at rates as fast as any in nearly 20 years. The national unemployment rate is 5.4 percent, which is lower than the average of the 1970s, 1980s, and 1990s. The unemployment rate in the State of New Hampshire is 3.7 percent.

I believe the most solemn duty of the American President is to protect the American people. If America shows uncertainty and weakness in this decade, the world will drift toward tragedy. This will not happen on my watch.

Audience members. Four more years! Four more years! Four more years!

The President. I am running for President with a clear and positive plan to build a safer America, a safer world, and a more hopeful America. I am running with a compassionate conservative philosophy that Government should help people improve their lives, not try to run their lives. I believe this Nation wants steady, consistent, principled leadership and that is why, with your help, we'll carry New Hampshire again and win a great victory in November.

But I understand the world in which we're living is changing. It wasn't all that long ago that a person in the workplace would have one job and one career, one pension plan, one retirement system, and that person was usually a man. The workplace has changed. Think about it. People are changing jobs. People are changing careers. Women are working inside the house and outside the house in America today. And yet, the fundamental systems of our Government, the Tax Code, the pension plans, health coverage, and worker training, were designed for the world of yesterday, not tomorrow. I'm running to transform these systems so that all citizens are equipped, prepared, and truly free to be able to make your own choices and pursue your own dreams.

A hopeful country is one that has a growing economy. In order to keep jobs here in America, America must be the best place in the world to do business. If you want jobs here, this has got to be the best place in the world to risk capital. That means less regulations. That means legal reform to stop the frivolous lawsuits that are plaguing our employers.

We want to keep this economy growing and have jobs here in America, Congress needs to pass my energy plan. It's a plan that encourages conservation. It's a plan that spends money to make sure we do a better job with renewables like ethanol and biodiesel. It's a plan that uses technology to burn coal in clean ways. It's a plan that uses technology to explore for natural gas in environmentally friendly ways. It is a plan that recognizes this fact: To keep this economy growing, we must be less dependent on foreign sources of energy.

In order to keep jobs here in America, we must open up markets to U.S. products.

We've opened up our markets for goods from overseas for a reason. It's good for our consumers. Think about this. If you've got more products to choose from, you're likely to get that which you want at a better price. That's how the market works. So rather than falling prey to economic isolationism, I'm saying to countries like China and elsewhere, "You treat us the way we treat you." I say that because I know when the rules are fair, we can compete with anybody, anytime, anywhere in the world.

Finally, to make sure this economy continues to grow, we've got to be wise about how we spend your money in Washington, and we've got to keep your taxes low. Taxes are an issue in this campaign. I'm running against a fellow who lived right south from here. [*Laughter*] He's so far promised $2.2 trillion in new spending. That's a lot, even for a Senator from Massachusetts. [*Laughter*] So they said, "How are you going to pay for it?" He said, "That's easy. We're going to tax the rich." You've heard that before, haven't you?

Audience members. Yes!

The President. About every campaign. The problem with that, there's some flawed logic. You can't raise enough money by taxing the rich to pay for $2.2 trillion in new spending. There's what I would call a tax gap. Guess who gets to fill the tax gap?

Audience member. We do!

The President. Yes. I'll tell you something else about the rhetoric of taxing the rich. The rich hire lawyers and accountants for a reason, so they can avoid the bill and stick you with it. The good news is, we're not going to let him tax you. We're going to win in November.

Speaking about the Tax Code, it's a complicated mess. It's full of special interest loopholes. It's a million pages long. Americans spend 6 billion hours a year filling out their tax forms.° In order to make sure this Tax Code is fair and simple, I'm going to call Republicans and Democrats together

---

° White House correction.

to do something about an antiquated Tax Code that needs to be changed.

Listen, we'll help our workers gain the skills of the 21st century. In a changing economy, sometimes there's a skills gap. Jobs are available, but workers don't have the skills necessary to fill the jobs. That's why I'm such a strong believer in the community college system. I believe—and I know that most new jobs in a changing economy are filled by people with at least 2 years of college, yet one in four of our students gets there. In our high schools, we'll fund early intervention programs to help at-risk students. We'll emphasize math and science. Over time, there ought to be a rigorous exam before graduation. By raising performance in our high schools and by expanding Pell grants for low- and middle-income families, more Americans will start their career with a college diploma.

Let me talk about health care. There is a wide, philosophical divide when it comes to health care. Let me see if I can summarize it this way. My opponent wants the Government to run the health care——

Audience members. Boo-o-o!

The President. ——which would lead to high prices and rationing. I want you to make the decisions when it comes to health care. I have a practical, commonsense way of dealing with health care to make sure it's available and affordable. Let me give you some ideas.

First of all, most of the uninsured work for small businesses. Many small businesses are having trouble affording health care. We ought to change the law to allow small businesses to pool risk, so they can buy insurance at the same discounts big businesses can buy insurance for. We'll expand tax-free health savings accounts. We'll give small businesses tax credits to pay into health savings accounts for their employees. We'll help low-income, uninsured working Americans to afford health savings accounts. These are innovative ways to make sure people get good health care coverage with catastrophic coverage as well.

We will expand community health centers to every poor county in America so the poor and the indigent can get preventative and primary care in places other than emergency rooms of your hospitals. We'll make sure poor children are enrolled in our low-income children's programs. To make sure health care is available and affordable, we've got to do something about these junk lawsuits that are running good docs out of practice and running your costs of medicine up. In all we do reform health care, we'll make sure the decisions are made by doctors and patients, not by bureaucrats in Washington, DC.

In changing times, ownership helps bring stability to people's lives. The homeownership rate in America is at an alltime high during my administration. I love that statistic. Think about it. More and more people are opening up the door where they live and saying, "Welcome to my home. Welcome to my piece of property." Over the next 4 years, we'll expand homeownership to every corner of America.

And I want to implement a part of ownership into the retirement system as well. You might remember some of the rhetoric that took place in 2000 when I was running. They said, "If George W. gets elected, he's going to take away your Social Security check." I don't know if you remember that or not. Well, you still got the check; nothing happened. What I'm telling you is, is that when I talk about Social Security reform, if you're a senior citizen on Social Security, you don't have to worry about your check. That's that same old stale rhetoric that they're going to put out every year. You'll get your check. Baby boomers like me, we'll probably get our checks, because the Social Security trust is that solvent.

But we need to worry about our children and grandchildren when it comes to Social Security. I believe younger workers ought to be able to take some of their own money and set up a personal savings account to make sure Social Security fulfills its promise, a personal savings account you call your own, a personal savings account the Government can never take away.

Listen, in this world of change, there are some things that won't change, the values we try to live by, courage and compassion, reverence and integrity. In changing times, we'll support the institutions that give our lives direction and purpose, our schools, our families, our religious congregations. We stand for a culture of life in which every person matters and every being counts. We stand for marriage and family, which are the foundations of our society. And we stand for the appointment of Federal judges who know the difference between personal opinion and the strict interpretation of the law.

This election will also determine how America responds to continuing danger of terrorism. Since 2001—September the 11th, 2001, we have fought the terrorists across the Earth, not for pride, not for power, but because the lives of our citizens are at stake. Our strategy is clear. We're defending the homeland. We'll transform our military. We'll keep the All-Volunteer Army an all-volunteer army.

Audience member. [Inaudible]

The President. Yes. We'll strengthen the intelligence services. We'll stay on the offensive. We'll defeat the terrorists around the Earth so we do not have to face them here at home. We'll continue to advance liberty in the broader Middle East and throughout the world, and we will prevail.

Our strategy is succeeding. Think about this: Four years ago, Afghanistan was the home base of Al Qaida; Pakistan was a transit point for terrorists; Saudi Arabia was fertile ground for terrorist fundraising; Libya was secretly pursuing nuclear weapons; Iraq was a gathering threat; and Al Qaida was largely unchallenged as it planned attacks.

Because we acted, Afghanistan is fighting terror; Pakistan is capturing terrorist leaders; Saudi Arabia is making raids and arrests; Libya is dismantling its weapons programs; the army of a free Iraq is fighting terror; and three-quarters of Al Qaida's leadership have been brought to justice.

This progress involved careful diplomacy, clear moral purpose, and some tough decisions. The toughest came on Iraq. We knew Saddam Hussein's record of aggression and support for terror. We knew that. I want you to remember that he harbored Abu Nidal, the leader of a terrorist organization that carried out attacks in Europe and Asia. We knew he harbored Abu Abbas, who killed American Leon Klinghoffer because of his religion. Zarqawi was in and out of Baghdad. He ordered the killing of an American citizen from Baghdad. We knew Saddam Hussein's long history of pursuing and using weapons of mass destruction. We knew that he would hope the world would turn away and not pay attention to him. We also knew that we must think differently after September the 11th. This country must take threats seriously before they fully materialize. That is a lesson we must never forget.

So I went to the United States Congress. The Congress looked at the same intelligence I looked at, remembered the same history I remembered, and concluded Saddam Hussein was a threat, and voted to authorize the use of force. My opponent looked at the same intelligence I looked at. He concluded that Saddam Hussein was a serious threat. He voted yes when it came to the authorization of force. He may not want to admit it today.

Before the Commander in Chief commits troops into harm's way, he must try all options, before military options. And so I went to the United Nations in hopes that diplomacy would work, in hopes that somehow the free world would finally convince Saddam Hussein to listen to the demands. The United Nations Security Council debated the issue and voted 15 to nothing to say to Saddam Hussein, "Disclose, disarm, or face serious consequences." I believe that when an international body speaks, it must mean what it says, in order to keep this world peaceful. Saddam Hussein ignored the demands yet again.

Last night my opponent said, "Well, we probably should have"—not probably—"We should have taken more time and passed another resolution," as if number 18 would have convinced him. We sent inspectors in—the U.N. did—they were systematically deceived. That's what history shows. My opponent said, "We should have left the inspectors in there." Why? I don't know. Maybe Saddam could deceived them even more. The truth was diplomacy had failed. And so I now have a choice to make: Do I take the word of a madman and forget the lessons of September the 11th, or take action to defend this country? Given that choice, I will defend America every time.

We didn't find the stockpiles we thought would be there. We didn't find the stockpiles everybody thought would be there. But I want you to remember, Saddam still had the capability of making weapons of mass destruction. He could have passed that capability onto an enemy, and that is a risk we could not have afforded to have taken after September the 11th. Knowing what I know today, I would have made the same decision. And the world is safer with Saddam Hussein sitting in a prison cell.

Because we acted to defend our country, 50 million people now live in freedom in Afghanistan and Iraq. Remember what it was like in Afghanistan some 3 years ago. People were living under the brutal reign of the Taliban. These people are—when I talk about ideologues of hate, that's what I'm talking about, people just like them. They would not let young girls go to school. They'd whip their mothers in the public square if they disagreed with their ideology of hate. They executed women in sports stadiums. They were barbaric and backwards, and they were harboring Al Qaida.

Today, Afghanistan is an ally in the war on terror, and 10 million people, 41 percent of whom are women, have registered to vote in the upcoming October Presidential election. Think about that for a minute. This country has gone from darkness to light because of freedom, and America and the world are better for it.

In Iraq, we have got a plan to win this war against the terrorists. First of all, we've got an ally in the war and a strong leader in Prime Minister Allawi. Secondly, there will be national elections in January of 2005. We're continuing our reconstruction efforts over the next months to help rebuild that country. We'll continue to work with our allies and friends. There will be a donors summit in Japan next month. There will be a regional conference of neighbor— of countries in the neighborhood to work with Iraq. We will continue to train the Iraqis so they will do the hard work of defending their country against those who want to stop the advance of freedom. That is our strategy. We'll implement it as quickly as possible. We'll get this country on the road to stability and democracy, and then our troops will come home with the honor they have earned.

I am proud of our United States military, and I want to thank the veterans who are here for having set such a great example.

I believe in the transformational power of liberty. The other night, I said, "I am realistic about what's taking place in Iraq. I understand how hard it is. I'm optimistic we will succeed." I'm optimistic we'll succeed, and one of the main reasons why is because I do believe in the transformational power of liberty.

I'll tell you what I mean by that. Perhaps the best way to explain that to you is using this example. One of the leaders I enjoy meeting with is Prime Minister Koizumi of Japan—interesting fellow. I told him in New York when I saw him, I said, "Do you mind if I tell the people in my country that we've got a good relationship?" He said, "Fine." I didn't tell him I was going to tell you that his favorite singer was Elvis—[*laughter*]—interesting man and a friend.

Think about this, though, that I sit down and talk to this leader of Japan some 60 years after our Nation was at war with them. Sixty years isn't very long in the march of history. It's long if you're 58 years old. [*Laughter*] But I want you to think about that for a minute. My dad, your dads, your granddads fought against the Japanese, and yet today, I now sit down at the table with the Prime Minister.

See, fortunately, Harry Truman and other citizens of the country believed in the transformational power of liberty, that liberty could transform an enemy into an ally. And because they overwhelmed the skeptics and the doubters, I now sit at the table with a leader of a former foe talking about the peace we all want. Someday, an American President will be sitting down with a duly elected leader of Iraq, talking about keeping the peace. And our children and our grandchildren will be better off for it.

I believe millions in the Middle East plead in silence for their liberty. I believe women in the Middle East want to be free to realize their dreams, and they can raise their children in hopeful societies. I believe that if given the chance, people in the Middle East will embrace the most honorable form of government ever devised by man, democracy. I believe all these things because freedom is not America's gift to the world; freedom is the Almighty God's gift to each man and woman in this world.

This young century will be liberty's century. By promoting freedom at home and abroad, we'll build a safer world and a more hopeful America. By reforming our systems of Government, we will help more Americans realize their dreams. We'll spread ownership and opportunity to every corner of this country. We'll pass the enduring values of our country to a new generation. We will continue to make the world more peaceful and more free.

For Americans—for all Americans, these years in our history will always stand apart. There are quiet times in the life a nation when little is expected of its leaders. This isn't one of those times. This is a time when we need firm resolve, clear vision, and a deep faith in the values that makes this a great nation.

None of us will ever forget that week when one era ended and another began. On September the 14th, 2001, I stood in the ruins of the Twin Towers. It's a day I'll never forget. The memories are vividly etched in my mind. There were workers in hardhats yelling at the top of their lungs, "Whatever it takes." I remember working the line, trying to comfort people coming out of that rubble, and a guy grabbed me by the arm, and he said, "Do not let me down." Ever since that day, that fateful day, I've woken up doing whatever I can to protect this country. I will never relent in defending you, whatever it takes.

Four years ago as I had the honor of traveling your State, I made this pledge, I said if you gave me the chance to serve, I would uphold the honor and the dignity of the office. With your hard work, with your help, I will do so for 4 more years.

May God bless you, and may God bless our great country. Thanks for coming. Thank you all.

NOTE: The President spoke at 3:58 p.m. at the McIntyre Ski Area. In his remarks, he referred to Gov. Craig Benson of New Hampshire; New Hampshire State Senator Theodore L. Gatsas and his wife, Cassandra; Massachusetts State Representative Brian Paul Golden; entertainers the Oak Ridge Boys; senior Al Qaida associate Abu Musab Al Zarqawi; Prime Minister Ayad Allawi of the Iraqi Interim Government; and Prime Minister Junichiro Koizumi of Japan.

Remarks to the National Association of Home Builders in Columbus, Ohio
October 2, 2004

The President. Thank you all very much. Thank you all.

Audience members. Four more years! Four more years! Four more years!

The President. Thanks a lot. Thanks for the warm welcome. I appreciate being with the homebuilders from all across our country. It's a good way to spend a Saturday morning. [*Laughter*] I'm proud to be back in the State capital of Ohio.

I don't know if you know this or not, but my great grandfather built a home right here in Columbus, on Roxbury Road. The homebuilder they hired did a good job. [*Laughter*] The house still stands. [*Laughter*] My grandfather was born in this city back in 1895, so I hope a month from now the Ohio voters will send a home boy back to Washington.

For millions of our citizens, the American Dream starts with owning a home. Homeownership gives people a sense of pride and independence and confidence for the future. When you work hard, like you've done, and there are good policies coming out of our Nation's Capital, we're creating a home—an ownership society in this country where more Americans than ever will be able to open up their door where they live and say, "Welcome to my house. Welcome to my piece of property."

I was in Florida this week. And I've been there quite often because of the hurricanes, and I want to thank you for the good work that the homebuilders are doing for the people of that State. Homebuilders have collected donations of cash and building materials for families that have lost so much. They've established an online disaster contractor network to help put homeowners in touch with licensed contractors and with Government officials who can help those people that have been hurt by these storms.

The Federal Government is also doing its part, along with State and local authorities. Florida has been through a terrible time. And so have many communities here in Ohio, that have suffered severe flooding caused by the hurricanes. We've issued disaster declarations for 20 counties in Ohio, making residents whose homes have been damaged or destroyed eligible for assistance. In Florida, Ohio, and other storm-damaged—ravaged States, we will not rest until life is back to normal, the damage repaired, and the homes are rebuilt.

Laura sends her best. When I asked her to marry me, she was a public school librarian in Texas. [*Applause*] There you are. Just wanted to see if any of the home State folks are here. [*Laughter*] I know Conine is here. [*Laughter*] She said, "Fine, I'll marry you, just so long as I never have to give a political speech." [*Laughter*] I said, "Okay." [*Laughter*] Fortunately, she didn't hold me to that promise. The American people are learning what I know: She's a compassionate, decent, strong First Lady for our country.

I want to thank Bobby Rayburn and Annette for their invitation and their leadership of this important group. I appreciate the board of directors who are here today. I want to thank the guests who are here today.

I'm traveling today with Senator Mike DeWine from the State of Ohio, who is a fine United States Senator. I appreciate you coming, Mike. Congressman Dave Hobson and Carolyn are with us today. Thank you for coming, Congressman. I appreciate you being here. Congressman Pat Tiberi is here. Thank you for coming, Pat. I'm proud you're here. He brought his mother, Rina, with him.

Yesterday I was in New Hampshire speaking, and Mother showed up. [*Laughter*] Just wanted to make sure she could continue giving me some instructions. [*Laughter*] Tiberi, my only advice to you is do what I do, and that's listen to your mother. [*Laughter*] I appreciate your dad, Joe, being here, and your sister.

I want to thank the Lieutenant Governor from this State being here, Jennette Bradley, and happy birthday to you, Governor. I appreciate it. Betty Montgomery, the State auditor is here. I know there's other local officials and State officials. We all appreciate you being here today.

Today when I landed at the airport, I met Karen Kindron. You've probably never heard of Karen, but let me tell you about her. She is an active volunteer in what's called Rebuilding Together of Columbus. She is a soldier in the army of compassion. She is the kind of person who's heard the universal call to love a neighbor. She represents the true strength of America, which is the hearts and souls of our citizens. The program for which she volunteers helps low-income, elderly, and disabled home-owners. They help them obtain services such as weatherization and repair work. Since founded in 1988, over 2 million volunteers have rehabilitated 87,000 homes and facilities. America can change one heart and one soul at a time for the better because of the volunteers all across our country who are making a difference. And I want to thank Karen. Where are you, Karen? She's somewhere. Anyway, she's here, and I thank her for setting such a good example. Thank you, Karen, appreciate it.

We're nearing an historic national election in 31 days—who's counting? [*Laughter*] Americans will go to the polls to determine the direction of this great Nation for the next 4 years. I'm looking forward to these final weeks of the campaign. I really am. I like to get out amongst the people, and I'm going to tell you where I stand and what I believe and where I'll lead this Nation.

I believe it is the job of a President to confront problems, not pass them on to future Presidents and future generations. And in the last 4 years, we have faced some problems. We faced a recession, corporate scandal. We passed tough laws now that make it abundantly clear, we will not tolerate dishonesty in the boardrooms of America. We faced a terrorist attack and war. Because we confronted these challenges with focus and resolve, our Nation is on the path to a better future. If America shows weakness or uncertainty in this decade, the world will drift toward tragedy. This is not going to happen on my watch.

We're going after the terrorists. We will hunt them down where they plot and plan, and we're making progress. Today, more than three-quarters of Al Qaida's key members and associates have been brought to justice. I have the solemn duty to protect the homeland, and we'll do everything we can here at home to protect you. But the best way to protect the homeland is to stay on the offensive, fighting the terrorists overseas so we do not have to face them here in America.

But I understand this: To make sure our children and grandchildren grow up in a hopeful, peaceful world, this country must continue to spread freedom and liberty. Freedom in Afghanistan—10 million citizens in that country that was once ruled by the barbarians, the Taliban, have registered to vote, 41 percent of whom are women, in the upcoming Presidential elections. Freedom is on the march.

We'll continue to work for a free society in Iraq. It's hard work there. You know it's hard, and I know it's hard. It's hard for a reason, because the terrorists fear freedom. Liberty will transform societies. Someday, an American President will be sitting down with a duly elected leader of Iraq talking about the peace, and our children and grandchildren will be able to grow up in a more peaceful world. In the long run, our interests are served by spreading freedom and liberty and, therefore, spreading peace.

There are clear differences in this campaign. In the debate Thursday night, my opponent continued his pattern of confusing contradictions on Iraq. After voting for the war, after saying my decision to remove Saddam Hussein from power was the right decision, he now says it was all a mistake. Then he was asked if our troops were dying for a mistake. He said, "No." You can't have it both ways. You can't say it's a mistake and not a mistake. You can't be for getting rid of Saddam Hussein when things look good and against it when times are hard. You can't claim terrorists are pouring across the border into Iraq yet, at the same time, try to claim that Iraq is somehow a diversion from the war against terrorism. A President cannot keep changing his mind. A President must be consistent. A President must speak clearly, and a President must mean what he says.

In the debate, Senator Kerry also said something revealing when he laid out the Kerry doctrine. He said that America has to pass a "global test" before we can use American troops to defend ourselves.

Audience members. Boo-o-o!

The President. That's what he said. [*Laughter*] Think about this, Senator Kerry's approach to foreign policy would give foreign governments veto power over our national security decisions. I have a different view. When our country is in danger, the President's job is not to take an international poll. The President's job is to defend America. I'll continue to work every day with our friends and allies for the sake of freedom and peace. But our national security decisions will be made in the Oval Office, not in foreign capitals.

We have hard work ahead to do our duty. But by being steadfast and resolved, we will prevail. And as we defend our great country, we will continue strengthening our Nation here at home.

To grow this economy and unleash the spirit of enterprise, to overcome the obstacles I described earlier, we passed the largest tax relief in a generation. And that tax relief has made a big difference for a lot of you all. See, many homebuilders are small businesses. Many homebuilders are—represent the great entrepreneurial spirit of America. Among the members of the National Association of Home Builders, 63 percent of you are either Subchapter S or sole proprietorships, which means you pay your taxes at the individual income-tax rate. Just like a lot of other small businesses in America do.

And so when we passed tax relief by cutting rates on everybody who pay taxes, we helped our small businesses; we helped our homebuilders. We helped you with resources to build or grow and expand and hire more workers. By cutting taxes on dividends and capital gains, we encouraged savings and investment, which is crucial to your industry. Tax relief left more money in the hands of American workers so they could save, spend, invest, and help drive this economy forward.

The economic recovery plan of ours is working. The results are clear for all to see. Over the past year, America has added 1.7 million jobs. We've added 107,000 manufacturing jobs since January. The national unemployment rate is down to 5.4 percent, nearly a full point below the rate in the summer of 2003 and below the average of the 1970s, 1980s, and 1990s.

Inflation is low. Mortgage and interest rates are near historic lows. Our economy is growing at rates as fast as any in nearly 20 years, spreading opportunity and prosperity across this country. And the homebuilders of America have helped lead the recovery in America.

The tax relief has helped many be able to put money down to buy a home. As well, my administration has worked to expand homeownership in other ways. Last December, I signed the American Dream Downpayment Act, which will help thousands of low-income families afford the downpayment and closing costs on their first home. We want people in every corner of America owning a home.

We've doubled funding for education and counseling services to help first-time home-buyers navigate the lending process, understand the fine print, and avoid predatory lenders. Homeownership rates are an all-time high in America, nearly 70 percent. I love that statistic. [*Laughter*] Think about that. More and more people own a home in America. More and more people have a chance to realize the great dream of our country. Minority homeownership is at record levels as well. In 2002, I set a clear goal, 5.5 million new minority homeowners by the end of the decade. And in just 2 years, more than 1.6 million minorities have become homeowners. America is a stronger country every single time a family moves into a house of their own.

The fundamental question in this campaign is how do we make the recovery lasting—to lasting prosperity? To create more jobs in America, to make sure people can find work, America must be the best place in the world to do business. That means less regulations on the entrepreneurs. To create jobs here, Congress needs to pass my energy plan. It's a plan that encourages conservation and renewable sources, but it's a plan that uses technology so we can burn coal and explore for natural gas. To make sure our economy remains strong and people can find work in America, we must become less dependent on foreign sources of energy.

To make sure this economy remains strong, we've got to reject economic isolationism. We have opened up our markets for products from overseas, and that's good for the consumer. If a person has more choices, he or she is likely to get the product they want at better quality and lower price. That's how the marketplace works. So I'm saying to other countries like China and elsewhere, "Treat us the way we treat you. Open up your markets for our farmers, ranchers, and entrepreneurs." We can compete with anybody, anytime, anywhere, so long as the rules are fair.

To make sure that jobs exist here in America people can find work, we've got to protect our small-business owners and workers from the junk lawsuits that threaten jobs across America. I don't think you can be pro-homebuilder, pro-small-business, pro-entrepreneur, and pro-trial-lawyer at the same time. I think you have to choose. My opponent made a choice. He put a trial lawyer on the ticket. I made my choice. I'm for legal reform to make sure this economy continues forward.

I've worked with Congress to create opportunity zones, which will provide extra tax relief and regulatory relief and other incentives for businesses to help our communities that have lost manufacturing and textile and other jobs to get back on their feet. We'll keep this economy growing until prosperity reaches every corner of America.

And I've set another great goal, and that's to build an ownership society, where everyone has a chance to own a home and a retirement account or health care plan and to gain a permanent stake in the American Dream. I believe expanded ownership is necessary for a lot of reasons, and one of the main reasons is because the times in which we live and work are changing dramatically.

Think about our society today compared to the society of our grandparents and parents. The workers of our parents' and grandparents' generation typically had only one job, one skill, one career, often with one company that provided health care and a pension. Today, people are changing jobs and careers quite often, and the workforce has changed. Women work inside the house and now outside the house. Yet, the fundamental systems of Government, the health care plans, the pension plans, the Tax Code, the worker training programs, were designed for yesterday, not for tomorrow.

I'm running for office to help people be able to realize their dreams by changing the fundamental systems of Government. And in times of change, I understand that ownership brings stability to our neighborhoods and security to our families. In changing times, it helps if you own something. It helps bring security to you. By paying a mortgage instead of rent, by putting money into your own retirement plan, you're storing up wealth for your family. And that nest egg grows in value, and you can pass it on to your children or your grandchildren.

To build an ownership society, we'll help even more Americans buy homes. Some families are more than able to pay a mortgage but just don't have the savings to put money down. We'll continue to help them realize their dreams with a downpayment. So I'm asking Congress to pass my Zero-Downpayment Initiative. We should remove the 3 percent downpayment rule for first-time homebuyers with FHA-insured mortgages. This change could help as many as 150,000 people become homeowners in the first year alone.

To help low- to moderate-income rural families purchase homes, I've requested $2.7 billion in loan guarantees and 1.1 billion for direct loans to low-income borrowers that can't get bank loans. These initiatives will help thousands in rural communities across America achieve the dream of homeownership.

Adding more qualified buyers won't accomplish much if there are no affordable homes to buy. My administration has set a goal of 7 million more affordable homes in the next 10 years. To help reach that goal, I've asked Congress to pass the single family housing affordable tax credit to help you build between 40 and 50 thousand new affordable homes every year.

I understand that the regulatory barriers at the Federal, State, and local levels can add as much as 35 percent of the cost to the homes. In order to make sure there's more affordable homes, we must remove the regulatory barriers on our homebuilders. I understand there's a need for sensible regulation, but when you have overlapping regulations that send confusing signals, when you have the Federal Government, the State government, the local governments creating obstacles for homebuilding, it is time to reduce those regulations.

Finally, I believe that the mortgage interest deduction enables more Americans to achieve the goal of homeownership. It is an important part of our Tax Code.

To build an ownership society, we should help our fellow citizens get health care, especially coverage for themselves. More than one-half of the uninsured in America are small-business employees and their families. To make sure they get help, we must allow small firms to join together through association health plans so they can purchase insurance for their employees at the same discounts that big businesses are able to do so. And I appreciate your homebuilders—the homebuilders for supporting this initiative.

We will offer a tax credit to encourage small businesses and their employees to set up health savings accounts. We'll provide help—direct help for low-income Americans to purchase health savings accounts. Health savings accounts—and I urge you to look into them—give workers the security of insurance against major illness, the opportunity to save tax-free for routine health expenses, and the freedom of knowing that you own your own account that you can take with you wherever you—whenever you change jobs.

And finally, in order to make sure—and another practical commonsense way to make sure health care is available and affordable, is to stop these frivolous lawsuits that are running good docs out of business and running up the cost of your health care. By making this medical liability issue a significant part of the campaign, by talking about every single stop, by reminding people about what these lawsuits do to their health care, I am confident that in the next 4 years, we'll get medical liability reform out of the United States Senate and the House of Representatives. In all we do to improve health care, we'll make sure the decisions are made by doctors and patients, not by bureaucrats in the Nation's Capital.

To build an ownership society, we've got to reform and strengthen our retirement system. I remember campaigning in 2000, and people tell me where they saw the TV ad they were running that said, "If George W. gets elected, our seniors aren't going to get their Social Security checks." So I'm going around the country reminding the seniors they got their checks. [*Laughter*]

With the baby boomer generation approaching retirement, many of our children and grandchildren understandably worry whether Social Security will be there when they need it. Social Security is in good shape for our seniors, and Social Security is in good shape for baby boomers like me. But we need to worry about our children and grandchildren. And so I believe we ought to strengthen Social Security by allowing younger workers to save some of their taxes in a personal account, a nest egg they can call their own that the Government cannot take away.

In all these proposals, we seek to provide not just a Government program but a path to greater opportunity and more freedom and more control over your own life. And here, as on so many other issues, there's a big difference between my opponent and me. Senator Kerry voted against tax deductible health savings accounts. He voted against expanding personal retirement savings accounts. He opposes our proposals to strengthen Social Security by allowing younger workers to put some of their taxes into personal accounts that they control. He opposes our plan to allow small businesses to join together to purchase health insurance at the discounts available to big companies. There's a pattern here. [*Laughter*] On just about every proposal to empower the individual instead of Government, my opponent has voted no.

A few weeks ago, Senator Kerry gave a speech in Detroit to lay our his economic agenda. Not once in that speech did he mention expanding ownership, not a word on how we would help more Americans own their own homes or stocks or savings accounts. Instead, his agenda focuses on expanding the scope and power of the Government. He has decided to put his faith in the wisdom of the Government. I will always put my faith in the wisdom of the American people.

Senator Kerry has spent almost 20 years in the Federal Government, and he's concluded that it just isn't big enough. [*Laughter*] On the campaign trail, he has proposed more than 2 trillion in new Federal spending so far. [*Laughter*] And that's a lot, even for a Senator from Massachusetts. [*Laughter*] And he said—they asked him, "Well, how are you going to pay for it?" He said, "By raising taxes on the rich. By raising taxes on the wealthiest 2 percent of the population." We've heard that rhetoric before, "raising taxes on the rich." There's one problem with that, that the tax increase would bring only in about $600 billion of revenue. And he wants to spend more than 2 trillion, so there's a tax gap. And guess who gets to fill the tax gap? Yes, you do. That's what happens. People make wild promises, and they can't pay for it, and then they're going to raise your taxes to pay for it.

He also doesn't understand when he's saying tax the so-called-rich, he's raising the taxes on the small-business owners of America. My opponent's plan would raise taxes on over 900,000 small-business owners, the Subchapter S corporations, the sole proprietorships, people just like you. Small businesses are the engine of job creation in our country. Small businesses create 7 out of every 10 new jobs. It makes no sense to tax the job creators as our economy is getting stronger. We should not punish free enterprise. We ought to encourage free enterprise in America.

Now, I've got a plan to help this country move forward. I believe tax—the tax relief we passed ought to be made permanent. I've got a practical way to make sure Americans get health coverage without empowering the Federal Government. We've got a clear view of how to make sure Social Security fulfills its promise to our younger folks. We're going to help more families find dignity and independence in a home they call their own. We're going to build an ownership society, where everyone has a stake in the success of America and everyone has a chance to realize the great promise of our country.

And you're helping people realizing that success. It must be a fantastic feeling to be a part of the American Dream. It must be great to see—it must be magnificent to see somebody walk in to their home and feel the pride of ownership, the fantastic feeling of saying to a son or daughter,

"Here's your room. Here's our piece of property."

I want to thank you very much for what you're doing. I want to thank you for helping pull our economy through some tough times and helping this Nation get on that hopeful path for a bright future. I appreciate your hard work. I appreciate your optimism. I appreciate your love for America.

May God bless you, and may God continue to bless our country. Thank you all.

NOTE: The President spoke at 10:01 a.m. at the Greater Columbus Convention Center. In his remarks, he referred to C. Kent Conine, immediate past president, and Bobby Rayburn, president, National Association of Home Builders; Carolyn Hobson, wife of Representative David L. Hobson; and Lt. Gov. Jennette Bradley and Auditor of State Betty Montgomery of Ohio.

The President's Radio Address
October 2, 2004

Good morning. Next week in Iowa, I will proudly sign the Working Families Tax Relief Act. This bipartisan law is good news for America's families. It keeps in place major portions of the tax relief we passed over the last 3 years. It preserves marriage penalty relief, the $1,000 child tax credit, and the expanded 10-percent tax bracket. The law also increases the refund limit on the child tax credit, which means about 7 million low-income families will get higher refund checks next year.

Because we acted, 94 million Americans will have a lower tax bill again next year, including 70 million women and 38 million families with children. I met many families that are benefiting from tax relief, including Gary and Angela Brown, from Springfield, Missouri. Gary works at a manufacturing company, and Angela stays at home with

their four children. Last year, the Browns saved about $3,000 on their taxes. They used some of that money to put a downpayment on braces for their daughter. If Congress had not extended tax relief, the Brown's tax bill would have gone up $1,500 next year. Now, because we acted, they will be able to keep and use that money. Tax relief has helped millions of families, like the Browns, to spend, save, and invest for the future. Thanks to their hard work, America's economy is strong and getting stronger.

This week brought more evidence that tax relief is helping our entire economy move forward. The economy grew at an annual rate of 3.3 percent in the second quarter. America's economy has been growing at rates as fast as any in nearly 20 years. And for 12 consecutive months, our economy has been creating jobs. We've added 1.7 million jobs since August, 2003, including 107,000 manufacturing jobs since January.

The unemployment rate is now 5.4 percent, down almost a full point since June, 2003, and below the average rate of the 1970s, 1980s, and 1990s. The homeownership rate is at an alltime high, and new home sales are still rising. After-tax income is increasing, which means workers are keeping more of their paychecks. The tax relief we passed is working.

Having extended tax relief, we must take additional action to strengthen our economy so every American who wants to work can find a job. To create more jobs, we need to reduce the burden of regulation on small businesses. We need to end the junk lawsuits that keep entrepreneurs from creating new jobs. Congress needs to pass my energy plan to make America less dependent on foreign sources of oil. We need to open more foreign markets to American products and ensure that other countries play by the rules. We must continue to spend taxpayer dollars wisely in Washington, DC. And to help families and small businesses plan with confidence, we need to make all of the tax relief permanent.

Some politicians in Washington have a different view of tax relief. When I pro-posed tax relief for working families in 2001 and 2003, Senator Kerry and other Democratic leaders voted against it. In fact, Senator Kerry has voted consistently against marriage penalty relief, against increasing the child tax credit, and against expanding the 10-percent bracket. Now, Senator Kerry and the Democrat leaders are proposing a lot of new Federal spending, and the only way to pay for all their promises is to raise taxes on working families.

You know where I stand. Higher taxes are the wrong policy for this growing economy. Our families and our country are better off when Government lets people keep more of what they earn. And that is why I'll work with Congress to keep taxes low, and that is why I will proudly sign the Working Families Tax Relief Act of 2004 into law.

Thank you for listening.

NOTE: The address was recorded at 2 p.m. on October 1 in Bedford, NH, for broadcast at 10:06 a.m. on October 2. The transcript was made available by the Office of the Press Secretary on October 1 but was embargoed for release until the broadcast. The Office of the Press Secretary also released a Spanish language transcript of this address.

Remarks in a Discussion in Mansfield, Ohio
October 2, 2004

The President. Thank you all. Thank you all for coming. Thanks for being here.

Audience members. Four more years! Four more years! Four more years!

The President. Thank you all for coming. I'm proud you're here. Go ahead and be seated. Thank you all. Thanks for coming.

It's great to be here in Mansfield. It's an honor to be back in the State of Ohio. You might have noticed I'm spending some quality time here. [*Laughter*] And there's a reason. I believe you have to get out amongst the people and ask for the vote, and that's what I'm doing here today. I'm here to say, I'd like your vote. And I'm also here to ask for your help.

Audience member. You got it!

The President. I appreciate it. [*Laughter*] I want to thank all those who are involved in the grassroots politics here. I know our party chairman is here. I know there's a lot of people putting up the signs and making the phone calls. I know people worked hard to turn out such a great crowd, and I thank you for it.

I'm going to thank you now for what you're going to do, which is to register people to vote. Don't overlook discerning Democrats like Zell Miller when you do so. And then remind people that in our free society, we have an obligation to vote. And then when you get them headed to the polls, tell them if they want a safer America, a stronger America, and a better America, to put me and Dick Cheney back in office.

Audience members. Four more years! Four more years! Four more years!

The President. Thank you all. Got a lot of work to do here. [*Laughter*] I'm here to let you know I have a reason for wanting to serve for 4 more years. It's important for a person running for office to say, "Here's what I've done," but only to verify that which I'm going to do. And that's what we're here to talk about. I appreciate you giving me a chance to come. As you can tell, we've got some citizens from the area here who are going to help illuminate the points about the approach to Government that I take, which is, the role of Government is to help people realize their dreams, not tell people how to live their lives.

And that's a fundamental difference in this campaign. It's a fundamental difference. I'm running against a fellow who trusts Government. I trust the people. And we're going to spend some time talking about it.

Before I do so, I want to tell you, Laura sent her best. She was a public school librarian in Texas when I asked her to marry me. She said, "Okay, just so long as I never have to give a speech." [*Laughter*] I said, "You've got a deal." [*Laughter*] Fortunately, she didn't hold me to my promise. [*Laughter*] People of this country got to see her in New York City. They got to see the woman I know—decent, compassionate,

strong, and a great First Lady. She said, hi. I'm going to give you some reasons to put me back into office, but perhaps the most important one of all is so that Laura will be your First Lady for 4 more years.

I'm proud of my Vice President. He's been a great friend and a good adviser. I admit it, he doesn't have the waviest hair in the race. [*Laughter*] I didn't pick him for his hair. [*Laughter*] I picked him because he's got good judgment; he's got great experience. I picked him because he's getting the job done for the American people.

I'm proud Oxley's here. I know you're proud to have him as your Congressman. Mike Oxley is a fine, fine man. Thanks, Ox. And I see the chairman is with us, Ralph Regula. Thank you, Ralph, for coming as well. Appreciate both of you here. I just got off the bus, and Mike DeWine went up the road. He is the warm-up person for the next speech, but he sends his best. Mike's a great United States Senator, and I hope you understand what a great Senator you have in George Voinovich. Please put him back into office. Thanks for coming.

Let me—a couple of things I want to say to you. One, as you're gathering up the vote, it's important for you to remind your fellow citizens what this country has been through for the last 3½ years and the fact that we have taken decisive action to deal with the issues that have confronted us. Take the economy. When we got in there, the stock market had been in decline for a while. It was kind of an indication of things to come, and then there was a recession. Recession, of course, means that small-business owners have trouble making payroll, that people are just—great uncertainty, that people are worried about their jobs. And then, just as we were beginning to get our balance in the recession, we found out that some of our citizens were not responsible citizens. They didn't tell the truth, and that affected our economy. Make no mistake about it, those corporate scandals affected the economic vitality of this country. So we acted. It's called the Sarbanes-Oxley bill. It's a bill that says we're not going to tolerate dishonesty in the boardrooms of America. And then after that, the enemy hit us, and it cost us jobs. The attacks of September the 11th caused a lot of grief, a lot of concern. It caused us to change our—aspects of our foreign policy, which I'll talk about in a little bit, but it hurt our economy.

There have been major obstacles in the path for economic success, yet we've overcome them. We've overcome them because the entrepreneurial spirit in America is strong. We've overcome it because our small-business owners are optimistic people. We've overcome it because we've got great workers in America. And we've overcome it because of well-timed tax cuts.

We're going to talk a little bit today about how the tax relief helped individual families as well as the small-business owners. The economy of this country is strong, and it's getting stronger. The national unemployment rate is 5.4 percent, which is lower than the average of the 1970s, 1980s, and 1990s. We're growing at rates as fast as any in nearly 20 years. I understand there's pockets of unemployment here in Ohio. It's been tough on this State, and I know that. That's why progrowth policies will help. You'll hear other ways to help the people who are hurting here. So long as anybody is looking for work, I'll continue to make sure this economy has got what it takes to grow.

Now, let me tell you about our economy. It's one thing to have overcome obstacles; the question is, how do you make sure the growth we have now is lasting prosperity? It's really the issue in this campaign. The best way to make sure work stays here in America, the best way to make sure people can find work is to make sure America is the best place in the world to do business. That means less regulations on our businessowners. That means legal reform so frivolous lawsuits don't make it hard to hire.

We open up our markets to goods from other countries. It's happened in previous administrations. Both Republican and Democrat Presidents have done so, because it's in your interests. The more products you have to choose from, the more likely it is you're going to get that which you want at a better price and higher quality. That's how the marketplace works. So in return, rather than closing our markets and isolating ourselves from the world, I've said to other countries like China, "You treat America the way America treats you." The best trade policy is to work to open up markets around the world because we can compete with anybody, anytime, anywhere if the rules are fair.

In order to keep jobs here, make sure the doors of our businesses stay open, we need an energy plan. I submitted a plan to the United States Congress. Congress needs to get it to my desk. It's a plan that encourages conservation. We spend billions on research to make sure that we can find alternative sources of energy. I strongly believe we ought to be using ethanol and biodiesel in the energy mix, which we are. I know we can use technology to see to it that our coals burn more cleanly. We need to be using technology to explore for natural gas in environmentally friendly ways. But to keep jobs here in America, this country must become less dependent on foreign sources of energy.

We've also got to be wise about how we spend your money in Washington. In order to make sure this economy grows, we've got to be wise. We've got to set priorities and stick to those priorities, and we've got to keep your taxes low. If you want this economy to grow, it's important to keep your taxes low, and it's an issue in this campaign. My opponent has, so far, proposed $2.2 trillion of new Federal spending. That's with a "T." That's a lot, even for somebody from Massachusetts. [*Laughter*] And so they said, "How are you going to pay for it?" They asked him, "How are you going to pay for it?" He said, "I'll just tax the rich." We've heard that, haven't we, before. "Just tax the rich."

Today I'm going to talk to a small-business owner that is evidently a part of that equation. There's a tax gap in his plan. He says, well—he's going to propose $2.2 trillion, by—but by raising the two top brackets, you only raise a little over $600 billion. That's the tax gap. Guess what happens when there's a tax gap in Washington? Guess who gets to fill the tax gap?

Audience member. We do!

The President. Yes. As well, when you hear him say "tax the rich," just remember that the rich hire lawyers and accountants for a reason, to slip the bill and pass it to you. The good news is, we're not going to let him tax you. I'm going to win in November, with your help. [*Applause*]

Thank you all. Hold on. We've got to work here. Thank you all. Behave yourselves back there. [*Laughter*] They got the best view in the house. Not now. [*Laughter*]

A couple other things I want to talk about. I want to remind you I understand we're living in a changing world. And it's changed—just think about the workplace. It used to be where a person had one job, one career, worked for one company, one pension plan, one health care plan, and that person was a male—generally a male. Today, the workplace has changed a lot. People are changing jobs and careers quite frequently. Women are working inside the house and outside the house. And yet, when you think about it, the fundamental systems of our Government, like the Tax Code or the health care plans or the pension plans, were designed for yesterday, not tomorrow. I'm running to change those systems so that people have the opportunity to be able to realize the great promise of America.

Let me talk about health care right quick, and we're going to talk about an interesting example of what I'm talking

about. The health care system today, we've got a choice, it seems like to me, and the choice is whether or not the Government is going to run the health care or you're going to run the health care. I believe it's as simple and as stark as that. I've analyzed my opponent's plans, and when you think about it, everything he's going to do, it's going to cause the Government to be more intrusive in the health care system. To me, that's the wrong approach.

About 50 percent—so here's some practical ideas for you to talk to your neighbors about. First of all, there ought to be a safety net. There's a safety net when it comes to Medicare. I went to Washington to solve problems. I saw a problem in Medicare. Medicare would pay nearly $100,000 for heart surgery but not a dime for the prescription drugs which would prevent the heart surgery from being needed in the first place. That didn't make any sense. It certainly didn't make any sense for our seniors. It didn't make any sense for the taxpayers. We brought Republicans and Democrats together. We modernized Medicare, and our seniors will be getting a prescription drug benefit in the year 2006.

I believe in community health centers, places where the low-income Americans can get primary and preventative care in places other than your emergency rooms. And I believe every poor county in America ought to have a community health center. I believe in a children's health insurance program, but we've got to make sure all those who are eligible are signed up to do so.

But I also understand this reality: 50 percent of the working uninsured work for small businesses. Small businesses are having trouble affording health care. And in order to enable them to be able to better afford health care, I think small business ought to be able to pool risk so they can buy insurance at the same discount big businesses get to do. My opponent opposes that. I think it—I don't think it makes sense. I don't think it's practical, common-sense policy to not enable small businesses to be able to afford health insurance for their employees.

Another problem we have in America, and it's America-wide, is the fact that there's too many lawsuits which are running good docs out of business and running up the costs of your health care. You can't be pro-doctor and pro-patient, pro-hospital and pro-trial-lawyer at the same time. I think you have to choose. My opponent has made his choice, and he put a trial lawyer on the ticket. I made my choice. I'm for medical liability reform—now.

I believe in health savings accounts. We're going to talk about health savings accounts in a minute. A better way for me to describe it is to let somebody who owns one describe what they mean. But really, what they are is a chance for somebody to own their own health care account. And I believe good Government policy will encourage—needs to encourage small businesses to set up health savings accounts for their employees, accounts that you call your own. In a changing world, when people change jobs, it makes sense to have somebody be able to own their own health care account that they can take from job to job and that they can pass on to other generations. See, if you own something in a changing world, you have more stability in your life.

Let me talk about the retirement plans in America. It's really important, in my judgment, to think about ownership in the Social Security system, in order to make sure our younger workers have got a system that is viable. Now, let me make—let me say this to you. In 2000, when I campaigned, I clearly remember some of these television ads saying to our seniors, "If George W. gets in, you're not going to get your check." Well, you got your check. It's not going to happen. It didn't happen in 2000. It's not going to happen in 2005. Seniors will get their checks. Baby boomers, we'll get our checks.

But we need to be worried about our young kids, our children and grandchildren. There's a big bulge of us baby boomers getting ready to retire, and there's not enough people putting money in. That's the issue. And to make sure Social Security is viable for our younger workers, the money in the Social Security trust has got to be earning a higher rate of return. That's why I believe younger workers ought to be able to take some of their own tax money and set it aside in a personal savings account to help fulfill the promise of Social Security, an account they call their own and an account the Government cannot take away.

A couple other things I want to say to you about how to cope in a changing world. The labor laws were designed for yesterday. We need to change them so that people working outside the home are able to have flex-time or comp-time. They're able to be able to store up time so they can better juggle their needs of being a mom and a worker at the same time. The labor laws ought to be family-friendly. The labor laws ought to recognize times have changed and give people flexibility so they can manage both their home and their career.

Right quick about education. First of all, I went to Washington to challenge this system that sometimes, and too many times, just shuffled kids through, grade after grade, year after year without teaching the basics. It is not right to allow a child to go through the school system without having the tools necessary to be able to compete and work in the world of the 21st century. And so I said to Washington, "Let's do things differently. We'll increase Federal spending, particularly for the poor and disadvantaged, but in return, we'll start asking some basic questions, 'Have you taught the child how to read, write, and add and subtract?' "

And so, now, in return for increased Federal money, States must design accountability systems which are able to determine whether or not we're meeting the high standards we've set. You cannot solve a problem until you diagnose it. And so the idea is to determine early in a child's career whether or not he or she can read and correct the reading problem today, before it's too late. We're closing a minority achievement gap in America. The system's working, and we're not going to go back to the old days of no accountability and no excellence in the classrooms, some of the classrooms of America.

But there's more to do, more to do when it comes to education. You know, many of the new jobs of the 21st century require a college degree, but only one in four of our students gets there. That's why I believe we've got to have at-risk programs for high school students so they don't slip behind. We've got to emphasize math and science so that skills—kids have got the skills necessary for the jobs of the 21st century. Over time, I believe there ought to be accountability in the high school systems so we can say we've raised the standards. We need to increase Pell grants for low- and middle-income families. But all this means that more and more of our kids will be able to start their career with a college diploma, will be able to compete in the 21st century.

There's also a skills gap in America. Think about this. In many communities, some communities, the job base is changing from the way it was, of yesterday, and yet, many workers don't have the skills necessary to fill those jobs. We've got a comprehensive program to make sure the worker training programs fulfill the needs of the 21st century. I am a big believer in the community college system, where many of our workers have got the capacity and ability to be able to get the skills necessary to fill the jobs in their own neighborhoods, in their own communities.

And so what I'm telling you is, is I understand this world of ours is changing. And we've got plans to say, in a changing world, the systems of Government will change with it, not to tell people how to live their lives, but to say, "Here's your opportunity." Government can't make somebody be ambitious, but what Government can do is say, "Here's a chance." We'll give you the skills and opportunity to be able to realize the great dreams of this country. That's a hopeful America.

So I'm telling the American people, give me a chance to be President for 4 more years, to build a more hopeful America, an America based upon ownership. Do you realize, under my administration, the home-ownership rate is at an alltime high?

And we're about to talk to a homeowner. But before we do so, I want to talk to— Teresa Slaubaugh is with us. Thanks for coming, Teresa. Glad you're here. You're married?

Teresa Slaubaugh. Yes, I am.

The President. Husband's name, please?

Mrs. Slaubaugh. My husband is Paul Slaubaugh.

The President. Good. He is—[*laughter*]—just getting warmed up. [*Laughter*] How many kids you got?

Mrs. Slaubaugh. I have two beautiful children.

The President. Two beautiful children. Are they here?

Mrs. Slaubaugh. Yes.

The President. Let me see if I can pick them out here. No. [*Laughter*] I've asked Teresa to join us just so people understand what the tax relief meant. Now, when I talk about tax relief, first of all, we cut the taxes on everybody who pays taxes. See, if you pay taxes, you ought to get relief. And secondly, we raised the child credit. Two beautiful children meant that the child credit went up for Teresa and her husband, Paul. It is Paul?

Mrs. Slaubaugh. Yes.

The President. Whew. [*Laughter*] Whooo. [*Laughter*]

This family of four, because of the reduction in rates, the creation of a new rate, the 10-percent bracket, raising the child credit—and oh, by the way, just one other thing before I let Teresa speak—she's probably wondering if she's ever going to get a word in edgewise. [*Laughter*] The code penalizes marriage. It doesn't make any sense to penalize marriage. We ought to have a Tax Code that encourages marriage.

And so, how much relief—how much tax relief did you all get in '03? Do you know? I know. You saved $1,700. That's not a lot in Washington terms, I understand that. Did that mean anything to you and Paul?

Mrs. Slaubaugh. It meant quite a bit to us.

The President. Okay, like how?

Mrs. Slaubaugh. My husband, Paul, works as a high school teacher, and he serves our country as a Navy Reservist.

The President. Great.

Mrs. Slaubaugh. I'm a home-school mom. I'm a stay-at-home mom, and we have benefited from your administration. This has allowed us to purchase curriculum for our son, school supplies for our son. We have been able to supply piano lessons, physical education classes where we have to go outside the home environment to supplement his education. And we've been able to take field trips to various places.

The President. Good. Listen, I think it's important—let me just—this will help me make my point. After Government meets its obligations, after we set priorities and fund them, I think it makes sense to let Teresa and her husband, Paul, keep as much money as possible. She can spend her money better than the Government can spend her money. That's the philosophy. That's our philosophy in this campaign.

And think about what this means. Think about what the tax relief means. I'm so pleased you're here, because it gives me a great example. Think about what it means. It means that as a result of tax relief, the Slaubaugh family has got more choices. It provides more freedom, and they've chosen to educate their child at home. First of all, that's a—it's got to be really hard to be the mom and the teacher,

although moms should be teachers, but this is, mom, teacher, and teacher. [*Laughter*]

And yet, the money is freeing them up to do what they want to do. When you hear me talk about Government policy to create more freedom, that's what I'm talking about. They have the freedom to be able to make a choice that they want to choose, and I want to thank the Congress for making sure that the child credit, the 10-percent bracket, and the marriage penalty relief that we passed was made permanent for 5 more years. I appreciate your work. [*Applause*]

Wait a minute. Hold on. We've got a lot more work to do yet.

So one of the things I love is to hear a story about somebody who said, "I've started my own business." I think one of the—I know one of the strengths of this country of ours is the small-business sector of our economy, and today we've got Grant Milliron with us. [*Applause*] Pretty well known, evidently. Pretty soon you'll be running for mayor.

Grant E. Milliron. You never know.

The President. That's right. So tell the people at what age you started your business.

Mr. Milliron. I was 18 years old, and I was 9 days away from my 19th birthday. [*Laughter*]

The President. You talk about the entrepreneurial spirit, I mean—I can't tell you how many people I've talked to that said, "Well, I started my business at the kitchen table," or "in my garage." I don't know where you started yours?

Mr. Milliron. Very similar. We started with one acre of property and 12 automobiles.

The President. Really? So what do you do? Give people a sense of what your business does.

[*Mr. Milliron, president, Milliron Iron & Metal, Inc., made brief remarks.*]

The President. There you go. [*Applause*] Hold on. Hold on. He's doing great. A couple of points. He said something interesting; I want to remind you. He said, "Your policies have meant a lot to us recently." And he talked about capital-intensive business—that means machines, got to buy equipment. And one of the things he's referring to is the fact that we provided incentives for small businesses to make purchases and investments, and there's a reason why. I'll get to it in a minute.

So with this incentive, did you buy anything? What did you buy?

Mr. Milliron. We certainly have. We began a program in late 2003 of reentering the solid waste business. I was in that business too for about 15 years. The first thing we did is buy three brand new trucks. Those trucks are very expensive. We spent almost a half-a-million dollars for three trucks.

The President. Somebody had to make the trucks. See, he said—what the tax policy did was it increased demand; that good tax policy says to Grant, "Here's something to help you in the decisionmaking process," which is to make a capital investment. When he decides to make the capital investment, somebody has to make it for him. That's how the economy works. His decision, based upon tax relief, caused somebody else to be able to work and, at the same time, meant his own workers were more productive. That's why good tax policy is—that's how good tax policy happens.

Go ahead. How many workers have you got?

Mr. Milliron. In one company, the iron and metal company, we had 23 people going into the first of this year. We have added seven people. And once our shredder operation is up and running, we know we'll be hiring six or eight more people.

The President. Think about that. That's what's happening in this economy. Grant's got optimism. He sees a brighter future. He's making some capital investments to make his business more competitive, and he's hiring people. He's added seven people. He says he's going to add seven more.

It's happening all over America. The small-business sector of this country is leading this recovery. Seventy percent of new jobs are created by small-business owners just like Grant. Isn't that right?

[*Mr. Milliron made further remarks.*]

The President. See, the small-business sector of this economy is leading the recovery. But I want to tell you something interesting and why my opponent's policies are wrong, in my judgment. Grant's company is a Subchapter S. That means he pays tax at the individual income-tax level. About 90 percent of the small businesses pay individual income tax. They don't pay corporate tax. They pay individual tax. That's because they're a Subchapter S corporation or a sole proprietorship. So when you hear my opponent saying, "Oh, we're just going to tax the rich," remember this. Thousands of small-business companies are the so-called rich, in his vernacular. It makes no economic sense to tax this man as this economy is recovering. He just said he's thinking about hiring seven more people. It is less likely that Grant will hire people if he knows his taxes are going up.

Good economic policy rewards investment, rewards risktaking, and honors the fact that 70 percent of new jobs in this country are created by small-business owners just like Grant. John Kerry's economic policies will hurt this economy. You ready? Good job, thank you.

Joanna Williams. How are you?

Joanna Williams. Good.

The President. You are married to Taylor?

Mrs. Williams. Exactly. Very good.

The President. Where is old Taylor?

Mrs. Williams. Oh, he's right back there.

The President. Oh, yes. Hey, Taylor.

Mrs. Williams. You just made his day.

The President. I made his day. Well, I'm trying to get him on TV. [*Laughter*] Give him a, "Hi, Mom," Taylor. [*Laughter*]

I've asked Joanna here and Taylor, because, guess what? They bought their first home this year, isn't that right?

Mrs. Williams. Yes, we did.

The President. I told you homeownership rates are at an alltime high. And so, what was it like?

Mrs. Williams. To buy our home?

The President. Yes.

[*Mrs. Williams made brief remarks.*]

The President. Yes, one reason why people are able to afford homes today is because of—mortgage rates are low. Interest rates are low. This is not the effect of—this is caused by the Federal Reserve Board. I can't claim credit for that. But I can claim credit for this, a policy—a tax policy which left more money in the hands of those that earned it.

I presume that tax relief helped you afford the downpayment?

Mrs. Williams. Yes, it did. And it also helped with Noah's nursery, and we did home renovations around the house too.

The President. Yes, see? Did you have to buy something to do the home renovation?

Mrs. Williams. The home? [*Laughter*]

The President. No, I know. To do the renovation in the home. You had to buy the home, that's for sure. [*Laughter*]

Mrs. Williams. No hard questions. [*Laughter*]

The President. Did you go to your local store and—[*laughter*].

Mrs. Williams. Yes. Yes. [*Laughter*]

The President. You did? That's called stimulating demand. The tax relief helped them buy the home; it helped them renovate their home. And when they renovated the home, they had to buy something to renovate it with. That's how it works. That's how the economy works. That's why you want to unleash the individual decisionmaking. See, the economy works on the decisions made by consumers, not by Government people. That's how it works.

And so this good family's decisionmaking was affected by good tax policy. And she owns her own home. We've got plans that encourage others to own their own home. We've got a downpayment plan to help those who can't afford downpayments. We've got counseling programs to help people understand the fine print. You know, a lot of first-time homebuyers—I don't know if that affected you or not—but they take a look at that contract; you know, "I'm not so sure I want to sign." You need a magnifying glass to read the print. And so we've got counselors to help people, first-time homebuyers, to understand the contracts they're signing.

I love it when, in this country, more and more people are opening up the door where they live and saying, "Welcome to my home. Welcome to my piece of property."

Good job. Thanks for coming. Give Noah a hug.

Mrs. Williams. I will.

The President. Kevin is with us. He is—what do you do, Kevin?

Kevin McElligott. I'm an insurance agent.

The President. Good. So you know something about that which you're able to talk about.

Mr. McElligott. Well, property and casualty, but I do work with health care.

The President. Yes. Anyway, he's the owner of a health savings account. Explain to people what that means.

Mr. McElligott. It's an insurance policy. It's a high deductible, around $4,000. We recently just got a couple quotes, conventional versus HSA. Conventional is approximately 50 percent higher. My employer—thank you—takes that money in savings and gives it back to my family in a bank account that we can use for our deductible.

The President. Yes, okay, let me—let me help. [*Laughter*] He owns one. I don't yet. So what he's saying is, is that they purchased a high deductible insurance policy. In his case—I mean, you can get all kinds of deductibles—but in his case, they've chosen a 4,000—is that right——

Mr. McElligott. Correct.

The President. ——dollar deductible, meaning the insurance pays the cost of health care above $4,000. And when you have a high deductible policy, it costs you a lot less than a regular insurance policy does. In other words, you——

Mr. McElligott. About 50 percent.

The President. Fifty percent. So what does it cost you a month for your high deductible, roughly?

Mr. McElligott. Four hundred and ninety dollars a month.

The President. Yes. So the other one would have been——

Mr. McElligott. Seven hundred and forty.

The President. Something like that. So, in other words, you start paying this to buy this high deductible. And so you say to yourself what about—what happens between zero and 4,000, in his case? And what they've done, and what anybody in America can now do because of the new law, is set up a savings account that you call your own. Your company helps you with the savings?

Mr. McElligott. They take the money that they save from the conventional, from the HSA, and puts that right in your account.

The President. So they put it in an account. So here he's got—think about this now—a family has got $4,000 of cash, earning interest tax-free—it's put in the account tax-free; it comes out tax-free—that they call their own. If they have expenses above $4,000, the insurance policy kicks in. The company contributes the money into the account. Think about, now, what this means. It means he controls the decisionmaking process, not some, you know, insurance executive or insurance worker somewhere. But Kevin and his family makes the decisions.

If there—spends less than $4,000 in the year, the money rolls over to the next year tax-free. It's his money at this point in time.

He owns the account. If he changed jobs, the account goes with him. This is a new way for health insurance that does a lot of interesting things. It makes sure Kevin is the decisionmaker. Is that right?

Mr. McElligott. Yes, we have the freedom to choose which doctor, which hospital, which pharmacy we use.

The President. It's very important. Secondly, it provides an interesting incentive, doesn't it, for he and his family to make healthy choices, like walking every day or running every day or swimming every—exercising. It's proven that if you take time out to exercise, you'll have less disease. And as less disease happens, he's got more money in his account. This is an account that makes sure the decisionmaking is between Kevin and the doctors, not between bureaucrats in Washington, DC. What else can you say about it?

Mr. McElligott. Well, I have a wife and three kids. Just to let you know, we use our health care. I have a 3-year-old, Jack, 8-year-old, Laura, and a 10-year-old, Chris, so we do use the doctor. And we've been on this for 3 years, and I don't have one nickel out-of-pocket for medical care in 3 years.

The President. Yes, I want people to look at these.

Mr. McElligott. My wife, Michelle.

The President. It's a different way of doing things, as opposed to the Government telling him what to do or an insurance company saying, "Oh, we'll just cover it." The decisionmaking process is essential to making sure health care is available and is affordable. And this is a way to make sure people are directly involved with health care decisions. I urge everybody, small-business owners out there to look at these plans. It's a way to make sure health care is affordable for your workers. And we're going to make sure that low-income Americans have access to this, providing refundable tax credits that they can use in a health savings account. It's much better if somebody owns their own health account, than be reliant upon the Government for health care. It's much better for the system, and it's much better for the patient. Good job.

A couple of other things. In a changing world, things shouldn't change. We stand for a culture of life in which every person matters and every person counts. We stand for marriage and family, which are the foundations of this society. I also stand for putting Federal judges on the bench who know the difference between their personal opinion and the strict interpretation of the law. Okay.

Audience members. Four more years! Four more years! Four more years!

The President. Thank you all. Let me talk about one other subject. I want to talk about how to make sure this country is safer. I want to share some of the lessons I learned on September the 11th. First of all, that we face a determined enemy that has no conscience. These are—these people are—I call them ideologues of hate. They've hijacked a religion in order to justify their brutal vision of the world, and they are determined, and they are tough. The best way to do our duty to protect this country is to fight them overseas so we do not have to face them here at home, is to stay on the offense, never relent, use every asset at our disposal.

Second lesson of September the 11th is that this is a different kind of war. I wish I wasn't talking about war. It's a war that came on our shores. We didn't ask for it. Nobody wanted it, but it's the calling of our time, to protect this country. It's a different kind of war than we're used to. We face these ideologues who will hide in the cities or caves, and therefore, a doctrine—I laid out a doctrine that said, "You can't harbor these people. If you do, you're just as guilty." In order to protect ourselves, we have said to people around the world, "You will be held to account."

Now, when the President has said something, in order to sure this world stays peaceful, he better mean what he says.

That's why, in the course of politics, you can't keep changing your position. You can't react to the political situation and say, "Well, now I believe this," or, "I believe that." There has to be a steadiness when it comes to securing this country. And so when I said, "If you harbor terrorists," I was speaking directly to the Taliban who had been harboring Al Qaida—as a matter of fact, thousands trained in Afghanistan— I meant what I said. They didn't believe me, and they're no longer in power, and the world is better off for it.

I want you to think about what's happening in Afghanistan. Three years ago or a little over 3 years ago, many young girls didn't get to go to school because the Taliban had such a dim vision of the world. Women were taken into the public square and whipped, or sports stadiums and killed if they didn't adhere to the strict doctrine of hatefulness. That was the reality and the truth. Plus, they were dangerous, dangerous because Al Qaida, the parasite, was slowly but surely taking over the host.

Today, in Afghanistan, 10 million citizens, 41 percent of whom are women, have registered to vote in a Presidential election that will take place in 10 days. As a matter of fact, I think it's a week from today. If I'm not mistaken, the election is a week from today. I could be corrected. But think about that. People that once lived in darkness are now living in light. Freedom is coming to Afghanistan, and it's important for our future to understand the ramifications of a free Afghanistan. First of all, it serves as a beacon for others to see. Secondly, we now have an ally in the war on terror, not an enemy.

And in Iraq, it's been tough work there, just like the tough decision I had to make, which is the third lesson of September the 11th. When we see a threat, we must deal with it before it materializes. If we see a—this is an important lesson to remember—prior to September the 11th, it used to be we'd see a threat and say, "Well, we may deal with it or may not deal with it, but it certainly can't come home to hurt us." That changed on that day. Our history changed. It's essential that the President and the people of this country never forget that threats must be dealt with before they fully materialize.

I saw a threat in Saddam Hussein. I'll tell you why I saw a threat. First, he was a sworn enemy of the United States of America. We had been to war with Saddam Hussein. He was shooting missiles at our pilots who were enforcing the world's sanctions. He had terrorist connections, Abu Nidal, Abu Abbas. Zarqawi was in and out of Baghdad. He ordered the killing of an American citizen from Baghdad, Foley. This is before the—before we went in. Saddam Hussein had used weapons of mass destruction. I understood—I understand today that the connection between weapons of mass destruction and the terrorist network is the biggest threat we face.

So I saw a threat. And I went to the Congress. And they looked at the same intelligence I looked at and concluded Saddam was a threat, and they authorized the use of force. My opponent looked at the same intelligence and voted yes when it came time to authorize the use of force. I guess it matters what the definition of yes is in his mind. [*Laughter*]

Before the Commander in Chief commits troops into harm's way, he must try everything else, and I did. I understood the consequences of putting our kids in harm's way. That's why I went to the United Nations, and I said, "Well, here's a threat." They looked at the same intelligence and, as they had 16 different times, passed another resolution. And the resolution said, "Disclose, disarm, or face serious consequences." A President must mean what he says; international bodies must mean what they say, too, in order to make this world a peaceful place.

Saddam Hussein just didn't pay attention to it. He wasn't interested in resolutions. Why should he be? The first 16 didn't mean anything to him. My opponent the

other night said, "Well, we should have passed another resolution." What, the 18th resolution is going to all the sudden make sense to Saddam Hussein? No, he's just waiting for the world to turn a blind eye.

We didn't find the stockpiles we found— that we thought would be there. We thought they'd be there. Everybody thought they'd be. But he had that capability of making those weapons. And when the world turned a blind eye, you can bet he would have.

So the U.N. obviously wasn't interested in—I mean, Saddam wasn't interested in listening to the U.N. Diplomacy wasn't working. The other night, my opponent said, "Well, we should have let the inspectors work." The inspectors were being deceived. The facts are, as David Kay pointed out, the reality on the ground was that the inspectors were being deceived. How can the inspectors work if they're being deceived? So I have a choice at this time. Diplomacy has failed. Saddam Hussein is basically thumbing his nose at the world again, and the choice is this: Do I take the word of a madman, do I hope for the best with Saddam Hussein, do I forget the lessons of September the 11th, or take action necessary to defend this country? Given that choice, I will defend our country every time. [*Applause*]

Thank you all.

In the debate Thursday night, my opponent continued his pattern of confusing contradictions about Iraq. After voting for the war and after saying my decision to remove Saddam Hussein from power was right, he says, now, "It was all a mistake." He's changing. Then he was asked if our troops were dying for a mistake. He said, "No." See, you can't have it both ways. You can't say it was a mistake and then it was not a mistake. You can't be getting—you can't be for getting rid of Saddam Hussein when things look good and against it when things look bad. You can't claim that terrorists are pouring across the border into Iraq, yet at the same time, try to claim that Iraq is a grand diversion from the war against terror. A President cannot keep changing his mind. A President must be consistent. A President must speak clearly, and a President must mean what he says. [*Applause*]

Thank you all.

A couple of other things. A couple of other things.

Audience member. We love you, George!

The President. In the debate, my opponent said something really revealing when he laid out the Kerry doctrine. He said that America has to pass a "global test" before we can use American troops to defend ourselves.

Audience members. Boo-o-o!

The President. You might remember that part of the debate, what he said. See, Senator Kerry's approach to foreign policy would give foreign governments veto power over national security decisions. I have a different view. When our country is in danger, it's not the President's job to take an international poll. It's the President's job to defend this country. I work hard with our friends and allies. I just talked to my friend Tony Blair on the bus coming into Mansfield. We'll continue working with our friends and allies for the sake of freedom and peace, but our national security decisions will be made in the Oval Office, not in foreign capitals.

A couple of other points I want to make for you. The—we've got to support our military when they're in harm's way. It's really important. We owe it to the troops in uniform. We owe it to their loved ones too. That's why I went to the United States Congress and asked for $87 billion of supplemental funding in September of '03, and the response was great. Members of both political parties understood that we needed to support our troops in harm's way and voted overwhelmingly for my request. Four United States Senators voted for the authorization of force and against funding, four of a hundred, two of whom are my opponent and his runningmate. [*Laughter*]

Think about that, four Members said, "Yes, we'll authorize force, but we're not going to give you what you need." That's politics, isn't it? So they asked him, they said, "Well, why?" And he said, "Well, I actually did vote for the $87 billion, before I voted against it." [*Laughter*] Amazing statement. [*Laughter*] The other night he said it was a mistake to say it. No, the mistake was not voting yes to fund our troops. That was the mistake.

Somebody said, "Well, you know, this war of yours is creating more enemy." The enemy was plotting before we went into Iraq and Afghanistan. The enemy was being trained in Afghanistan. These ideologues of hate do not need an excuse for their killing. They're trying to shake our will, is what they're trying to do. They want us to withdraw.

We will stay on the offense against them two ways. One, we use every asset at our disposal. Our troops are doing a great job in Iraq. They are—and they're helping us implement our strategy. Our strategy was to transfer sovereignty, which we did early, to a Government run by a strong leader in Prime Minister Allawi. Our strategy is to train Iraqis so they can fight these folks who are trying to stop the advance of freedom, and we're making progress. We've trained 100,000. We'll have 125,000 trained by the end of this year, and these soldiers are doing good work. Look on your TV screens, what's taking place in Samarra. The Iraqi soldiers are working hard, and you shouldn't be surprised. They want to live in freedom. They understand a free society will mean a hopeful society for their children.

There's a reason why Zarqawi and others are fighting. They can't stand the thought of freedom. They understand how powerful a free society will be in contrast to their dark view of the world. The best way to defeat terrorism in the long term is to defeat hopelessness and poverty by spreading liberty and freedom, and that's why this battle is taking place in Iraq. And that's why it's important signal to our troops. The President should never send mixed signals. We should never send confusing signals to friends and foe alike.

We'll continue our rebuilding efforts to help these people get up and going. We've got $7 million obligated to be spent over the next months. There will be elections in January. It's one thing to be realistic, but I think you can be realistic and optimistic. I believe we're going to succeed. As a matter of fact, I'm confident we'll succeed so long as we don't lose our will. And when we succeed, we'll have done our duty to protect America. Not only will we have removed a tyrant that had been a source of great instability and danger to our country, we will have helped a country grow in democracy. And that's important, because I believe in the power of liberty to transform societies.

I tell people this so people can understand better what I'm talking about. I've got a great relationship with Prime Minister Koizumi of Japan, an interesting guy. I saw him in New York a while ago at the U.N., and I said, "I'm telling people in our country about our relationship. Do you mind?" He said, "No, not at all. It's okay." He likes Elvis. [*Laughter*] I didn't tell him that part. I don't think he would mind. Do you mind, friend? Anyway, it's interesting to think about this conversation—these conversations we have with him, though, in this context. Fifty years ago, we were fighting the Japanese. Think about that. They were a sworn enemy of the United States of America. Fifty years isn't all that long, unless, of course, you're 58 years old, which seems like—[*laughter*]—seems like an eternity. [*Laughter*]

Anyway, so we were at war with a sworn enemy. My dad fought there. I'm sure, confident, other relatives of yours fought there as well. And yet, after that war was over, Harry S. Truman and others said, "Why don't we help Japan become a democracy so it becomes a peaceful part of the world?" There were skeptics in America

then, of course. You can imagine, many of the families were saying, "Wait a minute." Many of the families of the deceased were saying, "Wait a minute. Why would we want to help an enemy that killed my loved one become a democracy? Why would we want to help them at all?" But we had a belief that still stands today, that liberty can transform societies, liberty can cause an enemy to become a friend.

And so, today, I sit down with Prime Minister Koizumi talking about the peace we all want, talking about how to make this world a more peaceful place. Someday, an American President will be sitting down with the duly elected leader of Iraq talking about the peace in the greater Middle East. And our children and our grandchildren will be better off for it.

I believe people throughout the world long to live in free societies. I believe the women of the Middle East want to be free. I believe if given a chance, people will choose the form of government which enables people to better realize their dream, democracy. I believe all these things not because freedom is America's gift to the world—it's not—freedom is the Almighty God's gift to each man and woman in this world.

And so I've come here to Mansfield, Ohio. I've come here to let you know I've got a reason for asking for the vote again. I clearly see where this country needs to go. I strongly believe that when I get 4 more years, this country will be a safer place, a stronger place, and a better place for everybody who lives here.

Thanks for coming. On to victory. God bless.

NOTE: The President spoke at 12:15 p.m. at the Renaissance Theater. In his remarks, he referred to Robert T. Bennett, chairman, Ohio Republican Party; Senator Zell Miller of Georgia, who made the keynote address at the 2004 Republican National Convention; senior Al Qaida associate Abu Musab Al

Zarqawi; David Kay, former CIA Special Advisor for Strategy Regarding Iraqi Weapons of Mass Destruction Programs; Prime Minister Tony Blair of the United Kingdom; Prime Minister Ayad Allawi of the Iraqi Interim Government; and Prime Minister Junichiro Koizumi of Japan. A portion of these remarks could not be verified because the tape was incomplete.

Remarks in Cuyahoga Falls, Ohio
October 2, 2004

The President. Thank you all for coming.

Audience members. Four more years! Four more years! Four more years!

The President. Thank you all. The sun is shining on Ohio. I'm thrilled to be here. I am the first sitting President ever to come to this fine city. The rest of them missed a great place. I'm so proud you all came out today.

I'm so honored to be standing up here with Chuck Canterbury to receive the endorsement of the Fraternal Order of the Police. It means a lot to get the endorsement from those who serve our country on a daily basis to make it safe. I'm proud of that endorsement. I want to thank Jim Pasco and Nick DiMarco as well as all the Fraternal Order of Police folks standing behind me.

I want to thank you all for coming. I'm here to ask for your vote. We're getting closer and closer to election day, and I'm here to ask for your help as well. Go out and register your friends and your neighbors. Tell them they have a duty in America to vote. In a free society, we have an obligation to go to the polls. Make sure you don't overlook those discerning Democrats, either—*[laughter]*—like Zell Miller. Or my friend the mayor of Youngstown, Ohio, George McKelvey. I'm proud you're here, Mr. Mayor. I'm proud to call you friend, and I'm proud to call you supporter. Thanks for coming.

Then after you get them registered to vote, get them headed to the polls. And remind them that if they want a safer America, a stronger America, and a better America, to put me and Dick Cheney back in office.

Listen, I have one regret, and that is that Laura isn't here with me.

Audience members. Aw-w-w!

The President. Yes, I know. I hear it all the time, "Why didn't you send Laura, and you stay at home?" *[Laughter]* True story. She said, "Fine, I'll marry you," when I asked her, but she said, "I don't ever want to have to give a speech." *[Laughter]* I said, "You got a deal." *[Laughter]* Fortunately, she didn't hold me to my word. The country got to see Laura speaking in New York City at that convention. They got to see a strong, decent, fine woman. Laura is a great First Lady. I'm really proud of her. I'm going to give you some reasons to put me back in, but perhaps the most important one of all is so that Laura is the First Lady for 4 more years.

And I'm proud of my Vice President, Dick Cheney. He's warming up. *[Laughter]* He'll be right around the corner pretty soon. He's not going to have the waviest hair on the set. *[Laughter]* I didn't pick him for his hair. *[Laughter]* I picked him because of his judgment and his sound experience. Dick Cheney is getting the job done for the American people.

I'm proud of your United States Senator Mike DeWine. Thanks for coming, Mike. I'm honored you're here. Speaking about Senators, you've got another good one in George Voinovich. You need to put him back in. He's doing Ohio good work. He's a good, solid man, a good, decent fellow. I want to thank Congressman Ralph Regula for being with us today too. Thank you, Chairman. I'm glad you're here.

Lieutenant Governor Jennette Bradley is with us. Today is her birthday. Yes. What a great way to celebrate your birthday. [*Laughter*]

I want to thank the mayor, Don Robart, who is here. Mr. Mayor, my only advice, my only advice—I know you didn't ask for any—but my only advice is, fill the potholes. [*Laughter*]

I want to thank the high school band that's here. Appreciate you coming. But most of all, thank you all. I want to thank those who work at the grassroots level for putting up the signs and making the phone calls. I appreciate you. I want to thank you for what you have done and what you're going to do coming down the stretch. With your help, there is no doubt in my mind we will carry Ohio again and win a great victory in November.

And I'm looking forward to this campaign. I love coming to your State. I've been spending some quality time here. [*Laughter*] I like to come because I want to tell people where I stand, what I believe, and where I'm going to lead this Nation.

I believe every child can learn and every school can teach. I went to Washington to challenge what I've called the soft bigotry of low expectations. That's a system that, in some cases, passes children through, grade after grade, year after year, without learning the basics. It's not right. It's not right for our country. We've raised the standards. We're now measuring early, so we can solve problems before they're too late. I believe in local control of schools. We're closing an achievement gap in America, and we're not going to go back to the old days.

I believe we have a moral responsibility to honor our seniors with good health care. I went to Washington to solve problems, not to pass them on to future Presidents and future generations. I saw a problem in Medicare. Medicine had changed, but Medicare hadn't. You know, we pay $100,000 or so for a heart surgery for a Medicare patient but not one dime for the prescription drugs to prevent the heart surgery from being needed in the first place. That doesn't make any sense for our seniors. It doesn't make any sense for the taxpayers. I brought Republicans and Democrats together. I signed a bill that modernizes Medicare. Seniors will get prescription drugs in 2006, and we're not going to go back to the old days.

I believe in the energy and innovative spirit of our workers, our small-business owners, our farmers, our ranchers, and that's why we unleashed that energy with the largest tax relief in a generation.

When you're out gathering up the vote, remind your friends and neighbors about what this economy has been through. The stock market started to decline before Dick Cheney and I got to Washington. Then we had a recession. Then we had some citizens forget what it means to be a responsible American. They didn't tell the truth. We passed tough laws. It is abundantly clear now in America, we will not tolerate dishonesty in the boardrooms of our country. And then the enemy hit us. And that hurt us. That hurt our economy. You know it hurt the economy.

But this economy is strong, and it is getting stronger. We've been growing at rates as fast as any in nearly 20 years. It's growing because of the spirit of the people. It's growing because of those tax cuts. We've added 1.7 million new jobs last year. We've added 107,000 manufacturing jobs since January. The national unemployment rate is 5.4 percent, which is lower than the average of the 1970s, the 1980s, and the 1990s.

There's still work to do in parts of Ohio. I understand that. That's why I support opportunity zones, places like Summit County, to give companies relief and incentives so that they can expand to places where the manufacturing sector has been hurt. No, there are things we're going to do, but this economy is strong, and it's growing stronger. We're not going to go back to the old days of tax and spend.

I believe the most solemn duty of the President is to protect the American people. If America shows uncertainty or weakness in this decade, the world will drift toward tragedy. This will not happen on my watch.

I'm running for President with a clear and positive plan to build a safer world and a more hopeful America. I am running with a compassionate conservative philosophy that Government should help people improve their lives, not try to run their lives. I believe this Nation wants steady, consistent, principled leadership, and that is why with your help, we're going to win a great victory in November.

Audience members. Four more years! Four more years! Four more years!

The President. The world in which we live and work is changing. I understand that. The generation of our dads and granddads, a man generally had one job and one career, and the company he worked for paid for the pension plan and health care. This world we're living in is different. The workforce is changing. Women are working inside the house and now outside the house. And many workers change careers and jobs over their lifetime.

And yet, the most fundamental of our systems, the Tax Code, health coverage, pension plans, and worker training, were created for yesterday, not tomorrow. I am running to change those systems so all citizens are equipped, prepared, and thus truly free to make your own choices so you can pursue your own dreams.

Now, I understand that a hopeful society is one that has got a growing economy. If we want to keep jobs here in America and expand the job base, America must be the best place in the world to do business. That means less regulations on our businessowners. That means we got to do something about these frivolous lawsuits that plague our small businesses.

If we want to keep jobs here, if we want to—Congress needs to pass my energy plan. It is a plan that encourages conservation. It is a plan that encourages the use of renewables like ethanol and biodiesel. It is a plan that says we'll explore technologies to make sure we consume energy in different ways. It is a plan that encourages clean coal technology. It is a plan that allows us to explore for natural gas in environmentally friendly ways. It is a plan that recognizes, to keep jobs here in America, we must be less dependent on foreign sources of energy.

To keep jobs in this country, we've got to reject economic isolationism. See, we've opened up our markets—just not me. Other Presidents, as well, from both parties, have opened up our markets because it's good for you, the consumer. See, if you've got more products to choose from, you're likely to get that which you want at a better price and higher quality. That's how the market works. And so what I'm saying to places like China, "You treat us the way we treat you." Opening up markets is good for our workers. It's good for our farmers. See, we can compete with anybody, anywhere, anytime, so long as the rules are fair.

To make sure we keep jobs here, we've got to be wise about how we spend your money in Washington, and we've got to keep your taxes low. Taxes are an issue in this campaign. I'll tell you why. The fellow I'm running against has so far proposed $2.2 trillion in new spending. Yes.

Audience members. Boo-o-o!

The President. No, I know. That's a lot, even for a Senator from Massachusetts. So they asked him how he's going to pay for it, and he said, "Well, we're just going to tax the rich." We've heard that before, haven't we? Let me tell you a couple things wrong with this "tax the rich."

First of all, you can't raise enough money by taxing the rich to pay for $2.2 trillion.

You raise about $680 billion. Therefore, there is a tax gap. Guess who always gets to fill the tax gap? Yes, you do. "Tax the rich," yes, we've heard it. The rich hire lawyers and accountants for a reason, because they want to stick you with the bill. We're not going to let John Kerry tax you; we're going to win in November.

Now that we're on taxes, let me say something about the Tax Code. It's a complicated mess. It's a million pages long. It takes 6 billion hours a year to fill out the tax forms in this country. In a new term, I'm going to bring Republicans and Democrats together to simplify this Tax Code so it's more fair for you.

In a changing world, the skills that are required for the jobs of the 21st century change. We have a skills gap in America in some communities. Some jobs are gone; new jobs arrive. In order to help our workers, I'm a big believer in the community college system, to make the systems available so people can gain the skills necessary to fill the jobs of the 21st century. As well in a changing world, most new jobs filled by people—are filled by people with at least 2 years of college, yet, one in four of our students gets there. That's why I believe in early intervention programs in high school to help our at-risk students. That's why I know we've got to place a new focus on math and science. Over time, we'll require a rigorous exam before graduation. See, by raising the performance in our high schools and by expanding Pell grants for low- and middle-income families, more Americans will start their career with a college diploma.

In this time of change, we've got to do something about the health care system. There's a big difference in this campaign on health care. You listen carefully to what my opponent's laying out, and it says one thing: The Federal Government's going to run it.

Audience members. Boo-o-o!

The President. I want you to run it. I want you to be the decisionmaker. So

here's some practical ways to help. First of all, we'll take care of the poor and the needy by expanding community health centers all around the country. We have a duty and an obligation to do so. It makes sense that those folks get good health care in these centers and not in the emergency rooms of our hospitals. Secondly, we'll continue to expand the children's health care program for low-income Americans.

In order to make sure health care is available and affordable, we're going to help our small-business owners. One-half of the uninsured, currently uninsured, work for small businesses. There's a reason why, small businesses can't afford health care. They ought to be allowed to pool together their risk so they can buy insurance at the same discount big businesses can. That makes sense. That's a commonsense way to make sure the control of health care is in your hands. My opponent opposes that.

I'll tell you another thing we need to do to make sure health care is available and affordable. We've got to do something about these junk lawsuits that are running up the cost of medicine and running good doctors out of practice. You cannot be pro-doctor, pro-patient, pro-hospital, and pro-trial-lawyer at the same time. See, I think you have to make a choice. My opponent made his choice, and he put a trial lawyer on the ticket.

Audience members. Boo-o-o!

The President. I made my choice. I'm standing with the docs and patients. I'm for medical liability reform—now. In all we do, we'll make sure the medical decisions are made by doctors and patients, not by bureaucrats in Washington, DC.

In a changing society, it helps bring stability in people's life if they own something. The homeownership rate under my administration is the highest it's ever been in America. Over the next 4 years, we'll continue to expand the homeownership policies to every corner of America. I love the idea of somebody opening up the door where they live and saying, "Welcome to my home. Welcome to my piece of property."

As well, we've got to think different about our retirement systems. You might remember the 2000 campaign, when people said, "Well, if George W. gets in, they're going to take away your Social Security check." You still got your check, didn't you? So here's my message to our seniors: Don't worry about what they tell you in the campaign; the Social Security obligation will be fulfilled. And for us baby boomers, there's enough money in the system to take care of us.

But because there's a lot of baby boomers getting ready to retire, we need to worry about our children and our grandchildren when it comes to Social Security. I believe younger workers ought to be allowed to take some of their own tax money and set up a personal savings account that they can call their own, that the Government cannot take away.

In this world of change, there are some things that do not change, the values we try to live by, courage and compassion, reverence and integrity. In changing times, we'll support the institutions that give our lives direction and purpose, our families, our schools, our religious congregations. We believe in a culture of life in which every person matters and every being counts. We stand for marriage and family, which are the foundations of our society. We stand for the appointment of Federal judges who know the difference between personal opinion and the strict interpretation of the law.

This election will also determine how America responds to the continuing danger of terrorism. Since the terrible morning of September the 11th, 2001, we've fought the terrorists across the Earth, not for pride, not for power, but because the lives of our citizens are at stake. Our strategy is clear. We're defending the homeland. We're reforming and strengthening our intelligence services. We're strengthening our All-Volunteer Army, which will remain an all-volunteer army. We are staying on the offensive. We are striking the terrorists abroad so we do not have to face them here at home.

We will continue to spread freedom and liberty in the broader Middle East and around the world, and we will prevail. Our strategy is—see, you think about the world the way it was a while back. Afghanistan was the home base of Al Qaida; Pakistan was a transit point for terrorist groups; Saudi Arabia was fertile ground for terrorist fundraising; Libya was secretly pursuing nuclear weapons; Iraq was a gathering danger; and Al Qaida was largely unchallenged as it planned attacks.

Because we acted, a free Afghanistan is fighting terror; Pakistan is capturing terrorist leaders; Saudi Arabia is making arrests; Libya is dismantling its weapons programs; the army of a free Iraq is fighting for freedom; and more than three-quarters of Al Qaida have been brought to justice. We've led. Many have joined, and America and the world are safer.

This progress involved careful diplomacy, clear moral purpose, and some tough decisions. And the toughest came on Iraq. Saddam Hussein was a threat. We knew his record of aggression, support for terrorist organizations. Saddam Hussein used weapons of mass destruction. He fired missiles at our pilots which were enforcing the world's sanctions. He slaughtered his own people. Saddam Hussein was a threat. And after September the 11th, we must always remember, we must take threats seriously, before the fully materialize.

That is the reality of the world in which we live. I recognized that reality, and I went to the Congress. Congress debated the issue. They voted overwhelmingly to authorize the use of force. They had looked at the same intelligence I did, remembered the same history I did, and voted overwhelmingly for force. My opponent looked at the same intelligence I did, and when the vote came to authorize force, he voted yes. I guess now it depends on what the meaning of "yes" is in his mind.

Audience members. Flip-flop! Flip-flop! Flip-flop!

The President. Before the Commander in Chief commits our troops into harm's way, he must try every other alternative. And so I went to the United Nations hoping that diplomacy would work. The United Nations debated the issue and voted 15 to nothing, the U.N. Security Council, to say to Saddam Hussein, "Disclose, disarm, or face serious consequences." I believe when an international body speaks, it must mean what it says.

As he had for 16 other resolutions, Saddam Hussein ignored the United Nations. The other night, my opponent suggested we probably should have passed the 18th resolution. [*Laughter*] What good would a resolution do after he ignored the first 17? As he had for a decade, he wasn't about to listen to the demands of the free world. As a matter of fact, when they sent inspectors in—it is now a fact that Saddam Hussein was systematically deceiving the inspectors. Part of my opponent's plan, as articulated in Miami, said, "Well, we should have let the inspectors work." They weren't working. He was deceiving them. He was hoping the world would turn away. So I had a choice to make at this point in time: Do I take the word of a madman, forget the lessons of September the 11th, or take action to defend this country? Given that choice, I will defend America every time.

We didn't find the stockpiles we all thought were there. But remember, Saddam Hussein had the capability of making weapons of mass destruction. He could have passed that capability onto a terrorist enemy, and that was a risk we could not afford to take after September the 11th. Knowing what I know today, I would have made the same decision. America and the world are better off with Saddam in a prison cell.

Because we acted to defend our country, 50 million people now live in freedom in Afghanistan and Iraq. I want you to remind your friends and neighbors about the Af-

ghan story. You realize, almost 3½ years ago, the Taliban, these ideologues of hate, would not yet—let many young girls go to school. Imagine a society in which young girls weren't allowed to go to school. When their mothers didn't toe the line on their ideology, they'd take them in the public square and whip them. Sometimes, they shot them in the sports stadium. It was a dismal, dark society.

Today, 10 million Afghan citizens have registered to vote, 41 percent of whom are women, and they're having a Presidential election later on this month. Think about that. Freedom is powerful. Freedom has converted a society that was dark and gloomy to one of hope and light.

In Iraq, there's a brave Prime Minister named Prime Minister Allawi. They're going to have elections in January. It's hard work there. I know it's hard work. But you can be realistic and optimistic at the same time. We got a good plan. We're training the Iraqis so they can do the hard work. A hundred-thousand of them are trained. They're taking action today against some of those terrorist thugs. Slowly but surely, their forces are getting up, and some point in time, they'll be ready to defend themselves.

We're helping to rebuild that country. Other nations are involved. They're having conferences here and conferences there. I'll tell you one thing, a summit isn't how you solve the problem. I've been to a lot of summits. I've never seen one that brought a terrorist to justice.

No, we've got a plan, and it's working. Mr. Zarqawi's got one—he's got one weapon, and that is to shake our will, because we've got good conscience, because we care about human life and human dignity. Every life is precious. That's his one weapon. But when America gives its word, America will keep its word, for the Iraqi and Afghan citizens. We'll help these people move toward elections. We'll get them on the path to stability and democracy as quickly as possible, and then our troops will come home with the honor they have earned.

We've got a great military. I'm proud of our military. And I want to thank the veterans who are here for having set such a great example for those who wear the uniform. I also want to thank the military families who are here today. We appreciate your sacrifice, and I made a commitment to our families and to those who wear the uniform that you'll have all the resources you need to complete your missions.

That's why I went to the Congress, September of 2003 and asked them for $87 billion of important funding, funding to support our troops in harm's way. We got great support there. As a matter of fact, the support was overwhelming for the $87 billion. All but 12 United States Senators voted for the funding, 2 of whom were my opponent and his runningmate. I want you to remind your friends and neighbors this: There was only four Members of the Senate that voted to authorize the use of force and didn't vote to fund our troops, two of whom would be my opponent and his runningmate.

Audience members. Boo-o-o!

The President. So they actually asked him, they said, "Why did you do that?" He said, in one of the famous quotes of the 2004 campaign—[*laughter*]—"I actually did vote for the $87 billion, right before I voted against it."

Audience members. Flip-flop! Flip-flop! Flip-flop!

The President. They kept pressing him. He said he was proud of the vote. Finally, he said, "It was a complicated matter," and, yet, incredibly enough, he came up with a new reason. Last week, he described his vote against funding the troops as a protest vote. He said it on national TV.

Audience members. Boo-o-o!

The President. When American troops are in harm's way and defending our country, they deserve better than to have a candidate for President use them as a protest vote. Oh, I forgot. I forgot. There's yet

another explanation since then, and it happened at the debate. He said he made a mistake in how he talked about that vote. The mistake wasn't what Senator Kerry said. The mistake is what Senator Kerry did.

In the debate, my opponent also said something revealing when he laid out the Kerry doctrine. [*Laughter*] He said this, that America has to pass a "global test"——

Audience members. Boo-o-o!

The President. ——before we can use troops to defend ourselves. Senator Kerry's approach to foreign policy would give foreign governments veto power over national security decisions.

Audience members. Boo-o-o!

The President. I have a different view. When our country is in danger, the President's job is not to take an international poll. The President's job is to defend America.

I believe in the transformational power of liberty. The heart of my conviction is that liberty can help change societies for the better. You know, I spend time with the Prime Minister of Japan. He's a good friend. I was in New York with him at the U.N. I said, "By the way, I'm talking about you on the campaign trail. Do you mind?" And he said, "No, not at all." I didn't tell him I was going to tell you that he likes Elvis. [*Laughter*]

Nevertheless, here's why I like to bring him up. Wasn't all that long ago that our country was at war with Japan. My dad fought them. Your dads and granddads fought them as well. They were the sworn enemy. And after World War II, Harry Truman and other Americans believed that liberty could transform an enemy into an ally and worked with Japan to promote democracy. Now, a lot of people then, I'm confident, were skeptical about that being able to happen. You understand why. We had just fought them. A lot of lives had been lost. But because Harry Truman stuck to those values, today, I sit down at the table with the head of a former enemy, talking about the peace we all want, talking about how to work together to keep the peace.

Liberty is powerful. It is powerful. I am confident that someday, an American President will be sitting down with a duly elected leader of Iraq talking about how to keep the peace in the greater Middle East, and our country will be better off for it. Our children and grandchildren will be able to grow up in a more peaceful world.

I believe that the women in the Middle East want to live in freedom. I believe that everybody wants their child to grow up in a free and peaceful society. I believe if given the chance, the people in that part of the world will embrace the most honorable form of government ever devised by man. And I'll tell you why I believe these things: Freedom is not America's gift to the world; freedom is the Almighty God's gift to each man and woman in this world.

This young century will be liberty's century. By promoting freedom at home and abroad, we'll build a safer world and a more hopeful America. By reforming our systems of Government, we'll help more Americans realize their dreams. We'll work to spread ownership and opportunity to every corner of our country. We'll pass the enduring values of our country on to a young generation. We'll continue to work for peace and freedom around the world.

You know, for all Americans, these years in our history will always stand apart. There are quiet times in the life of a nation when little is expected of its leaders. This isn't one of those times. It's a time that requires firm resolve, clear vision, and a deep faith in the values that make this a great nation.

None of us will ever forget that week when one era ended and another began. September the 14th, 2001, I stood in the ruins of the Twin Towers. I'll never forget it. There were workers in hardhats there yelling at me at the top of their lungs, "Whatever it takes." I remember trying to console some people coming out of that rubble. A guy grabbed me by the arm. He looked me straight in the eye, and he said, "You don't let me down." Waking up every morning since then, trying to figure out how best to protect America. I will defend the security of the people of this country, whatever it takes.

Four years ago, as I traveled your great State asking for the vote, I made this pledge. I said if I was honored to be able to hold the office of the Presidency, I would uphold the honor and the dignity of that office. With your help and with your hard work, I will do so again for 4 more years.

Thanks for coming. God bless you all. Thanks for being here. Thank you all.

NOTE: The President spoke at 3:51 p.m. at the Cuyahoga Falls Civic Center. In his remarks, he referred to Kenneth C. Canterbury, national president, James O. Pasco, Jr., executive director, and Nicholas DiMarco, Ohio State president, Fraternal Order of Police; Mayor Don L. Robart of Cuyahoga Falls, OH; Senator Zell Miller of Georgia, who made the keynote address at the 2004 Republican National Convention; senior Al Qaida associate Abu Musab Al Zarqawi; Prime Minister Ayad Allawi of the Iraqi Interim Government; and Prime Minister Junichiro Koizumi of Japan.

Remarks on Signing the Working Families Tax Relief Act of 2004 in Des Moines, Iowa
October 4, 2004

Thank you all. Thanks for coming today. Thank you all. Please be seated. Mr. Chairman—[laughter]—you probably think I've come here to sign an important piece of legislation. Actually, I'm here for a different reason. The South Lawn of the White House has a lot of grass—[laughter]—I'm looking for somebody to mow it. [Laughter] And so Mr. Chairman, you shall now be known as "Grass-mower." [Laughter] And by the way, when you're through using that car—[laughter]—I've always liked an old Olds. [Laughter] I appreciate you being here, Mr. Chairman; proud to call you friend.

Thanks for being here as well. It's a beautiful day here in Iowa. Iowa is such a beautiful place.

Today, with my signature, Federal law will extend vital tax relief for millions of American families and add momentum to our growing economy. Today here in Des Moines, Iowa, the Working Families Tax Relief Act of 2004 becomes the law of the land, and I appreciate you being here to watch it.

And I really do appreciate working with Mr. Chairman. He's had a remarkable tenure as chairman of the Finance Committee in the Senate. We have accomplished a lot together. I appreciate other Members of the congressional delegation who are with us today, the chairman of the Budget Committee in the House of Representatives, Jim Nussle—thank you for coming, Jim. Jim Leach, Congressman Jim Leach is with us. I appreciate my friend Jim Leach being here, as well as Congressman Tom Latham. I'm honored they are here.

Not here is head of the Ways and Means Committee in the House of Representatives, Chairman Bill Thomas of California. I appreciate his hard work on this bill, and I appreciate him working with Chuck Grassley to get the bill done. I also want to thank minority leader in the House of Representatives on the—in the Ways and Means Committee, Charlie Rangel, Democrat from New York, for working on this bill, as well as Senator Max Baucus, Democrat from Montana, for working with Chuck Grassley on the bill as well. I want to thank all the Members of Congress who worked hard to get this bill done.

I appreciate members of the ex-Governors club who've joined us today. I happen to be a member of that club as well. I'm a fellow member. [Laughter] Terry Branstad and Bob Ray have served your State so very well, and I appreciate their friendship. And I'm glad Billie Ray is with Bob. I'll tell Mother and Dad hello for both of you. Appreciate you coming.

I want to thank all the State and local officials who are here. I particularly want to thank the president and CEO of the YMCA, Vernon Delpesce, as well as Dave Hoak, who's the chairman of the Y, for letting us use this facility for this bill signing ceremony.

I want to thank the Patterson family who is with us here. They're beneficiaries of the tax relief. I spent some time with them backstage. I'll be speaking about another family here in a minute.

The law I sign this morning comes at just the right time for America. Some of the tax relief provisions we passed over the last 3 years were set to expire at the end of 2004. Unless we acted, a family of four earning $40,000 would have seen their Federal income taxes rise by more than $900. That would have been a burden for hardworking families across America. And it would have been a setback for our economy.

Today we're acting to keep vital tax relief in place. The bipartisan bill I sign today extends the $1,000 child tax credit, the marriage penalty relief, and the expanded 10-percent tax bracket. It also protects millions of families from having to pay the alternative minimum tax in 2005. That tax was designed over three decades ago to make sure wealthy Americans pay their fair share of taxes, but now it affects middle-income families. This bill will also increase the child credit refunds for almost 7 million low-income families in the 2004 tax year.

Overall, 94 million Americans will have a lower tax bill next year, including 70 million women and 38 million families with children. The money they keep will make it easier to save for their retirement or their children's education, invest in a home or a small business or pay off credit card debts.

One of those families is the Hintz family from Clive, Iowa. Thank you all for coming. It's a special day for Mike and Sharla, not because they're with the President or with Chairman Grassley, but because it's their 13th wedding anniversary. Theirs is a typical story. See, last year they received a child tax credit check for $1,600 for their four children. And under all the tax relief we've passed, they saved about $2,800 last year. With this extra money they bought a wood-burning stove to reduce their home heating costs. They made a decision for their family. They also made home repairs and improvements. They took the family on a vacation to Minnesota. Next year when you get your check, you may want to come to Texas. [*Laughter*]

Without the tax bill I'm signing today, the Hintzes would have paid $1,200 more in Federal taxes next year. Think about that. Here's a family of four, working hard to raise their kids; the money would have been going out of their pocket. I believe they can spend that $1,200 better than the Federal Government can.

This legislation will have good effects throughout the economy. The tax relief we passed in 2001 has helped our economy overcome a lot of challenges, a stock market decline, a recession, terrorist attacks, and war. By extending key portions of that tax relief, we will leave close to $50 billion next year in the hands of the people who earned it, and that money will help keep the economy moving forward and result in even more new jobs for American workers.

This act of Congress is essential, but it's only a start. Over the next few years, if we fail to take further action, the tax relief will expire and Federal income taxes will go up for every American who pays them. For the sake of our families and small businesses and farmers, investors, and seniors, we need to make all the tax relief permanent.

We need to make sure the death tax doesn't come back to life. We need to keep the tax relief we enacted for investors and small businesses. We need to reform the Tax Code to make it simpler, easier to understand, and progrowth. To keep the economy growing, we need to reduce the burden of regulation on small businesses. To keep our economy growing, we need to end the junk lawsuits that keep entrepreneurs from creating new jobs. To keep the economy growing, we need an energy plan to make sure America is less dependent on foreign sources of energy, by using alternative uses of energy like ethanol and biodiesel. We need to open up foreign markets for our products and to continue to ensure that other countries play by the rules. We need spending discipline in our Nation's Capital.

I look forward to working with the Congress to achieve all these goals. When we keep taxes low and trust our American families with their own money, they spend it far more wisely than we can. And when they do, they make the American economy stronger.

I appreciate the Members of Congress who are here today. I wish they'd come up and join me as, in the great city of Des Moines, Iowa, I sign into law the Working Families Tax Relief Act of 2004.

NOTE: The President spoke at 11:24 p.m. at the South Suburban YMCA. In his remarks, he referred to former Gov. Terry E. Branstad of Iowa; former Gov. Robert D. Ray of Iowa and his wife, Billie; and Vernon Delpesce, executive director, and David Hoak, chief volunteer officer, YMCA of Greater Des Moines, IA. H.R. 1308, approved October 4, was assigned Public Law No. 108–311. The Office of the Press Secretary also released a Spanish language transcript of these remarks.

Remarks in a Discussion in Clive, Iowa
October 4, 2004

The President. Thank you all. Thanks for coming. Thanks for being here. Please be seated. We've got to get started. I've got some things I want to tell you.

First thing I'm going to tell you is I'm here asking for the vote in Clive, Iowa. I'm enjoying this campaign. It gives me a chance to get out among the people and tell people what I believe and where I stand and where I'm going to lead this country for the next 4 years. I'm here also to ask for your help. There's no doubt in my mind, with your help, we'll carry Iowa and win a great victory in November. [*Applause*] Thank you all.

They tell me I'm the first sitting President ever to visit Clive. I don't know what took all the other ones so long to get here—[*laughter*]—but thanks for being here. I wish Laura were here. Imagine this conversation: "Will you marry me?" "Fine, just so long as I never have to give a speech." [*Laughter*] I said, "Okay." [*Laughter*] Fortunately, she didn't hold me to the promise, because when people see Laura, they see a strong, compassionate, fine, fine First Lady. I think in the course of the campaign you have to tell people why they should vote for you; that's what I'm here to do. But perhaps the most important reason of all is so that Laura will be the First Lady for 4 more years.

Today I'm going to talk to some of your fellow citizens about why our policies make sense, and I'd like to answer some questions if you have some. Before I do that, I do want to introduce some people traveling with me. First, I do want to thank the next Congressman from the Third Congressional District, Stan Thompson. He's a good Member, I hope you put him in office. I'm here to tell you he ought to be the next United States Congressman.

I appreciate Members of the U.S. Congress from the Iowa delegation for coming. From the east side of the State, Jim Nussle and Jim Leach, two really fine friends. And I appreciate you all being here. Thanks for coming. Leach is a longtime Member, one of the most decent men you'll ever meet. Chairman Nussle is the chairman of the Budget Committee, making sure that the Iowa taxpayers' monies is well-spent in Washington. I also want to thank Tom Latham from northwest Iowa for being here today. Congressman, thanks for coming. Proud you're here.

And I just signed an important piece of legislation making a lot of the tax relief—extending a lot of the tax relief for 5 years. And I was able to stand on stage with the chairman of the Senate Finance Committee, Chuck Grassley. He's a good man. He went back to Washington. I told him if he'd suffer through one of my speeches, I'd give him a ride back. [*Laughter*] But he's frugal. [*Laughter*] I also told the people, I said, "I'm really getting to be good friends with Chuck Grassley, for a reason. The south lawn of the White House"—[*laughter*]—"is mighty big, and we're looking for a good mower." [*Laughter*]

I want to thank the State auditor, David Vaudt, for being here. I appreciate you coming, David. I want to thank the Senate president, Lamberti, as well as my friend Stew Iverson, the majority leader. Thank you all for coming. Good to see you all. Big Stew, looking good. Stew has got that same hair style as the Vice President. [*Laughter*]

By the way, I didn't pick the Vice President because of his hair. [*Laughter*] I picked him because he's a man of great judgment, wonderful experience, a guy who can get the job done for the American people.

I want to thank David Roederer, the chairman of the Bush-Cheney campaign. I want to thank all the grassroots activists, the people putting up the signs and making the phone calls and registering the voters. I can't thank you enough for what you're going to do, which is to work as we're coming down the stretch. It really means a lot. It really means a lot.

I'm running because I want this country to be a safer country and a more hopeful country. I understand that we're living in changing times, and the institutions of Government must change with those times. See, my philosophy of Government is that Government ought to help people realize the great opportunities of our country, not tell you how to live your lives. There's a fundamental difference in this campaign about Government philosophy.

When I say "changing institutions," I'm talking about the labor laws need to change with the times. Think about this fact: 30 years ago, most women stayed at home; today, most women are working inside the house and outside the house. Yet the labor laws reflect yesterday, not tomorrow. I believe the labor laws ought to change and have flex-time for workers, so that they can better manage their families and their workloads.

The retirement systems were designed for yesterday. I believe they ought to be designed for tomorrow. Let me tell you about my plans for Social Security. First of all, you might remember the campaign in 2000. Latham reminded me of it. When they were running, they said, "If George W. gets elected, he's going to take away your Social Security check." Remember those ads? Well, you remind your friends and neighbors, you got your check. That's the same old stale political rhetoric. You'll hear it again this time too. And baby-boomers, we're in good shape when it comes to Social Security.

But it's the youngsters who have to pay for the baby-boomers' retirement we better worry about. That's why I believe we ought to allow young workers to take some of their own tax money and set up a personal savings account that will earn better interest than the Social Security trust today, so they can be able to more likely get the benefits of the Social Security System, a personal savings account they call their own, a personal savings account they can pass on to their kids or grandkids, and a personal savings account that the Government will not take away.

We've got to make sure that our worker training programs work. They were designed for yesterday. They need to be designed for tomorrow. Listen, in this changing world of ours, it requires—oftentimes requires new skills. These jobs are new jobs, the jobs of the 21st century. Just look at the health care industry. It's a booming part of our economy, yet, oftentimes, people don't have the skills necessary to fill those jobs. So one of the things Government must do is make sure the Workforce Investment program works, make sure there's access to our community college system, expand Pell grants, and expand Government help for workers.

This is the kind of thing that is necessary to make sure people have the skills necessary to fill the jobs of the 21st century. And do you realize that most new jobs in America now require at least 2 years of college, yet one in four of our students gets there? And that's why it's essential we keep working on No Child Left Behind, to make sure every child has got the skills necessary to read and write and add and subtract.

I'm looking forward to discussing No Child Left Behind with the American people. You might remember, there were times when they would just move kids through school, grade after grade, year after year, without teaching the basics. I don't think that's right. That's what I call—that's why I went to—when I say I went to Washington to challenge the soft bigotry of low expectations, that's what I'm talking about. Expectations were so low that they just moved kids through. We've changed that. We're raising the bar. We believe in local control of schools, but we're now saying, "In return for increased Federal spending, measure. Show us whether or not a child can read. Let's correct problems early, before it is too late."

We've got to stop this business about shuffling kids through school, and we are. There's an achievement gap in America that's beginning to close, but there's more to be done. I believe we ought to have intermediate help programs for at-risk students in high school. We ought to emphasize math and science. We ought to expand Pell grants for low- and middle-income families. We want more of the kids graduating from college being able to fill the jobs of the 21st century. That's how you make sure this country is a hopeful place.

In changing times, it helps to own something. It brings stability to your life. I'm proud of the fact that homeownership rates are at an alltime high in America under my administration. And so we got plans to make sure homeownership is spread to every corner of America.

Speaking about ownership, it helps when somebody owns their own health care account in changing times. There's a big difference of opinion about health care in this campaign. I believe the decisions ought to be made by you and your doctor. My opponent believes that the Federal Government ought to be making your decisions.

Audience members. Boo-o-o!

The President. Yes. That's what I call—he's got a system that's creeping toward "Hillary Care." [*Applause*]

I got a commonsense, practical way of making sure health care is available and affordable. I'm a big believer in community health centers. That's where the poor and the indigent can get primary and preventative care. I believe every poor county in America ought to have a community health center to make sure health care is available for people. I believe we ought to make sure that the children's health care program for low-income families is fully subscribed.

To make sure health care is affordable, I want to help the small businesses afford health care. Do you realize 50 percent of the uninsured today work for small businesses? Small businesses are having trouble affording health care. I believe they ought to be allowed to pool risk with other small businesses so they can afford insurance at the same discount big businesses get.

I believe in health savings accounts, individualized health savings accounts that provide for catastrophic care and tax-free savings for routine medical costs. It's a plan that you own. When you change jobs or if you change jobs, you take your health care with your—with wherever you go. These are innovative, commonsense ways to make sure that health care is available and affordable.

I'll tell you another thing we need to do about health care costs. We've got to do something about these frivolous lawsuits that are running up the costs on small businesses. You cannot be pro-doctor, pro-patient, and pro-trial-lawyer at the same time. [*Laughter*] I think you have to choose. My opponent made his choice, and he put a trial lawyer on the ticket. I made my choice. I'm for medical liability reform—now.

Let me talk about Medicare right quick. I went to Washington to fix problems, not to pass them on to future Presidents. I thought Medicare needed to be fixed. It's a very important program. Yet, as medicine modernized, Medicare was not modernizing with it. And I'll give you an example. Medicare would pay $100,000 or so for heart surgery but not one dime for the prescription drugs that would prevent the heart surgery from being needed in the first place. That didn't make any sense for our seniors. It did not make any sense for the taxpayers. So I worked with Democrats and Republicans to modernize Medicare, and starting in 2006, our seniors will get a prescription drug benefit in Medicare. And today, our seniors can sign up for a drug discount card; 4.4 million seniors have done so in order to derive substantial savings at their local pharmacies.

We're making a difference when it comes to health care. But all we do to make sure health care is available and affordable, we'll make sure the decisionmaking is between patient and doctor, not between bureaucrats in the Nation's Capital.

It's important to make sure America is a hopeful place, by growing our economy. I want you to tell your friends and neighbors and remind them what we have been through. The stock market was in significant decline prior to my arrival in Washington, DC. That was an indicator that something was taking place in the economy, and sure enough, we had a recession. And the recession hurt us, but so did the corporate scandals. You know, our economy is based upon trust. And when some of our citizens didn't tell the truth, it shook our confidence and hurt our economy. We passed tough laws, and that made it abundantly clear that we're not going to tolerate dishonesty in the boardrooms of America.

And then the attacks hurt us. And then we got attacked. On September the 11th, 2001, our Nation was brutally attacked, and those attacks cost us a million jobs during the 3 months after September the 11th. Think about what we've been through as an economy, recession, attack, corporate scandal. And yet, the economy is strong, and it's getting strong. It's growing at rates as fast as nearly in any 20 years. Your great State of Iowa has got a farm economy that's really strong. Unemployment rate in this State is 4.5 percent. The national unemployment rate is 5.4 percent, lower than the average of the 1970s, 1980s, and 1990s.

And people say, "How did it happen? How did we get out of this recession so quickly?" One reason is, we've got great workers. Secondly, the entrepreneurial spirit is strong in America. More and more people are owning their own small business. Thirdly, we had well-timed tax cuts. Those tax cuts left more money in the hands who earned it. People had more money to spend.

The tax cuts also helped to stimulate the job creators. Not only did we help to stimulate demand, but we helped to stimulate the job creators. See, 70 percent of new jobs in America are created by small-business owners. Ninety percent of small businesses pay tax at the individual income-tax rate, because they're either Subchapter S corporation or a sole proprietorship; those are legal terms which basically mean they pay an individual income tax. And so when you cut individual income taxes on everybody who pays taxes, you're really helping our small businesses. And when you help the small businesses, you help the job creators. And when you help the job creators, somebody is more likely to find work. We've added 1.7 million jobs since August of 2003. The tax relief plan is making a difference.

And there's a difference in taxes in this campaign. There's a big difference. I've lowered taxes, and my opponent wants to raise taxes.

Audience members. Boo-o-o!

The President. You may have noticed, he changes positions quite frequently—[*laughter*]—but not on taxes. [*Laughter*] During his 20 years in the Senate, he's voted to raise your taxes 98 times.

Audience members. Boo-o-o!

The President. Now, all of a sudden, he's saying, well, he's for a middle class tax relief. Except he voted against raising the child credit. He voted against reducing the marriage penalty. He voted against creating a 10-percent bracket, which helps low-income Americans. Plus, he's proposed $2.2 trillion in new Federal spending. And so how—they asked him, "How are you going to pay for it?" And he said, "Oh, I'll just tax the rich." We've heard that before, haven't we?

Well, I want you to remember one thing. We're about to talk to a businessowner that will be affected by the so-called tax-the-rich policy. If most small businesses pay individual income taxes and you raise the top two brackets, you're taxing job creators. And that's bad economic policy, to be taxing the people who are creating the new jobs. If you want more jobs, you keep people's taxes low, not run them up.

If you propose 2.2 trillion, and you only raise a little over 600 billion by raising the top two brackets, there's a gap. [*Laughter*] Two-point-two trillion in spending, a little over 600 billion in revenues raised, means you've got to fill the hole. You've got to find additional taxes if you're going to fulfill your promises. And guess who ends up paying? Every time somebody out of Washington makes the promises and falls short of being able to raise the revenues, they're going to tax the middle class every singe time, aren't they?

Let me tell you one other problem he has with that. He says, "Oh, I'm just going to tax the rich." Well, the rich hire lawyers and accountants for a reason; that's to stick you with the tab. But we're not going to let him tax you. We're going to carry Iowa and the country in November.

A couple other points I want to make and then I want to talk to some of our citizens. It's one thing to have overcome obstacles and get the economy growing, the fundamental question is, what do you intend to do to keep it growing? Now that we're on the track to recovery, how do you make sure the recovery is lasting? Here are some ideas for you.

In order to make sure jobs stay here in America, America must be the best place in the world to do business. That means less regulations. My opponent's plans increase regulations. I believe in providing regulatory relief. If you want to keep jobs here in America, there needs to be fewer frivolous lawsuits that make it hard for employers to expand the job base.

If we want to keep jobs here in America, Congress needs to pass my energy plan. You can't have a growing economy unless we have a reasonable energy plan, an energy plan that encourages conservation, that provides money for research and development, so that we can develop alternative sources of energy, an energy plan that relies upon ethanol and biodiesel to help us become less dependent on foreign sources of energy, an energy plan that uses technology so we can burn the coal of our country, an energy plan which encourages the exploration for natural gas in environmentally friendly ways. To keep jobs here, we must become less dependant on foreign sources of energy.

To keep jobs here, we've got to open up markets. One reason Iowa's farmers are doing so well—I fulfilled a promise. I said, "If you let me be President, I'll work to make sure you can sell your crops anywhere in the world," and it's making a difference. We're selling a lot of soybeans to China. And that's the task of the President.

See, you'll hear some talk about, you know, reviewing trade agreements. That's really kind of hinting about economic isolationism. That makes no sense for Iowa workers and farmers and small-business owners. It makes no sense to wall ourselves off from the world. What we ought to be doing is opening up markets. We've opened up our markets for foreign goods, and it's good for you. If you've got more products to choose from, you're likely to get what you want at a better price and higher quality. That's how the market works. So what the President ought to be doing is what I'm doing, which is saying, "China, you treat us the way we treat you," saying to the world, "Open up your markets the way we've opened up our markets." And I'm saying that with confidence because I know we can compete with anybody, anytime, anywhere so long as the rules are fair.

One thing I forgot to mention about the Medicare Plan that Chuck and I worked on, along with the Members of Congress, is that we understood, under Medicare Iowa's hospitals weren't being treated fairly. I remember that clearly when I campaigned here in 2000. When I was knocking on doors, I can remember a lot of the citizens here were saying, "Now, if you get up there, do something about the rural hospitals. Make sure Iowa's hospitals are treated fairly." I delivered. So did Chuck Grassley. So did these Members of Congress. Iowa's hospitals are being treated fairly under the new Medicare law.

In order to make sure this economy grows, we've got to keep people's taxes low. We need to make sure the tax relief we pass is permanent. Today I signed a piece of legislation that extended the child credit, marriage penalty, and the 10-percent bracket for 5 more years.

And we're about to talk to a family. Bobbi and Ricardo Ramirez are with us. Thanks for coming. I've asked them to join us because I want you to hear their story. You know a lot of times, politicians talk or economists talk about tax relief this, tax relief that—but I always think it's good to put a face on it. Let people know exactly what the tax relief has meant.

What do you do? What do you all do?

Bobbi Ramirez. My husband works for Knapp Properties. He's a residential maintenance worker, and I'm a stay-at-home mother.

The President. Very good. And how many kids we got?

Mrs. Ramirez. We have three girls.

The President. There they are. Hi, girls. Good to see you. Thanks for coming. And so tax relief?

Mrs. Ramirez. Tax relief has been a huge blessing for us.

The President. How much did you save?

Mrs. Ramirez. We saved about $1,700.

The President. Yes. That's probably not a lot when you're working up in Washington. [*Laughter*] It's a lot for this family. It's their money to begin with.

What did you do? What did you do with the money?

Mrs. Ramirez. We were able to use the money mostly for our children, to be able to get them school clothes and school supplies and extracurricular activities that maybe we normally would not have been able to do, like softball and dancing and things like that.

The President. Yes. They were able to use the money so they could do their job as a mom and dad. When you think about it, they were able to fulfill—begin to fill ambitions for their family. That's what tax relief means. It not only helps the economy—just remember they said, "We were able to go out and buy some school supplies." Well, when somebody shows up to buy school supplies, it means somebody has got to make those school supplies. Somebody makes them; somebody is going to work. But equally importantly, these people with more money were able to begin to realize dreams for their children. Tax relief was important.

You also did something with your home.

Mrs. Ramirez. We did. We refinanced our home, and we were able to—in the amount that we saved for interest, we didn't raise our monthly payment, but we were able to build on and put an addition onto our home.

The President. Right, and refinancing their home—low interest rates, good fiscal policy meant they were able to improve their home. Nothing better than hearing somebody stand up and say, "I'm improving my home. This is my piece of property."

That's what the American experience is all about, isn't it? And tax relief helps.

Do you realize that had we not extended the tax relief, this good family would have paid $600 additional in taxes last year—next year? See, that's $600. The fundamental question in this campaign is, who do you want spending the people's money? Now, look, I think we need to set priorities. That's why I work with Chairman Nussle, to set priorities. But I believe that after we fund our priorities, the Ramirez family can spend their money better than the Federal Government can.

I'd like to—Jeff Henning is with us. Jeff, thanks for coming.

Jeff Henning. Good afternoon, Mr. President.

The President. Straight out of Johnstown, Iowa. [*Laughter*]

Mr. Henning. Close, Mr. President.

The President. Good to have you.

Mr. Henning. You too.

The President. You run what?

Mr. Henning. Henning Construction Company.

The President. Henning Construction Company. That's—since your name is Jeff Henning, I presume you own it.

Mr. Henning. Yes, I own the store. [*Laughter*]

The President. That's good. Did you start it?

Mr. Henning. My grandfather started the business in 1924.

The President. Oh, fantastic. Isn't that interesting? And so give me a sense of the business.

Mr. Henning. We are general contractors. As I say, we have four generations. Our business and our customers have come to us as a result of the tax bonus act and said, "We need to make investment. We want to take advantage of this." Therefore, our business has grown by 60 percent this year.

The President. See, what he's saying is, is that part of the Tax Code incented small businesses to invest. If they invested, they got tax relief. Investment means spend money. And so one of the things they spent money on, I take it, was something you had to build.

Mr. Henning. That's correct. We build buildings and equipment for our customers, and we had to make substantial investments, ourselves, in order to equip those troops to do that work.

The President. Yes. So what did you buy?

Mr. Henning. We bought forklifts, equipment, trucks, vehicles——

The President. Somebody had to make them. See, here's how the economy works. Good tax policy says to Jeff or his customers, invest. And when he invests, somebody has to make the product he buys. And so it has a ripple effect. And we'd rather that ripple effect be done in the private sector. That's what we're beginning to see in this country.

Have you hired anybody?

Mr. Henning. Yes, we have. We've hired 56 people additional this year.

The President. This year? [*Applause*] Yes. All of them live in Johnston?

Mr. Henning. No, Mr. President, they're all over the United States of America.

The President. Really? This guy has got quite a far reach. [*Laughter*] He is a intercontinental businessman. [*Laughter*] Let me ask you this: You were talking to me about your concerns about the death tax, why?

Mr. Henning. Well, Mr. President, we just went through some estate planning. We have two daughters in the business, and in order for us to be able to pass this on, they would have to sell the business if something happened, if we didn't take care of it.

The President. See, this is a problem in America, and we're about to talk to a farmer who can relate to it as well. But it's a problem when you've got a family-owned business and the Tax Code forces you to sell it. I think we need to simplify the Tax Code, and one way to simplify it is to get rid of the death tax forever.

Good job. Oh, wait a minute. I got one other point. Hold on. I got one other thing to tell you about this good man. He's an S corp. That's one of those companies that pays taxes at the individual income-tax rate.

Mr. Henning. That's correct.

The President. Yes, see, I wasn't making it up. [*Laughter*] And so when you hear them say "tax the rich," think about Jeff. That's the so-called rich. He hired 54 people this year. And I'm going to tell you, when they start taking money out of employers' pockets, like him, he's going to be less likely to hire somebody. If we want to keep this job—this recovery growing and people being able to find work, we should not be taxing Jeff Henning's company. We ought to be encouraging his company to expand and grow. [*Applause*] Thank you.

And my opponent doesn't understand that. Either he doesn't understand it, or he doesn't care, because he wants more money for the Federal Government.

Let's talk to Craig Lang. Yarrabee Farms, straight out of Brooklyn, and I'm talking Brooklyn, Iowa. [*Laughter*]

Craig Lang. Yes, that's right.

The President. Thanks for coming.

Mr. Lang. Thank you.

The President. Tell us about your farm.

Mr. Lang. Well, I'm fifth generation farmer. My great-great grandfather walked from Ohio to Brooklyn, Iowa, back in 1860, and we've had that farm in our family ever since. And we not only own it; we also operate it.

The President. That's good, yes. How's the farm economy?

Mr. Lang. It's great. It was wonderful to hear you talk about world trade—in Iowa, 30 percent—everything that the farmer produces in Iowa is sold somewhere outside of our borders. It's just absolutely important that we're competitive as farmers in the world market, and your administration is allowing us to do that.

The President. Actually, our administration is creating the conditions for somebody who knows what they're doing to be able to succeed. We can't make you succeed. That's up to you. All we can do is create the conditions, the opportunity, by opening up markets and have good tax policy. Did the tax policy help you?

Mr. Lang. That's right, the reduction tax policy, the income expensing, all those things have been very important this year. We've had one of the best years—my brother, my father, and myself. In fact, it's been such a great year that we're—right now we're working with an attorney and CPA and insurance agent——

The President. That's a heck of a year if you've got to hire an attorney. [*Laughter*]

Mr. Lang. ——to make sure that at the time of a death, that the estate taxes aren't a burden on our family, so the next generation beside me can have the opportunity to operate that farm too.

The President. Yes, see, that's a problem, isn't it? Here's a good man who is trying to figure out ways to pass his farm on, so he has to hire a lawyer and an accountant to do it. And again, this is where the death tax makes a huge difference. And people have got to understand out there listening that if you own a farm, sometimes you don't have much liquidity. And in order to pay the tax, you actually have to sell the farm in order to be able to pay the tax.

I hope that's an unintended consequence of the fellows who wrote the death tax years ago, but it's a lousy consequence. And that's why we got to get rid of this death tax. We want farms to stay family to family, if that's what the owners choose to do. We want people to make decisions. I appreciate you.

Finally, Hank Evans is here. Hank, thanks for coming. We've got a mike headed your way. You are the owner of?

Hank Evans. A.F. Johnson Millwork Company.

The President. And where are you? Des Moines—right here.

Mr. Evans. We're in West Des Moines.

The President. Very good, thanks for coming. What do you do?

Mr. Evans. We custom build architectural millwork, and we build things like teller lines, reception desks, and nurses stations.

The President. Really?

Mr. Evans. Store fixtures.

The President. Must we doing well—a lot of nurses.

Mr. Evans. It's been a good year, sir.

The President. A couple of points that we want to talk to Hank about is, one, he's concerned about the health care costs of his company. At least you told me you were, backstage.

Mr. Evans. Yes, Mr. President, our health care has gone up about 20 percent on average over the last half dozen years. A number of years ago, through the Association of Business and Industry, we had a group health plan for all the members of that association, 2,000 of them.

When the law changed, we were no longer able to do that, and as a result the level of health care we've been able to offer is not only had the cost has gone up, but the quality has gone down. We would love to see the ability for that association to again offer health care. It would allow us hire and attract and keep better workers and offer them a better plan.

The President. Right. Was this a health care association plan just for Iowa?

Mr. Evans. It was, yes, the Iowa Association of Business and Industry.

The President. Basically what he's saying is—and here is what we're talking about, see—a stand alone purchaser of health, like Hank, means he's not going to be able to afford a policy relative to being able to have others bid with him. In other words, the more people you have to spread risk, the lower the cost of your insurance is going to be. That makes sense, doesn't it? And so if you're a smaller business and stand-alone trying to purchase insurance in the marketplace, it's going to be a lot higher than if you had others to share the risk

with you. And here in Iowa, evidently, you had the capacity to do that, but law changed.

Mr. Evans. Yes, it did.

The President. Yes. See, what I believe we need to do is let Hank and his company pool with people not only in Iowa but in other States. The bigger the pool, the less costly the insurance. But Federal law won't let us do that now. And my opponent doesn't want that to happen. I think it makes sense to have it happen, because I want Hank making the health care decisions. I don't want there to be a great Federal pool.

He's done something else very interesting. Remember I was talking about making sure the workforce training programs work, actually mean something. Explain what you've done. This is a fantastic story.

Mr. Evans. Well, trying to find cabinetmakers is about like trying to find hens teeth, Mr. President. They're very scarce.

The President. Really? [*Laughter*]

Mr. Evans. We've had difficulty for years finding good workers. So about 3 years ago, we went to the local community college, DMACC, up in Ankeny, and we set up on an architectural millworker training program. It's a year-long program. We're training 16 kids a year now to be architectural millworkers and cabinetmakers.

The President. Isn't that something? Community colleges are great. I'll tell you something really interesting. Think about the attractiveness of the community college system: Curriculum change if need be. In other words, if there's a demand for workers, the community college can change curriculum or adapt curriculum or come up with curriculum necessary to train those workers for the jobs which actually exist. And all of a sudden, here you have an employer that says, "I'm going to be creative. I'm going to work with the local education institute to help people get the skills necessary to actually work."

In the old days, some of these worker training programs, they'd train people for jobs which didn't exist. Now we got an opportunity to train people for jobs which actually exist. And that's why I'm going to ask Congress to spend $250 million to make sure industry-type programs with community colleges are expanded. People want to work. They don't have the skills sometimes, and we can do—provide skills in a creative way, just like Hank has done, so people can realize their dreams here in this country.

Thanks for coming.

Mr. Evans. Thank you.

The President. I want you to know that in changing times, some things don't change, the values we try to live by, courage and compassion, reverence and integrity. We stand for a culture of life in which every person matters and every person counts. We stand for marriage and family, which are the foundations of our society. And we stand for judges who know the difference between personal opinion and the strict interpretation of the law. [*Applause*]

Okay, a couple of other points. I got some other things I got to tell you. I just saw somebody stand up with an "Army Wife for Bush" shirt. I'm going to talk about—[*applause*]—thank you. That's what I want to talk about, a safer America. My most solemn duty is to protect you. My most solemn obligation as the President is to do everything in our power to prevent harm to the American people.

You know, as I was campaigning here in 2000, I never dreamt that we'd be attacked the way we were. Nobody asked for this attack in America. But since they came, we're going to deal with it. I want to share some thoughts with you. Let me share some thoughts with you.

Let me share some thoughts with you about what I have learned and what I hope the country has learned. First of all, we're dealing with an enemy that has no conscience. Today, if you noticed, there was a car bomb near a school. These people are brutal. They—they're the exact opposite of Americans. We value life and human dignity. They don't care about life and human dignity. We believe in freedom. They have an ideology of hate. And they're tough, but not as tough as America. It's really important for people to understand, you cannot negotiate with these people; you cannot hope for the best. We must—we must chase them down all around the world, so we do not have to face them here at home. That's the lesson number one: Be relentless and determined; never yield.

Secondly, that this is a different kind of war that requires a different kind of strategy. And it's really important for you to realize that these people—their ambition is beyond just a single attack. Their ambition is to take over countries from which they can spread their ideology of hate. That's why they were in Afghanistan. They're like a parasite, hopefully being able to overcome a weak host, and they were in the process of doing that.

And so I laid out a doctrine that said, "If you harbor a terrorist, you're equally as guilty as the terrorist." Now, when the President says something, I believe the President must speak clearly, and when he says something, he must mean what he says. I meant what I said, and thanks to our military, the Taliban got routed.

Now, let me tell you about the Taliban. Their vision was so dark that many young girls were not allowed to go to school. It's hard for people in America to imagine that, but that's the way it was. And if their mothers or if the women of that country didn't toe the line, they'd be taken out into the public square and whipped or killed. These people were barbarians. And by routing them out, by toppling their government, not only did we deny Al Qaida a safe haven, but we have liberated people.

And I want you to hear this statistic. I think it's one of the most powerful statistics of the 21st century. Because we acted, 10 million citizens in that country, 41 percent of whom are women, have registered to vote in the October 9th Presidential election. Amazing, isn't it? It's an amazing statistic. The way I like to describe it is people are emerging from darkness to light because of freedom. And it's in our interest that Afghanistan be free. It's in our interest that we have an ally in the war on terror. It's in our interest that we have a model of freedom in a part of the world where freedom is desperately needed.

The third lesson is, when we see threats, we must deal with them before they fully materialize. When we see a threat—see, in the old days, we'd see a threat, and we'd say, "Well, maybe this threat will—we need to deal with, or maybe we don't." But we never thought it would come to hurt us. Every threat now must be taken seriously. We scan the world, watching very carefully. If our job is to protect you, then we just got to watch every threat seriously.

And we saw, I saw, my administration saw—Congress saw, by the way—a unique threat in Saddam Hussein. You know, at the time, we thought he had stockpiles of weapons. Everybody did. Since then we have found that he has had the capability of making weapons. And here's the danger. Saddam Hussein was a sworn enemy of America. We had been to war with Saddam Hussein before. Saddam Hussein was a source of great instability in a volatile part of the world. Saddam Hussein had the capability of making weapons. At the time, of course, we knew he had used them, so we knew he had that mindset. Since then we've discovered he had the capability. And we knew that he had terrorist connections. Saddam Hussein—here's the danger. Saddam Hussein could have shared that capability of weapons of mass destruction with the enemy. And that's a risk we could not afford to take. Knowing what I know today, I would have made the same decision to remove Saddam Hussein from power.

We have a difference of opinion in this campaign. My opponent calls Iraq a "great diversion" from the war on terror. I strongly disagree. The reason why Zarqawi is fighting so hard—why this terrorist is fighting so hard, is because he understands the stakes. A free Iraq will be a devastating blow for the ideologues of hate. He's called it a "diversion" from the war on terror. I call it a battle in the war on terror.

You cannot be the Commander in Chief of this country and tell those fine troops in Iraq that they're participating in a "grand diversion" from the war on terror. You can't be the Commander in Chief and lead those troops and at the same time say, "Wrong war, wrong place, wrong time."

No, we have a difference of opinion. My opponent said that—in the debate—I didn't say this; he said it—that we must pass a "global test" before we commit troops into harm's way.

Audience members. Boo-o-o!

The President. Think about that now. Our most solemn duty is to protect you. Can you imagine taking an international poll of nations to determine whether or not we need to protect you?

I'll tell you what's was really interesting, in 1991, when my dad was President, he saw a threat, and that was that Saddam Hussein was going to overrun Kuwait. And he went to the Congress and the United Nations and put together a vast coalition that I think under any scrutiny would pass the "global test." My opponent voted against authorizing the use of force in 1991. So now he says, you know, Iraq would have been a—Iraq is a mistake, and voted against 1991—that means Saddam would not only have been in his palaces, that means he would have been in Kuwait as well. The policies of my opponent are dangerous for world peace. If they were implemented, they would make this world not more peaceful but more dangerous.

In Iraq we're going to have elections in January. In Iraq we're training people, Iraqis, so they can do the hard work of defending themselves. We're training and equipping army, national guard, police, border patrol. I don't know if you've seen any newspapers recently, but in Samarra, the

Iraqi soldiers performed brilliantly. Slowly but surely, they're getting the confidence and the training necessary for them to do the hard work. That's our strategy. They're willing to fight for freedom, and they need the help to do so. In Iraq we're going to spend money to help them rebuild that society. In Iraq we'll continue to work with our friends and allies, and we've got a great coalition. You can't lead a coalition by saying to the leaders of those countries, "Join me for the wrong war." [*Laughter*]

As a matter of fact, my opponent—in the debate they said—he kept saying, "I've got a plan." If you listen carefully to it, the plan was to call a summit. I've been to summits. You don't bring terrorists to justice at summits. I can imagine him walking in to the leaders of the world saying, "We need your help, but Iraq is a mistake. We need your help. Commit your troops into harm's way for the wrong war at the wrong time and the wrong place." He has no plan. A summit won't solve the problem. Strong consistent leadership is what this world needs. [*Applause*] Thank you all.

Two other points, real quick. I'm not trying to filibuster. [*Laughter*] Two points, to the Army wife, I say to you, one, thank you for your husband's sacrifice. And I—[*applause*]—hold on for a minute. You're filibustering. And we owe you and your loved one the full support of the Federal Government. And that's why I went to the Congress to ask for $87 billion of funding. And it was important funding. It was funding that would give our troops that which they needed for combat in both Afghanistan and Iraq. And the bipartisan support was overwhelming for the funding. Think about this fact: Only four United States Senators voted for the authorization of force and against funding the troops—only four—two of whom are my opponent and his runningmate.

Audience members. Boo-o-o!

The President. So they asked him about the vote, and he issued the famous quote of the campaign, "I actually did vote for the $87 billion, before I voted against it." [*Laughter*] And they pressed him. He's given about five different answers on the vote. He said, well, he was proud of the vote. Then he said, "It was a complicated matter." [*Laughter*] And then he said that it was a protest vote. On national TV, he said, "Well, that vote was a protest vote." Think about somebody who wants to be the Commander in Chief saying that he's going to vote against important support for the troops in combat and calling it a protest vote. Finally he said, oh, his vote—the other night on the debate, he said, "Well, the vote was a mistake." No, what was a mistake was—he said, "What I said was a mistake." No. What he said wasn't the mistake. His vote was the mistake.

Finally, let me share with you about my beliefs on liberty. I believe liberty has got the ability to transform societies. I do. And I believe that because I'm watching it happen in Afghanistan. But also I spend time with my friend Prime Minister Koizumi. He's an interesting guy. I saw him at the United Nations recently when I was up in New York, and I said, "I'm telling people all across the country about our relationship. Do you mind?" He said, "No." I didn't tell him I was going to tell you that Elvis is his favorite singer. [*Laughter*] It's true. [*Laughter*]

Think about this story, though—think about what I'm telling you. It wasn't all that long ago that my dad and your dads or granddads were fighting the Japanese. They were the sworn enemy of the United States of America. And after World War II, after we won, Harry Truman believed that liberty could transform an enemy into an ally. That's what he believed. And I bet there was a lot of skepticism, don't you? There was a lot of heartache, lot of anger at the Japanese. "Why help them, you know. They killed some of our sons. Why do we care?" But Harry Truman cared, because he had a vision that was a long-term vision about world peace. People in America cared, because they have deep faith in the values that makes us a unique nation. As a result of Harry Truman's faith in liberty, I now sit down at the table with the leader of a country that was a sworn enemy, talking about the peace we all want. Think about that. Think about what liberty can do.

People like Zarqawi know the power of liberty, and that's why they're resisting. He's got one weapon. They can't whip our military. He's got one weapon. His weapon is to shake our conscience. His weapon is to conduct such horrific acts against innocent people that America loses its will and our faith in liberty to change the world is shaken. My faith in liberty will not be shaken. I understand what we're doing has got a chance to change the world for the better. Someday, when we achieve our goal in Afghanistan, which is helping this country get up to be a democracy, someday, an American President will be sitting down with a duly elected leader from Iraq, talking about the peace, talking about how to keep the peace in a troubled part of the world. And our children and our grandchildren will be better off for it.

I want to thank you all for giving me the chance to share with you why I'm running. See, I believe somebody running for office can't just sit on their laurels. They've got to talk about what they are going to do. I'm here to tell you America will be a safer place, a stronger place, and a better place when you send me and Dick Cheney back into office for 4 more years.

All right, let me see if we got some time for some questions. I'm ready to take some questions if anybody has got a question. Yes, sir, holding the child right there. [*Applause*] Thank you all.

Freedom of Religion

Q. Mr. President, first, we just want to tell you that we pray for you every night, as our President.

The President. Thank you, sir.

Q. We thank God that we live in a representative republic, that we're able to home-school our children, and—a fact that we're sharing with Leon Mosley the other night at the Christian Coalition dinner what we're teaching our children about a representative republic, and he said maybe my little 7-year-old should come down here and share it with you. Can you tell the President what Noah Webster said about our republic?

Participant. It would do our system well to learn at an early age that the correct principles of our republic is the Holy Bible, the New Testament, and Christianity.

The President. Thank you. Thank you. Let me say something about religion. Let say something about religion. First of all, that was well done. Here's the strength of America. You can worship or not worship, and be equally patriotic. That's the strength of this country. Think about it. A free society—a truly free society is one in which people can worship the Almighty God or choose not to worship the Almighty God, and you're free to do so. And you're just equally an American, no matter what choice you make.

Let me tell you something else. If you choose to worship the Almighty, you're equally an American if you're a Christian, Jew, or Muslim. That's the strength of America. It's essential that we maintain that strength. Thank you for your prayers. Amazing nation when they pray for the President and his family. It strengthens us and sustains us, and for that, I'm really grateful. I appreciate it a lot.

All right, anybody got a question out here? Yes, ma'am.

Medicare

Q. Why is Medicare—[*inaudible*].

The President. She asked about Medicare going up 17 percent. I'll give you the answer right now. First of all, because there was a formula fixed by the United States Congress in 1996. This wasn't the administration saying, "Raise it." This went up because of a formula that my opponent voted for, for example. Secondly, because the cost for doctors went up. In other words, when they reimbursed doctors more for Medicare, your premium went up. Thirdly, it went up because there are additional benefits that you're going to realize as a result of the law we passed, preventative medicine. And it's the first time ever that Medicare—you as a Medicare patient can get a screening and preventative care. Never has that been done before, and now we've got it in the new law. In '06, you're going to get a drug benefit. But those are the reasons why. Thanks for asking.

Yes, sir.

Timing of Troop Withdrawal From Iraq

Q. [*Inaudible*]—my son was able to serve in Iraq, and by the grace of God has come home safe.

The President. Fantastic. Thank you. What branch of service?

Q. He's in the Army.

The President. Army. Good.

Q. My question is, is when can other parents rest easy, knowing their sons and daughters are on their way home?

The President. You bet. Thanks for asking. As soon as the mission is complete. As quickly as possible, but we've got to get the mission done. I'll tell you, it's—whether it be for the sake of your son who sacrificed or for a son who did not come home, we must complete the mission in their honor. In the honor of your son's sacrifice and service, and in the honor and the sacrifice of those who didn't make it, it's essential we finish the job. It's in our interest that Iraq become a free country.

Think about what a free country will do in the broader Middle East. Think about what the signal will send to the Palestinian people, who must reject corrupt leadership and embrace a peaceful form of government called democracy—true democracy. Think about the example that a free Iraq will set for women in the broader Middle East. I believe everybody desires to be free. I believe that, and it's essential that there be a—an example of freedom in a part

of the world that is desperate for freedom. If we want to win this war on terror, we not only need to stay on the offense, we need to help nations become free nations. I believe all these things because freedom is not America's gift to the world; freedom is the Almighty God's gift to each man and woman in this world.

Yes, ma'am. You're on.

Community Colleges/No Child Left Behind Act

Q. I was excited about your proposal about funding for community colleges.

The President. Yes.

Q. I, myself, have gone back to school.

The President. Good. Thank you.

Q. My daughter is 12 years old. She's been behind in reading all along, but since I went back to school, myself, last fall, she has increased and is reading above grade level at this point.

The President. Fantastic.

Q. My point is that that also—educated parents educate their children better. And that affects No Child Left Behind. Would this funding affect all of community colleges or merely the industrial aspect of community college?

The President. First of all, there's a lot of money going to help people get worker training. We spend billions for worker training programs. What I'm talking about is a specific program aimed at encouraging the job creators and the community colleges to come together to give people the skills necessary to fill the jobs. I mean, there's trade adjustment assistance. There is help. I don't know if you're receiving Federal help or not, but there is all——

Q. [*Inaudible*]

The President. Well, full scholarships help. [*Laughter*] Sounds like—full scholarship is more than half scholarship. [*Laughter*]

She said something interesting about No Child Left Behind. She said, "My daughter was not reading at grade level." Think about that. How do you know, unless you measure? How can a mom say, stand up in front of the President of the United States and say, "You know, my daughter wasn't reading at grade level, and now she's reading above grade level," unless you measure? If you do not measure, you cannot diagnose problems and solve them. That's what No Child Left Behind has done. It gives you the confidence to say, "My daughter is reading above grade level."

Think about a system in which you have no idea. And what happens in a system like that is—is that somebody gets out of high school, and they can't read. And all of a sudden, that person becomes disillusioned and can't find the work of the 21st century. No Child Left Behind is really a good piece of legislation. We start early in measuring. People say, "Oh, don't test." You've got to test. How can you tell whether or not the curriculum is working? How can a parent decide whether or not her child's school is measuring up to the next neighborhood school? This isn't a way to punish people. This is a way to solve problems. It's essential that we stay strong when it comes to accountability. That's how we make sure children are educated.

Listen, I was the Governor of Texas. I heard them say all the time, "All you're doing is teaching the test." No, we're teaching a child to read so they can pass the test, and we better determine whether or not that child can read. I appreciate you bringing it up. The first teacher—a child's first teacher is a mom or a dad. And you're right, and I appreciate you helping a young child.

Yes, sir.

Possible Reserve Callups/Future of Iraq/ Draft

Q. [*Inaudible*]—I am appreciative of your leadership. We have a son that was in Iraq, in the Marine Corps——

The President. You do?

Q. ——he went in——

The President. You don't look old enough. [*Laughter*]

Q. Thank you.

The President. Certainly, the mom doesn't look old enough. [*Laughter*]

Q. He went in with the invasion, did 7 months there, came back, and he went back again. He was in the Sunni Triangle, and he's back now, safely, at home.

The President. Good.

Q. I served under your father, in Desert Storm, in the Air Force.

The President. Thank you, sir.

Q. Right now I'm currently in the Air Force Reserve. And my question to you is, I know the Reserves have more commitment and more responsibilities, and I'm wondering how will that look in the next 4 years for the Reserves?

The President. Yes, I appreciate that. Let me talk about the military. Thanks for your service. He's wondering whether he's going to get called up. Let's get to the bottom line. [*Laughter*] Yes, that's what I thought. [*Laughter*]

Here's the goal. The goal is to train the Iraqi citizens so they can do the work. And it takes the—it will take away the need for us to rotate troops in. That's the goal. People say, "What's the timetable?" Let me tell you what's wrong with saying a timetable. You might remember my opponent said, "Well, we'll have them out of there in 6 months." I got on him for that, because you can't send a signal for 6 months. Well, 6 months—so the enemy says, "Fine, I'll wait them out for six months and one day." That doesn't do any good.

You know, if I tell the Iraqis, "Well, we're coming out whether we get the job done or not," then they'll quit. They need confidence that we'll help them do the job. These people have gone from a tyrannical situation to a freedom, and that's hard to do. And you need the confidence necessary to start assuming the obligations of a free society. And that's why it's essential we not send any mixed signals to them and that we're wise about, you know, talking about timetables.

My answer to you, as quickly as possible. But the way to relieve the pressure off of our troops and the coalition troops is to train Iraqis as quickly as possible. We've got 100,000 of them trained now. We've got 125,000 of them trained by—at the end of this year. We'll have nearly 200,000 trained by the end of next year, and that's a significant number of troops and folks to help.

You know, my opponent says, "Well, what we're going to do is get other nations to send troops in." They're not going to go in for the "wrong war." I know these people. [*Laughter*] I've talked to them a lot. They're our friends. They're not going to say, "Yes, let us sacrifice for the wrong war at the wrong place at the wrong time."

To answer your question, sir, we're going to do our job as quickly as we can and make sure we get the job done.

Now, secondly, I want to answer something. You didn't ask it, but I'm going to ask it myself. [*Laughter*] Are you going to keep the All-Volunteer Army volunteer? And the answer is, absolutely. That is why we increased pay to make the All-Volunteer Army work. That's why we increased housing benefits. That's why we're making sure these troops are skilled.

Secondly, in order to win the war on terror, we need specialized forces. This is specialty work. If you draft, you don't get the specialized force you need. We don't need a draft. We will not have a draft so long as I'm the President of the United States.

Yes, ma'am.

International Criminal Court/Partial-Birth Abortion

Q. I want to thank you, Mr. President, for not joining the International Criminal Court. And thank you for——

The President. Put the mike on that.

Q. Thank you for not joining the International Criminal Court, and thank you for signing into law the partial-birth abortion ban act, which was—[*applause*].

The President. Thank you. Thank you all. Thank you all. Listen, I understand the life debate. And I believe reasonable people who disagree on the issue can come together for commonsense policy. Banning partial-birth abortion was commonsense policy. People on both sides of that issue recognize the brutality of the practice. My opponent wasn't for the ban. He's out of the—really out of the mainstream, it seems like to me, on that issue.

The lady brought up the International Criminal Court. This is a court based in The Hague, where our troops or diplomats, could be brought before a foreign judge, an unaccountable foreign judge, because of decisions made by our country. I think that would be really bad. I think it would be bad for our troops to have to be, you know, facing an unaccountable prosecutor in a foreign land for decisions that the Commander in Chief made.

Listen, if somebody does something wrong in our country, we've got plenty of justice, and we don't need to be signing up for a Federal—international court. My opponent would join the International Criminal Court.

Audience members. Boo-o-o!

The President. You see, they talk about, you know, popularity. I don't think you should try to be popular and make bad decisions. That may be popular in certain European capitals to join the International Criminal Court, but I assure you it is unpopular with our military and the diplomats. It is bad policy, and my opponent is wrong in supporting the International Criminal Court.

Yes, ma'am. You. [*Laughter*]

President's Leadership

Q. [*Inaudible*] Okay, I'll speak louder. [*Laughter*] Thank you, President Bush, for your integrity. You're a man of honesty, and I trust you with my life and my family's.

The President. Thank you.

Q. [*Inaudible*] [*Laughter*]

The President. That's kind of boiling it down right there, you know? Thank you. I appreciate that.

My job as President is to do a lot of things and make a lot of tough decisions. The job also is to set the right example, to live, you know, a life that will make the people proud. I told the people of Iowa when I was campaigning that if I had the honor of serving this office—if I was given the honor of serving the office, I would uphold the honor and dignity of the office. And I'll do so for 4 more years.

Thank you, sir. Yes, ma'am. They've got a mike coming right behind you. Hope this one works.

Presidential Debates/North Korea

Q. I would like to know when you go in to the next debate, if you would just stand up and tell that opponent of yours exactly what you're saying today. We're behind you. We pray for you.

The President. Thank you. Thank you. You know, I appreciate that. It's what you—that's about the only thing to do, is tell people what you believe. I—the last debate was really interesting. I mean, here we had a fellow who said he's for a "global test" for U.S. policy, that he thought my decision on Korea was the wrong decision. See, let me talk about Korea right quick so you understand.

There was a bilateral relations between Korea and the United States before I became President. We had an agreement. We paid the Koreans, gosh, I think about $350 million in fuel oil in the hopes that they would honor the agreement they made. Part of the agreement was they couldn't enrich uranium, and they enriched uranium. And my administration found it out. So I figured that, well, if one bilateral relations failed, maybe the next one won't work, and tried to do something differently to get other nations—you might remember, I've been criticized as being a unilateralist, but here I am putting together a multilateral effort—that means more than one

voice saying to the North Koreans, give up your weapons. And perhaps the most important voice in that discussion is China.

And we went down to Crawford, and Jiang Zemin, the predecessor of Hu Jintao, and I sat down at the table and said, "Why don't we come up with a joint declaration, a joint statement that says that the United States and China both think the Korean Peninsula ought to be nuclear-weapons-free." And he agreed, and we said that. And so now we have China involved, not one voice but two. And then we got South Korea involved and then Japan involved and Russia involved. There's five countries now saying the same thing.

So this time if Kim Chong-il decides to renege on any agreement, he's not only showing disrespect for the United States, he's showing disrespect for China. And my opponent says we need to go back to the old days of unilateralism with North Korea. It failed once. It will fail again. And so I believe we're on the right path to convincing North Korea to give up its weapons.

Let me say what else in that last debate. I'm glad you brought up that last debate. He also said—they asked him, was it a mistake to go in—or he said it was a mistake to go into Iraq. And then when asked, "Well, then is it a mistake to have our troops dying there," he said, "No." You cannot have it both ways. You can't have it both ways. And if you try to have it both ways, it sends mixed messages. See, what I—listen, I understand tactics change. But what shouldn't change is someone's core beliefs, because of politics.

All right, I'm getting the hook. I got to go back to Washington. I can't thank you enough for coming. I'm honored to have your support. Work hard, and we'll carry Iowa and win a great victory in November.

NOTE: The President spoke at 12:21 p.m. at the 7 Flags Event Center. In his remarks, he referred to Stan Thompson, candidate for Congress in Iowa's Third Congressional District; Iowa State Auditor David A. Vaudt; Jeff

Lamberti, president, and Stewart E. Iverson, Jr., majority leader, Iowa State Senate; David Roederer, Iowa State chairman, Bush-Cheney, '04, Inc.; senior Al Qaida associate Abu Musab Al Zarqawi; Prime Minister Junichiro Koizumi of Japan; former President Jiang Zemin and President Hu Jintao of China; and Chairman Kim Chong-il of North Korea.

Statement on the Death of Gordon Cooper
October 5, 2004

Gordon Cooper was a pioneer of human space exploration. He was one of the original seven Mercury astronauts, logging more than 225 hours in space throughout his distinguished career. He also served his country in the United States Air Force and received numerous awards including the Distinguished Flying Cross. Laura joins me in sending our condolences to the entire Cooper family.

Statement on House of Representatives Action on Legislation To Reinstate the Draft
October 5, 2004

I applaud the House of Representatives for soundly rejecting the "Reinstate the Draft" bill, sponsored by Congressman Rangel in the House and Senator Hollings in the Senate. If this bill were presented to me, I would veto it. America's all-volunteer military is the best in the world, and reinstating the draft would be bad policy.

We have increased pay and benefits to ensure that our troops have the resources they need to fight and win the war on terror. I want every American to understand that, as long as I am President, there will be no draft.

NOTE: The statement referred to H.R. 163.

Letter to the Speaker of the House of Representatives Transmitting a Supplemental Budget Request To Support Comprehensive Response and Recovery Efforts After Hurricane Jeanne
October 5, 2004

Dear Mr. Speaker:

On September 8th, I signed into law Public Law 108–303, the Emergency Supplemental Appropriations for Disaster Relief Act, 2004, which provided $2 billion in supplemental funds for hurricane-related disaster relief. On September 14th and 27th, I submitted additional supplemental requests totaling $10.2 billion to continue immediate assistance to address the impact of Hurricanes Charley, Frances, Ivan, and Jeanne.

Due to the availability of better estimates regarding the damage resulting from Hurricane Jeanne, I am requesting additional emergency funds from the Congress to address this natural disaster. I now ask the Congress to consider the enclosed requests, totaling $691.2 million, for additional emergency resources for the Departments of Agriculture, Defense, the Interior, Transportation, and Veterans Affairs; as well as the Corps of Engineers, the Environmental Protection Agency, and International Assistance Programs.

I hereby designate these specific proposals in the amounts requested herein as emergency requirements. These additional requests will support response and recovery efforts to address the critical needs associated with the effects of Hurricane Jeanne. In addition to this enacted and requested emergency funding, Federal agencies will continue to use existing resources and programs for response and recovery efforts from all recent hurricanes and storms.

I urge the Congress to limit this emergency funding to those items directly related to the recovery efforts from the impact of these recent major disasters and to act expeditiously on this and my pending emergency supplemental requests.

The details of this request are set forth in the enclosed letter from the Director of the Office of Management and Budget.

Sincerely,

GEORGE W. BUSH

Remarks in Wilkes-Barre, Pennsylvania
October 6, 2004

The President. Thank you all. Thank you all very much. Thank you all. Thank you all for coming. Please be seated. Thank you all. Thank you. Please be seated. Gosh, thanks for such a great welcome. I appreciate it. It's great to be in Wilkes-Barre, Pennsylvania. It's such an honor to be back here. I'm glad to be in a part of the world where people work hard, they love their families. Good to be in a part of the world where people like to hunt and fish.

My regret is that Laura is not with me. She is——

Audience members. Aw-w-w!

The President. I know it. [*Laughter*] That's generally the reaction. [*Laughter*] Kind of like, "Why didn't you stay home and send Laura." [*Laughter*] You're not going to believe this; it's a true story— or kind of true. [*Laughter*] I said, "Will you marry me?" She said, "Fine, just so long as I never have to give a speech." [*Laughter*] I said, "Okay, you got a deal." [*Laughter*] Fortunately, she didn't hold me to that promise. Laura—when Laura speaks, people see a compassionate, decent, strong First Lady.

I had my morning briefing today with someone you're familiar with. That would be your former Governor Tom Ridge. So Laura sends her best, as does Tom Ridge.

Today I traveled with Don Sherwood. As we say in Crawford, he's a good one. He's a great Member of the United States House of Representatives. I'm proud to work with him. He cares deeply about the people of this important part of the State of Pennsylvania. He is a fine Representative who brings integrity to the office. I appreciate your service.

I want to thank all the State and local officials who are here. I want to thank the candidates who are here. I want to thank the grassroots activists who are here. I want to thank you for what you're going to do, which is to put up the signs, make the phone calls, turn out the vote. With your help, there's no doubt in my mind we'll carry Pennsylvania.

I am sure many of you stayed up to watch the Vice Presidential debate last night. America saw two very different visions of our country and two different hairdos. [*Laughter*] I didn't pick my Vice

President for his hairdo. I picked him for his judgment, his experience—a great Vice President. I'm proud to be running with him.

In less than a month, you'll have a chance to vote for Dick Cheney and me. Think about that—less than a month. I'm looking forward to coming down the stretch with a positive, strong message. As your President, I've worked to make America a more hopeful and more secure place. I've led our country with principle and resolve. And that's how I'll lead our Nation for 4 more years.

When I took office in 2001, the bubble of the nineties had burst. Our economy was headed into a recession. And because of the attacks of September the 11th, nearly a million jobs were lost in 3 months. It was a dangerous time for our economy. People were warning of potential deflation and depression. But I acted.

To stimulate the economy, I called on Congress to pass historic tax relief, which it did, without my opponent's yes vote. The tax relief was the fuel that got our economy growing again. Thanks to the efforts of our citizens and the right policies in the right place at the right time, we put the recession behind us and America is creating jobs once again.

We have built a broad and solid record of accomplishment. In the past year, the United States of America has added about 1.7 million new jobs, more than Germany, Japan, Great Britain, Canada, and France combined. Real tax—real after-tax income—that's the money in your pocket to spend on groceries or house payments and rent—is up more than 10 percent since I took office. Homeownership is at an all-time high in America. Farm income is up. Small businesses are flourishing. The entrepreneurial spirit is strong in the United States of America.

Ours is a record of accomplishment. Thanks to reforms in education, math and reading scores are increasing in our public schools. Ten million students will get record levels of grants and loans to help with college. Low-income seniors are getting $600 extra to help pay for medicine this year, in their drug discount cards. And soon Medicare will offer prescription drug coverage to every senior in America. We have made America a stronger, more hopeful country, and we're just getting started.

Listen, I like to travel our country because I have a chance to talk to our fellow citizens. I understand the challenges facing our Nation. People are living and working in a time of change. Workers switch jobs more than they used to, which means they often need new skills and benefits they can take with them from job to job. We're in a changing world, yet the systems of Government haven't changed. I'm running for 4 more years to change the systems of Government so people can better realize the great dreams of America.

Making sure people realize those dreams, it's essential that our education systems work. We're going to raise the standards and expectations in every high school. We'll invest in our Nation's fine community colleges so workers can be prepared to fill the jobs of the 21st century. We're going to expand health savings accounts so people can pay health expenses with tax-free money and keep the savings if they change jobs. We're going to improve Social Security to allow younger workers to own a piece of their own retirement, a nest egg that the Washington politicians can never take away.

To keep this economy strong and competitive, we must make sure America is the best place in the world to start a business and to do business. To make sure America is the best place in the world to start a business, our taxes must be low. Congress must make the tax relief we passed permanent. To keep jobs here, there need to be less regulations on our small businesses. To keep jobs here, we must pass an energy plan that makes us less dependent on foreign sources of energy. To make sure jobs exist here in America, we got to do something about these junk and frivolous lawsuits. Trial lawyers shouldn't be getting rich at the expense of our entrepreneurs and our doctors.

My opponent and I have a very different view on how to grow our economy. Let me start with taxes. I have a record of reducing them. He has a record of raising them.

Audience members. Boo-o-o!

The President. He voted in the United States Senate to increase taxes 98 times.

Audience members. Boo-o-o!

The President. That's a lot. [*Laughter*] He voted for higher taxes on Social Security benefits.

Audience members. Boo-o-o!

The President. In 1997, he voted for the formula that helped cause the increase in Medicare premiums.

Audience members. Boo-o-o!

The President. My opponent was against all of our middle class tax relief. He voted instead to squeeze another $2,000 per year from the average middle class family.

Audience members. Boo-o-o!

The President. Now the Senator is proposing higher taxes on more than 900,000 small-business owners. My opponent is one of the few candidates in history to campaign on a pledge to raise taxes. [*Laughter*] And that's the kind of promise a politician from Massachusetts usually keeps. [*Laughter*]

He says the tax increase is only for the rich. You've heard that kind of rhetoric before. The rich hire lawyers and accountants for a reason—to stick you with the tab. The Senator is not going to tax you because we're going to win in November.

The Senator and I have different views on another threat to our economy, frivolous lawsuits. He's been a part of the Washington crowd that has obstructed legal reform again and again. Meanwhile, all across America, unfair lawsuits are hurting small businesses. Lawsuits are driving up health care costs. Lawsuits are threatening ob-gyns all across our country. Lawsuits are driving good doctors out of practice. We need a President who will stand up to the trial lawyers in Washington, not put one on the ticket.

The Senator and I have very different views on health care. I've got a specific plan to help Americans find health care that's available and affordable, lawsuit reform, association health care plans to help our small businesses, health savings accounts, community health centers to help the poor, expanding health care for low-income children, using technology to drive down the cost of health care.

He has a different vision. Under his health plan, 8 million Americans would lose the private insurance they get at work, and most would end up on a Government program. Under his plan, 8 out of 10 people who get new insurance will get it from the Federal Government. My opponent's proposal would be the largest expansion of Government-run health care ever. And when Government pays the bills, Government makes the rules. His plan would put bureaucrats in charge of dictating coverage, which could ration care and limit your choice of doctor. Senator Kerry's proposal would put us on the path to "Clinton-care."

Audience members. Boo-o-o!

The President. I'll make sure doctors and patients are in charge of the decisions in America's health care.

The Senator and I have different views on Government spending. Over the years, he's voted 274 times to break the Federal budget limits. And in this campaign, Senator Kerry has announced more than $2 trillion of new spending. And that's a lot of money, even for a Senator from Massachusetts. [*Laughter*]

During his 20 years as a Senator, my opponent hasn't had many accomplishments. Of the hundreds of bills he submitted, only five became law. One of them was ceremonial. But to be fair, he's earned a special distinction in Congress. The nonpartisan National Journal analyzed his record and named John Kerry the most liberal Member of the United States Senate.

Audience members. Boo-o-o!

The President. And when the competition includes Ted Kennedy—[*laughter*]—that's really saying something. [*Laughter*] I'm telling you, I know that bunch. [*Laughter*] It wasn't easy for my opponent to become the single most liberal Member of the Senate. You might even say, it was hard work. [*Laughter*] But he earned that title by voting for higher taxes, more regulation, more junk lawsuits, and more Government control over your life.

And that sets up a real difference in this campaign. My opponent is a tax-and-spend liberal. I'm a compassionate conservative. My opponent wants to empower Government. I want to use Government to empower people. My opponent seems to think all the wisdom is found in Washington, DC. I trust the wisdom of the American people.

Our differences are also clear on issues of national security. When I took office in 2001, threats to America had been gathering for years. Then on one terrible morning, the terrorists took more lives than America lost at Pearl Harbor. Since that day, we have waged a global campaign to protect the American people and bring our enemies to account. Our Government has trained over a half a million first-responders. We tripled spending on homeland security. Law enforcement and intelligence have better tools to stop terrorists, thanks to the PATRIOT Act, which Senator Kerry voted for but now wants to weaken.

The Taliban regime that sheltered Al Qaida is gone from power, and the people of Afghanistan will vote in free elections this very week. A black market network that provided weapons materials to North Korea and Libya and Iran is now out of business. Libya, itself, has given up its weapons of mass destruction programs. We convinced Pakistan and Saudi Arabia to join the fight against the terrorists. And more than three-quarters of Al Qaida's key members and associates have been brought to justice.

After September the 11th, America had to assess every potential threat in a new light. Our Nation awakened to an even greater danger, the prospect that terrorists who killed thousands with hijacked airplanes would kill many more with weapons of mass murder. We had to take a hard look at everyplace where terrorists might get those weapons, and one regime stood out, the dictatorship of Saddam Hussein.

We knew the dictator had a history of using weapons of mass destruction, a long record of aggression, and hatred for America. He was listed by Republican and Democrat administrations as a state sponsor of terrorists. There was a risk, a real risk, that Saddam Hussein would pass weapons or materials or information to terrorist networks. In the world after September the 11th, that was a risk we could not afford to take.

After 12 years of United Nations Security Council resolutions, we gave him a final chance to come clean and listen to the demands of the free world. When he chose defiance and war, our coalition enforced the just demands of the world. And the world is better off with Saddam Hussein sitting in a prison cell.

We've had many victories in the war on terror, and that war goes on. Our Nation is safer but not yet safe. To win this war, we must fight on every front. We'll stay on the offensive against terrorist networks, striking them before they come to America to hurt us. We'll confront governments that support terrorists and could arm them, because they're equally guilty of terrorist murder.

And our long-term victory requires confronting the ideology of hate with freedom and hope. Our victory requires changing the conditions that produce radicalism and suicide bombers and finding new democratic allies in a troubled part of the region. America is always more secure when freedom is on the march. And freedom is on the march in Afghanistan and Iraq and elsewhere. There will be good days, and there will be bad days in the war on terror. But every day we will show our resolve, and we will do our duty. This Nation is determined. We will stay in the fight until the fight is won.

My opponent agrees with all this, except when he doesn't. [*Laughter*] Last week in our debate, he once again came down firmly on every side of the Iraq war. [*Laughter*] He stated that Saddam Hussein was a threat and that America had no business removing that threat. Senator Kerry said our soldiers and marines are not fighting for a mistake but also called the liberation of Iraq a "colossal error." He said we need to do more to train Iraqis, but he also said we shouldn't be spending so much money over there. He said he wants to hold a summit meeting so he can invite other countries to join what he calls "the wrong war in the wrong place at the wrong time." [*Laughter*] He said terrorists are pouring across the Iraqi border but also said that fighting those terrorists is a "diversion" from the war on terror. [*Laughter*] You hear all that, and you can understand why somebody would make a face. [*Laughter*]

My opponent's endless back-and-forth on Iraq is part of a larger misunderstanding. In the war on terror, Senator Kerry is proposing policies and doctrines that would weaken America and make the world more dangerous. Senator Kerry approaches the world with a September the 10th mindset. He declared in his convention speech that any attack will be met with a swift and certain response. That was the mindset of the 1990s, while Al Qaida was planning the attacks on America. After September the 11th, our object in the war on terror is not to wait for the next attack and respond but to prevent attacks by taking the fight to the enemy.

In our debate, Senator Kerry said that removing Saddam Hussein was a mistake because the threat was not imminent. The problem with this approach is obvious. If America waits until a threat is at our doorstep, it might be too late to save lives. Tyrants and terrorists will not give us polite notice before they launch an attack on our country. I refuse to stand by while dangers gather. In the world after September the 11th, the path to safety is the path of action. And I will continue to defend the people of the United States of America. [*Applause*] Thank you all. Thank you all.

My opponent has also announced the Kerry doctrine, declaring that American actions in the war on terror must pass a "global test."

Audience members. Boo-o-o!

The President. Under this test, America would not be able to act quickly against threats, because we'd be sitting around waiting for our grade from other nations and other leaders. [*Laughter*]

I have a different view. America will always work with allies for security and peace. But the President's job is not to pass a "global test." The President's job is to protect the American people. [*Applause*] Thank you all.

When my opponent first ran for Congress, he argued that American troops should be deployed only at the directive of the United Nations.

Audience members. Boo-o-o!

The President. Now, he's changed his mind. [*Laughter*] No, he has, in all fairness. But it is a window into his thinking. Over the years, Senator Kerry has looked for every excuse to constrain America's action in the world. These days he praises America's broad coalition in the Persian Gulf war. But in 1991, he criticized those coalition members as, quote, "shadow battlefield allies who barely carry a burden." Sounds familiar. At that time, he voted against the war. If that coalition didn't pass his "global test," clearly, nothing will. [*Laughter*] This mindset would paralyze America in a dangerous world. I'll never hand over America's security decisions to foreign leaders and international bodies that do not have America's interests at heart.

My opponent's doctrine has other consequences, especially for our men and women in uniform. My opponent supports the International Criminal Court, which would allow unaccountable foreign prosecutors and judges to put American soldiers on trial.

Audience members. Boo-o-o!

The President. That would be a legal nightmare for our troops. My fellow citizens, as long as I'm your President, Americans in uniform will answer to the officers and laws of the United States, not to the International Criminal Court in The Hague.

Audience members. Four more years! Four more years! Four more years!

The President. The Senator speaks often about his plan to strengthen America's alliances, but he's got an odd way of doing it. In the middle of the war, he's chosen to insult America's fighting allies by calling them "window dressing" and the "coalition of the coerced and the bribed." The Italians who died in Nasiriyah were not window dressing. They were heroes in the war on terror. The British and the Poles at the head of the multinational divisions in Iraq were not coerced or bribed. They have fought and some have died in the cause of freedom. These good allies and dozens of others deserve the respect of all Americans, not the scorn of a politician.

Instead, the Senator would have America bend over backwards to satisfy a handful of governments with agendas different from our own. This is my opponent's alliance-building strategy: Brush off your best friends; fawn over your critics. And that is no way to gain the respect of the world.

My opponent says he has a plan for Iraq. Parts of it should sound pretty familiar. It's already known as the Bush plan. [*Laughter*] Senator Kerry suggests we train Iraqi troops, which we've been doing for months. Just this week, Iraqi forces backed by coalition troops fought bravely to take the city of Samarra from the terrorists and Ba'athists and insurgents. Senator Kerry is proposing that we have—that Iraq have elections. [*Laughter*] Those elections are already scheduled for January. [*Laughter*] He wants the U.N. to be involved in those elections. Well, the U.N. is already there.

There was one element of the Senator Kerry's plan—it's a new element. He's talked about artificial timetables to pull our troops out of Iraq. He sent the signal that America's overriding goal in Iraq would be to leave, even if the job isn't done. That may satisfy his political needs, but it complicates the essential work we're doing in Iraq. The Iraqi people need to know that America will not cut and run when their freedom is at stake. Our soldiers and marines need to know that America will honor their service and sacrifice by completing the mission. And our enemies in Iraq need to know that they can never out last the will of America.

Senator Kerry assures us that he's the one to win a war he calls a "mistake," an "error," and a "diversion." But you can't win a war you don't believe in fighting. On Iraq, Senator Kerry has a strategy of retreat; I have a strategy of victory. We've returned sovereignty to the Iraqi people ahead of schedule. We've trained about 100,000 Iraqi soldiers, police officers, and other security personnel, and that total will rise to 125,000 by year-end. We've already allocated more than $7 billion for reconstruction efforts, so more Iraqis can see the benefits of freedom. We're working with a coalition of some 30 nations to provide security. Other nations are helping with debt relief and reconstruction aid for Iraqis. And although the terrorists will try to stop them, Iraq will hold free elections in January because the Iraqi people want and deserve to govern themselves.

I understand some Americans have strong concerns about our role in Iraq. I respect the fact that they take this issue seriously, because it is a serious matter.

I assure them we're in Iraq because I deeply believe it is necessary and right and critical to the outcome of the war on terror. If another terror regime were allowed to emerge in Iraq, the terrorists would find a home, a source of funding, vital support. They would correctly conclude that free nations do not have the will to defend themselves. If Iraq becomes a free society at the heart of the Middle East, an ally in the war on terror, a model of hopeful reform in a region that needs hopeful reform, the terrorists will suffer a crushing defeat, and every free nation will be more secure.

This is why Democratic Senator Joe Lieberman calls Iraq a "crucial battle in the global war on terrorism." This is why Prime Minister Tony Blair has called the struggle in Iraq "the crucible in which the future of global terrorism will be determined." This is why the terrorists are fighting with desperate cruelty. They know their own future is at stake. Iraq is no diversion. It is the place where civilization is taking a decisive stand against chaos and terror, and we must not waver.

Unfortunately, my opponent has been known to waver. [*Laughter*] His well-chosen words and rationalizations cannot explain why he voted to authorize force against Saddam Hussein and then voted against money for bullets and vehicles and body armor for the troops on the ground. He tried to clear it all up by saying, "I actually did vote for the $87 billion, before I voted against it." Now he says he made a mistake in how he talked about the war. The mistake here is not what Senator Kerry said. The mistake is what he did in voting against funding for Americans in combat. That is the kind of wavering a nation at war can never afford.

As a candidate, my opponent promises to defend America. The problem is as a Senator for two decades, he has built a record of weakness. The record shows he twice led efforts to gut our intelligence service budgets. The record shows he voted against many of the weapons that won the

cold war and are vital to current military operations. And the record shows he has voted more than 50 times against missile defense systems that would help protect us from the threats of a dangerous world.

I have a record in office as well, and all Americans have seen that record. On September the 14th, 2001, I stood in the ruins of the Twin Towers. It's a day I will never forget. There were workers in hardhats yelling at me, "Whatever it takes." I remember trying to console people coming out of that rubble, and a guy grabbed me by the arm, and he looked me in the eye and said, "Do not let me down." These men and women—the men and women there took it personally. You took it personally. I took it personally. I have a responsibility that goes on. I wake up every morning thinking about how to make our country more secure. I have acted again and again to protect our people. I will never relent in defending America, whatever it takes.

Audience members. Four more years! Four more years! Four more years!

The President. Twenty-seven days from today, Americans will make a critical choice. My opponent offers an agenda that is stuck in the thinking and the policies of the past. On national security, he offers the defensive mindset of September the 10th, a "global test" to replace American leadership, a strategy of retreat in Iraq, and a 20-year history of weakness in the United States Senate. Here at home, he offers a record and an agenda of more taxes and more spending and more litigation and more Government control over your life.

The race for President is a contest for the future, and you know where I stand. I'm running for President to keep this Nation on the offensive against terrorists, with the goal of total victory. I'm running for President to keep this economy moving so every worker has a good job and quality health care and a secure retirement. I'm running for President to make our Nation a more compassionate society, where no one is left out, where every life matters.

I have a hopeful vision. I believe this young century will be liberty's century. We'll promote liberty abroad, protect our country, and build a better world beyond the war on terror. We'll encourage liberty at home to spread the prosperity and opportunity of America to every corner of our country. I will carry this message to my fellow citizens in the closing days of this campaign, and with your help, we will win a great victory on November the 2d.

God bless. God bless our great country. Thank you all. Thanks for coming.

NOTE: The President spoke at 10:13 a.m. at the Kirby Center for the Performing Arts. In his remarks, he referred to Prime Minister Tony Blair of the United Kingdom.

Remarks in Farmington Hills, Michigan
October 6, 2004

The President. Thank you all for coming. You know what I think, Bill? I think that with the help of these good folks here, we'll carry Michigan. We'll win a great victory in November, and I'll be there in the White House when you come back.

Listen, I appreciate you coming. Thanks for coming today. We're coming down the stretch. I'm here to ask for your vote, and I'm here to ask for your help. Register your friends and neighbors. Make sure you don't overlook discerning Democrats, people like Zell Miller. Get people headed to the polls, and remind them, if they want a safer America, a stronger America, and a better America, to put me and Dick Cheney back in office.

Speaking about the Vice President, I'm sure some of you stayed up to watch the debate last night. America saw two different visions of our country and two different hair styles. [*Laughter*] America saw why I picked Dick Cheney to be the Vice President. He's strong. He's steady. He knows what he's talking about.

Laura sends her best. She's warming up for the Jay Leno show. He's lucky to have her as a guest, and I'm lucky to have her as a wife. She is a great First Lady. Perhaps the most important reason to put me back into office, is so that Laura will be the First Lady for 4 more years.

I appreciate Bill Laimbeer for being here. I also want to thank another great leader and sports figure of your great State, Bo Schembechler is with us today as well. I appreciate you bringing Cathryn.

I also want to thank the attorney general, Mike Cox. My longtime friend Brooks Patterson is with us today. I thank Ruth Johnson and other State and local officials. I want to thank Betsy DeVos and all the grassroots activists who are here. I appreciate what you're doing. I appreciate the hard work you're doing.

I want to thank Mary Spangler, the chancellor of the Oakland Community College, and Ed Callaghan, who's the president. Thank you all for having me.

I want to thank my friend Mark Wills, country and western singer, for being here. Most of all, thank you all for being here.

In less than a month, you'll have a chance to vote for Dick Cheney and me. As your President, I've worked to make America more hopeful and more secure. I've led our country with principle and resolve, and that is how I'll lead our Nation for 4 more years.

When I took office in 2001, the bubble of the nineties had burst and our economy was headed into a recession. Because of the attacks of September the 11th, nearly a million jobs were lost in 3 months. It was a dangerous time for our economy. People were warning of potential deflation and depression, but I led. To stimulate the economy, I called on Congress to pass historic tax relief, which it did. The tax relief was the fuel that got our economy growing again. Thanks to the efforts of our citizens and the right policies at the right place at the right time, we put the recession behind us, and America is creating jobs again.

We have built a broad and solid record of accomplishment. In the past year, the United States of America has added about 1.7 million new jobs, more than Germany, Japan, Great Britain, Canada, and France combined. Real tax—real after-tax income, the money in your pocket that you have to spend on groceries and house payments and rent, is up more than 10 percent since I took office. Homeownership is at an all-time high in America. The farm economy is strong. The entrepreneurial spirit is alive and well. The small-business sector of America is doing well.

Thanks to our reforms in education, math and reading scores are increasing in our public schools. Under my budget, 10 million students will get record levels of grants and loans to help with college. Low-income seniors are getting $600 extra to help pay for medicine this year, and soon Medicare will offer prescription drug coverage to every senior in America. We've made America stronger, and we're just getting started.

Listen, I understand we're living in changing times—people are living and working in a time of change. Workers switch jobs more often than they used to, which means they need, oftentimes need new skills and new benefits that they can take with them from job to job. Ultimately, in our competitive global economy, it's our people that make America successful, and that's why I believe education is so vital.

So we'll raise standards and expectations for every public school in America. We'll invest in our Nation's fine community colleges, like this one right here, so they pre-pare workers for the jobs of the 21st century. We'll expand health savings accounts so people can pay health expenses with tax-free money. We'll improve Social Security to allow younger workers to own a piece of their retirement, a nest egg that Washington, DC, politicians can never take away.

To keep our economy strong and competitive, we must make sure America is the best place in the world to do business. That's why we need to make our tax relief permanent for our small businesses and our families. To keep jobs here, we need to cut needless regulations. To keep jobs here, we need to pass an energy plan that makes our Nation less dependent on foreign sources of energy. To make sure we got jobs here, we need to stop these junk and frivolous lawsuits that badger our employers.

My opponent and I have a very different view as how to grow our economy. We have a difference of opinion. Let's start with taxes. I have a record of reducing them. He has a record of raising them.

Audience members. Boo-o-o!

The President. He voted in the United States Senate to raise taxes 98 times.

Audience members. Boo-o-o!

The President. That sounds like a lot to me. He voted for higher taxes on Social Security benefits.

Audience members. Boo-o-o!

The President. He voted in 1997 for the formula that has helped cause the increases in Medicare premiums.

Audience members. Boo-o-o!

The President. Remember when I proposed middle class tax relief in order to get this economy going? I asked Congress to raise the child credit, reduce the marriage penalty, and create a new 10-percent bracket for lower income Americans. He voted against every one of those taxes to help the middle class.

Audience members. Boo-o-o!

The President. Now he's proposing higher taxes—higher taxes on about 900,000 small-business owners.

Audience members. Boo-o-o!

The President. Remember when you hear him say "tax the rich," a lot of small businesses pay individual income taxes. As a matter of fact, 90 percent of small businesses do. And we've heard that rhetoric, haven't we, "tax the rich"? Yes. That's why the rich hire lawyers and accountants, to stick you with the bill, to stick those small-business owners with the bill. We're not going to let him tax you; we're going to win Michigan and win in November.

My opponent is one of the few candidates in history to campaign on a pledge to raise taxes. That's the kind of pledge a politician from Massachusetts usually keeps. [*Laughter*]

We have a different view on another threat to our economy, frivolous lawsuits. Senator Kerry has been a part of the Washington crowd that has obstructed legal reform again and again. Meanwhile, all across America, unfair lawsuits are hurting small businesses. Lawsuits are driving up the cost of your health care. Lawsuits are driving good doctors out of the practice of medicine. We need a President who will stand up to the trial lawyers in Washington, not put one on the ticket.

The Senator and I have very different views on health care. I believe we ought to help the poor with community health centers. We ought to fully subscribe to the children's health program for low-income families. We need association health plans to help our small businesses afford insurance. We need health savings accounts to help our workers and small businesses be able to better afford insurance. We need to make sure we use technology to help drive down the cost of medicine.

He has a different view. Under his health plan, 8 million Americans would lose the private insurance they get at work and most would end up on a Government program.

Audience members. Boo-o-o!

The President. Under his plan, 8 out of 10 people who get new insurance will get it from the Federal Government. My opponent's proposal would be the largest expansion of Government-run health care ever. And when Government pays the bills, Government makes the rules. His plan would put bureaucrats in charge of dictating coverage, which could ration your care and limit your choice of doctors. My opponent's plan would put us on the path to "Hillary-care."

Audience members. Boo-o-o!

The President. In everything we do to reform health care, we will make sure the decisions are made by patients and doctors, not by bureaucrats in Washington, DC.

My opponent and I have different views on spending—spending your money. Over the years he's voted 274 times to break Federal budget limits. And in this campaign, he's announced more than $2 trillion in new spending, and that's a lot of money, even for somebody from Massachusetts.

During his 20 years as a Senator, my opponent hasn't had many accomplishments. Of the hundreds of bills he submitted, only five became law. One of them was ceremonial. But to be fair, he's earned a special distinction in Congress. The nonpartisan National Journal analyzed his record and named John Kerry the most liberal Member of the United States Senate.

Audience members. Boo-o-o!

The President. And when the competition includes Ted Kennedy, that's really saying something. [*Laughter*] Listen, it wasn't easy for my opponent to become the single most liberal Member of the Senate. You might even say it was hard work. [*Laughter*] But he earned that title. He earned it by voting for higher taxes, more regulation, more junk lawsuits, and more Government control over your life.

And that sets up one of the real differences in this campaign. My opponent is a tax-and-spend liberal. I'm a compassionate conservative. My opponent wants to empower Government. I want to use Government to empower citizens. My opponent seems to think all the wisdom is found in

Washington, DC. I trust the wisdom of the American people.

Our differences are also clear on issues of national security. When I took office in 2001, the threats to America had been gathering for years. Then on one terrible morning, terrorists took more lives than America lost at Pearl Harbor. Since that day, we've waged a global campaign to protect the American people and bring our enemies to account. Our Government has trained over a half a million first-responders and tripled spending on homeland security. Law enforcement and intelligence have better tools to stop terrorists, thanks to the PATRIOT Act, which Senator Kerry voted for but now wants to weaken.

The Taliban regime that sheltered Al Qaida is gone from power, and the people of Afghanistan will vote in free elections this coming Saturday. A black market network that provided weapons materials to North Korea and Libya and Iran is now out of business. Libya, itself, has given up its weapons of mass destruction. Pakistan and Saudi Arabia are joining the fight against the terrorists, and more than three-quarters of Al Qaida's key members and associates have been brought to justice.

After September the 11th, America had to assess every potential threat in a new light. Our Nation awakened to an even greater danger, the prospect that terrorists who killed thousands with hijacked airplanes would kill many more with weapons of mass murder. We had to take a hard look at everyplace where terrorists might get those weapons.

One regime stood out, the dictatorship of Saddam Hussein. We knew the dictator had a history of using weapons of mass destruction, a long record of aggression and hatred for America, and was listed by Republican and Democrat administrations as a state sponsor of terror. There was a risk that Saddam Hussein would pass weapons or materials or information to terrorists networks. In a world after September the 11th, that was a risk we could not afford to take.

After 12 years of United Nations Security Council resolutions, we gave him a final chance to come clean and prove his disarmament. He chose defiance. And when he did, he chose war. Our coalition enforced the just demands of the free world, and the world is better off today with Saddam Hussein in a prison cell.

We have had many victories in the war on terror, and that war goes on. Our Nation is safer but not yet safe. To win this war, we must fight on every front. We will stay on the offensive against terrorist networks. We will strike them overseas so we do not have to face them here at home. We will confront governments that support terrorists and could arm them, because they're equally guilty of terrorist murder.

And our long-term victory requires confronting the ideology of hate with freedom and hope. Our long-term victory says we must change the conditions that produce radicalism and suicide bombers. Our long-term security depends upon finding new democratic allies in a troubled region of the world.

America is always more secure when freedom is on the march, and freedom is on the march in Afghanistan, in Iraq, and elsewhere. There will be good days, and there will be bad days in the war on terror. But every day we will show our resolve and do our duty to future generations of Americans. This Nation is determined. We will stay in the fight until the fight is won.

My opponent agrees with all this, except when he doesn't. [*Laughter*] Last week in——

Audience members. Flip-flop! Flip-flop! Flip-flop!

The President. Last week in our debate, he once again came down firmly on every side of the Iraq war. [*Laughter*] He stated that Saddam Hussein was a threat and that America had no business removing that threat. Senator Kerry said our soldiers and marines are not fighting for a "mistake," but he also called the liberation of Iraq a "colossal error."

Audience members. Boo-o-o!

The President. He said we need to do more to train Iraqis, but he also said we shouldn't be spending so much money over there. He said he wants to hold a summit meeting, so he wants—so he can invite other countries to join what he calls the "wrong war at the wrong place at the wrong time." He said terrorists are pouring across the Iraqi border but also said that fighting those terrorists is a "diversion" from the war on terror. If you hear all that, you can understand why somebody would make a face. [*Laughter*]

Audience members. Four more years! Four more years! Four more years!

The President. My opponent—my opponent's endless back-and-forth on Iraq is part of a larger misunderstanding. In the war on terror, Senator Kerry is proposing policies and doctrines that would weaken America and make the world more dangerous. Senator Kerry approaches the world with a September the 10th mindset. He declared in his convention speech that any attack will be met with a swift and a certain response. This was a mindset of the 1990s, while Al Qaida was planning attacks on America. After September the 11th, our object in the war on terror is not to wait for the next attack and respond, but to prevent attacks by taking the fight to the enemy.

Audience members. U.S.A.! U.S.A.! U.S.A.!

The President. In our debate, Senator Kerry said that removing Saddam was a mistake because the threat was not imminent. The problem with this approach is obvious. If America waits until a threat is at our doorstep, it might be too late to save lives. Tyrants and terrorists will not give us polite notice before they launch an attack on our country. I refuse to stand by while dangers gather.

My opponent has also announced the Kerry doctrine, declaring that American actions in the war on terror must pass a "global test."

Audience members. Boo-o-o!

The President. Under this test, America would not be able to act quickly against threats because we'd be sitting around waiting for our grade from other nations. I have a different view. America will always work with our allies for security and peace, but the President's job is not to pass a "global test." The President's job is to protect the American people.

When my opponent first ran for Congress, he argued that American troops should be deployed only at the directive of the United Nations.

Audience members. Boo-o-o!

The President. Now, look, he has changed his mind, but it is a window into his thinking. Over the years, Senator Kerry has looked for every excuse to constrain America's actions in the world. These days he praises America's broad coalition in the Persian Gulf war, but in 1991, he criticized those coalition members as, quote, "shallow battlefield allies who barely carry a burden." Sounds familiar. And that time, he voted against the war. If that coalition didn't pass his "global test," clearly nothing will. His mindset would paralyze America in a dangerous world. I will never hand over America's national security decisions to foreign leaders or international bodies.

The Kerry doctrine has other consequences, especially for our men and women in uniform. The Senator from Massachusetts supports the International Criminal Court——

Audience members. Boo-o-o!

The President. ——which would allow unaccountable foreign prosecutors and judges to put American soldiers on trial.

Audience members. Boo-o-o!

The President. And that would be a legal nightmare for our troops. My fellow citizens, as long as I'm your President, Americans in uniform will answer to the officers and laws of the United States, not to the International Criminal Court in The Hague.

The Senator speaks often about his plan to strengthen America's alliances, but he's got an odd way of going about it. In the middle of the war, he's chosen to insult America's fighting allies by calling them "window dressing" and a "coalition of the coerced and the bribed." The Italians who died in Nasiriyah were not window dressing. They were heroes in the war on terror. The British and Poles at the head of multinational divisions in Iraq were not coerced or bribed. They have fought and some have died in the cause of freedom. These good allies and dozens of others deserve the respect of all Americans, not the scorn of a politician.

Instead, the Senator would have America bend over backwards to satisfy a handful of governments with agendas different from our own. This is my opponent's alliance-building strategy: Brush off your best friend; fawn over your critics. And that's no way to gain respect in this world.

My opponent says he has a plan for Iraq. Parts of it sound pretty familiar. It's already known as the Bush plan. Senator Kerry suggests we train Iraqi troops. That's what we've been doing for months. Senator Kerry is proposing that Iraq have elections. Those elections are scheduled for January. He wants the U.N. to be involved in those elections. The U.N. is already there. There's one new element of Senator Kerry's plan. He talked about artificial timetables to pull the troops out of Iraq. He has sent the signal that America's overriding goal in Iraq would be to leave, even if the job isn't done. That may satisfy his political needs, but it complicates the essential work we're doing in Iraq.

The Iraqi people need to know that America will not cut and run, with their freedom at stake. Our soldiers and marines need to know that America will honor their service and sacrifice by completing the mission. Our enemies in Iraq need to know that they can never out last the will of America. Senator Kerry assures us that he's the one to win a war he calls a "mistake" or an "error" and a "diversion." But you can't win a war you don't believe in fight-

ing. On Iraq, Senator Kerry has a strategy of retreat; I have a strategy for victory.

We returned sovereignty to the Iraqi people ahead of schedule. We've trained about 100,000 Iraqi soldiers, police officers, and other security personnel. And the total will rise to 125,000 by the end of this year. These people are fighting for their freedom. They want to be free. They're being trained to be able to fight and stop these terrorists from preventing the march of freedom. We've allocated more than $7 billion for reconstruction efforts so more Iraqis can see the benefit of freedom. We're working with a coalition of some 30 nations to provide security. Other nations are helping with debt relief and reconstruction aid for Iraqis. And although terrorists will try to stop them, Iraq will hold free elections in January, because the Iraqi people want to be free.

I understand some Americans have strong concerns about our role in Iraq. I respect the fact that they take this issue seriously. It's a serious matter. I assure them we're in Iraq because I deeply believe it is necessary and right and critical to the outcome of the war on terror and critical for long-term peace for our children and grandchildren.

If another terror regime were allowed to emerge in Iraq, the terrorists would find a home and a source of funding and a source of support, and they would correctly conclude that free nations do not have the will to defend themselves. If Iraq becomes a free society at the heart of the Middle East, an ally in the war on terror, a model for hopeful reform in that region, the terrorists will suffer a crushing defeat.

And that is why Democratic Senator Joe Lieberman calls Iraq "a crucial battle in the global war on terrorism." And that is why Prime Minister Tony Blair has called the struggle in Iraq "the crucible in which the future of global terrorism will be determined." That is why the terrorists are fighting with desperate cruelty. They know their future is at stake. Iraq is no diversion. It's a place where civilization is taking a decisive stand against chaos and terror, and we must not waver.

Unfortunately, my opponent has been known to waver. His well-chosen words and rationalizations cannot explain why he voted to authorize force against Saddam Hussein and then voted against money for bullets and vehicles and body armor for the troops on the ground.

Audience members. Boo-o-o!

The President. He tried to clear it up by saying, "I actually did vote for the $87 billion, before I voted against it." Now he says he made a mistake in how he talked about that vote. The mistake is not what Senator Kerry said. The mistake is what Senator Kerry did in voting against funding for our troops in combat, and that is the kind of wavering a nation at war cannot afford.

As a candidate, my opponent promises to defend America. The problem is, as a Senator for two decades, he has built a record of weakness. The record shows he twice led efforts to gut our intelligence service budget. The record shows he voted against many of the weapons that won the cold war and are vital to current military operations. And the record shows he has voted more than 50 times against missile defense systems that would help protect us from the threats of a dangerous world.

I have a record in office as well, and all Americans have seen that record. Not all Americans agree with me, but they know where I stand.

On September the 14th, 2001, I stood in the ruins of the Twin Towers. It's a day I will never forget. There were workers in hardhats yelling to me at the top of their lungs, "Whatever it takes." A guy grabbed me by the arm; he said, "Do not let me down." Ever since that day I wake up every morning thinking about how to better protect our country. I've acted again and again to make America safe. I will never relent in defending the people of this country, whatever it takes.

Audience members. U.S.A.! U.S.A.! U.S.A.!

The President. Twenty-seven days from today, Americans will make a critical choice. My opponent offers an agenda that is stuck in the thinking and the policies of the past. On national security, he offers the defensive, reactive mindset of September the 10th, a "global test" to replace American leadership, a strategy of retreat in Iraq, and a 20-year history of weakness in the Senate. Here at home, he offers a record and an agenda of more taxes and more spending and more litigation and more Government control over your life.

A race for President is a contest for the future, and you know where I stand. I'm running for President to keep this Nation on the offensive against the terrorists, with the goal of total victory. I'm running for President to keep this economy moving so every worker has a good job and quality health care and a secure retirement. I'm running for President to make our strong Nation a more compassionate society, where no one is left out and every life is valued.

And I have a hopeful vision. I believe this young century will be liberty's century. We'll promote liberty abroad to protect our country and to build a better world beyond the war on terror. We'll encourage liberty at home to spread the prosperity and opportunity to every corner of this great land. I will carry this message to my fellow citizens in the closing days of this campaign, and with your help, we'll carry Michigan and win a great victory in November.

Thank you all for coming. God bless. Thank you all.

NOTE: The President spoke at 3:22 p.m. at the Oakland Community College-Orchard Ridge Campus. In his remarks, he referred to former professional basketball player William Laimbeer, Jr.; Senator Zell Miller of Georgia, who made the keynote address at the 2004 Republican National Convention; television talk show host Jay Leno; Glenn E.

"Bo" Schembechler, former head coach, University of Michigan football team, and his wife, Cathy; Michigan State Attorney General Mike Cox; Oakland County Chief Executive L. Brooks Patterson; Michigan State Representative Ruth Johnson; Betsy DeVos, chairman, Michigan Republican Party; and Prime Minister Tony Blair of the United Kingdom.

Statement on Senate Passage of the "National Intelligence Reform Act"
October 6, 2004

I commend the Senate for acting in a bipartisan way to pass landmark legislation that will help us meet our goal to better protect the American people by strengthening the intelligence community. The "National Intelligence Reform Act" is consistent with my proposal to establish a strong National Intelligence Director with full budget authority and the new National Counterterrorism Center. America is a nation at war, and this legislation is another important step forward as we do everything in our power to defeat the terrorist enemy and protect the American people. I urge the House to act quickly so that Congress can resolve any differences and send legislation to me as soon as possible.

NOTE: The statement referred to S. 2845.

Remarks on the Report on Iraq's Weapons of Mass Destruction
October 7, 2004

Chief weapons inspector Charles Duelfer has now issued a comprehensive report that confirms the earlier conclusion of David Kay that Iraq did not have the weapons that our intelligence believed were there.

The Duelfer report also raises important new information about Saddam Hussein's defiance of the world and his intent and capability to develop weapons. The Duelfer report showed that Saddam was systematically gaming the system, using the U.N. Oil for Food Programme to try to influence countries and companies in an effort to undermine sanctions. He was doing so with the intent of restarting his weapons program, once the world looked away.

Based on all the information we have today, I believe we were right to take action, and America is safer today with Saddam Hussein in prison. He retained the knowledge, the materials, the means, and the intent to produce weapons of mass destruction, and he could have passed that knowledge on to our terrorist enemies. Saddam Hussein was a unique threat, a sworn enemy of our country, a state sponsor of terror, operating in the world's most volatile region. In a world after September the 11th, he was a threat we had to confront, and America and the world are safer for our actions.

The Duelfer report makes clear that much of the accumulated body of 12 years of our intelligence and that of our allies was wrong, and we must find out why and correct the flaws. The Silberman-Robb Commission is now at work to do just that, and its work is important and essential. At a time of many threats in the world, the intelligence on which the President and Members of Congress base their decisions must be better, and it will be. I look forward to the intelligence reform commission's recommendations, and we will act on them to improve our intelligence, especially our intelligence about weapons of mass destruction.

Thank you all very much.

NOTE: The President spoke at 1:24 p.m. on the South Grounds at the White House prior to his departure for Wausau, WI. In his remarks, he referred to Charles Duelfer, Special Advisor to the Director of Central Intelligence; David Kay, former CIA Special Advisor for Strategy Regarding Iraqi Weapons of Mass Destruction Programs; and former President Saddam Hussein of Iraq. He also referred to the Commission on the Intelligence Capabilities of the United States Regarding Weapons of Mass Destruction, chaired by former Senator Chuck Robb and Judge Laurence Silberman. The Office of the Press Secretary also released a Spanish language transcript of these remarks. The report of September 30 was entitled "Comprehensive Report of the Special Advisor to the DCI on Iraq's WMD."

Remarks in Wausau, Wisconsin
October 7, 2004

The President. Thank you all for coming out. It's great to be back in Wisconsin. Listen, thanks for coming. It's great to be back in Wausau. It's an honor that so many came out to say hello. I'm so thankful you're here. Next time I come back I'd like to do some hunting and fishing.

I'm here to ask for your vote. I'm here to ask for your help. We're getting close to the stretch run here in this campaign, and I'd like to encourage you to get your friends and neighbors to register to vote and then go to the polls. And remind them when they head to the polls, if they want a safer America, a stronger America, a better America, to put Dick Cheney and me back in office.

Laura sends her very best. Last time I saw her, I was watching the Jay Leno rerun this morning. [*Laughter*] I am—you know, when I asked her to marry me, she said, "Fine, just so long as I never have to give a speech." [*Laughter*] I said, "Okay, you got a deal." Fortunately, she didn't hold me to that promise. The American people have gotten to see what I know: She is a strong, compassionate, great First Lady for this country.

I was proud of the job my Vice President did the other night.

I appreciate Tommy Thompson. He's a great leader. He's in my Cabinet, as you recall. And I appreciate you training him so well.

I'm glad to be here on the stage with the next United States Senator from Wisconsin, Tim Michels. You got a good one in Tim, and I hope you put him in office. It's important. And make no mistake about it, with your help, he's going to win.

I want to thank Jack Voight, who is the State treasurer. I want to thank the assembly speaker, John Gard, who is with us, Scott Walker is over here from Milwaukee County. I appreciate him coming. We call him Scott W. [*Laughter*] I want to thank the mayor of Wausau for being here, Mayor Tipple. Mr. Mayor, I'm proud you're here. My only advice, and I know you didn't ask for any—[*laughter*]—but my only advice is to fill the potholes. [*Laughter*]

I want to thank Scott Klug for emceeing this event, and I appreciate my friend Stan Orr. I want to thank John Conlee, the singer who was here. I appreciate you coming,

John, and thanks for entertaining everybody.

I particularly want to thank the grassroots activists who are here. Those are the people who put up the signs and make the phone calls and do all the hard work. You never hardly get thanked. I'm here to thank you for what you're going to do. I know with your hard work, I know when we turn out the vote, we will carry Wisconsin this year and win a great victory in November.

I have a strong, positive message. As your President, I have worked hard to make America more hopeful and more secure. I have led our country with principle and resolve, and that's how I'll lead this Nation for 4 more years.

Audience members. Four more years! Four more years! Four more years!

The President. When I took office—I want you to remind your friends and neighbors about what we have been through as a country. When I took office, the bubble of the 1990s had burst, and our economy was heading into recession. Because of the attacks of September the 11th, nearly a million jobs were lost in 3 months. It was a dangerous time for our economy. You might remember there were people warning of potential deflation and depression.

But we acted. To stimulate the economy, I called on the United States Congress to pass historic tax relief, which it did. And that tax relief was the fuel that got our economy growing again, thanks to the effort of our citizens and the right policies in the right place at the right time. That recession is behind us, and we're creating jobs again.

In the past year, the United States has added about 1.7 million new jobs, more than Germany, Japan, Great Britain, Canada, and France combined. Real after-tax income—the money you keep in your pocket—is up more than 10 percent since I took office. Homeownership is at an alltime high in America today. Small businesses are flourishing. Today we learned that America's welfare rolls are the lowest in 34 years.

Math and reading scores are increasing in our public schools. Ten million students will get record levels of grants and loans to help with college. We have modernized Medicare so our seniors will get a prescription drug coverage in 2006.

And this farm economy is strong. I understand farming is a priority in Wisconsin, and I made it a priority in my administration. My opponent has taken a different view. In the Senate career he's consistently voted against the interests of your dairy farmers.

Audience members. Boo-o-o!

The President. He supported the Northeast Dairy Compact.

Audience members. Boo-o-o!

The President. That puts your farmers at a distinct disadvantage. I believe farm policy should treat all farmers fairly. That's why I was proud to sign a good farm bill. We've opened up foreign markets for your products. We've increased funding for ethanol and biodiesel. Farm income is at an alltime high.

I know that the Milk Income Lost Contract program is important to the dairy farmers here in Wisconsin. The milk program is set to expire next fall. I look forward to working with Congress to reauthorize the program so Wisconsin dairy farmers and dairy farmers all across this country can count on the support they need.

We have made America stronger, and we're just getting started. Listen, we live in a time of change. It's a changing economy. People are changing jobs and careers often. Women are working inside the home and outside the home. And yet the fundamental systems of our Government haven't changed. They're stuck in the past.

I understand a hopeful society is one in which we challenge the soft bigotry of low expectations in our public schools and raise the standards and trust the local people to make sure they make the right decisions for the schools. We have an achievement gap in America that's closing, thanks to our education reforms, and we're not going to turn back.

We're going to invest in our Nation's fine community colleges so they prepare workers for the jobs of the 21st century. In a time of change, because people are changing jobs often, we'll expand health savings accounts so people can pay health expenses tax-free and keep the savings if they change jobs.

We'll improve Social Security. Listen, if you're—I remember the 2000 campaign here in Wisconsin. You might remember it too. They said, "If old George W. gets elected, he's going to take away your Social Security check." You remember those ads? Well, you got your check, didn't you? And you're going to get it again.

Nobody is going to take away the check of those who are on Social Security, and the baby boomers are in good shape. But we better worry about our children and our grandchildren when it comes to Social Security. In order to make sure Social Security is available for them, younger workers ought to be able to take some of their own money and set up a personal savings account that they can call their own, that the Government will not take away.

To keep our economy strong and competitive, we got to make sure America is the best place in the world to do business. That means we've got to have that tax relief we passed permanent. That means we got to do something about these needless regulations on small businesses. This country needs an energy plan if we want to keep jobs here in America. I submitted a plan to the Congress over 2 years ago. It's a plan that calls for more conservation, the use of renewable fuels like ethanol and biodiesel. It's a plan that says we can use our coal and natural gas wisely without hurting the environment. It's a plan that says if we want jobs here in America, we must be less dependent on foreign sources of energy.

We got to do something about the frivolous and junk lawsuits here in America that hurt our employers and make it hard to get jobs. We've got—my opponent and I have got different views on all these issues. We've got some fundamental differences on issues like taxes. See, I have a record of reducing them. He's got a record of raising them.

Audience members. Boo-o-o!

The President. He voted in the United States Senate 98 times to raise taxes.

Audience members. Boo-o-o!

The President. That sounds like he's developing a habit. [*Laughter*] He voted for higher taxes on Social Security benefits.

Audience members. Boo-o-o!

The President. He voted for the 1997 formula that helped cause the increases in Medicare.

Audience members. Boo-o-o!

The President. He's against all the tax relief we've passed. You might remember that tax relief. We raised the child credit. We reduced the penalty on marriage. We created a 10-percent bracket for low-income Americans. He voted against them all.

Audience members. Boo-o-o!

The President. My opponent is one of the few candidates in history to campaign on a pledge to raise taxes.

Audience members. Boo-o-o!

The President. And unfortunately, that's the kind of promise more politicians keep. [*Laughter*] He says the tax relief—the tax increase is only for the rich. Now, you've heard that before. The rich hire lawyers and accountants for a reason: to stick you with the bill. [*Laughter*] The good news is we're not going to let him tax us this year. We're going to carry Wisconsin and win a great victory in November.

Audience members. Four more years! Four more years! Four more years!

The President. The Senator and I have different views on health care, fundamentally different views on health care. I believe that we ought to make health care available and affordable. We'll make it available by making sure low-income Americans can go to a community health center to get good preventative care and good primary care. We'll make it available to make sure our children's health programs for low-income Americans are expanded to every corner of this country. We'll make it affordable by doing something about these frivolous lawsuits that are running good doctors out of business and running your costs up. We'll make it affordable by promoting technologies which will help wring out excessive costs in health care.

We'll make it affordable by allowing small businesses to pool risk across jurisdictional boundaries so they can buy insurance at the same discounts big companies can buy insurance. We'll make it affordable by expanding health savings accounts, and that stands in stark contrast to my opponent's plan. Under his plan, 8 million Americans would lose the private insurance they get at work and would end up on a Government program.

Audience members. Boo-o-o!

The President. Under his plan, 8 out of 10 people who'd get new insurance would get it from the Federal Government.

Audience members. Boo-o-o!

The President. My opponent's proposal would be the largest expansion of Government-run health care ever.

Audience members. Boo-o-o!

The President. And you know something, when the Government pays the bills, it makes the rules. His plan would put bureaucrats in charge of dictating coverage, which could ration your care and limit your choice of doctors. What I'm telling you is he's putting us on the path to "Hillarycare."

Audience members. Boo-o-o!

The President. I've got a different idea. In all we do to improve health care, we will make sure the decisions are made by patients and doctors, not by bureaucrats in our Nation's Capital.

During his 20 years as a Senator, my opponent hasn't had many accomplishments. Of the hundreds of bills he submitted, only five became law. That's in 20 years of service. One of them was ceremonial. But to be fair, he has earned a special distinction in the Congress. The nonpartisan National Journal analyzed his record and named John Kerry the most liberal Member of the United States Senate.

Audience members. Boo-o-o!

The President. Now, that's saying something when the competition is people like Ted Kennedy. [*Laughter*] It wasn't easy for him to be the single most liberal Member of the Senate. You might say it took hard work. [*Laughter*] But he earned that title by voting for higher taxes and more regulation and more junk lawsuits and more Government control of your life. And that's one of the real differences of this campaign. My opponent is a tax-and-spend liberal. I'm a compassionate conservative. My opponent wants to empower Government. I want to use Government to empower our citizens. My opponent seems to think all the wisdom is found in Washington, DC. I trust the wisdom of the American people.

You know, I say this, we're living in a changing world, and we do. There's some things that won't change, the values we try to live by, courage and compassion, reverence and integrity. We stand for a culture of life in which every person matters and every being counts. We stand for marriage and family, which are the foundations of our society. And I stand for appointing judges who know the difference between personal opinion and the strict interpretation of the law.

Our differences are also clear on issues like national security. When I took office in 2001, threats to America had been gathering for years. Then, on one terrible morning, the terrorists took more lives than America lost at Pearl Harbor.

Since that day, we have waged a global campaign to protect the American people and bring our enemies to account. Our

Government has trained over a half a million first-responders. We've tripled the spending for homeland security. Law enforcement and intelligence have better tools to stop the terrorists, thanks to the PATRIOT Act, which my opponent voted for but now wants to weaken.

The Taliban regime that sheltered Al Qaida is gone from power. And in 2 days' time, 10 million people, 41 percent of whom are women, have registered to vote in a Presidential election that will take place in 2 days' time. Think about that. Think about what's going on there. The black market network that weapons materials to North Korea and Libya and Iran is now out of business. Libya has given up its weapons of mass destruction programs. Pakistan and Saudi Arabia have joined the fight, and more than three-quarters of Al Qaida's key members and associates have been brought to justice. We have led, many have followed, and America and the world are safer.

After September the 11th, America had to assess every potential threat in a new light. Our Nation awakened to even a greater danger, the prospect that terrorists who killed thousands with hijacked airplanes would kill many more with weapons of mass murder. That's the threat we face. And so we had to take a hard look at every place where terrorists might get those weapons.

And one regime stood out, the dictatorship of Saddam Hussein. We knew the dictator had a history of using weapons of mass destruction, a long aggression and hatred for America, and was listed by Republican and Democratic administrations as a state sponsor of terror. There was a risk that Saddam would pass weapons or materials or information on to terrorist networks. And that was a risk, after September the 11th, this Nation could not afford to take. After 12 years of United Nations Security Council resolutions, we gave him a final chance to come clean and to listen to the demands of the free world. He chose defi-

ance and he chose war, and the world is better off with Saddam Hussein sitting in a prison cell.

Last week in our debate, Senator Kerry once again came down firmly on every side of the Iraq war. He stated that Saddam Hussein was a threat and that America had no business removing that threat. Senator Kerry said our soldiers and marines are not fighting for a "mistake" but also called the liberation of Iraq a "colossal error." He said we need to do more to train Iraqis but also said we shouldn't be spending so much money over there. He said he wants to hold a summit meeting so he can invite other countries to join what he calls the "wrong war in the wrong place at the wrong time."

Audience members. Boo-o-o!

The President. You hear all that, and you can understand why somebody would make a face. [*Laughter*]

Just a short time ago, my opponent held a little press conference and continued his pattern of overheated rhetoric. He accused me of deception. He's claiming I misled America about weapons when he, himself, cited the very same intelligence about Saddam's weapons programs as the reason he voted to go to war. Two years ago this Saturday, back when he was for the war—[*laughter*]—my opponent said on the floor of the United States Senate, and I quote, "Saddam Hussein sitting in Baghdad, with an arsenal of weapons of mass destruction is a different matter. In the wake of September the 11th, who among us can say with any certainty to anybody that those weapons might not be used against our troops or against allies in the region." John Kerry went on: "Who can say that this master of miscalculation will not develop a weapon of mass destruction even greater, a nuclear weapon, then re-invade Kuwait or push the Kurds out, attack Israel, any numbers of scenarios to try to further his ambitions. Can we afford to ignore that possibility that Saddam Hussein might accidentally as well as purposely allow those weapons to slide off to one group or another in a region where weapons are the currency or the trade." End quote.

Now today my opponent tries to say I made up reasons to go to war. Just who is the one trying to mislead the American people?

We have many victories in this war on terror so far, and the war goes on. Our Nation is safer but not yet safe. To win this war, we must fight it on every front. We will stay on the offensive against the terrorist networks. We will defeat them overseas so we do not have to face them here at home.

We will confront governments that support terrorists and could arm them because they're equally guilty of terrorist murder. And our long-term victory requires confronting the ideology of hate with freedom and hope, changing the conditions that produce radicalism and suicide bombers, and finding new democratic allies in a troubled region of the world. You see, America is always more secure when freedom is on the march.

And freedom is on the march in Afghanistan, in Iraq, and elsewhere. There will be good days and there will be bad days in the war on terror. But every day, we will show our resolve, and we will do our duty. This Nation is determined. We will stay in the fight until the fight is won.

Audience members. Four more years! Four more years! Four more years!

The President. My opponent and I have very different views on conducting the war on terror. Senator Kerry approaches the world with a September-the-10th mindset. Think about this. He declared at his convention speech that any attack will be met with a swift and certain response. That was the mindset of the 1990s, while Al Qaida was planning the attacks on America. After September the 11th, our object in the war on terror is not to wait for the next attack and respond but to prevent attacks by taking the fight to the enemy.

In our debate, Senator Kerry said that removing Saddam Hussein was a mistake because a threat was not imminent. Think about that. The problem with his approach is obvious. If America waits until a threat is at our doorstep, it might be too late to save lives. You see, terrorists and tyrants will not give us polite notice before they launch an attack on our country. I refuse to stand by while dangers gather.

My opponent also announced the Kerry doctrine, declaring that Americans' actions in the war on terror must pass a "global test."

Audience members. Boo-o-o!

The President. Under this test, America would not be able to act quickly against threats because we'd be sitting around waiting for a grade from other nations. I have a different view. America will always work with our allies for security and peace, but the President's job is not to pass an international test. The President's job is to protect the American people.

When my opponent first ran for Congress, he argued that American troops should be deployed only at the directive of the United Nations.

Audience members. Boo-o-o!

The President. You probably think I'm making that up. [*Laughter*] I thought it was wrong when I first read it. [*Laughter*] Now, to be fair, he's changed his mind, but it is a window into his thinking. [*Laughter*] Over the years, Senator Kerry has looked for every excuse to constrain America's action in the world. These days he praises America's broad coalition in the Persian Gulf war. But in 1991—I want to remind you what he said—he criticized coalition members as, quote, "shadow battlefield allies who barely carry a burden." That sounds familiar, doesn't it? And that time he voted against the war. If that coalition didn't pass his "global test," nothing will pass his "global test." [*Laughter*]

The Kerry doctrine has other consequences, especially for our men and women in uniform. The Senator from Massachusetts supports the International Criminal Court——

Audience members. Boo-o-o!

The President. ——which would allow unaccountable foreign prosecutors and foreign judges to put American soldiers on trial.

Audience members. Boo-o-o!

The President. You probably think I'm making that up. See, that would be a legal nightmare for our troops. My fellow citizens, as long as I'm your President, Americans in uniform will answer to the officers and law of the United States, not to the International Criminal Court in The Hague.

We have a different point of view on how to build alliances. The Senator speaks about his plan to strengthen America's alliances, but he's got an odd way of going about it. In the middle of the war, he's chosen to insult our fighting allies by calling them "window dressing" and "a coalition of the coerced and the bribed."

Audience members. Boo-o-o!

The President. Well, the Italians who died in Nasiriyah were not window dressing. They're heroes in the war on terror, as far as we're concerned. The British and the Poles at the head of the multinational divisions in Iraq were not coerced or bribed. They fought and some have died in the cause of freedom and peace. These good allies and dozens of others deserve the respect of all Americans, not the scorn of a politician. Instead, the Senator would have America bend over backwards to satisfy a handful of governments with different agendas. This is my opponent's alliance-building strategy: Brush off your best friend and fawn over your critics. And that's no way to gain respect in this world.

My opponent says he has a plan for Iraq, and part of it should sound pretty familiar because it's already known as the Bush plan. [*Laughter*] Senator Kerry suggests we train Iraqi troops. That's what we've been doing for months. [*Laughter*] He's proposing that Iraq have elections. That's

what's going to happen in January. He says the U.N. ought to be involved in the elections. Well, the U.N. is already there. [*Laughter*]

There was one new element of Senator Kerry's plan. He talks about artificial timetables to pull our forces out of Iraq. You see, he sent a signal that America's overriding goal in Iraq would be to leave, even if the job isn't done.

Audience members. Boo-o-o!

The President. That may satisfy his political needs, but his words complicate the essential work we're doing in Iraq. See, the Iraqi people need to know that America will not cut and run when their freedom is at stake. Our soldiers and marines need to know that America will honor their service and sacrifice by completing the mission. Our enemies in Iraq need to know that they can never outlast the will of America. Senator Kerry assures us that he's the one to win a war he calls a "mistake," a "diversion," an "error." But you can't win a war you do not believe in fighting for. On Iraq, Senator Kerry has a strategy for retreat, and I have a strategy for victory.

We returned the sovereignty to the Iraqi people ahead of schedule. We have trained and equipped about 100,000 Iraqi soldiers, police officers, and other security personnel, and the total will rise to 125,000 by the end of the year. See, the strategy ought to be clear. The Iraqi people must stand up and fight for their freedom. They must be the ones that take the hard risk. We've allocated about $7 billion for reconstruction efforts so more Iraqis can see the benefit of freedom. We're working with the coalition of some 30 nations to provide security. Other nations are helping with debt relief. And although the terrorists will try to stop them, Iraq will hold free elections in January.

I believe in the power of liberty to transform nations. I believe that freedom can bring peace. You know, I talk to Prime Minister Koizumi quite often—he's the Prime Minister of Japan. I know we've got some veterans here—first of all, I want to say thanks to all the veterans who set such a great example. I suspect we may have some veterans of World War II with us. My dad was such a veteran. There's a veteran right there. The reason I bring that up is because it wasn't all that long ago in the march of history we were fighting Japan. My dad was there; others were there as well. They were the sworn enemy of America.

After World War II, Harry Truman believed that liberty could transform an enemy into a friend. So we worked hard to help Iraq with democracy—I mean, Japan with democracy. And as a result, I sit down at the table today talking with the leader of a former enemy about how to keep the peace we all want. Think about that. That's what's happening in the world today. A free Iraq will help us keep the peace. A free Iraq will be an ally in the war against terror. And someday, an American President will be sitting down at the table with a duly elected leader from Iraq, talking about how to keep the peace. And our children and our grandchildren will be better off for it.

These are important times. It is important we complete the mission successfully. I know some of the citizens of our country have concerns over Iraq. I respect that. We ought to take this issue seriously because it's a serious matter.

I assure them we're in Iraq because I believe it is necessary for the—to get a positive outcome in this war on terror. That's what I believe. If another terror regime were allowed to emerge in Iraq, the terrorists would find a home and a new source of funding. They would correctly conclude that free nations do not have the will to defend themselves. If Iraq becomes a free society in the heart of the Middle East, we'll have an ally and a model for other nations to look at.

That's why Democratic Senator Joe Lieberman calls Iraq "a crucial battle in the global war on terrorism." That's why Prime Minister Tony Blair called the struggle in Iraq "the crucible in which the future of global terrorism will be determined." That's why the terrorists are fighting with desperate cruelty, because they know their own future is at stake. Iraq is no diversion. It is a place where civilization is taking a decisive stand against chaos and terror, and we must not waver.

Unfortunately, my opponent has been known to waver. [*Laughter*] His well-chosen words and his rationalizations cannot explain why he voted to authorize force against Saddam Hussein and then voted against money to support our troops in combat.

Audience members. Boo-o-o!

The President. He actually tried to clear it up initially by issuing the famous quote, "I actually did vote for the $87 billion, before I voted against it." [*Laughter*] I've been in politics for some time. I've never heard one of them put it that way before. [*Laughter*] He now says he made a mistake in how he talked about his vote. The mistake is not what Senator Kerry said. The mistake is what he did in voting against funding for our troops in harm's way. That is the kind of wavering a nation at war can never afford.

On September the 14th, 2001, I stood in the ruins of the Twin Towers. It helped shape my thinking about my duty to protect you. I'll never forget that day. There were workers in hardhats there yelling at me at the top of their lungs, "Whatever it takes." I was doing my best to console those who were coming out of that rubble. They had grime and dirt all over them. I looked a guy right in the eye—he had bloodshot eyes—and he said, "Don't let me down."

I wake up every morning since that day thinking about how to better protect America. I will never relent in doing what is necessary to secure this country and to protect you, whatever it takes.

A race for President is a contest for the future, and you know where I stand. I'm running for President to keep this Nation on the offensive against terrorists with the goal of total victory and peace for our children and our grandchildren. I'm running for President to keep this economy moving so every worker has a good job and quality health care and a secure retirement. I'm running for President to make our strong Nation a more compassionate society where no one is left out, because I believe everybody counts and everybody matters.

I have a hopeful vision—I have a optimistic vision about this country. You would have one too if you've seen what I've seen. I've seen the spirit of America under good times and bad times. I've seen the great character of this Nation rise up to help a fellow citizen who hurts. I've seen strangers put their arms around another person and say, "I love you, brother." "I love you, sister. What can I do to help you?"

I believe this young century will be liberty's century. We'll promote liberty abroad to protect our country and build a better world beyond terror. We'll encourage liberty here at home to spread prosperity and opportunity to every part of this land. I'm going to carry this message to my fellow citizens in these closing days of this campaign. I'm looking forward to it, and with your help, we'll carry Wisconsin and win a great victory on November the 2d.

Thank you all for coming. I'm glad you're here. God bless. Thank you all.

NOTE: The President spoke at 3:19 p.m. at Marathon Park. In his remarks, he referred to television talk show host Jay Leno; John Gard, speaker, Wisconsin State Assembly; Milwaukee County Executive Scott Walker; Mayor James E. Tipple of Wausau, WI; former Representative Scott L. Klug of Wisconsin; Prime Minister Junichiro Koizumi of Japan; and Prime Minister Tony Blair of the United Kingdom.

Presidential Debate in St. Louis, Missouri
October 8, 2004

Charles Gibson. Good evening from the Field House at Washington University in St. Louis. I'm Charles Gibson of ABC News and "Good Morning America." I welcome you to the second of the 2004 Presidential debates between President George W. Bush, the Republican nominee, and Senator John Kerry, the Democratic nominee. The debates are sponsored by the Commission on Presidential Debates.

Tonight's format is going to be a bit different. We have assembled a townhall meeting. We're in the "Show Me" State, as everyone knows Missouri to be, so Missouri residents will ask the questions, these 140 citizens who were identified by the Gallup Organization as not yet committed in this election. Now, earlier today each audience member gave me two questions on cards like this: One they'd like to ask of the President; the other they'd like to ask the Senator. I have selected the questions to be asked and the order. No one has seen the final list of questions but me—certainly not the candidates. No audience member knows if he or she will be called upon. Audience microphones will be turned off after a question is asked.

Audience members will address their question to a specific candidate. He'll have 2 minutes to answer. The other candidate will have a minute and a half for rebuttal. And I have the option of extending discussion for 1 minute, to be divided equally between the two men. All subjects are open for discussion. And you probably know the light system by now, green light at 30 seconds, yellow at 15, red at 5, and flashing red means you're done. Those are the candidates' rules. I will hold the candidates to the time limits forcefully, but politely, I hope.

And now please join me in welcoming, with great respect, President Bush and Senator Kerry.

Gentlemen, to the business at hand. The first question is for Senator Kerry, and it will come from Cheryl Otis, who is right behind me.

Consistent Leadership

Cheryl Otis. Senator Kerry, after talking to several coworkers and family and friends, I asked the ones who said they were not voting for you, why. They said that you were too wishy-washy. Do you have a reply for them?

Senator John F. Kerry. Yes, I certainly do. [*Laughter*] But let me just first, Cheryl, if you will, I want to thank Charlie for moderating. I want to thank Washington University for hosting us here this evening. Mr. President, it's good to be with you again this evening, sir.

Cheryl, the President didn't find weapons of mass destruction in Iraq, so he's really turned his campaign into a weapon of mass deception. And the result is that you've been bombarded with advertisements suggesting that I've changed a position on this or that or the other. Now, the three things they try to say I've changed position on are the PATRIOT Act—I haven't. I support it. I just don't like the way John Ashcroft has applied it. And we're going to change a few things. The chairman of the Republican Party thinks we ought to change a few things.

No Child Left Behind Act—I voted for it. I support it. I support the goals. But the President has underfunded it by $28 billion. Right here in St. Louis, you've laid off 350 teachers. You're 150—excuse me, I think it's a little more—about $100 million shy of what you ought to be under the No Child Left Behind Act to help your education system here. So I complain about that. I've argued that we should fully fund it. The President says I've changed my

mind. I haven't changed my mind. I'm going to fully fund it. So these are the differences.

Now, the President has presided over the economy where we've lost 1.6 million jobs, the first President in 72 years to lose jobs. I have a plan to put people back to work. That's not wishy-washy. I'm going to close the loopholes that actually encourage companies to go overseas. The President wants to keep them open. I think I'm right. I think he's wrong.

I'm going to give you a tax cut. The President gave—the top one percent of income earners in America got $89 billion last year, more than the 80 percent of people who earn $100,000 or less all put together. I think that's wrong. That's not wishy-washy, and that's what I'm fighting for—you.

Mr. Gibson. Mr. President, a minute and a half.

President Bush. Charlie, thank you, and thank our panelists. Senator, thank you. I can—and thanks, Washington U. as well.

I can see why people at your workplace think he changes positions a lot, because he does. He said he voted for the $87 billion and—or voted against it right before he voted for it. And that sends a confusing signal to people. He said he thought Saddam Hussein was a grave threat and now said it was a mistake to remove Saddam Hussein from power. No, I can see why people think that he changes position quite often, because he does.

You know, for a while, he was a strong supporter of getting rid of Saddam Hussein. He saw the wisdom, until the Democratic primary came along and Howard Dean, the antiwar candidate, began to gain on him. And he changed positions. I don't see how you can lead this country in a time of war, in a time of uncertainty, if you change your mind because of politics.

He just brought up the tax cut. You remember, we increased that child credit by $1000, reduced the marriage penalty, created a 10-percent tax bracket for the lower income Americans—that's right at the middle class. He voted against it, and yet he tells you he's for a middle-class tax cut. It's—you've got to be consistent when you're the President. There's a lot of pressures, and you've got to be firm and consistent.

Mr. Gibson. Mr. President, I would follow up, but we have a series of questions on Iraq, and so I will turn to the next questioner. The question for President Bush, and the questioner is Robin Dahle.

Iraqi Weapons of Mass Destruction

Robin Dahle. Mr. President——

Mr. Gibson. Can you get a microphone, Robin, I'm sorry.

Mr. Dahle. Mr. President, yesterday in a statement you admitted that Iraq did not have weapons of mass destruction but justified the invasion by stating, I quote, "He retained the knowledge, the materials, the means, and the intent to produce weapons of mass destruction and could have passed this knowledge to our terrorist enemies." Do you sincerely believe this to be a reasonable justification for invasion when this statement applies to so many other countries, including North Korea?

President Bush. Each situation is different, Robin. And obviously, we hope that diplomacy works before you ever use force. The hardest decision a President makes is ever to use force.

After 9/11, we had to look at the world differently. After 9/11, we had to recognize that when we saw a threat, we must take it seriously before it comes to hurt us. In the old days, we'd see a threat, and we could deal with it if we felt like it or not. But 9/11 changed it all.

I vowed to our countrymen that I would do everything I could to protect the American people. That's why we're bringing Al Qaida to justice. Seventy-five percent of them have been brought to justice. That's why I said to Afghanistan, "If you harbor a terrorist, you're just as guilty as the terrorist." And the Taliban is no longer in power, and Al Qaida no longer has a place to plan.

And I saw a unique threat in Saddam Hussein, as did my opponent, because we thought he had weapons of mass destruction. And the unique threat was that he could give weapons of mass destruction to an organization like Al Qaida, and the harm they inflicted on us with airplanes would be multiplied greatly by weapons of mass destruction. And that was a serious, serious threat.

So I tried diplomacy. I went to the United Nations. But as we learned in the same report I quoted, Saddam Hussein was gaming the Oil for Food Programme to get rid of sanctions. He was trying to get rid of sanctions for a reason. He wanted to restart his weapons programs.

We all thought there was weapons there, Robin. My opponent thought there was weapons there. That's why he called him a grave threat. I wasn't happy when we found out there wasn't weapons, and we've got an intelligence group together to figure out why. But Saddam Hussein was a unique threat, and the world is better off without him in power. And my opponent's plans lead me to conclude that Saddam Hussein would still be in power and the world would be more dangerous.

Thank you, sir.

Mr. Gibson. Senator Kerry, a minute and a half.

Senator Kerry. Robin, I'm going to answer your question. I'm also going to talk—respond to what you asked, Cheryl, at the same time.

The world is more dangerous today. The world is more dangerous today because the President didn't make the right judgments. Now, the President wishes that I had changed my mind. He wants you to believe that, because he can't come here and tell you that he's created new jobs for America. He's lost jobs. He can't come here and tell you that he's created health care for Americans because one-point—what, we've got 5 million Americans who have lost their health care, 96,000 of them right here in Missouri. He can't come here and tell you that he's left no child behind because he didn't fund No Child Left Behind.

So what does he do? He's trying to attack me. He wants you to believe that I can't be President, and he's trying to make you believe it because he wants you to think I change my mind.

Well, let me tell you straight up, I've never changed my mind about Iraq. I do believe Saddam Hussein was a threat. I always believed he was a threat—believed it in 1998 when Clinton was President. I wanted to give Clinton the power to use force if necessary. But I would have used that force wisely. I would have used that authority wisely, not rushed to war without a plan to win the peace. I would have brought our allies to our side. I would have fought to make certain our troops had everybody possible to help them win the mission.

This President rushed to war, pushed our allies aside, and Iran now is more dangerous, and so is North Korea with nuclear weapons. He took his eye off the ball, off of Usama bin Laden.

Mr. Gibson. Mr. President, I do want to follow up on this one, because there were several questions from the audience along this line.

President Bush. Are we going to have a rebuttal thing back and forth?

Mr. Gibson. Well, I was going to have you do it with the rebuttal. But you go ahead. [*Laughter*] You're up.

President Bush. Remember the last debate? My opponent said that America must pass a global test before we use force to protect ourselves. That's the kind of mindset that says sanctions were working. That's the kind of mindset that says let's keep it at the United Nations and hope things go well.

Saddam Hussein was a threat because he could have given weapons of mass destruction to terrorist enemies. Sanctions were not working. The United Nations was not effective at removing Saddam Hussein.

Mr. Gibson. Senator?

Senator Kerry. The goal of the sanctions was not to remove Saddam Hussein. It was to remove the weapons of mass destruction. And Mr. President, just yesterday the Duelfer report told you and the whole world they worked. He didn't have weapons of mass destruction, Mr. President. That was the objective. And if we had used smart diplomacy, we could have saved $200 billion and an invasion of Iraq, and right now Usama bin Laden might be in jail or dead. That's the war against terror.

Mr. Gibson. We're going to have another question now on the subject of Iraq. And I'm just going to turn to Anthony Baldi with a question for Senator Kerry.

Mr. Baldi.

Iraq/War on Terror

Anthony Baldi. Senator Kerry, the U.S. is preparing a new Iraq Government, and we'll proceed to withdraw U.S. troops. Would you proceed with the same plans as President Bush?

Senator Kerry. Anthony, I would not. I have laid out a different plan because the President's plan is not working. You see that every night on television. There's chaos in Iraq. King Abdullah of Jordan said just yesterday—or the day before, you can't hold elections in Iraq with the chaos that's going on today. Senator Richard Lugar, the Republican chairman of the Foreign Relations Committee, said that the handling of the reconstruction aid in Iraq by this administration has been "incompetent." Those are the Republican chairman's words. Senator Hagel of Nebraska said that the handling of Iraq is "beyond pitiful, beyond embarrassing. It's in the zone of dangerous." Those are the words of two Republicans, respected, both on the Foreign Relations Committee.

Now, I have to tell you, I would do something different. I would reach out to our allies in a way that this President hasn't. He pushed them away time and again, pushed them away at the U.N., pushed them away individually. Two weeks ago, there was a meeting of the North Atlantic Council, which is the political arm of NATO. They discussed the possibility of a small training unit or having a total takeover of the training in Iraq. Did our administration push for the total training of Iraq? No. Were they silent? Yes. Was there an effort to bring all the allies together around that? No—because they've always wanted this to be an American effort. You know, they even had the Defense Department issue a memorandum saying don't bother applying for assistance or for being part of the reconstruction if you weren't part of our original coalition.

Now, that's not a good way to build support and reduce the risk for our troops and make America safer. I'm going to get the training done for our troops. I'm going to get the training of Iraqis done faster, and I'm going to get our allies back to the table.

President Bush. Two days ago in the Oval Office, I met with the Finance Minister from Iraq. He came to see me, and he talked about how optimistic he was and the country was about heading toward elections. Think about it. They're going from tyranny to elections. He talked about the reconstruction efforts that are beginning to take hold. He talked about the fact that Iraqis love to be free. He said he was optimistic when he came here. Then he turned on the TV and listened to the political rhetoric, and all of a sudden he was pessimistic.

This is a guy who, along with others, has taken great risk for freedom, and we need to stand with him. My opponent says he has a plan—sounds familiar because it's called the Bush plan. We're going to train troops, and we are. We'll have 125,000 trained by the end of December. We're spending about $7 billion.

He talks about a grand idea: Let's have a summit; we're going to solve the problem in Iraq by holding a summit. And what is he going to say to those people that show up to the summit? "Join me in the wrong war at the wrong time at the wrong place"? Risk your troops in a war you've called a "mistake"? Nobody is going to follow somebody who doesn't believe we can succeed and somebody who says the war where we are is a "mistake." I know how these people think. I meet with them all the time. I talk to Tony Blair all the time. I talk to Silvio Berlusconi. They're not going to follow an American President who says, "Follow me into a mistake."

Our plan is working. We're going to make elections, and Iraq is going to be free, and America will be better off for it.

Mr. Gibson. Do you want to follow up, Senator?

Senator Kerry. Yes, sir, please.

Ladies and gentlemen, the right war was Usama bin Laden and Afghanistan. That was the right place, and the right time was Tora Bora, when we had him cornered in the mountains. Now, everyone in the world knows that there were no weapons of mass destruction. That was the reason Congress gave him the authority to use force, not after excuse to get rid of the regime.

Now we have to succeed. I've always said that. I have been consistent. Yes, we have to succeed, and I have a better plan to help us do it.

President Bush. First of all, we didn't find out he didn't have weapons until we got there, and my opponent thought he had weapons and told everybody he thought he had weapons. And secondly, it's a fundamental misunderstanding to say that the war on terror is only Usama bin Laden. The war on terror is to make sure that these terrorist organizations do not end up with weapons of mass destruction. That's what the war on terror is about.

Of course we're going to find Usama bin Laden. We've already got 75 percent of his people, and we're on the hunt for him. But this is a global conflict that requires firm resolve.

Mr. Gibson. The next question is for President Bush, and it comes from Nikki Washington.

President's Decisionmaking on Iraq

Nikki Washington. Thank you. Mr. President, my mother and sister traveled abroad this summer, and when they got back, they talked to us about how shocked they were at the intensity of aggravation that other countries had with how we handled the Iraq situation. Diplomacy is, obviously, something that we have to really work on. What is your plan to repair relations with other countries, given the current situation?

President Bush. No, I appreciate that. I—listen, I—we've got a great country. I love our values. And I recognize I've made some decisions that have caused people to not understand the great values of our country. I remember when Ronald Reagan was the President. He stood on principle. Some might have called that stubborn. He stood on principle, standing up to the Soviet Union. And we won that conflict, yet at the same time, he was very—we were very unpopular in Europe because of decisions he made.

I recognize that taking Saddam Hussein out was unpopular, but I made the decision because I thought it was in the right interests of our security.

You know, I've made some decisions on Israel. That's unpopular. I wouldn't deal with Arafat because I felt like he had let the former President down, and I don't think he's the kind of person that can lead toward a Palestinian state. And people in Europe didn't like that decision. And that was unpopular, but it was the right thing to do. I believe Palestinians ought to have a state, but I know they need leadership that's committed to democracy and freedom, leadership that will be willing to reject terrorism.

I made a decision not to join the International Criminal Court in The Hague, which is where our troops could be brought to—brought in front of a judge, an unac-

counted judge. I don't think we ought to join that. That was unpopular. And so what I'm telling you is, is that sometimes in this world you make unpopular decisions because you think they're right.

We'll continue to reach out. Listen, there's 30 nations involved in Iraq, some 40 nations involved in Afghanistan. People love America. Sometimes they don't like the decisions made by America, but I don't think you want a President who tries to become popular and does the wrong thing. You don't want to join the International Criminal Court just because it's popular in certain capitals in Europe.

Mr. Gibson. Senator Kerry, a minute and a half.

Senator Kerry. Nikki, that's a question that's been raised by a lot of people around the country. Let me address it but also talk about the weapons the President just talked about, because every part of the President's answer just now promises you more of the same over the next 4 years.

The President stood right here in this hall 4 years ago, and he was asked a question by somebody just like you: Under what circumstances would you send people to war? And his answer was: With a viable exit strategy and only with enough forces to get the job done. He didn't do that. He broke that promise. We didn't have enough forces. General Shinseki, the Army Chief of Staff, told him he was going to need several hundred thousand. And guess what? They retired General Shinseki for telling him that. This President hasn't listened.

I went to meet with the members of the Security Council in the week before we voted. I went to New York. I talked to all of them to find out how serious they were about really holding Saddam Hussein accountable. I came away convinced that if we worked at it, if we were ready to work at letting Hans Blix do his job and thoroughly go through the inspections, that if push came to shove, they'd be there with us.

But the President just arbitrarily brought the hammer down and said, "Nope, sorry, time for diplomacy is over. We're going." He rushed to war without a plan to win the peace. Ladies and gentlemen, he gave you a speech and told you he'd plan carefully, take every precaution, take our allies with us. He didn't. He broke his word.

Mr. Gibson. Mr. President.

President Bush. I remember sitting in the White House, looking at those generals, saying, "Do you have what you need in this war? Do you have what it takes?" I remember going down in the basement of the White House the day we committed our troops—as last resort—looking at Tommy Franks and the generals on the ground, asking them, "Do we have the right plan with the right troop level?" And they looked me in the eye and said, "Yes, sir, Mr. President." Of course I listened to our generals. That's what a President does. A President sets the strategy and relies upon good military people to execute that strategy.

Mr. Gibson. Senator.

Senator Kerry. You rely on good military people to execute the military component of the strategy, but winning the peace is larger than just the military component. General Shinseki had the wisdom to say you're going to need several hundred thousand troops to win the peace. The military's job is to win the war. The President's job is to win the peace. The President did not do what was necessary, didn't bring in enough nations, didn't deliver the help, didn't close off the borders, didn't even guard the ammo dumps. And now our kids are being killed with ammos right out of that dump.

Mr. Gibson. The next question is for Senator Kerry, and it comes from over here, from Randee Jacobs. You'll need a microphone.

Senator Kerry. Is it Randee? I'm sorry.

Iran/North Korea

Randee Jacobs. Yes, Randee. Iran sponsors terrorism and has missiles capable of hitting Israel and southern Europe. Iran will have nuclear weapons in 2 to 3 years' time. In the event that U.N. sanctions don't stop this threat, what will you do as President?

Senator Kerry. I don't think you can just rely on U.N. sanctions, Randee, but you're absolutely correct. It is a threat. It's a huge threat. And what's interesting is it's a threat that has grown while the President has been preoccupied with Iraq, where there wasn't a threat. If he'd let the inspectors do their job and go on, we wouldn't have 10 times the numbers of forces in Iraq that we have in Afghanistan chasing Usama bin Laden.

Meanwhile, while Iran is moving towards nuclear weapons—some 37 tons of what they call yellow cake, the stuff they use to make enriched uranium—while they're doing that, North Korea has moved from one bomb, maybe—maybe—to 4 to 7 bombs.

For 2 years the President didn't even engage with North Korea, did nothing at all, while it was growing more dangerous, despite the warnings of people like former Secretary of Defense William Perry, who negotiated getting television cameras and inspectors into that reactor. We were safer before President Bush came to office. Now, they have the bombs, and we're less safe.

So what do we do? We've got to join with the British and the French, with the Germans who've been involved in their initiative. We've got to lead the world now to crack down on proliferation as a whole. But the President has been slow to do that even in Russia. At his pace, it's going to take 13 years to reduce and get a hold of all the loose nuclear material in the former Soviet Union. I've proposed a plan that can capture it and contain it and clean it within 4 years.

And the President is moving toward the creation of our own bunker-busting nuclear weapon. It's very hard to get other countries to give up their weapons when you're busy developing a new one. I'm going to lead the world in the greatest counterproliferation effort, and if we have to get tough with Iran, believe me, we will get tough.

Mr. Gibson. Mr. President, a minute and a half.

President Bush. That answer almost made me want to scowl. [*Laughter*] He keeps talking about letting the inspectors do their job. It's naive and dangerous to say that. That's what the Duelfer report showed. He was deceiving the inspectors.

Secondly, of course we've been involved with Iran. I fully understand the threat. And that's why we're doing what he suggested we do, get the Brits, the Germans, and the French to go make it very clear to the Iranians that if they expect to be a party to the world, to give up their nuclear ambitions. We've been doing that.

Let me talk about North Korea. It is naive and dangerous to take a policy that he suggested the other day, which is to have bilateral relations with North Korea. Remember, he is the person who is accusing me of not acting multilaterally. He now wants to take the six-party talks we have—China, North Korea, South Korea, Russia, Japan, and the United States—and undermine them by having bilateral talks. That's what President Clinton did. He had bilateral talks with the North Korean, and guess what happened? He didn't honor the agreement. He was enriching uranium. That is a bad policy.

Of course, we're paying attention to these. That's a great question about Iran. That's why, in my speech to the Congress, I said there is an axis of evil, Iraq, Iran, and North Korea, and we're paying attention to it, and we're making progress.

Mr. Gibson. We're going to move on, Mr. President, with a question for you. And it comes from Daniel Farley.

Mr. Farley.

Possibility of Reinstating the Draft

Daniel Farley. Mr. President, since we continue to police the world, how do you intend to maintain a military presence without reinstituting a draft?

President Bush. Yes, great question. Thanks.

I hear there's rumors on the Internets that we're going to have a draft. We're not going to have a draft—period. The All-Volunteer Army works. It works particularly when we pay our troops well. It works when we make sure they've got housing, like we have done in the last military budgets. An all-volunteer army is best suited to fight the new wars of the 21st century, which is to be specialized and to find these people as they hide around the world. We don't need massed armies anymore.

One of the things we've done is we've taken the—we're beginning to transform our military. And by that I mean we're moving troops out of Korea and replacing them with more effective weapons. We don't need as much manpower on the Korean Peninsula to keep a deterrent.

In Europe, we have massed troops as if the Soviet Union existed and was going to invade into Europe, but those days are over with. And so we're moving troops out of Europe and replacing it with more effective equipment.

So the answer to your question is, we're withdrawing—not from the world—we're drawing manpower, so they can be stationed here in America, so there's less rotation, so life is easier on their families and therefore more likely to be—we'll be more likely to keep people in the All-Volunteer Army.

One of the most important things we're doing in this administration is transformation. There's some really interesting technologies. For example, we're flying unmanned vehicles that can send real-time messages back to stations in the United States. That saves manpower, and it saves equipment. It also means that we can target things easier and move more quickly, which means we need to be lighter and quicker and more facile and highly trained.

Forget all this talk about a draft. We're not going to have a draft so long as I'm the President.

Mr. Gibson. Senator Kerry, minute and a half.

Senator Kerry. Daniel, I don't support a draft. But let me tell you where the President's policies have put us. The President—and this is one of the reasons why I'm very proud in this race to have the support of General John Shalikashvili, former Chairman of the Joint Chiefs of Staff; Admiral William Crowe, former Chairman of the Joint Chiefs of Staff; General Tony McPeak, who ran the air war for the President's father and did a brilliant job—supporting me; General Wes Clark, who won the war in Kosovo—supporting me; because they all—and General Baca, who was the head of the National Guard—supporting me. Why? Because they understand that our military is overextended under this President.

Our Guard and Reserves have been turned into almost active duty. You've got people doing two and three rotations. You've got stop-loss policies so people can't get out when they were supposed to. You've got a backdoor draft right now, and a lot of our military are underpaid. These are families that get hurt. It hurts the middle class. It hurts communities, because these are our first-responders, and they're called up, and they're over there, not over here.

Now, I'm going to add 40,000 active duty forces to the military. And I'm going to make people feel good about being safe in our military and not overextended because I'm going to run a foreign policy that actually does what President Reagan did and President Eisenhower did and others. We're going to build alliances. We're not going to go unilaterally. We're not going to go alone like this President did.

Mr. Gibson. Mr. President, let's extend for a minute.

President Bush. Let me just—I've got to answer this.

Mr. Gibson. Exactly. And with Reservists being held on duty and some soldiers——

President Bush. Let me just answer what he just said about going alone.

Mr. Gibson. I wanted to get into the issue of the backdoor draft.

President Bush. You tell Tony Blair we're going alone. Tell Tony Blair we're going alone. Tell Silvio Berlusconi we're going alone. Tell Aleksander Kwasniewski of Poland we're going alone. We've got 30 countries there. It denigrates an alliance to say we're going alone, to discount their sacrifices. You cannot lead an alliance if you say you're going alone. And people listen. They're sacrificing with us.

Mr. Gibson. Senator.

Senator Kerry. Mr. President, countries are leaving the coalition, not joining. Eight countries have left it. If Missouri, just given the number of people from Missouri who are in the military over there today, were a country, it would be the third largest country in the coalition, behind Great Britain and the United States. That's not a grand coalition. Ninety percent of the casualties are American. Ninety percent of the costs are coming out of your pockets. I could do a better job. My plan does a better job, and that's why I'll be a better Commander in Chief.

Mr. Gibson. The next question, Senator Kerry, is for you, and it comes from Ann Bronsing, who I believe is over in this area.

Terrorist Attacks/Homeland Security

Ann Bronsing. Senator Kerry, we have been fortunate that there have been no further terrorist attacks on American soil since 9/11. Why do you think this is? And if elected, what will you do to assure our safety?

Senator Kerry. Thank you very much, Ann. I've asked in my security briefings why that is, and I can't go into all the answers, et cetera, but let me say this to you. This President and his administration have told you and all of us, "It's not a question of when, it's a question of"—excuse me, "not a question of if, it's a question of when." We've been told that. The "when" I can't tell you. Between the World Trade Center bombing in—what was it, 1993 or so—and the next time was 5 years, 7 years. These people wait. They'll plan. They plot.

I agree with the President that we have to go after them and get them wherever they are. I just think I can do that far more effectively because the most important weapon in doing that is intelligence. You've got to have the best intelligence in the world. And in order to have the best intelligence in the world, to know who the terrorists are and where they are and what they're plotting, you've got to have the best cooperation you've ever had in the world.

Now, to go back to your question, Nikki, we're not getting the best cooperation in the world today. We've got a whole bunch of countries that pay a price for dealing with the United States of America now. I'm going to change that.

And I'm going to put in place a better homeland security effort. Look at it, 95 percent of our containers coming into this country are not inspected today. When you get on an airplane, your cart—your bag is X-rayed, but the cargo hold isn't X-rayed. Do you feel safer? This President, in the last debate, said that, well, that would be a big tax gap if we did that. Ladies and gentlemen, it's his tax plan. He chose a tax cut for the wealthiest Americans over getting that equipment out into the homeland as fast as possible. We have bridges and tunnels that aren't being secured; chemical plants, nuclear plants that aren't secured; hospitals that are overcrowded in their emergency rooms. If we had a disaster today, could they handle it?

This President chose a tax cut over homeland security. Wrong choice.

Mr. Gibson. Mr. President.

President Bush. That's an odd thing to say since we've tripled the homeland security budget from 10 to 30 billion dollars. Listen, we'll do everything we can to protect the homeland. My opponent is right: We need good intelligence. It's also a curious thing for him to say, since right after 1993, he voted to cut the intelligence budget by $7.5 billion.

The best way to defend America in this world we live in is to stay on the offense. We've got to be right 100 percent of the time here at home, and they've got to be right once. And that's the reality. And there's a lot of good people working hard. We're doing the best we possibly can to share information. That's why the PATRIOT Act was important. The PATRIOT Act is vital, by the way. It's a tool that law enforcement now uses to be able to talk between each other. My opponent says he hasn't changed his positions on it. No, but he's for weakening it.

I don't think my opponent has got the right view about the world to make us safe. I really don't. First of all, I don't think he can succeed in Iraq. And if Iraq were to fail, it would be a haven for terrorists, and there would be money, and the world would be much more dangerous. I don't see how you can win in Iraq if you don't believe we should be there in the first place. I don't see how you can lead troops if you say, "It's the wrong war at the wrong place at the wrong time." I don't see how the Iraqis are going to have confidence in the American President if all they hear is that it was a "mistake" to be there in the first place.

This war is a long, long war, and it requires steadfast determination. And it requires a complete understanding that we not only chase down Al Qaida, but we disrupt terrorists' safe havens as well as people who could provide the terrorists with support.

Mr. Gibson. I want to extend for a minute, Senator, and I'm curious about something you said. You said, "It's not when but if." You think it's inevitable? Because the sense of security is a very basic thing with everybody in this country, worried about their kids.

Senator Kerry. Well, the President and his experts have told America that it's not a question of if, it's a question of when. And I accept what the President has said. These terrorists are serious. They're deadly, and they know nothing except trying to kill. I understand that. That's why I will never stop at anything to hunt down and kill the terrorists.

But you heard the President just say to you that we've added money. Folks, the test is not if you've added money. The test is, have you done everything possible to make America secure? He chose a tax cut for wealthy Americans over the things that I listed to you.

Mr. Gibson. Mr. President.

President Bush. Well, we'll talk about the tax cut for middle class here in a minute. But yes, I'm worried. I'm worried. I'm worried about our country. And all I can tell you is, every day I know that there's people working overtime, doing the very best they can. And the reason I'm worried is because there's a vicious enemy that has an ideology of hate. And the way to defeat them long-term, by the way, is to spread freedom. Liberty can change habits, and that's what's happening in Afghanistan and Iraq.

Mr. Gibson. Mr. President, we're going to turn to questions now on domestic policy, and we're going to start with health issues. And the first question is for President Bush, and it's from John Horstman.

Drug Imports From Canada/Health Care

John Horstman. Mr. President, why did you block the reimportation of safer and inexpensive drugs from Canada, which would have cut 40 to 60 percent off of the cost?

President Bush. I haven't yet. I just want to make sure they're safe. When a drug comes in from Canada, I want to make sure it cures you and doesn't kill you. And

that's why the FDA and that's why the Surgeon General are looking very carefully to make sure it can be done in a safe way. I've got an obligation to make sure our Government does everything we can to protect you. And one of—my worry is that it looks like it's from Canada, and it might be from a third world. We've just got to make sure, before somebody thinks they're buying a product, that it works. And that's why we're doing what we're doing. Now, it may very well be, here in December, you hear me say, "I think there's a safe way to do it."

Other ways to make sure drugs are cheaper: One is to speed up generic drugs to the marketplace quicker. Pharmaceuticals were using loopholes to keep brand drugs in place, and generics are much less expensive than brand drugs. And we're doing just that. Another is to get our seniors to sign up for these drug discount cards, and they're working. Wanda Blackmore, I met here from Missouri—the first time she bought drugs with her drug discount card she paid $1.14, I think it was, for about $10 worth of drugs. These cards make sense.

And you know, in 2006, seniors are going to get prescription drug coverage for the first time in Medicare, because I went to Washington to fix problems. Medicare—the issue of Medicare used to be called "Mediscare." People didn't want to touch it for fear of getting hurt politically. I wanted to get something done. I think our seniors deserve a modern medical system. And in 2006, our seniors will get prescription drug coverage.

Thank you for asking.

Mr. Gibson. Senator, a minute and a half.

Senator Kerry. John, you heard the President just say that he thought he might try to be for it. Four years ago, right here in this forum, he was asked the same question, "Can't people be able to import drugs from Canada?" Do you know what he said?

"I think that makes sense. I think that's a good idea"—4 years ago.

Now, the President said, "I'm not blocking that." Ladies and gentlemen, the President just didn't level with you—right now, again. He did block it, because we passed it in the United States Senate. We sent it over to the House that you could import drugs. We took care of the safety issues. We're not talking about third-world drugs. We're talking about drugs made right here in the United States of America that have American brand names on them, in American bottles, and we're asking they be able to allow you to get them. The President blocked it.

The President also took Medicare, which belongs to you, and he could have lowered the cost of Medicare and lowered your taxes and lowered the cost to seniors. You know what he did? He made it illegal—illegal—for Medicare to do what the VA does, which is bulk-purchase drugs so that you could lower the price and get them out to you lower. He put $139 billion of windfall profit into the pockets of the drug companies, right out of your pockets.

That's the difference between us. The President sides with the power companies, the oil companies, the drug companies. And I'm fighting to let you get those drugs from Canada, and I'm fighting to let Medicare survive. I'm fighting for the middle class. That's the difference.

Mr. Gibson. Mr. President.

President Bush. If they're safe, they're coming. I want to remind you that it wasn't just my administration that made the decision on safety. President Clinton did the same thing, because we have an obligation to protect you.

Now, he talks about Medicare. He's been in the United States Senate 20 years. Show me one accomplishment toward Medicare that he accomplished. I've been in Washington, DC, 3½ years and led the Congress to reform Medicare so our seniors have got a modern health care system. That's what leadership is all about.

Senator Kerry. Actually, Mr. President, in 1997, we fixed Medicare, and I was one of the people involved in it. We not only fixed Medicare and took it way out into the future, we did something that you don't know how to do. We balanced the budget. And we paid down the debt of our Nation for 2 years in a row, and we created 23 million new jobs at the same time. And it's the President's fiscal policies that have driven up the biggest deficits in American history. He's added more debt to the debt of the United States in 4 years than all the way from George Washington to Ronald Reagan put together. Go figure.

Mr. Gibson. Next question is for Senator Kerry, and this comes from Norma-Jean Laurent.

Tort Reform

Norma-Jean Laurent. Senator Kerry, you've stated your concern for the rising cost of health care. Yet you chose a Vice Presidential candidate who has made millions of dollars successfully suing medical professionals. How do you reconcile this with the voters?

Senator Kerry. Very easily. John Edwards is the author of the Patients' Bill of Rights. He wanted to give people rights. John Edwards and I support tort reform. We both believe that as lawyers—I'm a lawyer too—and I believe that we will be able to get a fix that has eluded everybody else, because we know how to do it. It's in my health care proposal. Go to johnkerry.com—you can pull it off the Internet—and you'll find a tort reform plan.

Now, ladies and gentlemen, important to understand, the President and his friends try to make a big deal out of it. Is it a problem? Yes, it's a problem. Do we need to fix it, particularly for ob-gyns ° and for brain surgeons and others? Yes. But it's less than one percent of the total cost of health care. Your premiums are going up.

° White House correction.

You've gone up in Missouri about $3,500. You've gone up 64 percent. You've seen co-pays go up, deductibles go up. Everything has gone up. Five million people have lost their health insurance under this President, and he's done nothing about it.

I have a plan. I have a plan to lower the cost of health care for you. I have a plan to cover all children. I have a plan to let you buy into the same health care Senators and Congressmen give themselves. I have a plan that's going to allow people 55 to 64 to buy into Medicare early. And I have a plan that will take the catastrophic cases out of the system, off your backs, pay for it out of a Federal fund, which lowers the premiums for everybody in America, makes American business more competitive, and makes health care more affordable.

Now, all of that can happen, but I have to ask you to do one thing. Join me in rolling back the President's unaffordable tax cut for people earning more than $200,000 a year. That's all. Ninety-eight percent of America, I'm giving you a tax cut, and I'm giving you health care.

Mr. Gibson. Mr. President, a minute and a half.

President Bush. Let me see where to start here. First, the National Journal named Senator Kerry[*] the most liberal Senator of all. And that's saying something in that bunch. You might say that took a lot of hard work.

The reason I bring that up is because he's proposed $2.2 trillion in new spending and he says he's going to tax the rich to close the tax gap. He can't. He's going to tax everybody here to fund his programs. That's just reality.

And what are his health programs? First, he says he's for medical liability reform, particularly for ob-gyns. There was a bill on the floor of the United States Senate that he could have showed up and voted for if he's so much for it. Secondly, he

_____
[*] White House correction.

says that medical liability costs only cause one percent increase. That shows a lack of understanding. Doctors practice defensive medicine because of all the frivolous lawsuits that cost our Government $28 billion a year.

And finally, he says he's going to have a novel health care plan. You know what it is? The Federal Government is going to run it. It is the largest increase in Federal Government health care ever, and it fits with his philosophy. That's why I told you about the award he won from the National Journal. That's what liberals do: They create Government-sponsored health care. Maybe you think that makes sense. I don't. Government-sponsored health care would lead to rationing. It would ruin the quality of health care in America.

Mr. Gibson. Senator Kerry, we got several questions along this line, and I'm just curious if you'd go further on what you talked about with tort reform. Would you be favoring capping awards on pain and suffering? Would you limit attorneys' fees—yes, to follow up on this for a minute. Thirty seconds.

Senator Kerry. Yes, I think we should look at the punitive, and we should have some limitations. But look, what's really important, Charlie, is the President's just trying to scare everybody here with throwing labels around. I mean, "compassionate conservative," what does that mean? Cutting 500,000 kids from after-school programs? Cutting 365,000 kids from health care? Running up the biggest deficits in American history? Mr. President, you're batting 0 for 2. I mean, seriously, labels don't mean anything. What means something is do you have a plan, and I want to talk about my plan some more. I hope we can.

Mr. Gibson. We'll get to that in just a minute. Thirty seconds.

President Bush. What does matter is the plan. He said he is for—you're now for capping punitive damages? That's odd. You should have shown up on the floor in the

Senate and voted for it then. Medical liability issues are a problem, a significant problem. He's been in the United States Senate for 20 years, and he hasn't addressed it. We passed it out of the House of Representatives. Guess where it stuck? It stuck in the Senate because the trial lawyers won't act on it, and he put a trial lawyer on the ticket.

Mr. Gibson. The next question is for President Bush, and it comes from Matthew O'Brien.

Federal Deficit

Matthew O'Brien. Mr. President, you have enjoyed a Republican majority in the House and Senate for most of your Presidency. In that time, you've not vetoed a single spending bill. Excluding 120 billion spent in Iran and Afghan—I'm sorry, Iraq and Afghanistan, there has been $700 billion spent and not paid for by taxes. Please explain how the spending you have approved and not paid for is better for the American people than the spending proposed by your opponent.

President Bush. Right. Thank you for that. We have a deficit. We have a deficit because this country went into a recession. You might remember the stock market started to decline dramatically 6 months before I came to office, and then the bubble of the 1990s popped. And that cost us revenue—that cost us revenue.

Secondly, we're at war. And I'm going to spend what it takes to win the war, more than just 120 billion for Iraq and Afghanistan. We've got to pay our troops more. We have. We've increased money for ammunition and weapons and pay and homeland security. I just told this lady over here we spent—went from 10 to 30 billion dollars to protect the homeland. I think we have an obligation to spend that kind of money.

Plus, we cut taxes for everybody. Everybody got tax relief, so that they'd get out of the recession. I think if you raise taxes during a recession, you head to depression.

I come from the school of thought that says when people have more money in their pocket during tough economic times, it increases demand or investment. Small businesses begin to grow, and jobs are added. We found out today that over the past 13 months, we've added 1.9 million new jobs in the last 13 months. I proposed a plan, detailed budget, that shows us cutting the deficit in half by 5 years.

And you're right, I haven't vetoed any spending bills because we worked together. Non-homeland, non-defense, discretionary spending was rising at 15 percent a year when I got into office. And today, it's less than one percent, because we're working together to try to bring this deficit under control. Like you, I'm concerned about the deficit. But I am not going to shortchange our troops in harm's way. And I'm not going to run up taxes which will cost this economy jobs.

Thank you for your question.

Mr. Gibson. Senator Kerry, a minute and a half.

Senator Kerry. Let me begin by saying that my health care plan is not what the President described. It is not a Government takeover. You have choice: Choose your doctor; choose your plan. The Government has nothing to do with it. In fact, it doesn't ask you to do anything. If you don't want to take it, you don't have to. If you like your high premiums, you keep them. That's the way we leave it.

Now, with respect to the deficit, the President was handed a $5.6 trillion surplus, ladies and gentlemen. That's where he was when he came into office. We now have a $2.6 trillion deficit. This is the biggest turnaround in the history of the country. He's the first President in 72 years to lose jobs. He talked about war. This is the first time the United States of America has ever had a tax cut when we're at war. Franklin Roosevelt, Harry Truman, others knew how to lead. They knew how to ask the American people for the right things.

One percent of America—the highest one percent of income earners in America got $89 billion of tax cut last year. One percent of America got more than the 80 percent of America that earned from $100,000 down. The President thinks it's more important to fight for that top one percent than to fight for fiscal responsibility and to fight for you.

I want to put money in your pocket. I am—I have a proposal for a tax cut for all people earning less than the $200,000. The only people affected in my plan are the top income earners of America.

Mr. Gibson. I both—I heard you both say—I have heard you both say during the campaign, and I just heard you say it—that you're going to cut the deficit by a half in 4 years. But I didn't hear one thing in the last 3½ minutes that would indicate how either one of you do that.

President Bush. Look at the budget. One is, make sure Congress doesn't overspend. But let me talk back about where we've been. The stock market was declining 6 months prior to my arrival. It was the largest stock market correction—one of the largest in history, which foretold a recession. Because we cut taxes on everybody—remember, we ran up the child credit by 1,000; we reduced the marriage penalty; we created the 10-percent bracket; everybody who pays taxes got relief—the recession was one of the shortest in our Nation's history.

Mr. Gibson. Senator Kerry, 30 seconds.

Senator Kerry. After 9/11, after the recession had ended, the President asked for another tax cut and promised 5.6 million jobs would be created. He lost 1.6 million, ladies and gentlemen, and most of that tax cut went to the wealthiest people in the country. He came and asked for a tax cut; we wanted a tax cut to kick the economy into gear. Do you know what he presented us with? A $25 billion giveaway to the biggest corporations in America, including a $254 million refund check to Enron. Wrong priorities. You are my priority.

Mr. Gibson. Senator Kerry, the next question will be for you, and it comes from James Varner, who I believe is in this section. Mr. Varner? You need a microphone.

Taxes

James Varner. Thank you. Senator Kerry, would you be willing to look directly into the camera and, using simple and unequivocal language, give the American people your solemn pledge not to sign any legislation that will increase the tax burden on families earning less than $200,000 a year during your first term?

Senator Kerry. Absolutely. Yes. Right into the camera—yes. I am not going to raise taxes. I have a tax cut, and here's my tax cut. I raise the child care credit by $1,000 for families to help them be able to take care of their kids. I have a $4,000 tuition tax credit that goes to parents and kids, if they're earning for themselves, to be able to pay for college. And I lower the cost of health care in the way that I described to you.

Every part of my program, I've shown how I'm going to pay for it. And I've gotten good people, like former Secretary of the Treasury Bob Rubin for instance, who showed how to balance budgets and give you a good economy, to help me crunch these numbers and make them work. I've even scaled back some of my favorite programs already, like the child care program I wanted to fund and the national service program, because the President's deficit keeps growing. And I've said, as a pledge, I'm going to cut the deficit in half in 4 years.

Now, I'm going to restore what we did in the 1990s, ladies and gentlemen: Pay as you go. We're going to do it like you do it. The President broke the pay-as-you-go rule. Somebody here asked the question about why haven't you vetoed something. It's a good question. If you care about it, why don't you veto it? I think John McCain called the energy bill the no lobbyist left behind bill. I mean, you've got to stand up and fight somewhere, folks.

I'm pledging I will not raise taxes. I'm giving a tax cut to the people earning less than $200,000 a year. Now, for the people earning more than $200,000 a year, you are going to see a rollback to the level we were at with Bill Clinton, when people made a lot of money. And looking around here at this group here, I suspect there are only three people here who are going to be affected: the President, me, and Charlie, I'm sorry, you too. [*Laughter*]

Mr. Gibson. Mr. President, 90 seconds.

President Bush. It's just not credible. When he talks about being fiscally conservative, it's just not credible. If you look at his record in the Senate, he voted to break the spending—the caps, the spending caps, over 200 times, and here he says he's going to be a fiscal conservative all of a sudden. It's just not credible. You cannot believe it.

And of course he's going to raise your taxes. You see, he's proposed $2.2 trillion of new spending. And so they said, "Well, how are you going to pay for it?" He said, well, he's going to raise the taxes on the rich. That's what he said, the top two brackets. That raises—he says 800 billion; we say 600 billion. We've got battling green eyeshades—somewhere in between those numbers. And so there is a difference, what he's promised and what he could raise. Now, either he's going to break all these wonderful promises he's told you about, or he's going to raise taxes. And I suspect, given his record, he's going to raise taxes.

Is my time up yet?

Mr. Gibson. No, you can keep going.

President Bush. Keep going, good. [*Laughter*]

Mr. Gibson. You're on——

President Bush. You looked at me like my clock was up.

I think that the way to grow this economy is to keep taxes low, is to have an energy plan, is to have litigation reform. As I told you, we just got a report that

said over the past 13 months, we've created 1.9 million new jobs. We're growing. And so the fundamental question of this campaign is, who's going to keep the economy growing so people can work? That's the fundamental question.

Mr. Gibson. I'm going to come back one more time to how these numbers add up and how you can cut that deficit in half in 4 years, given what you've both said.

Senator Kerry. Well, first of all, the President's figures of 2.2 trillion just aren't accurate. Those are the fuzzy math figures put together by some group that works for the campaign. That's not the number.

Number two, John McCain and I have a proposal, jointly, for a commission that closes corporate giveaway loopholes. We've got $40 billion going to Bermuda. We've got all kinds of giveaways. We ought to be shutting those down.

And third, credible? Ladies and gentlemen, in 1985, I was one of the first Democrats to move to balance the budget. I voted for the balanced budget in '93 and '97. We did it. We did it, and I was there.

Mr. Gibson. Thirty seconds—I'm sorry, thirty seconds, Mr. President.

President Bush. Yes, I mean, he's got a record. He's been there for 20 years. You can run, but you can't hide. He voted 98 times to raise taxes. I mean, these aren't make-up figures. And so people are going to have to look at the record—look at the record of the man running for the President. They don't name him the most liberal in the United States Senate because he hasn't shown up to many meetings. They named him because of his votes, and it's reality. It's just not credible to say he's going to keep taxes down and balance budgets.

Mr. Gibson. Mr. President, the next question is for you, and it comes from James Hubb, over here.

Action on the Environment/Kyoto Protocol to the United Nations Framework Convention on Climate Change

James Hubb. Mr. President, how would you rate yourself as an environmentalist? What specifically has your administration done to improve the condition of our Nation's air and water supply?

President Bush. Off-road diesel engines—we have reached an agreement to reduce pollution from off-road diesel engines by 90 percent. I've got a plan to increase the wetlands by 3 million. We've got an aggressive brownfield program to refurbish inner-city sore spots to useful pieces of property.

I proposed to the United States Congress a Clear Skies Initiative to reduce sulfur dioxide, nitrogen oxide, and mercury by 70 percent. I was—fought for a very strong title in the farm bill for the Conservation Reserve Program to set aside millions of acres of land for—to help improve wildlife in the habitat.

We proposed and passed a Healthy Forests bill, which was essential to working with—particularly in western States, to make sure that our forests were protected. What happens in those forests, because of lousy Federal policy, is they grow to be—they are not—they're not harvested. They're not taken care of, and as a result, they're like tinder boxes. And over the last summers I've flown over there. And so this is a reasonable policy to protect old stands of trees and, at the same time, make sure our forests aren't vulnerable to the forest fires that have destroyed acres after acres in the West. We've got a good, common-sense policy.

Now, I'm going to tell you what I really think is going to happen over time, is technology is going to change the way we live, for the good, for the environment. So I proposed a hydrogen automobile, a hydrogen-generated automobile. We're spending a billion dollars to come up with the technologies to do that.

That's why I'm a big proponent of clean coal technology, to make sure we can use coal but in a clean way. I guess you'd say I'm a good steward of the land. The quality of the air is cleaner since I've been the President; fewer water complaints since I've been the President; more land being restored since I've been the President.

Thank you for your question.

Mr. Gibson. Senator Kerry, a minute and a half.

Senator Kerry. Boy, to listen to that, the President I don't think is living in a world of reality with respect to the environment. Now, if you're a Red Sox fan, that's okay. But if you're a President, it's not. Let me just say to you, number one, don't throw the labels around. Labels don't mean anything. I supported welfare reform. I led the fight to put 100,000 cops on the streets of America. I've been for faith-based initiatives helping to intervene in the lives of young children for years. I was—broke with my party in 1985, one of the first three Democrats to fight for a balanced budget when it was heresy. Labels don't fit, ladies and gentlemen.

Now, when it comes to the issue of the environment, this is one of the worst administrations in modern history. The Clear Skies bill that he just talked about—it's one of those Orwellian names you pull out of the sky, slap it onto something—like No Child Left Behind, but you leave millions of children behind. Here they're leaving the skies and the environment behind.

If they just left the Clean Air Act all alone the way it is today, no change, the air would be cleaner than it is if you pass the cleaner skies act. We're going backwards. In fact, his environmental enforcement chief air quality person at the EPA resigned in protest over what they're doing to what are called the New Source Performance Standards for air quality. They're going backwards on the definition for wetlands. They're going backwards on the water quality. They pulled out of the global warming, declared it dead; didn't even accept the science. I'm going to be a President who believes in science.

Mr. Gibson. Mr. President?

President Bush. Well, had we joined the Kyoto treaty, which I guess he's referring to, it would have cost America a lot of jobs. It's one of these deals where in order to be popular in the halls of Europe, you sign a treaty. But I thought it would cost a lot of—I think there's a better way to do it. And I just told you the facts, sir. The quality of the air is cleaner since I've been the President of the United States. And we'll continue to spend money on research and development because I truly believe that's the way to get from how we live today to being able to live a standard of living that we're accustomed to and being able to protect our environment better—the use of technologies.

Mr. Gibson. Senator Kerry, 30 seconds.

Senator Kerry. The fact is that the Kyoto treaty was flawed. I was in Kyoto, and I was part of that. I know what happened. But this President didn't try to fix it. He just declared it dead, ladies and gentlemen, and we walked away from the work of 160 nations over 10 years. You wonder, Nikki, why it is that people don't like us in some parts of the world. You just say, "Hey, we don't agree with you. Goodbye." The President has done nothing to try to fix it. I will.

Mr. Gibson. Senator Kerry, the next question is for you. It involves jobs, which is a topic in the news today. And for the question, we're going to turn to Jane Barrow.

Trade Competitiveness/Jobs/Taxes

Jane Barrow. Senator Kerry, how can the U.S. be competitive in a manufacturing given—in manufacturing, excuse me, given the wage necessary and comfortably accepted for American workers to maintain the standard of living that they expect?

Senator Kerry. Jane, there are a lot of ways to be competitive. And unfortunately, again, I regret, this administration has not seized them and embraced them. Let me give you an example. There's a tax loophole right now—if you're a company in St. Louis working, trying to make jobs here, there's actually an incentive for you to go away. You get more money—you can keep more of your taxes by going abroad. I'm going to shut that loophole, and I'm going to give the tax benefit to the companies that stay here in America to help make them more competitive.

Secondly, we're going to create a manufacturing jobs credit and a new jobs credit for people to be able to help hire and be more competitive here in America.

Third, what's really hurting American business, more than anything else, is the cost of health care. Now, you didn't hear any plan from the President, because he doesn't have a plan to lower the cost of health care. Five million Americans have lost their health care; 620,000 Missourians have no health care at all; 96,000 Missourians have lost their health care under President Bush.

I have a plan to cover those folks, and it's a plan that lowers costs for everybody, covers all children. And the way I pay for it—I'm not fiscally irresponsible—is I roll back the tax cut that this President so fiercely wants to defend, the one for him and me and Charlie. I think you ought to get the break. I want to lower your cost of health care.

I want to fully fund education, No Child Left Behind, special needs education. And that's how we're going to be more competitive, by making sure our kids are graduating from school and college. China and India are graduating more graduates in technology and science than we are. We've got to create the products of the future.

That's why I have a plan for energy independence within 10 years. And we're going to put our laboratories and our colleges and universities to work, and we're going to get the great entrepreneurial spirit of this country, and we're going to free our-selves from this dependency on Mideast oil. That's how you create jobs and become competitive.

Mr. Gibson. Mr. President, minute and a half.

President Bush. Let me start with how to control the costs of health care: Medical liability reform, for starters, which he's op-posed. Secondly, allow small businesses to pool together so they can share risk and buy insurance at the same discounts big businesses get to do. Thirdly, spread what's called health savings accounts. It's good for small businesses, good for owners. You own your own account. You can save tax-free. You get a catastrophic plan to help you—own it. This is different from saying, "Okay, let me incent you to go on the Govern-ment."

He's talking about his plan to keep jobs here. You know, he calls it an outsourcing—to keep—stop outsourcing. Robert Rubin looked at his plan and said it won't work. The best way to keep jobs here in America is, one, have an energy plan. I proposed one to the Congress 2 years ago. It encourages conservation, en-courages technology to explore for environ-mentally friendly ways for coal and use coal and gas. It encourages the use of renew-ables like ethanol and biodiesel. It's stuck in the Senate. He and his runningmate didn't show up to vote when they could have got it going in the Senate. Less regu-lations if we want jobs here. Legal reform if we want jobs here. And we've got to keep taxes low.

Now, he says he's only going to tax the rich. Do you realize 900,000 small busi-nesses will be taxed under his plan because most small businesses are Subchapter S corps or limited partnerships, and they pay tax at the individual income-tax level. And so when you're running up the taxes like that, you're taxing job creators, and that's not how you keep jobs here.

Mr. Gibson. Senator, I want to extend for a minute. You talk about tax credits

to stop outsourcing. But when you have IBM documents that I saw recently, where you can hire a programmer for $12 in China, $56 an hour here, tax credits won't cut it in that area.

Senator Kerry. You can't stop all outsourcing, Charlie. I've never promised that. I'm not going to, because that would be pandering. You can't. But what you can do is create a fair playing field, and that's what I'm talking about.

But let me just address what the Presi-dent just said. Ladies and gentlemen, that's just not true, what he said. The Wall Street Journal said 96 percent of small businesses are not affected at all by my plan. And you know why he gets that count? The President got $84 from a timber company that he owns, and he's counted as a small business. Dick Cheney is counted as a small business. That's how they do things. That's just not right.

President Bush. I own a timber com-pany? That's news to me. [*Laughter*] Need some wood? [*Laughter*]

Most small businesses are Subchapter S corps. They just are. I met Grant Milliron, Mansfield, Ohio. He's creating jobs. Most small businesses—70 percent of the new jobs in America are created by small busi-ness. His taxes are going up when you run up the top two brackets. It's a fact.

Mr. Gibson. President Bush, the next question is for you, and it comes from Rob Fowler, who I believe is over in this area.

PATRIOT Act

Rob Fowler. President Bush, 45 days after 9/11, Congress passed the PATRIOT Act, which takes away checks on law en-forcement and weakens American citizens' rights and freedoms, especially Fourth Amendment rights. With expansions of the PATRIOT Act and PATRIOT Act II, my question to you is, why are my rights being watered down and my citizens around me, and what are the specific justifications for these reforms?

President Bush. Yes, I appreciate that. I really don't think your rights are being watered down. As a matter of fact, I wouldn't support it if I thought that. Every action being taken against terrorists requires a court order, requires scrutiny. As a matter of fact, the tools now given to the terrorist fighters are the same tools that we've been using against drug dealers and white-collar criminals. So I really don't think so. I hope you don't think that. I mean, I—because I think whoever is the President must guard your liberties, must not erode your rights in America.

The PATRIOT Act is necessary, for example, because parts of the FBI couldn't talk to each other. Intelligence gathering and the law enforcement arms of the FBI just couldn't share intelligence under the old law, and that didn't make any sense. Our law enforcement must have every tool necessary to find and disrupt terrorists at home and abroad before they hurt us again. That's the task of the 21st century.

And so I don't think the PATRIOT Act abridges your rights at all, and I know it's necessary. I can remember being in upstate New York talking to FBI agents that helped bust the Lackawanna cell up there. And they told me they could not have performed their duty, the duty we all expect of them, if they did not have the ability to communicate with each other under the PATRIOT Act.

Mr. Gibson. Senator Kerry, a minute and a half.

Senator Kerry. Former Governor Racicot, as chairman of the Republican Party, said he thought that the PATRIOT Act has to be changed and fixed. Congressman Jim Sensenbrenner—he's the chairman of the House Judiciary Committee—has said over his dead body before it gets renewed without being thoroughly rechecked. Whole bunch of folks in America concerned about the way the PATRIOT Act has been applied.

In fact, the Inspector General of the Justice Department found that John Ashcroft had twice applied it in ways that were inappropriate. People's rights have been abused. I met a man who spent 8 months in prison, wasn't even allowed to call his lawyer, wasn't allowed to—finally, Senator Dick Durbin of Illinois intervened and was able to get him out. This is in our country, folks, the United States of America. They've got sneak-and-peak searches that are allowed. They've got people allowed to go into churches now and political meetings, without any showing of potential criminal activity or otherwise.

Now, I voted for the PATRIOT Act. Ninety-nine United States Senators voted for it. And the President has been very busy running around the country using what I just described to you as a reason to say I'm wishy-washy, that I'm a flip-flopper. Now, that's not a flip-flop. I believe in the PATRIOT Act. We need the things in it that coordinate the FBI and the CIA. We need to be stronger on terrorism. But you know what we also need to do as Americans is never let the terrorists change the Constitution of the United States in a way that disadvantages our rights.

Mr. Gibson. Senator Kerry, the next question is for you, and it comes from Elizabeth Long.

Embryonic Stem Cell Research

Elizabeth Long. Senator Kerry, thousands of people have already been cured or treated by the use of adult stem cells or umbilical cord stem cells. However, no one has been cured by using embryonic stem cells. Wouldn't it be wise to use stem cells obtained without the destruction of an embryo?

Senator Kerry. You know, Elizabeth, I really respect your—the feeling that's in your question. I understand it. I know the morality that's prompting that question, and I respect it enormously. But like Nancy Reagan and so many other people—you know, I was at a forum with Michael J. Fox the other day in New Hampshire, who's suffering from Parkinson's, and he wants us to do stem cell—embryonic stem cell. And this fellow stood up, and he was quivering. His whole body was shaking from the nerve disease, the muscular disease that he had, and he said to me and to the whole hall, he said, you know, "Don't take away my hope because my hope is what keeps me going." Chris Reeve is a friend of mine. Chris Reeve exercises every single day to keep those muscles alive for the day when he believes he can walk again, and I want him to walk again.

I think we can save lives. Now, I think we can do ethically guided embryonic stem cell research. We have 100,000 to 200,000 embryos that are frozen in nitrogen today from fertility clinics. These weren't taken from abortion or something like that. They're from a fertility clinic, and they're either going to be destroyed or left frozen. And I believe if we have the option, which scientists tell us we do, of curing Parkinson's, curing diabetes, curing some kind of a paraplegic or quadriplegic or a spinal cord injury, anything—that's the nature of the human spirit. I think it is respecting life to reach for that cure. I think it is respecting life to do it in an ethical way.

And the President's chosen a policy that makes it impossible for our scientists to do that. I want the future, and I think we have to grab it.

Mr. Gibson. Mr. President, a minute and a half.

President Bush. Embryonic stem cell research requires the destruction of life to create a stem cell. I'm the first President ever to allow funding, Federal funding, for embryonic stem cell research. I did so because I too hope that we'll discover cures from the stem cells and from the research derived.

But I think we've got to be very careful in balancing the ethics and the science. And so I made the decision we wouldn't spend any more money beyond the 70 lines, 22 of which are now in action, because science is important but so is ethics,

so is balancing life. To destroy life to save life is one of the real ethical dilemmas that we face.

There is going to be hundreds of experiments off the 22 lines that now exist, that are active, and hopefully we find a cure. But as well we need to continue to pursue adult stem cell research. I helped double the NIH budget to $28 billion a year to find cures. And the approach I took is one that I think is a balanced and necessary approach, to balance science and the concerns for life.

Mr. Gibson. Senator, thirty seconds, let's extend.

Senator Kerry. When you talk about walking a waffle line, he says he's allowed it, which means he's going to allow the destruction of life up to a certain amount, and then he isn't going to allow it. Now, I don't know how you draw that line. But let me tell you pointblank, the lines of stem cells that he's made available, every scientist in the country will tell you, "Not adequate," because they're contaminated by mouse cells and because there aren't 60 or 70; there are only about 11 to 20 now, and there aren't enough to be able to do the research because they're contaminated.

We've got to open up the possibilities of this research. And when I am President, I'm going to do it, because we have to.

Mr. Gibson. Mr. President.

President Bush. Let me make sure you understand my decision. Those stem cell lines already existed. The embryo had already been destroyed prior to my decision. I had to make the decision: Do we destroy more life; do we continue to destroy life? I made the decision to balance science and ethics.

Mr. Gibson. Mr. President, the next question is for you, and it comes from Jonathan Michaelson.

Supreme Court

Jonathan Michaelson. Mr. President, if there were a vacancy in the Supreme Court and you had the opportunity to fill that position today, who would you choose, and why?

President Bush. I'm not telling. [*Laughter*] I really don't have—I haven't picked anybody yet. Plus, I want them all voting for me. [*Laughter*] I would pick somebody who would not allow their personal opinion to get in the way of the law. I would pick somebody who would strictly interpret the Constitution of the United States.

Let me give you a couple of examples, I guess, of the kind of person I wouldn't pick. I wouldn't pick a judge who said that the Pledge of Allegiance couldn't be said in a school because it had the words "under God" in it. I think that's an example of a judge allowing personal opinion to enter into the decisionmaking process, as opposed to strict interpretation of the Constitution.

Another example would be the *Dred Scott* case, which is where judges years ago said that the Constitution allowed slavery because of personal property rights. That's personal opinion. That's not what the Constitution says. The Constitution of the United States says we're all—it doesn't say that. It doesn't speak to the equality of America.

And so I would pick people that would be strict constructionists. We've got plenty of lawmakers in Washington, DC. Legislators make law. Judges interpret the Constitution. And I suspect one of us will have a pick at the end of next year—next 4 years. And that's the kind of judge I'm going to put on there—no litmus test except for how they interpret the Constitution.

Mr. Gibson. Senator Kerry, a minute and a half.

Senator Kerry. Thank you, Charlie. A few years ago, when he came to office, the President said—these are his words—"What we need are some good conservative judges on the courts." And he said also that his two favorite Justices are Justice Scalia and Justice Thomas. So you get a pretty good sense of where he's heading if he were to appoint somebody.

Now, here's what I believe. I don't believe we need a good conservative judge, and I don't believe we need a good liberal judge. I don't believe we need a good judge of that kind of definition on either side. I subscribe to the Justice Potter Stewart standard. He was a Justice on the Supreme Court of the United States, and he said the mark of a good judge, a good Justice, is that when you're reading their decision, their opinion, you can't tell if it's written by a man or a woman, a liberal or a conservative, a Muslim, a Jew, or a Christian. You just know you're reading a good judicial decision.

What I want to find, if I'm privileged to have the opportunity to do it—and the Supreme Court of the United States is at stake in this race, ladies and gentlemen, the future of things that matter to you in terms of civil rights, what kind of Justice Department you'll have, whether we'll enforce the law, will we have equal opportunity, will women's rights be protected, will we have equal pay for women, which is going backwards, will a woman's right to choose be protected. These are constitutional rights, and I want to make sure we have judges who interpret the Constitution of the United States according to the law.

Mr. Gibson. Going to go to the final two questions, now. And the first one will be for Senator Kerry, and this comes from Sarah Degenhart.

Federal Funding of Abortions

Sarah Degenhart. Senator Kerry, suppose you are speaking with a voter who believed abortion is murder, and the voter asked for reassurance that his or her tax dollars would not go to support abortion. What would you say to that person?

Senator Kerry. I would say to that person exactly what I will say to you right now. First of all, I cannot tell you how deeply I respect the belief about life and when it begins. I'm a Catholic, raised a Catholic. I was an altar boy. Religion has been a huge part of my life. It helped lead me through a war, leads me today. But I can't take what is an article of faith for me and legislate it for someone who doesn't share that article of faith, whether they be agnostic, atheist, Jew, Protestant, whatever. I can't do that.

But I can counsel people. I can talk reasonably about life and about responsibility. I can talk to people, as my wife, Teresa, does, about making other choices and about abstinence and about all these other things that we ought to do as a responsible society. But as a President, I have to represent all the people in the Nation, and I have to make that judgment.

Now, I believe that you can take that position and not be pro-abortion. But you have to afford people their constitutional rights. And that means being smart about allowing people to be fully educated, to know what their options are in life, and making certain that you don't deny a poor person the right to be able to have whatever the Constitution affords them if they can't afford it otherwise.

That's why I think it's important. That's why I think it's important for the United States, for instance, not to have this rigid ideological restriction on helping families around the world to be able to make a smart decision about family planning. You'll help prevent AIDS. You'll help prevent unwanted children, unwanted pregnancies. You'll actually do a better job, I think, of passing on the moral responsibility that is expressed in your question, and I truly respect it.

Mr. Gibson. Mr. President, a minute and a half.

President Bush. Trying to decipher that. [*Laughter*] My answer is we're not going to spend Federal taxpayers' money on abortion. This is an issue that divides America, but certainly reasonable people can agree on how to reduce abortions in America. I signed the ban on partial-birth abortion. It's a brutal practice. It's one way to help reduce abortions. My opponent voted against the ban. I think there ought to be

parental notification laws. He's against them. I signed a bill called the Unborn Victims of Violence Act. In other words, if you're a mom and you're pregnant, you get killed, the murderer gets tried for two cases, not just one. My opponent was against that. These are reasonable ways to help promote a culture of life in America.

I think it is a worthy goal in America to have every child protected by law and welcomed in life. I also think we ought to continue to have good adoption law as an alternative to abortion. And we need to promote maternity group homes, which my administration has done. Culture of life is really important for a country to have if it's going to be a hospitable society.

Thank you.

Mr. Gibson. Senator, do you want to follow up? Thirty seconds.

Senator Kerry. Well, again, the President just said categorically, "My opponent is against this. My opponent is against that." It's just not that simple. No, I'm not. I'm against the partial-birth abortion, but you've got to have an exception for the life of the mother and the health of the mother under the strictest test of bodily injury to the mother. Secondly, with respect to parental notification, I'm not going to require a 16- or 17-year old kid who's been raped by her father and who's pregnant to have to notify her father. So you've got to have a judicial intervention. And because they didn't have a judicial intervention where she could go somewhere and get help, I voted against it. It's never quite as simple as the President wants you to believe.

Mr. Gibson. And 30 seconds, Mr. President.

President Bush. It's pretty simple when they say, "Are you for a ban on partial-birth abortion? Yes or no." And he was given a chance to vote, and he voted no. And that's just the way it is. That's a vote. It came right up. It's clear for everybody to see. And as I said, you can run, but you can't hide. It's the reality.

Mr. Gibson. And the final question of the evening will be addressed to President Bush, and it will come from Linda Grabel. Linda Grabel is over here.

President Bush. Put a head fake on.

Mr. Gibson. I got faked out, myself. [*Laughter*]

Presidential Decisionmaking/Funding U.S. Troops

Linda Grabel. President Bush, during the last 4 years, you have made thousands of decisions that have affected millions of lives. Please give three instances in which you came to realize you had made a wrong decision, and what you did to correct it. Thank you.

President Bush. I have made a lot of decisions, some of them little, like appointments to a board you've never heard of, and some of them big. And in a war, there's a lot of tactical decisions that historians will look back and say, "You shouldn't have done that. You shouldn't have made that decision." And I'll take responsibility for them. I'm human.

But on the big questions about whether or not we should have gone into Afghanistan, the big question about whether we should have removed somebody in Iraq, I'll stand by those decisions because I think they're right. That's really what you're— when they ask about the mistakes, that's what they're talking about. They're trying to say, "Did you make a mistake going into Iraq?" And the answer is absolutely not. It was the right decision.

The Duelfer report confirmed that decision today, because what Saddam Hussein was doing was trying to get rid of sanctions so he could reconstitute a weapons program, and the biggest threat facing America is terrorists with weapons of mass destruction. We knew he hated us. We knew he had been a—invaded other countries. We knew he tortured his own people.

On the tax cut, it's a big decision. I did the right decision. Our recession was one of the shallowest in modern history.

Now, you ask what mistakes—I made some mistakes in appointing people, but I'm not going to name them. I don't want to hurt their feelings on national TV. But history will look back, and I'm fully prepared to accept any mistakes that history judges to my administration. Because the President makes the decisions, the President has to take the responsibility.

Mr. Gibson. Senator Kerry, a minute and a half.

Senator Kerry. I believe the President made a huge mistake, a catastrophic mistake, not to live up to his own standard, which was build a true global coalition, give the inspectors time to finish their job, and go through the U.N. process to its end and go to war as a last resort.

I ask each of you just to look into your hearts, look into your guts—gut-check time. Was this really going to war as a last resort? The President rushed our Nation to war without a plan to win the peace, and simple things weren't done. That's why Senator Lugar says "incompetent" in the delivery of services. That's why Senator Hagel, Republican, says, "beyond pitiful, beyond embarrassing, in the zone of dangerous."

We didn't guard 850,000 tons of ammo. That ammo is now being used against our kids. Ten thousand out of twelve thousand Humvees aren't armored. I've visited some of those kids with no limbs today because they didn't have the armor on those vehicles. They didn't have the right body armor. I've met parents who've, on the Internet, gotten the armor to send their kids.

There's no bigger judgment for a President of the United States than how you take a nation to war. And you can't say, "Because Saddam might have done it 10 years from now, that's a reason." That's an excuse.

Mr. Gibson. Mr. President.

President Bush. He complains about the fact our troops don't have adequate equipment, yet he voted against the $87 billion supplemental I sent to the Congress and then issued one of the most amazing quotes in political history: "I actually did vote for the $87 billion, before I voted against it."

Saddam Hussein was a risk to our country, ma'am. And he was a risk that—and this is where we just have a difference of opinion. The truth of the matter is, if you listen carefully: Saddam would still be in power if he were the President of the United States, and the world would be "a lot better off."

Mr. Gibson. And Senator Kerry, 30 seconds.

Senator Kerry. Not necessarily be in power. But here's what I'll say about the 87 billion: I made a mistake in the way I talked about it. He made a mistake in invading Iraq. Which is a worse decision?

Now, I voted the way I voted because I saw that he had the policy wrong, and I wanted accountability. I didn't want to give a slush fund to Halliburton. I also thought the wealthiest people in America ought to pay for it, ladies and gentlemen. He wants your kids to pay for it. I wanted us to pay for it, since we're at war. I don't think that's a bad decision.

Closing Statements

Mr. Gibson. That's going to conclude the questioning. We're going to go now to closing statements, 2 minutes from each candidate. And the first closing statement goes to Senator Kerry. I believe that was the agreement.

President Bush. Go ahead. Actually——

Senator Kerry. You want to go first?

President Bush. Either way. [*Laughter*]

Senator Kerry. Thank you. Charlie, thank you. And thank you all. Thank you, all of you, for taking part; thanks for your questions tonight very, very much.

Obviously, the President and I both have very strong convictions. I respect him for that, but we have a very different view about how to make America stronger and safer. I will never cede the authority of our country or our security to any other nation. I'll never give a veto of American security to any other entity, not a nation,

not a country, not an institution. But I know, as I think you do, that our country is strongest when we lead the world, when we lead strong alliances. And that's the way Eisenhower and Reagan and Kennedy and others did it. We are not doing that today. We need to.

I have a plan that will help us go out and kill and find the terrorists, and I will not stop in our effort to hunt down and kill the terrorists. But I also have a better plan on how we're going to deal with Iraq, training the Iraqi forces more rapidly, getting our allies back to the table with a fresh start, with new credibility, with a President whose judgment the rest of the world trusts.

In addition to that, I believe we have a crisis here at home, a crisis of the middle class that is increasingly squeezed, health care costs going up. I have a plan to provide health care to all Americans. I have a plan to provide for our schools so we keep the standards, but we help our teachers teach and elevate our schools by funding No Child Left Behind. I have a plan to protect the environment so that we leave this place in better shape to our children than we were handed it by our parents. That's the test.

I believe America's best days are ahead of us. I'm an optimist. But we have to make the right choices, to be fiscally responsible and to create the new jobs of the future. We can do this. And I ask you for the privilege of leading our Nation to be stronger at home and respected again in the world.

Thank you.

Mr. Gibson. Senator. And a closing statement from President Bush.

President Bush. Charlie, thanks. Thank you all very much. It's been enjoyable.

The great contest for the Presidency is about the future, who can lead, who can get things done. We've been through a lot together as a country, been through a recession, corporate scandals, war. And yet, think about where we are. We added 1.9

million new jobs over the past 13 months. The farm income in America is high. Small businesses are flourishing. Homeownership rate is at an alltime high in America. We're on the move.

Tonight I had a chance to discuss with you what to do to keep this economy going: Keep the taxes low, don't increase the scope of the Federal Government, keep regulations down, legal reform, a health care policy that does not empower the Federal Government but empowers individuals, and an energy plan that will help us become less dependent on foreign sources of energy.

And abroad, we're at war, and it requires a President who is steadfast and strong and determined. I vowed to the American people after that fateful day of September the 11th that we would not rest nor tire until we're safe. The 9/11 Commission put out a report that said America is safer, but not yet safe. There's more work to be done. We'll stay on the hunt on Al Qaida. We'll deny sanctuary to these terrorists. We'll make sure they do not end up with weapons of mass destruction. The great nexus, the great threat to our country is that these haters end up with weapons of mass destruction.

But our long-term security depends on our deep faith in liberty. We'll continue to promote freedom around the world. Freedom is on the march. Tomorrow Afghanistan will be voting for a President. In Iraq, we'll be having free elections, and a free society will make this world more peaceful.

God bless.

Mr. Gibson. Mr. President and Senator Kerry. That concludes tonight's debate.

I want to give you a reminder that the third and final debate, on issues of domestic policy, will be held next Wednesday, October 13th, at Arizona State University in Tempe, Arizona, hosted by Bob Schieffer of CBS News.

I want to thank President Bush and Senator Kerry for tonight. I want to thank these citizens of the St. Louis area who asked the questions, who gave so willingly of their time, and who took their responsibility very seriously. Thank you also to everyone at Washington. I want to thank everyone at Washington University in St. Louis for being such gracious hosts.

I'm Charles Gibson from ABC News. From St. Louis, good night.

NOTE: The debate began at 8:02 p.m. in the Field House at Washington University. In his remarks, the President referred to former Democratic Presidential candidate Howard Dean; Finance Minister Adil Abd al-Mahdi of the Iraqi Interim Government; Prime Minister Tony Blair of the United Kingdom; Prime Minister Silvio Berlusconi of Italy; Chairman Yasser Arafat of the Palestinian Authority; Gen. Tommy R. Franks, USA (Ret.), former combatant commander, U.S. Central Command; Chairman Kim Chong-il of North Korea; President Aleksander Kwasniewski of Poland; and Grant E. Milliron, president, Milliron Iron & Metal, Inc. The President also referred to the National Commission on Terrorist Attacks Upon the United States (9/11 Commission). Senator Kerry referred to Marc Racicot, former chairman, Republican National Committee; Usama bin Laden, leader of the Al Qaida terrorist organization; Charles Duelfer, Special Advisor to the Director of Central Intelligence; King Abdullah II of Jordan; Gen. Eric K. Shinseki, USA (Ret.), former Army Chief of Staff; Hans Blix, former Executive Chairman, United Nations Monitoring, Verification, and Inspection Commission (UNMOVIC); Lt. Gen. Edward Baca (Ret.), former chief, National Guard Bureau; and actors Michael J. Fox and Christopher Reeve. Senator Kerry also referred to the "Comprehensive Report of the Special Advisor to the DCI on Iraq's WMD," issued September 30. The names of participants who asked questions of the candidates were taken from the transcript produced by the Commission on Presidential Debates.

Remarks at a Presidential Debate Watch Party in Ballwin, Missouri
October 8, 2004

The President. Thank you all for coming. Thanks for staying up so late. Anybody got any questions? [*Laughter*]

Audience member. We love Laura!

The President. Thank you all for coming. Laura said, "Don't talk too long tonight." [*Laughter*] I said, "Okay." [*Laughter*] But I do want to thank you all very much. There's no doubt in my mind, with your help, we'll carry Missouri again and win in November.

So tonight I was telling the people why I think they ought to put me back in there for 4 more years, but I didn't get the line I really wanted to say, which was that the main reason to put me back in was so that Laura would be the First Lady for 4 more years.

Audience members. Laura! Laura! Laura!

Audience member. We love you, Laura!

The President. Tomorrow morning, I'm waking up first thing in the morning to help the next Governor of Missouri, Matt Blunt, and the next Lieutenant Governor of Missouri, Peter Kinder. I want to thank them both. See you in the morning. I'll see you in the morning. Make sure the eggs aren't runny. [*Laughter*]

Then we're off to Iowa, then Minnesota. I'm fired up. I'm looking forward to this.

I thank all the candidates who are here. I really want to thank those of you who are putting up the signs and making the phone calls and doing all the work.

We had a good debate tonight. There's clear differences of opinion. One thing I hope you could tell is I know what I believe. I know why I need to lead this country to make this world a safer place and a more hopeful place for every American—for every single American.

Our dream is for America to fulfill its promise for every single person who lives here. There's no doubt in my mind, over the next 4 years this world will be a safer place, that we'll achieve the peace that we long for, for our children and grandchildren, and that the great promise of America, the great hope of our great country will be extended to every corner of this great land.

I can't thank you all enough for being here.

Audience member. Thank you!

The President. May God bless you, and may God continue to bless our country. Thank you all.

NOTE: The President spoke at 10:26 p.m. at the Greensfelder Recreation Complex. In his remarks, he referred to Missouri Secretary of State Matt Blunt, candidate for Missouri Governor; and Missouri State Senator Peter Kinder, candidate for Missouri Lieutenant Governor. A tape was not available for verification of the content of these remarks.

Statement on the Terrorist Attacks in Egypt
October 8, 2004

I condemn in the strongest possible terms the vicious terrorist attacks in Egypt yesterday. By targeting Muslims and Jews, Egyptians and Israelis, and women and children, the terrorists have shown their total contempt for all human life and for all human values. These acts show yet again why the civilized world must stand together against the forces of terror and defeat this evil.

On behalf of the American people, I express condolences to all who lost loved ones and to the people of Egypt and of Israel. I commend the cooperation between Israel and Egypt to help the victims and their families. The United States stands ready to provide assistance to the Government of Egypt as it brings the perpetrators of these acts to justice.

Remarks at a Breakfast for Gubernatorial Candidate Matt Blunt in St. Louis, Missouri
October 9, 2004

Thank you all. Thanks for coming. Thank you all for coming. Please be seated. I appreciate that kind introduction, Governor. [*Laughter*] He said, "Are you doing anything for breakfast?" [*Laughter*] I said, "Waking up." [*Laughter*] He said, "Why don't you come by and have some eggs with some friends." [*Laughter*] I said, "More than happy to." I want to thank you all for coming. With your help, Matt Blunt will be the next Governor for the great State of Missouri.

It's good to be back in St. Louis, home of the mighty Cardinals. You might remember opening day. [*Laughter*] The Cardinals had a great season after that. I can't claim any credit—[*laughter*]—although I've always wanted to lead a baseball team into the playoffs. [*Laughter*]

I'm proud to be traveling with Laura. She is a—so when I asked her to marry me, she said, "Fine, just so long as I never have to give a speech." [*Laughter*] I said, "Okay, you got a deal." [*Laughter*] Fortunately, she didn't hold me to that promise. The American people have seen her speak and have come to know her as a strong, compassionate, great First Lady. We're off to Iowa and then Minnesota. And I'm going to remind the people of those States, like I'm reminding everybody, there's some reasons to put me back into office, but perhaps the most important one is so that Laura will have 4 more years.

We got a great family. I'm proud to be with my Uncle Bucky Bush and my Aunt Patty Bush. Thank you for your love and compassion.

I want to thank Melanie Blunt for her willingness to serve the State of Missouri as the next first lady of Missouri. Besides Matt, you've got another fine Missourian on the ticket, running for Federal office, and that's Kit Bond. You need to put him back into office. He's a great Senator. I know Brenda Talent is here. I appreciate you being here, Brenda. Thank you for coming. You know, that fine husband of yours, I didn't hold it against him that he missed another one of my speeches, but he's heard a lot of them before. [*Laughter*] He's doing a great job, and I know you're proud of him. I know the people of Missouri are proud of him as well. Congressman Todd Akin—I don't know if Todd made it this morning or not, but I'm proud of the job he's doing for the people of this area of Missouri.

I saw Peter Kinder last night. I don't know if Pete is here, but he's going to make a great Lieutenant Governor for the State of Missouri. Yes, Peter, thank you for coming. You've come a long way for a country boy. [*Laughter*] I want to thank Catherine Hanaway, who's going to be the next secretary of state for the great State of Missouri.

I want to thank Ann Wagner, who has done such a fine job as the cochairman of the RNC and as the chairman of the Missouri Republican Party. Thank you for being here, Annie, it's good to see you. I want to thank my friend Sam Fox and Marilyn Fox for helping to organize this breakfast today. And I want to thank you all for joining the Foxes in supporting this good man, Matt Blunt for Governor.

I know Sarah Steelman is here, running for State treasurer, and Chris Byrd, running for attorney general. Thank you both for running. Good luck. I'm all for you.

But most of all, thank you all for coming. Thank you for being here. Thank you for what you're going to do, which is turn out the vote. And thanks for supporting Matt. It takes a lot of work to get 750 people to show up for breakfast. [*Laughter*] It's a great organizational effort. And I want to thank Matt's friends for putting this breakfast on. It's an important election here in Missouri. Matt has everything it takes to lead this State.

In 2001, he became the first statewide elected official in Missouri history to be called up to active duty. Think about that. He served his Nation with honor in the United States Navy. He's still a member of the Navy Reserves, and I'm proud to be his Commander in Chief. He knows people in the "Show Me" State want Government that gets results, not Government that just spends money.

For the last 4 years, Matt has been getting results as the secretary of the State. He's a results-oriented person. That's what you need in your statehouse. I know something about being a Governor. I was one once. [*Laughter*] A Governor's job is to get things done for the people of their State, and that's what he's going to do as your Governor.

His top priority is education, and that's the way it should be. Anybody running for Governor must make sure the education of the State is the top priority. I used to say in Texas, education is to a State what national defense is to the Federal Government. Matt understands that, and he be-

lieves that. He's got good plans and good visions for the schools of this State. He'll make sure school funding gets to the teachers and the classrooms, so not any child, not one child is left behind in this State. He'll make sure this great State continues to create jobs. He understands that a good economy is one in which the farmers and ranchers do well.

And he'll do something else, what's needed. The high cost of medicine is making it hard for small businesses to expand, for people to keep their health care. He understands like I understand, these frivolous lawsuits are driving good doctors out of business and driving up your cost of medicine.

We both share a commitment to keep our economy growing and to keep the people safe. We have some things in common. We're both in the same line of work as our dads. [*Laughter*] But all the good advice comes from our mothers. [*Laughter*] I want to thank Matt's mom for being here. Roseanne, great to see you. God bless you.

We share the same values. We stand for a culture of life, which every person matters and every being counts. We stand for marriage and family, which are the foundations of our society. We believe in the power of faith, and we stand with the armies of compassion. We stand for judges who know the difference between personal opinion and the strict interpretation of the law. These values are shared by Republicans and Democrats and independents all over the State of Missouri. When the people of Missouri elect Matt Blunt, you'll get a Governor who stands up for those values every single day. Let's get him in office.

We're getting close to voting time here in this country. But who's counting the days? [*Laughter*] There was voting time elsewhere in this world today. A marvelous thing is happening in Afghanistan. Freedom is powerful. Think about a society in which young girls couldn't go to school and their mothers were whipped in the public square. And today they're holding a Presidential election.

The first person to vote in the Presidential election, 3 years after the Taliban ruled that country with such barbarism, was a 19-year-old woman, an Afghan refugee who fled her homeland during the civil war. Here's what she said: "I cannot explain my feelings, just how happy I am. I would never have thought I would be able to vote in this election." She's voting in this election because the United States of America believes that freedom is the Almighty God's gift to each man and woman in this world. And today is an appropriate day for Americans to remember and thank the men and women of our Armed Forces who liberated Afghanistan.

The people of Australia voted today as well. And I want to congratulate my good friend Prime Minister John Howard, who won a great victory.

Laura and I are here to ask for people's vote. We believe you've got to get out amongst the people and say, "I want your vote. I want your support." I'm looking forward to coming down the stretch, traveling this great country, talking about a strong and positive message for our country. I've worked hard to make this country more hopeful and secure. I've led our country with principle and resolve, and that's how I'll lead this country for the next 4 years.

It was good to be back at Washington University. If I spend any more time there, they might give me an honorary degree. [*Laughter*] But I enjoyed that debate last night, and I really appreciated the questions from the people of Missouri. They were good questions. And they helped highlight some fundamental differences on issues from jobs to taxes to health care to national security.

Much as he tried to obscure it, on issue after issue, my opponent showed why he's earned the ranking, the most liberal Member of the United States Senate. And several of the statements just don't pass the credibility test.

With a straight face, he said, "I've only had one position on Iraq." He must think we've been on another planet. [*Laughter*] In the spring of 2003, as I ordered the invasion of Iraq, Senator Kerry said, "It was the right decision." Now he says, "It's the wrong war." And he tries to tell us he's had only one position. Who is he trying to kid? He can run, but he cannot hide.

With another straight face, he tried to tell Americans that when it comes to his health care plan, quote, "The Government has nothing to do with it." [*Laughter*] Eight out of ten people who would get health insurance under Senator Kerry's plan will be placed on a Government program. He can run, but he cannot hide.

Then Senator Kerry was asked to look into the camera—[*laughter*]—and promise he would not raise taxes for anyone who earns less than $200,000 a year. The problem is, to keep that promise he would have to break almost all of his other ones. [*Laughter*] His plan to raise taxes on the top two income brackets will raise 600 billion by our count, 800 billion by his. But his health care plan alone costs more than $1.2 trillion. He can't have it both ways. To pay for the big spending program he's outlined during his campaign, he will have to raise your taxes. He can run, but he cannot hide.

Much of what my opponent said last night is contradicted by his own record, 20 years of votes that earned him the "most liberal" label. He voted 98 times to raise taxes, more than 200 times to break spending caps. He voted against tort reform, although last night he tried to claim he now supports it. On national security, he has a voting record—a record of voting against the weapons systems that helped our country win the cold war. He voted to cut America's intelligence budget by $7.5 billion.

And now he says he wants a "global test" before taking action to defend America's security. The problem is, Senator Kerry's own record shows we can never pass that test. In 1991, the United Nations Security Council passed a resolution supporting action to remove Saddam Hussein from Kuwait. The international community was united. Countries throughout the world joined our coalition. Yet in the United States Senate after the Security Council resolution, Senator Kerry voted no. I have a different view. I'll work with our allies. I'll continue to build a strong coalition, but I will never allow other nations to veto America's national security decisions.

After listening to the litany of complaints and the dour pessimism, I did all I could not to make a bad face. [*Laughter*] We got a better way to make sure this country is more hopeful and more safe.

When you're out counting—rounding up the votes, remind people what we've been through. We've been through a recession. And by the way, the stock market started to decline 6 months before I became President. And then we had a recession. Then we had some corporate scandals. We passed tough laws to make it clear that we're not going to tolerate dishonesty in the boardrooms of America. And then we got attacked, and that attack cost us 1 million jobs in the 3 months after September the 11th.

But I put the right policies in at the right time at the right place, right here at home. We cut the taxes on the people. We gave the people more money to stimulate consumption and encourage in investment. And because we acted, the recession we faced was one of the shortest in history. America is on the move.

Yesterday we learned we've created 1.9 million new jobs in the last 13 months. We're on the move. The national unemployment rate is 5.4 percent. That is lower than the average of the 1970s, 1980s, and 1990s. Farm income is up. Small businesses are flourishing. The entrepreneurial spirit is strong. Homeownership rates are at an alltime high in America.

There is more to do. To make sure jobs stay here in America and this economy grows, we need less regulations on our job creators. We need legal reform in America. We need to make sure we have an energy plan that encourages consumption, that works with renewables, that explores for coal by using technologies to protect our air. To make sure jobs are here in America, America must be less dependent on foreign sources of energy.

To make sure jobs remain here, we got to reject economic isolationism. You know, we open up our markets for goods from overseas, and that's good for consumers. If you have more goods to choose from, you're likely to get that which you want at a better price and higher quality. That's how the marketplace works. That's why I'm saying to China, "You treat us the way we treat you. Level the playing field." And I believe strongly that America can compete with anybody, anytime, anywhere, so long as the rules are fair.

To make sure we continue to grow this economy, we got to make sure our people get educated. I went to Washington to solve problems, not to pass them on to future Presidents and future generations. I knew something about public schools because I was the Governor of a State. I knew that people in leadership positions had to challenge the soft bigotry of low expectations, a system that just quit on certain kids, a system that thought certain kids couldn't learn so they just shuffled them through, grade after grade, year after year. We let down too many families with that kind of attitude.

Yes, we've increased spending at the Federal level, but excellence in the classrooms requires more than just spending increases. It requires a change of attitude. We've raised the standards. We now measure early, so we can solve problems before it's too late. We believe every child can learn, and when we find a problem, we provide extra resources. And guess what's happening in America. There was an achievement—there is an achievement gap in America, but it's closing. It's closing because the system now focuses on each child, provides resources for each child, and will not let any child get behind in America.

There's more to do. There's more to do. We got—in a changing world, most new jobs require a college degree, yet one in four of our students gets there. That's why I believe in intermediate help in high schools for at-risk students. That's why I know we got to put math and science in place. That's why I'm for extending Pell grants for low- and middle-income families, so more of our people start their career with a college diploma.

And in a changing world, the skill sets required for jobs in the 21st century change as well. That's why I'm a big believer in the community college systems, to make sure our workers have got the capacity to fill the jobs of the 21st century.

No, there's more to do. We've done a lot. We've had a record of accomplishment. But the only reason to look back is to tell the people I'm going to do what I'm telling you I'm going to do. The only reason to look back at the record is to say, "This man intends to accomplish more for the American people."

We got to make sure our health care system is available and affordable. I remember campaigning here in 2000, going to a community health center right here in St. Louis, Missouri. I saw the compassionate care being delivered to the people there, to those who can't afford insurance, to those who need help. I'm a big believer in community health centers to help the poor and the indigent. I believe every poor county in America ought to have a community health center. I believe we ought to extend and expand the low-income health program—the health program for low-income children. I know to make sure health care is more affordable, we must allow small businesses to pool risk across jurisdictional boundaries so they can buy insurance at the same discounts big companies can.

I strongly believe we need to expand health savings accounts, tax-free accounts, coupled with catastrophic care, so workers have got more affordable health care, so small businesses can better afford health care.

I know we need to introduce technologies into the medical system to wring out the inefficiencies in the system to reduce the cost of health care. And I agree with Matt Blunt: In order to make sure health care is available and affordable, we need medical liability reform—now. I don't think you can be pro-doctor, pro-patient, and pro-trial-lawyer at the same time.

No, there's more to do to make sure America is a hopeful place, and there's more to do to make sure America is a safer place as well. Our strategy is clear. We're defending the homeland. We're transforming and strengthening the All-Volunteer Army—and we will keep it an all-volunteer army. We're making sure we got the best intelligence in the world. We will stay on the offensive. We will strike the terrorists abroad so we do not have to face them here at home. We'll continue to work for freedom and peace in the broader Middle East and around the world. And we'll prevail.

Our strategy is succeeding. Think about the world some 3½ years ago. Afghanistan was the home base of Al Qaida. Pakistan was a transit point for terrorist groups. Saudi Arabia was fertile ground for terrorist fundraising. Libya was secretly pursuing nuclear weapons. Iraq was a gathering threat. And Al Qaida was largely unchallenged as it planned attacks.

Because we led, because we acted, Afghanistan is fighting terror and holding a Presidential election today; Pakistan is capturing terrorists; Saudi Arabia is making raids and arrests; Libya is dismantling its weapons programs; a army of a free Iraq is fighting for freedom; and more than three-quarters of Al Qaida's leaders and associates have been brought to justice. We've led. Many have joined, and America and the world are safer.

And we've got more work to do. Over the next 4 years, we'll pursue Al Qaida wherever they hide. Over the next 4 years, we'll continue to disrupt the flows of weapons of mass destruction. Over the next 4 years, we'll continue to spread freedom.

And that's what's happening in Iraq. Last night I talked about the Finance Minister who came to see me. Let me recount some of that conversation I had with him. I thought it was really interesting and illustrative. He walks in full of confidence. He says, "Mr. President, thank you for what you and your country have done for us. We're headed toward elections."

Think about that statement. A fellow shows up in the Oval Office of the President of the United States and says, "We're headed for elections." For most of us, that doesn't sound like much. But for a person who used to live under the—in a country that was ruled by a brutal tyrant, where there were torture rooms and mass graves, where people had no freedom at all, to say, "We're headed toward elections," is a powerful statement.

And our strategy is clear. We're going to help the Iraqis. We're going to train Iraqis so they can do the hard work necessary for a free society to emerge. It's their country. We just want to stand with them as democracy comes to that piece of the world. And so we're training the troops. We'll have 125,000 police, Iraqi° national army trained up by the end of December. It's an essential part of our strategy. We got $7 billion allocated for reconstruction efforts. We're working with a grand coalition. Some 30 nations are involved there in Iraq.

As an aside, you cannot lead a coalition in Iraq if you tell them, "This is the wrong war at the wrong place at the wrong time." Imagine my opponent's grand idea of a global summit, and he walks in, and there are the leaders around the world sitting there, waiting for the American President

_____
° White House correction.

to speak. And he says, "Follow me into a great mistake." Nobody is going to follow. You must have optimism. You must believe in what you're doing if you expect to lead. And I believe in what we're doing in Iraq. And in January, Iraq will have elections, and that's important. You see, I believe in the power of liberty to transform societies.

I tell people all the time about my relationship with Prime Minister Koizumi of Japan. I was with him at the United Nations a couple of weeks ago, and I said, "I don't know if you know this, but I'm traveling the country talking about you and talking about our relationship. Is that okay?" After having done it about 30 times, he had to say yes. [*Laughter*] He said, "Sure." I didn't tell him I was going to tell you his favorite singer is Elvis. [*Laughter*]

But think about that for a minute. He and I are friends, and we're talking about different issues confronting the world. And the reason I say "think about it" is because it wasn't all that long ago that we were at war with Japan. If you're 58 years old, like me, it seems like an eternity. But a lot of people in this country still remember that war. My dad does, Buck's brother. I'm sure you've got dads and granddads who fought against the Japanese. They were our sworn enemy.

And after we were victorious in World War II, Harry S. Truman, from the State of Missouri, believed that liberty could transform an enemy into an ally. And so did a lot of other citizens. Oh, there were some skeptics in those days, and you can understand why. We had just finished a war. A lot of people's lives had been hurt as a result of that war. A lot of Americans had lost a loved one. They weren't interested in worrying about Japan. They were interested in their own souls and their own hearts. I'm sure there was a lot of people here that said, "It's just impossible for an enemy to become a friend." But because my predecessor and other Americans believed in the power of liberty to transform societies, I sit at the table with Prime Minister Koizumi, talking about the peace we all want.

We'll get the job done in Iraq. Freedom is powerful. And when we succeed, an American President will be sitting down with a duly elected leader of Iraq, talking about the peace that we all want. And we will have known—this generation of Americans will have known we have done our duty to our children and our grandchildren to leave behind a better world.

The stakes are high. This is an historic opportunity. It's essential that we be resolute and clear in our vision and have faith in the values that make us a great nation. I believe this century will be liberty's century. I know that by spreading freedom abroad, we'll bring the peace. And by spreading freedom at home, opportunity will go into every single corner of this country.

It's my honor to represent you. I look forward to winning this election. I want to thank you for help. May God bless you all, and may God continue to bless our country.

NOTE: The President spoke at 8:34 a.m. at the America's Center. In his remarks, he referred to Melanie Blunt, wife of gubernatorial candidate Matt Blunt; Brenda Talent, wife of Senator James M. Talent; Missouri State Senator Peter Kinder, candidate for Missouri Lieutenant Governor; Prime Minister John Howard of Australia; and Prime Minister Junichiro Koizumi of Japan.

The President's Radio Address
October 9, 2004

Good morning. As your President, I have led this country with principle and resolve. We have confronted historic challenges and built a broad record of accomplishment. I have proposed and delivered four rounds of tax relief, and our economy is creating jobs again. We have added over 1.9 million jobs in the past 13 months, more than Germany, Japan, Great Britain, Canada, and France combined. The unemployment rate is 5.4 percent, lower than the average rate of the 1970s, 1980s, and 1990s. Thanks to our education reforms, math and reading scores are increasing in public schools. We have strengthened Medicare to help low-income seniors save money on their medicine. And soon every senior will have the option of prescription drug coverage.

We have more to do. We will transform our systems of Government to fit a changing world and to help more people realize the American Dream. We will expand health savings accounts and improve Social Security to allow younger workers to own a piece of their retirement. Because education is vital to our prosperity, we will raise expectations in public schools and invest in community colleges. And to make sure America is the best place in the world to do business and create jobs, we will cut regulations, end junk lawsuits, pass a sound energy policy, and make tax relief permanent.

Senator Kerry takes a very different approach to our economy. He was named the most liberal Member of the United States Senate, and that's a title he has earned. Over the past 20 years, Senator Kerry has voted to raise taxes 98 times. He opposed all our tax relief and voted instead to squeeze an extra $2,000 in taxes from the average middle-class family. Now he's running on an agenda of higher taxes and higher spending and more Government control over American life. My opponent wants to empower Government. I want to use Government to empower people.

Since September the 11th, 2001, I have led a global campaign to protect the American people and bring our enemies to account. We have tripled spending on homeland security and passed the PATRIOT Act to help law enforcement and intelligence stop terrorists inside the United States. We removed terror regimes in Afghanistan and Iraq, and now both nations are on the path to democracy. We shut down a black-market supplier of deadly weapons technology and convinced Libya to give up its weapons of mass destruction programs. And more than three-quarters of Al Qaida's key members and associates have been detained or killed.

In the middle of a war, Senator Kerry is proposing policies and doctrines that would weaken America and make the world more dangerous. He's proposed the Kerry doctrine, which would paralyze America by subjecting our national security decisions to a "global test." He supports the International Criminal Court, where unaccountable foreign prosecutors could put American troops on trial in front of foreign judges. And after voting to send our troops into combat in Afghanistan and Iraq, he voted against the body armor and bullets they need to win.

For all of Senator Kerry's shifting positions on Iraq, one thing is clear: If my opponent had his way, Saddam Hussein would be sitting in a palace today, not a prison, and Iraq would still be a danger to America. As chief weapons inspector Charles Duelfer testified this week, and I quote, "Most senior members of the Saddam Hussein regime and scientists assumed that the programs would begin in earnest when sanctions ended, and sanctions were eroding." Instead, because our coalition acted, Iraq is free; America is safer; and the world will be more peaceful for our children and our grandchildren.

I will keep this Nation on the offensive against terrorists, with the goal of total victory. I will keep our economy moving so every worker has a good job, quality health care, and a secure retirement.

Thank you for listening.

NOTE: The address was recorded at 10:20 a.m. on October 8 at a private residence in St. Louis, MO, for broadcast at 10:06 a.m. on October 9. The transcript was made available by the Office of the Press Secretary on October 8 but was embargoed for release until the broadcast. In his remarks, the President referred to Charles Duelfer, Special Advisor to the Director of Central Intelligence. The Office of the Press Secretary also released a Spanish language transcript of this address.

Remarks in Waterloo, Iowa
October 9, 2004

The President. Thank you all for coming.

Audience members. Four more years! Four more years! Four more years!

The President. Thank you all for being here. What a beautiful day here in the great State of Iowa. Thanks for coming out to say hello. It's good to be in the home of tall corn, good tractors, and great people.

You know, I remember coming to Waterloo quite a few times before—one or two times before, in the 2000 campaign. And it's always good to be back. The crowds are bigger, and so is the entourage. [*Laughter*]

You know, we're getting closer to voting time here, and I'm here to ask for your vote, and I'm here to ask for your help.

There's no doubt in my mind, with your help, we'll carry Iowa and win a great victory in November.

Some other people were voting today around the world. As we meet here this morning, a really great thing is happening in Afghanistan. The people of that country, who just 3 years ago were suffering under the brutal regime of the Taliban, are going to the polls to vote for President. Think about that. Just 3 years ago, women were being executed in the sports stadium. Today they're voting for a leader of a free country. A 19-year-old woman, an Afghan refugee who fled her homeland during its civil war, became the very first voter. Here is what she said. She said, "I cannot explain my feelings, just how happy I am. I would never have thought I would be able to vote in this election." Amazing, isn't it? Freedom is beautiful.

And today is an appropriate day for Americans to remember and thank the men and women of our Armed Forces who liberated Afghanistan.

And earlier today I had the opportunity to call and congratulate my friend the Prime Minister of Australia, who won his election as well. Australia is a great ally in the war on terror, and John Howard is the right man to lead that country.

As you can see, I'm keeping pretty good company today. So I said, "Laura, will you marry me?" She said, "Fine, just so long as I never have to give a speech." [*Laughter*] I said, "Okay, you've got a deal." Fortunately, she didn't hold me to that promise. When she speaks, the American people know they're looking at someone who has got great compassion, a great heart. She's a wonderful First Lady.

I'm proud of my runningmate, Dick Cheney. He did a fine job in the debate the other night. I admit, he didn't have the waviest hair in the race. [*Laughter*] I didn't pick him because of his hair. [*Laughter*] I picked him because of his judgment, his experience. He's getting the job done for the American people.

Before I came up here, I had the privilege of saying hello to Jay and Patrick Grassley; that would be the son and grandson of a really fine United States Senator. I told him the other day in Des Moines that we've got a big yard there at the White House. [*Laughter*] If he's looking for something to do—[*laughter*]—bring those mowers over. [*Laughter*]

I appreciate Congressman Jim Nussle for his leadership. He's a fine, fine, fine leader.

I appreciate Mayor Tim Hurley of Waterloo, Iowa. I appreciate you coming, Mr. Mayor. Now, I understand the mayor didn't ask me for any advice, but I'm going to give him some. [*Laughter*] Fill the potholes. [*Laughter*] I'm honored you're here, Mr. Mayor. Thank you for your service.

I want to thank all the other State and local officials. I want to thank the people who are running for office. I want to thank Dave Roederer, who is the Bush-Cheney State campaign chairman. I want to thank Leon Mosley. I want to thank the grassroots activists who are here. I want to thank the people who are putting up the signs and making the phone calls, doing the hard work to turn out this vote. I want to thank the Sonny Burgess Band for being here. I'm honored you all are here. Appreciate you coming.

We had a great debate last night. It highlighted some of the fundamental differences on issues from jobs to taxes to health care to our national security. Much as he tried to obscure it, on issue after issue my opponent showed why he earned the ranking of the most liberal Member of the United States Senate. Several of the statements last night simply don't pass the credibility test.

With a straight face, he said, "I have only had one position on Iraq." [*Laughter*] I could barely contain myself. [*Laughter*] He must think we've been on another planet. [*Laughter*] In the spring of 2003, as I ordered the invasion of Iraq, Senator Kerry said, "It was the right decision." Now he says, "It's the wrong war," and he tries to tell us he's had only one position. He can run, but he cannot hide.

With another straight face, he tried to tell Americans that when it comes to health care, his health care plan, and I quote, "The Government has nothing to do with it." Eight out of ten people who get health care under Senator Kerry's plan would be placed on a Government program. He can run, but he cannot hide.

And then Senator Kerry was asked to look into the camera and promise he would not raise taxes for anyone who earns less than $200,000 a year. The problem is, to keep that promise he would have to break almost all of his other ones. [*Laughter*] His plan to raise taxes on the top two income brackets would raise between $600 billion by our estimates and $800 billion by his. But his health care plan alone costs 1.2 trillion. See, you can't have it both ways. To pay for big spending programs he's outlined during his campaign, he will have to raise your taxes. He can run, but he cannot hide.

You know, after listening to the litany of complaints and the dour pessimism, it took all I could do not to make a bad face. [*Laughter*] Much of what my opponent said last night is contradicted by his own records. Twenty years of votes have earned him the "most liberal" label.

I have a different record and a very different philosophy. I am a compassionate conservative. As your President, I have worked to make America more hopeful and more secure. I have led our country with principle and resolve, and that is how I will lead this Nation for 4 more years.

Audience members. Four more years! Four more years! Four more years!

The President. I'm looking forward to the campaign coming down the stretch. I like to get out with the people. I like to tell the people what I believe and where I stand. I believe every child can learn and every school must teach. I went to Washington, DC, to challenge the soft bigotry of low expectations. We've raised standards.

We're measuring early, to solve problems before it's too late. We're ending the old practice of just shuffling students through school whether they can read and write and add and subtract. And we're making progress. We're closing an achievement gap in America, and we're not going to go back to the old days of failure and mediocrity.

I believe we have a moral responsibility to honor our seniors with good health care. I went to Washington to solve problems, not to pass them on to future Presidents and future generations. We had a problem in Medicare. Medicine was changing, but Medicare wasn't. For example, Medicare would pay tens of thousands of dollars for heart surgery but wouldn't pay a dime for the prescription drugs that would prevent the heart surgery in the first place. We worked together with Republicans and Democrats; I worked with Chuck Grassley to make sure Iowa's rural hospitals got help in the Medicare program. We've strengthened and modernized Medicare for our seniors. Beginning in 2006, all seniors can get prescription drug coverage. We're helping our seniors, and we're not turning back.

I believe in the energy, innovation, and spirit of America's workers and small-business owners and farmers. And that's why we unleashed that energy with the largest tax relief in a generation.

When you're out gathering up the vote, when you're out convincing people to come our way, remind them what we have been through. The stock market was in serious decline 6 months before Dick Cheney and I took office. It was an indication of a recession that was coming, and we went through that recession. Then we had some corporate scandals which affected our economy. We passed tough laws. It's now abundantly clear that we will not tolerate dishonesty in the boardrooms of America. And then we got attacked, and that attack cost us about a million jobs in the 3 months following September the 11th, 2001.

But we acted. We put tax relief in place. And now our economy has been growing at rates as fast as any in nearly 20 years. The recession was one of the shallowest in American history. The unemployment rate in America is at 5.4 percent, lower than the average of the 1970s, 1980s, and 1990s. The unemployment rate in Iowa is 4.5 percent. The farm economy is strong here in the State of Iowa. More people own a home than ever before in the United States of America. We're moving forward to a more hopeful country, and we're not going to turn back.

I believe the most solemn duty of the American President is to protect the American people. If America shows uncertainty or weakness in this decade, the world will drift toward tragedy. This will not happen on my watch. I'm running for President with a clear and positive plan to build a safer world and a more hopeful America. I'm running with a compassionate conservative philosophy that Government should help people improve their lives, not try to run their lives. And with your help, we're going to win.

Any hopeful society has a growing economy, and I've got a plan to keep our economy moving forward. To make sure jobs are here, to make sure people can find work, America must be the best place in the world to do business. To keep jobs here, we need to reduce the burden of regulations on our business creators and job creators. To create jobs, we got to stop these junk lawsuits that are threatening the small businesses which are creating most new jobs in America.

To create jobs, Congress needs to pass my energy plan. My plan encourages conservation. It encourages the use of renewables like ethanol and biodiesel. It encourages new technologies. It encourages clean coal technology. What I'm telling you is, to keep jobs here we must become less dependent on foreign sources of energy.

To keep jobs here, we got to reject economic isolationism and open up markets around the world for U.S. products, for Iowa farm products. I like it when I hear

people around the world are eating Iowa corn or Iowa soybeans. See, I believe that we can compete with anybody, anywhere, anytime, so long as the rules are fair. And that's why I'm telling countries like China, "You treat us the way we treat you."

To create jobs, we got to be wise about we spend your money. We're going to keep your taxes low. You heard the language last night, "All I'm going to do is tax the rich." We've heard that before in American politics. You know what that means, "tax the rich." The rich hire lawyers and accountants for a reason: to stick you with the tab. We're not going to let him tax you. We're going to win in November.

I'll tell you something else about the Tax Code: It's a complicated mess. It is a million pages long. Americans spend 6 billion hours a year working on their tax returns. In a new term, I'm going to bring people together and simplify this Tax Code and make it more fair for you.

Most new jobs are filled by people with at least 2 years of college. That's what happens in a changing world. Yet only one in four of our students gets there. That's why in our high schools, we'll fund early intervention programs to help at-risk students. We'll place a new focus on math and science. Over time, we'll require a rigorous examination. By raising performance in our high schools and expanding Pell grants for low- and middle-income families, we'll help more Americans start their career with a college diploma.

I'm a big believer in the community college system in America. I believe the community colleges can be used wisely to make sure our workers gain the skills necessary to fill the jobs of the 21st century.

In this time of change, we also need to reform our health care system. We had a spirited debate last night on health care. The differences are clear. When it comes to health care, my opponent wants Government to dictate. I want you to decide. I want you to be the decisionmaker. So we have a plan to make sure health care is available and affordable. I believe in community health centers, places where the poor and indigent can get care. I believe every poor county in America ought to have a community health center. I know we got to make sure our programs for low-income children are fully subscribed, to make sure America's health care system works.

But we've got to do more to make sure health care is affordable as well. Listen, most of the uninsured work for small businesses. Small businesses are having trouble affording health care. To more enable people to be able to afford health care, we ought to allow small businesses to pool risk, to join together across jurisdictional boundaries so they can buy insurance at the same discounts that big businesses can do.

To make sure health care is affordable, we've got to expand health savings accounts, so workers and small businesses are able to save on premiums and people can save tax-free for a health care plan they call their own. To make sure health care is available and affordable, we've got to do something about these junk lawsuits that are running up the costs of health care and running good docs out of practice. You can't be pro-patient, pro-doctor, and pro-trial-lawyer at the same time. You have to choose. My opponent made his choice, and he put a trial lawyer on the ticket. I made my choice. I am for medical liability reform—now. In all we do to improve health care, this administration will make sure the health decisions are made by patients and doctors, not by officials in Washington, DC.

In a time of change, some things don't change. Those are the values we try to live by, courage and compassion and reverence and integrity. In changing times, we'll support the institutions that give our lives direction and purpose, our families, our schools, our religious congregations. We stand for a culture of life in which every person matters and every being counts. We stand for marriage and family, which are the foundations of our society. We stand for the appointment of Federal judges who

know the difference between personal opinion and the strict interpretation of the law.

This election will also determine how America responds to the continuing danger of terrorism. Since that terrible morning, September the 11th, 2001, we have fought the terrorists across the Earth, not for pride, not for power, but because the lives of our citizens are at stake.

Our strategy is clear. We're defending the homeland. We're transforming our military. I will make sure the All-Volunteer Army remains the All-Volunteer Army. We're reforming and strengthening our intelligence. We're staying on the offensive. We're striking the terrorists abroad so we do not have to face them here at home. We will work to advance liberty in the broader Middle East and around the world, because we understand free societies are peaceful societies. And we'll prevail.

Our strategy is succeeding. Think about the world as it was about 3½ years ago. Afghanistan was the home base of Al Qaida. Pakistan was a transit point for terrorist groups. Saudi Arabia was fertile ground for terrorist fundraising. Libya was secretly pursuing nuclear weapons. Iraq was a dangerous place and a gathering threat. Al Qaida was largely unchallenged as it planned attacks.

Because we led, Afghanistan is fighting terror and held a Presidential election today; Pakistan is capturing terrorist leaders; Saudi Arabia is making raids and arrests; Libya is dismantling its weapons programs; the army of a free Iraq is fighting for freedom; and more than three-quarters of Al Qaida's key members and associates have been brought to justice. We have led. Many have joined. And America and the world are safer.

The progress involved careful diplomacy, clear moral purpose, and some tough decisions. And the toughest came on Iraq. We knew Saddam Hussein's record of aggression. We knew he harbored terrorists. We knew he hated America. We knew he had a long history of pursuing and even using weapons of mass destruction. We know that after September the 11th, we must take threats seriously before they come to haunt us, before they hurt us.

In Saddam Hussein, we saw a threat. I went to the Congress. They looked at the very same intelligence I looked at, and they came to the same conclusion: Saddam Hussein was a threat. And they authorized the use of force. Some Members of the Senate want to forget that vote—or want you to forget it.

Before the United States ever commits troops into harm's way, we must try all means to deal with a threat. I understand the consequences of putting troops into combat. I know what it means. And so I went to the United Nations in hopes that diplomacy would work. The United Nations looked at the issue and passed another resolution. And this resolution said to Saddam Hussein, "Disclose, disarm, or face serious consequences." When an international body speaks, it must mean what it says.

The free world gave Saddam Hussein another chance, a final chance, to meet his demands. And as he had for over a decade, he refused the demands of the free world. He systematically deceived inspectors. So I had a choice to make at this point in time: Do I forget the lessons of September the 11th and take the word of a madman——

Audience members. No-o-o!

The President. ——or take action to defend America? Given that choice, I will defend our country every time.

We did not find the stockpiles we thought were there. But I want you to remember what the Duelfer report said. It said that Saddam Hussein was gaming the Oil for Food Programme to get rid of sanctions. And why? Because he had the capability and the knowledge to rebuild his weapon programs. And the great danger we face in the world today is that a terrorist organization could end up with weapons of mass destruction. Knowing what I know today, I would have made the same deci-

sion. The world is safer with Saddam in a prison cell.

Because we acted, freedom is on the march. We know what's happening in Afghanistan. And despite ongoing acts of violence, Iraq has got a strong Prime Minister, a National Council, and national elections are scheduled for January. We're standing with the people in Afghanistan and in Iraq because when America gives its word, America must keep its word. But we're doing so as well because it will make us safer. Free societies in the Middle East will be hopeful societies which no longer feed resentments and breed violence for export. Free governments in the Middle East will fight terrorists instead of harboring them, and that helps us keep the peace.

So our mission in Afghanistan and our mission in Iraq is clear. We'll help those leaders train armies so the people of Afghanistan and Iraq can do the hard work of defending democracy. We will help them get on the path to stability and democracy as quickly as possible, and then our troops will come home with the honor they have earned.

We've got a great United States military, and I want to thank the veterans who are here today for having set such a great example. And I want to thank the military families who are here today. I want to assure you, we'll keep the commitment I have made to our troops that they will have all the resources they need to complete their missions. That's why, in September 2003, I went to the Congress and requested $87 billion in funding for body armor and spare parts, ammunition, fuel, and other supplies necessary for our troops in combat in both Afghanistan and in Iraq. It was really important funding. As a matter of fact, we received great bipartisan support in both the House and the Senate. As a matter of fact, only 12 United States Senators voted against the funding, 2 of whom are my opponent and his runningmate.

Audience members. Boo-o-o!

The President. When you're out talking up this election and reminding people about the difference in this campaign, remind them there were only four United States Senators who voted to authorize the use of force and then voted against providing the funding for our troops—only four, two of whom are my opponent and his runningmate.

Audience members. Boo-o-o!

The President. You might remember his famous quote, "I actually did vote for the $87 billion, before I voted against it." I don't suspect a lot of people in Waterloo, Iowa, speak that way. He's given a lot of explanations for that vote. One of my favorites is when he said, "Well, the whole thing is a complicated matter." There's nothing complicated about supporting our troops in harm's way.

On national security, my opponent has a record of voting against the weapons systems that helped our country win the cold war. He voted to cut America's intelligence budget by 7.5 billion after 1993. And now he says he wants a "global test" before taking action to defend America's security. The problem is, Senator Kerry's own record shows we can never pass that test. In 1990, the United Nations Security Council passed a resolution supporting action to remove Saddam Hussein from Kuwait. The international community was united. Countries throughout the world joined our coalition. Yet in the United States Senate, after the Security Council resolution, Senator Kerry voted no.

Let me tell you how I think the President ought to lead. The President will always work with our friends and allies. We've built strong coalitions. As a matter of fact, I can—I told you I congratulated Prime Minister John Howard today. But I will never allow other nations to veto America's national security decisions.

In the long run, the best way to defend our security is to spread freedom. I believe in the transformational power of liberty. I like to tell people about my friend Prime Minister Koizumi of Japan. I was with him recently in the United Nations in New York. I said, "By the way, I'm campaigning a lot, and I'm talking about you a lot on the campaign trail. Do you mind?" He said, "Not at all." I didn't ask him if I could tell you his favorite singer was Elvis, which it is. What's interesting about my meetings with him is that, one, we get along great, and Laura and I consider him a friend. But we're sitting down with the head of a country that was a sworn enemy of America not so long ago. My dad fought against the Japanese. I just know a lot of people out here's relatives fought against the Japanese. It was a bloody war. But after the war was over, Harry S. Truman, President of the United States, believed in the transformational power of liberty, believed that liberty could change an enemy into an ally.

Now, there were some people in the United States at that time who didn't agree with that. There were skeptics and pessimists. You can understand why. After a war, there was bitterness about what took place. Some, I'm confident, were saying, "Who cares about the enemy. We won." But fortunately, enough Americans didn't believe that way, and they helped Japan become a democracy. And today, I sit down with my friend Prime Minister Koizumi, talking about how to keep the peace, talking about the peace that we all want for our children and grandchildren.

We'll succeed in Iraq. We've got a plan that will work. I believe strongly the Iraqi people want to live in a free society, and someday a duly elected leader of Iraq will be sitting down with the President of the United States, talking about how to keep the peace. And our children and our grandchildren will be better off for it.

I believe that millions in the Middle East plead in silence for their freedom. I believe women want to grow up in a free society and raise their children in a free society. I believe that given a chance, the people in the Middle East will embrace the most honorable form of government ever devised by man. I believe all these things because freedom is not America's gift to the world; freedom is the Almighty God's gift to each man and woman in this world.

For all Americans, these years in our history will always stand apart. There are quiet times in the life of a nation when little is expected of its leaders. This is not one of those times. This is a time that requires firm resolve and clear vision and the deep faith in the values that make us a great nation.

None of us will ever forget that week when one era ended and another began. September the 14th, 2001, I stood in the ruins of the Twin Towers. It's a day I'll never forget. I'll never forget the workers in hardhats that were yelling at me at the top of their lungs, "Whatever it takes." I will never forget the man who had been in the rubble looking for a friend, who came out and grabbed me by the arm, and he said, "Do not let me down." Ever since that day, I wake up every morning thinking about how to better protect our country. I will never relent in defending America, whatever it takes.

You know, 4 years ago when I traveled your great State in the caucuses and then in the general election, I made a pledge that if you gave me the chance to serve, I would uphold the honor and the dignity of the office to which I had been elected. With your help, with your hard work, I will do so for 4 more years.

God bless. Thank you for coming. I'm honored you're here. Thank you all for being here.

NOTE: The President spoke at 11:13 a.m. at Riverfront Stadium. In his remarks, he referred to Prime Minister John Howard of Australia; David Roederer, Iowa State chair, Bush-Cheney '04, Inc.; Leon Mosley, State cochair, Republican Party of Iowa; entertainer Sonny Burgess; Charles Duelfer, Special Advisor to the Director of Central Intelligence; Prime Minister Ayad Allawi of the Iraqi Interim Government; and Prime Minister Junichiro Koizumi of Japan. He also referred to the "Comprehensive Report of the Special Advisor to the DCI on Iraq's WMD," issued September 30.

Remarks in Chanhassen, Minnesota
October 9, 2004

The President. Thank you all. Thank you all for being here. What a beautiful day.

Audience members. Four more years! Four more years! Four more years!

The President. Thank you all. It turns out I am the first sitting President ever to visit Chanhassen, Minnesota. All the other ones missed out on a beautiful part of America. Thank you for coming out today. I'm here asking for the vote, and I'm here to ask for your help in getting that vote out. There is no doubt in my mind, with your help, we will carry Minnesota and win a great victory in November.

We're getting close to voting time here in America, and today a great thing happened in Afghanistan. The people of that country, who just 3 years ago were suffering under the brutal regime of the Taliban, went to the polls to vote for their President. A 19-year-old woman, an Afghan refugee who fled her homeland during its civil war, became the very first voter. It's amazing, isn't it? She said, "I cannot explain my feelings, just how happy I am. I never would have thought I'd be able to vote in this election." Freedom is beautiful. Freedom is on the march.

So today is an appropriate day for Americans to remember and thank the men and women of America's Armed Forces who liberated Afghanistan. Because of their actions, America is safer, and the world is better off.

Australia had an election as well. And I was honored to call my friend John Howard, the Prime Minister, and congratulate him on a great victory. As you can see, I'm keeping good company today.

So here's the way I like to tell the day I asked Laura to marry me. I said, "Would you marry me?" She said, "Fine, just so long as I never have to give a political speech." [*Laughter*] I said, "Okay, you've got a deal." [*Laughter*] Fortunately, she didn't hold me to the promise. Americans, when they see Laura speak, see a compassionate, decent, warm, great First Lady.

I'm proud of my runningmate, Dick Cheney. I thought he did a great job in his debate. I admit it, he didn't have the waviest hair on the platform there. Of course, I didn't pick him for his hair. [*Laughter*] I picked him because of his experience and sound judgment. I picked him because he can get the job done for the American people.

I'm proud of your Governor, Tim Pawlenty. He's a good Governor, and I'm proud to call him friend.

Plus, I like working with Norm Coleman. He's a fine United States Senator. And I hope you put John Kline back in office, the United States Congressman from this district. They're not here. They're in Washington, still voting. I can't wait for them to get out of town. [*Laughter*]

I want to thank the mayor of Chanhassen, Tom Furlong, for being here. I'm proud you're here, Mr. Mayor. One of the things I'm proud of is there's all kinds of Democrats around the country supporting me. People like Zell Miller are supporting my candidacy. But so is my friend, the mayor of St. Paul, Randy Kelly.

I want to thank all the statehouse people who are here. I want to thank the Shooting Star Band. I want to thank all the grassroots activists for what you're going to do. I can see by the signs and the size of this crowd you have done a lot. But it's what you're going to do I want to thank you for, and that is turn out the vote, get people to the polls.

Audience members. Four more years! Four more years! Four more years!

The President. We had an interesting evening last night. It was a great debate. I thought the citizens did a fantastic job of asking good questions, and that debate highlighted some fundamental differences on issues from jobs and taxes and health care and national security. Much as he tried to obscure it, on issue after issue my opponent showed why he earned the ranking of the most liberal Member of the United States Senate. And several of his statements just don't pass the credibility test.

With a straight face, he said, "I've only had one position on Iraq." [*Laughter*] I could barely contain myself. [*Laughter*] He must have—he must think we're on a different planet. [*Laughter*] In the spring of '03, as I ordered the invasion of Iraq, Senator Kerry said, "It was the right decision." Now he says, "It was the wrong war." He tries to tell us he's had only one position. Who's he trying to kid? He can run, but he cannot hide.

Again, with a straight face, he tried to tell Americans that when it came to his health care plan, quote, "the Government has nothing to do with it." [*Laughter*] Eight out of ten people who get health insurance under Senator Kerry's plan will be placed on a Government program. He can run, but he cannot hide.

And then Senator Kerry was asked to look in the camera and promise he would not raise taxes on anyone who earns less than 200,000 a year.

Audience members. [*Inaudible*]

The President. I know. The problem is, to keep that promise he would have to break almost all of his other ones. [*Laughter*] You see, his plan to raise taxes on the top two income brackets will raise $600 billion a year by our estimate and $800 a year by—$800 million by his estimate—will raise $600 billion by our estimate and $800 billion by his estimate. I think I finally got it right. [*Laughter*] But his own health care plan costs $1.2 trillion. So you begin to see the problem. He can't have it both ways. To pay for the big spending programs he's outlined during his campaign, he's going to have to raise your taxes. And he can run, but he cannot hide.

You know, after listening to his litany of complaints and his dour pessimism, it was all I could do not to make a bad face. [*Laughter*] I have a very different philosophy from Senator Kerry. I'm a compassionate conservative. As your President, I've worked to make America more hopeful and more secure. I've led this country with principle and resolve, and that's how I will lead with—the next 4 years.

I'm looking forward to coming back to Minnesota before election day. I'm looking forward to this stretch run. I like to be with people. I like to tell people what I believe and where I stand. I believe every child can learn and every school must teach. I went to Washington to challenge the soft bigotry of low expectations. I felt strongly we needed to end this business about just shuffling the kids through, grade after grade, year after year, without teaching the basics. We've raised the standards. We measure early to solve problems before it's too late. We trust the local people to make the right choices for their schools. We're closing an achievement gap in America, and we're not going to go back.

I believe our seniors must have a good health care system. I went to Washington to fix problems, not pass them on to future Presidents. I saw a problem in Medicare. Let me give you an example. Medicare would pay thousands of dollars for a heart surgery but not one dime for the prescription drugs to prevent the heart surgery from being needed in the first place. That wasn't right for our seniors. It wasn't right

for the taxpayers. We came together and strengthened Medicare for our seniors. Seniors will get prescription drug coverage in 2006, and we're not going to go back.

I believe in the energy and innovation and spirit of our workers and small-business owners and farmers and ranchers. That's why we unleashed that energy with the largest tax relief in a generation. When you're out there gathering up the vote, remind people what we've been through, what this economy has been through. Six months prior to our arrival in Washington, DC, the stock market was heading down. Then we had a recession. Then we had some corporate scandals, which affected our economy. We passed laws that say to people, "We will not tolerate dishonesty in the boardrooms of this country." And then the enemy hit us. And that attack cost us a million jobs in the 3 months after September the 11th. We've been through a lot. You think about that.

But our economy has been growing at rates as fast as any in nearly 20 years. The national unemployment rate is 5.4 percent, which is lower than the average of the 1970s, 1980s, and 1990s. The unemployment rate in the great State of Minnesota is 4.8 percent. Farm income is high. The homeownership rate is at an alltime high in America. America is on the move, and we're not going to go back.

I believe the most solemn duty of the American President is to protect the American people. If America shows uncertainty and weakness in this decade, the world will drift toward tragedy. This will not happen on my watch.

Listen, I recognize that a hopeful society must have a growing economy, and I have a strategy to keep this economy moving forward. In order to keep jobs here in America, in order to make sure people can find work, America must be the best place in the world to do business. That means less regulations on our businesses. That means we've got to do something about these junk lawsuits that are hurting small-business owners in America.

If we want to keep jobs here in America, this country—Congress has got to pass my energy plan. It's a plan that encourages conservation. It's a plan that encourages the use of renewables like ethanol and bio-diesel. It's a plan that uses technologies to make sure we can explore for natural gas in environmentally friendly ways. It's a plan that promotes clean coal technology. It is a plan that recognizes to keep jobs here, America must be less dependent on foreign sources of energy.

In order to keep jobs here in America, we've got to open up markets for our products. Listen, we've opened up America's markets for products from overseas, and that's good for you. If you have more choices, you're likely to get the product you want at higher quality and better price. That's how the market works. So rather than shutting down our market and hurting consumers, my strategy is to tell places like China, "You treat us the way we treat you." And I'm confident in doing so, because I know we can compete with anybody, anytime, anywhere, so long as the rules are fair.

To create jobs in America, we must be wise about how we spend your money and keep your taxes low. You heard that rhetoric, "Oh, all he's going to do is tax the rich." In order to make sure he can—in order to make sure he fulfills a little bit of his promises, he said he's going to tax the rich. We've heard that kind of language before. Yes, the rich hire lawyers and accountants for a reason—to stick you with the bill. We're not going to let the Senator tax you; we're going to whip him in November.

We've got to do something about this health care system. Costs are rising rapidly. We need to make sure health care is available and affordable. Most of the people who are uninsured work for small businesses. I think we ought to allow small businesses to pool risk across jurisdictional boundaries so they can buy insurance at the same price and the same discounts big businesses get to buy insurance. We need to expand tax-free health savings accounts to help our small businesses and our workers.

We need to make sure that each poor community in—county in America has got a community health center for our poor and the indigent. We've got to make sure our children's—low-income children's health program is fully subscribed. We've got to use technology to wring excess costs out of the system. This is a practical, commonsense way to make sure health care is available and affordable.

And another thing we need to do is we've got to get rid of those frivolous lawsuits that are running good docs out of business and running up the cost of health care. You cannot be pro-doctor, pro-patient, pro-hospital, and pro-trial-lawyer at the same time. You have to choose. My opponent made his choice, and he put a trial lawyer on the ticket.

Audience members. Boo-o-o!

The President. I have made my choice. I'm standing with the patients and the docs. I'm for medical liability reform—now. In all we do to reform health care, my administration will make sure the decisionmaking is between the doctor and the patient, not by officials in the Nation's Capital.

You know, in changing times—and we do have changing times—it helps bring stability into your life if you own something. More and more people are owning their own home. We've got plans over the next 4 years to continue to expand homeownership all around America. I love the idea of somebody opening up the front door where they live and saying, "Welcome to my home. Come to my house. Welcome to my piece of property."

In changing times, we've got to do something about our retirement system. You might remember the campaign in 2000, when they said, "If George W. wins, you're not going to get your Social Security check." Remember those ads? Yes. Our seniors got their checks. You're hearing the same rhetoric this time. Baby boomers like me, we'll get the checks.

We need to worry about our children and our grandchildren when it comes to Social Security. We need to do something to make that system available for our children and grandchildren. That's why I think younger workers ought to be allowed to take some of their own money and set up a personal savings account, a personal savings account that will earn better interest, a personal savings account they can call their own, that Government cannot take away.

We have a difference in philosophy in this campaign. My opponent's programs expand the Federal reach—the reach of the Federal Government. My programs expand freedom and opportunity for every American. He trusts Government. I trust the people.

In a world of change, there's some things that will not change, the values we try to live by, courage and compassion, reverence and integrity. In times of change, we'll support the institutions that give our lives direction and purpose, our families, our schools, our religious congregations. We stand for a culture of life in which every person matters and every being counts. We stand for marriage and family, which are the foundations of our society. We stand for the appointment of Federal judges who know the difference between personal opinion and strict interpretation of the law.

This election will also determine how America responds to the continuing danger of terrorism. Since the terrible morning of September the 11th, 2001, we've fought the terrorists across the Earth, not for pride, not for power, but because the lives of our citizens are at stake. Our strategy is clear. We're defending the homeland. We're strengthening the intelligence services. We're transforming the All-Volunteer Army, which will stay an all-volunteer army. We will stay on the offensive. We will strike the terrorists abroad so we do not have to face them here at home. We will continue to work to spread liberty in the greater Middle East and around the world. And we'll prevail.

Our strategy is succeeding. Think about the world the way it was prior to September the 11th. Afghanistan was the home base of Al Qaida. Pakistan was a transit point for terrorist groups. Saudi Arabia was fertile ground for terrorist fundraising. Libya was secretly pursuing weapons. Iraq was a gathering threat, and Al Qaida was largely unchallenged as it planned attacks.

Because we led, Afghanistan is an ally in the war on terror, and they're having Presidential elections today; Pakistan is capturing terrorists; Saudi Arabia is making raids and arrests; Libya is dismantling its weapons program; the army of a free Iraq is fighting for freedom; and three-quarters of Al Qaida—three-quarters of key members and associates of Al Qaida have been brought to justice. America has led. Many have followed. And the world is safer.

This progress involved careful diplomacy, clear moral purpose, and some tough decisions. And the toughest came in Iraq. We knew Saddam Hussein's record of aggression and support for terror. We knew he had harbored terrorists. We knew his long history of pursuing and using weapons of mass destruction. We knew that the biggest threat we face is if a terrorist group were able to attain weapons of mass destruction. And we knew that after September the 11th, it's vital that we think differently about our security. We must take threats seriously before they fully materialize.

Saddam Hussein was a threat. I went to the Congress. They looked at the same intelligence I looked at. They remembered the same history of Saddam Hussein, and they concluded Saddam was a threat and authorized the use of force. My opponent was one of those who authorized the use of force.

Before the Commander in Chief commits troops into harm's way, we must try every option—every option—to solve a problem. I understand the consequences of sending people into combat. I know exactly what takes place. And so I went to the United Nations, hoping to solve this problem diplomatically. You know, they looked at the intelligence. They debated the issue, and they voted 15 to nothing, in the U.N. Security Council and said to Saddam Hussein, "Disclose, disarm, or face serious consequences." That's what they told him. I believe when international bodies speak, it must mean what it says. In order to make the peace, when you say something, you'd better mean it.

As he had for over a decade, Saddam Hussein wasn't about to listen to the demands of the free world. As a matter of fact, the report that came out the other day showed he didn't have the weapons we thought he had but, nevertheless, was gaming the system. He was using the Oil for Food Programme to weaken the sanctions. And you know why? Because he wanted to start his weapons programs up again. Saddam was a danger. He was a threat. We gave him a final chance. He ignored the demands of the free world. He deceived the inspectors. So I have a choice to make at this point: Do I trust the word of a madman and forget the lessons of September the 11th, or take action to defend our country? Given that choice, I will defend America every time.

Because we acted to defend ourselves, 50 million people now live in freedom. The world is seeing what's happening in Afghanistan. Despite ongoing acts of violence, Iraq is moving toward free elections in January. Iraq has a strong Prime Minister and a National Council. We're standing with the people in those countries because when America gives its word, America must keep its word.

And in standing with those people, we're making our country safer. Free societies in the Middle East will be hopeful societies which no longer feed resentments and breed violence for export. Free societies in the Middle East will fight terrorists instead of harboring them, and that makes us safer.

Our missions in Afghanistan and Iraq are clear. We will help the Afghan people and the Iraqi people by training them, so they can fight for their own freedom, so they can fight for the destiny of their people. We'll help them get on the path to stability and democracy as quickly as possible, and then our troops will come home with the honor they have earned.

We've got a great United States military. I want to thank the veterans who are here for having set such a great example for those who wear the uniform. I want to thank the military families who are with us here today. I made a commitment to our families and to our troops: They will have the resources they need to complete their missions. That's why I went to the Congress in September of 2003 and asked for $87 billion of vital funding to support our troops in both Afghanistan and Iraq. We got great support there in the Congress, strong bipartisan support. As a matter of fact, only 12 United States Senators voted against the funding for our troops, 2 of whom are my opponent and his runningmate.

Audience members. Boo-o-o!

The President. When you're out gathering up the vote, remind people of this fact: Only four Members of the United States Senate voted to authorize force and then voted against funding the troops—only four, two of whom are my opponent and his runningmate.

Audience members. Boo-o-o!

The President. So they asked him why. And he said, "Well"—in the most famous quote of the 2004 election, one that has befuddled millions of Americans, he said, "I actually did vote for the $87 billion, before I voted against it." They kept pressing him, and he's given, I don't know, six or seven answers. But one of the most interesting ones of all was he finally through up his hands and said, "It's just a complicated matter." [*Laughter*] There's nothing complicated about supporting our troops in combat.

On national security, my opponent has a record of voting against the weapons systems that helped our country win the cold war. Right after the bombing in 1993, he voted to cut America's intelligence budget by $7.5 billion. And now he says he wants a "global test"——

Audience members. Boo-o-o!

The President. ——before we take action to defend our security. Think about that. The problem is that the Senator can never pass his own test. [*Laughter*] In 1990, the United Nations Security Council passed a resolution supporting action to remove Saddam Hussein from Kuwait. The international community was united. Countries around the world joined that coalition. Yet in the United States Senate, after the Security Council resolution, Senator John Kerry voted no for the use of force. See, I have a different view. We'll do everything we can to solve problems before we commit our troops, and I'll continue to work with our friends and allies. But I will never allow other nations to veto America's national security decisions.

I believe in the transformational power of liberty. I like to share with people some of my talks with Prime Minister Koizumi. He's the Prime Minister of Japan. I saw him in New York. I said, "You know, I'm going around America telling people that you and I talk. Do you mind if I share some of our conversation?" He said, "No." I didn't tell him I was going to tell you that Elvis is his favorite singer—[*laughter*]—was his favorite singer—is his favorite singer on CD. [*Laughter*]

The reason I bring him up is because it wasn't all that long ago that we were fighting Japan. My dad fought there. I'm sure your dads and granddads, probably somebody here was there himself. See, they were the enemy, the sworn enemy. After we won World War II, though, Harry Truman believed in the power of liberty to transform an enemy into an ally. That's what he believed. A lot of people in this country doubted that, and you can understand why. There was a lot of bitterness toward the Japanese. A lot of people resented the fact that they were the enemy. But Harry Truman and other Americans stayed with that concept.

And today, because they believed in the power of liberty, Japan is a democracy, and I sit down at the table with Prime Minister Koizumi talking about the big issues of the day and talking about how to keep the peace we all want. Think about that. Someday, if we're resolved and steadfast and strong, Iraq will become a democracy. And someday, an American President will be sitting down with a duly elected leader of Iraq talking about the peace we all want. And our children and our grandchildren will grow up in a better world for it.

I believe millions plead in silence for liberty in the Middle East. I believe women in the Middle East want to grow up in a free society. I know they want to raise their children, their sons and daughters, so they can realize their dreams. I believe if given a chance, people in that part of the world will embrace the most honorable form of Government ever devised by man. I believe all these things because freedom is not America's gift to the world; freedom is the Almighty God's gift to each man and woman in this world.

For all Americans, these years in our history will always stand apart. There are quiet times in the life of a nation when little is expected of its leaders. This isn't one of those times. This is a time when we need firm resolve, clear vision, and a deep faith in the values that makes us a great nation.

None of us will ever forget that week when one era ended and another began. I stood in the ruins of the Twin Towers on September the 14th, 2001. It's a day I'll never forget. There were workers in hardhats yelling at me at the top of their lungs, "Whatever it takes." I remember seeing a man who had been in the rubble, looking for his buddy. He grabbed me by the arm, and he said, "Do not let me down." Ever since that day, I wake up trying to do my best to protect this country. I will never relent in defending America, whatever it takes.

Four years ago, as I traveled this great State asking for the vote, I made a pledge that if you gave me a chance to serve, I would uphold the dignity and the honor of the office to which I had been elected. With your hard work, I will do so for 4 more years.

Thanks for coming. God bless. God bless America. Thank you all.

NOTE: The President spoke at 3:10 p.m. at Center City Park. In his remarks, he referred to Prime Minister John Howard of Australia; Gov. Tim Pawlenty of Minnesota; Senator Zell Miller of Georgia, who made the keynote address at the 2004 Republican National Convention; Prime Minister Ayad Allawi of the Iraqi Interim Government; and Prime Minister Junichiro Koizumi of Japan. He also referred to the "Comprehensive Report of the Special Advisor to the DCI on Iraq's WMD," issued September 30.

Remarks in Hobbs, New Mexico
October 11, 2004

The President. Thank you all. Thanks for coming out. It's nice to be back in a part of the world that I know very well. I was raised right around the corner. It's good to be in a part of the world where the cowboy hats outnumber the ties. It's good to be in a part of the world where people believe in their family and their faith and their country.

I want to thank all the people from Lea County, New Mexico, for coming here today. I'm proud you're here. Thanks for organizing this great event. I want to thank the people from Eddy County who are here. When I was a little guy, I distinctly remember going to Carlsbad Caverns. I went with the Cub Scout troop. It just so happened the den mother was my mother. [*Laughter*] I think that's when her hair started to go white. [*Laughter*] Appreciate the people from Chaves being here as well.

I want to thank my friends who've come over from the great State of Texas. I'm proud you all are here. I really appreciate the Flying Eagles from Hobbs being here. Thank you for being here in the band. Still play pretty good basketball? [*Applause*] Yes. That's what I figured. [*Laughter*]

I'm here to ask for your vote. That's what I'm here to do. By the way, I don't know if you know this, but I'm the first sitting President to have ever visited Hobbs, New Mexico. I may just be the first sitting President to have visited, and the first person who's the President who's ever been here before he was President. [*Laughter*] All I can tell you is the other ones missed a lot by not coming to Hobbs, New Mexico.

I'm also here to ask for your help. You know, last time, in New Mexico, we lost by just a little over 600 votes. If every one of you all takes somebody to the polls come voting time, we'll win. So I'm here to thank you for what you're going to do. You're going to convince our fellow citizens to do their duty and vote. And when you're turning people out to the polls, don't overlook discerning Democrats, people like Zell Miller who understands that if you want a safer America, a stronger America, and a better America, to put me and Dick Cheney back in office.

I'm keeping really good company today. I'm proud to be traveling with one of our twin daughters, Jenna Bush. This is the camping trip I promised to take her on when she was a kid. [*Laughter*]

Jenna and I just said goodbye to a great First Lady. You know, when I asked Laura to marry me, she said, "Fine, just so long as I never have to give a political speech." I said, "You got a deal." [*Laughter*] Fortunately, she didn't hold me to that. The American people have seen not only a great speaker, when she speaks, but they've seen a graceful, compassionate, great First Lady. I like to tell people, you know, I'm going to give you some reasons to put me back in, but perhaps the most important one of all is so that Laura is the First Lady for 4 more years.

I'm real proud of George P. Bush. Now, his dad is my brother, and he's the Governor of Florida. So if he's listening, turn out that vote. [*Laughter*]

I want to thank my Vice President. I'm proud to be running with Dick Cheney. He's a good, solid, strong American.

I really am pleased to be working with a great United States Congressman from this part of the world. I'm proud of the job that Steve Pearce is doing. He brings that eastern New Mexico commonsense to Washington, DC. He's down-to-earth. He's smart. He's capable. He's doing you a great job in the House of Representatives. Laura and I are fond of Cynthia, his wife, and he kindly introduced me to his mother, Jane, today. I said to her, I said, "Is Steve still listening to you?" She said, "About half the time." [*Laughter*] I said, "Well, that sounds like me and my mother." [*Laughter*]

With us today as well is a fellow running for Congress across the State line, named Randy Neugebauer. I know Randy. I trust his judgment. He's a good, honest man. He's a man that I can work with. It is important that the people of west Texas send Randy Neugebauer back to the United States Congress.

I want to thank all the other State and local officials. I want to thank the members of my team who are here of Hispanic origin. The head of the SBA is here today, Hector Barreto; Rosario Marin, who's a former U.S. Treasurer; the White House Counsel, Alberto Gonzales, is with us today. These folks are here to help us inspire the Hispanic vote to come our way. *Con su apoyo, vamos a ganar.*

See, my message is for everybody. When I say a hopeful America, I'm just not talking about one segment of the country, I'm talking about every single person when it comes to a hopeful America.

I want to thank my friend Mark Wills. He's a good singer. Nice of him to be here today. I'm proud he's here.

I particularly want to thank all the grass-roots activists, the people involved with turning out the vote and making the phone calls. I know you've done a lot of hard work. First of all, it takes a lot of hard work to get this many people to show up. [*Laughter*] If you put the same amount of work you put into getting this rally going to getting people to the polls, there's no doubt in my mind we'll carry New Mexico and win a great victory in November.

We had a great debate on Friday night. As you can tell, I'm kind of working my way west for the final debate. Our debates have highlighted the clear differences between the Senator and me on issues ranging from jobs to taxes to health care and to the war on terror. Much as he tries to obscure it, on issue after issue he has shown why he earned the ranking as the most liberal Member of the United States Senate. Several of his statements the other night simply don't pass the credibility test.

With a straight face, he said he'd had only one position on Iraq. [*Laughter*] He must think we're on another planet. [*Laughter*] In the spring of 2003, as I ordered the invasion of Iraq, Senator Kerry said, "It was the right decision." Now he says, "It's the wrong war." In the same debate, he said Saddam was a threat. Then a few minutes later, he said there wasn't a threat in Iraq. And now he tries to tell us he's had only one position. Who's he trying to kid? [*Laughter*] He can run, but he cannot hide.

With another straight face, he tried to tell Americans that when it comes to his health care plan, and I quote, "The Government has nothing to do with it." [*Laughter*] The facts are that 8 out of 10 people who get health care under Senator Kerry's plan would be placed on a Government program. He can run, but he cannot hide.

Then he was asked to look into the camera—[*laughter*]—and promise he would not raise taxes for anyone who earns less than $200,000 a year. The problem is, to keep that promise he'd have to break almost all his other promises. [*Laughter*] His plan to raise taxes on the top two income brackets would raise about $600 billion according to our counters, about $800 billion according to his planners—counters. The problem is, is that his spending plans will cost almost four times as much, $2.2 trillion. You can't have it both ways. To pay for all the big spending programs he's outlined during his campaign, he's going to have to raise your taxes. See, he can run, but he cannot hide.

You know, listening—after listening to that litany of complaints and the dour pessimism, it took all I could do not to make a face. [*Laughter*] I have a different view, a different philosophy, and a strong record to be running on. I've worked hard to make this country a more hopeful place and a more secure place. I've led our country with principle and resolve, and that's how I'll continue to lead this Nation.

The world in which we live and work is changing. Workers switch jobs more than they used to. Women are working in the home and outside the home as well. That means they need new skills and benefits they can take with them from job to job. Yet many of the most fundamental systems of our Government, the Tax Code, the health care, pension plans, and worker training, were created for a world of yesterday, not tomorrow. I'm running for 4 more years to transform these systems to help citizens realize their dreams.

And a plan—any plan, any strategy for a hopeful America begins with a growing economy that creates good jobs. See, I believe in the energy and innovation and spirit of our workers and our small-business owners and our farmers and our ranchers. And that's why we unleashed that energy with the largest tax relief in a generation.

When you're out rounding up the vote, you might remind people of what we've been through, what this economy has been through. The stock market started to go down 6 months prior to my arrival in Washington, DC. See, and that was—that foretold the recession that came. So we had the stock market correction and a recession. We had some corporate scandals which affected our economy. By the way, we passed tough laws. We have made it abundantly clear that we will not tolerate dishonesty in the boardrooms of America. And then the enemy hit us. And that cost our economy one million jobs in the 3 months after September the 11th.

No, we've been through a lot, but we acted. Because we passed tax relief, this economy is growing. It's getting stronger, and we're not going to go back to the old days of tax and spend. The past 13 months, we've added 1.9 million new jobs. The national unemployment rate is 5.4 percent, which is lower than the average of the 1970s, the 1980s, and the 1990s. State unemployment rate in New Mexico is 5.4 percent. People are working. People are finding a way to make a living. Our farmers are doing well. Our ranchers are doing well. The homeownership rate in America is at an alltime high.

We're moving forward, and there's more to do. To make sure quality jobs are here, created here in America, America must be the best place in the world to do business. That means less regulations on the job creators. That means we got to do something about these frivolous lawsuits that are making it hard to expand the job base.

Listen, to make sure this economy continues to grow, Congress needs to pass my energy plan. I put a plan up there that encourages conservation, that understands we can use renewables like ethanol and biodiesel. It's a plan that also recognizes that we can explore for natural gas in environmentally friendly ways. It's a plan that recognizes we can use clean coal technology. At the heart of my plan is the understanding that in order to create jobs here, America must become less dependent on foreign sources of energy. And people around here know what I'm talking about.

To create jobs, we need to keep people and businesses safe from wildfires. That's why I worked with Congress to pass the Healthy Forests Restoration Act. It's an important piece of legislation for much of your State. This good law allows us to thin out the underbrush that damages our forests and serves as kindling for fires. It's a commonsense measure that's protected communities all across the West. I was proud to work on it, and I was proud to sign it into law. Both the Republican Senator from this State—and by the way, Pete Domenici is a good one. He's a fine man. Both the Republican Senator and the Democrat Senator from New Mexico supported the Healthy Forests bill. But my opponent was against it. Now he says he likes parts of the law. I guess it's not only the wildfires that shift in the wind. [*Laughter*]

To create jobs, we've got to reject economic isolationism and open up markets. Listen, we've opened up the markets for products from overseas, and it's good for you as consumers. See, here's the way the market works. If you've got more products to choose from, you're likely to get that which you want at a better price and higher quality. That's how it works. So what I'm saying to places like China, "You treat us the way we treat you. You open up your markets." And I'm saying that because I know we can compete with anybody, anytime, anywhere, so long as the rules are fair.

To create jobs here and to make sure this economy grows, we got to keep your taxes low. Taxes are an issue in this campaign. We talked about them in the last debate, and I hope we talk about them in the next debate. See, he's saying, "Oh, don't worry, I can pay for all my programs by taxing the rich." We've heard that before, haven't we?

Audience members. [Inaudible]

The President. Yes, you know how it works. First of all, as I told you, he doesn't have enough money to pay for all his programs. There's a tax gap, and guess who usually gets stuck filling the hole? Yes, you do. Something else about taxing the rich, the rich hire lawyers and accountants for a reason: to dodge the tax bill and stick you with it. We're not going to let him do it to you; we're going to win in November.

To build a more hopeful America, we've got to have the best prepared and most highly skilled workforce in the world. It all starts with education. I believe every child can learn and every school must teach. I went to Washington, DC, to challenge the soft bigotry of low expectations, to challenge those systems that would just shuffle the kids through, year after year, grade after grade, without teaching them the basics. See, we have a optimistic outlook. I learned it being out here where the sky is big. I believe every child can learn. I believe that. That's why we've raised the standards. That's why we believe in local control of schools. And that's why we measure, so we can solve problems early, before it is too late.

The achievement gap in America is closing. We're not going back to those old days of mediocrity in our schools. *No dejaremos a ningun nino atras*—we will leave no child behind.

Listen, most new jobs are filled by people with at least 2 years of college education, yet only one in four of our students gets there. That's why we've got to fund early intervention programs for at-risk students in high schools. That's why we've got to emphasize math and science. That's why, over time, we'll require a rigorous exam before graduation. By raising performance in our high schools and by expanding Pell grants for low- and middle-income families, we will help more Americans start their career with a college degree.

I'm a big supporter of the community college system here in America. See, I believe that community colleges can be used wisely to make sure our workers gain the skills necessary to fill the jobs of the 21st century.

And to make sure our country is more hopeful, we need to make health care more affordable and more available. We need a safety net for those with the greatest needs. I believe every poor county in America ought to have a community health center, places where the poor and the indigent can get the health care they need. I believe we've got to expand those community health centers. Since I've been President, we've opened more than 600—expanded or opened more than 600. There's more to do. We got more to do to make sure our poor children are fully subscribed in programs for low-income families so they get the health care they need.

There's more we can do to make sure health care is affordable. Most of the uninsured are employees of small businesses. In order to make sure families can get the insurance they need, we ought to allow small businesses to pool together, to pool risk across jurisdictional boundaries so they can buy insurance at the same discount that big companies can buy insurance. We'll make sure health savings accounts are available to all, so workers in small businesses are able to pay lower premiums and people can save tax-free in a health care account they call their own.

To make sure health care is available and affordable, we've got to do something about the junk lawsuits that are running good doctors out of practice and running up the costs of your health care. You can't be pro-doctor, pro-patient, pro-hospital, and pro-trial-lawyer at the same time. [*Laughter*] I think you have to choose. And my opponent made his choice, and he put a trial lawyer on the ticket.

Audience members. Boo-o-o!

The President. I made my choice. I am for medical liability reform—now. No, there's a big difference in health care. We'll talk about it Wednesday night. But in all we do to improve health care, we will make sure that the decisions are made by doctors and patients, not by officials in Washington, DC.

I went to Washington to solve problems, not to pass them on. And I felt we had a problem when it came to making sure our seniors got good, modern medicine. Medicare is a vital program, yet it wasn't keeping pace with the changes in medicine. Let me give you an example. We'd pay thousands of dollars for heart surgery but not one dime for the prescription drugs that could prevent the heart surgery from being needed in the first place. That didn't make any sense. It didn't make any sense for our seniors, and it didn't make any sense for the taxpayers. So I worked with Republicans and Democrats to strengthen Medicare. In 2006, our seniors will be able to get prescription drugs in the Medicare program. Medicare is changing for the better. Our seniors will get a modern health care program, and we're not going to go back to the old days.

Let me talk about the retirement systems for a second. In the 2000 campaign, I remember distinctly our seniors being told on television ads that, "If George W. gets elected, you won't get your check." I don't know if they ran those kinds of ads here in New Mexico or not. I bet they did—yes. Well, the seniors got their checks. See, and that's the same kind of rhetoric you're going to hear again, because I'm going to talk about strengthening Social Security. But when I do so, I want you to remember that if you're getting your Social Security check, nothing is going to change. No matter what the political rhetoric is, you're going to continue to get your check, just like we said you would. If you're a baby boomer, we're in pretty good shape when it comes to Social Security.

But when it—but for our younger folks here in America, for our children and grandchildren, we need to think differently about whether or not the Social Security system is going to be viable for them. I believe younger workers ought to be able to take some of their own tax money and set up a personal savings account so they can get a better rate of interest on the money being accumulated for their retirement.

In times of change, there are some things that don't change, the values we try to live by, courage and compassion, reverence and integrity. In changing times, we will support the institutions that give our lives direction and purpose, our families, our schools, our religious congregations. We stand for a culture of life in which every person matters and every being counts. We stand for marriage and family, which are the foundations of our society. And we stand for the appointment of Federal judges who know the difference between personal opinion and the strict interpretation of the law.

This election will also determine how America responds to the continuing danger of terrorism. I believe the most solemn duty of the American President is to protect the American people. If America shows uncertainty and weakness in this decade, the world will drift toward tragedy. This will not happen on my watch.

Since that terrible morning of September the 11th, 2001, we have fought the terrorists across the Earth, not for pride, not for power, but because the lives of our citizens are at stake. We've got a strategy that's clear. We're defending the homeland. We're transforming our military. I will make sure the All-Volunteer Army remains the All-Volunteer Army. We're reforming and strengthening our intelligence services. We're staying on the offensive. We are striking the terrorists abroad so we do not have to face them here at home.

Our strategy is succeeding. Four years ago, Afghanistan was the home base of Al Qaida; Pakistan was a transit point for terrorists; Saudi Arabia was fertile ground for terrorists' fundraising; Libya was secretly pursuing nuclear weapons; Iraq was a gathering threat; and Al Qaida was largely unchallenged as it planned attacks. That's the way the world was.

Because we acted, the Government of a free Afghanistan held Presidential elections last weekend and is an ally in the war on terror; Pakistan is capturing terrorist leaders; Saudi Arabia is making raids and arrests; Libya is dismantling its weapons programs; the army of a free Iraq is fighting for freedom; and more than three-quarters of Al Qaida's key members and associates have been detained or killed. We have led. Many have joined. And America and the world are safer.

After September the 11th, America had to assess every potential threat in a new light. It's one of the lessons of that fateful day. We confront an even greater danger, that the prospect of terrorists getting weapons of mass destruction would inflict great harm on America. We had to take a hard look at every place where terrorists might get those weapons.

And one regime stood out, the dictatorship of Saddam Hussein. We knew his record of aggression and support for terror. We knew he hated America. We knew he had used weapons of mass destruction. We know that after September the 11th, we must take threats seriously before they fully materialize. In Saddam, we saw a threat.

And I went to the United States Congress. They looked at the same intelligence I looked at. They remembered the same history I remembered. And they came to the same conclusion I came to, that Saddam Hussein was a threat. And they voted to authorize the use of force. My opponent looked at the same intelligence, and he voted to authorize the use of force.

Before the United States ever commits troops into harm's way, we must try all means to deal with the threat. No President ever wants to send America's sons and daughters to war. So I worked to avoid that. And I went to the United Nations in the hopes that diplomacy would work. The United Nations had a debate. They looked at the same intelligence we were looking at. They passed another resolution telling Saddam Hussein to "Disclose, disarm, or face serious consequences." I believe that when an international body speaks, it must mean what it says.

So we gave Saddam Hussein a final chance, and he continued to deceive the world. He was deceiving the weapons inspectors. And so I have a choice to make at this time in our history: Do I forget the lessons of September the 11th and take the word of a madman, or do I take action to defend our country? Given that choice, I will defend America every time.

Now, we didn't find the stockpiles that we all thought were there. But as the Duelfer report said, Saddam Hussein retained the intent and the capability to rebuild his weapons programs. He was gaming the Oil for Food Programme, using it to influence officials in other countries. Why? Because he wanted the world to look the other way, so he could restart his programs. The world is safer with Saddam Hussein sitting in a prison cell. Knowing what I know today, I would have made the same decision.

Because we acted in Afghanistan and Iraq, America is safer and 50 million people now live in freedom. Think about what took place in Afghanistan this past weekend. It's an unbelievable story. Just 3½ years ago, people lived under the brutal dictatorship of the Taliban. These were people that wouldn't let many young girls go to school, and when women didn't agree with them, they took them in the public square and whipped them and sometimes killed them in the sports stadium. These were brutal people. And because they're gone, Afghanistan held Presidential elections. The first voter was a 19-year-old woman who was able to express her opinion in the polls.

And Iraq has got a strong Prime Minister and a National Council, and national elections are scheduled for January. Think about how far that country has come from the days of torture chambers and mass graves. No, we're standing with the people of Afghanistan and Iraq, because when America gives its word, America must keep its word.

We're also standing with them because a free Afghanistan and Iraq will make our country safer. See, free societies in the Middle East will be hopeful societies which no longer feed resentments and breed violence for export. Free governments in the Middle East will fight the terrorists instead of harboring them, and that helps us keep the peace.

Our mission is clear. We will help those countries train armies so that the people of Afghanistan and Iraq can do the hard work of defending democracy. We'll help them get on the path to stability and self-govern as soon as possible, and then our troops will come home with the honor they have earned.

We've got a great United States military. And I want to thank the veterans who are here today for having set such a great example to those who wear the uniform. And I want to thank the military families who are here today. I've made a commitment to those who wear the uniform and to their families: They'll have all the resources they need to do their job.

That's why I went to the United States Congress in September of 2003 and asked for $87 billion in supplemental funding to support our troops in harm's way in Afghanistan and Iraq. And this was essential funding. This was really important funding. We received great bipartisan support for that funding. As a matter of fact, the support was so strong that only 12 United States Senators voted against it. Now, when you're out there rounding up the vote, remind people there were only four United States Senators who voted to authorize the use of force and then voted against money necessary to support our troops in harm's way, and two of those are my opponent and his runningmate.

Audience members. Boo-o-o!

The President. You might remember my opponent's famous quote, "I actually did vote for the $87 billion, before I voted against it." [*Laughter*] Now, I know something about eastern New Mexico and west Texas, and there are not many folks who talk like that in this part of the world. [*Laughter*] They kept pressing him, you know. He's given a lot of explanations for that vote. There are just too many to enumerate. [*Laughter*] One of my favorites is when he said, "Well, it's just a complicated matter." [*Laughter*] There's nothing complicated about supporting our troops in combat.

Now, on national security, my opponent has a record. He can run, but he can't hide from it. [*Laughter*] He voted against the weapons systems that helped our country win the cold war. He voted to cut America's intelligence budget by $7.5 billion after 1993. That's after the World Trade Center got bombed for the first time. He now says he wants a "global test" before taking action to defend America's security.

Audience members. Boo-o-o!

The President. That's what he said. I'm not putting words in his mouth, either. [*Laughter*] The problem is the Senator can never pass his own test. [*Laughter*] Think about that. In 1990, the United Nations Security Council passed a resolution supporting action to remove Saddam Hussein from Kuwait. The international community was united. Countries throughout the world joined our coalition. Yet in the United States Senate after the Security Council

resolution, Senator Kerry voted no on the authorization of force.

Audience members. Boo-o-o!

The President. See, if driving Saddam Hussein out of Kuwait with the support of the international community does not meet this test, then nothing will meet his test, and that's dangerous in the kind of world we live in. See, we have a different view of the world, a different view of America's role in confronting threats. Just this weekend, we saw new evidence that Senator Kerry fundamentally misunderstands the war on terror. Earlier he questioned whether it was really a war at all, describing it as primarily a law enforcement and intelligence gathering operation instead of a threat that demands the full use of American power.

Now, just this weekend, Senator Kerry talked of reducing terrorism to, quote, "nuisance," end quote, and compared it to prostitution and illegal gambling. See, I couldn't disagree more. Our goal is not to reduce terror to some acceptable level of nuisance. Our goal is to defeat terror by staying on the offensive, destroying terrorists, and spreading freedom and liberty around the world.

I'll always work with our friends and allies. Alliances are important, and over the next 4 years, we'll continue to build strong coalitions. But I will never turn over America's national security decisions to leaders of other countries.

I believe in the transformational power of liberty. I tell people about my relationship with Prime Minister Koizumi of Japan. I tell them that because it's an interesting lesson. You see, it wasn't all that long ago that we were fighting the Japanese. If you're 58 years old, it seems like an eternity, since it was 60 years ago. [*Laughter*] But my dad was in the war. I guarantee you there are people here in the audience who were touched by that war and had a granddad or a dad fight in that war.

And after we won, Harry S. Truman, President of the United States, believed in the power of liberty to transform societies, and he worked with the Japanese to help them develop a democracy. A lot of people questioned that. You know, there was a lot of pessimism after World War II. You can understand why. The Japanese were the enemy. Why do we care after we won? We had defeated them. A lot of people here's lives had been turned upside-down because a loved-one's life had been lost, and they didn't have—want to have anything to do with the enemy. But fortunately, there were people in this country who had the faith in the ability of liberty to transform societies. And so now I sit down at the table with Prime Minister Koizumi talking about the peace, talking about how to achieve the peace we want for our children and grandchildren.

I believe the same lessons apply for today. We will achieve a free Iraq. Iraq will be a democracy. And when we do so, at some point in time, an American President and a duly elected leader of Iraq will be sitting down talking about how to keep the peace. And our children and grandchildren will be able to live in a better world.

I believe that millions in the Middle East plead in silence for their freedom. I believe women want there to be a free society in the Middle East. I know they want their children to be able to grow up in a world in which they can realize their dreams. I believe that if given a chance, the people of the Middle East will embrace the most honorable form of government ever devised by man. I believe all these things because freedom is not America's gift to the world; freedom is the Almighty God's gift to each man and woman in this world.

For all Americans, these years in our history will always stand apart. There are quiet times in the life of a nation when little is expected of its leaders. This isn't one of those times. This is a time that requires firm resolve, clear vision, and a deep faith in the values that makes us a great nation.

None of us will ever forget that week when one era ended and another began. On September the 14th, 2001, I stood in the ruins of the Twin Towers. It's a day that is indelibly etched in my memory. I will never forget it. There were workers in hardhats yelling at me at the top of their lungs, "Whatever it takes." I remember a man grabbing me by the arm, and looked me in the eyes, and he said, "Do not let me down." Ever since that day, I have awakened, working as hard as I possibly can to protect this country. I will never relent in defending America, whatever it takes.

Four years ago, when I traveled your great State, I said if you gave me a chance to serve, I would uphold the honor and the dignity of the office to which I had been elected. With your help, with your hard work, I will do so for 4 more years.

Thanks for coming. God bless. God bless you all.

NOTE: The President spoke at 9:13 a.m. at the Lea County Event Center. In his remarks, he referred to Senator Zell Miller of Georgia, who made the keynote address at the 2004 Republican National Convention; Gov. Jeb Bush of Florida; Cynthia Pearce, wife of Representative Stevan Pearce; Randy Neugebauer, candidate for Texas's 19th Congressional District; entertainer Mark Wills; Senator Jeff Bingaman of New Mexico; Charles Duelfer, Special Advisor to the Director of Intelligence; Prime Minister Ayad Allawi of the Iraqi Interim Government; and Prime Minister Junichiro Koizumi of Japan. He also referred to the "Comprehensive Report of the Special Advisor to the DCI on Iraq's WMD," issued September 30.

Remarks at a Luncheon for Senatorial Candidate Pete Coors in Denver, Colorado
October 11, 2004

The President. Thank you all for coming. Thank you all for being here. I appreciate you coming. Nice to be back in Colorado. I've spent some quality time here in the past. I'm here asking for the vote. I'm here also asking—I'm here to say as clearly as I can say it, the right man for the United States Senate from the State of Colorado is Pete Coors.

And I want to thank you all for being here to help him. I like his judgment. I like his experience. I like his values. I like the fact that he is—will bring some commonsense to the Halls of the United States Senate. Oh, I might not get him to vote every way—every time the way I want him to—[laughter]—he's kind of an independent fellow. [Laughter] But I know I'll be able to count on him on the big issues.

Laura sends her best. We spent the evening in Crawford, which is a long way away from Washington, DC. [Laughter] And she is—she's resting up today, and she's going to take to the road tomorrow. She is a fabulous First Lady. I love her dearly. You know, when I met her she was a public school librarian. And she said, "Fine, I'll marry you"—after I asked her, of course—and she said, "just so long as I never have to give any speeches." [Laughter] I said, "You got a deal." [Laughter] Fortunately, she didn't hold me to that deal. She's speaking a lot, and the American people know her as a compassionate, warm, great First Lady.

And I'm proud of my runningmate, proud of Dick Cheney. I like to tell people, when he was debating John Edwards it was clear he didn't have the waviest hair on the platform. [Laughter] But I didn't pick him for his hair. [Laughter] I picked him because he's a man of great judgment, excellent experience, and he's doing a really good job as our Vice President.

And I appreciate Marilyn Coors for putting up with the race for the Senate. It's not easy when you're out there campaigning every day, but it's worthwhile, believe me. Public service, done the right way, is necessary for a good country. So thanks for doing what you're doing. It's good to see your mom, Pete. You and I share a strong-willed mother. [Laughter]

Pete's going to take the place of a good man in Ben Nighthorse Campbell. I like him. He's a good fellow, a good, solid citizen. And he'll serve side by side with another good man in Wayne Allard.

I appreciate your Governor. Bill Owens is doing a fine job. And Frances is one of our alltime favorites. Great to see you, Frances. Thank you for being here. I appreciate the fact that Congressman Joel Hefley is here, along with his wife, Lynn. Thanks for coming. That would be State Representative Lynn Hefley. Just don't challenge him in the primary sometime. [Laughter]

Audience member. [Inaudible]

The President. Yes, that's right.

Tom Tancredo and Jackie are with us. Thanks, Tom and Jackie. Thanks for coming. Beauprez is here somewhere. Oh, there he is, yes—and Claudia. Thank you all for coming. It's good to see you all. I appreciate you're here. Finally got out of town, didn't you? [Laughter]

I want to thank all the State leaders who are here. I want to thank Bruce Benson, the campaign chairman for Pete. I wish Greg Walcher all the best in his race for the Third District of Colorado. Where is he? There he is, good.

Listen, thank you all for coming. I'm going to give a speech a little later on this evening, so I don't want to get too repetitive. But it's really time to start ginning up these voter turnout organizations. It's time to make sure that people understand we have an obligation in our society to vote. And I want to thank you all for helping to turn out that vote. It matters whether or not people show up to the polls. I mean, it—and I'm confident in this State. We'll carry Colorado again.

I'm heading toward our final debate. I enjoy the debates. It's an interesting experience. [*Laughter*] It gives a chance to share ideas and talk about the big differences. And there are big differences. He's a fellow that I think had some credibility problems in the debates. He said with a straight face that he'd only had one position on Iraq. [*Laughter*] I could barely contain myself. [*Laughter*]

Audience member. We noticed. [*Laughter*]

The President. You might remember, in the spring of 2003 as I ordered troops into harm's way, he said, "It was the right decision." Then when the political heat gets on, he says, "It was the wrong war." He can run from his positions, but he cannot hide.

He said with another straight face that when it comes to health care plan, and I quote, "The Government has nothing to do with it." Unbelievable statement. The facts are that 8 out of 10 people who get health care under Senator Kerry's plan would be placed on a Government program. He can run from his position, but he cannot hide.

And then he said—and then they asked him to look in the camera, and he promised not to raise taxes for anyone who earns less than $200,000. The problem is, to keep that promise he'd have to break almost all his other ones. [*Laughter*] I'm looking forward to talking about taxes in this campaign. He's going to raise your taxes, pure and simple. Raising your taxes would be bad policy for our economy, bad policy as this economy is beginning to grow. He can run, but he cannot hide.

That's why these debates are important. You know, after listening to all his complaints and his dour pessimism, it took all I could do not to make a face. [*Laughter*] Yes. No, I'm looking forward to it. We have a different philosophy, different way of looking at things. And one reason I'm hopeful that Pete wins—and I believe he will—is that we've got to put policies in place that keep the economy growing.

You know, when you're out there gathering up the vote, remind people of what we've been through. This economy has been through a lot. Six months prior to our arrival, the stock market was in serious decline. And then we had a recession, and then we had corporate scandals, and then we got attacked. And that attack on America cost us one million jobs in the 3 months after September the 11th.

We faced some serious obstacles, but because we acted, because we cut the taxes on the people, the recession was one of the shortest in American history. And our economy is growing, and it's getting stronger. And the fundamental question is, how do we keep it growing. It really is the issue, isn't it?

I think the best way to keep the economy growing is to make sure America is the best place in the world to do business. That means less regulations. That means less lawsuits. That means an energy plan that encourages conservation, spends money on renewables, and uses technology, but it's an energy plan as well that recognizes we can explore for natural gas in environmentally friendly ways. It's a plan that says in order to keep jobs here, we've got to be less dependent on foreign sources of energy.

I think trade is an issue in this campaign. I tell the American people we've opened up our markets to foreign products, which is good for the consumers. If you've got more products to choose from, you're likely to get that which you want at a better price and higher quality. That's how the marketplace works. So rather than shutting down our market and falling prey to economic isolationism, which I believe will hurt jobs, I've got a different strategy, which is to go to places like China and say, "You treat us the way we treat you. You open up your markets." And we're doing that all around the world.

I believe Pete understands all this. I know he knows how to—that the role of Government is not to create wealth but an environment in which the entrepreneurial spirit flourishes. And the best way to do that is keep taxes low, regulations down, and do something about these trial lawyers that are running all over the business—[applause]. I don't think you can be pro-entrepreneur, pro-doctor, and pro-trial-lawyer at the same time. [Laughter] I think you have to choose. My opponent made his choice, and he put a trial lawyer on the ticket. I made my choice. I'm for legal reforms.

A more hopeful society is one in which we educate our people. It starts with making sure the youngsters can read, write, and add and subtract. I look forward to defending the No Child Left Behind Act. At the heart of the No Child Left Behind Act is my fervent belief that every child can learn in America. Think about a system where the expectations are so low that all they do is shuffle kids through, grade after grade, year after year, without teaching the basics. That's not good enough for this country.

See, when you hear me say we're going to challenge the soft bigotry of low expectations, what I'm saying is, is that the heart of my education reforms is the belief that everybody can learn, and we should expect everybody to learn. It's easy to quit on certain kids in American schools. You go into inner-city America, and it's easy to take a classroom full of the hard-to-educate and just move them through, or somebody's parent doesn't speak English as a first language. That's not the America I know. The America I know believes every child can learn.

And that's why we now have got, in return for increased Federal spending, a sys-tem that says, "Why don't you measure early to determine whether or not a child can read, and if not, we'll correct the problems before it's too late." And we're closing an achievement gap in America, and I need Pete Coors up there to make sure we don't go back to the old days of mediocrity.

No, there's a lot more we can do. On health care—we'll have intermediate programs for at-risk kids in high schools and emphasize math and science, keep raising the bar, expand Pell grants for low- and middle-income families, to make sure more of our kids are able to start their careers with a college diploma. I'm a big believer in community colleges, to be able to use the community college system to be able to train workers for the jobs which actually exist. I mean, if we want to be competitive in the 21st century, we've got to be right about education. And this administration has got us headed in the right direction, and we're not going to go backwards.

Health care is an issue. Health care is a big issue in the country. I like to tell people I went up there to solve problems and not just shuffle them on to other Presidents. And so I took on the Medicare issue. It was called "Medi-scare" for a long period of time. You talked about it, and you got whipped at the polls. But that's not my style. My style is to take on issues head on. And Medicare wasn't meeting the obligations to our seniors. It just wasn't. Medicine was being modernized, and Medicare was stuck.

Let me give you an example—and I'll continue to cite these kind of examples in our forums. We would pay thousands of dollars for a heart surgery in Medicare but not a single dime for the prescription drugs that could prevent the heart surgery from being needed in the first place. That did not make any sense for our seniors. It certainly didn't make any sense for our taxpayers. So we worked with Congress, and we've now strengthened and modernized Medicare. Seniors will get prescription drug coverage in the year 2006, and the health care for our seniors will vastly improve.

But inherent in the new Medicare reform is my basic belief that our seniors as well as all people in America ought to have more choices when it comes to health care. One of the key reforms was to make sure that seniors were able to choose different plans to be able to meet their needs. And that's the fundamental difference between me and my opponent. I told you, he said the other day with a straight face the Government doesn't have anything to do with his health care. That's wrong. He's going to expand Medicaid. That's a Government program. My fundamental—my health care plan addresses the fundamentals, which is availability and affordability.

Now, look, we need to take care of the poor in America, and that's why I'm for expansion of community health centers so the poor and the indigent can get good preventative care, good primary care in places other than emergency rooms in the hospitals. And I believe we ought to make sure our children—low-income children's health care programs are fully subscribed to. These are commonsense ways to take care of people who cannot help themselves.

But when it comes to overall health care, it's a vital mistake to increase the role of the Federal Government. That's why I'm for association health plans, to allow small businesses to pool together so they can buy insurance at the same discounts big businesses can. I'm for expanding health savings accounts, which enable workers and small businesses to pay low premium—buy low-premium catastrophic plans and, at the same time, set aside money on a tax-free basis. Many of the young in America are uninsured because they can't find insurance that fits their needs. A health savings account will allow a young worker to be able to design his or her own health care program that he or she can save money tax-free and take from job to job.

And finally, in order to make sure that health care works, we've got to do some-thing about the lawsuits. I'm telling you, these lawsuits are driving good docs out of business and driving up the cost of health care. It's a big issue. It is a big issue, and it's one that resonates. And my opponent got up there and said he's for it. My only question is, why didn't you vote for it when it was on the floor of the United States Senate? He's trying to run, but we're not going to let him hide. [*Laughter*]

I think values are an important part of this campaign—values for the Presidency as well as values for the Senate race. You know, in changing times—and they do change—it's important to have people understand certain things don't change, like the values we try to live by, courage and compassion, reverence and integrity. I believe we ought to stand for a culture of life in which every person matters and every being counts. We need to stand up for institutions like marriage and family, which are the foundations of our society. And I need Pete in the United States Senate to make sure that my judges are confirmed, judges who will make decisions not based upon personal opinion but the strict interpretation of the law.

And the other issue, of course, is how to make the world a safer place, what to do to protect this country. Our most solemn duty is to protect the American people. I'll tell people tonight like I've been telling them all over the country, if we show uncertainty or weakness in this decade, this world will drift toward tragedy. This isn't going to happen on my watch. We will——

Audience member. We're with you, Mr. President!

The President. Thank you. We will continue to work to protect this homeland. You know, we've got to be right 100 percent of the time. The enemy has got to be right once, and that's a challenge we face. So Pete will be working on smart ways to make sure the intelligence system works better and make sure the information flows between our different law enforcement agencies is not disrupted. That's why I believe we need to renew the PATRIOT Act. We'll make sure the ports and borders are protected as well as they can be. But the best way to defeat the terrorists is to stay on the offense. We got to beat them overseas so we don't have to face them here at home.

We have a fundamental difference in this campaign. My opponent says it's all about law enforcement and intelligence. This war on terror requires all of the might of the United States of America in order to protect the American people. Let me tell you some of the things I've learned since I've been your President. One, you cannot negotiate with these people, these ideologues of hate. You cannot hope for the best, you know, "Well, maybe if we only say some nice things, they'll change their mind." That's not how they think. The only way to deal with them is to find them and bring them to justice before they hurt us again.

And we're making progress. We're making progress because three-quarters of Al Qaida's—and their associates have been brought to justice. And as we speak, we're on the hunt, and we'll keep the pressure on them, unrelenting pressure to protect you.

Secondly, this is a new kind of war. It's different from what we're used to. And when we find somebody who harbors these people, they must be held to account as well. Now, let me tell you something about the Presidency. When you say something, you better mean what you say. And when I told the Taliban that they need to get rid of Al Qaida, I meant what I said. And when they didn't, we sent troops in and liberated the people of Afghanistan. In liberating the people of Afghanistan, we made ourselves safer. Remember, Al Qaida was training in Afghanistan. It was like they were the parasite, and the Taliban was a weak host. And the strategy of these ideologues of hate is to eventually take over

the host. They had just about done it. And so we're safer.

We've also done something different as well—we've accomplished something else as well, and that is, in protecting our own security, we've helped establish a democracy. One of the most remarkable things happened this past weekend. Think about what life was like for people under the Taliban. Young girls couldn't go to school. Their mothers were whipped in the public square if they didn't toe the line on this barbaric vision of mankind. Some were executed in sports stadiums. And yesterday— or 2 days ago, people showed up to vote for the President of that country. And the first voter—the first voter was a 19-year-old girl. Isn't that fantastic?

It's in our interests that freedom spread. Freedom is powerful. If just given a chance, freedom is a powerful notion. Everybody wants to be free, I think. I believe freedom is God's gift to every man and woman in this world. At the heart of much of what I say to the American people is that belief.

And then we went into Iraq. The biggest threat facing America is that a terrorist network like Al Qaida could end up with weapons of mass destruction. If you think the carnage was bad with airplanes, imagine what it would be with a weapon of mass destruction. And I saw a threat. Well, the second lesson of September the 11th is that when we see a threat, we must deal with it before it comes to hurt us. Remember the old days of prior to September the 11th. If we saw a threat, we felt safe, because oceans seemed to protect us. That's all changed. It's essential your President understand that, and we just can't hope threats go away. We must deal with them.

And so I saw a threat in Saddam. Remember, I went to the Congress, and the Congress saw the same threat. My opponent saw the same intelligence I saw and voted to authorize the use of force, something he's not too clear about these days. [*Laughter*]

And I went to the United Nations because committing our troops into harm's way is the last option for the President. I fully understand the consequences of war. You know, I wish I never had to commit troops. I was hoping diplomacy would work. But as it had for over a decade, diplomacy failed. The United Nations passed resolution after resolution after resolution, and Saddam just ignored them. I think it is reflective of my opponent's point of view when he says, "Well, what we should have done was passed another resolution"— [*laughter*]—precisely what Saddam was hoping would happen. He was hoping the world would turn away.

Listen, we didn't find any weapons when we got in there. We all thought there would be weapons. But let me tell you what we did find. We found that he had the capability and the intent and the expertise to reconstitute his weapons programs and, as the Duelfer report pointed out, that he was gaming the Oil for Food Programme, trying to influence governments to get rid of the sanctions which were already weakening, for one reason: to reconstitute his weapons. Knowing what I know today, I would have made the same decision, and the world is better off without Saddam.

And we're making progress. We're headed toward elections in January. Think about how far that society has come from the days of a brutal tyrant. I told the story about the seven men that came to see me in the Oval Office. I think I said it at the convention. These guys walk in, and they've all had their right hands cut off by Saddam Hussein and an X carved in their forehead. I'll tell you why. The currency had gone down. The Iraqi dinar had gone down, and he needed a scapegoat in order to, I guess, justify to other people who were watching that he wasn't at fault. So he plucked these small-business merchants out of society.

I asked one of them, I said, "Why you?" He said, well, he was a jeweler, and he happened to sell gold—or sell dinars to buy euros to buy gold in order to use to make jewelry. It was just a bad day for him to have made that transition—transaction. So Saddam pulls him out, cuts off his hand, carves an X into his forehead, and charges him for the operation. This is Saddam Hussein. This is the kind of person that used to run that country.

Fortunately for them, citizens from around the world, including people in Houston, Texas, saw their plight, flew them to Houston, and they have a new hand put on, free. What a contrast between a society as brutal as that run by Saddam and a compassionate society like the United States of America.

The terrorists are fighting us in Iraq because they cannot stand the thought of a free society in their midst. The fight in Iraq is integral to the war on terror. It's an essential battle. And by being resolved and firm, we will succeed in Iraq. And when we do, the world will be better off.

A couple other points I want to make, and then we'll liberate you. [*Laughter*] First, anytime we put our troops into harm's way, they need to have the full support of the Government. And we got good support in September of 2003 for the $87 billion supplemental request. And I'm telling you, this money was vital. It provided important resources for troops in harm's way, not only in Iraq, in Afghanistan. Twelve Members of the Senate voted against it. Four Members of the Senate voted to authorize the use of force and not to fund the troops, two of whom were my opponent and his runningmate. I think that is illustrative. I think it's a statement about this race for the Presidency.

And so was his answer to the first time he got asked the question, "I actually did vote for the $87 billion, before I voted against it." It's an astounding answer. [*Laughter*] But it's been one of seven explanations—[*laughter*]—as to why. One of them was, "The whole thing is a complicated matter." There's nothing complicated about supporting our troops in harm's way. I will continue, as your Commander in Chief, to make sure our troops have the best.

I tell people about my relationship with Prime Minister Koizumi. I just did so in Hobbs, New Mexico, and I'm going to do so tonight here in Denver. I'm going to do so tomorrow in Colorado Springs, for a reason—because I want people to understand what liberty can do to societies. I tell people I believe in the transformational power of liberty. The best way to make the case is to explain that one of my friends, with whom I deal, is the Prime Minister of Japan, Koizumi. I saw him in New York, and I said, "Listen, I'm telling everybody in the country about you. Do you mind if I continue doing it?" He said, "Fine." Of course, what I didn't ask him, if I could tell you that his favorite singer was Elvis. [*Laughter*] The guy's a good guy. I like him a lot.

But it wasn't all that long ago that we were fighting the Japanese. We were at war. They were the sworn enemy of America. My dad fought them. I'm sure your dads and granddads did as well. After we won, Harry S. Truman believed in the transformational power of liberty, that liberty can convert an enemy into an ally. He believed that. There was a lot of skeptics who said that couldn't happen. You can understand why. We had just fought them. Many lives had been changed as a result of the carnage of World War II. I'm sure a lot of moms and dads say, "Why even think about it. Why worry about it?"

But Harry Truman had that belief, as did a lot of other Americans. And so after the war was over, we worked with Japan to help them build a democracy. And today, I sit down at the table with Prime Minister

Koizumi, talking about the big issues confronting the world, talking about how to keep the peace we all want. Think about that. Sixty years or so after we had fought these people, I now sit down with the leader of their country talking about peace, talking about North Korea, talking about helping Iraq, talking about fighting terror, all aimed at keeping the peace.

Someday, an American President and a duly elected leader of Iraq will be sitting down at the table talking about the peace in the greater Middle East, talking about how to help women in the greater Middle East realize a free society, talking about how others have a chance to realize the great benefits of democracy.

That's what's happened. These are historic times. The world is changing for the better. I told the people in my convention speech, we've done the hard work and climbed the mountain; we see the valley below. It's a valley of peace, based upon freedom and liberty. And make no mistake about it—make no mistake about it—if this country has the right leadership and the right determination and the will to succeed, we will. And future generations of Americans will be better off for it.

Thanks for coming. God bless you all.

NOTE: The President spoke at 12:24 p.m. at the Wings Over the Rockies Air and Space Museum. In his remarks, he referred to Marilyn Coors, wife of senatorial candidate Pete Coors; Gov. Bill Owens of Colorado and his wife, Frances; Jackie Tancredo, wife of Representative Tom Tancredo; Claudia Beauprez, wife of Representative Bob Beauprez; Charles Duelfer, Special Advisor to the Director of Central Intelligence; and Prime Minister Junichiro Koizumi of Japan. He also referred to the "Comprehensive Report of the Special Advisor to the DCI on Iraq's WMD," issued September 30.

Remarks in Morrison, Colorado
October 11, 2004

The President. Thank you all for coming. Thank you all for being here. Go ahead and be seated. Thanks for coming. It's nice to be in a part of the world where the cowboy hats outnumber the ties.

Tommy and I were both raised in Midland, Texas. He went to Alamo Junior High, and I went to San Jacinto Junior High. So we're standing here, and he says to me, "This doesn't look like where we were raised." [*Laughter*] What a beautiful part of the world. Thanks for coming out to say hello.

I've come back to this beautiful part of our country to ask for the vote, and I'm here to ask for your help as well. We're getting close to voting time here in America. And I'm asking you to get your friends and neighbors to go to the polls. I'm asking you to find people from all walks of life to vote. As you get people to go to the polls, don't overlook discerning Democrats. Like you, they want a safer America, a stronger America, and a better America. There is no doubt with your help, we'll carry Colorado again and win a great victory in November.

I wish Laura was here. When I asked her to marry me, she said, "Fine, just as long as I never have to give a speech." [*Laughter*] I said, "Okay, you got a deal." Fortunately, she didn't hold me to the promise. She's given a lot of speeches. The American people see a compassionate, warm, great First Lady in Laura Bush. She didn't make it, but Jenna did. I'm proud of our daughters, Barbara and Jenna.

I'm also proud of my runningmate, Dick Cheney. He did a great job at his debate. You know, he didn't have the prettiest hair there at the debate. [*Laughter*] I didn't pick him for his hairdo. I picked him because of his judgment and his experience and his ability to get the job done for the American people.

I'm proud to be introduced by a great American, Tommy Franks. He'll go down in history as one of America's great generals. America is more secure and the world is better off because of the generalship of General Tommy Franks. And I'm proud his wife, Cathy, is with him too.

I want to thank my friend Mike Shanahan for being up on stage with me. I appreciate him taking the time. I said, "You got any suggestions?" He said, "Yes, stay on the offense." I appreciate Peggy coming. I want to thank all the Bronco players who are here today. Congratulations on a great victory this weekend.

I'm proud to call your Governor my friend, Bill Owens. He's doing a great job for Colorado. And I want to thank the fine first lady of Colorado, Frances, for being here as well.

Two Members of the United States Congress with us today, Bob Beauprez and Tom Tancredo. I appreciate their service. Thank you all for coming.

I'm proud to be with the next United States Senator from Colorado, Pete Coors.

Audience members. Pete! Pete! Pete!

The President. I want to thank my friend Gwyn Dieter. She's the Bush-Cheney W Stands for Women chairman.

Appreciate Collin Raye being here. I want to thank all the grassroots activists. Thank you for what you have done, and thank you for what you're going to do to turn out the vote.

I'm on my way to the third and final debate. We had a good debate last Friday. These debates have highlighted the clear differences between the Senator and me on issues ranging from jobs to taxes to health care to the war on terror. Much as he's strived to obscure it, on issue after issue my opponent has shown why he has earned his ranking as the most liberal Member of the United States Senate.

Audience members. Boo-o-o!

The President. Several statements he made the other night simply didn't pass the credibility test. With a straight face, he said he had had only one position on Iraq. [*Laughter*]

Audience members. Flip-flop! Flip-flop! Flip-flop!

The President. I could barely contain myself. [*Laughter*] He must think we've been on another planet. Spring of 2003, I ordered the invasion of Iraq. Senator Kerry said, "It was the right decision." Now he says, "It's the wrong war." In the same debate, he said Saddam was a threat. Then a few minutes later, he said there wasn't a threat in Iraq. And he tells us he's only had one position. He can run from his record, but he cannot hide.

With another straight face, he tried to tell Americans that when it comes to his health care plan, and I quote, "The Government has nothing to do with it." [*Laughter*] The facts are that 8 out of 10 people who get health care under Senator Kerry's plan would be placed on a Government program.

Audience members. Boo-o-o!

The President. He can run, but he cannot hide.

And then Senator Kerry was asked to look into the camera and promise he would not raise taxes for anyone who earns less than $200,000 a year. The problem is, to keep that promise he would have to break almost all of his other ones. His plan to raise taxes in the top two income brackets would raise about $600 billion. But his spending plans will cost almost 4 times as much, more than $2.2 trillion. You cannot have it both ways. To pay for all the big spending programs he's outlined during his campaign, he will have to raise your taxes. He can run from his record, but he cannot hide.

You know, after listening to his litany of complaints and his dour pessimism, it took all I could do not to make a face. [*Laughter*]

I have a very different philosophy than him. I'm a compassionate conservative. I have worked to make America more hopeful and more secure. I've led our country with principle and resolve, and with your help, that is how I will lead our Nation for 4 more years.

Audience members. Four more years! Four more years! Four more years!

The President. My plan for a hopeful America begins with a growing economy that creates good jobs. I believe in the energy and innovation and spirit of America's workers and small-business owners and farmers and ranchers. And that is why we unleashed that energy with the largest tax relief in a generation.

When you're out convincing people to vote our way, remind them what we've been through. The stock market was in serious decline 6 months prior to my arrival in Washington, DC. Then we had a recession. We had some corporate scandals which affected our economy. We passed tough laws to make it abundantly clear: We will not tolerate dishonesty in the boardrooms of America. And then we had the attacks of September the 11th, which cost us about a million jobs in the 3 months afterwards.

But we acted. We put tax relief in place. The recession was one of the shallowest in American history, and our economy has been growing at rates as fast as any in nearly 20 years.

The past 13 months, we've added more than 1.9 million new jobs. The unemployment rate in America is at 5.4 percent, lower than the average of the 1970s, 1980s, and 1990s. The unemployment rate in your State is at 5.1 percent. Farm income is up. Homeownership rate is at an alltime high. More of our minority citizens own their homes than ever before. America is moving forward, and there's much more to do.

To make sure jobs are here in America, to make sure you can find good paying jobs, America must be the best place in the world to do business. That means we need to reduce the burden of regulations on our job creators. We've got to end the junk lawsuits that are threatening small businesses that create most of the new jobs in America.

To create jobs, Congress needs to pass my energy plan. My plan encourages conservation. It encourages the use of renewables like ethanol and biodiesel. It will help modernize the electricity grid. It encourages clean coal technology. It recognizes we can explore for hydrocarbons in environmentally friendly ways. In order to keep jobs here in America, we must be less dependent on foreign sources of energy.

To create jobs, we need to reject economic isolationism and open up markets around the world for U.S. products. See, I know, with a level playing field, we can compete with anybody, anytime, anywhere, so long as the playing field is fair. And that's why I tell China, "You treat us the way we treat you." The best way to create jobs is to be selling our goods overseas.

To create jobs, we need to be wise about how we spend your money and keep your taxes low. My opponent says oh, don't worry, he's going to pay for all his promises by taxing the rich. We've heard that before, haven't we?

Audience members. Yes!

The President. The rich hire lawyers and accountants for a reason: to stick you with the bill. [*Laughter*] We're not going to let him tax you; we're going to win in November.

Speaking about the Tax Code, it's a complicated mess. It's full of special interest loopholes. In a new term, I'll lead a bipartisan effort to simplify the Tax Code and make it more fair for the American people.

Listen, to build a more hopeful America, we must have the best prepared and most highly skilled workforce in the world. This all starts with education. I believe every child can learn and every school must teach. I went to Washington, DC, to challenge the soft bigotry of low expectations.

I went to stop the practice of just simply shuffling the hard-to-educate through, grade after grade, year after year, without teaching the basics. We've raised the standards. We're measuring early so we can solve problems before they're too late. We trust the local people to make the right decisions for their schools. We're closing an achievement gap in America, and we're not going to go back to the days of mediocrity.

Most new jobs are filled by people with at least 2 years of college, yet only one in four of our students gets there. So we'll fund early intervention programs in our high schools for at-risk students. We'll place a new focus on math and science. Over time, we'll require a rigorous exam before graduation from high school. By raising performance in our high schools and by expanding Pell grants for low- and middle-income families, we will help more Americans start their career with a college diploma.

One of the cornerstones of my plan to make sure our workers get the skills necessary to fill the jobs of the 21st century is to support the community college system here in Colorado and around our country.

To build a more hopeful America, we need to make health care more affordable and available. We need a safety net for those with the greatest needs. I believe in community health centers, places where the poor can get care. I believe every poor county in America should have a community health center. And we need to do more to make sure our poor children are fully subscribed in our program for low-income families so they can get the health care they need.

We must do more to make sure health care is affordable. Most of the uninsured are employees of small businesses. Small businesses have trouble affording health care. To help more workers get health care, we should allow small businesses to join together so they can buy insurance at the same discounts big companies get to do.

To make sure health care is affordable, we will expand health savings accounts. We will give small businesses tax credits to pay into health savings accounts for their employees. We want workers to own their own accounts so they can base their medical decisions on advice from a doctor, not somebody in an HMO.

To make sure health care is available and affordable, we've got to do something about these junk lawsuits that are running up the costs of health care and running good doctors out of practice. You cannot be pro-doctor, pro-patient, and pro-trial-lawyer at the same time. You have to choose. My opponent made his choice, and he put a trial lawyer on the ticket.

Audience members. Boo-o-o!

The President. I made my choice. I'm standing with the doctors and the patients. I'm for medical liability reform—now.

In all we do to improve health care, this administration will make sure the health decisions are made by doctors and patients, not by Government officials in Washington, DC. I believe we have a moral responsibility to honor our seniors with good health care. See, I went to Washington to solve problems, not to pass them on to future Presidents and future generations. I saw a problem in Medicare. Medicine was modernizing, but Medicare wasn't.

For example, we paid thousands of dollars for heart surgery under Medicare but wouldn't pay a dime for the prescription drugs that would prevent the heart surgery from being needed in the first place. That didn't make any sense. It didn't make any sense for our seniors. It didn't make any sense for the taxpayers. So we called people together, and we modernized Medicare. And starting in 2006, our seniors will get prescription drug coverage. We're not going to go back to the days of not honoring our seniors when it comes to good health.

Let me talk about our retirement systems. We need to do something about Social Security. In 2000, when I ran, I remember those ads saying, "If George W.

gets to be the President, our seniors won't get their checks." You might remember those ads. Well, our seniors got their checks, and the seniors will continue to get their Social Security checks. Baby boomers are in pretty good shape when it comes to the Social Security trust.

But we need to worry about our children and our grandchildren when it comes to Social Security. And that's why I believe younger workers ought to be allowed to set aside some of their own tax money in personal accounts to get a better rate of return, personal accounts they call their own.

No, we're living in changing times, but some things don't change, the values we try to live by, courage and compassion, reverence and integrity. In changing times, we will support the institutions that give our lives direction and purpose, our families, our schools, our religious congregations. We stand for a culture of life in which every person matters and every being counts. We stand for marriage and family, which are the foundations of our society. And we stand for the appointment of Federal judges who know the difference between personal opinion and the strict interpretation of the law.

This election will also determine how America responds to the continuing danger of terrorism. The most solemn duty of the American President is to protect the American people. If America shows uncertainty or weakness in this decade, the world will drift toward tragedy. This will not happen on my watch.

Audience members. Four more years! Four more years! Four more years!

The President. Since that terrible morning, September the 11th, 2001, we have fought the terrorists across the Earth, not for pride, not for power, but because the lives our citizens are at stake.

Audience members. We love you, W!

The President. Our strategy is clear. We're defending the homeland. We're transforming our military. I will make sure the All-Volunteer Army remains the All-Volunteer Army. We're reforming and strengthening our intelligence. We're staying on the offensive. We're striking the terrorists abroad so we do not have to face them here at home. We'll continue to work to spread freedom and peace. And we will prevail.

Our strategy is succeeding. Think about the world as it was 3½ years ago. Afghanistan was the home base of Al Qaida. Pakistan was a transit point for terrorist groups. Saudi Arabia was fertile ground for terrorist fundraising. Libya was secretly pursuing nuclear weapons. Iraq was a dangerous place and a gathering threat, and Al Qaida was largely unchallenged as it planned attacks.

Because we acted, the Government of a free Afghanistan held elections this weekend and is an ally in the war on terror; Pakistan is capturing terrorist leaders; Saudi Arabia is making raids and arrests; Libya is dismantling its weapons programs; the army of a free Iraq is fighting for freedom; and more than three-quarters of Al Qaida's key members and associates have been brought to justice.

This progress involved careful diplomacy, clear moral purpose, and some tough decisions. And the toughest came on Iraq. We knew Saddam Hussein's record of aggression and support for terror. We knew he hated America. We knew he had a long history of pursuing and even using weapons of mass destruction. We know that after September the 11th, we must take threats seriously before they fully materialize.

In Saddam Hussein, we saw a threat. So I went to the United States Congress. Members of Congress looked at the very same intelligence I looked at and concluded that Saddam Hussein was a threat and authorized the use of force. My opponent looked at the very same intelligence and came to the same conclusion and voted yes when it came time to authorize the use of force.

Before the United States ever commits troops into harm's way, we must try all means—all means—to deal with any threat. No President ever wants to have to send our sons and daughters into harm's way. And so that's why I went to the United Nations. I was hopeful that diplomacy would solve the threat. The United Nations looked at the same intelligence, debated the issue, and passed a resolution by a 15-to-nothing vote in the United Nations Security Council that said Saddam Hussein must disclose, disarm, or face serious consequences. Now, I believe when an international body speaks, it must mean what it says.

Saddam Hussein deceived the inspectors. He wasn't about to listen to the demands of the free world. He was used to ignoring the demands. After all, he'd ignored resolution after resolution after resolution. We gave him his final chance. He chose to deceive and evade. And so I have a choice to make: Do I take the word of a madman and forget the lessons of September the 11th, or take action to defend our country? Given that choice, I will defend America every time.

Now, we did not find the stockpiles that we all thought were there. But the Duelfer report that came out last week said that Saddam Hussein retained the intent and the capability and the expertise to rebuild his weapons programs. It said he was gaming the system, using the Oil for Food Programme to try to influence officials in other nations to get rid of the sanctions. And why? Because he wanted the world to look the other way so he could restart his weapons programs. And that was a danger we could not afford to take. Knowing what I know today, I would have made the same decision.

Audience members. Four more years! Four more years! Four more years!

The President. Because we acted in our self-interest, not only are we safer, but 50 million people now live in freedom. Think about what happened in Afghanistan. Think about what happened in that country that was once ruled by the Taliban. It wasn't all that long ago that many young girls were not even allowed to go to school, and their mothers were whipped in the public square, sometimes executed in a sports stadium because they wouldn't toe the line of these ideologues of hate. And just this weekend, people by the thousands voted for their President. The first—3½ years ago, nobody would have thought that was possible. The first person to vote in the Presidential elections in Afghanistan was a 19-year-old girl. Iraq is headed toward democracy. Iraq has a strong Prime Minister and a National Council, and elections will be held in January.

We're standing with the people in those countries because when America gives its word, America must keep its word. We're standing with them because a free Afghanistan and a free Iraq will make us all safer. You see, free societies in the Middle East will be hopeful societies which no longer feed resentments and breed violence for export. Free governments in the Middle East will fight the terrorists instead of harboring them. And that helps us keep the peace.

Our mission is clear. We will help these countries train armies so their own people can do the hard work of defending democracy. We will help them get on the path of stability and democracy as quickly as possible, and then our troops will come home with the honor they have earned.

I'm proud to be the Commander in Chief of a such a great military. I want to thank the veterans who are here today for having set such a great example for those who wear the uniform. I want to thank the military families who are here today for your sacrifice. And I assure you, we'll keep the commitment I've made to our troops. We'll make sure they have the resources they need to complete their missions.

And that's why I went to the United States Congress, September of 2003, and requested $87 billion to support our troops in both Afghanistan and Iraq. It was essen-tial funding. It was vital for their missions. We received great bipartisan support. As a matter of fact, only 12 United States Senators voted against the funding, 2 of whom are my opponent and his runningmate.

Audience members. Boo-o-o!

The President. Even more startling is this statistic: There were only four Members of the United States Senate who voted to authorize the use of force and then voted against funding for our troops in harm's way, two of whom are my opponent and his runningmate.

Audience members. Boo-o-o!

The President. You might remember perhaps the most famous quote of this campaign: When asked to explain his vote, my opponent said, "I actually did vote for the $87 billion, before I voted against it."

Audience members. Flip-flop! Flip-flop! Flip-flop!

The President. Now, he's given a lot of explanations since then for that vote. One of my favorites is when he just threw up his hands and said, "The whole thing was a complicated matter." [*Laughter*] There's nothing complicated about supporting our troops in harm's way.

On national security, my opponent has a record. He has a record of voting against the weapons systems that helped our country win the cold war. He voted to cut America's intelligence budget by $7.5 billion after 1993. He now says he wants a "global test" before taking action to defend America's security.

Audience members. Boo-o-o!

The President. The problem is, the Senator can never pass his own test. In 1990, the United Nations Security Council passed a resolution supporting action to remove Saddam Hussein from Kuwait. The international community was united. Countries throughout the world joined our coalition, yet in the United States Senate after the Security Council resolution, my opponent voted no when it came time to authorize the use of force.

Audience members. Boo-o-o!

The President. If driving Saddam Hussein out of Kuwait with the support of the international community does not meet his test, nothing will. [*Laughter*] And in this dangerous world, that's the wrong position to take.

We have a very different view on how to protect America and our role in confronting threats in the world. Just this weekend, we saw new evidence that my opponent fundamentally misunderstands the war against terror. Earlier, he questioned whether it's really a war at all, describing it as primarily a law enforcement and intelligence gathering operation instead of a threat that demands the full use of American power. Now just this weekend, Senator Kerry talked of reducing terrorism to a, quote, "nuisance"—[*laughter*]—and compared it to prostitution and illegal gambling.

Audience members. Boo-o-o!

The President. Our goal is not to reduce terror to some acceptable level of nuisance. Our goal is to defeat terror by staying on the offensive, destroying the terrorist networks, and spreading freedom and liberty around the world.

I will always work with our friends and allies. For the next 4 years, we'll continue to build on our strong coalition, but I will never turn over America's national security decisions to leaders of other nations.

I believe in the transformational power of liberty. To make my point, I oftentimes talk about my friend Prime Minister Koizumi of Japan. I saw him at the United Nations meetings in early September. I said, "You know, I'm talking about you on the campaign trail. Is that okay?" He said, "Fine, go ahead and talk about me." I didn't ask permission, though, as to whether or not I could tell you that his favorite singer was Elvis. [*Laughter*]

What's interesting about my relationship is that it wasn't all that long ago that we were fighting Japan. Japan was the sworn enemy of the United States of America. My dad fought against the Japanese. Your dads and granddads, husbands, loved ones fought against the Japanese as well. After we defeated the Japanese in World War II, we had a President named Harry S. Truman who believed in the transformational power of liberty to convert an enemy into an ally. He worked with others to help Japan develop a democracy.

And there was a lot of skepticism in our country at that time, about whether we wanted Japan to become a democracy, about whether Japan could become a democracy. And you could understand why there was skepticism. We had just fought them, and many families' lives had been turned upside-down because of the death in the World War II.

But my predecessor and other citizens held to that belief that liberty could transform nations. And today, I sit down at the table with Prime Minister Koizumi of Japan talking about the peace, talking about how do we make the world a more peaceful place for generations to come. We will succeed in Iraq. Iraq will become a democracy. Someday, an American President will be sitting down with a duly elected leader of Iraq talking about the peace.

I believe that millions in the Middle East plead in silence for their freedom. I believe women want to grow up in a free society and raise their children in a free society. And I believe that if given the chance, the people in the Middle East will embrace the most honorable form of government ever devised by man. I believe all these things because freedom is not America's gift to the world; freedom is the Almighty God's gift to each man and woman in this world.

For all Americans, these years in our history will always stand apart. There are quiet times in the life of a nation when little is expected of its leaders. This isn't one of those times. It's a time that requires firm resolve, clear vision, and the deep faith in the values that makes us a great nation.

None of us will ever forget that week when one era ended and another began.

September the 14th, 2001, I stood in the ruins of the Twin Towers. It's a day I will never forget. There were workers in hardhats there yelling at me at the top of their lungs, "Whatever it takes." I remember a fellow coming out of the rubble, and I was trying to do my best to console them there at the site. And a guy grabbed me by the arm, and he said, "Don't let me down." Ever since that day, I wake up every morning thinking about how to better protect our country. I will never relent in defending America, whatever it takes.

Audience members. Four more years! Four more years! Four more years!

The President. Four years ago, when I traveled your great State, I made a pledge that if you gave me the chance to serve, I would uphold the honor and the dignity of the office to which I had been elected. With your help—with your help, I will do so for 4 more years.

God bless, and thank you for coming. Thank you all.

NOTE: The President spoke at 4:55 p.m. at Red Rocks Park & Amphitheater. In his remarks, he referred to Cathy Franks, wife of Gen. Tommy R. Franks, USA (Ret.), former combatant commander, U.S. Central Command; Mike Shanahan, head coach, National Football League Denver Broncos and his wife, Peggy; Gov. Bill Owens of Colorado and his wife, Frances; Gwynneth A.E. Dieter, Colorado State chairperson, W Stands for Women, Bush-Cheney '04, Inc.; entertainer Collin Raye; Charles Duelfer, Special Advisor to the Director of Central Intelligence; Prime Minister Ayad Allawi of the Iraqi Interim Government; and Prime Minister Junichiro Koizumi of Japan. He also referred to the "Comprehensive Report of the Special Advisor to the DCI on Iraq's WMD," issued September 30. The transcript released by the Office of the Press Secretary also included the remarks of Gen. Franks, who introduced the President.

Statement on the Death of Christopher Reeve
October 11, 2004

Laura and I are saddened by the death of Christopher Reeve. Mr. Reeve was an example of personal courage, optimism, and self-determination. He was brave in the face of adversity and was greatly admired by millions of Americans. He will be remembered as an accomplished actor and for his dedicated advocacy for those with physical disabilities. We send our prayers and condolences to his family and friends.

Remarks in Colorado Springs, Colorado
October 12, 2004

The President. Thank you all for coming. It's great to be back in Colorado Springs. I've come back to ask for your vote. I've come back to ask for your help in getting people to the polls on November the 2d. We have a duty in this country to participate in the democratic system. Remind your friends and neighbors about that duty. Get people from all the neighborhoods in Colorado Springs to show up to vote. Get them to do what all of us must do, to vote on election day. And when you get them headed to the polls, remind them if they want a stronger America, a safer

America, and a better America, to put me and Dick Cheney back in office.

It's an amazing line of work, isn't it, where you get your daughter to introduce you in front of thousands of people. I'm really proud of Jenna and Barbara. Laura and I love them dearly. I want to thank them for their help on the campaign trail. And it warms my heart and strengthens my spirit to be campaigning with somebody I love a lot.

I wish Laura were here today, speaking about loving somebody a lot. When I asked her to marry me, she was a public school librarian, didn't much care for politics or politicians. [*Laughter*] She said, "Fine, I'll marry you, just so long as I never have to give a speech." [*Laughter*] I said, "Okay, you've got a deal." Fortunately, she didn't hold me to that pledge. She's speaking a lot, and when she does, the American people get to see a compassionate, strong, great First Lady in Laura Bush.

I'm proud of my runningmate, Dick Cheney. He did a great job in his debate the other night. I admit it, he doesn't have the waviest hair. [*Laughter*] But I didn't pick him for his hairdo. I picked him because he's a man of sound judgment and great experience. I picked him because he's getting the job done for the American people.

I'm honored to be on the platform with the next United States Senator from Colorado, Pete Coors. I hope when you're turning out the vote for me, you turn out the vote for Pete as well. He'll be taking the place of a really fine fellow in Ben Nighthorse Campbell. I've enjoyed working with Senator Campbell. He's served your State well. And Pete will be serving alongside another fine United States Senator in Wayne Allard. I appreciate Wayne being here. Thanks for coming, Joan. It's good to see you.

I'm honored to be on the stage with a great Governor of the State of Colorado, Bill Owens. He's doing a fine job. I know something about being a Governor. I was one.

You've got a great Congressman from this district in Joel Hefley. I'm proud that he's here, and how about his wife, State Representative Lynn Hefley. I told Joel the other day, he better hope Lynn doesn't run him in the Republican primary. [*Laughter*]

You know, I got to meet your mayor when I came to give the graduation speech at the Air Force Academy, and I was very impressed by Lionel Rivera, Mr. Mayor. What a good man he is. And I want to thank his wife, Lynn, for being here as well. I want to thank all the State and local officials who have joined us.

I want to thank Sammy Kershaw for being here and entertaining. I want to thank The Walker Williams Band for being here and entertaining everybody. I appreciate the members of the Olympic team who've joined us today, Shane Hamman and Matt Emmons. I'm honored you all are here.

I appreciate those who are here serving in our United States military. I want to thank your families—of the men and women who wear the uniform. Thank you for your sacrifice and your dedication. I want to thank all the veterans who are here today. Thank you all for coming. Thank you all.

I want to thank the grassroots activists for what you're going to do, to put up the signs and make the phone calls, turn out the vote. There's no doubt we'll carry Colorado again and win a great victory in November.

I'm on my way to Arizona for the final debate. Those debates have highlighted the clear differences between the Senator and me on issues ranging from jobs to taxes to health care to the war on terror. Much as he's tried to obscure it, on issue after issue, my opponent has showed why he earned his ranking as the most liberal Member of the United States Senate.

Audience members. Boo-o-o!

The President. And several of his statements he made in the last debate simply do not pass the credibility test. With a straight face, he said he'd had only one position on Iraq. [*Laughter*] I could barely contain myself. In the spring of 2003, Senator Kerry said, "It was the right decision to remove Saddam Hussein from power." Now, he says, "It's the wrong war." In the same debate, he said Saddam was a threat, and then a few minutes later, he said there wasn't a threat in Iraq. And he tries to tell us he's had only one position. Who's he trying to kid? See, he can run from his record, but he cannot hide.

With another straight face, he tried to tell Americans that when it comes to his health care plan, and I quote, "The Government has nothing to do with it." The facts are, 8 out of 10 people who get health care under Senator Kerry's plan would be placed on a Government program, see. He can run, but he cannot hide.

Then he was asked to look into the camera—[*laughter*]—and promise he would not raise taxes for anyone who earns less than $200,000 a year. The problem is, to keep that promise, he would have to break almost all of his other ones. [*Laughter*] His plan to raise taxes on the top two brackets would raise, we think, about $600 billion. But his spending plan costs almost 4 times that much, about $2.2 trillion. See, you can't have it both ways. To pay for all the big spending programs he's outlined during his campaign, he's going to have to raise your taxes. He can run, but he cannot hide.

You know, after listening to the litany of complaints and the dour pessimism, it took all I could do not to make a face. [*Laughter*] See, I have a different philosophy. I'm a compassionate conservative. I think Government ought to help people realize their dreams, not tell them how to live their lives. I've led this country with principle and resolve, and that's how I'm going to lead it, with your help, for 4 more years.

Audience members. Four more years! Four more years! Four more years!

The President. My plan for a more hopeful America begins with a growing economy that creates good jobs. See, I believe in the energy and innovation and spirit of our workers, our small-business owners, our farmers, our ranchers. And that's why we unleashed that energy with the largest tax relief in a generation.

When you're out convincing people to vote and to come our way, remind them what this economy and this country has been through. Six months before we got to Washington, the stock market was in serious decline. It foreshadowed a recession. Then we found out some of our citizens forgot what it meant to be a responsible American, and they didn't tell the truth. We passed tough laws to make it abundantly clear we won't tolerate dishonesty in the boardrooms of America. Those scandals hurt our economy. And then we got attacked. And the attack cost America 1 million jobs in the 3 months after September the 11th.

But we acted. We put tax relief in place, and this recession was one of the shallowest in American history. The tax relief spurred consumption and investment. And as a result, our economy has been growing at rates as fast as any in nearly 20 years. In the past 13 months, we've added 1.9 million new jobs. The unemployment rate nationally is 5.4 percent—lower than the average rate of the 1970s, 1980s, and 1990s. The unemployment rate in the State of Colorado is 5.1 percent. The homeownership rate is at alltime high in America. More minorities own a home than ever before in the history of this country. The entrepreneurial spirit is strong. We're moving forward, but there's more work to be done.

In order to make sure jobs are here in America, in order to make sure there's hope in this country when it comes to finding work, America must be the best place in the world to do business. That means less regulations on our employers. That means legal reforms so these junk lawsuits don't make it hard for people to find a job.

In order to make sure jobs stay here, Congress needed to pass my energy plan. See, it's a plan that encourages conservation. We spend money on research and development to expand the use of renewables, technologies to help us live different ways at the same lifestyle we're accustomed to, technologies to help us use coal in environmentally friendly ways. I believe we can explore for hydrocarbons in environmentally friendly ways. What I'm telling you is, to keep jobs here, we must become less dependent on foreign sources of energy.

To keep jobs here, we got to open up markets for U.S. products. See, we don't want to be closing down markets. We're going to be opening markets. It's to your advantage that our market is open from products for overseas. See, if you've got more choices to choose from, you're likely to get that which you want at a better price and higher quality. That's how the marketplace works. So I'm telling places like China, "You treat us the way we treat you. You treat us in a way that opens up your markets," because we can compete with anybody, anytime, anywhere, so long as the rules are fair.

In order to make sure this economy grows, we've got to keep your taxes low. Raising taxes would be the wrong prescription for economic growth. You've heard my opponent—I talked a little bit a while ago about it—he said, oh, he's going to pay for all his programs by taxing the rich. We've heard that kind of rhetoric before. The rich hire lawyers and accountants for a reason—[*laughter*]—to pass the tax bill on to you. We're not going to let him tax you, because we're going to win in November.

Speaking about the Tax Code, it is a complicated mess. It's a million pages long. We spend 6 billion hours a year filling out taxes. I'm going to bring Republicans and Democrats together in a new term to simplify the Tax Code and make it more fair for the American people.

Listen, in order to make sure we can compete in a global war, we've got to educate our workforce. It all starts with making sure our youngsters can read and write and add and subtract. I went to Washington, DC, to challenge the soft bigotry of low expectations. That's what happened in too many classrooms in America, where they would just shuffle the kid through, you know, the so-called hard-to-educate, an inner-city kid, shuffle him through, or maybe a child whose parents didn't speak English as a first language. "Let's just move him through." See, that's not the America I know. I believe every child can learn. I expect every school to teach. That is why we now measure, so we can solve problems early, before they are too late—before it is too late. We can't have children coming out the back end of the school system that can't read and write and add and subtract anymore, if we expect to compete in the 21st century. Do you realize we're closing an achievement gap in America, and we're not going to go back to the days of mediocrity in our schools.

There is more work to be done. I believe we ought to fund at-risk programs in our high schools. I believe we ought to emphasize math and science. I believe, over time, we ought to have a rigorous exam before graduation. I know we'll continue to expand Pell grants for low- and middle-income families. We want more of our kids who graduate to start their career with a college diploma.

To build a more hopeful America, we've got to make sure health care is more available and affordable. We'll have a safety net for those with the greatest need. I'm a strong proponent of community health centers. These are places where the poor and the indigent can get preventative and primary care. It's best they get the care in these centers and not in the emergency rooms around our country. It is a compassionate way to make sure people get the help they need. We will continue to make sure our health programs for low-income children are fully subscribed to. But we also must address this issue of affordability.

Most of the uninsured are employees of small businesses. Small businesses are having trouble affording health care. We should allow small businesses to pool together so they can buy insurance at the same discounts that big companies can do. I know we need to continue to expand health savings accounts, accounts where people can buy low-premium policies to cover major medical expenses and can set money aside on a tax-free basis to be able to cover their health care needs.

These are vital plans which will help our small businesses, help our young uninsured. These are plans where workers will own their own accounts, so they can base their medical decisions on the advice from their doctor, not in negotiations with an HMO. These are some commonsense, practical ways to make sure health care is available and affordable, without increasing the reach of the Federal Government.

Let me tell you one other practical way to deal with the cost of health care. We've got to do something about these frivolous lawsuits that are running good docs out of practice, frivolous lawsuits that are running up the cost of health care. See, you can't be pro-lawyer—I mean, pro-doctor, pro-patient, and pro-trial-lawyer at the same time. You have to choose. My opponent made his choice, and he put a trial lawyer on the ticket.

Audience members. Boo-o-o!

The President. I made my choice. I'm standing with the doctors and the patients. I'm for medical liability reform—now. In all we'll do to improve health care, this administration will make sure that the decisions are made by patients and doctors, not by Government officials in Washington, DC.

You know, I went to Washington to solve problems, not to pass them on to future Presidents and future generations. And I saw a problem in Medicare. Medicine was modernizing, but Medicare wasn't. And I believe we have a moral responsibility to honor our seniors with good health care. Let me tell you what I'm talking about, about modernizing and Medicare wasn't. You realize we would pay thousands of dollars for heart surgery under Medicare but not one dime for the prescription drug that could prevent the heart surgery from being needed in the first place. That did not make any sense for our seniors, and it didn't make any sense for the taxpayers. And so I worked with Republicans and Democrats to modernize Medicare. And now, in 2006, our seniors will get prescription drug coverage for the first time under Medicare.

Let me talk about Social Security. You might remember the campaign rhetoric of 2000 when they said, "If old George W. gets elected, they're going to take away your check," to our seniors. You still got your check, didn't you? Just remember that, when we talk about how to make sure the Social Security system works for our youngsters. See, baby boomers are okay when it comes to the Social Security trust.

But we need to worry about our children and our grandchildren if we want to make sure Social Security is available to them. We've got to think differently. And so one of the good ideas that I believe is necessary—an idea by the way, that came out of a Commission I formed to take a look at Social Security, headed by the late Senator Daniel Patrick Moynihan, Democrat from New York—was that younger workers ought to be allowed to take some of their own tax money and set aside a personal savings account that will earn a better rate of return than the current Social Security system does, so they will have the capacity to be able to realize benefits from a retirement system, a personal account they call their own, and a personal account the Government cannot take away.

We're living in changing times, and that can be unsettling. That's why I've promoted an ownership society throughout our country. We're living in changing times, but there's some things that don't change, reverence and integrity, compassion and courage. The values we try to live by don't change. In changing times, we must support the institutions that give our lives direction and purpose, our families, our schools, our religious congregations. We stand for a culture of life in which every person counts and every being matters. We stand for marriage and family, which are the foundations of our society. We stand for the appointment of Federal judges who know the difference between personal opinion and the strict interpretation of the law.

This election will also determine how America responds to the continuing danger of terrorism. I believe the most solemn duty of the American President is to protect the American people. If America shows uncertainty or weakness in this decade, the world will drift toward tragedy. This will not happen on my watch.

Since that terrible morning of September the 11th, 2001, we have fought the terrorists across the Earth, not for pride, not for power, but because the lives of our citizens are at stake. We've got a clear strategy. We'll defend the homeland. We'll strengthen our intelligence gathering services. We'll transform our military so it can do its job. The All-Volunteer Army will remain an all-volunteer army. We're staying on the offensive. We will strike the terrorists abroad so we do not have to face them here at home. We will continue to work to spread liberty and peace. And we will prevail.

Our strategy is succeeding. Think of the world the way it was 3½ years ago. Afghanistan was the home base of Al Qaida. Pakistan was a transit point for terrorist groups. Al Qaida—Saudi Arabia was fertile ground for terrorist fundraising. Libya was secretly

pursuing nuclear weapons. Iraq was a dangerous place, run by a sworn enemy of America. Al Qaida was largely unchallenged as it planned attacks.

Because we acted, the Government of Afghanistan is an ally in the war on terror, and they held Presidential elections last weekend. Because we acted, Pakistan is capturing terrorist leaders; Saudi Arabia is making raids and arrests; Libya is dismantling its weapons programs; the army of a free Iraq is fighting for freedom; and more than three-quarters of Al Qaida's key members and associates have been brought to justice.

This progress involved careful diplomacy, clear moral purpose, and some tough decisions. And the toughest came on Iraq. We knew Saddam Hussein's record of aggression and his support for terror. We knew he hated our country. We knew he had invaded another country. We knew he was shooting missiles at American pilots who were enforcing the sanctions of the world. We knew he had a long history of pursuing and even using weapons of mass destruction. And we knew that after September the 11th, we must take threats seriously before they fully materialize. That's one of the key lessons that we must never forget in order to protect the American people.

In Saddam Hussein, I saw a threat. And I went to the United States Congress. They looked at the same intelligence I looked at. They remembered the same history my administration remembered. And they concluded that Saddam Hussein was a threat and authorized the use of force. My opponent looked at the same intelligence I looked at. And he came to the same conclusion, and he voted yes when it came time to authorize the use of force.

Before I ever commit troops into harm's way, or any President, we must try all means to deal with the threat. No President ever wants to send our young into harm's way. No President ever wants to have to do that. So I went to the United Nations in hopes that diplomacy would work. That was my hope. I hoped that the free world would come together and make its voice clear, which it did. The Security Council voted 15 to nothing and said to Saddam Hussein, "Disclose, disarm, or face serious consequences." Now, I believe that when an international body speaks, it must mean what it says. And that goes for the President as well.

Saddam Hussein had no intention of listening to the demands of the free world. He ignored the resolution. He deceived the inspectors that were trying to get into— that were in his country. Why should he change? This is resolution number 17. Resolution after resolution after resolution had been passed, and nothing happened. He wasn't about to listen. As a matter of fact, when we gave him the final chance, he continued to deceive and evade. So I have a choice to make at this point in our history: Do I forget the lessons of September the 11th and take the word of a madman, or do I take action to defend this country? Given that choice, I will defend America every time.

We did not find the stockpiles that we all thought were there. But I want to remind you what the Duelfer report said. It said that Saddam Hussein retained the intent, the knowledge, and therefore, the capability to rebuild his weapons programs. Now, think about that. It also said that he was gaming the system, using the Oil for Food Programme to try to convince— the polite way of saying it—[*laughter*]—officials of other nations to get rid of the sanctions that were already weakening. And why would he do that? Well, because he wanted the world to look the other way so he could restart his weapons programs. The greatest danger we face is weapons of mass destruction in the hands of a terrorist enemy. Knowing what I know today, I would have made the same decision. America and the world are safer with Saddam Hussein in a prison cell.

Because we acted in Afghanistan and Iraq, America is safer and 50 million people now live in freedom. Think about what happened in Afghanistan over the past weekend. You know, it wasn't all that long ago that young girls were not allowed to go to school. Their mothers were pulled out in the public square and whipped if they didn't toe the line of these ideologues of hate. The Taliban were backward and barbaric. They had a dark view of the world. This past weekend, millions of Afghan citizens voted for their President. The first voter was an Afghan woman, a 19-year-old woman. That society has gone from darkness to light because of freedom. Freedom is powerful.

Iraq will have elections in January. They got a strong Prime Minister. We're fighting off the terrorists who are trying to prevent the elections from happening. Freedom frightens these ideologues of hatred. They can't stand the thought of free societies.

It's in our interest that we expand freedom. It's in our interest that when we tell the Afghan people and the Iraq people we'll stand with them, that we keep our word. It's in our interest that free societies emerge in the broader Middle East, because they will be hopeful societies, societies which no longer feed resentments and breed violence for export. Free governments in the Middle East will fight the terrorists instead of harboring them. And that helps us keep the peace. Free societies are peaceful societies.

And so our mission is clear. We will help these countries, Afghanistan and Iraq, train their armies and their police so they can do the hard work of defending democracy. We'll help them get on the path of stability and democracy as quickly as possible, and then our troops will come home with the honor they have earned.

I made a commitment to our troops and their families that we'll make sure they have the resources they need to complete their missions. That's why I went to the United States Congress in September of 2003 and requested $87 billion of supplemental funding. This is really important money. This is money to help our troops in harm's way in both Afghanistan and Iraq. And I was pleased that we received strong bipartisan support for the funding request. It was so strong that only 12 Senators—United States Senators voted against it, 2 of whom are my opponent and his runningmate. [*Laughter*] Now, I want to tell you another statistic. Let me just tell you another revealing statistic. There were 4 United States Senators who voted to authorize the use of force and then voted against funding for our troops in harm's way, only 4 out of 100, 2 of whom are my opponent and his runningmate.

Audience members. Boo-o-o!

The President. That's got to tell you something. So they asked him why, and he issued perhaps the most famous quote of the 2004 campaign, "I actually did vote for the $87 billion, before I voted against it." [*Laughter*] Now, since then, he's given numerous explanations for why he made the vote. One of the most interesting was he just finally said, "The whole thing is a complicated matter." [*Laughter*] There's nothing complicated about supporting our troops in combat.

Listen, on national security, just like domestic policy, we've got big differences between us. I want you to remember that my opponent has had a record—a record in 20 years in the United States Senate. He's had a record of voting against the weapons systems that helped our country win the cold war. He had a record—in 1993, after we got the first World Trade Center attack, he voted to cut the intelligence budget by $7.5 billion. See, that's part of his thinking. That's record. That happened. He now says he wants a "global test" before taking action to defend America's security.

Audience members. Boo-o-o!

The President. Think about that, a "global test." The problem is he could never pass his own test. [*Laughter*] I want you to remember this, now, when you're out gathering people to vote. In 1990, the United Nations Security Council passed a resolution supporting action to remove Saddam Hussein from Kuwait. The international community was united. Countries throughout the world joined the coalition. Yet, in the United States Senate, after the Security Council resolution, after it became clear there was international support, Senator Kerry voted against the authorization of force. Listen, if driving Saddam Hussein out of Kuwait with the support of the international community does not meet his test, nothing will.

And that is dangerous, a dangerous way of thinking in the world in which we live. We have a different view of our role confronting threats. Just this weekend we saw new evidence that the Senator fundamentally misunderstands the war against terror. See, earlier he questioned whether this is really a war at all, describing it as primarily a law enforcement and intelligence gathering operation, instead of a threat that demands the full use of American power. And this weekend he talked of reducing terrorism to, quote, "nuisance"—his word—and compared it to prostitution and illegal gambling.

Our goal is not to reduce terror to some acceptable level of nuisance. Our goal is to defeat terror by staying on the offensive, destroying the networks, and spreading freedom and liberty.

During the next 4 years, I will work with our friends and allies. We'll continue to build strong coalitions. But I will never turn over America's national security decisions to leaders of other countries.

I believe in the transformational power of liberty. I like to use my friend Prime Minister Koizumi to explain what I mean by the transformational power of liberty. I saw him in New York in early September, and I—at the United Nations—and I said, "By the way, I'm talking about you on the campaign trail. Do you mind if I continue to do so?" He said, "Not at all." I didn't ask him whether or not I could tell you whether or not Elvis was his favorite singer.

[*Laughter*] It's true. [*Laughter*] One of his favorite movies is "High Noon," by the way.

Anyway—[*laughter*]—so I like to bring him up because he's the head of a country that some 60 years ago we were at war with. My dad fought against the Japanese. I'm sure there's some in this audience who did so, and I know some dads and granddads did as well.

And after the war, Harry S. Truman, President of the United States, believed in the transformational power of liberty to convert an enemy into an ally. That's what he believed. So did a lot of other Americans. But there was some great skepticism of what that could mean. You know, we were working for democracy in Japan. A lot of people in this country said, "Why do it? Why bother? Why should we care? They were the enemy." You could understand; families' lives had been turned upside down because of the death of a loved one during that war. People were questioning whether or not it was worthwhile.

But fortunately, they believed in the power of liberty, and today, I sit down at the table with Prime Minister Koizumi, the head of Japan, talking about the peace, talking about how the United States and Japan, former enemies and now allies, can work together to achieve the peace we all want for our children and our grandchildren.

I believe we'll succeed in Iraq. I believe there will be a democracy. And I envision the day, someday, when an American President and a duly elected leader of Iraq are sitting down at the table talking about achieving the peace, and our children and our grandchildren will be better off for it.

I believe that millions plead in silence in the Middle East for freedom. I believe that women in the Middle East want to have a free society and have their children grow up in a free society. I believe that if given a chance, the people in the Middle East will embrace the most honorable form of government ever devised by man. I believe all these things because freedom is not America's gift to the world; freedom is the Almighty God's gift to each man and woman in this world.

For all Americans, these years in our history will always stand apart. There are quiet times in the life of a nation when little is expected of its leaders. This isn't one of those times. This is a time that requires firm resolve and clear vision and a deep faith in the values that make this a great nation.

None of us will ever forget that week when one era ended and another began. On September the 14th, 2001, I stood in the ruins of the Twin Towers. It's a day I'll never forget. There was workers in hardhats there, yelling at me at the top of their lungs, "Whatever it takes." I remember doing my best to console those people coming out of the rubble. They were there lined up, and we were heading down the ropeline—Rudy Giuliani and Governor Pataki and I were going down the line thanking people and hugging them. And a guy grabbed me by the arm, and he said, "Do not let me down." Ever since that day, I wake up every morning thinking about how to better protect our country. I will never relent in defending America, whatever it takes.

Four years ago, when I traveled your great State, I made a pledge that if you gave me the chance to serve, I would uphold the honor and the dignity of the office to which I had been elected. With your help, I will do so for 4 more years.

God bless. Thank you all for coming. Thank you all.

NOTE: The President spoke at 9:37 a.m. at the Colorado Springs World Arena and Ice Hall. In his remarks, he referred to Joan Allard, wife of Senator Wayne Allard; Gov. Bill Owens of Colorado; Mayor Lionel Rivera of Colorado Springs, CO, and his wife, Lynn; entertainers Sammy Kershaw and the Walker Williams Band; Shane Hamman, weightlifter, and Matt Emmons, shooter,

U.S. Olympic team; Charles Duelfer, Special Advisor to the Director of Central Intelligence; Prime Minister Ayad Allawi of the Iraqi Interim Government; Prime Minister Junichiro Koizumi of Japan; Rudolph W. Giuliani, former mayor of New York City; and Gov. George E. Pataki of New York. He also referred to the "Comprehensive Report of the Special Advisor to the DCI on Iraq's WMD," issued September 30.

Remarks in Paradise Valley, Arizona
October 12, 2004

The President. Thank you all for coming. Thank you all for being here. I want to thank my friends Jon Kyl and John McCain for their leadership. They're good, honest people, and they're good to work with, and they do a great job representing Arizona. I presume you want me to sign the water bill. [*Laughter*] No wonder you're here.

Anyway, I finally made it to Arizona—back to Arizona. You know, we're kind of warming up for these debates. I'm looking forward to tomorrow night. It's a chance to point out major differences. For example, if the Senator has his way, this is the way every house will feel, because he doesn't have an energy policy. But it's going to be a lot of fun. I want to thank Arizona State for hosting the debate, and thank the good city of Phoenix and Tempe for being such gracious hosts.

I'm—will be teaming up here in a minute with Laura. She's been working her way from east to west. She and little Barbara are campaigning New Mexico today, and Jenna introduced me in Colorado Springs. And I was sitting there watching that gracious young lady introduce me in front of 10,000 people, saying, "My, does time fly," you know. [*Laughter*] It's an unbelievable feeling, really. I told the girls when they were young, I said, "Oh, don't worry, we'll go on the famous father-daughter camping trip," come to the Grand Canyon, maybe ride down the Colorado River. This is the grand camping trip we never took them on, campaigning for President.

[*Laughter*] But it's a lot of fun to have your family out there.

I tell people—and this is true—I think it's true; it's got some truth to it, at least—that either when I asked her or shortly thereafter, Laura said, you know, "I never want to have to give a political speech. I'll marry you, but I don't want to give a speech." I said, "Okay, you got a deal." And—but fortunately, she didn't hold me to the deal. The American people have gotten to see her as a warm, compassionate, great First Lady.

It's such an honor to serve the people. You know, people say, "Well, gosh, that's interesting. What's it like on your marriage, you know, being the President and First Lady?" I say, "It strengthened our marriage. After all, I've only got a 45-second commute." [*Laughter*] But we're representing the country together, and Laura has come to know what I know, that we have a chance to really do some good things for people. And I remember when she gave the radio address to the—and spoke to the women of Afghanistan, made it very clear that the American people were standing with them as they went from tyranny to freedom. And the feedback was fantastic, and she realized what I know as well, that just simple gestures and kind—moments of kindness can really make a difference in people's lives and can help lift spirits and make a valuable contribution to the future of the country.

I tell people that I'm going to give you some reasons why to put me back in. Tomorrow night, that's part of the purpose, but perhaps the most important one of all is so that Laura is the First Lady for 4 more years. [*Laughter*]

And my runningmate is doing just fine. I talk to him quite frequently. I think I'm going to see him tomorrow on a video—on a SVTS, we call it, which is a secure two-way conversation via video. We talk about national security needs. And he's doing great. He's holding his own. He did a wonderful job in the debate. I tell people he doesn't have the—I tell people plainly the fact, and that is, he doesn't have the waviest hair there amongst the candidates. But I didn't pick him for his hairdo. [*Laughter*] I picked him because he's a man of sound judgment and great experience, and he's getting the job done. And I'm real proud of Dick Cheney and proud to serve with him.

I want to thank Members of the Congress who are here. Trent and Josie Franks are with us. It's great to see you all. Thanks for coming. You're doing a fine job, and I'm proud you're here. Shadegg is with us. Where is John? Somewhere, anyway. Either that or he's outside trying to find some cool air. [*Laughter*] I want to thank J.D. and Mary Hayworth. They're with us today. Big J.D., appreciate you coming. Jeff and Cheryl Flake—there he is. Thanks for coming. I'm glad to see you all.

The mayor is with us, Ron Clarke, of the town of Paradise, Arizona. What a fantastic name, Paradise. What a great name. You know who is here? I'm a member of the ex-Governors club, and my old buddy, the ex-Governor of the State of Arizona is with us, Fife Symington. I appreciate you coming. You look great, for an older guy—no. [*Laughter*]

I want to thank my friend Jim Click. I appreciate his leadership. Several people came through the line and said, "I'm Click's friend." I said, well, "I'm sorry."

[*Laughter*] But thanks for coming. [*Laughter*]

I want to thank my—longtime friend of Mother and Dad's and mine, Jim Simmons. I appreciate Jim, and thank you for being here. I don't know if many people know this, but he used to live in Midland, Texas. And that's where Laura is from. That's where I'm from. Mother and Dad were living out there, and they became fast friends. You can't make it in this line of work unless your friends stay with you. That's just the way it is, and I appreciate Jim.

Bob Castellini and Susie are here. They've helped on this event. I want to thank my longtime friend Bob Castellini. I want to thank Dave Thompson. I want to thank the chairman of the Republican Party of Arizona, Bob Fannin, and his wife, Lisa.

Let's see here—21 days from today, the people will be going to the polls.

Audience member. You've got my vote!

The President. That's good. [*Laughter*] I certainly hope so. [*Laughter*] I don't know who is counting the days. I guess—but my spirits are high. I feel great. I really feel like the people—I got a good record to run on. I went to Washington to do some things.

You might remind people about what this economy has been through. The stock market was declining 6 months before I arrived in Washington, DC. We had one of the most significant stock market corrections in our history, and it foretold a recession. And then we got attacked, which cost us a million jobs. But we acted. I acted. I led the Congress. We cut the taxes in order to create consumption and investment, and this recession was one of the shallowest in American history.

We're on the move. Jobs are being created. There's a sense of optimism everywhere I go. Do you realize that there are more homeowners today than ever before? More minorities own their home than ever before in the history of the United States. What a fantastic, fantastic statistic.

The entrepreneurial spirit is strong. I mean, I meet small-business owners all over who feel like tomorrow will be a better day, in part because of the policies we have put in place. Listen, farmers are doing well, and that's good. When you got a good ag economy, you got a good economy. Think about that. The agricultural sector is doing well, which means rural America is doing well. There are bright spots all over this country.

And what I'm going to tell the people tomorrow night is we're not going to go back to the days of tax and spend. We're not going to go back to the days where—kind of the vision of economic policy is, "We're going to take your money, and we'll decide what to do with it." Running up the taxes on the American people right now would be bad for our economy, and we're not going to let him tax you. We're going to win in Arizona, and we're going to win in November.

So it's—you can't run on your record, see, you got to run on—the only reason you look at your record is to say, "I did what I said I was going to do, and now here's what I'm going to do." And the best way to make sure jobs stay here is to make sure America is the best place in the world to do business. That means less regulations. That means legal reform. That means a commonsense energy policy that will make us less dependent on foreign sources of energy. That means opening up markets for U.S. goods.

One of the interesting debates in this campaign is about trade. I go around telling the people, "Look, we open up our markets for foreign goods, and that's good for you." I explain to them that when you have more products to choose from, you're likely to get that which you want at a better price and higher quality. That's how the market works. So rather than preventing you from having more choices, I think what we ought to do is to say to countries, "You treat

us the way we treat you." Let's open up markets for U.S. products and U.S. goods and U.S. services. And that's how you keep jobs here in America.

And you keep jobs here in America by being wise about how we spend your money. I look forward to working with Senators McCain and Kyl about—to bring some fiscal sanity to Washington, DC. But you're not going to have fiscal sanity with John Kerry as the President. He's been the most liberal Member of the United States Senate, which means he likes to spend your money. That's what that means. Now, he can try to run from his record, but I'm not going to let him hide.

A couple of other quick points before people start to fall out here—[*laughter*]— including me. [*Laughter*] I can't wait for the health care debate. It's clear in this campaign; there's a difference of opinion. He said the other day, the Government doesn't have anything to do with his plan. When he said that I could barely contain myself. [*Laughter*] Of course, the Government has something to do with his plan. It's the cornerstone of his plan. It's the crux of his health care policy, to expand the Federal Government.

I have a different view. I mean, we've got to address costs with medical liability reform. We got to address costs with structural reforms by giving consumers more choice in the marketplace. That's how you begin to control costs. And that's why I'm such a big believer in health savings accounts. I could give you the whole litany, but what I'm telling you is, is that there is a vast difference of opinion about health care. And I'm absolutely confident our view is the way to help make sure health care is available and affordable.

I'm looking forward to talking about education. This is a subject about which I've got great passion. We reformed our—the way the Federal Government looks at schools. We measure now, in return for extra Federal money. You've got to measure if you want to save people's lives.

You've got to measure if you want to educate every child. If you don't diagnose the problem, you can't solve it.

Listen, I'm looking forward to debating tomorrow night on domestic issues that will make a difference. I'm looking forward to probably spending a little time, hopefully, on the war on terror because there's a big difference of opinion on the war on terror.

Let me tell you a couple of things, and we'll all go home and find some air-conditioning. First, you got to understand the nature of the enemy. They are coldblooded. They have no conscience, and you can't negotiate with them, and you can't hope for the best with these people. We must find them overseas so we don't have to face them here, and that's exactly what we're doing.

A couple of other things. Secondly is that in this different kind of war, it is important to send clear and understandable messages, such as, "If you harbor a terrorist, you're just as guilty as the terrorist." See, it's one thing to go after the terrorist networks, which we'll continue to do, but we also got to go after those people who harbor them and support them. And that's what I meant when I told the Taliban to get rid of Al Qaida or face serious consequences. They didn't listen, and they're no longer in power.

And I want you to remind your friends and neighbors about what took place this weekend. It is a phenomenal statement about democracy and freedom. Do you realize the first person that voted in the Presidential election was a 19-year-old girl? That's unbelievable. It's an unbelievable thought. Imagine what is happening in that society because of freedom. And it's in our Nation's interest that we promote freedom in places like Afghanistan and elsewhere, because Afghanistan is now an ally in the war on terror and such a bright example of what is possible in parts of the world that are desperate for free societies.

The third lesson is that we've got to deal with threats before they come to hurt us.

That's the reality of September the 11th. Saddam was a threat. We didn't find the stockpiles we thought were there, but remember what the report last week said. It said he was gaming the Oil for Food Programme to convince governments to get rid of—weaken or get rid of the sanction program for one reason, to use his expertise to rebuild his weapons. And what could he do with the weapons? He could share them with a terrorist enemy, which would make the harm done on September the 11th mild in comparison to what they could do. That's the true threat we face. And therefore, it's incumbent upon a President to face those threats before they come to hurt us. And that's exactly what we did in Iraq. Getting rid of Saddam Hussein was the right thing to do, and the world is safer for it.

And we'll succeed in Iraq. We've got a plan, and we're moving toward elections. Think about a—they're going to have elections in January. It's dangerous there, and there's a reason. These terrorists want to stop us. They want us to quit. They can't stand the thought of a free society in their midst. They understand how powerful Iraq will be as an example of people being able to live in a free society.

I believe everybody wants to be free. I believe women in the Middle East want to live in a free world. I know mothers from all walks of life and all religions want to raise their children in a free society. I know that, and at the core of my belief is that people want to be free because freedom is the Almighty God's gift to each man and woman in this world. That's what I believe.

Let me tell you one story—one story, and then we'll all go home here. [*Laughter*] There's already enough hot air in here to begin with. [*Laughter*] I tell people I believe in the transformational power of liberty. And I put it—I try to put it in terms so everybody can understand what I'm saying. And I use my friend Koizumi as an example about what I mean. Now, he's the

Prime Minister of Japan. Laura and I are very fond of him. He's an interesting, interesting man. His favorite singer is Elvis— [*laughter*]—one of his favorite—pretty unusual. And one of his favorite movies is "High Noon." [*Laughter*]

And I sit down with him and talk to him quite frequently. And what I find amazing is that I am talking to him at all, because it wasn't all that long ago in the march of history that we were at war with Japan. Japan was the sworn enemy. My dad fought the Japanese. McCain's dad fought the Japanese. Your dads, granddads were at war with the Japanese.

And after we won, Harry S. Truman, President of the United States, believed in the power of liberty to transform an enemy into an ally. Think about what that must have been like for the President, to stand up to the American people and say, "We're going to help our enemy become a democracy. We'll help Japan, not hurt Japan, the enemy, but we'll help lift up Japan as a free nation."

And there were great doubters and skeptics, and you can understand why. Many lives had been turned up-side-down. "Who wants to help an enemy," some probably asked. But Truman and other Americans stood true to the belief that liberty is a powerful, powerful concept.

And so today, as a result of their belief, I sit down with Prime Minister Koizumi, talking about the peace that we all want. We talk about how to keep the peace on the Korean Peninsula. We're talking about how to spread democracy and freedom. We talk about how to help the people of Afghanistan and Iraq realize their dreams to live in a free society. He knows what I know: Free societies will yield a more peaceful world. And I'm talking to a former enemy about peace.

Someday, an American President will be sitting down with a leader from Iraq, elected by the people, talking about how to keep the peace in a troubled part of the world, talking about how to spread liberty to corners of the world that need liberty, talking about how to make sure the example of a free society shines brightly for all. And our children and our grandchildren will be better off for it.

The stakes are high. The stakes are high in this campaign. We have a competing different—competing visions on Government, and we have a different view of the war on terror. It's not just to be reduced as a "nuisance." It is to be defeated by using all the might of the United States and spreading freedom as an alternative. And make no mistake about it, with the firm resolve and clear vision, we will prevail.

And I want to thank you for your help. God bless you. Thank you all.

NOTE: The President spoke at 12:46 p.m. at the Sanctuary on Camelback Mountain. In his remarks, he referred to Josephine Franks, wife of Representative Trent Franks; Mary Hayworth, wife of Representative J.D. Hayworth; Cheryl Flake, wife of Representative Jeff Flake; Mayor Ron Clarke of Paradise Valley, AZ; and Prime Minister Junichiro Koizumi of Japan. He also referred to the "Comprehensive Report of the Special Advisor to the DCI on Iraq's WMD," issued September 30.

Presidential Debate in Tempe, Arizona
October 13, 2004

Bob Schieffer. Good evening from Arizona State University in Tempe, Arizona. I'm Bob Schieffer of CBS News. I want to welcome you to the third and last of the 2004 debates between President George Bush and Senator John Kerry.

As Jim Lehrer told you before the first one, these debates are sponsored by the Commission on Presidential Debates. Tonight the topic will be domestic affairs, but the format will be the same as that first debate. I'll moderate our discussion under detailed rules agreed to by the candidates, but the questions and the areas to be covered were chosen by me. I have not told the candidates or anyone else what they are.

To refresh your memory on the rules, I will ask a question. The candidate is allowed 2 minutes to answer. His opponent then has a minute and a half to offer a rebuttal. At my discretion, I can extend the discussion by offering each candidate an additional 30 seconds. A green light will come on to signal the candidate has 30 seconds left; a yellow light signals 15 seconds left; a red light means 5 seconds left. There is also a buzzer if it is needed. The candidates may not question each other directly. There are no opening statements, but there will be 2-minute closing statements.

There is an audience here tonight, but they have agreed to remain silent, except for right now, when they join me in welcoming President George Bush and Senator John Kerry.

Gentlemen, welcome to you both. By coin toss, the first question goes to Senator Kerry.

Homeland Security

Senator, I want to set the stage for this discussion by asking the question that I think hangs over all of our politics today and is probably on the minds of many people watching this debate tonight, and that is: Will our children and grandchildren ever live in a world as safe and secure as the world in which we grew up?

Senator John F. Kerry. Well, first of all, Bob, thank you for moderating tonight. Thank you, Arizona State, for welcoming us. And thank you to the Presidential Commission for undertaking this enormous task. We're proud to be here. Mr. President, I'm glad to be here with you again to share similarities and differences with the American people.

Will we ever be safe and secure again? Yes, we absolutely must be. That's the goal. Now, how do we achieve it is the most critical component of it. I believe that this President, regrettably, rushed us into a war, made decisions about foreign policy, pushed alliances away, and as a result, America is now bearing this extraordinary burden where we are not as safe as we ought to be.

The measurement is not: Are we safer? The measurement is: Are we as safe as we ought to be? And there are a host of options that this President had available to him, like making sure that at all our ports in America, containers are inspected. Only 95 percent of them—95 percent come in today uninspected. That's not good enough. People who fly on airplanes today—the cargo hold is not X-rayed, but the baggage is. That's not good enough. Firehouses don't have enough firefighters in them. Police officers are being cut from the streets of America because the President decided to cut the COPS program.

So we can do a better job of homeland security. I can do a better job of waging a smarter, more effective war on terror and guarantee that we go after the terrorists. I will hunt them down, and we'll kill them. We'll capture them. We'll do what's ever necessary to be safe. But I pledge this to you, America: I will do it in the way that Franklin Roosevelt and Ronald Reagan and John Kennedy and others did, where we build the strongest alliances, where the world joins together, where we have the best intelligence, and where we are able, ultimately, to be more safe and secure.

Mr. Schieffer. Mr. President, you have 90 seconds.

President Bush. Bob, thank you very much. I want to thank Arizona State as well.

Yes, we can be safe and secure if we stay on the offense against the terrorists and if we spread freedom and liberty around the world. I have got a comprehensive strategy to not only chase down Al Qaida, wherever it exists—and we're making progress; three-quarters of Al Qaida leaders have been brought to justice—but to make sure that countries who harbor terrorists are held to account. As a result of securing ourselves and ridding the Taliban out of Afghanistan, the Afghan people had elections this weekend. And the first voter was a 19-year-old woman. Think about that. Freedom is on the march. We held to account a terrorist regime in Saddam Hussein.

In other words, in order to make sure we're secure, there must be a comprehensive plan. My opponent, just this weekend, talked about how terrorism could be reduced to a "nuisance," comparing it to prostitution and illegal gambling. I think that attitude and that point of view is dangerous. I don't think you can secure America for the long run if you don't have a comprehensive view as to how to defeat these people.

At home, we'll do everything we can to protect the homeland. I signed the homeland security bill to better align our assets and resources. My opponent voted against it. We're doing everything we can to protect our borders and ports. But absolutely, we can be secure in the long run. It just takes good, strong leadership.

Mr. Schieffer. Anything to add, Senator Kerry?

Senator Kerry. Yes. When the President had an opportunity to capture or kill Usama bin Laden, he took his focus off of him, outsourced the job to Afghan warlords, and Usama bin Laden escaped. Six months after he said, "Usama bin Laden must be caught, dead or alive," this President was asked, "Where is Usama bin Laden?" He said,

"I don't know. I don't really think about him very much. I'm not that concerned." We need a President who stays deadly focused on the real war on terror.

Mr. Schieffer. Mr. President.

President Bush. Gosh, I don't think I ever said I'm not worried about Usama bin Laden. That's kind of one of those exaggerations. Of course, we're worried about Usama bin Laden. We're on the hunt after Usama bin Laden. We're using every asset at our disposal to get Usama bin Laden.

My opponent said this war is a matter of intelligence and law enforcement. No, this is a—war is a matter of using every asset at our disposal to keep the American people protected.

Flu Vaccine Shortage/Health Care

Mr. Schieffer. New question, Mr. President, to you. We're talking about protecting ourselves from the unexpected, but the flu season is suddenly upon us. Flu kills thousands of people every year. Suddenly we find ourselves with a severe shortage of flu vaccine. How did that happen?

President Bush. Bob, we relied upon a company out of England to provide about half of the flu vaccines for the United States citizen, and it turned out that the vaccine they were producing was contaminated. And so we took the right action and didn't allow contaminated medicine into our country. We're working with Canada to, hopefully—that they'll produce a—help us realize the vaccine necessary to make sure our citizens have got flu vaccinations during this upcoming season.

My call to our fellow Americans is, if you're healthy, if you're younger, don't get a flu shot this year. Help us prioritize those who need to get the flu shot, the elderly and the young. The CDC, responsible for health in the United States, is setting those priorities and is allocating the flu vaccine accordingly. I haven't gotten a flu shot, and I don't intend to, because I want to make sure that those who are most vulnerable get treated.

We have a problem with litigation in the United States of America. Vaccine manufacturers are worried about getting sued, and so, therefore, they have backed off from providing this kind of vaccine. One of the reasons I'm such a strong believer in legal reform is so that people aren't afraid of producing a product that is necessary for the health of our citizens and then end up getting sued in a court of law.

But the best thing we can do now, Bob, given the circumstances with the company in England, is for those of us who are younger and healthy, don't get a flu shot.

Mr. Schieffer. Senator Kerry.

Senator Kerry. This really underscores the problem with the American health care system. It's not working for the American family, and it's gotten worse under President Bush over the course of the last years. Five million Americans have lost their health insurance in this country. You got about a million right here in Arizona—just shy, 950,000—who have no health insurance at all. Eighty-two thousand Arizonians lost their health insurance under President Bush's watch. Two hundred and twenty-three thousand kids in Arizona have no health insurance at all. All across our country—go to Ohio, 1.4 million Ohioans have no health insurance; 114,000 of them lost it under President Bush; Wisconsin, 82,000 Wisconsinites lost it under President Bush.

This President has turned his back on the wellness of America, and there is no system. In fact, it's starting to fall apart, not because of lawsuits—though they are a problem, and John Edwards and I are committed to fixing them—but because of the larger issue that we don't cover Americans. Children across our country don't have health care. We're the richest country on the face of the planet, the only industrialized nation in the world not to do it. I have a plan to cover all Americans. We're going to make it affordable and accessible. We're going to let everybody buy into the same health care plan the Senators and Congressmen give themselves.

Mr. Schieffer. Mr. President, would you like to add something?

President Bush. I would, thank you. I want to remind people listening tonight that a plan is not a litany of complaints, and a plan is not to lay out programs that you can't pay for. He just said he wants everybody to be able to buy into the same plan that Senators and Congressman get. That costs the Government $7,700 per family. If every family in America signed up like the Senator suggested, it would cost us $5 trillion over 10 years. It's an empty promise. It's called bait and switch.

Mr. Schieffer. Time is up.

President Bush. Thank you.

Senator Kerry. Actually, it's not an empty promise. It's really interesting because the President used that very plan as a reason for seniors to accept his prescription drug plan. He said, "If it's good enough for the Congressmen and Senators to have choice, seniors ought to have choice."

What we do is we have choice. I choose Blue Cross/Blue Shield. Other Senators, other Congressman choose other programs. But the fact is we're going to help Americans be able to buy into it. Those that can afford it are going to buy in themselves. We're not giving this away for nothing.

Paying for New Federal Spending/Taxes

Mr. Schieffer. All right, Senator Kerry, a new question. Let's talk about economic security. You pledged during the last debate that you would not raise taxes on those making less than $200,000 a year. But the price of everything is going up, and we all know it. Health care costs, as you all are talking about, is skyrocketing, the cost of the war. My question is, how can you or any President, whoever is elected next time, keep that pledge without running this country deeper into debt and passing on more of the bills that we're running up to our children?

Senator Kerry. I'll tell you exactly how I can do it: by reinstating what President Bush took away, which is called pay as you go. During the 1990s, we had pay-as-you-go rules. If you were going to pass something in the Congress, you had to show where you were going to pay for it and how.

President Bush has taken—he's the only President in history to do this. He's also the only President since—in 72 years to lose jobs, 1.6 million jobs lost. He's the only President to have incomes of families go down for the last 3 years, the only President to see exports go down, the only President to see the lowest level of business investment in our country as it is today.

Now, I'm going to reverse that. I'm going to change that. We're going to restore the fiscal discipline we had in the 1990s. Every plan that I have laid out, my health care plan, my plan for education, my plan for kids to be able to get better college loans, I've shown exactly how I'm going to pay for those. And we start—we don't do it exclusively, but we start by rolling back George Bush's unaffordable tax cut for the wealthiest people, people earning more than $200,000 a year, and we pass, hopefully, the McCain/Kerry commission, which identified some $60 billion that we can get. We shut the loophole which has American workers actually subsidizing the loss of their own job. They just passed an expansion of that loophole in the last few days, $43 billion of giveaways, including favors to the oil and gas industry and to people importing ceiling fans from China.

I'm going to stand up and fight for the American worker, and I'm going to do it in a way that's fiscally sound. I show how I pay for the health care, how we pay for the education. I have a manufacturing jobs credit. We pay for it by shutting that loophole overseas. We raise the student loans. I pay for it by changing the relationship with the banks. This President has never once vetoed one bill, the first President in 100 years not to do that.

Mr. Schieffer. Mr. President.

President Bush. Well, his rhetoric doesn't match his record. He's been a Senator for 20 years. He voted to increase taxes 98 times. When they tried to reduce taxes, he voted against that 127 times. He talks about being a fiscal conservative or fiscally sound, but he voted over—he voted 277 times to waive the budget caps, which would have cost the taxpayers $4.2 trillion. He talks about pay-go—I'll tell you what pay-go means when you're a Senator from Massachusetts, when you're a colleague of Ted Kennedy: Pay-go means you pay, and he goes ahead and spends.

He's proposed $2.2 trillion of new spending, and yet the so-called tax on the rich, which is also a tax on many small-business owners in America, raises 600 million by our account—billion—800 billion by his account. There is a tax gap. And guess who usually ends up filling the tax gap? The middle class.

I proposed a detailed budget, Bob. I sent up my budget man to the Congress, and he says, "Here's how we're going to reduce the deficit in half by 5 years." It requires pro-growth policies that grow our economy and fiscal sanity in the Halls of Congress.

Jobs/Education

Mr. Schieffer. Let's go to a new question, Mr. President, 2 minutes. And let's continue on jobs. You know, there are all kind of statistics out there, but I want to bring it down to an individual. Mr. President, what do you say to someone in this country who has lost his job to someone overseas who is being paid a fraction of what that job paid here in the United States?

President Bush. I say, Bob, "I've got policies to continue to grow our economy and create the jobs of the 21st century, and here's some help for you to go get an education. Here's some help for you to go to a community college. We've expanded trade adjustment assistance. We want to help pay for you to gain the skills necessary to fill the jobs of the 21st century."

You know, there's a lot of talk about how to keep the economy growing, and we talk about fiscal matters. But perhaps the best way to keep jobs here in America and to keep this economy growing is to make sure our education system works.

I went to Washington to solve problems. And I saw a problem in the public education system in America. They were just shuffling too many kids through the system, year after year, grade after grade, without learning the basics. And so we said, "Let's raise the standards. We're spending more money, but let's raise the standards and measure early and solve problems now, before it's too late."

You know, education is how to help the person who has lost a job. Education is how to make sure this—we've got a workforce that's productive and competitive. You got—4 more years, I've got more to do to continue to raise standards, to continue to reward teachers and school districts that are working, to emphasize math and science in the classrooms, to continue to expand Pell grants, to make sure that people have an opportunity to start their career with a college diploma.

And so to the person you talked to, I say, "Here's some help. Here's some trade adjustment assistance money for you to go to a community college in your neighborhood, a community college which is providing the skills necessary to fill the jobs of the 21st century." And that's what we'd say to that person.

Mr. Schieffer. Senator Kerry.

Senator Kerry. I want you to notice how the President switched away from jobs and started talking about education principally. Let me come back in one moment to that, but I want to speak for a second, if I can, to what the President said about fiscal responsibility. Being lectured by the President on fiscal responsibility is a little bit like Tony Soprano talking to me about law and order in this country. [*Laughter*]

This President has taken a $5.6 trillion surplus and turned it into deficits as far as the eye can see. Health care costs for the average American have gone up 64 percent. Tuitions have gone up 35 percent, gasoline prices up 30 percent. Medicare premiums went up 17 percent a few days ago. Prescription drugs are up 12 percent a year. But guess what, America? The wages of Americans have gone down. The jobs that are being created in Arizona right now are paying about $13,700 less than the jobs that we're losing, and the President just walks on by this problem.

The fact is that he's cut job training money. A billion dollars was cut. They only added a little bit back this year because it's an election year. They've cut the Pell grants and the Perkins loans to help kids be able to go to college. They've cut the training money. They've wound up not even extending unemployment benefits and not even extending health care to those people who are unemployed. I'm going to do those things because that's what right in America: Help workers to transition in every respect.

Outsourcing Jobs

Mr. Schieffer. New question to you, Senator Kerry, 2 minutes, and it's still on jobs. You know, many experts say that a President really doesn't have much control over jobs. For example, if someone invents a machine that does the work of five people, that's progress. That's not the President's fault. So I ask you, is it fair to blame the administration entirely for this loss of jobs?

Senator Kerry. I don't blame them entirely for it. I blame the President for the things the President could do that has an impact on it. Outsourcing is going to happen. I've acknowledged that in union halls across the country. I've had shop stewards stand up and say, "Will you promise me you're going to stop all this outsourcing?" And I've looked them in the eye and I've said, "No, I can't do that."

What I can promise you is that I will make the playing field as fair as possible, that I will, for instance, make certain that with respect to the tax system, that you as a worker in America are not subsidizing the loss of your job. Today, if you're an American business, you actually get a benefit for going overseas. You get to defer your taxes. So if you're looking at a competitive world, you say to yourself, "Hey, I do better overseas than I do here in America." That's not smart. I don't want American workers subsidizing the loss of their own job. And when I'm President, we're going to shut that loophole in a nanosecond, and we're going to use that money to lower corporate tax rates in America for all corporations 5 percent. And we're going to have a manufacturing jobs credit and a job hiring credit so we actually help people be able to hire here.

The second thing that we can do is provide a fair trade playing field. This President didn't stand up for Boeing when Airbus was violating international rules with subsidies. He discovered Boeing during the course of this campaign after I've been talking about it for months. The fact is that the President had an opportunity to stand up and take on China for currency manipulation. There are companies that wanted to petition the administration. They were told, "Don't even bother. We're not going to listen to it."

The fact is that there have been markets shut to us that we haven't stood up and fought for. I'm going to fight for a fair trade playing field for the American worker. And I will fight for the American worker just as hard as I fight for my own job. That's what the American worker wants. And if we do that, we can have an impact. Plus, we need fiscal discipline. Restore fiscal discipline, we'll do a lot better.

Mr. Schieffer. Mr. President.

President Bush. Whoo! Let me start with the Pell grants. In his last litany of misstatements, he said we cut Pell grants. We've increased Pell grants by a million students. That's a fact.

Here he talks to the workers; let me talk to the workers. You got more money in your pocket as a result of the tax relief we passed and he opposed. If you have a child, you got a $1,000 child credit. That's money in your pocket. If you're married, we reduced the marriage penalty. The code ought to encourage marriage, not discourage marriage. We created a 10-percent bracket to help lower income Americans. A family of four making 40,000 received about $1,700 in tax relief. It's your money. The way my opponent talks, he said we're going to spend the Government's money. No, we're spending your money. And when you have more money in your pocket, you're able to better afford things you want. I believe the role of Government is to stand side by side with our citizens to help them realize their dreams, not tell citizens how to live their lives.

My opponent talks about fiscal sanity. His record in the United States Senate does not match his rhetoric. He voted to increase taxes 98 times and to bust the budget 277 times.

Mr. Schieffer. Senator Kerry.

Senator Kerry. Bob, anybody can play with these votes; everybody knows that. I have supported or voted for tax cuts over 600 times. I broke with my party in order to balance the budget, and Ronald Reagan signed into law the tax cut that we voted for. I voted for IRA tax cuts. I voted for small-business tax cuts.

But you know why the Pell grants have gone up in their numbers? Because more people qualified for them, because they don't have money. But they're not getting the $5,100 the President promised them. They're getting less money. There are more people who qualify. That's not what we want.

President Bush. Senator, no one is playing with your votes. You voted to increase taxes 98 times. When they voted—when they proposed reducing taxes, you voted against it 126 times. You voted to violate the budget caps 277 times. You know, there's a mainstream in American politics. You sit right on the far left bank. As a matter of fact, your record is such that Ted Kennedy, your colleague, is the conservative Senator from Massachusetts.

Same-Sex Marriage

Mr. Schieffer. Mr. President, let's get back to economic issues. But let's shift to some other questions here. Both of you are opposed to gay marriage. But to understand how you have come to that conclusion, I want to ask you a more basic question. Do you believe homosexuality is a choice?

President Bush. You know, Bob, I don't know. I just don't know. I do know that we have a choice to make in America, and that is to treat people with tolerance and respect and dignity. It's important that we do that. I also know, in a free society, people, consenting adults, can live the way they want to live. And that's to be honored.

But as we respect someone's rights and as we profess tolerance, we shouldn't change—or have to change our basic views on the sanctity of marriage. I believe in the sanctity of marriage. I think it's very important that we protect marriage as an institution between a man and a woman.

I proposed a constitutional amendment. The reason I did so was because I was worried that activist judges are actually defining the definition of marriage. And the surest way to protect marriage between a man and woman is to amend the Constitution. It has also the benefit of allowing citizens to participate in the process. After all, when you amend the Constitution, State legislatures must participate in the ratification of the Constitution.

I'm deeply concerned that judges are making those decisions and not the citizenry of the United States. You know, Congress passed a law called DOMA, the Defense of Marriage Act. My opponent was against it. It basically protected States from the action of one State to another. It also defined marriage as between a man and a woman. But I'm concerned that that will get overturned, and if it gets overturned,

then we'll end up with marriage being defined by courts. And I don't think that's in our Nation's interest.

Mr. Schieffer. Senator Kerry.

Senator Kerry. We're all God's children, Bob, and I think if you were to talk to Dick Cheney's daughter, who is a lesbian, she would tell you that she's being who she was. She's being who she was born as. I think if you talk to anybody, it's not choice. I've met people who've struggled with this for years, people who were in a marriage because they were living a sort of convention, and they struggled with it. And I've met wives who are supportive of their husbands, or vice versa, when they finally sort of broke out and allowed themselves to live who they were, who they felt God had made them. I think we have to respect that.

The President and I share the belief that marriage is between a man and a woman. I believe that. I believe marriage is between a man and a woman. But I also believe that because we are the United States of America, we're a country with a great, unbelievable Constitution, with rights that we afford people, that you can't discriminate in the workplace. You can't discriminate in the rights that you afford people. You can't disallow someone the right to visit their partner in a hospital. You have to allow people to transfer property, which is why I'm for partnership rights and so forth.

Now, with respect to DOMA and the marriage laws, the States have always been able to manage those laws, and they're proving today, every State, that they can manage them adequately.

Abortion

Mr. Schieffer. Senator Kerry, a new question for you. The New York Times reports that some Catholic archbishops are telling their church members that it would be a sin to vote for a candidate like you because you support a woman's right to choose an abortion and unlimited stem cell research. What is your reaction to that?

Senator Kerry. I respect their views. I completely respect their views. I am a Catholic, and I grew up learning how to respect those views. But I disagree with them, as do many. I believe that I can't legislate or transfer to another American citizen my article of faith. What is an article of faith for me is not something that I can legislate on somebody who doesn't share that article of faith. I believe that choice is a woman's choice. It's between a woman, God, and her doctor, and that's why I support that.

Now, I will not allow somebody to come in and change *Roe* v. *Wade*. The President has never said whether or not he would do that, but we know from the people he's tried to appoint to the court, he wants to. I will not. I will defend the right of *Roe* v. *Wade*.

Now, with respect to religion, you know, as I said, I grew up a Catholic. I was an altar boy. I know that throughout my life, this has made a difference to me. And as President Kennedy said when he ran for President, he said, "I'm not running to be a Catholic President. I'm running to be a President who happens to be Catholic."

Now, my faith affects everything that I do and choose. There's a great passage of the Bible that says, "What does it mean, my brother, to say you have faith, if there are no deeds? Faith without works is dead." And I think that everything you do in public life has to be guided by your faith, affected by your faith, but without transferring it in any official way to other people. That's why I fight against poverty. That's why I fight to clean up the environment and protect this Earth. That's why I fight for equality and justice. All of those things come out of that fundamental teaching and belief of faith.

But I know this, that President Kennedy, in his Inaugural Address, told all of us that, "Here on Earth, God's work must truly be our own." And that's what we have to—so I think that's the test of public service.

Mr. Schieffer. Mr. President.

President Bush. I think it's important to promote a culture of life. I think a hospitable society is a society where every being counts and every person matters. I believe the ideal world is one in which every child is protected in law and welcomed to life. I understand there's great differences on this issue of abortion, but I believe reasonable people can come together and put good law in place that will help reduce the number of abortions.

Take, for example, the ban on partial-birth abortion. It's a brutal practice. People from both political parties came together in the Halls of Congress and voted overwhelmingly to ban that practice. It made a lot of sense. My opponent, in that he's out of the mainstream, voted against that law.

What I'm saying is, is that as we promote life and promote a culture of life, surely there are ways we can work together to reduce the number of abortions: Continue to promote adoption laws—that's a great alternative to abortion; continue to fund and promote maternity group homes. I will continue to promote abstinence programs. At the last debate, my opponent said his wife was involved with those programs. That's great, and I appreciate that very much. All of us ought to be involved with programs that provide a viable alternative to abortion.

Health Care Costs

Mr. Schieffer. Mr. President, let's have a new question. It goes to you, and let's get back to economic issues. Health insurance costs have risen over 36 percent over the last 4 years, according to the Washington Post. We're paying more; we're getting less. I would like to ask you, who bears responsibility for this? Is it the Government? Is it the insurance companies? Is it the lawyers? Is it the doctors? Is it the administration?

President Bush. Gosh, I sure hope it's not the administration. [*Laughter*] No, there is a—look, there's a systemic problem. Health care costs are on the rise because the consumers are not involved in the decisionmaking process. Most health care costs are covered by third parties, and therefore, the actual user of health care is not the purchaser of health care. And there's no market forces involved with health care. It's one of the reasons I'm a strong believer in what they call health savings accounts. These are accounts that allow somebody to buy a low-premium, high-deductible catastrophic plan and couple it with tax-free savings. Businesses can contribute; employees can contribute on a contractual basis. But this is a way to make sure people are actually involved with the decisionmaking process on health care.

Secondly, I do believe the lawsuits—I don't believe, I know—that the lawsuits are causing health care costs to rise in America. That's why I'm such a strong believer in medical liability reform. At the last debate, my opponent said, "Well, they only—these lawsuits only cause costs to go up by one percent." Well, he didn't include the defensive practice of medicine that costs the Federal Government some $28 billion a year and costs our society between 60 and 100 billion dollars a year.

Thirdly, one of the reasons why there's still high costs in medicine is because this is the—they don't use information technology. It's like if you looked at the—it's the equivalent of the buggy-and-horse days compared to other industries here in America. And so we've got to introduce high technology into health care. We're beginning to do it. We're changing the language. We want there to be electronic medical records to cut down on error as well as to reduce costs. People tell me that when the health care field is fully integrated with information technology, it will wring some 20 percent of the costs out of the system.

And finally, moving generic drugs to the market quicker. So, those are four ways to help control the costs in health care.

Mr. Schieffer. Senator Kerry.

Senator Kerry. The reason health care costs are getting higher—one of the principal reasons is that this administration has stood in the way of commonsense efforts that would have reduced the costs. Let me give you a prime example. In the Senate, we passed the right of Americans to import drugs from Canada. But the President and his friends took it out in the House, and now you don't have that right. The President blocked you from the right to have less expensive drugs from Canada.

We also wanted Medicare to be able to negotiate bulk purchasing. The VA does that. The VA provides lower cost drugs to our veterans. We could have done that in Medicare. Medicare is paid for by the American taxpayer. Medicare belongs to you. Medicare is for seniors who are—many of them—on fixed income, to lift them out of poverty. But rather than help you, the taxpayer, have lower cost, rather than help seniors have less expensive drugs, the President made it illegal—illegal—for Medicare to actually go out and bargain for lower prices. Result: $139 billion windfall profit to the drug companies coming out of your pockets. That's a large part of your 17-percent increase in Medicare premiums. When I'm President, I'm sending that back to Congress, and we're going to get a real prescription drug benefit.

Now, we also have people sicker because they don't have health insurance. So whether it's diabetes or cancer, they come to the hospitals later, and it costs America more. We've got to have health care for all Americans.

Mr. Schieffer. Go ahead, Mr. President.

President Bush. I think it's important, since he talked about the Medicare plan—he's been in the United States Senate for 20 years. He has no record on reforming of health care, no record at all. He introduced some 300 bills, and he's passed 5— no record of leadership.

I came to Washington to solve problems. I was deeply concerned about seniors having to choose between prescription drugs and food, and so I led. And in 2006, our seniors will get a prescription drug coverage in Medicare.

Mr. Schieffer. Senator Kerry, 30 seconds.

Senator Kerry. Once again, the President is misleading America. I've actually passed 56 individual bills that I've personally written. And in addition to that, they're not always under my name; there is amendments on certain bills.

But more importantly, with respect to the question of "no record," I helped write—I did write—I was one of the original authors of the early childhood health care and the expansion of health care that we did in the middle of the 1990s. And I'm very proud of that. So the President's wrong.

Senator's Health Care Plan

Mr. Schieffer. Let me direct the next question to you, Senator Kerry, and again, let's stay on health care. You have, as you have proposed and as the President has commented on tonight, proposed a massive plan to extend health care coverage to children. You're also talking about the Government picking up a big part of the catastrophic bills that people get at the hospital. And you have said that you can pay for this by rolling back the President's tax cut on the upper two percent.

Senator Kerry. That's correct.

Mr. Schieffer. You heard the President say earlier tonight that it's going to cost a whole lot more money than that. I just ask you, where are you going to get the money?

Senator Kerry. Well, two leading national news networks have both said the President's characterization of my health care plan is incorrect. One called it fiction. The other called it untrue. The fact is that my health care plan, America, is very simple. It gives you the choice. I don't force you to do anything. It's not a Government plan. The Government doesn't require you to do anything. You choose your doctor. You choose your plan. If you don't want to take the offer of the plan that I want to put forward, you don't have to. You can keep what you have today, keep a high deductible, keep high premiums, keep a high co-pay, keep low benefits. But I got a better plan, and I don't think a lot of people are going to want to keep what they have today.

Here's what I do. We take over Medicaid children from the States so that every child in America is covered. And in exchange, if the States want to—they're not forced to; they can choose to—they cover individuals up to 300 percent of poverty. It's their choice. I think they'll choose it, because it's a net plus of $5 billion to them.

We allow you—if you choose to; you don't have to—but we give you broader competition to allow you to buy into the same health care plan that Senators and Congressmen give themselves. If it's good enough for us, it's good enough for every American. I believe that your health care is just as important as any politician in Washington, DC. If you want to buy into it, you can. We give you broader competition. That helps lower prices.

In addition to that, we're going to allow people 55 to 64 to buy into Medicare early. And most importantly, we give small business a 50-percent tax credit so that after we lower the cost of health care, they also get, whether they're self-employed or a small business, a lower cost to be able to cover their employees.

Now, what happens is, when you begin to get people covered like that—for instance, in diabetes, if you diagnose diabetes early, you could save $50 billion in the health care system of America by avoiding surgery and dialysis. It works, and I'm going to offer it to America.

Mr. Schieffer. Mr. President.

President Bush. In all due respect, I'm not so sure it's credible to quote leading news organizations about—well, never mind. Anyway—[*laughter*]—let me quote the Lewin report. The Lewin report is a group of folks who are not politically affiliated. They analyzed the Senator's plan. It costs $1.2 trillion. The Lewin report accurately noted that there are going to be 20 million people—over 20 million people added to Government-controlled health care. It will be the largest increase in Government health care ever.

If you raise the Medicaid to 300 percent, it provides an incentive for small businesses not to provide private insurance to their employees. Why should they insure somebody when the Government is going to insure for them? It's estimated that 8 million people will go from private insurance to Government insurance.

We have a fundamental difference of opinion. I think Government-run health will lead to poor quality health, will lead to rationing, will lead to less choice. Once a health care program ends up in a line item in the Federal Government budget, it leads to more controls. And just look at other countries that have tried to have federally controlled health care. They have poor quality health care. Our health care system is the envy of the world because we believe in making sure that the decisions are made by doctors and patients, not by officials in the Nation's Capital.

Mr. Schieffer. Senator.

Senator Kerry. The President just said that Government-run health care results in poor quality. Now, maybe that explains why he hasn't fully funded the VA, and the VA hospital is having trouble, and veterans are complaining. Maybe that explains why Medicare patients are complaining about being pushed off of Medicare—he doesn't adequately fund it.

But let me just say to America, I am not proposing a Government-run program. That's not what I have. I have Blue Cross/ Blue Shield. Senators and Congressmen have a wide choice. Americans ought to have it too.

Mr. Schieffer. Mr. President.

President Bush. You talk about the VA. We've increased VA funding by 22 billion in the 4 years since I've been President. That's twice the amount that my predecessor increased VA funding. Of course, we're meeting our obligation to our veterans, and the veterans know that. We're expanding veterans' health care throughout the country. We're aligning facilities where the veterans live now. Veterans are getting very good health care under my administration, and they will continue to do so during the next 4 years.

Social Security

Mr. Schieffer. Mr. President, the next question is to you. We all know that Social Security is running out of money, and it has to be fixed. You have proposed to fix it by letting people put some of the money collected to pay benefits into private savings accounts. But the critics are saying that's going to mean finding a trillion dollars over the next 10 years to continue paying benefits as those accounts are being set up. So where do you get the money? Are you going to have to increase the deficit by that much over 10 years?

President Bush. Bob, first let me make sure that every senior listening today understands that when we're talking about reforming Social Security, that they'll still get their checks. I remember the 2000 campaign; people said, "If George W. gets elected, your check will be taken away." Well, people got their checks, and they will continue to get their checks.

There is a problem for our youngsters, a real problem, and if we don't act today, the problem will be valued in the trillions. And so I think we need to think differently. We'll honor our commitment to our seniors, but for young—for our children and our grandchildren, we need to have a different strategy. In recognizing that, I called together a group of our fellow citizens to study the issue. It was a committee chaired by the late Senator Daniel Patrick Moynihan of New York, a Democrat. And they came up with a variety of ideas for people to look at.

I believe that younger workers ought to be allowed to take some of their own money and put it in a personal savings account, because I understand that they need to get better rates of return than the rates of return being given in the current Social Security trust. And the compounding rate of interest effect will make it more likely that the Social Security system is solvent for our children and our grandchildren.

I will work with Republicans and Democrats. This will be a vital issue in my second term. It is an issue that I'm willing to take on. And so I'll bring Republicans and Democrats together, and we're of course going to have to consider the costs. But I want to warn my fellow citizens the cost of doing nothing, the cost of saying the current system is okay, far exceeds the cost of trying to make sure we save the system for our children.

Mr. Schieffer. Senator Kerry.

Senator Kerry. You just heard the President say that young people ought to be able to take money out of Social Security and put it in their own accounts. Now, my fellow Americans, that's an invitation to disaster. The CBO said very clearly that if you were to adopt the President's plan, there will be a $2 trillion hole in Social Security, because today's workers pay into the system for today's retirees. And the CBO said—that's the Congressional Budget Office; it's bipartisan—they said that there would have to be a cut in benefits of 25 to 40 percent.

Now, the President has never explained to America—ever; hasn't done it tonight— where does the transitional money, that $2 trillion, come from? He's already got $3 trillion, according to the Washington Post, of expenses that he's put on the line from his convention and the promises of this campaign, none of which are paid for— not one of them are paid for.

The fact is that the President is driving the largest deficits in American history. He's broken the pay-as-you-go rules. I have a record of fighting for fiscal responsibility. In 1985, I was one of the first Democrats— broke with my party—we balanced the budget in the nineties. We paid down the debt for 2 years. And that's what we're going to do. We're going to protect Social Security. I will not privatize it. I will not cut the benefits. And we're going to be fiscally responsible, and we will take care of Social Security.

Mr. Schieffer. Let me just stay on Social Security with a new question for Senator Kerry, because Senator Kerry, you have just said you will not cut benefits. Alan Greenspan, the Chairman of the Federal Reserve, says there's no way that Social Security can pay retirees what we have promised them unless we recalibrate. What he's suggesting, we're going to have to cut benefits or we're going to have to raise retirement age; we may have to take some other reform. But if you've just said you've promised no changes, does that mean you're just going to leave this as a problem, another problem, for our children to solve?

Senator Kerry. Not at all. Absolutely not, Bob. This is the same thing we heard— I remember I appeared on "Meet the Press" with Tim Russert in 1990-something—we heard the same thing. We fixed it. In fact, we put together a $5.6 trillion surplus in the nineties that was for the purpose of saving Social Security. If you take the tax cut that the President of the United States has given—President Bush gave to Americans in the top 1 percent of America, just that tax cut that went to the top 1 percent of America would have saved Social Security until the year 2075. The President decided to give it to the wealthiest Americans in a tax cut.

Now, Alan Greenspan, who I think has done a terrific job in monetary policy, supports the President's tax cut. I don't. I support it for the middle class, not that part of it that goes to people earning more than $200,000 a year. And when I roll it back and we invest in the things that I've talked about to move our economy, we're going to grow sufficiently that we begin to cut the deficit in half, and we get back to where we were at the end of the 1990s when we balanced the budget and paid down the debt of this country. Now, we can do that.

Now, if later on, after a period of time, we find that Social Security is in trouble, then we'll pull together the top experts of the country. We'll do exactly what we did in the 1990s, and we'll make whatever adjustment is necessary. But the first and most important thing is to start creating jobs in America. The jobs the President is creating pay $9,000 less than the jobs that we're losing. And this is the first President in 72 years to preside over an economy in America that has lost jobs—1.6 million jobs. Eleven other Presidents—six Democrats and five Republicans—had wars, had recessions, had great difficulties. None of them lost jobs the way this President has.

I have a plan to put America back to work. And if we're fiscally responsible and put America back to work, we're going to fix Social Security.

Mr. Schieffer. Mr. President.

President Bush. He forgot to tell you he voted to tax Social Security benefits more than one time. I didn't hear any plan to fix Social Security. I heard more of the same. He talks about middle-class tax cuts; that's exactly where the tax cuts went. Most of the tax cuts went to low- and middle-income Americans. And now the Tax Code is more fair; 20 percent of the upper income people pay about 80 percent of the taxes in America today because of how we structured the tax cuts. People listening out there know the benefits of the tax cuts

we passed. If you have a child, you got tax relief. If you're married, you got tax relief. If you pay any tax at all, you got tax relief, all of which was opposed by my opponent. And the tax relief was important to spur consumption and investment to get us out of this recession.

People need to remember, 6 months prior to my arrival, the stock market started to go down, and it was one of the largest declines in our history. And then we had a recession, and we got attacked, which cost us one million jobs. But we acted. I led the Congress. We passed tax relief. And now this economy is growing. We added 1.9 million new jobs over the last 13 months.

Sure, there's more work to do. But the way to make sure our economy grows is not to raise taxes on small-business owners. It's not to increase the scope of the Federal Government. It's to make sure we have fiscal sanity and keep taxes low.

Immigration/Border Security

Mr. Schieffer. Let's go to a new question, Mr. President. I got more e-mail this week on this question than any other question, and it is about immigration. I'm told that at least 8,000 people cross our borders illegally every day. Some people believe this is a security issue, as you know. Some believe it's an economic issue. Some see it as a human rights issue. How do you see it, and what do we need to do about it?

President Bush. I see it as a serious problem. I see it as a security issue; I see it as an economic issue; and I see it as a human rights issue. We're increasing the border security of the United States. We've got 1,000 more Border Patrol agents on the southern border. We're using new equipment. We're using unmanned vehicles to spot people coming across, and we'll continue to do so over the next 4 years. This is a subject I'm very familiar with. After all, I was a border Governor for a while.

Many people are coming to this country for economic reasons. They're coming here to work. If you can make 50 cents in the heart of Mexico, for example, or make $5 here in America—5.15—you're going to come here if you're worth your salt, if you want to put food on the table for your families. And that's what's happening.

And so, in order to take pressure off the border, in order to make the borders more secure, I believe there ought to be a temporary-worker card that allows a willing worker and a willing employer to mate up—so long as there's not an American willing to do the job—to join up in order to be able to fulfill the employer's needs. That has the benefit of making sure our employers aren't breaking the law as they try to fill their workforce needs. It makes sure that the people coming across the border are humanely treated, that they're not kept in the shadows of our society, that they're able to go back and forth to see their families. See, the card will have a period of time attached to it.

It also means it takes pressure off the border. If somebody is coming here to work with a card, it means they're not going to have to sneak across the border. It means our Border Patrol will be more likely to be able to focus on doing their job.

Now, it's very important for our citizens to also know that I don't believe we ought to have amnesty. I don't think we ought to reward illegal behavior. There are plenty of people standing in line to become a citizen, and we ought not to crowd these people ahead of them in line. If they want to become a citizen, they can stand in line too. And here's where my opponent and I differ. In September 2003, he supported amnesty for illegal aliens.

Mr. Schieffer. Time's up.

Senator.

Senator Kerry. Let me just answer one part of that last question quickly, and then I'll come to immigration. The American middle-class family isn't making it right now, Bob, and what the President said about the tax cuts have been wiped out by the increase in health care, the increase in gasoline, the increase in tuitions, the increase in prescription drugs. The fact is the take-home pay of a typical American family as a share of national income is lower than it's been since 1929. And the take-home pay of the richest 1 percent of Americans is the highest it's been since 1928. Under President Bush, the middle class has seen their tax burden go up, and the wealthiest tax burden has gone down. Now, that's wrong.

Now, with respect to immigration reform, the President broke his promise on immigration reform. He said he would reform it. Four years later, he's now promising another plan. Here's what I'll do. Number one, the borders are more leaking today than they were before 9/11. The fact is we haven't done what we need to do to toughen up our borders, and I will.

Secondly, we need a guest-worker program, but if it's all we have, it's not going to solve the problem. The second thing we need is to crack down on illegal hiring. It's against the law in the United States to hire people illegally, and we ought to be enforcing that law properly.

And thirdly, we need an earned legalization program for people who've been here for a long time, stayed out of trouble, got a job, paid their taxes, and their kids are American. We've got to start moving them toward full citizenship, out of the shadows.

Mr. Schieffer. Do you want to respond, Mr. President?

President Bush. Well, to say that the borders are not as protected as they were prior to September the 11th shows he doesn't know the borders. They're much better protected today than they were when I was the Governor of Texas. We've got much more manpower, much more equipment there. He just doesn't understand how the borders work, evidently, to say that. That is an outrageous claim. And we'll continue to protect our borders. We'll continue to increase manpower and equipment.

Mr. Schieffer. Senator.

Senator Kerry. Four thousand people a day are coming across the border. The fact is that we now have people from the Middle East—allegedly—coming across the border. And we're not doing what we ought to do in terms of the technology. We have iris identification technology. We have thumbprint, fingerprint technology today. We can know who the people are, that they're really the people they say they are, when they cross the border. We could speed it up. There are huge delays. The fact is, our borders are not as secure as they ought to be, and I'll make them secure.

Minimum Wage/Education/Jobs

Mr. Schieffer. Next question to you, Senator Kerry. The gap between rich and poor is growing wider. More people are dropping into poverty. Yet the minimum wage has been stuck at, what, $5.15 an hour now for about 7 years. Is it time to raise it?

Senator Kerry. Well, I'm glad you raised that question. It's long-overdue time to raise the minimum wage. And America, this is one of those issues that separates the President and myself. We have fought to try to raise the minimum wage in the last years. But the Republican leadership of the House and Senate won't even let us have a vote on it. We're not allowed to vote on it. They don't want to raise the minimum wage.

The minimum wage is the lowest minimum wage value it has been in our Nation in 50 years. If we raise the minimum wage, which I will do over several years to $7 an hour, 9.2 million women who are trying to raise their families would earn another $3,800 a year. The President has denied 9.2 million women $3,800 a year, but he doesn't hesitate to fight for $136,000 to a millionaire. One percent of America got $89 billion last year in a tax cut. But people working hard, playing by the rules, trying

to take care of their kids—family values that we're supposed to value so much in America—I'm tired of politicians who talk about family values and don't value families. What we need to do is raise the minimum wage.

We also need to hold onto equal pay. Women work for 76 cents on the dollar for the same work that men do. That's not right in America. And we have an initiative that we were working on to raise women's pay. They've cut it off. They've stopped it. They don't enforce these kinds of things. I think that it is a matter of fundamental right that if we raise the minimum wage, 15 million Americans would be positively affected. We'd put money into the hands of people who work hard, who obey the rules, who play for the American Dream. And if we did that, we'd have more consumption ability in America, which is what we need right now in order to kick our economy into gear. I will fight tooth and nail to pass the minimum wage.

Mr. Schieffer. Mr. President.

President Bush. Actually, Mitch McConnell had a minimum wage plan that I supported that would have increased the minimum wage.

But let me talk about what's really important for the worker you're referring to, and that's to make sure the education system works, is to make sure we raise standards. Listen, the No Child Left Behind Act is really a jobs act when you think about it. The No Child Left Behind Act says, "We'll raise standards. We'll increase Federal spending, but in return for extra spending, we now want people to measure—States and local jurisdictions to measure, to show us whether or not a child can read or write or add and subtract." You cannot solve a problem unless you diagnose the problem, and we weren't diagnosing problems. And therefore, just kids were being shuffled through the school. And guess who would get shuffled through? Children whose parents wouldn't speak English as first language, just moved through; many inner-city kids, just moved through. We've stopped that practice now by measuring early, and when we find a problem, we spend extra money to correct it.

I remember a lady in Houston, Texas, telling me reading is the new civil right. And she's right. In order to make sure people have jobs for the 21st century, we've got to get it right in the education system. And we're beginning to close a minority achievement gap now. You see, we'd never be able to compete in the 21st century unless we have an education system that doesn't quit on children, an education system that raises standards, an education that makes sure there's excellence in every classroom.

Judicial Nominations/Education Funding

Mr. Schieffer. Mr. President, I want to go back to something Senator Kerry said earlier tonight and ask a followup of my own. He said—and this will be a new question to you—he said that you had never said whether you would like to overturn *Roe* v. *Wade.* So I'd ask you directly, would you like to?

President Bush. What he's asking me is will I have a litmus test for my judges, and the answer is no, I will not have a litmus test. I will pick judges who will interpret the Constitution, but I'll have no litmus test.

Mr. Schieffer. Senator Kerry, you'd like to respond?

Senator Kerry. Is that a new question, or a 30-second question?

Mr. Schieffer. That's a new question for President Bush.

Senator Kerry. Which time limit are we——

Mr. Schieffer. You have 90 seconds.

Senator Kerry. Thank you very much. Well, again, the President didn't answer the question. I will answer it straight to America. I'm not going to appoint a judge to the court who is going to undo a constitutional right, whether it's the first amendment or the fifth amendment or some other right that's given under our courts today—under the Constitution. And I believe that the right of choice is a constitutional right. So, I don't intend to see it undone. Clearly, the President wants to leave an ambivalence or intends to undo it.

Let me go a step further. We have a long distance yet to travel in terms of fairness in America. I don't know how you can govern in this country when you look at New York City and you see that 50 percent of the black males there are unemployed, when you see 40 percent of Hispanic children, of black children in some cities dropping out of high school. And yet the President, who talks about No Child Left Behind, refused to fully fund—by $28 billion—that particular program, so you can make a difference in the lives of those young people.

Now, right here in Arizona, that difference would have been $131 million to the State of Arizona to help its kids be able to have better education and to lift the property tax burden from its citizens. The President reneged on his promise to fund No Child Left Behind. He will tell you he's raised the money, and he has, but he didn't put in what he promised. And that makes a difference in the lives of our children.

Mr. Schieffer. Yes, sir.

President Bush. Two things: One, he clearly has a litmus test for his judges, which I disagree with.

And secondly, only a liberal Senator from Massachusetts would say that a 49-percent increase in funding for education was not enough. We've increased funds, but more importantly, we've reformed the system to make sure that we solve problems early, before they're too late. He talked about the unemployed. Absolutely, we've got to make sure they get educated. He talked about children whose parents don't speak English as a first language. Absolutely, we've got to make sure they get educated.

And that's what the No Child Left Behind Act does.

Mr. Schieffer. Senator.

Senator Kerry. You don't measure it by a percentage increase. Mr. President, you measure it by whether you're getting the job done. Five hundred thousand kids lost after-school programs because of your budget. Now, that's not in my gut. That's not my value system—and certainly not so that the wealthiest people in America can walk away with another tax cut: $89 billion last year to the top 1 percent of Americans, but kids lost their after-school programs. You be the judge.

Addressing the Needs of the Military

Mr. Schieffer. All right, let's go to another question, and it is to Senator Kerry. You have 2 minutes, sir. Senator, at the last debate, President Bush said he did not favor a draft. You agreed with him. But our National Guard and Reserve forces are being severely strained because many of them are being held beyond their enlistments. Some of them say that it's a backdoor draft. Is there any relief that could be offered to these brave Americans and their families? If you became President, Senator Kerry, what would you do about this situation of holding National Guard and Reservists for these extended periods of time and these repeated callups that they're now facing?

Senator Kerry. Well, I think the fact that they're facing these repeated callups, some of them two and three deployments, and there's a stop-loss policy that prevents people from being able to get out when their time was up, is a reflection of the bad judgment this President exercised in how he has engaged in the world and deployed our forces. Our military is overextended. Nine out of ten Active Duty Army divisions are either in Iraq, going to Iraq, or have come back from Iraq. One way or the other, they're wrapped up in it.

Now, I've proposed adding two active-duty divisions to the Armed Forces of the United States, one combat, one support. In addition, I'm going to double the number of special forces so that we can fight a more effective war on terror with less pressure on the National Guard and Reserve. And what I would like to do is see the National Guard and Reserve be deployed differently here in our own country. There's much we can do with them with respect to homeland security. We ought to be doing that, and that would relieve an enormous amount of pressure.

But the most important thing to relieve the pressure on all of our Armed Forces is, frankly, to run a foreign policy that recognizes that America is strongest when we are working with real alliances, when we are sharing the burdens of the world by working through our statesmanship at the highest levels and our diplomacy to bring other nations to our side.

I've said it before; I say it again: I believe the President broke faith with the American people in the way that he took this Nation to war. He said he would work through the—a real alliance. He said in Cincinnati, "We would plan carefully. We would take every precaution." Well, we didn't, and the result is our forces today are overextended. The fact is that he did not choose to go to war as a last resort. And America now is paying already 120 billion, up to 200 billion before we're finished and much more, probably, and that is the result of this President taking his eye off of Usama bin Laden.

Mr. Schieffer. Mr. President.

President Bush. The best way to take the pressure off our troops is to succeed in Iraq, is to train Iraqis so they can do the hard work of democracy, is to give them a chance to defend their country, which is precisely what we're doing. We'll have 125,000 troops trained by the end of this year.

I remember going on an airplane in Bangor, Maine, to say thanks to the Reservists and Guard that were headed overseas from

Tennessee and North Carolina and Georgia. Some of them had been there before. The people I talked to, the spirits were high. They didn't view their service as a backdoor draft. They view their service as an opportunity to serve their country.

My opponent, the Senator, talks about foreign policy. In our first debate, he proposed America pass a "global test." In order to defend ourselves, we have to get international approval. That's one of the major differences we have about defending our country. I work with allies. I work with friends. We'll continue to build strong coalitions. But I will never turn over our national security decisions to leaders of other countries. We'll be resolute. We'll be strong, and we will wage a comprehensive war against the terrorists.

Mr. Schieffer. Senator.

Senator Kerry. I have never suggested a test where we turn over our security to any nation. In fact, I've said the opposite. I will never turn the security of the United States over to any nation. No nation will ever have a veto over us. But I think it makes sense—I think most Americans in their guts know that we ought to pass a sort of truth standard. That's how you gain legitimacy with your own countrypeople, and that's how you gain legitimacy in the world. But I will never fail to protect the United States of America.

President Bush. In 1990, there was a vast coalition put together to run Saddam Hussein out of Kuwait. The international community, the international world, said this is the right thing to do. But when it came time to authorize the use of force on the Senate floor, my opponent voted against the use of force. Apparently, you can't pass any test under his vision of the world.

Assault Weapons Ban

Mr. Schieffer. Mr. President, new question, 2 minutes. You said that if Congress would vote to extend the ban on assault weapons, that you'd sign the legislation. But you did nothing to encourage the Congress to extend it. Why not?

President Bush. Actually, I made my intentions—I made my views clear. I did think we ought to extend the assault weapons ban and was told the fact that the bill was never going to move because Republicans and Democrats were against the assault weapon ban, people of both parties.

Now, I believe law-abiding citizens ought to be able to own a gun. I believe in background checks at gun shows or anywhere to make sure that guns don't get in the hands of people that shouldn't have them. But the best way to protect our citizens from guns is to prosecute those who commit crimes with guns. And that's why, early in my administration, I called the Attorney General and the U.S. attorneys and said, "Put together a task force all around the country to prosecute those who commit crime with guns." And the prosecutions are up by about 68 percent, I believe is the number. Neighborhoods are safer when we crack down on people who commit crimes with guns. To me, that's the best way to secure America.

Mr. Schieffer. Senator.

Senator Kerry. I believe it was a failure of Presidential leadership not to reauthorize the assault weapons ban. I am a hunter. I'm a gun owner. I've been a hunter since I was a kid, 12, 13 years old. And I respect the second amendment, and I will not tamper with the second amendment. But I'll tell you this. I'm also a former law enforcement officer. I ran one of the largest district attorney offices in America, one of the 10 largest. I've put people behind bars for the rest of their life. I've broken up organized crime. I know something about prosecuting. And most of the law enforcement agencies in America wanted that assault weapons ban. They don't want to go into a drug bust and be facing an AK–47.

I was hunting in Iowa last year with the sheriff from one of the counties there, and he pointed to a house in back of us and said, "See that house over there? We just did a drug bust a week earlier, and the guy we arrested had an AK–47 lying on the bed right beside him."

Because of the President's decision today, law enforcement officers will walk into a place that will be more dangerous. Terrorists can now come into America and go to a gun show and, without even a background check, buy an assault weapon today. And that's what Usama bin Laden's handbook said, because we captured it in Afghanistan, and it encouraged them to do it.

So I believe America is less safe. If Tom DeLay or someone in the House said to me, "Sorry, we don't have the votes," I'd have said, "Then we're going to have a fight." And I'd have taken it out to the country, and I'd have had every law enforcement officer in the country visit those Congressmen. We'd have won what Bill Clinton won.

Affirmative Action

Mr. Schieffer. Let's go to a new question. For you, Senator Kerry, 2 minutes. Affirmative action—do you see a need for affirmative action programs, or have we moved far enough along that we no longer need to use race and gender as a factor in school admissions and Federal and State contracts, and so on?

Senator Kerry. No, Bob, regrettably, we have not moved far enough along. And I regret to say that this administration has even blocked steps that could help us move further along. I'll give you an example.

I'm the—I served on the Small Business Committee for a long time. I was chairman of it once; now I'm the senior Democrat on it. We used to—we have a goal there for minority set-aside programs to try to encourage ownership in the country. They don't reach those goals. They don't even fight to reach those goals. They've tried to undo them.

The fact is that in too many parts of our country, we still have discrimination, and affirmative action is not just something that applies to people of color. Some people have a mistaken view of it in America. It also is with respect to women. It's with respect to other efforts to try to reach out and be inclusive in our country. I think that we have a long way to go, regrettably. If you look at what's happened, we've made progress; I want to say that at the same time.

During the Clinton years, as you may recall, there was a fight over affirmative action. And there were many people, like myself, who opposed quotas, who felt there were places where it was overreaching. So we had a policy called "mend it, don't end it." We fixed it. And we fixed it for a reason, because there are too many people still in this country who feel the stark resistance of racism. And so we have a distance to travel. As President, I will make certain we travel it.

Now, let me just share something. This President is the first President ever, I think, not to meet with the NAACP. This is a President who hasn't met with the Black Congressional Caucus. This is a President who has not met with the civil rights leadership of our country. If a President doesn't reach out and bring people in and be inclusive, then how are we going to get over those barriers? I see that as part of my job as President, and I'll make my best effort to do it.

Mr. Schieffer. Mr. President.

President Bush. Well, first of all, it is just not true that I haven't met with the Black Congressional Caucus. I met with the Black Congressional Caucus at the White House.

And secondly, like my opponent, I don't agree we ought to have quotas—I agree, we shouldn't have quotas. But we ought to have an aggressive effort to make sure people are educated, to make sure when they get out of high school there's Pell grants available for them, which is what we've done. We've expanded Pell grants by a million students. Do you realize, today in America, we spend $73 billion to help

10 million low- and middle-income families better afford college? That's the access I believe is necessary, is to make sure every child learns to read, write, add, and subtract early, to be able to build on that education by going to college so they can start their careers with a college diploma.

I believe the best way to help our small businesses is not only through small-business loans, which we have increased since I've been the President of the United States, but to unbundle Government contracts so people will have a chance to be able to bid and receive a contract to help get their business going.

Minority ownership of businesses are up because we created an environment for the entrepreneurial spirit to be strong. I think—I believe part of a hopeful society is one in which somebody owns something. Today in America more minorities own a home than ever before. And that's hopeful, and that's positive.

Candidates' Faith

Mr. Schieffer. Mr. President, let's go to a new question. You were asked before the invasion—or after the invasion of Iraq if you had checked with your dad. And I believe—I don't remember the quote exactly—but I believe you said you had checked with a higher authority. I would like to ask you, what part does your faith play on your policy decisions?

President Bush. First, my faith plays a lot—a big part in my life. And that's—when I was answering that question, what I was really saying to the person was that I pray a lot, and I do. And my faith is a very—it's very personal. I pray for strength. I pray for wisdom. I pray for our troops in harm's way. I pray for my family. I pray for my little girls. But I'm mindful, in a free society, that people can worship if they want to or not. You're equally an American if you choose to worship an Almighty and if you choose not to. If you're a Christian, Jew, or Muslim, you're equally an American. That's the great thing about America, is the right to worship the way you see fit.

Prayer and religion sustain me. I've received calmness in the storms of the Presidency. I love the fact that people pray for me and my family all around the country. Somebody asked me one time, "Well, how do you know?" I said, "I just feel it." Religion is an important part. I never want to impose my religion on anybody else, but when I make decisions, I stand on principle. And the principles are derived from who I am. I believe we ought to love our neighbor like we love ourself. That's manifested in public policy through the Faith-Based Initiative, where we've unleashed the armies of compassion to help seal—heal people who hurt.

I believe that God wants everybody to be free. That's what I believe. And that's part of my foreign policy. In Afghanistan, I believe that the freedom there is a gift from the Almighty, and I can't tell you how encouraged I am to see freedom on the march. And so my principles that I make decisions on are a part of me, and religion is a part of me.

Mr. Schieffer. Senator Kerry.

Senator Kerry. Well, I respect everything that the President has said, and certainly I respect his faith. I think it's important, and I share it. I think that he just said that freedom is a gift from the Almighty. Everything is a gift from the Almighty. And as I measure the words of the Bible—and we all do; different people measure different things, the Koran, the Torah, or—Native Americans who gave me a blessing the other day had their own special sense of connectedness to a higher being, and people all find their ways to express it.

I was taught—I went to a church school, and I was taught that the two greatest commandments are "Love the Lord, your God, with all your mind, your body, and your soul" and "Love your neighbor as yourself." And frankly, I think we have a lot more loving of our neighbor to do in this country and on this planet.

We have a separate and unequal school system in the United States of America. There's one for the people who have, and there's one for the people who don't have. And we're struggling with that today. The President and I have a difference of opinion about how we live out our sense of our faith. I talked about it earlier when I talked about the works and faith without works being dead. I think we've got a lot more work to do. And as President, I will always respect everybody's right to practice religion as they choose or not to practice, because that's part of America.

Era of Divisiveness

Mr. Schieffer. Senator Kerry, after 9/11—and this is a new question for you—it seemed to me that the country came together as I've never seen it come together since World War II. But some of that seems to have melted away. I think it's fair to say we've become pretty polarized, perhaps because of the political season. But if you were elected President or whoever is elected President, will you set a priority in trying to bring the Nation back together? Or what would be your attitude on that?

Senator Kerry. Well, very much so. Let me pay a compliment to the President, if I may. I think in those days after 9/11, I thought the President did a terrific job. And I really was moved as well as impressed by the speech that he gave to the Congress. And I think the hug Tom Daschle gave him at that moment was about as genuine a sense of there being no Democrats, no Republicans; we were all just Americans. That's where we were.

That's not where we are today. I regret to say that the President, who called himself a uniter, not a divider, is now presiding over the most divided America in the recent memory of our country. I've never seen such ideological squabbles in the Congress of the United States. I've never seen members of a party locked out of meetings the way they're locked out today.

We have to change that, and as President, I am committed to changing that. I don't care if the idea comes from the other side or this side. I think we have to come together and work to change it. And I've done that. Over 20 years in the United States Senate, I've worked with John McCain, who's sitting here. I've worked with other colleagues. I've reached across the aisle. I've tried to find the common ground, because that's what makes us strong as Americans.

And if Americans trust me with the Presidency, I can pledge to you, we will have the most significant effort—openly, not secret meetings in the White House with special interests, not ideologically driven efforts to push people aside, but a genuine effort to try to restore America's hope and possibilities by bringing people together.

And one of the ways we're going to do it is, I'm going to work with my friend John McCain to further campaign finance reform so we get these incredible amounts of money out of the system and open it up to average people so America is really represented by the people who make up America.

Mr. Schieffer. Mr. President.

President Bush. My biggest disappointment in Washington is how partisan the town is. I had a record of working with Republicans and Democrats as the Governor of Texas, and I was hopeful to be able to do the same thing. And we made good progress early on. The No Child Left Behind Act, incredibly enough, was good work between me and my administration and people like Senator Ted Kennedy. And we worked together with Democrats to relieve the tax burden on the middle class and all who pay taxes in order to make sure this economy continues to grow.

But Washington is a tough town, and the way I view it is there's a lot of entrenched special interests there, people who are on one side of the issue or another, and they spend enormous sums of money, and they convince different Senators to tout their way or different Congressmen to talk about their issue, and they dig in.

I'll continue in the 4 years to continue to try to work to do so. My opponent said this is a bitterly divided time. It was pretty divided in the 2000 election. So, in other words, it's pretty divided during the 1990s as well. We're just in a period, and we've got to work to bring it out.

My opponent keeps mentioning John McCain, and I'm glad he did. John McCain is for me for President because he understands I have the right view in winning the war on terror and that my plan will succeed in Iraq, and my opponent has got a plan of retreat and defeat in Iraq.

Wives and Daughters of the Candidates

Mr. Schieffer. We've come, gentlemen, to our last question. And it occurred to me, as I came to this debate tonight, that the three of us share something. All three of us are surrounded by very strong women. We're all married to strong women. Each of us have two daughters that make us very proud. I'd like to ask each of you, what is the most important thing you've learned from these strong women?

President Bush. To listen to them— [*laughter*]—to stand up straight and not scowl. [*Laughter*] I love the strong women around me. I can't tell you how much I love my wife and our daughters. I am— you know, it's really interesting, I tell the people on the campaign trail, when I asked Laura to marry me, she said, "Fine, just so long as I never have to give a speech." I said, "Okay, you got a deal." Fortunately, she didn't hold me to that deal, and she's out campaigning, along with our girls, and she speaks English a lot better than I do. [*Laughter*] I think people understand what she's saying.

But they see a compassionate, strong, great First Lady in Laura Bush. I can't tell you how lucky I am when I met her in the backyard at Joe and Jan O'Neill in Midland, Texas. It was the classic backyard barbecue. O'Neill said, "Come on over. I

think you'll find somebody who might interest you." So I said, "All right," popped over there. There was only four of us there, and not only did she interest me, I guess you could say it was love at first sight.

Mr. Schieffer. Senator Kerry.

Senator Kerry. Well, I guess the President and you and I are three examples of lucky people who married up. [*Laughter*] And some would say maybe me more so than others. [*Laughter*] But I can take it. [*Laughter*]

Can I say, if I could just say a word about a woman that you didn't ask about, but my mom passed away a couple years ago, just before I was deciding to run. And she was in the hospital, and I went in to talk to her and tell her what I was thinking of doing. And she looked at me from her hospital bed, and she just looked at me, and she said, "Remember, integrity, integrity, integrity." Those are the three words that she left me with.

And my daughters and my wife are people who just are filled with that sense of what's right, what's wrong. They also kick me around. [*Laughter*] They keep me honest. They don't let me get away with anything. I can sometimes take myself too seriously. They surely don't let me do that. And I'm blessed, as I think the President is blessed. As I said last time, I've watched him with the First Lady, who I admire a great deal, and his daughters—he's a great father. And I think we're both very lucky.

Closing Statements

Mr. Schieffer. Well, gentlemen, that brings us to the closing statements. Senator Kerry, I believe you're first.

Senator Kerry. My fellow Americans, as you heard from Bob Schieffer a moment ago, America is being tested by division. More than ever, we need to be united as a country. And like Franklin Roosevelt, I don't care whether an idea is a Republican idea or a Democrat idea. I just care whether it works for America and whether it's going to make us stronger.

These are dangerous times. I believe I offer tested, strong leadership that can calm the waters of a troubled world. And I believe that we can, together, do things that are within the grasp of Americans. We can lift our schools up. We can create jobs that pay more than the jobs we're losing overseas. We can have health care for all Americans. We can further the cause of equality in our Nation.

Let me just make it clear: I will never allow any country to have a veto over our security. Just as I fought for our country as a young man, with the same passion I will fight to defend this Nation that I love. And with faith in God and with conviction in the mission of America, I believe that we can reach higher. I believe we can do better. I think the greatest possibilities of our country, our dreams and our hopes, are out there just waiting for us to grab onto them.

And I ask you to embark on that journey with me. I ask you for your trust. I ask you for your help. I ask you to allow me the privilege of leading this great Nation of ours, of helping us to be stronger here at home and to be respected again in the world and, most of all, to be safer forever.

Thank you. Good night, and God bless the United States of America.

Mr. Schieffer. Mr. President.

President Bush. In the Oval Office, there's a painting by a friend of Laura and mine named—by Tom Lea. It's a west Texas painting, a painting of a mountain scene. And he said this about it, he said, "Sarah and I live on the east side of the mountain. It's the sunrise side, not the sunset side. It's the side to see the day that is coming, not to see the day that is gone." I love the optimism in that painting because that's how I feel about America.

You know, we've been through a lot together during the last 3¾ years. We've come through a recession, a stock market

decline, an attack on our country. And yet, because of the hard work of the American people and good policies, this economy is growing. Over the next 4 years, we'll make sure the economy continues to grow.

We reformed our school system, and now there's an achievement gap in America that is beginning to close. Over the next 4 years, we'll continue to insist on excellence in every classroom in America so that our children have a chance to realize the great promise of America.

Over the next 4 years, we'll continue to work to make sure health care is available and affordable. Over the next 4 years, we'll continue to rally the armies of compassion to help heal the hurt that exists in some of our country's neighborhoods.

I'm optimistic that we'll win the war on terror, but I understand it requires firm resolve and clear purpose. We must never waver in the face of this enemy that—these ideologues of hate. And as we pursue the enemy wherever it exists, we'll also spread freedom and liberty. We've got great faith in the ability of liberty to transform societies, to convert hostile—a hostile world to a peaceful world. My hope for America is a prosperous America, a hopeful America, and a safer world.

I want to thank you for listening tonight. I'm asking for your vote. God bless you.

Mr. Schieffer. Thank you, Mr. President. Thank you, Senator Kerry. Well, that brings these debates to a close, but the campaign goes on. I want to wish both of you the very best of luck between now and election day.

That's it for us from Arizona State University in Tempe, Arizona. I'm Bob Schieffer of CBS News. Good night, everyone.

NOTE: The debate began at 6 p.m. in Gammage Auditorium at Arizona State University. In his remarks, the President referred to former President Saddam Hussein of Iraq. Senator Kerry referred to Usama bin

Laden, leader of the Al Qaida terrorist organization.

Remarks at a Presidential Debate Watch Party in Phoenix, Arizona
October 13, 2004

The President. Thank you all.

Audience members. Four more years! Four more years! Four more years!

The President. Thank you all very much. I've been to a lot of ballparks in my day, but I've never been to a ballpark filled with so many people who are going to go out and work the vote and make sure we can win in November.

I am so honored you came out tonight. I cannot thank you enough for greeting me and Laura and Barbara and Jenna. It warms our heart and lifts our spirit to be here with so many great American citizens. Thanks for coming. You know, when I got here, Laura said, "Stand up straight. Don't scowl, and keep your speech short." [*Laughter*]

I meant what I said about Laura. I love her dearly. She's a great First Lady. Tonight I tried to give the people a reason to put me back in for 4 more years, but perhaps the most important reason of all is so that Laura is the First Lady for 4 more years. I'm proud to be here with Barbara and Jenna. I told them, I said, "Get you some sleep tonight, and get back out on the campaign trail." [*Laughter*]

But thank you all for coming. I love my family. I love my country. I love working with John McCain. I'm so proud to be standing with him here today. He is—he and I are going to go to Nevada tomorrow. We're going to Las Vegas. We're going to Reno. We're going to Oregon. We're going to travel this country with a message that's hopeful and optimistic, and we're going to win.

I want to thank Cindy McCain as well for being here. I want to thank my friend Senator Jon Kyl and Caryll Kyl for being here as well. I want to thank the Members of Congress who are here.

I want to thank my friend Aaron Tippin for providing some—[*applause*]—yes. I want to thank the Arizona Diamondbacks for opening up this fantastic facility for us here today. I want to thank the players who are here.

I want to thank the grassroots activists, the people who are going to put up the signs and make the phone calls and turn out the people to vote.

I know you know this, but you can now cast your ballot for Dick Cheney and me. Make sure you do so, and get your friends and neighbors to do so. We need your help. We need your vote. We're going to win in November.

I enjoyed the debate tonight. It gave me a chance to tell the American people where I want to lead for the next 4 years. We'll continue to create jobs. We'll continue to make sure our schools work. We'll work on health care. We'll make sure that America is safe and secure by staying on the offensive. We'll defeat the terrorists overseas so we do not face them here at home.

And finally, we will never forget the values of this country, our faith, our families. We will make sure that we continue to hold true to our beliefs that liberty can transform the world. We long for peace. We will spread the peace by spreading freedom.

I'm honored that you're here. Thank you for coming. May God bless you, and may God bless America.

NOTE: The President spoke at 8:12 p.m. at the Bank One Ballpark. In his remarks, he referred to Cindy McCain, wife of Senator John McCain; Caryll Kyl, wife of Senator Jon L. Kyl; and entertainer Aaron Tippin.

Statement on Signing the Military Construction Appropriations and Emergency Hurricane Supplemental Appropriations Act, 2005
October 13, 2004

Today, I have signed into law H.R. 4837, the "Military Construction Appropriations and Emergency Hurricane Supplemental Appropriations Act, 2005." This Act provides funding for construction to support the operations of the U.S. Armed Forces and for military family housing. The Act also provides the funds I requested to help citizens in Florida and elsewhere rebuild their lives in the aftermath of multiple hurricanes and other natural disasters.

Sections 107, 110, 113, 118, and 303 of the Act provide for notice to the Congress of relocation of activities between military installations, initiation of a new installation abroad, U.S. military exercises involving $100,000 in construction costs, specific actions to encourage foreign nations to assume a greater share of the common defense burden, and initiation of certain types of programs. The Supreme Court of the United States has stated that the President's authority to classify and control access to information bearing on national security flows from the Constitution and does not depend upon a legislative grant of authority. Although notice can be provided in most situations as a matter of comity, situations may arise, especially in wartime, in which the President must act promptly under his constitutional grants of executive power and authority as Commander in Chief while protecting sensitive national security information. The executive branch shall construe these sections in a manner consistent with the constitutional authority of the President.

Section 128 of the Act purports to require Department of Defense officials to respond in writing within 21 days to any question or inquiry from the congressional military construction appropriations subcommittees. The executive branch shall construe section 128 in a manner consistent with the President's constitutional authority to supervise the unitary executive branch and to withhold information the disclosure of which could impair foreign relations, the national security, the deliberative processes of the Executive, or the performance of the Executive's constitutional duties.

The executive branch shall construe section 110(d)(2) of the Alaska Natural Gas Pipeline Act as contained in Division C of the Act, relating to submission of legislative recommendations, in a manner consistent with the President's exclusive constitutional authority to recommend for the consideration of the Congress such measures as the President judges necessary and expedient.

GEORGE W. BUSH

The White House,
October 13, 2004.

NOTE: H.R. 4837, approved October 13, was assigned Public Law No. 108–324. This statement was released by the Office of the Press Secretary on October 14.

Exchange With Reporters Aboard Air Force One
October 14, 2004

The President. How is everybody? Ballsky [Dan Balz, Washington Post].

Q. Mr. President, how are you?

The President. Were you anticipating my arrival? [*Laughter*] Listen, 19 days to go, and I'm looking forward to it. I enjoyed myself last night. The debate phase of the campaign is over, and now it's a sprint to the finish. And the good news is I'm not going to be sprinting alone. I'll have a lot of support from people like Senator McCain and Governor Lingle. We'll be seeing Governors today in Las Vegas, and they're going to spread out all across the country, and I'm excited about it. It's—my spirits are high. I'm enthusiastic about my chances.

I'll answer a couple of questions, and then we'll let you have your coffee.

Presidential Debate in Tempe

Q. Some of the early polls say Kerry won last night. What do you have to say?

The President. Well, the voters will decide. They'll decide on November the 2d who they want to be the President.

Q. Has Kerry helped himself with these debates, if you have an opinion?

The President. The voters will decide that. You know, that's—the great thing about a campaign, all the speculation ends on election day.

Senator John McCain. Can I just say, on substance, there is no doubt. When you talk about Social Security, they all want to reform it. You don't know how to pay for it. You can't answer the question, and people notice that. On substance, the President won, and that's what the people think about when they go into the ballot booth.

Can I also say at that event afterwards, 40,000 citizens of Arizona showed up at Bank One Ballpark. There has never been an event like that in the history of our State, not only the numbers but the enthusiasm.

Q. Mr. President, what do you think your best moment was last night?

The President. Telling people what I think. You know, the pundits and the spinners and the—they'll all have their opinion, but there's only one opinion that matters, and that's the opinion of the American people on November the 2d. I feel great about where we are. There's lot of enthusiasm for my candidacy. People have seen me lead, and they also know that I've got plans for the next 4 years. And as you'll hear me today, I'm optimistic about the future of this country.

Governor Linda Lingle. I thought that a great moment was the question about jobs. It's more than statistics. I think the President made a key point when he said the important point is that a solid education for the children in America is the best way to ensure a sound economy over the long term. It's common sense. It's why No Child Left Behind is not just important for education, it's important for the sustained economic progress of this Nation.

And personally, the part I liked is when the President talked about his feelings for Mrs. Bush and his daughters. I thought that was just so touching. I think people across America felt how close they were as a family, and I thought it was a really important part of the debate as well.

The President. All right, I'm going to let you all go back to your breakfast.

Senator McCain. Can I just mention one thing? Again, on Social Security, the President has pledged to reform Social Security and bring America together on that issue. You can't just say that the status quo will prevail on Social Security. Millions and millions of baby boomers are going to be facing retirement. This is an issue that has got to be the highest priority. The President has pledged to address it and not be satisfied with the status quo.

Q. Mr. President, one question that you were asked last night about the cost, the transition cost of——

The President. Well, that's part of bringing people together, to figure out how to address the costs. The point is, is that I'm the President who understands Social Security needs to be reformed.

Listen, thank you. Good to see you, Dan. Get a smile on your faces, everybody, 18 days left.

Q. Will you come visit us again?
Senator McCain. Every day. [*Laughter*]
The President. I'm a better person for it, of course. [*Laughter*]

NOTE: The exchange began at 9:07 a.m. while en route to Las Vegas, NV. Gov. Linda Lingle of Hawaii participated in the exchange. A tape was not available for verification of the content of this exchange.

Remarks in Las Vegas, Nevada
October 14, 2004

The President. I appreciate it. Thank you. Thank you all for coming. I appreciate you all being here. With only 19 days to the election, the finish line is in sight, and Nevada will be a part of a great nationwide victory in November, the 2d.

I'm proud to be on stage with so many of the Governors, the Nation's Governors. I'm a member of the ex-Governors club. They'll be a member of that club one day soon. [*Laughter*] I know these folks really well. They're hard-working. They bring people together to get the job done in their States. They focus on results, and that's what I've done as your President, and that's what I'll do for 4 more years.

I want to thank our host, Governor Kenny Guinn, for his hospitality. It wasn't very hard to get the Governors to come to Vegas—[*laughter*]—to begin a road trip. The next 2 days, they're going to travel our country to tell people that leadership matters. They're going to tell the people that the best way to make sure America has strong and steady and principled leadership is to put Dick Cheney and me back into office.

It's great to be in the home of the Running Rebels. And that's what I'm doing:

I'm running, and I'm not going to stop until election day. Look, my only regret is that Laura is not here to see this crowd. She's right around the corner at the AARP convention. So the convention said, "Send your best speaker." [*Laughter*] When I married Laura, she said, "Fine, I'll marry you, so long as I never have to give a speech." [*Laughter*] I said, "Okay, you got a deal." Fortunately, she didn't hold me to that deal. When the people see her speak, they see a compassionate, strong, great First Lady.

I'm proud of my runningmate, Dick Cheney. He did a really good job in his debate. I admit it, he doesn't have the—he didn't have the waviest hair there on the set. [*Laughter*] I didn't pick him because of his hairdo. [*Laughter*] I picked him because of his experience, his judgment, his ability to get the job done for the American people.

After this we're going to Reno, and then we're going up to Oregon, and I'm proud to be traveling with a great American in John McCain. I like traveling with John. We have a lot of fun. We laugh. We enjoy each other's company, and we share something in common: We both love our Nation.

I want to thank Senator John Ensign, the great Senator from Nevada, for being here today, and Congressman Jon Porter—make sure you put him back into office. Congressman Jim Gibbons from the northern part of this State is with us today as well. Congressman, thanks for coming. I want to thank all the State and local officials who are here.

I want to thank my friend Lee Greenwood for entertaining the folks. Thank you for coming.

I particularly want to thank the grassroots activists who are here, the people who are going to put up the signs and make the phone calls. I'm here to thank you in advance for what you're going to do over the course of the next 19 days. You're going to tell people they have a duty in our democracy to vote. Get them headed to the polls. But don't overlook discerning Democrats, people like Zell Miller. And when you get them headed to the polls, tell them if they want a safer America, a stronger America, and a better America, to put me and Dick Cheney back into office.

We had a great debate last night. Those debates, all three debates, clarified the differences in our records, our approaches, and our plans for the future. I'm proud of my record. My opponent seemed to want to avoid talking about his. My record is one of lowering taxes, reforming education, providing prescription drugs to seniors, improving our homeland protection, and waging an aggressive war against the terrorists.

The Senator's record is 20 years of out-of-the-mainstream votes without many significant reforms or results.

Audience members. Boo-o-o!

The President. Our very different records are a window into what we believe and what we'll do in the next 4 years. The Senator believes in a bigger Government. I believe in more freedom and choices for our citizens. The Senator believes Government should dictate. I believe you should make the decisions.

Sometimes it's a little hard to tell exactly what he believes—*[laughter]*—because he tries to obscure his votes. Take health care. Once again, last night, with a straight face—*[laughter]*—the Senator tried to say his health care plan is not a Government plan. *[Laughter]* Yet, 22 million new people will be enrolled in a Government program under his plan, the largest expansion of Government health care ever. Eighty percent of the newly insured on his plan would be placed on a Government program like Medicaid. The Senator claimed his plan would help small businesses, yet a study conducted by small-business groups this week concluded Senator Kerry's plan is an overpriced albatross.

I have a different view. I want to make health care more available and affordable by helping small businesses, not saddling them with a bunch of Government rules.

And once again, last night, with a straight face, the Senator, shall we say, refined his answer on the proposed "global test" he would administer before acting to defend America.

Audience members. Boo-o-o!

The President. After trying to say it wasn't really a test at all, last night he once again defended his approach, saying, "I think it makes sense." *[Laughter]* The Senator now says we have to pass some international truth standard. Those are his words. The truth is, we should never turn over America's national security decisions to international bodies or leaders of other countries.

In the last few years, the American people have gotten to know me. They know my blunt way of speaking. I get that from Mom. They know I sometimes mangle the English language. *[Laughter]* I get that from Dad. *[Laughter]* Americans also know that I tell you exactly what I'm going to do and I keep my word.

When I came into office, the stock market had been in serious decline for 6 months. The American economy was sliding into a recession. To help families and get this economy growing again, I pledged to reduce taxes. I kept my word, and the results are clear. The recession was one of the shallowest in American history.

Over the last 3 years, our economy has grown at the fastest rate of any major industrialized nation. In the past 13 months, we've added 1.9 million new jobs. The unemployment rate in America is at 5.4 percent, lower than the average of the 1970s, 1980s, and 1990s. The unemployment rate in Nevada is 4 percent. The mining sector is strong. Farm and ranch income is up. More people are owning their own home.

We're moving forward, and there is much more to do. To make sure quality jobs are created in America and to make sure people can find work, America must be the best place in the world to do business. That means we need to reduce the regulations on our job creators. We must end junk lawsuits, which are threatening the small businesses which create most new jobs.

To keep jobs here, Congress needs to pass my energy plan. My plan encourages conservation, encourages the use of renewables like ethanol and biodiesel. It encourages new technologies. It encourages clean coal technology and increased domestic production. To keep jobs here, our Nation must become less dependent on foreign sources of energy.

To protect jobs and communities in the West, we need to reduce the risk of devastating wildfires. That's why I was proud to sign the Healthy Forests Restoration Act. Under this good law, we are cleaning the underbrush that serves as fuel for fires. Because we acted, our forests are healthier; residents and small businesses are safer; and people across the West are better off.

To create jobs, we need to reject economic isolationism and open up markets around the world for U.S. products. Americans can compete with anybody, anytime, anywhere, so long as the rules are fair. To create jobs, we need to be wise about how we spend your money and keep your taxes low.

My opponent has his own history on the economy.

Audience members. Boo-o-o!

The President. In 20 years as a Senator from Massachusetts, he's built up quite a record—of a Senator from Massachusetts. [*Laughter*] He's voted to raise taxes 98 times.

Audience members. Boo-o-o!

The President. That is a vote for a tax increase about five times every year.

Audience members. Boo-o-o!

The President. I think that qualifies as a pattern. [*Laughter*] He can run from his record, but he cannot hide. Now he's promising not to raise taxes for anyone who earns less than $200,000 a year. The problem is, to keep that promise he would have to break almost all of his other ones. [*Laughter*] His plan to raise taxes in the top two income brackets would raise about $600 billion. But his spending promises will cost about 4 times that much, more than 2.2 trillion. That's with a "T." [*Laughter*] That's a lot even for somebody from Massachusetts. [*Laughter*] See, you can't have it both ways. To pay for all the big spending promises he made, he'll have to raise your taxes.

Audience members. Boo-o-o!

The President. The choice in this election is clear. My opponent has a history of voting for higher taxes, and he promised to raise them in this campaign. And that's the kind of promise a Washington politician usually keeps. [*Laughter*] I believe our families and our economy are better off when Americans keep more of what they earn. We will keep your taxes low.

When I came into office, the public schools had been waiting for decades for hopeful reform. Too many of our children were shuffled through school without learning the basics. I pledged to restore accountability to the schools and end the soft bigotry of low expectations, and I kept my word. Seeing the results—our children are making sustained gains in reading and math. We're closing the achievement gap for minority students. We're making progress for our families. We will leave no child behind.

To build a more hopeful America, we must have the best prepared and most highly skilled workforce in the world. Most new jobs are filled by people with at least 2 years of college education, yet only about one in four of our students gets there. So we'll fund early intervention programs in our high schools to help at-risk students. We'll place a new focus on math and science. Over time, we'll require a rigorous examination before graduation from high school. By raising performance in our high schools and by expanding Pell grants for low- and middle-income families, we'll help more Americans start their career with a college diploma.

My opponent has a history on education issues, a history of doing almost nothing. [*Laughter*] The Senator has pledged to weaken the No Child Left Behind Act.

Audience members. Boo-o-o!

The President. He has proposed diluting the accountability standards and looking at measures like teacher attendance to judge whether students are learning.

Audience members. Boo-o-o!

The President. His proposals would undermine the high standards and accountability we worked hard to pass. We're moving beyond the old days of failure and mediocrity and low standards, and we're not going to go back.

When I came to office, we had a problem in Medicare. Medicine was changing, but Medicare wasn't. For example, Medicare would pay tens of thousands of dollars for heart surgery but wouldn't pay a dime for the prescription drugs that could prevent the heart surgery from being needed in the first place. It didn't make any sense for our seniors, and it didn't make any sense for our taxpayers. I pledged to bring Republicans and Democrats together to strengthen and modernize Medicare for our

seniors, and I kept my word. The results are clear. Seniors are already getting discounts on medicines, and beginning in 2006, all seniors will be able to get prescription drug coverage under Medicare.

We're moving forward on health care, and there's much more to do. We need to make health care more affordable and more available for all our people. We need a safety net for those with the greatest needs. I believe in community health centers, places where the poor and the indigent can get care. In a new term, we'll make sure every poor county in America has a community health center. We need to do more to make sure more children are fully subscribed in our programs for low-income families.

We must do more to make sure health care is affordable. You know, most of the uninsured are employees of small businesses. Small businesses have trouble affording health care. To help more workers get health care, we should allow small businesses to join together so they can buy insurance at the same discounts that big companies do.

To make sure health care is affordable, we have got to expand health savings accounts so workers in small businesses are able to pay lower premiums and people can save tax-free in a health care account they call their own.

To make sure health care is available and affordable, we have got to do something about the junk lawsuits that are running up the costs of your health care. All the lawsuits force doctors to practice defensive medicine, which costs our Government about $28 billion a year. They cost our Nation's economy anywhere from 60 to 100 billion dollars a year. The lawsuits drive up insurance premiums, which drive good doctors out of practice.

Today I met Dr. James Barber. Three years ago, Dr. Barber paid $27,000 in insurance premiums as an ob-gyn in Henderson. Last year's premiums would have been more than $100,000. He had to stop delivering babies in Nevada. He's now practicing in California, where they have reasonable medical liability laws. His premiums in California are $33,000, 70 percent of what they would cost in Nevada.

I also met one of his former patients, Nicole Byrne. She said Dr. Barber saved her life during a previous pregnancy. Now she's pregnant again, and she is devastated that Dr. Barber won't be able to deliver her babies. Nicole and Dr. Barber understand that you cannot be pro-patient and pro-doctor and pro-trial-lawyer at the same time. You have to choose. My opponent made his choice, and he put a trial lawyer on the ticket.

Audience members. Boo-o-o!

The President. I made my choice. I'm standing with the docs and patients. I am for medical liability reform—now.

The choice in this election is clear. My opponent wants to move in the direction of Government-run health care. I believe health decisions ought to be made by doctors and patients, not by officials in Washington, DC. I've set out policies that move America toward a positive and optimistic vision. I believe our country can and must be an ownership society. There's a saying that no one ever washes a rental car. [*Laughter*] There's a lot of wisdom in that statement. [*Laughter*] When you own something, you care about it and you have a vital stake in the future of our country.

So we're encouraging entrepreneurship, because every time a small business is started, someone is achieving the American Dream. We're encouraging health savings accounts so people have the security of owning their own health care plan. We're promoting homeownership. More and more Americans own a home today. I love it when somebody opens the door of the place they live and says, "Welcome to my home. Welcome to my piece of property."

In a new term, I will take the next great step to build an ownership society by strengthening Social Security. Our Social Security system needs fixing. First, we'll make sure we keep the promise to those who are on Social Security today. I remember, in the 2000 campaign, those ads saying, "If George W. gets elected, they're going to take away your check." Our seniors got their checks. Nobody is going to take away our seniors' checks. Baby boomers like me are going to be just fine when it comes to Social Security.

But our children and our grandchildren are understandably worried about whether Social Security will be around when they need it, and we need to be concerned about them. For their sake, we must strengthen Social Security by allowing younger workers to save some of their payroll taxes in a personal account that Washington politicians can never take away. My opponent wants to maintain the status quo when it comes to Social Security.

Audience members. Boo-o-o!

The President. That is unacceptable. He's against Social Security—these Social Security reforms. And he's just about against just about every other reform that gives more authority and control to individuals. On issue after issue, from Medicare without choices to schools with less accountability to higher taxes, he takes the side of more centralized control and more bureaucracy. There's a word for that attitude. It's called liberalism. Now, he dismisses that as a label—must have seen it differently when he said to a newspaper, "I'm a liberal and proud of it." [*Laughter*]

Others have noticed. The nonpartisan National Journal magazine did a study and named him the most liberal member of the United States Senate. And that's saying something. [*Laughter*] Another group known as the Americans for Democratic Action have given Senator Kerry a higher lifetime liberal rating than Senator Ted Kennedy, and that's an accomplishment.

Audience members. Boo-o-o!

The President. See, I have a different record and a different philosophy. I don't believe in big Government, and I don't believe in indifferent Government. I am a compassionate conservative. I believe in policies that empower people to improve their lives, not try to run their lives.

In this time of change, some things do not change. Those are the values we try to live by, courage and compassion, reverence and integrity. In changing times, we will support the institutions that give our lives direction and purpose, our families, our schools, our religious congregations. We stand for a culture of life in which every person matters and every being counts. We stand for marriage and family, which are the foundations of our society. We stand for the appointment of Federal judges who know the difference between personal opinion and the strict interpretation of the law.

My opponent's words on these issues are a little muddy, but his record is plenty clear. [*Laughter*] He says he supports the institution of marriage, but he voted against the Defense of Marriage Act, which a bipartisan Congress overwhelmingly passed and my predecessor signed into law. He voted against the ban on the brutal practice of partial-birth abortion.

Audience members. Boo-o-o!

The President. He called himself the candidate of conservative values, but he has described the Reagan years as a time of moral darkness.

Audience members. Boo-o-o!

The President. There is a mainstream in American politics, and my opponent sits on the left bank. He can run, but he cannot hide.

This election will also determine how America responds to the continuing danger of terrorism. I believe the most solemn duty of the American President is to protect the American people. If America shows uncertainty or weakness in this decade, the world will drift toward tragedy. This will not happen on my watch.

Since that terrible morning of September the 11th, 2001, we have fought the terrorists across the Earth, not for pride, not for power, but because the lives of our citizens are at stake. Our strategy is clear. We will defend the homeland. We'll strengthen our intelligence services. We'll transform the All-Volunteer Army, and we'll keep it an all-volunteer army. We will stay on the offensive. We will strike the terrorists abroad so we do not have to face them here at home. We will continue to spread freedom and liberty, and we will prevail.

Our strategy is succeeding. Think about the world as it was 3½ years ago. Afghanistan was the home base of Al Qaida. Pakistan was a transit point for terrorist groups. Saudi Arabia was fertile ground for terrorist fundraising. Libya was secretly pursuing nuclear weapons. Iraq was a dangerous place and a gathering threat. And Al Qaida was largely unchallenged as it planned attacks.

Because we acted, Afghanistan is a free nation fighting terror. And last Saturday, the people of Afghanistan voted for a President. Pakistan is capturing terrorist leaders. Saudi Arabia is making raids and arrests. Libya is dismantling its weapons programs. The army of a free Iraq is fighting for freedom. And more than three-quarters of Al Qaida's leaders and associates have been brought to justice.

We've got an aggressive strategy to keep us safe, and we'll stand with the people of a free Afghanistan and Iraq. Think about what happened in Afghanistan. It wasn't all that long ago that the Taliban ran that country. Young girls couldn't even go to school. They were not only harboring terrorists; they had this dark ideology of hate. And people showed up in droves to vote. Freedom is powerful. People have gone from darkness to light, because of liberty. The first voter in the Afghan Presidential election was a 19-year-old woman.

Iraq is headed toward elections. See, free societies in the Middle East will be hopeful societies which no longer feed resentments and breed violence for export. Free governments in the Middle East will fight the terrorists instead of harboring them, and that helps us keep the peace. Our mission is clear. We'll help the countries train their armies and their police so they can do the hard work of defending democracy. We'll help them get on the path to stability and democracy as quickly as possible, then our troops will come home with the honor they have earned.

We have got a great United States military. I want to thank all the veterans who are here for having set such a great example for those who wear today's uniform. I want to thank the military families who are with us today for their sacrifices. And I want to assure the families, we'll keep the commitment I made to our troops. We will make sure they have all the resources they need to complete their missions.

And that's why I went to the United States Congress in September of 2003 and asked for an $87 billion supplemental request, money necessary to support those troops in Afghanistan and Iraq. We received great bipartisan support. As a matter of fact, only 12 United States Senators voted against the supplemental request, the funding, 2 of whom are my opponent and his runningmate.

Audience members. Boo-o-o!

The President. When you're out gathering the vote, remind your fellow citizens that only four United States Senators voted to authorize the use of force and then against sending the money to support them in harm's way, two of whom—two of those four—are my opponent and his runningmate.

Audience members. Boo-o-o!

The President. You might remember my opponent's famous quote, when asked about that vote. He said, "I actually did vote for the $87 billion, before I voted against it."

Audience members. Boo-o-o!

The President. Now, he's given a lot of explanations since that one. One of the most interesting ones is when he finally said, "Well, the whole thing is a complicated matter." [*Laughter*] There's noth-

ing complicated about supporting our troops in combat.

I believe in the transformational power of liberty. I believe that millions in the Middle East plead in silence for their freedom. I believe women want to grow up in a free society and raise their children in a free society. I believe that if given a chance, the people of the Middle East will embrace the most honorable form of government ever devised by man. I believe all these things because freedom is not America's gift to the world; freedom is the Almighty God's gift to each man and woman in this world.

For all Americans, these years in our history will always stand apart. You know, there are quiet times in the life of a nation when little is expected of its leaders. This isn't one of those times. It's a time that requires firm resolve and clear vision and a deep faith in the values that makes us a great nation.

None of us will ever forget that week when one era ended and another began. September the 14th, 2001, I stood in the ruins of the Twin Towers. It's a day I will never forget. There were workers in hardhats yelling at me at the top of their lungs, "Whatever it takes." Governor Pataki was with me. He knows—he remembers those workers and those police and firefighters coming out of the rubble, bloodshot eyes. A guy grabbed me by the arm, and he said, "Do not let me down." Ever since that day, I wake up every morning trying to figure out how best to defend this country. I will never relent in defending America, whatever it takes.

Four years ago, when I traveled your State asking for the vote, I made this pledge: If you gave me a chance to serve, I would uphold the honor and the dignity of the office to which I had been elected. With your help, I will do so for 4 more years.

God bless. Thanks for coming. Thank you all.

NOTE: The President spoke at 10:05 a.m. at the Thomas & Mack Center. In his remarks, he referred to Gov. Kenny C. Guinn of Nevada; entertainer Lee Greenwood; Senator Zell Miller of Georgia, who made the keynote address at the 2004 Republican National Convention; and Gov. George E. Pataki of New York.

Remarks in Reno, Nevada
October 14, 2004

The President. Thank you all for coming out today. It's great to be back in Nevada. It's such a beautiful day. I'm proud to be here in the "Biggest Little City in the World." I'm really pleased to be in a place where the cowboy hats outnumber the suits.

Thank you all for coming. I'm here to ask for the vote. And I want your help. Tell your friends and neighbors to go to the polls on November the 2d. Everybody ought to vote in this country. And tell them if they want a safer America, a stronger America, and a better America to put me and Dick Cheney back in office.

I'm sorry Laura is not here.

Audience members. Aw-w-w!

The President. I know it. We were in Las Vegas earlier, and they had an AARP convention there. And the head of the AARP said, "Send your family's best speaker." [*Laughter*] So Laura went. [*Laughter*] You know, when I married her, I said— she said, "Fine, I'll marry you, just so long as I never have to give a speech." I said, "Okay, you've got a deal." [*Laughter*] Fortunately, she didn't hold me to that deal. When she speaks, America sees a compassionate, warm, great First Lady.

I'm proud of my runningmate, Dick Cheney. He's a fine man with good judgment and great experience. He's getting the job done for the American people. I'm proud to be introduced by a unique and strong and great American in John McCain. When he says he's for you, he's really for you. Las Vegas this morning, Reno right now, and then we're headed to Medford, Oregon. He's by my side. He's campaigning hard, and I'm proud to have his support.

And I'm proud of the job that Senator John Ensign is doing for the great State of Nevada. He's a really fine man. I want to thank Jim Gibbons for his service as well. Old Congressman Greg Walden from Oregon snuck across the State line. He's with us today. Thanks for coming, Greg. I appreciate you being here.

I'm really proud that Dema Guinn is with us, the first lady of the great State of Nevada. Thank for coming, Dema. I'm proud you're here. How about your attorney general, Brian Sandoval? What a class act he is. I want to thank Brian Krolicki, the State treasurer, for being with us today. I want to thank—Dean Heller is with us today. I'm proud he's here.

I want to thank all the State and local officials. But mainly, I want to thank the grassroots activists, the people who are putting up the signs, the people making the phone calls, the people turning out the vote. With your help, we'll carry Nevada and win a great victory in November.

I enjoyed the debate last night. You know, those debates clarify the differences in our record, our approach, and our plans for the future. I'm proud of my record. My opponent seemed to want to avoid talking about his. [*Laughter*] My record is one of lowering taxes, reforming education, providing prescription drug coverage to seniors, improving homeland protections, and waging an aggressive war against the ideologues of hate.

The Senator's record is 20 years of out-of-the-mainstream votes without many significant reforms or results. Our very different records are a window into what we believe and what we'll do for the next 4 years. The Senator believes in a bigger Federal Government. I believe in more freedom and more choices for individual Americans. The Senator believes Government should dictate. I believe you should decide.

Sometimes it's a little hard to tell exactly what he believes—[laughter]—as he tries to obscure his approach to Government. Take health care. Once again, last night, with a straight face—[laughter]—the Senator tried to say his health care plan is not a Government plan. [Laughter] I could barely contain myself. [Laughter] Yet 22 million new people would enroll on a Government program under his plan, the largest expansion of Government health care ever. Eighty percent of the newly insured on his plan would be placed on a Government program like Medicaid. The Senator claimed his plan would help small business, yet a study conducted by small-businesses groups concluded Senator Kerry's plan is an overpriced albatross that would saddle small businesses with 225 new mandates.

I have a different view. I want health care to be available and affordable by helping small businesses, not by saddling them with a bunch of new Government rules.

Once again last night, with a straight face, the Senator, shall we say, refined his answer on the proposed "global test" he would administer before acting to defend America. See, after trying to say it really wasn't a test at all, last night he once again defended his approach by saying, "I think it makes sense." Now he says we have to pass some international truth standard.

Audience members. Boo-o-o!

The President. The truth is, we should never turn America's national security decisions over to international bodies or leaders of other countries.

The last few years, the American people have gotten to know me. They know my blunt way of speaking. I get that from Mom. [Laughter] They know I sometimes mangle the English language. I get that from Dad. [Laughter] Americans also know I tell you exactly what I'm going to do, and I keep my word.

When I came to office, the stock market had been in serious decline for 6 months. The American economy was sliding into recession. To help families, to get this economy growing again, I pledged to reduce taxes. I kept my word, and the results are clear. The recession was one of the shallowest in American history. And over the last 3 years, America's economy has grown at the fastest rate of any major industrialized nation.

In the past 13 months, we've added more than 1.9 million new jobs. The unemployment rate in America is at 5.4 percent, below the average rate of the 1970s, the 1980s, and the 1990s. The unemployment rate in your State is 4 percent. Mining sector is strong. Farm and ranch income is up. Homeownership is at an alltime high in America. We're moving forward, and there's more to do.

To make sure quality jobs are created here in America, America must be the best place in the world to do business. That means less regulations on the job creators. That means we've got to do something about these frivolous lawsuits that make it hard to expand employment.

To create jobs, Congress needs to pass my energy plan. It encourages conservation. It encourages the use of renewables like ethanol and biodiesel. It encourages new technologies. It encourages clean coal technology and increased domestic production. To keep jobs here, we must become less dependent on foreign sources of energy.

To protect jobs and communities in the West, we need to reduce the risk of devastating wildfire. I was proud to sign the Health Forests Restoration Act. I want to thank the three Members of Congress for working on that act. Under this good law, we're clearing the underbrush that serves as fuel for fires. Because we acted, our forests are healthier, residents and small businesses are safer, and people across the West are better off.

To create jobs here in America, we need to reject economic isolationism and open up markets around the world for U.S. products. America can compete with anybody, anytime, anywhere, so long as the rules are fair.

To create jobs, we've got to be wise about how we spend your money and keep your taxes low. My opponent has his own history on the economy—20 years as a Senator from Massachusetts, he's built a record of a Senator from Massachusetts. [*Laughter*] He voted to raise taxes 98 times.

Audience members. Boo-o-o!

The President. That's a vote for a tax increase about five times every year.

Audience members. Boo-o-o!

The President. I think that qualifies as a pattern. [*Laughter*] He can run from his record, but he cannot hide.

Now the Senator—he looked in the camera last Friday night and promised not to raise taxes for anyone who earns less than $200,000 a year. The problem is, to keep that promise he would have to break almost all of his other ones. [*Laughter*] His plan to raise taxes on the top two income brackets would raise about $600 billion, but his spending promises cost about 4 times that much—about 2.2 trillion. That's with a "T." [*Laughter*] See, you can't have it both ways. To pay for all his big spending promises he's made, he's going to have to raise your taxes.

Audience members. Boo-o-o!

The President. The choice in this election is clear when it comes to taxes. My opponent has a history of voting for higher taxes, and he's promised to raise them on the campaign trail, and that's a promise politicians usually keep.

I believe our families and our economy are better off when Americans keep more

of what they earn. In a new term, I'll work with Congress to keep your taxes low.

When I came into office, our public schools had been waiting decades for hopeful reform. Too many of our children were shuffled through schools, grade after grade, year after year, without learning the basics. I pledged to restore accountability to the schools and end the soft bigotry of low expectations, and I kept my word. We're now seeing results. Our children are making sustained gains in reading and math. We're closing the achievement gap for minority students. We're making progress for America's families. We will leave no child behind.

To make sure jobs are here and to build a more hopeful America, we must have the best prepared and most highly skilled workforce in the world. Most new jobs are filled by people with at least 2 years of college, yet only one in four of our students gets there. So we'll fund early intervention programs in our high schools to help at-risk students. We'll place a new focus on math and science. Over time, we'll require a rigorous examination before graduation. By raising performance in our high schools and expanding Pell grants for low- and middle-income families, we'll help more Americans start their career with a college diploma.

My opponent has a history on education issues, a history of doing almost nothing. [*Laughter*] The Senator has pledged to weaken the No Child Left Behind Act. He's proposed diluting the accountability standards and looking at measures like teacher attendance to judge whether students are learning. His proposals would undermine the high standards and accountability we worked hard to pass. We've moved beyond the old days of failure and mediocrity and low standards, and we're not going to go back.

When I came into office, we had a problem in Medicare. Medicine was changing, but Medicare wasn't. Think about this: Medicare would pay tens of thousands of dollars for a heart surgery but wouldn't pay a dime for the prescription drugs that could prevent the heart surgery from being needed in the first place. That wasn't fair to seniors. It certainly wasn't fair to taxpayers. I brought Republicans and Democrats together to strengthen and modernize Medicare for our seniors. And I kept my word.

We're moving forward on health care, and there's more to do. We need to make health care more affordable and more available for all our people. We'll have a safety net for those with the greatest need. I believe in community health centers, places where the poor and the indigent can get primary preventative care. In a new term, we'll make sure every poor county in America has a community health center. We'll do more to make sure poor children are fully subscribed in our programs for low-income families.

We'll do more to make sure health care is affordable. Most of the uninsured are employees of small businesses. Small businesses are having trouble affording health care. To help workers get the health care, we should allow small businesses to join together so they can buy insurance at the same discounts big companies can do. We've got to expand health savings accounts so workers and small businesses are able to pay lower premiums, and people can save tax-free in a health care account that they call their own.

And to make sure health care is available and affordable, we must do something about the junk lawsuits that are running up the cost of health care. By forcing doctors to practice defensive medicine, medical lawsuits cost the Government about $28 billion a year. They cost our Nation's economy anywhere from 60 to 100 billion dollars a year. They drive up insurance premiums, which drive good doctors out of practice.

Today in Las Vegas, I met Dr. James Barber. Three years ago, Dr. Barber paid $27,000 in insurance premiums as an ob-gyn in Henderson, Nevada. Last year's premiums would have been more than $100,000. So he had to stop delivering babies here, and he moved his practice to California. Because the medical liability laws in California have reasonable caps, that good doctor's premiums cost him about $33,000 a year. I also met one of his former patients, Nicole Byrne. Nicole Byrne said that Dr. Barber saved her life during a previous pregnancy. Now she's pregnant again, and she's devastated that Dr. Barber will not be around to deliver her baby. Nicole and Dr. Barber understand you can't be pro-patient, pro-doctor, and pro-plaintiff-attorney at the same time. You have to choose. My opponent made his choice, and he put a personal injury lawyer on the ticket.

Audience members. Boo-o-o!

The President. I made my choice. I'm standing with the docs and the patients. I'm for medical liability reform—now. The choice is clear in this election. My opponent wants to move in the direction of Government-run health care. I believe the health decisions ought to be made by patients and doctors, not by officials in Washington, DC.

I've set out policies that move our country toward an optimistic and positive vision. I believe our country can become an ownership society. You know, there's an old saying that no one ever washes a rental car. [*Laughter*] There's a lot of wisdom in that statement. When you own something, you care about it; you have a vital stake in the future of our great country.

So we're encouraging entrepreneurship, because every time a small business is started, someone is achieving the American Dream. We're encouraging health savings accounts so people have the security of owning and managing their own health care. We're promoting homeownership. I love the fact that more citizens than ever are able to open up the door where they live and say, "Welcome to my home. Welcome to my piece of property."

In a new term, I'll take the next great step to build an ownership society by strengthening Social Security. Now, listen, our Social Security system needs fixing. I want the seniors out here to hear me loud and clear: You'll get your check. I remember when I was running in 2000, they said, "If George W. gets elected, you won't get your Social Security check." You got your checks. You'll continue to get your check. When you hear them talk about reform, don't let them fool you and say you're not going to get your check. Baby boomers are in pretty good shape when it comes to the Social Security trust.

But we need to worry about our children and our grandchildren. They are understandably worried about whether Social Security will be around when they need it. And for their sake, we must strengthen Social Security by allowing younger workers to save some of their own payroll taxes in a personal savings account that will earn compounded rate of interest, an account that Washington cannot take away.

My opponent wants to maintain the status quo when it comes to Social Security.

Audience members. Boo-o-o!

The President. He's against these Social Security reforms. As a matter of fact, he's just about against about every other reform that gives more authority and control to individuals. On issue after issue, from Medicare without choices to schools with less accountability to higher taxes, he takes the side of more centralized control and bigger Government. There's a word for that attitude. It's called liberalism. [*Laughter*] My opponent dismisses that as a label. He must have seen it differently when he said to a newspaper, "I'm a liberal and proud of it." [*Laughter*]

Others have noticed. The nonpartisan National Journal magazine did a study and named him the most liberal Member of the United States Senate. That's hard work. [*Laughter*] A group known as the Americans for Democratic Action have given Senator Kerry a higher lifetime liberal rating than Ted Kennedy. That's an accomplishment. [*Laughter*]

I have a different record and a different philosophy. I don't believe in big Government, and I don't believe in indifferent Government. I'm a compassionate conservative. I believe in policies that empower people to improve their lives, not try to run their lives. We're helping men and women find the skills and tools necessary to prosper in a time of change. We're helping all Americans to have a future of dignity and independence, and that is how I will lead our country for 4 more years.

Audience members. Four more years! Four more years! Four more years!

The President. In this time of change, some things do not change. These are the values we try to live by, courage and compassion, reverence and integrity. In the times of change, we'll support the institutions that give our lives direction and purpose, our families, our schools, our religious congregations. We stand for a culture of life in which every person counts and every being matters. We stand for marriage and family, which are the foundations of our society. We stand for the appointment of Federal judges who know the difference between personal opinion and the strict interpretation of the law.

My opponent's words on these issues are a little muddy, but his record is clear. [*Laughter*] He says he supports the institution of marriage, but he voted against the Defense of Marriage Act, which a bipartisan Congress overwhelmingly passed and which President Clinton signed. He voted against the ban on the brutal practice of partial-birth abortion.

Audience members. Boo-o-o!

The President. He calls himself the candidate of conservative values, but he described the Reagan years as a time of moral darkness.

Audience members. Boo-o-o!

The President. There is a mainstream in American politics, and my opponent sits on the left bank. He can run, but he cannot hide.

This election will also determine how America responds to the continuing danger of terrorism. The most solemn duty of the American President is to protect the American people. If America shows uncertainty or weakness in this decade, the world will drift toward tragedy. This will not happen on my watch.

Since that terrible morning, September the 11th, 2001, we have fought the terrorists across the Earth, not for pride, not for power, but because the lives of our citizens are at stake. Our strategy is clear. We'll defend the homeland. We'll strengthen our intelligence services. We'll transform the All-Volunteer Army—we'll keep the All-Volunteer Army an all-volunteer army. We're staying on the offensive. We'll strike the terrorists abroad so we do not have to face them here at home. We'll spread freedom and liberty. And we'll prevail.

Our strategy is succeeding. Think about the world as it was 3½ years ago. Afghanistan was the home base of Al Qaida. Pakistan was a transit point for terrorist groups. Saudi Arabia was fertile ground for terrorist fundraising. Libya was secretly pursuing nuclear weapons. Iraq was a dangerous place and a gathering threat. And Al Qaida was largely unchallenged as it planned attacks.

Because we led, Afghanistan is a free society and is an ally in fighting the war against terror; Pakistan is capturing terrorist leaders; Saudi Arabia is making raids and arrests; Libya is dismantling its weapons programs; the army of a free Iraq is fighting for freedom; and more than three-quarters of Al Qaida's key leaders and associates have been brought to justice.

Free societies in the Middle East will be hopeful societies which no longer feed resentments and breed violence for export. Free governments in the Middle East will fight terrorists instead of harboring them. And that's why I think it's so significant that because we defended ourselves, we liberated 50 million people in Afghanistan and Iraq.

Freedom helps us keep the peace. That's why it was so uplifting to see what took place in Afghanistan. Remember what that society was like. These people lived under the brutal darkness of the Taliban regime. Young girls weren't allowed to go to school. Their mothers were whipped in the public squares if they didn't toe the ideology of hate.

But because we acted, there's light in Afghanistan. Thousands and thousands of people voted in the Presidential elections. The first voter was a 19-year-old woman in Afghanistan. Iraq will have elections in January. Our mission is clear. We will help these countries train armies and police so they can do the hard work of defending freedom and democracy. We'll help them get on the path to stability as quickly as possible, and then our troops will come home with the honor they have earned.

We've got a great United States military. I want to thank the veterans who are here for having set such a great example for those who wear the uniform. I want to thank the military families who are here for the sacrifices they have made. And I want to assure you, we'll keep our commitments to our troops. We will make sure they have the resources they need to complete their missions.

And that's why I went to the Congress in September of 2003 and asked for $87 billion, supplemental request to help our troops in combat both in Afghanistan and Iraq. We received great bipartisan support. As a matter of fact, only 12 United States Senators voted against the funding request, 2 of whom are my opponent and his runningmate.

Audience members. Boo-o-o!

The President. When you're out rounding up the vote, remind people there's only 4 United States Senators who voted to authorize the use of force and then voted against the support of our troops——

Audience members. Boo-o-o!

The President. ——only 4 of 100, 2 of whom are my opponent and his runningmate.

Audience members. Boo-o-o!

The President. So they asked him how he could have made that vote. You might remember perhaps the most famous quote of the 2004 campaign, "I actually did vote for the $87 billion, right before I voted against it."

Audience members. Boo-o-o!

The President. I suspect a lot of people in Reno don't talk that way. [*Laughter*] He's given several explanations since then. One of my favorites is, he said, "The whole thing is a complicated matter." [*Laughter*] There's nothing complicated about supporting our troops in harm's way.

I believe in the transformational power of liberty. I want you to explain this to your friends and neighbors this way. One of my friends in the world is Prime Minister Koizumi of Japan. What's interesting about that, it wasn't all that long ago that Japan was a sworn enemy of the United States of America. My dad fought against the Japanese. John's dad—I'm sure your dads and granddads did as well. They were our sworn enemy. But because Harry S. Truman, President of the United States then, believed in the power of liberty to transform an enemy into an ally, we worked to help Japan become a democracy. There were a lot of people in our country that didn't agree with that. "Why bother? They're the enemy. Why help them? They hurt my family." There was a lot of reasons, a lot of pessimism that Japan couldn't conceivably become a self-governing democracy. But she did.

And as a result of that, I sit down at the table today with Prime Minister Koizumi talking about the peace we all want. He's an ally.

And someday, an American President will be sitting down with a duly elected leader of Iraq, talking about keeping the peace in the Middle East, and our children and our grandchildren will be better off for it.

I believe that millions in the Middle East plead in silence for their freedom. I believe women in the Middle East want to grow up in a free society. I believe if given a chance, the people in that region will embrace the most honorable form of government ever devised by man. I believe all these things because freedom is not America's gift to the world; freedom is the Almighty God's gift to each man and woman in this world.

For all Americans, these years in our history will always stand apart. There are quiet times in the life of a nation when little is expected of its leaders. This is not one of those times. This is a time that requires firm resolve, clear vision, and the deep faith in the values that makes us a great nation.

None of us will ever forget that week when one era ended and another began. September the 14th, 2001, I stood in the ruins of the Twin Towers. It's a day I will never forget. There were workers in hardhats there yelling at me at the top of their lungs, "Whatever it takes." I remember trying to console the folks coming out of the rubble. A guy grabbed me by the arm, and he said, "Do not let me down." Ever since that day, I wake up trying to figure out how best to protect our country. I will never relent in defending America, whatever it takes.

Four years ago, when I traveled your great State, I made a pledge that if you gave me a chance to serve, I would uphold the honor and the dignity of the office to which I had been elected. With your hard work, I will do so for 4 more years.

God bless. Thank you for coming. On to victory. I appreciate you all.

NOTE: The President spoke at 1:41 p.m. at Rancho San Rafael Park. In his remarks, he referred to Dema Guinn, wife of Gov. Kenny C. Guinn of Nevada; State Attorney General Brian Sandoval, State Treasurer Brian K. Krolicki, and Secretary of State Dean Heller of Nevada; and Prime Minister Junichiro Koizumi of Japan.

Remarks in Central Point, Oregon
October 14, 2004

The President. Thank you all very much. It's great to be back in Oregon. It's great to be back in Jackson County, Oregon. Laura and I are staying at the Jacksonville Inn tonight. Last President to stay there was Rutherford B. Hayes. [*Laughter*] I understand Rutherford complained about the tab. [*Laughter*] I'm not going to. We're thrilled to be here.

I want to thank not only you all coming from Jackson County, I want to thank the folks from the Klamath Basin who are here as well. It's great to be in a part of the world where the boots outnumber the suits.

I've come to ask for your vote, and I'm here to ask for your help. Tell your friends and neighbors we have a duty in our country to vote. Head them to the polls, Republicans and independents and discerning Democrats like Zell Miller. And when you get them heading to the polls, tell them if they want a safer America, a stronger America, and a better America to put me and Dick Cheney back into office.

I am keeping great company with the First Lady. She is—we were in Las Vegas earlier today, and they had the AARP convention, and so they said, "Why don't you send your best speaker to that convention." So Laura spoke there, and I went to the rally. [*Laughter*] She was a public school librarian when I met her again. We went to the seventh grade together at San Jacinto Junior High in Midland, Texas.

Audience members. Aw-w-w!

The President. Yes, how about that? [*Laughter*] And she said, "Fine, I'll marry you. I just never want to have to give a speech." I said, "Okay, you've got a deal." Fortunately, she didn't hold me to the deal, and the people of America see a compassionate, decent, strong woman when she gets up and gives a speech.

I'm proud of my runningmate, Dick Cheney. He's a good, strong man. I'm proud

to be up here with a fine American, a great friend, John McCain. I thank you, John, for coming. We have a lot of fun traveling together. It makes a big difference that he's campaigning for me. I can't thank him enough for doing so.

I'm also proud to be up on the stage with a fine United States Senator in Gordon Smith. We're real fond of Greg Walden and Mylene, his wife. You're well represented in the Halls of Congress by Greg. He's a good, solid man. All he does is talk about water—[*laughter*]—and forests and the people of this district.

I want to thank all the other State and local officials. I want to thank the grassroots activists who are here, the people who are putting up the signs and turning out the vote. With your help, we'll carry Oregon and win a great victory in November.

I enjoyed the debate last night. You know, these debates clarify the differences in our records, our approaches, and our plans for the future. I'm proud of my record. My opponent seemed to want to avoid talking about his. [*Laughter*] My record is one of lowering taxes, of reforming education, providing prescription drug coverage to seniors, improving our homeland protections, and waging an aggressive war against the ideologues of hate.

The Senator's record is 20 years of out-of-the-mainstream votes without many significant reforms or results. Our very different records are a window into what we believe and what we do—we'll do for the next 4 years. That's why these debates are important. See, the Senator believes in a bigger Government. I believe in more freedom and choices for the citizens of this country. The Senator believes Government ought to dictate. I believe you ought to decide.

And sometimes it's a little hard to tell exactly what he believes. [*Laughter*] He tries to obscure his philosophy. Take health care. Once again, last night, with a straight face, the Senator tried to say his health care plan is not a Government plan. I could barely contain myself when I heard that. Yet 22 million people would enroll on a Government program under his plan. That would be the largest expansion of Government health care ever. Eighty percent of the newly insured on his plan would be placed on a Government program like Medicaid. He claimed his position would help small business. It's not what the people who studied his plan say. They say his plan would be an overpriced albatross that would saddle small business with 225 new mandates.

I have a different view. I want to make health care more affordable and available by helping small businesses, not by saddling them with a bunch of regulations.

Once again, last night, with a straight face, the Senator said—well, shall we say, refined his answer on his proposed "global test." That's the test he would administer before defending America. After trying to say it really wasn't a test at all, last night he once again defended his approach, saying, "I think it makes sense." [*Laughter*] The Senator now says we'd have to pass some international truth standard. The truth is we should never turn America's national security decisions over to international bodies or leaders of other countries.

The last few years, the American people have gotten to know me. They know my blunt way of speaking. I get that from my mom. [*Laughter*] They know I sometimes mangle the English language. [*Laughter*] I get that from my dad. [*Laughter*] Americans also know I tell you exactly what I'm going to do, and I keep my word.

When we came into office, the stock market had been in serious decline for 6 months and the American economy was sliding into a recession. To help families and get this economy growing again, I pledged to reduce taxes. I kept my word.

The results are clear. The recession was one of the shallowest in American history.

Over the last 3 years, our economy has grown at the fastest rate as any in nearly 20 years. The homeownership rate in America is at an alltime high. Farm and ranch incomes are up.

The past 13 months, we've added 1.9 million new jobs in America. The unemployment rate across our country is 5.4 percent, lower than the average of the 1970s, 1980s, and 1990s. Here in Oregon, I understand that some of the areas are lagging behind, but we're making progress. This State has added more than 40,000 jobs since January of 2002. So long as somebody is looking for work and can't find a job, means we'll continue to expand the economy with pro-growth, pro-entrepreneur, pro-farmer, pro-small-business policies.

To make sure we can find job—people can find jobs here, America must be the best place in the world to do business. If you want jobs to create, you've got to be a good place to create jobs. That means we need less regulations on our small businesses. We need to do something about these frivolous lawsuits that are making it harder for our employers to expand the job base.

To create jobs, Congress needs to pass my energy plan. It encourages conservation. It encourages the use of renewables like ethanol and biodiesel. It encourages new technologies. It encourages clean coal technology. It encourages increased domestic production. To create jobs here in America, we must become less dependent on foreign sources of energy.

To protect jobs in communities in the West, we need to reduce the risk of devastating wildfires. That's why I was proud to work on and sign the Healthy Forests Restoration Act. Under this good law, we're clearing the underbrush that serves as fuel for fire. Because we acted, our forests are healthier, residents and small businesses are safer, and people across the West are better off.

My opponent says he's in touch with the West, but sometimes I think he means western Massachusetts. [*Laughter*] When the Healthy Forests bill came up in the Senate, it had the support of both Senators from Oregon, one Republican and one Democrat. It had the strong support of your Congressman. And Senator Kerry was against it.

Audience members. Boo-o-o!

The President. When I signed the Healthy Forests Act last December, he said, "We're taking a chainsaw to public forests."

Audience members. Boo-o-o!

The President. Now it's time to campaign in the West. He's kind of turning his position around a little bit. [*Laughter*] He's actually—he's now saying that he actually likes a lot of part of the law. I guess it's not only the wildfires that shift in the wind.

To create jobs, we need to reject economic isolationism and open up markets for U.S. products. Listen, we can compete with anybody, anytime, anywhere, so long as the rules are fair. To create jobs, we need to be wise about how we spend your money and keep your taxes low. My opponent has his own history on the economy. In 20 years as a Senator from Massachusetts, he's built the record of a Senator from Massachusetts. [*Laughter*] He's voted to raise taxes 98 times.

Audience members. Boo-o-o!

The President. That's a vote for a tax increase about five times every year he's served in the Senate. I think that qualifies as a pattern. He can run from his record, but he cannot hide.

You might remember the debate last Friday. The Senator looked in the camera and promised not to raise taxes on anyone who earns less than $200,000 a year. The problem with that is to keep that promise, he must break all his other ones. His plan to raise taxes on the top two income brackets will raise about $600 billion, but his spending promises will cost almost four times as much, more than 2.2 trillion.

That's with a "T." See, you can't have it both ways. To pay for all his promises, his spending promises, he's going to have to raise your taxes. The choice in this election is clear when it comes to taxes.

He's had a—tell your friends and neighbors he's had a history of voting to raise taxes, and he has promised to raise them in this campaign. And that's the kind of promise a Washington politician usually keeps. [*Laughter*]

I believe our families and our economy are better off when Americans keep more of what they earn. In a new term, I will work with the United States Congress to keep your taxes low.

When I came to office, our public schools had been waiting for decades for hopeful reform. Too many of our children were shuffled through school, year after year, grade after grade, without learning the basics. I pledged to restore accountability to our schools and end the soft bigotry of low expectations. I kept my word. We're now seeing the results of our reforms. Our children are making sustained gains in reading and math. We're closing the achievement gap for minority students. We're making progress for our families. We will leave no child behind in America.

To build a more hopeful America, we must have the best prepared and most highly skilled workforce in the world. Most new jobs are filled by people with at least 2 years of college, yet one in four of our students gets there. So we'll fund early intervention programs in our high schools to help at-risk students. We'll place a new focus on math and science. Over time, we'll require a rigorous exam before graduation. By raising the performance in our high schools and by expanding Pell grants for low- and middle-income families, we will help more Americans start their careers with a college diploma.

When I came into office, we had a problem with Medicare. Medicine was changing, but Medicare was not. For example, Medicare would pay tens of thousands of dollars for a heart surgery but not one dime for the prescription drugs that might prevent the heart surgery from being needed in the first place. That didn't make any sense for our seniors. It didn't make any sense for our taxpayers. I pledged to bring Republicans and Democrats together to strengthen and modernize Medicare for our seniors, and I kept my word. Seniors are already getting discounts on medicine, and beginning in 2006, all seniors will be able to get prescription drug coverage under Medicare.

No, we're moving forward on health care, and there's much more to do. We need to make health care more affordable and available for all our people. We need a safety net for those with the greatest needs. I believe in community health centers, a place where the poor and the indigent can get primary and preventative care. In a new term, we'll make sure every poor county in America has a community health center. We need to do more to make sure poor children are fully subscribed in our programs for low-income families so they can get the health care they need.

We must do more to make sure health care is affordable. Most of the uninsured in America are employees of small businesses. Small businesses are having trouble affording health care. To help more workers get health care, we should allow small businesses to join together so they can buy insurance at the same discounts as big businesses can do. We must expand health savings accounts so workers and small businesses are able to pay lower premiums and people can save tax-free in a health care account they call their own.

To make sure health care is available and affordable, we've got to do something about the junk lawsuits that are running up the cost of health care. By forcing doctors to practice defensive medicine, medical lawsuits cost the Government about $28 billion a year. They cost our Nation's economy anywhere from 60 to 100 billion dollars a year. They drive up insurance premiums,

which drives good docs out of practice. You cannot be pro-patient and pro-doctor and pro-plaintiff-attorney at the same time. You have to choose. My opponent made his choice, and he put a plaintiff attorney on the ticket. I made my choice. I'm standing with the doctors and patients. I'm for medical liability reform—now.

The choice for health care is clear in this election. My opponent wants to move in the direction of Government-run health care. I believe health decisions should be made by patients and doctors, not by officials in Washington, DC.

I've set out policies that move America toward a positive and optimistic vision. I believe our country can be an ownership society. You know, there's an old saying: No one ever washes a rental car. [*Laughter*] A lot of wisdom in that statement. When you own something, you care about it. When you own something, you have a vital stake in the future of our country. We're encouraging entrepreneurship, because every time a small business is started, someone is achieving the American Dream. We're encouraging health savings accounts so people have the security of owning their own health care plan. We're providing—promoting homeownership. Listen, I love it when more and more people open up the door where they live and say, "Welcome to my home. Welcome to my piece of property."

In a new term, I'll take the next great step to build an ownership society by strengthening Social Security. Our Social Security system needs fixing. We'll keep the promise of Social Security to our seniors. You might remember the 2000 campaign, when they ran those ads that said, "If George W. gets in, the seniors won't get their checks." The seniors got their checks, and our seniors will continue to get checks. And the baby boomers are in pretty good shape when it comes to the Social Security trust.

But we need to worry about our children and our grandchildren. We need to be worried about whether Social Security will be around when they need it. For their sake, we must strengthen Social Security by allowing younger workers to save some of their payroll taxes in a personal savings account that they can call their own, that the Government will not take away.

When it comes to Social Security, my opponent wants to maintain the status quo.

Audience members. Boo-o-o!

The President. That's unacceptable. He's against these Social Security reforms. He's against just about every reform that gives more authority and more control to the individual. On issue after issue, from Medicare without choices to schools with less accountability to higher taxes, he takes the side of more centralized control and more bureaucracies. And there's a word for that attitude. It's called liberalism.

Audience members. Boo-o-o!

The President. He dismisses that as a label, but he must have seen it differently when he said to a newspaper, "I am a liberal and proud of it."

Audience members. Boo-o-o!

The President. The nonpartisan National Journal magazine did a study and named him the most liberal Member of the United States Senate. That takes a lot of hard work. [*Laughter*] Another group known as the Americans for Democratic Action has given Senator Kerry a higher lifetime liberal rating than that given to Ted Kennedy. And that's an accomplishment. [*Laughter*]

I have a different record and a different philosophy. I don't believe in big Government, and I don't believe in indifferent Government. I'm a compassionate conservative. I believe in policies that empower people to improve their lives, not in policies that try to run their lives.

These are changing times, but in a time of change, some things do not change, the values we try to live by, courage and compassion, reverence and integrity. In changing times, we will support the institutions that give our lives direction and purpose, our families, our schools, our religious congregations. We stand for a culture of life in which every person counts and every being matters. We stand for marriage and family, which are the foundations of our society. We stand for the appointment of Federal judges who know the difference between personal opinion and a strict interpretation of the law.

My opponent's words on these issues are a little muddy, but his record is pretty clear. He says he supports the institution of marriage, but he voted against the Defense of Marriage Act.

Audience members. Boo-o-o!

The President. He voted against the ban on partial-birth abortion.

Audience members. Boo-o-o!

The President. One time he called himself the candidate of conservative values, but he has described the Reagan years as a period of moral darkness.

Audience members. Boo-o-o!

The President. There is a mainstream in American politics, and my opponent sits on the far left bank. [*Laughter*] He can run, but he cannot hide.

Audience members. Four more years! Four more years! Four more years!

The President. This election will also determine how America responds to the continuing danger of terrorism. The most solemn duty of the American President is to protect the American people. If America shows uncertainty or weakness in this decade, the world will drift toward tragedy. This will not happen on my watch.

Since that terrible morning of September the 11th, 2001, we have fought the terrorists across the Earth, not for pride, not for power, but because the lives of our citizens are at stake. Our strategy is clear. We'll defend the homeland. We're strengthening our intelligence. We're transforming our military. We will keep the All-Volunteer Army an all-volunteer army. We're staying on the offensive. We're striking the terrorists abroad so we do not have to face them here at home. We will spread freedom and liberty. And we will prevail.

Our strategy is succeeding. Think about the world as it was 3½ years ago. Afghanistan was the home base of Al Qaida. Pakistan was a transit point for terrorist groups. Saudi Arabia was fertile ground for terrorist fundraising. Libya was secretly pursuing nuclear weapons. Iraq was a dangerous place and a gathering threat. And Al Qaida was largely unchallenged as it planned attacks.

Because we acted, because the United States of America led, Afghanistan is an ally in the war on terror; Pakistan is capturing terrorist leaders; Saudi Arabia is making raids and arrests; Libya is dismantling its weapons programs; the army of a free Iraq is fighting for freedom; and more than three-quarters of Al Qaida's key members and associates have been brought to justice.

In defending ourselves, we have freed 50 million people. Think about what happened recently in Afghanistan. It wasn't all that long ago that the country was ruled by brutal ideologues of hate who had a dark vision of the world. Young girls were not allowed to go to school—many young girls were not. Their moms, if they didn't toe the ideological line, were taken into the public square and whipped, sometimes killed in a sports stadium. Recently, thousands and thousands of Afghan citizens once under the rule of the Taliban voted in a Presidential election. The first voter in that election was a 19-year-old woman.

Iraq will have elections in January. We're standing with the people of Afghanistan and Iraq. When America gives its word, America must keep its word. And we're standing with them because we understand that free societies in the Middle East will be hopeful societies which no longer feed resentments and breed violence for export. Free governments in the Middle East will fight terrorists instead of harboring them, and that helps us keep the peace.

Our mission is clear. We'll help those countries train their armies and police forces so the citizens of Afghanistan and Iraq can do the hard work of defending democracy. We will help them get on the path to stability and democracy as quickly as possible, and then our troops will come home with the honor they have earned.

I see some folks who wear the uniform. Thank you for your service. I want to thank the veterans who are here for having set such a great example to those who wear the uniform. I want to thank the military families who have joined us today. I assure you, we'll keep the commitment I made to our troops and their loved ones. We'll make sure they have all the resources they need to complete their missions.

And that's why I went to the United States Congress in September of 2003 and requested $87 billion for important funding to support our troops in combat. We received great support for that funding request. As a matter of fact, only 12 United States Senators voted against the funding for our troops in harm's way, 2 of whom are my opponent and his runningmate.

Audience members. Boo-o-o!

The President. As you round up the vote, remind people of this fact: Only four United States Senators voted to authorize the use of force, and then voted against funding the troops, two of whom are my opponent and his runningmate.

Audience members. Boo-o-o!

The President. You might remember perhaps one of the most famous quotes of the 2004 campaign. When asked to explain his vote, my opponent said, "I actually did vote for the $87 billion, before I voted against it."

Audience members. Boo-o-o!

The President. I suspect a lot of people in Jackson County, Oregon, don't speak that way. And they kept pressing him, and he had all kinds of different explanations. One of the most interesting was, he finally said, "It is a complicated matter." [*Laughter*] There's nothing complicated about supporting our troops in combat.

I believe in the transformational power of liberty. Let me tell you a story that will help make the point. One of our good friends is Prime Minister Koizumi of Japan. That doesn't sound unusual, probably, except for think about what life was like some 60 years ago with the Japanese. They were our mortal enemy. My dad fought against the Japanese. Senator McCain's dad fought against the Japanese. I'm confident there are people here whose dad or granddad saw combat against the Japanese. It was a tough war.

After we won the war, Harry S. Truman believed in the transformational power of liberty to convert an enemy into an ally, and so he worked to build a democracy in Japan. There were a lot of citizens here who, I'm confident, weren't very happy about that decision. "Why would you want to work with an enemy? The enemy can't possibly convert to a democracy. Too many of our lives were lost during the war." But we had great faith in the ability of liberty to transform a nation. And today, because of that faith, I sit down with Prime Minister Koizumi talking about the peace we all want, talking about how to deal with the issues of the world to make the world more peaceful.

Someday, a duly elected leader of Iraq will be sitting down with an American President talking about the peace in the Middle East, and our children and our grandchildren will be better off for it.

I believe millions in the Middle East plead in silence for freedom. I believe women in the Middle East want to grow up in a free society and raise their children in freedom. I believe that if given a chance, the people of the Middle East will embrace the most honorable form of government ever devised by man. I believe all these things because freedom is not America's gift to the world; freedom is the Almighty God's gift to each man and woman in this world.

For all Americans, these years in our history will always stand apart. There are quiet times in the life of a nation when little is expected of its leaders. This isn't one of those times. This is a time that requires firm resolve, clear vision, and the deep faith in the values that makes us a great nation.

None of us will ever forget that week when one era ended and another began. As John mentioned, I stood in the ruins of the Twin Towers on September the 14th, 2001. It is a day I will never forget. Workers in hardhats yelling at the top of their lungs, "Whatever it takes." A guy grabbed me by the arm, and he looked me in the eye, and he said, "Do not let me down." Ever since that day, I wake up working hard to figure out how best to protect America. I will never relent in defending the security of this country, whatever it takes.

Four years ago, when I traveled your beautiful State asking for the vote, I said if you gave me a chance to serve, I would uphold the honor and the dignity of the office to which I had been elected. With your help, with your hard work, with your vote, I will do so for 4 more years.

Thanks for coming. May God bless. Thank you all very much.

NOTE: The President spoke at 6:16 p.m. at the Jackson County Fairgrounds. In his remarks, he referred to Senator Zell Miller of Georgia, who made the keynote address at the 2004 Republican National Convention; and Prime Minister Junichiro Koizumi of Japan.

Remarks in Cedar Rapids, Iowa
October 15, 2004

The President. It is great—thank you all. It is great to be back in Iowa. This isn't the first time we've been here. [*Laughter*] It's not going to be our last, either. I want to thank you for putting up the signs and doing the hard work. I want to thank you for what you're going to do over the next couple of weeks, and that is turn out the vote. There's no doubt in my mind, with your help, we will carry Iowa and win a great victory on the 2d of November.

And I just told the chairman—I call him the chairman. You call him Chuck. [*Laughter*] I said, "I got a job for him over the next 4 years." He said, "What's that?" I said, "Well, get those lawn mowers cranked up; there's a lot of grass on the South Lawn."

And tell your friends and neighbors, if they want a safer America, a stronger America, and a better America, to put me and Dick Cheney back in office.

The President. I'm pleased——

Audience member. [*Inaudible*]

The President. I'm pleased that Laura is traveling with me today. She is—we were in Las Vegas yesterday, and there was an important conference. The AARP was having a convention, and they said, "Send your best speaker over." So I went to the rally, and Laura went to the AARP. [*Laughter*] People have come to know her like I know her. She's warm. She's compassionate. She's a strong woman. She is a great First Lady.

I'm proud of my runningmate. Dick Cheney is doing a fine job. In the debate the other night, I admit he didn't have the waviest hair. [*Laughter*] I didn't pick him because of his hairdo. I picked him because of his experience, his judgment, and he's getting the job done for the American people.

I appreciate working with the chairman. He always talks about Iowa. Chuck Grassley is a good friend. He's a really good United States Senator. And so is your Congressman, Jim Leach. I appreciate Jim. What a decent and honorable man Jim Leach is. And I'm proud that the chairman of the Budget Committee in the House of Representatives, Jim Nussle, is with us as well.

I want to thank the grassroots activists, all the people who are doing all the hard work. You never get thanked enough, and so here's my chance to thank you before election day. Keep putting up the signs. Keep making the phone calls. Turn out the vote, and we will win.

I enjoyed our debates. I enjoyed standing up there with my opponent, talking about our differences, and we have big differences. We have very different records and different plans for the future. My record is one of reforming education, of lowering taxes, of providing prescription drug coverage for seniors, for improving homeland protections, and for waging an aggressive war against the ideologues of hate. The Senator's record is 20 years of out-of-the-mainstream votes without many significant reforms or results to show for those 20 years. The records are important because our country faces many challenges, and the next President must recognize the need for reform and must be able to lead to achieve them.

On issue after issue, from jobs to health care to the need to strengthen Social Security, Senator Kerry's policies fail to recognize the changing realities of today's world and the need for fundamental reforms. In our final debate, when I talked about the vital link between education and jobs, the Senator didn't seem to get it. He said I switched away from jobs and started talking about education. No, good jobs start with good education. At a time when most new jobs require at least 2 years of college, I understand that one of the best ways to keep jobs in America is to make sure our workforce is educated, the most highly skilled, the most creative, and the most innovative in the world. That's how we create jobs here in America.

When it comes to health care, once again, the other night, with a straight face—[laughter]—the Senator said his health care was not a Government plan.

Audience members. Boo-o-o!

The President. I could barely contain myself. Twenty-two million new people would enroll in a Government program under his plan, the largest expansion of Government health care ever. Eighty percent of the newly insured would be placed on a Government program like Medicaid. He claims his plan would help small businesses. Yet studies conducted by people who understand small businesses concluded that his plan is an overpriced albatross that would saddle small businesses with 225 new mandates.

I have a different view. We'll work to make sure health care is available and affordable. We'll help our small businesses. The decisions will be made by doctors and patients, not by officials in Washington, DC.

The Senator said about Social Security, if, later on, after a period of time, we find that Social Security is in trouble, then he'll call a meeting of experts. [Laughter] See, it seems that he likes meetings. [Laughter] Younger workers understandably worry whether Social Security will be there when they need it. We have plans for the future. We will solve problems before they—before it's too late. As I said in the debate the other night, our seniors have nothing to worry about when it comes to their Social Security check. You might remember the 2000 campaign, and those ads said, "If George W. gets in, you're not going to get your check." You got your checks. You will continue to get your check.

But for the sake of our children and our grandchildren, we must confront the Social Security problem now. Younger workers

must be able to take some of their own payroll taxes and set up a personal savings account that will earn better interest, an account they can call their own.

The last few years, the people have gotten to know me. They know my blunt way of speaking. I get that from Mom. [Laughter] They know I sometimes mangle the English language. I get that from Dad. [Laughter] Americans also know I tell you what I'm going to do and that I keep my word.

Audience members. Four more years! Four more years! Four more years!

The President. Thank you all. When I came into office, the stock market had been in serious decline for 6 months, and the American economy was sliding into a recession. To help families, to get this economy growing again, I pledged to reduce taxes. I kept my word. Because we acted—and I include the Senator and Members of Congress here from Iowa, not all of them but most of them—because we acted, the recession was one of the shallowest in American history.

Over the last 3 years, our economy has grown at the rate—at the fastest rate of any major industrialized nation. The homeownership rate in America is at an alltime high. I remember campaigning in Iowa, and I made it clear to the farmers here that I understand a healthy economy requires a healthy farm economy. And today, farm and ranch income is up. In the past 13 months, we've added more than 1.9 million new jobs. The unemployment rate in America is 5.4 percent, lower than the average of the 1970s, the 1980s, and the 1990s. The unemployment rate in Iowa is down to 4.5 percent. This economy is moving forward, and we're not going back to the old days of tax and spend.

Listen, to make sure jobs stay here in America and people can find work, America must be the best place in the world to do business. That means less regulations on the job creators. That means we've got to do something about the frivolous lawsuits that make it hard for people to expand their businesses.

To keep jobs here, Congress needs to pass my energy plan. The plan encourages conservation. It focuses on renewables like ethanol and biodiesel. It encourages new technologies. It encourages clean coal technology and increased domestic production. To create jobs here in America, we must be less dependent on foreign sources of energy.

To create jobs, to make sure people can find work, we've got to reject economic isolationism. We need to open up markets for Iowa farm products, for example. See, America can compete with anybody, anytime, anywhere, so long as the playing field is level. To create jobs, we've got to be wise about how we spend your money and keep your taxes low.

My opponent has his own history on the economy. In 20 years as a Senator from Massachusetts, he's built the record of a Senator from Massachusetts. He has voted to raise taxes 98 times.

Audience members. Boo-o-o!

The President. That's a vote for a tax increase about five times every year he has served in the Senate. That qualifies as a pattern. [*Laughter*] He can run from his record, but he cannot hide.

He looked in the camera, and he promised not to raise taxes on anyone who earns less than $200,000 a year. The problem is, to keep that promise he would have to break almost all of his other ones. [*Laughter*] You see, he's promised about $2.2 trillion in new Federal spending. That's trillion with a "T." And he says he's going to raise the top two brackets, which raises between 600 billion and 800 billion. There is a tax gap. That's the difference between what he could raise and what he's promised to spend. You can't have it both ways. To pay for all his big spending promises he's made, he's going to have to raise your taxes.

Audience members. Boo-o-o!

The President. But we're not going to let him; we're going to carry Iowa and win the Nation.

When I came into office, our public schools had been waiting decades for hopeful reform. Too many of our children were being shuffled through school without learning the basics. I pledged to restore accountability to our schools and end the soft bigotry of low expectations. And I kept my word. We passed the No Child Left Behind Act, and we're now seeing results. Our children are making sustained gains in reading and math. We are closing the achievement gap for minority students. We're making progress in America, and we will leave no child behind.

There is more work to be done. We'll fund early intervention programs in our high schools to help at-risk students. We'll place a new focus on math and science. Over time, we'll require a rigorous examination before graduation from high school. By raising performance in our high schools and by expanding Pell grants for low- and middle-income families, we will help more Americans start their career with a college diploma.

My opponent has a history on education issues—a history of almost doing nothing. The Senator has pledged to weaken the No Child Left Behind Act. He's proposed diluting the accountability standards and looking at measures like teacher attendance to judge whether students are learning. His proposals would undermine the high standards and accountability we worked hard to pass. We've moved beyond the old days of failure and mediocrity and low standards, and we're not going back.

When I came into office, we had a problem with Medicare. See, medicine was changing, but Medicare wasn't. For example, Medicare would pay tens of thousands of dollars for heart surgery but wouldn't pay a dime for the prescription drugs that could prevent the heart surgery from being needed in the first place. That didn't make any sense for our seniors. It didn't make any sense for the taxpayers. I pledged to bring Republicans and Democrats together to strengthen and modernize Medicare for our seniors, and I kept my word.

We strengthened Medicare. Seniors are getting discounts on medicine through prescription drug cards. Rural hospitals and doctors are being treated fairly in the State of Iowa because of the Medicare law we passed. Beginning in 2006, all seniors will be able to get prescription drug coverage under Medicare.

Moving forward on health care, and there's much more to do. We need to make health care more available and affordable. We need a safety net for those with the greatest needs. I believe in community health centers, places where the poor and the indigent can get care. In a new term, we'll make sure every poor county in America has a community health center. We'll make sure our poor children are fully subscribed in our programs for low-income families.

We'll do more to make sure health care is affordable. Most uninsured work for small businesses. Small businesses are having trouble affording health care. To help our workers get the health care they need, we should allow small businesses to join together so they can buy insurance at the same discounts that big businesses are able to do. We will expand health savings accounts.

We will make sure that health care is available and affordable by doing something about the junk lawsuits that threaten our docs, running up the cost of medicine. By forcing doctors to practice defensive medicine, medical lawsuits cost the Government about $28 billion a year. They cost our economy anywhere from 60 to 100 billion dollars a year. They're driving up insurance premiums, which drives good doctors out of practice. You cannot be pro-patient, pro-doctor, and pro-trial-lawyer at the same time. You have to choose. My opponent made his choice, and he put a personal injury lawyer on the ticket. I made my

choice. I'm standing with the doctors and patients. I am for medical liability reform—now.

I believe our country can be an ownership society. You know, there's a saying that says, no one ever washes a rental car. [Laughter] There's some wisdom in that statement. See, when you own something, you care about it. When you own something, you have a vital stake in the future of our country. So we encourage entrepreneurship. Every time a small business is starting, someone is achieving a part of the American Dream. We encourage homeownership in America. I love the fact that more and more people are owning up—opening up the front door of their home, saying, "Welcome to my piece of property. Welcome to my home."

You know, on issue after issue, from Medicare without choices to schools with less accountability to higher taxes, my opponent takes the side of more centralized control and more Government.

Audience members. Boo-o-o!

The President. There's a word for that attitude. It's called liberalism. [Laughter] He dismisses that as a label, but he must have seen it differently when he said to a newspaper, "I am a liberal and proud of it." He's been rated by the National Journal as the most liberal Member of the United States Senate. That's hard to do. [Laughter] He's had some serious competition. [Laughter]

See, I have a different record and a very different philosophy. I don't believe in big Government, and I don't believe in indifferent Government. I'm a compassionate conservative. I believe in policies that empower people to improve their lives. I do not believe in policies that try to run people's lives. And so we're helping men and women find the skills and tools to prosper in a time of change. We're helping all Americans to have a future of dignity and independence. And that is how I will continue to lead our country for 4 more years.

Audience members. Four more years! Four more years! Four more years!

The President. In this time of change, some things do not change, the values we try to live by, courage and compassion, reverence and integrity. In changing times, we must support the institutions that give our lives direction and purpose, our families, our schools, our religious congregations. We stand for a culture of life in which every person matters and every being counts. We stand for marriage and family, which are the foundations of our society. We stand for the appointment of Federal judges who know the difference between personal opinion and the strict interpretation of the law.

Listen, my opponent's words on these issues are a little muddy, but his record is plenty clear. He says he supports the institution of marriage, but he voted against the Defense of Marriage Act. He voted against the ban on partial-birth abortion.

Audience members. Boo-o-o!

The President. He calls himself—at one time in the race called himself the candidate of conservative values.

Audience members. Boo-o-o!

The President. But he has described the Reagan years as a time of moral darkness.

Audience members. Boo-o-o!

The President. There is a mainstream in American politics, and my opponent sits on the far left bank. He can run, but he cannot hide.

This election will also determine how America responds to the continuing danger of terrorism. The most solemn duty of the American President is to protect the American people. If America shows uncertainty or weakness in this decade, the world will drift toward tragedy. This will not happen on my watch.

Since that terrible morning of September the 11th, 2001, we've fought the terrorists across the Earth, not for pride, not for power, but because the lives of our citizens are at stake. Our strategy is clear. We're defeating the—we're defending our homeland. We're strengthening the intelligence

services. We're modernizing and transforming our United States military so we can keep the All-Volunteer Army an all-volunteer army. We're staying on the offensive. We will strike the terrorists abroad so we do not have to face them here at home. We will spread liberty and freedom. And we will prevail.

Our strategy is succeeding. Think about the world as it was about 3½ years ago. Afghanistan was the home base of Al Qaida. Pakistan was a transit point for terrorist groups. Saudi Arabia was fertile ground for terrorist fundraising. Libya was secretly pursuing nuclear weapons. Iraq was a dangerous place and a gathering threat. And Al Qaida was largely unchallenged as it planned attacks.

Because we led, Afghanistan is free and is now an ally in the war on terror; Pakistan is capturing terrorist leaders; Saudi Arabia is making raids and arrests; Libya is dismantling its weapons programs; the army of a free Iraq is fighting for freedom; and more than three-quarters of Al Qaida's key members and associates have been brought to justice. We have led. Many have joined. And America and the world are safer.

And part of our strategy for a safe and peaceful world is to continue to spread freedom, and freedom is on the march. As we worked to secure ourselves in Afghanistan and Iraq, 50 million people have been freed from the clutches of brutal tyranny— 50 million.

Think about what happened in Afghanistan. I want the youngsters here to realize what took place recently in history. It wasn't all that long ago that young girls couldn't go to school. Their mothers were pulled in the public square and whipped because they wouldn't toe the line to an ideology of hate. These people lived in darkness. Because we acted, people were freed. Thousands and thousands of people went to vote for a President. The first person to vote in the Afghan Presidential election was a 19-year-old woman. Freedom is powerful. Can you imagine a society that's gone from darkness to light in 3 short years? Freedom is on the move.

There will be elections in Iraq. It hadn't been all that long ago that there was torture chambers and mass graves. Then the people will be having a chance to vote for President and Prime Minister of that country. Free societies in the Middle East will be hopeful societies which no longer feed resentments and breed violence for export. Free governments in the Middle East will fight the terrorists instead of harboring them. Freedom will help us keep the peace. Freedom will make America more secure.

So our mission is clear. We will help Afghanistan and Iraq train armies and police so their people can do the hard work of defending democracy. We will help them get on the path to stability and democracy as quickly as possible, and then our troops will come home with the honor they have earned.

It's a high honor to be the Commander in Chief of such a great military. We're a great military because it's full of great people. I'm proud of our military. I'm proud of our military families. And I want to thank the veterans who are here for having set such a great example for those who wear the uniform.

We will continue to make sure our troops have all the resources they need to complete their missions. That's why I went to the United States Congress in September of 2003 and asked for $87 billion of supplemental funding to support our troops in both Iraq and Afghanistan. It was really an important piece of legislation. The bipartisan support was very strong. As a matter of fact, only 12 United States Senators voted against the $87 billion, 2 of whom are my opponent and his runningmate.

Audience members. Boo-o-o!

The President. Now, when you're out gathering the vote, when you're out convincing people to go to the polls and getting them to be for us, remind them of this fact. Only 4 United States Senators

voted to authorize the use of force and then voted against providing the funding necessary to support our troops in combat—only 4 of 100—2 of whom, 50 percent of whom, are my opponent and his runningmate.

Audience members. Boo-o-o!

The President. So they asked him why he made the vote. You might remember one of the most famous quotes in this campaign season. He said, "I actually did vote for the $87 billion, right before I voted against it."

Audience members. Boo-o-o!

The President. Yes. He's given a lot of explanations for that vote since. One of the most interesting ones of all, he said, "Well, the whole thing is a complicated matter." There's nothing complicated about supporting our troops in combat.

In our debate, Senator Kerry proposed that we should pass a "global test" before we defend ourselves.

Audience members. Boo-o-o!

The President. The problem with that "global test" is that the Senator can't ever pass it. I say that because in 1990, the United Nations Security Council passed a resolution supporting action to remove Saddam Hussein from Kuwait. The international community was united. Countries throughout the world joined the coalition. Yet, even after the United Nations' approval, in the United States Senate, Senator Kerry voted against authorization for the use of force. He couldn't pass his own test.

In this campaign, you might remember he said that removing Saddam Hussein was a mistake. He actually said he would have done it differently. He would have had the U.N. pass another resolution. [*Laughter*] If Senator Kerry had his way, not only would Saddam Hussein still be in a palace in Baghdad, he'd be occupying Kuwait. This world of ours is safer with Saddam Hussein sitting in a prison cell.

We'll continue to build strong alliances. I talked with Tony Blair today, on Air Force One. He's a great ally. And we'll build on those alliances, and we'll strengthen our coalitions. But I will never turn over America's national security decisions to leaders of other countries.

I believe in the transformational power of liberty. Perhaps I can explain it to you this way. Prime Minister Koizumi is a good friend of mine and Laura's. But it wasn't all that long ago that we were at war with the Japanese. My dad fought in World War II. I know dads and granddads of the people out here fought in World War II as well, against a sworn enemy. And it was a tough war. It was a brutal war, like all war.

And after World War II, Harry S. Truman, President of the United States, believed in the power of liberty to transform an enemy into an ally. That's what he believed. So after the war was over, we worked with the Japanese to build a democracy. There's a lot of people in this country who were skeptical about that action, skeptical about whether an enemy could ever become an ally, skeptical about whether Japan would become a democracy, skeptical about efforts to help them after they had hurt many of our citizens. But people believed. And as a result of that belief, today, I sit down with Prime Minister Koizumi, talking about how to keep the peace that we all want.

Someday, a duly elected leader of Iraq will sit down with an American President, talking about how to keep the peace in the Middle East, and our children and our grandchildren will be better off for it.

I believe that millions in the Middle East plead in silence for freedom. I believe that women in the Middle East want to grow up in a free society, and they want to raise their children in a free society. I believe that if given a chance, the people of the Middle East will embrace the most honorable form of government ever devised by man: democracy. I believe all these things because freedom is not America's gift to the world; freedom is the Almighty God's gift to each man and woman in this world.

For all Americans, these years in our history will always stand apart. There are quiet times in the life of a nation when little is expected of its leaders. This isn't one of those times. This is a time that requires firm resolve, clear vision, and a deep faith in the values that make us a great nation.

None of us will ever forget that week when one era ended and another began. September the 14th, 2001, I stood in the ruins of the Twin Towers. It is a day I will never forget. Workers in hardhats were there yelling at me at the top of their lungs, "Whatever it takes." I remember a fellow grabbed me by the arm, and he looked me in the eye, and he said, "Do not let me down." Ever since that day, I wake up every morning thinking about how to better protect our country. I will never relent in defending America, whatever it takes.

Four years ago, as I traveled your great State in the caucuses and then in the general election, I pledged that if you honored me with the high office of President, I would uphold the honor and the dignity. With your help, with your hard work, I will do so for 4 more years.

God bless. Thank you all for coming. Thank you all for being here. On to victory.

NOTE: The President spoke at 1:55 p.m. at the U.S. Cellular Center. In his remarks, he referred to Prime Minister Tony Blair of the United Kingdom; and Prime Minister Junichiro Koizumi of Japan.

Remarks in Oshkosh, Wisconsin
October 15, 2004

The President. Thank you all. Okay. It's great to be back in Oshkosh. My only regret is I don't have time to drive by Leon's. Laura and I are thrilled to be here. We're glad to be back in Wisconsin. The enthusiasm in this State is high. With your help, with your hard work, there is no doubt in my mind we will carry Wisconsin on November the 2d.

I want to—I am traveling with very good company today. So when I asked Laura to marry me, when I asked her to marry me, she said, "Okay, I will, just so long as I never have to give a speech." [*Laughter*] I said, "Okay, you got a deal." Fortunately, she didn't hold me to the deal. She's giving a lot of speeches. The American people have come to know Laura as a compassionate, warm, great First Lady.

Audience members. Laura! Laura! Laura!

The President. I know my opponent * has been in the neighborhood recently.

Audience members. Boo-o-o!

The President. He thought he was going over to Lambert Field. [*Laughter*] One of these days I'm going to make it to Lambeau Field and thank the Packers for being—setting such good examples for our kids.

I'm proud of Dick Cheney. Now, look, I admit it, he doesn't have the waviest hair in the race. [*Laughter*] I didn't pick him because of his hair. I picked him because of his judgment, his experience, his ability to get the job done for the American people.

I want to thank your Congressman, Tom Petri. He's a fine man. I appreciate you coming, Congressman. I see the chairman over there, Jim Sensenbrenner. Thanks for coming, Chairman. Finely, we're proud to be here with Mark Green, Congressman Mark Green. I appreciate you guys coming.

———
* White House correction.

You need to vote for Tim Michels for the United States Senate. He wisely married Barbara. [*Laughter*] I know somebody else who made the right choice. [*Laughter*]

I really appreciate the Experimental Aircraft Association for allowing us to use this hangar. You're famous in Oshkosh, by gosh. [*Laughter*] One reason why is your airplanes. Another reason why is because of the good people who live here. I'm honored you all came out to say hello. Thanks for being here.

I want to thank Jack Voight, the State treasurer. I appreciate the speaker being here. I want to thank all the local officials.

I want to thank my friend Rick Graber. I want to thank the grassroots politics—politicians, the people who are putting up the signs and making the phone calls, the volunteers. I know many of you are working hard, and I thank you for that. It's takes a lot of hard work to get this many people out. But there's more hard work to be done. Laura and I will be campaigning alongside of you. Work hard. We will win in November.

Audience members. Four more years! Four more years! Four more years!

The President. We're working—we're coming from the West. We were in Oregon this morning. Then we stopped off in Iowa, and fortunately, get to come to Wisconsin today. And one of the reasons we're coming west to east is, you might remember, we had a debate or two recently. I enjoyed those debates. Those debates give us a chance to express our opinions, and they show the stark differences between my opponent and me. See, we have different records, and we have different plans for the future.

My record is one of reforming education, lowering taxes, providing prescription drugs for our seniors, improving homeland protections, and waging aggressive war against the ideologues of hate. The Senator's record is 20 years of out-of-the-mainstream politics, out-of-the-mainstream votes without many significant reforms or results to show for it. The records are important because our country faces many challenges, and the next President must recognize the need to reform and to be able to achieve reform. On issue after issue, from jobs to health care to the need to strengthen Social Security, my opponent has failed to recognize the changing realities of today's world and the need for fundamental reforms.

You know, in the final debate, I talked about the link between jobs and education. I believe when you're talking about jobs, you need to be talking about educating the people so they can fill the jobs of the 21st century. He said during that debate, I switched away from jobs and started talking about education. Well, yes, good jobs start with good education in America.

When it comes to health care, once again, the other night, he said with a straight face that his health care plan was not a Government plan. I could barely contain myself. Twenty-two million new people would enroll on a Government program under his plan. That would be the largest increase in Government health care ever.

Audience members. Boo-o-o!

Audience member. Who pays for it?

The President. Yes. Eighty percent of the newly insured for his plan would be placed on a Government program like Medicaid. That's not the way to handle health care in America.

Audience members. Boo-o-o!

The President. He said, well, his plan would help small businesses. Yet when you look at his plan, just like some of these analysts have done, they concluded that Senator Kerry's plan would be an overpriced albatross which would saddle small businesses with 225 new mandates.

Audience members. Boo-o-o!

The President. I have a different view. Health care must be available and affordable and portable to help small businesses, and we don't need to saddle them with a bunch of Government rules.

Finally, talking about change, we need to do something about Social Security. And yet in the debate, my opponent said if later on, after a period of time, we find that Social Security is in trouble, well, then he'll call a meeting of experts. [*Laughter*] Social Security is fine for our seniors. You might remember the 2000 campaign here in Wisconsin, when they said, "If George W. gets elected, the seniors won't get their checks." Do you remember that?

Audience members. Yes!

The President. Well, the seniors got their checks, and the seniors will continue to get their checks.

But we have trouble for our children and our grandchildren when it comes to Social Security. I think we need to think differently from the status quo. Youngsters ought to be able to take some of their own payroll taxes and set up a personal savings account, an account they call their own. It is the President's job to confront problems, not to pass them on to future generations and future Presidents.

The last few years, the American people have got to know me. They know my blunt way of speaking. I get that from my mother. [*Laughter*] They know I sometimes mangle the English language. [*Laughter*] I get that from my father. [*Laughter*] Americans also know I tell you exactly what I'm going to do, and I keep my word.

When I came into office, the stock market had been in serious decline for 6 months, and the economy was headed into a recession. To help families and to get this economy going again, I pledged to reduce taxes. I kept my word. The recession was one of the shallowest in American history.

Over the last 3 years, our economy has grown at the fastest rate of any major industrialized nation. The homeownership rate in America is at an alltime high. Incomes are up. Farm incomes are up. The past 13 months, we've added 1.9 million new jobs. The unemployment rate across America is 5.4 percent. That's lower than the average of the 1970s, the 1980s, and the 1990s. The unemployment rate in the great State of Wisconsin is 4.8 percent.

This economy is moving forward, and we have more work to do. To keep this economy strong, I'll continue to stand behind our farmers, like our dairy farmers. I signed a good farm bill. It's a farm bill that promoted conservation on our farms and ranches. It's a farm bill that recognizes that by opening up markets, our farmers can make a good living. We want to be selling Wisconsin products all around the world. I'll continue to promote good agricultural policy. I'll work with Congress to renew the milk-income-loss contract, the milk program, which is vital to Wisconsin's dairy farmers.

We'll also make sure America is the best place in the world to do business. If you want jobs here in America, it's got to be the best place in the world to do business. That means less regulations on our job creators. We've got to do something about the junk lawsuits that are threatening the job creators in America.

To keep jobs here, we need an energy plan. The Congress needs to pass the plan I sent up there a couple of years ago. It is a plan that encourages conservation. It's a plan that encourages the use of renewables like ethanol and biodiesel. It encourages clean coal technology. It encourages increased domestic production in environmentally friendly ways. To keep jobs here in America, we must be less dependent on foreign sources of energy.

To keep jobs here, we've got to reject economic isolationism and open up markets. We've opened up our markets for products from overseas, and it's good for you as a consumer. If you've got more to choose from in the marketplace, you're likely to get that which you want at a better price and higher quality. That's how the market works. That's why I'm saying to places like China, "You treat us the way we treat you. You open up your markets." See, we can compete with anybody, anytime, anywhere, so long as the rules are fair.

To create jobs here and to keep this economy growing, we've got to be wise about how we spend your money and we've got to keep your taxes low.

Now, my opponent has his own history on the economy.

Audience members. Boo-o-o!

The President. In 20 years as a Senator from Massachusetts, he has built the record of a Senator from Massachusetts. [*Laughter*] He has voted to raise taxes 98 times.

Audience members. Boo-o-o!

The President. That's in 20 years. That's nearly five times a year. I'd call that a pattern. [*Laughter*] See, he can run from his record, but he cannot hide. Now he's promising not to raise taxes for anyone who earns less than $200,000 a year. The problem is, to keep that promise he'd have to break all of his other ones. [*Laughter*] You see, he's proposed $2.2 trillion in new Federal spending. That's with a "T." And yet he says he's going to raise it by taxing the rich. That only raises between 600 billion and 800 billion dollars. And so you can see there's a tax gap. [*Laughter*] Guess who usually fills the tax gap?

Audience members. We do!

The President. Yes. Let me say one other thing about this business about taxing the rich. The rich hire lawyers and accountants for a reason: to stick you with the tab. We're not going to let him tax you; we're going to carry Wisconsin and win a great victory.

Audience members. Four more years! Four more years! Four more years!

The President. When I came into office, our public schools had been waiting for decades for hopeful reform. Too many of our children were being shuffled through, grade after grade, year after year, without learning the basics. I pledged to restore accountability in our schools and end the soft bigotry of low expectations, and I kept my word. The No Child Left Behind Act is working. Our children are making sustained gains in reading and math. We're closing achievement gaps all around this country. We're making progress for our families. We will leave no child behind.

There is more work to do. We'll fund early intervention programs in our high schools to help at-risk students. We'll place a new focus on math and science. Over time, we'll require a rigorous exam before graduation. By raising performance in our high schools and by expanding Pell grants for low- and middle-income families, we will help more Americans start their careers with a college diploma.

My opponent has a history on education issues, a history of doing almost nothing. The Senator's pledged to weaken the No Child Left Behind Act.

Audience members. Boo-o-o!

The President. He's proposed diluting the accountability standards and looking at measures like teacher attendance to judge whether students are learning.

Audience members. Boo-o-o!

The President. We must have high standards. We must have strong accountability measures. We must not undermine what we have passed. We have worked to move beyond the old days of mediocrity and excuses, and we're not going to go back.

When I came into office, we had a problem with Medicare. Medicine was changing. Medicare wasn't. Take, for example this: Medicare would pay hundreds—nearly $100,000 for a heart surgery but would not pay one dime for the prescription drugs that could prevent the heart surgery from being needed in the first place. Think about that. It's not right for our seniors. It's certainly not right for our taxpayers. I pledged to bring Republicans and Democrats together to strengthen and modernize Medicare for our seniors, and I kept my word. Seniors are already getting discounts on their medicines. Rural doctors and rural hospitals are being treated more fairly. And beginning in 2006, all seniors will be able

to get prescription drug coverage in Medicare.

We're moving forward on health care, and there's more to do. We need to make sure health care is affordable and available for all our people. We need a safety net for those with the greatest needs. I'm a big believer in community health centers, where the poor and the indigent can get good primary and preventative care. We'd much rather them getting care in a community health center than an emergency room of a local hospital. We'll do more to make sure poor children are fully subscribed in our programs for low-income families.

Most of the uninsured here in America work for small businesses. Small businesses are having trouble affording health care. In order to help our small businesses and help their workers and their families, small businesses ought to be able to pool together to be able to—so they can buy insurance at the same discounts big businesses are able to do. We'll expand health savings accounts so workers and small businesses are able to pay lower premiums and people can save tax-free in a health care account they call their own.

In order to make sure health care is available and affordable, we will do something about the junk lawsuits that are running up the cost to your health care. To make sure health care works, we've got to do something about the lawsuits that cause the Federal Government's tab to go up. You see, doctors practice what's called defensive medicine because of all the lawsuits. It costs our Government about $28 billion a year. It costs our economy 60 to 100 billion dollars a year.

I don't think you can be pro-doctor, pro-patient, and pro-plaintiff-attorney at the same time. You have to choose. My opponent made his choice, and he put a personal injury lawyer on the ticket.

Audience members. Boo-o-o!

The President. I made my choice. I'm standing with the doctors and the patients. I am for medical liability reform–now. In all we do to reform health care, this administration will make sure the decisions are made by doctors and patients, not by officials in Washington, DC.

You know, there's an old saying here: No one ever washes a rental car. [*Laughter*] A lot of wisdom in that statement. [*Laughter*] When you own something, you care about it. When you own something, you have a vital stake in the future of your country. That's why I will continue to promote an ownership society in America. We want our younger workers to be able to own a piece of the Social Security system so it will be available for them when they retire. We want more people owning their own business. Every time somebody starts a small business in America, they are achieving a piece of the American Dream. We will continue to expand ownership to every corner of our country. I've told you homeownership rates are at an alltime high. We want more people opening up the door where they live, saying, "Welcome to my home. Welcome to my piece of property."

On issue after issue, from Medicare without choices to schools with less accountability to higher taxes, my opponent takes the side of more centralized Government. There's a word for that attitude. It's called liberalism.

Audience members. Boo-o-o!

The President. Now, he dismisses that as a label. He must have seen it differently when he told a newspaper, "I'm a liberal, and I'm proud of it." [*Laughter*] The nonpartisan National Journal did a study that named him the most liberal Member of the United States Senate. And that's going a long way with that bunch. [*Laughter*]

I have a different record and a different view and a different philosophy. I don't believe in big Government, and I don't believe in indifferent Government. I'm what you would call a compassionate conservative. I believe in policies that empower people to improve their lives. I don't believe in policies that try to run people's lives. I trust the people. My opponent trusts the Government.

Audience members. Boo-o-o!

The President. We've done everything we can to help people, stand beside people, to help them have a future of dignity and independence. And that's how I'll continue to lead our Nation for 4 more years.

Audience members. Four more years! Four more years! Four more years!

The President. In this time of change, there are some things that do not change, the values we try to live by, reverence and integrity, courage and compassion. In a time of change, we all must support the institutions that give our lives direction and purpose, our families, our schools, and our religious congregations. We stand for a culture of life in which every person matters and every being counts. We stand for marriage and family, which are the foundations of our society. We stand for the appointment of Federal judges who know the difference between personal opinion and the strict interpretation of the law.

My opponent's words on these issues are a little muddy, but his record is plenty clear. He says he supports the institution of marriage, but he voted against the Defense of Marriage Act. He voted against the ban on partial-birth abortions.

Audience members. Boo-o-o!

The President. One time on his campaign, he called himself the candidate of conservative values, but he described the Reagan years as a period of moral darkness.

Audience members. Boo-o-o!

The President. There is a mainstream in American politics, and my opponent sits on the far left bank. He can run, but he cannot hide.

This election will also determine how America responds to the continuing danger of terrorism. The most solemn duty of the American President is to protect the American people. If America shows uncertainty or weakness in this decade, the world will drift toward tragedy. This will not happen on my watch.

Since that terrible morning of September the 11th, 2001, we have fought the terrorists across the Earth, not for pride, not for power, but because the lives of our citizens are at stake. Our strategy is clear. We'll protect the homeland. We'll strengthen our intelligence. We'll transform our All-Volunteer Army and keep it an all-volunteer army. We're staying on the offensive. We will strike the terrorists abroad so we do not have to face them here at home. We will continue to spread freedom and liberty. And we will prevail.

Our strategy is succeeding. Think about the world as it was some 3½ years ago. Afghanistan was the home base of Al Qaida. Pakistan was a transit point for terrorists. Saudi Arabia was fertile ground for terrorist fundraising. Libya was secretly pursuing nuclear weapons. Iraq was a dangerous place and a gathering threat. And Al Qaida was largely unchallenged as it planned attacks.

Because we acted, because the United States of America led, Afghanistan is free and is now an ally in the war on terror; Pakistan is capturing terrorist leaders; Saudi Arabia is making raids and arrests; Libya is dismantling its weapons programs; and an army of a free Iraq is fighting for freedom; and more than three-quarters of Al Qaida's key members and associates have been brought to justice.

We are conducting a broad strategy to keep America safe. By defending ourselves, 50 million people in Afghanistan and Iraq are now free. Think about that. I want our youngsters here to recognize they're watching incredible history unfold.

Take a look at Afghanistan. It wasn't all that long ago that many young girls were not allowed to go to school. That country was run by barbarians. They were backwards. They had an ideology based upon hatred. Their mothers would be pulled into the public square and whipped, some of them killed in a sports stadium because they wouldn't toe the line of their ideology. It was a dim and dark society. But because

we acted in our self-interest, we freed the people of Afghanistan. And they had Presidential elections. Thousands of people came out to vote. The first voter in the Presidential elections in Afghanistan was a 19-year-old woman. Think about that. Freedom is on the march, and the world is better for it.

In Iraq, elections are scheduled for January. Think about how far that society has come from the days of torture chambers and mass graves. See, it's in our interests. It's in our security interests that we stand with the people of Afghanistan and Iraq. Free societies in the Middle East will be hopeful societies which no longer feed resentments and breed violence for export. Free governments in the Middle East will fight the terrorists instead of harboring them. And that will help us keep the peace.

So the mission is clear. We will help these countries train armies and police and security forces, so the people of Afghanistan and Iraq can do the hard work of defending their freedom and democracy. We will help them get on the path to stability and self-government as quickly as possible, and then our troops will come home with the honor they have earned.

I am proud to be the Commander in Chief of a great military. And it is a great military because of the character and the decency of those who wear our Nation's uniform. I want to thank the veterans who are here tonight for having set such a good example for those who wear the uniform. I want to thank the military families who are here for having made such great sacrifices for our freedom.

We will continue to make sure that our military has all the resources they need to complete their missions. That is why I went to the United States Congress and asked for $87 billion of supplemental funding to support our troops in combat in both Iraq and Afghanistan. It was a really important request, and it received great bipartisan support. As a matter of fact, only 12 United States Senators voted against the funding request, 2 of whom are my opponent and his runningmate.

Audience members. Boo-o-o!

The President. And when you're out there gathering up the vote, remind people of this fact: Only 4 Members of the United States Senate—only 4 out of 100—voted to authorize the use of force and then voted against funding the troops sent into harm's way, 2 of whom are my opponent and his runningmate.

Audience members. Boo-o-o!

The President. So they asked him, how could he have made that vote? And perhaps the most famous quote of the 2004 campaign—[*laughter*]—he said, "I actually did vote for the $87 billion, before I voted against it."

Audience members. ——before I voted against it! [*Laughter*]

The President. Now, he's given a lot of answers since then. One of the most interesting ones is when he said, "Well, the whole thing was just a complicated matter." [*Laughter*] There's nothing complicated about supporting our troops in combat.

We have a difference of opinion when it comes to making this country secure. And in one of our debates, Senator Kerry proposed that this Nation should pass a "global test" before we send our troops.

Audience members. Boo-o-o!

The President. You know, the problem with his "global test" is that he could never pass it. [*Laughter*] In 1990, the United Nations Security Council passed a resolution supporting action to remove Saddam Hussein from Kuwait. The international community was united. Countries throughout the world joined our coalition. Yet even after United Nations approval, in the United States Senate, Senator Kerry voted against the authorization of the use of force.

Audience members. Boo-o-o!

The President. Think about that, and think about what he said in one of the debates when he said it was a "mistake" to remove Saddam Hussein. He said he

would have tried it differently. He would have had another United Nations Security Council resolution. That's exactly what Saddam Hussein would have wanted. The truth of the matter is, Saddam would still be in power in Baghdad if Senator Kerry had his way, and he would have been in Kuwait.

Audience members. Yes!

The President. And the world would be worse off. The world is better off with Saddam sitting in a prison cell.

Listen, I'll continue to build strong alliances during the next 4 years. Today, when I was flying in from out west, I had a good visit with Tony Blair, our strong ally. Alliances are important. Coalitions are important. But I will never turn over America's national security decisions to leaders of other countries.

Audience members. Four more years! Four more years! Four more years!

The President. I believe in the transformational power of liberty. I'll tell you what I mean by that. I'll use an example. Prime Minister Koizumi of Japan is my friend. He's Laura's friend as well. That probably doesn't seem unusual to some, but think about this. It wasn't all that long ago in the march of history that we were at war with Japan. They were the sworn enemy of the United States of America. They attacked us. My dad fought against the Japanese. I'm confident people's relatives out here went to World War II against the Japanese.

And after we won that war, President Harry S. Truman believed in the transformational power of liberty to convert an enemy into an ally. And so they worked to build a democracy in Japan. And there were a lot of skeptics in America then. You can imagine why. Japan was the enemy. How could an enemy possibly become a democracy? Why do we want to work with somebody who killed our sons—great skepticism.

But fortunately, he believed in the power of liberty to transform. And as a result of that belief, I sit down at the table today with Prime Minister Koizumi of Japan, talking about the peace we all want, talking about how we can work together to confront the problems of the world so our children can live in a more peaceful world.

We will succeed in Iraq, and someday, an American President will sit down with a duly elected leader of Iraq, and they'll be talking about the peace in the Middle East, and our children and our grandchildren will be better off for it.

I believe that millions plead in silence for their freedom in the Middle East. I believe women want to live in a free society. I believe the moms in the Middle East want their children to grow up in a free world. I believe that if given a chance, the people of the Middle East will embrace the most honorable form of government ever devised by man: democracy. I believe all these things because freedom is not America's gift to the world; freedom is the Almighty God's gift to each man and woman in this world.

For all Americans, these years in our history will always stand apart. There are quiet times in the life of a nation when little is expected of its leaders. This is not one of those times. This is a time that requires firm resolve, clear vision, and a deep faith that makes us a great nation.

None of us will ever forget that week when one era ended and another began. September the 14th, 2001, I stood in the ruins of the Twin Towers. It's a day I will never forget. There were workers in hardhats there yelling at me at the top of their lungs, "Whatever it takes." I remember trying to console a fellow. He looked me in the eye, and he said, "Do not let me down." Ever since that day, I wake up every morning thinking about how to better protect our country. I will never relent in defending America, whatever it takes.

When I traveled your great State 4 years ago, I made a pledge that if I had a chance to serve, I would uphold the honor and the dignity of the office to which I had been elected. With your help, with your hard work, I will do so for 4 more years.

God bless. Thank you all for coming. Thank you all.

NOTE: The President spoke at 4:58 p.m. at the Experimental Aircraft Association, Exhibit Hangar B. In his remarks, he referred to Tim Michels, senatorial candidate in Wisconsin, and his wife, Barbara; Wisconsin State Treasurer Jack C. Voight; John Gard, speaker, Wisconsin State Assembly; Richard W. Graber, chairman, Republican Party of Wisconsin; Prime Minister Tony Blair of the United Kingdom; and Prime Minister Junichiro Koizumi of Japan.

Message on the Observance of Ramadan
October 15, 2004

I send warm greetings to Muslims in the United States and around the world as they begin observance of Ramadan, the holiest season in their faith.

Ramadan commemorates the revelation of the Qur'an to Muhammed. By teaching the importance of compassion, justice, mercy, and peace, the Qur'an has guided many millions of believers across the centuries. Today, this holy time is still set aside for Muslims to remember their dependence on God through fasting and prayer, and to show charity to those in need.

American history has taught us to welcome the contributions of men and women of all faiths, for we share the fundamental values of religious freedom, love of family, and gratitude to God. Americans who practice the Islamic faith enrich our society and help our Nation build a better future.

Laura joins me in sending our best wishes.

GEORGE W. BUSH

NOTE: An original was not available for verification of the content of this message.

The President's Radio Address
October 16, 2004

Good morning. Over the past 4 years, I have brought a straightforward approach to the Presidency. I tell you what I'm going to do, and I keep my word. When I came into office 4 years ago, the economy was sliding into recession. Then terrorist attacks cost our Nation nearly a million jobs in 3 months. To help families and to get this economy growing again, I pledged to reduce taxes, and I kept my word. Now the results are clear. Over the last 3 years, America's economy has grown at the fastest rate of any major industrialized nation. The homeownership rate is at an alltime high, and we have added more than 1.9 million new jobs in the past 13 months.

My opponent has a different approach. Over the last 20 years, he has voted to raise taxes 98 times. Now he is promising over $2.2 trillion in new spending, and paying for it would require broad tax increases on small businesses and the middle class. I have a better plan. I will continue to be wise with taxpayers' money, and I will keep your taxes low.

When I came into office, too many of our children were shuffled through school without learning the basics. I pledged to restore accountability and end the soft bigotry of low expectations, and I kept my word. Now our children are making sustained progress in reading and math, and we are closing the achievement gap for minority students.

My opponent has pledged to weaken the No Child Left Behind Act. His proposals would undermine the accountability we worked so hard to pass. I have a better plan. We will keep demanding results for all our children, and we will leave no child behind.

When I came into office, Medicare wasn't paying for the prescription drugs that can reduce health costs and save a lot of lives. I pledged to strengthen and modernize Medicare for our seniors, and I kept my word. Now seniors are saving money with drug discount cards. And in 2006, all seniors will be able to get prescription drug coverage.

On health care, my opponent has a history of opposing needed reforms. He voted against the Medicare bill even though it was supported by the AARP and other seniors groups. He has voted 10 times against medical liability reform, and now his health care proposal calls for bigger, more intrusive Government. Eight out of ten people who get health care under his plan would be placed on a Government program. I have a better plan. I will protect doctors and patients from junk lawsuits, help employees in small businesses afford health coverage, make sure every poor county has a community health center. And I will make sure health decisions are always made by patients and doctors, not by officials in Washington, DC.

In this time of change, some things do not change. Those are the values we try to live by, courage and compassion, reverence and integrity. I stand for a culture of life in which every person matters and every being counts. I stand for marriage and family, which are the foundations of our society. I stand for the appointment of Federal judges who know the difference between personal opinion and the strict interpretation of the law.

My opponent says he supports the institution of marriage, but he voted against the Defense of Marriage Act, which Congress passed by an overwhelming majority and my predecessor into law. My opponent has voted against sensible bipartisan measures like parental notification laws. He voted against the ban on partial-birth abortion.

On issues that are vital to this Nation's future, all Americans know where I stand. I'm a compassionate conservative. I believe in policies that empower people to improve their lives, not try to run their lives. I believe in helping men and women find the skills and tools to prosper in a changing world. I have worked to help all Americans build a future of dignity and independence. And that is how I will continue to lead this Nation for 4 more years.

Thank you for listening.

NOTE: The address was recorded at 10:45 a.m. on October 15 at the Jacksonville Inn in Jacksonville, OR, for broadcast at 10:06 a.m. on October 16. The transcript was made available by the Office of the Press Secretary on October 15 but was embargoed for release until the broadcast. The Office of the Press Secretary also released a Spanish language transcript of this address.

Remarks in Sunrise, Florida
October 16, 2004

The President. Thank you all. Nothing like spending a Saturday morning in Florida. Thank you. I'm proud you all are here. Thanks for coming.

I'm really proud of my brother Jeb. Your State has been tested recently—not one hurricane but four hurricanes. Jeb was a strong leader during these times. I had the honor of visiting Florida's families with him, those who hurt with him. I had an honor of traveling your State and seeing the great compassion of Florida arise as people hurt and suffered. You know, when times are tough is when you see where strong leaders emerge. Strong leadership emerged not only in your Governor, but strong leadership emerged all throughout your great State. We'll continue to help Florida rebuild. But one thing about this State you never have to worry about is the spirit of the people.

Listen, Laura and I are here to ask for the vote. We're traveling in Florida, and we're here to ask for your help. Make sure you get people to the polls. Starting Monday, people can vote. Listen, don't overlook discerning Democrats when you get them headed to the polls, people like Zell Miller. Remind people that if they want a safer America, a stronger America, and a better America, to put me and Dick Cheney back in office.

And one reason you need to put me back in office is so that Laura will have 4 more years as the First Lady. When I asked her to marry me, she said, "Fine, I'll marry you, just so long as I never have to give a political speech." [*Laughter*] I said, "Okay, you've got a deal." Fortunately, she didn't hold me to that deal. When people see her speak, they see a compassionate, strong, warm First Lady. I am really proud of her.

And I am really proud of my runningmate, Dick Cheney. Now, look, I admit he doesn't have the waviest hair in the race. [*Laughter*] I didn't pick him because of his hair. I picked him because of his judgment, his experience, and his ability to get the job done.

I appreciate so very much Wendell Hays joining me, Laura, and Jeb up here. Wendell, thank you for your service. Thank you for your courage, and thank you for your understanding the vision of peace that we're spreading.

I appreciate Congressman Clay Shaw joining us today. I want to thank Congresswoman Ileana Ros-Lehtinen for joining us today. My friend Mel Martinez is not here, but you need to put him in the United States Senate. I want to thank Attorney General Charlie Crist joining us today. Mr. General, I appreciate you being here. Listen, the mayor of Fort Lauderdale is with us today—Mr. Mayor.

I thank all the grassroots activists. You never get thanked enough for putting up the signs or making the phone calls. I'm here to thank you for what you're going to do over the next 2 weeks. Turn out the vote. We'll win Florida again and win a great victory in November.

Audience members. Four more years! Four more years! Four more years!

The President. In the last few years, the American people have gotten to know me. They know my blunt way of speaking. I get that from my mom. They know that I sometimes mangle the English language. [*Laughter*] I get that from my dad. [*Laughter*] Americans also know that I tell you exactly what I'm going to do, and I keep my word.

Those debates were interesting experiences. I enjoyed them. They highlighted the stark differences between my opponent and me. We have very different records and very different plans for the future. My record is one of reforming education, of lowering taxes, of providing prescription drug coverage for our seniors, for improving homeland security, and for waging an aggressive war against the ideologues of hate.

The Senator's record is 20 years of out-of-the-mainstream votes without many significant reforms or results.

Audience members. Boo-o-o!

The President. When I came into office, the stock market had been in serious decline for 6 months. And then the country was headed into a recession. To help families and to get this economy growing again, I pledged to reduce taxes. I kept my word.

Because we acted, the recession was one of the shallowest in American history. Over the last 3 years, our economy has grown at the fastest rate of any major industrialized nation. Today, the homeownership rate in America is at an alltime high. More minorities own a home than ever before in our Nation's history. Farm income is up. Our ranchers are doing well.

In the past 13 months, we've added more than 1.9 million new jobs. The unemployment rate in America is at 5.4 percent. That is lower than the average rate of the 1970s, the 1980s, and the 1990s. The unemployment rate in your State is at 4.5 percent. This economy is moving forward, and we're not going to go back to the days of tax and spend.

To make sure quality jobs are created right here in America, we've got to make sure America is the best place in the world to do business. We need to reduce the burden of regulations on our job creators. We must end the junk lawsuits that are threatening our small businesses, which create most new jobs.

To create jobs here, Congress must pass my energy plan. The plan encourages conservation. It encourages the use of renewables like ethanol and biodiesel. It encourages new technologies. It encourages clean coal technology and increased domestic production in environmentally friendly ways. To keep jobs here, we must become less dependent on foreign sources of energy.

To keep jobs here, we've got to reject economic isolationism and open up markets for U.S. products. We've opened up our market for products from overseas, and that's good for you as a consumer. If you've got more products to choose from, you're likely to get that which you want at a better price and higher quality. That's how the marketplace works. That's why I'm saying to China, "You treat us the way we treat you." See, we can compete with anybody, anytime, anywhere, if the markets are open and the rules are fair.

To create jobs, we got to be wise about how we spend your money, and we've got to keep your taxes low. My opponent has his own history on the economy. [*Laughter*] In 20 years as Senator from Massachusetts, he's built a record of a Senator from Massachusetts. [*Laughter*] He's voted to raise taxes 98 times in the Senate.

Audience members. Boo-o-o!

The President. Now, he's been there 20 years. That means, on average, he's voted nearly five times a year to raise taxes. I'd call that a pattern. [*Laughter*] He can't run—he can run from his record, but he cannot hide.

Now the Senator is promising not to raise taxes for anyone who earns less than $200,000 a year. The problem is, to keep that promise he would have to break almost all of his other ones. [*Laughter*] See, he's proposed $2.2 trillion in new spending. That's with a "T." Yet, his plan to tax the rich only raises about 600 billion or 800 billion. See, there's a gap. There's a gap between the difference of what he's promising and what he can raise. And guess who usually gets to fill that gap?

Audience members. Boo-o-o!

The President. Let me say one other thing about taxing the rich. You've heard that language all the time, but the rich hire lawyers and accountants for a reason: to slip the bill and pass it to you. We're not going to let him tax you; we're going to carry Florida and win a great victory.

When I came into office, our public schools had been waiting decades for hopeful reform. Too many of our children were shuffled through school, year after year,

grade after grade, without learning the basics. I pledged to restore accountability to the schools and end the soft bigotry of low expectations. I kept my word. We're seeing results. Our children are making sustained gains in reading and math. We're closing an achievement gap all across this country. We're making progress for our families. We will leave no child behind in America.

To build a more hopeful America, we must have the best prepared, most highly skilled workforce in the world. See, most new jobs are filled by people with at least 2 years of college education, yet only one in four of our students gets there. That's why we'll fund early intervention programs in our high schools to help at-risk students. We'll emphasize math and science. Over time, we'll require a rigorous exam before graduation. By raising performance in our high schools and expanding Pell grants for low- and middle-income families, more of our students will start their career with a college diploma.

My opponent has a history on education issues, a history of doing almost nothing. [*Laughter*] The Senator has pledged to weaken the No Child Left Behind Act.

Audience members. Boo-o-o!

The President. See, he's proposed diluting the accountability standards and looking at measures like teacher attendance to judge whether or not our students are learning. His proposals would undermine high standards and accountability. We've moved beyond the old days of failure and mediocrity and low standards, and we're not going back.

When I came into office, we had a problem in Medicare. See, medicine was modernizing and medicine was changing, but Medicare was not. Let me give you this example. Medicare would pay tens of thousands of dollars for heart surgery but wouldn't pay a dime for the prescription drugs that could prevent the heart surgery from being needed in the first place. That was not fair to our seniors. It wasn't fair to the taxpayers. I pledged to bring Republicans and Democrats together to strengthen and modernize Medicare for our seniors, and I kept my word. The results are clear. Seniors are already getting discount on their medicines. Rural hospitals are being treated more fairly. And beginning in 2006, all seniors will be able to get prescription drug coverage under Medicare.

We're moving forward on health care, and there's more to do. We need to make sure health care is available and affordable to all our people. I believe in a safety net for those with the greatest needs. I believe in community health centers, places where the poor and the indigent can get primary and preventative care. I believe every poor county in America ought to have a community health center. We will do more to make sure poor children are fully subscribed in our programs for low-income families.

We will do more to make sure health care is affordable. Most of the uninsured work for small businesses. Small businesses are having trouble affording health care insurance. We ought to allow small businesses to pool together so they can buy insurance at the same discounts that big businesses can do. We must expand health savings accounts so workers and small businesses are able to pay lower premiums and people can save tax-free in a health care account they call their own.

To make sure health care is available and affordable, we must do something about the junk lawsuits that are running up the cost of health care. By forcing doctors to practice defensive medicine, medical lawsuits cost the Federal Government about $28 billion a year. That means it costs you $28 billion a year. It costs our economy anywhere from 60 to 100 billion dollars a year. They drive up insurance premiums, which drives good doctors out of business. I've met many ob-gyns and patients of ob-gyns who understand the harm that lawsuits are doing to our system. I've met women who have had to drive miles to go see an ob-gyn. See, you cannot be pro-patient and pro-doctor and pro-personal-injury-lawyer at the same time. You have to choose. My opponent made his choice, and he put a personal injury lawyer on the ticket.

Audience members. Boo-o-o!

The President. I made my choice. I'm standing with the doctors, and I'm standing with the patients. We're for medical liability reform—now.

My opponent has a health care proposal of his own, and it's a plan for a bigger and more intrusive role for the Federal Government. The other day, he looked in the television camera and he said the Government has nothing to do with his health care plan. I could barely contain myself. [*Laughter*] Of course his plan has got something to do with the Federal Government. Eight out of ten people who get health care under Senator Kerry's plan would be placed on a Government program.

Audience members. Boo-o-o!

The President. Eight million Americans would lose their private insurance at work, and most would have to go on a Government plan.

Audience members. Boo-o-o!

The President. He claimed his plan would help small businesses, yet groups who've studied his plan have called it an overpriced albatross that would saddle small businesses with 225 new mandates.

I have a different view. Instead of moving health care to the Federal Government, I believe health care decisions ought to be made by doctors and patients, not by officials in Washington, DC.

I've set out policies that move America toward a positive and optimistic future. I believe our country can be an ownership society. You know, there's a saying that says: No one ever washes a rental car. [*Laughter*] There's some wisdom in that statement. When you own something, you care about it. When you own something, you have a vital stake in the future of the United States of America.

Our policies encourage entrepreneurship because every time a small business is started, someone is achieving the American Dream. We are encouraging health savings accounts so people have the security of owning and managing their own health care account. We're continuing to spread ownership. I love the idea when more and more Americans from all walks of life open up the door where they live and say, "Welcome to my home. Welcome to my piece of property."

In a new term, I'll take the next great step to build an ownership society by strengthening Social Security. Our Social Security system needs fixing. You might remember the 2000 campaign, all those ads that told our seniors, "If George W. gets elected, he's going to take away your check." I want the seniors to remember they got their checks. No one is going to take away our seniors' checks. The Social Security system is solvent for those who relied upon Social Security. And baby boomers like me are in pretty good shape when it comes to Social Security.

We need to worry about our children and our grandchildren. We need to be worried—and many are—about whether Social Security will be around when they need it. For the sake of our children, we must strengthen Social Security by allowing younger workers to save some of their payroll taxes in a personal account, an account they can call their own, an account the Government cannot take away.

When it comes to Social Security, you heard my opponent the other night. He wants to maintain the status quo.

Audience members. Boo-o-o!

The President. He's against these Social Security reforms I talk about, and he's against just about every other reform that gives more authority and more control to the individual. On issue after issue, from Medicare without choices to schools with less accountability to higher taxes, he takes the side of more centralized control and more Government. There's a word for that attitude. It's called liberalism.

He dismisses that word as a label, but he must have seen it differently when he told a newspaper, "I am a liberal, and I am proud of it." The nonpartisan National Journal magazine did a study and named him the most liberal Member of the United States Senate. That takes hard work. [*Laughter*] That's an accomplishment, if you're more liberal than Ted Kennedy. [*Laughter*]

I have a different record and a different philosophy. I do not believe in big Government, and I do not believe that Government should be indifferent. That's called compassionate conservatism. I believe in policies that empower people to improve their lives. I reject policies that tell people how to run their lives. We're helping men and women find the skills and tools to prosper in a time of change. We're helping all Americans to have a future of dignity and independence. And that's how I will continue to lead our Nation for 4 more years.

Audience members. Four more years! Four more years! Four more years!

The President. In a time of change, some things do not change, the values we try to live by, courage and compassion, reverence and integrity. In a time of change, we must support the institutions that give our lives direction and purpose, our families, our schools, our religious congregations. We stand for a culture of life in which every person matters and every being counts. We stand for marriage and family, which are the foundations of our society. We stand for the appointment of Federal judges who know the difference between personal opinion and the strict interpretation of the law.

My opponent's words on these issues are a little muddy, but his record is plenty clear. [*Laughter*] He says he supports the institution of marriage, but he voted against the Defense of Marriage Act, which my predecessor signed.

Audience members. Boo-o-o!

The President. He voted against the ban on the brutal practice of partial-birth abortion.

Audience members. Boo-o-o!

The President. One time in this campaign, he claimed he was a candidate of conservative values, but he's described the Reagan years as a time of moral darkness.

Audience members. Boo-o-o!

The President. There is a mainstream in American politics, and my opponent sits on the far left bank. He can run, but he cannot hide.

This election will also determine how America responds to the continuing danger of terrorism. I believe the most solemn duty of the American President is to protect the American people. If America shows uncertainty or weakness in this decade, the world will drift toward tragedy. This will not happen on my watch.

Since that terrible morning of September the 11th, 2001, we have fought the terrorists across the Earth, not for pride, not for power, but because the lives of our citizens are at stake. Our strategy is clear. We're defending the homeland. We're transforming our military. We will keep the All-Volunteer Army an all-volunteer army. We're strengthening our intelligence capacities. We're staying on the offensive. We will strike the terrorists abroad so we do not have to face them here at home. We will spread freedom and liberty. And we will prevail.

Our strategy is succeeding. Think about the world as it was 3½ years ago. Afghanistan was the home base of Al Qaida. Pakistan was a transit point for terrorist groups. Saudi Arabia was fertile ground for terrorist fundraising. Libya was secretly pursuing nuclear weapons. Iraq was a dangerous place and a gathering threat. Al Qaida was largely unchallenged as it planned attacks.

Because we led, Afghanistan is an ally in the war on terror; Afghanistan held elections; Pakistan is capturing terrorist leaders; Saudi Arabia is making raids and arrests;

Libya is dismantling its weapons programs; the army of a free Iraq is fighting for freedom; and more than three-quarters of Al Qaida's key members and associates have been brought to justice.

In defending ourselves, in upholding doctrine, 50 million people in Afghanistan and Iraq are free. And that's important to our security. Free nations will be peaceful nations. Free nations will help us reject terror. Free nations will no longer feed resentments and breed violence for export. When America gives its word, America must keep its word. And that's why we're standing with the people of Afghanistan and Iraq.

I want the youngsters here to recognize what's happened in the world. It wasn't all that long ago in Afghanistan that people lived under the brutal dictatorship of the Taliban. The Taliban had this grim ideology of hate. People lived in darkness. Young girls weren't allowed to go to school. Their mothers were taken into the public square and whipped if they wouldn't toe the ideological line. Because we acted in our own self-interest, millions of Afghan citizens went to vote for a President. The first voter was a 19-year-old woman. Freedom is on the march. That society has gone from darkness to light because of freedom.

And the same thing is happening in Iraq. The terrorists are trying to stop the advance of freedom because they understand a free society in the midst of the Middle East will defeat their ideology of hate. But freedom is on the march. There will be elections in Iraq in January. Think how far that society has come from the days of mass graves and torture chambers.

Our mission is clear. We'll help these countries train armies so their people can do the hard work of defending democracy. We'll help them get on the path to stability and self-government as quickly as possible, and then our troops will come home with the honor they have earned.

I'm proud to be the Commander in Chief of such a great United States military. And it's a great military because of the character of those who serve. I want to thank the veterans who are here today for having set such a great example for those who wear the uniform. I want to thank the military families who are here today.

And we will make sure that your loved ones have all the resources they need to win the war on terror. And that's why I went to the United States Congress in September of 2003 and requested $87 billion in funding for our troops in harm's way. It was important funding. It was necessary funding, so necessary that the bipartisan support was overwhelming. As a matter of fact, only 12 United States Senators voted against supporting our troops in harm's way, 2 of whom are my opponent and his runningmate.

Audience members. Boo-o-o!

The President. When you're out there getting people to vote, remind people of this startling statistic: There were only four Members of the United States Senate who voted to authorize the use of force and then voted against funding our troops in combat—only four—two of whom are my opponent and his runningmate.

Audience members. Boo-o-o!

The President. You might remember perhaps the most famous quote of the 2004 campaign. When asked why he made his vote, my opponent said, "I actually did vote for the 87 billion, right before I voted against it."

Audience members. Boo-o-o!

The President. He's been giving a lot of explanations since that explanation. One of the most interesting of all is he said, "The whole thing was a complicated matter." There's nothing complicated about supporting our troops in combat.

Tomorrow is the one-year anniversary of Senator Kerry's vote against funding our troops. He's had many and conflicting positions on the issue, and it's a case study into why his contradictions call into question his credibility and his ability to lead our Nation. In September 2003, as the $87 billion funding package was being debated, Senator Kerry said, "It would be irresponsible to abandon our troops by voting against the measure." Just one month later, he did exactly that irresponsible thing, and he abandoned our troops in combat by voting against the funding.

Audience members. Boo-o-o! Flip-flop! Flip-flop! Flip-flop!

The President. What happened to change the Senator's mind so abruptly in one short month? His opponent in the Democrat primary, Howard Dean, was gaining ground as an antiwar candidate. Senator Kerry apparently decided supporting the troops, even while they were in harm's way, was not as important as shoring up his own political position.

Audience members. Boo-o-o!

The President. At a time of great threat to our country, at a time of great challenge in the world, the Commander in Chief must stand on principle, not the shifting sands of political convenience.

We have differences when it comes to defending our country. Take, for example, the proposed "global test" that the Senator proposed before we defend ourselves.

Audience members. Boo-o-o!

The President. The problem with his "global test" is that the Senator can never pass it. [*Laughter*] In 1990, the United Nations Security Council passed a resolution supporting action to remove Saddam Hussein from Kuwait. The international community was united. Countries throughout the world joined the coalition. Yet, even after United Nations approval, in the United States Senate, Senator Kerry voted against the authorization for the use of force.

Audience members. Boo-o-o!

The President. If that action didn't pass his "global test," nothing will pass his "global test."

In this campaign, in one of our debates, you might remember that he said removing Saddam Hussein was a "mistake." When he said how he would have done it differently, he said, "Well, all we needed to do was pass another United Nations Security Council resolution."

Audience members. Boo-o-o!

The President. If the Senator had his way, not only would Saddam Hussein be still sitting in a palace in Baghdad, he'd be occupying Kuwait. The world is better off with Saddam Hussein sitting in a prison cell.

We will continue to build strong alliances. We'll continue to work to strengthen our coalitions. But I will never turn over America's national security decisions to leaders of other countries.

I believe in the transformational power of liberty. I'll tell you what I mean by that. One of our friends—I say "our"—Laura and my friends—is Prime Minister Koizumi of Japan. That doesn't sound like much, except when you think about it wasn't all that long ago that we were at war with the Japanese. In the march of history, 60 years isn't much. My dad fought against the Japanese. Your dads fought against—and granddads fought against the Japanese. They were the sworn enemy of America.

After World War II, President Harry S. Truman believed in the power of liberty to transform an enemy into an ally. There was a lot of skeptics then; a lot of people doubted that. You can understand why. Why would you want to waste time on an enemy? Many lives had been upset as a result of that war, and people were bitter. Some people just said the Japanese couldn't possibly self-govern. But we worked to help them build a democracy.

And today, I sit down at the table with Prime Minister Koizumi, talking about how to keep the peace. Someday, an American President will be sitting down with a duly elected leader of Iraq, talking about the peace in the Middle East. And our children and our grandchildren will be better off for it.

See, I believe that millions in the Middle East plead in silence for their freedom. I believe women want to live in a free society. I believe that moms and dads want to raise their children in freedom and peace. I believe all these things, because freedom is not America's gift to the world; freedom is the Almighty God's gift to each man and woman in this world.

Extending freedom also means confronting the evil of anti-Semitism. Today I signed the Global Anti-Semitism Review Act of 2004. This law commits a government to keep a record of anti-Semitic acts throughout the world and also a record of responses to those acts. This Nation will keep watch. We will make sure that the ancient impulse of anti-Semitism never finds a home in the modern world.

For all Americans, these years in our history will always stand apart. There are quiet times in the life of a nation when little is expected of its leaders. This isn't one of those times. This is a time that requires firm resolve, clear vision, and a deep faith in the values that make us a great nation.

None of us will ever forget that week when one era ended and another began. On September the 14th, 2001, I stood in the ruins of the Twin Towers. It's a day I will never forget. There were workers in hardhats there yelling at the top of their lungs, "Whatever it takes." I remember trying to do my best to console those coming out of the rubble. A guy grabbed me by the arm, and he looked me square in the eye, and he said, "Do not let me down." Ever since that day, I wake up thinking about how to better protect our country. I will never relent in defending America, whatever it takes.

Audience members. Four more years! Four more years! Four more years!

The President. Four years ago, when I traveled your great State, I made a pledge that if you gave me a chance to serve, I would uphold the honor and the dignity of the office to which I had been elected. With your help, I will do so for 4 more years.

Thanks for coming. God bless. Thank you all.

NOTE: The President spoke at 10:33 a.m. at the Office Depot Center. In his remarks, he referred to Gov. Jeb Bush of Florida; Senator Zell Miller of Georgia, who made the keynote address at the 2004 Republican National Convention; Wendell B. Hays, 1st Lt., Florida Army National Guard; Mel R. Martinez, senatorial candidate in Florida; Florida State Attorney General Charlie Crist; Mayor Jim Naugle of Fort Lauderdale, FL; and Prime Minister Junichiro Koizumi of Japan.

Remarks in West Palm Beach, Florida
October 16, 2004

The President. Thank you all for coming. Thank you all for being here. It lifts our spirits that so many came out to say hello on a Saturday afternoon. Laura and I are grateful that you're here, and we appreciate you being here.

We're here to ask for your vote and your help. As Jeb mentioned, we're coming close to voting time, and it's time to go to your friends and neighbors and remind them they have a duty in this country to vote. And when you get them headed to the polls, tell them, if they want a safer America, a stronger America, and a better America, to put me and Dick Cheney back in office.

I'm going to give you some reasons to put me back in office today, but perhaps the most important one of all is so that Laura is the First Lady for 4 more years. When I asked her to marry me, she said, "Fine, I'll marry you, just as long as I never have to give a political speech." [*Laughter*] I said, "Okay, you got a deal." Fortunately, she didn't hold me to that promise. She's given a lot of speeches, and when she does, the American people see a warm, compassionate, great First Lady.

I'm proud of my runningmate. I admit, Dick Cheney doesn't have the waviest hair in the race——

Audience members. Laura! Laura! Laura!

The President. Dick Cheney is a great Vice President.

I'm proud of brother Jeb. You know, you can determine the character of a person when times are tough, and times are really tough for you all here in Florida—not one hurricane but four. Jeb stepped up, as did a lot of other people, including, I hope, the Federal Government to your satisfaction, to provide help for people who hurt. But you know what we saw in those storms was the great character of the people of Florida, neighbor loving neighbor, neighbor helping neighbor. There's no doubt in my mind that the people of this State showed the people of the world that there's great character amongst you. And I'm proud of you, and I want to thank you for doing everything you can to help rebuild this State.

What an honor it is to be sharing the stage with Jack Nicklaus. He gave me a chance—I asked for a few putting lessons. [*Laughter*] He said, "Your game is beyond repair." [*Laughter*] But I'm proud to have his support, proud for him—to be able to call him friend.

I also want to thank Congressman Mark Foley, who is with us today. I appreciate you being here, Congressman. Congressman Clay Shaw and Emilie Shaw are with us today. Thanks for coming. Tom Gallagher is with us today. I appreciate him being here. I want to thank all the other statehouse officials and local officials.

But most of all, I want to thank the grassroots activists who are here. I want to thank all the volunteers who are getting ready to walk the vote across not only Florida but all across our country today. See, what's happening is, we've got people all over the country heading out into neighborhoods to knock on doors and putting in a good word for the Bush-Cheney ticket. Some volunteers are watching on the Internet right now, and I hope they're stretching for their walk. [*Laughter*] I want to thank them for their hard work. With your help, with their help, we're going to win a great victory in Florida and win on November the 2d.

In the last few years, the American people have gotten to know me. They know my blunt way of speaking. I got that from Mother. [*Laughter*] They know I sometimes mangle the English language. I got that from Dad. [*Laughter*] Americans also know I tell you exactly what I'm going to do, and I keep my word.

You know, I enjoyed the debates against my opponent, and they showed stark differences between his views and mine. We have different records. We have very different plans for the future. My record is one of reforming education, of lowering taxes, of providing prescription drug coverage for our seniors, improving homeland protection, and waging an unrelenting fight against the ideologues of hate.

My opponent's record is 20 years of out-of-the-mainstream votes without many significant reforms and results to show for it.

Audience members. Boo-o-o!

The President. These records are important. They are important because our country faces challenges. And the next President must recognize the need to lead and reform. On issue after issue, from jobs to health care to the need to strengthen Social Security, Senator Kerry's policies fail to recognize the changing realities of today's world and the need for fundamental reforms.

See, when I came into office, the stock market had been in serious decline for 6 months. The American economy was sliding into a recession. To help families and to get this economy growing again, I pledged to reduce your taxes. I kept my word. The results are clear. The recession was one of the shallowest in American history.

Over the last 3 years, our economy has grown at the fastest rate as any in nearly 20 years. The homeownership rate in America is at an alltime high. Farm and ranch income is up. In the past 13 months, we have added 1.9 million new jobs. The national unemployment rate is 5.4 percent, lower than the average of the 1970s, 1980s, and 1990s. Your unemployment rate is 4.5 percent. This economy is moving forward, and we're not going to go back to the days of tax and spend.

To make sure quality jobs are created right here in America, we've got to make sure America is the best place in the world to do business. That means less regulations on our job creators. That means we've got to do something about these lawsuits that threaten small businesses that are creating most new jobs.

To create jobs in America, Congress needs to pass my energy plan. It's a plan that encourages conservation. It encourages the use of renewables like ethanol and biodiesel. It encourages clean coal technology. It encourages the exploration for natural gas in environmentally friendly ways. To make sure this economy stays strong and people can find work, we must become less dependent on foreign sources of energy.

To create jobs, we need to reject economic isolationism and open up markets around the world for U.S. products. We open up our markets for goods from overseas, and that's good for you. If you've got more choices in the marketplace, you're likely to get that which you want at a better price and higher quality. So, rather than shutting our markets, I'm saying to countries like China, "Treat us the way we treat you." Americans compete with anybody, anytime, anywhere, so long as the rules are fair.

To create jobs, we've got to be wise about how we spend your money and keep your taxes low. My opponent has his own history on the economy. In 20 years as a Senator from Massachusetts, he's built up a record of a Senator from Massachusetts. [*Laughter*] He's voted to raise taxes 98 times.

Audience members. Boo-o-o!

The President. Think about that. He's been in the United States Senate for 20 years. That's about five times a year. [*Laughter*] That's a pattern. [*Laughter*] That's an indication of what's going to come. See, he can run from his record, but he cannot hide.

He's now promising not to raise taxes on anybody who earns less than $200,000 a year. The problem is, to keep that promise he would have to break almost all of his other ones. [*Laughter*] He's promised $2.2 trillion in new spending. That's with a "T." And yet his plan to pay for it is to tax the rich. But you can't raise enough money to tax the rich to pay for 2.2 trillion. There's a tax gap between his promises and what he can raise. And guess who usually has to fill the tax gap.

Audience members. Boo-o-o!

The President. Yes. Let me say something else about the rhetoric of taxing the rich. The rich hire lawyers and accountants for a reason: to slide the tab and stick you with the bill. We're not going to let the Senator tax you; we're going to carry Florida again and win in November.

When I came into office, our public schools had been waiting for decades for hopeful reform. Too many of our children were shuffled through school, year after year, without learning the basics. I pledged to restore accountability to our schools and raise standards and end the soft bigotry of low expectations, and I kept my word.

To build a more hopeful America, we must have the best prepared and most highly skilled workforce in the world. Most new jobs are filled with people—by people with at least 2 years of college, yet one in four of our students gets there. So that's why we'll fund early intervention programs in our high schools to help at-risk students. We'll place a new focus on math and science. Over time, we'll require a rigorous examination before graduation. By raising performance in our high schools and expanding Pell grants for low- and middle-income families, we will help more Americans start their career with a college diploma.

When I came into office, we had a problem in Medicare. Medicine was changing; Medicare was not. For example, Medicare would pay tens of thousands of dollars for a heart surgery but would not pay a dime for the prescription drugs that can prevent the heart surgery from being needed in the first place. That was not fair to our seniors, and it was not fair to the taxpayers. I pledged to bring Republicans and Democrats together to strengthen and modernize Medicare for our seniors, and I kept my word. Seniors are getting discounts on medicine. Docs are being treated fairly. Rural hospitals are being reimbursed. And beginning in 2006, all seniors will be able to get prescription drug coverage under Medicare.

We have more work to do. We have more work to do to make sure health care is available and affordable. We need a safety net for those with the greatest needs. I believe in community health centers, places where the poor and the indigent can get primary and preventative care, places where people can get the help they need without burdening the emergency rooms of our hospitals. In a new term, we'll work to make sure every poor county in America has a community health center. We'll need to do more to make sure poor children are fully subscribed in our program for low-income families.

We've got to do more to make sure health care is affordable. Most of the uninsured work for small businesses. Small businesses are having trouble affording health care. To help our workers get the health care they need, we must allow small businesses to join together so they can purchase insurance at the same discounts big companies are able to do. We will expand health savings accounts so workers in small businesses are able to pay low premiums and can save tax-free for a health care account they manage and call their own.

To make sure health care is available and affordable, we must do something about the junk lawsuits that are running good doctors out of practice and running the premiums up. By forcing doctors to practice defensive medicine, medical lawsuits cost the Government about $28 billion a year. That means they cost you $28 billion a year. The lawsuits cost our Nation's economy anywhere from 60 billion to 100 billion dollars a year. They drive up insurance premiums, which drives good doctors out of practice. You cannot be pro-patient and pro-doctor and pro-plaintiff-attorney at the same time. You have to choose. My opponent made his choice, and he put a personal injury trial lawyer on the ticket.

Audience members. Boo-o-o!

The President. I have made my choice. I'm standing with the doctors. I'm standing with the patients. I'm for medical liability reform—now.

My opponent says he has a health care plan.

Audience members. Four more years! Four more years! Four more years!

The President. My opponent has a health care plan. It's a plan for bigger and more intrusive Government. The other day in the debate, he said, "The Government has nothing to do with it." He was talking about his health care plan. I could barely contain myself. [*Laughter*] Of course, the Government has things to do with it. The facts are, 8 out of 10 people who get health care under Senator Kerry's plan would be placed on a Government program.

Audience members. Boo-o-o!

The President. Eight million Americans would lose their private health insurance, and most would go on Medicaid. That is a Government program. Senator Kerry claimed his plan would help small businesses. Those who've studied his plan call it an overpriced albatross which would saddle small businesses with 225 new mandates.

I have a different view of health care. I'm not for increasing the Federal role in health care. I want to make sure health decisions are made by doctors and patients, not by officials in Washington, DC.

I've set out policies that move America toward a positive and optimistic vision. We're headed toward an ownership society in America. There's a saying that no one ever washes a rental car. [*Laughter*] There's a lot of wisdom in that statement. [*Laughter*] When you own something, you care about it. When you own something, you have a vital stake in the future of your country.

That's why we're encouraging entrepreneurship. Every time a small business is started, someone is achieving the American Dream. We're encouraging health savings accounts so people have the security of owning and managing their own health care account. We're promoting homeownership. I love it when more and more people from all walks of life open up the door where they live and say, "Welcome to my home. Welcome to my piece of property."

In a new term, we'll take the next step to build an ownership society by strengthening Social Security. Our Social Security system needs fixing. First, let me talk to those who are on Social Security today. You might remember the 2000 campaign when they said in these TV ads, "If George W. wins, you will not get your check." I won, and you got your checks. You will continue to get your checks. The problem in Social

Security is not for those on Social Security today or baby boomers like me.

The problem is for our children and our grandchildren. People are understandably worried about whether our children and grandchildren will have Social Security around when they need it. For their sake, we must be bold and think about how to reform Social Security. For our children's sake, we must strengthen Social Security by allowing younger workers to save some of their payroll taxes in a personal savings account that they call their own and that the Government cannot take away.

My opponent wants to maintain the status quo when it comes to Social Security. He's against the Social Security reforms I just discussed, and he's just—against about every other reform that gives more authority and control to individuals. On issue after issue, from Medicare without choices to schools with less accountability to higher taxes, he takes the side of more Government control. There is a word for that attitude. It's called liberalism.

Audience members. Boo-o-o!

The President. He dismisses that as a label, but he must have been thinking differently when he told a newspaper, "I am a liberal and proud of it." As a matter of fact, the nonpartisan National Journal magazine did a study and named him the most liberal Member of the United States Senate. That takes hard work. [*Laughter*]

I have a different record and a different philosophy. I do not believe in big Government, and I do not believe Government should be indifferent. That is called compassionate conservatism. I believe in policies that empower people to improve their lives, not try to run their lives. So we're helping men and women find the skills and tools they need to prosper in a time of change. We're helping all Americans to have a future of dignity and independence, and that is how I will continue to lead our Nation for 4 more years.

In a time of change, some things do not change, the values we try to live by, cour-

age and compassion, reverence and integrity. We stand for a culture of life in which every person matters and every being counts. We stand for marriage and family, which are the foundations of our society. We stand for the appointment of Federal judges who know the difference between personal opinion and the strict interpretation of the law.

My opponent's words on these issues are a little muddy, but the record is real clear. [*Laughter*] He says he supports the institution of marriage, but he voted against the Defense of Marriage Act, which my predecessor signed into law. He voted against the ban on the brutal practice of partial-birth abortion.

Audience members. Boo-o-o!

The President. He described the Reagan years as a time of moral darkness.

Audience members. Boo-o-o!

The President. There is a mainstream in American politics, and my opponent sits on the far left bank. He can run, but he cannot hide.

This election will also determine how America responds to the continuing danger of terrorism. The most solemn duty of the American President is to protect the American people. If America shows uncertainty or weakness in this decade, the world will drift toward tragedy. This will not happen on my watch.

Since that terrible morning of September the 11th, 2001, we have fought the terrorists across the Earth, not for pride, not for power, but because the lives of our citizens are at stake. Our strategy is clear. We're defending the homeland. We're transforming our military. The All-Volunteer Army will remain an all-volunteer army. We're strengthening our intelligence. We're staying on the offensive. We will strike the terrorists abroad so we do not have to face them here at home. We will spread freedom and liberty. And we will prevail.

Our strategy is succeeding. Think about the world as it was some 3½ years ago.

Afghanistan was the home base of Al Qaida. Pakistan was a transit point for terrorist groups. Saudi Arabia was fertile ground for terrorist fundraising. Libya was secretly pursuing nuclear weapons. Iraq was a dangerous place and a gathering threat. And Al Qaida was largely unchallenged as it planned attacks.

Because we acted, because the United States led, Afghanistan is free and an ally in the war on terror; Pakistan is capturing terrorist leaders; Saudi Arabia is making raids and arrests; Libya is dismantling its weapons programs; the army of a free Iraq is fighting for freedom; and more than three-quarters of Al Qaida's key members and associates have been brought to justice. Because we acted to defend ourselves, more than 50 million people are now free, and that makes us more secure.

Think about what happened in Afghanistan. I want the youngsters here to understand the significance of what took place in 3½ short years. It wasn't all that long ago that the people of that country lived under the barbaric regime of the ideologues of hate. They lived in a period of darkness. Young girls were not allowed to go to school. Their mothers were pulled in the public square and whipped if they didn't toe their ideological line of these people. Because we acted to secure ourselves and to remove Al Qaida's ability to train, the people of Afghanistan are free. They went to the polls. They went to the polls to vote for President in the millions. The first voter in Afghanistan was a 19-year-old woman. Freedom is on the march. The people of Afghanistan no longer live in darkness. They now live in light because of democracy.

And we're making progress in Iraq. The people of Iraq will have elections in January. Think how far that society has come from the days of torture chambers and mass graves and brutality. No, we will stand with the people of Afghanistan and Iraq, because when America gives its word, America will keep its word. And we will

stand with those people because we understand free societies in the Middle East will be hopeful societies which no longer feed resentment and breed violence for export. Free governments in the Middle East will fight the terrorists instead of harboring them. Freedom will help us keep the peace we all want.

So our mission is clear. We'll help the countries train armies so that the people of Afghanistan and Iraq can do the hard work of defending their democracies. We'll help them get on the path of stability and self-government as quickly as possible, and then our troops will come home with the honor they have earned.

It is a great honor to be the Commander in Chief of a great military. And we're a great military because of the character of the people who wear our Nation's uniform. I want to thank the veterans who are here today for having set such a great example for those who wear the uniform. I want to thank the military families who are here today for their sacrifices.

We will make sure that our troops have all the resources they need to complete their missions. That's why I went to the United States Congress and asked for $87 billion of supplemental funding in September of '03. It was a very important request. We were there to support our troops in harm's way, and I received great bipartisan support for my request. As a matter of fact, the support was so strong that only 12 Members of the United States Senate voted against funding for our troops in combat, 2 of whom are my opponent and his runningmate.

Audience members. Boo-o-o!

The President. When you're out rounding up the vote, remind people of this startling statistic: Only four United States Senators voted to authorize the use of force and then voted against funding for our troops—only four—two of whom are my opponent and his runningmate.

Audience members. Boo-o-o!

The President. So they asked him why—you might remember the most famous quote of the 2004 campaign, when he said, "I actually did vote for the $87 billion, right before I voted against it."

Audience members. Boo-o-o!

The President. He's had several explanations since then of his vote. One of them was, "The whole thing was a complicated matter." There's nothing complicated about supporting our troops in harm's way.

Tomorrow is the one-year anniversary of Senator Kerry's vote against funding for our troops. My opponent's many and conflicting positions on this issue are a case study into why his contradictions call into question his credibility and his ability to lead our Nation. In September 2003, as the $87 billion funding package was being debated, Senator Kerry said on national TV, "It would be irresponsible to abandon our troops by voting against it." Just one month later, he did exactly that irresponsible thing, and he abandoned our troops in combat by voting against the funding. What happened to change the Senator's mind so abruptly in one short month? His opponent in the Democrat primary, Howard Dean, was gaining ground as an antiwar candidate. Senator Kerry apparently decided supporting our troops, even while they were in harm's way, was not as important as shoring up his political position.

Audience members. Boo-o-o!

The President. At a time of great threat to our country, at a time of great challenge to the world, the Commander in Chief must stand on principle, not on the shifting sands of political convenience.

There are big differences of opinion about how best to lead in this world. Senator Kerry proposed that we should pass a "global test" before we defend ourselves.

Audience members. Boo-o-o!

The President. The problem is with that "global test," the Senator can never pass it. Remember what happened in 1990. The United Nations Security Council passed a resolution supporting action to remove Saddam Hussein from Kuwait. The international community was united. Countries throughout the world joined our coalition. Yet, even after United Nations approval, in the United States Senate, Senator Kerry voted against the authorization for the use of force. If that coalition didn't pass his "global test," nothing will pass a "global test."

During the debate, you might remember he said that removing Saddam Hussein was a "mistake." He actually said he would have done it differently by supporting another United Nations Security Council resolution.

Audience members. Boo-o-o!

The President. Precisely what Saddam Hussein wanted. He wanted the world to look the other way. If my opponent had his way, Saddam Hussein would not only be sitting in a palace in Baghdad, he'd be in Kuwait. The world is better off with Saddam in a prison cell.

Listen, I'll continue to work to build strong alliances to keep our coalition strong. I talked to Prime Minister Tony Blair yesterday on Air Force One as I was heading from Iowa to Wisconsin. Alliances are important. Friendships are important in this dangerous world. But I will never turn over America's national security decisions to leaders of other countries.

I believe in the transformational power of liberty. I'll tell you what I mean by that. One of Laura and my best friends or closest friends in the international scene is Prime Minister Koizumi of Japan. That doesn't sound like much until you think about the fact that we were at war with them 60 years ago. Japan was a sworn enemy of the United States of America. My dad fought against the—our dad fought against the Japanese. I'm sure your dads and granddads probably did as well. They were a mortal enemy.

Yet, after we won in World War II, Harry S. Truman, President of the United States, believed in the transformational power of liberty. He believed that liberty could change an enemy into an ally. There was a lot of skeptics about that in America then, and you can understand why. Why would you want to work with the enemy? People lost lives, had their families turned upside down, were wondering why we even cared about a former enemy. But fortunately, enough citizens and the President believed in the power of liberty. And today, I sit down with Prime Minister Koizumi, as a result of Japan being a democracy, talking about the peace we all want.

Someday, an American President will be sitting down with a duly elected leader of Iraq. They'll be talking about the peace in the Middle East, and our children and our grandchildren will be better off for it.

I believe that millions in the Middle East plead in silence for their freedom. I believe that women in the Middle East want to live in a free society. I believe moms in the Middle East want to raise their child in a free world. I believe all these things, because freedom is not America's gift to the world; freedom is the Almighty God's gift to each man and woman in this world.

Extending freedom means confronting the evil of anti-Semitism. Today, I signed the Global Anti-Semitism Review Act of 2004. This law commits the Government to keep a record of anti-Semitic acts throughout the world and also a record of responses to those acts. This Nation will keep watch and make sure the ancient impulse of anti-Semitism never finds a home in the modern world.

For all Americans, these years in our history will always stand apart. There are quiet times in the life of a nation when little is expected of its leaders. This isn't one of those times. This is a time that requires firm resolve, clear vision, and the deep faith in the values that makes this a great nation.

None of us will ever forget that era when one—that week when one era ended and another began. On September the 14th, 2001, I stood in the ruins of the Twin Towers. It's a day I will never forget. There were workers in hardhats there yelling at the top of their lungs, "Whatever it takes." I remember trying to console people, and a guy grabbed me by the arm, and he said, "Do not let me down." Ever since that day, I wake up every morning thinking about how to better protect our country. I will never relent in defending America, whatever it takes.

Four years ago, when I traveled your great State, I made a pledge that if you gave me a chance to serve, I would uphold the honor and the dignity of the office to which I had been elected. With your help, I will do so for 4 more years.

Thanks for coming. God bless. On to victory. Thank you all.

NOTE: The President spoke at 1:20 p.m. at the Sound Advice Amphitheater. In his remarks, he referred to Gov. Jeb Bush of Florida; professional golfer Jack Nicklaus; Emilie Shaw, wife of Representative Clay Shaw; Tom Gallagher, chief financial officer, Florida Department of Financial Services; former President Saddam Hussein of Iraq; Prime Minister Tony Blair of the United Kingdom; and Prime Minister Junichiro Koizumi of Japan.

Remarks in Daytona Beach, Florida
October 16, 2004

The President. Thank you all for coming. Thank you all for being here on a beautiful Florida Saturday afternoon. Laura and I are honored so many came out to say hello.

We're here to ask for your vote and ask for your help. As Jeb said, it's nearly voting time, and we're counting on you to get your friends and neighbors to the polls. Everybody ought to vote in this country. In a democracy, we have a duty to vote. So round up everybody you can find, head them to the polls, and remind them, if they want a safer country, a stronger country, and a better country, to put me and Dick Cheney back in office.

And perhaps the reason why you should put me back in is so that Laura will be First Lady for 4 more years. I love her dearly, and she's a great First Lady.

I'm proud of my Vice President. I recognize he doesn't have the waviest hair in the race. [*Laughter*] I didn't pick him for his hair. I picked him because of his experience and sound judgment.

I'm proud of my brother Jeb. You've been through a lot of hardship in this State—not one hurricane, not two, but four. The people of this State rose to the occasion, as did your Governor. It's amazing what happens in hard times. The compassion of this country comes forth, and the compassion of the people of Florida came forth, neighbor helping neighbor, people putting their arm around somebody who hurts. I hope the Federal Government did—recognized that we did as much as we can possibly do, and we'll continue to help the people of this State get its feet back on the ground.

I want to thank Monty for his service to the country and for his introducing Jeb up here today. The Lieutenant Governor is with us, and I appreciate Toni Jennings. I appreciate all the State and local folks who are here.

I want to thank my friend Bill France. He's got something to do with cars over here. [*Laughter*] I'm proud he's here. One of the most amazing events of my life, at least as the Presidency, was to go to the NASCAR race here at the Daytona 500.

Most of all, I want to thank the grassroots activists who are here, the people who are putting up all the signs, turning out crowds like this at this rally, the people who are making the phone calls. There is no doubt in my mind that with your help, we'll carry Florida again and win a great victory on November the 2d.

The last few years, the American people have come to know me. They know my blunt way of speaking. I get that from Mother. [*Laughter*] They know that sometimes I mangle the English language. I get that from Dad. [*Laughter*] Americans also know that I tell you exactly what I'm going to do, and I keep my word.

When I came into office, the stock market had been in serious decline for 6 months. And then we had a recession. To help families and to get this economy going again, I pledged to reduce taxes. I kept my word.

Because we acted, the recession was one of the shallowest in American history. Over the last 3 years, our economy has grown at the fastest rate of any major industrialized nation. The national unemployment rate is at 5.4 percent, lower than the average of the 1970s, 1980s, and 1990s. The unemployment rate in your State is 4.5 percent. Farm income is up. Homeownership rate is at an alltime high. This economy is moving forward, and we're not going to go back to the days of big Government, tax and spend.

To make sure quality jobs are created here in America, America must be the best place in the world to do business. That means less regulations on our job creators. That means we've got to do something about these junk lawsuits that are hurting small-business owners.

Listen, to keep jobs here, Congress needs to pass my energy plan. It's a plan that encourages conservation and encourages the use of renewables like ethanol and biodiesel. It encourages clean coal technology. It encourages the exploration for natural gas in environmentally friendly ways. To keep jobs here, America must be less dependent on foreign sources of energy.

To create jobs here, we need to open up markets for U.S. products. Listen, we open up our markets for goods from overseas, and that's good for you. When you've got more products to choose from, you're likely to get that which you want at a better price and higher quality. That's how the market works. And so, therefore, I'm saying to other countries like China, "Treat us the way we treat you." See, we can compete with anybody, anytime, anywhere, if the playing field is level.

To create jobs, we've got to be wise about how we spend your money and keep your taxes low.

My opponent has his own history on the economy.

Audience members. Boo-o-o!

The President. In 20 years as a Senator from Massachusetts, he's built a record of a Senator from Massachusetts. [*Laughter*] He has voted to raise taxes 98 times.

Audience members. Boo-o-o!

The President. That's in 20 years. That's about five times a year. I'd call that a pattern. I'd call that an indicator. He can run from his record, but he cannot hide.

He looked in the camera the other night, and he said he promised not to raise taxes on anybody earning—that earns less than $200,000 a year. He said it with a straight face. [*Laughter*] The problem is, to keep that promise he would have to break almost all of his other ones. See, he's promised $2.2 trillion of new spending. That's with a "T."

Audience members. Boo-o-o!

The President. He said he's going to pay for it by taxing the rich, but you raise only about 600 billion if you raise the top two brackets. So there's a gap between what he's going to spend and what money he can collect. And so guess who usually pays—fills that gap.

Audience members. We do!

The President. There's something else wrong with taxing the rich. The rich hire lawyers and accountants for a reason: to slip the bill and stick you with it. [*Laughter*] We're not going to let him tax you;

we're going to carry Florida and win in November.

When I came into office, our public schools had been waiting decades for hopeful reform. Too many of our children were shuffled through school, year after year, without learning the basics. I pledged to restore accountability to our schools, to raise the standards, and to end the soft bigotry of low expectations. And I kept my word. Our children are making sustained gains in reading and math. We're closing an achievement gap, and we're not going to go back to the days of mediocrity and low expectations.

To build a more hopeful America, we must have the best prepared and most highly skilled workforce in the world. We live in a global economy. Most new jobs are filled by people with at least 2 years of college, yet only one in four of our students gets there. So we'll fund early intervention programs in our high schools to help at-risk students. We'll place a new focus on math and science. Over time, we'll require a rigorous exam before graduation. By raising performance in our high schools and by expanding Pell grants for low- and middle-income families, we will help more Americans start their career with a college diploma.

When I came to office, we had a problem in Medicare. Medicine was changing; Medicare was not. Let me give you an example. Medicare would pay hundreds of thousands of dollars—tens of thousands of dollars for heart surgery but not one single dime for the prescription drug coverage—for the prescription drugs that would prevent the heart surgery from being needed in the first place. That wasn't fair to our seniors and didn't make any sense for the taxpayers. I pledged to bring Republicans and Democrats together to strengthen and modernize Medicare for our seniors. I kept my word.

We're moving forward on health care, and there's more to do. We need to make sure health care is available and affordable for all our people. We need a safety net for those with the greatest needs. I believe in community health centers, where low and poor can get their preventative care. See, I'd rather them get the care there at a place of compassion rather than your emergency rooms in your hospitals here. It doesn't make any sense to have pressures on your emergency rooms. We can do a better job for the poor and the indigent. I believe every poor county in America ought to have a community health center. We'll make sure our poor children are fully subscribed in our programs for low-income families so they can get the health care they need.

We also ought to make sure health care is affordable. Listen, most of the uninsured work for small businesses. Small businesses are having trouble affording health care. We ought to allow small businesses to join together in associations so they can purchase insurance at the same discounts that big companies get to do. We got to expand health savings accounts so workers in small businesses are able to pay low premiums and people can save tax-free for a health care account they manage, a health care account they can call their own.

To make sure health care is available and affordable, we must do something about the junk lawsuits that are running up the cost of health care. By forcing doctors to practice defensive medicine, medical lawsuits cost the Government $28 billion a year. That means those lawsuits cost you $28 billion a year. Lawsuits—medical lawsuits cost our economy anywhere from 60 to 100 billion dollars a year. They drive up the insurance premiums, which drive good doctors out of practice. I have talked to too many ob-gyns that are having trouble practicing. I've talked to too many expectant moms who are having to drive mile after mile because of these lawsuits. You cannot be pro-doctor, pro-patient, and pro-plaintiff-attorney at the same time. You have to make a choice. My opponent made

his choice, and he put a personal injury trial lawyer on the ticket.

Audience members. Boo-o-o!

The President. I made my choice. I'm standing with the docs and the patients. I'm for medical liability reform—now.

We have a difference when it comes to health care. My opponent has a plan that calls for bigger and more intrusive Government. In one of our debates, he actually said about his health care plan, the Government has nothing to do with it. I could barely contain myself. [*Laughter*] The facts are that 8 out of 10 people who get health care under Senator Kerry's plan would be placed on a Government program. Eight million Americans would lose their private health insurance at work, and most would have to go on a Government plan like Medicaid. He claimed his plan would help small businesses. But upon analysis, small-business groups concluded that his plan is an overpriced albatross that would saddle small businesses with 225 new mandates.

The choice in this election is clear. My opponent wants to move in the direction of Government-run health care. I believe health decisions ought to be made by doctors and patients, not by officials in Washington, DC.

We're moving toward an ownership society in America. There's an old saying that says no one ever washes a rental car—[*laughter*]—a lot of wisdom in that. [*Laughter*] When you own something, you care about it. When you own something, you have a vital stake in the future of our country. That's why we're promoting entrepreneurship, creating an environment where the small-business owner can flourish. Every time a small business is started someone is realizing the American Dream. We're encouraging health savings accounts, so people have the security of owning their own health care that they could take with them from job to job. We're promoting homeownership. I love the idea that more and more Americans from all walks of life are opening up the door where they live and saying, "Welcome to my house. Welcome to my piece of property."

In a new term, we'll take the next step to build an ownership society by strengthening Social Security. The Social Security system needs fixing. I came to Washington to solve problems, not to pass them on to future Presidents and future generations. Now, those who are on Social Security don't need to worry. Remember in the 2000 campaign when I was running, they said, "If George W. gets elected, he's going to take away your checks." Well, our seniors got their checks. They will continue to get their checks. Baby boomers are in pretty good shape when it comes to Social Security.

But we need to worry about our children and our grandchildren. We need to worry about whether or not Social Security will be around when they need it. For their sake, we must strengthen Social Security by allowing younger workers to save some of their payroll taxes in a personal savings account that will earn a better rate or interest than the current trust, a personal savings account they can call their own, an account the Government can never take away.

When it comes to Social Security, as you heard the other night, my opponent wants to maintain the status quo. He's against the Social Security reforms I outlined. As a matter of fact, he's against just about every reform that gives more authority and more control to the individual. On issue after issue, from Medicare without choices to schools with less accountability to higher taxes, he takes the side of more Government.

There's a word for that attitude. It is called liberalism. He dismisses that as simply a label. He must have seen it differently when he said to a newspaper, "I'm a liberal and proud of it." [*Laughter*] The nonpartisan National Journal magazine did a study, named him the most liberal Member of the United States Senate. That's hard work. That's hard to do. [*Laughter*] It's

hard to make Ted Kennedy the conservative Senator from Massachusetts. He can run, but he cannot hide.

I have a different point of view, a different philosophy. I do not believe in big Government, and I do not believe that Government should be indifferent. I'm a compassionate conservative. I believe in policies that empower people to improve their lives, not try to run their lives. We're helping men and women find the skills and tools to prosper in a time of change. We'll help all Americans have a future of dignity and independence. That is how I have led, and that is how I will continue to lead for 4 more years.

Audience members. Four more years! Four more years! Four more years!

The President. In this time of change, some things do not change, the values we try to live by, courage and compassion, reverence and integrity. In times of change, we all must support the institutions that give our lives direction and purpose, our families, our schools, our religious congregations. We stand for a culture of life in which every person matters and every being counts. We stand for marriage and family, which are the foundations of our society. We stand for the appointment of Federal judges who know the difference between personal opinion and the strict interpretation of the law.

Now, my opponent's words on these issues are a little muddy—[*laughter*]—but his record is plenty clear. He says he supports the institution of marriage, but he voted against the Defense of Marriage Act, which my predecessor signed into law.

Audience members. Boo-o-o!

The President. He voted against the ban on the brutal practice of partial-birth abortion.

Audience members. Boo-o-o!

The President. He called the Reagan years a time of moral darkness.

Audience members. Boo-o-o!

The President. There is a mainstream in American politics, and my opponent sits on the far left bank. He can run, but he cannot hide.

This election will also determine how America responds to the continuing danger of terrorism. The most solemn duty of the American President is to protect the American people. If America shows uncertainty or weakness in this decade, the world will drift toward tragedy. This will not happen on my watch.

Since that terrible morning of September the 11th, 2001, we have fought the terrorists across the Earth, not for pride, not for power, but because the lives of our citizens are at stake. Our strategy is clear. We're defending the homeland. We are reforming and strengthening our intelligence capabilities. We are transforming our military. Our All-Volunteer Army will remain an all-volunteer army.

My opponent seems to be willing to say almost anything he thinks will benefit him politically. After standing on the stage, after the debates, I made it very plain, we will not have an all-volunteer army. And yet, this week—we will have an all-volunteer army. Let me restate that. [*Laughter*] We will not have a draft. No matter what my opponent tries to tell people and scare them, we will have an all-volunteer army. The only person talking about a draft is my opponent. The only politicians who have supported a draft are Democrats. And the best way to avoid a draft is to vote for me.

As part of our strategy, we will stay on the offensive. We will strike the terrorists abroad so we do not have to face them here at home. We will spread freedom and liberty. And we will prevail.

The strategy is succeeding. Think about the world as it was 3½ years ago. Afghanistan was the home base of Al Qaida. Pakistan was a transit point for terrorist groups. Saudi Arabia was a fertile ground for terrorist fundraising. Libya was secretly pursuing nuclear weapons. Iraq was a dangerous place and a gathering threat. And

Al Qaida was largely unchallenged as it planned attacks.

Because we led, Afghanistan is free and is now an ally in the war on terror; Pakistan is capturing terrorist leaders; Saudi Arabia is making raids and arrests; Libya is dismantling its weapons programs; the army of a free Iraq is fighting for freedom; and more than three-quarters of Al Qaida and its associates have been brought to justice.

In defending ourselves, in fighting for our security, we have freed over 50 million people in Afghanistan and Iraq. Think about what has happened in Afghanistan. I want the youngsters to understand what has taken place in about 3½ years. It used to be, those people lived under—in Afghanistan lived under the brutal reign of the Taliban. They lived in darkness. These people were so backward and so barbaric that young girls couldn't go to school. Their mothers were whipped in the public square if they didn't toe the ideological line. Because we protected ourselves, we liberated the people of Afghanistan from the Taliban. And by millions, they showed up at the polls to vote. The first voter in the Presidential election was a 19-year-old woman.

Iraq will be holding Presidential elections. Think how far that country has come in a short period of time from the days of mass graves and torture chambers to a country beginning—a democracy beginning to grow. And it's in our interests to promote freedom. It's in our interests these countries become free, because free societies in the Middle East will be hopeful societies which no longer feed resentment and breed violence for export. Free societies and free governments in the Middle East will fight the terrorists instead of harboring them. Freedom will help us keep the peace.

And so our mission is clear. We will help these countries train the armies and police so the people of Afghanistan and Iraq can do the hard work of defending democracy. We will help them get on the path of stability as quickly as possible, and then our troops will return home with the honor they have earned.

We have a great United States military, and I'm proud to be their Commander in Chief. I want to thank the veterans who are here for having set such a great example for those who wear the uniform. I want to thank the military families who are here for their sacrifices. And I assure you, we'll keep the commitments I have made to our troops. We will make sure they have all the resources they need to complete their missions. That's why I went to the Congress in September of 2003 and requested $87 billion of supplemental funding to support our troops in harm's way in both Afghanistan and Iraq. The support was strong for that request, so strong that only 12 Members of the United States Senate voted against the funding, 2 of whom are my opponent and his runningmate.

Audience members. Boo-o-o!

The President. When you're out gathering the vote, remind your fellow citizens that only four Members of the Senate voted to authorize the use of force and voted against funding for our troops—only four— two of whom are my opponent and his runningmate.

Audience members. Boo-o-o!

The President. You might remember my opponent's famous quote when asked about his vote. He said, "I actually did vote for the $87 billion, before I voted against it."

Audience members. Boo-o-o!

The President. He's given a lot of explanations since then. One explanation was, "The whole thing was just a complicated matter." There's nothing complicated about supporting our troops in combat.

Tomorrow is the one-year anniversary of Senator Kerry's vote against funding for our troops. My opponent's many and conflicting positions on this issue are a case study into why his contradictions call into question his credibility and ability to lead our Nation. In September of 2003, as the $87 billion funding package was being debated in Congress, Senator Kerry said, "It would be irresponsible to abandon our troops by voting against it." Just one month later, he did exactly that irresponsible thing and voted not to fund our troops. And so, what happened to change the Senator's mind so abruptly in one month? His opponent in the Democrat primary, Howard Dean, was gaining ground as an antiwar candidate. Senator Kerry apparently decided supporting the troops, even while they were in harm's way, was not as important as shoring up his political position.

Audience members. Boo-o-o!

The President. At a time of great threat for our country, at a time of great challenge in the world, the Commander in Chief must stand on principle, not on the shifting sands of political convenience.

The differences are clear when it comes to defending the country. Senator Kerry proposed that we should pass a "global test" before we defend ourselves.

Audience members. Boo-o-o!

The President. The problem with that "global test" is that the Senator can never pass it. [*Laughter*] In 1990, the United Nations Security Council passed a resolution supporting action to remove Saddam Hussein from Kuwait. The international community was united. Countries throughout the world joined the coalition. Yet, even after the United Nations' approval, Senator Kerry voted against the authorization of the use of force. If the 1991 gulf war didn't pass his "global test," nothing will pass his "global test."

Audience members. Boo-o-o!

The President. And that makes America more dangerous. It makes the world less secure. I'll work with our allies. I'll build coalitions. But I will never turn over our national security decisions to leaders of other countries.

I believe in the transformational power of liberty. You know, one of our friends is Prime Minister Koizumi of Japan. That probably doesn't sound too unusual, except think back some 60 years ago when we were at war with the Japanese. They were our mortal enemy. My dad fought against the Japanese. I'm confident many relatives out here fought against the Japanese. And it was a tough war, a brutal war.

After the war was over, Harry S. Truman, President of the United States, believed in the power of liberty to transform an enemy into an ally. So did other Americans. There was a lot of skepticism as we worked with Japan to build a democracy. You can understand that. "This enemy could never become a democracy," some said. "Why do we want to help somebody who hurt so many of our citizens? Why do we care about a country that attacked us?" However, because people had belief in the power of liberty to transform, today, I sit down with Prime Minister Koizumi as a friend, talking about keeping the peace we all want.

Someday, a duly elected leader from Iraq will be sitting down with the President of the United States talking about peace in the Middle East, and our children and our grandchildren will be better off for it.

Extending freedom also means confronting the evil of anti-Semitism. Today I signed the Global Anti-Semitism Review Act of 2004. This law commits the Government to keep a record of anti-Semitic acts throughout the world and also a record of responses to them. This Nation will keep watch and will make sure that the ancient impulse of anti-Semitism never finds a home in the modern world.

For all Americans, these years in our history will always stand apart. There are quiet times in the life of a nation when little is expected of its leaders. This is not one of those times. This is a time that requires firm resolve and clear vision and the deep faith in the values that makes this a great nation. And one of those deep faiths we believe and understand is that we know that freedom is not America's gift to the world; freedom is the Almighty God's gift to each man and woman in this world.

None of us will ever forget that week when one era ended and another began. On September the 14th, 2001, I stood in the ruins of the Twin Towers. It's a day I will never forget. There were workers there in hardhats yelling at the top of their lungs, "Whatever it takes." A fellow grabbed me by the arm. He looked me right in the eye, and he said, "Do not let me down." Ever since that day, I wake up every morning thinking about how to better protect our country. I will never relent in defending our security, whatever it takes.

Four years ago, when I traveled your great State asking for the vote, I made a pledge that if you gave me a chance to serve, I would uphold the honor and the dignity of the office to which I had been elected. With your help, with your hard work, I will do so for 4 more years.

God bless. Thank you all for coming. I appreciate you. Thank you all.

NOTE: The President spoke at 4:10 p.m. outside the office building at 525 Fentress Blvd. near the Daytona International Speedway. In his remarks, he referred to Gov. Jeb Bush and Lt. Gov. Toni Jennings of Florida; Bill France, Jr., former president, NASCAR; and Prime Minister Junichiro Koizumi of Japan.

Remarks to the 2004 United States Olympic and Paralympic Teams
October 18, 2004

Thank you all for coming. Please be seated. It's such an honor for Laura and me to welcome the mighty United States Olympic team to the White House. We're really proud of our athletes. We want to welcome the U.S. Olympians and the Paralympians here on the South Lawn. We welcome the coaches and the team leaders who are here today. We welcome the former Olympians and Paralympians who are with us today. We want to welcome Herman Frazier and Jeanne Picariello. We want to welcome the family members here. But most of all, we're thrilled the athletes are here.

To qualify for Team USA, you had to set high goals, devote long hours to training, and outperform talented athletes from all across our country. In Athens, you faced the toughest competition and the highest pressure in all of sports. And when the games were over, America had earned more than 100 medals, the most in the world. We heard our national anthem played 35 times to honor gold medalists. Our athletes created lasting memories for millions of Americans who followed the games.

We'll always remember Paul Hamm coming from behind to win the gold in the men's gymnastics, and Carly Patterson winning the women's gold the next night. We'll remember Rulon Gardner leaving his shoes in the ring after winning his last match as an Olympic wrestler. We'll remember our many incredible swimmers, swimmers like Michael Phelps and the 4 by 200 women's freestyle relay team that set a world record. We'll remember the Paralympians who earned a remarkable 88 medals for the United States of America. Including Royal Mitchell and Karissa Whitsell, each of who earned two gold medals. We'll remember all the American teams that came together to win gold in the Olympics and Paralympics—men's rowing and sailing, women's soccer, softball, basketball—[*laughter*]—beach volleyball, and the women's wheelchair basketball team. Your success has showed the power of discipline and persistence.

These games came at an historic time for the world. You and your fellow Olympians showed why we have such great hope in this world. Think about what happened at the opening ceremonies. Our teams marched alongside men and women from Afghanistan and Iraq, nations that just 4 years ago knew only tyranny and repression.

With millions watching, you showed the best values of America. You were humble in victory, gracious in defeat. You showed compassion for your competitors. You showed the great tolerance and diversity of our people. You're great athletes. Most importantly, you showed great character. You made us all proud, and I want to thank you for being such fine ambassadors of our Nation to the world.

You also understand your responsibility to be champions away from the field as well. Appreciate the good examples you set for millions of children who dream about becoming Olympians or Paralympians themselves.

In the years ahead, I hope you'll continue to give back to your communities. I hope you'll consider mentoring a child or coaching a child. With your generosity and decency, you'll make this country a more hopeful place.

Once again, welcome to the White House. Congratulations. May God continue to bless our country.

NOTE: The President spoke at 10:07 a.m. on the South Lawn at the White House. In his remarks, he referred to Herman Frazier, Chef de Mission, 2004 U.S. Olympic team; Jeanne Picariello, Chef de Mission, 2004 U.S. Paralympic team; Paul Hamm, gymnast, Carly Patterson, gymnast, Rulon Gardner, wrestler, and Michael Phelps, swimmer, U.S. Olympic team; and Royal Mitchell, runner, and Karissa Whitsell, cyclist, U.S. Paralympic team.

Remarks in Marlton, New Jersey
October 18, 2004

The President. Thank you all. Thanks for coming. Thanks for the warm welcome. It is great to be back in the State of New Jersey. Oh, I know it might surprise some to see a Republican Presidential candidate in New Jersey in late October. The reason why I'm here, with your help, we'll carry the State of New Jersey in November.

We are now 15 days away from a critical election. Many important domestic issues are at stake. I have a positive, hopeful agenda for job creation, broader health coverage, and better public education. Yet all the progress we hope to make depends on the security of our Nation. America is in the middle of a global war on terror, a struggle unlike any we have ever known before. We face an enemy that is determined to kill the innocent and make our country into a battlefield. In the war on terror, there is no place for confusion and no substitute for victory. For the sake of our future and our freedom, we will fight this war with every asset of our national power, and we will prevail.

Laura sends her best. So I asked her to marry me; she said, "Fine, just so long as I never have to give a political speech." [*Laughter*] I said, "Okay, you got a deal." Fortunately, she didn't hold me to that deal. The American people—a lot of Americans have seen her give a speech, and when they do, they see a compassionate, strong, warm woman.

I'm proud to have been standing on the stage with Bernie Kerik. He knows something about security. He's lived security all his life, and I want to thank him for his dedication and his service to the people of this country.

I want to thank Congressman Jim Saxton for being here today. And thank you for bringing your daughter, Jennifer. I want to thank Congressman Scott Garrett for joining us today. Congressman, thank you.

Congressman Frank LoBiondo—thanks for coming, Frank and Tina. I want to thank Congressman Chris Smith and Marie for joining us. The chairman of the Republican Party was born and raised in this county. He's doing a fabulous job. Welcome my friend Ed Gillespie. Thanks for coming, Ed.

I want to thank all the State senators and statehouse members who are here. I want to thank the grassroots activists. I want to thank you for what you're going to do during the next 15 days. Put up the signs. Call the phones. Get the people out to vote. We're going to win the State of New Jersey and win a great victory in November.

Audience members. Four more years! Four more years! Four more years!

The President. During the decade of the 1990s, our times often seemed peaceful on the surface. Yet, beneath that surface were currents of danger. Terrorists were training and planning in distant camps. In 1993, terrorists made their first attack on the World Trade Center. In 1998, terrorists bombed American Embassies in Kenya and Tanzania. And then came the attack on the U.S.S. *Cole* in 2000, which cost the lives of 17 American sailors. In this period, America's response to terrorism was generally piecemeal and symbolic. The terrorists concluded this was a sign of weakness, and their plans became more ambitious,* and their attacks became more deadly.

Most Americans still felt that terrorism was something distant and something that would not strike on a large scale in America. That is the time that my opponent wants to go back to——

Audience members. Boo-o-o!

The President. ——a time when danger was real and growing, but we didn't know

---

* White House correction.

it, a time when some thought terrorism was only a "nuisance."

Audience members. Boo-o-o!

The President. But that very attitude is what blinded America to the war being waged against us. And by not seeing the war, our Government had no comprehensive strategy to fight it. September the 11th, 2001, changed all that. We realized that the apparent security of the 1990s was an illusion.

The people of New Jersey were among the first to understand how the world changed. On September the 11th, from places like Hoboken and Jersey City, you could look across the Hudson River and see the Twin Towers burning. We will never forget that day, and we will never forget our duty to defend America.

Out of the horror of that day, we also saw good emerge. America has seen a new generation of heroes, police, firefighters, members of the military. Americans have felt a new sense of community in neighborhoods and across our country. We've been reminded that all of us are a part of a great American story that is larger than our individual lives, and we have been reminded of our solemn responsibility to defend freedom.

September the 11th also changed the way we should look at national security, but not everyone realizes it. The choice we face in this election, the first Presidential election since September the 11th, is how our Nation will defeat this threat. Will we stay on the offensive against those who want to attack us——

Audience members. Yes!

The President. ——or will we take action only after we are attacked?

Audience members. No-o-o!

The President. Will we make decisions in the light of September the 11th or continue to live in the mirage of safety that was actually a time of gathering threats? And in this time of choosing, I want all Americans to know you can count on me

to fight our enemies and defend our freedom.

Winning the war on terror requires more than tough-sounding words repeated in the election season. America needs clear moral purpose and leaders who will not waver, especially in the tough times. And winning the war on terror requires a strategy for victory. Unlike my opponent, I understand the struggle America faces, and I have a strategy to win.

Our first duty in the war on terror is to protect the homeland. This morning at the White House, I signed a strong law that will make our Nation more secure. With the 2005 Homeland Security Appropriations Act, we are providing essential funding for Coast Guard patrols and port security, for the Federal air marshal program, and for technology that will defend aircraft against missiles. We're adding new resources to patrol our borders and to verify the identity of foreign visitors to America. We need to know who's coming in and out of our country.

The new law includes vital money for first-responders and for better security of chemical facilities and nuclear plants and water treatment plants and bridges and subways and tunnels. All these measures show the unwavering commitment of our Government. We will do everything in our power to protect the American people.

The law I signed today is part of a broad effort to defend America against new dangers. After September the 11th, we created the Department of Homeland Security to make sure our Government agencies are working together. We're transforming the FBI into an agency whose primary focus is stopping terrorism. Through Project BioShield, we are developing new vaccines and treatments against biological attacks. We've trained more than a half million first-responders across America.

To protect America, we passed the PATRIOT Act, giving law enforcement many of the same tools to fight terrorists that they already had to fight drug cartels and organized crime. Since September the 11th, law enforcement professionals have stopped terrorist activities in Columbus, Ohio; San Diego, California; Portland, Oregon; Seattle, Washington; Buffalo, New York; and other places, including New Jersey, where we apprehended an arms dealer who was allegedly trying to sell shoulder-fired missiles to terrorists.

My opponent voted for the PATRIOT Act, but now he wants to weaken it. There are plenty of safeguards in this law, making sure that civil liberties are protected and searches are authorized by court order. By seeking to dilute the PATRIOT Act, my opponent is taking the eye off the ball. The danger to America is not the PATRIOT Act or the good people who use it; the danger to America is the terrorists. And we will not let up in this fight.

To protect America, our country needs the best possible intelligence. Chairman Tom Kean and other members of the September the 11th Commission made thoughtful and valuable recommendations on intelligence reform. We are already implementing the vast majority of those recommendations that can be enacted without a vote of Congress. We're expanding and strengthening the capabilities of the CIA. We've established the Terrorist Threat Integration Center so we can bring together all the available intelligence on terrorist threats to one place.

But other changes require new laws. Congress needs to create the position of the National Intelligence Director and take other measures to make our intelligence community more effective. These reforms are necessary to stay ahead of the threats. I urge Congress to act quickly so I can sign them into law.

My opponent has taken a different approach, and it shows in his record. Just one year after the first attack on the World Trade Center in 1993, Senator Kerry proposed a $6 billion cut in the Nation's intelligence budget.

Audience members. Boo-o-o!

The President. But the majority of his colleagues ignored his irresponsible proposal. In 1995, he tried to cut intelligence funding again, and this time he could not get a single Member of the United States Senate to support his bill. And that's an important difference between us. Senator Kerry has a record of trying to weaken American intelligence. I am working every day to strengthen American intelligence.

In a free and open society, it is impossible to protect against every threat. So second, we must pursue a comprehensive strategy against terror. The best way to prevent attacks is to stay on the offense against the enemy overseas. We are waging a global campaign from the mountains of central Asia to the deserts of the Middle East and from the Horn of Africa to the Philippines.

These efforts are paying off. Since September the 11th, 2001, more than three-quarters of Al Qaida's key members and associates have been brought to justice. The rest of them know we're coming after them.

After September the 11th, we set a new direction for American policy and enforced a doctrine that is clear to all: "If you support or harbor terrorists, you're equally guilty of terrorist murder." We destroyed the terror camps that trained thousands of killers in Afghanistan. We removed the Taliban from power. We have persuaded Governments in Pakistan and Saudi Arabia to recognize the enemy and join the fight. We ended the regime of Saddam Hussein, which sponsored terror. Iraq's new Government under Prime Minister Allawi is hunting down terrorists in Iraq. We sent a message to Libya, which has now given up weapons of mass destruction programs and handed nuclear materials and equipment over to the United States. We have acted, through diplomacy and force, to shrink the area where the terrorists can operate freely, and that strategy has the terrorists on the run.

My opponent has a fundamental misunderstanding on the war on terror. A reporter recently asked Senator Kerry how September the 11th changed him. He replied, "It didn't change me much at all."

Audience members. Boo-o-o!

The President. His unchanged worldview is obvious from the policies he still advocates. He has said this war is primarily an intelligence and law enforcement operation. He has declared, we should not respond to threats until they are, quote, "imminent." He has complained that my administration, quote, "relies unwisely on the threat of military preemption against terrorist organizations." Let me repeat that. He says that preemptive action is "unwise," not only against regimes but even against terrorist organizations.

Audience members. Boo-o-o!

The President. Senator Kerry's approach would permit a response only after America is hit.

Audience members. Boo-o-o!

The President. This kind of September the 10th attitude is no way to protect our country. The war on terror is a real war with deadly enemies, not simply a police operation. In an era of weapons of mass destruction, waiting for threats to arrive at our doorsteps is to invite disaster. Tyrants and terrorists will not give us polite notice before they attack our country. As long as I'm the Commander in Chief, I will confront dangers abroad so we do not have to face them here at home.

The case of one terrorist shows what is at stake. The terrorist leader we face in Iraq today, the one responsible for beheading American hostages, the one responsible for many of the car bombings and attacks against Iraqis, is a man named Zarqawi. Before September the 11th, Zarqawi ran a camp in Afghanistan that trained terrorists in the use of explosives and poisons—until coalition forces destroyed that camp. He fled to Saddam Hussein's Iraq, where he received medical care and set up operations with some two dozen terrorist associates. He operated in Baghdad and worked with associates in northern Iraq who ran camps to train terrorists and conducted chemical and biological experiments—until coalition forces arrived and ended those operations. With nowhere to operate openly, Zarqawi has gone underground and is making a stand in Iraq.

Here, the difference between my opponent and me is very clear. Senator Kerry believes that fighting Zarqawi and other terrorists in Iraq is a "diversion" from the war on terror. I believe that fighting and defeating these killers in Iraq is a central commitment in the war on terror.

If Zarqawi and his associates were not busy fighting American forces in Iraq, does Senator Kerry think they would be leading productive and peaceful lives? [*Laughter*] Clearly, these killers would be plotting and acting to murder innocent civilians in free nations, including our own. By facing these terrorists far away, our military is making the United States of America more secure.

Third, to win the war on terror, America must work with allies and lead the world with clarity. And that is exactly what we are doing. The flags of 64 nations fly at U.S. Central Command Headquarters in Tampa, Florida, representing coalition countries that are working openly with us in the war on terror. Dozens more are helping quietly in important ways. Today, all 26 NATO nations have personnel either in Iraq, Afghanistan, or both. America's allies are standing with us in the war on terror, and we are grateful.

My opponent promises that he would do better with our allies, yet he's decided that the way to build alliances is to insult our friends. As a candidate for President, Senator Kerry has managed to offend or alienate almost every one of America's fighting allies in the war on terror. He has called the countries serving alongside us in Iraq, quote, "a trumped-up coalition of the bribed, the coerced, the bought, and the extorted."

Audience members. Boo-o-o!

The President. He has dismissed the sacrifice of 14 nations that have lost forces in Iraq, calling those nations "window dressing." In our debate a few weeks ago, he declared, "When we went in, there were three countries: Great Britain, Australia, and the United States." He left out Poland, one of the first countries to see combat on the first days of hostilities in Iraq. He never shows respect for some of the 30 nations that are serving courageously in Iraq today.

Senator Kerry even has disregarded the contributions of Iraqis who are fighting for their freedom. When he speaks of coalition casualties in Iraq, he doesn't count the hundreds of Iraqis who have given their lives fighting the terrorists and the insurgents. When Iraq's Prime Minister came to Washington to address Congress last month, Senator Kerry did not show up. Instead, he called a press conference and questioned the Prime Minister's credibility. The Prime Minister of Iraq is a brave man who survived the assassins of Saddam. The Prime Minister of Iraq deserves the respect of the world, not the scorn of a politician.

As part of his foreign policy, Senator Kerry has talked about applying a "global test."

Audience members. Boo-o-o!

The President. As far as I can tell, it comes down to this: Before we act to defend ourselves, he thinks we need permission from foreign capitals.

Audience members. Boo-o-o!

The President. Yet, even the gulf war coalition in 1991 did not pass Senator Kerry's "global test." Even with the United Nations approval, he voted against removing Saddam Hussein from Kuwait.

Audience members. Boo-o-o!

The President. If that vast, U.N.-supported operation did not pass his test, nothing ever could. Senator Kerry's "global test" is nothing more than an excuse to constrain the actions of our own country in a dangerous world.

I believe in strong alliances. I believe in respecting other countries and working with them and seeking their advice. But I will never submit our national security decisions to a veto of a foreign government.

Audience members. U.S.A.! U.S.A.! U.S.A.!

The President. Fourth, we will win the war on terror and make America safer by advancing the cause of freedom and democracy. Free societies are hopeful societies which do not nurture bitterness or the ideologies of terror and murder. Free governments in the broader Middle East will fight the terrorists instead of harboring them. And this is why a free Iraq and a free Afghanistan are vital to peace in that region and vital to the security interests of our country.

After decades of tyranny in the broader Middle East, progress toward freedom will not come easily. Yet, that progress is coming faster than many would have said possible. Across a troubled region, we are seeing a movement toward elections, greater rights for women, and open discussion of peaceful reform. The election in Afghanistan less than 2 weeks ago was a landmark event in the history of liberty. That election was a tremendous defeat for the terrorists.

My opponent has complained that we are trying to, quote, "impose" democracy on people in that region. Is that what he sees in Afghanistan, unwilling people having democracy forced upon them? We removed the Taliban by force, but democracy is rising in that country because the Afghan people, like everywhere, want to live in freedom.

No one forced them to register by the millions or stand in long lines at polling places. On the day of that historic election, an Afghan widow brought all four of her daughters to vote alongside her. She said this, she said, "When you see women here lined up to vote, this is something profound. I never dreamed this day would come." But that woman's dream finally arrived, as it will one day across the greater Middle East. [*Applause*] Thank you.

The dream of freedom is moving forward in Iraq. The terrorists know it, and they hate it, and they fight it. And we can expect more violence as Iraq moves toward free elections. Yet, every day in Iraq, our coalition is defeating the enemy's strategic objectives. The enemy seeks to disrupt the march toward democracy. But an Iraqi independent electoral commission is up and running, political parties are planning campaigns, voter registration will begin next month, and free and fair Iraqi elections will be held on schedule this coming January.

The enemy seeks to establish sanctuaries in Iraq from which to commit acts of terror. But Iraqi and coalition forces are on the offensive in Fallujah and North Babil and have restored Government control in Samarra, Tall 'Afar, and Najaf.

The enemy wants to make Iraqis afraid to join security forces. But every week, more and more Iraqis answer the call to arms. More than 100,000 soldiers, police, and border guards are already trained, equipped, and bravely serving their country. And well over 200,000 will be in place by the end of 2005.

The enemy seeks to break the will of the Iraqi people. But as Prime Minister Allawi told the Congress, Iraqis are hopeful, optimistic, and determined to prevail in their struggle for liberty.

After the enemy has failed in so many goals, what can these killers do now? They can fill up our TV screens with horrible images of suicide bombings and beheadings. These scenes are chaotic and horrific, but they're not a complete picture of what's happening in Iraq. A recent poll found that more than 75 percent of Iraqis want to vote, and they have confidence in the electoral progress. And more than 75 percent are hopeful about the future of their country. The violent acts of a few will not divert Iraqis and our coalition from the mission

we have accepted. Iraq will be free. Iraqis will be secure. And the terrorists will fail.

My opponent has a different outlook. While America does the hard work of fighting terror and spreading freedom, he has chosen the easy path of protest and defeatism. He refuses to acknowledge progress or praise the growing democratic spirit in Iraq. He has not made democracy a priority of his foreign policy. But what is his strategy, his vision, his answer? Is he content to watch and wait as anger and resentment grow for more decades in the Middle East, feeding more terrorism until radicals without conscience gain the weapons to kill without limit?

Giving up the fight might seem easier in the short run, but we learned on September the 11th that if violence and fanaticism are not opposed at their source, they will find us where we live. America is safer today because Afghanistan and Iraq are fighting terrorists instead of harboring them. And I believe future generations of Americans will be spared violence and fear as democracy and hope and governments that oppose terror multiply across the Middle East.

Victory in the war on terror requires victory in Iraq. If a terror regime were allowed to reemerge in Iraq, the terrorists would find a home, a source of funding, and vital support. They would correctly conclude that free nations do not have the will to defend themselves. When Iraq becomes a free society at the heart of the Middle East, an ally in the war on terror, and a model for hopeful reform in a region that needs hopeful reform, the terrorists will suffer a crushing defeat and every free nation will be more secure.

Unfortunately, Senator Kerry does not share our commitment to victory in Iraq. For 3 years, depending on the headlines, the poll numbers, and political calculation, he has taken almost every conceivable position on Iraq.

Audience members. Flip-flop! Flip-flop! Flip-flop!

The President. First, he said Saddam Hussein was a threat, and he voted for the war. Then he voted against funds for bullets and body armor for the troops he had voted to send into battle.

Audience members. Boo-o-o!

The President. He declared himself an antiwar candidate. Months later, he said that knowing everything we know now, he would have still voted for the war. Then he said the war was a "mistake," an "error," or "diversion." Having gone back and forth so many times, the Senator from Massachusetts has now flip-flopped his way to a dangerous position. My opponent finally has settled on a strategy, a strategy of retreat.

Audience members. Boo-o-o!

The President. He has talked about artificial timetables to pull our troops out of Iraq. He has sent the signal that America's overriding goal in Iraq would be to leave, even if the job is not done.

Audience members. Boo-o-o!

The President. And that approach would lead to a major defeat in the war on terror. So long as I'm the Commander in Chief, America will never retreat in the face of the terrorists. [*Applause*] Thank you.

We will keep our word to the Iraqi people. We'll make sure Iraqi forces can defend their country, and then American troops will return home with the honor they have earned.

On each of the four commitments needed to prevail in the war on terror, there is a clear choice before the American people. My opponent wants to weaken the PATRIOT Act and has a history of trying to undermine our intelligence services. I will take every necessary measure to protect the homeland. The Senator wants to wage the war on terror on the defensive. I will take the fight to the enemy. The Senator insults our friends in the world and wants to please a few critics. I'm working with our friends for the sake of freedom and security. The Senator is skeptical and pessimistic about democracy in Iraq and critical of our efforts in the broader Middle East.

I know that the advance of freedom is the path to security and peace.

In all these areas, my opponent's views would make America less secure and the world more dangerous. And none of these positions should come as a surprise. Over a 20-year career in the United States Senate, Senator Kerry has been consistently wrong on the major national security issues facing our country. The Senator who voted against the $87 billion for our troops in Afghanistan and Iraq is the same Senator who has voted against vital weapons systems during his entire career. He tried to cancel the Patriot missile, which shot down Scud missiles in Operation Desert Storm. He opposed the B–1 bomber, which was critical to victory in the Afghan campaign. He opposed the B–2 stealth bomber, which delivered devastating air strikes on Taliban positions. He opposed the modernized F–14D, which we used against terrorists in Tora Bora. He opposed the Apache helicopter, which destroyed enemy tanks and anti-aircraft missile launchers in Iraq.

The Senator who is skeptical of democracy in Iraq also spoke with sympathy for a communist dictator in Nicaragua in the 1980s and criticized the democracy movement as "terrorism." His misguided policies would have impeded the spread of freedom in Central America. The Senator who claims the world is more dangerous since America started fighting the war on terror is the same Senator who said that Ronald Reagan's policies of peace through strength actually made America less safe——

Audience members. Boo-o-o!

The President. ——the same Senator who said the Reagan Presidency was 8 years of "moral darkness."

Audience members. Boo-o-o!

The President. In this campaign, Senator Kerry can run from his record, but he cannot hide. [*Applause*] Thank you.

The Senator's long record shows a clear pattern on national security. He has consistently opposed a stronger military. He has consistently looked for excuses to constrain

American power. He has consistently shown poor judgment on the great issues of war and peace. When one Senator among a hundred holds a policy of weakness, it doesn't make a lot of difference. But the Presidency is an office of great responsibility and consequence.

I have a record in office as well, and all Americans have seen that record. September the 14th,° 2001, I stood in the ruins of the Twin Towers. It's a day I will never forget. Bernie might remember the workers in hardhats that were yelling at me and yelling at us, "Whatever it takes." A man grabbed me by the arm, just coming out of the rubble, and he said, "Do not let me down." I have a responsibility that goes on. I wake up every morning thinking about how to make our country more secure. I acted again and again to protect the American people. I will never relent in defending our country, whatever it takes.

In a new term——

Audience members. Four more years! Four more years! Four more years!

The President. In a new term as your President, we will finish the work we have

started. We will stand up for terror—we will stand up for freedom. And on November the 2d, my fellow Americans, I ask that you stand with me.

God bless. Thank you all.

NOTE: The President spoke at 1:21 p.m. at the Evesham Recreation Center. In his remarks, he referred to Bernard B. Kerik, former commissioner, New York City Police Department; Tina LoBiondo, wife of Representative Frank A. LoBiondo; Marie Smith, wife of Representative Christopher H. Smith; Edward W. Gillespie, chairman, Republican National Committee; Thomas H. Kean, Chairman, National Commission on Terrorist Attacks Upon the United States (9/11 Commission); former President Saddam Hussein of Iraq; Prime Minister Ayad Allawi of the Iraqi Interim Government; senior Al Qaida associate Abu Musab Al Zarqawi; and former President Daniel Ortega of Nicaragua. The Office of the Press Secretary also released a Spanish language transcript of these remarks.

Remarks in Marlton
October 18, 2004

Listen, thank you all for coming. So you're wondering what a Republican Presidential candidate is doing in New Jersey 15 days until the election? I'll tell you, what I'm doing here is I'm sending a strong message that with your help, we can carry New Jersey on November the 2d.

I'm so honored you all came out to say hello. Thank you so very much for your friendship, for your support. Make sure your friends go to the polls. Make sure your neighbors go to the polls. And tell them if they want a safer America, a

stronger America, and a better America, to put me and Dick Cheney back into office.

God bless you all. I'm headed down to Florida. I'm working. We're going to win. God bless. Thanks for coming.

NOTE: The President spoke at 2:18 p.m. at the Evesham Recreation Center. A tape was not available for verification of the content of these remarks.

° White House correction.

Statement on Signing the North Korean Human Rights Act of 2004
October 18, 2004

Today, I have signed into law H.R. 4011, the "North Korean Human Rights Act of 2004." The Act is intended to help promote human rights and freedom in the Democratic People's Republic of Korea.

Section 107 of the Act purports to direct negotiations with foreign governments and international organizations. The executive branch shall implement section 107 in a manner consistent with the Constitution's grant to the President of the authority to conduct the foreign affairs of the United States.

GEORGE W. BUSH

The White House,
October 18, 2004.

NOTE: H.R. 4011, approved October 18, was assigned Public Law No. 108–333.

Statement on Signing the Department of Homeland Security Appropriations Act, 2005
October 18, 2004

Today, I have signed into law H.R. 4567, the "Department of Homeland Security Appropriations Act, 2005." The Act provides funds to protect the United States against terrorism and to carry out other departmental functions.

The executive branch shall construe as calling solely for notification the provisions of the Act that purport to require congressional committee approval for the execution of a law. Any other construction would be inconsistent with the principles enunciated by the Supreme Court of the United States in *INS v. Chadha*. Such provisions include the purported approval requirements in the appropriations for expenses for the development of the United States Visitor and Immigrant Status Indicator Technology project; customs and border protection automated systems; immigration and customs enforcement automated systems; operations, maintenance, and procurement of marine vessels, aircraft, and other related equipment of the air and marine program; United States Secret Service protective travel; and in sections 504 relating to unobligated balances, 508 relating to training facilities, and 510 relating to prospectuses.

Under the heading "Customs and Border Protection," the Act purports to require the Bureau of Customs and Border Protection to relocate its tactical checkpoints in the Tucson, Arizona, sector at least an average of once every 14 days. Decisions on deployment and redeployment of law enforcement officers in the execution of the laws are a part of the executive power vested in the President by Article II of the Constitution. Accordingly, the executive branch shall construe the relocation provision as advisory rather than mandatory.

The executive branch shall construe the provision relating to the Coast Guard under the heading "Acquisition, Construction, and Improvements" that purports to require inclusion of an amount for a particular purpose in the President's proposed budget for fiscal year 2006, in a manner consistent with the President's exclusive authority under the Constitution to recommend for the consideration of the Congress such measures, including proposals for appropriations, as the President judges necessary and expedient.

To the extent that provisions of the Act, including section 514, call for submission of legislative recommendations to the Congress, the executive branch shall construe such provisions in a manner consistent with the President's constitutional authority to supervise the unitary executive branch and to recommend for the consideration of the Congress such measures as the President shall judge necessary and expedient. Accordingly, the affected departments and agencies shall ensure that any reports or recommendations submitted to the Congress are subjected to appropriate executive branch review.

Section 518 of the Act purports to direct the conduct of security and suitability investigations. To the extent that section 518 relates to access to classified national security information, the executive branch shall construe this provision in a manner consistent with the President's exclusive constitutional authority, as head of the unitary executive branch and as Commander in Chief, to classify and control access to national security information and to determine whether an individual is suitable to occupy a position in the executive branch with access to such information.

To the extent that section 522 of the Act purports to allow an agent of the legislative branch to prevent implementation of the law unless the legislative agent reports to the Congress that the executive branch has met certain conditions, the executive branch shall construe such section as advisory, in accordance with the constitutional principles enumerated in the *Chadha* decision.

As is consistent with the text of the Act, the executive branch shall construe section 528 as relating to the integrity and supervision of the United States Secret Service only within the Department of Homeland Security. The executive branch therefore shall construe section 528 neither to affect the functions and supervision of personnel of the Secret Service assigned or detailed to duty outside the Department of Homeland Security nor to limit participation by the Secret Service in cooperative command and other arrangements with other governmental entities for the conduct of particular operations.

GEORGE W. BUSH

The White House,
October 18, 2004.

NOTE: H.R. 4567, approved October 18, was assigned Public Law No. 108–334.

Statement on Signing the District of Columbia Appropriations Act, 2005
October 18, 2004

Today, I have signed into law H.R. 4850, the "District of Columbia Appropriations Act, 2005." The bill appropriates funds for the Government of the District of Columbia and other activities chargeable against the revenues of the District.

The provision of the Act relating to the Federal payment to the office of the District's Chief Financial Officer makes funds available for the projects and in the amounts specified in the statement of managers accompanying the conference report on the Act. While the specifications of projects and amounts in the statement of managers cannot satisfy the constitutional requirements of bicameral approval and presentment to the President needed to give them the force of law, the executive branch shall treat the specifications in a manner reflecting the comity between the executive and legislative branches on such matters.

Section 309 of the Act purports to require the use of particular revenue estimates in the budget request for fiscal year 2006. The executive branch shall construe section 309 in a manner consistent with the President's constitutional authority to recommend for congressional consideration such measures, including requests for appropriations, as he judges necessary and expedient.

Section 331(5) of the Act purports to require congressional committee approval prior to obligation or expenditure of appro-priated funds. The executive branch shall construe this provision to require only prior notification to the congressional committees, as any other construction would be contrary to the constitutional principles set forth by the Supreme Court of the United States in 1983 in *INS v. Chadha.*

GEORGE W. BUSH

The White House,
October 18, 2004.

NOTE: H.R. 4850, approved October 18, was assigned Public Law No. 108–335.

Remarks in St. Petersburg, Florida
October 19, 2004

The President. Thank you all for coming. Nothing like spending a Tuesday morning at the ballpark. I can't thank you enough for coming. It lifts our spirits to see so many people here.

It's close to voting time, and I'm here to ask for your vote. We're going to travel your State today, and we'll be back quite often, asking the people of Florida for their vote. I'm also here to ask for your help. See, you can vote now in Florida. So get your friends and neighbors to do their duty. We have a duty in this country to vote. And remind them when you get them headed to the polls, if they want a safer America, a stronger America, and a better America, to put me and Dick Cheney back in office.

As I travel your State giving people a reason why they ought to put me back in office, perhaps the most important one of all is so that Laura is the First Lady for 4 more years. I'm really proud of her. I love her a lot. She is a warm, compassionate, great First Lady for this country.

And I'm proud of my runningmate, Dick Cheney. He does not have the waviest hair in this race. [*Laughter*] I didn't pick him because of his hairdo. [*Laughter*] I picked him because of his experience, his judgment, his ability to get the job done for the American people.

And I'm proud of my brother Jeb. In this time of need, he has risen to the occasion. I have seen him comfort those who have been hurt because of these hurricanes. I've seen him put his arms around those who worry about their future. We're doing everything we can to help this State get back on its feet. The Governor of your State is providing strong and necessary leadership to help.

And I know there are some here who are worried about the flu season. I want to assure them that our Government is doing everything possible to help older Americans and children get their shots, despite the major manufacturing defect that caused this problem. We have millions of vaccine doses on hand for the most vulnerable Americans, and millions more will be shipped in the coming weeks. We're stockpiling more than 4 million doses of flu vaccine for children. We're working closely with State and local officials to make sure we distribute vaccines to the most vulnerable Americans throughout our country.

I am grateful to the healthy Americans who are deciding a flu shot—who are declining a flu shot this year so that the most vulnerable of our citizens will get the vaccine. Here in Florida and across the Nation, we will continue to do everything possible to help our citizens.

I want to thank Lance Corporal Taylor Pancake for introducing Jeb and being on the stage. I want to thank him for his service to our country.

By the way, our brother Marvin is with us today. I appreciate you coming, big Marv. There he is, right there. See, we love our family. We've got a great family. There's nothing like being on the campaign trail with a brother you love. I've been looking forward to this day. Not only do I have one brother I love, I've got two brothers I love traveling the great State of Florida.

I'm proud to be able to work with Congressman Bill Young, the great Congressman from Florida. Your attorney general, Charlie Crist, is with us today. Thanks for coming, General. Our Government is working with Charlie to make sure anybody who tries to gouge the seniors of this State when it comes to the flu vaccines is going to be held to account.

I'm honored that the mayor took time to come by and say hello. Mr. Mayor, Rick Baker, is with us today. Thank you for coming, Mayor, proud you're here. I want to thank all the State and local officials. I'm proud to be on the stage with the next United States Senator from Florida, Mel Martinez. I know him well. He's the right man for the right State at the right time for the United States Senate. Kitty is here too, Kitty Martinez. She's going to make a great First Senator's wife. Thanks for coming, Kitty, great to see you.

I want to thank my friend Lee Greenwood, who's here. I want to thank all the grassroots activists for what you're going to do today and for the next 2 weeks to turn out the vote. There is no doubt in my mind, with your help, we'll carry Florida again and win a great victory in November.

Audience members. Four more years! Four more years! Four more years!

The President. In the last few years, the American people have gotten to know me. They know my blunt way of speaking. I get that from Mother. They know I sometimes mangle the English language. [*Laughter*] I get that from Dad. [*Laughter*] They also know I tell you exactly what I'm going to do, and I keep my word.

You know, our debates highlighted the stark differences between Senator Kerry's views and mine. We have different records. We have different plans for the future. My record is one of reforming education, of lowering taxes, of providing prescription drug coverage for our seniors, for improving homeland protections, and for waging an aggressive war against the ideologues of hate.

My opponent's record is 20 years of out-of-the-mainstream votes.

Audience members. Boo-o-o!

The President. Instead of articulating a vision or positive agenda for the future, the Senator is relying on a litany of complaints and old-style scare tactics.

Audience members. Boo-o-o!

The President. As proven by his record and a series of contradictions in this campaign, my opponent will say anything he thinks that will benefit him politically at the time. I will do what I've said I will do. We will keep the promise of Social Security for all our seniors. We will not have a draft. We'll keep the All-Volunteer Army. With your help on November 2d, the people of America will reject the politics of fear and vote for an agenda of hope and opportunity and security for all Americans.

When I came into office, the stock market had been in serious decline for 6 months, and the American economy was sliding into a recession. To help families and to get this economy growing again, I pledged to reduce taxes, and I kept my word. And we have gotten results for the American people. The recession was one of the shallowest in American history.

Over the last 3 years, our economy has grown at the fastest rate of any major industrialized nation. The homeownership rate in America is at an alltime high. Farm and ranch income is up. In the past 13 months we've added more than 1.9 million new jobs. The unemployment rate in America is 5.4 percent, lower than the average rate of the 1970s, 1980s, and 1990s. The unemployment rate in Florida is 4.5 percent. This economy is moving forward, and we're not going to go back to the days of tax and spend.

To make sure jobs are here in America, to make sure we continue to be a place where people can realize their dreams, America must be the best place in the world to do business. We need to reduce the burden of regulations on our job creators. We need to do something about the junk lawsuits that are threatening the small-business job creators.

To create jobs here in America, Congress needs to pass my energy plan. It's a plan that encourages the use of renewables like ethanol and biodiesel. It's a plan that encourages conservation. It encourages new technologies like clean coal technologies. It encourages increased domestic production in environmentally friendly ways. We will not drill off the coast of Florida. To keep jobs here, we must become less dependent on foreign sources of energy.

To create jobs here, we need to reject economic isolationism. See, we open up our markets for products from overseas, and that's good for you. If you have more products to choose from, you're likely to get that which you want at a better price and higher quality. That's how the market works. Rather than shutting down our market, we're working to convince others to open up theirs. I'm saying to China, "You treat us the way we treat you." We can

compete with anybody, anytime, anywhere, so long as the rules are fair.

To make sure this economy grows, we've got to be wise about how we spend your money and keep your taxes low. Now, my opponent has his own history on the economy.

Audience members. Boo-o-o!

The President. In 20 years as a Senator from Massachusetts, he has built a record of a Senator from Massachusetts. [*Laughter*] He's voted to raise taxes 98 times.

Audience members. Boo-o-o!

The President. Think about that. He's been there 20 years. That's a vote for a tax increase about five times every year.

Audience members. Boo-o-o!

The President. I would call it a pattern. He can run from his record, but he cannot hide.

Now, the Senator is promising not to raise taxes for anyone who earns less than $200,000 a year. He said that with a straight face. The problem is, to keep that promise, he would have to break almost all of his other ones. See, he has promised more than $2.2 trillion of new Federal spending. That's trillion, with a "T." And to pay for it he said, aw, he's just going to tax the rich. You know, we've heard that before. You can't raise enough money by taxing the rich to pay for $2.2 trillion of new spending, so there's a gap—a gap between the promise and a gap between what he can deliver. And guess who usually has to fill that gap?

Audience members. We do!

The President. Yes. I'll tell you what else is wrong with taxing the rich. The rich hire lawyers and accountants for reason: to slip the bill and pass it on to you. We're not going to let him tax you; we're going to carry Florida and win a great victory in November.

When I came into office, our public schools had been waiting decades for hopeful reform. Fortunately, you had a Governor that did not allow the wait. See, he knows what I know, that too many of our children were being shuffled through, grade after grade, year after year, without learning the basics. I pledged to restore accountability to our schools and end the soft bigotry of low expectations, and I kept my word. Our children are making sustained gains in reading and math. We're closing an achievement gap for minority students. We're making progress in our schools, and we're not going to go back to the old days of mediocrity and low standards.

We have a changing world, and most new jobs are filled by people with at least 2 years of a college education. Yet, only one in four of our students gets there. That's why we will fund early intervention programs at our high schools to help at-risk students. That's why we'll place a new focus on math and science. Over time, we'll require a rigorous exam before graduation. By raising performance in our high schools, by increasing and expanding Pell grants for low- and middle-income families, we will help more Americans start their career with a college diploma.

When I came into office, we had a problem with Medicare. Medicine was changing, but Medicare was not. Let me give you an example. Medicare would pay tens of thousands of dollars for heart surgery but would not pay a dime for the prescription drugs that could prevent the heart surgery from being needed in the first place. That wasn't fair to our seniors. It certainly was not fair to the taxpayers. I pledged to bring Republicans and Democrats together to strengthen and modernize Medicare for our seniors, and I kept my word. Seniors and—getting discounts on medicine. And beginning in 2006, all seniors will be able to get prescription drug coverage under Medicare.

We're moving forward on health care, and there's more to do. We need to make sure health care is available and affordable for our people. We need a safety net for those with the greatest needs. I believe in community health centers, places where the poor and the indigent can get health care. In a new term, we'll make sure every poor county in America has a community health center. We'll do more to make sure poor children are fully subscribed in our programs for low-income families.

We'll do more to make sure health care is affordable. Listen, most of the uninsured are employees of small businesses. Small businesses are having trouble affording health care. To help workers get the health care they need, we should allow small businesses to join together so they can buy insurance at the same discount that big businesses get to do. We will expand health savings accounts so workers and small businesses are able to pay lower premiums and people can save tax-free in an account they call their own.

To make sure health care is available and affordable, we will do something about the junk lawsuits that are running up the cost of health care and running good docs out of practice. By forcing doctors to practice defensive medicine, medical lawsuits cost the Government about $28 billion a year.

Audience members. Boo-o-o!

The President. When we say "cost the Government," that means they're costing you, the taxpayer.

Audience members. Boo-o-o!

The President. These lawsuits drive up insurance premiums, which drive good doctors out of practice. I've met ob-gyns that are—say, "I can't practice. I can't practice medicine anymore." I met the patients of ob-gyns, anxious women who drive miles to meet a doc. The system is not working. There's a big difference in this campaign. My opponent has voted against medical liability reform. I am for medical liability reform—now. And I will work with Senator Mel Martinez to get it done.

My opponent has a health care proposal of his own, a plan for bigger and more intrusive Government.

Audience members. Boo-o-o!

The President. Now, the other day in the debate he said, when it comes to his health care plan, and I quote, "The Government has nothing to do with it." I could barely contain myself. [*Laughter*] The facts are that 8 out of 10 people who get health care under Senator Kerry's plan would be placed on a Government program.

Audience members. Boo-o-o!

The President. He said the plan would help small businesses. Yet a small-business group studied the plan and concluded it was an overpriced albatross that would saddle small businesses with 225 new mandates. I want to help small businesses; I don't want to saddle them with Government mandates.

Listen, the choice is clear when it comes to health care. My opponent wants to move in the direction of Government-run health care. I believe the health decisions ought to be made by patients and doctors, not by officials in Washington, DC. He can run, but he cannot hide.

I've set out policies that move America toward an optimistic vision. I believe our country can and must become an ownership society. There's an old saying, no one ever washes a rental car. [*Laughter*] You see, when you own something, you care about it. When you own something, you have a vital stake in the future of our country.

That's why we're encouraging entrepreneurship. Every time a small business is started, someone is achieving the American Dream. We're encouraging health savings accounts so people have the security of managing and owning their own health care account. We will continue to encourage homeownership. I love the idea that more and more Americans from all walks of life are opening up the door where they live and saying, "Welcome to my home. Welcome to my piece of property."

In a new term, we'll take the next, great step to build an ownership society by strengthening Social Security. In the 2000 campaign, you might remember the ads that were saying, "If George W. gets in, the seniors will not get their checks." The seniors got their checks, and our seniors will continue to get their checks. Baby boomers are in pretty good shape when it comes to Social Security. We're okay.

But we need to worry about our children and our grandchildren. People are understandably worried about whether Social Security will be around when our children and grandchildren need it. We must think differently. To strengthen Social Security, we must allow younger workers to save some of their payroll taxes in a personal savings account, a personal savings account they call their own.

I believe it is the President's problem to solve problems—the President's job to solve problems, not to pass them on to future generations. My opponent has a different point of view. He wants to maintain the status quo when it comes to Social Security.

Audience members. Boo-o-o!

The President. He's against the reforms we're talking about when it comes to Social Security, and he's against just about every other reform that gives more authority and control to the individual. On issue after issue, from Medicare without choices to schools with less accountability to higher taxes, he takes the side of more government control.

There's a label for that. There's a word for that. It's called liberalism. That's what it's called. He doesn't like that label. He dismisses it as just a word. He must have seen it differently when he told a newspaper, "I am a liberal and proud of it." See, he's the kind of—got a voting record that makes Ted Kennedy look like the senior—the conservative Senator from Massachusetts. He can run, but he cannot hide.

I have a different record and a different philosophy. I do not believe in big government, and I do not believe that government should be indifferent. I'm a compassionate conservative. I believe in policies that empower people to improve their lives, not try to run their lives. I believe we ought to help men and women find the skills and tools necessary to prosper in a time of change. So we're helping all Americans to have a future of dignity and independence, and that is how I will continue to lead our country for 4 more years.

In a time of change, some things do not change, the values we try to live by, courage and compassion, reverence and integrity. In times of change, we must support institutions that give our lives direction and purpose, our families, our schools, our religious congregations. We stand for a culture of life in which every person matters and every being counts. We stand for marriage and family, which are the foundations of our society. We stand for the appointment of Federal judges who know the difference between personal opinion and the strict interpretation of the law.

My opponent's words on these issues are a little muddy, but his record is plenty clear. He says he supports the institution of marriage but voted against the Defense of Marriage Act.

Audience members. Boo-o-o!

The President. He voted against the ban on the brutal practice of partial-birth abortion.

Audience members. Boo-o-o!

The President. He described the Reagan years as a time of moral darkness.

Audience members. Boo-o-o!

The President. There is a mainstream in American politics, and my opponent sits on the far left bank. He can run, but he cannot hide.

This election will also determine how America responds to the continuing threat of terrorism. The most solemn duty of the American President is to protect the American people. If America shows uncertainty or weakness in this decade, the world will drift toward tragedy. This will not happen on my watch.

Since that terrible morning of September the 11th, 2001, we fought the terrorists across the Earth, not for pride, not for power, but because the lives of our citizens are at stake. Our strategy is clear. We're defending the homeland. We're reforming and strengthening our intelligence capabilities. We're transforming our military. I repeat, the All-Volunteer Army will remain an all-volunteer army. We are staying on the offensive. We will strike the terrorists abroad so we do not have to face them here at home. We will spread freedom and liberty. And we will prevail.

Our strategy is succeeding. Think about the world as it was some 3½ years ago. Afghanistan was the home base of Al Qaida. Pakistan was a transit point for terrorist groups. Saudi Arabia was fertile ground for terrorist fundraising. Libya was secretly pursuing nuclear weapons. Iraq was a dangerous place and a gathering threat. And Al Qaida was largely unchallenged as it planned attacks.

Because we acted, because the United States of America led, Afghanistan is a free nation and an ally in the war against terror; Pakistan is capturing terrorist leaders; Saudi Arabia is making raids and arrests; Libya is dismantling its weapons programs; the army of a free Iraq is fighting for freedom; and more than three-quarters of Al Qaida's key members and associates have been brought to justice.

We are standing with the peoples of a free Afghanistan and Iraq. It's amazing to say the words "free Afghanistan" and a "free Iraq." I want you to remind your children and grandchildren what has taken place in Afghanistan in the 3½ short years. It wasn't all that long ago that young girls couldn't go to school in Afghanistan, or their mothers were taken into the public square and whipped because they wouldn't toe the line of the ideologues of hate. And yet, because we acted in our self-interest, because we acted to secure our country, the people of Afghanistan are liberated, and by the millions, showed up to vote in a Presidential election. The first voter in the Presidential election in Afghanistan was a 19-year-old woman. Freedom is on the march. Freedom is taking hold in a part of the world that no one ever dreamed would be free, and that makes America more secure.

There will be elections in Iraq this January. Think how far that country has come from the days of torture chambers and mass graves and the brutal dictates of a brutal tyrant. You see, it's important that we continue to spread freedom, because free societies will help us keep the peace. Free societies will no longer feed resentments and breed violence for export. Free governments in the Middle East will fight the terrorists instead of harboring them, and that will help us keep the peace and make America more secure.

And so our mission is clear. We will help these countries train armies and police so the people of Afghanistan and Iraq can do the hard work of defending their freedom. We will help them get on the path to stability and democracy as quickly as possible, and then our troops will come home with the honor they have earned.

We have a great United States military. It is great because of the dedication and the character of those who wear the uniform. I want to thank the veterans who are here today for having set such a great example to those who wear the uniform. I want to thank the military families who are here today for their sacrifices. You can be certain of this: Your loved ones are answering one of the great calls of American history. They're defending our country against ruthless enemies. They're spreading freedom and hope. They are winning the war on terror.

And our Nation is keeping our commitments to those who serve and to their families. We have increased basic pay in the military by 21 percent since I've been the Commander in Chief. We've increased health benefits and Federal support for schools on bases across the country. We've reduced out-of-pocket expense for off-base housing to zero for our military families. We are supporting our Guard and our Reserve troops and families. We're spending 14 billion for construction and maintenance

on Guard and Reserve facilities. We're extending military health benefits to those in the Guard and Reserves. We're increasing—we will increase monthly education benefits for those in the Guard and Reserves.

Our single most important responsibility is to make sure our military families are well-treated and our military has all the tools necessary to do their missions. And that's why in September of 2003, I went to the United States Congress and asked for $87 billion of supplemental funding to support our troops in harm's way. This was essential funding. Most Members of the United States Congress understood how important the funding was. As a matter of fact, only 12 Members of the United States Senate voted against the funding for our troops——

Audience members. Boo-o-o!

The President. ——two of whom are my opponent and his runningmate.

Audience members. Boo-o-o!

The President. When you're out rounding up the vote, remind people of this startling statistic: Only 4 Members of the Senate— 4 out of 100—voted to authorize the use of force and then voted against providing funding for our troops.

Audience members. Boo-o-o!

The President. And two of those four were my opponent and his runningmate.

Audience members. Boo-o-o!

The President. You might remember my opponents famous quote. When they asked him about his vote, he said, "I actually did vote for the $87 billion, right before I voted against it."

Audience members. Boo-o-o!

The President. He's given a lot of explanations for that vote since. One of the most interesting ones of all, he said, "Well, the whole thing was a complicated matter." There's nothing complicated about supporting our troops in harm's way.

Last Sunday was the one-year anniversary of Senator Kerry's vote against funding for our troops. My opponent's many and conflicting positions on this issue are a case study into why his contradictions call into question his credibility and ability to lead our Nation.

In September 2003, as the $87 billion funding package was being debated, Senator Kerry said this on national TV: "It would be irresponsible to abandon our troops by voting against it." That is, against the $87 billion. And then, of course, just one month later, he did exactly the opposite. You know, it's important for our fellow citizens to wonder what changed his mind in one short month. Well, his opponent in the Democrat primary, Howard Dean, was gaining ground as an antiwar candidate, just about the time he changed his mind. See, apparently, my opponent decided supporting the troops, even while in harm's way, was not as important as shoring up his political position.

Audience members. Boo-o-o!

The President. At a time of great threat to our country, at a time of great challenge in the world, the Commander in Chief must stand on principle, not on the shifting sands of political convenience.

Senator Kerry's vote against supporting our troops in combat is part of a pattern. He has consistently opposed the weapons our troops are using to win the war on terror. He opposed the B–1 bomber. He opposed the B–2 stealth bomber. He opposed the modernized F–14D. He opposed the Apache helicopter. He opposed the antimissile launchers that we've been using, the Patriot missile system. He has a 20-year history of weakness. He can run from his record, but he cannot hide.

Let me just give you one more piece of evidence about why my opponent is not prepared and equipped to be the Commander in Chief. He believes that America should pass a "global test" before we defend ourselves.

Audience members. Boo-o-o!

The President. That's what he said. See, the problem with a "global test" is the Senator can never pass it. In 1990, the United Nations Security Council passed a resolution supporting action to remove Saddam Hussein from Kuwait. The international community was united. Countries throughout the world joined our coalition. Yet, even after United Nations approval, Senator Kerry voted against the authorization for the use of force.

Audience members. Boo-o-o!

The President. You might remember during the debates in the campaign he said it was a mistake to remove Saddam Hussein. He would have done it differently. He would have passed another United Nations Security Council resolution——

Audience members. Boo-o-o!

The President. ——as if the first 16 or 17, you know, had an effect. [*Laughter*]

See, we'll continue to build strong alliances. We'll work with friends. But I will never turn over America's national security decisions to leaders of other countries.

Audience members. Four more years! Four more years! Four more years!

The President. In this time of uncertainty and challenge, the Commander in Chief must be steadied and principled and must use every asset at our disposal to protect the American people.

I believe in the transformational power of liberty. I'll tell you what I mean by that. One of our friends, Laura and my friends in the international community is Prime Minister Koizumi of Japan. That probably doesn't seem like much of a big deal to you, except for the fact that 60 years ago, Japan was a sworn enemy of the United States of America. We were at war with the Japanese. My dad—our dad fought against the Japanese. Your dads and granddads did as well. It was a brutal war.

And after the war was over, Harry S. Truman, President of the United States, believed that liberty could transform an enemy into an ally. There were a lot of skeptics during that time, and you can imagine why. Japan was the enemy. Many families had been turned upside down because of death in World War II. But there was this belief in the country that if we helped Japan become a democracy, the world would be better off for it. Today, because people held that belief, I sit at the table with the Prime Minister of a former enemy, talking about how to keep the peace we all want.

Someday, someday, an American President will be sitting down with the duly elected leader from Iraq, talking about the peace, and our children and our grandchildren will be better off for it.

I believe that millions in the Middle East plead in silence for their freedom. I believe women in the Middle East want to live in a free society. I believe mothers and dads want to raise their children in a free world. I believe all these things because freedom is not America's gift to the world; freedom is the Almighty God's gift to each man and woman in this world.

For all Americans, these years in our history will always stand apart. There are quiet times in the life of a nation when little is expected of its leaders. This isn't one of those times. This is a time that requires firm resolve, clear vision, and a deep faith in the values that makes this a great nation.

None of us will ever forget that week when one era ended and another began.

On September the 14th, 2001, I stood in the ruins of the Twin Towers. It's a day I will never forget. There were workers in hardhats yelling at me at the top of their lungs, "Whatever it takes." I remember the fellow who grabbed me by the arm. He looked me straight in the eye, and he said, "Do not let me down." Ever since that day, I wake up every morning thinking about how to better protect America. I will never relent in defending our country, whatever it takes.

Four years ago, when I traveled your great State, I made a pledge that if you gave me the chance to serve, I would uphold the honor and the dignity of the office to which I had been elected. With your help, I will do so for 4 more years.

Thanks for coming. God bless. Thank you all.

NOTE: The President spoke at 9:15 a.m. at Al Lang Field at the Progress Energy Park. In his remarks, he referred to Gov. Jeb Bush of Florida; Florida State Attorney General Charlie Crist; Mayor Rick Baker of St. Petersburg, FL; Kitty Martinez, wife of Florida senatorial candidate Mel R. Martinez; entertainer Lee Greenwood; and Prime Minister Junichiro Koizumi of Japan.

Remarks in New Port Richey, Florida
October 19, 2004

The President. Thank you all for coming. If you're looking for sunshine, Florida is the place to come. I'm looking for votes, and Florida is the place to come. Thank you all for coming out. I'm here to ask for not only your vote, I'm here to ask for your help. Get your friends and neighbors to go to the polls. And when you get them headed to the polls, remind them, if they want a stronger America, a safer

America, and a better America, to put me and Dick Cheney back in office.

I've got a lot of reasons why you ought to put me back in, but perhaps the most important one of all is so that Laura will have 4 more years as the First Lady. When I asked her to marry me, she said, "Fine, just so long as I never have to give a speech." [*Laughter*] I said, "Okay, you got a deal." Fortunately, she didn't hold me to that deal. She's giving a lot of speeches, and the American people see a warm, compassionate, strong First Lady.

I'm proud of my runningmate, Dick Cheney. Now, look, I admit it, he doesn't have the waviest hair in the race. [*Laughter*] I didn't pick him because of his hairdo. [*Laughter*] I picked him because of his judgment, his experience. I picked him because he can get the job done for the American people.

I'm proud of my brother Jeb. What a great Governor for Florida. I appreciate the strength and compassion he showed during the hurricanes. Florida showed that out of adversity can come good, neighbors loving neighbors, people helping people who hurt. We'll continue to do everything we can to help the people of Florida get back on their feet.

By the way, brother Marvin is with us too. [*Applause*] Yes. We love our family. And I love campaigning with my family.

I want to thank Sam for his service to the United States of America. He was in the first gulf war. He's in the second incursion into Iraq. And our country is more secure because of his service.

I want to thank Sheriff Bob White for joining us today. Sheriff, thanks. Appreciate it. I want to thank Daron Norwood, the country music singer, for being with us today.

I want to thank Al Cardenas and all the grassroots activists who are here today. Thank you for putting up the signs. Thank you for making the phone calls. Thank you for working the polls. With your help, we will carry Florida again and win a great victory in November.

In the last few years, the American people have gotten to know me. They know my blunt way of speaking. I get that from Mother. [*Laughter*] They know that I occasionally mangle the English language. [*Laughter*] I get that from my father. [*Laughter*] They also know that I tell you exactly what I'm going to do, and I keep my word.

I enjoyed our debates. They showed the big differences between my opponent and me. We have different records. We have different views of the future. My record is one of reforming education, lowering taxes, providing prescription drug coverage for our seniors, improving homeland protections, and waging an aggressive war against the ideologues of hate.

The Senator's record of 20 years is out of the mainstream. Instead of articulating a vision or a positive agenda for the future, the Senator is relying on a litany of complaints and old-style scare tactics. As proven by his record and a series of contradictions in this campaign, my opponent will say anything he thinks will benefit him politically at the time.

I will do what I've said I will do. We will keep the promise of Social Security for our seniors. We will not have a draft; we will have an all-volunteer army. On November 2d, the people of America will reject the politics of fear and vote for an agenda of hope and opportunity and security for every American.

When I came into office, the stock market had been in decline for 6 months. And then we had a recession. To help families and to get this economy growing again, I pledged to reduce taxes. I kept my word, and the results are clear. The recession was one of the shallowest in American history.

Over the last 3 years, our economy has grown at a rate faster than any major industrialized nation. Homeownership rate is at an alltime high in America. We added 1.9 million new jobs since August of 2003. The national unemployment rate is 5.4 percent, lower than the average of the 1970s, 1980s, and 1990s. The unemployment rate in Florida is 4.5 percent. This economy is moving forward, and we're not going to go back to the old days of tax and spend.

To make sure jobs are here in America, America must be the best place in the world to do business. We need to reduce the regulations on our job creators. We need to do something about these frivolous lawsuits that hurt the small businesses.

Listen, to keep jobs here, Congress needs to pass my energy plan. It encourages conservation. It encourages the use of renewables. It encourages clean coal technology. It encourages environmentally friendly ways to explore for natural gas. We will not explore off the coast of Florida. What I'm telling you is in order to keep jobs here, we must become less dependent on foreign sources of energy.

To keep jobs here, we've got to reject economic isolationism. I believe in free trade. I believe in fair trade. I know Americans compete with anytime—anybody, anytime, anywhere, so long as the rules are fair.

To keep jobs here, we've got to be wise about how we spend your money and keep your taxes low. My opponent has his own history on the economy.

Audience members. Boo-o-o!

The President. In 20 years as a Senator from Massachusetts, he's built the record of a Senator from Massachusetts. [*Laughter*] He voted to increase taxes 98 times in his 20 years. That's about five times a year. I would call that a pattern—[*laughter*]—a predictable pattern. He can run from his record, but he cannot hide.

Now he's promising not to raise taxes for anyone who earns less than $200,000 a year. He said that with a straight face. [*Laughter*] The problem with that is, to keep that promise you'd have to break all the other ones. See, he's promised over $2.2 trillion in new spending. That's with a "T." In order to pay for it, he said, well, all he's going to do is tax the rich. You can't raise enough money by taxing the rich to pay for $2.2 trillion. There is a gap between what he's promised and what he can raise. Guess who generally fills the gap? You do.

Let me tell you what else is wrong with taxing the rich. The rich hire lawyers and accountants for a reason: to slip the bill and to pass it on to you. We're not going

to let Senator Kerry tax you; we're going to carry Florida and win a great victory on November the 2d.

When I came into office, our public schools had been waiting decades for hopeful reform. Fortunately, you had a Governor here in Florida who enacted hopeful reform. Too many of our children were shuffled through school without learning the basics. I pledged to restore accountability to our schools and to end the soft bigotry of low expectations. I kept my word. We're seeing results. Children are making sustained gains in reading and math. We're closing achievement gaps all over this country, and we're not going to go back to the days of low expectations and mediocrity.

When I came into office, we had a problem in Medicare. Medicine was changing; Medicare was not. For example, Medicare would pay tens of thousands of dollars for heart surgery but not one dime for the prescription drugs that could prevent the heart surgery from being needed in the first place. It was not fair to our seniors. I pledged to bring Republicans and Democrats together to strengthen and modernize Medicare for our seniors. I kept my word.

We're moving forward on health care. There is more to do. We need to make sure health care is available and affordable. We need a safety net for those with the greatest needs. I believe in community health centers, places where the poor and the indigent can get health care. We will make sure that poor children are fully subscribed in our programs for low-income families so they can get the health care they need.

To make sure health care is affordable, we must recognize that most of the uninsured work for small businesses. Small businesses are having trouble affording health care. To help our workers get health care, we should allow small businesses to join together so they can buy insurance at the same discounts as big companies get to do. We will expand health savings accounts so workers and small businesses are able to pay lower premiums and people can save tax-free in a health care account they call their own.

To make sure health care is available and affordable, we must do something about the junk lawsuits that are running up the cost of medicine and running good doctors out of practice. There is a clear difference in this campaign. My opponent has consistently voted against medical liability reform. I stand for medical liability reform, and I know I can work with the next Senator from Florida, Mel Martinez, to get that reform done.

The Senator has a health care proposal of his own, a plan for bigger and more intrusive Government. The other day, he tried to tell Americans that when it comes to his health care plan, and I quote, "The Government has nothing to do with it." [*Laughter*] I could barely contain myself. [*Laughter*] The facts are that 8 out of 10 people who get health care under Senator Kerry's plan would be placed on a Government program. He says his plan would help small businesses. Yet, groups that studied this plan concluded it was an overpriced albatross that would saddle small businesses with 225 new mandates.

I have a different view. I want to help our small businesses, not saddle them with a bunch of Government rules. The choice is clear. My opponent wants to move in the direction of Government-run health care. I believe health decisions should be made by doctors and patients, not by officials in Washington, DC. He can run, but he cannot hide.

I've set out policies that move our country toward a more hopeful and optimistic vision. I believe our country can and must be an ownership society. There's an old saying: No one ever washes a rental car— [*laughter*]—a lot of wisdom in that statement. When you own something, you care about it. When you own something, you have a vital stake in the future of your country. That's why we're encouraging en-

trepreneurship. Every time a small business is started, someone is achieving the American Dream.

We're encouraging health savings accounts so people have the security of owning and managing their own health care. We will continue to encourage homeownership in America. I love it when somebody opens the door where they live and says, "Welcome to my home. Welcome to my piece of property."

In a new term, we'll take the next step to build an ownership society by strengthening Social Security. Let me talk about Social Security right quick. In 2000, people traveled this State saying, "If George W. gets elected, our seniors will not get their checks."

Audience members. Boo-o-o!

The President. Our seniors must remember, you got your checks. You will continue to get their checks, no matter what they try to tell you. And baby boomers, we're in pretty good shape when it comes to Social Security.

But we need to worry about our children and our grandchildren. The job of the President is to confront problems, not to pass them on to future generations and future Presidents. To make sure Social Security is around when our children grow up, we must allow younger workers to save some of their own payroll taxes in a personal savings account that earns better interest, a personal savings account they call their own and an account the Government cannot take away.

When it comes to Social Security, my opponent wants to maintain the status quo. That is not leadership. He's against these Social Security reforms. He's against just about every other reform that gives more authority and control to the people. On issue after issue, from Medicare without choices to schools without accountability to higher taxes, he takes the side of more bureaucracy and more Government.

There is a word for that attitude. It is called liberalism. He dismisses that as a label. He must have seen it differently when he told a newspaper, "I am a liberal, and I'm proud of it."

Audience members. Boo-o-o!

The President. The nonpartisan National Journal did a study and named him the most liberal Member of the United States Senate. That takes a lot of hard work. [*Laughter*]

I have a different record and a different philosophy. I do not believe in big Government, and I do not believe that Government should be indifferent. That is called compassionate conservatism. I believe in policies that empower people to improve their lives, not try to run their lives. I believe we must continue to help men and women find the schools—skills and tools to prosper in a time of change. And so we're helping all Americans find dignity and independence. And I will continue to lead our country for 4 more years with that philosophy in mind.

Audience members. Four more years! Four more years! Four more years!

The President. In this time of change, some things do not change, the values we try to live by, courage and compassion, reverence and integrity. In a time of change, we must support the institutions that gives our lives purpose and direction, our families, our schools, our religious congregations. We stand for a culture of life in which every person matters and every being counts. We stand for marriage and family, which are the foundations of our society. We stand for the appointment of Federal judges who know the difference between personal opinion and the strict interpretation of the law.

My opponent's words on these issues are a little muddy, but his record is plenty clear. He says he supports the institution of marriage but voted against the Defense of Marriage Act. He voted against a ban on the practice of partial-birth abortion.

Audience members. Boo-o-o!

The President. He's described the Reagan years as a time of moral darkness.

Audience members. Boo-o-o!

The President. There is a mainstream in American politics, and my opponent sits on the far left bank. He can run, but he cannot hide.

This election will also determine how America responds to the continuing danger of terrorism. The most solemn duty of the American President is to protect the American people. If America shows uncertainty or weakness in this decade, the world will drift toward tragedy. This will not happen on my watch.

Our strategy is clear. We are defending the homeland. We are reforming and strengthening our intelligence services. We are transforming our military. The All-Volunteer Army will remain an all-volunteer army. We are staying on the offensive. We're striking the terrorists abroad so we do not have to face them here at home. We will spread freedom and liberty. And we will prevail.

Our strategy is succeeding. Think about the world as it was 3½ years ago. Afghanistan was the home base of Al Qaida. Pakistan was a transit point for terrorist groups. Saudi Arabia was fertile ground for fundraising. Libya was secretly pursuing nuclear weapons. Iraq was a dangerous place and a gathering threat. And Al Qaida was largely unchallenged as it planned attacks.

Today, because we acted, Afghanistan is free and is an ally on the war on terror; Pakistan is capturing terrorist leaders; Saudi Arabia is making raids and arrests; Libya is dismantling its weapons programs; the army of a free Iraq is fighting for freedom; and more than three-quarters of Al Qaida's key members and associates have been brought to justice.

We're standing with the peoples of a free Afghanistan and Iraq. I want you to remind your children about the historic moment that took place when the Afghan citizens went to vote. It was all but 3 years ago that these people lived under the brutal, brutal reign of the Taliban. Young girls couldn't go to school. Mothers were taken and whipped in the public square because they didn't toe the line of these ideologues of hate. But because we acted in our self-defense, millions went to the polls. The first voter in Afghan—in the Afghanistan Presidential election was a 19-year-old woman. Freedom is on the march.

There will be elections in Iraq in January. Think about how far that country has come from the days of mass graves and torture chambers and the brutal reign of a tyrant who hated America. It's important that freedom be on the march. We're more secure when societies are free. Free societies will be hopeful societies which no longer feed resentments and breed violence for export. Free governments in the Middle East will fight the terrorists instead of harboring them. Free societies will be peaceful societies. Freedom means America will be more secure.

And so our mission is clear. We will help the people in these countries, in Afghanistan and Iraq, train their armies, train their police, so they can do the hard work of defending freedom. We will help the countries get on the path of stability and democracy as quickly as possible, and then our troops will return home with the honor they have earned.

I want to thank those who wear our uniform. I want to thank the veterans who have set such a great example for those who wear the uniform. I want to thank the military families who are with us today.

Under my leadership and working with the Congress, our Nation is keeping our commitments to those who serve and to their families. We've increased basic pay in the military by 21 percent. We've increased health benefits and Federal support for schools on our bases. We've reduced the out-of-pocket expenses for off-base housing to zero for our military families. We're supporting our Guard and our Reserves. We're spending 14 billion for construction and maintenance for Guard and Reserve facilities. We've extended military health care to our Guard and Reserve families. We're making sure that our troops have what they need in order to complete their missions.

And that's why I went to the Congress and requested $87 billion of funding in September of 2003. And the support in the Congress was strong, except for 12 Senators voted against funding for our troops——

Audience members. Boo-o-o!

The President. ——2 of whom were my opponent and his runningmate.

Audience members. Boo-o-o!

The President. When you're out rounding up the vote, remind the people of this startling statistic: There were only four Members of the Senate who voted to authorize the use of force and voted against supporting our troops in combat—only four—two of whom are my opponent and his runningmate.

Audience members. Boo-o-o!

The President. So they asked him about the vote, and he said, in perhaps the most famous quote of the 2004 campaign, "I actually did vote for the $87 billion, before I voted against it."

Audience members. Boo-o-o!

The President. Sunday was the one-year anniversary of Senator Kerry's vote against funding for our troops. My opponent's many and conflicting positions on this issue are a case study into why his contradictions call into question his credibility and his ability to lead our Nation.

In September 2003, as the $87 billion funding package was being debated, Senator Kerry, on national TV, said it would be "irresponsible to abandon our troops by voting against it." That's what he said. Just one month later, he did exactly the opposite. And so you wonder why. What happened to change the Senator's mind so abruptly in one month? Well, his opponent in the Democrat primary, Howard Dean, was gaining ground as an antiwar candidate. Senator Kerry apparently decided supporting the troops, even while they were in harm's way, was not as important as shoring up his own political position.

Audience members. Boo-o-o!

The President. At a time of great threat to our country, at a time of great challenge in the world, the Commander in Chief must stand on principle, not on the shifting sands of political convenience.

His vote against supporting our troops in combat is part of a pattern. He opposed the B–1 bomber. He opposed the B–2 stealth bomber. He opposed modernization of the F–14D, all of which helped us secure our country in Afghanistan and Iraq. He opposed the Apache helicopter. He opposed the Patriot missile system. My opponent has built a 20-year record of military weakness. He can run from his record——

Audience members. But he can't hide!

The President. In our debate, Senator Kerry proposed we should pass a "global test" before we defend ourselves.

Audience members. Boo-o-o!

The President. I'm not making that up. That's exactly what he said. I was standing right there. [*Laughter*] The problem with a "global test" is the Senator cannot ever pass it. In 1990, the United Nations Security Council passed a resolution supporting action to remove Saddam Hussein from Kuwait. The international community was united. Countries throughout the world joined our coalition. Yet even after United Nations approval, Senator Kerry voted against authorization for the use of force.

Audience members. Boo-o-o!

The President. If that didn't pass a "global test," nothing will pass a "global test." Listen, I'll continue to build strong alliances. We'll work with our friends and allies. But I will never turn over America's national security decisions to leaders of other countries.

I believe in the transformational power of liberty. After World War II, after we defeated the Japanese, Harry Truman believed in the transformational power of liberty to convert an enemy into an ally. A lot of people doubted that. A lot of people wondered whether an enemy could ever become a democracy. But there were strong beliefs. And as a result of that belief, today, I sit down at the table with the head of a former enemy, Prime Minister Koizumi of Japan, talking about the peace we all want.

Someday, a duly elected leader of Iraq will be sitting down with an American President, talking about the peace in the greater Middle East, and our children and our grandchildren will be better off for it.

I believe that millions in the Middle East plead in silence for their freedom. I believe women in the Middle East want to live in a free society. I believe mothers and dads in the Middle East want their children to grow up in a free and peaceful world. I believe all these things because freedom is not America's gift to the world; freedom is the Almighty God's gift to each man and woman in this world.

For all Americans, these years in our history will always stand apart. There are quiet times in the life of a nation when little is expected of its leaders. This isn't one of those times. This is a time that requires firm resolve and clear vision and a deep faith in the values that makes this a great nation.

None of us will ever forget that week when one era ended and another began. On September the 14th, 2001, I stood in the ruins of the Twin Towers. It's a day I will never forget. I will never forget the workers in hardhats who were yelling at me at the top of their lungs, "Whatever it takes." I'll never forget the man that grabbed me by my arm and looked me in the eye, and he said, "Do not let me down." Ever since that day, I wake up every morning thinking about how to better protect our country. I will never relent in defending America, whatever it takes.

Four years ago, when I traveled your great State, I made a pledge that if you gave me a chance to serve, I would uphold the honor and the dignity of the office to which I had been elected. With your help, I will do so for 4 more years.

God bless. Thank you for coming. Thank you all. Thanks for coming.

NOTE: The President spoke at 11:34 a.m. at Sims Park. In his remarks, he referred to Gov. Jeb Bush of Florida; Bob White, sheriff, Pasco County, FL; Al Cardenas, former chair, Republican Party of Florida; Mel R. Martinez, senatorial candidate in Florida; and Prime Minister Junichiro Koizumi of Japan.

Remarks in The Villages, Florida
October 19, 2004

The President. Thank you all for coming today. I am proud to be the first sitting President ever to have visited The Villages. The other ones missed out on a lot. Thanks for having me. Thanks for coming. This is a huge crowd, for which I am grateful. I told Jeb it looks like a beautiful day in The Villages. He said, "It's always a beautiful day in The Villages."

I'm traveling your State to ask for the vote. I think you got to get out amongst the people and say, "I want your vote." I'm going to give you some reasons to put me back into office. I also want your help. You need to go to your friends and neighbors. Tell them we have a duty in our free society to vote. When you get them headed to the polls, remind them, if they want a safer America, a stronger America, a better America, to put me and Dick Cheney back in office.

My one regret is that Laura is not with me today.

Audience members. Aw-w-w!

The President. I know, that's generally the reaction. [*Laughter*] I'm going the give you some reasons, as I said, to put me in, but perhaps the most important one of all is so that Laura is the First Lady for 4 more years. When I met her again— see, we went to the seventh grade together in San Jacinto Junior High in Midland, Texas. When I met her again, she was a public school librarian. I said, "Will you marry me?" She said, "Fine, just so long as I never have to give a speech." [*Laugh-

ter*] I said, "Okay, you got a deal." Fortunately, she did not hold me to that promise. She's giving a lot of speeches, and when she does, the American people see a strong, warm, compassionate, great First Lady.

I am proud of my runningmate, Dick Cheney. I readily concede, he does not have the waviest hair in the race. [*Laughter*] I did not pick him for his hairdo. [*Laughter*] I picked him because of his experience and sound judgment.

I am very proud of my brother, the Governor of Florida, Jeb Bush. He is a strong, consistent leader. You do not have to worry about him shifting his political thoughts because of a poll or a focus group. And when times were tough during the four hurricanes, Jeb led this State with resolve and compassion. Brother Marvin is with us today as well, and I want to thank Marv for coming. I love to be with my family. I get great strength from my faith, my family, and my friends.

I want to thank Carey Baker for his service, not only in the Armed Forces but in the statehouse. As I came up on the stage, Mrs. Baker informed me they'll be having a child tomorrow. [*Laughter*] Let's just make sure it's tomorrow. [*Laughter*]

I want to thank Congressman Cliff Stearns for his leadership in the House of Representatives. I appreciate the service of the State chief financial officer, Tom Gallagher. I want to thank all the other State and local officials who are here.

I want to thank Ralph Reed, the Bush-Cheney '04 southeast regional chair, for his leadership and friendship. I want to thank Carole Jean Jordan, who's the Republican Party Florida chairman. I want to thank all the people who are involved in grassroots politics. I want to thank those of you who are putting up the signs. I want to thank those of you who are making the phone calls. With your help, there is no doubt in my mind, we will carry Florida again and win a great victory on November the 2d.

Finally, I want to thank my friend Mark Wills, the country singer who has been entertaining you today.

In the last few years, the American people have come to know me. They know my blunt way of speaking. I get that from my mother. [*Laughter*] They know that sometimes I mangle the English language. I get that from my father. [*Laughter*] Americans also know that I tell you exactly what I'm going to do, and I keep my word.

I enjoyed telling the people what I was going to do, during our three debates. Those were important debates because they showed the clear differences between my opponent and me. We have different records. We have very different plans for the future. My record is one of reforming education, of lowering taxes, of providing prescription drug coverage for our seniors, of improving homeland protections, and of waging an aggressive war against the ideologues of hate. I enjoyed the chance to lay out my vision for the future.

Instead of articulating a vision or a positive agenda for the future, the Senator, my opponent, is relying on a litany of complaints and an old-style scare tactic.

Audience members. Boo-o-o!

The President. As proven by his record and a series of contradictions in this campaign, my opponent will say anything he thinks will benefit him politically at the time. I will do what I have said I will do. We will keep the promise of Social Security for our seniors. And there will be no draft, as long as I'm the President. On November the 2d, the people of America will reject the politics of fear and vote for an agenda of hope and opportunity and security.

When I came into office, the stock market had been in serious decline for 6 months. And then we headed into a recession. To help families and to get this economy growing again, I pledged to reduce taxes. I kept my word. The results are clear. The recession was one of the shallowest in American history.

Over the last 3 years, our economy has grown at rates as fast as any in nearly 20 years. Today, the homeownership rate in America is at an alltime high. In the past 13 months, we've added more than 1.9 million new jobs. The unemployment rate in America is 5.4 percent, lower than the average rate of the 1970s, the 1980s, and the 1990s. The unemployment rate in Florida is 4.5 percent. This economy of ours is moving forward, and we're not going to go back to the days of tax and spend.

To make sure quality jobs are created here in America, America must be the best place in the world to do business. That means less regulations on our job creators. That means we will do something about the frivolous lawsuits that plague our small-business owners.

To keep jobs here, Congress needs to pass my energy plan. It's a plan that encourages conservation, a plan that encourages renewables, encourages new technologies. It's a plan that recognizes we can explore for natural gas in environmentally friendly ways. We will not drill off the coast of Florida. It's a plan that uses clean coal technology. To keep jobs here in America, America must be less dependent on foreign sources of energy.

To create jobs, we need to reject economic isolationism. We've opened up our markets from products for overseas, and that is good for the American consumer. See, the market works this way. If you have more products to choose from, you're likely to get that which you want at a better price and higher quality. So instead of shutting down our market, what we'll continue to do is open up other people's markets. I say to China, "You treat us the way we treat you." We can compete with anybody, anytime, anywhere, so long as the playing field is level.

To make sure this economy continues to grow, we've got to be wise about how we spend your money and keep your taxes low. My opponent has his own history on the economy. In 20 years as a Senator from Massachusetts, he has built the record of a Senator from Massachusetts. [*Laughter*] He voted for higher taxes 98 times in his 20 years. That's about five times a year. I would call that a predictable pattern. [*Laughter*]

Now the Senator is promising not to raise taxes for anyone who earns less than $200,000 a year. He said that with a straight face. [*Laughter*] The problem is, to keep that promise, he would have to break almost all of his other ones. He's made a lot of promises. He's promised over $2.2 trillion a program—of new spending. He said he's going to raise the money by taxing the rich. You can't raise enough money by taxing the rich to raise 2.2 trillion. There is a gap, a gap between what he's promised and what he can raise. And guess who usually gets to fill the gap?

Audience members. We do!

The President. Yes. You've also heard that talk before about taxing the rich. The rich hire lawyers and accountants for a reason: to slip the bill and pass it on to you. We're not going to let him tax you; we're going to carry Florida and win on November the 2d.

When I came in this office, our public schools had been waiting decades for hopeful reform. Fortunately, you had a Governor who had been providing hopeful reform. But too many of our children were shuffled through school, year after year, grade after grade, without learning the basics. I pledged to restore accountability to our schools and end the soft bigotry of low expectations, and I kept my word. We're seeing the results. Our children are making sustained gains in reading and math. We're closing achievement gaps all across America. And we're not going to go back to the days of low standards and mediocrity in the public schools in America.

When we came into office, we had a problem with Medicare. Medicine was changing; Medicare was not. And let me give you an example. Many here understand what I'm talking about. Medicare would pay hundreds of thousands of dollars for heart surgery but not one dime for the prescription drugs that could prevent the heart surgery from being needed in the first place. That did not make any sense for people on Medicare. It didn't make any sense for the taxpayers of the country. I pledged to bring Republicans and Democrats together to strengthen and modernize Medicare for our seniors. I kept my word. Seniors are getting discounts on medicine. And beginning in 2006, all seniors will be able to get prescription drug coverage under Medicare.

We have more work to do when it comes to moving forward with health care. I have practical plans to make sure health care is available and affordable. We need a safety net for those with the greatest need. I believe in community health centers, places where the poor and the indigent can get good preventative and primary care. In a new term, we'll make sure every poor county in America has a community health center. We will do more to make sure poor children are fully subscribed in our programs for low-income families.

Do you realize that half of the working uninsured work for small businesses? Small businesses are having trouble affording health care. In order to help our workers get health care, in order to help small businesses, we must allow small businesses to pool together, to join together, so they can buy insurance at the same discounts big companies are able to do. We will continue to expand health savings accounts so workers and small businesses are able to pay lower premiums and people can save tax-free in a health care account they call their own.

To make sure health care is available and affordable, we must do something about the junk lawsuits that are running up the cost of health care and running good docs out of practice. By forcing doctors to practice defensive medicine, medical lawsuits cost the Government, and therefore you, about $28 billion a year. Lawsuits drive up insurance premiums, which drive good doctors out of practice. I have met too many ob-gyns who are worried about being able to stay in practice. I have met too many of their patients, women who are worried about getting the health care they need.

See, you can't be pro-doctor, pro-patient, and pro-personal-injury-lawyer at the same time. You have to choose. My opponent made his choice, and he put a personal injury lawyer on the ticket. I made my choice. I'm standing with the docs and the patients. I am for medical liability reform—now.

And I urge you to vote for Mel Martinez in the Senate. He will join us in fighting for medical liability reform—now.

My opponent has a health care plan, a plan for bigger, more intrusive Government. The other day, he tried to tell the Americans that when it comes to his health care plan, and I quote, "The Government has nothing to do with it." I could barely contain myself. [*Laughter*] Facts are 8 out of 10 people who get health care under Senator Kerry's plan would be placed on a Government program. He said his plan helps small businesses, but yet, further study concluded that it is an overpriced albatross that would saddle small businesses with 225 new mandates.

I have a better idea. I want to help small businesses afford health care, not saddle them with new Government rules. The choice in this election is clear. My opponent wants to move in the direction

of Government-run health care. I believe health decisions should be made by patients and doctors, not by officials in Washington, DC. He can run, but he cannot hide.

I have set out policies that move this country toward a positive and optimistic vision. I believe our country can and must become an ownership society. You know, there's an old saying, no one ever washes a rental car—[*laughter*]—a lot of wisdom in that statement. When you own something, you care about it. When you own something, you have a vital stake in the future of your country.

That's why we'll continue to encourage ownership. Every time a small business is started, someone is achieving the American Dream. That's why we're encouraging health savings accounts, so people have the security of owning their own health care plan. That's why we'll continue to spread the ownership of homes all across America. I love it when more and more people from all walks of life open up the door where they live and say, "Welcome to my home. Welcome to my piece of property."

In a new term, we'll take the next step toward building an ownership society by strengthening Social Security. Now, let me remind you of something that took place in the 2000 campaign. They said in those political ads that, "If George W. gets elected, our seniors will not get their Social Security checks." You might remember those ads. I want you to remind your friends and neighbors, they got their checks. Nobody is going to take away the checks of those who are now on Social Security. And baby boomers like me, we're in pretty good shape when it comes to Social Security.

But we need to worry about our children and our grandchildren. We need to make sure Social Security is available for them. That is why I believe younger workers ought to be allowed to take some of their own payroll taxes and put it in a personal savings account that will earn better interest, a personal savings account they can call their own, an account the Government cannot take away.

My opponent wants to maintain the status quo when it comes to Social Security. That is unacceptable for younger Americans. I believe a President should solve problems, not pass them on to future generations or future Presidents. On issue after issue, from Medicare without choices to schools with less accountability to higher taxes on working Americans, my opponent takes the side of more centralized control and bigger Government.

There's a word for that attitude. It's called liberalism.

Audience members. Boo-o-o!

The President. He dismisses it as simply a label. He must have seen it differently when he told a newspaper, "I am a liberal and proud of it." Don't take my word for it. Take the word of the nonpartisan National Journal magazine that did a study of voting records and named him the most liberal Member of the United States Senate. That takes a lot of hard work. [*Laughter*] It's hard to be more liberal than the likes of Ted Kennedy. He can run, but he cannot hide.

I have a very different record and a different philosophy. I do not believe in big Government, and I do not believe that Government should be indifferent. I am a compassionate conservative. I believe in policies that empower people to improve their lives, not try to run their lives. I believe we should help men and women find the skills and tools needed to prosper in a time of change. We're helping all Americans to have a future of dignity and independence, and that is how I will lead our Nation for 4 more years.

Audience members. Four more years! Four more years! Four more years!

The President. In this time of change, some things do not change, the values we try to live by, courage and compassion, reverence and integrity. In a time of change, we must support the institutions that give our lives direction and purpose, our families, our schools, our places of worship. We stand for a culture of life in which every person matters and every being counts. We stand for marriage and family, which are the foundations of our society. We stand for the appointment of Federal judges who know the difference between personal opinion and the strict interpretation of the law.

This election will also determine how America responds to the continuing danger of terrorism. The most solemn duty of the American President is to protect the American people. If America shows uncertainty or weakness in this decade, the world will drift toward tragedy. This will not happen on my watch.

Since that terrible morning of September the 11th, 2001, we have fought the terrorists across the Earth, not for pride, not for power, but because the lives of our citizens are at stake. Our strategy is clear. We're defending the homeland. We're reforming and strengthening our intelligence capabilities. We're transforming our military so the All-Volunteer Army will remain an all-volunteer army. We're staying on the offensive. We will strike the terrorists abroad so we do not have to face them here at home. We will spread freedom and liberty. And we will prevail.

Our strategy is succeeding. Think about the world the way it was some 3½ years ago. Afghanistan was the home base of Al Qaida. Pakistan was a transit point for terrorist groups. Saudi Arabia was fertile ground for terrorist fundraising. Libya was secretly pursuing nuclear weapons. Iraq was a dangerous place and a gathering threat. And Al Qaida was largely unchallenged as it planned attacks.

Because we led, because the United States of America was firm in our resolve, Afghanistan is free and is now an ally in the war on terror; Pakistan is capturing terrorist leaders; Saudi Arabia is making raids and arrests; Libya is dismantling its weapons programs; the army of a free Iraq is fighting for freedom; and more than three-quarters of Al Qaida's key members and associates have been brought to justice.

We're standing with the people in Afghanistan and Iraq. I want the youngsters here to understand how profound history has changed because of the actions we took to defend ourselves. Think about Afghanistan. It wasn't all that long ago that the Taliban ran that country. These ideologues of hatred would not even allow young girls to go to school, and their mothers were taken into the public square and whipped if they didn't toe their line. Because we acted, because we upheld doctrine that said, "If you harbor a terrorist, you're equally as guilty as the terrorist," millions of citizens went to vote in a Presidential election. The first voter in Afghanistan for the election of a President was a 19-year-old woman. Freedom is on the march. Freedom is on the march in a part of world that no one ever dreamt would be free.

In Iraq, there will be Presidential elections in several months. Think how far that country has come from the days of torture rooms and mass graves. No, we're standing with those people. When American gives its word, America must keep its word. And we're standing with them. And we're standing with them because we understand that free societies in the Middle East will be hopeful societies which no longer feed resentments and breed violence for export. Free governments in the Middle East will fight the terrorists instead of harboring them. And that will help us keep the peace.

Our strategy and our mission in Afghanistan and Iraq should be clear. We'll train the armies and the police in those countries so the people of Afghanistan and the people of Iraq can do the hard work of defending their freedom. We will get those countries on the path of stability and democracy as quickly as possible, and then our troops will come home with the honor they have earned.

I am proud to be the Commander in Chief of a great United States military. I want to thank the veterans who are here for having set such a great example for those who wear the uniform. I want to thank the military families who are here.

The single most important responsibility is to make sure our military has all the tools and resources they need to complete their missions. That's why I went to the United States Congress in September of 2003 and asked for $87 billion of funding to support our troops in combat. I was very pleased with the overwhelming bipartisan support for that initiative. The support was so strong that only 12 Members of the United States Senate voted against the funding, 2 of whom were my opponent and his runningmate.

Audience members. Boo-o-o!

The President. As you're out gathering the vote, remind people of this startling fact: There were only four Members of the United States Senate who voted to authorize the use of force and then voted against funding our troops in harm's way—only four members—two of whom were my opponent and his runningmate.

Audience members. Boo-o-o!

The President. You might remember his famous quote when they asked him about his vote, he said, "I actually did vote for the $87 billion, right before I voted against it."

Audience members. Boo-o-o!

The President. Sunday was the one-year anniversary of Senator Kerry's vote against funding for our troops. My opponent's many and conflicting positions on this issue are a case study into why his contradictions call into question his credibility and his ability to lead our Nation.

September of 2003, as the $87 billion funding package was being debated in Congress, he said on national TV, "It would be irresponsible to abandon our troops by voting against it"—his words. And yet one month later, he did exactly that irresponsible thing. He voted against the funding. And so we say, why? What happened to change the Senator's mind so abruptly in one month? Well, his opponent in the

Democrat primary, Howard Dean, was gaining ground as an antiwar candidate. Senator Kerry apparently decided supporting the troops, even while in harm's way, was not as important as shoring up his own political position.

Audience members. Boo-o-o!

The President. At a time of a great threat to our country, at a time of great challenge in the world, the Commander in Chief must stand on principle, not on the shifting sands of political convenience.

We have big differences when it comes to how to protect America. You might remember in one of the debates Senator Kerry proposed that we must pass a "global test" before we defend ourselves.

Audience members. Boo-o-o!

The President. I didn't make that up. I was standing right there. I heard him. [*Laughter*] The problem with the "global test" is that the Senator can never pass it. And that's dangerous in the world in which we live. I say he can't because remember 1990; the United Nations Security Council passed a resolution supporting action to remove Saddam Hussein from Kuwait. The international community was united. Countries throughout the world joined the coalition. And yet even after United Nations approval, Senator Kerry voted against the authorization for the use of force. He says removing Saddam Hussein was a "mistake," during one of the debates.

Audience members. Boo-o-o!

The President. He said—well, here's how he would have solved the problem. He would have asked the United Nations to pass another United Nations Security Council resolution.

Audience members. Boo-o-o!

The President. Precisely what Saddam Hussein wanted to hear, another resolution. Had the Senator had his way; Saddam Hussein not only would be sitting in a palace; he would have occupied Kuwait. And the world would be dangerous for it. America is better off with Saddam Hussein sitting in a prison cell.

I'll work to build alliances. We'll work to make sure our coalition remains strong. But I will never turn over America's national security decisions to leaders of other countries.

I believe in the transformational power of liberty. I'll tell you what I mean by that. One of our friends in the international community is the Prime Minister of Japan, Koizumi. I saw him at the United Nations and said, "You know, I'm talking about you everywhere you go across the country." I said, "I hope you don't mind." He said, "No." I didn't tell him I was going to tell you, though, that his favorite singer was Elvis. [*Laughter*] Shows we're getting to know each other quite well. Doesn't seem like much, does it, that the head of Japan is a friend. But think about the history. Wasn't all that long ago, 60 years ago, that we were at war with the Japanese. Perhaps some here in the crowd was in that war. My dad—our dad was fighting the Japanese. I guarantee you people had relatives fighting the Japanese who are here. They were the sworn enemy of the United States of America.

After we won that war, Harry S. Truman, President of the United States, along with other Americans, believed in the power of liberty to transform an enemy into an ally. And there was a lot of skepticism about that. You can imagine why. "Japan conceivably becoming a democracy," people would ask. "Why do we worry about an enemy that has upset so many families in America?" But people believed, and as a result of people having firm belief, I sit down now at the table with the Prime Minister of Japan, talking about the peace we all want.

Someday, an American President will be sitting down with the duly elected leader of Iraq, talking about keeping the peace in the Middle East, and our children and our grandchildren will be better off for it.

I believe that millions in the Middle East plead in silence for their freedom. I believe women in the Middle East want to live in a free society. I believe the mothers and the fathers of the Middle East want to bring their children up in a free and peaceful world. I believe all these things, because freedom is not America's gift to the world; freedom is the Almighty God's gift to each man and woman in this world.

For all Americans, these years in our history will always stand apart. There are quiet times in the life of a nation when little is expected of its leaders. This is not one of those times. This is a time that requires firm resolve, clear vision, and a deep faith in the values that makes this a great nation.

None of us will ever forget that week when one era ended and another began. On September the 14th, 2001, I stood in the ruins of the Twin Towers. It's a day I will never forget. I will never forget the voices of those in hardhats yelling at me at the top of their lungs, "Whatever it takes." I will never forget the look in the man's eyes as he grabbed me by the arm, and he said, "Do not let me down." Ever since that day, I wake up every morning thinking about how to better protect our country. I will never relent in defending America, whatever it takes.

Four years ago, when I traveled your great State, 4 years ago, when I came to The Villages, for that matter, I made this pledge, that if you gave me a chance to serve, I would uphold the honor and the dignity of the office to which I had been elected. With your help, I will do so for 4 more years.

God bless. Thanks for coming. Thank you all. Thank you all.

NOTE: The President spoke at 2:25 p.m. at the Lake Sumter Landing Market Square. In his remarks, he referred to Florida State Representative Carey Baker and his wife, Lori; Mel R. Martinez, senatorial candidate in Florida; former President Saddam Hussein of Iraq; and Prime Minister Junichiro Koizumi of Japan.

Statement on the Anniversary of the Allied Landing on Leyte Island
October 19, 2004

On October 20, we commemorate the 60th anniversary of the Allied landing on Leyte Island's shores, a pivotal moment in the history of the War in the Pacific and in the human struggle for liberty. The Leyte landing is a central event in the long history of friendship between the peoples of the Philippines and the United States.

This year we are privileged that American, Filipino, and Australian veterans once again stand on the very beach where they fought for the liberation of the Philippines six decades ago. Many of those brave Allied soldiers made the ultimate sacrifice on these shores in the cause of freedom. MacArthur, Osmena, Romulo, and all those heroes commemorated in bronze on Leyte's shores were tenacious and brave.

Veterans of the Leyte landing: Know that we will continue to recognize this date as a day to draw renewed inspiration from your courage and sacrifice in the cause of freedom. We will pass on to our children what your great generation has passed to us, a world where liberty is the right of all humankind, and where men and women will remain vigilant in its defense.

Letter to Congressional Leaders on Continuation of the National Emergency With Respect to Significant Narcotics Traffickers Centered in Colombia
October 19, 2004

Dear Mr. Speaker: (*Dear Mr. President:*)

Section 202(d) of the National Emergencies Act, 50 U.S.C. 1622(d), provides for the automatic termination of a national emergency unless, prior to the anniversary date of its declaration, the President publishes in the *Federal Register* and transmits to the Congress a notice stating that the emergency is to continue in effect beyond the anniversary date. In accordance with this provision, I have sent the enclosed notice, stating that the emergency declared with respect to significant narcotics traffickers centered in Colombia is to continue in effect beyond October 21, 2004, to the *Federal Register* for publication. The most recent notice continuing this emergency was published in the *Federal Register* on October 20, 2003 (68 *Fed. Reg.* 60023).

The circumstances that led to the declaration on October 21, 1995, of a national emergency have not been resolved. The actions of significant narcotics traffickers centered in Colombia continue to pose an unusual and extraordinary threat to the national security, foreign policy, and economy of the United States and to cause extreme violence, corruption, and harm in the United States and abroad. For these reasons, I have determined that it is necessary to maintain economic pressure on significant narcotics traffickers centered in Colombia by blocking their property or interests in property that are in the United States or within the possession or control of United States persons and by depriving them of access to U.S. commercial and financial markets.

Sincerely,

GEORGE W. BUSH

NOTE: Identical letters were sent to J. Dennis Hastert, Speaker of the House of Representatives, and Richard B. Cheney, President of the Senate. An original was not available for verification of the content of this letter. The notice is listed in Appendix D at the end of this volume.

Remarks in Mason City, Iowa
October 20, 2004

The President. Thank you all for coming. Thank you all for coming out to say hello. It is great to be in Mason City, Iowa. I appreciate the warm welcome. It's the home of fine corn, fine people, and fine music.

I'm here to ask for your help. We're less than 2 weeks away from voting time. And I'd like for you to get your friends and neighbors and remind them we have a duty in democracy to vote. And get them headed to the polls, and remind them, if they want a safer America and a stronger America and a better America, to put me and Dick Cheney back in office.

My only regret is that Laura is not traveling with me today.

Audience members. Aw-w-w!

The President. That is generally the reaction. [*Laughter*] "Why didn't you send her, and you stay at home?" [*Laughter*] She was a public school librarian when I met her for the second time. See, we were in the seventh grade together in San Jacinto Junior High in Midland, Texas. She became a public school librarian, and I met her again. I said, "Will you marry me?" She said, "Fine, just so long as I never have to give a speech." [*Laughter*] I said, "Okay, you got a deal." Fortunately, she didn't hold me to that deal. She is giving a lot of speeches, and when she does the American people see a warm, compassionate, great First Lady. I am traveling in Iowa today to give you reasons why I think you ought to put me back into office, but perhaps the most important one of all is so that Laura is the First Lady for 4 more years.

This morning in the Oval Office, I met with our fine Vice President, Dick Cheney. I was there, of course, to discuss national security matters before we hit the campaign trail today. I'm proud of my Vice President. I admit to you, he does not have the waviest hair in the race. [*Laughter*] You'll be happy I didn't pick him because of his hairdo. [*Laughter*] I picked him because of his judgment, his experience, and his ability to get the job done.

I am proud of your United States Congressman, Tom Latham. He is doing an excellent job. You're proud to call him Congressman. I'm proud to call him friend. And I appreciate his wife, Kathy, as well. She's a fine, fine lady.

I'm also proud to be working with your United States Senator, Charles Grassley. I told him when I saw him—I saw him the other day in Cedar Rapids. I took him aside, and I said, "Listen, the South Lawn at the White House has got a lot of grass." [*Laughter*] I'm proud to work with him, and with your help, I'll continue to work with him for 4 more years.

I want to thank the house majority leader, Chuck Gipp, who's with us. I want to thank all those who serve in State and local government.

I appreciate the mayor being here. I'm honored that the mayor is taking time out

to be here. My only advice to the mayor is to pave the potholes. [*Laughter*] I appreciate your service, Mayor.

I want to thank all the grassroots activists. I thank you for what you have done and what you're going to do. Put up the signs. Get on the phone. Turn people out to vote. Talk to your friends and neighbors. Go to your community centers. Go to your coffee shops. Go to your houses of worship. Remind people we have a duty. With your help, we will carry Iowa and win a great victory in November.

Listen, in the last few years, the American people have come to know me. They know my blunt way of speaking. I got that from my mother. [*Laughter*] They know that sometimes I mangle the English language. I got that from my dad. [*Laughter*] Americans also know I tell you exactly what I'm going to do, and I keep my word.

When I came into office, the stock market had been in serious decline for 6 months. That had been an indication that our economy was sliding into a recession. To help families and to get this economy growing again, I pledged to reduce taxes. I kept my word. The results are clear. The recession was one of the shallowest in American history.

Over the last 3 years, our economy has grown at rates as fast as any in nearly 20 years. Today, the homeownership rate is at an alltime high in America. In the past 13 months, we've added more than 1.9 million new jobs. The unemployment rate in America is 5.4 percent, lower than the average rate of the 1970s, 1980s, and the 1990s. Farm income is up. The unemployment rate in Iowa is 4.5 percent. This economy is moving forward, and we're not going to go back to the days of tax and spend.

To keep this economy strong, we'll continue to stand with our farmers. I understand a good national economy depends on a good farm economy. I signed a good farm bill that's helping our farmers. We're phasing out the death tax to help our farmers keep their farms from generation to generation. We have extended contracts in the Conservation Reserve Program to help protect our wildlife, to help improve land, and to help our farm families. We're expanding broadband technology to make high-speed Internet access available to all Americans by 2007. We're opening up markets for Iowa farmers all across the world.

We are pursuing an energy strategy that encourages conservation, increased domestic production, and renewables like ethanol and biodiesel. When I campaigned in your State in 2000, I told the people of Iowa I support ethanol. I kept my word. To make sure jobs remain here, America must be the best place in the world to do business. That means less regulations on our job creators. That means we must do something about the frivolous lawsuits that make it hard for small-business owners to expand their companies. We will open up markets around the world. We will make sure that we're wise about how we spend your money. And to make sure this economy continues to grow, we must keep your taxes low.

Now, my opponent has his own history on the economy. [*Laughter*] In 20 years as a Senator from Massachusetts, he has built a record of a Senator from Massachusetts. [*Laughter*] He has voted to raise taxes 98 times.

Audience members. Boo-o-o!

The President. I want to remind you, he voted to tax Social Security benefits.

Audience members. Boo-o-o!

The President. He's been there for 20 years. That's about five tax increases every year. I'd call that a predictable pattern. I'd call that an indicator. He looked in the camera the other night with a straight face and said he's not going to raise taxes on anyone who earns less than $200,000. The problem with that is to keep that promise, he would have to break almost all of his other ones. He has proposed more than $2.2 trillion in new Federal spending. That's trillion with a "T." [*Laughter*] And

so they asked him, "How are you going to pay for it?" He said, "Oh, I'll just tax the rich." Now, we've heard that before, haven't we?

Audience members. Yes!

The President. See, you can't raise enough money by raising the top two brackets to pay for $2.2 trillion of new spending. There is a gap between what he has promised and what he can deliver, and guess who usually has to fill that gap?

Audience members. We do!

The President. There's also something else wrong with taxing the rich. The rich hire lawyers and accountants for a reason—[*laughter*]—to slip the tab and stick you with the bill. The good news is, we're not going to let him tax you; we're going to carry Iowa and win in November.

When I came into public office, too many of our public schools were passing children, grade to grade, year after year, without learning the basics. So I pledged to restore accountability to our schools and to end the soft bigotry of low expectations. I kept my word. The No Child Left Behind Act is a solid piece of reform. We're now seeing results. Our children are making sustained gains in reading and math. We're closing achievement gaps all across our country, and we're not going to go back to the days of low expectations and mediocrity in our classrooms.

When I came into office, we had a problem in Medicare. Medicine was changing, but Medicare was not. And that was a problem. Let me give you an example. Medicare would pay tens of thousands of dollars for heart surgery but not one dime for the prescription drug that could prevent the heart surgery from being needed in the first place. That was not fair to our seniors or our taxpayers. In 2002, I remember campaigning around your State saying that we were going to reform Medicare so rural hospitals would be treated more fairly in the State of Iowa. I kept my pledge. I kept my word. Iowa's rural hospitals are being treated fairly. Thanks to the good work of Senator Chuck Grassley and Congressman Tom Latham, beginning in 2006, all seniors will be able to get prescription drug coverage under Medicare.

There's more to do in health care. We need to make sure health care is available and affordable for all our citizens. We need a safety net for those with the greatest needs. We'll do more to make sure our poor children are fully subscribed in our programs for low-income families so they get the health care they need. I believe in community health centers, places where the poor and the indigent can get health care. Since I took office, we have opened or expanded more than 600 community health centers. We've provided care to more than 3 million patients, including many from farm communities. In a new term, we'll open or expand another 600 centers, and we will make sure every poor county in America has a community or rural health center.

Most of the uninsured today work for small businesses. Small businesses are having trouble affording health care. To help workers get the health care they need, we must allow small businesses to join together so they can buy insurance at the same discounts that big companies can buy insurance. We will expand health savings accounts so workers and small businesses are able to pay lower premiums, and people can save tax-free in a health care account they call their own.

To make sure health care is available and affordable, we must do something about the junk lawsuits that are running up the cost of medicine and running good doctors out of practice. By forcing doctors to practice defensive medicine, these medical lawsuits cost the Federal Government $28 billion a year. That means they cost you $28 billion a year. Lawsuits drive up insurance premiums, which drives good doctors out of practice. I've talked to too many ob-gyns, for example, who are having to leave their practice because of lawsuits. And I've met too many women who are worried about the quality of the health care they receive because of lawsuits. You cannot be pro-doctor and pro-patient and pro-trial-lawyer at the same time. I think you have to choose. My opponent made his choice, and he put a personal injury trail lawyer on the ticket.

Audience members. Boo-o-o!

The President. I made my choice. I'm standing with the docs and the patients. I'm for medical liability reform—now.

We have big differences in this campaign when it comes to health care. My opponent has laid out one that calls for a bigger and more intrusive Government. Now, the other day, in the debate, he looked right in the camera again, and he said this, he said, "The Government has nothing to do with it." I could barely contain myself. [*Laughter*] The facts are that 8 out of 10 people who get health care under Senator Kerry's plan would be placed on a Government program. Those are the facts.

Audience members. Boo-o-o!

The President. He said his plan would help small businesses, yet upon analysis, small-business groups have concluded that it is an overpriced albatross that would saddle small businesses with 225 new mandates. I want to help our small businesses and will through association health plans, but we're not going to saddle them with a bunch of new Government regulations. My opponent wants to move in the direction of Government health care. Health decisions, in my plan, will be made by doctors and patients, not by officials in Washington, DC. He can run from his plan, but he cannot hide.

We'll continue to promote an ownership society in America. You know, there's a saying that says no one ever washes a rental car. [*Laughter*] There's a lot of wisdom in that statement. See, when you own something, you care about it. And when you own something, you have a vital stake in the future of our country. That's why we will continue to promote entrepreneurship.

Every time a small business is started, someone is achieving the American Dream.

That's why we're encouraging health savings accounts, so people can have the security of managing and owning their own health care account. That's why we'll continue to promote homeownership in America. I love it when more and more people open up the door where they live and say, "Welcome to my home. Welcome to my piece of property."

In a new term, we'll take the next step to build an ownership society by strengthening Social Security. Now, I want to take you back to the 2000 campaign, if I might, when they ran all those ads that said, "If George W. gets elected, you will not get your check." You remember those? I want you to remind your friends and neighbors that they got their Social Security checks. No one is going to take the Social Security check away from our seniors. And as far as the baby boomers like me go, we're in pretty good shape when it comes to Social Security.

But we need to worry about our children and our grandchildren when it comes to the Social Security system. We need to worry about whether or not Social Security will be around when they need it. I believe we need to think differently about Social Security for our youngsters. For their sake, we must strengthen the system by allowing younger workers to save some of their own payroll accounts—payroll taxes in a personal savings account that they can call their own, that the Government cannot take away.

The other night, my opponent said he's going to maintain the status quo when it comes to Social Security. That is unacceptable. The job of a President is to confront problems, not to pass them on to future Presidents and future generations.

We have a different philosophy of Government. On just about every issue, my opponent is for more authority to the United States Government. I'm for more authority to the people. On issue after

issue, from Medicare without choices to schools with less accountability to higher taxes, he takes the side of bigger Government.

And there's a word for that attitude. It is called liberalism. Now, he just dismisses that word as a label. He must have seen it differently when he told a newspaper, "I am liberal and proud of it." [*Laughter*] There have been people who have judged people's records in politics—the nonpartisan National Journal Magazine did a study and named him the most liberal Member of the United States Senate. That takes hard work. [*Laughter*] See, he can run, but he cannot hide.

I have a different record and a different philosophy. I do not believe in big Government, and I do not believe Government should be indifferent. I'm a compassionate conservative. I believe in policies that empower people to improve their lives, not try to run their lives. So we're helping men and women find the skills and tools to prosper in a time of change. We're helping people realize their dreams so they can find dignity and independence in America, and that is how I will continue to lead our country for 4 more years.

Audience members. Four more years! Four more years! Four more years!

The President. In a time of change—in this time of change, some things do not change, the values we try to live by, courage and compassion, reverence and integrity. In a time of change, we must support the institutions that give our lives direction and purpose, our families, our schools, our houses of worship. We stand for a culture of life in which every person matters and every being counts. We stand for marriage and family, which are the foundations of our society. We stand for the second amendment, which protects every American's individual right to bear arms. We stand for the appointment of Federal judges who know the difference between personal opinion and the strict interpretation of the law.

My opponent's words on these issues are a little muddy, but his record is plenty clear. [*Laughter*] He says he supports the institution of marriage, but he voted against the Defense of Marriage Act. He says he's—he called himself the candidate with conservative values, but he voted against the ban on the brutal practice of partial-birth abortion.

Audience members. Boo-o-o!

The President. He described the Reagan years as a time of moral darkness.

Audience members. Boo-o-o!

The President. There is a mainstream in American politics, and my opponent sits on the far left bank. In this campaign, he can try to run from his record and his philosophy, but he cannot hide.

This election will also determine how America responds to the continuing danger of terrorism. The most solemn duty of the American President is to protect the American people. If America shows uncertainty or weakness in this decade, the world will drift toward tragedy. This will not happen on my watch.

Since that terrible morning of September the 11th, 2001, we've fought the terrorists across the Earth, not for pride, not for power, but because the lives of our citizens are at stake. Our strategy is clear. We're reforming and strengthening our intelligence gathering capabilities. We're defending the homeland. We're transforming our military. The All-Volunteer Army will remain an all-volunteer army. We're staying on the offensive. We will strike the terrorists abroad so we do not have to face them here at home. We will spread freedom and liberty. And we will prevail.

Our strategy is succeeding. Think about the world the way it was some 3½ years ago. Afghanistan was the home base of Al Qaida. It's where terrorists were training to inflict great harm on America and the free world. Pakistan was a transit point for terrorist groups. Saudi Arabia was fertile ground for terrorist fundraising. Libya was secretly pursuing nuclear weapons. Iraq was

a dangerous place and a gathering threat. And Al Qaida was largely unchallenged as it planned horrific attacks.

But because we acted, because the United States of America was steadfast and resolved, Afghanistan is now a free nation and an ally in the war on terror; Pakistan is capturing terrorist leaders; Saudi Arabia is making raids and arrests; the army of a free Iraq is fighting for freedom; and more than three-quarters of Al Qaida's key members and associates have been brought to justice.

Now we're standing with the people of Afghanistan and Iraq. When America gives its word, America must keep its word. But I want the youngsters here to hear what is happening in the world in which you live. Think about Afghanistan 3½ years ago. There were young girls there who couldn't go to school, and their mothers were pulled in the public square and whipped if they didn't toe the line of these ideologues of hate who ran the country. They were called the Taliban. These were barbaric, brutal people.

Because we acted in our own self-interest, because we upheld the doctrine that said, "If you harbor a terrorist, you're equally as guilty as the terrorist," today, Afghanistan is free. Millions of people voted in a Presidential election. The first voter in the Afghan Presidential election was a 19-year-old woman. Freedom is on the march. People want to be free. That's what you've got to know. People desire to be free.

In Iraq, there will be elections in January. Think how far that society has come from the days of torture chambers, the days of a brutal dictator who was willing to cut the hands off people arbitrarily. Think about the difference that is from the days of the mass graves. See, free societies help us keep the peace. Free societies will be hopeful societies which no longer feed resentments and breed violence for exports. Free countries will join us in fighting these ideologues of hate instead of supporting them. And that helps us keep the peace we all long for.

And so our mission is clear. We will help train police and armies in Afghanistan and Iraq so people in those countries can do the hard work of defending their own freedom. We will get those countries on the path to stability and democracy as quickly as possible, and then our troops will come home with the honor they have earned.

It is such an honor to be the Commander in Chief of such a great military. And it is a great military because of the character of the people who wear our Nation's uniform. And I want to thank the veterans who are here today for having set such a great example.

And I want to thank the military families who are here. And I want you to know that we will keep our commitment to those who wear the uniform and their families by making sure that our troops have all they need to complete their missions. That's why I went to the United States Congress in September of 2003 and asked for $87 billion in supplemental funding to support our troops in harm's way, in both Iraq and Afghanistan. I was very pleased with the overwhelming bipartisan support for that important funding request. As a matter of fact, the support was so strong that only 12 Members of the United States Senate voted against the funding to support our troops in combat, 2 of whom were my opponent and his runningmate.

Audience members. Boo-o-o!

The President. Now, let me remind you of a startling statistic, and I want you to remind your friends and neighbors of this startling statistic. There were only 4 Members of the United States Senate—4 out of 100—who voted to authorize the use of force and then voted against the funding to support our troops in combat. Two of those four were my opponent and his runningmate.

Audience members. Boo-o-o!

The President. So I asked him why. I asked him about that vote. And that's when

he said, "I actually did vote for the $87 billion, before I voted against it." Now, I don't know if a lot of folks around the coffee shops in this part of the world talk like that. [*Laughter*] I doubt they do. They continued to press him. He's given them a bunch of answers as to why he made that vote. One of the most interesting ones of all is he finally just said, "It was a complicated matter." [*Laughter*] There's nothing complicated about supporting our troops in combat.

This is America's first Presidential election since September the 11th, 2001. The security of our country is at risk in ways different from any we have before faced. We are in the midst of a global war against a well-trained, highly motivated enemy, an enemy who hates America for the very freedoms and values we cherish most. The next Commander in Chief must lead us to victory in this war, and you cannot lead a war when you don't believe you're fighting one.

Senator Kerry was recently asked how September the 11th had changed him. He replied, "It didn't change me much at all." And this unchanged world view becomes obvious when he calls the war against terror primarily an intelligence and law enforcement operation, rather than what I believe, a war which requires the full use of American power to keep us secure.

Senator Kerry's top foreign policy adviser has questioned whether this is even a war at all. Here's what he said, and I quote, "We're not in a war on terror in the literal sense. It is like saying 'the war on poverty.' It is just a metaphor." End quote. Confusing food programs with terrorist killings reveals a fundamental misunderstanding of the war we face, and that is very dangerous thinking.

My opponent also misunderstands our battle against insurgents and terrorists in Iraq, calling Iraq a "diversion" from the war on terror. The case of one terrorist shows how wrong his thinking is. The terrorist leader we face in Iraq today, the one responsible for planting car bombs and be-heading Americans, is a man named Zarqawi. Zarqawi ran a terrorist training camp in Afghanistan until our military coalition destroyed that camp. He then fled to Iraq, where he got medical treatment and continued his plotting and planning. To confirm where he's coming from, just the other day, Zarqawi publicly announced his sworn allegiance to Usama bin Laden.

If Zarqawi and his associates were not busy fighting American forces in Iraq, does Senator Kerry think he would be leading a productive and peaceful life? Of course not. And that's why Iraq is no "diversion" but a central commitment in the war on terror, a place where our military is confronting and defeating terrorists overseas so we do not have to face them here at home.

You cannot lead our Nation to decisive victory, on which the security of every American family depends, if you do not see the true dangers of a post-September the 11th world. The war against terror requires all our resources, all our strength. We will stay on the offense. We will improve our homeland protections. And of course, we'll continue to work with our allies and our coalition to keep us safe.

Senator Kerry's view of alliance-building is to call them "the coerced and the bribed," is to insult the friends who stands with us and try to placate countries who disagree with us. No, we'll work hard with all our friends and allies, but I will never give a country a veto power over our national security.

I believe in the transformational power of liberty. That's what I believe. You know, I have had many conversations with Prime Minister Koizumi of Japan. That may not seem like much to some here. But it wasn't all that long ago, when you think about it, that we were at war with Japan. Japan was the sworn enemy of the United States of America. My dad fought against the Japanese. I'm confident many out here's relatives fought against the Japanese as well. And after we won that war, Harry S. Tru-

man, President of the United States, believed in the power of liberty to transform an enemy into an ally.

There was a lot of skepticism about that during that period in our history. You can understand why. "Japan couldn't conceivably become a democracy," people would say. "Why do we want to help a country that inflicted such harm on the United States of America," others would say. There was pessimism and doubt.

But fortunately, predecessors of ours believed in the power of liberty to transform, and as a result of that belief and because we helped Japan become a democracy, I now sit at the table with Prime Minister Koizumi, talking about how to keep the peace we all want.

Someday, an American President will be sitting down the a duly elected leader of Iraq, talking about keeping the peace in the Middle East. And our children and our grandchildren will be better off for it.

I believe that millions in the Middle East plead in silence for their freedom. I believe women in the Middle East want to live in a free society. I believe mothers and dads in the Middle East want to raise their children in a free and peaceful environment. I believe all these things because freedom is not America's gift to the world; freedom is the Almighty God's gift to each man and woman in this world.

We have climbed the mountain, and we see the valley below. And the valley below is one of peace and hope and optimism. You know, for all Americans, these years in our history will always stand apart. There are quiet times in the life of a nation when little is expected of its leaders. This isn't one of those times. [*Laughter*] This is a time that requires firm resolve, clear vision, and a deep faith in the values that makes us a great nation.

None of us will ever forget that week when one era ended and another began. On September the 14th, 2001, I stood in the ruins of the Twin Towers. I will never forget the day. I will never forget the voices of those in their hardhats yelling at me at the top of their lungs, "Whatever it takes." I will never forget the look in the man's eye who grabbed me by the arm, and he said, "Do not let me down." Ever since that day, I wake up every morning thinking about how to better protect our country. I will never relent in defending America, whatever it takes.

Four years ago, when I traveled your great State in the caucuses and then in the general election, I made a pledge that if you gave me a chance to serve, I would uphold the honor and the dignity of the office to which I had been elected. With your help, with your hard work coming

down the stretch, I will do so for 4 more years.

God bless. Thank you all for coming. I appreciate you being here. Thank you all.

NOTE: The President spoke at 10 a.m. at the North Iowa Fairgrounds. In his remarks, he referred to Chuck Gipp, majority leader, Iowa State House of Representatives; Mayor Jean Marinos of Mason City, IA; former President Saddam Hussein of Iraq; senior Al Qaida associate Abu Musab Al Zarqawi; Usama bin Laden, leader of the Al Qaida terrorist organization; and Prime Minister Junichiro Koizumi of Japan.

Remarks in a Discussion in Rochester, Minnesota
October 20, 2004

The President. Thank you all for coming. Thank you all. Please be seated. I might just decide to take off my jacket. We've got some work to do.

As you can see, I'm joined on the platform here with some of your fellow citizens. We're going to talk about economic policy and ownership and ways to make America a more hopeful place. And we'll be having a dialog here in a minute, but I've got something I want to tell you first.

I'd like your help in this election. We're coming down the stretch, and I'm here to ask for your help in turning out the vote. Get your friends and neighbors to go to the polls. We have a duty in this country to participate in our democratic system by voting. And get them going to the polls, and when you get them headed there, remind them that if they want a safer America and a stronger America and a better America, put me and Dick Cheney back in office.

It is nice to be back in Rochester, and it's great to be back in the great State of Minnesota. And there is no doubt, with

your help, we will carry Minnesota and win a great victory on November the 2d.

Laura said for me to send her best. I'm sorry she's not here. You know, when I— we went to the seventh grade together at San Jacinto Junior High in Midland, Texas. And then we got to know each other again later on, and she was a public school librarian. And I asked her to marry me, of course, and she said, "Fine, but never make me give a political speech." [*Laughter*] I said, "Okay, if that's one of the conditions, you got a deal." Fortunately, she didn't hold me to that promise. She's giving a lot of speeches, and when she does, the American people see a strong, compassionate, warm, great First Lady. I love her dearly. We are enjoying ourselves on this campaign. It's really a lot of fun to travel with her, and it's really a lot of fun to travel with our daughters, Barbara and Jenna. They're now out campaigning. You know, I told them when they were kids, "We'll go on the great family camping trip." This is it. [*Laughter*]

I'm proud to be here with your United States Senator, Norm Coleman. I appreciate you, Senator. He's a good man. I enjoy working with him. He represents Minnesota in fine fashion. And I'm also proud to be here with Gil Gutknecht, the United States Congressman for this area, and Mary—where is Mary? Oh, hi, Mary, good to see you again. Thanks for coming.

I want to thank—the Governor is not with us. He's doing a great job, though. I appreciate Tim. I enjoy him. I like him. I trust him, and so should you. He's doing you a good job. I'm sure he's out working a phone bank, turning out that vote. I want to thank all the local and State officials who are here.

I really want to thank the grassroots activists. You never get thanked enough for putting up the signs, for making the phone calls, for doing all the hard work. I know how hard you are working. I want to thank you in advance for the great victory we're going to have here in the State of Minnesota.

I met Sister Chabanel Hayunga today. Where are you, Sister? I know she's—you got a terrible seat. [*Laughter*] You would have thought a soldier in the army of compassion would have gotten a better seat. I'm going to talk to the advance person here. [*Laughter*] The reason I bring her up is because she is active with the Senior Companion Program through Catholic Charities.

The strength of this country is the hearts and souls of our citizens. That is the strength of America. We've got a great military, and we'll keep it strong. We've got a world-class economy that's growing. We'll keep it strong. But the true strength of this society of ours is the fact that there are millions among us who love a neighbor just like they'd like to be loved themselves. America can change and will change, one heart, one soul, one conscience at a time, because of the deep compassion of people like the Sister. She, of course, says—typical of a true soldier in the army of compas-

sion—out here on the runway when we had our picture taken at Air Force One, she said, "I am here representing the thousands of people in Minnesota who volunteer to make society a better place."

You have set such a clear example, for which we are grateful. Thank you, Sister, for what you do.

The President's job is to solve problems. We had a serious problem when it came to our economy. The stock market had been in significant decline 6 months prior to my arrival—I want you to remind your friends and neighbors of that—which foretold a recession that took place. And then we had some corporate scandals which affected our economy. We passed tough laws that made it clear to people we will not tolerate dishonesty in the boardrooms of America. That ought to be now abundantly clear. And then we got attacked, and those attacks cost our economy one million jobs in the weeks after September the 11th.

But we acted. I led; the Congress responded with tax relief. And the tax relief was vital. The tax relief encouraged consumption. It encouraged investment. And the recession was one of the shallowest in American history.

And the facts are clear. When you get through all the political noise, the facts are clear. Our economy is growing at rates as fast as any in nearly 20 years. We've added 1.9 million new jobs since August of 2003. The national unemployment rate is 5.4 percent, which is lower than the average rate of the 1970s, the 1980s, and the 1990s. Your unemployment rate in Minnesota is 4.5 percent. The farm income is up. Homeownership is at an alltime high. We're moving forward. We have overcome problems. There's more work to be done, but think about where we have been and where we're going. And we're not going to go back to the days of tax and spend. We're not going to go back to the days of the policies that stifle the entrepreneurial spirit.

So the fundamental question in this campaign, after I've shown people I can lead and solve problems is, what else are we going to do? I'll tell you what else we're going to do. We're going the make sure we get an energy policy to my desk. I proposed a plan over 2 years ago that encourages conservation, that uses renewables like ethanol and biodiesel, that uses technologies for clean coal technology, that says we can explore for environmentally friendly ways for natural gas, a plan that recognizes we must become less dependent on foreign sources of energy.

In order to make sure this economy grows, we've got to keep opening up markets for Minnesota farmers and entrepreneurs and small-business owners. See, the tendency in American politics is to fall prey to economic isolationism. That would be bad for our workers. It would be bad for our consumers. The Presidents before me have opened up our markets, and I'm happy to open up markets too. It's in our consumers' interests. If you have more products to choose from, you're likely to get that which you want at a better price and better quality. See, it's in your interests. And so I'm saying to places like China, "You treat us the way we treat you. You open up your markets just like we've opened up our markets." And I say that with confidence because we can compete with anybody, anytime, anywhere, so long as the rules are fair.

And I want our soybean growers here in Minnesota to understand that one reason your prices are such that you can make a living is because you're selling soybeans to China. See, they're using your soybeans. It's essential you have a President who understands what free trade means to people from all sectors of our economy.

I'll tell you what else we need to do to make sure jobs stay here in America and the entrepreneurial spirit is strong. We've got to do something about the regulations that plague our business and job creators and something about these frivolous lawsuits that are making it hard for small businesses to expand their businesses.

To keep jobs here, we've got to be wise about how we spend your money and keep your taxes low. And taxes are an issue in this campaign. See, I'm running against a fellow who has promised $2.2 trillion worth of new spending. That's a lot. That's with a "T." [Laughter] That's a lot even for a Senator from Massachusetts. [Laughter] So they asked him, "How are you going to pay for it? How are you going to pay for it?" He said, "Oh, we'll just tax the rich, raise the top two brackets." Let me tell you at least two things—three things wrong with that. First of all, you got to believe him that he's going to tax. You know, he's one of the first—one of the few Presidential candidates to ever promise raising taxes in a Presidential campaign, and that's a promise most politicians are happy to keep.

First of all, you can't pay for $2.2 trillion worth of new spending by raising the top two brackets. You fall short by about $800 billion. There's a gap between what is promised and what is deliverable. Actually, it's 1.4 trillion you fall short, beg your pardon, and so guess who usually gets to fill that gap between what is promised and what is capable of delivering? You do.

Secondly, when you're taxing the rich, you're taxing about 900,000 small-business owners. Most small businesses are Subchapter S corporations or limited partnerships. And they pay tax at the individual income-tax level, which means you're running up the taxes on the job creators. We're about to talk to somebody, you know, one of these people who are going to be affected by the top two brackets.

Thirdly, the rich hire lawyers and accountants for a reason: to stick you with the tab. We're not going to let him tax you, because we're going to win Minnesota on November the 2d and carry this country.

Let me talk about a couple of other issues. I want to talk about health issues. This is a good place to talk about health. Mayo Clinic, one of the great clinics—we always want our country to be on the leading edge of change when it comes to providing good medicine for our people. My mother keeps telling me what to say when it comes to Mayo Clinic. [*Laughter*]

So there is a fundamental difference of philosophy in this campaign about health care. I believe health care ought to be a commonsense approach, not one that increases the scope and power of the Federal Government. We ought to be worried about a health care system that moves people from private care to federally controlled health care because what that will lead to is rationing, bad decisionmaking. It will take the consumer totally out of the equation. Other countries have tried centralized health care, and it has failed. And the health care systems have slowly but surely declined in the quality of health care.

I have a different—and make no mistake about it, my opponent's program does that. He actually—he said in the camera at one of our debates, he said, "My plan is not a Government plan." You know, I could barely contain myself. [*Laughter*] I understand the nature of his plan. When you increase Medicare—Medicaid availability, it provides an excuse for small-business owners to no longer provide insurance for their employees because the Government will pick it up. See, 8 out of 10 new people subscribed to health care under his plan would end up on Federal rolls. That is an increase in the role of the Federal Government.

Here's a different approach. One, we'll make sure health care is available. We'll take care of the poor and the indigent through community health centers. Every poor county in America ought to have a community health center, places where people can get good preventative and primary care. It is a good use of your money to make sure the poor and the indigent get good primary and preventative care. We'll make sure our programs for children in low-income families are fully subscribed to. But to make sure health care is afford-

able—that's what we need to address, the cost of health care.

Part of the reason health care costs are high is because third-party payers make the payment. There is no market discipline. There is no real demand—focus on demand in health care. That's why I believe in health savings accounts, tax-free plans to allow the decisionmaker to be you, a plan you own, a plan you carry with you from job to job, a plan in which you're totally in charge of.

Secondly, health care costs are up because of lawsuits. Make no mistake about it, junk lawsuits against our doctors are running up the cost of your health care. They're making it hard for small businesses to be able to afford insurance, and they're running good doctors out of practice. You cannot be pro-doctor, pro-patient, and pro-trial-lawyer at the same time. You have to choose. You have to choose. My opponent made his choice, and he put a personal injury trial lawyer on the ticket. I made my choice. I am standing with our doctors and our patients. I support medical liability reform—now.

Two other ways to address the cost of health care: One is speed up generic drugs to the market. Plus, I support these Minnesota Congressman and Senator's idea of importation of drugs from Canada, so long as it's safe. We want you to take drugs that cure you, not harm you. I have a duty—it's easy for some in Congress to be calling for importation. I'm just going to make sure, before they come in, we know exactly what we're importing. You want to make sure that that which comes in from Canada is actually manufactured in Canada. You don't want to be buying something from a Third World country. And so we want to be safe. We want to make sure we do the right thing.

And fourthly, medicine, in all due respect, is like going back to the horse-and-buggy days when it comes to the use of information technology. I mean, you know, there's a lot of files that are handwritten still, and you can't even read a doctor's writing most of the time. [*Laughter*] So I believe in electronic medical records. I know we need to have a common language all across the medical field. They estimate that over 20 to 30 percent of the costs can be wrung out of the system with the proper use of information technology. This is an exciting new era available for medicine. You just need a President who understands how to address the root causes of costs going up. And that's how you avoid federalizing health care, and that's how you put in place commonsense policies that makes sure the decisions are always made by doctor and patient, not by officials in our Nation's Capital.

A couple of other points I want to make very quickly—kind of getting wound up here—[*laughter*]—you notice the temperature in the room is rising. [*Laughter*] One, education is vital to make sure that we have a hopeful America. The No Child Left Behind Act that we passed is a great piece of legislation. It challenges the soft bigotry of low expectations. It increases Federal spending but in return says, "Show us. Measure and let us know whether a child can read and write and add and subtract." And we've got to find that out early. We cannot have a system that just simply shuffles kids through the system and hope we get it right. We need to know if we're getting it right. You can't solve a problem unless you've diagnosed it, and now we're diagnosing problems early. We're providing extra money for at-risk students and students who need extra help.

And there's an achievement gap closing in America, and it's vital. You know how we know? We measure. We can determine whether a child can read. And reading scores are going up for kids that have generally been shuffled through the school system. And we're not going to go back to the days of mediocrity and low standards. We're making progress, and America is better off for it.

So we're going to talk about education today. See, one of the things we've got to do is make sure education is not only strong for our kids; we've got to make sure education is available for all our citizens, because in a changing world—and the world is changing—the jobs of the 21st century oftentimes require a new skill set. For those of you involved with medicine know exactly what I'm talking about. Medicine is changing, and there constantly needs to be an upgrading of skills. And a great place to do that and a wonderful way to make sure people have got the skills necessary to fill the jobs of the 21st century is through our community college system. I'm a big backer of the community college system, and we're going to talk to a community college student here today about what it means to go back to school.

One other thing I want to talk about right quick, and that is Social Security. A President must solve problems, must confront problems, not pass them on to future Presidents or future generations. We have a problem in Social Security, and that is, when baby boomers like me retire, younger workers are going to have trouble paying for us and, therefore, have money available when they retire. That's just the facts.

Now, first, I want to address kind of the typical old-style, stale politics, and that is the politics of scare tactics towards Social Security. When I ran in 2000, I suspect here in the State of Minnesota—I know in other States—they ran ads saying, "If George W. gets elected, the seniors will not get their checks." I want you to remind your friends and neighbors, the seniors got their checks. Nobody's going to take away the Social Security check from our seniors. The fund has got enough money, and baby boomers like me are in good shape.

But we need to worry about our children and our grandchildren when it comes to Social Security. Social Security will not be there when they need it if we don't think differently. That is why I believe younger workers ought to be able to take some of their payroll taxes and set up a personal savings account, a personal savings account that will earn a better rate of return than the current Social Security trust, an account they call their own, an account the Government cannot take away.

You know, I like to tell people that no one ever washes a rental car. [*Laughter*] There's wisdom in that. If you own something, you tend to wash it. If you own something, you have a vital stake in the future of our country. You know, one of the most heartwarming things about our society is when I hear people own something. They've started their own business, for example, or own their own home. We're going to talk to an owner right here, and that would be Jon Eckhoff.

Jon, thank you for coming. Please tell us the name of your company, and are you the owner? And if you're the owner, how did you end up owning it? [*Laughter*]

Jon Eckhoff. Thank you for the introduction. Thank you. I am the owner of Venture Computer Systems, along with three other people, two of which are in the audience. And how did it get started? Well, that could be a complex story, but let's just say that I came to Rochester 16 years ago to work for the Mayo Clinic, a dream job for a kid from Iowa. And it was a great job, but I was always restless. I always wanted to do something on my own. So in an unfinished corner of my basement, I put up a whiteboard, and I bought a computer, and I started meeting. Some of the people in this room probably were in my basement in the beginning of Venture Computer Systems.

The President. It's a classic, right, the old kitchen table, the garage, in this case, the basement. [*Laughter*] That's what happens. Don't you love to live in a country where old Jon says, you know, "I've got a dream. I want to start my own business"? The role of the Government is to create an environment.

What do you do? I mean, like, here's your chance to sell some products. [*Laughter*] It's a marketing opportunity.

Mr. Eckhoff. Let's take it. Well, Venture Computer Systems sells computers, network security products to businesses like the ones that people in this room own. In fact, I recognize many of my customers, and if you're not my customer, give me a call after the—[*laughter*].

The President. No wonder he's successful. He gets on the President's time and sells some products. [*Laughter*]

So, let me ask you something. How many employees you got?

Mr. Eckhoff. We have 30 employees in Venture Computer Systems.

The President. See, that's classic small business, isn't it? Thirty employees. Did you hire any this year?

Mr. Eckhoff. We're going to add three more before December 31st.

The President. Three more? For the year?

Mr. Eckhoff. For the year.

The President. Yes, see, that's what's happening all across America, by the way. When the entrepreneurial spirit is strong, when people are upbeat about the future, they hire people. Do you realize 70 percent of new jobs in America are created by small businesses like Jon's—70 percent. The job creators in America are the small-business owners of America. So let me ask you something. How are you organized legally?

Mr. Eckhoff. Well, we're an S corporation.

The President. S corp. See, now let me explain what that means. That's legalese. I'm not even a lawyer. Anyway—but I do understand facts. If you're an S corporation, they pay tax at the individual income-tax level. So when you hear my opponent say, "Oh, we're just going to tax the rich"— that means anybody that's got income over $200,000 a year—I want you to remind your friends and neighbors he's talking about taxing job creators. It makes no sense to run up the taxes on somebody like Jon and his company as they're gaining steam, as they're hiring new people. If you take money out of his treasury, it's less likely he's going to hire somebody.

Let me ask you something—one other point I want to make. Part of good tax policy encourages good decisionmaking. And so part of the tax policy we had, we said, if you invest—in other words, if you purchase something—you're going to get a little tax break for small businesses.

Did you purchase anything?

Mr. Eckhoff. Yes, sir, we did. We purchased a variety of things. We used that money to buy a new truck. A lot of people have seen the Venture Computer Systems truck in the neighborhood.

The President. Always selling. Go ahead. [*Laughter*] Go ahead, what else did you buy?

[*At this point, Mr. Eckhoff made further remarks.*]

The President. What he's doing is he's buying equipment to make his workforce more productive. And when the workforce becomes more productive, A, it means the worker is going to make more money, and B, it means he's going to stay in business. See, a open market is one where you compete, and you're constantly trying to get better. It's in the consumer's interest that he gets better. It means he gives a better product. Tax policy encouraged him to make certain decisions. He said he bought a truck. Well, remember, somebody has to make the truck. And when somebody makes the truck, it means the decision he made means that somebody is more likely to keep a job.

The tax policy we passed not only helped in a large sense; the tax policy we passed made the entrepreneurial spirit shine even more brightly in America. And more and more people are starting their small businesses today, which is great for our country.

Michele Clements is with us. All right, Michele, what did you used to do?

Michele Clements. I was a full-time employee at a local electronics manufacturing plant here in Rochester. And in February of 2003, they laid us all off and sent our jobs overseas.

The President. Right. So this is the classic case of somebody being affected by jobs going overseas. The fundamental question is what does society do about it without harming our markets and our economy? What do you do about it? Well, the first thing you do about it is you make sure this is the best place in the world to do business. You make sure it's the best place for jobs to continue to grow here. You make sure Jon is optimistic so he continues to grow his jobs. But also, you've got to help people.

And so what happened?

Mrs. Clements. Well, after we found out we were losing our jobs, we—shortly after that we found out we qualified for retraining programs through the Dislocated Worker Program, if we wanted to go back to school to further our education and get back into the workforce.

The President. Right. Right. And so, like, you hadn't been in school for a while. I'm not going to ask you how long. [*Laughter*]

Mrs. Clements. It's been a while.

The President. It's been a while. You had a husband and two daughters, been a mom and everything, and you go back to school. Where?

Mrs. Clements. Right here at RCTC in Rochester.

The President. Yes, very good. So what was it like? I mean, I'm sure people are listening out there who wonder whether or not they could go back to school at this point in their life. Was it as tough as you thought?

Mrs. Clements. It was a big step.

The President. Yes.

Mrs. Clements. It was not easy to go back, but it was well worth it. I'm in the law enforcement program here at RCTC. Law enforcement was something that I always wanted to get into, but because of financial and family commitments, I wasn't able to do so. And if it wasn't for the funding I received through the retraining program——

The President. Trade adjustment assistance, retraining programs—listen, the Federal Government has got ample money to help people go back to school. [*Applause*] Don't clap for me; clap for her. She's the one who made the decision to go back to school. Yes, we can't pass a law that says somebody has got to want to improve themselves. But the role of Government is to say, "Here's an opportunity. Here's a chance."

And so, you're now doing something— you're being trained for something you've always wanted to do, law enforcement. Well, it's a noble profession. Thank you for doing it.

And secondly, what's interesting is, I asked her—kind of none of my business, but you know, anyway—I asked her anyway, "Are you going to make more money?"

Mrs. Clements. Yes, sir, hopefully at least 50 percent more than what I was making at the plant.

The President. Yes, listen to that. I want everybody to hear that. With a little education—in other words, improving skill sets, you make more money. By going back to a community college, with Government help, you become a more productive worker. And when you become a more productive worker, your wage goes up. And her wage went up.

Let me tell you something else interesting. You know, when we cut the taxes, we cut them for everybody who paid taxes. I was one—I'm a fellow who believes, if you pay taxes, you ought to get relief. We ought not to try to pick and choose winners when it comes to tax relief. But we also helped our families. We raised the child credit to $1,000 a child. We reduced the penalty on marriage. The code ought to encourage marriage, not discourage marriage.

And this family saved $1,700 a year in tax relief, see, and the fundamental question in this campaign is who can spend the $1,700 better, this family or the Government? I believe this family can spend their money better.

Good job. Thank you.

The homeownership rate in America is an alltime high. More and more people from all walks of life are owning their homes for the first time. And Jill Wooten is with us. She is a first-time homeowner. First of all, you work.

Jill Wooten. I work. I'm a teacher at Gage Elementary School—love it.

The President. Fabulous. Thank you for teaching. Husband, Jesse.

Mrs. Wooten. He's the cute guy in the front row right there. [*Laughter*]

The President. Having trouble finding one. Oh, there he is. [*Laughter*] I agree, yes. It's an election year—anyway. [*Laughter*] We just embarrassed Jesse——

Mrs. Wooten. I know. He's beet-red. Shouldn't I be the one red up here?

The President. No, you're doing great. So why did you all decide to buy a home?

[*Mrs. Wooten made further remarks.*]

The President. Isn't that wonderful to hear? You know, there's nothing better in a society, where more and more people open up the door where they live and say, "Welcome to my home. Welcome to my piece of property." If you own something, you care a lot about a lot of things, like your future. That's why we want to have people own their own savings account— health savings account, so they can manage their health care, or own a piece of their retirement, if you're a younger American, or own your own business or own your own home. A hopeful America is one in which ownership is spread throughout all our society.

We've got good plans to help people own their home. By the way, this family will save $2,500 in 2004 on tax relief. You know, you hear this—it matters. The tax relief helps. It helps the American family be able to realize their dreams like owning their own home. And by the way, my opponent voted against every one of these tax reliefs that I talked about—voted no when American families were on the line, voted no when it came to raising the child credit, voted no when it came to reducing the marriage penalty.

Audience members. Boo-o-o!

The President. There is a big difference in this campaign. Make no mistake about it. Make no mistake about it. There is a different philosophy, a different attitude. He trusts Government. I trust the people.

Good job. Really good job.

The platform wouldn't be complete without a farmer, Duane Alberts, Pine Shelter Farms.

Duane Alberts. That's correct.

The President. Good, yes. And you do what?

Mr. Alberts. Well, Mr. President, it's time to kill the death tax. I just want to start out that way.

The President. Well, he's got—the man's got an opinion. We've got it—it's on its way to extinction. Unfortunately, it pops back up. It's going to be an odd year in 2010. You can imagine people—I mean, it goes away in 2010; it pops back up in 2011. So people are going to have some weird choices in 2010 when it comes to the death tax, but never mind. [*Laughter*] It's a little morbid.

So why are you that concerned about it? Here's a farmer, a dairy farmer, got a lot of money tied up in inventory and land.

Mr. Alberts. That's correct. I farm in— I'm a fifth-generation farmer, a fifth-generation dairy farmer. Some of the sixth generation is sitting out here in the second row.

The President. Let me guess. Oh, yeah.

Mr. Alberts. I farm in partnership with my—in partnership with my father and my two brothers, and we milk 550 cows. Now, I used to have——

The President. By hand?

Mr. Alberts. Not anymore. Not anymore. [*Laughter*] You could ask my father about that, I suppose.

The President. Good. I just wanted to tell you there's a new kind of way to milk if you do.

Mr. Alberts. But we—but I used to have another partner. My uncle passed away 7 years ago, 7 years ago now. It's hard to believe it's been that long. But while my Uncle Myron was alive, he paid all the taxes, income taxes, Social Security taxes, payroll taxes, property taxes, sale taxes. He was loaded with taxes. And when he died, the estate tax bill came, and that came to $1,000 per cow.

The President. See, you can understand why people who farm the land or small-business owners that have got their assets— I mean, their money tied up in assets are worried about a tax that causes them to have to liquidate a herd to pay for it, I guess is what you're saying.

Mr. Alberts. That's right. That's right. It's hard to believe that a tax can be so huge, actually, that farmers, ranchers, and small-business men have to buy insurance to pay for it.

The President. Yes. And so what we've done is we've put the death tax on its way to extinction. But I'm telling you, it's coming back, unless you have the right President. I think we need to get rid of the death tax forever—once and for all.

People talk about simplifying the code. By the way, the Tax Code needs to be simplified. It's a complicated mess. A major portion of the Tax Code is the death tax. Once we get rid of that once and for all, it will help simplify the code. We need to do more work, don't get me wrong. But I want to thank you for sharing.

People have got to understand the death tax hurts our farmers, hurts our small-businessmen. People say we've got to protect the family farmer. You can't be a family farmer if you have to liquidate your farm in order to pay the death tax.

You got something else you want to say? Good job.

Mr. Alberts. I do want to stress that my uncle did his estate tax planning. He did everything right. He bought the insurance, but the annual premiums were $25,000 a year.

The President. Yes, see, when you get rid of the death tax, you don't have to worry about lawyers, and you don't have to worry about premiums and insurance. All you've got to worry about is who you want to leave your property to. And that is a fundamental American right. You ought to be able to leave your property to whoever you want to leave your property to. Thank you, sir.

I've got something else on my mind—two other things on my mind. I told you it's a changing world. Some things don't change, the values we try to live by, courage, compassion, reverence, and integrity. Our basic beliefs don't change. We stand for a culture of life in which every person matters and every being counts. We stand for marriage and family, which are the foundations of our society. And we stand for the appointment of Federal judges who know the difference between personal opinion and the strict interpretation of the law.

Let me talk about the security of our country right quick. Please be seated. This may take a little longer than you hope. [*Laughter*] The most solemn duty of the American President is to protect you, is to protect the American people. In this dangerous world—in this dangerous world, if our country shows uncertainty or weakness, this world will drift toward tragedy. This will not happen on my watch.

I want to share with you some of the lessons of September the 11th. First, we face an enemy that has no conscience. They are coldblooded killers. They would just as soon kill in a schoolhouse as they would bomb the Twin Towers with our airplanes. Therefore, we can never negotiate with them. We can never hope for the best. We can never say, "Oh, gosh, well, maybe if we change our behavior, they'll change their ways." The only way to deal with them is to find them and bring them to justice before they hurt us again.

Secondly, we are fighting a different kind of war, but it is a—this war requires a complete strategy. Not only will we continue bringing Al Qaida and like terrorists to justice—and by the way, three-quarters of them have been brought to justice, and we're after the rest of them—but we also must make it clear to others that if you harbor a terrorist, you're just as guilty as the terrorist. And when the President says something, I think the President must speak clearly and mean what he says in order to keep the peace.

And so I meant what I said to the Taliban who were harboring Al Qaida. Remember, thousands of people had been trained in Afghanistan under the—with the consent of the Taliban. And so I said to the Taliban, "Get rid of Al Qaida. Join the community of free nations." They ignored our demand, and as a result of the brave actions of the United States military, the Taliban have been routed from power, Al Qaida training camps were destroyed, and 25 million people lived in a free society.

I want our youngsters here to think about what has happened over a course of 3½ years. Something amazing has taken place, truly amazing, in Afghanistan. You know, it wasn't all that young ago that young girls couldn't go to school. Two-and-a-half years is really nothing in the march of history, when you think about it. And their mothers were taken into the public squares and whipped if they didn't toe the ideological line of the Taliban, those ideologues of hate. Because we acted in our self-interest, because we upheld doctrine, the people of Afghanistan went to the polls to vote for a President. The first voter was a 19-year-old woman. Think about that.

There weren't a lot of people who believed 3½ years ago that Afghanistan would ever be free, but Afghanistan is free now.

And it's in our interests that they are free. Not only did we uphold doctrine, but a free society is one that is now an ally in the war on terror. A free society sets such a hopeful example for others. Free societies do not export terror. Free societies help defeat the hopelessness that enables terrorists to breed. Free societies equal peaceful societies.

The second—the third lesson is that when we see a threat, we must deal with it before it fully materializes. Saddam Hussein was a threat. He was a threat because he hated America. He was a threat because he was shooting missiles at American airplanes. He was a threat because he harbored terrorists. He was a threat because he invaded his neighbors. He was a threat because he had used weapons of mass destruction. He was a threat.

Now, we didn't find the stockpiles we all thought were there. That includes me and my opponent. But we did realize that he was gaming the Oil for Food Programme to get the world to turn a blind eye, to continue to weaken the sanctions so he could reconstitute his weapons programs. And the danger America faces is the nexus of terrorist organizations and weapons of mass destruction. That's a danger. It is a threat.

We cannot hope for the best in this world—in the post-September the 11th world. We must deal with every threat. Military is always the last option. That's why I went to the United Nations. I was hopeful that diplomacy would work. But the 17th resolution failed just like the first 16 resolutions. We passed the resolution, but Saddam wasn't afraid of a resolution. He wasn't worried about the United Nations or the will of the free world, because the will didn't mean anything to him in the past. And so he ignored the demands. I have a choice to make: Do I trust a madman and forget the lessons of September the 11th, or take action to defend this country? Given that choice, I will defend America every time.

And now we're—Iraq is headed toward elections. Remember the skepticism about elections in Afghanistan? I do. Well, the same skepticism exists about Iraq. Can they ever be free? Do they ever want to vote? Of course they do. People want to be free. People love the idea of a free society. And so we're headed toward elections, and there are people there who are trying to stop them. Freedom is the greatest fear these terrorists have. That's why Zarqawi is fighting—Zarqawi who had been in Afghanistan, routed out of Afghanistan when his training camp was destroyed, comes to Baghdad, gets medical help in Baghdad, working with people in northern Iraq, prior to our arrival, on poisons and chemicals, and he's now fighting to stop the advance of freedom. He's a known killer.

And this is where my opponent and I disagree. He said, after September the 11th he wasn't fundamentally changed. I mean—and it reflects in his policies. He believes that this is a war only for intelligence and law enforcement. It is a limited point of view, which is a dangerous point of view in the world in which we live. He said that Iraq is a "diversion" from the war on terror. What does he think, Zarqawi has become a peaceful citizen? Does he think Zarqawi is going to change his ways? Zarqawi wants to destroy American life. Zarqawi was plotting and planning to attack us. It is essential we defeat Zarqawi there so we don't have to face the likes of him here at home.

You cannot win a war when you don't believe we're fighting a war, and that's the problem with my opponent's policies. They're limited in view, and that would lead to a danger for America. We must use every asset at our disposal. We must fully understand the nature of the enemy. We must take threats seriously before they materialize in order to do our duty to protect the American people. If we should uncertainty or weakness, this world will drift toward tragedy. And the American people can count on me to show no uncertainty or weakness in protecting you.

A couple of other points I want to make, and then we'll get out of here. When you have troops in harm's way, we have a duty to support them. That's why I went to the Congress and asked for $87 billion of supplemental funding to support our troops in combat, really important money. I want you to remind your friends and neighbors that there were only 4 United States Senators—4 out of 100—that voted to authorize the use of force and voted against supporting our troops in combat, 2 of whom were my opponent and his runningmate.

Audience members. Boo-o-o!

The President. Voted to authorize force and wouldn't support the troops. People wonder why he made the vote. Well, I'll tell you why: Howard Dean was gaining in the Democrat primary. A Commander in Chief has got to stand on principle, not on the shifting sands of political convenience.

Audience member. Whoo!

The President. Undecided voter. [*Laughter*]

I want to share one other thing with you. I have a firm belief in the power of liberty to transform societies. At the heart of much of what I believe is this strong and unshakeable belief in the ability of freedom to change the world.

Let me share an experience with you that I've had over time as your President, and that is my relationship with the Prime Minister of Japan, Prime Minister Koizumi. He's a friend of Laura and mine, really interesting guy. I like him a lot. He's a lot of fun to be around. When I saw him at the United Nations, I said, "You know, I'm traveling our country talking about you. I hope you do not mind." He said, "No, go ahead and talk about me." I didn't ask his permission to tell you Elvis was his favorite singer, though—but anyway. [*Laughter*]

And it probably doesn't sound too unusual to you that I would say that the Prime Minister of Japan is a friend, but think about our history, our recent history. Japan was the sworn enemy of the United States of America some 60 years ago. My dad fought against the Japanese. I suspect somebody in this crowd might have fought against the Japanese. I know somebody's relative fought against the Japanese. They were the sworn enemy of the United States of America, and it was a brutal war. All war is brutal, and we suffered a lot in that war. Families were disrupted. Loved ones were lost. Hearts were broken.

And after World War II, Harry S. Truman, one of my predecessors, believed that liberty could transform an enemy into an ally. And so he set policy to say we'll help Japan become a democracy.

Now, there were a lot of skeptics in America about that, and you can understand why, about that decision. "Why would you want to help an enemy," some probably said. "How could an enemy possibly become a peaceful, self-governing nation? These people can't be a democracy," others would say. There was enormous skepticism.

But my predecessor and others had belief. And as a result of believing that liberty could transform an enemy into an ally, I now sit down at the table with my friend Prime Minister Koizumi, talking about how to keep the peace we all want, talking about how to make this troubled world a more stable, peaceful place.

Someday, an American President will be sitting down with a duly elected leader from Iraq, and they will be talking about the peace in the Middle East, and our children and our grandchildren will be better off for it.

I believe people want to live in a free society. I believe women in the Middle East want to live in freedom. I know moms and dads want to raise their children in a free and peaceful world. I believe millions plead in silence for their liberty. And I believe this not because freedom is America's gift to the world; I believe this because freedom is the Almighty God's gift to each man and woman in this world.

I'm running again because I want to make sure hope and opportunity spread throughout the land, through good economic policy, through encouraging ownership for all people in our society. I'm running again because I hold certain values dear that I think are important for this country. And I'm running again because I fully understand the risks we face, and I have a strategy to protect the American people.

We're going to win on November the 2d, with your help. May God bless you. May God bless our great country. Thank you all for coming.

NOTE: The President spoke at 12:10 p.m. in the Rochester Aviation Hangar at Rochester International Airport. In his remarks, he referred to Mary Gutknecht, wife of Representative Gilbert W. Gutknecht; Gov. Tim Pawlenty of Minnesota; former President Saddam Hussein of Iraq; senior Al Qaida associate Abu Musab Al Zarqawi; and Prime Minister Junichiro Koizumi of Japan.

Remarks in a Discussion in Eau Claire, Wisconsin
October 20, 2004

The President. Thank you all. Please be seated. Listen, thanks for coming today. It's good to be back here in Eau Claire, Wisconsin. We're getting closer and closer to voting time. I'm here to ask for your help. I saw—somebody has been helping—I saw a lot of signs up coming in. I want to thank you for putting up the signs. I know some of you are making phone calls, reminding your fellow citizen to go to the polls. I need your help. And with your help, we will carry Wisconsin and win a great victory in November.

So today I'm here to talk about reasons why I think your fellow citizens ought to put me in office for 4 more years. We're going to talk about some issues, and we've got some fellow citizens up here to help talk about the plans and policies of my administration.

Perhaps the most important reason for you to put me back in for 4 more years is so that Laura will be the First Lady for 4 more years. She sends her best. She's doing great. She was a public school librarian when I met her for the second time. The first time I ever met her, we were at San Jacinto Junior High, seventh grade,

in Midland, Texas. The second time I met her, she was a public school librarian. She said, "Fine, I'll marry you, but you have to make me a promise." I said, "What's that?" She said, "I never want to have to give a speech." [*Laughter*] Well, fortunately, she didn't hold me to that promise. [*Laughter*] She is giving a lot of speeches, and when she does, the American people see a warm, compassionate, strong First Lady.

I'm proud of my runningmate, Dick Cheney. He's doing a great job.

And I'm proud of my Cabinet Secretary for Health and Human Services; that would be former Governor Tommy Thompson. He's doing a great job. I like to tell the people of Wisconsin, you did a fine job of training him. He's a good man.

I want to thank the Redetzkes for letting us come here today, Don and Diana. I'm proud you—these are some of the products they manufacture here. I said, "How is your business doing?" He said, "Just fine." He said, "We've added 30 employees this year. We're thinking about adding more." There's an optimism around. Our policies are working. And I want to thank the

Redetzkes for letting us come and visit this important plant.

I want to thank Jack Voight, the State treasurer, for joining us today. Appreciate you being here, Mr. Treasurer. I want to thank Scott Walker from Milwaukee County. I'm proud Scott is here. I call him Scott W. I want to thank John Gard for joining us today. Speaker, where are you? Appreciate you, Speaker. Good to see you again. I've been in your State a lot, and he's been there all the time, for which I'm grateful.

I want to thank very much Dale Schultz for being here. He is a good man. I know him well. He will make a great Member of the United States Congress. And finally, Tim Michels. Good to see you, Tim—and Barbara. I know something about Barbaras. Thank you all for coming.

We've been through some challenges together in this country, really have been. And when you're out gathering up the vote, remind people about what this economy has been through. Six months prior to my arrival in Washington, the stock market was in serious decline, and that foretold a recession. And then we had some corporate scandals, and we passed tough laws, and we made it abundantly clear to people in this country that we will not tolerate dishonesty in the boardrooms of America. We expect citizens to be responsible citizens.

And then we got attacked. We got attacked. And those attacks hurt us; they really did. And we responded to those attacks with good policy. We cut the taxes, and by cutting the taxes people had more money to spend and more money to invest. When you increase consumption and increase investment, the economy tends to grow. The recession we had was one of the shallowest in American history.

Our economy has been growing at rates as fast as any in nearly 20 years. We've added 1.9 million new jobs since August of 2003. The unemployment rate is at 5.4 percent. That's the national unemployment rate—lower than the average of the 1970s, 1980s, and 1990s. And your unemployment rate in Wisconsin is 4.8 percent. Think about that. When people go to the polls, I want them to remember the people of this State are working because of good policy. Farm income is up. Homeownership rates are at an alltime high. We're moving forward. We've overcome these challenges, and we're not going to go back to the days of tax and spend.

A good economic policy means good farm policy. I told the people when I was running, I understand that we've got to have good agricultural policy in this country. And the agricultural sector of our country is doing fine, is doing well. Income is up. As a matter of fact, farm income is at a record high under my administration.

Audience member. [*Inaudible*]

The President. We're going to talk to some farmers up here, but dairy farm income is up. We're selling more and more of Wisconsin crops overseas. See, to make sure this economy continues to grow, we've got to continue to open up markets for U.S. products. It's easy to say we're going to shut down markets, but shutting down markets will hurt you. See, when you've got more products to choose from as a consumer, you're likely to get that which you want at a better price and higher quality. That's how the market works. So shutting down our markets, which would hurt you— my policy is let's open up everybody else's markets. We can compete with anybody, anytime, anywhere, so long as the playing field is level.

And farm exports are at an alltime high. We want to be using Wisconsin farm products to feed the world. If you're good at something, let's promote it, and we're really good at growing corn and soybeans.

I signed a good farm bill which is helping the agricultural sector, and part of the farm bill is the conservation title, which encourages farmers and landowners to set aside land for wildlife restoration, for land protection. We're going to talk about somebody who knows what he's talking about when it comes to good conservation policy.

I tell everybody, "If you own the land, every day is Earth Day." If you make a living off the land, the best person to look after the land is the person making a living off of it, not some bureaucrat in Washington, DC.

Keeping jobs here means good energy policy. See, we've got to become less dependent on foreign sources of energy if we expect to keep this economy growing. And I submitted a plan to the United States Congress 2 years ago, and it's stuck, of course, because of politics. But it's a plan that encourages conservation. It's a plan that uses our technologies to be able to burn coal cleanly. It says we can explore for natural gas in environmentally friendly ways. But it also recognizes the valuable contribution that ethanol and biodiesel make to the energy mix here in America. Congress needs to pass that plan. We've got to become less dependent on foreign sources of energy.

To make sure jobs stay here, we've got to have less regulations on the job creators. To make sure jobs stay here, we've got to do something about these lawsuits that are making it hard for the small businesses all across our country. You see, these lawsuits make it hard for a small business to expand. They're tending to having to fight these lawsuits off and not hiring people.

To keep jobs here, we've got to be wise about how we spend your money and keep your taxes low. Taxes are an issue. I'm running against a fellow who's promised $2.2 trillion in programs that cost—that's how much they cost the Government, 2.2 trillion. That's with a "T." That's a lot even for a Senator from Massachusetts. So they asked him how he was going to pay for it. He said, oh, he's just going to tax the rich, going to raise the top two brackets. Well, the only problem with that is it raises about 600 billion or 800 billion, depending on whose numbers you look at. In either case, it's far short of 2.2 trillion, so there's a gap. There's a gap between what he promised and how he's going to pay for

it. Guess who usually fills that gap? Yes, you do. You understand how tax policy works.

Let me tell you what else is wrong with raising the top two brackets. We're going to talk to some small-business owners. Most small businesses are Subchapter S corporations, limited liability corps. They pay tax at the individual income-tax rate. So you hear him talking about running up the taxes, taxing the rich—they're taxing the job creators.

And the third thing wrong with it, the rich hire lawyers and accountants for a reason: to slide the tab and stick you with it. We're not going to let him tax you; we're going to win Wisconsin and win on November the 2d.

Audience members. Four more years! Four more years! Four more years!

The President. Thank you. Before we get to our guests here, I want to talk about a couple of other issues. We're in a changing world. Times are changing. And in a changing world, it helps to promote an ownership society in America to bring stability into people's lives. And I told you, homeownership rates are at an alltime high. We've got policies to continue to expand that. I can't tell you how it warms my heart to know more and more Americans from all walks of life are opening up the door where they live, saying, "Welcome to my home. Welcome to my piece of property."

In order to make sure we're hopeful, we've got to promote ownership when it comes to health care accounts. See, health care is an issue in this campaign too. There is a fundamental divide.

My opponent is proposing bigger Government health care. Now, he looked in the TV cameras the other night and said no Government was involved. I could barely contain myself. [*Laughter*] I looked at the fine print of his plan. Eight out of ten get signed up to a Government health care plan. See, if you raise the Medicaid limits to 300 percent, it provides incentives for small-business owners to stop providing insurance for their employees because the Government will pay for it. And so you're shifting people from the private sector to the public policy. And Government health care programs do not work. They may sound good, but they have failed in every country that has tried them. The quality of health care will decline. There will be rationing. If you end up as a line item in the Government budget, you can rest assured there will be Government controls over your health care.

I have a different point of view. We will take care of those who cannot help themselves through community and rural health centers. Those will be places where the poor and the indigent can get primary and preventative care. That's a good use of your taxpayers' money. It's best that people get care there and not in the emergency rooms of local hospitals. We will make sure that the program for children of low-income families is fully subscribed. That makes sense.

But to make sure health care is affordable, we ought to allow small businesses to pool risk, to join together so they can buy insurance at the same discounts that big businesses get to do.

To make sure health care is affordable, we will continue to expand health savings accounts, which will enable somebody to pay a low-premium, high-deductible major medical liability policy, coupled with a tax-free savings. These health care plans will reduce the cost of health care for the average citizen or the small business. They will be a health care plan in which the decision-maker is the owner of the health care plan. They're a health care plan that you own, you control, and you can take with you from job to job throughout your entire life. This is a way to make sure health care is more affordable.

Also to make sure health care is more available and affordable, we've got to do something about the junk lawsuits that are running up the cost of medicine. See, I looked at the cost to the Federal Govern-ment on these lawsuits. Lawsuits cause doctors to have to practice defensive medicine. In other words, they're practicing medicine in anticipation of getting sued because there's so many suits, and that runs up the cost of health care. And the lawsuits run up the cost of premiums for docs, which run good docs out of business. I can't tell you the number of ob-gyns I've met who are anxious and upset by the fact that they, many times, cannot practice. And then you can imagine, if the ob-gyn can't practice, what it does to many pregnant women. It is stressful. It is not right. These lawsuits are a damage to our economy and to our society and to health care. You cannot be pro-doctor, pro-patient, and pro-personal-injury-lawyer at the same time. You have to choose. You have to choose. My opponent made his choice, and he put a personal injury lawyer on the ticket. I made my choice. I'm for medical liability reform—now.

Let me talk about one other form of ownership, and that's Social Security. See, the job of a President is to solve problems, not to pass them on to future Presidents or future generations. At least that's what I think it is. I think you come to Washington, DC—if you see a problem, you solve it as best as you can. Now, others have chosen a different attitude. They just say, "We'll pass it on and let somebody else take care of it." We have a problem with Social Security.

Now, I remember the 2000 campaign, particularly here in Wisconsin, when they told the seniors, "If old George W. gets in, you're not going to get your check." You might remember that aspect of the 2000 campaign. [*Laughter*] Well, I want you to remind your friends and neighbors of all political parties, George W. got in, and our seniors got their checks. And our seniors will continue to get their checks. The seniors have nothing to worry about when it comes to the Social Security check. Neither do baby boomers like me.

But our children and our grandchildren have got a problem because of the nature of the Social Security system. There will be more recipients than payers. More baby boomers like me retire with not enough people putting money into the system, and therefore, the system is going to be in trouble for our children and our grandchildren.

In order to make sure our children and grandchildren have got a retirement system that works when they need it, we ought to allow younger workers to set aside some of their own payroll taxes in a personal savings account they call their own, a personal savings account that will earn a better rate of return than the current Social Security trust, a personal savings account that the Federal Government can never take away.

My opponent says he's for the status quo in Social Security. I think it—I don't think that's leadership. We have a problem. In a new term, I'm going to bring Republicans and Democrats together and solve the problem.

In times of change, some things do not change—now, while I'm here, I got something else I want to say, and then I want to talk to our guests here. [Laughter] The values we try to live by don't change, courage and compassion, reverence and integrity. We stand for a culture of life in which every person matters and every being counts. [Applause] Thank you all. We stand for marriage and family, which are the foundations of our society. We stand for judges who know the difference between personal opinion and the strict interpretation of the law. Go ahead and sit down.

And we stand for the second amendment to the United States Constitution, which gives every American individual the right to bear arms. And today I'm proud that Wayne LaPierre and Chris Cox from the National Rifle Association are with us. I appreciate you all coming. They have endorsed my candidacy for President of the United States, for which I'm grateful. I also am grateful for their gun safety programs as well as their understanding that the best way to protect the American people is to firmly prosecute those who commit crimes with guns, to hold them to account, and bring them to justice.

With us today is Bill Bruins. Bill, thank you for coming. What do you do to make a living? Or do you make a living? [Laughter]

Bill Bruins. You'd have to check with my bookkeeper, my wife.

The President. That's true. [Laughter]

[At this point, Mr. Bruins made brief remarks.]

The President. By the way, they set up their farm as a limited liability corporation, which means, under Senator Kerry's plan, he's going to get a tax increase. See, he's part of the—when they raise those top two brackets, if you've got income over $200,000 a year and you're a limited liability corp or a Subchapter S corp, you're taxed. I don't think it makes any sense to be taxing our farmers right now, as they're getting ready to make some money. I'd rather have him have the money so he can expand his farm.

How are you doing? Are you making a living?

Mr. Bruins. Yes, we are. It's been a good year. It's been a good year. Milk prices are strong. Beef prices are up. And it's just really exciting, the possibilities that we're looking at, given the climate that you've created here in Wisconsin.

The President. Well, thanks. We met back there. He asked about supporting the MILC Program. I do. I'm for the extension of the MILC Program, which would help the dairy farmers here in Wisconsin.

Mr. Bruins. Absolutely. That little program that you have endorsed and have endorsed extending has already put $413 million in the pockets of dairy farmers in the State of Wisconsin.

The President. That's good, yes. Glad to help out. What else are you concerned about? I can tell you what you're concerned about because you told me, but why don't you tell the people to make it look—[*laughter*].

Mr. Bruins. Well, because of your farm bill and the conservation provisions and the countercyclical payments that are provided with it, because of your lowering the taxes, and because of your continued commitment to making agriculture better, you have made a positive difference on agriculture in the State of Wisconsin. And as president of Wisconsin Farm Bureau, the largest farm organization in the State, I am endorsing you for a second term as President of the United States.

The President. Thank you very much. I accept. Thank you, I appreciate that. Thank you all. I was hoping that would come. [*Laughter*] I'm proud to get the Farm Bureau endorsement. It means a lot. It really does. In a State where it's heavily agricultural, that's a big endorsement to get, and I'm proud to receive it. Thank you, sir.

Doug Mueller is with us. Welcome. And what do you do to make a living?

Doug Mueller. I milk cows twice a day. We have a family corporation.

The President. Hopefully not by hand. [*Laughter*]

Mr. Mueller. No, sir, not anymore.

The President. I would say there's some new technology that's come along. [*Laughter*]

Mr. Mueller. And I'm not old enough that I ever milked cows by hand when I was younger, either.

The President. You boys have got big hands, though, I'll tell you. [*Laughter*] What's on your mind? Tell me—tell the folks what's on your mind about——

Mr. Mueller. Well, I think the energy policy is one thing that really can be a benefit to agriculture and the entire economy. The use of more—more use of ethanol, biodiesel I think is great for farmers all over the country. And the use of the ethanol, cleaner emissions and everything, too, has got to be positive for the country.

The President. Yes, it is. See, it's interesting. What's happening is that we're spending money on research and development so that we can diversify away from old usage, old habits. We've got to get away from dependency upon crude oil coming in from overseas. And one way to do so is to better use ethanol and biodiesel. I mean, can you imagine someday a President sitting in the Oval Office, they come in and say, "On crops, we've got a great corn crop," and the first reaction is, "We're less dependent on foreign sources of energy." And so we're spending a lot of money on research and development to better use crops—soybeans, like biodiesel, as well as one of—in the State of the Union Address I talked about spending money to research—to develop a hydrogen-powered automobile.

I mean, technology is going to enable us to evolve away from our current energy usage. And one way to do so is through, as Doug mentioned, through the use of agricultural products. And there's more to learn, and there's more research to be done. And that's what we're promoting. But right now we're using ethanol in significant quantities, and it's helping our farmers.

What else?

Mr. Mueller. Thank you. And the death tax is an issue that is heavily on farmer and small-business owners' minds.

[*Mr. Mueller made further remarks.*]

The President. Let me talk about that right quick. It's an issue in this campaign. I suggested that the Members of the United States Senate vote to repeal the death tax forever. Of course, I couldn't get my opponent's vote. [*Laughter*] We got quite a few votes. As a matter of fact, we put the death tax on its way to extinction. The problem is it pops back up in 2011, which is going to make some interesting estate planning decisions at that point in time.

We need to get rid of the death tax totally. It's important for our small-business owners and our farmers and ranchers to get rid of the death tax forever, so a person can pass their farm on from one generation to the next without losing the farm. People talk about—if you got your assets tied up in land and inventory, in his case, cows and equipment, and you have to pay high death taxes, there's nothing to liquidate except for the farm itself, and that's unfair. I believe a person shouldn't be taxed twice, once during life and once after life. And I believe a person ought to be able to pass their assets on to whomever they want to pass it on to.

Thank you, Doug.

Mr. Mueller. Thank you.

The President. Lee Christenson is with us.

Audience member. [*Inaudible*]

The President. You got a fan base out there. [*Laughter*] I first got to know him because he tied some bass fishing flies for me. The flies did better than the fisherman. I was fishing, but I wasn't catching. [*Laughter*] He's got an interesting story to tell when it comes to preserving land.

Lee Christenson. I have a small family farm that I live on in rural Eleva, Wisconsin, just south of Eau Claire, and I took it over in 1994 from my parents. And I've converted that farm from a dairy farm into kind of a wildlife preserve, where I've utilized a lot of the Government programs that you've helped us get going. The CRP program is just the greatest program in the world.

The President. Conservation Reserve Program.

Mr. Christenson. Yes, Conservation Reserve Program. And that program allows us to take the real highly erodible land, the steep lands that are marginal farmlands, and preserve them by putting them into trees, into prairie plantings, and into solid vegetative cover that keeps our streams a lot cleaner. And I've been able to get a WHIP, which is the Wildlife Habitat Improvement grant; EQUIP, which is the Environmental Quality Incentive Program

grant through the Government; all sorts of assistance, technical assistance from the Fish and Wildlife Service. In fact, on our farm, we've taken the ditches, plugged the ditches, pulled all the tiles out of the prior converted farm fields that historically were wetlands at one time, and now we've created, just on our little farm, over 15 acres of wetlands.

So, you know, that's great that you do that, and we're able to turn the tides and create wetlands, instead of having lost them in the past.

The President. Yes, see, one of the—we used to have a policy of no new net loss—no net loss. How could you have a new net loss—no net loss of wetlands. I've now changed that policy to an increase in the number of wetlands all across the country to 3 million acres. Here's part of the way we're able to do so.

[*Mr. Christenson made further remarks.*]

The President. See, good environmental policy doesn't mean you have to be a lawyer in Washington, DC. Good environmental policy brings conservation groups together, brings hunting and fishing groups together, brings local community together, brings local environments into play, brings farmers into play. It's a collaborative effort, so we all work together to achieve national goals such as better air, cleaner water, and more wildlife preserve areas. And we're doing that. We're making very solid progress with a commonsense way of approaching environmental issues.

[*Mr. Christenson made further remarks.*]

The President. All right, I want to talk about one other thing. Thank you, sir. He doesn't hunt and fish all the time. You actually have a business.

Mr. Christenson. Yes, I forgot about that. [*Laughter*]

The President. What do you do?

Mr. Christenson. I have fun on the farm making wetlands and habitat and all that stuff, but I have to pay the bills. So I have a small Subchapter S corporation with about 50 employees, and we collect deer hides all across the United States and export them to China. So we, you know, we're bringing some money back to the United States. And with these great tax breaks that we've had in the last few years, we've been able to buy more semis, more forklifts. We've put a lot of good people to work. We've hired more people. And the interest rates—my gosh, just look at what the interest rates have been the last few years. They've really, really helped us by being able to expand our credit lines and do a lot of beneficial things for business.

The President. See, the tax policy we passed, I want you to remember what it was, which my opponent voted against every aspect of the tax policy. We raised the child credit to help people's families. We reduced the marriage penalty. We believe we ought to encourage marriage, not discourage marriage through the Tax Code.

We said, "If you pay tax, you ought to get relief," instead of trying to pick and choose winners in the Tax Code. But we also provided incentives for small businesses to invest. If you invest as a small business, there is a—there's a benefit. You heard him say he bought forklifts. Good tax policy encourages certain behavior, and one of the behaviors we're trying to encourage is for people to invest more and to spend money, to spend capital, because when he buys a forklift, somebody has got to make the forklift. When somebody is making the forklift, it means somebody is going to get work. That's how the economy works. It ripples throughout the economy.

He says he's a Subchapter S corporation. He's adding jobs. It is bad policy to tax the job creators. Do you realize 70 percent of new jobs in America are created by small businesses just like this guy's? And my opponent, in order to pay for his promises, is, at the minimum, going to run up the taxes on about 900,000 Subchapter S and

LLC corporations, going to tax the job creators. That is lousy economic policy.

Let me talk about one other aspect of this campaign in your life, and that is how to make sure we keep America secure. The most solemn responsibility of the American President is to protect the American people. If we show uncertainty or weakness in this decade, this world of ours will drift toward tragedy. That's not going to happen on my watch.

I understand the world in which we live. This is an important issue in this campaign. Let me tell you some of the lessons I have learned about the post-September the 11th world in which we live. The first lesson is, we face an enemy that is ruthless and has no conscience. They will kill just like that, whether it be in airplanes on the World Trade Center or in a schoolhouse in the Caucasus region of the world. That's what they'll do, and therefore, you cannot negotiate with these people. You cannot hope for the best with these people. You can't say, "Well, oh, gosh, we'll change the way we conduct foreign policy and hope they change their ways." The only way to deal with them is to find them and bring them to justice before they hurt us again.

Secondly, this is a different kind of war than we're used to, and therefore, it's important to think differently about how to protect the American people. One way to do so is to make it very clear that if a country harbors a terrorist, they're just as guilty as the terrorist. And when the President says something, it is important that the President speak clearly, so everybody understands, and mean what he says.

And I meant what I said to the Taliban in Afghanistan. See, they were the ones harboring Al Qaida. Thousands of people were trained there. It's kind of the classic case of the host and the parasite—the Al Qaida was the parasite, and the host was becoming weaker and weaker and—in the sense that Al Qaida had free will, doing what they wanted to do inside the country. There was no restrictions whatsoever. And they ignored our demands until the Taliban no longer is in power. We took them out of power, thanks to a great United States military.

I want the youngsters here to understand what has taken place. It's a phenomenal moment in history, phenomenal. See, it wasn't all that long ago—3½ years ago is hardly anything in the march of history— that the people in Afghanistan were living under a brutal reign of people whose vision is so dark and dim that it's hard for Americans to comprehend. And when you hear me talk about the ideologues of hate, I'm talking about the Taliban and the people like Al Qaida. Young girls were not allowed to go to school. See, that's their vision of the world. And if their moms didn't toe the line, they were taken into the public square and whipped, in some cases killed in the sports stadium. These people were grim.

But because we acted in our own self-interest, because we acted to uphold doctrine and make this world a safer place and to protect the American people, millions of Afghan citizens went to the polls to vote for a President of their country. The first voter was a 19-year-old woman at the polls. It's amazing. Because we acted in our self-interest, the poor people living in that country have been liberated from the clutches. They no longer live in darkness. They live in light, because freedom is on the march.

And that's important for our long-term security. It's important because free societies are peaceful societies. A free society will become an ally in the war on terror. A free society will set a incredibly hopeful example for others who long for freedom.

Thirdly, when we see a threat, we've got to deal with it. You know, we used to think oceans could protect us. We'd see a threat overseas, and if we didn't deal with it, it could be okay because it wouldn't come home to hurt us. That all changed on September the 11th.

I saw a threat with Saddam Hussein. I saw a threat because he was a sworn enemy of the United States. I saw a threat because we had been at war with him. I saw a threat because he invaded his neighborhood. I saw a threat because he was shooting missiles at our airplanes who were trying to enforce the world's sanctions. I saw a threat—he paid suicide bombers; he harbored Abu Nidal and Abu Abbas. Terrorist Zarqawi was in and out of his country. I saw a threat because he had used weapons of mass destruction. Saddam Hussein was a threat.

The Congress looked at the same intelligence I looked at and concluded he was a threat. My opponent looked at the very same intelligence, the very same data, and concluded that Saddam Hussein was a threat and voted to authorize his removal. Now, before the President ever commits troops into harm's way—listen, I understand the consequences. To commit our troops is the last option for me. To put somebody in harm's way is the very last choice, not the first, second, or third. It is the last. And so I went to the United Nations in hopes that diplomacy would solve the threat. And as—they passed a resolution 15 to nothing, and Saddam Hussein just ignored it, just like he had done 16 different resolutions.

You know, we didn't find the stockpiles we thought we found—that we thought we would find, that everybody thought we'd find. But we did find that he had the capability to restart a weapons programs—he still hated us—that he was using the Oil for Food Programme to game the system, to get the world to look the other way, to get rid of the sanctions so he could restart his programs. The biggest danger we face is a terrorist network ending up with weapons of mass destruction. Knowing what I know today, I would have made the same decision. [*Applause*] Thank you.

My opponent was recently interviewed, and he said September the 11th, in quotes, his words, "did not change me much at all." See, and it's reflected in his attitude and his policies. He says, "Well, this is just a intelligence and law enforcement matter." No, this is a matter that requires all the assets of the United States of America in order to protect you.

He said that Iraq is a "diversion" from the war on terror. That's a fundamental misunderstanding of the nature of the world in which we live, and it's a dangerous misunderstanding. Mr. Zarqawi, who is fighting us in Iraq, was in Afghanistan, in terror training camps. He then got run out of Afghanistan because of us and moved to Iraq. He then was working with a poisons factory in northern Iraq. And now we've got him on the run inside of Iraq, and he's fighting us. And he says this is a diversion? Does he think if we weren't in Iraq that Mr. Zarqawi would become a peaceful citizen of the world? [*Laughter*] He's a dangerous man. He hates what we stand for. He intends to inflict harm. It is best we defeat Zarqawi in Iraq so we do not have to face him here at home.

You cannot win a war when you don't believe we're fighting one, and that's my opponent. The most solemn duty of the American President is to protect the American people. If we show uncertainty or weakness in this decade, the world will drift toward tragedy. It's not going to happen on my watch.

The third lesson—fourth lesson is when we put somebody in harm's way, they deserve the full support of our Government. And that's why I went to the United States Congress and asked for $87 billion of very important funding, funding to support our troops in combat. And we received great support, strong bipartisan support. I want you to tell your friends and neighbors of this startling statistic. Of the 100 Members of the United States Senate, only 4 voted to authorize the use of force and then did not vote for the funding to support the troops in combat, 2 of whom are my opponent and his runningmate.

Audience members. Boo-o-o!

The President. They asked him, they said, "How did you make that vote?" He said, "Well, I actually did vote for the $87 billion, right before I voted against it." It may be the most famous quote of the 2004 campaign. They then kept pressing him and pressing him, and he finally said, "The whole thing is a complicated matter." There is nothing complicated about supporting the men and women who wear the United States uniform in harm's way. [*Applause*] Thank you all.

I want to thank the family members of our military who are here. I want to thank the veterans who are here who have set such a great example for those who wear the uniform.

I want to share one more thing with you that I think is important for you to know about me. I believe in the power of liberty to transform societies. Let me tell you what I mean by that. Perhaps an example is the best way to make my point. Laura and I have a great friend in Prime Minister Koizumi of Japan. We like him. He's a fun guy to be around. He's a good friend. I saw him in New York at the United Nations in early September. I said, "You know, I'm talking about you when I get out there on the campaign trail. I hope you don't mind." He said, "Fine, go ahead and talk about me." I didn't ask him permission to tell you what I'm about to tell you, and that is, Elvis is his favorite singer—truthfully—[*laughter*]—and "High Noon" is his favorite movie. [*Laughter*]

Anyway, so, you know, it doesn't sound that—must not sound—to some it probably doesn't sound that profound that the Prime Minister of Japan and I are friends. But remember this part of history: 60 years ago, they were the sworn enemy of the United States of America. We were at war with the Japanese. And a lot of relatives of yours, I'm confident, fought in that war. My dad did, and other dads and granddads did as well. And it was a tough war, and we lost a lot of folks.

Yet, after we won the war, President Harry S. Truman believed in the power of liberty to transform an enemy into an ally. That's what he believed. So did a lot of other Americans. A lot of other Americans didn't agree with him, though. Why help the enemy? And the enemy couldn't become a democracy. You know, there was a lot of excuses and a lot of pessimism about the helping the Japanese. But fortunately, they stuck to it. Japan became a democracy. And today I sit down at the table with Prime Minister Koizumi, talking about how to keep the peace we all want, talking about keeping the peace.

Someday, an American President will be sitting down with the duly elected leader from Iraq, talking about the peace in the greater Middle East, and our children and our grandchildren will be better off for it.

I believe people in the Middle East want to live in freedom. That's what I believe. The people of Afghanistan showed what freedom can mean. Do you realize women stood in line for hours waiting to vote, after having lived in a society where they had no rights. And they stood in line to vote, even though the Taliban were threatening them with death and destruction. People want to be free. I believe women in the greater Middle East want to live in a free society. I believe moms and dads want to raise their children in a free and peaceful world. I believe all these things because freedom is not America's gift to the world; freedom is the Almighty God's gift to each man and woman in this world.

It's the last time I'm going to be in Eau Claire before the election, but I do want to thank you for coming. And when I campaigned in your State in 2000, I said if you gave me a chance to serve, I would uphold the honor and the dignity of the office to which I had been elected. With your help, we will carry Wisconsin, and I will do so for 4 more years.

God bless. Thank you all for coming. Thank you for coming.

NOTE: The President spoke at 2:49 p.m. at J&D Manufacturing. In his remarks, he referred to Don and Diana Redetzke, founders, J&D Manufacturing; Milwaukee County Executive Scott K. Walker; John Gard, speaker, Wisconsin State Assembly; Dale Schultz, candidate in Wisconsin's Third Congressional District; Tim Michels, senatorial candidate in Wisconsin, and his wife, Barbara; Wayne LaPierre, Jr., executive vice president and chief executive officer, and Chris W. Cox, Institute for Legislative Action executive director, National Rifle Association; former President Saddam Hussein of Iraq; senior Al Qaida associate Abu Musab Al Zarqawi; and Prime Minister Junichiro Koizumi of Japan.

Statement on Signing the Belarus Democracy Act of 2004
October 20, 2004

The Belarus Democracy Act of 2004, which I signed into law earlier today, will help the cause of freedom in Belarus. This bipartisan legislation demonstrates America's deep concern over events in Belarus and a commitment to sustain those Belarusians who must labor in the shadows to return freedom to their country.

At a time when freedom is advancing around the world, Aleksandr Lukashenko and his Government are turning Belarus into a regime of repression in the heart of Europe, its Government isolated from its neighbors and its people isolated from each other. We will work with our allies and partners to assist those seeking to return Belarus to its rightful place among the Euro-Atlantic community of democracies. There is no place in a Europe whole and free for a regime of this kind.

On October 17, Mr. Lukashenko claimed victory for referendum results that swept away constitutional limits on his term in office. The referendum campaign and concurrent Parliamentary elections were conducted in a climate of abuse and fear. OSCE and other observers have determined that this victory was achieved by fraudulent means.

These actions are the latest in a series of measures designed to stifle independent voices within Belarus. Since 2001, Belarusian authorities have systematically repressed independent media, trade unions, civic organizations, and religious congregations. The Lukashenka regime has repeatedly responded to the peaceful expression of opposition with beatings, arrests and, in a number of cases, the disappearance of opposition leaders.

The Belarus Democracy Act will help us support those within Belarus who are working toward democracy. We welcome this legislation as a means to bolster friends of freedom and to nurture the growth of democratic values, habits, and institutions within Belarus. The fate of Belarus will rest not with a dictator, but with the students, trade unionists, civic and religious leaders, journalists, and all citizens of Belarus claiming freedom for their nation.

NOTE: H.R. 854, approved October 20, was assigned Public Law No. 108–347.

Remarks in Downingtown, Pennsylvania
October 21, 2004

The President. Thank you all for coming. I appreciate you all being here. Thanks for coming. Thanks for coming. I appreciate such a warm welcome. I'm proud to be back in Chester County, Pennsylvania. I'm here to ask for your help. We're less than two weeks away, when the people get to go express their opinion in the polls. And I believe with your help, we're going to win the State of Pennsylvania.

I know a lot of people are working hard in this campaign, and I am here to thank you. I want to thank you for putting up the signs. I want to thank you for making the phone calls. I want to thank you for reminding our fellow citizens we have a duty to go to the polls in a democracy. And when you get them headed to the polls, remind them if they want a safer America, a stronger America, and a better America, to put me and Dick Cheney back in office.

So ever since Barbara and Jenna were young, I've been telling them we're going to go on the great family camping trip. [*Laughter*] I'm sure they envisioned the Colorado River or the wilds of Alaska, but no, the great family camping trip turned out to be the campaign of 2004. And I can't tell you—I cannot tell you how great it is to have my daughter introduce me in front of you all. I'm proud of Barbara. I love her dearly. And I thank you for joining me, darling.

My only regret, which is I'm sure your regret, is that Laura is not here—and Jenna, of course, but she's with Laura. See, when I asked Laura to marry me, she said, "Fine, I will marry you, so long as I never have to give a speech." [*Laughter*] I said, "Okay, you've got a deal." Fortunately, she did not hold me to that deal. Laura is giving a lot of speeches, and when she does, the American people see a warm, compassionate, strong First Lady.

Audience members. Four more years! Four more years! Four more years!

The President. Thank you all.

I am proud of my runningmate. I met with the Vice President this morning at our national security briefing. It—taking a look at him reminded me I didn't pick him because of his hairdo. [*Laughter*] He does not have the waviest hair in the race. [*Laughter*] But I picked him because of his experience and sound judgment. He's doing a great job for the American people.

By the way, a fellow you trained is doing a great job in Washington, and that would be your former Governor, Tom Ridge. He is a fine member of a very strong Cabinet. And he is doing a fine job of helping protect this homeland.

I want to thank your two United States Senators for their service to your State. First, I hope you put Arlen Specter back into office. He's a good Senator. And I'm proud to work with your other Senator, Rick Santorum.

I want to thank Congressman Jim Gerlach for his service to this district. I appreciate you, Congressman. He's somewhere around here. Where—there you are, Congressman. Good to see you. I see you're sitting next to a good fellow in Congressman Joe Pitts—appreciate you coming, Joe. And Congressman Tom Feeney from the State of Florida is with us. Feeney— yes, what are you doing here? Get back to your district and turn out the vote. [*Laughter*] I'll see you down there Saturday. [*Laughter*]

I want to thank all the local folks who are here. I want to thank my friend Alan Novak, who is the party chairman. I want to thank—[*applause*].

Barbara and I just had a chance to meet with four doctors from the area and a patient, Charlene Ware. And the docs were all telling me you got a problem here. We're going to talk about health care here today. I want to thank the docs for taking time to visit with me to share their concerns. And part of my address today is to share their concerns with you, because in order to make sure we've got a good health care system, we've got to make sure you have good professionals remain right here in your neighborhood to help solve the problems you have.

We have a lot at stake in this election. There are big issues that we're discussing. When I ran for President 4 years ago, none of us could have ever envisioned the horror of September the 11th. Since that day, I have led a comprehensive strategy to defeat the terrorists, to keep the homeland safe and secure. I pledged to the American people, we would be resolute and determined and do our duty to protect you, and I kept my pledge.

Our economy has been through a lot. When you're out rounding up the vote, remind people about what we have been through. The stock market was in serious decline 6 months prior to my arrival in Washington, DC. And then we went through a recession. We had some corporate scandals. We passed tough laws, by the way. We have made it abundantly clear we will not tolerate dishonesty in the board rooms of America. And then we got attacked. It cost us about a million jobs in the 3 months after September the 11th. I pledged to the American people, we would reduce your taxes to get our economy going again. I kept my word. Our economy is strong, and it is getting stronger.

I promised to reform our public schools and to challenge the soft bigotry of low expectations. I kept my word. We passed the No Child Left Behind Act, and we're closing an achievement gap all across America. And we're not going to go back to the days of mediocrity and low standards.

Another major area that needs reform is health care. We have made a good start. And in a new term, I will build on our efforts to improve America's health care. Health care is an essential issue in this campaign. And it's an essential issue in

Pennsylvania, and that's why I'm delighted to come here to talk about it.

Across America, small-business owners are struggling with the high cost of providing health insurance for their employees. Some workers have lost good coverage because they have changed jobs. Women have lost doctors they trust because of frivolous lawsuits. We need to act on these concerns. And we need to act in a practical, responsible way.

Here, America faces a clear choice. When it comes to health care, Senator Kerry's prescription is bigger Government with higher costs. My reforms will lower costs and give more control and choices to the American people.

The United States of America has a world-class health care system that leads the world in providing amazing treatments and cures for millions of people. As a candidate for President, I had pledged to double the budget of the National Institutes of Health to make sure we stay on the leading edge of change and reform. I kept my word. We have the most advanced hospitals in the world who do the most innovative research. We have the finest, most highly trained health care professionals in the world. We lead the world because we believe in a system of private medicine that encourages innovation and change.

Yet, rising costs and changes in the way Americans live and work are putting affordable health care out of the reach of too many of our citizens. Today I want to talk about a commonsense way to make health care more affordable and accessible while preserving America's system of private medicine.

Our reforms will help our families and individuals afford health insurance and save for health care expenses. They will help more small businesses provide health care coverage for their employees. And that's important, because more than one-half of the uninsured working Americans work for small businesses. My reforms will make sure low-income Americans, especially chil-

dren, get the health care they need. They will ensure preventative care and prescription drug coverage for our seniors on Medicare and provide quality health care for our Nation's veterans. And my reforms address the root causes of rising health care costs, which make health care more expensive for everyone.

In a new term, we'll take five practical steps to make health care more affordable and accessible in America. And here they are.

First, we'll expand health savings accounts or HSAs. An HSA is an innovative approach to health care that gives you affordable coverage for major illness and allows you to save money, tax-free, up to a set limit to use for routine medical expenses. You can make a contribution to this account; your government can make a contribution to the account; or your employer can make a contribution to the account. If you don't use all the money in a year, you can roll it over, tax-free, to meet future expenses.

Health savings accounts protect you against catastrophic medical expenses. Because you can take your savings account from job to job, it provides you more security if you change jobs. This approach will help our Nation confront the rising cost of health care, and this is how.

One of the reasons why health care costs are on the rise is that consumers are not involved in the decisionmaking process. Most health care costs are covered by third parties, and therefore, the user of health care is really not the purchaser of health care. With HSAs, we introduce market forces. It means you can shop around for the health care that's best for you. It means you'll be able to get better health care at better prices, because you're the decisionmaker.

To help more people own HSAs, I proposed allowing individuals to deduct the cost of their insurance premiums from their taxes. To help employers cover more workers, I proposed tax credits for small businesses to pay into HSAs for their employees. To help the uninsured, I proposed a $3,000 refundable tax credit to help low-income families buy their own HSAs. These incentives will allow many more of our fellow citizens to have a health care account that they manage and that they call their own.

To help people afford health care, we will pass association health plans, which allows small firms to join together, to pool risk so they can buy insurance at the same discounts big companies are able to do. That means a stand-alone family restaurant in Pennsylvania can join together with other small restaurants all around the country so they can spread the risk, so they don't have to buy insurance in the market as a stand-alone entity. This is a practical way to enable small businesses to better afford health care for their employees.

I view a health savings account or an association health plan as commonsense ideas. It makes sense. Yet my opponent is against both of them. He doesn't agree. And there's a reason why. Senator Kerry's idea of reform always involves bigger and more intrusive Government.

Audience members. Boo-o-o!

The President. And his health care proposal proves my point. In one of our debates, Senator Kerry looked into the television camera with a straight face and said, quote, "Government has nothing to do with it." That was in reference to his health care plan. I could barely contain myself. In fact, Government has a whole lot to do with his plan, and that's important for you to know. Senator Kerry's proposal would expand the Government health care rolls by nearly 22 million Americans. That would be the largest expansion of Government health care in American history. Eight out of ten people who get health coverage under his plan would be placed on a Government program.

He would make Medicaid a large—a program so large that employers would have the incentive to drop private coverage so the Government would pick up the insurance tab for their employees. Now, think about that. When you make Medicaid more accessible, the small business will have the incentive to say, "Well, the Government will provide the insurance, so I don't have to." That's why I say that some 8 million Americans will go from private insurance to Government-run insurance. And Medicaid is a Government-run program.

The Senator wants the Federal Government to pick up the tab for large medical bills that private employer-sponsored plans now pay for. In other words, the Federal Government is going to become like an insurance company, a re-insurer, which sounds fine on the surface except remember this, when the Federal Government writes the check, the Federal Government also writes the rules. And when the Federal Government starts to write the rules, the Government decides who's covered and who gets the coverage and how much care you get.

In addition, an independent study estimates that John Kerry's plan would impose at least 225 new regulatory mandates on small businesses. One group looked at the plan and described it as an overpriced albatross. [*Laughter*] That's being kind. [*Laughter*] This is a plan that will create burdens that our job creators cannot afford and do not deserve.

And the plan costs a lot: $1.2 trillion. That's with a "T." That's a lot. [*Laughter*] And he says, "Oh, don't worry, I'm going to pay for it all by taxing the rich." You can't raise enough money by taxing the rich to pay for a $1.2 trillion health care plan. Matter of fact, if you run up the top two brackets, it raises between 600 billion and 800 billion dollars, so there is a gap between what he promises and how he says he's going to pay for it. And guess who usually fills the gap? Yes, you do.

There's also something else wrong with saying "to tax the rich." The rich hire lawyers and accountants for a reason: to slip the tab to you. We're not going to let him tax you; we're going to carry Pennsylvania on November the 2d.

Audience members. Four more years! Four more years! Four more years!

The President. Thank you all.

When you're out there campaigning and rounding up the vote, remind people about the facts of his plan. The Kerry plan would move America down the road toward Federal control of health care, which would lead to lower quality and health-care rationing. Other countries have tried centralized health care, and it didn't work. We have great quality health care in America because it is a private-center system. And I intend to keep it that way. Health care decisions ought to be between doctors and patients, not by officials in Washington, DC.

Third, we must fix our broken legal system. Junk lawsuits are expensive for doctors and hospitals to fight in court. They are expensive to settle out of court. They drive up the cost of liability insurance for every doctor, and they increase the cost of health care for all Americans.

To avoid junk lawsuits, many doctors practice defensive medicine. They order tests and write prescriptions that aren't really necessary just to protect themselves from lawsuits. That's what happens in a society that has too many lawsuits. The practice of defensive medicine raises costs for patients and small businesses and adds about $28 billion a year to the Federal budget. Remember, the Federal budget takes care of Medicare and Medicaid and veterans, and the practice of defensive medicine runs up the cost to the Federal Government, which really runs up your tab. See, you pay for it. When we're talking about the Government's money, we're really talking about your money. We want our doctors focused on fighting illness, not on having to fight lawsuits.

The effects of the litigation culture are real in the State of Pennsylvania. They are hurting the quality of life in this State. Medical liability premiums are skyrocketing in this State, as they are in other States. For specialists in high-risk fields like ob-gyn, those premiums have doubled or tripled in some counties since 2000. And guess what happens? Docs leave the practice of medicine.

In the past 2 years, Mercy and Methodist Hospitals in Philadelphia both stopped delivering babies. The quality of life is deteriorating because of these lawsuits. Brandywine's only trauma center was forced to close. The quality of life is deteriorating because of these junk lawsuits. According to a recent poll, one in four people in Pennsylvania have been forced to change doctors in the last year because liability costs have forced their doctor to move, to stop practicing, or to discontinue procedures. And every time a good doctor is forced out of a community by lawsuits or the fear of lawsuits, the quality of life deteriorates.

Not long ago, I met Mary Coar from Honesdale. Her ob-gyn had to give up delivering babies because of liability concerns. When Mary was 4 months pregnant, she started driving 50 miles each way to see a different doctor. When Mary's daughter arrived this summer, she was delivered by a doctor she had never met. When a mother is looking forward to having a baby, the last thing she needs is uncertainty about her health care. For the sake of women and families across this State and this country, we need medical liability reform.

The difference between my opponent's point of view and mine is very clear on this issue. He has voted 10 times against medical liability reform during his Senate career. This year, when the Senate considered bills to protect ob-gyns and trauma physicians, Senator Kerry opposed them. Now, I know we're in a campaign, and he's paying lip service to legal reform. But it's his votes and his actions, not his words, that really count. He can run from his record, but he cannot hide.

In a new term, we'll pass real caps on noneconomic damages. This is a national problem requiring a national solution. And I will lead the United States Congress to pass medical liability reform.

Fourth, we'll reduce health care costs by applying modern information technology to our medical system. Many doctors' offices practice 21st century medicine; many hospitals practice 21st century medicine but still have 19th century filing systems. And in hospitals, there's more risk of medical error when all the records are handwritten on paper instead of cross-checked on a computer. That makes sense. Doctors don't write very well, anyway. [*Laughter*] They write about as well as I speak English. [*Laughter*]

The current system is costly and is wasteful and sometimes horrible—sometimes harmful. And we're on our way to fixing it. I've set a goal to make electronic medical records available for most Americans within the next decade. We're working with States and private hospitals to set standards for information storage and sharing. When the health care community fully maximizes the use of information technology, we will reduce medical costs by as much as 20 percent. We will cut medical errors, and we will save lives.

Fifth, we're cutting health care costs by moving cheaper generic drugs to the market faster. My administration is making sure that drug companies do not use delaying tactics to keep cheaper generic equivalents from getting to the consumers. Our actions will save Americans at least $35 billion on the medicine over the next 10 years. And that will make lifesaving drugs more affordable to our seniors.

As we move forward and make health care more affordable and accessible, we'll also keep the commitments we've made, commitments necessary for a compassionate country. We have strengthened and modernized Medicare. I told the American people we had a problem with Medicare when I was campaigning. I brought Republicans and Democrats together, and I kept my word in modernizing Medicare.

Listen, Medicare would pay thousands of dollars for a heart surgery but not one dime for the prescription drug that could prevent the heart surgery from being needed in the first place. It didn't make any sense. And so we've strengthened and modernized Medicare. I signed a bill to strengthen the system. Now seniors are getting discounts on their medicine with drug discount cards. And low-income seniors are getting $600 worth of help a year to buy those medicines. And beginning in 2006, all seniors will be able to get prescription drug coverage under Medicare.

We have another difference of opinion on this issue. My opponent voted against the Medicare bill that included prescription drug coverage for seniors, even though that bill was supported by AARP and other seniors' groups. Later, he said, quote, "If I'm the President, we're going to repeal that phony bill." Then he said—then he said a little later——

Audience members. Boo-o-o!

The President. ——"No, I don't want to repeal it." That sounds familiar.

Audience members. Flip-flop! Flip-flop! Flip-flop!

The President. As President for the next 4 years, I will defend the reforms we have worked so hard to pass so we can keep the promise to our seniors.

We'll keep our commitment to America's children by helping them get a healthy start in life. I'll work with Governors and community leaders and religious leaders to make sure every eligible child is enrolled in our Government's low-income health insurance program. We will not allow a lack of attention or information to stand between millions of children and the health care they need.

I know some of you here are worried about the upcoming flu season. I want to assure our seniors and families with young children that our Government is doing everything possible to help seniors and children get their shots, despite the major manufacturing defect that has caused this problem. We have millions of vaccine doses on hand, and millions more will be shipped in the coming weeks. We're working closely with State and local officials to get the flu vaccine to the most vulnerable Americans throughout our country. If you're feeling healthy, like I'm feeling healthy these days, don't get in line for the flu shot.

To make sure health care is available, we will keep our commitment to low-income Americans by expanding America's community health centers. Community health centers take the pressure off of local emergency rooms, improve care for the needy, and lower costs for us all. Since I took office, we have opened or expanded more than 600 community health centers. In a new term, we'll open or expand 600 more and bring healing to areas with the greatest need. Every poor county in America should have a rural or community health center.

And finally, we will keep our commitment to American veterans who have served our country so well. We have increased spending for the veterans during my time by $22 billion, which is double the amount my predecessor did in the 8 years he served as President of the United States. We're reducing the backlog in veterans' health care claims. We're modernizing our VA health centers and building new ones. Men and women who wore this Nation's uniform deserve first-class medical care, and we are getting the job done.

Health care is one of the most important issues facing our country. I'm glad you came today to let me talk about it. I'm passionate in understanding there is a right way to make sure health care is available and affordable and a wrong way. I feel strongly that the way I have proposed is the right way for Americans.

There is a big difference of philosophy in this campaign. If you think about it, on issue after issue after issue, my opponent wants the Government to dictate to the American people. I want the American people to decide. He trusts Government; I trust the people.

I'm ready for the work ahead. I know what we need to do to make sure this country is a more hopeful country and a more secure country. I've set out a set of clear priorities based upon a political philosophy that says Government will help people realize their dreams, not tell them how to live their lives.

We'll move forward on a health care system that makes sure we got the best health care system in the world, a health care system where the decisions will be made by doctors and patients, not by officials in our Nation's Capital. We'll continue to promote excellence in every public school, so no child is left behind. I'll continue to promote a pro-growth, pro-entrepreneur, pro-small-business, pro-farmer economic agenda so people can find work.

But all progress ultimately depends on the security of our Nation. We're in the middle of a global war on terror. We face an enemy that is determined to kill the innocent and convert our country into a battlefield. In this war on terror, there is no place for confusion, no substitute for victory.

Audience members. Four more years! Four more years! Four more years!

The President. The most solemn duty of the American President is to protect the American people. If America shows uncertainty or weakness in this decade, the world will drift toward tragedy. This will not happen on my watch.

Since that terrible morning of September the 11th, 2001, we've fought the terrorists across the Earth, not for pride, not for power, but because the lives of our citizens are at stake. Our strategy is clear. We'll defend the homeland. We'll strengthen our intelligence services. We will transform our All-Volunteer Army—I will keep our All-Volunteer Army an all-volunteer army. We will be relentless. We will stay on the offense. We will strike the terrorists abroad so we do not have to face them here in America. We will spread freedom and liberty. And we will prevail.

I want to tell you—I want to talk about two quick examples of what I'm talking about, about spreading freedom and liberty. I want you to remind people, particularly the young, about what is taking place in Afghanistan. Three-and-a-half years ago, the Taliban ran that country and Al Qaida was using Afghanistan as a place to train killers, some of whom came and took lives here in America—3 ½ years ago. Three-and-a-half years ago, young girls couldn't go to school because the vision of the Taliban was so dark. Three-and-a-half years ago, women were pulled in the public square and whipped if they didn't toe the ideological line of those ideologues of hatred. It was a grim world. And we acted to defend ourselves.

Remember, I set out a doctrine—and when the American President speaks, the American President better mean what he says. And I said, "If you harbor a terrorist, you're just as guilty as the terrorists." And I meant what I said. And we removed the Taliban for our own security. But because we did, millions of citizens of Afghanistan voted in the Presidential election that took place a couple of weeks ago. The first voter in the Presidential election was a 19-year-old woman. Afghanistan has gone from darkness to light because freedom is on the march. And America is better off for it. Free nations will be an ally on the war on terror. Free nations will serve as a great example for others.

Iraq will have Presidential elections in January. Think about how far that society has come. It's gone from torture chambers and mass graves to elections. Freedom is on the march.

One of my friends—one of our friends— Laura and my friends in the world is Prime Minister Koizumi of Japan. That probably doesn't sound like much—so what. Well, let me tell you what the "so what" is. It wasn't all that long ago that we were at war with the Japanese. It's an eternity if you're 58 years old, but really, in the march of history it wasn't all that long. And after we won the war against the Japanese—and it was a brutal war; my dad fought there; your dads and granddads fought there as well—Harry S. Truman believed in the power of liberty to transform an enemy into an ally.

There was a lot of people that were skeptical about that. A lot of people said, "Why do we want to care about an enemy?" or, "This enemy can't conceivably become an democracy. Why should we pay attention to somebody who—some country that killed a lot of our citizens?"

But there was great faith in the power of liberty to transform. That's what I believe. I believe in the power of liberty to transform societies. And as a result of that belief, I sit down with Prime Minister Koizumi, talking about how to achieve the peace we all want, talking about tough problems in the world so we can make a better world for our children and our grandchildren.

Someday, an American President will sit down with a duly elected leader from Iraq, talking about the peace in the Middle East. And our children and our grandchildren will be better off for it.

I believe in the power of liberty. I believe that people in the Middle East want to be free. I believe women in the Middle East long to live in a free society. I believe mothers and dads in the Middle East want to raise their children in a free and peaceful world. I believe all these things because freedom is not America's gift to the world; freedom is the Almighty God's gift to each man and woman in this world.

Over the past nearly 4 years, we've done a lot of hard work together. We climbed the mountain, and we see the valley below. The valley below is of a more peaceful world, of a hopeful America. You know, when I campaigned in your State in 2000,

I said if you gave me the chance to serve, I would uphold the honor and the dignity of the office. With your help, I will do so for 4 more years.

Thanks for coming. God bless. Thank you all. I appreciate your coming.

NOTE: The President spoke at 1:37 p.m. at the United Sports Training Center. In his remarks, he referred to Alan Novak, chairman, Republican State Committee of Pennsylvania; and Prime Minister Junichiro Koizumi of Japan.

Remarks in Hershey, Pennsylvania
October 21, 2004

The President. Thank you all. Thank you all for coming. So he said, "A couple of hundred people might show up if you came." I came—thousands are here, and I'm grateful. You know what this tells me. With your help, we will carry Pennsylvania on November the 2d.

Listen, we have a duty in our country to vote. And I'm asking you to turn to your friends and neighbors, go to your coffee shops, your houses of worship, your community centers, and tell people that we have a duty. And as you get people going to the polls, don't overlook discerning Democrats, people like Senator Zell Miller from Georgia. Our message is for everybody. If you want a safer America, a stronger America, and a better America, put me and Dick Cheney back in office.

Audience members. Four more years! Four more years! Four more years!

The President. Thank you all for coming. I am so grateful so many came. It means a lot. My only regret is that Laura is not here to see this crowd. She was a public school librarian when I met her for the second time. See, we went to the seventh grade together, San Jacinto Junior High in Midland, Texas. When I met her the second time and I finally asked her to marry me, she said, "Fine, just so long as I never have to give a speech." [*Laughter*] I said, "Okay, you got a deal." Fortunately, she didn't hold me to that promise. She's giving a lot of speeches, and when she does, the American people see a compassionate,

strong, great First Lady. She is not with me today, but one of our twin daughters, Barbara, has come. Thank you for coming, baby. There's nothing better than campaigning for a President with a daughter you love.

I'm proud of my Vice President, Dick Cheney. Now, look, I admit it, he does not have the waviest hair in the race. [*Laughter*] I did not pick him because of his hairdo. [*Laughter*] I picked him because of his experience, his judgment. I picked him because he can get the job done.

I am proud to have been introduced to this great crowd by Major Dick Winters, an American hero who commanded Easy Company in World War II.

I want to thank Congressman Todd Platts for joining us today. I'm proud you're here, Congressman. I want to thank the folks who are here from the statehouse and local office. I'm here to say as clearly as I can that Scott Paterno needs to be the next Congressman from the 17th Congressional District. I appreciate Tom Corbett, who is going to be the next attorney general, and Jean Craige Pepper, who's running for treasurer.

But most of all, I want to thank you all for coming. It's getting close to voting time. It's time to crank up the phones. It's time to put up the signs. It is time to carry Pennsylvania.

In the last few years, the people have come to know me. They know my blunt way of speaking. I get that from my mother. They know I mangle the English language sometimes. I get that from my dad. [*Laughter*] Americans also know I tell you exactly what I'm going to do, and I keep my word.

When I came into office, the stock market had been in serious decline for 6 months. And the American economy was sliding into a recession. To help families and to get this economy growing again, I pledged to reduce taxes. I kept my word. The results are clear. The recession was one of the shallowest in American history.

Over the last 3 years, our economy has grown at rates as fast as any in nearly 20 years. The homeownership rate in America is at an alltime high. The past 13 months, we've added 1.9 million new jobs. The unemployment rate across our country is 5.4 percent—lower than the average rates of the 1970s, the 1980s, and the 1990s. Farm income is up. This economy is moving forward, and we're not going to go back to the days of tax and spend.

To make sure jobs are here in America, to make sure people can find work, America must be the best place in the world to do business. That means less regulations on our job creators. That means we've got to do something about these frivolous lawsuits that are plaguing small-business owners.

To keep jobs here in America, Congress needs to pass my energy plan. It's a plan that encourages conservation and encourages renewables. It's a plan that encourages clean coal technology. It is a plan that recognizes, to keep jobs in America, we must be less dependent on foreign sources of energy.

To keep jobs here in America, we must open up markets for U.S. products. Listen, we can compete with anybody, anytime, anywhere, so long as the rules are fair.

To make sure this economy continues to grow, we've got to be wise about how we spend your money and keep the taxes low. Taxes are an issue in this campaign.

Now, my opponent has his own history on the economy.

Audience members. Boo-o-o!

The President. Yes. In 20 years as a Senator from Massachusetts, he's built a record of a Senator from Massachusetts. [*Laughter*] He's voted—he has voted to raise taxes 98 times.

Audience members. Boo-o-o!

The President. Yes. He voted to tax Social Security benefits.

Audience members. Boo-o-o!

The President. Ninety-eight times in twenty years—that's about five times a year. I would call that a predictable pattern. See, he can run from his record, but he cannot hide.

Now he's promising not to raise taxes for anyone who earns less than $200,000 a year. He said that with a straight face. [*Laughter*] The problem is, to keep that promise he'd have to break all his other promises. He has promised $2.2 trillion in new Federal spending. That's trillion with a "T." And so they said, "How are you going to pay for it?" And he said, fine, he's just going to raise taxes on the rich. Now, you've heard that before. When you try to raise taxes on the rich, that raises between 600 billion and 800 billion. There's a gap between what he's promised and how he says he's going to pay for it. And guess who usually gets to fill the gap?

Audience members. Boo-o-o!

The President. There's something else wrong with the "tax the rich" slogan. The rich hire lawyers and accountants for a reason: to slip the bill and pass it to you. We are not going to let him tax you; we will carry Pennsylvania and win on November the 2d.

Audience members. Four more years! Four more years! Four more years!

The President. When I came into office, our public schools had been waiting decades for hopeful reform. Too many of our children were being shuffled through school without learning the basics. I pledged to restore accountability in the school and to challenge the soft bigotry of low expectations. I kept my word. We passed the No Child Left Behind Act, and we're seeing results. Our children are making sustained gains in reading and math. We're closing achievement gaps all around this country, and we're not going to go back the days of low standards and accepted mediocrity.

When I came into office, we had a problem in Medicare. Medicine was changing, but Medicare was not. For example, we'd pay hundreds—tens of thousands of dollars for heart surgery but not one dime for the prescription drugs that could prevent the heart surgery from being needed in the first place. That did not make any sense to our seniors. It wasn't right. I pledged to bring Republicans and Democrats together to strengthen and modernize Medicare. I kept my word. Seniors are getting discounts on medicine. And beginning in 2006, all seniors will be able to get prescription drug coverage under Medicare.

We got more to do on health care. We've got to make sure health care is available and affordable. We'll have a safety net for those with the greatest needs. That's why I believe in community health centers for the poor and the indigent. We'll do more to make sure poor children are fully subscribed in our programs for low-income families.

Most of the uninsured in America work for small businesses. Small businesses are having trouble affording health care. To enable small businesses to afford health care, we must allow them to pool together so they can buy insurance at the same discount big companies get to do. We will expand health savings accounts so workers and small businesses are able to pay lower premiums and people can save tax-free in a health care account they manage and call their own.

To make sure health care is available and affordable, we have to do something about the frivolous lawsuits that are running up the cost of medicine and running good doctors out of practice. You have a problem here in the State of Pennsylvania because of these junk lawsuits. You're losing too many good docs. Too many ob-gyns are leaving the practice. Too many pregnant women are wondering whether or not they're going to get the health care they need in order to bring their child into this world. The system is broken. You cannot be pro-doctor, pro-patient, and pro-personal-injury-lawyer at the same time. You have to make a choice. My opponent put a personal injury lawyer on the ticket.

Audience members. Boo-o-o!

The President. He voted against medical liability reform 10 times. I'm standing with the doctors. I'm standing with the patients. I'm standing with the people of Pennsylvania. I'm for medical liability reform—now.

I laid out a health care plan that's sensible and reasonable. Now, my opponent has got his health care plan of his own. And it's a plan for bigger Government.

Audience members. Boo-o-o!

The President. Now, the other day in the debate, he looked right in the camera again, and he said this about his health care plan: "The Government has nothing to do with it." I remember him saying that. I was standing right there. [*Laughter*] I could barely contain myself. The Government has got a lot to do with his health care plan. Eight out of ten Americans would end up on a Government health insurance program. Eight million Americans would lose their private health insurance at work, and most would go on a Government plan. He says his plan helps small businesses. That's what—that's not what small-business groups think. They've called it an overpriced albatross that would saddle small businesses with 225 new mandates.

I have a different view. We've got to help small businesses afford insurance, not saddle them with a bunch of rules and regulations from Washington, DC. In all we do to reform health care, I believe the health decisions need to be made by doctors and patients, not by officials in our Nation's Capital.

I'll continue to set out policies for an optimistic and hopeful America. I believe this country should be an ownership society. You know, there's a saying, no one ever washes a rental car. [Laughter] There's a lot of wisdom in that statement. When you own something, you care about it. When you own something in America, you care about the future of our country.

That's why we promote entrepreneurship in this administration. Every time a small business is started in America, somebody is achieving the American Dream. We're encouraging health savings accounts so people have the security of owning and managing their own health care account. We're encouraging homeownership. Listen, more and more people are able to open up the door where they live and say, "Welcome to my home. Welcome to my piece of property." And America is better off for it.

In a new term, we'll take the next step to build an ownership society by strengthening Social Security. Now, let me speak to the seniors who are here. You remember the 2000 campaign when they were running the TV ads that said, "If George W. gets elected, the seniors will not get their checks." That's old-style scare politics. I want you to remind your friends and neighbors, they got their checks. They'll continue to get their checks. And baby boomers like me are in pretty good shape when it comes to the Social Security trust fund.

But we need to worry about our children and our grandchildren. See, we need to worry about whether or not the Social Security trust will be solvent when they need help in retirement. I think younger workers ought to be allowed to take some of their payroll taxes and set up a personal savings account that earns a better rate of return, an account they call their own, an account the Government cannot take away.

When it comes to Social Security, as you heard the other night in the debates, my opponent wants to maintain the status quo.

Audience members. Boo-o-o!

The President. The job of a President is to confront problems, not pass them on to future generations or future Presidents. He's against the Social Security reforms I laid out, and he's against about every other reform that gives more authority and control to the individual. On issue after issue, from Medicare without choices to schools with less accountability to raising taxes, he takes the side of more centralized control and more Government.

There is a word for that attitude. There is a word for that philosophy. It is called liberalism. Now, he dismisses that word as a label. He must have seen it differently when he said, "I'm a liberal and proud of it." [Laughter] The others have noticed as well. There's a nonpartisan National Journal magazine that did a study and named him the most liberal Member of the United States Senate. That takes a lot of hard work in that bunch. [Laughter] Can you imagine being more liberal than Ted Kennedy?

Audience members. No-o-o!

The President. He can run—he can even run in camo—but he cannot hide.

I have a different record. I have a different philosophy. I do not believe in big Government, and I do not believe Government should be indifferent. I'm what I call a compassionate conservative. I believe in policies that empower people to improve their lives, not try to run their lives. We'll continue to help men and women all across this country find the skills and tools they need to prosper in a time of change, skills and tools necessary to realize the great promise of our country. That's how I have led, and that's how I will continue to lead for 4 more years.

Audience members. Four more years! Four more years! Four more years!

The President. In this time of change, some things do not change. Those are the values we try to live by, courage and compassion, reverence and integrity. In changing times, we will support the institutions that give our lives direction and purpose, our families, our schools, our religious congregations. We stand for a culture of life in which every person matters and every being counts. We stand for marriage and family, which are the foundations of our society. We stand for the second amendment, which protects every American's individual right to bear arms. We stand for the appointment of Federal judges who know the difference between personal opinion and the strict interpretation of the law.

My opponent's words on these issues are a little muddy, but his record is plenty clear. He says he supports the institution of marriage but voted against the Defense of Marriage Act.

Audience members. Boo-o-o!

The President. He voted against the ban on the brutal practice of partial-birth abortion.

Audience members. Boo-o-o!

The President. He called the Reagan years as a period of moral darkness.

Audience members. Boo-o-o!

The President. There is a mainstream in American politics, and my opponent sits on the far left bank. During this campaign, he can run, but he cannot hide.

This election will also determine how America responds to the continuing danger of terrorism. I believe the most solemn duty of the American President is to protect the American people. If America shows uncertainty or weakness in this decade, the world will drift toward tragedy. This will not happen on my watch.

Since that terrible morning of September the 11th, 2001, we have fought the terrorists across the Earth, not for pride, not for power, but because the lives of our citizens are at stake. Our strategy is clear. We are defending the homeland. I thank the first-responders who are here with us today. We're strengthening our intelligence. We're transforming our military. We will

not have a draft. The All-Volunteer Army will remain an all-volunteer army. We are staying on the offensive. We will strike the terrorists abroad so we do not have to face them here at home. We will spread freedom and liberty. And we will prevail.

Our strategy is succeeding. Think about the world, the way it was some 3½ years ago—think about this. Afghanistan was the home base of Al Qaida. Pakistan was a transit point for terrorist groups. Saudi Arabia was fertile ground for terrorist fundraising. Libya was secretly pursuing nuclear weapons. Iraq was a dangerous place and a gathering threat. And Al Qaida was largely unchallenged as it planned horrific attacks.

Because the United States of America led, Afghanistan is an ally in the war on terror and is now a free nation; Pakistan is capturing terrorist leaders; Saudi Arabia is making raids and arrests; Libya is dismantling its weapons programs; the army of a free Iraq is fighting for its country's freedom; and more than three-quarters of Al Qaida's associates and members have been brought to justice.

We are standing with the people of Afghanistan and Iraq. I want the youngsters here to understand what has taken place during a brief period of your life. It wasn't all that long ago that young girls couldn't go to school in Afghanistan. It wasn't all that long ago that their mothers were taken into the public square and whipped because they wouldn't toe the line of these ideologues of hate called the Taliban. It wasn't all that long ago that the people of that country lived in darkness. Because we acted in our own self-interest, because we acted to destroy the Al Qaida terrorists' training camps, because we worked to secure ourselves, 25 million people live in freedom. They had Presidential elections a couple of weekends ago in Afghanistan. The first voter in Afghanistan was a 19-year-old girl. Freedom is on the march, and the people of Afghanistan have gone from darkness to light.

The people of Iraq will be voting for a President in January. Think how far that society has come from the day of torture chambers and mass graves. It's in our interest that we spread freedom. Free societies will be hopeful societies which no longer feed resentments and breed violence for export. Free governments in the Middle East will fight the terrorists instead of harboring them. Freedom will help us keep the peace we all want. Freedom is on the move, and America is more secure for it.

So our mission is clear—our mission is clear. We will help these countries train armies and police forces and security forces in Afghanistan and Iraq so they can do the hard work of defending their freedom, so they can stand up and fight these terrorists who are trying to stop the advance of freedom. We'll help the countries get on the path of stability and democracy as quickly as possible, and then our troops will come home with the honor they have earned.

We have a great United States military because those who wear the uniform are people of such great character and service and duty and honor. And I want to thank the veterans who are here today for having set such a great example for those who wear the uniform. And I want to thank the military families who are here for the sacrifices you have made. And I assure you, we'll keep the commitment we have made to the troops and their families. They will have the resources they need to complete their missions.

That's why I went to the Congress in September of 2003 and asked for $87 billion of supplemental funding to support our troops in harm's way. I received great bipartisan support. Your Senators, Senator Specter and Santorum, voted with me on that bill. It was an important piece of legislation. Most people up in Congress understood how important it was. As a matter of fact, only 12 Members of the United States Senate voted against funding for our troops, 2 of whom were my opponent and his runningmate.

Audience members. Boo-o-o!

The President. Now, I want to tell you another startling statistic. When you're out gathering the vote—I want to tell you another startling statistic, a true fact. There were only 4 Members of the United States Senate—4 out of 100—that had voted to authorize the use of force and then voted against the funding to support our troops in harm's way, 2 of whom are my opponent and his runningmate.

Audience members. Boo-o-o!

The President. So they asked him how he could have made that vote. They asked him how he could have made that vote. And you might remember perhaps the most famous quote of the 2004 campaign. Here is what he said: "I actually did vote for the $87 billion, before I voted against it."

Audience members. Boo-o-o!

The President. They kept asking him, and he kept answering. He must have given five or six different explanations. One of the most interesting ones of all is he finally said, "The whole thing was a complicated matter." [*Laughter*] There's nothing complicated about supporting our troops in harm's way.

All elections come down to a choice, and in this, America's first Presidential election since September the 11th, the security of our country is at risk in many ways different than we have ever faced before. We're in the midst of a global war against a well-trained, highly motivated enemy, an enemy that has no conscience, an enemy that hates Americans because of the very freedoms we love. The next Commander in Chief must lead us to victory in this war. Yet, you cannot win a war when you do not believe you are fighting one.

Senator Kerry was recently asked how September the 11th had changed him. And he replied this: "It did not change me much at all." End quote.

Audience members. Boo-o-o!

The President. His unchanged world becomes obvious when he calls the war against terror primarily an intelligence and law enforcement operation rather than a war which requires the full use of American strength. Senator Kerry's top foreign policy advisor questioned this is even a war at all. And here's what he said: "We're not in a war on terror in a literal sense. It's like saying 'the war on poverty'—it's just a metaphor." End quote. It's a different mindset, a different attitude. Confusing food programs with terrorist killings reveals a fundamental misunderstanding of the world we live in, of the world we face. And this is very dangerous thinking.

Senator Kerry also misunderstands our battle against insurgents and terrorists in Iraq. He called Iraq a "diversion" from the war on terror. Let me talk about the case of one terrorist to show you how wrong this thinking is. The terrorist leader we face today in Iraq, the one responsible for car bombings and beheadings of Americans, is a man named Zarqawi. Zarqawi ran a terrorist training camp in Afghanistan until our military arrived. He then went to Iraq. He received medical care in Iraq. He plotted and planned in Iraq. To confirm where he's coming from, just the other day Zarqawi announced his allegiance to Usama bin Laden. Zarqawi and his associates were not busy fighting American forces in Iraq, does my opponent think they would be living peaceful and productive lives? Course not. That's why Iraq is not a diversion but a central commitment in the war on terror.

The Senator the other day talked about the need for America to pass a "global test" when it comes to committing our troops.

Audience members. Boo-o-o!

The President. I'm not making that up. He was standing right there when he said it. No, we'll work with our friends and allies. I'll continue to build alliances and strong coalitions. But I will never turn over America's national security decisions to leaders of other countries.

Audience members. U.S.A.! U.S.A.! U.S.A.!

The President. I believe in the transformational power of liberty. That's what I believe. I believe liberty can transform nations. One of our friends—Laura and my friends is Prime Minister of Japan. He's a friend. I saw him at the United Nations in New York. I said, "Listen, I'm going to be talking about you on the campaign trail. Do you mind?" He said, "No, go ahead and talk about me." I said, "Okay." What he didn't—I didn't ask him permission to tell you that Elvis is his favorite singer. [*Laughter*] We've gotten to know him quite well.

It probably doesn't sound much to folks out there, that I would call him my friend. But remember, 60 years ago, we were at war with Japan. They were the sworn enemy of the United States of America. My dad, like many of his generation, like many of the Band of Brothers, fought against the Japanese—people of that generation served. And your dads and granddads did the same, I'm confident.

After we won the war, Harry S. Truman, President of the United States, believed that liberty could transform an enemy into an ally. That's what he believed. There was a lot of skepticism about that, a lot of doubt. There was a lot of anger because of the war, and you can understand why. Families' lives have been turned upside down because of death during the war. A lot of people just said, "Well, the enemy can't possibly become a democracy." But our predecessors stayed with it. And as a result of that belief, I sit down at the table today talking about how to keep the peace with Prime Minister Koizumi.

Someday, an American President will be sitting down with a duly elected leader of Iraq, talking about peace in the Middle East. And our children and our grandchildren will be better off for it.

I believe that millions in the Middle East plead in silence for their liberty. I believe women in the Middle East want to live in a free society. I believe mothers and fathers in the Middle East want to raise their children in a free and peaceful world. I believe all these things because freedom is not America's gift to the world; freedom is the Almighty God's gift to each man and woman in this world.

For all Americans, these years in our history will always stand apart. There are quiet times in the life of a nation when little is expected of its leaders. This isn't one of those times. This is a time that requires firm resolve, clear vision, and a deep faith in the values that makes us a great nation.

None of us will ever forget that week when one era ended and another began. On September the 14th, 2001, I stood in the ruins of the Twin Towers. It is a day I will never forget. I will never forget the voices of those in hardhats yelling at me at the top of their lungs, "Whatever it takes." I will never forget the police or firefighter coming out of the rubble who grabbed me by the arm, and he looked me square in the eye, and he said, "Do not let me down." Ever since that day—ever since that day, I wake up every morning thinking about how to better protect our country. I will never relent in defending America, whatever it takes.

Four years ago, when I traveled your great State asking for the vote, I made a pledge that if you gave me a chance to serve, I would uphold the honor and the dignity of the office to which I have been elected. With your help, with your hard work, I will do so for 4 more years.

God bless. Thanks for coming. Thank you all.

NOTE: The President spoke at 4:20 p.m. at Hershey Park Stadium. In his remarks, he referred to Tom Corbett, candidate for Pennsylvania State Attorney General; Jean Craige Pepper, candidate for Pennsylvania State Treasurer; senior Al Qaida associate Abu Musab Al Zarqawi; Usama bin Laden, leader of the Al Qaida terrorist organization; and Prime Minister Junichiro Koizumi of Japan.

Remarks in Wilkes-Barre, Pennsylvania
October 22, 2004

The President. Thank you all for coming. It seems like yesterday I was here in Wilkes-Barre. Come to think of it, I was. [*Laughter*] I figure if I keep coming back, I'll meet everybody in town.

I'm coming back because I want you to know how important your vote is. That's why I'm here. We're close to voting time. I've come back to tell you how important your help is in this election. Find your friends and neighbors. Convince them to go to the polls on November the 2d. Do not overlook discerning Democrats, people like Senator Zell Miller. And remind your friends and neighbors, if they want safer America, a stronger, and a better America, to put me and Dick Cheney back in office.

I regret that Laura is not traveling with us today.

Audience members. Aw-w-w!

The President. Yes, that is generally the reaction—[*laughter*]—kind of like, "Why didn't you stay home and let her come?" [*Laughter*] You know, we were in the same grade at San Jacinto Junior High in Midland, Texas. That would be the seventh grade. And then I became reacquainted with her when she was a public school librarian. [*Laughter*] And when I asked her to marry me, she said, "Fine, but make me a promise." I said, "What is it?" "Promise me I'll never have to give a speech." [*Laughter*] I said, "Okay, you got a deal." Fortunately, she didn't hold me to that promise. She's giving a lot of speeches. And when she does, the American people see a warm, compassionate, great First Lady.

I love traveling with my daughters on the campaign trail. There's nothing better than being with somebody who, well, tells you to keep your tie straight. [*Laughter*] "Don't spill your food before you get out there and talk to the people." [*Laughter*] You know, I used to tell Barbara and Jenna that one of these days we'll go on a camping trip together, the great family camping experience. I'm sure they envisioned the Colorado River or somewhere. Well, darling, this is it. This is the great—[*laughter*]. We're traveling this country asking for the vote, and I'm glad Barbara is by my side.

I spoke with our great Vice President this morning. His spirits are high. He's working hard. I admit that Vice President Cheney does not have the waviest hair in the race. [*Laughter*] I didn't pick him because of his hairdo. [*Laughter*] I picked him because of his experience, his sound judgment, and his ability to get the job done for the American people.

I'm pleased to be sharing the platform with Congressman Don Sherwood. He's doing a great job. And Congressman Jim Greenwood is traveling today. He comes up from the suburbs of Philadelphia. I'm proud to have his support, and I'm proud to call him friend. Thanks for coming, Congressman.

Specter is out there working on behalf of his own campaign, and Santorum is out there working for mine. They're two fine United States Senators. I hope you put Arlen Specter back in office.

I want to thank all the State and local officials. I want to thank Jean Craige Pepper for being here, the candidate for treasurer of the State. I appreciate people who are running for office. I want to thank my friend Sammy Kershaw, country singer.

Most of all, I want to thank the grassroots activists who are here, the people putting up all the signs, making the phone calls, writing the letters. I'm here to thank you for what you're going to do as we're coming down the stretch. There is no doubt in my mind, with your hard work and with your help, we will carry Pennsylvania and win a great victory in November.

With just 11 days left in this campaign— who's counting? [*Laughter*] Voters are focusing on the issues that matter most for their families and for our country. You've heard the debates. You know where I stand. Sometimes you even know where my opponent stands. [*Laughter*] You've had a chance to see both of us in action, to measure our consistency, our resolve, our values, and our ability to lead. This election comes down to five clear choices for the American families, five choices on issues of great consequence: your family's security, your budget, your quality of life, your retirement, and the bedrock values that are so critical to our families and our future.

The first clear choice is very important because it concerns the security of your family. All progress on every other issue depends on the safety of our citizens. This will be the first Presidential election since September the 11th, 2001. Americans will go to the polls in a time of war and ongoing threat to our country. The enemies who killed thousands of innocent people are still dangerous and determined to strike us again. The outcome of this election will set the direction of the war against terror, and in this war, there is no place for confusion and no substitute for victory.

The most solemn duty of the American President is to protect the American people. If America shows uncertainty or weakness in this decade, the world will drift toward tragedy. This will not happen on my watch.

Since that terrible morning of September the 11th, 2001, we have fought the terrorists across the Earth, not for pride, not for power but because the lives of our citizens are at stake. Our strategy is clear. We're defending the homeland. We're strengthening our intelligence capabilities. We are transforming our All-Volunteer

Army to make sure it remains an all-volunteer army. We are staying on the offensive.

And we are succeeding. More than three-quarters of Al Qaida's key members and associates have been brought to justice, and the rest of them know we're after them. We are in a real war, and the only strategy must lead to victory.

My opponent has a different approach. He says that September the 11th, quote, "didn't change me much at all."

Audience members. Boo-o-o!

The President. And that's pretty clear. He considers the war on terror primarily a law enforcement and intelligence gathering operation. His top foreign policy adviser has questioned whether it's even a war at all, saying that's just a metaphor, like the "war on poverty." I've got news. Anyone who thinks we are fighting a metaphor does not understand the enemy we face and has no idea how to win the war and keep America secure. My opponent also misunderstands our battle against insurgents and terrorists. He's called it a "diversion" from the war on terror. My opponent used to recognize Saddam Hussein as a threat. That's until he started to slide in the polls.

Saddam Hussein was a threat to the United States. He hated America. He had a long history of pursuing and even using weapons of mass destruction. He had ties to terrorists. He was firing missiles at American pilots enforcing the sanctions of the world. He paid families of suicide bombers. He was a threat.

We didn't find the stockpiles that we thought were in Iraq, that I thought was there, that my opponent thought was there, that the United Nations thought was there, that the world thought was there. But I want you to remember—tell your friends and neighbors what the Duelfer report did find. It said that Saddam Hussein had the intent and capability and the expertise to rebuild a weapons program, that he was gaming the system, he was using the Oil for Food Programme to try to influence officials of other nations to get rid of the sanctions. And why? Because he wanted the world to look the other way so he could restart his programs. That was a risk we could not afford to take. Knowing what I know today, I would have taken the same action. America and the world are safer with Saddam Hussein sitting in a prison cell.

Remember, my opponent called our action a "mistake." That's after he started slipping in the polls. [*Laughter*]

Iraq is still dangerous because terrorists there are trying to stop the advance of freedom and elections. A man named Zarqawi is responsible for planting car bombs and beheading Americans in Iraq. He ran a terrorist training camp in Afghanistan until our coalition forces destroyed that camp. He then fled to Iraq where he's fighting us today. To confirm where he's coming from, he recently announced his allegiance to Al Qaida. If Zarqawi and his associates were not busy fighting American forces in Iraq, does my opponent think they would be peaceful citizens of the world? [*Laughter*] Does he think they'd be opening a small business somewhere? [*Laughter*] Fighting the likes of Zarqawi in Iraq is not a "diversion" from the war on terror; it is the way we will win the war on terror.

When it comes to your security, the choice in this election could not be clearer. You cannot lead our Nation to decisive victory on which the security of every American family depends if you do not see the true dangers of the post-September the 11th era. My opponent has a September 10th point of view. At his convention, he declared his strategy was to respond to attacks after America had been hit.

Audience members. Boo-o-o!

The President. As we learned on September the 11th, it's too late to respond. In our debates, he said we can defend America only if we pass a "global test."

Audience members. Boo-o-o!

The President. I'm not making that up. He was standing right there when he said it. No, we'll work with friends and allies, but I will never turn over America's national security decisions to leaders of other countries.

For the sake of our freedom and for your security, we'll fight this war with every asset of our national power. We will protect America by striking the terrorists abroad so we do not have to face them here at home. And we will prevail.

Audience members. Four more years! Four more years! Four more years!

The President. We've got another powerful asset at our disposal, and that's liberty. And that's freedom.

I want the youngsters here listening to think about what has happened in a brief period of time, some 3½ years in Afghanistan. It wasn't all that long ago in that country that young girls were not allowed to go to school, and their mothers were taken into the public square and whipped or sometimes taken to a sports stadium and executed because they refused to toe the line of the ideologues of hate, the Taliban, which ran Afghanistan. In working to secure ourselves, in ridding that country of terrorist camps, of upholding a doctrine that said, "If you harbor a terrorist, you're just as guilty as the terrorist," we liberated over 25 million people in Afghanistan. And just a couple of weekends ago, millions of Afghan citizens voted in a Presidential election, and the first voter was a 19-year-old woman.

Freedom is on the march. That society has gone from darkness to light because of liberty, and America is more secure because of it. Free societies are peaceful societies. Free societies will not harbor terrorists. Free societies will be hopeful places where people can realize their dreams.

Iraq will have elections in January. Iraq is changing. Think how far that country has come from the days of mass graves and torture chambers and the brutal reign of one man. I believe liberty has the capacity to transform societies and make the world a more peaceful place.

One of our friends in the world is Prime Minister Koizumi. I said "our"—I'm talking about Laura and me. He is—he's a good man. He's a person with whom I work. It wasn't all that long ago that we were at war with the Japanese. See, 60 years ago, we were fighting the Japanese. My dad was in that war. I'm confident many other people were in that war, or families represented here were—had fathers and grandfathers in the war against the Japanese.

After World War II, Harry Truman—after we won that war, Harry Truman believed in the power of liberty to transform an enemy into an ally. There were a lot of skeptics then. There were a lot of doubters, the Japanese—the enemy—could never become a democracy. "Why do we even want to help them," some would say. After all, they destroyed a lot of the U.S. lives. But there was faith and belief in the power of liberty to transform societies. And today, because of that belief, I sit down with the Prime Minister of Japan talking about keeping the peace that we all want, talking about dealing with the world's problems.

Someday, a duly elected leader from Iraq will be sitting down with the President of the United States of America, talking about the peace in the Middle East, and our children and our grandchildren will be better off for it.

Freedom is on the march in this world. I believe everybody in the Middle East desires to live in freedom. I believe women in the Middle East want to live in a free society. I believe mothers and fathers want to raise their children in a free and peaceful world. I believe all these things because freedom is not America's gift to the world; freedom is the Almighty God's gift to each man and woman in this world.

The second clear choice in this election concerns your family budget. When I ran for President 4 years ago, I pledged to lower taxes for American families, and I kept my word. To help our families, we doubled the child credit to $1,000 per child. We reduced the marriage penalty. Our Tax Code should encourage marriage, not discourage marriage. We dropped the lowest tax bracket to 10 percent so working families, working Americans can keep more of their paychecks. We reduced income taxes for everyone that pays taxes. That's the fair way of doing things.

As a result of our policies, real after-tax income, money in your pocket that you can spend, is up about 10 percent since I took office. Because of tax relief, because we increased consumer spending and investment, our economy is overcoming the tough times we've been through.

Remind your friends and neighbors that when I got in office, the stock market had been in serious decline for 6 months prior to our arrival. Then we were in a recession. And the attacks of September the 11th, 2001, cost us nearly a million jobs in the 3 months after the attacks.

But because we acted, this economy of ours is strong and it's getting stronger. Our economy is growing at rates as fast as any in nearly 20 years. We've added 1.9 million new jobs in the last 3 months. The State of Pennsylvania has added 4,600 jobs in the month of September 2004. The unemployment rate across America is at 5.4 percent, lower than the average rates of the 1970s, the 1980s, and the 1990s. And the new unemployment rate figure in the State of Pennsylvania released today is 5.3 percent.

My opponent has a very different plan for your budget. He intends to take a bigger chunk out of it.

Audience members. Boo-o-o!

The President. He voted against the— he voted against a higher child tax credit. He voted against marriage penalty relief. He voted against lowering the tax rates. If his vote had prevailed, an average middle-class family would be paying $2,000 more a year to the IRS.

Audience members. Boo-o-o!

The President. That's a fact. It's also part of a pattern. See, the Senator voted 10 times to raise taxes on gasoline. All told, during his 20 years in the United States Senate, my opponent has voted to raise taxes 98 times. That's about five times a year. When he does something that often, he must really enjoy it. [*Laughter*] During his campaign, my opponent has made a lot of big, expensive promises. He promised about $2.2 trillion of new spending. That's with a "T." [*Laughter*] That's a lot even for a Senator from Massachusetts. So they said, "How are you going to pay for it?" He said, "Oh, we'll just tax the rich." We've heard that before, haven't we? He's going to raise the top two brackets. There's three things—a lot of things wrong with it, but let me give you three right off the bat.

One is, by raising individual rates, you're taxing many, many small businesses. Seventy percent of the new jobs in America are created by small businesses. Most small businesses pay tax at the individual income-tax level. And by running up the top two brackets, you're taxing the job creators. And that's bad economic policy.

Secondly, there's a gap between what he's promised and what he can deliver. By raising the top two brackets, you raise about 600 billion to 800 billion dollars, and he's promised 2.2 trillion. So there's a gap, a gap between the promises and what he can deliver. Guess who gets to usually fill those gaps?

Secondly—or thirdly, the rich hire lawyers and accountants for a reason when it comes to taxes. That's to slip the bill and stick you with it. But we're going to protect the family budgets; we're going to carry Pennsylvania and win a great victory on November the 2d.

When it comes to your budget, you have a clear choice. My opponent has earned— and I mean earned—his rank as the most liberal Member of the United States Senate. He'll raise your taxes to fund bigger Government. I'm going to keep your taxes low. This is the road to prosperity. It's a road to economic vitality. Now, when it comes to taxes, he may try to run in a camouflaged outfit—[*laughter*]—but he cannot hide.

The third choice in this election involves the quality of life for our families. I believe a good education and quality health care are important for successful lives. When I ran for President 4 years ago, I promised to end the soft bigotry of low expectations by reforming our public schools, and I kept my word. We passed good education reform. We're raising the standards. We're making sure our schools are accountable, accountable to our parents. We're seeing progress. Math and reading scores are on the rise. We're closing the achievement gap all across this country. We will build on these reforms. We will extend them to our high schools so that not one single child in America is left behind.

We will continue to improve life for our families by making health care more affordable and more accessible. We'll expand health savings accounts and create association health plans so small businesses can cover their workers, so more families are able to get health insurance plans they manage and they call their own. We'll help families in need by expanding community health centers. We'll make sure every eligible child is enrolled in our Government's low-income health insurance program.

To make sure health care is available and affordable for the American citizens, we're going to do something about the junk lawsuits that run up the cost of medicine and run good doctors out of practice.

Doctor Linda Barrasse is with us today, a cardiologist. She's got a group practice in Scranton. She's just like the docs I met yesterday in Chester County, Pennsylvania. Doctors are concerned about the quality of health care in Pennsylvania because of all these junk lawsuits. They're running good docs out of practice. There are too many ob-gyns being run out of practice and too many Pennsylvania women having to drive for miles to get the care they need and deserve. Linda talks about the—needing to close offices. They're having trouble recruiting new doctors. Medical liability is an issue in the Pennsylvania. It is an issue across this country. It is a national problem that requires a national solution. I am for medical liability reform.

Senator Kerry has a different point of view on our schools and our health care system. Now, he voted for the No Child Left Behind Act, but now wants to weaken the accountability standards. He's proposed including measures like teacher attendance in the accountability measures to judge whether students can read and write and add and subtract. He voted against health savings accounts. He opposed association health care plans that would help our small businesses. He has voted 10 times against medical liability reform on the floor of the United States Senate.

Audience members. Boo-o-o!

The President. The other day, he said, well, he's for some kind of plan.

Audience members. Boo-o-o!

The President. He put a trial lawyer on the ticket.

Audience members. Boo-o-o!

The President. He can run, but he cannot hide.

He's proposed a big Government health care plan that would cause 8 million families to lose the private coverage they get at work and have to go on a Government plan. Eighty percent of the people who get coverage under his proposal would be enrolled on a Government program. You might remember one of our debates. He tried to tell the Americans when it comes to his health care plan, and I quote, "The Government has nothing to do with it." I could barely contain myself when I heard that. My opponent's plan would move America down the road to Federal control of health care, and that is the wrong road to take for American families.

In all we do to reform health care, we will make sure the decisions are made by doctors and patients, not by officials in Washington, DC.

Fourth clear choice in this election involves your retirement. Our Nation made a solid commitment to America's seniors on Social Security and on Medicare. When I ran for President 4 years ago, I promised to keep that commitment and improve Medicare by adding prescription drugs. I kept my word. Leaders in both political parties have talked about strengthening Medicare for years. We got the job done. Seniors are now getting discounts on medicine with drug discount cards. Low-income seniors are getting $600 to help them with their prescription drugs this year, another $600 next year. And beginning in 2006, all seniors will be able to get prescription drug coverage under Medicare.

My opponent voted against the Medicare bill that included prescription drugs, even though it was supported by AARP and other seniors groups. During this campaign, he said, quote, "If I'm President, we're going to repeal that phony bill," end quote. Then, of course, later on, he said, "No, I don't want to repeal it." Sounds familiar. [*Laughter*] As your President for the next 4 years, I will defend the reforms we have worked so hard to pass, and we will keep the promise of Medicare for America's seniors.

We will keep the promise of Social Security for our seniors and strengthen Social Security for generations to come. Every election, politicians try to scare seniors about Social Security. It's predictable. In the 2000 campaign, they ran ads saying that, "If George W. gets elected, our seniors will not get their checks." You might remember those ads. As you round up the vote, would you please remind our seniors, George W. got elected, and our seniors got their checks. And when I get elected this time, the seniors will still get their checks.

But I know today's moms and dads and grandparents are concerned about their children and grandchildren when it comes to Social Security. Someday, our youngest workers, of course, will retire, and we need to make sure Social Security will be there

when they need it as well. I believe younger workers ought to take some of their own money and put it in a personal savings account, a personal savings account that will earn a greater rate of return than a Social Security trust, a personal savings account they can call their own, an account the Government cannot take away.

My opponent takes a different approach. He talks about protecting Social Security, but I want everybody to remember, he is the only candidate who has voted eight times for higher taxes on Social Security benefits.

Audience members. Boo-o-o!

The President. When it comes to the next generation, he has offered nothing to strengthen Social Security. American families have a clear choice in this election. My opponent wants to scare the seniors of today and do nothing to secure the system for seniors of tomorrow. I'll keep the promise of Social Security and Medicare and strengthen these great systems for our children and our grandchildren.

The fifth clear choice in this election is on the values that are so crucial to keeping America's families strong. Here, my opponent and I are miles apart.

I believe marriage is a sacred commitment, one of the most fundamental, most enduring, and most important institutions of our civilization. My opponent says he supports marriage, but his record shows he will not defend it. This isn't a partisan issue. The vast majority of Democrats, for example, supported the Defense of Marriage Act, which defined marriage as the union of a man and a woman—a bill which President Clinton signed into law. But Senator Kerry was a part of the far left bank, far left minority, that voted against that piece of legislation. I will always stand firm to protect the sanctity of marriage.

I believe it is important to work with people to find common ground on difficult issues. Republicans and Democrats, many citizens on both sides of the life issue, agreed we should ban the brutal practice of partial-birth abortion. But Senator Kerry was part of a far left minority that voted against the ban.

Audience members. Boo-o-o!

The President. He also voted against parental notification laws and voted against the Unborn Victims of Violence Act. I will continue to——

Audience members. Boo-o-o!

The President. I will continue to reach out to Americans of every belief and move this goodhearted Nation toward a culture of life.

My opponent has said that you can find the heart and soul of America in Hollywood. [*Laughter*] Most of us don't look to Hollywood as the source of values. The heart and soul of America is found right here in Wilkes-Barre, Pennsylvania.

All these choices make this one of the most important elections in our history. The security and prosperity of our country, the health and education of our citizens, the retirement of our seniors, and the direction of our culture are all at stake. The decision is in the best hands because the decision belongs to the American people.

I believe in the future of this country. We see a great day for the American people. One of my favorite quotes was written by a Texan, a friend of ours. He said, "Sarah and I live on the east side of the mountain. It's the sunrise side, not the sunset side. It is the side that sees the day

that is coming, not to see the day that is gone." My opponent has spent a lot of this campaign talking about the day that is gone. I see the day that's coming.

We've been through a lot together. We've been through a lot together in the last years. Because we've done the hard work of climbing that mountain, we see the valley below. We'll protect our families. We'll build on their prosperity. We'll defend our deepest values. We will spread freedom and peace, and as we do, America will be safer here at home.

Four years ago, when I traveled your great State asking for the vote, I made a pledge that if you honored me with this office, I would uphold the honor and the dignity. With your help, I will do so for 4 more years.

Thanks for coming. On to victory! Thank you all. Thank you all.

NOTE: The President spoke at 10:30 a.m. at the Wachovia Arena at Casey Plaza. In his remarks, he referred to Charles Duelfer, Special Advisor to the Director of Central Intelligence; former President Saddam Hussein of Iraq; senior Al Qaida associate Abu Musab Al Zarqawi; and Prime Minister Junichiro Koizumi of Japan. He also referred to the "Comprehensive Report of the Special Advisor to the DCI on Iraq's WMD," issued September 30.

Remarks in a Discussion in Canton, Ohio
October 22, 2004

The President. Thank you all for coming. Go ahead and be seated, please. We've got some work to do. Thank you all for coming today.

First of all, George, thank you for that strong endorsement. I am proud to have George in my corner, just like I'm proud to have thousands of Democrats all across

the State of Ohio who understand if they want a safer America, a stronger America, and a better America to put me and Dick Cheney back in office. Thank you, sir.

I'm keeping mighty good company today. So I don't know if you know this or not, but Laura and I were in the seventh grade together at San Jacinto Junior High in Midland, Texas. And then we became reacquainted when she was a public school librarian in Texas. I asked her to marry me. She said, "Fine, I will marry you, but make me one promise." I said, "What is it?" She said, "Never make me give a speech." [*Laughter*] I said, "Okay, you've got a deal." Fortunately, she didn't hold me to that promise. Laura is a great speaker, and when she does, the American people see a compassionate, warm, wonderful First Lady.

So I have been telling the girls, one of these days, we'll take the family camping trip. [*Laughter*] They envisioned the Grand Canyon, the wilds of Alaska. Girls, this is it, the 2004 campaign. [*Laughter*] We love them dearly. I'm proud of Barbara and Jenna. Thank you all for campaigning so hard.

Thanks for coming today. I'm back in the great city of Canton because I'm here asking for the vote. I'm here to describe to you what I intend to do over the next 4 years to make this country a better place. I believe you have to get out amongst the people and ask for the vote. We've got a very unusual way of making some points today. As you can see, I've been joined by some citizens from Ohio here on the stage. We will listen to their stories. I think it'll help the people of Ohio understand why I have made some of the decisions I have made.

Before I begin, though, I want to thank your Governor, Bob Taft, for joining us today. Governor, great to see you. I want to thank Jennette Bradley, the Lieutenant Governor. Thanks for coming, Governor. You look great.

Congressman Ralph Regula—appreciate you being here, Congressman. Laura and I were looking forward to seeing the wife, but, no, of course, she's probably out mowing the lawn like you should be doing. [*Laughter*]

Listen, you've got a great United States Senator in George Voinovich. He doesn't need a poll or a focus group to tell him what to think. He stands on principle. You know where he's coming from. He doesn't shift in the wind like some other United States Senators I know. [*Laughter*] Put him back in office. And I'm proud of Mike DeWine, a fine United States Senator as well. We're—Laura and I are proud to call both George and Mike friends.

Today, when I landed at the airport, I met Dan Yeric, who's sitting right there. Dan, why don't you wave your hand. Thanks for coming. Dan has been a volunteer at the Akron Children's Hospital for 12 years. The reason I bring him up is the strength of this country lies in the hearts and souls of our fellow citizens. The true strength of America is not our military might; it's not the size of our pocketbook. The true strength of America is in the hearts and souls of citizens who are working to change this country one person at a time, those who've heard the call to love a neighbor just like they'd like to be loved themselves. Dan is a soldier in the army of compassion. Thank you for your example. Thank you for your care.

We're getting close to voting time. Who's counting the days? [*Laughter*] And I'm here to ask for your help. I believe with your help, we will carry Ohio again and win a great victory in November.

So Laura and I and the girls are here to thank you for what you are going to do over the next less than 2 weeks: call the phone—get on the phone and call the voters; put up the signs; find those discerning Democrats like the mayor, independents, Republicans; get people to do their duty and vote.

And when you do, as you get them out to vote, remind them what this economy has been through. I know there's tough times here in Ohio. Remind everybody what we have been through. You might remind them, starting with this point: The stock market was in a serious decline 6 months prior to my arrival in Washington, DC. And then we had a recession. In other words, that stock market decline was an indicator that the economy was heading south, and it did. And then we had some corporate scandals. We passed tough law to make it abundantly clear we're not going to tolerate dishonesty in the boardrooms of America. And then we got attacked. And those attacks cost us nearly a million jobs in the 3 months after September the 11th, 2001.

Our economy has been through a lot. But we acted. We cut the taxes to spur consumption and investment, and our economy is growing. We raised the child credit to help people with kids. We lowered the marriage penalty. Listen, we don't want a Tax Code that penalizes marriage. We want a Tax Code that encourages marriage. We reduced rates on everybody who pays taxes. I don't think you ought to be trying to pick and choose winners when it comes to tax relief. If you pay taxes, you ought to get relief. We helped our small businesses. We encouraged investment.

Our economy has been growing at rates as fast as any in nearly 20 years. We've added 1.9 million new jobs since August of 2003. This month of September—in the last month, that being September, the State of Ohio added 5,500 new jobs. Your unemployment rate will drop from 6.3 to 6 percent. We're moving forward.

I signed a bill that's going to help our manufacturers. It will save $77 billion over the next 10 years for the manufacturing sector of America. That will help keep jobs here. It's a bill that extended the $100,000 expensing deduction, expensing allowance for small businesses. That will help keep jobs here in Ohio. It closes corporate loopholes. It repeals the 4.3 percent tax on railroad diesel and barge fuel. That will help keep jobs here in Ohio.

To keep jobs here, we've got to have less regulations on our job creators. To keep jobs growing in Ohio, we need to do something about the junk lawsuits that plague the job creators in the State of Ohio.

It's important for us to open up markets for U.S. products, for markets, for crops grown right here in the State of Ohio. Listen, we've opened up our market, and it's good for consumers. Here's the way the market works. If you have more products to choose from, you're like to get that which you want at a better price and higher quality. So rather than hurting our consumers, what I'm saying to places like China, "You treat us the way we treat you; you open up your markets," because we can compete with anybody, anytime, anywhere, so long as the rules are fair.

To keep jobs here, we need an energy plan. I proposed one to the United States Congress over 2 years ago. It's a plan that encourages conservation. It's a plan that encourages the use of renewables. It's a plan that recognizes we can use technology to protect our environment and, at the same time, burn coal and find natural gas. It is a plan that recognizes in order to keep jobs in Ohio, in order to expand the job base here in this State and other States, we must be less dependent on foreign sources of energy.

In order to make sure jobs are here, we've got to do a good job of educating our people. I told the people when I ran I was going to challenge the soft bigotry of low expectations, you know, the system that just shuffled kids through the schools, grade after grade, year after year, without teaching the basics. I kept my word. We passed the No Child Left Behind Act. It raises standards. It spends more money. But in return for more money, we're now measuring. You cannot solve a problem unless you've diagnosed the problem. We're diagnosing problems early now, and more and more of our children are learning to read and write and add and subtract, and we're not going to go back to the days of mediocrity in our classrooms.

Education is more than just elementary school. We'll extend high standards to our high schools. We'll emphasize math and science. We'll continue to expand Pell grants so low- and middle-income Americans can start their career with a college diploma. We're going to continue to expand access to community colleges so that people actually have the skills necessary to fill the jobs of the 21st century.

I'm going to also remind you that to make sure our economy grows, we've got to keep your taxes low. And taxes are an issue in this campaign. They are a significant issue, and I'll tell you why. My opponent has proposed $2.2 trillion of new spending thus far. That's trillion with a "T." [*Laughter*] That's a heck of a lot even for a Senator from Massachusetts. [*Laughter*]

So they asked him, "How are you going to pay for it?" And he pulled out that same old line, that class warfare line, "Don't worry, we'll pay for it by taxing the rich." You can't raise enough money to pay for $2.2 trillion of new spending by taxing the rich. He says he's going to raise the top two brackets. I'll tell you three things about that.

One, most small businesses are Subchapter S corporations or limited partnerships, which mean they pay tax at the individual income-tax level. And when you're running up the top two brackets, you're taxing about 900,000 to a million small businesses all across America. Guess what, 70 percent of new jobs in America are created by small businesses. It makes no sense to tax job creators.

Secondly, there is a tax gap. There is a difference between what he has promised, 2.2 trillion, and what he can raise. Now, guess who usually gets to fill that gap? Yes, you do.

Thirdly, the so-called rich hire lawyers and accountants for a reason when it comes to tax time: to slip the bill and pass it onto you. The good news is, we're not going to let him tax you. Taxes would be bad for our economy. If you want to make sure you keep jobs here in Ohio, you keep the taxes low. We're not going to let him tax the American people because we're going to win in November. He can run.

He can run—he can even run in camo—[*laughter*]—but he cannot hide.

A couple of other things I want to share with you, and then we're going to talk about health care, as you can see. I want to talk about promoting an ownership society in America. You know, it's said that no one ever washes a rental car. [*Laughter*] There's some wisdom in that. [*Laughter*] When you own something, you care about it. If you own your own small business, you care about the future of America. Do you realize that the homeownership rate under my administration is at an alltime high in America. We're going to talk about health savings accounts in a minute, but this is a way for people to own their own health care and manage their own health care in a way that makes sense for American families and American small businesses.

I want to talk about Social Security and ownership. The 2000 campaign, I remember it clearly. During that campaign, people ran advertisements that said, "If George W. gets elected, our seniors will not get their Social Security checks." You might remember those ads. It's kind of the old typical political scare tactic. Well, as you're out gathering up the vote, remind our senior citizens, I did get elected, and you got your checks. And I'm going to get elected again, and you're still going to get your checks.

The reason I bring that up is because I'm willing to talk about how to make sure the Social Security system is available for our children and our grandchildren. It is necessary to do so. See, we're in good shape as a baby boomer. The money in the trust—there's enough people paying in that we'll be taken care of. We need to worry about the children and grandchildren. We need to worry about whether or not Social Security will be available for them.

In order to make sure Social Security is available for our young, I believe younger workers ought to be allowed to take some of their payroll taxes and set up a personal savings account that will earn a greater rate of interest—rate of return on their money than it does in the current Social Security trust, a personal account they can call their own, a personal account they can pass on to whomever they want, and a personal account the Government will never take away.

And here we have another difference in this campaign. See, I believe a President ought to confront problems and not pass them on to future Presidents and future generations. And we have a problem in Social Security. You might remember one of our debates when my opponent said, "Well, the status quo was fine." Let me remind you of two things about that. One, he is the only person on that stage during the debate that voted to tax Social Security benefits, not once but eight times. And secondly, the status quo is not fine when it comes to our children. A President must be willing to confront problems. And in a new term, I'll bring Republicans and Democrats together to make sure Social Security is available for the younger generation.

Now, let me talk about health care. We have a clear choice when it comes to health care in this campaign. I have a common-sense approach to make sure health care is available and affordable. Available through places like community health centers, where the poor and the indigent can get health care and relieve pressure off of the emergency rooms of the hospitals all across the country. Available by making sure our children of low-income families are fully subscribed in the Government health care program for them.

Affordable by recognizing that most of the uninsured in America work for small businesses, and therefore, small businesses ought to be allowed to pool risk across jurisdictional boundaries so they can buy insurance at the same discounts that big companies are able to do. Affordable through health savings accounts, which we'll discuss. Health care more affordable by moving ge-

neric drugs quicker to the market so our seniors are able to better afford prescription drugs.

Affordable because I'm the first President to have taken on Medicare—I shouldn't say that; other Presidents have talked about Medicare. It used to be called "Medi-scare" because anytime you talked about it, somebody would club you over the head with it as an issue, political issue. But I went to Washington to solve problems. And we had a problem in Medicare. Medicine was changing. Medicine was modernizing; Medicare wasn't. We'd pay tens of thousands of dollars for a heart surgery for a Medicare patient but not a dime for the prescription drugs that could prevent the heart surgery from being needed in the first place. That didn't make any sense. So I brought Republicans and Democrats together. I signed a good Medicare bill that says, in 2006, our seniors will get prescription drug coverage.

To make sure health care is available and affordable, we have got to do something about these frivolous and junk lawsuits that are running up the cost of medicine and running good doctors out of practice. We're going to talk about that issue in a minute.

We're going to talk about that issue in a minute, but I do want to make it very clear there is a difference of opinion between me and my opponent on health care. In one of the debates he said—he looked right in the camera, he said, "The Government doesn't have anything to do with it," referring to his health care program. Stared right in the camera and said it. I could barely contain myself. [*Laughter*]

The Government has got a lot to do with it. Eight out of ten people that will be signed up for health insurance on his program will end up on a Government program. When you raise the limits of Medicaid, it provides an incentive for small-business owners to provide no insurance for their employees because the Government will pick it up. And therefore, millions of people will go from private insurance to the Government rolls. His is a plan that creates 225 new mandates for small businesses. Government-run health care does not work. We have got a great health care system in the world because it's innovative, because it's—private medicine is at the center of our health care system. And my opponent's plan would increase the scope and the size of the Federal Government when it comes to your health care decisions.

In all we do to make sure health care works, we'll make sure the decisions are between patients and doctors, not by officials in Washington, DC.

Up here with me is Michael Gordon. No, not Michael Gordon. He didn't make it. Michael Gordon was supposed to be here. He's a small-business owner. Let me talk about Michael Gordon right quick. He's stuck out there, probably behind a barricade chanting, "Four more years." [*Laughter*]

Audience member. Four more years!

The President. Oh, Michael, you made it. [*Laughter*]

Anyway, he's from Tendon Manufacturing. He's a small business. He's adding employees. He's optimistic—a small manufacturing company here in Ohio. He is a Subchapter S corporation. I wish Michael were sitting up here so you could see him. He's a Subchapter S. He's expanding his business. When you run up the top two brackets of the Tax Code, you're taxing Michael. You're taxing his company. It makes no sense to tax the small-business job creators, which is precisely what Senator Kerry will do.

Now, let me talk to you about Bruce, Bruce McDonnell. That's you.

Bruce McDonnell. That's me.

The President. Okay. [*Laughter*] What do you do, Bruce?

Mr. McDonnell. I'm a CPA.

The President. You are? Good. And he is here to discuss with us health savings accounts. Some of you have heard of health savings accounts; some of you haven't heard of health savings accounts. But it is an innovative way to make sure the health care costs are reasonable.

Describe to us, if you don't mind, for this great crowd how it works.

[*At this point, Mr. McDonnell made brief remarks.*]

The President. Let me stop you. That's to pay for major medical bills. So anything above 1,000 for an individual will be taken care of by the insurance company. Go ahead.

[*Mr. McDonnell made further remarks.*]

The President. Right. So here's the way it works. He says—what he just said is, a health savings account, one, is a combination of a tax-free saving account plus a high deductible insurance policy. So say you've got a $1,000 deductible, from zero to 1,000, you're responsible for paying, or in his case, his company contributes from the zero to 1,000 a portion of that. And then above 1,000, the insurance company pays for it.

But think about the benefits of that kind of plan. First of all, if you don't use all 1,000, it's rolled over to the next year tax-free, so that you begin to accumulate savings for your own health care. Secondly, if he were to start a new firm, which I'm not suggesting you're going to do, but if you were, and you moved, the health care account would go with you. It's yours. You own the health care account. You make the decisions. Decisionmaking between patient and doctor is a part of how we introduce market forces into a health care industry. One way to control cost is to let consumers have more decisionmaking, which is precisely what a health savings account does.

Isn't that right?

Mr. McDonnell. Absolutely right.

The President. Did we get it right?

Mr. McDonnell. You got it right.

The President. This is a very interesting way to help small businesses hold down—[*applause*].

Guess who else is a health savings account owner? Doc, you're a health savings account owner—Dr. Schwieterman. Where are you from, doc?

Tom Schwieterman. I'm from Mercer County, which is on the other side of the State, Mr. President.

The President. Welcome. Glad you're here. You are a doctor of?

Dr. Schwieterman. Family practice, and I provided obstetrics up until a month ago.

The President. Yes. We've got a problem. "Provided up until a month ago"—helps define what we're here to talk about, which is good health care for people.

Doc, tell me, you have been—you've told me something really interesting. I don't know if you know this, but my grandfather was raised in Columbus, Ohio. He ended up being a Senator from Connecticut—Connecticut, yes. My dad, as you know, was in politics. I'm in politics. Anybody in your family ever been a doctor before?

Dr. Schwieterman. I am the fourth generation family physician in the same town and actually in the same building in rural Mercer County.

The President. Yes. Nothing wrong with following the old family footsteps. [*Laughter*]

Dr. Schwieterman. Little easier, though.

The President. Right, girls. [*Laughter*] Oops.

So, we were backstage talking. I mean, this is, obviously, not the first time I met Tom, or the doc, I call him. We have a—he's a rural doc. Rural health care is really important for the quality of life in a State like Ohio. And so tell me, describe your problem.

Dr. Schwieterman. We have a family practice that has a very long heritage, of course, 113 years of providing general medical care and obstetrics. Over those 113 years, we have delivered over or near

10,000 children, and—[*applause*]. Thank you. See, my dad's right there. He delivered 5,000.

The President. Is that Dad?

Dr. Schwieterman. That's my dad.

The President. Hey, Dad. You raised a good boy.

Dr. Schwieterman. And during those 110–13 years, we have never had a claims made against our practice. We have retained a majority of those births within the practice. And unfortunately, last month, we were forced to do our last delivery, and this was a fourth generation patient. And she unfortunately ended the legacy that we have enjoyed for so long.

The President. And why? Tell people why. They need to know the truth. The people of Ohio need to understand what's taking place as a result of all these lawsuits.

Dr. Schwieterman. For the past 3 years, we've pretty much done ob at cost. What we took in is what we paid out in malpractice, and this year, we—our premiums went up 40 percent, and it became a point where we could not afford to maintain a small business with our employees, take care of our patients, with the premiums going from 25 to 80 thousand dollars in 48 months.

The President. Yes. Let me tell—people need to hear this. This is an issue in this campaign. The quality of life in the State of Ohio depends on whether or not you've got good docs and good, strong hospitals and people being able to find health care in cities and in rural America.

Let me talk to you about these lawsuits. First of all, docs practice what's called defensive medicine. If you've got a lawyer looming right behind you all the time, if you're worried about what happens in the court—in the—okay, fine. Everybody needs a good lawyer. I've got too many myself. Anyway—[*laughter*]—it's the difference between some lawyers and personal injury trial lawyers that are constantly out there trying to convert this legal system into what looks like a lottery. And guess who ends up paying for the ticket? The taxpayers and the people, because the quality of health care is going down.

If you've got a lawsuit, if you think you're going to get sued, you're going to practice more medicine than is needed so you can defend yourself in a court of law. That's what happens, and guess what that does to the Federal budget, for example. The defensive practice of medicine costs our budget about $28 billion a year. I say "our" budget, because when I talk about the Government budget, you pay for it. It's your money, 28 billion a year in excess costs in Medicaid and Medicare and veterans' health benefits. This is a national issue.

Secondly, because of the lawsuits, because many people just settle whether the suit has merit or not, premiums go up. And guess who pays the premiums? You do.

And thirdly, as a result of a lot of these lawsuits, people just can't simply practice medicine anymore. And you just talk—you just heard the story that unfortunately is being repeated over and over and over again in America. This country needs medical liability reform—now.

And this is an issue in this campaign. This is an issue in campaign—this campaign. Oh, I heard him in the debates, my opponent. I heard him talking about medical liability reform. But let me tell you something. We had a bill on the floor of the United States Senate to provide liability protection to ob-gyns, and my opponent voted "no." He's voted against medical liability reform 10 times in the United States Senate. He can run, but he cannot hide from that record.

Barb Coen is with us. Doc, thanks. Where do you work?

Barbara L. Coen. I work in Norton, Ohio, at a practice called Generations Women's Health Care, with my partner, Dr. Susan Clark, who's here.

The President. Where's the doc? Oh, there you go. Thanks for coming. I appreciate you. Very good. Dr. Clark?

Dr. Coen. Dr. Clark.

The President. Yes, Dr. Clark. Good to see you, doc. You must have drawn the short straw, so you're the one who had to actually get up here and talk in front of all the cameras. [*Laughter*] Tell us about your practice. Just give—tell people exactly what's happening.

[*Dr. Coen made brief remarks, concluding as follows.*]

Dr. Coen. And as all of you know who've had a baby, the relationship between an ob-gyn and a pregnant patient is pretty special. They trust you with not only their life but the life of their unborn child. I can't tell you what an honor it is to be the first person to touch a new life when it comes into the world. There is absolutely nothing like it.

The President. Listen, it was pretty cool to be the second person when I touched Barbara and Jenna. [*Laughter*] Go ahead. They'll be happy to hear I let the doc go first. [*Laughter*]

[*Dr. Coen made further remarks.*]

The President. Thank you, doc. I appreciate you. Thank you. [*Applause*] Okay, thanks, hold on. We've got more work to do here. Thank you. Stay right there. Thank you all. And not only do we need legislation, we need something that works. Legislation that doesn't work is not a good deal. We're not going to do that. We need to make sure that there is a real cap on noneconomic damages. If you want docs to be in practice, we need to make sure that the reform of the medical liability law works. That's why I believe in firm caps to keep docs in business.

Andy Kazar is with us. Andy, tell us your story. This is—just, again, I want people listening to understand the consequences of not getting a good medical liability law out of the United States Senate, a law that my opponent has consistently opposed. Please.

[*Aundria D. Kazar made brief remarks.*]

The President. See, this is—the story is being repeated all across the country. I was in Pennsylvania yesterday—ob-gyns can't practice. Women have to drive miles in order to find a doc. This is not the quality of life that we expect here in America. And it's caused by frivolous lawsuits. Make no mistake about it, it is a legal culture.

When you're out rounding up the vote or if you're listening and trying to determine who you're for, remember the stories up here, remember the stories of good-hearted docs who are worried about practicing their skill. And remember the story about moms who are deeply concerned about their child. This is a big issue in this campaign.

Now, I want to talk about a couple of other issues, and then we'll all go home and start working. Actually, I'm going down to Florida; you're going to go home and start working. [*Laughter*] The—and I'm not going down there to sit on the beach, either. [*Laughter*] I'm going down there to campaign.

Two other—a couple of other things. I talk about time of change, and these are changing times. Some things don't change. The values we try to live by don't change, courage and compassion, reverence and integrity. And we stand for a culture of life in which every person matters and every being counts. We stand for institutions like family and marriage, which are the foundations of our society. And we stand for judges—Federal judges who know the difference between personal opinion and the strict interpretation of the law.

Talking about education and health care, these are very important issues. But let me say to you that it all goes to naught if we don't secure this country, that the security of the American people is the most important responsibility of the President. If we show any uncertainty or weakness in this decade, this world of ours will drift toward tragedy. This isn't going to happen so long as I'm your President.

Let me talk to you—I want to talk to you about some of the lessons that I've learned as your President after September the 11th. First of all, we face an enemy which has no conscience. They are cold-blooded. Therefore, you can never hope for the best with them. You cannot negotiate with them. You can't say, "Oh, well, maybe we'll sign a peace treaty, and therefore, they'll change their ways." The only way to secure America, to keep us safe, is to find them and bring them to justice before they hurt us again. And therefore, any strategy has got to be one that is consistent, firm, and resolved and never relenting. [*Applause*]

Hold on a second. Hold on for a—I've got some more I've got to tell you.

Secondly, this is a different kind of war. You've got to understand, I wish I wasn't talking about war. No President ever wants to be the President of a country—of our country during war. War is horrible. But it's necessary to be realistic during these times. Our most solemn duty is to protect you, and it's a different kind of war than we're used to. It's a kind of war when you say something, you need to speak clearly and mean what you say.

And so when I said, "If you harbor a terrorist, you're just as guilty as the terrorist," I meant what I said. I was speaking to the Taliban in Afghanistan. And see, I was talking to the Taliban because they were providing safe haven for Al Qaida. Al Qaida was training there. And we said, "Listen, get rid of Al Qaida." They didn't believe the United States of America. But because of a great military and because I meant what I said, Al Qaida and—the Taliban is no longer in control of Afghanistan and Al Qaida is on the run.

We're making progress. Three-quarters of Al Qaida and their associates have been brought to justice. I assure you, we're after the rest of them. And the Taliban no longer is in power. And as a result of our action, America and the world are safer.

But I want to tell your sons and daughters about what has taken place in an incredibly brief period of time. It wasn't all that long ago in Afghanistan that young girls were not allowed to go to school. Think about a society that was run by such barbarians that girls were not allowed to be educated. These ideologues of hate had a dark vision about the future. As a matter of fact, if their moms didn't toe the line, they'd be whipped in the public square and sometimes executed in a sports stadium. In defending ourselves and upholding doctrine, we liberated the people of Afghanistan. Twenty-five million people now live in freedom. Millions went to the polls to vote for their President, and the first voter was a 19-year-old woman.

Three-and-a-half years ago, if you would have asked anybody whether or not women would be voting in Afghanistan for President, they would have said, "You're crazy. You're wrong." And freedom is on the march. Darkness has turned to light in Afghanistan, and America is better off for it. We're better off to have an example of freedom in that part of the world. We're better off to have an ally in Afghanistan, an ally in the war on terror. And we're making progress in Iraq.

The third lesson of September the 11th, by the way, is we've got to take threats seriously before they fully materialize. You can't hope—you cannot hope for the best. It used to be, prior to September the 11th, that if we saw a threat, we could deal with it or not deal with it because we didn't ever think it would come home to hurt us. That's what we thought. That all changed on September the 11th. You better have a President who fully understands that.

My opponent in his convention speech said, "Oh, we'll respond if attacked." That is a pre-September the 11th mindset that is dangerous in the world in which we live. We've got to take threats seriously before they come to hurt us.

And I saw a threat in Saddam Hussein. The world is better off with Saddam Hussein sitting in a prison cell. [Applause] Thank you all.

There will be Presidential elections there in January. Think how far that society has come from the days of mass graves and torture chambers.

You know, I told the story one time about the seven—there's a lot of docs here and healers here. One of the most poignant stories of my Presidency was when the Oval Office door opened and in came seven men from Iraq, all of whom had had their right hand cut off by Saddam Hussein because the currency of that country had devalued and he needed scapegoats. It's a true story, I'm telling you. And I asked one of the men there, I said, "Why you?" He said he was a small merchant who needed gold to make jewelry, and he sold dinars to buy another currency so he could buy the gold, and it just happened to be on the day that Saddam was looking for a scapegoat. He found seven small merchants, seven individuals, hauled in, Xs carved in their foreheads, and their right hands cut off.

They had come to see me in the Oval Office because, guess what happened? Great compassion existed for them when their stories were known. They had been to Houston, Texas, to get new hands put on. And the guy who did it is a guy I know, and he said, "Would you mind welcoming these citizens of the world into the Oval Office," which I was more than happy to do. They came in; they were in awe of the Oval Office, of course. You know, I'm kind of a weeper at times; and they were weeping; I was semi-weeping. The guy grabs a Sharpie with his new hand and folds it and writes a prayer in Arabic blessing the United States of America. I told the guy, I told him, I said, "Freedom is on the march in your country. There will be institutions greater than the people there. One of the great things about the American Presidency is the office is always greater than the person. And someday in your country, the institutions will be bigger than the individuals, so that no leader will ever be able to pluck you out of society and cut off your right hand again."

People want to be free in this world. There will be elections in Iraq. Listen, these enemies are trying to stop us. This guy Zarqawi, he's trying to stop the march of freedom. Freedom frightens these ideologues of hate. It is the worst thing that can happen to them. They can't stand the thought of free societies.

I love to tell the story about our friend Koizumi. I'm getting kind of wound up here, yes. [*Laughter*] She wants me to— all right, hold on a second. I kind of felt the invisible hook, you know. [*Laughter*]

I want to share this with you, though, because it's important for you to know my thinking about how to make this world a better place. I have a deep desire for your children to grow up in a peaceful world. I understand my duty to protect this country. I believe that liberty can transform societies. I believe that, and living proof of that is the fact that Prime Minister Koizumi is a good friend of Laura and mine. That probably doesn't seem much to some, but remember, it wasn't all that long ago, 60 years ago, that we were at war with the Japanese. The Japanese were the sworn enemy of the United States of America. My dad fought against the Japanese. I'm confident many of your relatives fought against the Japanese.

And after we won the war in World War II, Harry S. Truman, President of the United States, and others in our country believed in the power of liberty to transform an enemy into an ally. There was a lot of skeptics then. You can understand why. "An enemy couldn't conceivably become a democracy," some would say. "Why do we even care about working with a country that had inflicted * so much harm on the citizens of this country?" But there was great faith in this view. And as a result

---

* White House correction.

of that and as a result of helping Japan become a democracy, I sit down at the table with the Prime Minister of a former enemy, talking about how to keep the peace in a troubled world, talking about doing what we all want, and that is to extend the peace.

Someday, an American President will be sitting down with the duly elected leader of Iraq talking about the peace in the Middle East, and our children and our grandchildren will be better off for it. [*Applause*]

Hold on for a second. I have a—I believe that people want to be free. Freedom is not America's gift to the world; freedom is the Almighty God's gift to each man and woman in this world.

In the closing days of this campaign, it's very important for you to remind your friends and neighbors we have—my opponent and I have a different vision about how to keep America secure. He talks in terms of a "global test" before we commit troops. I didn't make that up. The man was standing right there when he said it—well, right here to my right during the debate. He wasn't there physically right now. I saw a lot of heads turn. [*Laughter*]

Listen, I work with our friends and allies. We'll continue to build alliances. But I will never turn over America's national security decisions to leaders of other countries.

I want to thank you all for coming to greet us. I want to thank you for your help. I know where I want to lead this country. I know what it takes to continue to expand this economy so people can find work. I've got a vision for a health care plan that empowers patients and docs. I believe in high standards in our schools, and we'll continue to press for educational excellence for every child. And I understand that the President of the United States must be consistent and firm and resolved in these troubling times.

You know, when I campaigned across your State, I said if you gave me—in 2000—if you gave me a chance to serve, I would uphold the honor and the dignity of the office to which I had been elected. With your hard work, with your help, I will do so for 4 more years.

God bless. And thank you all for coming.

NOTE: The President spoke at 2:06 p.m. at the Canton Palace Theatre. In his remarks, he referred to Mayor George M. McKelvey of Youngstown, OH, who introduced the President; Gov. Bob Taft and Lt. Gov. Jennette B. Bradley of Ohio; Mary Regula, wife of Representative Ralph Regula; former President Saddam Hussein of Iraq; senior Al Qaida associate Abu Musab Al Zarqawi; and Prime Minister Junichiro Koizumi of Japan.

The President's Radio Address
October 23, 2004

Good morning. In the 3 years since September the 11th attacks, our Government has acted decisively to protect the homeland.

This week, I took another important step by signing the 2005 Homeland Security Appropriations Act. This bill provides essential resources for Coast Guard patrols and port security, for the Federal Air Marshal program, and for technology that will defend aircraft against missiles. With this law, we are adding new resources to patrol our borders and to verify the identity of foreign visitors to America. The new law also includes vital money for first-responders and for better security of chemical facilities and nuclear plants and water treatment plants and bridges and subways and tunnels.

All these measures show the unwavering commitment of our Government. And since 2001, we have tripled overall spending for homeland security. We are doing everything in our power to protect the American people. There is more to do, and we are moving forward.

To protect America, our country needs the best possible intelligence. Chairman Tom Kean and other members of the 9/11 Commission made thoughtful and valuable recommendations on intelligence reform. My administration is already implementing the vast majority of those recommendations that can be enacted without a vote of Congress. We are expanding and strengthening the capabilities of the CIA. We are transforming the FBI into an agency whose primary focus is stopping terrorism. We have established the Terrorist Threat Integration Center so we can bring together all the available intelligence on terrorist threats in one place.

But other changes require new laws. Congress needs to create the position of the National Intelligence Director, with strong authority over the personnel and budgets of our intelligence agencies. These and other reforms are necessary to make our intelligence community more effective and to stay ahead of the threats. My administration has sent proposed legislation to Capitol Hill, and we are working with Congress to pass a good bill. I urge Congress to act quickly, so I can sign these needed reforms into law.

The surest way to defend our country is to stay on the offensive against terrorists. In an era of weapons of mass destruction, waiting for threats to arrive at our doorsteps is to invite disaster. Tyrants and terrorists will not give us polite notice before they attack our country. As long as I am the Commander in Chief, I will confront dangers abroad so we do not have to face them here at home.

My opponent has a fundamental misunderstanding of the war on terror. Senator Kerry was recently asked how September the 11th had changed him. He replied, quote, "It didn't change me much at all," end quote. And his unchanged world view becomes obvious when he calls the war on terror primarily an intelligence and law enforcement operation. That is very dangerous thinking.

We must fight the war on terror with every asset of our national power. We are waging a global campaign from the mountains of central Asia to the deserts of the Middle East and from the Horn of Africa to the Philippines. These efforts are paying off. Since September the 11th, 2001, more than three-quarters of Al Qaida's key members and associates have been killed, captured, or detained. The rest of them know we will hunt them down.

America faces a grave threat, and our Government is doing everything in its power to confront and defeat that threat.

We're making progress in protecting our homeland and progress against the terrorists who seek to harm our Nation. And by staying focused and determined, we will prevail.

Thank you for listening.

NOTE: The address was recorded at 7:46 a.m. on October 22 in the Cabinet Room at the White House for broadcast at 10:06 a.m. on October 23. The transcript was made available by the Office of the Press Secretary on October 22 but was embargoed for release until the broadcast. In his remarks, the President referred to Thomas H. Kean, Chairman, National Commission on Terrorist Attacks Upon the United States (9/11 Commission). The Office of the Press Secretary also released a Spanish language transcript of this address.

Remarks in Fort Myers, Florida
October 23, 2004

The President. Thank you all. Thank you all for coming.

Audience members. Four more years! Four more years! Four more years!

The President. It's getting close to voting time, and I am here to ask for your help. Get your friends and neighbors to go to the polls. Remind people we have a duty to vote. And when you get them headed to the polls—and by the way, don't overlook discerning Democrats—*[laughter]*—people like Senator Zell Miller. When you get them headed to the polls, remind them, if they want a safer America, a stronger America, and a better America, to put me and Dick Cheney back in office.

I want to thank you all for coming. It's a great way to start a Saturday morning, at the ballpark with a lot of great Americans. I'm so happy that Laura is traveling with me today. Today I'm going to talk about why I think you need to put me

back in office for 4 more years, but perhaps the most important reason of all is so that Laura is the First Lady for 4 more years.

My runningmate, Dick Cheney, is out working hard. Listen, I readily concede, he does not have the waviest hair in the race. *[Laughter]* You'll be happy to hear I didn't pick him because of his hairdo. *[Laughter]* I picked him because of his judgment and his experience, and he's getting the job done for the American people.

I'm proud of my brother Jeb. When the hurricanes hit this part of your State, I came by to try to lend my support, to remind people that the Federal Government will do everything we can do to help the people of this part of the world get their feet back on the ground. But your Governor showed great compassion and great leadership.

I want to thank Connie Mack for joining us today. He represented this State and this district with such class and dignity. I'm proud that his son, Connie Mack IV, is running for the United States Congress. Nothing—there's nothing wrong with a son following in a father's footsteps. When you're in there voting for Connie, make sure you put Mel Martinez in the United States Senate.

I want to thank my friend Congressman Mark Foley for joining us today. I appreciate the mayor of Fort Myers being here. Mayor Humphrey, thanks for coming. I want to thank the attorney general for joining us. I want to thank the house speaker. Listen, I want to thank all the people who are serving for coming here today.

I thank my friend Daron Norwood for singing to help entertain you before the—before we made it here.

Most of all, I want to thank you. I want to thank the people putting up the signs, making the phone calls, doing all the hard work at the grassroots level. With your help, we'll carry Florida again and win a great victory.

We've just got 10 days to go in this campaign. And voters have a clear choice between two very different candidates with different approaches and different records. You know where I stand, and sometimes—and sometimes, you even know where my opponent stands. [*Laughter*] We both have records. I am proudly running on mine. The Senator is running from his—[*laughter*]—and there's a reason why. There's a reason why. There is a mainstream in American politics, and my opponent sits on the far left bank. [*Laughter*] I'm a compassionate conservative and proudly so.

This election comes down to five clear choices for American families, five choices on issues of great consequence: your family's security; your family's budget; your quality of life; your retirement; and the bedrock values that are so critical to our families and to our future.

The first clear choice is very important because it concerns the security of our country and the security of your family.

All our progresses on every issue depends on the safety of our citizens. This will be the first Presidential election since September the 11th, 2001. Americans will go to the poll in a time of war and ongoing threats unlike any we have faced before. The terrorists who killed thousands of innocent people are still dangerous and determined to strike us again. The outcome of this election will set the direction of the war against terror. The most solemn duty of the American President is to protect the American people. If America shows uncertainty or weakness in this decade, the world will drift toward tragedy. This will not happen on my watch.

Since that terrible morning of September the 11th, 2001, we have fought the terrorists across the Earth, not for pride, not for power, but because the lives of our citizens are at stake. Our strategy is clear. We've strengthened protections for our homeland. We're reforming our intelligence capabilities. To meet the changing threats in today's world, we are transforming our All-Volunteer Army—I will keep it an all-volunteer army. We're on the offensive. We will stay on the offensive. And we're succeeding. More than three-quarters of Al Qaida's key members and associates have been brought to justice, and the rest of them know we're on their trail.

My opponent has a very different approach. He says that September the 11th— he says that September the 11th, quote, "didn't change me much at all," end quote.

Audience members. Boo-o-o!

The President. And that's pretty clear. He considers the war on terror primarily a law enforcement and intelligence gathering operation.

Audience members. Boo-o-o!

The President. His top foreign policy adviser questioned it is even a war at all, saying, "It's just like a metaphor, like the war on poverty."

Audience members. Boo-o-o!

The President. Anyone who thinks we are fighting a metaphor does not understand the enemy we face. You cannot win a war if you are not convinced we're even in one.

Senator Kerry also misunderstands our battle against the insurgents and terrorists in Iraq. After voting to authorize force against Saddam Hussein, after calling it the right decision when I sent troops into Iraq, the Senator now calls it the "wrong war."

Audience members. Boo-o-o!

The President. The Senator used to recognize that Saddam Hussein was a gathering threat who hated America. After all, he said so. He used to recognize that Saddam was a state sponsor of terror with a history of pursuing and even using weapons of mass destruction. After all, he said so. He used to understand that Saddam was a major source of instability in the Middle East. After all, he said so. And when he voted to authorize force, the Senator must have recognized the nightmare scenario that terrorists might somehow access weapons of mass destruction. Senator Kerry seems to have forgotten all of that, as his position has evolved during the course of the campaign. You might call it election amnesia. I know then and I know now that America and the world are safer with Saddam Hussein sitting in a prison cell.

Senator Kerry now calls Iraq a "diversion."

Audience members. Boo-o-o!

The President. But the case of just one terrorist shows how wrong his thinking is. It's a man named Zarqawi. He's responsible for planting car bombs and beheading Americans in Iraq. I want you to remember, he ran a terrorist camp, a terrorist training camp in Afghanistan until our forces arrived to destroy that camp. He then fled to Iraq. He recently publicly announced his allegiance to Usama bin Laden. If Zarqawi and his associates were not busy fighting American forces in Iraq, what does Senator Kerry think, that he'd be a small-business man? [*Laughter*] That he'd be living a peaceful life, making positive contributions to society somewhere? I don't think so. Our troops will defeat them

there so we do not have to face them in our own cities.

The choice in this election cannot be clearer. You cannot lead our Nation to the decisive victory on which the security of every American family depends if you do not see the true dangers of the post-September 11th world. My opponent has a September the 10th point of view. At his convention, he declared that his strategy will be to respond to attacks after America is hit.

Audience members. Boo-o-o!

The President. That would be too late. In our debates, he said with a straight face, we can defend America only if we pass a "global test."

Audience members. Boo-o-o!

The President. I'm not making that up. I heard him. He was standing right there when he said it. I will work with our friends and allies, but I will never turn over our national security decisions to leaders of other countries.

I want to thank the veterans who are here. I want to thank the military families who are here. I want to thank those who wear the uniform who are here. You will have the full support of our Government. That's why I went to Congress and proposed $87 billion of funding. I want—as you gather up the vote, I want you to remind your fellow citizens of this startling statistic. Four Members of the United States Senate voted to authorize the use of force and then voted against funding for our troops in combat—only four Members—two of whom were my opponent and his runningmate.

Audience members. Boo-o-o!

The President. My opponent is a person who said he actually did vote for the $87 billion, right before he voted against it. He then said, "The whole thing was a complicated matter." There's nothing complicated about supporting our troops in harm's way.

I believe in the transformational power of liberty. I want you to recognize what's happened in Afghanistan. That country has gone from darkness to light. Young girls couldn't go to school some 3½ years ago. Their mothers were whipped in the public square if they didn't toe the line of these barbaric Taliban. Today, because we defended ourselves, freedom is on the march. Millions voted in a Presidential election. The first voter was a 19-year-old woman. And the world is better off for it.

Despite ongoing violence, Iraq has an Interim Government. It's building up its own security forces. We're headed toward elections in January. You see, we're safer, America is safer with Afghanistan and Iraq on the road to democracy. We can be proud that 50 million citizens of those countries now live as free men and women. We must understand that free societies help us keep the peace. I believe strongly in freedom. Freedom is not America's gift to the world; freedom is the Almighty God's gift to each man and woman in this world.

The second clear choice in this election concerns your family budget. When I ran for President 4 years ago, I pledged to lower taxes for America's families. I kept my word. We doubled the child credit to $1,000 per child. We reduced the marriage penalty. Our Tax Code ought to encourage marriage, not penalize marriage. We dropped the lowest bracket to 10 percent to help our families. We reduced income taxes for everybody who pays taxes. As a result of these good policies, real after-tax income, the money in your pocket, the money you get to use, is up about 10 percent since I took office.

Our economy has been through a lot. See, that stock market was in serious decline 6 months prior to my inauguration. That stock market decline foretold a recession. And then we had some corporate scandals. By the way, we made it clear, we're not going to tolerate dishonesty in the boardrooms of this country. And then we got attacked, and those attacks hurt our economy. We lost about a million jobs in the 3 months after September the 11th.

But our economic policies have led us back to growth, and that's good for American families. Our economy is growing at rates as fast as any in nearly 20 years. We've added 1.9 million new jobs since August of 2003. The national unemployment rate is 5.4 percent, lower than the average of the 1970s, the 1980s, and the 1990s. The unemployment rate in your great State is 4.5 percent. We're moving forward.

My opponent has different plans for your budget. He intends to take a big chunk out of it.

Audience members. Boo-o-o!

The President. When I asked Congress to help grow this economy and help our American families, he voted against the higher child credit; he voted against marriage penalty relief; he voted against lower taxes. If he had had his way, the average middle-class family would be paying 2,000 more a year to the Federal Government.

Audience members. Boo-o-o!

The President. It's kind of part of a pattern. He voted 10 times to raise taxes on gasoline as a United States Senator. And all told, during his 20 years in the Senate, he voted 98 times to raise taxes.

Audience members. Boo-o-o!

The President. Think about it. It's about five times a year he's voted to raise taxes. When a Senator does something that often, he must really enjoy it. [*Laughter*] And that's a warning. That's a predictable pattern. During the campaign, he's made a lot of big, expensive promises. He's promised about $2.2 trillion worth of new spending. That's with a "T." [*Laughter*] That's a lot, even for a Senator from Massachusetts. [*Laughter*]

So they said, "How are you going to pay for it?" And he said, "Oh, I'm just going to tax the rich." We have heard that before. First of all, when you raise the top two brackets, you know who you're taxing;

you're taxing job creators. Most small businesses pay tax at the individual income-tax rate. Seventy percent of new jobs in America are created by small businesses. Raising taxes on small businesses is lousy economic policy.

When you talk about running up the top two brackets or taxing the rich, you raise about 600 billion or 800 billion dollars, depending on who's counting, but remember, that's far short of the 2.2 trillion he promised. So there's a gap, a gap between what he's promised and how he's going to raise the money. And guess who usually gets to fill the gap?

Audience member. We do!

The President. That's exactly right. And finally, the rich hire lawyers and accountants during tax time for a reason; that's to slip the tab and stick you with the bill. We're not going to let him raise your taxes; we're going to carry Florida and win a great victory in November.

Audience members. Four more years! Four more years! Four more years!

The President. The third clear choice in this election involves the quality of life for our Nation's families. I believe a good education and quality health care are important to a successful life. When I ran for President 4 years ago, I promised to end the soft bigotry of low expectations by reforming our public schools. I kept my word. We passed the No Child Left Behind Act, meaningful education reforms to bring high standards to our classrooms and to make schools more accountable to our parents. We're making progress. Math and reading scores are rising. We're closing an achievement gap by helping all students. We will build on these reforms. We will extend them to our high schools so that no child is left behind in America.

We will continue to improve life for our families by making health care more available and more affordable. We'll expand health savings accounts so more small businesses can cover their workers and more families will be able to get health care ac-

counts they can manage and call their own. We will create association health plans so small businesses can join together to buy insurance at the same discounts big companies get.

We will help families in need by expanding community health centers and making sure every eligible child is enrolled in our Government's low-income health programs. We'll help patients and doctors everywhere by doing something about the frivolous lawsuits that run up the cost of your practice and run good doctors out of business. We want our doctors focusing on fighting illnesses, not on fighting frivolous lawsuits. These lawsuits are a national problem that require a national solution. I am for medical liability reform.

Senator Kerry has a different point of view on our schools and health care system. Listen, he voted for the No Child Left Behind Act but now wants to weaken the accountability standards. He's proposed including measures like teacher attendance to judge whether students can read or write or add and subtract.

Audience members. Boo-o-o!

The President. He voted against health savings accounts. He opposes association health plans. He has voted 10 times against medical liability reform.

Audience members. Boo-o-o!

The President. You heard him in the debates the other day, mouth something about helping our docs and patients. Remember, he put a personal injury trial lawyer on the ticket. He can run from his record, but he cannot hide.

Now he's proposing a big Government health care plan that would cause 8 million families to lose private coverage they get at work and have to go onto a Government plan. Eighty percent of the people who get coverage under his idea would be enrolled in a Government program. In one of our debates, he tried to tell America that when it comes to his health care plan, and I quote, "The Government has nothing to do with it." [*Laughter*] I could barely contain myself. [*Laughter*] He can run from his record, but he cannot hide.

My opponent's plan would move America down the road to Federal control of health care, and that is the wrong road for American families. In all we do to improve health care in a new term, we will make sure the decisions are made by doctors and patients, not by officials in Washington, DC.

The fourth clear choice in this election involves your retirement. Our Nation has made a solemn commitment to our seniors on Medicare and Social Security. When I ran for President 4 years ago, I promised to keep that commitment. I promised to improve Medicare by adding prescription drug coverage for our seniors. I kept my word. You remember those endless debates; leaders on both political parties have talked about strengthening Medicare for years. We got the job done. Seniors are now getting discounts on medicine through drug discount cards. Low-income seniors are getting $600 to help them this year and next year. And beginning in 2006, all seniors will be able to get prescription drug coverage under Medicare.

My opponent voted against the Medicare bill that included prescription drug coverage, even though it was supported by AARP and other senior groups. Later he said, quote, "If I'm the President, we're going to repeal that phony bill." Then a little later, he said, "No, I don't want to repeal it." Sounds familiar.

As your President for the next 4 years, I will defend the reforms we have worked so hard to pass and keep the promise to America's seniors. And we will keep the promise of Social Security for our seniors, and as we do so, we will strengthen Social Security for generations to come. Every election, desperate politicians try to scare our seniors about Social Security. It's just predictable. You remember in the 2000 campaign, they ran the ads telling our seniors, "If George W. gets elected, you won't get your Social Security check." Well, when you're out gathering up the vote, remind our seniors that George W. did get elected and our seniors did get their checks. And our seniors will continue to get their checks. And baby boomers are in pretty good shape when it comes to the Social Security trust.

But we all must be concerned about our children and our grandchildren. Someday, our youngest workers will retire, and we've got to make sure the Social Security system will be there when they need it. I believe younger workers ought to be able to take some of their own money and put it into a personal savings account, a personal savings account that will earn a better rate of return, a personal savings account they can call their own, an account the Government cannot take away.

Once again, my opponent takes a different point of view. He talks about protecting Social Security, but he's the only candidate in this race who voted eight times for higher taxes on Social Security benefits.

Audience members. Boo-o-o!

The President. And when it comes to the next generation, he has offered nothing. The job of the President is to confront problems, not to pass them on to future generations and future Presidents. In a new term, I will bring Republicans and Democrats together to strengthen Social Security for an upcoming generation of Americans.

The fifth choice in this election is on the values that are so crucial to keeping our families strong. And here, my opponent and I are miles apart. I believe marriage is a sacred commitment, a pillar of our civilization, and I will defend it. This is not a partisan issue. When Congress passed the Defense of Marriage Act, defining marriage as a union of a man and a woman, the vast majority of Democrats supported it. My predecessor, President Clinton, signed it into law. But Senator Kerry was part of an out-of-the-mainstream minority that voted against the Defense of Marriage Act.

Audience members. Boo-o-o!

The President. I believe that reasonable people can find common ground on difficult issues. Republicans and Democrats and many citizens on both sides of the life issue came together and agreed that we should ban the brutal practice of partial-birth abortion. Senator Kerry was part of an out-of-the-mainstream minority that voted against the ban.

Audience members. Boo-o-o!

The President. He voted against parental notification laws——

Audience members. Boo-o-o!

The President. ——against the Unborn Victims of Violence Act.

Audience members. Boo-o-o!

The President. I will continue to reach out to Americans of every belief and move this goodhearted Nation toward a culture of life.

My opponent has said that the heart and soul of America can be found in Hollywood.

Audience members. Boo-o-o!

The President. Most American families do not look to Hollywood as a source of values. The heart and soul of America is found right here in Fort Myers, Florida.

All these choices make this one of the most important elections in our history. The security and prosperity of our country, the health and education of our families, the retirement of our seniors, and the direction of our culture are all at stake. The decision is in the best hands, because the decision belongs to the American people.

I see a bright future for America. I see a better day for all of us. One of my favorite quotes was written by a fellow Texan, Tom Lea. He said, "Sarah and I live on the east side of the mountain. It's the sunrise side, not the sunset side. It is the side to see the day that is coming, not to see the day that is gone." If you listen carefully to this campaign, my opponent has spent much of this campaign talking about the day that is gone. I see the day that is coming.

We've been through a lot together in the last 4 years. Because we've done the hard work of climbing that mountain, we can see the valley below. We'll protect our families. We'll build their prosperity. We will defend the deepest values. We'll spread freedom in this world, and as we do so, we'll keep America safe and spread the peace.

Four years ago, when I traveled your great State asking for the vote, I made this pledge. I said if I was elected, I would uphold the honor and the dignity of the office to which I had been elected. With your help, I will do so for 4 more years.

God bless. Thanks for coming.

NOTE: The President spoke at 10:10 a.m. at City of Palms Park. In his remarks, he referred to Senator Zell Miller of Georgia, who made the keynote address at the 2004 Republican National Convention; Gov. Jeb Bush of Florida; former Senator Connie Mack III of Florida; Connie Mack IV, candidate in Florida's 14th Congressional District; Mel R. Martinez, senatorial candidate in Florida; Mayor Jim Humphrey of Fort Myers, FL; State Attorney General Charlie Crist of Florida; Johnnie Byrd, speaker, Florida State House of Representatives; entertainer Daron Norwood; senior Al Qaida associate Abu Musab Al Zarqawi; and Usama bin Laden, leader of the Al Qaida terrorist organization.

Remarks in Lakeland, Florida
October 23, 2004

The President. Thank you all for coming.

Audience members. Four more years! Four more years! Four more years!

The President. Thank you all for coming today. Laura and I are so honored that so many came out to say hello. We really appreciate it. It is a beautiful day to be campaigning in the great State of Florida. Of course, according to your Governor, every day is a beautiful day in Florida.

I'm here to ask for your vote, and I'm here to ask for your help. We're close to voting time. As a matter of fact, in your State, voting time is already here. Please go to your friends and neighbors, people from all parties—don't overlook discerning Democrats—[*laughter*]—people like Zell Miller. They want a better country too. Tell them we have a duty in this country to vote. Tell them we have an obligation in a free society to go to the polls. And when you get them headed to the polls, remind them, if they want a safer America and a stronger America and a better America, to put me and Dick Cheney back in office.

I think it's important to go around this country telling people what you're going to do. I'm here to tell you why I think you need to put me in office for 4 more years. But perhaps the most important reason of all is so that Laura is the First Lady for 4 more years.

Audience members. Laura! Laura! Laura!

The President. I'm sure some of you all will appreciate this, when I tell you that Laura and I knew each other in the seventh grade in San Jacinto Junior High in Midland, Texas. We became reacquainted. She was a public school librarian at the time. I said, "Will you marry me?" She said, "Fine, so long as you make me a promise." I said, "What is it?" She said, "I never want to have to give a political speech." [*Laughter*] I said, "Okay, you got a deal." Fortunately, she didn't hold me to that deal. She is giving a lot of speeches, and when she speaks, the American people see a compassionate, warm, strong First Lady.

I'm proud of my runningmate, Dick Cheney. He's doing a great job. I see some others out here who are follically challenged. [*Laughter*] See, I admit he doesn't have the waviest hair in the race. [*Laughter*] You'll be pleased to hear I didn't pick him because of his hairdo. [*Laughter*] I picked him because he can get the job done. I picked him because of his judgment. I picked him because of his experience.

I'm proud to be traveling with my brother. Jeb Bush is a great Governor for Florida. He's led with conviction. You know, one thing about him, you don't have to worry about where he stands. In other words, he's not one of these politicians who is going to take a poll or run a focus group, trying to figure out what to tell you. He stands on principles. That's how we were raised. You stand for what you believe. And Jeb showed great courage and compassion during the times of these storms. I came over to try to lend a hand and show the people of this important State that the Federal Government cared, people around the country cared for you. But I was incredibly impressed by two things, one, Jeb's leadership, and two, the great compassion of the people of Florida.

I'm proud to be up here with Adam Putnam. I call him Red; you call him Congressman. [*Laughter*] We went over and saw some orange growers the other day, and it was my honor to be in that citrus grove, telling the orange growers of this part of the State, we're going to help them get their feet back on the ground.

I want to thank—listen, while you're out there voting, voting for me and Dick Cheney, make sure you vote for Mel Martinez for the United States Senate. He'll be a fine United States Senator, no doubt in my mind.

I want to thank Lieutenant Governor Toni Jennings for being here. I want to thank the State Senate majority whip. I want to thank all the local and State officials who are here.

I want to thank Trini Triggs for performing for you all.

I want to thank the grassroots activists, the people putting up the signs, the people making the phone calls, the people who have encouraged this rally. I want to thank you for what you've done. I want to thank you for what you're going to do. With your help, we will carry Florida and win a great victory in November.

We just got 10 days to go in the campaign. Who's counting? The voters have a clear choice between two very different candidates with dramatically different approaches and records. You know where I stand. And sometimes, you even know where my opponent stands. We both have records. We both have records.

Audience members. Flip-flop! Flip-flop! Flip-flop!

The President. We both have records. I'm proudly running on mine. And the Senator is running from his, and there's a reason why. There is a mainstream in American politics, and Senator John Kerry sits on the far left bank. I'm a compassionate conservative and proudly so. At a time when our country has much to accomplish and much more to do, I offer a record of reform and results, and my opponent offers a long list of out-of-the-mainstream votes.

This election comes down to five clear choices for American families, five choices on issues of great consequence: your family's security; your family's budget; your quality of life; your retirement; and the bedrock values that are so critical to our families and our future.

The first choice is the most important because it concerns the security of your family. All progress on any of the other issues depends on the safety of our citizens. This will be the first Presidential election since September the 11th, 2001. Americans will go to the polls in a time of war and ongoing threats unlike any° we have seen before. The terrorists who killed thousands are still dangerous, and they are determined to strike again. The outcome of this election will set the direction of the war against terrorism.

I believe the most solemn duty of the American President, the most solemn duty, is to protect the American people. If America shows uncertainty or weakness, the world will drift toward tragedy. This will not happen on my watch.

Since that terrible morning, September the 11th, 2001, we've fought the terrorists across the Earth, not for pride, not for power, but because the lives of our citizens are at stake. Our strategy is clear. We're strengthening the homeland. We're reforming our intelligence services. We are transforming our All-Volunteer Army. We will not have a draft. We are staying on the offensive against these terrorists. We are relentless and we are determined, and our strategy is paying off. More than three-quarters of Al Qaida's key members and associates have been brought to justice, and the rest of them know we're on their trail.

My opponent has a different approach. He says that September the 11th, quote, "didn't change me much at all," end quote.

Audience members. Boo-o-o!

The President. And that's pretty clear. He considers the war on terror primarily a law enforcement and intelligence gathering operation.

Audience members. Boo-o-o!

The President. His top foreign policy adviser questioned it is even a war at all, saying, "It's just like a metaphor, like the war on poverty." Anyone who thinks we're fighting a metaphor does not understand the enemy we face. You cannot win a war

---

° White House correction.

if you are not convinced we are even in one.

Senator Kerry also misunderstands our battle against insurgents and terrorists in Iraq. After voting to authorize force against Saddam Hussein, after calling it the right decision when I sent troops into Iraq, the Senator now calls it the "wrong war."

Audience members. Boo-o-o!

The President. The Senator used to recognize that Saddam Hussein was a gathering threat who hated America. After all, he said so. He used to recognize that Saddam was a state sponsor of terror with a history of pursuing and even using weapons of mass destruction. After all, he said so. He used to understand that Saddam was a major source of instability in the Middle East. After all, he said so. And when he voted to authorize force, the Senator must have recognized the nightmare scenario that terrorists might somehow gain access to weapons of mass destruction. Senator Kerry seems to have forgotten all of that as his position has evolved during the course of this campaign. You might call it election amnesia. [*Laughter*] I know then and I know now that the world and America are safer with Saddam Hussein sitting in a prison cell.

Senator Kerry now calls Iraq a "diversion." But the case of just one terrorist shows how wrong his thinking is. A man named Zarqawi is responsible for the car bombs and beheading Americans in Iraq. He ran a terrorist training camp in Afghanistan until coalition troops arrived. He then ran to Iraq, where he's fighting today. He supports and swore allegiance to Usama bin Laden. If Zarqawi and his associates were not busy fighting American forces and Iraqi forces in Iraq, what does my opponent think he'd be doing, a peaceful businessman somewhere? Leading a benevolence campaign? [*Laughter*] Of course not. Our troops will defeat them there so we do not have to face them in our own cities.

The choice in this election could not be clearer when it comes to the security of our families. You cannot lead our Nation to decisive victory, on which the security of every American family depends, if you do not see the true dangers of a post-September the 11th world. My opponent has a September 10th point of view. You might remember, at his convention he declared that his strategy would be to respond to attacks after America is hit.

Audience members. Boo-o-o!

The President. That would be too late. In our debates, he said we can defend America only if we pass a "global test."

Audience members. Boo-o-o!

The President. I'm not making that up. He was standing right there when he said it. I work with our friends and allies. We will strengthen our coalitions. But I will never turn over America's national security decisions to leaders of other countries.

I saw some of our troops coming in. I want to thank them for their service. I want to thank the veterans who are here for having set such a great example for those who wear the uniform. I want to thank our military families who are here for supporting our troops fighting for freedom and security. And I want to assure you your loved ones will have the full support of our Government.

That's why I went to Congress and asked for $87 billion of supplemental funding. This was money to support our troops in harm's way. When you're out gathering up the vote, I want you to remind your fellow citizens of this startling statistic. There were 4 Members in the United States Senate— only 4 out of 100—that voted to authorize the use of force and then voted against funding for our troops in harm's way. And four of those—two of those four were my opponent and his runningmate.

Audience members. Boo-o-o!

The President. They asked him about that vote. He said, "I actually did vote for the 87 billion, right before I voted against it." You know—I bet you don't hear many people talking like that around the coffee shops here. They pressed him even further, and he finally just threw up his hands. He said, "The whole thing is a complicated matter." My fellow Americans, there is nothing complicated about supporting our troops in combat.

And to protect America, we will lead the cause of freedom. I believe in the transformational power of liberty. I want the youngsters here to understand what has taken place in a short period of time. Afghanistan was once ruled by the Taliban. Young girls couldn't go to school. If their mothers didn't toe the ideological line of the haters, they'd be whipped in the public squares and sometime shot in the stadiums. Because we acted in our own self-defense, millions of Afghan citizens went to the polls to vote for the President, and the first voter was a 19-year-old woman. Freedom is on the march. Freedom is precious. Freedom is powerful. And we're better off for it.

Iraq will have Presidential elections in January. Think how far that country has come from the days of torture chambers and the brutality of Saddam Hussein. Fifty million people now live in freedom because we acted to secure ourselves. We're more secure. The world is better off as freedom is on the march. I believe everybody yearns to be free in this world. Freedom is not America's gift to the world; freedom is the Almighty God's gift to each man and woman in this world.

The second clear choice in this election concerns your family budget, your wallet. When I ran for President 4 years ago, I pledged to lower taxes for American families. I have kept my word. We raised the child credit. We reduced the marriage penalty. The Tax Code ought to encourage marriage, not penalize marriage. We created a 10-percent bracket to help working families. We reduced income taxes for everybody who pays taxes. We're helping our small-business owners. And as a result of these policies, real after-tax income, the money in your pocket, is up by about 10 percent since I got into office.

Think about what this economy has been through. Tell your friends and neighbors what we have overcome. Six months prior to my arrival, the stock market was in serious decline, indicating the recession that came. Then we had some corporate scandals. And then we got attacked, and those attacks cost us about a million jobs in the 3 months after September the 11th.

Our economic policies are working. They've led us back to growth. Our economy is growing at rates as fast as any in nearly 20 years. We've added more than 1.9 million new jobs since August of 2003. The unemployment rate is 5.4 percent, lower than the average of the 1970s, 1980s, and 1990s. Farm income is up. Homeownership rates are at an alltime high. The unemployment rate in Florida is 4.5 percent. We're moving forward, and we're not going to go back to the old days.

My opponent has very different plans for your budget. He intends to take a big chunk out of it.

Audience members. Boo-o-o!

The President. When I proposed the tax relief to help our families and get this economy going again, he voted against the higher child tax credit. He voted against the marriage penalty relief. He voted against lower taxes. He voted against the help to small businesses. If he had had his way, the average middle-class family in America would have been paying $2,000 more in Federal income taxes.

Audience members. Boo-o-o!

The President. It's part of a pattern. The Senator has voted 10 times to raise gasoline taxes since he's been in the Senate. And all told, during his 20 years in the United States Senate, my opponent has voted 98 times to raise taxes.

Audience members. Boo-o-o!

The President. Think about that. That's about five times every year he served. When a Senator does something that often, he must really enjoy it. [*Laughter*]

During this campaign, he's made a lot of big promises. As a matter of fact, he's promised about $2.2 trillion in new spending. That's with a "T." [*Laughter*] That's a lot even for a Senator from Massachusetts. [*Laughter*] So they said, "How are you going to pay for it?" He said, "Oh, we'll just tax the rich." We've heard that before, haven't we?

By running up the top two brackets, guess who he's taxing? He's taxing job creators. Seventy percent of new jobs are created by small businesses in America. Most small businesses pay tax at the individual income-tax level. It's a bad idea to tax the job creators in this country.

Raising the top two brackets will raise between 600 and 800 billion dollars, so as you can tell, there's a tax gap. There's a difference between what he has promised and what he can deliver. Now, you know who gets to fill that tax gap, don't you? I'll tell you one other thing about taxing the rich. The rich, during tax time, hire lawyers and accountants for a reason: to slip the tab and to stick you with the bill. We're not going to let him tax you; we're going to carry Florida and win a great victory on November the 2d.

Audience members. Four more years! Four more years! Four more years!

The President. The third clear choice in this election involves the quality of life for our families. A good education and quality health care are important for a successful life. When I ran for President 4 years ago, I promised to end and to challenge the soft bigotry of low expectations in our schools. I kept my word, passed the No Child Left Behind Act, which is a great piece of legislation. It brings high standards to our classrooms and makes our schools accountable to our parents. We're seeing progress. Math and reading scores are rising. We are closing an achievement gap all across America. We will build on these reforms. We'll extend them to our high schools so that no child is left behind in America.

We'll continue to improve life—the life of our families by making health care more affordable and accessible. We'll expand health savings accounts so small businesses can cover their workers and more families are able to get health care accounts they can manage and call their own. We'll create association health plans so small businesses can join together and buy insurance at the discounts that big companies are able to do. We will help our families in need by expanding community health centers. We'll make sure every child eligible is enrolled in our Government's low-income health insurance program.

And we'll help patients and doctors everywhere by doing something about these frivolous lawsuits that are running up the cost of health care and running good doctors out of practice. I met too many obgyns that are having trouble making ends meet, and so they're quitting the practice. I met too many women who are driving miles to get the good health care they need for themselves and their child. And this isn't right for America. You can't be pro-trial-lawyer and pro-doctor and pro-patient at the same time. You have to pick. My opponent made his pick. He put a personal injury trial lawyer on the ticket. I stand for medical liability reform—now.

Senator Kerry has a different point of view on our schools and health care system. Listen, he voted for the No Child Left Behind Act, but now he wants to weaken the accountability standards. He has proposed including measures like teacher attendance to judge whether students can read or write or add and subtract. He voted against health savings accounts. He opposes association health plans that will help our small businesses. He voted 10 times against medical liability reform.

Audience members. Boo-o-o!

The President. He can run from his record, but he cannot hide.

Now he's proposing a big Government health care plan that would cause 8 million families to lose private coverage they get at work and have to go onto a Government plan. Eighty percent of the people who get coverage under his proposal would be enrolled in a Government plan. In one of our debates, he said with a straight face that when it comes to his health care plan, and I quote, "The Government has nothing to do with it." I could barely contain myself when I heard that. [*Laughter*] The Government has a lot to do with it. His plan would move America down the road to Federal control of health care, and that's the wrong road for American families. He can run from his record, but he cannot hide.

In all we do to improve health care, we will make sure decisions are made by doctors and patients, not by officials in Washington, DC.

Fourth clear choice in this election involves your retirement. Our Nation has made a solemn commitment to America's seniors on Social Security and Medicare. When I ran for President 4 years ago, I promised to keep that commitment and improve Medicare by adding prescription drug coverage. I have kept my word. You know, leaders in both political parties have talked about Medicare for years—for years. We got the job done. Seniors are now getting discounts on medicine with drug discount cards. Low-income seniors are getting $600 on their card this year and 600 next year. And beginning in 2006, all seniors will be able to get prescription drug coverage under Medicare.

My opponent voted against the Medicare bill that included prescription drug coverage, even though it was supported by the AARP and other seniors groups. Later he said, quote, "If I am President, we're going to repeal that phony bill." A little later on, he said, "No, I don't want to repeal it." Kind of sounds familiar. As your President for the next 4 years, I will defend the reforms we have worked so hard to pass and keep the promise of Medicare for our senior citizens.

And we will keep the promise of Social Security for our seniors, and we'll strengthen Social Security for generations to come.

Every election, desperate politicians try to scare our seniors about Social Security. It is predictable, and it's beginning to happen again. I want you to tell your friends and neighbors about what happened in the 2000 campaign. They said, "If George W. gets elected, our seniors will not get their checks." Now, you might remember that. Well, tell them George W. did get elected, and our seniors did get their checks. And our seniors will continue to get their checks, and baby boomers like me are in pretty good shape when it comes to the Social Security trust.

But we need to think about our children and our grandchildren. We need to make sure that when they retire, there's a Social Security system available to meet their needs. And that is why I believe younger workers ought to be allowed to take some of their own money and put it in a personal account. It will earn a better rate of return, a personal account they call their own, a personal account the Government cannot take away.

My opponent is taking a different approach. He talks about protecting Social Security. He's the only candidate in this race that voted to tax Social Security benefits eight times.

Audience members. Boo-o-o!

The President. He can run, but he cannot hide. And when it comes to the next generation, he has offered no reform. The job of a President is to confront problems, not to pass them on to future Presidents and future generations. In a new term, I'll bring Republicans and Democrats together to make sure Social Security is around when a younger generation of America needs it.

The fifth clear choice in this election is on the values that are so critical to keeping America's families strong. And my opponent and I are miles apart. I believe marriage is a sacred institution. Marriage is a pillar of our civilization, and I will always defend it. This is not a partisan issue. When Congress passed the Defense of Marriage Act, defining marriage as the union of a man and a woman, the vast majority of Democrats supported it, and my predecessor, President Bill Clinton, signed it into law. Senator Kerry was part of an out-of-the-mainstream minority that voted against the Defense of Marriage Act.

Audience members. Boo-o-o!

The President. I believe that reasonable people can find common ground on the most difficult of issues. Republicans and Democrats and many citizens on both sides of the life issue came together and agreed we should ban the brutal practice of partial-birth abortion. Senator Kerry was part of an out-of-the-mainstream minority that voted against the ban.

Audience members. Boo-o-o!

The President. He voted against parental notification laws.

Audience members. Boo-o-o!

The President. He voted against the Unborn Victims of Violence Act.

Audience members. Boo-o-o!

The President. I'll continue to reach out to Americans of every belief and move this goodhearted Nation toward a culture of life.

My opponent has said that the heart and soul of America can be found in Hollywood.

Audience members. Boo-o-o!

The President. I understand most American families do not look to Hollywood as a source of values. The heart and soul of America is found in communities like Lakeland, Florida.

All of these choices make this one of the most important elections in our history. The security and prosperity of our country, the health and education of our families, the retirement of our seniors, and the direction of our culture are all at stake. And this decision is in the best of hands, because the decision rests with the American people.

I can't tell you how optimistic I am about the future of this country. I see a better day for everybody. You know, one of my favorite quotes was written by a fellow Texan named Tom Lea. He said, "Sarah and I live on the east side of the mountain. It's the sunrise side, not the sunset side. It is the side to see the day that is coming, not the side to see the day that is gone." My opponent has spent much of this campaign talking about the day that is gone. I see the day that is coming.

We've been lot—we've been through a lot together in the last nearly 4 years. Because we've done the hard work of climbing the mountain, we can see the valley below. We'll protect our families and build their prosperity and defend our deepest values. We'll spread freedom in the world and the peace we all want.

Four years ago, when I traveled your State asking for the vote, I pledged to restore honor and dignity to the office to which I had been elected. With your help, I will do so for 4 more years.

God bless. Thank you all. Thank you all. On to victory!

NOTE: The President spoke at 11:55 a.m. at Ty Cobb Field. In his remarks, he referred to Senator Zell Miller of Georgia, who made the keynote address at the 2004 Republican National Convention; Lt. Gov. Toni Jennings of Florida; Paula Dockery, majority whip, Florida State Senate; entertainer Trini Triggs; former President Saddam Hussein of Iraq; and senior Al Qaida associate Abu Musab Al Zarqawi.

Remarks in Melbourne, Florida
October 23, 2004

The President. Thanks for coming today.
Audience members. Four more years! Four more years! Four more years!

The President. Thank you all. Thanks for coming today. We're getting close to voting time—actually, you already are voting here. We're traveling your State not only asking for the vote, I'm here to ask for your help. I'm asking you to get your friends and neighbors and remind them they have a duty to vote in a democracy. And as you're getting people to do their duty, don't overlook discerning Democrats, people like Senator Zell Miller from Georgia. Remind people that if they want a safer America, a stronger America, and a better America, put me and Dick Cheney back in office.

I really enjoy campaigning. I like to be out with the people. I like to tell people why I'm running and what I intend to do as your President for 4 more years. Perhaps the most important reason of all for you to put me back into office is so that Laura will be the First Lady for 4 more years.

Audience members. Laura! Laura! Laura!

The President. Listen, some of you all may appreciate this—I think some of you will appreciate this. When I asked Laura to marry me—well, we'd been to the seventh grade together at San Jacinto Junior High in Midland, Texas. We became reacquainted later on. She was a public school librarian at the time. And when I asked her to marry me, she said, "Fine, but make me a promise." I said, "What is it?" She said, "Promise me that I'll never have to give a political speech." [*Laughter*] I said, "Okay, you got a deal." Fortunately, she didn't hold me to that promise. [*Laughter*] She is giving a lot of speeches, and when she does, the American people see a compassionate, warm, strong First Lady.

I'm proud of my runningmate, Dick Cheney. I fully admit it, he doesn't have the most hair in the race. [*Laughter*] I didn't pick him because of his hairdo. I picked him because of his judgment, his experience. He's getting the job done for the American people.

And I'm proud of brother Jeb. The thing I like about him is you know where he stands. He's not one of these people that takes a poll or a focus group to kind of find his way. And not only that, when times were tough here in the State of Florida, I saw firsthand his steady leadership. Though I came and tried to remind the people of this State the Federal Government would do everything we can to help the people, the truth of the matter is, Florida's great strength is not only your Governor but the fact that neighbor loved neighbor, neighbor helped neighbor. Florida showed great character during these times of testing.

I'm honored to call Buzz Aldrin friend. I appreciate him being here today. He's one of the great pioneers of America. I appreciate you, Buzz, coming. I want to thank you for the example you have set for future pioneers.

I want to thank Congressman Dave Weldon for his service to the great State of Florida. I appreciate you being here, Dave. When you go to the polls, make sure you vote for Mel Martinez. He'll make a great United States Senator. I want to thank all the State and local officials who are here. I want to thank my friends in Little Texas for having played for you all today.

Most of all, I want to thank the grassroots activists who are putting up the signs and making the phone calls, who have worked so hard to make this rally such a fantastic rally. I want to thank you for what you have done and what you're going to do, and that is turn out the vote. And with your help, we'll carry Florida again and win a great victory on November the 2d.

We have just 10 days to go in this election, and voters have a clear choice between two very different candidates and dramatically different approaches and records. You know where I stand, and sometimes, you even know where my opponent stands. [*Laughter*] We both have records. I am proudly running on my record. And the Senator is running from his, and there is a reason why. There is a mainstream in American politics, and my opponent sits on the far left bank. I'm a compassionate conservative and proudly so. At a time when our country has much to accomplish and much more to do, I offer a record of reform and results.

This election comes down to five clear choices for America's families, five choices on issues of great consequence: your family's security; your family's budget; your quality of life; your retirement; and the bedrock values that are so critical to our families and to our future.

The first clear choice is the most important because it concerns the security of your family. All our progress on every other issue depends on the safety of our citizens. This will be the first Presidential election since September the 11th, 2001. Americans will go to the polls in a time of war and ongoing threats unlike any we have faced before. Terrorists who killed thousands are still dangerous. They are determined to strike us again. The outcome of this election will set the direction of the war against terror. The most solemn duty of the American President is to protect the American people. If America shows uncertainty or weakness in this decade, the world will drift toward tragedy. This will not happen on my watch.

Audience members. Four more years! Four more years! Four more years!

The President. Since that terrible morning of September the 11th, 2001, we have fought the terrorists across the Earth, not for pride, not for power, but because the lives of our citizens are at stake. Our strategy is clear. We've strengthened protections for our homeland. We're reforming and strengthening our intelligence services. We're transforming our military. We will not have a draft. We will have an all-volunteer army. We're staying on the offensive. We are resolute, and we are determined to protect the people.

And we're succeeding. More than three-quarters of Al Qaida's key members and associates have been brought to justice, and the rest of them know we're on their trail.

My opponent has a very different approach. He says that September the 11th, quote, "didn't change me much at all"——

Audience members. Boo-o-o!

The President. ——end quote. And that's pretty clear. He considers the war on terror primarily a law enforcement and intelligence gathering operation.

Audience members. Boo-o-o!

The President. His top policy adviser has questioned whether it is even a war at all, saying that, "It's just a metaphor, like the war on poverty."

Audience members. Boo-o-o!

The President. Anyone who thinks we're fighting a metaphor does not understand the enemy we face. You cannot win a war if you are not convinced we are even in one.

Senator Kerry also misunderstands our battle against insurgents and terrorists in Iraq. After voting to authorize force against Saddam Hussein, after calling it the right decision when I sent troops into Iraq, the Senator now calls it the "wrong war."

Audience members. Boo-o-o!

The President. The Senator used to recognize that Saddam Hussein was a gathering threat who hated America. After all, the Senator said so. He used to recognize that Saddam was a state sponsor of terror with a history of pursuing and even using weapons of mass destruction. After all, the Senator said so. He used to understand that Saddam was a major source of instability in the Middle East. After all, the Senator said so. And when he voted to authorize force, the Senator must have recognized the nightmare scenario that terrorists might somehow access weapons of mass destruction. Senator Kerry seems to have forgotten all that as his position has evolved over the course of this campaign. You might call it election amnesia.

I knew it then, and I know it now, that America and the world are safer with Saddam Hussein sitting in a prison cell.

Senator Kerry now calls Iraq a "diversion." But the case of just one terrorist shows how wrong his thinking is. A man named Zarqawi is responsible for planting car bombs and beheading Americans in Iraq. He ran a terrorist training camp in Afghanistan—until we arrived. And then he fled to Baghdad, where he plotted and planned and where he's fighting us today. He publicly announced his allegiance to Usama bin Laden. See, if Zarqawi and his associates were not busy fighting American and Iraqi forces in Iraq, what does my opponent think they'd be doing? Peaceful small-business men? [*Laughter*] Working for benevolent societies? Our troops will defeat the likes of Zarqawi so we do not have to face him in our own cities.

The choice in this election could not be clearer. You cannot lead our Nation to the decisive victory on which the security of every American family depends if you do not see the true dangers of the post-September the 11th era. My opponent has a September 10th point of view. At his convention, he declared his strategy would be to respond to attacks after America is hit. And that would be too late. America—in our debates, he said we can defend America only if we pass a "global test."

Audience members. Boo-o-o!

The President. I'm not making that up. He was standing about this far from me when he said it. Listen, I'll work with our friends and allies. We'll build strong coalitions. But I will never turn over America's national security decisions to leaders of other countries.

I want to thank those who wear the uniform who are here today. Thank you for your service. I want to thank the veterans who are here for having set such a great example for those who wear the uniform. I want to thank the military families who are here.

And I assure you, we will continue to support our troops in harm's way. That is why I went to the United States Congress and proposed $87 billion in supplemental funding, to make sure our troops had that which they need to complete their missions in Afghanistan and Iraq.

We received great bipartisan support for that funding. As you gather the vote, I want you to remind your friends and neighbors of this startling statistic: Only 4 Members of the United States Senate—4 out of 100—voted to authorize the use of force and then voted against providing the funding necessary to supporting our troops in harm's way, and 2 of those 4 were my opponent and his runningmate.

Audience members. Boo-o-o!

The President. So they asked him, "Why did you make the vote?" And you might remember the most famous quote of the 2004 campaign, "I actually did vote for the $87 billion, right before I voted against it." They kept pressing him, and he finally said, "The whole thing was a complicated matter." There is nothing complicated about supporting our troops in combat.

We will continue to protect America by spreading freedom and liberty. I believe in the transformational power of liberty. Free nations do not breed resentment and export terror. Free nations become allies against these ideologues of hate.

Think about what's happened in Afghanistan. Because we acted to defend ourselves, that society has gone from darkness to light. Three-and-a-half years ago, young girls couldn't go to school. Their mothers were taken to the public square and whipped if they did not toe the line of the barbarians who ran that country. Because we acted, millions voted in a Presidential election. The first voter in the Afghan Presidential election was a 19-year-old woman. Freedom is on the march.

Audience members. Four more years! Four more years! Four more years!

The President. Iraq has a strong Prime Minister. They'll be holding Presidential elections in January. Think how far that society has come from the days of torture chambers and mass graves. I believe people in the Middle East want to be free. Freedom is not America's gift to the world; freedom is the Almighty God's gift to each man and woman in this world.

The second clear choice in this election concerns your family budget, your wallet. When I ran for President 4 years ago, I pledged to lower taxes for American families. I kept my word. We doubled the child credit to $1,000 to help our moms and dads. We reduced the marriage penalty. We believe the Tax Code ought to encourage marriage, not penalize marriage. We dropped the lowest tax bracket to 10 percent to help our working families. We reduced taxes on everybody who paid taxes. As a result of these good policies, real after-tax income—that's the money you have left in your pocket—is about—is up about 10 percent since I've been your President.

When you're out gathering up the vote, remind the people what we have been through in this country. Six months prior to my arrival, the stock market was in serious decline—6 months before getting there. That foretold a recession. Then we had some corporate scandals. Then those attacks on our country cost us about a million jobs in the 3 months after September the 11th.

But our economic policies are working. This economy is growing. We're growing at rates as fast as any in nearly 20 years. We've added 1.9 million° new jobs since August of 2003. The unemployment rate

---

° White House correction.

is 5.4 percent. That's lower than the average rate of the 1970s, the 1980s, and the 1990s. Farm income is up. The home-ownership rate in America is at an alltime high. And your unemployment rate in the great State of Florida is 4.5 percent.

My opponent has very different plans for your family's budget. He intends to take a bigger chunk out of it.

Audience members. Boo-o-o!

The President. He voted against the higher child tax credit. He voted against the marriage penalty relief. He voted against lower taxes. If he had had his way, an average middle-class family would be paying 2,000 more dollars a year to the Federal Government.

Audience members. Boo-o-o!

The President. It's part of a pattern. See, he's voted 10 times to raise taxes on gasoline. All told, during his 20 years as a United States Senator, my opponent has voted 98 times to raise taxes.

Audience members. Boo-o-o!

The President. That's about five times a year. When a Senator does something that often, he must really enjoy it. [*Laughter*] During this campaign, he's also made a lot of big, expensive promises. He's promised about $2.2 trillion of new Federal spending. That's with a "T"—trillion with a "T." That's a lot even for a Senator from Massachusetts. [*Laughter*]

So they said, "How are you going to pay for it?" He said, "Well, oh, don't worry. We'll just tax the rich." You've heard that before, haven't you? See, there's a gap. When he says "tax the rich," he can raise about 600 to 800 billion dollars. So there's a gap between what he has promised and what he can raise, and guess who usually gets to fill that gap?

Audience members. We do!

The President. We're not going to let him tax you; we're going to carry Florida and win a great victory in November.

The third choice in this election involves the quality of life for our families. A good education and quality health care are important to successful life. When I ran for President 4 years ago, I promised to end the soft bigotry of low expectations by reforming our public schools. I kept my word. We passed education reforms to bring high standards to our classrooms and to make schools accountable to our parents. We're seeing progress. Math and reading scores are rising. We're closing an achievement gap amongst minority students. We'll build on these reforms and extend them to our high schools so that no child is left behind in America.

We'll continue to improve our lives—lives for our families, by making health care more affordable and accessible. We'll expand health savings accounts so small businesses can cover their workers and more families are able to get health care accounts they own and manage themselves. We'll create association health plans so small businesses can join together and buy insurance at the same discounts that big companies are able to do. We will help families in need by expanding community health centers. We'll make sure every eligible child is enrolled in our Government's low-income health insurance program to make sure health care is available and affordable to you.

We will do something about these junk lawsuits that are running up the cost of medicine and driving good doctors out of practice. I've met too many ob-gyns who are being driven out of practice because of these lawsuits. And I've met too many women who are worried about whether they're going to get the quality health care they need to bring their baby into life. We have a national problem with health care and these lawsuits. You cannot be pro-doctor and pro-patient and pro-personal-injury-lawyer at the same time. You have to choose. My opponent has made his choice, and he put a personal-injury trial lawyer on the ticket.

Audience members. Boo-o-o!

The President. I have made my choice. I'm standing with the doctors and patients. I am for medical liability reform—now.

Senator Kerry has a different point of view on our schools. He voted for the No Child Left Behind Act but now wants to weaken the accountability standards. He's proposed including measures like teacher attendance to judge whether students can read and write and add and subtract. He voted against health savings accounts. He opposes association health plans. He voted 10 times against medical liability reform. He can run from his record, but he cannot hide.

Now he's proposing a big-Government health care plan that would cause 8 million families to lose the private coverage they get at work, put them on the health—the Government plan. Eighty percent of the people who would get coverage under his proposal would be enrolled in a Government program.

In one of our debates, he tried to tell Americans, when it comes to his health care plan, and I'd like to quote him, "Government has nothing to do with it." I could barely contain myself. My opponent's plan would move America down the road to Federal control of health care, and that is the wrong road for America's families. He can run—he can run in camo, but he cannot hide.

In all we do to improve health care, we will make sure the decisions are made by doctors and patients, not by officials in Washington, DC.

The fourth clear choice in this election involves your retirement. Our Nation has made a solemn commitment to America's seniors on Social Security and Medicare. When I ran for President 4 years ago, I promised to keep that commitment and improve Medicare by adding prescription drug coverage. I kept my word. Leaders in both political parties have talked about strengthening Medicare for years. We got the job done. Seniors are now getting discounts on medicine with drug discount cards. Our low-income seniors are getting $600 this year and another $600 next year to help pay for their prescriptions. And beginning in 2006, all seniors will be able to get prescription drug coverage under Medicare.

My opponent voted against the Medicare bill that included prescription drug coverage, even though it was supported by AARP and other seniors groups. Campaigning, he said, "If I am the President, I am going to repeal that phony bill." Then a little later on, he said, "No, I don't want to repeal it." That sounds familiar.

As your President for the next 4 years, I will defend the reforms we worked so hard to pass, and we will keep the promise of Medicare for America's seniors. And we will keep the promise of Social Security for our seniors. And we will strengthen Social Security for a younger generation.

Every election, desperate politicians try to scare seniors about Social Security. You might remember the campaign in 2000. They were saying, "If George W. gets elected, our seniors will not get their checks." Remind your friends and neighbors that George W. got elected and our seniors got their checks. You will continue to get your checks. Baby boomers like me are in good shape when it comes to the Social Security trust.

But we need to worry about our children and our grandchildren. We need to make sure Social Security will be there when they need it. And that is why I believe younger workers ought to be able to take some of their own money and put it in a personal savings account, a personal savings account they call their own, that the Government cannot take away.

My opponent takes a different approach about Social Security. He talks about protecting Social Security. But he's the only candidate in this race who voted eight times for higher taxes on Social Security benefits. That's his record. He can run from it, but he cannot hide.

And when it comes to the next generation, he's offered nothing. American families have a clear choice. My opponent wants to scare the seniors of today and do nothing to secure the system for the seniors of tomorrow. I will keep the promise of Social Security and Medicare and strengthen these great systems for our children and our grandchildren.

The fifth clear choice in this election is on the values that are so crucial to keeping our families strong. And here, my opponent and I are miles apart. I believe marriage is a sacred commitment, a pillar of our civilization, and I will defend it. This isn't a partisan issue. You know, when Congress passed the Defense of Marriage Act, defining marriage as the union of a man and a woman, the vast majority of Democrats supported it and my predecessor, Bill Clinton, signed the bill into law. Senator Kerry was part of an out-of-the-mainstream minority that voted against the Defense of Marriage Act.

Audience members. Boo-o-o!

The President. I believe that reasonable people can find common ground on difficult issues. Republicans and Democrats and many citizens on both sides of the life issue came together and agreed we should ban the brutal practice of partial-birth abortions. I proudly signed that bill. But Senator Kerry was part of an out-of-the-mainstream minority that voted against the ban.

Audience members. Boo-o-o!

The President. He voted against parental notification laws.

Audience members. Boo-o-o!

The President. He voted against the Unborn Victims of Violence Act.

Audience members. Boo-o-o!

The President. I'll continue to reach out to Americans of every belief and move this goodhearted Nation toward a culture of life.

In the course of this campaign, my opponent has said that the heart and soul of America can be found in Hollywood.

Audience members. Boo-o-o!

The President. Most American families don't look to Hollywood as the source for values. The heart and soul of America is found in communities like Melbourne, Florida.

All of these choices make this one of the most important elections in our history. The security and prosperity of our country, the health and education of our families, the retirement of our seniors, and the direction of our culture are all at stake. The decision is in the best hands, because the decision belongs to the American people.

I see a great day for America. One of my favorite quotes was written by a Texan named Tom Lea. He said, "Sarah and I live on the east side of the mountain. It's the sunrise side, not the sunset side. It's the side that sees the day that is coming, not to see the day that is gone." You know, my opponent has spent much of this campaign talking about the day that is gone. I see the day that is coming.

We've been through a lot together over the last 3¾ years. Because we've done the hard work of climbing the mountain, we see the valley below. We'll protect our families and build on their prosperity. We'll defend the deepest values of our country. We will spread freedom and the peace we all want. We'll do everything I can to make America safer.

Four years ago when I traveled this great State, I made this pledge, that if I was honored with the office, I would uphold the honor and the dignity of that office. With your help, I will do so for 4 more years.

Thanks for coming. God bless. On to victory. Thank you all.

NOTE: The President spoke at 1:39 p.m. at the Space Coast Stadium. In his remarks, he referred to Senator Zell Miller of Georgia, who made the keynote address at the 2004 Republican National Convention; Gov. Jeb Bush of Florida; Apollo 11 astronaut Edwin "Buzz" Aldrin; Mel R. Martinez, senatorial candidate in Florida; entertainers Little Texas; Usama bin Laden, leader of the Al Qaida terrorist organization; and Prime Minister Ayad Allawi of the Iraqi Interim Government.

Remarks in Jacksonville, Florida
October 23, 2004

The President. Thank you all. Thank you so much for coming today. Brother Jeb said, "Why don't we go to Jacksonville; maybe a couple of folks will show up to say hello." Laura and I thank you so very much for coming out on a Saturday afternoon. I'm here to ask for your vote, and I'm here to ask for your help. People are voting here in Florida. You need to get your friends and neighbors to go to the polls. And by the way, when you're getting people to go to the polls, don't overlook discerning Democrats, people like Senator Zell Miller from Georgia. With your help, we'll carry Florida again and win a great victory in November.

So when I asked Laura to marry me, she said, "Fine, just so long as you—I never have to give a political speech." I said, "Okay, you got a deal." Fortunately, she didn't hold me to the promise. Laura is giving a lot of speeches, and when people see her speak, they see a warm, compassionate, great First Lady. I'm going to give you some reasons to put me back into office. Perhaps the most important one of all is so that Laura is the First Lady for 4 more years.

I'm proud of my runningmate, Dick Cheney. I admit it, he doesn't have the waviest hair in the race. [*Laughter*] I didn't pick him because of his hairdo. I picked him because of his judgment, his experience, and his ability to get the job done for the American people.

I'm proud of my brother, your Governor, Jeb Bush. You don't have to worry about where he stands. He doesn't take a poll or focus group to find out what he should believe. Jeb Bush stands on principle, and when times are tough, he leads this State with compassion. He has done a masterful job of helping to bring comfort for those who have been afflicted by the four hurricanes. Florida showed its true strength not only in your Governor but because people cared for people who were hurting in this State. I am really proud of how Florida handled the four hurricanes.

Mel Martinez is the right man for the United States Senate from Florida. And when you vote for him and put him in office, he'll be joining a fine United States Senator who has joined us today from the State of Utah, Senator Orrin Hatch. Thank you, Senator.

Congressman Ander Crenshaw is doing a great job in the House of Representatives. Thank you, Ander. Congressman Cliff Stearns is with us today. I appreciate you coming, Cliff.

I want to thank the State chief financial officer, Tom Gallagher, for joining us today. I want to thank the mayor of the great city of Jacksonville, Florida, Mayor John Peyton.

When I came in, I had the opportunity to say hello to Nelson Cuba, who's the president of the Jacksonville Fraternal Order of Police. I am proud to have the endorsement of the FOP. I'm proud to be standing with the policemen all across this country.

I want to thank Bill Cerveny and Aaron Tippin for providing such wonderful entertainment here for this great crowd.

I want to thank the people who put on this event. It takes a lot of work to get this many people to come. I want to thank the grassroots activists, the people who are putting up the signs, making the phone calls, turning out the vote. With your help, we will win a great victory on November the 2d.

We have just 10 days to go in this campaign, and voters have a clear choice between two very different candidates and dramatically different approaches and records. You know where I stand, and sometimes, you even know where my opponent stands. [*Laughter*] We both have records. I'm running on my record. Senator Kerry's running from his record, and there is a reason why. There is a reason why. There is a mainstream in American politics, and my opponent sits on the far left bank. I am a compassionate conservative and proudly so. At a time when our country has much to accomplish and much more to do, I offer a record of reform and results.

This election comes down to five clear choices for America's families, five choices on issues of great consequence: your family's security; your family's budget; your quality of life; your retirement; and the bedrock values that are so critical to our families and to our future.

The first clear choice is the most important because it concerns the security of your family. All our progress on every other issue depends on the safety of our citizens. The most—this is the first Presidential election since September the 11th, 2001. Americans will go to the polls in a time of war and ongoing threats unlike any we have faced before. The terrorists who killed thousands of innocent people are still dangerous. They are determined to strike us again. The outcome of this election will set the direction of the war against terror. I believe the most solemn duty of the American President is to protect the American people. If America shows uncertainty or weakness in this decade, the world will drift toward tragedy. This will not happen on my watch.

Since that terrible morning of September the 11th, 2001, we have fought the terrorists across the Earth, not for pride, not for power, but because the lives of our citizens are at stake. Our strategy is clear. We've strengthened protections for the homeland. We're reforming and strengthening our intelligence capabilities. We're transforming our All-Volunteer Army. We will not have a draft. We will keep the All-Volunteer Army an all-volunteer army. We are staying on the offensive. We are relentless. We are determined to protect the American people, and we're succeeding. More than three-quarters of Al Qaida's key members and associates have been brought to justice, and the rest of them know we are on their trail.

My opponent has a different approach. He says that September the 11th, quote, "didn't change me much at all," end quote.

Audience members. Boo-o-o!

The President. And that's pretty clear. He considers the war on terror primarily a law enforcement and intelligence gathering operation.

Audience members. Boo-o-o!

The President. His top foreign policy adviser has questioned whether it's even a war at all, saying "That's just a metaphor, like the war on poverty."

Audience members. Boo-o-o!

The President. Anyone who thinks we're fighting a metaphor does not understand the enemy we face, and you cannot win a war if you're not convinced we're even in one.

Senator Kerry misunderstands our battle against insurgents and terrorists in Iraq. After voting to authorize force against Saddam Hussein, after calling it the right decision when I sent troops into Iraq, the Senator now calls it the "wrong war."

Audience members. Boo-o-o!

The President. The Senator used to recognize that Saddam Hussein was a gathering threat who hated America. After all, the Senator said so. He used to recognize that Saddam was a state sponsor of terror with a history of pursuing and even using weapons of mass destruction. After all, the Senator said so. He used to understand that

Saddam was a major source of instability in the Middle East. After all, the Senator said so. And when he voted to authorize force, the Senator must have recognized the nightmare scenario that terrorists might somehow access weapons of mass destruction. Senator Kerry seems to have forgotten all that as his position has evolved during the course of this campaign. You might call it election amnesia. [*Laughter*]

I knew then and I know now that America and the world are safer with Saddam Hussein sitting in a prison cell.

Senator Kerry now calls Iraq a "diversion."

Audience members. Boo-o-o!

The President. But the case of just one terrorist shows how wrong his thinking is. A man named Zarqawi is responsible for planting car bombs and beheading Americans in Iraq. He ran a terrorist training camp in Afghanistan until American troops arrived. Then he fled to Baghdad, where he's fighting us today. He publicly announced his allegiance to Usama bin Laden. If Zarqawi and his associates were not busy fighting Iraqi and American forces in Iraq, what does Senator Kerry think they would be doing? Simple shopkeepers? [*Laughter*] Running benevolence societies? I don't think so. And our troops will defeat Zarqawi and his friends and allies overseas so we do not have to face them in America.

The choice in this election could not be clearer. You cannot lead our Nation to decisive victory, on which the security of every American family depends, if you do not see the true dangers of the post-September the 11th world. My opponent has a September the 10th point of view. At his convention, he declared that his strategy will be to respond to attacks after America is hit.

Audience members. Boo-o-o!

The President. That would be too late. In our debates, he said we can defend America only if we pass a "global test."

Audience members. Boo-o-o!

The President. I'm not making that up. He was standing about that far away from me when he said it. I'll work with our friends and allies. We'll continue to build strong coalitions. But I will never turn over America's national security decisions to leaders of other countries.

I want to thank those who wear the uniform who have joined us today. I want to thank the veterans who are here today for having set such a great example. I want to thank the military families who are here today. And I'm going to assure you, so long as I'm the Commander in Chief, our Federal Government will make sure your loved ones have what is necessary to complete their missions.

And that's why I went to the United States Congress in September of 2003, asking for $87 billion in supplemental funding to support our troops in combat in Iraq and Afghanistan. I appreciate the strong bipartisan support for this very important request. When you're out gathering up the vote, I want you to remind your friends and neighbors that only four Members of the United States Senate voted to authorize the use of force and then voted against the funding necessary to support our troops in harm's way, and two of those four were my opponent and his runningmate.

Audience members. Boo-o-o!

The President. They asked him, "Why did you make the vote?" And he issued perhaps the most famous quote of the 2004 campaign, "I actually did vote for the $87 billion, right before I voted against it."

Audience members. Boo-o-o!

The President. They've asked him time and time again, and he must have given five or six explanations of that vote. At one point, he said, "The whole thing is a complicated matter." There is nothing complicated about supporting our troops in combat.

We'll protect America by leading the cause of freedom. I believe in the transformational power of liberty. I want you to remember what has taken place in Af-

ghanistan in a short period of time. That country has gone from darkness to light. Three-and-a-half years ago, young girls couldn't go to school. If their mothers did not toe the line of the ideologues of hate who ran Afghanistan, they were whipped in the public square and sometimes executed in a sports stadium. Because we acted in our self-interest, because we upheld doctrine, 25 million people in Afghanistan are free. Millions went to vote in a Presidential election. The first voter was a 19-year-old woman in Afghanistan.

Iraq will be holding elections in January. Think about how far that country has come from the days of torture chambers and mass graves. Freedom is on the march, and America is more secure because of it.

I believe every person in the world wants to be free. I believe this because freedom is not America's gift to the world; freedom is the Almighty God's gift to each man and woman in this world.

On September the 14th, 2001, I stood in the ruins of the Twin Towers. It is a day I will never forget. There were workers there in hardhats yelling at me at the top of their lungs, "Whatever it takes." I remember the man coming out of the rubble—we were doing our best to console people—he grabbed me by the arm; he looked me in the eye; and he said, "Do not let me down." Ever since that day, I wake up every morning thinking about how to better protect our country. I will never relent in defending America, whatever it takes.

The second clear choice in this election concerns your family budget. When I ran for President 4 years ago, I pledged to lower taxes for American families. I kept my word. We raised the child credit. We reduced the marriage penalty. Listen, our Tax Code ought to encourage marriage, not penalize marriage. We dropped the lowest bracket to 10 percent to help our working families. We reduced income taxes for everyone who pays taxes. As a result of these good policies, after-tax income, money in your pocket that you can spend, is up by about 10 percent since I became your President.

We've been through a lot together. When you're out rounding up the vote, remind your friends and neighbors that the stock market had been in serious decline for 6 months prior to my arrival in Washington, DC. And then we had a recession and corporate scandals and the attacks on our country. We lost nearly one million jobs in the 3 months after September the 11th.

But our economic policies are working. Our economy is growing at rates as fast as any in nearly 20 years. We've added more than 1.9 million new jobs in the last 13 months. The unemployment rate is 5.4 percent, lower than the average rate of the 1970s, 1980s, and 1990s. Our farmers and ranchers are making a living. The small businesses are flourishing. The entrepreneurial spirit is strong. Homeownership rate is at an alltime high, and the unemployment rate in Florida is 4.5 percent.

My opponent has very different plans for your family's budget. He intends to take a big chunk out of it.

Audience members. Boo-o-o!

The President. He voted against the higher child tax credit. He voted against the marriage penalty relief. He voted against lower taxes. If he had had his way, an average middle-class family would be paying 2,000 more dollars a year to the Federal Government.

Audience members. Boo-o-o!

The President. It's part of a pattern. See, the Senator voted 10 times to raise taxes on gasoline. All told, during his 20 years in the United States Senate, he has voted 98 times to raise your taxes.

Audience members. Boo-o-o!

The President. That's about five times a year. When a Senator does something that often, he must really enjoy it. [*Laughter*] During this campaign, he's also made a lot of big, expensive promises. He's promised $2.2 trillion of new Federal spending. That's trillion with a "T." That's a lot even

for a Senator from Massachusetts. [*Laughter*]

They asked him how he's going to pay for it. He said, "Oh, we'll just pay for it by taxing the rich." There's a problem with that promise. When you run up the top two brackets, you're taxing many small businesses. Most small businesses pay tax at the individual income-tax level. Seventy percent of new jobs are created by small businesses in America. Taxing small businesses is bad economic policy.

And there's a gap between what he's promised and what he can deliver. Running up the top two brackets like he wants to do raises between 600 and 800 billion dollars. And remember, there's $2.2 trillion of spending promises. So there's a gap, a gap between what he's promised and what he says he's going to pay. And guess who usually fills the gap?

Audience member. We do!

The President. You do. The good news is, we're not going to let him tax you; we are going to carry Florida and win on November the 2d.

Third clear choice in this election involves the quality of life for our Nation's families. A good education and quality health care are important to a successful life. When I ran for President 4 years ago, I promised to end the soft bigotry of low expectations by reforming our public schools. I have kept my word. We passed good, sound education reforms to bring high standards to the classroom and make our schools more accountable to parents and teachers. We're seeing progress. Math and reading scores are rising. We're closing the achievement gap by helping minority students. We will build on these reforms and extend them to our high schools so that no child in America is left behind.

And we'll continue to improve our—life for our families by making health care more affordable and accessible. We'll expand health savings accounts so more small businesses can cover their workers and more families are able to get health care accounts they manage and they call their own. We'll create association health plans so small businesses can join together and buy insurance at the same discounts that big companies are able to do. We will help our families in need by expanding community health centers. We'll make sure every eligible child is enrolled in our Government's low-income health insurance program.

And we'll help patients and doctors all across this Nation by doing something about the frivolous and junk lawsuits that are running up your costs and running good doctors out of practice. I have met too many good docs being run out of practice because of these junk lawsuits. I met too many ob-gyns who are not able to practice their skill. I met too many pregnant women who are having to drive miles, which isn't right. Our expectant moms need good, quality health care, and these lawsuits are making it tough for them to find good, quality health care. You cannot be pro-doctor, pro-patient, and pro-personal-injury-lawyer at the same time. You have to make a choice. My opponent made his choice, and he put a personal injury trial lawyer on the ticket.

Audience members. Boo-o-o!

The President. I have made my choice. I'm standing with the docs and the patients. I am for medical liability reform—now.

Senator Kerry has a different point of view on our schools and health care. Listen, he voted for the No Child Left Behind Act, but now he wants to weaken the accountability standards. He's proposed including measures like teacher attendance to judge whether students can read and write and add and subtract. He voted against health savings accounts. He opposes association health plans. He has voted 10 times against medical liability reform. He can run from his record, but he cannot hide.

Now he's proposing a health care plan in this campaign, a big Government health care plan that would cause 8 million families to lose private coverage they get at work and have to go on a Government plan. Eighty percent of the people who get coverage under his proposal would be enrolled in a Government program.

Audience members. Boo-o-o!

The President. In one of our debates, he looked in that camera and he told the Americans that when it comes to his health care plan, and I quote, "The Government has nothing to do with it." I could barely contain myself. [*Laughter*] My opponent's plan would move America down the road to Federal control of health care. It's the wrong road for American families. He can run from his plan——

Audience members. But he cannot hide!

The President. In all we do to improve health care, we will make sure the decisions are made by doctors and patients, not by officials in Washington, DC.

The fourth clear choice in this election involves your retirement. Our Nation has made a solemn commitment to America's seniors on Social Security and Medicare. When I ran for President 4 years ago, I promised to keep that commitment and improve Medicare by adding prescription drug coverage. I have kept my word. Seniors are now getting discounts on medicine with drug discount cards. Low-income seniors are getting $600 this year and $600 next year to help pay for prescriptions. And beginning in 2006, all seniors will be able to get prescription drug coverage under Medicare.

My opponent voted against the Medicare bill that includes prescription drug coverage, even though it was supported by AARP and other seniors groups. This campaign, he said, "If I'm the President, we're going to repeal that phony bill." A little later he said, "No, I don't want to repeal it." That sounds familiar. As your President for the next 4 years, I will defend the reforms we have worked so hard to pass and keep the promise of Medicare for our country's seniors.

We'll keep the promise of Social Security for our seniors, and we will strengthen Social Security for generations to come. Every campaign is predictable. It is predictable that you'll hear once again that our seniors will lose their checks. I want you to remind our seniors that in the 2000 campaign, they said, "If George W. gets elected, the seniors will not get their Social Security checks." You might remember that. Well, remind them of this: George W. got elected, and the seniors got their checks. And the seniors will continue to get their checks. And baby boomers like me are just fine when it comes to the Social Security trust.

But we need to be concerned about children and our grandchildren. We need to make sure that the Social Security system will be there when they need it too. And that is why I believe younger workers ought to be able to take some of their own money and put it in a personal savings account, a savings account they call their own, a savings account the Government cannot take away.

My opponent takes a different approach. He talks about protecting Social Security, but he's the only candidate in this race who has voted eight times for higher taxes on Social Security benefits.

Audience members. Boo-o-o!

The President. He can run——

Audience members. But he cannot hide!

The President. And when it comes to the next generation, he's offered nothing in terms of Social Security reform. The job of the President is to confront problems, not to pass them on to future Presidents and future generations. In a new term, I'll bring Republicans and Democrats together and strengthen Social Security so a younger generation can count on it.

The fifth clear choice in this election is on the values that are so crucial to keeping America's families strong, and here my opponent and I are miles apart. I believe marriage is a sacred commitment. I believe marriage is a pillar of our civilization, and I will always defend it. This is not a partisan issue. When Congress passed the Defense of Marriage Act, defining marriage as the union of a man and a woman, the vast majority of Democrats supported it, and Bill Clinton signed it into law. But Senator Kerry was part of an out-of-the-mainstream minority that voted against the Defense of Marriage Act.

Audience members. Boo-o-o!

The President. I believe that reasonable people can find common ground on the difficult issues. Republicans and Democrats and many citizens on both sides of the life issue came together and agreed we should ban the brutal practice of partial-birth abortion. I was honored to sign that bill. But Senator Kerry was part of the out-of-the-mainstream minority that voted against the ban.

Audience members. Boo-o-o!

The President. He also voted against parental notification laws——

Audience members. Boo-o-o!

The President. ——and against the Unborn Victims of Violence Act.

Audience members. Boo-o-o!

The President. I will continue to reach out to Americans of every belief and move this goodhearted Nation toward a culture of life.

During this campaign, my opponent has said that you can find the heart and soul of America in Hollywood.

Audience members. Boo-o-o!

The President. Most American families do not look to Hollywood as a source of values. I believe the heart and soul of America is found in communities like Jacksonville, Florida.

All of these choices make this one of the most important elections in our history. The security, the prosperity of our country, the education of our children, and the health of our families, the retirement of our seniors, and the direction of our culture are—all are at stake. And the decision is in the best hands, the hands of the American people.

I see a positive future for this country. I see a better day. One of my favorite quotes was written by a fellow Texan. He said, "Sarah and I live on the east side of the mountain. It's the sunrise side, not the sunset side. It's the side to see the day that is coming, not to see the day that is gone." During this campaign, my opponent has spent much of his campaign talking about the day that is gone. I see the day that is coming.

We have been through a lot together in the last nearly 4 years. Because we have done the hard work of climbing the mountain, we can see the valley below. We'll protect our families, build up the prosperity of this country, and defend our deepest values. We will spread freedom in this world and achieve the peace we all long for.

When I campaigned in your State 4 years ago, I said if you gave me the honor of serving, I would uphold the honor and the dignity of the office to which I had been elected. With your help, I will do so for 4 more years.

God bless. Thank you for coming. Thank you all.

NOTE: The President spoke at 4:20 p.m. at Alltel Stadium. In his remarks, he referred to Gov. Jeb Bush of Florida; Senator Zell Miller of Georgia, who made the keynote address at the 2004 Republican National Convention; Mel R. Martinez, senatorial candidate in Florida; entertainers Billy Cerveny and Aaron Tippin; former President Saddam Hussein of Iraq; senior Al Qaida associate Abu Musab Al Zarqawi; and Usama bin Laden, leader of the Al Qaida terrorist organization.

Remarks in Alamogordo, New Mexico
October 24, 2004

The President. Thank you all. Thanks for coming out on a beautiful Sunday afternoon. Laura and I are so pleased to be here in Alamogordo. It's great to be back in the great State of New Mexico.

We're getting close to voting time, and I'm here to ask for your vote and for your help. Tell your friends and neighbors in the coffee shops and community centers and places of worship, we have a duty to vote in the United States. Get them headed to the polls. Don't overlook discerning Democrats like Zell Miller of Georgia. And when you get them headed to the polls, remind them if they want a safer America, a stronger America, and a better America, to vote for Bush-Cheney.

I'm keeping really good company in the First Lady. You know, when I—I don't know if you know this or not, we both grew up kind of around the corner. As a

matter of fact, we were in the seventh grade together at San Jacinto Junior High in Midland. And then we became reacquainted. She was a public school librarian when I met her again.

Audience member. [*Inaudible*]—moment!

The President. It sure was. When I asked her to marry me, she said, "Fine, just make me a promise." I said, "Okay, what is it?" She said, "Promise me I'll never have to give a political speech." [*Laughter*] I said, "Okay, you got a deal." Fortunately, she did not hold me to that promise. She's giving speeches all over the country, and when people see her speak, they see a compassionate, warm, strong First Lady.

And I'm proud of my runningmate, Dick Cheney. Now, look, I admit it—I admit it, he does not have the waviest hair in the race. [*Laughter*] I didn't pick him because of his hairdo. I picked him because of his judgment, his experience. He's getting the job done for the American people.

I'm proud to be sharing this platform with a great United States Senator in Pete Domenici. You know, if you had to describe Senator Domenici, you would call him a class act. And he is. I know you're proud of him, and Laura and I are proud to call him friend. I want to thank Congressman Steve Pearce and his wife, Cynthia.

I want to thank the Alamogordo Tiger Band for being here today. It's good to be in country where the cowboy hats outnumber the ties. I want to thank the people who have helped put on this rally and are putting up the signs, making the phone calls, turning people out to vote. There is no doubt in my mind that with your help, we will carry New Mexico and win a great victory in November. *Con su apoyo, vamos a ganar.*

You know, we've just got 9 days to go. And the voters have a clear choice between two very different candidates with dramatically different approaches and records. You know where I stand, and sometimes you even know where my opponent stands. [*Laughter*] We both have records. I'm proudly running on mine. The Senator is running from his. [*Laughter*] And there's a reason why. There is a mainstream in American politics, and my opponent sits on the far left bank. I'm a compassionate conservative and proudly so. At a time when our country has much to accomplish and much more to do, I offer a record of reform and a record of results.

This election comes down to five clear choices for America's families, five choices on issues of great consequence: your family's security; your family's budget; your quality of life; your retirement; and the bedrock values that are so critical to our families and our future.

The first clear choice is the most important, because it concerns the security of your family. All progress on every other issue depends on the safety of our citizens. This will be the first Presidential election since September the 11th, 2001. Americans will go to the polls in a time of war and ongoing threats unlike any we have faced before. The terrorists that killed thousands of innocent people are still dangerous, and they are determined to strike us again. The outcome of this election will set the direction of the war against terror. The most solemn duty of the American President is to protect the American people.

If America shows uncertainty or weakness in this decade, the world will drift toward tragedy. This will not happen on my watch. Since that terrible morning of September the 11th, 2001, we've fought the terrorists across the Earth, not for pride, not for power but because the lives of our citizens are at stake. Our strategy is clear. We've strengthened the protections for our homeland. We're reforming and strengthening our intelligence services. We're transforming our All-Volunteer Army. There will not be a draft. We're staying on the offensive. We're relentless. We are determined to protect the American people. And we're succeeding. More than three-quarters of Al Qaida's key members and associates have been brought to justice, and the rest of them know we're on their trail.

My opponent has a very different approach. He says that September the 11th, quote, "didn't change me much at all"——

Audience members. Boo-o-o!

The President. ——end quote. [*Laughter*] And that's pretty clear. He considers the war on terror primarily a law enforcement and intelligence gathering operation. His top foreign policy advisers question whether we're even in a war at all, saying, "The war on terror is just like a metaphor, kind of like the war on poverty." Anyone who thinks we're fighting a metaphor does not understand the enemy we face. You cannot win a war if you are not convinced we are even in one.

My opponent also misunderstands our battle against insurgents and terrorists in Iraq. After voting to authorize force against Saddam Hussein, after calling it the right decision when I sent troops into Iraq, the Senator now calls it the "wrong war." The Senator used to recognize that Saddam Hussein was a gathering threat who hated America. After all, he said so. He used to recognize that Saddam was a state sponsor of terror with a history of pursuing and even using weapons of mass destruction. Even so, he said so. He used to understand that Saddam was a major source of instability in the Middle East. He said so. And when he voted to authorize force, the Senator must have recognized the nightmare scenario that terrorists might somehow access weapons of mass destruction.

Senator Kerry seems to have forgotten all that as his position has evolved during the course of this campaign. You might call it election-year amnesia. [*Laughter*] I know then—I knew then and I know now that America and the world are safer with Saddam Hussein sitting in a prison cell. We have a different point of view when it comes to defending America. Senator Kerry now calls Iraq a "diversion." But the case of just one terrorist shows how wrong his thinking is. A man named Zarqawi is responsible for planting car bombs and beheading Americans in Iraq. He ran a terrorist training camp in Afghanistan—until coalition forces arrived. And then he fled to Iraq, where he's fighting us today. He swore his allegiance to Usama bin Laden. If Zarqawi and his associates were not busy fighting Iraqi and American forces in Iraq, what does Senator Kerry think they would be doing? Peaceful small-business owners? [*Laughter*] Running a benevolent society? [*Laughter*]

Our troops will defeat Zarqawi and his likes overseas in Iraq so we do not have to face them here at home.

The choice in this election could not be clearer. You cannot lead our Nation to decisive victory on which the security of every American family depends if you do not see the true dangers of the post-September the 11th world. My opponent has a September 10th point of view. At his convention, he declared that his strategy will be to respond to attacks after America is hit.

Audience members. Boo-o-o!

The President. Those were his words. That would be too late. In our debates, he said we can defend America if we pass a "global test."

Audience members. Boo-o-o!

The President. I'm not making that up. He was standing right about right there. Listen, I'll work with our friends and allies. We'll continue to build strong coalitions to keep us secure. But I will never turn over America's national security decisions to leaders of other countries.

I want to thank those who wear our Nation's uniform. I want to thank our great United States military. It's such an incredible honor to be the Commander in Chief of such a great military. And our military is great because of the character of the men and women who wear our uniform. I want to thank the veterans who are here today for having set such a great example. I want to thank the military families who are here for your sacrifice.

And I want to assure you that we'll make sure our troops have got all the tools necessary to complete their missions in Afghanistan and Iraq. That's why I went to the Congress and asked for $87 billion in supplemental funding to support our troops in harm's way. It was a vital request. It was necessary. And we got great bipartisan support. I want you to tell your friends and neighbors this startling statistic: Only 4 Members of the United States Senate— 4 out of 100—voted to authorize the use of force and then voted against the funding necessary to support our troops in combat, and 2 of those 4 were my opponent and his runningmate.

Audience members. Boo-o-o!

The President. You might remember, when asked to explain his vote he said, and I quote, "I actually did vote for the $87 billion, before I voted against it." [*Laughter*] I've spent quite a bit of time in New Mexico. I've never heard anybody talk that way in this State. [*Laughter*] They kept pressing him, and he's given a lot of answers about his vote. One of the most interesting ones of all was he said, "It's a complicated matter." There's nothing complicated about supporting our troops in harm's way.

And we will continue to protect in America by spreading freedom. I believe in the transformational power of liberty. I believe that free nations do not breed resentments and export terror. Free nations become allies in the war against terror.

I want you to tell your children what has taken place in a brief period of time. Tell them what happened in Afghanistan. Because we defended ourselves, because we upheld the doctrine that said, "If you harbor a terrorist, you're as equally guilty as the terrorists," 25 million people live in freedom in Afghanistan. It wasn't all that long ago that young girls couldn't go to school because the ideologues of hate, the Taliban, had such a dim view of the world. And if their mothers didn't toe their line, they were taken into public squares and whipped and sometimes killed in a sports stadium. Because we acted, millions of people in Afghanistan went to vote in a Presidential election. The first voter was a 19-year-old woman. Freedom is on the march.

Iraq will have Presidential elections. Think how far that country has come from the days of torture chambers and mass graves. It is in our interests that we spread liberty. It's in our interests that we help societies become free. I believe people want to be free. Freedom is not America's gift to the world; freedom is the Almighty God's gift to each man and woman in this world.

The second clear choice in this election concerns the family's budget. When I ran for President 4 years ago, I pledged to lower taxes for American families. I kept my word. We doubled the child credit to $1,000 per child. We want to help people raise their children. We reduced the marriage penalty. The Tax Code ought to encourage marriage, not penalize marriage. We dropped the lowest bracket to 10 percent to help our working families. We reduced income taxes for everybody who pays taxes. As a result of our policies, real, after-tax income—that's money in your pocket—has gone up by about 10 percent since I became the President.

When you're out there rounding up the vote, remind your friends and neighbors about what this economy has been through. Six months prior to my arrival in Washington, the stock market was in serious decline. Then we had a recession. Then we had corporate scandals. And then we got attacked. And that attack cost us about a million jobs in the 3 months after September the 11th.

But our economic policies are working. This country is on the road to growth. We're growing at rates as fast as any in 20—nearly 20 years. The homeownership rate is at an alltime high in America. Our farmers and ranchers are making a living. Small businesses are flourishing. The entrepreneurial spirit is strong. We've added 1.9 million new jobs in the past 13 months. The national unemployment rate is 5.4 percent, lower than the average rate of the 1970s, 1980s, and 1990s. And the unemployment rate in New Mexico is 5.3 percent. This economy is getting stronger.

Now, my opponent has a different plan for your budget. He intends to take a big chunk out of it. You know, he voted against the higher child credit and the marriage penalty relief, and he voted against lower tax rates. I want the people to understand that if he had had his way, the average middle class family would be paying $2,000 more in taxes to the Federal Government.

Audience members. Boo-o-o!

The President. It's part of a pattern. All told, during his 20 years in the United States Senate, he's voted to increase taxes 98 times. That's five times for every year he's been in the Senate. I'd call that a predictable pattern. [*Laughter*] If a Senator does something that often, he must really enjoy it. [*Laughter*] During this campaign, he's made a lot of big promises too—a lot of them. As a matter of fact, he's promised about $2.2 trillion worth of new spending. That's trillion with a "T." That's a lot even for a Senator from Massachusetts. [*Laughter*]

So they asked him, "How you going to pay for it?" He said, "Oh, we'll just tax the rich." The problem is, is that his ledger doesn't add up, see. If you run up the top two brackets like he said, it's going to raise about 600 to 800 billion dollars. That's far short of 2.2 trillion. And when there's a gap like that, guess who usually gets stuck with the bill?

Audience member. We do!

The President. The good news is, we're not going to let him tax you; we're going to carry New Mexico and win a great victory on November the 2d.

The third clear choice in this election involves the quality of life for our Nation's families. A good education and quality health care are important for a successful life. When I ran for President 4 years ago, I promised to challenge the soft bigotry of low expectations by reforming our public schools. I kept my word. We passed the No Child Left Behind Act, which is bringing high standards to our classrooms and making schools accountable to our parents. We're seeing great progress across this country. Math and reading scores are on the rise. We're closing the achievement gap. More and more Latino youngsters are learning how to read and write and add and subtract. And the country is better off for it. We'll build on these reforms. We'll extend them to our high schools so that no child is left behind in America.

We'll continue to improve lives for our families by making health care more affordable and more accessible. We'll expand health savings accounts so small businesses can cover their workers and more families are able to get the health care accounts that they manage and own. We'll expand—create association health plans so small

businesses can join together and buy insurance at the same discounts that big companies are able to do. We'll help families in need by expanding community health centers, make sure every eligible child is enrolled in our Government's low-income health insurance programs.

And we're going to help patients and doctors everywhere by doing something about these junk lawsuits that are running up the cost of medicine and running good docs out of practice. You cannot be pro-doctor and pro-patient and pro-personal-injury-lawyer at the same time. You have to choose. And my opponent made his choice. He put a personal-injury trial lawyer on the ticket.

Audience members. Boo-o-o!

The President. I have made my choice. I'm standing with the doctors and patients of New Mexico. I am for medical liability reform—now.

We have a difference when it comes to health care. My opponent voted against health savings accounts. He's voted against association health plans. He's voted 10 times against medical liability reform. He can run from his record, but he cannot hide.

And now he's proposing a new plan, a new idea, which is a big-Government health care plan. That's what it is. It would cause about 8 million families to lose private coverage they get at work and have to go on a Government plan. Eighty percent of the people who get coverage would be enrolled with the Federal Government. We just have a different philosophy. You know, in one of the debates, he actually looked in the camera with a straight face and he said, when it comes to his health care plan, and I quote, "The Government has nothing to do with it." I could barely contain myself. [*Laughter*] His plan would move America down the road to Federal control of health care, and that is wrong road for America's families.

In all we do to improve health care, we will make sure the decisions are made by doctors and patients, not by officials in Washington, DC.

The fourth clear choice involves your retirement. Our Nation has made a solemn commitment to our seniors on Social Security and Medicare. When I ran for President 4 years ago, I promised to keep that commitment and improve Medicare. By adding prescription drug coverage, I kept my word. Seniors are now getting discounts on medicine with drug discount cards. Low-income seniors are getting $600 worth of help this year and next year. And beginning in 2006, all seniors will be able to get prescription drug coverage under Medicare.

We'll keep the promise of Social Security for our seniors. And we'll strengthen Social Security for generations to come. Listen, every election there is a predictable event that takes place, and that is they run TV ads saying to our seniors, "If George W. gets elected, you're not going to get your checks." That's what happened in 2000. They said, "If George W. gets elected, our seniors will not get their Social Security checks." You might remember that. In this campaign, as we're coming down the stretch, tell your friends, George W. got elected and the seniors got their checks. And the seniors will continue to get their checks. And baby boomers like me, we're in pretty good shape when it comes to the Social Security Trust.

But we need to worry about our children and our grandchildren. We need to worry about whether or not Social Security will be there when they retire. So I believe younger workers ought to be able to take some of their own money and put it in a personal savings account that they own and that the Government cannot take away.

Once again, my opponent takes a different approach. You know, he talked about protecting Social Security. I want to remind you and I want you to remind your friends and neighbors that he voted eight times to tax Social Security benefits. That's his record. He can run, but he cannot hide.

It's the job of the President to confront problems, not to pass them on to future Presidents and future generations. The other night at the debates, when I talked about Social Security, he defended the status quo. He had nothing to offer to our younger workers. In a new term, I'll bring Republicans and Democrats together and strengthen Social Security so our children and our grandchildren will have a system available for them when they retire.

And the fifth clear choice in this election is on the values that are so crucial to keeping America's families strong. And here, my opponent and I are miles apart. I stand for the appointment of Federal judges who know the difference between personal opinion and the strict interpretation of the law. I believe marriage is a sacred commitment. It is a pillar of our civilization, and I will always defend it. This is not a partisan issue. When Congress passed the Defense of Marriage Act during my predecessor's time, defining marriage as a union of a man and a woman, the vast majority of Democrats supported that bill and my predecessor signed it into law. But Senator Kerry was part of an out-of-the-mainstream minority that voted against the Defense of Marriage Act.

Audience members. Boo-o-o!

The President. I believe reasonable people can find common ground on difficult issues. Republicans and Democrats and many citizens on both sides of the life issue came together and agreed we should ban the brutal practice of partial-birth abortion. I signed that law. But Senator Kerry was part of an out-of-the-mainstream minority that voted against the ban.

In the course of this campaign, he said the heart and soul of America can be found in Hollywood.

Audience members. Boo-o-o!

The President. No, most American families do not look to Hollywood as a source of values. The heart and soul of America is found in places like Alamogordo, New Mexico.

All these choices make this one of the most important elections in our history. The security and prosperity of our country, the health and the education of families, the retirement of our seniors, the direction of our culture are all at stake. And the decision is in the best of hands; it's in the hands of the American people.

I see a good day for America. I clearly see a better tomorrow for all of us. One of my favorite quotes was written by a Texan from right down the road in El Paso, Texas. He said, "Sarah and I live on the east side of the mountain. It's the sunrise side, not the sunset side. It's the side to see the day that is coming, not to see the day that is gone." You know, when you really listen to the words in this campaign, my opponent has spent much of this campaign talking about the day that is gone. I'm talking about the day that is coming.

We've been through a lot together over the last 3¾ years. Because we've done the hard work of climbing the mountain, we see the valley below. We'll protect our families. We'll build on our prosperity. We'll defend our deepest values. We will spread freedom and liberty around the world, and that will help us keep the peace we all want.

You know, when I campaigned in New Mexico 4 years ago asking for the vote, I said that if you gave me the honor to serve, I would uphold the honor and the dignity of the office to which I had been elected. With your help, I will do so for 4 more years.

God bless. Thanks for coming. I appreciate you all.

NOTE: The President spoke at 3:50 p.m. at Alamogordo High School. In his remarks, he referred to Senator Zell Miller of Georgia, who made the keynote address at the 2004 Republican National Convention; former President Saddam Hussein of Iraq; senior Al Qaida associate Abu Musab Al Zarqawi; and Usama bin Laden, leader of the Al Qaida terrorist organization.

Statement on the Death of James Cardinal Hickey
October 24, 2004

Cardinal James Hickey was an inspirational spiritual leader who brought comfort to the sick and help and hope to those in need. He was a caring and compassionate man. For 20 years, he led the Archdiocese of Washington with great dignity and conviction. He will be deeply missed by his church, the Washington community, and all of the people throughout America whose lives he touched so deeply. Laura and I send our prayers and condolences to his family, friends, and loved ones.

Remarks in Greeley, Colorado
October 25, 2004

The President. Thank you all. Thanks for coming today. Laura and I are so honored so many came out to say hello. You have lifted our spirits. Thank you for being here. It's great to be here in Greeley, Colorado.

You know, I am told the last sitting President to visit Greeley was Franklin D. Roosevelt, who came right before he won his second term. With your help, history will be repeated.

And that's what we are here to do; we're here to ask for your help. We'd like you to get your friends and neighbors to go to the polls. Remind them we have a duty in our democracy to vote. When you get them headed to the polls, tell them if they want a safer America, a stronger America, and a better America, to put me and Dick Cheney back in office.

So Laura and I were in the seventh grade together in west Texas. And then we became reacquainted when she—she was a public school librarian at the time. I asked her to marry me. She said, "Fine, but make me one promise." I said, "What is that?" She said, "Promise me I'll never have to give a political speech." [*Laughter*] I said, "Okay, you've got a deal." Fortunately, she didn't hold me to that promise. She's given a lot of speeches, and when she does, the American people see a strong, compassionate, great First Lady.

I am proud of my runningmate, Dick Cheney. Look, I readily concede that he does not have the waviest hair in the race. [*Laughter*] But you'll be pleased to know I didn't pick him because of his hairdo. I picked him because of his judgment, his experience. He's getting the job done for the American people.

You know, Laura, and I were able to welcome the Giulianis to our ranch in Crawford, Texas, last night. We know him more—I know him better than I knew him as mayor. I know him as a person, a compassionate, strong leader. I am proud to have Rudy and Judith Giuliani traveling with us. I'm proud to have your support, Mr. Mayor. And I appreciate your great service to our country.

And like the mayor, I recognize that you've got a great Governor in Governor Bill Owens, I want to thank his wife, Frances, and daughter, Monica, and son, Brett, for being with us today.

I want to thank Senator Wayne Allard for his great service to the State of Colorado, and his wife, Joan, is with us today. I'm proud to stand with the next Senator

from Colorado, Pete Coors. I appreciate Marilyn being here. And when he wins, he'll be taking the place of a fine man in Senator Ben Nighthorse Campbell. And I know you're proud of the Congresswoman from this district, Marilyn Musgrave. We're proud you're here, Marilyn. I appreciate Steve being here.

I want to thank the Lieutenant Governor. I want to thank all the State and local officials who are here. I appreciate Congressman Bob Schaffer for being here. Congressman, I appreciate working together to make sure this party stays united coming down the stretch.

I want to thank Mark Wills, the country and western singer who is here. He likes to sing in a part of the world where the cowboy hats outnumber the ties. I want to thank Kenny Cordova & The Olde Rock Band. I'm proud to be up here with a man who can hit that baseball in Todd Helton. We got to know him a little while back; we had he and his wife to the White House for dinner. And he can sure play. [*Laughter*]

I want to thank those who wear the uniform who are with us here today. Thank you for your service. I want to thank the veterans who are here today for having set such a great example. I want to thank the military families who are here today for your sacrifice.

But most of all, I want to thank the rest of you for coming. I appreciate what you have done on behalf of our campaign and what you're going to do. Keep putting up the signs, making the phone calls, turning out the vote, and we're going to win a great victory on November the 2d.

We're coming down the stretch in the last week of this campaign. I will continue to talk about my vision for a more hopeful America. I am committed to low taxes, spending discipline. I'm committed to a sound energy policy that makes us less dependent on foreign sources of energy.

In a new term, we'll continue to work to make sure our farmers and ranchers can make a decent living. In a new term, we'll continue to work to make sure the entrepreneurial spirit in America is strong so small businesses can thrive and succeed. In a new term, we'll stay on the path of reform and results in our schools so no child is left behind in America. In a new term, we'll make sure health care is more affordable and accessible for all our families and small businesses. In a new term, we'll keep the promise of Social Security for our seniors and strengthen the system for our children and our grandchildren. We will protect marriage and family, which are the foundations of our society. And I'll name judges who know the difference between personal opinion and the strict interpretation of the law.

And all the progress we hope to make depends on the security of our Nation. We face enemies who hate our country and would do anything to harm us. I'll fight these enemies with every asset of our national power, and we will do our duty and protect the American people.

In the last 4 years, we've been through a lot of history. We saw a ruthless, sneak attack on the United States. We learned of heroism on doomed airplanes. We saw the bravery of rescuers running toward danger. We've seen our military bring freedom to the oppressed and justice to our enemies. Our Nation has shown our character to the world. We are proud to be Americans.

Now we are nearing the first Presidential election since September the 11th, 2001. The people of the United States will choose the leader of the free world in the middle of a global war. The choice is not only between two candidates; it is between two directions in the conduct of the war on terror. Will America return to the defensive, reactive mindset that sought to manage the dangers to our country?

Audience members. Boo-o-o!

The President. Or will we fight a real war with the goal of victory?

In every critical aspect, in every critical respect, my opponent and I see the war on terror differently, and the Americans need to consider these differences as they make a vital choice. First, I believe that America wins wars by fighting on the offensive. When I saw those images of the fire and death on September the 11th, I made a decision: Our country will not sit back and wait for future attacks; we will prevent those attacks by going after the enemy.

We are waging a global campaign from the mountains of central Asia to the deserts of the Middle East, from the Horn of Africa to the Philippines. And those efforts are succeeding. Since September the 11th, 2001, more than three-quarters of Al Qaida's key members and associates have been brought to justice, and the rest of them know we're on their trail.

After September the 11th, we set a new direction for American policy and enforced a doctrine that is clear to all: "If you supported or harbored terrorists, you are equally guilty of terrorist murder." We destroyed the terror camps that trained thousands of killers in Afghanistan. We removed the Taliban from power. We have persuaded Governments in Pakistan and Saudi Arabia to recognize the enemy and to join the fight. We ended the regime of Saddam Hussein, which sponsored terror. America and the world are safer with Saddam Hussein sitting in a prison cell. We sent a clear message to Libya, which has now given up its weapons of mass destruction programs. We have acted through diplomacy and force to shrink the area where the terrorists can freely operate. And that strategy has the terrorists on the run.

My opponent has a different view.

Audience members. Boo-o-o!

The President. He says that fighting terrorists in the Middle East, America has, quote, "created terrorists where they did not exist," end quote.

Audience members. Boo-o-o!

The President. This is his argument, that terrorists are somehow less dangerous or fewer in number if America avoids provoking them.

Audience members. Boo-o-o!

The President. But this represents a fundamental misunderstanding of the enemy. We are dealing with killers who have made the death of Americans the calling of their lives. If America were not fighting these killers west of Baghdad and in the mountains of Afghanistan and elsewhere, what does Senator Kerry think they would do? Would they be living productive lives of service and charity? [*Laughter*] Would the terrorists who behead innocent people on camera just be quiet, peaceful citizens if we had not liberated Iraq?

Audience members. No-o-o!

The President. We are fighting these terrorists with our military in Afghanistan and Iraq and beyond so we do not have to face them in the streets of our own cities.

America is not to blame for terrorist hatred, and no retreat by America would appease them. We don't create terrorists by fighting them. We defeat the terrorists by fighting them.

Our second big difference concerns Iraq. Victory in Iraq is essential to victory in the war on terror. We have a strategy to achieve that victory. The stakes in that country are high. If a terror regime were allowed to reemerge in Iraq, terrorists would again find a home, a source of funding, and vital support; they would correctly conclude that free nations do not have the will to defend themselves.

As Iraq succeeds as a free society in the heart of the Middle East, an ally in the war on terror, and a model of hopeful reform in a troubled region, the terrorists will suffer a crushing defeat, and every free nation will be more secure.

We are still confronting serious violence from determined enemies. Yet, the Iraqi Interim Government, with American and coalition support, is making progress week by week. Along with Iraqi forces, we're on the offensive in Fallujah, north Babil. We've restored Government control in

Samarra, Tall 'Afar, and Najaf. More than 100,000 Iraqi soldiers, police, and border guards are already trained, equipped, and bravely serving their country. More than 200,000 will be in place by the end of next year. An Iraqi independent electoral commission is up and running. Political parties are planning campaigns. A free and fair Iraq elections will be held on schedule this January.

The desperate executions of unarmed Iraqi security forces show the evil nature of the terrorists we fight. It proves these terrorists are enemies of the Iraqi people and the American people and everyone who loves freedom. The terrorist insurgents hate our progress, and they fight our progress, but they will not stop our progress. We will stay on the offense against these terrorists, and we will prevail. We will help the Iraqis get on the path to stability and democracy as quickly as possible, and then our troops will return home with the honor they have earned.

My opponent has a different view.

Audience members. Boo-o-o!

The President. The Senator calls America's missions in Iraq a "mistake," a "diversion," a "colossal error."

Audience members. Boo-o-o!

The President. And then he says he's the right man to win the war?

Audience members. Boo-o-o!

The President. You cannot win a war you do not believe in fighting.

On Iraq, my opponent has a strategy of pessimism and retreat.

Audience members. Boo-o-o!

The President. He's talked about artificial timetables to pull our troops out. He has sent the signal that America's overriding goal in Iraq would be to leave, even if the job is not done.

Audience members. Boo-o-o!

The President. That sends the wrong message. It sends the wrong message to Iraqis who need to know that America will not cut and run. That sends the wrong message to the troops of our coalition who need to know that we will honor their sacrifice by completing the mission. My opponent has the wrong strategy for the wrong country at the wrong time.

On this vital front of the war on terror, protest is not a policy, retreat is not a strategy, and failure is not an option. As long as I'm the Commander in Chief, America will never retreat in the face of the terrorists.

Audience members. Four more years! Four more years! Four more years!

The President. Third, American leadership is indispensable to winning the war on terror. Ever since September the 11th, 2001, America has sounded a certain trumpet. We've stated clearly the challenge to civilization. We've rallied many nations to oppose it. More than 90 nations are actively engaged in the war on terror. All 26 nations of NATO have personnel in either Iraq, Afghanistan, or both. NATO has taken leadership of an international force in Afghanistan, the first out-of-area deployment in the history of our Alliance. Japan has deployed forces in Iraq, the first overseas mission in the history of their democracy. Forces from South Korea are there. America has led. Many have joined. And America and the world are safer.

My opponent takes a different approach.

Audience members. Boo-o-o!

The President. He believes that instead of leading with confidence, America must submit to what he calls a "global test."

Audience members. Boo-o-o!

The President. I'm not making that up. [*Laughter*] I was standing right here when he said it. As far as I can tell, that means our country must get permission from foreign capitals before we act in our own defense.

Audience members. Boo-o-o!

The President. As President, I will always work with other countries. I will seek their advice. But there is a world of difference between working with good allies and giving a few reluctant nations veto power over our national security. I will never, never submit our national security decisions to veto of a foreign government.

In addition to a "global test," my opponent promises what he calls a "golden age" of diplomacy, to charm critical governments all over the world.

Audience members. Boo-o-o!

The President. I don't see much diplomatic skill in Senator Kerry's habit of insulting America's closest friends. He's called the countries serving alongside us in Iraq, quote, "a trumped up coalition of the bribed, the coerced, the bought, and the extorted."

Audience members. Boo-o-o!

The President. Even last week, my opponent said that we have, quote, "hardly anyone with us in Iraq." That is a deeply offensive way to treat some 30 nations that are in Iraq, and especially the 14 nations that have lost forces in our cause. How can Senator Kerry denigrate the contributions led by the likes of Tony Blair of Great Britain, John Howard of Australia, Silvio Berlusconi of Italy, Aleksander Kwasniewski of Poland, and then expect other leaders to stand with America in the future? You cannot expand an alliance by showing contempt for those already in it. In this time of challenge to civilization, America has found strong and responsible allies, and they deserve the respect of all Americans, not the scorn of a politician.

Fourth, I believe that America will gain long-term security by promoting freedom and hope and democracy in the broader Middle East. Our country needs to look ahead. And 20 years from now, if the Middle East is dominated by dictators and mullahs who build weapons of mass destruction and harbor terrorists, our children and grandchildren will live in a nightmare world of danger. That doesn't have to happen.

By taking the side of reformers and democrats in the Middle East, we'll gain allies in the war on terror and isolate the ideology of murder and help defeat the despair and hopelessness that feeds terror. By spreading freedom, by spreading liberty, the world will become a much safer place for future generations. Progress in the broader Middle East toward freedom will not come easily. Yet, that progress is coming faster than many would have said possible. Across a troubled region, we're seeing a movement toward elections, greater rights for women, and open discussion of peaceful reform. The election in Afghanistan this month and the election in Iraq next January will be counted as landmark events in the history of liberty.

My opponent looks at things differently.

Audience members. Boo-o-o!

The President. He's not only skeptical of democracy in Iraq; he has not made democracy a priority for his foreign policy. But what is his long-term answer to the threat of terror? Is he content to watch and wait as anger and resentment grow for more decades? Is he content to wait as more and more people are angry and hostile and turn to terrorism? Is he content to wait until radicals without conscience gain the weapons to kill without limit? Ignoring the root causes of terror, turning a blind eye to the oppression and despair of millions may be easier in the short run, but we learned on September the 11th, if violence and fanaticism are not opposed at their source, they will find us where we live.

Instead of offering his own agenda for freedom, my opponent complains that we are trying to, quote, "impose democracy on the people of the broader Middle East." Is that what he sees in Afghanistan, unwilling people having democracy forced upon them? We did remove the Taliban by force, but democracy is rising in that country because the Afghan people, like people everywhere, want to live in freedom. No one forced them to register by the millions or to stand in long lines waiting to vote. For many people, that historic election was a day they will never forget. One man in western Kabul arrived to vote at 7 a.m. He said, "I don't want"—he said, "I didn't

sleep all night. I wanted to be the first in my polling station." My fellow citizens, freedom is on the march, and it is changing the world.

We are witnessing big and hopeful events. Yet, my opponent refuses to see them. I believe that people across the Middle East are weary of poverty and oppression. I believe everybody wants to be free. Freedom is not America's gift to the world; freedom is the Almighty God's gift to each man and woman in this world.

Our fifth great difference concerns the role of the Presidency. A President has to lead with consistency and strength. In a war, sometimes your tactics will change, but not your principles. Americans have seen how I do my job. Even when you might not agree with me, you know what I believe, where I stand, and what I intend to do. On good days and on bad days, whether the polls are up or down, I am determined to win the war on terror, and I will always support the men and women who do the fighting.

My opponent has taken a different approach.

Audience members. Boo-o-o!

The President. It's fair to say that consistency has not been his strong point. [*Laughter*] Senator Kerry says that we are better off with Saddam Hussein out of power, except when he declares that removing Saddam made us less safe.

Audience members. Boo-o-o!

The President. Senator Kerry stated in our second debate that he always believed that Saddam Hussein was a threat, except a few questions later, when he said Saddam Hussein was not a threat. [*Laughter*] He says he was right when he voted to authorize the use of force against Saddam Hussein, but that I was wrong to use force against Saddam Hussein. [*Laughter*] Now my opponent is throwing out the wild claim that he knows where bin Laden was in the fall of 2001—[*laughter*]—and that our military had a chance to get him in Tora

Bora. This is an unjustified and harsh criticism of our military commanders in the field. This is the worst kind of Monday morning quarterbacking, and it is what we've come to expect from Senator Kerry.

In fact, our Commander in Afghanistan, General Tommy Franks recently wrote, quote, "The Senator's understanding of events do not square with reality." He was talking about Tora Bora. The General says that American Special Forces were actively involved in the search of terrorists in Tora Bora and that intelligence reports at the time placed bin Laden in any of several countries.

Before Senator Kerry got into political difficulty and revised his views, he saw Tora Bora differently. In the fall of 2001, on national TV, Senator Kerry said, quote, "I think we have been doing this pretty effectively, and we should continue to do it that way." At the time, Senator Kerry said about Tora Bora, "I think we've been smart. I think administration leadership has done well, and we are on the right track," end quote. All I can say is that I am George W. Bush, and I approve of that message.

Yet, Senator Kerry's record on national security has a far deeper problem than election-year flip-flopping. On the largest national security issues of our time, he has been consistently and dangerously wrong. When Ronald Reagan was confronting the Soviet Union at the height of the cold war, Senator Kerry said that President Reagan's policy of peace through strength was making America less safe.

Audience members. Boo-o-o!

The President. And he voted against many of the weapons systems critical to our defense buildup. History has shown that Senator Kerry was wrong, and President Reagan was right.

When former President Bush led a coalition against Saddam Hussein in 1991, Senator Kerry voted against the use of force to liberate Kuwait.

Audience members. Boo-o-o!

The President. If his view had prevailed, Saddam Hussein today would dominate the Middle East and possess the world's most dangerous weapons. History has shown that Senator Kerry was wrong, and former President Bush was right.

In 1994, just one year after the first bombing of the World Trade Center, Senator Kerry proposed massive cuts in America's intelligence budget——

Audience members. Boo-o-o!

The President. ——so massive that even his Massachusetts colleague, Ted Kennedy, opposed them. [*Laughter*] History has shown that Senator Kerry was wrong and— we've got to be fair—[*laughter*]—Senator Kennedy was right.

Just last year, American troops in Iraq and Afghanistan needed $87 billion for body armor, hazard pay, vehicles, weapons, and bullets. First, Senator Kerry said, "It would irresponsible to vote against the troops." Then he voted against the troops.

Audience members. Boo-o-o!

The President. Then he said, "I actually did vote for the $87 billion, before I voted against it." [*Laughter*] History has shown that Senator Kerry was right, then wrong— [*laughter*]—then briefly right—[*laughter*]— then wrong again. [*Laughter*]

Since then, the Senator has said the whole matter about the $87 billion is a complicated matter. There's nothing complicated about supporting our troops in combat.

During the last 20 years, in key moments of challenge and decision for America, Senator Kerry has chosen the position of weakness and inaction. With that record, he stands in opposition not just to me but to the great tradition of the Democratic Party. The party of Franklin Roosevelt and Harry Truman and John Kennedy is rightly remembered for confidence and resolve in times of war and in hours of crisis. Senator Kerry has turned his back on "pay any price" and "bear any burden." And he has replaced those commitments with "wait and see" and "cut and run."

Audience members. Boo-o-o!

The President. Many Democrats in this country do not recognize their party anymore. Today I want to speak to every one of them: If you believe that America should lead with strength and purpose and confidence in our ideals, I would be honored to have your support, and I ask for your vote.

All the differences I outlined today add up to one big difference: Senator Kerry says that September the 11th did not change him much at all.

Audience members. Boo-o-o!

The President. And his policies make that clear. He says the war on terror is primarily a law enforcement and intelligence gathering operation. His top foreign policy adviser says, "The war is just a metaphor, like the war on poverty." The Senator's goal is to go back to the mindset of the 1990s, when terrorism was seen as a nuisance, and we fought with subpoenas and a few cruise missiles.

Audience members. Boo-o-o!

The President. There is a major problem with that. The era of calm he longs for was only a shallow illusion of peace. We know that throughout the 1990s, the terrorists were training and plotting against us. They saw our complacency as weakness. And so their plans became more ambitious and their attacks more deadly, until, finally, the Twin Towers became Ground Zero and the Pentagon was in flames. My outlook was changed on September the 11th.

A few days after the attacks, I stood with Rudy where the buildings fell. He'll never forget that day, and neither will I. I'll never forget the evil of the enemy and the suffering of our people. I know we're not fighting a metaphor. And I remember the hard—workers in hardhats there yelling at the top of their lungs, "Whatever it takes." A fellow grabbed me by the arm, and he said, "Do not let me down." From that day forward, I have gotten up every morning thinking about how to better protect our country. I will never relent in defending America, whatever it takes.

In a new term, we will finish the work we have started. We will stand against terror. We will stand for freedom and peace. And on November 2d, my fellow Americans, I ask you stand with me.

God bless. Thank you all.

NOTE: The President spoke at 10:14 a.m. at the Island Grove Regional Park Community Events Center. In his remarks, he referred to former Mayor Rudolph W. Giuliani of New York City, and his wife, Judith; Gov. Bill Owens and Lt. Gov. Jane Bergman Norton of Colorado; Marilyn Coors, wife of Colorado senatorial candidate Pete Coors; Steven E. Musgrave, husband of Representative Marilyn N. Musgrave; former Representative Bob Schaffer, senatorial candidate in Colorado; professional baseball player Todd Helton and his wife, Christy; Prime Minister Tony Blair of the United Kingdom; Prime Minister John Howard of Australia; Prime Minister Silvio Berlusconi of Italy; President Aleksander Kwasniewski of Poland; Usama bin Laden, leader of the Al Qaida terrorist organization; and Gen. Tommy R. Franks, USA (Ret.), former combatant commander, U.S. Central Command.

Remarks in Council Bluffs, Iowa
October 25, 2004

The President. Thank you all for coming. Thank you all. Thanks for coming. I appreciate you being here. Laura and I are so honored so many came out to say hello. You're lifting our spirits.

I want to thank all the Iowans who are here. Thank you for coming. I want to thank those of you from the great State of Nebraska who took the—[applause]. We are here to not only ask for the vote in this part of the world; we're here to ask for your help. We're here to say that we need your help coming down the stretch. We need you to make the phone calls, find your friends and neighbors and encourage them to go to the polls. With your help, we will carry Iowa and win a great victory on November the 2d.

So when I asked Laura to marry me, she was a public school librarian, and she said—and some of you will probably be able to relate to this—she said, "Fine, I will marry you, but make me a promise." I said, "What is it?" She said, "Promise me I'll never have to give a political speech." [Laughter] I said, "You've got a deal." Fortunately, she didn't hold me to that promise. She's giving a lot of speeches, and when she speaks the American people see a warm, strong, great First Lady.

Audience members. Laura! Laura! Laura!

The President. I'm proud of my runningmate, Dick Cheney. Now, look, I fully admit he does not have the waviest hair in this race. [Laughter] But I want to assure you, I didn't pick him because of his hairdo. [Laughter] I picked him because of his experience. I picked him because of his judgment.

We had breakfast with Rudy at our ranch in Crawford. We've just come from Greeley, Colorado. We're headed to Davenport, Iowa. I tell you, it's a great joy to travel with Rudy Giuliani. I'm proud to have his support, and I'm honored to call him friend. And by the way, his wife, Judith, is traveling with us too.

So the last time I saw Senator Grassley, I turned to Laura and said, "Laura, you know the South Lawn has got a lot of grass on it, and we're looking for somebody to come and mow it." [Laughter] Let me tell you something about your Senator. When it came time to cut the taxes on the work-

ing people of this country, Senator Grassley led the charge in the United States Senate. When it came time to strengthen Medicare to make sure our seniors got prescription drug coverage and rural hospitals were treated fairly, Senator Grassley led the United States Senate. I know the people of Iowa are proud to call him Senator. I'm proud to call him Mr. Chairman.

I want to thank Congressman Steve King from Iowa for joining us today. Congressman, you're doing a fine job. I appreciate you being here.

I want to thank all the grassroots activists who are here. I want to thank those of you who are putting up the signs. I want to thank those of you who are making the phone calls. I want to thank you for what you're going to do, which is turn out a big vote on November the 2d.

I want to thank my friend Michael W. Smith for singing for you this evening.

I want to thank all of you who are here who wear our Nation's uniform. Thank you for your service. I want to thank the veterans who are here for having set such a great example for our military. And I want to thank our military families for the sacrifices you have made.

In the last week of this campaign, I will continue to talk about my vision for a more hopeful America. I'm committed to low taxes and spending discipline. We'll talk about how to make sure the entrepreneurial spirit is strong in America. I'll talk about how to make sure our farm economy remains strong in America.

In the next 4 years, we'll stay on the path of reform and results in our schools, so no child is left behind in America. I'll remind people we have a plan to make sure health care is more affordable and accessible and that in all we do to reform health care, we'll make sure the decisions are made between doctors and patients, not by officials in Washington, DC. I will remind the people that over the next 4 years, we'll keep the promise of Social Security for our seniors, and we'll strengthen the system for our children and our grand-children.

I will tell the people we'll continue to promote a culture of life in which every person matters and every being counts. I will remind them that we'll protect family and marriage, which are the foundations of our society. And I will tell the people that I'll name Federal judges who know the difference between personal opinion and the strict interpretation of the law.

Yet, all progress we hope to make depends on the security of our Nation. We face enemies who hate our country and would do anything to harm us. We will fight these enemies with every asset of our national power. We will do our duty and protect the American people.

And that's what I want to talk to you and the good people of Iowa and Nebraska about today, our national security. In the last 4 years, we've been through a lot of history. We saw a ruthless sneak attack on the United States. We learned of heroism on doomed airplanes. We saw the bravery of rescuers rushing toward danger. We have seen our military bring freedom to the oppressed and justice to our enemy. Our Nation has shown its character to the world. We are proud to be Americans.

We are now nearing the first Presidential election since September the 11th, 2001. People of the United States will choose the leader of the free world in the middle of a global war. The choice is not only between two candidates; it's between two directions in the conduct of the war on terror. The American voters must answer these questions: Will America return to the defensive, reactive mindset that sought to manage the dangers to our country?

Audience members. Boo-o-o!

The President. Or will we fight a real war, with the goal of victory? In every critical aspect, my opponent and I see the war on terror differently, and Americans need to consider those differences as they make a vital choice.

First, I believe that America wins wars by fighting on the offensive. When I saw all those images of fire and death on September the 11th, I made a decision: Our country will not sit back and wait for future attacks; we will prevent those attacks by going after the enemy.

And so since that day, we are waging a global campaign from the mountains of central Asia to the deserts of the Middle East, from the Horn of Africa to the Philippines. And those efforts are succeeding. Since September the 11th, 2001, more than three-quarters of Al Qaida's key members and associates have been brought to justice, and the rest of them know we're on their trail.

After September the 11th, we set a new direction for American policy and endorsed a doctrine that is clear to all: If you support or harbor terrorists, you're equally guilty of terrorist murder.

We destroyed the terror camps that trained thousands of killers in Afghanistan. We removed the Taliban from power. We persuaded the Governments in Pakistan and Saudi Arabia to recognize the enemy and to join the fight. We ended the regime of Saddam Hussein, which sponsored terror, and we know that America and the world are safer with Saddam Hussein sitting in a prison cell.

Audience members. U.S.A.! U.S.A.! U.S.A.!

The President. We sent a message to Libya—we sent a clear message to Libya, which has now given up its weapons of mass destruction programs. We have acted through diplomacy and force to shrink the area where the terrorists can freely operate. And our strategy has the terrorists on the run.

My opponent has a different point of view.

Audience members. Boo-o-o!

The President. He says that by fighting terrorists in the Middle East, America has, quote, "created terrorists where they did not exist."

Audience members. Boo-o-o!

The President. This is his argument, that terrorists are somehow less dangerous or fewer in number if America avoids provoking them.

Audience members. Boo-o-o!

The President. But this represents a fundamental misunderstanding of the enemy. We're dealing with killers who have made the death of Americans the calling of their lives. If America were not fighting these killers west of Baghdad and in the mountains of Afghanistan and elsewhere, what does Senator Kerry think they would do? Would they begin leading productive lives of service and charity?

Audience members. No-o-o!

The President. Would the terrorists who behead innocent people on camera just be quiet and peaceful citizens if we had not liberated Iraq?

Audience members. No-o-o!

The President. We are fighting the terrorists with our military in Afghanistan and Iraq and beyond so we do not have to face them in the streets of our cities.

Audience members. Four more years! Four more years! Four more years!

The President. America is not to blame for terrorist hatred, and no retreat by America would appease them. We don't create terrorists by fighting them; we defeat the terrorists by fighting them.

Our second difference concerns Iraq. I believe victory in Iraq is essential to victory in the war on terror, and we have had a strategy to achieve that victory. The stakes in that country are high. If a terror regime were allowed to reemerge in Iraq, terrorists would again find a home, a source of funding, and vital support. They would correctly conclude that free nations do not have the will to defend themselves. As Iraq succeeds as a free society at the heart of the Middle East, an ally in the war on terror, and a model for hopeful reform in a troubled region, the terrorists will suffer a crushing defeat and every free nation will be more secure.

We are still confronting serious violence from determined enemies. Yet, the Iraqi Interim Government, with American and coalition support, is making progress, week by week. Along with Iraqi forces, we're on the offensive in Fallujah and north Babil. We've restored Government control in Samarra and Tall 'Afar and Najaf. More than 100,000 Iraqi soldiers, police, and border guards are already trained and equipped and bravely serving their country. And more than 200,000 will be in place at the end of next year. An Iraqi independent electoral commission is up and running. Political parties are planning campaigns, and free and fair Iraqi elections will be held on schedule this coming January.

The despicable executions of unarmed Iraqi security forces show the evil nature of the terrorists we fight and prove those terrorists are enemies of the Iraqi people and the American people and the civilized world. The terrorists and insurgents hate our progress and fight our progress, but they will not stop our progress.

We will stay on the offense, and we will prevail. We will help Iraqis get on the path to stability and democracy as quickly as possible, and then our troops will return home with the honor they have earned.

My opponent has a different view.

Audience members. Boo-o-o!

The President. The Senator calls America's mission in Iraq a "mistake," a "diversion," a "colossal error."

Audience members. Boo-o-o!

The President. And then says he's the right man to win the war.

Audience members. Boo-o-o!

The President. You cannot win a war you do not believe in fighting.

On Iraq, my opponent has a strategy of pessimism and retreat. He has talked about artificial timetables to pull our troops out. He has sent the signal that America's overriding goal in Iraq would be to leave, even if the job is not done.

Audience members. Boo-o-o!

The President. That sends the wrong message. It sends the wrong message to Iraqis, who need to know that America will never cut and run. That sends the wrong message to our troops and the troops of our coalition, who need to know that we will honor their sacrifice by completing the mission. My opponent has the wrong strategy for the wrong country at the wrong time. On this vital front of the war on terror, protest is not a policy, retreat is not a strategy, and failure is not an option. As long as I am the Commander in Chief, America will never retreat in the face of terrorism.

Third, I believe that American leadership is indispensable to winning the war on terror. Ever since September the 11th, 2001, America has sounded a certain trumpet. We have stated clearly the challenge to civilization, and we have rallied many nations to oppose it. More than 90 nations are actively engaged in the war on terror. All 26 NATO nations have personnel in either Iraq, Afghanistan, or both. NATO has taken leadership of an international force in Afghanistan, the first out-of-area deployment in the history of our Alliance. Japan has deployed forces to Iraq, the first overseas mission in the history of their democracy. Forces from South Korea are in Iraq as well. America has led. Many have joined. And America and the world are safer.

My opponent takes a different approach. He believes that instead of leading with confidence, America must submit to what he calls a "global test."

Audience members. Boo-o-o!

The President. I'm not making that up. [*Laughter*] He was standing right about just there when I heard him say it. As far as I can tell, that means our country must get permission from foreign capitals before we act in our own self-defense.

Audience members. Boo-o-o!

The President. As President, I will always work with other countries and seek their advice. But there is a world of difference between working with good allies and giving a few reluctant nations veto power over our role in the world. I will never submit our national security decisions to the veto of a foreign government.

In addition to a "global test," my opponent promises what he calls a "golden age" of diplomacy to charm critical governments all over the world.

Audience members. Boo-o-o!

The President. I don't see much diplomatic skill in Senator Kerry's habit of insulting America's closest friends. He has called the countries serving alongside us in Iraq, quote, "a trumped-up coalition of the bribed, the coerced, the bought, and the extorted."

Audience members. Boo-o-o!

The President. Even last week, my opponent said that we have, quote, "hardly anyone with us in Iraq."

Audience members. Boo-o-o!

The President. That is a deeply offensive way to treat some 30 nations that are in Iraq, especially the 14 nations that have lost forces in our cause. How can Senator Kerry denigrate the contributions of countries led by the likes of Tony Blair of Great Britain, John Howard of Australia, or Silvio Berlusconi of Italy or Aleksander Kwasniewski of Poland and then expect other leaders to stand with America in the future? You cannot expand an alliance by showing contempt for those already in it. In this time of challenge to civilization, America has found strong and responsible allies. They deserve the respect of all Americans, not the scorn of a politician.

Fourth, I believe that America will gain long-term security by promoting freedom and hope and democracy in the broader Middle East. The job of a leader is to look ahead, and our country must look ahead. In 20 years from now, if the Middle East is dominated by dictators and mullahs who build weapons of mass destruction and harbor terrorists, our children and grandchildren will live in a nightmare world of danger. That does not have to happen. By taking the side of reformers and democrats in the Middle East, we will gain allies in the war on terror; we'll isolate the ideology of murder; and we will help defeat the despair and hopelessness that feeds terror. By spreading freedom and liberty, the world will become a much safer place for future generations.

Progress in the broader Middle East toward freedom will not come easily. Yet, that progress is coming faster than many would have said possible. Across a troubled region, we're seeing a movement toward elections and greater rights for women and open discussions for peaceful reform. The election in Afghanistan this month and the election in Iraq next January will be counted as landmark events in the history of liberty.

My opponent looks at things differently. He is not only skeptical of—about democracy in Iraq; he's not made democracy a priority of his foreign policy. But what is his long-term answer to the threat of terror? Is he content to watch and wait as anger and resentment grow for more decades in the Middle East, feeding more terrorism until radicals without conscience gain the weapons to kill without limit? Ignoring the root causes of terror, turning a blind eye to the oppression and despair of millions may be easier in the short run. But we learned on September the 11th that if violence and fanaticism are not opposed at their source, they will find us where we live.

Instead of offering his own agenda for freedom, my opponent complains that we're trying to, quote, "impose democracy on people in the broader Middle East." Is that what he sees in Afghanistan, unwilling people having democracy forced upon them? We did remove the Taliban by force, but democracy is rising in that country because the Afghan people, like people everywhere, want to live in freedom.

No one forced them to register by the millions or to stand in long lines to vote. For many people, that historic election was a day they will never forget. One man in western Kabul arrived to vote at 7 a.m. He said, "I didn't sleep all night. I wanted to be the first in my polling station." My fellow citizens, freedom is on the march, and it's changing the world.

We are witnessing big and hopeful events. I believe that people across the world, people in the Middle East want to live in freedom. I believe this because freedom is not America's gift to the world; freedom is the Almighty God's gift to each man and woman in this world.

Our fifth great difference concerns the role of the Presidency. A President has to lead with consistency and strength. In a war, sometimes your tactics have to change but not your principles. Americans have seen how I do my job. Even when you might not agree with me, you know what I believe and where I stand and what I intend to do.

Audience members. Four more years! Four more years! Four more years!

The President. Thank you all. On good days and on bad days, whether the polls are up or the polls are down, I am determined to win the war on terror, and I will always support the men and women who do the fighting.

My opponent has taken a different approach.

Audience members. Boo-o-o!

The President. It's fair to say that consistency has not been his strong point.

Audience members. Flip-flop! Flip-flop! Flip-flop!

The President. Senator Kerry says that we're better off with Saddam Hussein out of power, except when he declares that removing Saddam made us less safe. He stated in our second debate that he always believed that Saddam was a threat, except, a few questions later, when he said Saddam Hussein was not a threat.

Audience members. Flip-flop! Flip-flop! Flip-flop!

The President. He says he was right when he voted to authorize the use of force against Saddam Hussein but that I was wrong to use force against Saddam Hussein. [*Laughter*] Now my opponent is throwing out the wild claim that he knows where bin Laden was in the fall of 2001 and that our military passed up the chance to get him in Tora Bora. This is an unjustified criticism of our military commanders in the field. This is the worst kind of Monday morning quarterbacking. And that's what we've come to expect from Senator Kerry.

In fact, our commander in Afghanistan, General Tommy Franks recently wrote this about Tora Bora: "The Senator's understanding of events does not square with reality." The General said that American Special Forces were actively involved in the search for terrorists in Tora Bora and that intelligence reports at the time placed bin Laden in any of several countries.

Before Senator Kerry got into political difficulty and revised his views, he saw our actions in Tora Bora differently. In the fall of 2001, on national TV, Senator Kerry said this, "I think we have been doing this pretty effectively, and we should continue to do it that way." At the time, the Senator said about Tora Bora, "I think we've been smart. I think the administration leadership has done it well, and we are on the right track." Well, all I can tell you is that I am George W. Bush, and I approve of that message.

Yet, Senator Kerry's record on national security has a far deeper problem than election-year flip-flopping. On the largest national security issues of our time, he has been consistently and dangerously wrong. When Ronald Reagan was confronting the Soviet Union at the height of the cold war, Senator Kerry said that President Reagan's policy of peace through strength was making America less safe.

Audience members. Boo-o-o!

The President. He voted against many of the weapons systems critical to our defense buildup.

Audience members. Boo-o-o!

The President. History has shown that Senator Kerry was wrong and President Reagan was right.

When former President Bush led a coalition against Saddam Hussein in 1991, Senator Kerry voted against the use of force to liberate Kuwait.

Audience members. Boo-o-o!

The President. If his view had prevailed, Saddam Hussein today would dominate the Middle East and possess the world's most dangerous weapons. History has shown that Senator Kerry was wrong and former President Bush was right.

In 1994, just one year after the first bombing of the World Trade Center, Senator Kerry proposed massive cuts in America's intelligence budget, so massive that even his Massachusetts colleague, Ted Kennedy, opposed them.

Audience members. Boo-o-o!

The President. History has shown that Senator Kerry was wrong and—we've got to be fair—Senator Kennedy was right.

Just last year, American troops in Iraq and Afghanistan needed $87 billion for body armor and hazard pay, vehicles, weapons, and bullets. First, Senator Kerry said, "It would be irresponsible to vote against the troops." Then he voted against the troops.

Audience members. Boo-o-o!

The President. You might remember perhaps the most famous quote of the 2004 campaign when he said, "I actually did vote for the $87 billion, before I voted against it." History has shown that Senator Kerry was right, then wrong—[*laughter*]—then briefly right, and wrong again. Since then, on the 87 billion, my opponent has said, "The whole thing is a complicated matter." There's nothing complicated about supporting our troops in combat.

During the last 20 years, in key moments of challenge and decision for America, Senator Kerry has chosen the position of weakness and inaction. With that record, he stands in opposition not just to me but to the great tradition of the Democratic

Party. The party of Franklin Roosevelt and Harry Truman and John Kennedy is rightly remembered for confidence and resolve in times of war and hours of crisis. Senator Kerry has turned his back on "pay any price" and "bear any burden." He's replaced those commitments with "wait and see" and "cut and run."

Audience members. Boo-o-o!

The President. Many Democrats in this country do not recognize their party anymore. Today I want to speak to every one of them. If you believe that America should lead with strength and purpose and confidence in our ideals, I would be honored to have your support, and I'm asking for your vote.

All the differences I outlined today add up to one big difference, and it's important for our fellow citizens to understand that difference. Senator Kerry says that September the 11th did not change him much at all.

Audience members. Boo-o-o!

The President. His policies make that clear. He says the war on terror is primarily a law enforcement and intelligence gathering operation.

Audience members. Boo-o-o!

The President. His top foreign policy adviser says, "The war is just like a metaphor, like the war on poverty." The Senator's goal is to go back to the mindset of the 1990s, when terrorism was seen as a nuisance and was fought with subpoenas and a few cruise missiles.

Audience members. Boo-o-o!

The President. There's a major problem with that. The calm—the era of calm he longs for was only a shallow illusion of peace. We now know that throughout the 1990s, the terrorists were training and plotting against us. They saw our complacency as weakness. And so their plans became more ambitious and their attacks became more deadly until, finally, the Twin Towers became Ground Zero and the Pentagon was in flames.

My outlook was changed on September the 11th. A few days after the attacks, I stood with Rudy where buildings fell. I will never forget the evil of our enemy and the suffering of our people. I know we are fighting a war. And I remember the workers in the hardhats there at Ground Zero, yelling at me at the top of their lungs, "Whatever it takes." A fellow grabbed me by the arm, and he looked me in the eye, and he said, "Do not let me down." From that day forward, I've gotten up every morning thinking about how to better protect our country. I will never relent in defending America, whatever it takes.

In a new term, we will finish the work we have started. We will stand against terror and stand for freedom and peace we all want. And on November the 2d, my fellow Americans, I ask you to stand with me.

God bless. On to victory. Thank you all.

NOTE: The President spoke at 2:51 p.m. at the Mid-America Center. In his remarks, he referred to former Mayor Rudolph W. Giuliani of New York City, and his wife, Judith; entertainer Michael W. Smith; Prime Minister Tony Blair of the United Kingdom; Prime Minister John Howard of Australia; Prime Minister Silvio Berlusconi of Italy; President Aleksander Kwasniewski of Poland; Usama bin Laden, leader of the Al Qaida terrorist organization; and Gen. Tommy R. Franks, USA (Ret.), former combatant commander, U.S. Central Command.

Remarks in Davenport, Iowa
October 25, 2004

The President. Thank you all. Thanks for coming. It is great to be back in the great city of Davenport, Iowa. Laura and I are—[*applause*]. Thanks for coming. You've lifted our spirits today. We really appreciate you being here.

We're heading down the stretch. I'm here to ask for your vote. I'm here to ask for your help. I need you to go to your friends and neighbors and remind them we have a duty in this great democracy to vote. Don't overlook discerning Democrats when you get people going to the polls, by the way, people like Senator Zell Miller. Remind your friends and neighbors if they want a safer country, a stronger country, and a better country, to put me and Dick Cheney back in office.

Laura and I were in the seventh grade together in San Jacinto Junior High, in Midland, Texas, and then we became reacquainted. She was a public school librarian when I met her again. I said, "Will you marry me?" She said, "Fine, if you make me one promise." I said, "What is it?" "Promise me I'll never have to give a political speech." [*Laughter*] I said, "Okay, you've got a deal." [*Laughter*] Fortunately, she didn't hold me to that promise. She's giving a lot of speeches, and when she does, the American people see a strong, compassionate First Lady.

And I'm proud of my runningmate, Dick Cheney. You know, I'm looking around, and I can see a few folks out there have got the same hairstyle he does. [*Laughter*] I did not pick the Vice President because of his hairdo. [*Laughter*] And I admit, he doesn't have the waviest hair in the race. [*Laughter*] I picked him because he can get the job done for the American people.

How about Rudy? We love traveling with Rudy. Rudy is a great American. We woke up, and we had breakfast with Rudy and Judith at our place in Crawford. Then we

went to Greeley, Colorado. Then we went to the western part of your State, and we're finishing a great day here in Davenport. And I want to thank Rudy—I want to thank him for joining me. I appreciate his support.

So I was telling Laura, I said, "You know something, the South Lawn at the White House has got a lot of grass on it, and we need somebody to come and mow it." [*Laughter*] "I can't think of anybody better than the chairman, Chuck Grassley, to be mowing our lawn." What a good man Chuck Grassley is. He's a great United States Senator. I know you're proud of him.

And I'm proud of your Congressman, Jim Nussle, the budget chairman. He's watching your money like a hawk—eye. He's a good man. And I know you're proud of a Congressman who was raised right here, former Congressman. He moved up the road a little bit, but a man we call friend, and that's Congressman Jim Leach, and his wife, Deb, is here.

I want to thank all the grassroots activists who are here, the people putting up the signs, the people making the phone calls, the people organizing a rally just like this one. I want to thank you for what you have done and what you're going to do. With your hard work, with your help, we will carry Iowa and win a great victory on November the 2d.

Audience members. Four more years! Four more years! Four more years!

The President. We have just 8 days to go in this campaign, and voters have a clear choice between two very different candidates with dramatically different approaches and different records. You know where I stand, and sometimes, you even know where my opponent stands. [*Laughter*] We both have records. I'm proudly running on mine. The Senator is running from his. [*Laughter*] And there's a reason why. There is a mainstream in American politics, and my opponent sits on the far left bank. I'm a compassionate conservative and proudly so. In a time when our country has much to accomplish and much to offer, I proudly offer my record of reform and results.

This election comes down to five clear choices for America's families, five choices on issues of great consequence: your family's security; your family's budget; your quality of life; your retirement; and the bedrock values that are so critical to our country's future.

The first clear choice is the most important because it concerns the security of your family. All our progress on every other issue depends on the safety of our citizens. This will be the first Presidential election since September the 11th, 2001. Americans will go to the polls in a time of war and ongoing threats unlike any we have faced before. The terrorists who killed thousands are still dangerous, and they're determined. The outcome of this election will set the direction of the war against terror. The most solemn duty of the American President is to protect the American people. If America shows uncertainty or weakness in this decade, the world will drift toward tragedy. This will not happen on my watch.

Since that terrible morning of September the 11th, 2001, we have fought the terrorists across the Earth, not for pride, not for power, but because the lives of our citizens are at stake. Our strategy is clear. We've strengthened the protections for our homeland. We're reforming our intelligence capabilities. We're transforming our army. There will be no draft. We will keep the All-Volunteer Army. We are determined. We are relentless. We are staying on the offensive, and we're succeeding. The 9/11 Commission report said, "America is safer, not yet safe." More than three-quarters of Al Qaida's key members and associates have been brought to justice. The rest of them know we're on their trail.

The American President, in these times of danger, must lead with consistency and strength. In a war, sometimes your tactics change but not your principles. Americans have seen how I do my job. Even when you might not agree with me, you know what I believe and where I stand and what I intend to do. On good days and on bad days, whether the polls are up or the polls are down, I am determined to win the war on terror, and I will always support the men and women who wear the uniform.

Audience members. Four more years! Four more years! Four more years!

The President. My opponent has taken a different approach. It's fair to say that consistency has not been his strong point. [*Laughter*] Senator Kerry says we're better off with Saddam Hussein out of power, except when he declares that removing Saddam has made us less safe. He stated in our second debate that he always believed Saddam was a threat, except a few questions later, when he said Saddam Hussein was not a threat. [*Laughter*] He says he was right when he voted to authorize the use of force against Saddam Hussein, but that I was wrong to use force against Saddam Hussein. [*Laughter*]

Now my opponent is throwing out the wild claim that he knows where bin Laden was in the fall of 2001, and that our military passed up the chance to get him in Tora Bora. This is unjustified criticism of our military commanders in the field. This is the worst kind of Monday morning quarterbacking. And it's what we've come to expect from my opponent during this campaign.

In fact, our Commander in Afghanistan, General Tommy Franks, recently wrote about Tora Bora, and he said, "The Senator's understanding of events does not square with reality." The General said that American Special Forces were actively involved in the search for the terrorists in Tora Bora and that intelligence reports at the time placed bin Laden in several countries.

Before Senator Kerry got into political difficulty and revised his views, he saw our actions in Tora Bora differently. In the fall of 2001, on national TV, he said this about Tora Bora, "I think we've been doing this pretty effectively, and we should continue to do it that way." At the time, the Senator said about Tora Bora, "I think we've been smart. I think the administration leadership has done it well, and we are on the right track." End quote. All I can say about that is, I am George W. Bush, and I approve of that message.

Senator Kerry's record on national security has a far deeper problem than election-year flip-flopping. On the largest national security issues of our time, he has been consistently wrong. When Ronald Reagan was confronting the Soviet Union at the height of the cold war, Senator Kerry said that President Reagan's policy of peace through strength was making America less safe.

Audience members. Boo-o-o!

The President. He voted against many weapons systems critical to our defense buildup. History has shown that Senator Kerry was wrong, and President Ronald Reagan was right.

When former President Bush led a coalition against Saddam Hussein in 1991, Senator Kerry voted against the use of force to liberate Kuwait.

Audience members. Boo-o-o!

The President. If his view had prevailed, Saddam Hussein today would dominate the Middle East and possess the world's most dangerous weapons. History has shown that Senator Kerry was wrong, and former President George Bush was right.

In 1994, just one year after the first bombing of the World Trade Center, Senator Kerry proposed massive cuts in America's intelligence budget.

Audience members. Boo-o-o!

The President. So massive that even his Massachusetts colleague, Ted Kennedy, opposed them. [*Laughter*] History has shown that Senator Kerry was wrong and—we've

got be fair—Senator Kennedy was right. [*Laughter*]

Just last year, American troops in Iraq and Afghanistan needed $87 billion for important funding to help them complete their missions. First, my opponent said, "It would be irresponsible to vote against the troops." Then he voted against the troops.

Audience members. Boo-o-o!

The President. You might remember perhaps the most famous quote of the 2004 campaign. They asked him about his vote, and he said, "I actually did vote for the $87 billion, right before I voted against it." History has shown that Senator Kerry was right, then wrong—[*laughter*]—then briefly right—[*laughter*]—then wrong again. [*Laughter*] Since then, he said, "The whole thing was a complicated matter." My fellow Americans, there's nothing complicated about supporting our troops in harm's way.

During the last 20 years, in key moments of challenge and decision for America, Senator Kerry has chosen a position of weakness and inaction. With that record, he stands in opposition not just to me but to the great tradition of the Democratic Party. The party of Franklin Roosevelt and Harry Truman and John Kennedy is rightly remembered for confidence and resolve in times of war and hours of crisis. Senator Kerry has turned his back on "pay any price" and "bear any burden." And he's replaced those commitments with "wait and see" and "cut and run." Many Democrats in this country do not recognize their party anymore. And today I want to speak to every one of them. If you believe that America should lead with strength and purpose and confidence in our ideals, I would be honored to have your support, and I'm asking for your vote.

Audience members. Four more years! Four more years! Four more years!

The President. The second clear choice in this election concerns your family's budget. When I ran for President 4 years ago, I pledged to lower taxes for American families, and I kept my word. I enjoyed working with Chairman Chuck Grassley to keep a pledge I made. We doubled the child credit to $1,000 per child. We reduced the marriage penalty. The Tax Code should encourage marriage, not penalize marriage. We dropped the lowest bracket to 10 percent so working families could keep more of their paychecks. We reduced taxes for everybody who pays taxes. After-tax income is up—that's money in your pocket to spend—it's up by about 10 percent since I became your President.

I want you to remind your friends and neighbors what this economy has been through. Six months prior to our arrival in Washington, DC, the stock market was in serious decline. And then we faced the recession and corporate scandals and the attacks of September the 11th, 2001, which cost us about a million jobs in the 3 months after that fateful day.

But our economic policies have put us back on the road to growth. Our economy is growing at rates as fast as any in nearly 20 years. The homeownership rate is at an alltime high. Our farmers are making a good living. The entrepreneurial spirit is strong. Small businesses are flourishing all across our country. We've added more than 1.9 million new jobs in the last 13 months. The national unemployment rate is 5.4 percent, lower than the average rate of the 1970s, the 1980s, and the 1990s. The unemployment rate in the great State of Iowa is 4.7 percent. This economy is strong, and it is getting stronger.

My opponent has very different plans for your budget—for your family's budget, and that's to take a big chunk out of it.

Audience members. Boo-o-o!

The President. You tell your friends and neighbors, he voted against the child credit, marriage penalty relief, lower tax rates. If his vote had prevailed, an average middle-class family would be paying $2,000 more a year to the Federal Government.

Audience members. Boo-o-o!

The President. It's part of a pattern. He's been in the United States Senate for 20

years, and he's voted for tax increases 98 times. That's about five times every year. That's predictable. When a Senator does something that often, he must really enjoy it. [*Laughter*] During his campaign, he's made a lot of big promises—big spending promises too. He's promised $2.2 trillion of new spending. That's trillion with a "T." That's a lot even for a Senator from Massachusetts. [*Laughter*]

So they asked him, "How are you going to pay for it?" He said, "Oh, we'll just tax the rich." You've heard that before, haven't you? When you run up the top two brackets, one, he's taxing a lot of small businesses. Seventy percent of job—new jobs in America are created by small businesses. Most small businesses pay individual income-tax rates. And when you're running up the taxes, you're taxing the job creators, and that is bad economic policy. When you raise the top two brackets, you raise between 600 billion and 800 billion dollars. That's far short of the 2.2 trillion. There is a gap. And guess who usually pays that gap?

Audience members. We do!

The President. You do. The good news is, we're going to carry Iowa. We're going to win on November the 2d, and he's not going to tax you.

The third clear choice in this election involves the quality of life for our Nation's families. A good education and quality health care are important to a successful life. When I ran for President 4 years ago, I promised to challenge the soft bigotry of low expectations in every school in America, and I kept my word. We passed good reforms. The No Child Left Behind Act has raised standards. It believes in local control of schools. Schools are now more accountable. Our children are learning to read and write and add and subtract. We're closing achievement gaps all across this country for minority students. We'll build on these reforms. We'll extend high standards to our high schools, so that no child is left behind in America.

And we'll continue to improve lives for our families by making health care more affordable and accessible. We'll expand health savings accounts so more small businesses can cover their workers and more families are able to get health care accounts they can manage and call their own. We will help our small businesses afford health insurance by allowing them to pool together so they can buy insurance at the same discounts that big companies are able to do. We will expand community health centers and rural health centers to help the poor and the indigent. We'll make sure every eligible child is enrolled in our Government's low-income health insurance program.

And to make sure health care is available and affordable, we will do something about these frivolous lawsuits that are running up the cost of medicine. I've met too many ob-gyns around this Nation that are having trouble practicing medicine because the lawsuits are running up their premiums and driving them out of business. I've met too many pregnant women who are worried about the quality of the health care they're receiving because their ob-gyn can't practice in the local community. This is a national problem that requires a national solution. You cannot be pro-doctor and pro-patient and pro-trial-lawyer at the same time. You have to make a choice. My opponent made his choice, and he put a personal-injury trial lawyer on the ticket.

Audience members. Boo-o-o!

The President. I made my choice. I have made my choice. I'm standing with the doctors, and I'm standing with the patients. I'm for medical liability reform—now.

My opponent has a different point of view when it comes to schools and health care. He voted for the No Child Left Behind Act but now wants to weaken the accountability standards. For example, he's proposed including measures like teacher attendance to judge whether a student can read or write or add and subtract. We need to keep high standards in our schools.

We've got to expect the best for the children. And he voted against health savings accounts. He opposes association health plans. He voted 10 times against medical liability reform. He can run from his record, but he cannot hide.

No, he's laid out a plan for health care, and it would be a big-Government health care plan. Eighty percent of the people who get coverage under his proposal would be enrolled in a Government program. Now, listen, I remember those debates when he looked right in the camera with a straight face and said, "The Government has nothing to do with it." I could barely contain myself. [*Laughter*] The Government has got a lot to do with it. It's a plan that will lead us down the road to Federal control of health care. In all we do to improve health care, we will make sure the decisions are made by doctors and patients, not by officials in Washington, DC.

The fourth clear choice in this election involves your retirement. Our Nation has made a solemn commitment to America's seniors on Social Security and Medicare. When I ran for President 4 years ago, I promised to keep that commitment and improve Medicare by adding prescription drug coverage. I kept my word. I want you to remember the history on Medicare. Leaders in both political parties have talked about strengthening and modernizing Medicare for years. We got the job done. And I want to thank Chairman Chuck Grassley for his hard work on this issue. Seniors are getting discounts on medicine with drug discount cards. Low-income seniors are getting $600 of help this year and $600 of help next year. And beginning in 2006, all seniors will be able to get prescription drug coverage under Medicare.

Here we have another difference in this campaign. My opponent voted against the Medicare bill that included prescription drug coverage, even though it was supported by AARP and other seniors groups. In this campaign, he said, "If I'm President, we're going to repeal that phony bill." Then he went on to say, "No, I don't want to repeal it." [*Laughter*] Sounds familiar. [*Laughter*] As your President for the next 4 years, I will defend the reforms we have worked so hard to pass and keep the promise of Medicare for America's seniors. And I will keep the promise of Social Security for our seniors, and we will strengthen Social Security for generations to come.

Now, I want to remind you all what took place in the 2000 election and may be taking place in this election already, and that is that every—every campaign cycle it seems like somebody is trying to scare our seniors. See, in 2000, they said, "If George W. gets elected, our seniors will not get their checks." As you're out rounding up the votes, I want you to remind people, George W. did get elected, and our seniors did get their checks. And I plan on getting reelected, and our seniors will continue to get their checks. And baby boomers like me, we're in pretty good shape when it comes to the Social Security trust.

But we need to worry about our children and our grandchildren. We need to worry about whether or not a retirement system—a viable retirement system in Social Security will be there when they need it. And that's why I believe younger workers ought to be allowed to take some of their own payroll taxes and put it in a personal savings account that will earn a better rate of return, an account they own, an account the Government cannot take away.

My opponent takes a different approach. He said he talks about protecting Social Security, but he's the only candidate in this race who has voted eight times for higher taxes on Social Security benefits.

Audience members. Boo-o-o!

The President. He might not want us to remind him of that. He can run, but he cannot hide.

And when it comes to a younger generation, he offered nothing, no reforms. The job of the President is to confront problems, not to pass them on to future Presi-

dents and future generations. I will bring Republicans and Democrats together to make sure Social Security is viable for a younger generation of Americans.

And the fifth and final clear choice in this election is on the values that are so crucial to keeping America's families strong. And here, my opponent and I are miles apart. I stand for the appointment of Federal judges who know the difference between personal opinion and the strict interpretation of the law. I believe marriage is a sacred commitment. Marriage is a pillar of civilization, and I will defend it. This is not a partisan issue. When Congress passed the Defense of Marriage Act, which defined marriage as a union of a man and a woman, the vast majority of Democrats supported it, and the bill was signed by my predecessor.

But Senator Kerry was part of an out-of-the-mainstream minority that voted against the Defense of Marriage Act.

Audience members. Boo-o-o!

The President. I believe that reasonable people can find common ground on the difficult issues. Republicans and Democrats, many citizens on both sides of the life issue came together and agreed we should ban the brutal practice of partial-birth abortion. I proudly signed that bill.

Senator Kerry was part of the out-of-the-mainstream minority that voted against the ban.

Audience members. Boo-o-o!

The President. He also voted against parental notification laws. He voted against the Unborn Victims of Violence Act. I'll continue to reach out to Americans of every belief and move this goodhearted Nation toward a culture of life.

My opponent has said that the heart and soul of America can be found in Hollywood.

Audience members. Boo-o-o!

The President. I know. Most American families do not look to Hollywood for a source of values. [*Laughter*] The heart and soul of America is found in caring and loving communities like Davenport, Iowa.

All these choices make this one of the most important elections in our history. The security and prosperity of our country, the health and education for our families, the retirement of our seniors, and the direction of our culture are all at stake. And the decision is in the best of hands; it's in the hands of the American people.

I see a great day coming for America. One of my favorite quotes was written by a fellow Texan named Tom Lea. He said, "Sarah and I live on the east side of the mountain. It's the sunrise side, not the sunset side. It is the side to see the day that is coming, not to see the day that has gone." My opponent has spent much of this campaign talking about the day that has gone. I'm talking about the day that's coming.

You know, we have been through a lot together over the past years. Because we've done the hard work of climbing the mountain, we can see the valley below. We'll protect our families. We'll build on their prosperity. We'll defend our Nation's deep-est values. We'll spread freedom in the world, and as we do, we'll achieve the peace we all long for.

When I traveled your State in 2000, asking for the vote, first in the caucuses and then in the general election, I made this pledge: I pledged that I would uphold the honor and the integrity of the office to which I had been elected. With your help, I will do so for 4 more years.

God bless. Thanks for coming. Thank you all. Thank you all.

NOTE: The President spoke at 5:30 p.m. at the RiverCenter. In his remarks, he referred to Senator Zell Miller of Georgia, who made the keynote address at the 2004 Republican National Convention; former Mayor Rudolph W. Giuliani of New York City, and his wife, Judith; Usama bin Laden, leader of the Al Qaida terrorist organization; and Gen. Tommy R. Franks, USA (Ret.), former combatant commander, U.S. Central Command. He also referred to the National Commission on Terrorist Attacks Upon the United States (9/11 Commission).

Remarks in Onalaska, Wisconsin
October 26, 2004

The President. Thank you all. What a great way to spend a Tuesday, and that's to be on a bus traveling throughout the great State of Wisconsin. Thank you all for coming out to say hello. It's such an honor to be here. Laura and I are—our spirits are lifted up because so many have come out to say hello. We're honored you are here. I'm here to ask for your vote. I'm here to ask for your help. There's no doubt in my mind, if we turn out our vote in Wisconsin, we'll win a great victory on November the 2d.

I don't know if you know the history of me and Laura. We were in the seventh grade together in San Jacinto Junior High in Midland, Texas, and then we became reacquainted years later when she was a public school librarian. And I asked her to marry me—I'm sure some of you can relate to this. She said, "Fine, but make me a promise." I said, "What is it?" "Well, promise me I'll never have to give a political speech." [*Laughter*] I said, "Okay, you've got a deal." [*Laughter*] Fortunately, she didn't hold me to that promise. She's giving a lot of speeches, and when she does the American people see a warm, compassionate, great First Lady. I have been traveling your State a lot, talking about the reasons why I think people ought to put me back into office. But perhaps the most important one is so that Laura will be First Lady for 4 more years.

I am proud of my runningmate, Dick Cheney. In all due respect to those who are here who are follically challenged—[*laughter*]—I readily concede my runningmate does not have the waviest hair in the race. You'll be pleased to know I did not pick him because of his hairdo. [*Laughter*] I picked him because of his experience and his judgment and his ability to get the job done.

And I'm proud of your friend Tommy Thompson. He has done a great job. I gave him one of the toughest jobs in Washington, DC, and he has responded. He has done a fabulous job to help those who hurt. Just take the issue of Medicare. Tommy and I went to Washington to solve problems, not to pass them on to future Presidents and future generations. That's our job, to tackle the tough problems. Medicare was a problem. See, Medicare hadn't changed, but medicine had. For example, they pay nearly $100,000 for heart surgery, but not one dime for the prescription drugs that could prevent the heart surgery from being needed in the first place. Tommy recognized that wasn't fair. I recognized it wasn't fair. We brought Republicans and Democrats together. We did what other Presidents and other Secretaries couldn't do: We modernized Medicare, and starting in 2006, our seniors will get prescription drug coverage.

Let me say one other thing to our seniors here in Wisconsin. You might remember the 2000 campaign, when they ran those ads that said, "If George W. gets elected, our seniors are not going to get their Social Security checks." Remember those? Yes. Well, I want you—as you're gathering up the vote, remind your friends and neighbors that George W. did get elected and our seniors did get their Social Security check. And our seniors will continue to get their Social Security checks. But we're also

going to strengthen Social Security for our younger generation. Our youngsters ought to be allowed to take some of their payroll taxes and set up a personal savings account they call their own, an account the Government cannot take away.

I want to thank Congressman Mark Green, who is with us today. Congressman, I appreciate you coming. He's a fine, good, young Member of the House of Representatives. I want to thank the mayor of Onalaska with us today. Mr. Mayor, I'm proud you're here. Thanks for coming. Fill the potholes. [*Laughter*]

I'm proud to be standing with the next United States Senator from Wisconsin, Tim Michels. He married a lady named Barbara. [*Laughter*] I know some Barbaras. [*Laughter*] One of them is still telling me what to do. [*Laughter*] And I'm still listening, I want you to know.

I'm very impressed by a candidate for Wisconsin's Third Congressional District, a man I hope you support, the next Congressman, Dale Schultz.

I want to thank the grassroots activists who are here, the people who are putting up the signs, making the phone calls, the people who helped turn out such a huge crowd here. I'm honored to have your support. Now is the time to keep the work up. Now is the time to find every single voter and tell them we have a duty, a duty in this country to vote. When you get them headed to the polls, remind them if they want a safer America, a stronger America, and a better America, to put me and Dick Cheney back in office.

Audience members. Four more years! Four more years! Four more years!

The President. We're only one week away from the vote, and I'm focusing on the big issues that are facing our country's families. This election comes down to five clear choices for our families: your family's security; your family's budget; your quality of life; your retirement; and the bedrock values that are so critical to our country's future.

First and foremost, I've talked about the quality retirement. When I'm talking about Medicare and making sure it exists and strong, that helps our families. When I'm talking about Social Security and making sure it's around today as well as around tomorrow, that helps our families.

But the first, biggest concern of any President is your security. Our Nation is at war against a terrorist enemy unlike any we have faced before. The most solemn duty of the American President is to protect the American people. We will be relentless, determined, steadfast, and strong. We will not relent. We will stay on the offensive until the fight is won.

Another big issue, of course, is our economy. It affects the quality of life. It affects your budget. It affects how much money you have in your wallet. We will expand and strengthen our economic recovery to make sure opportunity spreads throughout every corner of this country. This campaign offers a clear choice when it comes to the economy and our vision for how to create jobs. My policies support and strengthen the small businesses, which are creating most new jobs in America.

I'm going to spend a little time talking about the vision of enhancing the entrepreneurial spirit. My opponent promises to raise your taxes.

Audience members. Boo-o-o!

The President. And unfortunately for our small-business owners, that's a promise most politicians tend to keep. [*Laughter*]

Our economy has been through a lot. When you're out there rounding up the vote, I want you to remind people that 6 months prior to my arrival, the stock market was in serious decline. Our economy was declining in the last half of the year 2000. We fell into a recession. We had corporate scandals which affected our economy. By the way, we passed tough laws. We have made it abundantly clear, we will not tolerate dishonesty in the boardrooms of America.

We were attacked. And those attacks cost us about a million jobs in the 3 months after September the 11th. But, see, I understand something. I understand the engine of growth that this economy has found with the entrepreneurs and workers of America. And that's why we passed the largest tax relief in a generation, tax relief which encouraged consumption and investment.

And it's working. The economic stimulus plan we passed is working. This country created about 1.9 million jobs in the last 13 months. The national unemployment rate is down to 5.4 percent. And let me remind you of where that stands: That's lower than the average rate of the 1970s, the 1980s, and the 1990s. The unemployment rate in Wisconsin is down to 5 percent. That is down almost a full point since the summer of 2003. We're headed in the right direction in America.

Our farmers are doing well. Farm income is up, and that's good for our economy. The homeownership rate is at an all-time high in America. We're on the move. We're going forward, and we're not going to go back to the days of tax and spend.

This is a time of fantastic opportunity. The job of Government is to create an environment in which the entrepreneurial spirit can flourish, in which people are willing to work hard to realize their dreams. Government doesn't create wealth. Government creates the environment that says, "Take a risk. Start a business if you choose to. Own something."

Today Joan Shelley is with us. I want you to hear her story. Joan is right there. First of all, she is a mom. She and her husband have got eight children. Listen to her story. She didn't think she was spending enough time—she worked as a nurse—didn't spend enough time at home. First of all, she's got her priorities straight. If you are fortunate enough to be a mom or a dad, your most important responsibility is to love your child with all your heart and all your soul.

So guess what happened? Six years ago, she decided to start an online business selling cabinet hardware from the basement of her home. How many times have you heard that story? You know, "I sat around the kitchen table and came up with an idea and started a business." "I started a business in my garage." She started hers in her basement. Today, KnobGallery employs 20 people, most of them moms who wanted more flexibility for their families. This administration believes in flex-time. The world has changed. Our labor laws ought to change with them. Moms and dads ought to be able to have the flex-time in the workplace so they can balance family and the need to work.

KnobGallery is a thriving, $1.4 million business. Her family is working in the business: Kristina, it turns out, designs the company's web page. Joan is living the American Dream. She has started her own business. She owns her own company. And she—I said, "Are you going to increase the jobs?" She said, "I'm intending to add more people to work." See, the more Joans that start up their own business, the more likely that somebody is going to find a job in America. The role of the Government is to create an environment for the Joan Shelleys to feel comfortable in starting and expanding their business.

Ric Hartman is with us. There he is. Hi, Ric. He managed at one time the in-house design shop of a large packaging firm for 15 years. Last October, about a year ago, he learned the company was going to close his operation. So guess what he did? He got some of those people he worked with, put them in a van, went to a local flour mill and said, "This is where we're going to start our new company." See, the entrepreneurial spirit must be strong if America is going to be a hopeful place. Five came with him. Today, he runs a profitable small business called Hartman Design. Here's what he said: "Deep down, I think every design person wants to run their own shop." Deep down, a lot of peo-

ple in America want to run their own shop. Deep down, people have a desire to start their own business, and when they do, somebody is more likely to find a job.

A hopeful America and one that's good for your budget is one in which small businesses are thriving, in which people from all walks of life feel comfortable about starting their own business. Do you realize minority businesses are up in America? That is hopeful and positive for the future of this country. Seven out of ten new jobs in America are created by small businesses. And there is a source of upward mobility in America that comes with ownership. When a woman owns her own business, she's upwardly mobile. When a Latino or an African American starts his or her own business, they become upwardly mobile. Ownership is a powerful part of the American Dream.

And so the fundamental question in this campaign, who's got the best strategy to make sure the entrepreneurial spirit is strong? Who's got the idea, who understands, and who can best make sure that more small businesses grow in America? First, in order to make sure the entrepreneurial spirit is strong, America must be the best place in the world to do business. If you want businesses to start, this must be the best place in the world to do business. And secondly, to make sure this is a hopeful world, we've got to make sure the workforce is the best trained in the world. A lot of good jobs and a lot of good hopes start with good education.

First, let me talk about how to make sure this is the best place in the world to do business. One, we've got to keep your taxes low. We passed good tax relief. We raised the child credit. That helps if you're a mom or a dad. We reduced the marriage penalty. I believe strongly the Tax Code ought to encourage marriage, not penalize marriage. We created a 10 percent bracket. That helps the working families. But we also said, "If you pay taxes, you ought to get relief." If you're going to have tax relief, everybody who pays taxes ought to get relief. That's only fair.

But guess what happens? What most Americans don't know, and evidently what my opponent doesn't know, is that most small businesses are either a Subchapter S corporation like the two small businesses I just mentioned or sole proprietorships, which means you pay tax at the individual income-tax rate. Ninety percent of businesses in America pay individual income taxes, which says when you cut the taxes on everybody who pays taxes, you're helping the small businesses. See, there is a connection between good tax relief and growth in the small-business sector.

And so to encourage small-business investment, not only did we say, "You can have more money in your coffers so you can expand your business or pay more money or better afford health care," but we encouraged investment by increasing the small-business expensing deduction from $25,000 to $100,000. See, I understand if you create the demand for goods and services and provide incentives for investment, the economy grows. That's what you've got to understand. It's a difference of opinion. It's a difference of philosophy. My opponent believes the economy grows by growing the size of the Federal Government. I believe the economy grows by growing the size of the coffers of small businesses.

Here's what Paul Schoeneck of New Berlin, Wisconsin, said. See, his business, like the other two, were Subchapter S corporations. He said about tax relief, "We have doubled our workforce. We've increased pay. We have consistently paid out bonuses. We've significantly increased our gross and net income. We've increased our production lines by nine, remodeled our offices, and significantly improved our infrastructure." That's what he said. Those aren't my words. That is what a small-business owner from Wisconsin has said about the tax relief. He said, "Without tax relief, this would not have been possible."

I want you, when you hear these people talking about tax relief, about how it only benefited certain people—this tax relief has helped our small businesses grow and prosper, and this economy is on the move because the entrepreneurial spirit is strong.

And taxes are an issue in this campaign. I'm running against a fellow who's promised $2.2 trillion of new Federal spending. That's with a "T." That is—that's a lot even for a Senator from Massachusetts. [*Laughter*] So they said, "How are you going to pay for it?" He said, "Oh, we'll just tax the rich." That means raise the top two brackets. By raising the top two brackets, he's taxing the small-business sector of America. That's bad economic policy. Just as the economy is beginning to grow, just as the small businesses are feeling confident—I talked to the two small-business owners here. I said, "Are you going to hire somebody?" They said, "We're thinking about hiring new people." But running up the taxes on them would make it less likely they'd hire somebody. It's bad economic policy to tax the small-business owners of America, which is precisely what my opponent's plan would do.

See, when you say you're going to run up the top two brackets, you raise about $600 billion, maybe 800 billion, depending on whose accountant you use. [*Laughter*] But the point is, in either case you're far short of the $2.2 trillion that he has promised. There is a gap. There is a gap between what he's promised and what he can deliver. And guess who usually gets to fill the gap?

Audience members. We do!

The President. Yes, you do. But we're not going to let him tax you. We're going to win on November the 2d.

The bottom line about our economic visions is this: To pay for all his new spending he's proposed, my opponent will have to raise taxes not just on small-business owners but on everyone who's ever worked for a small business, shopped at a small business, or walked by a small business.

[*Laughter*] We're not going to let him tax you; we're going to win.

Audience members. Four more years! Four more years! Four more years!

The President. To make sure that this economy is strong and the small businesses can flourish, we've got to do something about the frivolous and junk lawsuits. These kind of lawsuits cost our economy about $230 billion a year. This amounts to about $3,000 a year for the average family. They're expensive, and they're really expensive on small businesses. If part of the vision is to make sure the small-business sector of our economy flourishes, we've got to do something about the liability. The average cost of tort liability for a small business is about $150,000. That's money that could be better used for employees, worker training, health care, expanding the business, creating new jobs.

My opponent and I have a different approach. He's sided with the personal-injury trial lawyers time and time again. They're powerful in Washington, make no mistake about it. It's hard to get good legal reform out of the United States Senate because they're influential. As a matter of fact, he's raised more money from lawyers than any other Member of the United States Senate. That's about $22 million so far since 1989, and still counting. And there's a reason why. He's voted five times against protecting small businesses on punitive damages. He's made it clear where he stands. He's made it abundantly clear. He's put a personal-injury trial lawyer on the ticket.

Audience members. Boo-o-o!

The President. Now, I'm going to stand with our small-business owners and continue to be for legal reforms in Washington, DC.

We need less regulations on our small businesses. We need reasonable regulations. I can't guarantee that anybody in Washington has ever read the forms small businesses have to fill out. I wish I could say they have; I doubt it. But one way to make sure we reduce the burden on our—not only our small businesses but our—the working people here in America is to reform the Tax Code. It's a complicated mess. It is too complex. I'm going to bring people together. Listen, I recognize the—first of all, the code is a million pages long. American workers and small-business owners and families spend 6 billion hours a year filling out the forms. We can do a better job. We can make this Tax Code pro-growth, pro-family, and fair. And I will bring Republicans* and Democrats together to do so.

A couple of other quick points on how to make sure the environment is good for business growth so that you've got more money, so that you can manage your budget better, so that people can find a job. We need—Congress needs to pass my energy plan. It's a plan that makes sense. It's common sense. It encourages conservation. It encourages the use of renewables like ethanol and biodiesel. It uses technologies to help us burn coal more cleanly. It encourages exploration for natural gas in environmentally friendly ways. To make sure that this environment for growth is strong, we need to be less dependent on foreign sources of energy.

Let me talk right quick about education, because I believe a good economy requires this workforce of ours to be educated. I think the two go hand in hand. I don't think you can have a hopeful environment for growth if our people aren't educated. It all starts with the younger kids. That's why I went to Washington, to challenge the soft bigotry of low expectations. You know, this business about just shuffling the children through, grade after grade, year after year, without learning the basics was not good enough for America, as far as I'm concerned. I believe every child can learn, and I believe every school must teach. And so we increased funding, particularly for Title I students. But we said, "In return for extra funding, show us

—————————
* White House correction.

whether or not a child can read and write and add and subtract."

See, I understand you can't solve a problem until you diagnose a problem. You can't fix a problem until you fully understand the nature of the problem. By measuring, we now know where the problems exist in America, and we're providing the extra money to solve them. And guess what's happening? Kids are learning to read and write and add and subtract. Because we're measuring, we now know the benchmarks. We're seeing progress. We're closing the achievement gap amongst minority students in America. And we're not going to go back to the old days of mediocrity and low standards.

I think one of the country's greatest assets is the community college system. Community colleges are able to adjust their curriculum to meet the needs of the job providers. I've met small businesses who have told me about helping set up a curriculum in our community colleges so our workers can gain the skills necessary to fill the jobs of the 21st century. You just heard about Joan's company, where in her basement, she started a company over the Internet. In other words, we need new skill sets as this economy of ours changes. And a great place for America's workers to gain new skill sets is in the community college system all across our country.

Most of the uninsured in America work for small businesses. Small businesses are having trouble affording health care. That's why I believe small businesses ought to be allowed to pool risk to join together so they can buy insurance at the same discount that big companies are able to do.

We'll expand health savings accounts to help our families and small businesses to be able to better afford health insurance and, at the same time, provide a health account that you can own and you can manage, you can take with you from job to job. And we'll make sure we do something about these frivolous lawsuits that are running up the cost of health care. This

is a national issue. I have met too many ob-gyns who are being driven out of practice because the lawsuits are running up their cost of doing business, their premiums. And I've met too many patients of ob-gyns who are having to drive for miles, wondering whether or not they and their child will get the health care they need.

Medical liability is a crisis in America, and it's a crisis because we can't get anything done in the United States Senate because the trial bar is too strong. My opponent has voted against medical liability reform not once, not twice but 10 times. In a new term, I'm going to bring people together and say, "The people have spoke. We need medical liability reform now to make sure health care is affordable and available."

We have a big difference when it comes to health care in this campaign. And it is a big difference. I remember that debate when my opponent stood up there with a straight face and he said, "The Government has nothing to do with it,"—"it" being his health care plan. I could barely contain myself. [*Laughter*] The Government has got a lot to do with it—a lot to do with it. Eight out of ten people would end up on the Government health care. Think about this: When you run up the Medicaid, make Medicaid more eligible for people, it's going to provide an incentive for small businesses to not provide insurance for their employees because the Government will. That doesn't make any sense, to be moving people from private insurance to the Government. When the Government writes the check, the Government starts setting the rules, and you don't want the Federal Government making the rules when it comes to your health care.

I've come here to Wisconsin to tell the people I understand how this economy works, and my policies are standing square with the workers, the families, and the small-business owners of America. I also want to tell you in changing times, some things do not change, the values we try to live by, courage and compassion, reverence and integrity. In changing times, we will support and must support the institutions that give our lives direction and purpose, our families, our schools, and our religious congregations. We stand for a culture of life in which every person matters and every being counts. We stand for marriage and family, which are the foundations of our society. We stand for the appointment of Federal judges who know the difference between personal opinion and the strict interpretation of the law.

My opponent takes a different approach. His words on these issues are a little murky, but his record is really clear. [*Laughter*] He says he supports the institution of marriage but voted against the Defense of Marriage Act, which overwhelmingly passed with Democrat and Republican votes. My predecessor signed that bill into law, which defined marriage as a union between a man and a woman, and my opponent voted against it. He says—you know, he says he's got a personal view on the issue of life, but he voted against the ban on the brutal practice of partial-birth abortion.

Audience members. Boo-o-o!

The President. He's called the Reagan years a time of moral darkness.

Audience members. Boo-o-o!

The President. There is a mainstream in American politics, and my opponent sits on the far left bank. My fellow Americans, he can run from his views, but he cannot hide.

All the progress we hope for in America and all the prosperity and opportunity we want for every family and for our children ultimately depends on the security of our Nation. We're in the middle of a global war on terror. We face a determined enemy. In the war on terror, there's no place for confusion, no place for weakness, no substitute for victory. I believe if America shows uncertainty or weakness in this decade, the world will drift toward tragedy. This will not happen on my watch.

Audience members. Four more years! Four more years! Four more years!

The President. Since that terrible morning of September the 11th, 2001, we fought the terrorists across the Earth, not for pride, not for power but because the lives of our citizens are at stake. Our strategy is clear. We're defending the homeland. We're strengthening our intelligence services. We're transforming our military. There will be no draft. The All-Volunteer Army will remain an all-volunteer army. We're on the offensive. We will strike the terrorists abroad so we do not have to face them here at home.

We're promoting democracy and liberty, the great alternatives to despair and terror. I want you to tell your children about what took place in Afghanistan. It wasn't all that long ago that young girls lived under the reign of the Taliban, a brutal, barbaric people. They would not let young girls go to school, and if their mothers didn't toe their ideological line, they were taken in the public square sometimes and whipped. These people were dark and dim. There was darkness in Afghanistan. Because we defended ourselves, because we believe in freedom, the Afghanistan people went by the millions to the polls to vote for their President. The first voter—the first voter—was a 19-year-old woman.

Iraq will have a Presidential election. Think how far that country has come from the days of torture chambers and mass graves. Freedom is on the march. Freedom is on the move, and our country is better for it.

A President must lead with consistency and strength in these troubling times. In war, sometimes you change your tactics, but you never change your principles. And Americans have seen how I do my job. [*Applause*] Thank you. Even when you might not agree with me, you know where I stand, what I believe, and what I intend to do. On good days and on bad days, whether the polls are up or the polls are down, I am determined to win this war on terror, and I will always support the men and women of the United States military.

My opponent has taken a different approach. It's fair to say that consistency has not been his strong point. [*Laughter*] Senator Kerry says we're better off with Saddam Hussein out of power, except when he declared that removing Saddam made us less safe. He stated in our second debate that he always believed that Saddam was a threat except, a few questions later, when he said Saddam Hussein was not a threat. [*Laughter*] He says he was right when he voted to authorize the use of force against Saddam Hussein, but that I was wrong to use force against Saddam Hussein. [*Laughter*]

And now he's throwing out a wild claim that he knows where bin Laden was in the fall of 2001, and that our military passed up a chance to get him at Tora Bora. It is unjustified criticism of the military commanders in the field. It is the worst kind of Monday morning quarterbacking. Our commander in Afghanistan at the time was General Tommy Franks, and he wrote this about Tora Bora, he said, "The Senator's understanding of events does not square with reality." [*Laughter*] That's what the man who was there said. He says the American Special Forces were actively involved in the search for the terrorists in Tora Bora, and that intelligence reports at the time placed bin Laden in one of several countries. They didn't know whether he was here, there, or otherwise. In other words, they didn't have hard intelligence. Maybe my opponent has seen something we all haven't seen.

As a matter of fact, Senator Kerry, before he got into political difficulty and revised his views, he said this about Tora Bora on national TV, in the fall of 2001, he said, "I think we have been doing this pretty effectively, and we should continue to do it that way." At the time, the Senator said about Tora Bora, "I think we have been smart. I think the administration leadership has done it well, and we are on the right track." All I can say about that is, I am George W. Bush, and I approve of that message.

My opponent's record on national security has a far deeper problem than election-year flip-flopping. On the largest national security issues of our time, he has been consistently wrong. When Ronald Reagan was confronting the Soviet Union at the height of the cold war, Senator Kerry said that President Reagan's policy of peace through strength was making America less safe. History has shown that Senator Kerry was wrong and President Ronald Reagan was right.

When former President Bush led a coalition against Saddam Hussein in 1991, Senator Kerry voted against the use of force to liberate Kuwait, even though the United Nations had passed a resolution and there was a strong coalition and agreement with U.S. policy. History has shown that Senator Kerry was wrong, former President Bush was right.

In 1994, just one year after the first bombing of the World Trade Center, my opponent proposed massive cuts in America's intelligence budget, so massive that even his Massachusetts colleague, Ted Kennedy, opposed them. History has shown that Senator Kerry was wrong—we've got to be fair—Senator Kennedy was right. [*Laughter*]

The President must be consistent and strong in these difficult times. Just last year, when American troops were in combat in Afghanistan and Iraq, I proposed $87 billion of increased funding to support our troops in harm's way. It was important funding. Bipartisan support for that funding was very strong. As you round up the vote, I want you to remind your friends and neighbors of this startling statistic: Only 4 members of the United States Senate—4 out of 100—voted to authorize the use of force and then voted against funding for our troops in harm's way, and 2 of those 4 were my opponent and his runningmate.

Audience members. Boo-o-o!

The President. You might remember, when they asked him about the vote, he said this, he said, "I actually did vote for the $87 billion, right before I voted against it." History has shown that Senator Kerry was right, then wrong, then briefly right, then wrong again. [*Laughter*] They finally kept pressing him. He said the whole thing about the $87 billion was a complicated matter. My friends, there is nothing complicated about supporting our men and women in combat.

And speaking about those men and women, we have got a fantastic military and I'm proud to be their Commander in Chief. And I want to thank the military families who are here today for your sacrifice. And I want to thank the veterans who are here today for having set such a great example.

During the last 20 years, in key moments of challenge and decision for America, Senator Kerry has chosen a position of weakness and inaction. With that record, he stands in opposition not just to me but to the great tradition of the Democratic Party. The party of Franklin Roosevelt and Harry Truman and John Kennedy is rightly remembered for confidence and resolve in times of war and hours of crisis. Senator Kerry has turned his back on "pay any price" and "bear any burden." He's replaced those commitments with "wait and see" and "cut and run." Many Democrats in this country do not recognize their party anymore, and today I want to speak to every one of them: If you believe America should lead with strength and purpose and confidence and resolve, I'd be honored to have your support, and I'm asking for your vote.

Our differences on keeping the security of the country and protecting our families are vast. My opponent says that September the 11th did not change him much at all.

Audience members. Boo-o-o!

The President. And his policies make that clear. He says the war on terror is primarily a law enforcement and intelligence gathering operation. Well, my outlook was changed on September the 11th. I'll never forget going to the Ground Zero on September the 14th, 2001. There were workers in hardhats there yelling at the top of their lungs, "Whatever it takes." I'll never forget the sights and sounds. I'll never forget the person looking me straight in the eye and saying, "Do not let me down." Ever since that day, I wake up every morning trying to figure out how best to protect our country. I will never relent in defending America, whatever it takes.

When I traveled your State 4 years ago, I made a pledge that if I was elected, I would uphold the honor and the dignity of the office to which I had been elected. With your help, with your hard work, I will do so for 4 more years.

Thanks for coming. God bless. Thank you all.

NOTE: The President spoke at 8:30 a.m. at the Onalaska Omni Center. In his remarks, he referred to Mayor James Bialecki of Onalaska, WI; Kristina Shelley, daughter of KnobGallery owner Joan Shelley; former President Saddam Hussein of Iraq; Usama bin Laden, leader of the Al Qaida terrorist organization; and Gen. Tommy R. Franks, USA (Ret.), former combatant commander, U.S. Central Command.

Remarks in a Discussion in Richland Center, Wisconsin
October 26, 2004

The President. Thank you all for being here. Laura and I are—we're glad you came, and we are glad we came. I'm here to give you some reasons why I think you ought to put me back into office. I'm here to talk about issues that matter to our future. We're going to have—we're going to do it a little interesting way today. I've asked some of your fellow citizens to come up and talk about how our policies have affected their lives. And this will perhaps give people a clear view of why I have made some of the decisions I have made.

Perhaps the most important reason why people ought to put me back into office is so that Laura will be the First Lady for 4 more years. I'm going to take my jacket off. Okay. Some of you all may relate to this. When I asked her to marry me—actually, we had gone—I don't know if you know this or not, but we were in seventh grade together in San Jacinto Junior High in Midland, Texas. We became reacquainted—are you from Midland?

Audience member. Lubbock.

The President. Lubbock, Texas, 150 miles south of Midland. Anyway, thank you, welcome.

When we became reacquainted, she was a public school librarian. It's fitting we're in a school here, by the way. We want to thank the teachers who work in this school to help every child realize their dreams. Thank you.

She said, "Fine, I will marry you"—this is after I asked her, of course—"only if you make me one promise." I said, "What is the promise?" "Promise me I'll never have to give a political speech." [*Laughter*] I, of course, said, "Okay, you've got a deal." She didn't hold me to the promise, thankfully. She's giving a lot of speeches, and when she does, the American people see a warm and compassionate and great First Lady.

I want to thank our friend Tommy Thompson. I want to thank him for his service to our country, and I want to thank him for his friendship. Tommy has done a great job in Washington. You trained him well. [*Laughter*] He was a wonderful Governor of Wisconsin; I knew that when I was looking for a Cabinet Secretary. I gave him a tough assignment, and he's handled it brilliantly. And I want to thank you, Tommy, for your service. Appreciate you.

You know, Tommy and I went to Washington to get some things done, and one of the things we had to do was to make sure our seniors had quality health care. Medicine was changing; Medicare was not. For example, the Government would pay thousands of dollars for a heart surgery under Medicare but not one dime for the prescription drugs that could prevent the heart surgery from being needed in the first place. And Tommy and I understood that didn't make any sense for our seniors and it didn't make any sense for the taxpayers, so we worked together with both Republicans and Democrats to strengthen Medicare, to keep the promise to our seniors. And beginning in the year 2006, all seniors will be able to get prescription drug coverage under Medicare. I think it's important for you to know that when I say something, I mean it, and I'm going to get the job done.

I want to thank thank Congressman Mark Green. I appreciate you coming, Congressman, a fine young Congressman from Wisconsin. He's not from this part of the world, but you'll get to know him, and when you do, you'll like him. He's a good, honest man.

I want to thank Jack Voight for being here, the State treasurer of the great State of Wisconsin. Jack, thank you, sir. Good to see you again. And I want to thank the mayor. Madam Mayor, thanks for coming.

I'm proud you're here. I appreciate you being here. It means a lot.

I want to thank U.S. Senate candidate Tim Michels and his wife, Barbara. You need to put him in the Senate. He's a good man. He's got good values. He'll make you a fine United States Senator. And I'm going to tell you who's going to make you a fine United States Congressman, and that would be Dale Schultz. Appreciate you—Schultz. He's working. He's shaking a lot of hands. He's putting up a lot of signs. I know firsthand. See, I'm taking the bus throughout this part of the world. [*Laughter*] And I've seen a lot of the signs, and that's a good sign. And I also want to thank Rachel—Rachel Schultz, who happens to be the district superintendent of the schools. And I want to thank you for your—being in education. I want to thank John Cler and all the folks associated with the high school for letting us come here today. I appreciate you coming. I want to thank the students. Thanks for coming, letting me come. All right. Study more than you watch TV. [*Laughter*] And if you're 18, make sure you vote.

See, that's what I'm here to do. I'm here to ask people for the vote and for their help. We have a duty in this country to vote. We have a duty in democracy to go to the polls. People need to exercise their right in a free society. And I'm asking you for your help to get people to go to the polls. I know you've done a lot of work in this part of the world. I've seen a lot of signs for me, too, and I appreciate it. But those signs are important, but they don't pull the lever. And so coming down the stretch, I'm here to ask for your help in turning out the vote. And there's no doubt in my mind, with your help, we're going to carry the State of Wisconsin.

We've really enjoyed our bus trips through Wisconsin. Today we stopped off and saw John and Connie Turgasen.

Audience members. [*Inaudible*]

The President. Evidently you've heard of them. That's good. [*Laughter*] Well, I won-der if they'd reconsider when they saw four buses pull up in their front yard. [*Laughter*] But they're dairy farmers. There were four generations of Turgasens right there, making a living off that one farm. It reminds me about how important it is to support our small businesses, our farmers, our ranchers. When you're getting people to go to the polls, remind them of this, that under the Bush administration, the farmers are doing just fine. The income is up, and people are making a living. And that's good for people all across this part of the world. We enjoyed going to that farm, and we enjoyed meeting that great Wisconsin family.

You know, we've overcome a lot in this country. I pledged to make this country a more hopeful place, and that means hopeful for everybody. But we've had to overcome a lot in order to make it more hopeful. When you're out rounding up the vote, remind people about what this economy has been through. You know, a hopeful country is one in which people can make a living, people can stay on the farm, people who say to me, "Mr. President, we've been able to support four generations of Turgasens on this farm."

But we've been through a lot in this economy. You know, the stock market was in serious decline 6 months prior to my arrival in Washington, DC. And then we had a recession. And then we had some corporate scandals, and that affected our economy. It's now abundantly clear that we're not going to tolerate dishonesty in the boardrooms of America. We expect people to be responsible citizens in this country. And we got attacked. And that attack of September the 11th cost us nearly a million jobs in the 3 months after the attack. We've had some obstacles put in our path.

But we acted. I understand that when somebody's got more money in their pocket, they're likely to demand an additional good or a service. And when you demand an additional good or a service in our marketplace, somebody is going to produce it. When somebody produces it, somebody is likely to find a job. The tax relief we passed is working. The tax relief we passed has got this economy growing again.

And the facts are clear. We've added 1.9 million jobs in the last 13 months. We're growing at rates as fast as any in nearly 20 years. Our farmers are doing well. Homeownership rate is at an alltime high. The unemployment rate nationally is 5.4 percent. Let me put that in perspective for you: 5.4 percent is lower than the average of the 1970s, the 1980s, and the 1990s. The unemployment rate in the State of Wisconsin is 5 percent. We're moving forward, and we're not going to go back to the days of tax and spend. That's not an economic policy; that's a way to get in your wallet and grow the size of the Federal Government.

So there's more to do. It's one thing to talk about a record, but the only reason to look back is to be able to say to people, "Here's what we're going to do as we move forward." The job of the President is to make sure the entrepreneurial spirit is strong, the environment for small-business creation is good, that people have a chance to make a living.

So what does it take? One, it means we've got to keep your taxes low. I'm about to talk to some small-business owners here who know what it means to pay high taxes and what it means to have their taxes lowered. But taxes are an issue in this campaign. As you travel in your district and travel talking to people, remind people that taxes are an issue. The fellow I'm running against has proposed $2.2 trillion of new Federal spending. That's trillion with a "T." That's a lot. Even for a Senator from Massachusetts, that's a lot.

And so they said—and you know the legitimate question is, "Fine, you made all these promises; how are you going to pay for them?" And he threw out that same old line we've heard almost every campaign: "Oh, we're just going to tax the rich." Now, we've heard that before. Let me tell you the two things wrong with that.

One is that when you tax the rich—in other words, when you're running up the top two income brackets—you're going to tax small-business owners. Many small businesses pay tax at the individual income-tax rate because they're called Subchapter S corporations or sole proprietorships. Those are fancy legal and accounting words which mean they pay income tax at the individual rate. That's just the truth. About 90 percent of all small business pay individual income taxes. So when you hear somebody say, "Oh, we're just going to tax the rich," I want you thinking about the truth. And the truth is they're talking about taxing about 900,000 to a million small businesses. You know what the problem with that is? Seventy percent of new jobs are created by small businesses in America. It makes no sense to be taxing the job creators.

And here is the other thing wrong with it. If you promise 2.2 trillion, but your tax plan only raises between 600 and 800 billion, there is a gap between what is promised and what can be delivered. Now, there is a—my opponent has a history; it's a record. I like to tell people I'm running on my record. He's not running on his; he's running from his record. And part of his record—in his 20 years as Senator, part of his record is he's voted to raise taxes 98 times. That's a record; that's what he's done. I'm not making it up. That's five times every year he's been in the Senate. That's a predictable pattern. And so when you're trying to find out who's going to fill the tax gap, think about predictable patterns. In order to fill that gap, in order to make the difference between what he's promised and what he can deliver, guess who's going to get stuck with the bill? Yes, that's always what happens.

We're not going to let him tax you; we're not going to let him tax the small businesses, because we're going to carry Wisconsin and win on November the 2d.

A couple of other things that I want to talk to you right quick about to make sure this economy continues to grow. First, we will continue with good farm policy. I'm for the MILC program—MILC, which is helping our dairy farmers. I'm for the reauthorization of that. Ask your dairy farmers whether that means something to them, and you're going to find out it does.

We'll continue to open up markets, opening up markets for agriculture products and manufacturing products and high-tech products. They're good for the job creation and the job creators. Listen, we've opened up our market for goods from overseas, and that's good for you as a consumer. Think about how the market works. If you have more products to choose from, you're likely to get that which you want at a better price and higher quality. That's how the market works. So instead of shutting down our market when it comes to trade and hurting our consumers, our strategy is to say to places like China, "You treat us the way we treat you," is to open up markets, is to demand that others are fair to us. And the reason why I do that is because I know we can compete with anybody, anytime, anywhere, so long as the rules are fair.

If you want jobs to stay here, we've got to do something about the energy situation. I submitted a plan to the United States Congress 2 years ago that encourages conservation, that encourages the use of ethanol and biodiesel. Think about the idea of being able to say as the President, "The corn crop is up, and we're less dependent." Think about that, that someday it's going to happen. We're going to continue to spend research and development dollars so we can grow our way toward less reliance.

We're promoting clean coal technology so that your powerplants can have power. We're going to modernize the electricity grid. We're going to explore for natural gas in environmentally friendly ways. What I'm telling you is this: In order to make sure that jobs continue to grow, that people can make a living, this country must become less dependent on foreign sources of energy.

We're going to talk to a small-business manufacturer here. He told me he's had a problem with health care. Small businesses are having trouble affording health care. Most of the uninsured in America work for small businesses. So here's some commonsense ways to help you on health care.

Small businesses ought to be able to pool together, pool risk so they can buy insurance at the same discounts that big companies get to do. You know, there needs to be economies of purchase in the marketplace. If you're a stand-alone small business, it costs you a lot of money to afford health care. If you're able to pool across jurisdictional boundaries, if you get more people to spread the risk, you're able to get insurance at better prices for your workers. That's a commonsense way of helping small businesses.

We'll expand health savings accounts, which are commonsense ways of enabling people to be able to manage their own health care account, low-premium, high-deductible accounts where you can save tax-free. It will help your families. If you change jobs, you can take your health account with you from year to year. If you save money, you can roll over your savings in your health account tax-free. It's a way to make sure the decisionmaking is between you and your doctor, not between some insurance person and your doctor. The more you're able to have—the more you're involved with your health care decisions, the more likely it is there's a cost discipline in the marketplace.

Listen, we'll take care of the needy. We have an obligation in our society to do so.

I'm a big believer in community health centers, places where the poor and the indigent can get good primary and preventative care. My pledge, I said in the convention speech and I'm saying all over the country, is that in a new term, we'll make sure every poor county in America has got a community health center to take the pressure off our emergency rooms and our hospitals.

But let me tell you another practical way to make sure health care is available and affordable. We must do something about the litigious nature of our society. There's too many lawsuits. Lawsuits are running up the cost of doing business. Lawsuits are running good doctors out of practice. Lawsuits are hurting people who need health care. I have met too many ob-gyns around this country that are having to leave their practice because these lawsuits are running up their premiums. They cannot afford to practice medicine. I've met too many women who are deeply concerned about their health care and the health of their child because their local doctor no longer practices. And that's not right for America.

If we're interested in our quality of life, we'd better do something about all these lawsuits. You cannot be pro-doctor, pro-patient, and pro-personal-injury-trial-lawyer at the same time. You have to choose in life. My opponent made his choice, and he put a personal injury trial lawyer on the ticket. I have made my choice. I am standing with the Wisconsin docs and patients and small-business owners. I am for medical liability reform—now.

We have a difference of opinion when it comes to health care. I remember the debate when my opponent—they asked him about his health care plan, and he actually looked in the camera and said, "The Government has nothing to do with it." You know, I could barely contain myself when he said that. [*Laughter*]

The Government has a lot to do with his plan, and that's what I want you to understand. His plan is one—for example, when you run up Medicaid, run up the eligibility for Medicaid, it provides an incentive for small businesses to not provide insurance for their employees because the Government will. It's estimated some 8 million people will go from private insurance to Government insurance. Eight out of ten people will be signed up to a Government program under his plan. I just strongly disagree. You don't want the Federal Government running your health care. When the Government starts paying, the Government starts deciding. And then the Government rations, and the Government chooses your doctor. It is not the right way to go when it comes to making sure there's quality health care for the people.

Let me talk about another issue, and then we're going to talk to our guests. I have made a commitment to our seniors not only to good-quality Medicare but to Social Security. And Tommy and I were talking about the 2000 campaign. We were coming down the stretch, and they ran some ads here in this State that said to the seniors of Wisconsin, "If George W. gets elected, you're not going to get your check." I don't know if you remember those. Tommy sure remembered them. Well, I want you to tell your friends and neighbors this: George W. did get elected, and the seniors got their checks. And the seniors will continue to get their checks. The Social Security trust, no matter what the politicians say, is in good shape for our seniors. It's going to meet—the seniors have nothing to worry about. Every 4 years, the scare tactics come out. I just assure you, you're going to get your checks. And baby boomers like me, we're in pretty good shape when it comes to the Social Security trust.

But a President must deal with problems—you want a President who confronts problems, not passes them on to future generations and future Presidents. We have a problem with Social Security when it comes to our children and our grand-children. When the baby boomer genera-tion retires, there is a question as to wheth-er or not the children will have a—Social Security accounts available for them unless we think differently. I believe younger workers ought to be allowed to take some of their payroll taxes and set up a personal savings account, a personal savings account that will earn a greater rate of return than the current Social Security trust, an account they call their own, an account the Govern-ment cannot take away.

Eric Sauey is with us. Eric, you ready to say something?

Eric Sauey. Yes, sir.

The President. Good. [*Laughter*] I hope so. I call him "Mr. President." He's the president of?

Mr. Sauey. Seats, Incorporated.

The President. Based in?

Mr. Sauey. Reedsburg, Wisconsin.

The President. What do you do?

Mr. Sauey. We manufacture seating for vehicles with wheels or tracks, other than passenger cars.

The President. Okay. [*Laughter*]

Mr. Sauey. Some of the markets that we serve are off-highway equipment, semi trac-tors, commercial turf mowers, firetrucks, delivery vans, many different custom-types of seats.

The President. Are you making a living?

Mr. Sauey. We're making a living.

The President. Good. Tell me—first of all, I want you to know—how are you orga-nized?

Mr. Sauey. We're an S corporation. We're a family-run, family-owned business. We're an S corporation. We're in the proc-ess of trying to expand here into Richland Center. Some of the things that we have, from the basic values that we have—[*ap-plause*].

The President. Sounds like they want you here. [*Laughter*]

Mr. Sauey. We have some values of a small business that were passed on to me by my father, who helped start this busi-ness, and my mother, that—we can't take all the profits out of the business. We have to put them back into the business to grow the business, to nurture it. I'm second gen-eration. I hope to pass it—the business goes to my kids or nieces and nephews, and we can't do that if we're paying taxes. We need to invest that back into the busi-ness for capital, reinvestment, R&D.

The President. Perfect. Let me—so here's the tax relief. Remember all the rhetoric about the tax relief, "only certain people benefit." When you cut the taxes for everybody who pays taxes, you're bene-fiting small-business owners like Subchapter S corporations. Have you hired anybody this year?

Mr. Sauey. We've hired a lot of people this year. We're up to about 380 people right now; we're looking to hire more.

The President. Yes, see, they're hiring. They're expanding. They're growing. One reason why they're doing well, they've got innovative leadership. Isn't that right?

Mr. Sauey. Yes, sir. [*Laughter*]

The President. Another reason why is they've got more money. See, the money is not going to the Federal Government; the money is staying with his company, which gives him the optimism and con-fidence to expand. Seventy percent of new jobs are created by small businesses. Our economic policies recognize that and we say to people like Eric, "Go for it. Expand. Here's some extra money, your money to begin with." And he says he's going to hire. He may come here to Richland Center.

And so my opponent says, oh, he's just going to tax the rich. You're looking at the rich. [*Laughter*] You're looking at a man who said, "We may come to Richland Cen-ter. We may hire new people." They're less likely to expand and to hire new people if the Federal Government takes money from them. That just makes sense. That's just simple economics.

Let me ask you something. Do you ever invest?

Mr. Sauey. We invest a lot. Every year we invest in excess of $1½ million. This last year we've invested more than $2 million in capital equipment. We are in the process right now of installing a computerized—[*inaudible*]—machine, a computerized—[*inaudible*], a 400-ton punch press—[*laughter*].

The President. That sounded like a big one to me. [*Laughter*] You see, good tax policy says to businessowners, "Invest," because you know what investment means? Investment means jobs. And so in our tax policy we said to small-business owners that you're able to deduct up to $100,000 for equipment expensing in the year in which you buy it, as opposed to $25,000. And why did we do that? Because we want to encourage Eric to invest. And so he says he buys a 400-ton——

Mr. Sauey. Punch press.

The President. Punch press. [*Laughter*] Kind of hard to say if you're from Texas—[*laughter*]—punch press. But guess what, because of the decision he made, two things happened: One, his business is more productive; it's more likely that he can compete. He's bought a piece of equipment that makes him more competitive. And we live in a competitive world, and the more competitive he is, the more likely it is someone is going to work for his company. The more competitive he is, the more likely it is he's going to expand his business here. But guess what else, because he bought the 400-ton punch press, somebody had to make it. And when somebody makes it, somebody is more likely to find work at the punch press manufacturing business.

This economy is moving because people like Eric are confident about the future. He's sitting here in front of all these cameras and these people saying, "I'm going to expand my business." That's what you want to hear. And the question is, which one of the Presidential candidates, one, understands the importance of small businesses and the entrepreneurial spirit, and which one of us has the plans to make

sure Eric feels comfortable investing and expanding his business? And I make the case to the people of Wisconsin, it is George W. Bush who understands that.

Ready to go, Greeley?

Jim Greeley. I'm ready for you, I think.

The President. All right. Jim Greeley, small-business owner. What do you do?

Mr. Greeley. Thank you.

The President. Greeley Signs, yes.

Mr. Greeley. Yes.

The President. Tell us what you do.

Mr. Greeley. Well, Mr. President, I have a sign company that I started about 30 years ago. And I'm at the point now where I'm passing it along to my son. But in the last 2 years, we've expanded with a 20,000 square foot addition. We've added new printing equipment so we can print giant posters, such as political posters. If you need any, you know where to look. [*Laughter*]

The President. It's a little late. You should have gotten your order in early. But anyway. [*Laughter*]

Mr. Greeley. We've added a laser engraver, and we've added several other such printing equipment——

The President. So you've been investing.

Mr. Greeley. Pardon?

The President. You've been investing.

Mr. Greeley. I've been investing, and we've been putting our money where our mouth is. We have to. We have to have confidence in the future of America——

The President. Right.

Mr. Greeley. ——and confidence in the future of this country.

The President. See, he's investing $140,000 this year. I hope you didn't mind me saying that. [*Laughter*] And he saved $27,000 as a result of the tax relief package, because of the investments. See, good tax policy says to Jim, "If you make a capital investment, there's an incentive to do so." And it's very important for people to understand that the reason we passed tax policy when we did was to help move this economy forward, and the best way to move it forward is to talk—is to address the needs of small-business owners. If 70 percent of the new jobs in America are created by the Jims of the world, then we ought to encourage him, and we ought to provide incentives for him to expand his business.

Did you hire anybody? Are you going to hire anybody? Tell me.

Mr. Greeley. Oh, yes, we'll keep hiring.

The President. Good. Well, it says here you hired three in 2004.

Mr. Greeley. Say again?

The President. You hired three people in 2004.

Mr. Greeley. Yes, we've hired three in 2004, and we'll hire more because we have plans of continuing to expand. In fact, we have dibs on another acre and a half of land.

The President. There you go.

Mr. Greeley. We want to keep on——

The President. See, here's what's happening in America. Small businesses hire 3 people there, 100 here, 50 there, and it's the real vitality of our economy, when you think about it.

I want to say something else about small-business ownership, two other things. And this relates to our farmers too. You heard both these men say they're thinking about passing their business on to their family members, but our Tax Code discourages that. The Tax Code makes it really hard for somebody—the Turgasens were talking about it, how hard it is to pass their dairy farm on to the next generation. You know why? Because this Tax Code of ours taxes a person twice, once when they're living and once when they die. And the death tax is hard on our small-business owners and really hard on our farmers. If you're interested in keeping family farms alive, then you need to support me when it comes to getting rid of the death tax forever. If you want there to be a small business—[*applause*].

Thank you, sir. You did a great job.

Mr. Greeley. Did you see the Packer-Dallas game? [*Laughter*]

The President. I saw that, and I know the Wisconsin Badgers are undefeated, you know. And let me tell you what else I know. I know the Packers beat Dallas at Lambeau Field. Who invited you? [*Laughter*]

Anyway, you know, one of the things we did—good tax policy also helps families. And part of our tax plan was to help families be able to better afford life and better enable them to raise their children.

Margie Seamans is with us. When people are arguing about this Tax Code, remind them we raised the child credit to 1,000. We reduced the marriage penalty. By the way, there is a—I can't imagine a Tax Code that penalizes marriage. The Tax Code ought to encourage marriage.

And so what do you do?

Margie Seamans. I work at Land's End, and I do payroll and scheduling.

The President. Very good company. Yes. And David—your husband, David?

Mrs. Seamans. Yes. My husband, David, is not employed right now.

The President. Right.

Mrs. Seamans. He has a back injury that he had in the service.

The President. Service, right.

Mrs. Seamans. And so he currently stays home right now.

The President. You're bringing home the money.

Mrs. Seamans. I'm bringing home the money.

The President. And children?

Mrs. Seamans. I have two children—Danielle, 13, and Megan, 11.

The President. Fabulous. Teenage years, I remember them fondly. [*Laughter*] The tax relief we passed saved this family $1,700 a year. Now that may not sound a lot to people in Washington, DC. It's a lot for this family.

Mrs. Seamans. It was a blessing when we received the child tax credit. My husband had outstanding medical bills, and we used those—used that money to pay for those. And just having that lower tax from my paycheck each week, it makes a big difference, a noticeable difference.

The President. See, here's the fundamental difference in the campaign. By the way, my opponent voted against all this tax relief. It would have cost the average family—middle-class family $2,000 extra in Federal taxes, and that's the philosophical difference. Who do you want spending your own money?

See, we're setting priorities in Washington, and we'll meet those priorities. You're going to hear me talk about a big priority here pretty soon, which is defending the homeland. But I believe this family can spend their money better than the Federal Government can spend their money.

Thanks for coming, Margie. I appreciate you being here.

Finally, we've got Corey Kanable. Welcome.

Corey Kanable. Thank you. [*Applause*]

The President. You've got quite a following here. [*Laughter*] I'll tell you why he's here. He bought a home. You know, one of the greatest things in America is when somebody opens up the door where they live and says, "Welcome to my home. Welcome to my piece of property." Do you realize the homeownership rate is at an all-time high under my administration.

So when did you buy it?

Mr. Kanable. We bought our home in July 2003.

The President. Good. What's it like? You like it?

Mr. Kanable. Oh, we love it. It's a three-bedroom ranch on the west side of town. It's a nice quiet neighborhood—most of the town is. It's real comfortable to be in your hometown. My wife, Gretchen, and I both grew up in this area and wanted to come back here and——

The President. Fantastic. Good.

Mr. Kanable. It allowed us to do so.

The President. And you were a renter before?

Mr. Kanable. We rented 2 years out of the area. And I mean, the American Dream of owning your own home was realized to us because of the tax credit and the interest rate. We couldn't go wrong.

The President. Well, this is important for, I think, for the future of this country, is to encourage owner—homeownership as well as ownership. We want youngsters being able to own and manage their own Social Security account. We want businesses flourishing and people to own their own small business. And we want people owning their own home. You know why? Because when you own something, you have a vital stake in the future of your country. I like to tell people, no one ever washes a rental car. [*Laughter*]

Mr. Kanable. Absolutely.

The President. So how has it changed your life? If somebody is watching and hears—says, "Gosh, I don't know whether I want to buy a home or not," how has it changed your life?

Mr. Kanable. Oh, it's great. I mean, you have something of your own, something you've invested in. We've had the privilege of doing some remodeling to it, things that, you know, it would be great to be able to do. We would like to do this. We recently were able to get a FEMA grant to fix our basement; it had a water problem. So now we can finish that off. You know, we're looking at new siding, new roofing, and maybe adding a garage on. We're planning on building a deck this spring, things that we just—you know, in an apartment, you can't do that.

The President. Right, it's your home.

Mr. Kanable. That's right.

The President. The tax relief saved this family $1,000 this year and last year. So you hear a person say, "Gosh, I'm thinking about adding a garage," you know, "I'm thinking about doing something to my piece of property." Tax relief has helped people realize their dreams. Tax relief is a vital part not only of helping this economy recover, but it's a vital part of enhancing the quality of life of our citizens. And that's why I'm going to keep your taxes low.

I've got a couple other things—if you've got time, I've got a couple other things on my mind.

First, I've been talking about a changing world, and it's important that we know the world is changing. In a changing world, jobs change, the nature of jobs change, the skill sets necessary to fill jobs change. That's why education is so vital. That's why we've got to make sure we get it right. The No Child Left Behind Act is a great piece of legislation because we believe in high standards and accountability. We're challenging the soft bigotry of low expectations. We want to make sure the high school diploma means something. We'll expand Pell grants for lower and middle-income families so more children are able to start their career with a college diploma. I'm a big believer in the community college system, because community colleges are able to devise curriculum for the jobs which actually exist, to be able to help people get the skills necessary to fill the new jobs which are being created.

But in times of change, some things do not change, the values we try to live by, courage and compassion, reverence and integrity. We stand for a culture of life in which every person matters and every being counts. We stand for marriage and families, which are the foundations of our society. And we stand for judges who know the difference between personal opinion and the strict interpretation of the law.

And on these issues, there is a difference of opinion. My opponent's words on values issues are a little murky—[laughter]—but his record is clear. You know, the Congress in the mid-nineties voted on what was called the Defense of Marriage Act. It's an act that defined marriage as between a man and a woman. It received big bipartisan support. Republicans voted for it. Democrats voted for it. President Clinton signed the bill into law. My opponent was one of a few out-of-the-mainstream Democrats that voted against the Defense of Marriage Act. He voted against the ban on the brutal practice of partial-birth abortion. He has said that the Reagan years were a period of moral darkness. There is a mainstream in American politics, and he sits on the far left bank. He can try to run, but he cannot hide from his record.

And finally, I want to talk to you about how to keep the peace. I want to talk to you about the overriding issue in this campaign, which is the security of the American people. See, all we've talked about is really important, but unless we're secure, unless we're able to achieve the peace, we won't be able to achieve a hopeful America. And the people are confronted with a clear choice in this campaign on this issue.

Let me tell you what I have learned and what I know about the post-September the 11th world. First, that we're fighting against a ruthless enemy that has no conscience, which means you cannot negotiate with them, you cannot appease them, you cannot hope for the best with them. The way to deal with them and protect the American people is to stay on the offense, find them where they hide, defeat them overseas so we do not have to face them here at home. Secondly—[applause]. Thank you. Thank you all.

I tell people that if we show uncertainty or weakness during these troubled times, this world of ours will drift toward tragedy. It's not going to happen so long as I'm your President. I understand that we must not show weakness. We must be certain in our resolve. The terrorists must absolutely understand they can't intimidate us; they can't force us to not defend our freedom.

Second lesson is that when the President says something, he better mean what he says in order to keep this world peaceful. And I meant what I said when I said, "If you harbor a terrorist, you're equally as guilty as the terrorists." In other words, this is a different kind of—we have a different challenge to defend our country.

And I was speaking at that moment in time specifically to the Taliban in Afghanistan.

Why was I doing that? Because you might remember, some 3½ years ago, Al Qaida was training in Afghanistan. They were like the parasite, and the host was slowly but surely being overcome by the parasite, it seemed like to me. But there was a—kind of a convenience of philosophy. These people are ideologues of hate. They have a backward, dim vision of the world. I want the kids here to understand what life was like in Afghanistan. Young girls could not go to school. There was a grim ideology that expected certain things, particularly out of women. And if the women did not toe the line, they were taken to the public square and whipped and sometimes executed in a sports stadium.

These are barbaric people, the Taliban. This is their view of the world and Al Qaida's view of the world. They've hijacked a great religion. They hate what we stand for because we're the opposite. We believe in freedom. We believe people can express their opinion anyway they see fit, that you can worship the Almighty or not worship the Almighty in America and you're equally American. And if you choose to worship the Almighty, you're just as American if you're a Muslim, Jew, or Christian. That's what we believe in our country. And that's the opposite of them. They don't believe that.

And so I said, you know, "If you harbor a terrorist, you're equally as guilty." And they just ignored what we said. And we removed the Taliban from power, thanks to a great United States military, and as a result—it's important to uphold doctrine when you say it—sent a message throughout the world that when America says something, we mean it. When we say we're going to defend ourselves, we mean it.

And as a result of the Taliban being removed from power, Al Qaida no longer trains in Afghanistan. As a result of the Taliban no longer being in power, millions of citizens registered to vote and voted in a Presidential election. And the first voter was a 19-year-old woman, the first voter in the Afghanistan election. Unbelievable moment.

Think about how far that society has come in a brief period of time. You know, I'm confident there were a lot of doubters as to whether or not democracy would take hold in Afghanistan. You can understand why. I mean, who would have ever thought that people that had been subjected to such a brutal life would conceivably want to vote. But they forgot what we know: Freedom lurks in everybody's heart. People want to be free in the world. Freedom is on the march, and America is more secure for it.

Thirdly, when we see a threat, we must take it seriously before it comes to hurt us. Prior to September the 11th, if we saw a threat, we could deal with it or not deal with it because we felt secure. We felt oceans could protect us. But we learned a different lesson on September the 11th. It's essential the American people and the American President understand that when we see a threat, we must take it seriously. Elsewise, it might come and hurt us. I saw a threat in Saddam Hussein, and the world is better off with Saddam Hussein sitting in a prison cell.

And our strategy in Iraq is clear. We'll train Iraqi citizens so they can do the hard work of defending their freedom against the likes of Zarqawi. You know, I've heard the critics say, "Well, if we hadn't been on the offensive, the terrorists wouldn't be as active as they are." Well, Zarqawi was planning in Afghanistan; he was in a training camp until we arrived and closed the camp down. Then he moved to Baghdad, where he's beheading people and setting off car bombs. What do these people think Zarqawi would be doing? Do they think he'd be kind of a peaceful small-business owner? [*Laughter*] He hates America. It is best we defeat Zarqawi in Iraq so he doesn't come here and hurt us. It is best we secure our country by defeating the enemy overseas.

And we're training the Iraqis to do the hard work. I remember the debates. He said, "Well, America is suffering all the casualties." That excludes and ignores the casualties being lost by the Iraqi people as they defend their own country. We mourn every single life in America, and we mourn the lives of those brave souls who are defending freedom in Iraq as well.

Iraq is going to have elections. Think about how far that country has come in a brief period of time from the days of torture chambers and mass graves, the days of a brutal tyrant. We're better off with America helping to promote liberty around the world. And so we'll get those countries on the path to stability and democracy as quickly as we can. And then our troops will come home with the honor they have earned.

I want to thank those who are here who have set such a great example for those who wear the uniform, our veterans. I appreciate your service to our country. I want to thank the military families who are here for your sacrifice. I want to thank those who wear the uniform. We got a great United States military. [Applause] And I want to assure—please be seated, thank you. We've still got a lot—a little work left to do. Just a little, then we're heading on the bus to Cuba City.

So I want to assure the loved ones of those who wear the uniform that so long as I'm the Commander in Chief, we'll give your loved ones all the support they need to complete their missions. That's why I went to the Congress and asked for $87 billion of vital funding for our troops in harm's way, and it was important. It was important—such an important request that we got great bipartisan support. I want you tell your friends and neighbors of this startling statistic: 4 Members of the United States Senate, 4 out of 100, voted to authorize the use of force and then voted against the funding to support our troops

in combat—4 people, 2 of whom were my opponent and his runningmate. Think about that—voted yes for the authorization but voted no when it came time to support the troops.

They asked him why, and he said, "I actually did vote for the $87 billion, right before I voted against it." [Laughter] I haven't been in any coffee shops in this part of the world; I suspect not a lot of people talk like that. [Laughter] He's given a lot of explanations since, a lot of them. One of the most interesting ones of all is, he finally said about the $87 billion vote, "The whole thing was a complicated matter." There is nothing complicated about supporting our men and women in harm's way.

I believe that liberty has the power to transform societies. It's etched in my very being. Let me help make my case by describing our relationship to Prime Minister Koizumi of Japan. We like him a lot—I say, "we"; Laura and I do. We've had him to our ranch. He's a good man. I saw him in the U.N. I said, "You know, I'm out on the campaign trail, and I'm telling people about my relationship with you. I hope you don't mind." He said, "Oh, fine, go ahead and talk about it." What I didn't ask him was permission to tell you that Elvis was his favorite singer—[laughter]—true.

Anyway, so we have got a good relationship with him. And that's—I'm sure to some doesn't seem odd. "So what, the President of the United States and the Prime Minister of Japan working together; it's happened with other Presidents." That's right, except it wasn't all that long ago that we were at war with the Japanese. Some 60 years ago, Japan was the sworn enemy of the United States of America. There's a generation of Americans still alive today that fought in that war. My dad was one; your dads—I'm sure somebody here did that very same thing. There's a gentleman right there. Thank you, sir. There's another man. Yes, sir. There's another gentleman.

Thank you. Another one—well, they're everywhere. Yes, sir, thanks. It makes my point. It wasn't all that long ago that we were at war with the Japanese. They were the bitter enemy of the United States.

And after we won that war, Harry S. Truman, President of the United States, believed in the power of liberty to transform an enemy into an ally and worked to build a democracy in Japan. Now, there was a lot of skeptics. You can understand why. Why should we help an enemy? A lot of people's lives were turned upside down as a result of that war with the Japanese, and they weren't interested at all about helping the Japanese. I'm sure there were skeptics saying the enemy couldn't conceivably become a democracy—a lot of doubters. There was also people in this country had faith in the ability of liberty to transform societies. As a result of that faith, I sit down at the table with Prime Minister Koizumi, talking about how to keep the peace that we all want.

Think about that. Think about what liberty can do to a society. And that's what I want the young to understand, what's taking place in the world today. Someday, an American President will be sitting down with a duly elected leader from Iraq, talking about the peace in the broader Middle East. And our children and our grandchildren will be better off for it.

I believe everybody yearns to be free. I believe people in the broader Middle East want to be free. I believe that because freedom is not America's gift to the world; freedom is the Almighty God's gift to each man and woman in this world.

So I've come to your good city to ask for the vote and ask for your help. I know why I'm running again. I want to extend prosperity and hope to every corner of the country. I want to promote an ownership society where more and more citizens from all walks of life can say, "I own my home. I own my business." I want people to be able to realize a great tomorrow by making sure this country is safe and secure from an enemy. I know where I want to take us. We've done the hard work together over 3¾ years. We've climbed the mountain, and now we can see the valley below, a valley which is hopeful and prosperous and peaceful. And with your help, we will get there together.

God bless. Thank you for coming. I appreciate you being here. Thank you all. Thank you, sir.

NOTE: The President spoke at 11:43 a.m. at Richland Center High School. In his remarks, he referred to Mayor Rita Kidd of Richland Center, WI; Dale Schultz, candidate in Wisconsin's Third Congressional District, and his wife, Rachel, district administrator, Richland School District; John Cler, principal, Richland Center High School; senior Al Qaida associate Abu Musab Al Zarqawi; and Prime Minister Junichiro Koizumi of Japan.

Remarks in Cuba City, Wisconsin
October 26, 2004

The President. Thank you all for coming. I am honored you're here. Thanks for coming today. You know, Cuba City is known as the City of the Presidents. Kind of makes sense that a President stops in to say hello, doesn't it? A few months ago,

I was the first sitting President to pass through Cuba City. Today I'm the first sitting President to stop in and give a speech. And I'm looking forward to signing my name to the shield of the 43d President.

As I'm traveling your beautiful State asking for the vote and I'm asking for your help, I'd like to encourage you to get your friends and neighbors to go to the polls. We have a duty in this democracy to vote. We have an obligation. When you get them headed to the polls, don't overlook discerning Democrats—[laughter]—people like Zell Miller, the Senator from Georgia who is strongly for my candidacy. Remind people if they want a safer America, a stronger America, and a better America, to put me and Dick Cheney back in office.

Listen, I'm going to give you—I've been traveling Wisconsin a lot, giving people reasons to put me back into office. But perhaps the most important one of all is so that Laura is the First Lady for 4 more years. When I asked her to marry me, she said, "Fine, just make me a promise." I said, "What is it?" She said, "Promise me I'll never have to give a political speech." [Laughter] I said, "Fine, you know, you've got a deal." Fortunately, she didn't hold me to the deal. [Laughter] She is giving a lot of speeches. And when she does, the American people see what I know, that she is compassionate; she is warm; she is a strong, great First Lady.

I asked Tommy to take on a tough job in Washington, DC, and he's done a heck of a job. I'm proud of Tommy Thompson. My only problem with being around Tommy, all he wants to do is talk about Wisconsin football. And of course he did have to bring up the Packers-Cowboy game as well, played right there at Lambeau Field. [Laughter]

I want to thank Steve Freese for his introduction. I appreciate his service to your community in the statehouse. I want to thank my friend Mark Green, Congressman Mark Green, who's traveling with us. Thanks for coming, Mark.

I want to thank the mayor, Dick Davis. Thank you, Mr. Mayor, for being here. It's kind for you to come. I want to thank the members of the City of Presidents Committee—right there. Thank you all.

I'm traveling with a fine man and his wife, Tim and Barbara Michels. He is going to make a great United States Senator. I appreciate him coming. And I want to thank my friend Dale Schultz, who will also make a great Congressman in the Third Congressional District.

I want to thank Sam McGrew, the superintendent of schools. Appreciate you being here, Mr. Superintendent. I want to remind you, Mr. Superintendent, when it came time to pick a Secretary of Education, I picked a superintendent of schools. And the reason why I did is because I understand local control of schools is important, and I understand a superintendent of a school district understands education firsthand. And I appreciate your service.

And I want to thank Tim Hazen, the principal of the Cuba City High School. Thank you, sir. [Applause] That's a good sign, when the students are cheering for you. [Laughter] I want to thank the—Danielle Wallenhorst, the student council president. Madam President, thank you for greeting me. Oh, there she is. Yes, there she is, good. Listen, I understand the football team has got a game tonight. I wish you all the best. Good luck to you. And as Tommy pointed out, the volleyball team here is really good too. I appreciate you being here.

Listen, thanks for coming. We're coming down the stretch in this campaign. And there are different candidates running with different points of view. You know where I stand, and sometimes, you even know where my opponent stands. [Laughter]

Now, we both have records. I'm running on mine. He's running from his, and there's a reason why. There is a mainstream in American politics. The fellow I'm running against sits on the far left bank. I'm a compassionate conservative and proudly so.

I have a positive and optimistic vision for our future, a comprehensive strategy for victory in Iraq and for victory in the wider war against terror, a plan to make sure our economy continues to grow so that hope spreads its wings in every corner of America. My opponent has no plan, no vision, just a long list of complaints. But a Monday morning quarterback has never led any team to victory.

This election comes down to five clear choices for your families, for America's families: your family's security; your family budget; your quality of life; your retirement; and the bedrock values that makes this a great country.

The first clear choice is the most important one because it concerns the security of your family. All progress on every other issue depends on the safety of our citizens. This will be the first Presidential election since September the 11th, 2001. Americans will go to the polls in a time of war and ongoing threats. The terrorists who killed thousands of innocent people are still dangerous, and they're determined. The outcome of this election will set the direction of the war on terror. The most solemn duty of the American President is to protect the American people. If America shows weakness or uncertainty in this decade, this world of ours will drift toward tragedy. That's not going to happen on my watch.

Our strategy is clear. We've strengthened the protections of our homeland. We're reforming our intelligence capabilities. We're transforming our military. There will be no draft. The All-Volunteer Army will remain the All-Volunteer Army. We are relentless. We are determined. We're staying on the offensive. We're defeating the terrorists overseas so we do not have to face them here in our own country. And we're making progress. More than three-quarters of Al Qaida's key members and associates have been brought to justice, and the rest of them can be certain of this: We're on their trail.

A President has to lead with consistency and strength. In war, your tactics change but never your principles. Americans have seen how I do my job. Even when you don't agree with me, you know what I believe, where I stand, and what I intend

to do. On the good days and on the bad days, when the polls are up or the polls are down, I am determined to win this war on terror, and I will always support the men and women who wear our Nation's uniform.

My opponent in this campaign has taken a different approach. It's fair to say that consistency has not been his strong point. [*Laughter*] Senator Kerry says we're better off with Saddam Hussein out of power, except when he declares that removing Saddam makes us less safe. In our second debate, he said he always believed that Saddam was a threat, except a few questions later when he said Saddam was not a threat. [*Laughter*] He says he was right when he voted to authorize the use of force against Saddam Hussein, but that I was wrong to use force against Saddam Hussein. [*Laughter*]

Now he's saying he knew where bin Laden was in the fall of 2001 and that our military passed up a chance to get him at Tora Bora. Let me talk about that for a minute. That's unjustified criticism of our military commanders in the field. This is the worst kind of Monday morning quarterbacking. In fact, our commander in Afghanistan, General Tommy Franks, recently wrote this about Tora Bora: "The Senator's understanding of events does not square with reality." The general says that American Special Forces were actively involved in the search for the terrorists in Tora Bora, and the intelligence reports at the time placed bin Laden in any of several countries.

Before Senator Kerry got into political difficulty and revised his views, he saw our actions in Tora Bora differently. In the fall of 2001, on national TV, he said this about Tora Bora: "I think we have been doing this pretty effectively, and we should continue to do it that way." At the time, the Senator said this about Tora Bora: "I think we've been smart. I think the administration leadership has done it well, and we are on the right track." All I can say to that is, I am George W. Bush, and I approve of that message. [*Laughter*]

Audience members. Four more years! Four more years! Four more years!

The President. I want to thank those who wear the Nation's uniform that have joined us today. I appreciate your service. I want to thank the veterans who are here, who have set such a great example for those who wear the uniform. And I want to thank the military families who are with us today as well.

And I made a pledge to our troops and their families that they would have all they need to do their jobs and to complete their missions. That's why I went to the United States Congress and proposed $87 billion of supplemental funding to support our troops in harm's way. It was necessary funding. It was really important and so important that we got great bipartisan support for the vote—on the vote to fund the money. As a matter of fact, it was so strong that only 12 Members of the United States Senate voted against it. As you're out rounding up the vote, I want you to remind the people of this important part of the State of this startling statistic: 4 Members of the United States Senate, 4 out of 100, voted to authorize the use of force and then voted against supporting our troops in harm's way—only 4, 2 of whom are my opponent and his runningmate.

Audience members. Boo-o-o!

The President. They asked him, they said, "Well, how could you have made that vote?" And he said perhaps the most famous quote of the 2004 campaign—[*laughter*]—"I actually did vote for the $87 billion, before I voted against it." [*Laughter*] Now, look, I didn't spend any time in the coffee shops around Cuba City, but I suspect you're not going to find many people who talk that way here. [*Laughter*]

He's given several explanations—you can't be calibrating the polls when it comes time to be supporting our troops. They said, well, when did he start changing his mind? Well, he started changing his mind

about his position when it looked like he was losing to Howard Dean in the Democrat primary, right about the time this vote came up. See, earlier on TV, prior to the vote, he said it would be irresponsible not to support our troops in combat. And sure enough, he took a look at the polls and decided not to support our troops in combat. A President must be consistent. A President must be willing to stand for what he believes.

In the last 20 years, in key moments of challenge—now remember, my opponent opposed President Ronald Reagan's doctrine of peace through strength. He didn't support removing Saddam Hussein from Kuwait, even though the international community united in concert. In moments of challenge and decision, he has chosen the path of weakness and inaction. Now, look, his record not only stands in opposition to me but in opposition to the great tradition of the Democrat Party of America. The party of Franklin Roosevelt and Harry Truman and John Kennedy is rightly remembered for confidence and resolve in times of crisis. Senator Kerry has turned his back on "pay any price" and "bear any burden," and he has replaced those commitments with "wait and see" and "cut and run."

Many Democrats in this country do not recognize their party anymore. Today I want to speak to every one of them: If you believe that America should lead with strength and purpose and confidence in our ideals, I'd be honored to have your support, and I'm asking for your vote.

We have big differences—we have differences in this campaign about how to keep you secure, and the differences are clear. Senator Kerry says that September the 11th did not change him much at all. Those are his words. And the policies make it clear. He said that the war on terror is primarily a law enforcement and intelligence gathering operation. Well, I want to tell you something. My outlook changed on September the 11th. I understand the stakes. I understand the consequences of inaction. I understand the consequence of sending mixed signals.

I remember standing in the ruins of the Twin Towers on September the 14th, 2001. It's a day I will never forget. I will never forget the sights and the sounds. I will never forget the hardhats yelling at me at the top of their lungs, "Whatever it takes." I remember the guy looking at me straight in the eye, and he said, "Do not let me down." Ever since that day, I wake up every morning trying to figure out how to better protect our country. I will never relent in defending our security, whatever it takes.

The second clear choice involves your budget. When I ran for President 4 years ago, I pledged to lower taxes for American families, and I kept my word. And remember what we have been through as an economy. Six months prior to my arrival, the stock market was in serious decline. And then we had a recession and corporate scandals and the attack on America, which cost us about a million jobs in the 3 months after September the 11th.

But we acted. I led the Congress to reduce your taxes, and our economic policies have led us back to growth. Think about these statistics and remind your friends and neighbors about these statistics. We've created 1.9 million jobs in the last 13 months. Farm incomes are up all across America. The farmers are making a good living. Homeownership rate is at an alltime high. The entrepreneurial spirit is strong in America. Small businesses are flourishing. The national unemployment rate is 5.4 percent. Let me put that in perspective for you: That's lower than the average rate of the 1970s, 1980s, and 1990s. The unemployment rate in Wisconsin is 5 percent.

And one of the reasons Wisconsin is doing so well is because your small businesses are flourishing and because the farmers are making a living. In 4 years, we'll—the next 4 years, we'll continue to help our dairy farmers. I support the MILC program to help the dairy farmers here in Wisconsin. We will make sure—we'll continue to open up markets for Wisconsin's farmers. I understand a good farm economy is necessary for a good national economy.

Look, we have a different point of view when it comes to taxes. My opponent has a different economic plan. It starts with the fact that he said he's going to raise taxes. And that's a promise most politicians keep. [*Laughter*] He's promised to spend $2.2 trillion in new money—spending. That's trillion with a "T." That's a lot even for a Senator from Massachusetts. [*Laughter*] And they asked him, "How you going to pay for all that new spending?" And he said, "Oh, we're just going to tax the rich." You've heard that before, haven't you? See, there's a difference between what he's promised and how much he can raise. He's promised 2.2 trillion, but by running up the top two brackets, he only raises about 600 to 800 billion dollars. There's a gap. Guess who usually fills the gap? The good news is, we're not going to let him tax you because we're going to carry Wisconsin and win a great victory on November the 2d.

A third issue about the quality of our families and the life of our families is education and health care. When I ran for President 4 years ago, I promised to end the soft bigotry of low expectations in our schools. And I kept my word. The No Child Left Behind Act is a good, solid piece of legislation. It says in return for extra Federal money, schools must measure to show us whether or not our children are learning to read and write and add and subtract. You can't solve a problem until you diagnose the problem. And so by measuring early, we're correcting problems before they become too acute, before it is too late. And an achievement gap in America is closing all over America. People are learning to read and write and add and subtract, and we're not going to go back to the old days of mediocrity and low expectations in our schoolhouses.

And I've got a commonsense way to help on health care. Most of the uninsured work for small businesses. Small businesses ought to be allowed to pool together to extend risk so they can buy insurance at the same discounts big companies get to do. I believe we ought to expand health savings accounts, low-premium, high-deductible, tax-free policies that enable people to manage and control their own health care. I know we're going to help the poor and the needy through community health centers and rural health centers. We're going to help sign up people for our low-income children's programs.

But also to make sure health care is available and affordable to you, we've got to do something about these junk lawsuits that are running good doctors out of practice and running up the cost of medicine. I've met too many ob-gyns around our country that are quitting the practice of medicine because these lawsuits are running their premiums up too high on their insurance policy. They just can't practice. I met too many women who are wondering whether or not they're going to get the quality health care for themselves and their baby because ob-gyns are being run out of practice. This isn't right for America. You cannot be pro-doctor and pro-patient and pro-plaintiff-attorney at the same time. You've got to make a choice. My opponent made his choice, and he put a personal-injury trial lawyer on the ticket.

Audience members. Boo-o-o!

The President. I have made my choice. I'm standing with the doctors and the patients and the hospitals and the small-business owners. I am for medical liability reform—now.

You know, in one of our debates, my opponent looked right in the camera and said his health care plan—about his health care plan, "The Federal Government has nothing to do with it." You know, I could barely contain myself. [*Laughter*] See, I understand his plan. The Federal Government has got a lot to do with it. Eight out of

ten people will be signed up on a Federal program. When you make it easier to get on Medicaid, small businesses will drop insurance for their employees because the Government will pay for it, and that will cause about 7 or 8 million people to get on Medicaid. And when the Government starts writing the checks, the Government starts writing the rules. And then when the Government starts writing the rules, the Government starts making decisions for you. They start rationing health care. They decide what doctor you can go see. To me, that is the wrong prescription for health care in America.

Here's what I believe. I believe when it comes to health care, the decisions ought to be between patients and doctors, not by officials in Washington, DC.

The fourth clear choice involves your retirement. Our Nation has made a solemn commitment to our seniors on Social Security and Medicare. When I ran for President 4 years ago, I promised to keep that commitment and improve Medicare by adding prescription drugs. I kept my word. And I want to thank Tommy Thompson for his help. You know, you've heard this issue debated for years. Matter of fact, it became such a political hot potato they called Medicare, "Medi-scare." But Tommy and I ignored all that, and we decided to do what was right for our seniors. Seniors are now getting discounts on medicines with drug discount cards. Low-income seniors are getting $600 this year to help them on their cards and $600 next year. And beginning in 2006, all seniors will be able to get prescription drug coverage under Medicare.

Let me talk about Social Security. You all might remember the 2000 campaign here in Wisconsin, the ads that said, "If George W. gets elected, our seniors are not going to get their checks." That's the old-style scare tactics. When you're out there talking to your friends and neighbors, remind them, George W. did get elected, and our seniors got their checks. And our seniors will continue to get their checks. And baby boomers like me, we're in pretty good shape when it comes to the Social Security trust.

But we need to worry about our children and our grandchildren when it comes to Social Security. When the baby boomers retire, it's going to be hard for the next generation to support us and then have a retirement system for their own. That's why we need a President to think differently about Social Security. I think younger workers ought to be allowed to take some of their own money and set up a personal savings account, an account that earns better interest, an account they call their own, an account the Government cannot take away.

You know, we have a difference of opinion on Social Security. My opponent said he's going to protect Social Security, but what he forgot to tell you is he's voted eight times for higher taxes on Social Security benefits. That's part of that record. See, that's just—see, he doesn't want you to know the record. He can run, but he cannot hide. That's what I say. He can run from it, but he can't hide from it.

And then he said, when it comes to Social Security, things are okay for the next generation. I think the job of a President[*] is to confront problems, not to pass them on to future Presidents and future generations. You've got to expect from your President somebody who is willing to take on the tough issue, not have their finger stuck in the wind trying to figure out which way the winds are blowing but somebody who is going to do what is right. And what is right is to protect Social Security for our seniors and make it viable for the younger citizens of this country.

And finally, the final clear choice in this election is on the values that are crucial to keeping our families strong. And here my opponent and I are miles apart. I stand for the appointment of Federal judges who

---

[*] White House correction.

know the difference between personal opinion and the strict interpretation of the law. I believe marriage is a sacred commitment, a pillar of our civilization. I don't believe this is a partisan issue. As a matter of fact, when Congress passed the Defense of Marriage Act, defining marriage as the union between a man and a woman, the vast majority of Democrats supported it, and President Bill Clinton signed it into law. But Senator Kerry was part of an out-of-the-mainstream minority that voted against the Defense of Marriage Act.

Audience members. Boo-o-o!

The President. Listen, reasonable people can find common ground on the most difficult of issues. Republicans and Democrats came together and agreed we should ban the brutal practice of partial-birth abortion. I proudly signed that bill. But my opponent was part of an out-of-the-mainstream minority that voted against the ban.

Audience members. Boo-o-o!

The President. See, we just have a difference of opinion, a big difference of opinion. I'll continue to reach out to Americans of every belief and move this goodhearted Nation toward a culture of life.

My opponent said the heart and soul of America can be found in Hollywood. [*Laughter*] Most American families don't look to Hollywood as a source of values. [*Laughter*] The heart and soul of America is found in communities like Cuba City, Wisconsin.

You know, one of my favorite quotes that I hope tells you what I believe and how I lead is by a fellow Texan named Tom Lea, and here's what he said. He said, "Sarah and I live on the east side of the mountain. It is the sunrise side, not the sunset side. It is the side to see the day that is coming, not to see the day that has gone." That's how I feel about this country, optimistic and hopeful. I know we can achieve anything we set our mind to. You know, in the last 4—nearly 4 years, we've come through a lot together. Because we've done the hard work of climbing the mountain, we see the valley below. And that valley is a valley full of prosperity and hope, a valley where people in this country feel comfortable about owning something, a valley where the entrepreneurial spirit is strong, where our families are strong. We're going to continue to spread freedom and liberty so we can achieve the peace that we all want for generations to come.

Four years ago, when I traveled your State asking for the vote, I made you this pledge: I said I would restore the integrity to the Oval Office. With your help and with your hard work, I will do so for 4 more years.

Thanks for coming. God bless. I appreciate it. Now I'm going to sign this shield.

NOTE: The President spoke at 2:43 p.m. at Cuba City High School. In his remarks, he referred to Wisconsin State Representative Stephen J. Freese; Mayor Richard Davis of Cuba City, WI; Samuel McGrew, district administrator, School District of Cuba City; former President Saddam Hussein of Iraq; Usama bin Laden, leader of the Al Qaida terrorist organization; and Gen. Tommy R. Franks, USA (Ret.), former combatant commander, U.S. Central Command.

Remarks in Dubuque, Iowa
October 26, 2004

The President. Thank you all for coming. Listen, Laura and I are glad to be back in Dubuque and so honored so many came out to say hello. You lift our spirits. Really appreciate you coming. We're here, of course, asking for the vote and asking for your help. We need you to get your friends and neighbors to go to the polls, find our fellow Republicans, find independents, find discerning Democrats and remind them if they want a safer America, a stronger America, and a better America, to put me and Dick Cheney back in office.

When I asked Laura to marry me, she said, "Fine, so long as you make me a promise." I said, "What is it?" She said, "Promise me I'll never have to give a political speech." [*Laughter*] I said, "Okay, you've got a deal." Fortunately, she is not holding me to that promise. She's giving a lot of speeches, and when she does, the American people see a compassionate, strong, great First Lady.

And I'm proud of my runningmate, Dick Cheney. He's doing a wonderful job. You know, I admit it, he does not have the waviest hair in the race. [*Laughter*] You'll

be happy to hear I didn't pick him because of his hairdo; I picked him because of his experience, his judgment, his ability to get the job done.

I'm proud to be on the stage with Congressman Jim Nussle, and I want to thank his wife, Karen, for being here. He's the chairman of the Budget Committee. He's watching your money like a hawk—eye. Nussle is a good man, good, solid citizen from the State of Iowa and I'm proud to call him friend.

You know, we love your Senator, Chuck Grassley. I saw him the other day, and I said, "Say, Chuck, you know, the South Lawn has got a lot of grass"—[*laughter*]—"and we're looking for somebody to give us a hand." [*Laughter*] He's done a wonderful job as the chairman of the Finance Committee. I know the people of Iowa are proud that he's the Senator; I know you're going to put him back into office for 6 more years.

I want to thank Dale Schultz for coming. Dale is right there. He's from the Third Congressional District in the great State of Wisconsin. He's been traveling with me all

 Photographic Portfolio

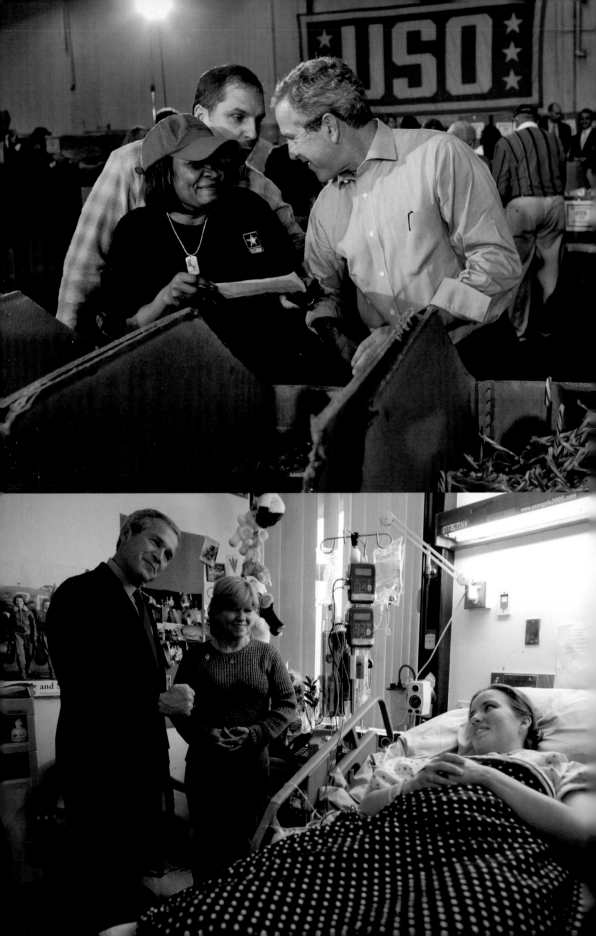

Overleaf: Waving at the crowd gathered at a Victory 2004 rally at Alltel Stadium in Jacksonville, Florida, October 23.

Left: Visiting the USO care package stuffing facility at Fort Belvoir, VA, December 10.

Below left: Visiting Sgt. Clara Best, USA, and her mother, Vickie Ebeling, at Walter Reed Army Medical Center, November 9.

Right: Attending a puppet show at the children's Christmas program in the East Room, December 6.

Below right: Signing H.R. 1308, the Working Families Tax Relief Act of 2004, at the South Suburban YMCA in Des Moines, Iowa, October 4.

TAX RELIEF
FOR
WORKING FAMILIES

Left: Exchanging greetings with President Alvaro Uribe of Colombia at a news conference at the Escuela Naval de Cadetes "Almirante Padilla" in Cartagena, Colombia, November 22.

Below left: Arriving at La Moneda for a social dinner with President Ricardo Lagos of Chile in Santiago, Chile, November 21.

Right: Meeting with President Olusegun Obasanjo of Nigeria in the Oval Office, December 2.

Below: Meeting with President Pervez Musharraf of Pakistan in the Oval Office, December 4.

Left: Attending a victory celebration at the Ronald Reagan Building and International Trade Center, November 3.

Right: Waiting in the Center Hall of the Private Residence at the White House on election night. November 3.

Below: Receiving the concession phone call from Senator John F. Kerry in the Oval Office, November 3.

Overleaf: In the Blue Room with Mrs. Bush, December 5.

day. Just in case anybody from Wisconsin is watching on TV, put this good man in as a Congressman.

I want to thank Dave Vaudt for being here. I want to thank Dave Roederer. I want to thank Doug Gross. I want to thank the Wil Gravatt Band for entertaining you all. I want to thank the grassroots activists who are here, the people putting up all the signs and making the phone calls and helping turn out people to rallies in the Dubuque area. With your help, there is no doubt in my mind we're going to carry Iowa and win a great victory in November.

We have just one week to go. Voters have a clear choice between two very different candidates with dramatically different approaches and records. Now, you know where I stand. And sometimes— sometimes you even know where my opponent stands. [*Laughter*] We both have records. I'm proudly running on mine. The Senator is running from his, and there's a reason why. There's a mainstream in American politics, and my opponent sits on the far left bank.

I'm a compassionate conservative and proudly so. I have a positive, optimistic vision for our future and a comprehensive strategy for victory in Iraq and the wider war against terror. My opponent has no plan, no vision, just a long list of complaints. [*Laughter*] But a Monday morning quarterback has never led any team to victory.

This election comes down to five clear choices for America's families: your family's security; your family's budget; your quality of life; your retirement; and the bedrock values that are so critical to our families and to our future.

The first clear choice is the most important because it concerns the security of your family. All progress on every other issue depends on the safety of our citizens. This will be the first Presidential election since September the 11th, 2001. Americans will go the polls in a time of war and ongoing threats. The terrorists who killed thousands are still dangerous and determined to strike us again. And this outcome—the outcome of this election will set the direction of the war against the terrorists. The most solemn duty of the American President is to protect the American people. If America shows uncertainty or weakness in this decade, the world will drift toward tragedy. This will not happen on my watch.

Since that terrible morning of September the 11th, 2001, we fought the terrorists across the Earth, not for pride, not for power but because the lives of our citizens are at stake. Our strategy is clear. We've strengthened the protections for the homeland. We're reforming our intelligence capabilities. We're transforming our military. There will be no draft; the All-Volunteer Army will remain an all-volunteer army. We're staying on the offensive. We are relentless. We are determined. We will strike the terrorists abroad so we do not have to face them here at home. We will continue to spread freedom and liberty. And we will prevail.

The President has to lead with consistency and strength. In a war, sometimes your tactics change but not your principles. Americans have seen how I do my job. Even when you might not agree with me, you know what I believe, you know where I stand, and you know what I intend to do.

Audience members. Four more years! Four more years! Four more years!

The President. On good days and on bad days, whether the polls are up or the polls are down, I am determined to protect the American people and I will always support the men and women who do.

My opponent has taken a different approach. It's fair to say that consistency has not been his strong point. Senator Kerry says we're better off with Saddam Hussein out of power, except when he declares that removing Saddam made us less safe. He said in our second debate that he always believed Saddam was a threat, except a few questions later when he said Saddam Hussein was not a threat. [*Laughter*] He says he was right when he voted to authorize the use of force against Saddam Hussein, but that I was wrong to use force against Saddam Hussein. [*Laughter*] Now my opponent is throwing out a wild claim that he knows where bin Laden was in the fall of 2001, that our military passed up a chance to get him at Tora Bora. It's an unjustified criticism of the military commanders in the field. It is the worst kind of Monday morning quarterbacking.

Tommy Franks was our commander in Afghanistan, and here's what he said about Tora Bora. He said, "The Senator's understanding of events does not square with reality." Tommy was there. Tommy says that Special Forces were actively involved in the search for the terrorists in Tora Bora and that intelligence reports at the time placed bin Laden in any of several countries.

Now, before Senator Kerry got into political difficulty and revised his views, here's what he said about Tora Bora on national TV in the fall of 2001. He said, "I think we've been doing this pretty effectively, and we should continue to do it that way." At the time, the Senator said about Tora Bora, "I think we've been smart. I think the administration leadership has done it well, and we are on the right track." Well, all I can say to that is, I am George W. Bush, and I approve of that message.

Yet, my opponent's record on national security has a far deeper problem than election-year flip-flopping. On the largest national security issues of our time, he has been consistently wrong. When Ronald Reagan was confronting the Soviet Union at the height of the cold war, Senator Kerry said that President Reagan's policy of peace through strength was making America less safe. Well, history has shown that Senator Kerry was wrong and President Ronald Reagan was right.

When former President Bush led a coalition against Saddam Hussein in 1991, Sen-

ator Kerry voted against the use of force to liberate Kuwait. If his view had prevailed, Saddam Hussein today would dominate the Middle East and possess the world's most dangerous weapons. History has shown that Senator Kerry was wrong and former President Bush was right.

In 1994, just one year after the first bombing of the World Trade Center, Senator Kerry proposed massive cuts in America's intelligence budget, so massive that even his colleague from Massachusetts opposed them. Well, history has shown that Senator Kerry was wrong and—got to be fair—Senator Kennedy was right.

Just last year, American troops in Iraq and Afghanistan needed $87 billion to help them on their missions, to make sure they had all that was necessary in harm's way. First, Senator Kerry said it would be irresponsible to vote against the troops, then he voted against the troops. You might remember perhaps the most famous quote of the 2004 campaign when he said, "I actually did vote for the $87 billion, before I voted against it." [*Laughter*] History has shown that Senator Kerry was right, then wrong, then briefly right, then wrong again. [*Laughter*]

You know, he's given quite a few answers about that vote, and finally, at one time he just said, "The whole thing was a complicated matter." My fellow Americans, there is nothing complicated about supporting our troops in combat. I thank our troops. I thank the families of our troops. And I thank the veterans who have set such a great example to our troops.

During the last 20 years, in key moments of challenge and decision for America, my opponent has chosen the position of weakness and inaction. With that record, he stands in opposition not just to me but to the great tradition of the Democratic Party. The party of Franklin Roosevelt, of Harry Truman, of John Kennedy is rightly remembered for confidence and resolve in times of war and hours of crisis. Senator Kerry has turned his back on "pay any price" and "bear any burden," and he has placed those commitments—replaced those commitments with "wait and see" and "cut and run." Many Democrats in this country do not recognize their party anymore. Today I want to speak to every one of them: If you believe that America should lead with strength and purpose and confidence in our ideals, I'd be honored to have your support, and I'm asking for your vote.

Audience members. Four more years! Four more years! Four more years!

The President. All the difference—all the differences I've outlined today add up to one big difference. My opponent says that September the 11th, in his words, did not change him much at all. And his policies make that clear. He says the war on terror is primarily a law enforcement and intelligence gathering operation.

My outlook was changed on September the 11th. A few days after the attacks, I stood where the buildings fell, in Ground Zero. It's a day I'll never forget—the workers in hardhats yelling at me at the top of their lungs, "Whatever it takes." I remember a guy grabbed me by the arm, he looked me square in the eye, and he said, "Do not let me down." After that morning, I wake—I've wakened up every morning thinking about how to better protect America. I will use every asset at our disposal. I will never relent in defending the security of the American people, whatever it takes.

The second clear choice concerns your family's budget. When I ran for President 4 years ago, I pledged to lower taxes for American families. And I kept my word. We doubled the child credit to help mothers and dads raise their children. We reduced the marriage penalty. Listen, I think the Tax Code ought to encourage marriage, not penalize marriage. We created the lowest bracket of 10 percent, so to help families. We're reduced income taxes for everybody who pays taxes.

Now, I want you to remind your friends and neighbors what we have overcome, the obstacles this economy has overcome. You know, the stock market had been in decline for 6 months prior to my arrival. We were headed into a recession. And these corporate scandals which affected the economy—we passed tough laws, by the way, and we made it abundantly clear we're not going to tolerate dishonesty in the boardrooms of America. And then we got attacked, and those attacks cost us about a million jobs in the 3 months after September the 11th. But because we cut your taxes, because we encouraged consumption and investment, because we recognized the contributions small-business owners make in this country, our economic policies have led us on the path to growth.

Our economy has been growing at rates as fast as any in nearly 20 years. We've added 1.9 million new jobs since August of 2003. The national unemployment rate is 5.4 percent. Let me put that in perspective for you: That's lower than the average rate of the 1970s, the 1980s, and the 1990s. Our farm economy is strong. I campaigned here in the caucuses, and I campaigned in 2000, and I've been coming back to your State saying, "I support ethanol." We're supporting ethanol. I said, "I'm going to come back and open up markets so Iowa farm products are all around the world." We've opened up markets. Our farmers are making a good living. The entrepreneurial spirit is strong. Small businesses are flourishing. The homeownership rate is at an alltime high. And the unemployment rate in the State of Iowa is 4.7 percent. Our policies are working, and we're not going to go back to the days of Federal spending and Federal taxes.

We have a different point of view on the budget. My opponent has different plans. He's going to take a big chunk out of your budget. Listen, he's promised $2.2 trillion in new spending in this campaign. That's trillion with a "T." [*Laughter*] That's a lot even for a Senator from Massachusetts. [*Laughter*]

And they asked him how he's going to pay for it. And he threw out the same old tired line, "We're going to tax the rich." Well, first of all, when you run up the top two brackets, you're taxing job creators. Do you realize most of the small businesses in America pay individual income taxes because they're either a Subchapter S or a sole proprietorship? Seventy percent of new jobs are created by small businesses. Senator Kerry's plan would tax the job creators of America, and that is bad economic policy.

And secondly, by taxing people who have earned over $200,000 or entities that have earned over $200,000, you raise between 600 and 800 billion dollars. It doesn't take much math to figure out that's far short of the 2.2 trillion he's promised. So there's a gap, a gap between what he's promised and how he's going to pay for it. And guess who usually fills the gap?

Audience members. We do!

The President. You do. The good news is, he's not going to tax you, because we're going to win Iowa and win a great victory.

The third clear choice involves the quality of life for our Nation's families. A good education and quality health care are important for our country's families. When I ran for President 4 years ago, I promised to challenge the soft bigotry of low expectations by reforming our public schools. I kept my word. We passed education reform to bring high standards into the classrooms and to make our schools accountable to our parents. We're seeing progress. Math and reading scores are rising. We are closing achievement gaps for minority students all across America. We'll build on these reforms. We'll extend them to our high schools so that no child is left behind in America.

We'll make sure health care is available and affordable. We'll expand health savings accounts so small—more small businesses can cover their workers and more families can get health care accounts they call their own and manage. In order to make sure our small businesses can afford health care, we ought to allow them to pool together, pool risk so they can afford insurance at the same discount that big companies get. We're going to make sure we take care of the poor and the indigent through community and rural health centers. We'll work hard to make sure every eligible child is enrolled in our Government's low-income health insurance program.

To make sure health care is available and affordable for you, we will do something about the frivolous lawsuits that are running up the cost of medicine and running good doctors out of practice. I have met too many good doctors who have quit practicing medicine. Some of the saddest tales are those of ob-gyns. These lawsuits are running up the cost of premiums to the point where they can't afford to stay in business. So they leave their community. Some of them quit the practice of medicine. And that means there are expectant moms who are desperate—desperately worried about whether or not they'll get the health care they need for their child and for themselves.

You cannot be pro-doctor and pro-patient and pro-personal-injury-lawyer at the same time. You have to make a choice. My opponent made his choice, and he put a personal-injury trial lawyer on the ticket. I have made my choice. I'm standing with the patients. I'm standing with doctors. I'm standing with small-business owners. I'm standing with hospitals. I'm for medical liability reform—now.

There is a big difference of opinion when it comes to health care between me and my opponent. I remember that debate when he looked right in the camera, and they asked him about his health care plan, and he said, "The Government doesn't have anything to do with it." I could barely contain myself. [*Laughter*]

The Government has got a lot to do with it. Eight out of ten people end up on a

Government program under his health care. Listen, when you make Medicaid more attractive, small businesses will stop providing insurance for their employees because the Government will. And that moves people from private care—private insurance to Government insurance. And you know what I know: When the Government starts writing the checks, the Government starts making the rules; and the Government starts making the rules, the Government starts making your decisions. They ration care; they decide what doctors you go to. No, Federal health care is the wrong prescription for health care in America. In all we do, we'll make sure the health decisions are made by doctors and patients, not by officials in Washington, DC.

The fourth clear choice in this election involves your retirement. We made a solemn commitment to America's seniors on Social Security and Medicare. When I ran for President 4 years ago, I promised to keep that commitment and improve Medicare by adding prescription drug coverage. I kept my word. You might remember the Medicare issue. People in Washington have been debating Medicare for years, and nothing got done. Well, thanks to working with Senator Grassley and Congressman Nussle, we got the job done for our seniors. Beginning in 2006, all seniors will be able to get prescription drug coverage under Medicare.

I remember coming to eastern Iowa during the congressional campaigns in 2002. I said that I understand Iowa's hospitals are not being treated fairly under Medicare. Nussle, you might remember—I stood and looked right in the camera. I said, "I'm going to work with Congressman Nussle and Senator Grassley to make sure Iowa's rural hospitals, in particular, are treated fairly." The bill I signed not only helps our seniors but it helps Iowa hospitals. I kept my word.

And we will keep the promise of Social Security for our seniors. And I want to remind you what happened in the 2000 campaign. I don't know if it's happened here yet or not, but it certainly happened in 2000, when they made it abundantly clear to people that if I got elected, our seniors were not going to get their Social Security checks. That's the old scare tactics that they like to use. You might remember those ads. As you gather up the vote, I want you to remind people, George W. did get elected, and our seniors did get their checks. I don't care how they put it or how they try to scare you, our seniors will continue to get their checks. And baby boomers like me, I think we're in pretty good shape when it comes to getting the checks when we retire.

But we need to worry about our children and our grandchildren when it comes to Social Security. We need to worry about whether or not there will be a Social Security system available for them when they retire. And that's why I think we ought to allow younger workers to take some of their own payroll taxes and set them in a personal savings account, an account that earns a better rate of return, an account that they can call their own.

My opponent has taken a different approach on this issue. He said he is going to protect Social Security, but he forgot to tell you he's the only candidate in this race who voted eight times for higher taxes on Social Security benefits.

Audience members. Boo-o-o!

The President. You're wondering why you got those taxes on your Social Security benefits—there's one reason why, Senator John Kerry. And then when he talks about reforming the system for our youngsters, he had nothing to offer. The job of a President is to confront problems, not pass them on to future Presidents and future generations. In a new term, I'll bring people together to strengthen the Social Security system for a younger generation.

And the final clear choice in this election is on the values that are so crucial to keeping our families strong. And here my opponent and I are miles apart. I stand for the appointment of Federal judges who know the difference between personal opinion and the strict interpretation of the law. I believe marriage is a sacred commitment, a pillar of our civilization, and I will defend it. This isn't a partisan issue. You know, when Congress passed the Defense of Marriage Act, which defined marriage as a union of a man and a woman, the vast majority of Democrats supported it and President Bill Clinton signed it into law. But Senator Kerry was part of the out-of-the-mainstream minority that voted against the Defense of Marriage Act.

Audience members. Boo-o-o!

The President. I believe reasonable people can find common ground on difficult issues. Republicans and Democrats came together and agreed we should ban the brutal practice of partial-birth abortion. I proudly signed that bill. But Senator Kerry was part of the out-of-the-mainstream minority that voted against the ban on partial-birth abortion. As a matter of fact, he voted against parental notification laws. He voted against the Unborn Victims of Violence Act. I'll continue to reach out to Americans of every belief and move this goodhearted Nation toward a culture of life.

I don't know if you remember this in the campaign, but at one point my opponent said you can find the heart and soul of America in Hollywood.

Audience members. Boo-o-o!

The President. Most families don't look to Hollywood for a source of values. The heart and soul of America is found in communities like Dubuque, Iowa.

All of these choices make this one of the most important elections in our history. The security and prosperity of our country is at stake. The health and education for families are important. The retirement of our seniors, the direction of our culture—they're all at stake. And the decision is in the best of hands; it's in the hands of the American people.

I've got a—I see a great America coming. I see a hopeful day. One of my favorite quotes—I hope it helps capture how I feel about America—is what a fellow Texan named Tom Lea wrote. He said, "Sarah and I live on the east side of the mountain. It's the sunrise side, not the sunset side. It is the side to see the day that is coming, not to see the day that has gone." In the course of this campaign, my opponent has spent much of the time talking about the day that has gone. I'm talking about the day that is coming. I'm talking about a great day for America.

We've been through a lot together in the last nearly 4 years. Because we've done the hard work of climbing the mountain, we can see the valley below. We'll protect our families. We'll build on their prosperity. We'll defend the deepest values. We'll continue to spread liberty and freedom, achieving the peace we all long for.

You know, when I campaigned in your State—around your State in the caucuses and in the 2000 general election, I made you this pledge: I said if I was honored to be elected, I would uphold the honor and the dignity of the office. With your help, with your hard work, I will do so for 4 more years.

Thanks for coming. God bless. We're on to victory. Thank you all.

NOTE: The President spoke at 4:03 p.m. at the Grand River Center. In his remarks, he referred to Dale Schultz, candidate in Wisconsin's Third Congressional District; Auditor of State Dave Vaudt of Iowa; David Roederer, Iowa State chair, Bush-Cheney '04, Inc.; former President Saddam Hussein of Iraq; Usama bin Laden, leader of the Al Qaida terrorist organization; and Gen. Tommy R. Franks, USA (Ret.), former combatant commander, U.S. Central Command.

Remarks in Lititz, Pennsylvania
October 27, 2004

The President. Listen, before I want to say something, I'm traveling with a guest and a friend who represents thousands of people all across this country who are affiliated with the Democrat Party. My friend has come from Georgia to share a message with you about how we're going to work with Republicans and Democrats and independents to carry the great State of Pennsylvania. Please welcome my friend Senator Zell Miller. [*Applause*] I'm thrilled to be traveling with him.

I told Zell when we landed, I said, "This is a good size crowd here, and there's a reason why: because we're going to carry Pennsylvania on November the 2d." And that's what I'm here to do. I'm here to ask for your vote and ask for your help. I'm asking that you turn out your friends and neighbors to the polls. I'm asking you to continue to make the phone calls and put up the signs. I'm asking you to do everything you can because with your help, we'll make America a safer country, a stronger country, and a better country for every single citizen.

Perhaps the most important reason to put me back into office is so that Laura will be the First Lady for 4 more years. When I asked her to marry me, she said, "Fine, just make me a promise." I said, "What is it?" "Promise me I'll never have to give a political speech." [*Laughter*] I said, "Okay, you got a deal." Fortunately, she didn't hold me to that deal. She is giving a lot of speeches, and when she does, the American people see a fine, compassionate, strong First Lady.

I'm proud of my runningmate, Dick Cheney. I admit it, he does not have the waviest hair in the race. [*Laughter*] You'll be happy to hear I didn't pick him because of his hairdo. I picked him because of his judgment. I picked him because of experi-ence. He's getting the job done for the American people.

What a great United States Senator Rick Santorum is. He and Zell serve in the Senate together. I'm proud to have Rick Santorum as my campaign manager for the State of Pennsylvania. I'm proud to—excuse me—call him friend, and I know you're proud to call him Senator. And I hope you put Arlen Specter back in there. We need to work with him for 6 more years.

I'm honored to be on the stage with Joe Pitts, Congressman from this area. I appreciate you being here, Joe. Thanks for your service. I want to thank Pat Toomey for the class he showed during the primary campaign. I appreciate his leadership and his service to the Congress.

I want to thank all the candidates who are here, people running for office. I wish you all the best coming down the stretch. I want to thank my friend Daron Norwood and the Matt Goss Band for singing.

Most of all, I want to thank you all. You've lifted our spirits for being here. You're kind with your time, and I want to thank you for coming. This election comes down to some clear choices——

Audience members. Four more years! Four more years! Four more years!

The President. This election comes down to some clear choices, clear choices for our families. We have issues of great consequence. The first clear choice is the most important because it concerns the security of your family. All the progress on every other issue depends on the safety of our citizens. It will be the first Presidential election since September the 11th, 2001. Americans will go to the polls in a time of war, an ongoing threat unlike any we have ever faced before. The terrorists who killed thousands are still dangerous, and they are determined to strike again. And the outcome of this election will set the direction of the war against the terrorists.

The most solemn duty of the American President is to protect the American people. If America shows uncertainty or weakness in this decade, the world will drift toward tragedy. This will not happen on my watch.

Since that terrible morning of September the 11th, 2001, we fought the terrorists across the Earth, not for pride, not for power but because the lives of our citizens are at stake. Our strategy is clear. We've strengthened the protection of the homeland. Tom Ridge, the former Governor of your State, is doing a great job as the Secretary of Homeland Security. We're strengthening our intelligence capabilities. We're transforming our military. There will be no draft. The All-Volunteer Army will remain an all-volunteer army. We're staying on the offensive. We're relentless. We are determined. We will strike the terrorists abroad so we do not have to face them here at home.

And part of our strategy is to spread liberty. We believe in the transformational power of liberty to change societies. Think what happened in Afghanistan; think about what's happened there. It wasn't all that long ago that young girls couldn't go to school, and if their mothers didn't toe the line of the ideologues of hate which ran that country, they were whipped in the public square and sometimes executed in a sports stadium. Because we acted in our self-interest, because we acted to destroy Al Qaida's capacity to train in Afghanistan, millions of people went to vote in a Presidential election. The first voter in that election was a 19-year-old woman. Freedom is on the march, and America is more secure for it.

Iraq will be having Presidential elections in January. That society has come a long way from the days of torture chambers and mass graves. Free societies are hopeful societies. By spreading freedom and liberty, we not only secure ourselves in the short

term, we spread the peace that we all long for so our children and our grandchildren can grow up in a hopeful tomorrow.

A President has to lead with consistency and strength. In a war, sometimes your tactics have to change but not your principles. Americans have seen how I do my job. Even when you might not agree with me, you know what I believe and where I stand and where I intend to lead our country. On good days and on bad days, whether the polls are up or the polls are down, I am determined to win this war on terror and to protect the American people. And I will always support the men and women who wear their Nation's uniform.

I want to thank those who wear the uniform. I want to thank the families of our military. And I want to thank the veterans who are here who have set such a great example. We have a duty to support those in harm's way with all the resources they need, necessary for them to do their job. That's why I went to the United States Congress and asked for $87 billion of supplemental funding to support our troops in combat. And we got good support in the Congress. Matter of fact, the support was so strong that only 12 United States Senators voted against the supplemental funding request, 2 of whom were my opponent and his runningmate.

Audience members. Boo-o-o!

The President. As you're out gathering the vote and as you're out talking to people about this election, remind people of this startling statistic: Only four members of the United States Senate voted to authorize the use of force and then voted against providing the funding for our troops in combat—only four, two of whom were my opponent and his runningmate.

Audience members. Boo-o-o!

The President. So they asked him—they asked him—I'm sure the people of Lancaster, Pennsylvania, are just as surprised as people all around the country when he gave his famous answer about his vote. He said, "I actually did vote for the $87 billion, right before I voted against it." [*Laughter*] He's given a lot of explanations since then, a lot of them. One of the most interesting ones of all was that it was just a complicated matter. There's nothing complicated about supporting our troops in combat.

After repeatedly calling Iraq the "wrong war" and a "diversion," Senator Kerry this week seemed shocked to learn that Iraq was a dangerous place full of dangerous weapons. [*Laughter*] The Senator used to know that, even though he seems to have forgotten it over the course of the campaign. But after all, that's why we're there. Iraq was a dangerous place run by a dangerous tyrant who had a lot of weapons. We have seized or destroyed more than 400,000 tons of munitions, including explosives, at more than a—thousands of different sites, and we're continuing to round up more weapons every day. I want to remind the American people, if Senator Kerry had his way, we would still be taking our "global test." Saddam Hussein would still be in power. He would control all those weapons and explosives and could have shared them with our terrorist enemies.

Now, the Senator is making wild charges about missing explosives when his top foreign policy adviser admits, quote, "We do not know the facts." Think about that. The Senator is denigrating the action of our troops and commanders in the field without knowing the facts. Unfortunately, that's part of a pattern of saying almost anything to get elected, like when Senator Kerry charged that our military failed to get Usama bin Laden at Tora Bora, even though our top military commander, General Tommy Franks, said, "The Senator's understanding of events does not square with reality." And our intelligence reports placed bin Laden in any of several different countries at the time.

Our military is now investigating a number of possible scenarios, including that the explosives may have been moved before our troops even arrived at the site. This investigation is important, and it's ongoing. And a political candidate who jumps to conclusions without knowing the facts is not a person you want as your Commander in Chief.

When it comes to your security—when it comes to the security of our families, my opponent takes a very different approach. He says that September the 11th did not change him much at all.

Audience members. Boo-o-o!

The President. And his policies make that clear. He says the war on terror is primarily a law enforcement and intelligence gathering operation. Well, September the 11th changed me. I remember the day I was in the—at Ground Zero, on September the 4th, 2001. It's a day I will never forget. There were workers in hardhats there yelling at me at the top of their lungs, "Whatever it takes." I remember a man grabbed me by the arm, he looked me square in the eye, and he said, "Do not let me down." Ever since that day, I wake up every morning trying to figure out how to better protect America. I will never relent in defending America, whatever it takes.

The second clear choice in this election concerns your family budget. When I ran for President 4 years ago, I pledged to lower taxes for American families. And I kept my word. We've doubled the child credit to $1,000 per child. We reduced the marriage penalty. The Tax Code should encourage marriage, not penalize marriage. We created the lowest—a lower tax bracket of 10 percent so working families would get help. We reduced income taxes for everybody who paid income taxes. We helped our farmers. We helped our ranchers. We helped our small-business owners. After-tax income—that's the money in your pocket—increased by about 10 percent since I became your President.

Our economy has been through a lot, and I want you to remind your friends and neighbors about these facts. First, 6 months prior to our arrival in Washington, the stock market was in serious decline, and then we had a recession. Then we had corporate scandals, and then the attacks of September the 11th cost us about a million jobs in the 3 months after that fateful day.

But we acted. By cutting the taxes, we spurred consumption and investment, and our economic policies have led us back to growth. Our economy is growing faster than in any nation in the industrialized world. We've added 1.9 million new jobs since August of 2003. The national unemployment rate is 5.4 percent, which is lower than the average rate of the 1970s, the 1980s, and the 1990s. The unemployment rate in Pennsylvania is 5.3 percent. Home-ownership rate is at an alltime high. Farm income is up. The small-business sector of our economy is flourishing. The entrepreneurial spirit is strong, and we're not going to go back to the days of tax and spend.

My opponent has very different plans for your budget. He's going to take a big chunk out of it. He voted against all the tax relief that I suggested Congress pass. If he'd had his way, the average family in America would be paying $2,000 more in taxes to the Federal Government.

Audience members. Boo-o-o!

The President. All told, during his 20 years in the United States Senate, he has voted to raise taxes 98 times. That's five times a year. I would call that a predictable pattern. [*Laughter*] When a Senator does something that often, he must really enjoy it. [*Laughter*] During this campaign, he's proposed $2.2 trillion of new spending. Now, that is a trillion with a "T." That's a lot even for a Senator from Massachusetts. [*Laughter*]

So they said, "How are you going to pay for it?" And he said, "Oh, we're just going to tax the rich." Now, you've heard that before. Be wary when you hear, "Oh, we're just going to tax the rich." My opponent has promised 2.2 trillion, but when you run up the top two brackets, you only raise between 600 and 800 billion. There is a

gap between that which he promised and that which he can deliver. And guess who usually fills that gap?

Audience members. We do!

The President. We're not going to let him tax you; we're going to carry Pennsylvania on November the 2d and win a great victory.

Audience members. Four more years! Four more years! Four more years!

The President. The third clear choice in this election involves the quality of life of our families. A good education and quality health care are important to a successful life. As a candidate, I pledged to challenge the soft bigotry of low expectations by reforming our public schools. And as President, I kept my word. We passed education reforms to bring high standards to our classrooms and to make schools accountable to our parents. We're seeing progress all across America. Math and reading scores are on the rise. Achievement gaps, particularly for minority students, are closing all across our country. We're building on these reforms. We'll extend them to our high schools so that no child is left behind in America.

We'll continue to improve our lives. We're making health care more accessible and affordable. We will expand health savings accounts so small businesses can cover their workers and more families are able to get health care accounts they manage and call their own. We will create association health plans so small businesses can join together and buy insurance at the same discounts that big companies are able to do. We will help families in need by expanding community health centers. We'll make sure every eligible child is enrolled in our Government's low-income health insurance programs.

And to help the families of Pennsylvania, we will do something about the frivolous lawsuits that are running up the cost of medicine and running good doctors out of practice. Like other States, you've got an issue when it comes to these medical liability lawsuits. I met too many good ob-gyns who have been run out of practice because their premiums have gone up too high. I have met expectant mothers here in Pennsylvania who are worried about whether they and their baby will get the health care they need. You cannot be pro-doctor and pro-patient and pro-personal-trial-lawyer at the same time. You have to make your choice. My opponent made his choice, and he put a personal injury trial lawyer on the ticket. I have made my choice. I'm standing with the doctors of Pennsylvania, with the patients of Pennsylvania. I'm for medical liability reform—now.

My opponent has got a different view when it comes to health care. I remember our debate, when he looked right in the camera and he said his health care plan, "the Government has nothing to do with it." I could barely contain myself. [*Laughter*]

The Government has got a lot to do with it. Eight out of ten people would be signed up to a Government program. Think about the idea of making it easier for people to sign up for Medicaid. It means small businesses will no longer provide coverage for their employees because the Government will. And people would be moved from private insurance to Government insurance. You see, when the Government writes the checks, the Government starts making the rules. And when it comes to health care, when the Government makes the rules, the Government starts making your decisions. And they start making the decisions for you, and they start making the decisions for the doctors.

His plan is a big Government-run health care plan. It is the wrong prescription for American families. In all we do to reform health care, we'll make sure the decisions are made by doctors and patients, not by officials in Washington, DC.

The fourth clear choice in this election involves your retirement. Our Nation has made a solemn commitment to America's seniors on Social Security and Medicare. When I ran for President 4 years ago, I promised to keep that commitment and improve Medicare by adding prescription drug coverage. I kept my word. Seniors are now getting discounts on medicine with drug discount cards. Low-income seniors are getting $600 of help this year and $600 of help next year to help them afford prescription drugs. And beginning in 2006, all seniors will be able to get prescription drug coverage under Medicare.

And we'll keep the promise of Social Security for our seniors, and as we do so, we'll strengthen Social Security for generations to come. I want you to remember what happened in the 2000 campaign. It is—it's pretty predictable what takes place when it comes to elections. You might remember, they said, "If George W. gets elected, our seniors will not get their checks." Well, I want you to remind your friends and neighbors when you're out gathering up the vote that George W. did get elected, and our seniors did get their checks. And our seniors will continue to get their checks under Social Security, no matter what the politicians try to scare you with. Baby boomers like me are in pretty good shape when it comes to the Social Security trust.

But we need to worry about our children and our grandchildren. We need to worry about whether the Social Security system will be there when they need it. And that's why I think younger workers ought to be able to take some of their own money and put it in a personal savings account, a savings account that will earn a better rate of return, a savings account they call their own, a savings account that the Government cannot take away.

My opponent takes a different approach when it comes to Social Security. He declared he will protect Social Security. But I want you to remind people that he voted eight times for higher taxes on Social Security benefits. And when it comes to the next generation, he hasn't offered anything at all when it comes to strengthening Social Security. The job of a President is to confront problems, not to pass them on to future generations and future Presidents. In a new term, I'll bring people together and strengthen the Social Security system for generations to come.

In this campaign, I'm speaking to the hopes of all Americans. The President's job is not to lead one party, but to serve the entire Nation. I'm proud to have lifelong Democrats like Zell Miller by my side, and he's joined by millions of other Democrats across our country who are supporting our ticket. As the citizens of this Nation prepare to vote, I want to speak directly to the Democrats. I'm a proud Republican, but I believe my policies appeal to many Democrats. In fact, I believe my opponent is running away from some of the great traditions of the Democrat Party. If you're a Democrat and you want America to be strong and confident in our ideals, I'd be honored to have your vote.

The Democratic Party has a great tradition of leading this country with strength and conviction in times of war and crisis. I think of Franklin Roosevelt's commitment to total victory. I think of Harry Truman's clear vision at the beginning of the cold war. I think of John Kennedy's brave declaration of American ideals. President Kennedy said, "The rights of man come not from the generosity of the state but from the hand of God."

Many Democrats look at my opponent and wonder where the—that great tradition of their party has gone. My opponent takes a narrow, defensive view of the war on terror. As the United States of America hunts down the terrorists and liberates millions from tyranny and aids the rise of liberty in distant lands, my opponent counsels retreat, votes against supporting our troops in combat, downplays the power of democracy, and accepts and adopts a narrow so-called realism that is little more than defeatism.

I believe American leadership is the hope of the repressed, the source of our great security, and the greatest force for good in this world. I believe the liberation of captive peoples is a noble achievement that all Americans can be proud of. If you are a Democrat who wants America to lead with strength and idealism, I would be honored to have your vote.

The Democratic Party has a tradition of support for our public schools. The party of Lyndon Johnson and Hubert Humphrey always stood up for the right of poor and minority children to get the best education America could offer. Many Democrats look at my opponent and wonder where that firm conviction has gone. Just as teachers and principals across America are lifting the sights of our schools and raising the test scores of minority children, my opponent is talking about weakening the standards and going back to the old days of stagnation and excuses for failure.

I got into politics and I ran for Governor of Texas because I wanted to challenge that soft bigotry of low expectations. I didn't want to stand by and watch another generation of students miss out on the opportunity of our great country. When I came to Washington, I made schools my first domestic priority. We've increased funding to record levels. We're demanding results for our children of every background. If you're a Democrat who believes in strong public schools that teach every child, I'd be honored to have your vote.

Americans of both political parties have always had respect and reverence for the institution of marriage. Never in our history has marriage been a partisan issue; it's not a partisan issue today. Yet, many Democrats look at my opponent and wonder, where is his commitment to defending the basic institution of civilization? He says he supports marriage, but he'll do nothing to defend it. My opponent even voted against the Defense of Marriage Act, which defined marriage as between a man and a woman. More than two-thirds of Democrats in the Senate supported that act, and President Bill Clinton signed it into law. On the issue of protecting marriage, the Senator from Massachusetts is outside the mainstream of America and outside the mainstream of the Democratic Party.

I believe that our society must show tolerance and respect for every individual, yet I do not believe this commitment of tolerance requires us to redefine marriage. If you are a Democrat who believes that marriage should be protected from activist judges, I'd be honored to have your vote.

The Democrat Party has also a great tradition of defending the defenseless. I remember the strong conscience of the late Democratic Governor from Pennsylvania, Robert Casey, who once said that when we look to the unborn child, the real issue is not when life begins but when love begins. I remember the moral clarity of the late Senator Daniel Patrick Moynihan, Democrat of New York, who said that partial-birth abortion is, quote, "as close to infanticide as anything I have ever come upon." Many Democrats look at my opponent and see an attitude that is much more extreme. He says that life begins at conception but denies that our caring society should prevent even partial-birth abortion.

Preventing partial-birth abortion is an ethical conviction shared by many people of every faith and by people who have no religion at all. I understand good people disagree on the life issue, so I've worked with Republicans and Democrats to find common ground on difficult questions and to move this goodhearted Nation toward a culture of life. If you're a Democrat who believes that our society must always have room for the voiceless and the vulnerable, I would be honored to have your vote.

There are Democrats all over America, north and south, east and west, who believe their party's nominee does not share their deepest values. I know the Democrats are not going to agree with me on every issue. Yet on the big issues of our country's security, victory in the war against terror, improving our public schools, respecting marriage and human life, I hope people who usually vote for the other party will take a close look at my agenda. If you're a Democrat and your dreams and goals are not found in the far left wing of the Democrat Party, I'd be honored to have your vote. And next Tuesday, I ask you to stand with me.

And I want to thank each and every one of you who have come today for standing with me. I appreciate your support. I appreciate your convictions. I appreciate your good work. I believe in the future of this country.

One of my favorite quotes was written by a Texan named Tom Lea. He said this, he said, "Sarah and I live on the east side of the mountain. It is the sunrise side, not the sunset side. It is the side to see the day that is coming, not to see the day that is gone." During the course of this campaign, my opponent has spent much of the time talking about the day that is gone. I'm talking about the day that is coming.

We've been through a lot together in the last 4 years. Because we've done the hard work of climbing that mountain, we can see the valley below. For the next 4 years, we'll protect our families. We'll build on the prosperity of our Nation. We will defend our deepest values. We will spread freedom and liberty around the world and continue to work for the peace we all long for.

You know, when I campaigned across this great State in 2000, I said if you gave me a chance to serve, I would uphold the honor and the integrity of the office to which I have been elected. With your help, with your hard work, I will do so for 4 more years.

Thanks for coming. God bless. Thank you all.

NOTE: The President spoke at 11:12 a.m. at the Lancaster Airport. In his remarks, he referred to entertainer Daron Norwood;

Usama bin Laden, leader of the Al Qaida terrorist organization; and Gen. Tommy R. Franks, USA (Ret.), former combatant commander, U.S. Central Command.

Remarks in Vienna, Ohio
October 27, 2004

The President. Thank you all for coming. Thanks so much for coming. My fellow Republicans, discerning Democrats, wise independents, I'm here to ask for your vote and ask for your help.

We're getting close to voting time here in Ohio. It's coming close to time for people to get out and exercise their responsibility in a free society. And so I'm asking you to get people to go to the polls. I'm asking you to get your friends and neighbors to do their duty. Don't overlook discerning Democrats, people like the mayor and Senator Miller. Don't overlook people who understand that I stand for all of America, that my vision is a vision for everybody. And when you get them headed to the polls, remind them, if they want a safer America, a stronger America, and a better America, to put me and Dick Cheney back in office.

Perhaps the most important reason why your fellow citizens ought to vote for me is so that Laura is the First Lady for 4 more years. I'm sure many of you will relate to this. When I asked Laura to marry me, she said, "Fine, but make me a promise." I said, "Okay, what is it?" She said, "Promise me I'll never have to give a political speech." [*Laughter*] I said, "Okay, you got a deal." Fortunately, she didn't hold me to that promise. She's giving a lot of speeches, and when she speaks, the American people see a warm, compassionate, strong First Lady.

I'm proud of my runningmate, Dick Cheney. Now, look, I admit it, he does not have the waviest hair in the race. [*Laughter*] I see some others who are follically challenged. [*Laughter*] But you'll be happy to hear I did not pick the man because of his hairdo. [*Laughter*] I picked him because of his experience. I picked him because of his judgment. I picked him because he can get the job done for the American people.

Nothing better than traveling throughout Ohio with Zell Miller. What a good man, good, down-to-earth, solid citizen of the United States of America. Zell, we're proud you're here.

And I want to thank George McKelvey, the mayor of Youngstown, Ohio. I can't thank him enough for his friendship and his strong support.

I'm proud to be with your fine Governor, Bob Taft. Governor, thanks for being here. I want to thank all the State and local officials, all the candidates who are running for different offices.

I want to thank my friend Sammy Kershaw. I appreciate you, Sammy. And I want to thank Lorrie Morgan as well. We're honored you're here. I want to thank the Boardman High School marching band for being here.

Most of all, I want to thank you all for coming. You're lifting my soul and lifting my spirits. It is so great to see such a big crowd. I want to thank you for putting up the signs. I want to thank you for making the phone calls. I want to thank you for what you're going to do as we're coming down the stretch, which is to turn out that vote. With your help, there is no doubt in my mind, we will carry Ohio again and win a great victory.

Audience members. Four more years! Four more years! Four more years!

The President. Thank you all. This election comes down to some clear choices for America's families, choices on issues of great consequence.

The first clear choice is the most important because it concerns the security of your family. All progress on every other issue depends on the safety of our citizens. This will be the first Presidential election since September the 11th, 2001. Americans will go to the polls in a time of war and ongoing threats to our Nation. The terrorists who killed thousands are still dangerous, and they're determined. The outcome of this election will set the direction of the war against terror.

The most solemn duty of the American President is to protect the American people. If America shows uncertainty or weakness in this decade, the world will drift toward tragedy. This will not happen on my watch.

Since that terrible morning of September the 11th, 2001, we have fought the terrorists across the Earth, not for pride, not for power, but because the lives of our citizens are at stake. Our strategy is clear. We've strengthened the protections for the homeland. We're reforming our intelligence services. We're transforming our military. There will be no draft; the All-Volunteer Army will remain an all-volunteer army. We are relentless. We are steadfast. We are pursuing the enemy across the Earth so we do not have to face them here at home.

And we are spreading liberty. I want you to tell your children what a monumental event has taken place in Afghanistan. It wasn't all that long ago that young girls couldn't go to school, and if their mothers didn't toe the line of the ideologues of hate, the Taliban, they were pulled out in the public square and whipped and sometimes executed. But because we acted in our self-defense, because we acted to remove terrorist training camps in Afghanistan, because we upheld doctrine that said, "If you harbor a terrorist, you're equally as guilty as the terrorist," millions of people in Af-

ghanistan went to the polls to vote for a President. The first voter was a 19-year-old woman. Freedom is on the march.

Iraq will have Presidential elections. Think how far that country has come from the days of torture chambers and mass graves. We believe everybody wants to be free. We believe in the power of liberty to transform societies. And we believe that not because freedom is America's gift to the world; freedom is the Almighty God's gift to each man and woman in this world.

A President must lead with consistency and strength. In war, sometimes you change your tactics but never your principles. Americans have seen how I do my job. Even when you might not agree with me, you know where I stand, you know what I believe, and you know where I intend to lead this country. On good days and on bad days, whether the polls are up or the polls are down, I am determined to protect the American people. I will continue to lead with resolve. And I can assure you, I will always stand by the men and women who wear our Nation's uniform as they protect us.

And that's why I went to the United States Congress in September of 2003, asking for $87 billion to support our troops in harm's way. It was vital funding request. We got good support for that request except from a handful of people. I see we got a lot of veterans here. I want to thank you for serving and setting such a great example. You all know what I'm talking about when I say "support our troops in harm's way." You know how important that is. Well, most of them in Congress understood how important it was. I want you to tell your friends and neighbors, Republicans, Democrats, independents, about this startling statistic: There were only four Members of the United States Senate that voted to authorize the use of force and then did not provide the funding to our troops in combat—only four, two of whom were my opponent and his runningmate.

Audience members. Boo-o-o!

The President. So they asked him about that vote, and you might remember perhaps the most famous quote of the 2004 campaign when John Kerry said, "I actually did vote for the $87 billion, right before I voted against it."

Audience members. Boo-o-o!

The President. You know, I haven't spent as much time in Youngstown as the mayor has, but you know, I talked to the mayor, and he assures me not many people in Youngstown, Ohio, talk like that. [*Laughter*] People in this part of the world like somebody who shoots straight with them.

They finally pressed him, and Senator Kerry finally said, after about four or five different answers as to—about why he made the vote he made, he said, "The whole thing was a complicated matter." My fellow Americans, there is nothing complicated about supporting our troops in combat.

A President must be consistent. After repeatedly calling Iraq the "wrong war" and a "diversion," Senator Kerry this week seemed shocked to learn that Iraq was a dangerous place full of dangerous weapons. [*Laughter*] The Senator used to know that, even though he seems to have forgotten it over the course of this campaign. But after all, that's why we went into Iraq. Iraq was a dangerous place run by a dangerous tyrant who hated America and who had a lot of weapons. We've seized or destroyed more than 400,000 tons of munitions, including explosives, at more than thousands of sites. And we're continuing to round up the weapons almost every day.

I want to remind the American people, if Senator Kerry had his way, we would still be taking our "global test."

Audience members. Boo-o-o!

The President. Saddam Hussein would still be in power.

Audience members. Boo-o-o!

The President. He would control all those weapons and explosives and could have shared them with our terrorist enemies.

Audience members. Boo-o-o!

The President. Now the Senator is making wild charges about missing explosives, when his top foreign policy adviser admits, "We don't know the facts," end quote. Think about that. The Senator is denigrating the actions of our troops and commanders in the field without knowing the facts. Unfortunately, that's part of the pattern of saying anything it takes to get elected, like when he charged that our military failed to get Usama bin Laden at Tora Bora, even though our top military commander, General Tommy Franks, said, "The Senator's understanding of events does not square with reality," and intelligence reports place bin Laden in any of several different countries at the time.

See, our military is now investigating a number of possible scenarios, including this one: that explosives may have been moved before our troops even arrived—even arrived at the site. The investigation is important and ongoing. And a political candidate who jumps to conclusions without knowing the facts is not the person you want as the Commander in Chief.

We have a very different perspective when it comes to protecting the American people. Senator Kerry says that September the 11th did not change him much at all.

Audience members. Boo-o-o!

The President. Those were his words. That's what he said. And his policies make that clear. He says the war on terror is primarily a law enforcement and intelligence gathering operation. My outlook was changed on September the 11th. It changed my view of risks we face.

I'll never forget the day when I was at Ground Zero on September the 14th, 2001. The sights and sounds of that day will never escape my memory. Workers in hardhats were yelling at me at the top of their lungs, "Whatever it takes." I remember the man coming out and grabbing me by the arm and looking me square in the eye, and he said, "Do not let me down." Ever since that day, I have awakened wondering how best to protect this country, trying to figure out everything we can do to protect you. I will never relent in defending America, whatever it takes.

The second clear choice in this election concerns your families' budget, your wallet. When I ran for President 4 years ago, I pledged to lower taxes for American families. I kept my word. We doubled the child credit to $1,000 per child to help you raise your kids. We reduced the marriage penalty. We believe the Tax Code ought to encourage marriage, not penalize marriage. We dropped the lowest tax bracket to 10 percent to help the working Americans. We reduced income taxes for everybody who pays taxes.

I want you to tell your friends and neighbors, remind them before they go to the polls, what our economy has been through. Six months prior to my arrival in Washington, the stock market was in serious decline—six months prior to my arrival. Then we had a recession. Then we had some corporate scandals. We passed laws, tough laws that now make it abundantly clear we will not tolerate dishonesty in the boardrooms of America. We lost nearly one million jobs after the attacks on our country on September the 11th, 2001. We have been through a lot.

But our economic policies, our policies of helping the small businesses and helping the families, have led us back to growth. Our economy is growing as fast as any in nearly 20 years. Homeownership rate is at an alltime high in America. We have added 1.9 million new jobs in the last 13 months. The national unemployment rate is 5.4 percent. That's lower than the average rate of the 1970s, 1980s, and 1990s. I understand you've had tough times in Ohio. I know that. I've traveled your State a lot. But let me remind you, things are getting better here. The unemployment rate dropped from 6.3 percent to 6 percent last month. We added 5,500 new jobs in one month here in the State of Ohio.

But there's more work to be done. There's more work to be done. I signed a bill last week to help our manufacturing sector here in Ohio and across the country. We'll continue to support our community colleges. We've expanded trade adjustment assistance to make sure our workers have got the skills necessary to fill the jobs of the 21st century. We have overcome a lot together. Our economy is strong, and it is getting stronger.

My opponent has a different point of view, a different view about your family's budget. To put it bluntly, he intends to take a big chunk out of it.

Audience members. Boo-o-o!

The President. He voted for all the tax relief—against all the tax relief. We put the tax relief up there to stimulate the economy, to encourage consumption, to help investment, to stimulate our small businesses. And he voted "no." If he had had his way, the average family in America would be paying 2,000 more dollars in income taxes to the Federal Government.

Audience members. Boo-o-o!

The President. He's been in the United States Senate 20 years, and he's voted to raise taxes 98 times. That's five times a year. I would call that a predictable pattern. [*Laughter*] I would call that as an indicator. When a Senator does something that often, he must really enjoy it. [*Laughter*] I also want to remind you, he's promised $2.2 trillion of new Federal spending. That's trillion with a "T." That's a lot even for a Senator from Massachusetts.

So they asked him, "How are you going to pay for it?" He threw out that same old, tired line we've heard every 4 years: "Oh, I'll pay for it by taxing the rich." The problem is, is that when you raise the top two brackets, you only raise between 600 and 800 billion dollars. There is what I would call a tax gap. That would be the difference between what he's promised and what he can pay for. And when you have a tax gap like that and you've got a man of his record running for President, guess who usually gets to pay?

Audience members. We do!

The President. Here's the good news. We're not going to let him tax you; we're going to carry Ohio and win a great victory. Senator Kerry can run from his record, but he cannot hide.

Third clear choice in this election involves the quality of life for our families. A good education and quality health care are important for our families. As a candidate, I pledged to challenge the soft bigotry of low expectations by reforming our public schools. I kept my word. We passed education reforms to bring high standards to our schools. We increased Federal spending, but instead—in return for Federal spending, increases of Federal spending, we said, "Measure. Show us." We believe in accountability. You cannot solve a problem unless you diagnose a problem. We are diagnosing and solving problems all across America. Math and reading scores are up. The achievement gap for minority students across our country is closing. We'll extend these kind of reforms and high standards to our high schools so that no child is left behind in America.

We'll improve our lives for our families by making sure health care is affordable and accessible. We'll take care of the low-income and the needy by expanding community health centers across our country. We will work to make sure our low-income children's health program is fully subscribed. To make sure health care is affordable, we will promote health savings accounts, which will help our families and small businesses better afford insurance. We will allow small businesses to pool risk, to join together so they can buy insurance at the same discounts big companies are able to do.

And to help families and small businesses afford health care, we will do something about the frivolous lawsuits that are running up the cost of health care. We have a problem when it comes to these lawsuits. I have met too many ob-gyns that are being run out of the practice of medicine because their premiums are too high. I have met too many pregnant moms who are worried about their health care and the health care of their child because they can't find an ob-gyn that's close to the community in which they live. This is a national problem that requires a national solution. You cannot be pro-doctor, pro-patient, and pro-personal-injury-trial-lawyer at the same time. You have to choose. My opponent made his choice, and he put a personal-injury trial lawyer on the ticket.

Audience members. Boo-o-o!

The President. I have made my choice. I'm standing with the doctors of Ohio, the patients of Ohio. I'm for medical liability reform—now.

I remember one of those debates when my opponent looked straight in the camera and said—when asked about his health care plan, he said, "The Government doesn't have anything to do with it." I could barely contain myself. [*Laughter*]

The Government has got a lot to do with it. About 80 percent of the people who sign up for health insurance under his plan will end up on the Government. Do you realize, when you make it easier for people to get on Medicaid, small businesses will no longer provide insurance because the Government will provide insurance, moving people from the private sector to the Government? Now, listen, when the Government starts writing checks, the Government starts making rules. And when the Government starts making rules, the Government starts making decisions on behalf of the people, and the Government starts to ration health care, and they decide your doctors, and then they start telling your doctors what to do. Federally-run health care is the wrong prescription for America's families. In all we do to improve health care, we'll make sure the decisions are made by doctors and patients, not by officials in Washington, DC.

The fourth clear choice in this election involves your retirement. Our Nation has made a solemn commitment to our seniors on Social Security and Medicare. When I ran for President 4 years ago, I promised to keep that commitment and improve Medicare by adding prescription drugs. I kept my word. We are strengthening Medicare. Seniors are now getting discounts on medicine with drug discount cards. Poor seniors can get $600 worth of help on their drug discount card this year and next year. And beginning in 2006, all seniors will be able to get a prescription drug benefit when it comes to Medicare.

And we'll keep our promise of Social Security for our seniors. Let me remind you about what took place in the 2000 campaign. That same old, tired scare tactic was unleashed—probably being done today too, who knows. People said, "If George W. gets elected, our seniors will not get their checks." Now, I want you to remind your friends and neighbors, George W. did get elected, and the seniors did get their checks. And our seniors will continue to get their checks. And baby boomers like me and a couple of others I see out there, we're in pretty good shape when it comes to the Social Security trust.

But we need to worry about our children and our grandchildren. We need to worry about whether or not Social Security will be available for them when they retire. I believe younger workers ought to be able to take some of their own money and set up a personal savings account, an account that earns a better rate of return, an account they call their own, an account the Government cannot take away.

My opponent takes a different approach. He has said that he is going to protect Social Security, but I want you to remind your friends and neighbors of this fact: He's the only candidate in this race who has voted eight times for higher taxes on Social Security benefits.

Audience members. Boo-o-o!

The President. He can run from that record, but I'm not going to let him hide.

And when it comes to the next generation, when it comes to our children and our grandchildren, he hasn't offered any

reform. See, the job of a President is to confront problems, not to pass them on to future generations and future Presidents. In a new term, I'll bring Republicans and Democrats together to strengthen Social Security so our children will be able to have a Social Security system that works.

In this campaign, I'm speaking to the hopes of all Americans. The President's job is not to lead one party but to serve one Nation. I'm proud to have lifelong Democrats like Zell and George by my side in this campaign, and they're joined by millions of other Democrats all across this country. As the citizens of this Nation prepare to vote, I want to speak directly to the Democrats. I'm a proud Republican, but I believe my policies appeal to many Democrats. In fact, I believe my opponent is running away from some of the great traditions of the Democratic Party. If you're a Democrat and you want America to be strong and confident in our ideals, I would be honored to have your vote.

The Democratic Party has a great tradition of leading this country with strength and conviction in times of war. I think of Franklin Roosevelt's commitment to total victory. I think of Harry Truman's clear vision at the beginning of the cold war. I think of John Kennedy's brave declaration of American ideals. President Kennedy said, "The rights of man come not from the generosity of the state, but from the hand of God."

Many Democrats look at my opponent and wonder where that great tradition of their party has gone. My opponent takes a narrow, defensive view of the war on terror. As the United States of America hunts down the terrorists and liberates millions from tyranny and aids the rise of liberty in distant lands, my opponent counsels retreat. He votes against supporting our troops in combat. He downplays the power of democracy and adopts a narrow so-called realism that is little more than defeatism.

I believe—I believe that American leadership is the hope of the oppressed, the source of security, and the greatest force for good in this world. I believe the liberation of captive peoples is a noble achievement that all Americans can be proud of. I believe that our troops in the field need our support 100 percent of the time.

If you are a Democrat who wants America to lead with strength and idealism, I would be honored to have your support. The Democratic party has a tradition for support of our public schools. I think about Lyndon Johnson and Hubert Humphrey, who always stood up for the right of the poor and minority children to get the best education America could offer. Many Democrats look at my opponent and wonder where that firm conviction has gone. Just as teachers and principals across America are lifting the sights of our schools and raising the test scores of minority children, my opponent is talking about weakening the standards and going back to the old days of stagnation and excuses for failure.

Audience members. Boo-o-o!

The President. I got into politics and I ran for Governor of my State because I would not stand by and watch another generation of students miss out on the opportunity of America. And when I came to Washington, I made schools my top domestic priority. If you are a Democrat who believes in strong public schools that teach every child, I'd be honored to have your vote.

Americans of both political parties have always had respect and reverence for the institution of marriage. Never in our history has marriage been a partisan issue, and it's not a partisan issue today. Yet, many Democrats look at my opponent and wonder, where is his commitment to defending the basic institution of civilization?. He says he supports marriage, but he will do nothing to defend it.

Audience members. Boo-o-o!

The President. My opponent even voted against the Defense of Marriage Act, which defined marriage as between a man and a woman. And two-thirds of the Democrats

in the Senate supported it, and my predecessor, Bill Clinton, signed it into law. On the issue of protecting marriage, the Senator from Massachusetts is outside the mainstream of America and outside the mainstream of the Democratic Party.

I believe that our society must show tolerance and respect for every individual. Yet, I do not believe this commitment to tolerance requires us to redefine marriage. If you are a Democrat who believes that marriage should be protected from activist judges, I'd be honored to have your vote.

The Democrat Party is also a great tradition of defending the defenseless. I remember the strong conscience of the late Democratic Governor of Pennsylvania, Robert Casey, who once said that when he looked to an unborn child, the real issue is not when life begins but when love begins. I remember the moral clarity of the late Senator Daniel Patrick Moynihan, Democrat of New York, who said that partial-birth abortion is, quote, "as close to infanticide as anything I have come upon."

Many opponents—many Democrats look at my opponent and see an attitude that is much more extreme. He says that life begins at conception but denies that our caring society should prevent even partial-birth abortion.

Audience members. Boo-o-o!

The President. He voted against the ban on partial-birth abortion.

Audience members. Boo-o-o!

The President. I proudly signed the ban on partial-birth abortion. Preventing partial-birth abortion is an ethical conviction shared by many people of every faith and by people who have no religion at all. I understand good people disagree on the life issue, and I'll continue to work with Republicans and Democrats to find common ground on the difficult questions and move this goodhearted Nation toward a culture of life. If you are a Democrat who believes that our society must always have room for the voiceless and the vulnerable, I would be honored to have your vote.

I know that Democrats are not going to agree with me on every issue, yet on the big issues of our country's security, victory in the war against terror, improving our public schools, respecting marriage and human life, I hope people who usually vote for the other party will take a close look at my agenda. If you are a Democrat and your dreams and goals are not found on the far left wing of the Democratic Party, I'd be honored to have your vote. And next Tuesday, I ask you to stand with me.

Audience members. Four more years! Four more years! Four more years!

The President. I am optimistic about our great land. I love my country. The great strength of America is found in the hearts and souls of our people. What a fantastic land we have. One of my favorite quotes was written by a fellow Texan, a fellow named Tom Lea. And here's what he said, he said, "Sarah and I live on the east side of the mountain. It is the sunrise side, not the sunset side. It is the side to see the day that is coming, not to see the day that is gone." You know, my opponent has spent much of this campaign talking about the day that is gone. I'm talking about the day that is coming.

Because we have done the hard work of climbing that mountain, we can see the valley below. Over the next 4 years, we'll work to protect our families; we'll build our prosperity; we will defend the deepest values. Over the next 4 years, we'll continue to spread liberty so we can achieve the peace we want for our children and our grandchildren.

When I traveled your State 4 years ago, I made you this pledge: I said if I was— if I happened to win that election, I would uphold the honor and the dignity of the office to which I had been elected. With your help, I will do so for 4 more years.

God bless. Thank you all for coming. Thank you all.

NOTE: The President spoke at 2:16 p.m. at the Youngstown-Warren Regional Airport. In his remarks, he referred to entertainers Sammy Kershaw and Lorrie Morgan; former President Saddam Hussein of Iraq; Usama bin Laden, leader of the Al Qaida terrorist organization; and Gen. Tommy R. Franks, USA (Ret.), former combatant commander, U.S. Central Command.

Remarks in Findlay, Ohio
October 27, 2004

The President. Thank you all for coming. You know, it is such a beautiful day in Flag City, I think I'll just take off my jacket and stay a while. Thanks for coming out. You are lifting our spirits. We're honored you're here. And Laura and I have come with the great Senator from Georgia to not only ask for your vote but to ask for your help. We need your help coming down the stretch to get your friends and neighbors to go to the polls.

We have a duty in our democracy to vote. We have an obligation to vote. So I'm asking you to tell your friends and neighbors about that obligation. Get our Republicans to go out there. Get independents to go out there. And find those discerning Democrats like Zell Miller and head them to the polls. And when you get them to the polls, remind them, if they want a safer America and a stronger America and a better America, to put me and Dick Cheney back in office.

Audience members. Four more years! Four more years! Four more years!

The President. I have been traveling your State a lot, and I enjoy it. I have had a chance to say hello to a lot of the citizens from Ohio. And I've been telling them why they ought to put me back in office. But perhaps the most important reason why I ought to have 4 more years is so that Laura is the First Lady for 4 more years. I'm sure some will be able to relate to this story. You know, Laura and I went to the seventh grade together in San Jacinto Junior High in Midland, Texas. We became reacquainted. She was a public school librarian, and when I asked her to marry me, she said, "Fine, but make me a promise." I said, "Okay, what is it?" She said, "Promise me I'll never have to give a political speech." [*Laughter*] I said, "Okay, you got a deal." Fortunately, she did not hold me to that promise. She is giving a lot of speeches, and when she does, the American people see a warm, compassionate, strong First Lady.

I'm looking around. I see some people out there who are follically challenged. [*Laughter*] And think about that, it reminds me of my Vice President. [*Laughter*] Dick Cheney is a great Vice President. He does not have the waviest hair in the race. [*Laughter*] But you all will be pleased to hear, I didn't pick him because of his hairdo. I picked him because of his judgment. I picked him because of his experience. I picked him because he's getting the job done for the American people.

It's a joy to travel with my friend Zell Miller. He's strong. He is courageous. He puts party aside and puts his country first, and for that, I am grateful.

I call him Ox; you call him Congressman. Mike Oxley is as fine as they are in the House of Representatives. He's a good man, and I appreciate his service. And I want to thank his wife, Pat, for joining us as well. And I am proud to be up here, or close by, with the fine United States Senator, Michael DeWine. He's doing a good job for the people of Ohio, as is George Voinovich. Make sure you put

George back in. And I appreciate Fran DeWine joining us. I want to thank Congressman Paul Gillmor for being here today.

I want to thank your Governor, Bob Taft, for joining us today. Mr. Governor, I appreciate your service to the State of Ohio. I want to thank Jennette Bradley for joining us today, the Lieutenant Governor of the State of Ohio.

I appreciate Mayor Iriti for joining us today. Mr. Mayor, you didn't ask me for any advice, but I'm going to give you some: Fill the potholes. Mayor Iriti is a good man, and I appreciate him being here. And I want to thank you, Mr. Mayor, for serving. I want to thank all the other State and local officials.

I want to thank the Findlay High School Marching Band for joining us. I want to thank Wil Gravatt Band for joining us today.

Most of all, I want to thank you all. I want to thank the grassroots activists, the people who are putting up the signs, the people making the phone calls, the people who have worked so hard to make this rally such a successful rally. I want to thank you for what you have done, and I want to thank you for what you are going to do, which is turn out that vote. And with your help, there is no doubt in my mind, we'll carry Ohio again and win a great victory on November the 2d.

This election comes down to some clear choices for America's families, choices on issues of great consequence. The first clear choice is the most important because it concerns the security of your family. All progress on every other issue depends on the safety of our citizens. This will be the first Presidential election since September the 11th, 2001. Americans will go to the polls in a time of war and of ongoing threat unlike any we have faced before. The terrorists who kill thousands of innocent people are still dangerous, and they are determined to strike. The outcome of this election will set the direction of the war against terror. The most solemn duty of the American President is to protect the American people. If America shows uncertainty or weakness in this decade, the world will drift toward tragedy. This will not happen on my watch.

Since that terrible morning of September the 11th, 2001, we have fought the terrorists across the Earth, not for pride, not for power but because the lives of our citizens are at stake. Our strategy is clear. We have strengthened the protections for the homeland. We're reforming our intelligence capabilities. We're transforming the United States military. We will keep the All-Volunteer Army an all-volunteer army. There will be no draft. We are relentless. We are determined. We are staying on the offensive so we do not have to face these terrorists here at home.

And we're spreading freedom and liberty. Some amazing things have happened in a short period of time. I want the youngsters here to understand what has happened in the world. In Afghanistan, 3½ years ago, young girls couldn't go to school. And if their mothers did not toe the line of the ideologues of hate who ran that country, they were whipped in the public square, sometimes executed in a sports stadium. We acted to defend ourselves. We upheld the doctrine that said, "If you harbor a terrorist, you're equally as guilty as the terrorist." And in so doing, we liberated people from the clutches of those barbaric people called the Taliban. Millions of people went to vote in a Presidential election. The first voter was a 19-year-old woman. Freedom is on the march.

It's never easy to go from tyranny to liberty, but that's where we're headed. There will be elections in Iraq. Think how far that country has come from the days of mass graves and torture chambers. I believe everybody in the world yearns to be free. I believe people deep in their soul want to live in a free society. I believe that because freedom is not America's gift to the world; freedom is the Almighty God's gift to each man and woman in this world.

A President must lead with consistency and strength. In a war, sometimes you have to change your tactics but never your principles. Americans have seen how I do my job. Even when you might not agree with me, you know what I believe, you know where I stand, and you know what I intend to do. On good days and on bad days, whether the polls are up or the polls are down, I will do everything we can do to defend the American people and win this war against the terrorists. And I will always support the men and women who wear our Nation's uniform.

We have got a great United States military. And I am proud to be their Commander in Chief. I want to thank the families of those who wear our Nation's uniform. I want to thank you for your sacrifices. I want to thank the veterans who are here today for having set such a great example for those who wear the uniform.

As I've told families all across this country, we will make sure your loved ones have the support necessary to complete their missions. And that's why I went to the United States Congress and asked for $87 billion of supplemental funding in September of 2003, necessary funding, important funding to support our troops in harm's way. And we received good support for that. As a matter of fact, the support was so strong that only 12 Members of the United States Senate voted against funding for our troops, 2 of whom were my opponent and his runningmate.

Audience members. Boo-o-o!

The President. Now, I would like for you to share this startling statistic with your friends and neighbors as you get them going to the polls: There were only 4 Members of the United States Senate—4 out of 100—that voted to authorize the use of force and then voted against supporting our troops in harm's way, and 2 of those 4 were my opponent and his runningmate.

Audience members. Boo-o-o!

The President. Now, you might remember his—Senator Kerry's explanation about that vote. He said, "I actually did vote for the $87 billion, right before I voted against it." Now, I haven't spent much time in the coffee shops of Findlay, but I suspect you're not going to find many people in this part of the world who talk that way.

They kept pressing him about it. He's given four or five different explanations about the vote. One of the most interesting ones of all that speaks to my opponent, said, "Well, the whole thing was just a complicated matter." [*Laughter*] There's nothing complicated about supporting our troops in harm's way.

After repeatedly calling Iraq the "wrong war" and a "diversion," Senator Kerry, this week, seemed shocked to learn that Iraq was a dangerous place full of dangerous weapons. [*Laughter*] The Senator used to know that, even though he seems to have forgotten it over the course of the campaign. But that's why we went there. See, Iraq was a dangerous place run by a dangerous tyrant who hated the United States. And he had a lot of weapons. And we've seized or destroyed more than 400,000 tons of munitions, including explosives at thousands of sites. And we're continuing to round up weapons nearly every day.

Now, I want to remind you all, if Senator Kerry had had his way, we would still be taking our "global test."

Audience members. Boo-o-o!

The President. And Saddam Hussein would still be in power, and he would control all those weapons and explosives and could have shared them with a terrorist enemy. Now, the Senator is making wild charges about missing explosives. One of his top foreign policy advisers admits he doesn't know the facts. He said, "I don't know the truth," end quote. Well, think about that. The Senator is denigrating the actions of our troops and commanders in the field without knowing the facts. Our military is now investigating a number of possible scenarios, including that the explosives may have been moved before our troops even arrived at the site. This investigation is important, and it is ongoing. And a political candidate who jumps to conclusions without knowing the facts is not the person you want as the Commander in Chief.

Unfortunately, that is part of a pattern. My opponent is throwing out the wild claim that he knows where bin Laden was in the fall of 2001 and that our military passed up a chance to get him at Tora Bora. You might remember that. He kept repeating that in the debates. Well, this is unjustified criticism of our military commanders in the field. This is the kind of—worst kind of Monday morning quarterbacking, what we've come to expect from him, however.

In fact, our commander in Afghanistan, General Tommy Franks, recently wrote this about Tora Bora: "The Senator's understanding of events does not square with reality." He went on to say—the General says, "American Special Forces were actively involved in the search for the terrorists at Tora Bora" and that "intelligence reports at the time placed bin Laden in any of several countries." That's what Tommy Franks, who knew what he's talking about, said.

Before Senator Kerry got into political difficulty and revised his views, he saw our actions in Tora Bora differently. In the fall of 2001, on national television, he said this about Tora Bora: "I think we've been doing this pretty effectively, and we should continue to do it that way." At the time, the Senator said about Tora Bora: "I think we have been smart. I think the administration leadership has done it well, and we are on the right track," end quote. All I can say about that is, I am George W. Bush, and I approve of that message.

The security of our families is vital, and it's important to our people of this country to understand the records. Senator Kerry's record on national security has the far deeper problem than election-year flip-flopping. On the largest national security issues of our time, he has been consistently wrong. When Ronald Reagan was confronting the Soviet Union at the height of the cold war, Senator Kerry said that President Reagan's policy of peace through strength was making America less safe. History has shown that Senator Kerry was wrong and President Ronald Reagan was right.

When former President Bush led a coalition against Saddam Hussein in 1991, Senator Kerry voted against the use of forces to liberate Kuwait. History has shown that Senator Kerry was wrong and former President Bush was right.

In 1994, just one year after the first bombing of the World Trade Center, Senator Kerry proposed massive cuts in America's intelligence budget, so massive that even his Massachusetts colleague, Ted Kennedy, opposed them. History has shown that Senator Kerry was wrong and—we have got to be fair—that Senator Kennedy was right.

During the last 20 years, in key moments of challenge and decision for America, Senator Kerry has chosen the position of weakness and inaction. With that record, he stands in opposition not just to me but to the great tradition of the Democratic Party. The party of Franklin Roosevelt, the party of Harry Truman, the party of John Kennedy is rightly remembered for confidence and resolve in times of war and hours of crisis. Senator Kerry has turned his back on "pay any price" and "bear any burden," and he has replaced those commitments with "wait and see" and "cut and run."

Many Democrats in this country do not recognize their party anymore. And traveling Ohio, I want to speak to every one of them: If you believe that America should lead with strength and purpose and confidence in our ideals, I would be honored to have your support, and I'm asking for your vote.

Audience members. Four more years! Four more years! Four more years!

The President. The second clear choice in this election concerns your family's budget. When I ran for President 4 years ago, I pledged to lower taxes for American families. And I kept my word. We doubled the child credit to $1,000 per child to help our families. We reduced the marriage penalty. I believe the Tax Code ought to encourage marriage, not penalize marriage. We dropped the lowest bracket to 10 percent. We reduced income taxes for everybody that pays income taxes. After-tax income—that's money in your pocket—has gone up by about 10 percent since I became your President.

And I want you to remind your friends and neighbors, when you're out there getting people to the polls, what this economy has been through. Six months prior to my arrival, the stock market was in serious decline. Then we had a recession. Then we had corporate scandals. But we passed what's called the Sarbanes-Oxley bill, a bill that makes it abundantly clear that we will not tolerate dishonesty in the boardrooms of America. And I want to thank Congressman Oxley for authoring this legislation. And then we got attacked on September the 11th. Those attacks cost us about a million jobs in the 3 months after that fateful day.

But our economic policies have led us back to growth. Our economy is growing at rates as fast as any in nearly 20 years. Homeownership in America is at an alltime high. We saw a lot of good farmland, flying in today. The farm incomes are up all across America. Our small businesses are flourishing. The entrepreneurial spirit is strong. We've added 1.9 million new jobs since August of 2003. The national unemployment rate is 5.4 percent. Let me put that in perspective for you: That's lower than the average rate of the 1970s, the 1980s, and the 1990s.

I know there are placed hurting here in Ohio. I've traveled into those neighborhoods. I've talked about an economic plan to continue growth. But I want to remind you that just last month, the unemployment rate in the State of Ohio went from 6.3 percent to 6 percent, and this great State added 5,500 new jobs in 1 month. We're on the move. We're moving forward.

My opponent has very different plans for your budget. He's going to take a big chunk out of it.

Audience members. Boo-o-o!

The President. He voted against the child tax credit. He voted against marriage penalty relief. He voted against lower taxes. And if his way had prevailed, the average family in America would have been paying 2,000 more in taxes to the Federal Government.

Audience members. Boo-o-o!

The President. That may not seem like a lot to folks in Washington. It means a lot to people in Findlay, Ohio.

He served in the United States Senate for 20 years, and he's voted for higher taxes 98 times. That's five times every year he served in the Senate. I would call that a predictable pattern—[*laughter*]—a reliable indicator. [*Laughter*] When a Senator does something that often, he must really enjoy it. [*Laughter*] Around the campaign, he's been promising $2.2 trillion in new Federal spending. That's trillion with a "T." That's a lot even for a Senator from Massachusetts. [*Laughter*]

So they asked him, "How are you going to pay for it?" And he said that same old, tired line you've heard over and over again, "We're going to tax the rich." Well, there's a problem with that. When you run up the top two brackets, you only raise between 600 and 800 billion dollars. That's far short of the 2.2 trillion he has promised. I would call that a tax gap. And guess who gets to usually fill that tax gap?

Audience member. We do!

The President. You do. The good news is we're going to carry Ohio, and we're not going to let him tax you.

The third choice in this election involves the quality of life for our Nation's families. A good education and quality health care

are important for your future. As a candidate, I pledged to end the soft bigotry of low expectations by reforming our public schools. I kept my word. We passed a really good piece of reform legislation. We're raising the standards. We've increased Federal spending, but now we're asking for results. We want to measure. See, you can't solve a problem unless you've diagnosed the problem. And we're diagnosing problems all across America, and we're beginning to solve them. Our test scores in reading and math are up. We're closing achievement gaps for minority students all across America. We'll build on these reforms and extend them to our high schools so that no child is left behind in our country.

We'll continue to improve life for our families by making health care more affordable and accessible. We'll make sure the poor and the indigent get health care in what's called community health centers. We'll make sure our low-income—our program for low-income—children in low-income families is fully subscribed so they get health care. To make sure health care is affordable, we'll help our small businesses. We'll allow them to pool together so they can spread risk and buy insurance at the same discounts big companies are able to do. We will expand health savings accounts, which will help our families and small-business owners.

Let me tell you what else we need to do. We need to do something about these frivolous lawsuits that are running up the cost of medicine and running good doctors out of practice. I was in Canton the other day talking to a ob-gyn who got run out of business because these lawsuits made her premiums too high to practice medicine. And I met too many citizens not only in your State but across the country, too many moms, expectant moms, who are worried about their health care and the health care of their baby because these lawsuits have made ob-gyn care more scarce. This is a national problem. You cannot be pro-doctor, pro-patient, and pro-plaintiff-injury-attorney at the same time. You've got to make a choice. My opponent made his choice, and he put a personal injury trial lawyer on the ticket.

Audience members. Boo-o-o!

The President. I have made my choice. I'm standing with the doctors of Ohio. I'm standing with the patients of Ohio. I'm for medical liability reform—now.

In one of our debates, my opponent looked straight in the camera when they asked him about his health care plan, and he said, "The Government doesn't have anything to do with it." I'll be frank with you, I could barely contain myself. The Government has got a lot to do with his plan. Eighty percent of the people who sign up on his plan would end up on the Government. See, if you make it easier for people to sign up for Medicaid, it means small businesses are likely not to provide insurance for their employees because the Government will provide insurance for their employees. That's logical. And when the Government starts writing the checks, the Government starts making the rules. And when it comes to health care when the Government's making the rules, the Government starts making decisions for you and decisions for your doctor. The wrong prescription for health care in America is to increase the role of the Federal Government. In all we do to improve health care, we'll make sure the decisions are made by patients and doctors, not by officials in Washington, DC.

The fourth clear choice in this election comes to your retirement. Our Nation has made a solemn commitment to America's seniors on Social Security and Medicare. When I ran for President 4 years ago, I promised to keep that commitment and improve Medicare by adding prescription drug coverage. I kept my word. We have modernized Medicare for our seniors. Beginning in 2006, all seniors will be able to get prescription drug coverage under Medicare.

And we'll keep our promise for Social Security for our seniors, and we will strengthen Social Security for generations to come. I remember the campaign in 2000. I remember those ads they were running. You might remember them. They said, "If George W. gets elected, the seniors are not going to get their checks." They may be doing it again this year. I want you to remind your friends and neighbors as you get them to the polls that George W. did get elected, and our seniors did get their checks. And our seniors will continue to get their checks. Nobody's going to take away your check. Baby boomers like me, we're in pretty good shape when it comes to the Social Security trust. We'll probably get our checks.

But we need to worry about our children and our grandchildren. We need to worry about whether or not the Social Security system will be there for them when they retire. That's why I believe younger workers ought to be able to take some of their own money—some of their own payroll taxes—and put it in a personal savings account, an account they call their own, an account the Government cannot take away.

Now, my opponent takes a different approach. He says he's going to strengthen Social Security; he's going to protect it. But you might remember, he is the only candidate in this race who has voted eight times for higher taxes on Social Security benefits.

Audience members. Boo-o-o!

The President. He doesn't like talking about that. He can run, but he cannot hide.

And he offered nothing for the younger generation in terms of reform. The job of a President is to confront problems, not to pass them on to future Presidents and future generations. In a new term, I will bring Republicans and Democrats together to strengthen the Social Security system for generations to come.

And the final choice in this election is on the values that are so crucial to keeping our families strong. And here, my opponent and I are miles apart. I stand for the appointment of Federal judges who know the difference between personal opinion and the strict interpretation of the law. I believe marriage is a sacred commitment, a pillar of our civilization, and I will defend it. This is not a partisan issue. When Congress passed the Defense of Marriage Act, defining marriage as a union of a man and a woman, the vast majority of Democrats supported it and President Bill Clinton signed it into law. But Senator Kerry was part of an out-of-the-mainstream minority that voted against the Defense of Marriage Act.

Audience members. Boo-o-o!

The President. I believe that reasonable people can find common ground on difficult issues. Republicans and Democrats came together and agreed we should ban the brutal practice of partial-birth abortion. I proudly signed that bill. But Senator Kerry was part of an out-of-the-mainstream minority that voted against the ban.

Audience members. Boo-o-o!

The President. He voted against parental notification laws and against the Unborn Victims of Violence Act. I will continue to reach out to Americans of every belief and move this goodhearted Nation toward a culture of life.

At one point in this campaign, you might remember this: My opponent said that the heart and soul of America can be found in Hollywood.

Audience members. Boo-o-o!

The President. Most American families do not look toward—to Hollywood as a source of values. The heart and soul of America is found in communities like Flag City, Ohio.

All these choices make this one of the most important elections in our history. The security and prosperity of our country, the health and education of our families, the retirement of our citizens, and the direction of our culture are all at stake. And the decision is in the best of hands. It is in the hands of the American people.

It is in your hands. You get to decide. And that gives me great confidence.

See, I'm optimistic about this country and our future. One of my favorite quotes is from a fellow Texan named Tom Lea. He said this, he said, "Sarah and I live on the east side of the mountain. It is the sunrise side, not the sunset side. It is the side to see the day that is coming, not to see the day that is gone." During the course of this campaign, my opponent has spent much of his campaign talking about the day that is gone. I'm talking about the day that's coming.

We've been through a lot together. We have been through a lot together during the last nearly 4 years. Because we've done the hard work of climbing the mountain, we can see the valley below. The next 4 years, we'll work to protect our families, build our prosperity, and defend our values. We will work hard to spread freedom and liberty so we can achieve the peace we want for generations to come.

Four years ago, when I traveled your great State asking for the vote, I made you this pledge, that if I was elected to the office I hold, I would uphold the honor and its dignity. With your help, with your hard work, I will do so for 4 more years.

Thanks for coming. God bless. Thank you all. Thanks for coming.

NOTE: The President spoke at 4:20 p.m. at the Hancock County Fairgrounds. In his remarks, he referred to Senator Zell Miller of Georgia, who made the keynote address at the 2004 Republican National Convention; Frances DeWine, wife of Senator Mike DeWine; Gov. Bob Taft and Lt. Gov. Jennette B. Bradley of Ohio; Mayor Anthony P. Iriti of Findlay, OH; entertainers the Wil Gravatt Band; former President Saddam Hussein of Iraq; Usama bin Laden, leader of the Al Qaida terrorist organization; and Gen. Tommy R. Franks, USA (Ret.), former combatant commander, U.S. Central Command.

Remarks in Pontiac, Michigan
October 27, 2004

The President. Thank you all for coming. Laura and I appreciate you all being here. You're lifting our spirits, and we're grateful. I'm so honored you're here. I'm here in Michigan today and tomorrow. I'll be back on Saturday. I'm here to ask for the vote and to ask for your help. It is important for all of us to vote. In a free society we have a duty to go to the polls. And so I'm asking you to get your friends and neighbors to go to the polls and exercise their duty. And as you get them headed to the polls, make sure you don't overlook discerning Democrats like my friend Zell Miller from the great State of Georgia. Make sure you talk to independents and, of course, our fellow Republicans. And when you get them to the polls, remind them that if they want a safer America, a stronger America, and a better America, to put me and Dick Cheney back in office.

You know, Laura and I love to campaign, and I like to tell people why I think people ought to put me back in. And perhaps the most important reason of all is so that Laura is the First Lady for 4 more years.

Audience members. Laura! Laura! Laura!

The President. I am proud of my runningmate, Dick Cheney. I see some folks out here who are follically challenged, kind of like the Vice President. I admit it, he doesn't have the waviest hair in the race. You'll be pleased to hear, I did not pick him because of hairdo. I picked him because of his judgment. I picked him because of his experience. I picked him because he's the got the ability to get the job done for the American people.

I want to thank my friend Michael Williams for joining us today. And I want to thank the other African American leaders I'm proud to call friend, who have joined me on this stage, including the Lieutenant Governor from the State of Maryland,

Lieutenant Governor Michael Steele. I appreciate you coming, Michael.

I want to thank Joe Knollenberg and Thad McCotter, Members of the United States Congress from Michigan. I particularly want to thank Congresswoman Candice Miller for leading my campaign in Michigan. I want to thank Terri Lynn Land. I want to thank Betsy DeVos. I want to thank the entertainers who were here today.

And I want to thank all the grassroots activists who are here, the people who put up the signs and made the phone calls and helped turn out this huge crowd. I want to thank you for what you have done and what you are going to do as we come down the stretch. With your help, with your hard work, there is no doubt in my mind we will carry Michigan and win a great victory on November the 2d.

This election comes down to some clear choices for our families, issues of great consequence. The first clear choice is the most important because it concerns the security of your family. All progress on every other issue depends on the safety of our citizens. This will be the first Presidential election since September the 11th, 2001. Americans will go to the polls in a time of war and ongoing threats. The outcome of this election will set the direction of the war against terror. The most solemn duty of the American President is to protect the American people. If America shows uncertainty or weakness in this decade, the world will drift toward tragedy. This will not happen on my watch.

Our strategy is clear. We're strengthening protections for the homeland. We're reforming our intelligence capabilities. We're transforming the United States military. There will be no draft. We will keep the All-Volunteer Army an all-volunteer army. We are determined. We are relentless. We will fight the terrorists overseas so we do not have to face them here at home. And we understand that our long-term security comes from spreading freedom.

I want some of the younger folks here to understand how far the world has come in about 3¾ years. It wasn't all that long ago that young girls were not able to go to school in Afghanistan because the Taliban was so barbaric, and if their mothers didn't toe the line of the ideologues of hate, they'd be taken in the public square and sometimes killed in a sports stadium. Because we acted to defend ourselves, because we upheld a doctrine that said, "If you harbor a terrorist, you're equally as guilty as the terrorist," millions of people went to the polls to vote for a President. The first voter in the Afghan Presidential election was a 19-year-old woman.

There will be Presidential elections in Iraq in January. Think how far that country has come from the days of torture chambers and mass graves. Freedom is on the march, and we're more secure for it. Free societies are peaceful societies, and we believe everyone desires to live in freedom. Freedom is not America's gift to the world; freedom is the Almighty God's gift to each man and woman in this world.

A President must lead with consistency and strength. In a war, sometimes our tactics have to change but never your principles. Americans have seen how I do my job. Even when you might not agree with me, you know what I believe, where I stand, and where I intend to lead this Nation. On good days and on bad days, when the polls are up or when the polls are down, I will do everything I can to defend the American people, and I will support our troops in combat.

I am honored to be the Commander in Chief of such a fine group of people, the people in the United States military. I want to thank the veterans who are here today for having set such a great example. I want to thank the military families who are here. And I will assure you that so long as I'm the Commander in Chief, our troops will have that which is necessary to complete their missions.

That's why I went to the United States Congress and asked for $87 billion of supplemental funding to support our troops in combat. As you gather the vote, I want you to remind people of this startling statistic: There were only four Members of the United States Senate that voted to authorize the use of force and then voted against funding for our troops in harm's way—only four Members—two of whom were my opponent and his runningmate.

Audience members. Boo-o-o!

The President. They asked him why he made his vote, and Senator Kerry uttered perhaps the most famous statement of the 2004 campaign when he said, "I actually did vote for the $87 billion, right before I voted against it."

Audience members. Boo-o-o!

The President. The Commander in Chief must be consistent. After repeatedly calling Iraq the wrong war and a diversion, Senator Kerry this week seemed shocked to learn that Iraq was a dangerous place full of dangerous weapons. The Senator used to know that, even though he seems to have forgotten it over the course of the campaign. Of course, that's why we went into Iraq. Iraq was a dangerous place run by a dangerous tyrant who hated America and who had a lot of weapons. And we have seized or destroyed more than 400,000 tons of munitions, including explosives, at thousands of different sites. And we're continuing to round up more weapons almost every day.

I want to remind the American people if Senator Kerry had had his way, we would still be taking our "global test."

Audience members. Boo-o-o!

The President. We would be waiting for yet another United Nations resolution to make us more safe.

Audience members. Boo-o-o!

The President. Saddam Hussein would be in power. He would control all those weapons and explosives and could have shared them with the terrorist enemy.

Audience members. Boo-o-o!

The President. Now, the Senator is making wild charges about missing explosives, when his top foreign policy adviser admits he does not know the facts. He said, quote, "I don't know the truth," end quote. But think about that. The Senator is denigrating the actions of our troops and commanders in the field without knowing the facts.

Audience members. Boo-o-o!

The President. Our military is now investigating a number of possible scenarios, including that the explosives may have been moved before our troops arrived. This investigation is important. It's ongoing. And a political candidate who jumps to conclusions without knowing the facts is not a person you want as Commander in Chief. Unfortunately——

Audience members. Four more years! Four more years! Four more years!

The President. Unfortunately, that is part of a pattern of a candidate who will say anything to get elected. My opponent is throwing out the wild claim that he knows where bin Laden was in the fall of 2001 and that our military passed up a chance to get him at Tora Bora. You might remember that discussion during our debates. I think this is unjustified criticism of our military commanders in the field. This is the worst kind of Monday morning quarterbacking.

Our commander in Afghanistan, General Tommy Franks, recently wrote this about Tora Bora, quote, "The Senator's understanding of events doesn't square with reality." That's what the man knows what—who knows what he's talking about said. The general says that American Special Forces were actively involved in the search for terrorists in Tora Bora and that intelligence reports at the time placed bin Laden in any of several countries.

Before Senator Kerry got into political difficulty and revised his views, he saw our actions in Tora Bora differently. In the fall of 2001, on national TV, he said, quote, "I think we have been doing this pretty effectively, and we should continue to do it that way." He went on to talk about Tora Bora. The Senator said this: "I think we have been smart. I think the administration leadership has done it well, and we are on the right track." All I can say to this is, I am George W. Bush, and I approve of that message.

Audience members. Four more years! Four more years! Four more years!

The President. The security of our families is very important. And my opponent's record on national security has far deeper problems with just election-year flip-flopping. On the largest national security issues of our time, he has been consistently wrong. He has a record. When Ronald Reagan was confronting the Soviet Union at the height of the cold war, Senator Kerry said that President Reagan's policy of peace through strength was making America less safe.

Audience members. Boo-o-o!

The President. History has shown that Senator Kerry was wrong and President Ronald Reagan was right.

When former President Bush led a coalition against Saddam Hussein in 1991, Senator Kerry voted against the use of force to liberate Kuwait.

Audience members. Boo-o-o!

The President. History has shown that Senator Kerry was wrong and former President Bush was right.

In 1994, just 1 year after the first bombing of the World Trade Center, Senator Kerry proposed massive cuts in America's intelligence budget, so massive that even his colleague from Massachusetts, Ted Kennedy, opposed them. [*Laughter*] History has shown that Senator Kerry was wrong and—we've got to be fair—Senator Kennedy was right.

During the last 20 years, in key moments of challenge and decision for America, Senator Kerry has chosen the position of weakness and inaction. With that record, he stands in opposition not just to me but to the great tradition of the Democrat Party. The party of Franklin Roosevelt, the party of Harry Truman, the party of John Kennedy is rightly remembered for confidence and resolve in times of war and in hours of crisis. Senator Kerry has turned his back on "pay any price" and "bear any burden," and he's replaced those commitments with "wait and see" and "cut and run."

Audience members. Boo-o-o!

The President. Many Democrats in this country do not recognize their party anymore, and today I want to speak to every one of them here in the State of Michigan. If you believe America should lead with strength and purpose and confidence in our ideals, I would be honored to have your support, and I'm asking for your vote.

The second clear choice in this election concerns your family's budget. When I ran for President 4 years ago, I pledged to lower taxes for American families. I kept my word. We doubled the child credit to $1,000 per child to help moms and dads. We reduced the marriage penalty. We believe the Tax Code ought to encourage marriage, not penalize marriage. We lowered—we dropped the lowest tax bracket to 10 percent to help our working families. We reduced income taxes for everybody who pays taxes. After-tax income in America is up by 10 percent since I've become the President.

We have overcome a lot. I want you to remind your friends and neighbors about what this economy has been through. Six months prior to my arrival in Washington, the stock market was in serious decline. Our economy was slowing. We had a recession. We had corporate scandals. And then the attacks on September the 11th cost us nearly a million jobs in the 3 months after those attacks.

But our economic policies are working. They've led us back to the path of growth. We're growing—our economy is growing faster than any in the major industrialized world. Small businesses are flourishing. The entrepreneurial spirit is strong in America. Michigan farmers are making a good living under the Bush administration. We've added more than 1.9 million jobs in the last 13 months. The national unemployment rate is 5.4 percent. That's lower than the average rate of the 1970s, the 1980s, and the 1990s. There is more work to be done to make sure this economy continues to grow so people in Michigan can find work, but one thing is certain: This economy of ours is strong, and it is getting stronger.

My opponent has a very different view about your budget. He intends to take a big chunk out of it.

Audience members. Boo-o-o!

The President. He voted against the higher child tax credit. He voted against the marriage penalty relief. He voted against lower taxes. If he had had his way over the last 3 years, the average American family would have been paying $2,000 more in Federal taxes.

Audience members. Boo-o-o!

The President. That may not sound like a lot to people in Washington. It's a heck of a lot for people living in Michigan.

You know, my opponent has been in the United States Senate for 20 years. And hear this fact: He voted for increased taxes 98 times. That's five times for every year he's been in the Senate—nearly five times. I would call that a predictable pattern. I'd call that a indicator. [*Laughter*] When a Senator does something that often, he must really enjoy it. [*Laughter*] The problem is you won't enjoy it. If he raises your taxes—as a matter of fact, here's another indicator. He's promised $2.2 trillion of new spending. That's trillion with a "T." That's a lot even for a senator from Massachusetts. [*Laughter*]

And they said, "How are you going to pay for it? How are you going to pay for it?" He said, "Oh, we'll just tax the rich." Now, we have heard that before. Let me tell you two things wrong with that. One, most small businesses pay tax at the individual income tax. Ninety percent of small businesses are what they call Subchapter S corporations and sole proprietorships, and they pay tax at the individual income-tax rate. Seventy percent of new jobs are created by small businesses. And so when you start running up the top two income brackets, guess who you're taxing? You're taxing the job creators in America, and that makes no economic sense.

And secondly, by taxing the rich you raise about 600 to 800 billion dollars. So you can see there is a gap between that which he has promised and that which he can deliver. I would call it a tax gap. And guess who usually gets to fill the tax gap?

Audience member. We do!

The President. The good news is we're not going to let him tax you. We're going to carry Michigan and win a great victory.

The third clear choice in this election improves the quality of life for our families. A good education and quality health care are important to a successful life. As a candidate, I pledged to end the soft bigotry of low expectations in our schools. And as President, I have kept my word. We passed the No Child Left Behind Act, which is an historic achievement for public education. We are raising the standards in our schools. We've increased Federal spending, especially for poor students. But in return for an increase of Federal spending, we're now saying, "Show us whether or not a child can read or write, and add and subtract. Show us whether or not children are becoming literate. Show us whether or not we're ending that practice of just shuffling kids through school, year after year, without learning the basics."

You cannot solve a problem until you diagnose a problem, and we are diagnosing problems, and we're solving more and more problems, so that our children are learning to read and write. We're closing an achieve-ment gap in America, and we're not going to go back to the days of low expectations and mediocre results.

We will continue to improve life by making sure health care is affordable and available. To make sure health care is available, we will expand community health centers so the poor and the indigent can get good primary and preventative care. We will make sure our low-income—children for low-income family program for health care is fully subscribed.

To make sure health care is affordable, here are three commonsense ways to help the American family. First, we'll expand health savings accounts to help our small businesses and families have an affordable health care account that you manage and you call your own. Secondly, we will help our small businesses by allowing them to pool risk across jurisdictional boundaries so they can buy insurance at the same discounts that big companies are able to do. And thirdly, we will do something about these frivolous lawsuits that are running up the cost of health care and running good docs out of practice.

You cannot be pro-doctor and pro-patient and pro-trial-lawyer at the same time. I think you have to make a choice. My opponent made his choice, and he put a personal-injury trial lawyer on the ticket.

Audience members. Boo-o-o!

The President. I have made my choice. I am standing with the families of Michigan. I am standing with the docs of Michigan. I'm standing with the hospitals of Michigan. I am for real medical liability reform—now.

We have a difference of opinion when it comes to your health care. I don't know if you remember that debate when he— my opponent, when they asked him about his health care plan, looked straight in the camera, and he said, "The Government doesn't have anything to do with it." You know, I could barely contain myself. [*Laughter*] The Government has got a lot to do with his health care plan. Eighty percent of the people would end up on a Government-run health program. See, if you increase Medicaid eligibility, it provides an incentive for many small businesses to drop private coverage because the Government will be providing coverage for their employees. That's moving people from the private sector to the public sector. And when the Government writes a check, the Government makes the rules. And when it comes to your health care, when the Government makes the rules, the Government starts making decisions for you and for your doctors. Federalizing health care is the wrong prescription for America's families.

In all we do to reform health care, we will make sure the health decisions are made by doctors and patients, not by officials in Washington, DC.

The fourth clear choice in this election involves your retirement. Our Nation has made a solemn commitment to America's seniors on Social Security and Medicare. When I ran for President 4 years ago, I promised to keep that commitment and improve Medicare by adding prescription drug coverage. I kept my word. Beginning in 2006, all seniors will be able to get prescription drug coverage under Medicare.

And we'll keep the promise of Social Security for our seniors and strengthen it for generations to come. I don't know if you remember the 2000 campaign, when they were running ads that said, "If George W. gets elected, our seniors will not get their checks." They may be running some here in Michigan now for all I know, trying to scare our seniors again. As you're rounding up the vote, I want you to remind your friends and neighbors that George W. did get elected, and our seniors got their checks. And our seniors will continue to get their checks. Nobody is going to take away the Social Security checks of our seniors. And baby boomers like me, and like a couple others out there I see—[laugh-

ter]—we're in pretty good shape when it comes to Social Security.

But we need to worry about our children and our grandchildren. We need to worry about whether the Social Security system will be there when they need it. And that's why I believe younger workers ought to be able to take some of their own payroll account—some of their payroll taxes and set up a personal savings account, an account they call their own, an account that will earn better interest, an account the Government cannot take away.

My opponent takes a different approach on the Social Security issue. He talks about protecting Social Security. But I want you to remind your friends and neighbors about this fact: He's the only candidate in the race who has voted eight times for higher taxes on Social Security benefits.

Audience members. Boo-o-o!

The President. He can run, but he cannot hide. And when it comes to offering help for the next generation, he's offered nothing. The job of a President is to confront problems, not to pass them on to future Presidents and future generations. In a new term, I will bring Republicans and Democrats together to strengthen the Social Security system for generations to come.

The fifth clear choice in this election is on the values that are so crucial to keeping America's families strong. I stand for the appointment of Federal judges who know the difference between personal opinion and the strict interpretation of the law. I stand for marriage and family, which are the foundations of our society. When Congress passed the Defense of Marriage Act, the vast majority of Democrats supported it, and my predecessor, Bill Clinton, signed it into law. But Senator Kerry was part of an out-of-the-mainstream minority that voted against the Defense of Marriage Act.

Audience members. Boo-o-o!

The President. Reasonable people can find common ground on difficult issues. Republicans and Democrats came together and agreed we should ban the brutal practice of partial-birth abortions. I proudly signed that bill into law. My opponent was part of an out-of-the-mainstream minority that voted against the ban on partial-birth abortion.

Audience members. Boo-o-o!

The President. I'll continue to reach out to Americans of every belief and move this good-hearted Nation to a culture of life.

At one point in this campaign you might remember that my opponent said the heart and soul of America can be found in Hollywood.

Audience members. Boo-o-o!

The President. No, I agree. I understand. I understand most American families do not look to Hollywood as a source of values. The heart and soul of America is found in places like Oakland County, Michigan.

No, this election is an important election. It's about important choices, and the decision is in the best of hands. It is in the hands of the American people. I am optimistic about the future of this country. I believe so strongly in what we stand for, and I understand the strength of this country. It lies in the hearts and souls of our fellow citizens. That's the true strength of America.

You know, one of my favorite quotes was written by a fellow Texan named Tom Lea, and here's what Tom said. He said, "Sarah and I live on the east side of the mountain. It is the sunrise side, not the sunset side. It is the side to see the day that is coming, not to see the day that is gone." During this campaign, my opponent has spent much of the campaign talking about the day that is gone. I'm talking about the day that is coming.

I see a day that's coming where America is more safe and our families are more secure, a day when this country is prosperous in every corner of the land, a day in which every child can read and write and add and subtract, a day in which we defend the bedrock values that make our society such a compassionate, decent place.

When I campaigned across your State 4 years ago, I made this pledge, that if I got elected, I would uphold the honor and the dignity of the office to which I had been elected. With your help, I will do so for 4 more years.

Thanks for coming. God bless. Thank you all.

NOTE: The President spoke at 6:33 p.m. at the Pontiac Silverdome. In his remarks, he referred to Senator Zell Miller of Georgia, who made the keynote address at the 2004 Republican National Convention; Michael L. Williams, commissioner, Railroad Commission of Texas; Lt. Gov. Michael S. Steele of Maryland; Secretary of State Terri Lynn Land of Michigan; Betsy DeVos, chairman, Michigan Republican Party; former President Saddam Hussein of Iraq; Usama bin Laden, leader of the Al Qaida terrorist organization; and Gen. Tommy R. Franks, USA (Ret.), former combatant commander, U.S. Central Command.

Remarks in Saginaw, Michigan
October 28, 2004

The President. Thank you all. Thanks for coming out to say hello. I got to tell me, you have lifted my spirits, for which I am grateful. It's good to be back in Saginaw.

I'm grateful so many of you came out to say hello.

Listen, I'm traveling your State asking for the vote and asking for your help. It is close to voting day. We have a duty in our country to vote. In our free land, free citizens must vote. And so I'm asking you to get your friends and neighbors to go to the polls, turn out our fellow Republicans, find independents who understand we have a better tomorrow ahead of us, and don't overlook discerning Democrats. Tell your fellow citizens that if they want a safer country, a stronger country, and a better country, to put me and Dick Cheney back in office.

My only regret is that Laura is not here to see this fantastic crowd. She headed off to campaign today in Florida. You know, when I asked her to marry me, she said, "I'll marry you, but make me a promise." I said, "What is it?" She said, "Promise me I will never have to give a political speech." [*Laughter*] I'm sure some of you can relate to that. I said, "Okay, you got a deal." Fortunately, she didn't hold me to that deal. She is giving a lot of speeches, and when she does, the American people see a strong, compassionate, great First Lady. Perhaps the most important reason why people ought to put me back in office is so that Laura will be the First Lady for 4 more years.

Audience members. Four more years! Four more years! Four more years!

The President. I am proud of my runningmate, Dick Cheney. He is doing a great job. Although, I admit, he does not have the waviest hair in the race. [*Laughter*] You will be pleased I didn't pick him because of his hairdo. I picked him because of his experience. I picked him because of his judgment. I picked him because he can get the job done for the American people.

I'm proud to call Dave Camp my friend, and I know you're proud to call him Congressman. And I want to thank Terri Lynn Land for joining us, the secretary of state for the great State of Michigan. And I wish Myrah Kirkwood all the best in her run for the United States Congress. I want to thank Betsy DeVos and all the grassroots activists who are here. I want to thank the Saline Fiddlers. I want to thank the Saginaw Area Band. I want to thank the Wil Gravatt Band for joining us. Thank you for entertaining this good crowd.

Most of all, I want to thank you all. I want to thank you for what you have done on behalf of my candidacy and what you're going to do. By working the phones, by getting people to—by reminding people of their duty to vote, by putting up the signs, by turning out that vote, there is no doubt in my mind, we will carry Michigan and win a great victory in November.

Five days from now, the people go to the polls. We are choosing the leader of our country at a time of great consequence to our Nation. We're at war against a terrorist enemy unlike any we have ever seen. We have much more to do to win a decisive victory against the terrorists. The most important duty of the American President is to protect the American people. If America shows uncertainty or weakness in these troubling times, the world will drift toward tragedy. This will not happen on my watch.

Our economy is in the midst of change and challenge. It can be a great time of opportunity if we have the right policies that strengthen rather than stall our economic growth. We have much more to do to create jobs, to improve our children's education, to make health care available and affordable, and to strengthen Social Security for our seniors and for generations to come. And I am ready for the job.

My years as your President have confirmed some lessons and have taught me some new ones. A President must have a vision. A President must set goals and bring people together to achieve those goals. A President must surround himself with strong, capable people. And I have done so. A President must make America's priorities crystal-clear in this uncertain world. I've learned to expect the unexpected, because history can deliver sudden horror from a soft autumn sky. I found you better know what you believe or risk being tossed to-and-fro by the flattery of friends or the chorus of the critics.

I've been grateful for the lessons I have learned from my parents: Respect every person; do your best; and live every day to its fullest. I have been strengthened by my faith and humbled by its reminder that my life is part of a much bigger story. I've learned firsthand how hard it is to send young men and women into battle, even when the cause is right. I've been reminded that the world looks to America for leadership and that it is crucial for an American President to be consistent.

Perhaps most of all, I've learned the American President must make decisions on principle, core convictions from which you must not waver. The issues vary; the challenges are different every day. Tactics and strategy must be flexible, but a President's convictions must be steady and true. As Presidents from Abraham Lincoln to Franklin Roosevelt to Ronald Reagan so clearly demonstrated, a President cannot blow in the wind. A President has to make tough decisions and stand by them.

A President must follow the—must not follow the path of the latest polls. A President must lead based on conviction and conscience. Especially in a time of war, mixed signals only confuse our friends, embolden our enemies. Mixed signals are the wrong signals for the American President to send.

When America chooses a President, you choose not just a set of positions on issues or a philosophy or record; you choose a human being who comes with strengths and weaknesses. One of the things I've learned about the Presidency is, whatever your strengths are, you're going to need them, and whatever your shortcomings are, people are going to notice them. Sometimes I'm a little too blunt. I get that from my mother. Sometimes I mangle the English language. [*Laughter*] I get that from my dad. [*Laughter*] But Americans have learned that when you disagree with me,

at least you know what I believe and where I stand.

Audience members. Four more years! Four more years! Four more years!

The President. You cannot say that about my opponent. [*Laughter*] Senator Kerry has taken a lot of different positions, but he rarely takes a stand. He's run a campaign of contradictions. I think it's fair to say consistency is not the Senator's strong suit. [*Laughter*] He was for the PATRIOT Act and the No Child Left Behind Act, until he was against key provisions of both of them. He voted to authorize the use of force in Iraq and then said I was wrong to use that force.

Audience members. Boo-o-o!

The President. When I sent troops into Iraq to remove Saddam Hussein from power, he said it was the right decision. Now he says it was the "wrong war."

Audience members. Boo-o-o!

The President. During one of our debates, he said Saddam Hussein was a threat. And then a couple of answers later, he said there was no threat in Iraq.

Audience members. Boo-o-o!

The President. Just last year, American troops in Afghanistan and Iraq needed $87 billion for body armor, hazard pay, vehicles, weapons, and bullets—necessary funding, funding that would keep a commitment we have made to our soldiers and their loved ones. They will have what is necessary to complete their mission. Something the veterans in this crowd understand, the Government must support those in harm's way. And I say thanks to our veterans from the bottom of a grateful heart.

Back to the 87 billion. First Senator Kerry said, "It would be irresponsible to vote against the troops." That's what he said on TV, national TV. Then he did the irresponsible thing and voted against the funding for our troops.

Audience members. Boo-o-o!

The President. Now, they asked him about that vote, and you might remember perhaps the most famous quote of the 2004 campaign when he said, "I actually did vote for the 87 billion, before I voted against it." Pressed further to explain his vote, he's given several explanations. One of the most interesting was this: "The whole thing was a complicated matter." [*Laughter*] There's nothing complicated about supporting our troops in combat.

You have to wonder why my opponent has taken such different positions at different places and different times in this campaign. I think you'll find two reasons why. Senator Kerry changes positions because he's willing to say anything he thinks will help him politically at the time. And he does so to try to obscure a 20-year record, 20 years of out-of-the-mainstream votes. That leads to an inescapable conclusion. Senator Kerry has been wrong—on the wrong side of the defining national security and domestic policy debates for the last two decades. He can run from his record, but he cannot hide.

Several times during the course of this campaign, the Senator has changed his positions for political convenience. The Senator recognized Saddam Hussein was a threat and authorized force to remove him, until his Democratic opponent Howard Dean began gaining ground as an antiwar candidate. And then he decided he had to appeal to that wing of his party, so he voted against the troops—after voting to put them at risk in the first place. See, he looked at the polls and changed positions. The Senator was all for removing Saddam Hussein when we went into Baghdad. He was very supportive when we captured him. After all, the polls showed that that was very popular at the time. When the going got tough and when we faced determined opposition and things weren't quite so popular, the Senator suddenly wasn't quite so supportive. In fact, he changed his mind entirely, deciding it was the "wrong war at the wrong place at the wrong time."

Audience members. Boo-o-o!

The President. It's important for the citizens of Michigan to think about this. What does that lack of conviction say to our troops who are risking their lives in a vital cause? What does it say to our allies who have joined us in that cause? What does that lack of conviction signal to our enemies, that if you make things uncomfortable, if you stir up trouble, John Kerry will back off? And that's a very dangerous signal to send during this time.

This week Senator Kerry is again attacking the actions of our military in Iraq, with complete disregard for the facts. Senator Kerry will say anything to get elected. The Senator's willingness to trade principle for political convenience makes it clear that John Kerry is the wrong man for the wrong job at the wrong time.

And there's another reason the Senator changes positions. He doesn't want you to know where he really stands. [*Laughter*] He doesn't want you to know where he stands on national security, because he has a record of weakness. When Ronald Reagan was confronting the Soviet Union at the height of the cold war, Senator Kerry proposed cancellation of critical defense weapons systems and said that President Reagan's policy of peace through strength was making America less safe.

Audience members. Boo-o-o!

The President. History has shown that Senator Kerry was wrong and President Ronald Reagan was right.

Former President Bush led a coalition against Saddam Hussein in 1991. Senator Kerry voted against using force to liberate Kuwait. If his view had prevailed, Saddam Hussein today would dominate the Middle East, possess the world's most dangerous weapons. History has shown that John Kerry was wrong and former President Bush was right.

In 1994, just one year after the first bombing of the World Trade Center, Senator Kerry proposed massive cuts in America's intelligence budgets, cuts so extreme that even his Massachusetts colleague, Ted

Kennedy, opposed them. History has shown that Senator Kerry was wrong and—we have got to be fair—Senator Kennedy was right. [*Laughter*]

When you are one Senator among 100, you can be wrong without consequence. But the President's opinion decides the security and the fate of our country. And while the Senator's 20-year record of votes is long, it's also lacking of significant reform or achievement. He talks about bringing new allies to the war against terror—if somehow countries that have not yet been involved might want to join what he calls the "wrong war." [*Laughter*] Yet he has no history of convincing even his colleagues in the United States Senate to join him on signature reforms or achievements.

The next 4 years, I will work with our friends and allies. We will strengthen our coalition, but I will never turn over America's national security decisions to leaders of other countries.

Audience members. Four more years! Four more years! Four more years!

The President. The security of our country is at stake. Senator Kerry says September the 11th, in his words, "did not change him much at all." That's what he said.

Audience members. Boo-o-o!

The President. And his policies make that clear. The Senator says the war on terror is primarily a law enforcement and intelligence gathering operation. He says his goal is to go back to the days of the 1990s when terrorism was seen as a "nuisance"——

Audience members. Boo-o-o!

The President. ——fought with subpoenas and cruise missiles.

Well, September the 11th changed my outlook for the world. It made it crystal-clear to me the dangers we face. A few days after the attacks, I went to Ground Zero, September 14th, 2001. I stood in the ruins of the Twin Towers. It's a day I will never forget. The sights and sounds of that day are always in my mind. Workers in

hardhats there yelling at the top of their lungs, "Whatever it takes." A man coming out of the rubble grabbed me by the arm. He looked me in the eye, and he said, "Do not let me down." Ever since that day, I wake up every morning thinking how to—thinking about how to better protect our country. I will never relent in defending America, whatever it takes.

There are other things about his views and his ideas the Senator really doesn't want you to know about. You might remember the debate when they asked him about his health care plan. He looked straight in the camera and said, "The Government doesn't have anything to do with it." I could barely contain myself. [*Laughter*]

The Government has got a lot to do with it. Eighty percent of the people end up, under his idea, on a Government plan. When you increase Medicaid eligibility, it means small businesses will likely stop writing insurance because the Government will provide the insurance. That moves people from the private sector to the public sector when it comes to health care. And see, when the Government starts paying the money, the Government starts writing the rules. And when the Government starts writing the rules when it comes to your health care, the Government starts making decisions for you and decisions for your doctors and rationing care. Senator Kerry's plan for health care for America is the wrong prescription.

We will make health care more affordable and available for our citizens. We will expand community health centers to help the poor and the indigent. We'll make sure our program for low-income children is fully subscribed. We'll expand health savings accounts to help our businesses and families with innovative ways to manage— so you can manage your own health care account. We understand small businesses provide important insurance to the workers, and yet, many small businesses are having trouble affording health care, so we'll allow small businesses to join together so they can buy insurance at the same discounts that big companies are able to do.

And we understand that these frivolous lawsuits are running up the cost of health care for small businesses, for patients, and they're running good doctors out of practice. You cannot be pro-doctor, pro-patient and pro-personal-injury-trial-lawyer at the same time. You have to make a choice. My opponent made his choice, and he put a personal-injury trial lawyer on the ticket.

Audience members. Boo-o-o!

The President. I made my choice. I'm standing with the doctors of Michigan. I'm standing with the patients of Michigan. I am for medical liability reform—now.

This campaign, the Senator doesn't want you to know where he really stands on taxes. He's going to raise them. To be fair, raising taxes is one of the few things that he's been consistent about. You might say he's made a habit out of it. See, he's been in the United States Senate 20 years, and he's voted to raise taxes 98 times. That's five times for every year he's been in the Senate. I'd call it a predictable pattern, an early-warning indicator. [*Laughter*]

You know, when we reduced the taxes for our families by raising the child credit and doing something about the marriage penalty, he voted against it. He voted against that tax relief at a vital time. Plus, he's decided to raise $2.2 trillion° in new Federal spending. He's going to spend it. That's what he said. He said, "I'm going to spend 2.2 trillion new money," when you add up all his promises. He doesn't really want to clarify that. That's 2.2 trillion with a "T." That's a lot. That is a lot even for a Senator from Massachusetts. [*Laughter*]

And so they asked him, "How are you going to pay for it?" They said, "How are you going to pay for it?" He said, "Oh, I'm just going to tax the rich." Now, people in Saginaw, Michigan, have heard that be-

---

° White House correction.

fore. You see, if you raise the top two brackets, it raises 600 to 800 billion dollars. That is short of the 2.2 trillion. That's called a tax gap. [*Laughter*] And guess who usually has to fill that tax gap?

Audience member. We do!

The President. Yes, you do. The good news is, we're not going to let him tax you; we're going to carry Michigan and win a victory.

No, the Senator doesn't really want to talk about his record, and there is a reason why. There is a mainstream in American politics, and he sits on the far left bank. I'm a compassionate conservative and proudly so. I'm more than happy to travel our country talking about my record, talking about a record that has made America a stronger place and a safer place and a better place.

When you're rounding up the vote, remind people what this economy has been through. Six months prior to my arrival in Washington, the stock market was in serious decline, which foretold a recession. And then we had some corporate scandals, passed—we passed tough laws, and we have made it abundantly clear that we're not going to tolerate dishonesty in the boardrooms of America. And then the attacks came, and they cost us about a million jobs in the 3 months after September the 11th.

But we acted. I led the Congress to cut the taxes on the American people to encourage consumption and investment, to stimulate the small-business sector of our economy. And our policies are paying off. We're growing at rates as fast as any in nearly 20 years. We have added 1.9 million jobs in the last 13 months. The farmers in Michigan are making a living. The small-business owners are alive and well. The entrepreneurial spirit is strong. The home-ownership rate in America is at an alltime high. More minorities own a home than ever before in our Nation's history. The national unemployment rate is 5.4 percent. Let me put that in perspective for you:

That is lower than the average rate of the 1970s and the 1980s and the 1990s.

I understand there are some people hurting in Michigan, but that's not a reason to go back to tax and spend. The best way to make sure people can find work is to continue to promote a pro-growth, pro-entrepreneur, pro-small-business economic policy, which is what we have done. Our economy is strong, and it is getting stronger.

When I ran—when I was running for President 4 years ago, I promised to do something about the public schools. I told the American people I was troubled by a system that would shuffle children through, grade after grade, year after year, without teaching the basics. I call that the soft bigotry of low expectations. So I promised to reform our system. I kept my word. We've increased spending, particularly for minority students and poor students. But in return, we've now said, "Show us whether or not a child can read and write and add and subtract." See, you can't solve a problem until you diagnose the problem. And as a result of the system in place, the system that says we're going to set high standards for every child, we're diagnosing problems and we're solving them. Math and reading scores are up across this country. We are closing an achievement gap for minority students. And we're not going to go back to the days of mediocrity and excuses for failure in our public schools.

When I ran for President 4 years ago, I promised to improve Medicare by adding prescription drugs. I kept my word. You might remember the old Medicare debates. They would call it "Medi-scare" because politicians wouldn't talk about it. I came to Washington to solve problems. We had a problem in Medicare. Medicare would pay thousands of dollars for the heart surgery but not one dime for the prescription drugs that could prevent the heart surgery from being needed in the first place. Now we've strengthened Medicare. We've modernized Medicare. Beginning in 2006, all seniors will be able to get prescription drug coverage under Medicare.

My opponent voted against that bill that provided prescription drug coverage for our seniors——

Audience members. Boo-o-o!

The President. ——even though AARP and other senior groups supported it. As your President the next 4 years, I will defend the reforms we put in place for our seniors. We will keep our promise to America's seniors with modern medicine.

When I ran for President, I said we would help those who need help in America, we would help those who could not help themselves. I said Government should not discriminate against faith-based and community groups who provide compassionate care for the broken heart. And now our Government welcomes those groups as partners in meeting the needs of those who need hope and those who need help.

I said we would help the poor and the indigent with health care, and we've expanded community health centers all across this country, and we will continue to do so. We've doubled funding for medical research into new cures and diseases, just like I said I would do during the campaign. As we pursued threats around the world, as we have used our might to protect ourselves and to protect others, we have also delivered American compassion. We've dramatically increased funding to combat AIDS and to help developing countries who are making good governance decisions and investing in their future.

We're pursuing a forward strategy of freedom around the world. We're promoting democracy. I want you to tell your children about what has taken place in a brief period of time in this world. You know, it wasn't all that long ago that young girls couldn't go to school in Afghanistan because the country was run by ideologues of hate called the Taliban. And if their mothers didn't toe the line, they would be pulled into the public squares and whipped and sometimes shot in a sports stadium.

They were backward. The society was grim and dark. Because we acted to defend ourselves, because we upheld the doctrine that said, "If you harbor a terrorist, you're equally as guilty as the terrorist," millions of people in Afghanistan went to the polls to vote for a President. And the first voter was a 19-year-old woman.

There will be elections in Iraq in January. Think how far that society has come from the days of torture chambers and mass graves. Freedom is on the march. Liberty will transform societies. I believe everybody yearns to be free. I believe this not because freedom is America's gift to the world, I believe this because freedom is the Almighty God's gift to each man and woman in this world.

The role of a President is to confront problems, not to pass them on to future generations and future Presidents. That is how I have led, and that is how I will continue to lead our great Nation. We will keep your taxes low so this economy continues to grow. We will work on the education reforms and take them to our high schools. We will expand Pell grants for low- and middle-income families so more of our children can start their career with a college degree. We'll make sure that health decisions are made by doctors and patients, not by officials in Washington, DC.

We'll keep the promise of Social Security for our seniors. You might remember the 2000 campaign. Perhaps the same thing is happening in this campaign. It's kind of the old, tired scare tactics. They said, "If George W. gets elected, our seniors aren't going to get their checks." That's what they said 4 years ago. Please tell your friends and neighbors, George W. did get elected, and our seniors did get their checks. Our seniors will continue to get their checks. Baby boomers like me and a couple others out there I see—we're in pretty good shape when it comes to the Social Security trust.

But we need to worry about our children and our grandchildren. We need to worry about whether or not a—Social Security

will be available for them when they retire. I believe younger workers ought to be able to take some of their payroll taxes and set up a personal savings account, a personal savings account that earns a better rate of return than the Social Security trust, an account they call their own, an account the Government cannot take away.

Over the next 4 years, I'm going to work with Republicans and Democrats to do something about the Tax Code. It is a complicated mess. It is a million pages long. We need to make the Tax Code easier to understand and more fair for the American people.

Over the next 4 years, I will defend the values that are important for our families and our Nation. Marriage and family are the foundations of our society, and we will keep them strong. I believe that this society must promote a culture of life. I was proud to sign the ban on partial-birth abortion. I stand and will continue to stand for the appointment of Federal judges who know the difference between personal opinion and the strict interpretation of the law.

My opponent and I differ on these issues. Look at his record. He voted against the Defense of Marriage Act and voted against the ban on partial-birth abortion.

Audience members. Boo-o-o!

The President. He said he—he said there would be a litmus test for his judges. And at one point in this campaign, he said that you can find the heart and soul of America in Hollywood.

Audience members. Boo-o-o!

The President. The heart and soul of America is found in caring communities like Saginaw, Michigan.

Now, I'm looking forward to the rest of this campaign. I like talking about what we have done to make it clear to the American people I intend to do what I say I'm going to do during the next 4 years. I got a hopeful vision for this country. I see a better day coming. That stands in contrast with my opponent, who has offered a long litany of complaints without a significant record.

One of my favorite quotes that I hope helps you understand how I feel about our great country comes from a fellow Texan named Tom Lea. He said, "Sarah and I live on the east side of the mountain. It's the sunrise side, not the sunset side. It is the side to see the day that is coming, not to see the day that is gone." During the course of this campaign, my opponent has spent much time talking about the day that is gone. I'm talking about the day that is coming.

I see a prosperous America where people are able to realize their dreams. I see an education system that challenges our children so that no child is left behind. I see a compassionate health care system run by you, where doctors aren't being sued every day. I see a world that is free and therefore peaceful. I see the peace that we all long for our children and our grandchildren.

When I traveled your State 4 years ago, I made you this pledge, that if I was elected, I would uphold the honor and the dignity of the office. With your help and with your hard work, I will do so for 4 more years.

Thanks for coming. God bless. Thank you all.

NOTE: The President spoke at 9:16 a.m. at the Dow Event Center. In his remarks, he referred to Myrah Kirkwood, candidate in Michigan's Fifth Congressional District; Betsy DeVos, chairman, Michigan Republican Party; the Saline Fiddlers, a student musical group from Saline High School, Saline, MI; and former President Saddam Hussein of Iraq.

Remarks in Dayton, Ohio
October 28, 2004

The President. Thank you all. Thanks for coming. Thanks for coming out today. You're lifting my spirits. I'm honored you're here. I have come back to the great city of Dayton, Ohio, to ask for your vote and ask for your help. We have a duty in our country to vote. I'm asking for you to remind your friends and neighbors of that duty. We have an obligation in a free society to show up to the polls.

I've come to Dayton to ask you to get our fellow Republicans to vote, to find independents to go to the polls, and don't overlook discerning Democrats like Mayor McKelvey from the great city of Youngstown, Ohio. And when you get them headed to the polls, remind them, if they want a safer America, a stronger America, and a better America for all of us, to put me and Dick Cheney back in office.

My regret is that Laura is not with me today.

Audience members. Aw-w-w!

The President. It's obviously your regret as well. [*Laughter*] So we were in the seventh grade together at San Jacinto Junior High in Midland, Texas. And then we became reacquainted when she was a public school librarian. And I asked her to marry me, and she said, "Fine, but make me a promise." I said, "Okay, what is it?" She said, "Promise me I'll never have to give a political speech." [*Laughter*] I said, "Okay, you got a deal." Fortunately, she is not holding me to that promise. She is giving a lot of speeches, and when she does, the American people see a strong, a warm, a compassionate First Lady. I love her dearly. And, as a matter of fact, just as we pulled into the parking lot I got a phone call from three other members of my family. Barbara and Jenna, our twins, are out campaigning, and guess who they're with? They're with old Number 41. That would be former President Bush. And they send their best to the good people of Dayton, Ohio.

And they send their best to my buddy, the Senator from Ohio, George Voinovich. I tell you, you're lucky to have a man of this caliber serving you in the United States Senate. What a fine American, and I hope you put him back in office with a resounding vote. Plus he married well.

I want to thank my friend George McKelvey, the—from Youngstown, Ohio. We had a rally there yesterday. A lot of people showed up to see the Mayor. [*Laughter*] They wanted to see their leader. I'm proud that George has stood up by me—by side—side by side with me. There's a lot of Democrats that are for my candidacy. There's a lot of people around this country who know that the Democrat Party has left them. And I welcome every Democrat's support. You are welcome on our team.

I want to thank the other United States Senator from Ohio for joining us today. Mike DeWine and his wife, Fran, are with us. Thanks, Mike, for coming. I know you're proud of Congressman Mike Turner. Mike, you're doing a great job. And my friend John Boehner is with us, Congressman John Boehner—and his wife, Debbie—the author of the No Child Left Behind Act in the House of Representatives.

I want to thank Chief Justice Tom Moyer for joining us today. Mr. Judge, thanks for being here. I want to thank your mayor, the mayor of Trotwood, Ohio, for joining us today. Thanks for coming, Don. I'm proud you're here. I want to thank all the local and State officials, all the candidates.

But most of all, I want to thank you all. I want to thank the grassroots activists, the people putting up the signs, the people making the phone calls, the people doing all the hard work. I want to thank you

for what you have done, and I want to thank you for what you're going to do. With your help, with your hard work in turning out that vote, there is no doubt in my mind we'll carry Ohio again and win a great victory on November the 2d.

Five days from today, the people of America will go to the polls. We're choosing the leader of our country at a time of great consequence in our world. We're at war against a terrorist enemy unlike any we have seen. We have much more to do to win a decisive victory in the war on terror. The most solemn duty of the American President is to protect the American people. If America shows uncertainty or weakness in these troubled times, the world will drift toward tragedy. This is not going to happen on my watch.

Our economy is in the midst of change and challenge. It can be a time of great opportunity if we have the right policies to strengthen rather than stall our economic recovery. We have much more to do to improve our children's education, to make health care more accessible and affordable, to strengthen our Social Security for our children and our grandchildren. And I'm ready for the job.

My 4 years as your President have confirmed some lessons and have taught some new ones. A President must have a vision in order to lead this country. You cannot lead if you don't know where you're going. A President must set clear goals and bring people together to achieve those goals. A President must surround himself with smart and capable people who are willing to express their opinion. I have surrounded myself with smart and capable people.

A President must make America's priorities crystal-clear, especially in an uncertain world. I've learned to expect the unexpected, because history can deliver sudden horror from a soft autumn sky. I have found you better know what you believe or risk being tossed to-and-fro by the flattery of friends or the chorus of critics. I've been grateful for the lessons I've learned from my parents: Respect every person; do your best; live every day to its fullest. And I've been strengthened by my faith and humbled by its reminder that my life is part of a much bigger story.

I have learned firsthand how hard it is to send young men and women into battle, even when the cause is right. I've been reminded that the world looks to America for leadership and that it is crucial for the American President to be consistent. I have learned America's President must base decisions on principle, core convictions from which you will never waver. The issues vary; the challenges are different every day in this job. Tactics and strategy must be flexible, but a President's convictions must be steady and true. As Presidents from Abraham Lincoln to Franklin Roosevelt to Ronald Reagan so clearly demonstrated, a President cannot blow in the wind. A President has to make the tough decisions and stand by them.

The President must not follow the path of the latest polls. The President must lead based on conviction and conscience. Especially at a time of war, mixed signals only confuse our friends, embolden our enemies. Mixed signals are the wrong signals for an American President to send.

When America chooses a President, you choose not just a set of positions on issues of philosophy or record; you choose a human being who comes with strengths and weaknesses. One of the things I've learned about the Presidency is, whatever your strengths are, you're going to need them, and whatever your shortcomings are, people are going to notice them. [*Laughter*] Sometimes I'm a little too blunt. I get that from my mother. Sometimes I mangle the English language. [*Laughter*] I get that from my dad. But Americans have learned this, that even when you disagree with me, at least you know what I believe and where I stand. And you cannot say that about my opponent.

Audience members. Boo-o-o!

The President. Senator Kerry has taken a lot of different positions, but he rarely takes a stand. He has run a campaign of contradictions. I think it's fair to say that consistency has not been the Senator's long suit. [*Laughter*] He was for the PATRIOT Act and the No Child Left Behind Act—until he was against key provisions of both of them. He voted to authorize the use of force in Iraq, then said I was wrong to use that force. When I sent troops into Iraq to remove Saddam Hussein from power, he said it was the right decision. Now he says it was the "wrong war."

Audience members. Boo-o-o!

The President. During one of our debates, he said Saddam Hussein was a threat. Then a couple of answers later, he said there was no threat in Iraq. Just last year, American troops in Afghanistan and Iraq needed $87 billion to help them complete their missions. This was vital support. First, Senator Kerry said, "It would be irresponsible to vote against the troops." He said that on national TV. Then he did that irresponsible thing and he voted against the funding for our troops.

Audience members. Boo-o-o!

The President. You might remember perhaps the most famous quote of the 2004 campaign. When they asked him about his vote, he said, "I actually did vote for the 87 billion, before I voted against it." He's given several explanations of that vote since then, but perhaps one of the most interesting is, he said, "The whole thing was a complicated matter." There's nothing complicated about supporting our troops in combat.

I will always stand with our troops. I want to thank the military families who have joined us today. And I want to thank the veterans who have set such a great example to those who wear the uniform.

Now, you have to wonder why the Senator has taken such different positions at different places and different times in this campaign. Well, let me give you two reasons. It's important for the people of

Ohio to understand this. Senator Kerry changes positions because he's willing to say anything he thinks that will help him politically at the time. And he does so to try to obscure a 20-year trail of out-of-the-mainstream votes that leads to an inescapable conclusion: Senator Kerry has been on the wrong side of the defining national security and domestic policy debates of the last 2 years. He can run, but he cannot hide.

Several times during the course of the campaign, the Senator has changed his positions for political convenience. The Senator recognized Saddam Hussein was a threat and authorized force to remove him, until his Democratic opponent, Howard Dean, began gaining ground as an antiwar candidate. The Senator decided he had to appeal to that wing of his party, so he voted against the troops—after voting to put them in risk in the first place.

Audience members. Boo-o-o!

The President. The Senator was all for removing Saddam Hussein when we went into Baghdad, and he was very supportive when we captured him. After all, the polls showed that he was—that that was very popular at the time. People liked that. When the going got tough and when we faced determined opposition and things weren't quite so popular, the Senator suddenly wasn't quite so supportive. In fact, he changed his mind entirely, saying that Iraq was the "wrong war at the wrong place at the wrong time."

Audience members. Boo-o-o!

The President. What does that lack of conviction say to our troops who are risking their lives in this vital cause? Think about what that says to our allies who have joined our cause. Think about what that says, that lack of conviction, say to our enemies, that if you make things uncomfortable, if you stir up trouble, John Kerry will back off. And that's a very dangerous signal in the world in which we live.

Just this week Senator Kerry showed his willingness to put politics ahead of facts and the truth. He criticized our military's handling of explosives in Iraq, when his own advisers admitted he didn't know what had happened. His spokesman has now had to acknowledge that the explosives may have been moved before our troops arrived. A President needs to get all the facts before jumping to politically motivated conclusions. The Senator's willingness to trade principle for political convenience makes it clear that John Kerry is the wrong man for the wrong job at the wrong time.

There's another reason the Senator changes positions. He doesn't want you to know where he stands. He has a history. He doesn't want you to know where he really stands on national security because he has a record of weakness. When Ronald Reagan was confronting the Soviet Union at the height of the cold war, Senator Kerry proposed cancellation of critical defense weapons systems and said that President Reagan's policy of peace through strength was making America less safe.

Audience members. Boo-o-o!

The President. History has shown that Senator Kerry was wrong and President Ronald Reagan was right.

When former President Bush led a coalition against Saddam Hussein in 1991, Senator Kerry voted against using force to liberate Kuwait.

Audience members. Boo-o-o!

The President. History has shown that Senator Kerry was wrong and former President Bush was right.

In 1994, just one year after the first bombing of the World Trade Center, Senator Kerry proposed massive cuts in America's intelligence budget, cuts so extreme that even his Massachusetts colleague, Ted Kennedy, opposed them. History has shown that Senator Kerry was wrong and—we've got to be fair—Senator Kennedy was right.

When you are one Senator among 100, you can be wrong without consequence. But the President's opinion decides the security and the fate of the American people.

We have a different point of view when it comes to your security. Senator Kerry says September the 11th did not change him much. That's what he said.

Audience members. Boo-o-o!

The President. And his policies make that clear. The Senator says the war on terror is primarily a law enforcement and intelligence gathering operation.

Audience members. Boo-o-o!

The President. September the 11th changed me a lot. In the days after the attacks, I went to Ground Zero. On September the 14th, 2001, I stood where those buildings used to stand. I'll never forget that day, workers in hardhats yelling at me at the top of their lungs, "Whatever it takes." I remember the man—I remember one person in particular, who grabbed me by the arm. His eyes were bloodshot, and he looked me square in the eye and he said, "Do not let me down." Ever since that day, I've gotten up every morning thinking about how to better protect our country. I will never relent in defending America, whatever it takes.

There are other things about my opponent's positions he doesn't want you to know. I don't know if you remember the debate—one of the debates, they were talking about health care. And he looked square in the camera and he said, "My plan—the Government doesn't have anything to do with it." [*Laughter*] I could barely contain myself. [*Laughter*]

The Government has got a lot to do with it. Eighty percent of the people in his plan end up on a Government plan. You see, if you make it easier for people to get on Medicaid, small businesses will drop coverage for their employees because the Government will provide the insurance. That's moving people from the private sector to the public sector. When the Government starts writing the checks, the Government starts making the rules. And when it comes to your health care, when the Government starts making the rules, the Government starts making your decisions,

and they start deciding for the docs. Federal control of health care is the wrong prescription for American families.

I've got a better idea. We'll make sure health care is available and affordable. We'd take care of the poor and the indigent by expanding community health centers across this country. We'll help make sure low-income children are signed up for the health programs available for them. We're also going to help our families. We'll expand health savings accounts so small businesses and families can better afford insurance and manage their own account. We will allow small businesses to come together so they can buy insurance at the same discounts that big companies are able to do.

And to make sure health care is available and affordable, we're going to do something about these frivolous lawsuits that are running up the cost of medicine. I have met too many doctors, here in Ohio and elsewhere, too many ob-gyns that are getting run out of practice because these lawsuits are causing their premiums to go up. And that hurts the people of Ohio when that happens. I have met too many expectant moms who are worried about the quality of the health care for their baby. See, these lawsuits are making it hard for you to afford health care. You cannot be pro-doctor and pro-patient and pro-personal-injury-trial-lawyer at the same time. You have to choose. My opponent made his choice, and he put a personal-injury trial lawyer on the ticket.

Audience members. Boo-o-o!

The President. I have made my choice. I'm standing with the patients of Ohio. I'm standing with the doctors of Ohio. I am for medical liability reform—now.

The Senator really doesn't want you to know where he stands on taxes, because he's going to raise them. Listen, to be fair, raising taxes is one of the few things that he has been consistent about. You might say he's made a habit of it. He's been in the Senate for 20 years. He's voted to raise taxes 98 times.

Audience members. Boo-o-o!

The President. That is five times for every year he's been in the Senate. I would call that a predictable pattern, a leading indicator. [*Laughter*] During the campaign, he's promised a lot of new spending, $2.2 trillion of new spending. That's trillion with a "T." That's a lot even for a Senator from Massachusetts. They asked him how he's going to pay for it, and he said, "That's simple. We'll just tax the rich." Most small businesses in Ohio pay tax at the individual income tax. One of the reasons why people are finding work here is because the small-business sector of your economy is strong and getting stronger. Seventy percent of new jobs are created by small businesses. And by raising the top two brackets, my opponent would be taxing the job creators of Ohio, and that's bad economic policy.

The other thing is, is that by raising the top brackets, you only raise between 600 and 800 billion. That is far short of 2.2 trillion. I would call that a tax gap. That would be the difference between what he has promised to spend and what he can deliver. Guess who usually gets to fill the tax gap? You do. But the good news is, we're not going to let him tax you; we're going to carry Ohio and win nationally on November the 2d.

You know where I stand when it comes to taxes. When I campaigned for the Presidency in 2000, I said we're going to provide our families tax relief. I kept my word. We increased the child tax credit to help our families. We reduced the marriage penalty. We believe the Tax Code should encourage marriage, not penalize marriage. We provided help for our small businesses.

This economy of ours is strong, and it is getting stronger. We're growing at rates as fast as any in nearly 20 years. The number of jobs have been increased by 1.9 million since August of 2003. The national unemployment rate is 5.4 percent. Let me put that in perspective for you: That's lower than the average rate of the 1970s, the 1980s, and the 1990s. Ohio's farmers are

making a living. The entrepreneurial spirit is strong in the State of Ohio. Homeownership rate is at an alltime high. More minority families own a home today than ever before in our Nation's history.

I understand times are tough here in Ohio in certain parts of your State. I know that. That's why I've been coming to your State, listening to people, talking about how to make sure this economy continues to grow. The unemployment rate went from 6.3 percent to 6 percent last month. Ohio added 5,500 new jobs last month. We're on our way to recovery. And the question the Ohio people have got to answer: Who's got the plan to make sure this economy continues to grow? I do: Low taxes; less regulation; and tort reform.

When I ran for President 4 years ago, I promised to challenge the soft bigotry of low expectations in our public schools. And I kept my word. We passed the No Child Left Behind Act. We are spending more money for Title I students, trying to help low-income students. But now we're asking the question, "Can you read and write and add and subtract?" See, in return for excess money, we want to know whether or not people are learning. We believe every child can learn. We believe everybody has got potential, and we expect every child to learn in America.

You cannot solve a problem until you diagnose the problem. And now we're diagnosing, and we're beginning to solve them. Math and reading scores are going up. The achievement gap amongst minority students is closing in America. And we're not going to go back to the old days of low expectations and mediocrity in our schoolhouses.

When I ran for President 4 years ago, I promised to improve Medicare by adding prescription drug coverage for our seniors. I kept my word. You might remember the old debates of Medicare. They called it "Medi-scare." [*Laughter*] People weren't willing to really take on the issue. I took on the issue. I was joined by Senator

Voinovich and Senator DeWine, Congressman Boehner, Congressman Turner. We go to Washington to do things for the people. Medicare needed to be strengthened. Medicare needed to be modernized. You see, Medicare would pay thousands of dollars for a heart surgery but not one dime for the prescription drugs that could prevent the heart surgery from being needed in the first place. That wasn't fair to our seniors. We got the job done, and beginning in 2006, all seniors will be able to get prescription drug coverage in Medicare.

My opponent voted against the Medicare bill.

Audience members. Boo-o-o!

The President. In a new term, I will defend the reforms we have put in place and keep our promise to our America's seniors.

And speaking about our seniors, let me talk about Social Security, now that you got me on a roll. [*Laughter*] When you're out gathering up the vote, remind your friends and neighbors that in the 2000 campaign, it was said that if George W. got elected, the seniors would not get their checks. I don't know if you remember that. It may be happening here in Ohio now. You remind them that George W. did get elected, and our seniors got their checks. And our seniors will continue to get their checks. And baby boomers like me, we'll probably get our checks.

But we need to worry about our children and our grandchildren. We need to worry about whether or not Social Security will be there for them when they retire. I believe younger workers ought to be allowed to take some of their payroll taxes and set up a personal savings account, an account they call their own, an account the Government cannot take away.

The job of a President is to confront problems, not to pass them on to future Presidents and future generations. My opponent said he's going to protect Social Security, but remind your friends and neighbors, he voted eight times to tax Social Security benefits.

Audience members. Boo-o-o!

The President. And he's offered nothing for the younger generation. In a new term, I'll bring Republicans and Democrats together to strengthen Social Security for generations to come.

Let me tell you what else we're going to do in a new term. We're going to simplify the Tax Code. It is a complicated mess. It's a million pages thick. We're going to make it fair for our workers, fair for our business, and fair for America.

Now, there's more to do. I'm asking for your vote because I know where I want to lead this country. I see a more hopeful America. I want to work with you to make sure our education system fulfills its promise and to make sure health care is available and affordable without the Federal Government taking it over. I want to make sure we do our duty to younger generations of Americans, and I want to continue to work to spread freedom and liberty so the world is more peaceful.

I want you to understand what has taken place in a brief period of time, particularly the youngsters who are here. The Taliban ran Afghanistan, and young girls could not go to school because they had a dark vision of the world. And if their mothers did not toe their ideological line of hatred, they would be pulled in the public square and whipped and sometimes killed in a sports stadium. These people were barbaric people. Because we acted to defend ourselves, because we upheld doctrine that said, "If you harbor a terrorist, you're equally as guilty as the terrorist," because we acted in our self-interest to defend ourselves and eradicated those Al Qaida training camps that were in Afghanistan, millions of people were able to go to the polls and vote for a President of Afghanistan. And the first voter was a 19-year-old woman. Think about that.

There will be elections in Iraq. Think how far Iraq has come from the days of torture chambers and mass graves. Freedom is on the march, and we're better off for it. We believe that people want to be free. Freedom is not America's gift to the world; freedom is the Almighty God's gift to each man and woman in this world.

Over the next 4 years, we've got work to do to make sure our families are secure and prosperous and our children are educated. And we've also got work to do to defend the values that are important for our country. I believe marriage is a sacred commitment. I believe marriage and family are the foundations of our society. I believe in a culture of life in America. I proudly signed the ban on partial-birth abortion. I will name judges who know the difference between personal opinion and the strict interpretation of the law.

My opponent has a different view. He voted against the Defense of Marriage Act, and he voted against the ban on partial-birth abortion.

Audience members. Boo-o-o!

The President. The way I heard it, he says he's going to have a litmus test for his judges. He also went on to say that, one time in this campaign, that the heart and soul of America can be found in Hollywood.

Audience members. Boo-o-o!

The President. The heart and soul of America is found in caring communities like Dayton, Ohio.

I'm optimistic about the future of this country. I know we can overcome any problem that faces us, because I know the American people. I know the strength and courage and compassion of the people who live in this land.

You know, one of my favorite quotes is written by a fellow Texan named Tom Lea. He said, "Sarah and I live on the east side of the mountain. It is the sunrise side, not the sunset side. It is the side to see the day that is coming, not to see the day that is gone." You know, in the course of this campaign, my opponent has been talking about the day that is gone. I'm talking about the day that is coming.

And I see a great day coming for America. I see a hopeful day. And I see the fact that the hard work we've done is paying off. I see peace coming as well, peace for our children and our grandchildren.

You know, when I campaigned across your State, I made this pledge, that if I won in 2000, I would uphold the honor and the dignity of the office to which I had been elected. With your help, with your hard work, I will do so for 4 more years.

God bless. Thank you for coming. Thank you all.

NOTE: The President spoke at 12:10 p.m. at the Hara Complex. In his remarks, he referred to Mayor George M. McKelvey of Youngstown, OH; Chief Justice Thomas J. Moyer of the Supreme Court of Ohio; Mayor Donald K. McLaurin of Trotwood, OH; and former President Saddam Hussein of Iraq.

Remarks in Westlake, Ohio
October 28, 2004

The President. Thank you all for coming. Thank you all for being here today. I am so honored so many came out to say hello. You've lifted my spirits. I am here in Westlake, Ohio, asking for your vote and your help. I am asking you during the next couple of days to get on the telephone, to tell your friends and neighbors we have a duty in our free society to vote. We have an obligation to vote. Tell them they need to go to the polls, and when you get them headed to the polls, tell them that if they want a safer America, a stronger America, and a better America, to put me and Dick Cheney back in office.

I am so honored you are here. My only regret on this beautiful day is that Laura is not here to see the size of this crowd.

Audience members. Aw-w-w!

The President. I know it. That is generally the reaction. [*Laughter*] "Why didn't you stay at home and send her?" [*Laughter*] I don't know if you know this or not, but Laura and I went to the seventh grade together, San Jacinto Junior High. By the way, she went to the same high school at the same time that Tommy Franks did, in Midland, Texas. He's older, and she's prettier. [*Laughter*] And so, I met her again—we became reacquainted—and she was a public school librarian when I did so. And she said—I said, "Will you marry me?" She said, "Fine, but make me a promise." I said, "What is it?" She said, "Promise me I will never have to give a political speech." [*Laughter*] I said, "You got a deal." Fortunately, she didn't hold me to that promise. She's giving a lot of speeches—she's speaking in Florida today—and when she does, the American people see a strong, compassionate, great First Lady.

I'm proud of my runningmate, Dick Cheney. I readily concede he does not have the waviest hair in the race. [*Laughter*] You'll be happy to hear I did not pick him because of his hairdo. [*Laughter*] I picked him because of his judgment. I picked him because of his experience, and he is getting the job done for the American people.

I'm proud and I am honored to be supported by General Tommy Franks. America is safer and the world is better off because of the leadership of this fine American. God bless you, Tommy. And I'm proud to be here with Senator Bob Dole and all the retired officers who are on this stage who represent hundreds of people, former military leaders who are supporting my candidacy. It means a lot. It means a lot to be standing on the stage with people who have served our country so courageously.

Thank you all for coming today, and thank you for your support.

I've been traveling today with a fine United States Senator in George Voinovich. Send him back to Washington. He's doing a great job for you. And so is Mike DeWine. I'm proud to call him friend. I know you're proud to call him United States Senator.

I want to thank Lieutenant Governor Jennette Bradley. I want to thank Mayor Hruby for joining us. And guess who else is with us today, a buddy of mine I've been traveling with across the State of Ohio, the Democrat mayor of Youngstown, Ohio, George McKelvey. He represents a lot of Democrats that are supporting my candidacy. There are a lot of people who understand and remember the great Democrat tradition of Franklin Roosevelt and Harry Truman and John Kennedy, of standing strong in times of crisis. As the mayor puts it, he didn't leave the Democrat Party; the Democrat Party under John Kerry left him. And I welcome every Democrat to my campaign, and I'm honored you're here.

I want to thank all the State and local officials. I appreciate so very much the Fraternal Order of Police folks who are here today. I want to thank you for the endorsement of my candidacy for President.

I know the great Cleveland Indian, Bob Feller, is with us today. I'm honored you're here. I appreciate my friend Sammy Kershaw for being here today. Thank you, Sammy and Lorrie Morgan, his wife, for coming; thanks for entertaining everybody.

But most of all, thank you all. I'm here to thank you for what you have done and what you're going to do over the next 5 days. Get on that phone. Tell your friends and neighbors to vote. There's no doubt in my mind, with your help, we will carry Ohio again and win a great victory on November the 2d.

When people go to the polls, we'll be choosing the leader of our country at a time of great consequence in our world. We're at war against the terrorist enemy unlike any we have seen. We have much more to do to win this war on terror. The primary job of the President of the United States is to protect the American people. If America shows any uncertainty or weakness in these troubling times, the world will drift toward tragedy. This is not going to happen on my watch.

Our economy is in the midst of change and challenge. It can be a time of great opportunity if we have the right policies to strengthen, rather than stall, the economic recovery. We have more to do to make sure people can find work in places like Ohio, more to do to improve our children's education, more to do to make sure health care is available and affordable, more to do to strengthen Social Security for a generation to come, and I am ready for the job.

My 4 years as your President have confirmed some lessons and taught me some new ones. The President must have a vision. You must understand where you're going in order to lead this Nation. A President must set clear goals and bring people together to achieve those goals. A President must surround himself with good, capable, strong people, and I have done so.

I have learned to expect the unexpected. History can deliver sudden horror from a soft autumn sky. I've found you better know what you believe or you risk being tossed to-and-fro by the flattery of friends or the chorus of the critics. I've been grateful for the lessons I've learned from my parents, respect every person, do your best, live every day to its fullest. I have been strengthened by my faith and humbled by its reminder that my life is part of a much bigger story.

I have learned firsthand how hard it is to send young men and women into battle, even when the cause is right. I've been reminded that the world looks to America for leadership and that it is crucial for America's President to be consistent. I've learned America's President must base decisions on principle, core convictions from which you will not waver. The issues vary; the challenges are different every day as your President. Tactics and strategy will be flexible, but a President's convictions must be steady, and they must be true.

As Presidents from Abraham Lincoln to Franklin Roosevelt to Ronald Reagan so clearly demonstrated, a President cannot blow in the wind. A President has to make tough decisions and stand by them. That is how I have led our country, and that is how I will continue to lead our country for 4 more years.

Audience members. Four more years! Four more years! Four more years!

The President. The President must not follow the path of the latest polls. The President must lead based on conviction and conscience. Especially in a time of war, mixed signals only confuse our friends, embolden our enemies. Mixed signals are the wrong signals for an American President to send.

When America chooses a President, you choose not just a set of positions on issues or a philosophy or record; you choose a human being who comes with strengths and weaknesses. One of the things I've learned about the Presidency is whatever your strengths are, you are going to need them, and whatever your shortcomings are, people are going to notice them. [*Laughter*] Sometimes I'm a little too blunt. I get that from my mother. [*Laughter*] Sometimes I mangle the English language. I get that from my father. [*Laughter*] But Americans have learned that even when you disagree with me, at least you know what I believe and where I stand.

You cannot say that about my opponent. Senator Kerry has taken a lot of different positions, but he rarely takes a stand. He has run a campaign of contradictions. I think it's fair to say consistency has not been the Senator's strong suit. He was for the PATRIOT Act and the No Child Left Behind Act until he was against key provisions of both of them. He voted to authorize the use of force in Iraq and then said

I was wrong to use that force. When I sent troops to Iraq to remove Saddam Hussein from power, he said it was the right decision. Now he says it's the wrong war. During one of our debates, he said Saddam Hussein was a threat. Then a couple of answers later, he said there was no threat in Iraq.

This last year, American troops in Afghanistan and Iraq needed $87 billion to support them in their missions. First, Senator Kerry said on national TV, "It would be irresponsible to vote against the troops." Then he did that irresponsible thing and voted against the troops.

Audience members. Boo-o-o!

The President. You might remember perhaps the most famous quote of the 2004 campaign when they asked him about that vote, when he said this: "I actually did vote for the 87 billion, before I voted against it." I haven't spent nearly as much time in these parts as you have, but I think you're going to have trouble finding anybody in Westlake who talks that way.

He's given a lot of answers about that vote. One of the most interesting ones of all is when he said, "The whole thing was a complicated matter." My fellow Americans, there's nothing complicated about supporting our troops in combat.

You have to wonder why he's taken such dramatically different positions in different places in different times in this campaign. Well, here's two reasons why, and it's important for the Ohio voters to understand this. Senator Kerry changes positions because he's willing to say anything he thinks will help him politically at the time. And he does so to try to obscure a 20-year record of out-of-the-mainstream votes that leads to this conclusion: Senator Kerry has been on the wrong side of defining national security and domestic policy debates for the last two decades. That is his record. He can run, but he cannot hide.

Several times during the course of this campaign, the Senator has changed his position for political convenience. The Senator recognized Saddam Hussein was a threat and authorized the use of force, until his Democratic opponent Howard Dean began gaining ground as an antiwar candidate. The Senator decided he had to appeal to that wing of his party. So he voted against the troops after voting to put them at risk in the first place. The Senator was all for removing Saddam Hussein when we went into Baghdad and very supportive when we captured him. After all, the polls showed that was popular at the time. [*Laughter*] When the going got tough, when we faced determined opposition and things were not quite so popular, the Senator suddenly wasn't quite so supportive. In fact, he changed his mind entirely, deciding it was the "wrong war at the wrong place and the wrong time."

Audience members. Boo-o-o!

The President. The voters of Ohio must ask these questions. What does that lack of conviction say to our troops who are risking their lives in the vital cause? What does it say to our allies who have joined that cause? And what does his lack of conviction signal to our enemies? That if you make things uncomfortable, if you stir up trouble, John Kerry will back off. And that's a very dangerous signal in a world of grave threats. The President must be consistent. The President must stand for something.

Just this week, Senator Kerry showed his willingness to put politics ahead of the facts and the truth. He criticized our military's handling of explosives in Iraq, when his own advisers admitted he did not know what had happened. His spokesman has now had to acknowledge that the explosives may have been moved before our troops ever arrived. A President needs to get all the facts before jumping to politically motivated conclusions. The Senator's willingness to trade principle for political convenience makes it clear that John Kerry is the wrong man for the wrong job at the wrong time.

And there's another reason why the Senator changes positions. He doesn't want you to know where he really stands. He doesn't want you to know where he stands on national security because he has a record of weakness. When Ronald Reagan was confronting the Soviet Union at the height of the cold war, Senator Kerry said President Reagan's policy of peace through strength was making America less safe. History has shown that Senator Kerry was wrong, and President Ronald Reagan was right.

When former President Bush led a coalition against Saddam Hussein in 1991, Senator Kerry voted against using force to liberate Kuwait. History has shown that Senator Kerry was wrong, and former President Bush was right.

In 1994, just one year after the first bombing of the World Trade Center, Senator Kerry proposed massive cuts in America's intelligence budget, cuts so extreme that even his Massachusetts colleague, Ted Kennedy, opposed them. History has shown that Senator Kerry was wrong and—we've got to be fair—[laughter]—Senator Kennedy was right. When you are one Senator among 100, you can be wrong without consequence. The President's opinion—the President's decision decides the security and the fate of our country.

My opponent and I have a different view about how to protect you, about how to make this country secure. He's got a limited, narrow view of the war on terror. Senator Kerry said September the 11th did not change him much at all.

Audience members. Boo-o-o!

The President. Those are his words, not mine. And his policies make that clear. The Senator says the war on terror is primarily a law enforcement and intelligence gathering operation.

Audience members. Boo-o-o!

The President. My outlook was changed by September the 11th. I clearly see the threats that we face. A few days after the attack, I stood where the buildings fell. I'll never forget the evil of the enemy and the suffering of our people. I remember that day—clearly remember that day. I remem-

ber the sights and sounds. I remember the workers in hardhats yelling at me at the top of their lungs, "Whatever it takes." I remember looking in the eyes of a man coming out of that rubble who said to me, "Do not let me down." Ever since that day, I've waken up every morning trying to figure out how to better protect our country. I will never relent in defending America, whatever it takes.

There are other things about my opponent's views he doesn't want you to know. I don't know if you remember that in one of those debates. He looked square in the camera when they asked him about his health care plan, and he said, "The Government doesn't have anything to do with it." I could barely contain myself. [*Laughter*] The Government has got a lot to do with his health care plan. Eighty percent of the people would end up on Government insurance. If you increase the Medicaid limits, it provides an incentives for small businesses not to provide insurance for their employees, because the Government is going to provide insurance for their employees. You're moving people from the private sector to the Government when it comes to health insurance, and when the Government writes the checks, the Government makes the rules. And when it comes to your health care, when the Government makes the rules, the Government starts making decisions for you and starts deciding for your doctors. The wrong prescription for our families' health care is the Federal control of health care.

I have got a better idea. We'll take care of the poor and the indigent through community health centers. We'll make sure low-income children are fully subscribed into the health programs aimed for them. I understand that most of the uninsured work for small businesses. Small businesses ought to be allowed to pool risk so they can buy insurance at the same discounts that big companies can do. We'll expand health savings accounts to help our small businesses and our families. And to make sure health care is available and affordable, we will do something about the junk lawsuits that are running good docs out of practice and running your bills up.

I was in Canton a while ago and met ob-gyns that could no longer deliver babies. They had to get out of practice because these lawsuits had run their insurance up so high they couldn't afford to stay in practice. I've met too many women around our country who are worried about their baby. They're worried that they can't get the quality of health care that they need. Too many people are driving too far to get good health care because these lawsuits are ruining medicine, as far as I'm concerned. You can't be pro-doctor and pro-patient and pro-personal-injury-trial-lawyer at the same time. You have to make a choice. My opponent made his choice, and he put a personal injury trial lawyer on the ticket.

Audience members. Boo-o-o!

The President. I have made my choice. I'm standing with the doctors of Ohio. I'm standing with the patients of Ohio. We are for medical liability reform.

The Senator doesn't want you to really know where he stands on taxes, because he's going to raise them. Listen, to be fair, raising taxes is one of the view things that he has been consistent about. [*Laughter*] You might say he's made a habit out of it. He's been in the Senate 90—he's been in Senate 20 years, and he's voted to raise your taxes 98 times.

Audience members. Boo-o-o!

The President. That's five times every year he's been in the Senate. I would call that a predictable pattern—[*laughter*]—a leading indicator—tells you what he thinks about your wallet. He's also proposed $2.2 trillion in new spending. That's a lot. That's a lot even for a Senator from Massachusetts. So they asked him, "How are you going to pay for it?" And he threw out that same old tired line, you know, "We're just going to tax the rich." Well, the problem is, is that by running up the top two brackets you raise between 600 and 800

billion dollars, and that's far short of the 2.2 trillion worth of promises. I would call that a tax gap. That would be the gap between what he's promised and what he can deliver. And guess who usually fills the tax gap.

Audience member. We do!

The President. The good news is we're not going to let him tax you. We're going to carry Ohio and win on November the 2d.

The Senator's record is clear. There is a mainstream in American politics, and he sits on the far left bank. I'm a compassionate conservative and proudly so. I am glad to talk about my record. You know, when I ran for office, I said we would cut the taxes on the American people, and I kept my word. We increased the child credit. We reduced the marriage penalty. We believe that the Tax Code ought to encourage marriage, not penalize marriage. We created a 10-percent bracket to help our working families. We cut the taxes on everybody who pays taxes. We're helping our small businesses, and our economic policies are paying off. This economy is strong, and it is getting stronger.

You remind your friends and neighbors, when you're out gathering the vote, what we have been through. Six months prior to my arrival in Washington, DC, the stock market was in serious decline. That foretold a recession. Then we had some corporate scandals. We passed good law that make it abundantly clear we're not going to tolerate dishonesty in the boardrooms of America. And finally, those attacks cost us about a million jobs in the 3 months after September the 11th.

But our plans are working. We've added 1.9 million new jobs since August of 2003. Homeownership rate is at an alltime high in America. More minorities own a home today than ever before in our Nation's history. Ohio's farmers are making a living. The entrepreneurial spirit is strong in the State of Ohio. Our small businesses are creating jobs.

I know there's pockets of problems here in this State. I understand that. I've been traveling your State. I know it well. But I want to remind you, in the month of September, the unemployment rate went from 6.3 percent to 6 percent in the State of Ohio. You added 5,500 new jobs in this State. We're making progress. We're going forward, and we're not going to go back to the days of tax and spend.

No, I'm proud to run on my record. When I campaigned for President 4 years ago, I promised to challenge the soft bigotry of low expectations in our public schools. I kept my word. We passed the No Child Left Behind Act, which is a fine piece of legislation. In return for increased Federal spending, we're now measuring. You know why? Because we believe every child can learn in America, and we expect every school to teach. You cannot solve a problem unless you diagnose the problem, and we're now diagnosing problems all across America, and our children are learning to read and write and add and subtract. The math scores are up. The English scores are up. We're closing an achievement gap among minority students, and we are not going to back to the day of low standards and mediocrity in our classrooms.

When I ran for President 4 years ago, I promised to improve Medicare by adding prescription drug coverage for our seniors. I kept my word. Medicine was changing, and Medicare wasn't. We pay thousands of dollars for heart surgery but not one dime for the prescription drugs that could prevent the heart surgery from being needed in the first place. I brought Republicans and Democrats together. We have strengthened and modernized Medicare. Beginning in 2006, all seniors will be able to get prescription drug coverage under Medicare.

Now that you've got me on a roll, let me talk about Social Security. [*Laughter*] I promised our seniors we would keep the promise of Social Security, and we did. In the 2000 campaign, I remember those— some of those television ads, the fliers that went out to our seniors that said, "If George W. gets elected, our seniors are not going to get their checks." You might remember those, the shameless scare tactics. Well, George W. did get elected, and our seniors got their checks. And our seniors will continue to get their checks. And baby boomers like me—I see a few of us out there—don't admit it—[*laughter*]— we're going to get our checks.

But we need to worry about our children and our grandchildren. We need to worry about whether Social Security will be there for them when they need it. That's why I think younger workers ought to be allowed to take some of their payroll taxes and set up a personal savings account, a personal savings account they call their own, that the Government cannot take away.

During the debate, I remember my opponent standing up there saying, well, he's going to protect Social Security. But what he forgot to tell you was, he voted eight times to raise taxes on Social Security benefits.

Audience members. Boo-o-o!

The President. The good thing about a campaign is, you can run, but you cannot hide.

He also offered nothing for the younger generation. The job of a President is to confront problems, not to pass them on to future Presidents and future generations. In a new term, I will bring Republicans and Democrats together to make sure the Social Security system is strengthened for generations to come.

There's more work to be done. I'm here to ask for the vote and let you know I want to make sure education systems continue to work. We'll expand the high standards to our high schools and expand Pell grants for low- and middle-income families so more children can start their career with a college degree. We'll continue to expand our economy and create an environment for the entrepreneur to flourish, by keeping your taxes low and doing something about regulations and lawsuits. We're going to make sure that the compassion of America continues to be unleashed through our faith-based and community-based initiatives. And we'll work hard to make sure this country is secure, by not only chasing the terrorists abroad so we do not have to face them here at home but by spreading freedom and liberty.

I want to thank you all for bringing your children here today. I want to tell the children something, and I hope parents reinforce this. We—we're changing the world because of our belief in liberty. It wasn't all that long ago in Afghanistan where young girls could not go to school. Think about a society that way. Think about how barbaric and backward the Taliban were. And if their mothers didn't toe their ideological line of hatred, they would be pulled in the public square and whipped; some cases, killed in a sports stadium.

We acted in our own self-interest in Afghanistan. We acted to uphold a doctrine that I explained to the world, that said, "If you harbor a terrorist, you're equally as guilty as the terrorist." When the President says something, he needs to speak clearly and mean what he says in order to keep the peace. And I meant what I said, and Tommy knew I meant what I said. We acted in our interest and removed the Taliban—Al Qaida can no longer train there—but in so doing, millions of people voted in a Presidential election. The first voter in the Afghanistan Presidential election was a 19-year-old woman. Think about that. Think about how that society has gone from darkness to light because of freedom.

Iraq will hold elections in January. Think how far that society has come from the days of torture chambers and mass graves. Freedom is on the march, and America is more secure because of it. And freedom will stay on the march so long as I am your President. I believe everybody yearns to be free. Freedom is not America's gift to the world; freedom is the Almighty God's gift to each man and woman in this world.

Over the next 4 years, we will work to protect and defend the values that make our country such a unique place. I stand for judges who know the difference between personal opinion and the strict interpretation of the law. I stand for a culture of life in which every being matters and every person counts. I proudly signed the ban on partial-birth abortion. I stand strongly for marriage and family, which are the foundations of our society.

My opponent and I disagreed on these issues. He voted against the ban on partial-birth abortion.

Audience members. Boo-o-o!

The President. He voted against the Defense of Marriage Act.

Audience members. Boo-o-o!

The President. As a matter of fact, at one time during this campaign, he actually said he thought you could find the values—find the heart and soul of America in Hollywood.

Audience members. Boo-o-o!

The President. The heart and soul of America is found right here in places like Westlake, Ohio.

It's an important election. I want to thank you all for coming out and giving me a chance to encourage you to vote and to work the crowd, work the folks—work the folks in your neighborhood and communities—community centers and your coffee shops. Tell the people we have an obligation, and when you're talking to them, tell them I see such a bright future for America. I see a great day ahead for our citizens.

One of my favorite quotes is written by a fellow Texan named Tom Lea. Here's what he said. He said, "Sarah and I live on the east side of the mountain. It is the sunrise side, not the sunset side. It is the side to see the day that is coming, not to see the day that is gone." The course of this campaign, my opponent has spent much of the time talking about the day that is gone. I'm talking about the day that's coming, a better day for all Americans, a prosperous America, an educated America, a compassionate America, and a peaceful world that we all want.

You know, when I campaigned across your State 4 years ago, I made you this pledge, that if I got elected, I would uphold the honor and the integrity of the office. With your help, with your hard work, I will do so for 4 more years.

God bless. Thank you all for coming. Thank you all.

NOTE: The President spoke at 2:50 p.m. at the Westlake Recreation Center. In his remarks, he referred to Gen. Tommy R. Franks, USA (Ret.), former combatant commander, U.S. Central Command; former Senator Bob Dole; Mayor Jerry N. Hruby of Brecksville, OH; and Baseball Hall of Fame pitcher Bob Feller.

Remarks in Yardley, Pennsylvania
October 28, 2004

The President. Thank you all for coming. I have had a fabulous day today. What a great way to end it. Thanks for lifting my spirits. It is such an honor to be back in Bucks County.

First, I want to thank Ruth Wright, who's the owner of this beautiful farm. And I want to thank her for enrolling the land in the Conservation Reserve Program, to help preserve the open spaces of Bucks County. What a great citizen. What a fantastic contribution to this beautiful part of the world. Ms. Wright, we are honored that you let us all come here. Some of us will stay over afterwards and help clean up. [*Laughter*] I, of course, will be going to another State to keep putting the message out.

I'm here to ask for your vote, and I'm here to ask for your help. We're coming down the stretch. There's not many days left. We have a duty in this country to vote, and I'm asking you to get your friends and neighbors to go to the polls. Tell your friends and neighbors that in a free society, all of us have an obligation to participate in our democracy. Make sure our fellow Republicans get the word. Make sure independents get the word. And don't overlook discerning Democrats. They too want what

we want, which is a safer America, a stronger America, and a better America.

I am sorry that Laura is not with me this evening.

Audience members. Aw-w-w!

The President. That is generally the reaction. I take it like, "Why didn't you stay home and send her?" [*Laughter*] What a fabulous woman she is. You know, when I asked her to marry me, she was a public school librarian. She said, "Fine, I'll marry you, but make me a promise." I said, "What is the promise?" She said, "Promise me I'll never have to give a political speech." [*Laughter*] I said, "Okay, you got a deal." Fortunately, she didn't hold me to that promise. She was in Florida today giving speeches. When the people see Laura Bush give a speech, they see a strong, compassionate, great First Lady.

I'm proud of my runningmate, Dick Cheney. I do not want to offend anybody here who's follically challenged, but I admit my runningmate does not have the best hairdo in the race. [*Laughter*] I didn't pick him because of his hairdo. I picked him because of his judgment, his experience. He is getting the job done for the American people.

I'm honored to be introduced by Chad Lewis. No, I know you know him as a fine football player. Michele knows him as a loving dad and a great husband. I know him as a man of character. I'm proud to be standing on stage with Chad, and I want to thank the other Eagles for coming here today. I'm honored you all are here. Congratulations on a great season. Just don't be too tough on the Cowboys. [*Laughter*]

I want to thank my friend Arlen Specter for being here today. I hope you put him back in for 6 more years. And I enjoy the other Senator from Pennsylvania, a good friend of mine, I know a friend of yours, Rick Santorum.

I'm a little angry at your Congressman. He's leaving. I've enjoyed working with Jim Greenwood. He cares deeply about the people of Pennsylvania and Bucks County. He has done a fine job as a Member of the United States Congress, and I wish him all the best in this new venture. And I urge you to support Mike Fitzpatrick to take his place.

I welcome Melissa Brown here. She too is running for the United States Congress from the Thirteenth Congressional District. I wish Melissa all the best. I want to thank all the other candidates who are here. I appreciate the entertainers who are here.

Most of all, I thank you all for coming. Thanks for putting up the signs. Thanks for making the phone calls. Thanks for working hard to turn out such a big crowd. I want to thank you for what you're going to do. Turn out the vote—no doubt in my mind, we can carry and will carry Pennsylvania and win a victory on November the 2d.

Audience members. Four more years! Four more years! Four more years!

The President. And one other person I want to recognize, and that's Sam Evans. Sam Evans is 101 years young. He is with us tonight. He is the chairman of the American Foundation of Negro Affairs. I am proud to have his support. Mr. Evans, God bless you, and thanks for coming.

The election comes down to some clear choices for America's families, and that's what I'm here to talk about. The first clear choice is the most important because it concerns the security of your family. All progress on every issue depends on the safety of our citizens. This will be the first election since September the 11th, 2001. Americans will go to the polls in a time of war and ongoing threats. The terrorists who killed thousands of innocent people are still dangerous, and they are determined. The outcome of this election will set the direction of the war on terror. The most solemn duty of the American President is to protect the American people. If America shows uncertainty or weakness in these troubled times, the world will drift toward tragedy. This will not happen on my watch.

Since that terrible morning of September the 11th, 2001, we've fought the terrorists across the Earth, not for pride, not for power but because the lives of our citizens are at stake. Our strategy is clear. We're strengthening the protections of our homeland. The former Governor of Pennsylvania, Tom Ridge, is doing a great job as the Secretary of Homeland Security. We're reforming our intelligence capabilities. We are transforming our military. There will be no draft. The All-Volunteer Army works, and we'll keep it an all-volunteer army. We are relentless. We are determined. We are staying on the offense against these terrorists so we do not have to face them here at home.

And we're making progress. More than three-quarters of Al Qaida's key members and associates have been brought to justice, and the rest of them know we're on their trail. And at the same time, we use all our assets to protect ourselves.

We've got one other asset, and that's our deep belief in liberty and freedom. We believe in the power of liberty to transform societies. I want you to tell your children and grandchildren about the astonishing events that are taking place.

In a short period of time, Afghanistan has gone from a country ruled by barbarians who would not let young girls go to school. And if their mothers didn't toe their line of hatred, they were taken into the public squares and whipped and sometimes executed in a sports stadium. Because we defended ourselves, because we upheld the doctrine that said, "If you harbor a terrorist, you're equally as guilty as the terrorist," millions of people voted in a Presidential election in Afghanistan. And the first voter was a 19-year-old woman. Because of freedom, that society has gone from darkness to light, and America is more secure to have Afghanistan as an ally in the war on terror.

Iraq will hold Presidential elections in January. Think how far that society has come from the days of mass graves and torture chambers, from the days of a brutal dictator, Saddam Hussein. Freedom is on the march. The world is changing because of our deep belief in freedom. We believe everybody wants to be free. Freedom is not America's gift to the world; freedom is the Almighty God's gift to each man and woman in this world.

A President must lead with consistency and strength. In a war, sometimes your tactics change but not your principles. Americans have seen how I do my job. Even when you might not agree with me, you know what I believe, you know where I stand, and you know where I'm going to lead this country. On good days and on bad days, whether the polls are up or the polls are down, I am determined to protect the American people, and I will always support the men and women who wear our uniform.

I see a sign that says "Moms of Military." I want to thank the families who are here— the families of our military who are here for their sacrifices. I want to thank the veterans who are here for having set such a great example for those who wear the uniform. And I want to assure those who wear the uniform and their loved ones, we will make sure they have all the resources they need to complete their missions. That's why I went to the United States

Congress in September of 2003 and asked the Congress for support—to support our men and women in harm's way. We asked for $87 billion, and it was necessary. It was important funding.

The bipartisan support for that measure was overwhelming. Republicans and Democrats both understood the need to support our troops in harm's way. It was so strong that only 12 Members of the United States Senate voted against the funding, 2 of whom are my opponent and his runningmate. As you're out gathering up the vote, as you find people who wonder about which candidate can lead, you might remind them of this startling statistic: Four Members of the United States Senate voted to authorize the use of force and voted against providing the funding necessary to support our troops in combat—only 4 out of 100—4 Members of the Senate, 2 of whom are my opponent and his runningmate.

Audience members. Boo-o-o!

The President. They asked him why, and you might remember the famous quote of the 2004 campaign, when he said, "I actually did vote for the $87 billion, right before I voted against it." He's given several explanations since then about that vote. Perhaps the most interesting and telling of all is when he finally said, "Well, the whole matter was a complicated matter." There is nothing complicated about supporting our troops in combat.

Senator Kerry's record on national security has a far deeper problem than election-year flip-flopping. On the largest national security issues of our time, he has been consistently wrong. When Ronald Reagan was confronting the Soviet Union at the height of the cold war, Senator Kerry said that President Reagan's policy of peace through strength was making America less secure. Well, history has shown that Senator Kerry was wrong and President Ronald Reagan was right.

When former President Bush led a coalition against Saddam Hussein in 1991, Senator Kerry voted against the use of force to liberate Kuwait. Well, history has shown that Senator Kerry was wrong and former President Bush was right.

In 1994, just one year after the first bombing of the World Trade Center, Senator Kerry proposed massive cuts in America's intelligence budget, so massive that even his Massachusetts colleague, Ted Kennedy, opposed them. Well, history has shown that Senator Kerry was wrong and— we've got to be fair—[*laughter*]—Senator Kennedy was right.

During the last 20 years, in key moments of challenge and decision for America, Senator Kerry has chosen the position of weakness and inaction. With that record, he stands in opposition not just to me but to the great tradition of the Democratic Party. The party of Franklin Roosevelt and Harry Truman and John Kennedy is rightly remembered for confidence and resolve in times of war. Senator Kerry has turned his back on "pay and price" and "bear any burden," and he has replaced those commitments with "wait and see" and "cut and run."

Many Democrats in this country do not recognize their party anymore. And today, here in the great State of Pennsylvania, I want to speak to every one of them: If you believe that America should lead with strength and purpose and confidence in our ideals, I would be honored to have your support, and I am asking for your vote.

Audience members. Four more years! Four more years! Four more years!

The President. The security of our families is at stake. Senator Kerry says that September the 11th did not change him much at all. That's what he said. His policies make that clear. He says the war on terror is primarily a law enforcement and intelligence gathering operation.

September the 11th changed me, and changed my outlook. I'll never forget the day that I stood in the ruins of the Twin Towers, September the 14th, 2001. I'll never forget the sights and sounds of that day, the workers in hardhats yelling at me at the top of their lungs, "Whatever it takes." I remember the firefighter or police officer, I'm not sure which one, who'd come out of the rubble. He grabbed me by the arm. He looked me square in the eye, and he said, "Do not let me down." Ever since that morning, I've gotten up thinking about how to best protect America. I will never relent in defending our country, whatever it takes.

The second clear choice in this election concerns your family's budget. When I ran for President 4 years ago, I pledged to lower taxes for American families. I kept my word. We doubled the child credit to $1,000 per child to help the moms and dads. We reduced the marriage penalty. I believe the Tax Code ought to encourage marriage, not penalize marriage. We dropped the lowest bracket to 10 percent so working families can take—keep more of their paychecks. We reduced income taxes for everybody who pays income taxes. And real after-tax income, the money you have in your pocket, is up by about 10 percent since I've been your President.

When you're out gathering the vote, remind people about what this economy has been through. Six months prior to my arrival in Washington, the stock market was in serious decline. It foretold a recession that we went through. And then we had some corporate scandals. But we acted. We passed good legislation that made it abundantly clear we will not tolerate dishonesty in the boardrooms of America. And then we got attacked, and those attacks cost us about a million jobs in the 3 months after September the 11th.

But our economic policies are working. By stimulating consumption and increasing investment, this economy is strong, and it is getting stronger. Think about what's taken place. Homeownership is at an all-time high in America. More minority families own a home than ever before in our

Nation's history. Pennsylvania farmers, like farmers everywhere, are making a good living under the Bush administration. Small businesses are flourishing. The entrepreneurial spirit is strong in America.

We've added 1.9 million new jobs in the last 13 months. The national unemployment rate is 5.4 percent. Let me put that in perspective for you: That's lower than the average rate of the 1970s, the 1980s, and the 1990s. The unemployment rate in Pennsylvania is 5.3 percent. This economy is moving forward, and we're not going to go back to the days of tax and spend.

My opponent has a different plan for your family's budget. He's going to take a big chunk out of it. You remind your friends and neighbors about these facts. He voted against the child—increasing the child credit. He voted against the marriage penalty relief. He voted against lower taxes. If he had had his way, the average American family would be paying 2,000 more in Federal income taxes.

Audience members. Boo-o-o!

The President. That probably doesn't seem like a lot to people in Washington. It's a lot to people who are trying to make ends meet in Bucks County, Pennsylvania. It matters to families right here in this part of the world.

He's been in the United States Senate 20 years, and he's voted for higher taxes 98 times. That is five times a year. I would call that a predictable pattern, a leading indicator. When a Senator does something that often, he must really enjoy it. [*Laughter*]

I want you to couple that fact with this one: He's proposed about $2.2 trillion in new Federal spending. That's trillion with a "T." That's a lot. That's a lot even for a Senator from Massachusetts. [*Laughter*] And so they asked him, "How are you going to pay for it?" And he threw out that same old tired line we've heard before. He's going to tax the rich.

Let me tell you two things about that. One, most small businesses are sole propri-etorships or Subchapter S's. They pay tax at the individual income-tax level. Seventy percent of new jobs in America are created by small businesses. By running up the top two brackets, you're taxing the job creators. You're taking money out of the coffers of small businesses, and that is bad economic policy.

This may interest you as well. By raising the top two brackets, by taxing the rich, you raise about 600 billion to 800 billion dollars. That is far short of the 2.2 trillion that he had promised. That's what we call a tax gap. That's the difference between what's promised and what's delivered. Guess who usually fills the tax gap? You do. But the good news is, we're not going to let him tax you; we're going to carry Pennsylvania and win on November the 2d.

The third clear choice in this election involves the quality of life for our families. A good education and quality health care are important to our families. As a candidate, I pledged to challenge the soft bigotry of low expectations by reforming our public schools. I kept my word. I signed the No Child Left Behind Act and proudly so. We're raising the standards. We're spending more money, but in return, we're asking for results. We believe every child can learn, and we expect every school to teach.

You cannot solve a problem until you diagnose the problem, and we're now diagnosing problems and we're solving them. Test scores are up in reading and math. We're closing an achievement gap for minority students all across America. And we're not going to go back to the days of low standards and mediocrity in our classrooms.

We'll continue to improve life for our families by making health care more affordable and available. We'll make it available by making sure the poor and the indigent are able to get care in community health centers, places where people can get good preventative care and good primary care without burdening the emergency rooms of your local hospitals. We'll make sure that children of low-income families are—subscribe to the programs aimed to help them, to make sure health care is affordable.

We'll help our small businesses. Small businesses ought to be allowed to pool risk across jurisdictional boundaries so they can buy insurance at the same discounts that big companies are able to do. We will expand health savings accounts to help our small-business owners and families afford health insurance and manage their own health care plans.

To make sure health care is available and affordable in a State like Pennsylvania and others, we will do something about the frivolous lawsuits that are running up the cost of medicine and running good doctors out of practice. We have a problem in this Nation when it comes to medical liability. There are too many lawsuits. I have met too many ob-gyns from the State of Pennsylvania who are being driven out of practice because their premiums are so high because of the lawsuits. And I, unfortunately, have met too many patients of ob-gyns who are deeply concerned about the quality of health care for not only the mom but the baby. This is a national problem.

You cannot be pro-doctor and pro-patient and pro-personal-injury-trial-lawyer at the same time. You have to make a choice. My opponent made his choice, and he put a personal-injury trial lawyer on the ticket.

Audience members. Boo-o-o!

The President. He's voted against medical liability reform 10 times in the United States Senate. I made my choice. I'm standing with the doctors of Pennsylvania. I'm standing with the patients of Pennsylvania. I am for real medical liability reform.

My opponent proposed a plan. You might remember, at one of our debates, he looked straight in the camera and he said about his plan, "The Government doesn't have anything to do with it." I could barely contain myself. [*Laughter*]

The Government's got a lot to do with it. Eighty percent of the people in this plan will end up on a Government plan. If you make it easier for people to get on Medicaid, it is likely small-business owners will stop providing insurance for their employees because the Government will cover them. That's moving people from the private sector to the public sector when it comes to health care. And when the Government writes the checks, the Government makes the rules. And when the Government starts making the rules for your family's health care, they start making decisions for you. And they make decision for the docs. And they start making decisions on rationing of care.

Countries that have tried centralized health care can't get away from it quick enough. The wrong prescription for American families is to federalize health care in America. In all we do to make sure health care is available and affordable, we will make sure the decisions are made by doctors and patients, not by officials in Washington, DC.

The fourth clear choice in this election involves your retirement. Our Nation has made a solemn commitment to America's seniors on Social Security and Medicare. When I ran for President 4 years ago, I promised to keep that commitment and improve Medicare by adding prescription drug coverage. I kept my word.

We reformed Medicare. The system need to be fixed. We would pay thousands of dollars for a heart surgery but not one dime for the prescription drugs that could prevent the heart surgery from being needed in the first place. And that was not fair to our seniors, and it certainly wasn't fair to the taxpayers. And so we modernized Medicare. I brought Republicans and Democrats together. I proudly signed the Medicare bill. And beginning in 2006, all seniors in America will be able to get prescription drug coverage under Medicare.

We'll keep the promise of Social Security for our seniors, and we'll strengthen Social Security for generations to come. In the 2000 campaign, I remember some of those ads that said, "If George W. gets elected, our seniors won't get their checks." You might remember those. When you're out gathering up the vote, remind people George W. got elected, and the seniors got their checks. Those scare tactics are not going to work in 2004. They're too old, and they're too tired. Seniors will always get their checks. Baby boomers like me, like some of you, are in pretty good shape when it comes to the Social Security trust.

But we need to worry about our children and our grandchildren. We need to worry about whether the Social Security system will be there when they retire, and that's why I think younger workers ought to be allowed to take some of their own payroll taxes and set up a personal savings account, a personal savings account that will earn a better rate of return, a personal savings account they call their own, a personal savings account the Government cannot take away.

My opponent takes a different approach. He said he's going to protect Social Security, but tell your friends and neighbors about this fact: He voted eight times for higher taxes on Social Security benefits.

Audience members. Boo-o-o!

The President. And when it comes to the next generation, he has offered no reform. See, the job of a President is to confront problems, not to pass them on to future Presidents and future generations. In a new term, I'll bring people together to strengthen Social Security for generations to come.

The fifth clear choice in this election is on the values that are so crucial to keeping a family strong. I stand for the appointment of Federal judges who know the difference between personal opinion and the strict interpretation of the law. I stand for marriage and family, which are the foundations of our society. I stand for a culture of life in which every person matters and every being counts. And I proudly signed the ban on partial-birth abortion.

My opponent has taken a different position. He voted against the Defense of Mar-

riage Act. He voted against the ban on partial-birth abortion. And at one point in this campaign, he actually said that the heart and soul of America can be found in Hollywood.

Audience members. Boo-o-o!

The President. That's what he said. Most Americans do not look to Hollywood as a source of values. The truth of the matter is, the heart and soul of America is found in communities in Bucks County, Pennsylvania.

I'm running for a reason. I see clearly where this country needs to go.

Audience members. Four more years! Four more years! Four more years!

The President. I thank you all. I know where I want to lead us. You know, one of my favorite quotes is from a fellow Texan named Tom Lea, and he said, "Sarah and I live on the east side of the mountain. It is the sunrise side, not the sunset side. It is the side to see the day that is coming, not to see the day that is gone." The course of this campaign, my opponent has spent much of it talking about the day that is gone. I'm talking about the day that's coming.

I'm talking about a day in which our families are able to realize their dreams for their children. I'm talking about a day where prosperity reaches every corner of America, a day in which every school sets high standards so every child can realize the great promise of America. I'm talking about a day when we achieve the peace we all desperately want.

When I campaigned across Pennsylvania 4 years ago, I made this pledge, that I would uphold the honor and the dignity of the office. With your help, I will do so for 4 more years.

God bless. On to victory. Thank you all.

NOTE: The President spoke at 6:25 p.m. at Broadmeadows Farm. In his remarks, he referred to professional football player Chad Lewis and his wife, Michele; Mike Fitzpatrick, candidate in Pennsylvania's

Eighth Congressional District; and former President Saddam Hussein of Iraq.

Statement on Signing the Ronald W. Reagan National Defense Authorization Act for Fiscal Year 2005
October 28, 2004

Today, I have signed into law H.R. 4200, the "Ronald W. Reagan National Defense Authorization Act for Fiscal Year 2005." The Act authorizes funding for defense of the United States and its interests abroad, for military construction, and for national security-related energy programs.

Section 326 of the Act, amending sections 3551, 3552, and 3553 of title 31, United States Code, purports to require an executive branch official to file with the Comptroller General a protest of a proposed contract for private sector performance of agency functions previously performed at higher cost by Federal employees, whenever a majority of those Federal employees so requests, unless the official determines, free from any administrative review, that no reasonable basis exists for the protest. The executive branch shall construe section 326 in a manner consistent with the President's constitutional authority to supervise the unitary executive branch, including the making of determinations under section 326.

Section 574 of the Act amends sections 3037, 5046, 5148, and 8037 of title 10, United States Code, to prohibit Department of Defense personnel from interfering with the ability of a military department judge advocate general, and the staff judge advocate to the Commandant of the Marine Corps, to give independent legal advice to the head of a military department or chief of a military service or with the ability of judge advocates assigned to military units to give independent legal advice to unit commanders. The executive branch shall construe section 574 in a manner consistent

with: (1) the President's constitutional authorities to take care that the laws be faithfully executed, to supervise the unitary executive branch, and as Commander in Chief; (2) the statutory grant to the Secretary of Defense of authority, direction, and control over the Department of Defense (10 U.S.C. 113(b)); (3) the exercise of statutory authority by the Attorney General (28 U.S.C. 512 and 513) and the general counsel of the Department of Defense as its chief legal officer (10 U.S.C. 140) to render legal opinions that bind all civilian and military attorneys within the Department of Defense; and (4) the exercise of authority under the statutes (10 U.S.C. 3019, 5019, and 8019) by which the heads of the military departments may prescribe the functions of their respective general counsels.

The executive branch shall construe section 1021, purporting to place restrictions on the use of the U.S. Armed Forces in certain operations, and sections 1092 and 1205, relating to captured personnel and to contractor support personnel, in a manner consistent with the President's constitutional authority as Commander in Chief and to supervise the unitary executive branch.

Section 1203 of the Act creates a Special Inspector General for Iraq Reconstruction, under the joint authority of the Secretaries of State and Defense, as a successor to the Inspector General of the Coalition Provisional Authority under title III of Public Law 108–106. Title III as amended by section 1203 shall be construed in a manner consistent with the President's constitutional authorities to conduct the Nation's foreign affairs, to supervise the unitary executive branch, and as Commander in Chief of the Armed Forces. The Special Inspector General shall refrain from initiating, carrying out, or completing an audit or investigation, or from issuing a subpoena, which requires access to sensitive operation plans, intelligence matters, counter-intelligence matters, ongoing criminal investigations by administrative units of the Department of Defense related to national security, or other matters the disclosure of which would constitute a serious threat to national security. The Secretary of State and the Secretary of Defense jointly may make exceptions to the foregoing direction in the public interest.

The executive branch shall construe as advisory section 1207(b)(1) of the Act, which purports to direct an executive branch official to use the U.S. voice and vote in an international organization to achieve specified foreign policy objectives, as any other construction would impermissibly interfere with the President's constitutional authorities to conduct the Nation's foreign affairs and supervise the unitary executive branch. The executive branch also shall construe the phrase "generally recognized principles of international law" in sections 1402(c) and 1406(b) to refer to customary international law as determined by the President for the Nation, as is consistent with the President's constitutional authority to conduct the Nation's foreign affairs.

The executive branch shall construe section 3147 of the Act, relating to availability of certain funds if the Government decides to settle certain lawsuits, in a manner consistent with the Constitution's commitment to the President of the executive power and the authority to take care that the laws be faithfully executed, including through litigation and decisions whether to settle litigation.

Several provisions of the Act, including sections 315, 343(2) amending section 391 of Public Law 105–85, 506(b), 517(c), 571(b), 574(d)(8), 576(c), 577(c), 643(c) and (e), 651(g)(2), 666(c), 841(c), 3114(d)(2), and 3142(c) call for executive branch officials to submit to the Congress proposals for legislation. The executive branch shall implement these provisions in a manner consistent with the President's constitutional authority to supervise the unitary executive branch and to recommend for the consideration of the Congress such measures as the President judges necessary and expedient. Also, the executive branch shall construe section 1511(d) of the Act, which purports to make consultation with specified Members of Congress a precondition to the execution of the law, as calling for, but not mandating such consultation, as is consistent with the Constitution's provisions concerning the separate powers of the Congress to legislate and the President to execute the laws.

A number of provisions of the Act, including sections 112(b)(6), 213(c), 513(e)(1), 912(d), 1021(f), 1022(b), 1042, 1047, 1202, 1204, 1207(c) and (d)(2), 1208, 1214, and 3166(a) amending section 3624 in Public Law 106–398, call for the executive branch to furnish information to the Congress, a legislative agent, or other entities on various subjects. The executive branch shall construe such provisions in a manner consistent with the President's constitutional authority to withhold information the disclosure of which could impair foreign relations, national security, the deliberative processes of the Executive, or the performance of the Executive's constitutional duties.

Section 3161 expands the categories of atomic weapons industry employees who may receive direct compensation from the United States for their work-related illnesses. As a result, some claimants from the private sector who have occupationally caused asbestos-related diseases may be able to receive direct Federal compensation under the Energy Employees Occupational Illness Compensation Act Program. As a general matter, Federal taxpayers should bear no additional burdens arising from the tort liabilities of private sector defendants, including contractors of the United States. The limited extension of Federal responsibility here is unique because it is solely a replacement for no-fault workers' compensation payments not otherwise available, in the unique situation in which the Federal Government may have encouraged its contractors to resist workers' compensation claims brought by atomic weapons industry employees with occupational illnesses.

GEORGE W. BUSH

The White House,
October 28, 2004.

NOTE: H.R. 4200, approved October 28, was assigned Public Law No. 108–375. This statement was released by the Office of the Press Secretary on October 29. An original was not available for the verification of the content of this statement.

Remarks in Manchester, New Hampshire
October 29, 2004

The President. Thank you all. Thank you all for coming. Thanks for coming. We are honored you are here. Thanks for being here today. You've lifted our spirits. And with your help, we'll carry New Hampshire and win a great victory next Tuesday.

I want to thank my friends Senator Judd Gregg and Kathy. I want to thank Senator Sununu, Congressman Bradley, Congressman Bass, Governor Benson—put him back in. Put Gregg back in too. Most of all, thank you for coming.

Laura and I are thrilled you are here. You know, I'm here to tell the people of New Hampshire, you need to put me back in for a reason. Perhaps the most important one of all is so that Laura is the First Lady for 4 more years. I love her dearly. She is a great First Lady.

In the final 4 days of this historic campaign, I'm taking my vision of a more hopeful America directly to the people of this country. That's what I've come to New Hampshire about, to talk about a hopeful future for all of us. Today, our economy is strong, and it is getting stronger. The tax relief we passed is working. Think about this: Homeownership rate is at an alltime high in America. More minority families own a home than ever before in our Nation's history. Our farmers are making a good living. The entrepreneurial spirit is strong in America.

In the course of traveling your State, I met a lot of small-business owners who are making a good living because of our tax relief and because of their ingenuity and vision. And because they're making a good living, they're hiring people. We've added 1.9 million new jobs across this country in the last 13 months. The national unemployment rate is 5.4 percent. Let me put that in perspective for you. That's lower than the average rate of the 1970s, the 1980s, and the 1990s. The unemployment rate in the great State of New Hampshire is 3.5 percent. Our economic policies are working.

In a new term, we'll keep your taxes low. We'll reduce the regulations. We'll do something about these lawsuits. We will put plans in place to make sure the entrepreneurial spirit is strong so people can continue to work.

When I campaigned in 2000, I promised to challenge the soft bigotry of low expectations in our public schools. I kept my word. In a new term, we'll stay on the path of reform and results in all our schools so no child is left behind in America. In a new term, we'll make sure health care is more affordable and accessible for our families. In all we do to reform health care, we will make sure the health care decisions are made by doctors and patients, not by officials in Washington, DC. In a new term, we'll keep the promise of Social Security for our seniors and strengthen the system for our children and our grandchildren. In a new term, we'll protect marriage and family, which are the foundations of our society.

And all the progress we hope to make depends on the security of our Nation. We face enemies who hate our country and would do anything to harm us. I will fight these enemies with every asset of our national power. We will do our duty, and we will protect the American people.

Audience members. Four more years! Four more years! Four more years!

The President. On September the 11th, 2001, our Nation suffered terrible harm, and the pain was greatest for our families of the lost. With us today are Ernie Strada and his wife, Mary Ann, who lost their son, Tom, at the World Trade Center. Please welcome the Stradas. The September 11th families will always be in our thoughts and always be in our prayers. This Nation must never forget their pain.

On the day of that tragedy, I made a decision: America will no longer respond to terrorist murder with half-measures and empty threats. We will no longer look away from gathering dangers and simply hope for the best. We are pursuing a comprehensive strategy to fight the terrorist enemy and defend America. We will not relent, and we will prevail.

First, we're on the offensive against the terrorist networks. The best way to prevent future attacks is to go after the enemy. We will confront the terrorists abroad so we do not have to face them here at home. We are waging a global campaign from the mountains of central Asia to the deserts of the Middle East, from the Horn of Africa to the Philippines. We're getting results. Since September the 11th, more than three-quarters of Al Qaida's key members and associates have been detained or killed, and the rest of them know we are on their trail.

Secondly, we are confronting regimes that harbor terrorists and feed the terrorists and support the terrorists. I set a doctrine that these regimes are equally as guilty as the terrorists. When a President speaks, he must speak clearly and he must mean what he says. I meant what I said, and the Taliban regime in Afghanistan doubted our commitment. The regime is no more, and America and the world are safer.

Third, we're confronting outlaw regimes that pursue weapons of mass destruction, have ties to terror, and defy the world. A lesson of September the 11th is we must never allow the terrorists to gain the world's most dangerous weapons. Saddam Hussein chose to defy the world. He doubted our resolve, and America and the world are safer because he is sitting in a prison cell. And that message was heard in Libya, which has now given up its weapons of mass destruction programs, and that has made America and the world safer.

Fourth, we're promoting freedom and democracy in the broader Middle East. If 20 years from now the Middle East is dominated by dictators and mullahs who build weapons of mass destruction and harbor terrorists, our children and our grandchildren will grow up in a nightmare world of danger. This does not have to happen. We have a duty to protect ourselves and to protect future generations of Americans.

By taking the side of reformers and democrats in the Middle East, we will gain allies in the war on terror, and we'll isolate the ideology of hatred, and we'll help defeat the despair and hopelessness that feeds terror. So we're helping to build free societies in Afghanistan and Iraq and across that troubled region. Freedom is on the march, and America and the world are more secure.

Our strategy to win the war on terror is succeeding. We are shrinking the area where terrorists can operate freely. We have the terrorists on the run. And so long as I am your President, we'll be determined and steadfast, and we will keep the terrorists on the run.

Audience members. Four more years! Four more years! Four more years!

The President. To win the war on terror, to do our duty, America needs an unwavering commitment to see the task through. In any war, there are good days and there are bad days, but everyday, you need the same resolve.

When I took the oath of office 4 years ago, none of us could have envisioned what these years would bring. We've been through a lot together. My years as your President have confirmed some lessons and have taught me some new ones. One of the things I've learned about the Presidency is that whatever your strengths are, you're going to need them, and whatever your shortcomings are, people are going to notice them. [*Laughter*] Sometimes, I'm a little too blunt. I get that from my mother. Sometimes, I mangle the English language. [*Laughter*] I get that from my dad. But all the times, you know where I stand, what I believe, and where I'm going to lead this country.

A President must make America's priorities absolutely clear, especially in our uncertain world. I've learned firsthand how hard it is to send young men and women into battle, even when the cause is right. I've been reminded that the world looks to America for leadership, and it is crucial for the American President to be consistent. I have learned a President must base decisions on principle, core convictions from which he will never waver. The issues vary. The challenges are different every day. The polls go up; the polls go down. But a President's convictions must be consistent and true.

And through these 4 years, I have learned anew the enduring character of this great Nation. I have met exceptional men and women during my time as your President. I have seen their strength and their sacrifice, and their examples have confirmed there is no limit to the greatness of America. I have seen the character in people like Cheryl McGuinness, Debra Burlingame, and Elizabeth Kovalcin, who are with us today.

Cheryl's husband, Tom, and Debra's brother, Charles, were both pilots who lost their lives on September the 11th. Elizabeth's husband, David, was a passenger on Flight 11. These women have shown that hope can be found even in the worst tragedy. Cheryl says this: "While those terrorists may have killed almost 3,000 of our husbands and wives, mothers and fathers, children and friends on that day, they did not take away our spirit, our hope, or the promise of tomorrow." There is hope beyond the ashes of September the 11th, and nobody can take that away from us.

I've seen the character of America in people like Lisa Beamer and the husband she lost. Todd Beamer and other passengers on Flight 93 rushed those hijackers and led the first counterattack in the war on terror. Todd's final words captured the spirit of a nation. He said a prayer, and then he said, "Let's roll." Todd's dad, David Beamer, is with us today. I have been honored to have met Lisa as well. In terrible sadness, this family has been a model of grace, their own and the grace of God.

Just over a month after her husband's death, Lisa decided to take the same Newark-to-San Francisco flight that Todd had taken. And she explained, "I won't be held captive by fear." In the years to come, Lisa's words must be remembered by all Americans. As we fight the terrorists, they will try to frighten us. They will test our will by their barbaric tactics. We must be resolved. So long as I'm your President, we will not be held captive by fear.

The enemies who hit our country on September the 11th thought Americans would be fearful and weak. Instead, the world saw courageous rescuers, like New York City firefighters Michael Boyle and Tim and Tom Haskell, who ran toward danger. Michael's father, Jimmy, is with us today. Also with us is Ken Haskell, brother of Tim and Tom. America honors the courage of our first-responders. And we must always be grateful to those who carry out the great tradition of bravery and courage in the likes of Michael, Tim, and Tom.

After September the 11th, the world saw strangers comforting each other and a nation united in pride and defiance. For 3 years, the people of this country have shown patience and purpose in the hard tasks of history. We've risen to great challenges, and every American can be proud of their country.

I have seen the spirit of our country in those who wear our Nation's uniform, people like Mike McNaughton. Mike is a platoon sergeant from the Louisiana National Guard. He enlisted after September the 11th. He fought in Afghanistan and lost two fingers and a leg. I remember visiting Mike in the hospital. I said, "What do you like to do?" He said, "I like to run." I said, "Well, someday, you and I are going to run on the South Lawn of the White House." I don't know if he believed me at the time, but one day he showed up at the South Lawn of the White House, and we ran. I will never forget his determination and his courage and his sacrifice for our freedom.

I've spoken with so many of our people in uniform, from bases across America to a Thanksgiving in Baghdad. And I know their courage and their honor. They have fought our enemies with skill. They have treated the innocent with kindness, and they have delivered millions from oppression.

I have returned the salute of the wounded who told me they were only doing their duty. I've tried my best to comfort the families of the lost who told me to honor their loved ones by completing the mission. Like the men of Normandy and Iwo Jima before them, another great generation is serving America today, and our Nation is proud to stand with them.

All Americans must always remember the debt this Nation owes to the men and women who defend us. Those who wear the uniform are people of great character and service and duty and honor. We are thankful. And as we remember those who wear the uniform today, we must always remember the veterans who have set such a good example for today's men and women. And we are grateful to our military families for their sacrifice. And as long as I am the Commander in Chief, I assure you, we will keep our commitment we have made to our troops and their families. They will have the resources they need to complete their missions. As America saw on the $87 billion supplemental request, when I say something, I mean it.

We are not in this war alone. We must remember, our cause has been joined by many great nations and strong leaders. I've seen the determination of allies like Prime Minister Tony Blair of Great Britain. The Prime Minister and I come from different political backgrounds and traditions, yet we share a clear understanding of the threat we face and our duty to defeat it. I remember a phone call I had with Prime Minister Blair on a Sunday morning early last year. I called him when he was facing a political crisis at home. I told him I wanted him as an ally, but if politics was such that he could not commit British troops to combat in Iraq, I would understand. The Prime Minister replied that he believed our cause was right, and because it was right, Britain would join us. He said, "I am with you, and I mean it." That day I heard the spirit of Winston Churchill in the Prime Minister of Britain.

More than 90 countries share this commitment in the war on terror, because they understand this is civilization's fight. All 26

NATO nations have personnel in Iraq, Afghanistan, or both. And 14 of the countries that have joined our coalition in Iraq have lost forces in our vital work. In the war on terror, America has led; many have joined; and America and the world are safer.

We must always remember the steadfast conviction of our good allies. Their contributions and their sacrifice must never be dismissed or denigrated. They have earned the gratitude of the American people. In a new term, in order to secure America, I will continue to work with our allies. We will strengthen our alliances. But I will never turn over America's national security decisions to leaders of other countries.

As the President, I've also seen the spirit of the people we have liberated. I will never forget the day when seven Iraqi men came into the Oval Office. Coming into the Oval Office can be sometimes a awe-inspiring experience. It's a magnificent shrine to democracy. They came in—they had all had their right hands cut off by Saddam Hussein. They had had their hands cut off because his currency had been devalued and he needed a scapegoat. These men had been discovered in Iraq, had been flown to America to get a prosthesis, a new hand.

I told them, I said, "Welcome to the Oval Office. As we helped secure liberty in your country, we'll make sure—and you need to make sure—the institutions are bigger than the people who occupy the offices." That's certainly the case of the Oval Office. The institution of the President is always bigger than the person. I told them that by having the institutions bigger than the people, never again will somebody be able to pluck them out of society and arbitrarily cut off their right hands.

I will never forget the moment when one of those Iraqi men grabbed a Sharpie and in his new hand that he was just learning to use, slowly wrote out in Arabic a prayer for God to bless America. America should always be proud that our country remains the hope of the oppressed and the greatest force for good on this Earth.

Just last month, I welcomed Iraq's Prime Minister Allawi to the White House. For decades, he was a fearless critic of Saddam Hussein. As a matter of fact, in 1978, a team of assassins sent by the dictator attacked Dr. Allawi and his wife with axes and nearly killed him. He is a courageous man. Saddam Hussein knows the man he tried to murder is the leader of a free Iraq. Prime Minister Allawi is now confronting the enemies of freedom with strong determination. In the Rose Garden, he said that his nation would fight the terrorists in Iraq, room to room and house to house, so that the people of Iraq would never again have to live in tyranny.

Our mission in Iraq is clear. We are helping Iraq's new Government train armies and police forces and security forces so they can do the hard work of defending their freedom, so they can stand up and fight the terrorists who are trying to stop the advance of liberty. We'll help Iraq get on the path to stability and democracy as quickly as possible, and then our troops will come home with the honor they have earned.

The will of the Iraqis is strong, and their dream for freedom is moving forward. The terrorists are brutal and cruel. Yet everyday, Iraq and coalition forces are defeating the enemy's strategic objectives. The enemy in Iraq wants to establish terrorist bases from which to operate. We are on the offensive. We are denying them sanctuary. The enemy wants to intimidate Iraqis from joining the security forces, yet more 100,000 Iraqi soldiers and police and border guards are bravely serving their country. The enemy seeks to disrupt the march toward democracy, but Iraqis are preparing for free elections on schedule this coming January. The violent acts of a few will not divert Iraqis or our coalition from the mission we have accepted. Iraq will be free. Iraqis will be secure. And the terrorists will fail.

The Afghan people are also showing their character. The terrorists did everything they could to stop this month's elections, but the will of the Afghan people was more powerful than the hatred of the killers. Millions of Afghans lined up at the polls. The first vote in the Presidential election—the first voter was a 19-year-old woman. Imagine what the Taliban would have said about that. [*Laughter*]

The new President, Hamid Karzai, is a brave, respected leader who traveled southern Afghanistan by horseback to rally forces against the Taliban. Three years ago, his country was the training camp of Al Qaida. Now it is a democracy, a friend of America, and an ally in the war on terror.

By acting in Afghanistan and Iraq, we removed threats. We're making our country safer. We are also living up to the highest calling of our history. We're the Nation that freed Europe and lifted up former enemies in Germany and Japan. And we gave hope to captive peoples behind the Iron Curtain. The liberation of more than 50 million people in our time is a noble achievement, and every American can be proud of that achievement.

We must always remember the principles of our founding and the hope that our country has brought to the world. As long as I'm your President, this Nation will stand for freedom and stand by our friends and never cut and run. I believe everybody wants to be free. Freedom is not America's gift to the world; freedom is the Almighty God's gift to each man and woman in this world.

These experiences have helped shape my view of the world and the kind of leader I am. And one of the most powerful and defining experiences took place on September the 14th, 2001. George Howard, an officer with the Port Authority of New York and New Jersey, was off-duty on Sep-

tember the 11th. But when he learned the news, he went right to the Twin Towers. He died trying to save others. On that day of September the 14th, I met his mom, Arlene, who is with us today. She gave me George's police shield. She asked me not to forget the fallen. I carry Shield Number 1012. I will never forget the fallen. God bless you, Arlene.

Time passes, but we must always remember the enemy that kills without shame or mercy. I will always remember the men in hardhats at Ground Zero shouting at me at the top of their lungs, "Whatever it takes." My determination has not faded since that day. My determination is wrong—strong. I will never relent in defending America, whatever it takes.

We have come so far. We've accomplished so much. Yet, our work is not finished. All of us are part of a great historic endeavor. We will lead our country through a time of danger. We will build a world of freedom and peace beyond the war of terror. I know we'll succeed. I know the character of the American people.

The polls open in Manchester at 6 a.m. on Tuesday. For a safer America, for a stronger America, and for a better America, I ask the people of New Hampshire to vote for me.

God bless you, and God bless America. Thank you all.

NOTE: The President spoke at 10:56 a.m. at the Verizon Wireless Arena. In his remarks, he referred to Kathleen MacLellan Gregg, wife of Senator Judd Gregg; Gov. Craig Benson of New Hampshire; former President Saddam Hussein of Iraq; Prime Minister Tony Blair of the United Kingdom; Prime Minister Ayad Allawi of the Iraqi Interim Government; and President Hamid Karzai of Afghanistan.

Remarks in Portsmouth, New Hampshire
October 29, 2004

The President. Thank you all for coming. We are honored to be back. Such a beautiful day here in the great State of New Hampshire. Thank you all for coming out to say hello.

We are here in your State today asking for your vote and asking for your help. I'm asking you to get your friends and neighbors to do their duty, and that is to vote. We have a duty in this society of ours, in our free land, to vote. And so will you please find fellow Republicans and wise independents—[*laughter*]—discerning Democrats and head them to the polls. And when you get them going that way, remind them, if they want a safer America, a stronger America, and a better America, to put Dick Cheney and me back in office.

Perhaps the most important reason to put me back in is so that Laura will be the First Lady for 4 more years.

I'm proud of my runningmate, Dick Cheney. I don't want to offend anybody here who is follically challenged—[*laughter*]—but the Vice President doesn't have the prettiest hair in the race. [*Laughter*] You'll be happy to hear I didn't pick him because of his hairdo. I picked him because he's a man of sound judgment, excellent experience. He's getting the job done for the American people.

Two of our favorite people in Washington, DC, is Judd and Kathy Gregg. We're proud to call him friend. I know you're proud to call him Senator, and you should be. He's doing a great job for the people of New Hampshire. And we're fond of your junior Senator, John Sununu. What a good job he's doing. Congressman Jeb Bradley, your Congressman, is doing a great job in the House of Representatives. And Congressman Charlie Bass is with us. I appreciate you coming, Congressman. He's a good one.

And finally, I'm fond of your Governor. I know something about being a Governor. I was one—once one. He's doing a great job for the people of New Hampshire. You got to put Governor Benson back into office.

I want to thank Paul Needham for joining us. He's the former Democrat Derry town councilor. He was John Edwards for President State cochair. He's now a Democrat for Bush, and I'm proud he's here. And he's not alone. A lot of Democrats want a secure America. A lot of Democrats want a prosperous America. With your help, we're going to carry New Hampshire, and we're going to win a great victory in November.

I want to thank the grassroots activists who are here. We made a lot of friends in our travels throughout New Hampshire. I see Barbara. I know Ruthie is here, people who have been friends of ours for a long time. I want to thank you for putting up the signs. I want to thank you for making the phone calls. I want to thank you for what you have done and what you're going to do over the course of the next 5 days, and that is gather up the vote and turn them out for a great victory.

The voters have a clear choice between two very different candidates with dramatically different approaches and different records. You know where I stand. And sometimes, you even know where my opponent stands. [*Laughter*] We both have records. I'm proudly running on mine. The Senator is running from his. [*Laughter*]

This election comes down to clear choices for our families, issues of great consequence. The first clear choice is the most important because it concerns the security of your family. All our progress on every other issue depends on the safety of our citizens. Americans will go to the polls in a time of war and ongoing threats unlike with any we have faced before. The terrorists who killed thousands of innocent people are still dangerous, and they're determined to strike us again. The outcome of this election will set the direction of the war against terror. The most solemn duty of the American President is to protect the American people. If America shows uncertainty or weakness during these troubled times, the world will drift toward tragedy. This will not happen on my watch.

Since that terrible morning of September the 11th, 2001, we've fought the terrorists across the Earth, not for pride, not for power, but because the lives of our citizens are at stake. Our strategy is clear. We've strengthened the protections for the homeland. We're reforming our intelligence services. We're transforming our All-Volunteer Army. There will be no draft. We are relentless. We are determined. We're staying on the offensive. We're defeating the terrorists abroad so we do not have to face them here at home.

Because we have led, Afghanistan is a free nation and an ally in the war on terror. Because we led, Pakistan is capturing terrorists, and Saudi Arabia is making raids and arrests. Because we led, Libya is dismantling its weapons programs. Because we led, the army of a free Iraq is fighting for freedom, and more than three-quarters of Al Qaida's key members and associates have been brought to justice.

And I'll protect America by leading the cause of freedom. I believe in the transformational power of liberty. I believe liberty can transform societies and help us keep the peace. I want you to remind your sons and daughters about the amazing history that has taken place in a relatively short period of time. Three-and-a-half years ago, young girls could not go to school in Afghanistan because of the brutality and dark vision of the Taliban. And if their mothers didn't toe their line of ideological hatred, they were whipped in the public square and sometimes executed in a sports stadium. Because we acted to protect our-

selves, because we upheld the doctrine that said, "If you harbor a terrorist, you're equally as guilty as the terrorist," millions voted in the Presidential election in Afghanistan. And the first voter was a 19-year-old woman.

Iraq will have Presidential elections in January. Think how far that country has come from the days of torture chambers and mass graves. Freedom is on the march, and America is better for it. Freedom is on the move around the world.

I believe everybody yearns to be free. That's what I believe. And it drives much of my foreign policy. Listen, I understand freedom is not America's gift to the world; freedom is the Almighty God's gift to each man and woman in this world.

The President has to lead with consistency and strength. In a war, sometimes your tactics change but not your principles. And Americans have seen how I do my job. Even when you might not agree with me, you know what I believe and where I stand and what I intend to do. On good days and on bad days, whether the polls are up or the polls are down, I am determined to protect the American people, and I will always support our men and women who wear our Nation's uniform. I want to thank those who wear our uniform. I want to thank the military families who are here today. And I want to thank the veterans who are here who have set such a great example for the men and women of the military.

We have made a commitment to support our troops in combat. I'm the kind of fellow, when I say something, I mean it. I want the military families to know I mean what I said. That's why I went to the United States Congress in September of 2003 and requested $87 billion of important funding to support our troops in combat. We received great support from people of both political parties. As a matter of fact, only 12 Members of the United States Senate voted against supporting our troops in harm's way. Only 12 voted against the

$87 billion, 2 of whom were my opponent and his runningmate.

Audience members. Boo-o-o!

The President. When you're out gathering up the vote, I want you to remind people of this startling statistic: Only four Members of the United States Senate voted to authorize the use of force and then voted against supporting our troops in combat—four Members, two of whom were my opponent and his runningmate.

Audience members. Boo-o-o!

The President. You might remember perhaps the most famous quote of the 2004 campaign. When they asked my opponent about his vote, he said, "I actually did vote for the $87 billion, right before I voted against it." [*Laughter*] You know, I spent some time here in New Hampshire. I've been to the coffee shops. I've been to the community centers. I haven't heard anybody talk that way. [*Laughter*] They asked him several times about that vote, and he's given several different answers. Perhaps the most revealing of all was when he said about his vote against the $87 billion, "The whole thing was a complicated matter." [*Laughter*] My fellow Americans, there's nothing complicated about supporting our troops in combat.

Senator Kerry's record on national security has a far deeper problem than election-year flip-flopping. On the largest national security issues of our time, he has been consistently wrong. When Ronald Reagan was confronting the Soviet Union at the height of the cold war, Senator Kerry said that President Reagan's policy of peace through strength was making America less safe. He voted against many of the weapons systems critical to our defense buildup to help us keep the peace. History has shown that Senator Kerry was wrong and President Ronald Reagan was right.

When former President Bush led a coalition against Saddam Hussein in 1991, Senator Kerry voted against the use of force to liberate Kuwait. If his view had prevailed, Saddam Hussein today would domi-

nate the Middle East and would possess the most dangerous weapons. History has shown that Senator Kerry was wrong and former President Bush was right.

In 1994, just one year after the first bombing of the World Trade Center, Senator Kerry proposed massive cuts in Americans' intelligence budget, so massive that even his Massachusetts colleague, Ted Kennedy, opposed them.

Audience members. Boo-o-o!

The President. History has shown that Senator Kerry was wrong and—we've got to be fair—Senator Kennedy was right.

During the last 20 years, in moments of challenge and decision for America, Senator Kerry has chosen the position of weakness and inaction. With that record, he stands in opposition not just to me but to the great tradition of the Democratic Party. The party of Franklin Roosevelt, the party of Harry Truman, the party of John Kennedy is rightly remembered for confidence and resolve in times of war and hours of crisis. Senator Kerry has turned his back on "pay any price" and "bear any burden," and he has replaced those commitments with "wait and see" and "cut and run."

Many Democrats in this country do not recognize their party anymore. Today I want to speak to every one of them. If you believe that America should lead with strength and purpose and confidence in our ideals, I would be honored to have your support, and I am asking for your vote.

Audience members. Four more years! Four more years! Four more years!

The President. There are big differences between us as to how to best protect our country. The security of our families is at stake during this election. Senator Kerry says that the war on terror is primarily a law enforcement and intelligence gathering operation. He says that America must submit to what he calls a "global test."

Audience members. Boo-o-o!

The President. I'm not making that up. [*Laughter*] He was standing right about here when he said it during one of the debates. [*Laughter*] As far as I can tell, that means our country must get permission from foreign capitals before we act in our own defense. That's what the "global test" says to me.

Audience members. Boo-o-o!

The President. Listen, I'll always work with our friends and allies. But I will never turn over America's national security decisions to leaders of other countries.

We have a big difference of opinion. Recently the Senator was quoted as saying about 9/11 that it didn't change him much at all. It changed me. It changed my outlook. A few days after the attacks, I stood where the buildings fell. I will never forget that day. There were workers in hardhats there yelling at me at top of their lungs, "Whatever it takes." I remember the policeman or fireman—I don't know which one, where he worked, but he came out of the rubble, and he looked me square in the eye, and he said, "Do not let me down." Ever since that day, I've gotten up every morning thinking about how to better protect our country. I will never relent in defending America, whatever it takes.

The second clear choice in this election concerns your family's budget. When I ran for President 4 years ago, I pledged to lower taxes for American families, and I kept my word. We doubled the child credit to $1,000 per child. We reduced the marriage penalty. We think the Tax Code ought to encourage marriage, not penalize marriage. We dropped the lowest bracket to 10 percent. We reduced income taxes for everybody who pays income taxes. And after-tax income in America is up by about 10 percent since I have been your President. That means more money in your pocket.

When you're out gathering the vote, remind people about what we have been through. The stock market was in serious decline 6 months prior to my arrival in Washington. Then we had a recession. Then we had corporate scandals. And then we had the attacks of September the 11th that cost us about a million jobs in the 3 months after September the 11th.

But our economic policies are working. We're on the path to growth. Our economy is growing at rates as fast as any in 20 years. Homeownership is at an alltime high in America. Our farmers are making a good living. The small-business sector of our economy is strong. The entrepreneurial spirit is flourishing across New Hampshire. Listen, we've added 1.9 million new jobs in the last 13 months. The national unemployment rate is 5.4 percent. Let me put that in perspective for you. That's lower than the average rate of the 1970s, the 1980s, and the 1990s. The unemployment rate in New Hampshire is 3.5 percent. We've overcome the obstacles. This economy is strong, and it is getting stronger.

Now, my opponent has very different plans for your budget. He intends to take a big chunk out of it. He voted against the higher child tax credit, and he voted against the marriage penalty relief. He voted against lower taxes. If he had had his way, the average family in America would be paying $2,000 more to the Federal Government.

Audience members. Boo-o-o!

The President. That may not sound like a lot to people in Washington. It's a lot to families right here in New Hampshire. It means a lot to you. It means a lot to a mom or a dad who are trying to raise their children. It means a lot to a small-business owner who's expanding his or her company. All told, during my opponent's 20-year career in the United States Senate, he voted to raise taxes 98 times.

Audience members. Boo-o-o!

The President. That is five times for every year he's been in the Senate. That's what I would call a predictable pattern—[*laughter*]—a leading indicator. [*Laughter*] When a Senator does something that often, he must really enjoy it. [*Laughter*] He's also promised $2.2 trillion of new spending in this campaign. That's trillion with a "T."

That's a lot even for a Senator from Massachusetts. [*Laughter*]

So they asked him—they asked him, how are you going to pay for it? And he trotted out that same old, tired line we hear every campaign. He said, "Well, I'm just going to tax the rich."

Well, first of all, most small businesses in New Hampshire and around the country are sole proprietorships or Subchapter S corporations, which means they pay tax at the individual income-tax level. Most small businesses create most new jobs in America. Seventy percent of new jobs in this country are created by the small-business sector. And so when you're running up the top two tax brackets, you're taxing the job creators. And that makes no economic sense.

Secondly, raising the top two brackets raises about 600 billion or 800 billion, depending on who's doing the counting. In either case, that's far short of $2.2 trillion of spending. See, there's a gap—[*laughter*]—a gap between what has been promised and what can be delivered. I would call it a tax gap, and you know who usually gets to fill the gap. [*Laughter*] You do. The good news is, we're not going to let him tax you; we're going to carry New Hampshire and win on November the 2d.

The third clear choice in this election involves the quality of life for our Nation's families. A good education and quality health care are important to a successful life. As a candidate, I pledged to challenge the soft bigotry of low expectations by reforming our public schools. I kept my word. I worked with Senator Gregg and others, and we passed the No Child Left Behind Act, a fine piece of reform. We're increasing spending at the Federal level, but in return, we're asking for results. See, we believe every child can learn to read and write and add and subtract, and we expect every school to teach. You cannot solve a problem until you diagnose the problem. We're diagnosing the problems all across our country, and the test scores are improv-

ing. Scores in reading and math are on the rise, and an achievement gap for minority students is closing. In a new term, we'll build on these reforms. We'll extend them to high schools so that no child is left behind in America.

We'll continue to improve the lives of our families by making health care more accessible and affordable. We'll promote and extend community health centers to help the poor and the indigent get good primary and preventative care. We'll make sure our programs for children from low-income families will be fully subscribed to help people get the health care they need. In order to make sure health care is affordable, small business ought to be allowed to pool together across jurisdictional boundaries so they can buy insurance at the same discounts big companies get to buy insurance. We'll expand health savings accounts, which will help our small businesses and families with more affordable health care.

To make sure health care is available and affordable, not only in New Hampshire but across this country, we must do something about the frivolous lawsuits that are running up the cost of health care. I have met too many ob-gyns that have been driven out of practice because of high premiums as a result of these lawsuits. I have met too many moms, expectant moms, who are concerned about the health care they and their baby will receive because their doctor no longer is in practice. This is a national problem that requires a national solution. You cannot be pro-doctor, pro-patient, and pro-personal-injury-trial-lawyer at the same time. You have to choose. My opponent made his choice. He's voted against medical liability reform 10 times in the United States Senate, and he put a personal injury trial lawyer on the ticket.

Audience members. Boo-o-o!

The President. I made my choice. I'm standing with New Hampshire's docs. I'm standing with New Hampshire's families. I'm standing with the patients. I'm for medical liability reform—now.

My opponent has a different point of view when it comes to health care. I don't know if you remember the debate. They asked him about his health care plan. He stared straight in the camera, and he said his plan—"The Government has nothing to do with it." That's in reference to his health care plan. I could barely contain myself. [*Laughter*] The Government has got a lot to do with it. Eighty percent of the people under his plan will go to a Government-run plan. If you make it easier for people to get on Medicaid, small businesses will start dropping insurance because the Government is going to pay for it, and that moves people from private care to public care. When the Government starts writing a check, when it comes to your health care, then they start making the rules. And when the Government starts making the rules, when it comes to your health care, they start making decisions for you, and they start making decisions for your docs, and they start rationing care. Government-run health care is the wrong prescription for health care for America's families. In all we do to improve health care for our families, we'll make sure the decisions are made by doctors and patients, not by officials in Washington, DC.

The fourth clear choice concerns your retirement. Our Nation has made a solemn commitment to America's seniors on Social Security and Medicare. When I ran for President 4 years ago, I promised to keep that commitment and improve Medicare by adding prescription drugs for our seniors. I kept my word. Medicare needed to be fixed. See, we would pay thousands of dollars for a heart surgery but not one dime for the prescription drugs that could prevent the heart surgery from being needed in the first place. I didn't think that made sense for our seniors. It didn't make sense for the taxpayers. We brought people together, and I signed a Medicare law. And beginning in 2006, all seniors will be able to get prescription drug coverage under Medicare.

And we'll keep the promise of Social Security for our seniors. And we'll strengthen Social Security for generations to come. Now, I remember the 2000 campaign, clearly remember it. They said in TV ads in those days and through mailers and word of mouth that, "If George W. got elected, the seniors wouldn't get their checks." When you're out rounding up the vote, please remind people that George W. did get elected and our seniors got their checks. And our seniors will continue to get their checks. And baby boomers like me and Senator Gregg, we're in pretty good shape when it comes to the Social Security trust.

But we need to worry about our children, and we need to worry about our grandchildren. We need to worry about whether or not Social Security will be there when they need it. And that is why I believe in personal savings accounts, that a worker ought to take some of their money and set aside a personal savings account, an account they call their own, an account the Government cannot take away.

Now, my opponent takes a different approach. He talks about protecting Social Security. But he's the only candidate in this race who voted eight times for higher taxes on Social Security benefits.

Audience members. Boo-o-o!

The President. On issue after issue, he tries to run, but we're not going to let him hide. When it comes to the next generation, he hasn't offered anything about fixing the system. See, the job of a President is to confront problems, not to pass them on to future Presidents and future generations. In a new term, I'll bring people together, and we will strengthen Social Security for generations to come.

The fifth clear choice in this election is on the values that are crucial to keeping America's families strong. I stand for the appointment of Federal judges who know the difference between personal opinion and the strict interpretation of the law. I stand for marriage and family, which are the foundations of our society. I stand for a culture of life, and I proudly signed the ban on partial-birth abortions.

My opponent has taken a different approach. He voted against the Defense of Marriage Act. He voted against the ban on partial-birth abortion. At one time in his campaign, he actually said, "The heart and soul of America can be found in Hollywood."

Audience members. Boo-o-o!

The President. The heart and soul of America is found in communities all across New Hampshire.

I'm asking for your vote based upon my plans for the future, my record, and my philosophy. My opponent's views are out of the mainstream. I share your values. In a new term, I will stand for bedrock values of strengthening our economy every day. And I will do everything in my power to keep our country safe.

I'm sure Senator Kerry means well, but his policies are the wrong policies at this time of threat. He'll raise your taxes to pay for his promises, and that will stall our economy. He cannot lead our troops to victory in a war he does not agree with, a war he has called wrong. He cannot attract or keep allies in a cause he's labeled a diversion.

As your President, I'll rally the world. I will lead our troops. I commit our Nation to decisive victory in the war against terror. And my fellow citizens, against this threat to our founding values of freedom and tolerance and equality, victory is our only option.

One of my favorite quotes that I hope helps capture my feeling about our country and about our future came from a fellow Texan named Tom Lea. He said, "Sarah and I live on the east side of the mountain. It is the sunrise side, not the sunset side. It is the side to see the day that is coming, not to see the day that is gone." During the course of this campaign, my opponent has spent much of this campaign talking about the day that is gone. I'm talking about the day that is coming.

I see a great day coming for America. And with your help and with your hard work, I'll be honored to lead this Nation for 4 more years.

God bless. Thanks for coming. Thank you all.

NOTE: The President spoke at 1:07 p.m. at the Pease International Tradeport Airport. In his remarks, he referred to Gov. Craig Benson of New Hampshire; Republican Party activist Barbara Russell; Ruth L. Griffin, councilor, District 3, Executive Council of New Hampshire; and former President Saddam Hussein of Iraq.

Remarks in Toledo, Ohio
October 29, 2004

The President. Laura and I are so honored so many came out to say hello. We appreciate it very much. I'm honored—we thank you for taking time out of your day.

I've got something to tell you. I'm traveling Ohio a lot. I'm asking for the vote, and I'm asking for your help. We have a duty in this country to vote. You may have heard, the election is right around the corner. [*Laughter*] And I'm asking you, get your friends and neighbors to go to the polls. Make sure our fellow Republicans vote. Make sure independents vote. Find some discerning Democrats, and there's a lot across the State of Ohio. And get them headed to the polls and remind them, if they want a safer America, a stronger

America, and a better America, to put me and Dick Cheney back in office.

One of the most important reasons why I think you ought to put me back into office is so that Laura is the First Lady for 4 more years.

Audience members. Laura! Laura! Laura!

The President. I don't want to offend anybody who is follically challenged, but I admit my great Vice President doesn't have the waviest hair in the race. [*Laughter*] The people of Toledo will be proud to know that I didn't pick him because of his hairdo. [*Laughter*] I picked him because of his judgment, his experience. He's getting the job done for the American people.

I want to thank Senator Mike DeWine for joining us today. I'm proud to call him friend. You're proud to call him Senator. I urge you to put George Voinovich back in the United States Senate. I want to thank your Governor for joining us. I want to thank Paul Gillmor, Congressman Paul Gillmor, for being here today. I want to thank Betty Montgomery for joining us. And I want to thank the next Congressman from the Ninth Congressional District, Larry Kaczala, for joining us.

I want to thank the Wil Gravatt Band. I want to thank the Anthony Wayne High Marching Generals for being here. I will try to keep my speech short so you can get home and do your homework.

Audience members. Boo-o-o!

The President. I want to thank the grassroots activists. I want to thank my friend Bernadette Noe and Tom Noe for their leadership in Lucas County. I remember our breakfast. She had me flipping pancakes. [*Laughter*]

I want to thank those of you who are putting up the signs and making the phone calls. I want to thank those of you who are working long hours. We're almost there. Election Day is almost here. I urge you to continue working to turn out that vote. With your help, we'll win Ohio again and win a great victory.

We've just got 4 days to go, and the voters have a clear choice between two very different candidates and different approaches and different records. You know where I stand, and sometimes, you even know where my opponent stands. [*Laughter*] We both have records. I'm proudly running on mine. My opponent has an interesting idea of how to win friends. During this campaign, he's insulted our allies and he questioned the good work of our troops in combat.

Audience members. Boo-o-o!

The President. Earlier today, my opponent even insulted the American people, saying you need to, quote, "wake up."

Audience members. Boo-o-o!

The President. Well, the American people are awake. Their eyes are wide open. They are seeing more clearly every day the critical choices in this election: The Senator's failed, out-of-the-mainstream policies or my commitment to defend our country, to build our economy, and to uphold our bedrock values.

This election comes down to some clear choices, five clear choices for America's family. The first clear choice is the most important because it concerns the security of your family. All progress on every other issue depends on the safety of our citizens. This will be the first Presidential election since September the 11th, 2001. Americans will go to the polls in a time of war and ongoing threats unlike any we have faced before. The terrorists who killed thousands of innocent people are still dangerous, and they are determined.

The outcome of this election will set the direction of the war against terror. The most solemn duty of the American President is to protect the American people. If America shows uncertainty or weakness during these troubling times, the world will drift toward tragedy. This is not going to happen on my watch.

Since that terrible morning of September the 11th, we've fought the terrorists across the Earth, not for pride, not for power but because the lives of our citizens are at stake. Our strategy is clear. We're strengthening the protections for our homeland. We're reforming our intelligence capabilities. We are transforming the All-Volunteer Army. There will be no draft. We are determined. We are relentless. We are staying on the offensive. We're chasing the terrorists overseas so we do not have to face them here at home.

Because we led, Afghanistan is a free nation and an ally in the war on terror; Pakistan is capturing terrorist leaders; Saudi Arabia is making raids and arrests. Because we led, Libya is dismantling its weapons programs; the army of a free Iraq is fighting for freedom; and more than three-quarters of Al Qaida's key members and associates have been brought to justice. We have led. Many have joined. And America and the world are safer.

And part of our strategy is to spread liberty and peace. I believe in the transformational power of liberty to change societies. I want you to remind your sons and daughters what has taken place in a relatively quick period of time in Afghanistan. It wasn't all that long ago that young girls could not go to school or their mothers were taken into the public square and whipped and sometimes into a sports stadium and killed because of the barbaric vision of the Taliban. Because we acted in our self-interest, because we acted to uphold the doctrine which I laid out that said, "If you harbor a terrorist, you're equally as guilty as the terrorist," millions of people—millions of people in Afghanistan voted in a Presidential election. The first voter was a 19-year-old woman.

Free societies will be peaceful societies. Free societies will help us keep the peace. Iraq is going to have elections in January. Think how far that society has come from the days of mass graves and torture chambers. Freedom is on the march. I believe everybody yearns to be free. I believe people long for freedom. I believe this. I understand freedom is not America's gift to the world; freedom is the Almighty God's gift to each man and woman in this world.

A President must lead with consistency and strength. In a war, sometimes your tactics change but not your principles. Americans have seen how I do my job. Even when you might not agree with me, you know what I believe. You know where I stand, and you know where I'm going to lead our Nation. On good days and on bad days, when the polls are up or the polls are down, I am determined to protect the American people.

And I'll support our troops in harm's way. You know, I want to thank those who wear our Nation's uniform. I want to thank the military families who sacrifice on behalf of our Nation's freedom. I want to thank the veterans who have set such a great example to those who wear the uniform. And I assure you, we will keep the commitment we have made. Our troops will have what they need to complete their missions.

That's why I went to the Congress and asked for $87 billion of supplemental funding in September of 2003. And we received great bipartisan support for this necessary and critical funding. As a matter of fact, the support was so strong that only 12 Members of the United States Senate voted against the funding, 2 of whom were my opponent and his runningmate.

Audience members. Boo-o-o!

The President. But let me give you a more startling statistic, one that I would hope you would use as you're gathering up the vote: Four Members of the United States Senate—only four—voted to authorize the use of force and then voted against the funding necessary to support our troops in combat. Two of those four were my opponent and his runningmate.

Audience members. Boo-o-o!

The President. So they asked him why he made that vote, and you might remember this quote. He said, "I actually did vote for the 87 billion, before I voted against it." Now, look, I haven't spent all that much time in Toledo, but I doubt I'm going to find many people who talk that way here in Toledo, Ohio.

He has given several answers about why he made the vote. Perhaps the most revealing was when he said, "The whole matter was a complicated matter." My fellow Americans, there is nothing complicated about supporting our troops in combat.

Senator Kerry's record on national security has a far deeper problem than election-year flip-flopping. On the largest national security issues of our time, he has been consistently wrong. When Ronald Reagan was confronting the Soviet Union at the height of the cold war, Senator Kerry said that President Reagan's policy of peace through strength was making America less safe.

Audience members. Boo-o-o!

The President. Well, history has shown that Senator Kerry was wrong and President Reagan was right.

When former President Bush led a coalition against Saddam Hussein in 1991 because he had invaded Kuwait, Senator Kerry voted against the use of force to liberate Kuwait.

Audience members. Boo-o-o!

The President. Well, history has shown that Senator Kerry was wrong and former President Bush was right.

In 1994, just one year after the first bombing of the World Trade Center, Senator Kerry proposed massive cuts in America's intelligence budget, so massive that even his Massachusetts colleague, Ted Kennedy, opposed them. [*Laughter*] History shows that Senator Kerry was wrong—and let's be fair about it—Senator Kennedy was right. [*Laughter*]

During the last 20 years in key moments of challenge and decision for America, Senator Kerry has chosen the position of weakness and inaction. With that record, he stands in opposition not just to me but to the great tradition of the Democratic Party. The party of Franklin Roosevelt, the party of Harry Truman, the party of John Kennedy is rightly remembered for confidence and resolve in times of war and hours of crisis. Senator Kerry has turned his back on "pay any price" and "bear any burden," and he's replaced those commitments with "wait and see" and "cut and run."

Many Democrats in this country do not recognize their party anymore. And today, I want to speak to every one of them: If you believe that America should lead with strength and purpose and confidence in our ideals, I would be honored to have your support, and I'm asking for your vote.

Audience members. Four more years! Four more years! Four more years!

The President. In this campaign, there are big differences about how to protect America's families. One time in our debate, my opponent said America must submit to what he calls a "global test" before we commit force.

Audience members. Boo-o-o!

The President. I'm not making that up. [*Laughter*] I heard it. [*Laughter*] As far as I can tell, that means our country must get permission before we act in our own defense. As President, I'll always work with friends and allies. I'll always build coalitions. But I will never turn over America's national security decisions to leaders of other countries.

My opponent says that September the 11th did not change him much at all. And that's clear in his policies. He believes that the war on terror is primarily a law enforcement and intelligence gathering operation. September the 11th changed me. I remember that day when I was at Ground Zero on September the 14th, 2001. I'll never forget the sights. I'll never forget the sounds. I remember the workers in hardhats yelling at me at the top of their lungs, "Whatever it takes." I remember the first-responder—I can't remember if he was a firefighter or a policeman—who came out of the rubble, and he grabbed me by the arm, and he looked me square in the eye, and he said, "Do not let me down." Ever since that day, I've gotten up every morning thinking about how to better protect our country. I will never relent in defending America, whatever it takes.

The second clear choice in this election concerns your family budget. When I ran for President 4 years ago, I pledged to lower taxes for American families. And I kept my word. We doubled the child credit to $1,000 per child. We want to help the moms and dads of America do their duty. We reduced the marriage penalty. We believe the Tax Code ought to encourage marriage, not penalize marriage. We dropped the lowest bracket to 10 percent. We reduced income taxes for everybody who pays taxes. Real after-tax income is up 10 percent since I've been the President. That's money in your pocket. That's money you can spend.

I want you to remind your friends and neighbors that the stock market was in serious decline 6 months prior to my arrival in Washington. And then we had a recession, and we had some corporate scandals. We passed tough laws. We have made it abundantly clear we will not tolerate dishonesty in the boardrooms of America.

The attacks of September the 11th cost us nearly a million jobs in the 3 months after that attack. But our economic policies are working. They have led us back to the path of growth and recovery. Our economy is growing at rates as fast as any in nearly 20 years. We've added 1.9 million new jobs in the last 13 months. Homeownership rates are at an alltime high. Minorities are owning their home at rates greater than ever before in our history. Farm income is up. The entrepreneurial spirit is strong in America. Small businesses are flourishing. The national unemployment rate is 5.4 percent. Let me put that in perspective for you: That's lower than the average rate of the 1970s, the 1980s, and the 1990s.

I know people are still struggling here in Ohio. I understand that. I've traveled your State a lot. I've spoken to people. But that doesn't mean we should get away

from pro-growth economic policies. Quite the contrary. We need to keep your taxes low. We need to do something about lawsuits. We need to do something about regulatory reform. To keep this economy going, I will empower our small businesses, our consumers, and American families by keeping the taxes low.

Speaking about taxes, my opponent has got some plans for your budget. He's going to take a big chunk out of it. He voted against the higher child tax credit, and he voted against the marriage penalty relief. He voted against lower taxes. If he'd have had his way, the average middle-class family would be paying 2,000 more dollars a year in taxes.

Audience members. Boo-o-o!

The President. That's probably not a lot for some of the folks in Washington. It's a lot for the folks in Toledo, Ohio. That means a lot to the people in this part of the world. That money helps moms and dads. It helps our families.

You know, he's been in the United States Senate for 20 years, and he's voted to raise taxes 98 times. That's five times for every year he's been in the Senate. I would call that a predictable pattern—[*laughter*]—a leading indicator. [*Laughter*] When a Senator does something that often, he really must like it. [*Laughter*] And he's proposed $2.2 trillion in new spending. That is trillion with a "T." That's a lot. That's a lot even for a Senator from Massachusetts. [*Laughter*]

So they asked him how he's going to pay for it. He said, well, he's going to tax the rich. You know, by raising the top two brackets, you're taxing small-business creators. Most small businesses pay tax at the individual income-tax rate. Seventy percent of new jobs in America are created by small businesses. It makes no sense to tax the job creators in America. Running up the tax is lousy economic policy.

Let me tell you what else is wrong, and you need to tell this to your friends and neighbors. He's proposed 2.2 trillion in new spending, but when you raise the top two brackets, you only raise between 600 and 800 billion. So there's a gap. I would like to call it a tax gap, a gap between what he's promised and what he can pay. And guess who usually fills the tax gap.

Audience member. We do!

The President. You do. The good news is, we're not going to let him tax you; we're going to carry Ohio and win on November the 2d.

The third clear choice in this election involves the quality of life for our families. A good education and quality health care are important to a successful life. As a candidate, I pledged to challenge the soft bigotry of low expectations by reforming our public schools. I kept my word. We passed strong education reforms in Washington. We're increasing spending, particularly for low-income students. But in return for increased spending, we're now asking whether or not a child can read or write and add and subtract. See, we realize—or we think every child can learn, and we expect every school to teach.

You cannot solve a problem unless you diagnose the problem, and we are diagnosing and solving problems all across America. Our test scores in reading and math are up. We are closing a achievement gap for minority students all across America. And we're not going to go back to the old days of mediocrity and low expectations in our Nation's schoolrooms.

We will continue to work to make sure health care is available and affordable. We'll make sure health care is available by expanding community health centers so the poor and the indigent can get good primary and preventative care in places other than your emergency rooms. We're going to make sure that children of low-income families are subscribed to our health programs. We want to make sure people get health care in America that can't afford it. We also want to make sure it's affordable. Most of the uninsured work for small businesses. Small businesses ought to

be allowed to join together, to spread risk, so they can buy insurance at the same discount that big companies are able to do.

We will expand health savings accounts, which will help our families and our small businesses. And to make sure health care is available and affordable in this good State, we will do something about the frivolous lawsuits that are running up the cost of health care and running doctors out of business.

I was campaigning in Canton the other day, and I met two docs who are no longer practicing medicine because their premiums got so high because of the lawsuits. I have met too many ob-gyns who are leaving practice because of the lawsuits. And I have met too many young expectant moms who are concerned about their health care because they don't have a doc close by. And that's not right for America. This is a national problem that requires a national solution. You cannot be pro-doctor, pro-patient and pro-personal-injury-trial-lawyer at the same time. My opponent has made his choice. He voted against medical liability reform 10 times in the Senate, and he put a personal-injury trial lawyer on the ticket.

Audience members. Boo-o-o!

The President. I have made my choice. I'm standing with the doctors of Ohio. I'm standing with the patients of Ohio. I'm standing with the families of Ohio. I'm for medical liability reform.

My opponent has got a different point of view when it comes to health care. You might remember one of the debates when they asked him about his health care plan, and he said, with a straight face, "The Government doesn't have anything to do with it." I could barely contain myself. [*Laughter*] The Government has got a lot to do with it. Eighty percent of the people would be signed up to a Government program under his vision. When you make it easier for people to sign up for Medicaid, it means the small-business owners will stop writing insurance for their employees because the Government is going to. That moves people from the private sector to the public sector. Now, when the Government starts writing the checks when it comes to health care, they start making the rules when it comes to health care. And when they start making the rules when it comes to health care, they start making the decisions for you when it comes to health care and they make decisions for your doctors when it comes to health care. The wrong prescription for American families is to federalize health care.

In all we do to improve health care for our families, we'll make sure the decisions are made by doctors and patients, not by officials in Washington, DC.

The fourth clear choice in this election involves your retirement. Our Nation has made a solemn commitment to America's seniors on Social Security and Medicare. When I ran for President 4 years ago, I promised to keep that commitment and improve Medicare by adding prescription drugs. I kept my word.

We got the job done for our seniors. Medicare needed to be modernized. Medicare would pay thousands of dollars for a heart surgery but not one dime for the prescription drugs that might prevent the heart surgery from being needed in the first place. That didn't make any sense to people on Medicare. And so I brought Republicans together and Democrats together. I signed a Medicare law. And beginning in 2006, all seniors will be able to get prescription drug coverage under Medicare. And we will keep our promise of Social Security for our seniors. And we'll strengthen Social Security for generations to come.

Now, you might remember the 2000 campaign, when they were running the ads and the fliers and the mailers that said, "If George W. gets elected, our seniors will not get their checks." Well, as you gather up the vote, please remind your friends and neighbors that George W. did get elected, and the seniors got their checks.

And the seniors will continue to get their checks. And baby boomers like me and a couple other people I see out there, we'll get our checks.

But we need to worry about our children and our grandchildren. We need to worry about whether the Social Security system will be there when they need it. And that's why I believe younger workers ought to be able to take some of their own payroll taxes and set up a personal savings account, a personal savings account that will earn a better rate of return, a personal savings account they call their own, a personal savings account the Government cannot take away.

My opponent's taken a different approach on this issue. He said he's going to protect Social Security. I want you to remind your friends and neighbors that he has voted eight times for higher taxes on Social Security benefits. He can run from his record, but he cannot hide.

And when it comes to the young generation, he's offered nothing. The job of a President is to confront problems, not pass them on to future generations and future Presidents. In a new term, I'll bring people together and make sure the Social Security system is strong for generations to come.

The fifth clear choice in this election is on the values that are so crucial to keeping our families strong. I stand for the appointment of Federal judges who know the difference between personal opinion and the strict interpretation of the law. I stand for marriage and family, which are the foundations of our society. I will promote a culture of life, and I proudly signed the ban on partial-birth abortion.

My opponent's taken a different point of view. He voted against the Defense of Marriage Act. He voted against the ban on partial-birth abortion.

Audience members. Boo-o-o!

The President. And at one time in this campaign, he actually said the heart and soul of America can be found in Hollywood.

Audience members. Boo-o-o!

The President. Most families do not look to Hollywood as a source of values. The heart and soul of America is found in caring communities like Toledo, Ohio.

All these choices make this one of the most important elections in our history. The security and prosperity of our country are at stake. The health and education for our families and our children are at stake. The direction of our culture is at stake. The decision is in the best of hands. It's in the hands of the American people. It's in your hands.

Our country is a strong country. It is a great country. I see a great day coming for all Americans. One of my favorite quotes is from a fellow Texan named Tom Lea. And he said, "Sarah and I live on the east side of the mountain. It is the sunrise side, not the sunset side. It is the side to see the day that is coming, not to see the day that is gone." In the course of this campaign, my opponent has spent much of the campaign talking about the day that is gone. I'm talking about the day that is coming, a prosperous day, a hopeful day, a compassionate day, and a day when we can achieve the peace we so long for for our children and our grandchildren.

When I campaigned across Ohio 4 years ago, I made this pledge, that if I was elected, I would uphold the honor and the dignity of the office. With your help, with your hard work, I will do so for 4 more years.

Thanks for coming. God bless. Thank you all.

NOTE: The President spoke at 4:30 p.m. at the SeaGate Convention Centre. In his remarks, he referred to Gov. Bob Taft and Auditor of State Betty Montgomery of Ohio; Bernadette Restivo Noe, chairman, Lucas County Republican Party, and her husband, Tom; and former President Saddam Hussein of Iraq.

Remarks on Al Jazeera Videotape of Usama bin Laden
October 29, 2004

Earlier today I was informed of the tape that is now being analyzed by America's intelligence community. Let me make this very clear: Americans will not be intimidated or influenced by an enemy of our country. I'm sure Senator Kerry agrees with this.

I also want to say to the American people that we're at war with these terrorists, and I am confident that we will prevail.

Thank you very much. Thank you.

NOTE: The President spoke at 5:53 p.m. at the Toledo Express Airport in Toledo, OH. A tape was not available for verification of the content of these remarks.

Statement on Signing the Ronald W. Reagan National Defense Authorization Act for Fiscal Year 2005
October 29, 2004

Protecting the American people is my most solemn responsibility, and a superior U.S. military is essential to that effort and to fighting and winning the global war on terrorism. The Defense Authorization Act of 2005 will continue to strengthen our security and ensure that our troops are the best paid, best trained, and best equipped fighting force in the world.

We have increased military pay by over 20 percent since I came into office, and this legislation includes the fourth consecutive pay raise for our service men and women. It funds more protective equipment like body armor and reinforced Humvees to keep our troops as safe as possible.

This bill also continues the transformation of our military and funds the technology and advanced weapons systems we need. And it keeps our commitment to our troops, military retirees, reservists, and their families by ensuring they get the health, housing, and other benefits that they deserve. This bill will help us continue to strengthen our All-Volunteer Military.

NOTE: H.R. 4200, approved October 28, was assigned Public Law No. 108–375.

Remarks in Columbus, Ohio
October 29, 2004

The President. Thank you all. Thanks for coming. Thank you all for being here. Thank you all for coming. Laura and I are honored so many of you came out to say hello. You've lifted our spirits.

I also want to thank Governor Schwarzenegger for coming. It's such an honor to have him here in Columbus and campaigning on my behalf. You know, he and I share some things in common. We both married well. [*Laughter*] We both have trouble speaking the English language. [*Laughter*] We both got big biceps. [*Laughter*] Well, two out of three ain't bad. [*Laughter*]

It's great to be back in Columbus. I don't know if you know this or not, but my grandfather was raised here. So why don't you send a home boy back to Washington? We love campaigning in your State. Ohio is a wonderful place. I'm campaigning hard to let people know that I've got an agenda for 4 more years.

Perhaps the most important reason why you ought to put me back into office is so that Laura is the First Lady for 4 more years.

I'm proud of my runningmate, Dick Cheney. I readily concede that he does not have the waviest hair in the race. You'll be happy to hear I didn't pick him because of his hairdo. [*Laughter*] I picked him because he's a man of sound judgment, excellent experience. He's getting the job done for the American people.

Laura and I are pleased that your Governor, Bob Taft, and First Lady Hope Taft are with us today. Thank you all for coming.

Senator Mike DeWine is with us. Senator, thank you for being here. You need to put George Voinovich back in the United States Senate. I want to thank Congressman Pat Tiberi for his leadership. I want to thank Congressman Dave Hobson and Carolyn for being with us today. We're honored you are here. I want to thank my friend Deborah Pryce in the United States Congress, who is here.

I want to thank the Lieutenant Governor, who is with us. The Supreme Court of Ohio Chief Justice is with us. We've got a lot of State and local officials here. We are honored with your presence.

I want to thank all the grassroots activists who are here. I want to thank my friend Jo Ann Davidson and Doug Preisse. I want to thank you all, all of you who are making the phone calls, putting up the signs, and turning out the vote.

I'm here to not only ask for your vote; I'm here to ask for your help. I'm here to ask you to get your friends and neighbors to go to the polls. Turn out our fellow Republicans, fine independents, and discerning Democrats. Four days to go, and we're counting on your help. There's no doubt in my mind, with your help, we will carry Ohio again and win a great victory on Tuesday.

We have a clear choice—or you have a clear choice in this campaign, a clear choice between two very different candidates, dramatically different approaches and different records. You know where I stand, and sometimes, you even know where my opponent stands. [*Laughter*] We both have records. I am proudly running on mine.

This election comes down to some clear choices for America's families. The first choice is the most important because it concerns the security of your family. All progress on every issue depends on the safety of our families. Americans will go to the polls in a time of war and ongoing threats unlike any we have faced before. The terrorists who killed thousands of innocent people are still dangerous and determined to strike. The outcome of this election will set the direction of the war against terror. The most solemn duty of the American President is to protect the American people. If America shows uncertainty or weakness in this decade, the world will drift toward tragedy. This will not happen on my watch.

Since that terrible morning, we have fought the terrorists across the Earth, not for pride, not for power but because the lives of our citizens are at stake. Our strategy is clear. We have strengthened our homeland. We're reforming and strengthening our intelligence capabilities. We are transforming the All-Volunteer Army. There will be no draft. We are relentless. We are determined. We are staying on the of-

fense. We're chasing the terrorists across the globe so we do not have to face them here at home.

Because we led, Afghanistan is a free Nation and an ally in the war on terror; Pakistan is capturing terrorist leaders; Saudi Arabia is making raids and arrests. Because we led, Libya is dismantling its weapons programs; the army of a free Iraq is fighting for freedom; and more than three-quarters of Al Qaida's key members and associates have been brought to justice.

And we've got another asset at our disposal: freedom. We believe—I believe in the power of liberty. Think about what has happened in a short period of time. Young girls in Afghanistan couldn't go to school because the Taliban was so barbaric and backward. And if their mothers didn't toe the line of ideological hatred, they were taken into the public square and whipped and sometimes executed in a sports stadium. Because we acted in our own interests, because we acted to protect ourselves, because we upheld a doctrine that said, "If you harbor a terrorist, you're just as guilty as the terrorist," millions of people went to the polls to vote for the President of Afghanistan. The first voter was a 19-year-old woman.

Iraq will have elections in January. Think how far that country has come from the days of torture chambers and mass graves. Freedom is on the march. Freedom is taking place around this world, and America is more secure for it. I believe everybody longs to be free. I believe deep in everybody's soul, there's a yearning to live in a free society. I believe all these things because freedom is not America's gift to the world; freedom is the Almighty God's gift to each man and woman in this world.

A President has to lead our country with consistency and strength. In a war, sometimes your tactics change but not your principles. Americans have seen how I do my job. Even when you might not agree with me, you know what I believe and where I stand and where I intend to lead this country. On good days and on bad days, whether the polls are up or the polls are down, I am determined to lead this Nation and win the war on terror.

And I will always support the United States military. I want to thank those who wear our Nation's uniform. I want to thank our military families who are here. I want to thank the veterans who have set such a great example for our military. And I want to assure our military and their families and our veterans, we will make sure our troops have that which they need to complete their missions.

That's why I went to the United States Congress and asked for $87 billion of supplemental funding, necessary funding to support our troops in harm's way. We got great bipartisan support for that request. Only 12 United States Senators voted against the funding for our troops, 2 of whom were my opponent and his runningmate.

Audience members. Boo-o-o!

The President. When you're out gathering the vote over the next 4 days, when you're rounding up people to go to the polls, remind them of this statistic: Only four Members of the United States Senate voted to authorize the use of force and then voted against providing the funding necessary for our troops in combat. Two of those four were my opponent and his runningmate.

Audience members. Boo-o-o!

The President. You might remember the most famous quote of the 2004 campaign. When asked about his vote on the $87 billion, Senator Kerry said, "I actually did vote for the 87 billion, before I voted against it."

Audience members. Boo-o-o!

The President. Now, I haven't spent a lot of time in Columbus, but I doubt we're going to find many people here who talk that way. [*Laughter*] He's given several explanations since about his $87 billion vote. Perhaps the most illustrative one of them all was when he said, "The whole thing was a complicated matter." [*Laughter*] My fellow citizens, there is nothing complicated about supporting our troops in combat.

Unfortunately, my opponent, tonight, continued to say things he knows are not true, accusing our military of passing up a chance to get Usama bin Laden in Tora Bora. As the commander in charge of that operation, Tommy Franks, has said, "It's simply not the case." It's the worst kind of Monday morning quarterbacking. It is especially shameful in the light of a new tape from America's enemy. Our commander in Afghanistan, Tommy Franks, recently said, "The Senator's understanding of events does not square with reality." General Franks said America's Special Forces were actively involved in the search for the terrorists in Tora Bora. And intelligence reports at the time placed bin Laden in any of several different countries. As General Franks said, "If we'd ever known where bin Laden was, we would have gotten him."

Before Senator Kerry got into political difficulty and revised his views, he saw our actions in Tora Bora differently. In the fall of 2001, on national TV, he said, quote, "I think we have been doing this pretty effectively, and we should continue to do it that way." Senator Kerry also went on to say about Tora Bora on national TV, "I think we've been smart. I think the administration leadership has done it well, and we are on the right track." I couldn't have said it better myself.

Senator Kerry's record on national security has a far deeper problem than election-year flip-flopping. On the largest national security issues of our time, he has been consistently wrong. When Ronald Reagan was confronting the Soviet Union at the height of the cold war, Senator Kerry said that President Reagan's policy of peace through strength was making America less safe.

Audience members. Boo-o-o!

The President. History has shown that Senator Kerry was wrong and President Ronald Reagan was right.

When former President Bush led a coalition against Saddam Hussein in 1991, Senator Kerry voted against the use of force to liberate Kuwait.

Audience members. Boo-o-o!

The President. History has shown that Senator Kerry was wrong and former President Bush was right.

In 1994, just one year after the first bombing of the World Trade Center, Senator Kerry proposed massive cuts in America's intelligence budget, so massive that even his Massachusetts colleague, Ted Kennedy, opposed them.

Audience members. Boo-o-o!

The President. History has shown that Senator Kerry was wrong—and we have got to be fair—Senator Kennedy was right. [*Laughter*]

During the last 20 years, in key moments of challenge and decision for America, Senator Kerry has chosen the position of weakness and inaction. With that record, he stands in opposition not just to me but to the great tradition of the Democratic Party. The party of Franklin Roosevelt, the party of Harry Truman, the party of John Kennedy is rightly remembered for confidence and resolve in times of war and hours of crisis. Senator Kerry has turned his back on "pay any price" and "bear any burden," and he's replaced those commitments with "wait and see" and "cut and run."

Audience members. Boo-o-o!

The President. Many Democrats in this country do not recognize their party anymore, and today, I want to speak to every once of them: If you believe that America should lead with strength and purpose and confidence in our ideals, I would be honored to have your support, and I am asking for your vote.

We have a difference of opinion. We have a difference of opinion how—as how to protect our families. My opponent said America must submit to what he calls a "global test" before we commit our troops.

Audience members. Boo-o-o!

The President. I'm not making that up. [*Laughter*] He was standing about three yards away when he said it. I couldn't believe it either. As far as I tell, that means our country must get permission before we act in our own defense. As President, I'll build on alliances. We'll continue to work with our friends and allies, but I will never turn over America's national security decisions to leaders of other countries.

We have a difference of opinion as to how to protect you on this crucial issue. My opponent said that September the 11th did not change him much at all. September the 11th changed me a lot. I'll never forget the day I stood in the ruins of the Twin Towers on September the 14th, 2001. I'll never forget the sights and sounds of that day, the workers in hardhats who were yelling at me at the top of their lungs, "Whatever it takes." The worker came out of the rubble—policeman or a fireman, I'm not sure which one—who grabbed me by the arm. He looked me square in the eye. He said, "Do not let me down." From that day forward, I get up every morning thinking about how to better protect our families. I will never relent in defending America, whatever it takes.

The second clear choice in this election concerns your family's budget. When I ran for President 4 years ago, I pledged to lower taxes for America's families. I kept my word. We doubled the child credit to $1,000 per child to help moms and dads. We reduced the marriage penalty. We believe the Tax Code ought to encourage, not penalize marriage. We dropped the lowest tax bracket to 10 percent. We reduced income taxes on everybody who pays income taxes.

I want you to remind your friends and neighbors about this fact: When I came into office, the stock market had been in serious decline for 6 months; and we faced a recession and corporate scandals; and the attacks of September the 11th cost us about a million jobs in the 3 months after that fateful day.

But our economic policies are working. Because we increased consumption and encouraged investment, our economy is growing at rates as fast as any in nearly 20 years. We added 1.9 million new jobs in the last 13 months. The entrepreneurial spirit in America is strong. Small businesses are flourishing all across Ohio. Farm income is up in Ohio. The homeownership rate is at an alltime high. More minority families own a home than ever before in our Nation's history. The national unemployment rate is 5.4 percent. Let me put that in perspective for you: That's lower than the average rate of the 1970s, the 1980s, and the 1990s.

I fully understand there are still people hurting in the great State of Ohio, but we're heading in the right direction. Your unemployment rate dropped from 6.3 percent to 6 percent in the month of September, and we added 5,500 new jobs. We're headed in the right direction.

My opponent has plans for your family budget. He intends to take a big chunk out of it.

Audience members. Boo-o-o!

The President. He voted against the higher child tax credit. He voted against marriage penalty relief. He voted against lower taxes. If he'd have had his way, the average American family would be paying $2,000 more in Federal taxes.

Audience members. Boo-o-o!

The President. That may not sound like a lot to some of them in Washington, but it's a lot for families right here in Columbus, Ohio. It helps moms and dads. It helps the small-business owners. You know, my opponent has been in the Senate for 20 years and he voted to raise taxes 98 times.

Audience members. Boo-o-o!

The President. That's five times for every year in the Senate. I'd call that a predictable pattern, a leading indicator. During this campaign, he's also made a lot of promises. He's promised $2.2 trillion in new Federal spending. That's trillion with a "T." That's a lot even for a Senator from Massachusetts.

So they asked him, "How are you going to pay for it?" And he said, "Oh, we'll just tax the rich." You've heard that before. Be wary. See, you raise, when you run up the top two brackets, between 600 and 800 billion dollars. That is far short of the 2.2 trillion he's promised. I would call that a tax gap. That's the gap between what he's promised and what he says he can deliver. And guess who usually gets to fill the tax gap?

Audience members. We do!

The President. Yes, you do. The good news is, he is not going to tax you; we're going to carry Ohio and win a great victory.

Third—the third clear choice in this election involves the quality of life for our Nation's families. A good education and quality health care are important to a successful life. As candidate for President, I pledged to end the soft bigotry of low expectations by reforming our public schools. I kept my word. We passed good education reforms. We believe every child can learn, and we expect every child, every school to teach. We increased Federal spending. But in return for Federal increases, we now expect State and local jurisdictions to measure. We understand you cannot solve a problem until you diagnose the problem. And we are diagnosing and we are solving problems all across America. Test scores are up in reading and math. We're closing an achievement gap for minority students. And we will not go back to the days of low expectations and mediocrity in our classrooms.

We'll continue to improve life for our families by making health care affordable and accessible. We'll make sure the poor and the indigent get good health care in community health centers. We'll make sure our program for children of low-income families is fully subscribed. To make sure health care is affordable, we must allow small businesses to join together across jurisdictional boundaries so they can buy insurance at the same discounts big companies are able to do. We will expand health savings accounts to help our small businesses and our families.

And to make sure health care is available and affordable for citizens of Ohio, we will do something about the frivolous lawsuits that are running up the cost of health care. I have met too many ob-gyns who are having to leave practice because of increased premiums due to lawsuits. I have met too many expectant moms who are deeply concerned about getting the health care they need. This litigation problem is a national problem. You cannot be pro-doctor, pro-patient, and pro-personal-injury-trial-lawyer at the same time. My opponent has made his choice. He voted against medical liability reform 10 times and he put a personal-injury trial lawyer on the ticket.

Audience members. Boo-o-o!

The President. I have made my choice. I'm standing with the doctors of Ohio. I'm standing with the families of Ohio. I'm for medical liability reform.

Senator Kerry has got a different idea about health care. You might remember in the debate when he looked square in the camera and he said about his health care plan, "The Government didn't have anything to do with it." I could barely contain myself. [*Laughter*] The Government has got a lot to do with it. Eighty percent of the people who are signed up under his program end up on a Government plan. If you make it easier for people to be on Medicaid, it is likely small-business owners will drop insurance for their employees because the Government will provide it. See, you're moving people from the private sector to Government plans. When the Government writes the check, the Government makes the rules. And when the Government is making the rules about your health care, the Government starts making decisions for you and they make decisions for your doctors. The wrong prescription for

American families is to federalize our health care. In all we do to improve our family's health care, we will make sure the decisions are made by doctors and patients, not by officials in Washington, DC.

The fourth clear choice involves your retirement. Our Nation has made a solemn commitment to America's seniors on Social Security and Medicare. When I ran for President 4 years ago, I promised to keep that commitment and improve Medicare by adding prescription drug coverage. I kept my word. Medicare needed to be changed. See, we would pay thousands of dollars for a heart surgery but not one dime for the prescription drugs that could prevent the heart surgery from being needed in the first place. That didn't make any sense to our seniors. So I brought Republicans and Democrats together. We modernized Medicare for our seniors, and beginning in 2006, seniors will get prescription drug coverage under Medicare.

And we'll keep the promise of Social Security for our seniors, and we will strengthen Social Security for generations to come. Now, you might remember the 2000 campaign when they started running those ads and putting out the leaflets and flyers that said this to our seniors: "If George W. gets elected, our seniors will not get their checks." So when you're out there rounding up the vote, when you're working hard over the next 4 days, remind your friends and neighbors that George W. did get elected, and the seniors did get their checks. And our seniors will continue to get their checks. And baby boomers like me and Arnold—[*laughter*]—we're in pretty good shape when it comes to Social Security.

But we need to worry about our children and our grandchildren. We need to worry about whether Social Security will be there for them. And that is why I believe younger workers ought to be allowed to take some of their payroll taxes and set up a personal savings account, an account that earns a greater rate of interest, an account you own and an account the Government can never take away.

My opponent takes a different approach. You know, he said he's going to protect Social Security. But tell your friends and neighbors that he voted eight times for higher taxes on Social Security benefits.

Audience members. Boo-o-o!

The President. Like on other issues, he can run, but he cannot hide.

And he's offered nothing for the next generation when it comes to Social Security. The job of the President is to confront problems, not to pass them on to future Presidents and future generations. In a new term, I will bring people together so that we modernize and strengthen Social Security for generations to come.

The final choice in this election is on the values that are crucial to keeping our families strong. I believe marriage is a sacred institution. I will promote a culture of life and proudly signed the ban on partial-birth abortion. And I stand for the appointment of Federal judges who know the difference between personal opinion and the strict interpretation of the law.

All these choices make this one of the most important elections in our history. The security and prosperity of our country are at stake. The health of our families is at stake. The education of our children is at stake. And the direction of our culture is at stake. And the decision is in the best of hands. The decision is in the hands of the American people.

One of my favorite quotes was written by a fellow Texan named Tom Lea. He said, "Sarah and I live on the east side of the mountain. It is the sunrise side, not the sunset side. It is the side to see the day that is coming, not to see the day that is gone." My opponent has spent much of this campaign talking about the day that is gone. I'm talking about the day that's coming.

I see a day where prosperity reaches every corner of America. I see a day where every child is able to read and write and add and subtract. I see a day in which this world becomes more peaceful and we're able to achieve the peace we all dream for for our children and our grandchildren.

When I campaigned across your State in 2000, I made you this pledge, that if I got elected, I would uphold the honor and the integrity of the office. With your help, with your hard work, I will do so for 4 more years.

God bless. Thanks for coming. Thank you all.

NOTE: The President spoke at 7:27 p.m. at the Nationwide Arena. In his remarks, he referred to Gov. Arnold Schwarzenegger of California; Gov. Bob Taft of Ohio and his wife, Hope; Carolyn Hobson, wife of Representative David Hobson; Lt. Gov. Jennette B. Bradley of Ohio; Chief Justice Thomas J. Moyer of the Supreme Court of Ohio; Jo Ann Davidson, Ohio Valley regional chairman, Bush-Cheney '04, Inc.; Doug Preisse, chairman, Franklin County Republican Party Executive Committee; Gen. Tommy R. Franks, USA (Ret.), former combatant commander, U.S. Central Command; Usama bin Laden, leader of the Al Qaida terrorist organization; and former President Saddam Hussein of Iraq.

Remarks in Grand Rapids, Michigan
October 30, 2004

The President. Thank you all for coming. Thanks for taking time out of your Saturday morning to come by and say hello. Laura and I are honored to be back in western

Michigan. You've lifted our spirits. We're proud to be in a home of a fine former President, President Gerald Ford, and a great First Lady in Betty Ford. I know you honor their service to our country, as do Laura and I. We're here to ask for your vote, and I'm here to ask for your help.

Audience members. Four more years! Four more years! Four more years!

The President. We're close to voting time. We have a duty in our country to vote. In our free society, we have an obligation, I think, to go to the polls and express our opinions. So I'm here to ask you to convince your friends and neighbors to do their duty. Make sure our fellow Republicans go to the polls. Make sure independents go to the polls. Make sure discerning Democrats go to the polls. And when you get them headed to the polls, remind them, if they want a safer America and a stronger America and a better America, to put me and Dick Cheney back in office.

I enjoy traveling our country. I enjoy talking to the people. I love to tell the people what I am going to do for the next 4 years. Perhaps the most important reason to put me in, though, is to make sure Laura is the First Lady for 4 more years.

Audience members. Laura! Laura! Laura!

The President. I am proud of my runningmate, Dick Cheney. I readily concede he does not have the waviest hair in this race. [*Laughter*] But I know the people of western Michigan will be pleased to hear I didn't pick him because of his hairdo. I picked him because of his judgment. I picked him because of his experience. He's getting the job done for the American people.

I want to thank my friend Betsy DeVos for her leadership and her community spirit. I want to thank the DeVos family for joining us today.

I want to thank my friend Congressman Peter Hoekstra for joining us today. Pete, I'm glad you're here; his wife, Diane, is here; other family members are here. I look forward to working with the chairman of a really important committee to make sure our intelligence gathering works, to make sure America can stay secure. Appreciate your service, Pete. I want to thank Congressman Vern Ehlers for joining us today. Congressman, we're proud you're here. Thank you for representing this district with such distinction and honor.

I want to thank the attorney general, Mike Cox, and Secretary of State Terri Lynn Land for joining us.

I want to thank all the local and State officials who are here. I want to thank all the people who have thrown their hat in the ring and are running for office.

I want to thank the Sparta High School Marching Band for joining us today, the Western Michigan Home School Northern Lights Marching Band. I want to thank Daron Norwood for singing for you today. He's good, isn't he?

But most of all, I want to thank you all and the grassroots activists, the people putting up the signs, the people making the phone calls. I know how much work it requires to get a crowd this big, and I thank you for what you have done. I want to thank you for what you're going to do. You're going to turn out a big vote in western Michigan, and we'll carry this State on November 2d.

This election takes place in a time of great consequence. The person who sits in the Oval Office for the next 4 years will set the course of the war on terror and the direction of our economy. America will need strong, determined, optimistic leadership, and I'm ready for the work ahead.

My 4 years as your President have confirmed some lessons and taught me some new lessons. I've learned to expect the unexpected, because war and emergency can arrive on a quiet autumn morning. I've learned firsthand how hard it is to send young men and women into battle, even when the cause is right. I've been grateful for the lesson I've learned from my parents, respect every person and do your best and live every day to its fullest. I've been strengthened by my faith and humbled by its reminder that every life is a part of a larger story. I've learned how a President needs to lead, as Presidents from Lincoln to Roosevelt to Reagan so clearly demonstrated.

A President must not shift in the wind. A President has to make tough decisions and stand by them. The role of the American President is not to follow the path of the latest polls. The role of the President is to lead based upon principle and conviction and conscience. Especially in dangerous times, mixed signals only confuse our friends and embolden our enemies. Mixed signals are the wrong signals for the American President to send.

The last 4 years, Americans have learned a few things about me as well. Sometimes, I'm a little too blunt. [*Laughter*] I get that from my mother. [*Laughter*] Sometimes I mangle the English language. I get that from my father. [*Laughter*] But Americans have learned also that even when you might not agree with me, you know where I stand. You know what I believe, and you know where I'm going to lead.

You cannot say that about my opponent.

Audience members. Boo-o-o!

The President. I think it's fair to say, consistency is not his long suit. And next Tuesday, the American people will go to the polls. They will be voting for vision. They will be voting for consistency. They will be voting for conviction. And no doubt in my mind,° they'll be voting for Bush/Cheney.

This election comes down to five clear choices for the American people. The first clear choice is the most important because it concerns the security of your family. All progress on every other issue depends on the safety of our citizens. The will—this will be the first Presidential election since September the 11th, 2001. Americans will go to the polls in a time of war and ongoing threats unlike any we have faced before.

° White House correction.

The terrorists who killed thousands of innocent people are still dangerous, and they are determined. The outcome of this election will set the direction of the war against terror. The most solemn duty of the American President is to protect the American people. If America shows any uncertainty or weakness in this decade, the world will drift toward tragedy. This will not happen on my watch.

Since that terrible morning of September the 11th, 2001, we have fought the terrorists across the Earth, not for pride, not for power but because the lives of our citizens are at stake. Our strategy is clear. We have strengthened protections for the homeland. We're reforming and strengthening our intelligence services. We are transforming our military. There will be no draft. The All-Volunteer Army will remain an all-volunteer army. We are determined. We are steadfast. We are staying on the offensive against the terrorists across the globe so we do not have to face them here at home.

Our strategy is succeeding. As the September the 11th Commission pointed out, we are safer but not yet safe. But because we led, Afghanistan is a free nation and now an ally in the war on terror. Because we led, Pakistan is capturing terrorists; Saudi Arabia is making raids and arrests; Libya is dismantling its weapons programs; the army of a free Iraq is fighting for freedom; and more than three-quarters of Al Qaida's key members and associates have been brought to justice.

And part of our strategy to make sure our children and our grandchildren grow up in a peaceful world is to spread freedom. I believe in the transformational power of liberty. I believe liberty can transform societies.

Think about what has happened in Afghanistan in a relatively brief period of time. It wasn't all that long ago that young girls were not allowed to go to school and their mothers were taken into the public square and whipped because of these ideologues of hate called the Taliban. Because we acted in our own self-interest, because we acted to uphold a doctrine I outlined which said, "If you harbor a terrorist, you're equally as guilty as the terrorist," because we acted to secure the American people, millions of citizens voted in a Presidential election in Afghanistan. And the first voter was a 19-year-old woman.

Despite the horrific acts of the terrorists in Iraq, there are going to be free elections in Iraq in January. And think how far that country has come from the days of torture chambers and mass graves. Freedom is on the march. Freedom is on the move around the world, and that's important. Free societies will be peaceful societies. Free societies will join us in fighting the terrorists instead of harboring the terrorists. I believe every soul wants to be free in this world. Freedom is not America's gift to the world; freedom is the Almighty God's gift to each man and woman in this world.

A President must lead this country with consistency and strength. In a war, sometimes your tactics change but never your principles. Americans have seen how I do my job. On good days and on bad days, when the polls are up or the polls are down, I am determined to protect this country. And I will always support the men and women who wear our Nation's uniform. I am proud to be the Commander in Chief of a great military, and I want to thank those who wear our uniform for your service to our country. I want to thank the military families who are here, for your sacrifice and service. And I want to thank the veterans who are here who have set such a great example for those who wear the uniform. And I will assure you, in a new term, I will keep the commitment I have made to support our troops in harm's way.

I went to the Congress in September of 2003, asking for $87 billion to support our troops in combat. It was very important funding. We got great support—Pete might

remember—overwhelming bipartisan support. Only 12 Members of the United States Senate voted against it, 2 of whom were my opponent and his runningmate. I want you——

Audience members. Boo-o-o!

The President. When you're out gathering up the vote, remind people of this statistic, this fact: Four Members of the Senate voted to authorize force and then voted against the funding necessary to support our troops in harm's way, two of whom—two of those four—were my opponent and his runningmate.

Audience members. Boo-o-o!

The President. You might remember what he said when they asked him about why he made the vote. Senator Kerry said, "I actually did vote for the 87 billion, before I voted against it." I haven't spent nearly as much time in this part of the world as you have, but I can assure you, you're not going to find many people in Grand Rapids, Michigan, who talks that way.

You know, he's given several answers on that vote since then. Perhaps the most revealing of all was when he just said, "The whole thing was a complicated matter." My fellow Americans, there's nothing complicated about supporting our troops in combat.

My opponent has had a propensity to change positions in this campaign. His positions are like the weather here in western Michigan. [*Laughter*] You don't like it, wait a little bit, and it will change.

Senator Kerry said that we're better off with Saddam Hussein out of power, except when he declares that removing Saddam Hussein made us less safe. He stated in our second debate he always believed Saddam was a threat—except, a few questions later, when he said Saddam Hussein was not a threat. He says he was right when he voted to authorize the use of force against Saddam Hussein, but I was wrong to use force against Saddam Hussein.

His record on national security has a far deeper problem than election-year flip-flops. One of the largest national security issues of our time—on the largest national issues of our time, he has been consistently wrong. When Ronald Reagan was confronting the Soviet Union at the height of the cold war, Senator Kerry said that President Reagan's policy of peace through strength was making America less safe. Well, history has shown that Senator Kerry was wrong and President Reagan was right.

When former President Bush led a coalition against Saddam Hussein in 1991, Senator Kerry voted against the use of force to liberate Kuwait. History has shown that Senator Kerry was wrong and former President Bush was right.

In 1994, just one year after the first bombing of the World Trade Center, Senator Kerry proposed massive cuts in America's budget, so massive that even his Massachusetts colleague, Ted Kennedy, opposed them. History has shown that Senator Kerry was wrong and—let's be fair about it—Senator Kennedy was right.

During the last 20 years, in key moments of challenge and decision, Senator Kerry has chosen the path of weakness and inaction. With that record, he stands in opposition not just to me but to the great tradition of the Democratic Party. The party of Franklin Roosevelt, the party of Harry Truman, the party of John Kennedy is rightly remembered for confidence and resolve in times of war and in hours of crisis. Senator Kerry has turned his back on "pay any price" and "bear any burden," and he has replaced those commitments with "wait and see" and "cut and run."

Many Democrats in this country do not recognize their party anymore, and today, I want to speak to every one of them. If you believe that America should lead with strength and purpose and confidence in our ideals, I would be honored to have your support, and I am asking for your vote.

Audience members. Four more years! Four more years! Four more years!

The President. There are big differences in this campaign when it comes to your family's security. Senator Kerry said that America must submit to what he calls a "global test."

Audience members. Boo-o-o!

The President. I'm not making that up. He said it in a debate. I was surprised, like you were. [*Laughter*] As far as I can tell, it means our country must get permission from foreign capitals before we act in our own defense. I will work with our allies. I will strengthen our alliances. I will work with our friends, but I will never turn over America's national security decisions to leaders of other countries.

We have a difference of opinion. My opponent was quoted as saying that September the 11th did not change him much at all. His policies make that clear. He says the war on terror is primarily a law enforcement and intelligence gathering operation. September the 11th changed my outlook. I remember the day I went to the ruins of the Twin Towers on September the 14th, 2001. The sights and sounds will be with me forever. I remember the workers in hardhats yelling at me at the top of their lungs, "Whatever it takes." I remember looking the man square in the eye who came out of the rubble. He grabbed me by my arm, and he said, "Do not let me down." Ever since that day, I wake up every morning trying to better figure out how to better protect America. I will never relent in defending our country, whatever it takes.

The second clear choice in this election concerns your family's budget. When I ran for President 4 years ago, I pledged to lower taxes for America's families. I kept my word. We doubled the child credit to $1,000 per child. We reduced the marriage penalty. We think the Tax Code ought to encourage marriage, not penalize marriage. We dropped the lowest bracket to 10 percent. We reduced income taxes for everybody who pays taxes. Our plans are working.

When you round up the vote, remind people about what this economy has been through. Six months prior to my arrival in Washington, the stock market was in serious decline. Then we had a recession. Then we had corporate scandals. And then the attacks of September the 11th cost us a million jobs in the 3 months after those attacks.

But our economic policies have led us back to growth. This economy of ours is growing at rates as fast as any in nearly 20 years. We've added 1.9 million new jobs in the last 13 months. The national unemployment rate is 5.4 percent. That's lower than the average rate of the 1970s, the 1980s, and the 1990s. Homeownership rate is at an alltime high in America. More minority families own their own home, and that's better for our country. Michigan farmers are making a living. The entrepreneurial spirit is strong. The small-business sector is alive and well in America.

People are still hurting in the State of Michigan. I know that. I've traveled here a lot. I've heard the stories. But the fundamental question is, which candidate can continue to grow this economy? Who's got the pro-growth, pro-entrepreneur, pro-small-business plan? And that's George W. Bush.

My opponent has very different plans for your family's budget. He intend to take a big chunk out of it.

Audience members. Boo-o-o!

The President. He voted against the higher child tax credit. He voted against marriage penalty relief. He voted against reducing income taxes. If he had had his way over the past 3 years, the average Michigan family would be paying $2,000 per year more to the Federal Government.

Audience members. Boo-o-o!

The President. Now, I know that doesn't sound like a lot to some of them in Washington, but it's a lot for families right here in Grand Rapids. It helps moms and dads. That money helps our small businesses create new jobs. My opponent has been in the Senate for 20 years, and he's voted to raise taxes 98 times. That's about five times per year in the Senate. I'd call that a predictable pattern—[*laughter*]—a leading indicator. [*Laughter*] A Senator does something that often, he must really like it. [*Laughter*] During this campaign, he's also promised $2.2 trillion in Federal spending. That's trillion with a "T." [*Laughter*] That's a lot. Even for a Senator from Massachusetts, that's a lot. [*Laughter*] So they asked him, "How are you going to pay for it?" He said that same old thing, you know, "We're just going to tax the rich."

Two things wrong with that. One is, most small businesses pay individual income taxes. Most small businesses are sole proprietorships and Subchapter S corporations. Seventy percent of the new jobs in America are created by small businesses. So when you run up the top two brackets like he has promised to do, you're taxing the job creators, and that's lousy economic policy.

And here's something you need to be wary about. When you talk about top— raising the top two brackets, you're only raising between 600 and 800 billion dollars. I say "only" because he's promised 2.2 trillion. So there's a tax gap. That would be a gap between what he has promised and what he can deliver. And given his record, you probably can guess who is going to have to fill that tax gap. You are. But don't worry about it. We're going to carry Michigan, and he's not going to be able to tax you.

The third clear choice in this election involves the quality of life for our Nation's families. A good education and quality health care are important for a successful life. As a candidate, I pledged to challenge the soft bigotry of low expectations by reforming our public schools. As President, I kept my word.

The No Child Left Behind Act is substantial reform. In return for extra help from the Federal Government, we now demand accountability in our classrooms. You know why? Because we believe every child can learn, and we expect every school to teach. You cannot solve a problem until you diagnose the problem, and we're making diagnoses all across our country, and we're solving problems. Test scores are up in reading and math. We're closing achievement gaps for our minority students all across America. And we're not going to go back to the days of low standards and mediocrity in our classrooms.

We'll continue to improve life for our families by making health care more accessible and more affordable. We will take care of the poor and the indigent by spreading community health centers. We will make sure our programs for children with—from low-income families are fully subscribed. We want to help people get health care.

But we also understand we've got to make it more affordable, and here are three commonsense ways to do so. Small businesses ought to be allowed to join together to share risk, so they can buy insurance at the same discounts that big companies are able to do. We will expand health savings accounts to help our families and our small businesses better afford insurance and plans that enable you to manage your health care. And finally, we will do something about the frivolous lawsuits that are running good docs out of practice and running the cost of health care up.

I have met too many ob-gyns in our country who are having to quit the practice of medicine because these lawsuits have driven their premiums sky-high. I've met too many expectant moms who have told me about their concerns about getting quality health care because their doctor is no longer in practice. We have a national problem when it comes to medical liability reform. I don't think you can be pro-patient and pro-doctor and pro-personal-injury-trial-lawyer at the same time. I think you have to make a choice. My opponent has made his choice. He voted 10 times against

medical liability reform, and he put a personal-injury trial lawyer on the ticket.

Audience members. Boo-o-o!

The President. I have made my choice. I'm standing with the doctors of Michigan. I'm standing with the patients of Michigan. I am for real medical liability reform.

Senator Kerry's got a different point of view when it comes to health. You might remember one of the debates. And they asked him about his health care plan. He looked square in the camera, and he said, "The Government doesn't have anything to do with it." I could barely contain myself. [*Laughter*] The Government has got a lot to do with it. Eighty percent of the people under his plan would end up on a Government-run program. When you make it easier for people to sign up on Medicaid, it means small businesses are likely to drop coverage for their employees because the Government will provide the coverage. People move from the private sector to the Government sector under his plan. And when Government writes the checks when it comes to health care, they start writing the rules when it comes to health care. And when they start writing the rules when it comes to health care, they start making decisions for you when it comes to your health care and they start making decisions for the doctors when it comes to health care. The wrong prescription for American families when it comes to their health care is to federalize health care.

In all we do to improve health care, we will make sure the decisions are made by doctors and patients, not by officials in Washington, DC.

The fourth clear choice in this election involves your retirement. Our Nation has made a solemn commitment to America's seniors on Social Security and Medicare. When I ran for President 4 years ago, I promised to keep that commitment and improve Medicare by adding prescription drug coverage. I have kept my word. Medicare needed to be modernized. The Government would pay thousands of dollars for the heart surgery under Medicare but not a dime for the prescription drugs that could prevent the heart surgery from being needed in the first place. We brought people together. We strengthened and modernized the system. And beginning in 2006, our seniors will be able to get prescription drug coverage under Medicare.

And when it comes to Social Security, we will keep the promise of Social Security for our seniors, and we will strengthen Social Security for generations to come. When you're gathering up the vote, remind your friends and neighbors about what took place in the 2000 campaign. They said by TV and by flier and by word of mouth that, "If George W. got elected, our seniors would not get their checks." You might remember that aspect of the 2000 campaign. Well, George W. got elected, and our seniors got their checks. And our seniors will continue to get their checks. And baby boomers like me and a couple others out there I see, we will get our checks. The Social Security system is in good shape for the seniors and baby boomers.

But we need to worry about our children and our grandchildren when it comes to Social Security. We need to worry about whether or not Social Security will be there when they need it. And therefore, I think younger workers ought to be allowed to take some of their personal savings account—some of their payroll taxes and set up a personal savings account, an account they call their own, an account the Government cannot take away.

My opponent has taken a different approach about Social Security. He told the people he's going to strengthen Social Security, but remind your friends and neighbors, he voted to tax Social Security benefits eight times.

Audience members. Boo-o-o!

The President. And he hasn't offered anything for the younger Americans when it comes to modernizing the system. The job of a President is to confront problems, not to pass them on to future Presidents and future generations. In a new term, I will bring people together, and we will strengthen the Social Security system for generations to come.

The fifth clear choice in this election is on the values that are crucial to keeping our families strong. I believe marriage and family are the foundation of our society. I will promote a culture of life, and I proudly signed the ban on partial-birth abortion. I stand for the appointment of Federal judges who know the difference between personal opinion and the strict interpretation of the law.

My opponent and I differ. He voted against the ban on partial-birth abortion. He voted against the Defense of Marriage Act, and at one point in this campaign, he said that the heart and soul of America can be found in Hollywood.

Audience members. Boo-o-o!

The President. Most families do not look to Hollywood as a source for values. The heart and soul of America is found in communities like Grand Rapids, Michigan.

I'm optimistic about the future of our country. You know, when you're running for President, anger is not an agenda, and a litany of complaints is not a plan. I have a hopeful and positive vision. The President must see clearly where he intends to lead this Nation. Perhaps, let me define to you how I feel by quoting a friend from Texas, Tom Lea. Unfortunately, he's deceased recently, but here's what he said. He said, "Sarah and I live on the east side of the mountain. It is the sunrise side, not the sunset side. It is the side to see the day that is coming, not to see the day that is gone." In the course of this campaign, my opponent has spent much of the campaign talking about the day that is gone. I'm talking about the day that's coming.

I see a great day coming for our country. I see a day when prosperity reaches every corner of America. I see a day where every child is able to read and write. I see a day in which this world becomes more peaceful. I see a day in which we achieve the peace we all long for, for our children and our grandchildren.

When I campaigned across your State in 2000, I made this pledge: I said if I won, I would uphold the honor and the dignity of the office to which I had been elected. With your help, with your hard work, I will do so for 4 more years.

God bless. Thank you all.

NOTE: The President spoke at 9:55 a.m. at DeVos Place. In his remarks, he referred to Betsy DeVos, chairman, Michigan Republican Party; entertainer Daron Norwood; and former President Saddam Hussein of Iraq. He also referred to the National Commission on Terrorist Attacks Upon the United States (9/11 Commission).

The President's Radio Address
October 30, 2004

Good morning. In just a few days, Americans will choose who will lead our country during a time of war and economic opportunity. And the choice on Tuesday comes down to a few issues of great consequence. The first choice is the most important, because all our progress depends on our safety.

Since September the 11th, 2001, I have led a relentless campaign against the terrorists. We have strengthened homeland security. We removed terror regimes in Afghanistan and Iraq. We are on the offensive around the world, because the best way to prevent future attacks is to go after the enemy.

My opponent has a different view. Senator Kerry says September the 11th didn't change him much, and his policies make that clear. He says the war on terror is primarily an intelligence and law enforcement operation. He has proposed what he calls a "global test" that would give foreign governments a veto over American security decisions. And when our troops in Afghanistan and Iraq needed funding for body armor and bullets, Senator Kerry voted against it.

The direction of the war on terror is at stake in the election of 2004. And when you go to the polls on Tuesday, remember this: I will do whatever it takes to defend America and prevail in the war on terror,

and I will always support the men and women who do the fighting.

The second choice in this election concerns your family budget. As a candidate, I pledged to lower taxes for families, and I have kept my word. We doubled the child tax credit, reduced the marriage penalty, and dropped the lowest tax bracket to 10 percent. Now working families keep more of their paychecks, and America's economy is growing faster than any other among major industrialized nations.

My opponent voted against all our tax relief for working families. His votes would have squeezed about $2,000 more in taxes from the average middle-class family. Now Senator Kerry is promising to increase Federal spending by more than $2.2 trillion. And to pay for all that new spending, he would have to raise taxes on American families. I will keep your taxes low because I know it's not the Government's money; it's your family's money.

The third choice in this election involves your quality of life. As President, I signed historic education reforms to bring high standards to the classroom and make schools accountable to parents, and our children are making progress in reading and math. We've strengthened Medicare, created health savings accounts, and expanded community health centers to help more Americans get health care. I'm proposing a series of practical reforms to make health care more affordable and accessible by expanding health savings accounts, allowing association health plans, and protecting patients and doctors from junk and frivolous lawsuits.

My opponent has a different approach. Senator Kerry voted for the No Child Left Behind Act, but he has pledged to weaken the accountability standards. He's voted 10 times against medical liability reform. And now, he's proposing a big-Government health care plan that would do nothing about rising health costs and would cause millions of Americans to lose their private health insurance and end up on Government programs.

Finally, this election presents a choice on the values that keep our families strong. I believe marriage is a sacred commitment, and I will always defend it. I will continue to appoint judges who strictly interpret the law. And I will keep working to move this goodhearted nation toward a culture of life.

On these issues, my opponent and I are miles apart. Senator Kerry was part of an out-of-the-mainstream minority that voted against the Defense of Marriage Act. He believes there ought to be a liberal litmus test for judicial appointments. He voted against banning the brutal practice of partial-birth abortion. I believe that reasonable people can find common ground on difficult issues, and I will continue reaching out and bringing Americans together to protect our deepest held values.

All of these choices make this one of the most important elections in our history. These past 4 years, you have seen how I do my job. Even when you might not agree with me, you know where I stand, what I believe, and what I intend to do. Soon, the decision will be in your hands. And however you decide, I urge you to get out and vote on Tuesday.

Thank you for listening.

NOTE: The address was recorded at 7:50 a.m. on October 29 in the Cabinet Room for broadcast at 10:06 a.m. on October 30. The transcript was made available by the Office of the Press Secretary on October 29 but was embargoed for release until the broadcast. The Office of the Press Secretary also released a Spanish language transcript of this address.

Remarks in Ashwaubenon, Wisconsin
October 30, 2004

The President. Thank you all for coming. Thank you all. It's good to be with all the cheeseheads. It's great to be back in Brown County.

We're here to ask for your vote and here to ask for your help. It is close to voting time. We have a duty in our democracy to vote. And so I'm asking you to get your friends and neighbors and remind them of that duty. Find our fellow Republicans, and turn them out. Find independents, and turn them out. Find discerning Democrats, and head them to the polls. And when you get them going to the polls, remind them, if they want a safer America, a stronger America, and a better America, to put me and Dick Cheney back in office.

Perhaps the most important reason of all to put me back in for 4 more years is to make sure that Laura is the First Lady for 4 more years.

I'm proud of my runningmate. I don't want to offend anybody here who is follically challenged—[*laughter*]—but I admit it, Vice President Cheney doesn't have the waviest hair in the race. [*Laughter*] People in this part of the world will be happy I didn't pick him because of his hairdo. I picked him because of his judgment. I picked him because of his experience. He's getting the job done for the American people.

I'm proud of your former Governor, my friend and Cabinet Secretary, Tommy Thompson. He's done a great job. You know, one of the jobs of a President is to surround himself with smart, capable people. I obviously know how to do that when I picked Tommy Thompson.

I want to thank Congressman Mark Green for being such a fine Member of the United States Congress. I want to thank his wife, Sue. I want to thank Congressman Jim Sensenbrenner and wife, Cheryl, for joining us today. I want to thank Congressman Tom Petri for joining us today. I want to thank Congressman Paul Ryan for joining us today.

I want to thank your State treasurer, Jack Voight. I want to thank the assembly speaker for being here. I want to thank Milwaukee County Executive Scott Walker. I call him Scott W. I want to thank all the local officials, the mayors and the city council folks.

I want to thank Tina Danforth, the Oneida Nation chairwoman, for joining us today. I want to thank Bob Chicks, the Stockbridge tribal president, for joining us today. I am honored—I'm honored these tribal leaders are here, and I look forward to working on a government-to-government basis in the next 4 years to help build a more hopeful America for every citizen who lives in this country.

I hope you vote for Tim Michels for the United States Senate. Laura and I have come to know he and Barbara, and he is a fine, fine man. He'll make a great United States Senator.

I want to thank my friend Kayne Robinson, who's the president of the NRA, the National Rifle Association. I want to thank Wayne LaPierre for being with us today.

I'm proud to have the endorsement and support of so many of the sports men and women across the State of Wisconsin. I appreciate Jeff Schinkten, who's the Whitetails Unlimited founder and board president, for supporting my candidacy.

I want to thank Lee Greenwood for being here, my friend.

But most of all, Laura and I thank you all for coming. Thank you for taking time out of your Saturday afternoon to come by and say hello. I want to thank those of you who are putting up the signs. I want to thank those of you who are making the phone calls. I want to thank you for turning out such a huge crowd today. I want to thank you for what you have done and what you're going to do. By working hard and by turning out the vote, there is no doubt in my mind we will carry Wisconsin and win a great victory in November.

The person who sits in the Oval Office for the next 4 years will set the course of the war on terror and the direction of our economy. America will need strong, determined, optimistic leadership, and I am ready for the job. My 4 years as your President have confirmed some lessons and have taught me some new ones. I've learned to expect the unexpected because war and emergency can arrive suddenly on a quiet morning. I have learned firsthand how hard it is to send young men and women into battle, even if the cause is right. I've been grateful for the lessons I have learned from my parents: Respect every person; do your best; live life to its fullest. I've been strengthened by my faith and humbled by its reminder that every life is part of a larger story.

I know how a President must lead, as Presidents from Lincoln to Roosevelt to Reagan so clearly demonstrated. A President must not shift with the wind. A President has to make the tough decisions and stand by them. In the last 4 years, Americans have learned a few things about me.

Sometimes I am a little too blunt. [*Laughter*] I got that from my mother. [*Laughter*] Sometimes I mangle the English language. [*Laughter*] I got that from my father. [*Laughter*] But all the time, whether you agree with me or disagree with me, you know where I stand. You know what I believe, and you know where I'm going to lead.

You can't say that about my opponent. I think it is fair to say that consistency is not his long suit. [*Laughter*] Next Tuesday, the citizens of this country will vote. They will vote for conviction. They will vote for principle. They will vote for somebody who knows how to lead this country, and with your help, they'll be voting for George W. Bush.

This election comes down to five choices for America's families. And the first clear choice is the most important, because it concerns the security of your family. All progress on every other issue depends on the safety of our citizens. The terrorists who killed thousands of innocent people are still dangerous and determined to strike. The outcome of this election will set the direction of the war against terror. The most solemn duty of the American President is to protect the American people. And if our country, if America shows any uncertainty or any weakness in this decade, the world will drift toward tragedy. This is not going to happen on my watch.

Since that terrible morning of September the 11th, 2001, we fought the terrorists across the Earth, not for pride, not for power but because the lives of our citizens are at stake. Our strategy is clear. We're protecting the homeland. We're transforming—or reforming and strengthening our intelligence capabilities. We are transforming our military. The All-Volunteer Army will remain an all-volunteer army. There will be no draft. We are relentless. We are steadfast. We are determined. We will chase the terrorists around the globe so we do not have to face them here at home.

Because we led, Afghanistan is a free nation and now an ally in the war on terror. Because we led, Pakistan is capturing terrorist leaders; Saudi Arabia is making raids and arrests. Because we led, Libya is dismantling its weapons programs. Because we led, an army of a free Iraq is fighting for freedom; and more than three-quarters of Al Qaida's key members and associates have been brought to justice.

We will not only stay on the offense with all our assets; we will stay on the offense by spreading freedom and liberty. I believe in the power of liberty to transform societies. And I want the youngsters to know firsthand what I mean. Just look at what happened in Afghanistan. It wasn't all that long ago that the people of that country lived under the brutal reign of barbarians, ideologues of hate called the Taliban. Young girls were not allowed to go to school, and if their mothers did not toe the line, they were taken into the public square and whipped and sometimes executed in a sports stadium. Because we acted in our own self-defense, because we upheld a doctrine that I clearly laid out for the world which said, "If you harbor a terrorist, you're equally as guilty as the terrorist," because we did what we said we were going to do, millions of people in Afghanistan voted for President of that country. And the first voter was a 19-year-old woman. And America is better off to have freedom take the place of tyranny in Afghanistan.

And there are going to be elections in Iraq in January. Think how far that country has come from the days of torture chambers and the brutal reign of a hater of America who had mass graves for thousands of his citizens. Freedom is on the march, and America and the world are more secure because of it. I believe in my heart of hearts that every person in the world desires to live in a free society. I believe this because I understand that freedom is not America's gift to the world; freedom is the Almighty God's gift to each man and woman of this world.

A President must lead with consistency and strength. In a war, sometimes your tactics have to change but never your principles. Americans have seen how I do my job. On good days and on bad days, when the polls are up or the polls are down, I am determined to protect the security of the American people.

And I will always support the men and women who wear our Nation's uniform. I want to thank those who wear the uniform who are here today. I want to thank the military families who are here today for your sacrifice. And I want to thank the veterans who are here today for having set such a great example for the men and women of today's military. And we'll make sure our troops have got the full support of the Government.

That's why I went to the Congress and requested $87 billion of funding to support our troops in combat. It was important. This happened in September of 2003. And it was vital, a vital funding request. And we got good bipartisan support there in Washington. Only 12 Members of the Senate voted against the funding, 2 of whom are my opponent and his runningmate.

Audience members. Boo-o-o!

The President. But I want to tell you this fact. As you're gathering up the vote, remind your friends and neighbors about this. Only 4 Members of the United States Senate—4 out of 100—voted to authorize force and then voted against the funding to support the troops they authorized, and 2 of those 4 were my opponent and his runningmate. They kept asking him why he made the vote he did. And he uttered perhaps the most famous quote of the 2004 campaign, when he said, "I actually did vote for the $87 billion, right before I voted against it." [*Laughter*]

Now, I haven't spent a lot of time in the coffee shops here in Green Bay, but I suspect I'm not going to find many people who talk that way. [*Laughter*] They

kept pressing him. They kept asking for answers. He's given several answers since then, but perhaps the most revealing of all was that he said, "The whole thing was a complicated matter." [*Laughter*] My fellow Americans, there is nothing complicated about supporting our troops in combat.

My opponent's positions are kind of like the weather here in Green Bay—[*laughter*]—if you don't like it, wait a little bit, and it will change. [*Laughter*]

My opponent's record on national security has a far deeper problem than election-year flip-flopping. And it's important for you to understand the record. On the largest national security issues of our time, he has been consistently wrong. When Ronald Reagan was confronting the Soviet Union at the height of the cold war, Senator Kerry said that President Reagan's policy of peace through strength was making America less safe. History has shown that Senator Kerry was wrong and President Reagan was right.

When former President Bush led a coalition against Saddam Hussein in 1991 because the tyrant had invaded Kuwait and threatened the peace and stability of the world, Senator Kerry voted against the use of force to liberate Kuwait. History has shown that Senator Kerry was wrong and former President Bush was right.

In 1994, just one year after the first bombing of the World Trade Center, Senator Kerry proposed massive cuts in America's intelligence budget, so massive that even his colleague from Massachusetts, Ted Kennedy, voted against them. History has shown that Senator Kerry was wrong—and we have got to be fair—in this case, Senator Kennedy was right. [*Laughter*]

During the 20 years—during the last 20 years, in key moments of challenge and decision for America, Senator Kerry has chosen the position of weakness and inaction. With that record, he stands in opposition not just to me but to the great tradition of the Democratic Party. The party of Franklin Roosevelt and Harry Truman and John Kennedy is rightly remembered for confidence and resolve in times of crises and in times of war. Senator Kerry has turned his back on "pay any price" and "bear any burden," and he has replaced those commitments with "wait and see" and "cut and run."

Many Democrats in this country do not recognize their party anymore. And today, I want to speak to every one of them: If you believe that America should lead with strength and purpose and confidence in our ideals, I would be honored to have your support, and I'm asking for your vote.

We have big differences about how to approach the security of our country. You might remember one of our debates when my opponent said that America must pass a "global test" before we commit our troops.

Audience members. Boo-o-o!

The President. I'm not making that up. [*Laughter*] I heard it too. [*Laughter*] As far as I can tell, that means we've got to get permission from foreign capitals before we act in our own defense. That's——

Audience members. No-o-o!

The President. That is a dangerous policy in the world in which we live. I'll work with our friends. I will work with our allies. I understand how important these alliances are, but I will never turn over America's national security decisions to leaders of other countries.

The security of our families are—is at stake. We've got to be firm and resolved. My opponent was quoted about September the 11th, and he said it didn't change him much at all. Well, September the 11th changed me. It made me look at the world in a different light. I'll never forget the day I stood in the ruins of the Twin Towers—that was September the 14th, 2001. I'll never forget the sights and the sounds of that moment when the workers in hardhats were yelling at me at the top of their lungs, "Whatever it takes." And one of the first-responders—I don't know if he worked for the fire department of New York or the police department—he came out of the rubble, and he grabbed me by the arm, and he looked me right in the eye and he said, "Do not let me down." Ever since that day, I wake up every morning trying to figure out how to better protect America. I will never relent in defending this country, whatever it takes.

The second clear choice in this election concerns your family's budget. When I ran for President 4 years ago, I pledged to lower taxes for our families, and I kept my word. We raised the child credit. We lowered the penalty on marriage. We believe the code ought to encourage marriage, not penalize marriage. We created a 10-percent bracket. We reduced taxes on everybody who pays taxes, and we're overcoming obstacles because of that plan.

When you're out gathering the vote, remind your friends and neighbors that 6 months prior to my arrival the stock market was in serious decline. That would be 6 months prior to my arrival in January of 2001. And then we had a recession and corporate scandals and an attack that cost us about a million jobs in the 3 months after September the 11th.

But our economic policies are working. This economy of ours is strong, and it is getting stronger. We've added 1.9 million jobs in the last 13 months. Homeownership rate is at an alltime high in America. More minority families own a home than ever before in our Nation's history. Wisconsin farmers are making a living. The small-business sector in our country is strong. The entrepreneurial spirit is alive, and it is well. The national unemployment rate is 5.4 percent. Let me put that in perspective for you: That's lower than the average rate of the 1970s, the 1980s, and the 1990s. The unemployment rate in the great State of Wisconsin is 5 percent. We're overcoming the obstacles. We're strong, and we are getting stronger.

My opponent has different plans for your budget. He's going to take a big chunk out of it. He voted against the child cred-it—raising the child credit. He voted against reducing the marriage penalty. He voted against the tax relief. And had he had had his way, the average family in Wisconsin would be paying $2,000 more per year in taxes.

Audience members. Boo-o-o!

The President. Now, that probably doesn't seem like a lot to some of them in Washington, but I understand it's a lot for the families in Green Bay, Wisconsin. People can use that $2,000. It can help them raise their children, help them make a living—and if you're a small-business owner.

My opponent's been in the Senate for 20 years, and he voted to raise taxes 98 times. That's five times a year. Now, I would call that a leading indicator. [*Laughter*] He's also promised $2.2 trillion in new spending. That would be trillion with a "T." [*Laughter*] And that's a lot even for a Senator from Massachusetts. [*Laughter*]

So they asked him how he's going to pay for it, and he threw out that same old, tired line, "Oh, we'll pay for it by taxing the rich." That means he's going to raise the top two brackets. You know most small businesses are sole proprietorships or Subchapter S corporations, which means they pay tax at the individual income-tax level. Seventy percent of new jobs in America are created by small businesses. So therefore, when you run up the top two brackets, you're taxing job creators; you're taxing small-business owners. And that doesn't make any economic sense at all.

And secondly, when you top—raise the top two brackets, you raise between 600 and 800 billion dollars, which is far short of the 2.2 trillion he has promised. I call that a tax gap. [*Laughter*] And given his record, guess who gets to fill the tax gap? You do. The good news is, you're not going to get taxed; we're going to carry Wisconsin and win on November the 2d.

The third clear choice in this election involves the quality of life for our families.

That means good education and quality health care. As a candidate, I pledged to challenge the soft bigotry of low expectations by reforming our public schools. I kept my word. We passed the No Child Left Behind Act, which I proudly signed into law. In return for increased Federal spending, we're now expecting results because we believe every child can learn and we expect every school to teach. You cannot solve a problem unless you diagnose the problem. And so the new system enables us to diagnose and solve problems. The test scores are on the rise across this country in reading and math. We're closing an achievement gap for minority students all across this country. And we refuse to go back to the days of low standards and mediocrity in our classrooms.

And we will improve health care by making sure it is available and affordable. To make sure health care is available, we'll expand community health centers to help the poor and the indigent get primary and preventative care. We'll make sure our program for children of low-income families is fully subscribed. A compassionate society takes care of those who cannot help themselves. But I also recognize that most of the uninsured work for small businesses. And so to enable the small businesses to better afford insurance, we ought to allow them to join together to pool risk so they can buy insurance at the same discounts that big companies are able to do. We will expand health savings accounts to help our families and our entrepreneurs.

And to make sure health care is available and affordable, we will do something about the frivolous lawsuits that are running up the cost of medicine and driving too many doctors out of business. I have met too many ob-gyns as I've traveled our country who are having trouble staying in practice because these lawsuits are running up their premiums and running them out of practice. And I have met too many women who are concerned about whether or not they and their child will get the health care they need. Too many communities have been upset because doctors can no longer practice medicine.

This is a national problem, I'm telling you, that requires a national solution. You cannot be pro-doctor, pro-patient, and pro-personal-injury-trial-lawyer at the same time. I think you have to make a choice. My opponent made his choice. He has voted against medical liability reform not once but 10 times as a Senator. And he put a personal-injury trial lawyer on the ticket.

Audience members. Boo-o-o!

The President. I've made my choice. I'm standing with the doctors. I'm standing with the patients of Wisconsin. I am for medical liability reform—now.

My opponent has got a different point of view when it comes to health care. You might remember the debate when he said, well, the—they asked him about his plan, and he looked in the camera and he said, "The Government doesn't have anything to do with it." I could barely contain myself. [*Laughter*] The Government has got a lot to do with it. Eighty percent of the people that would be signed up for health insurance under his plan would go on the Government health care plan. If you make it easier for people to sign up for Medicaid, small businesses will drop insurance because the Government will provide the insurance. And so you're moving people from the private sector to the public sector. And when the Government starts writing the check, the Government starts making the rules. And when the Government starts making the rules for your family's health care, they start making the decisions for your family's health care and they start making the decisions for your doctors. Federalizing health care is the wrong prescription for American families.

In all we do to make sure health care is available and affordable, we will make sure the decisions are made by doctors and patients, not by officials in Washington, DC.

The fourth clear choice in this election involves your retirement. Our Nation has made a solemn commitment to America's seniors on Social Security and Medicare. When I ran for President 4 years ago, I promised to keep that commitment and improve Medicare by adding prescription drug coverage. I kept my word. The Medicare debate was one of those debates in which people said a lot of stuff but nothing ever got done. I worked with Republicans and Democrats to make the system work better. We would pay thousands of dollars for a heart surgery under Medicare but not one dime for the prescription drugs that could prevent the heart surgery from being needed in the first place. It didn't make any sense. The system wasn't working. We got the job done. And beginning in 2006, all seniors will get prescription drug coverage under Medicare.

And we'll keep our commitment in Social Security as well. Let me talk about Social Security—well, you don't have any choice. I'm going to talk about Social Security. [*Laughter*] You might remember the 2000 campaign when they ran the ads in Wisconsin that tried to scare our seniors by saying that, "If George W. gets elected, the seniors will not get their checks." Remind your friends and neighbors, George W. got elected, and the seniors got their checks. And the seniors will continue to get their checks. No matter how they try to scare Wisconsin seniors, the seniors will get their checks. And baby boomers like me and like some of the others I see out there—[*laughter*]—are in pretty good shape when it comes to Social Security.

But we need to worry about our children and our grandchildren. We need to worry about whether the Social Security trust will be available for them when they need it. And therefore, I think younger workers ought to be allowed to take some of their payroll taxes and set up a personal savings account, a personal saving account they call their own, a personal savings account the Government cannot take away.

My opponent takes a different approach about Social Security. He's promised he's going to protect the system, but what he didn't tell you was he voted eight times for higher taxes on Social Security benefits. He can run from his record, but he cannot hide. We're not going to let him hide.

And he didn't offer anything for the youngsters when it comes to strengthening Social Security. The job of a President is to confront problems, not to pass them on to future Presidents and future generations. In a new term, I will bring people together and strengthen Social Security for generations to come.

And the fifth clear choice is on the values that are crucial for our country. We stand for things. We stand for marriage and family, which are the foundations of our society. We stand for a culture of life in which every person matters and every being counts. I proudly signed the ban on partial-birth abortions. And we stand for the appointment of Federal judges who know the difference between personal opinion and the strict interpretation of the law.

My opponent has had a different point of view. He voted against the ban on partial-birth abortion. He voted against the Defense of Marriage Act. And at one point in this campaign, he said that the heart and soul of America can be found in Hollywood.

Audience members. Boo-o-o!

The President. The heart and soul of America is found in communities all across the great State of Wisconsin.

All these choices make this one of the most important elections in our history. And the decision is in the best of hands. It is in the hands of the American people. In less than 72 hours, the American people will be voting, and the decision comes down to who do you trust?

Audience members. You!

The President. I offer——

Audience members. Four more years! Four more years! Four more years!

The President. I offer leadership and results for a time of threat and a time of challenge. I ask for your trust. I ask for your vote. I ask for your help. I have a vision for this country that is clear. I know where I want to take us, and it's to a more hopeful tomorrow.

One of my favorite quotes is by a fellow Texan named Tom Lea. He said, "Sarah and I live on the east side of the mountain. It is the sunrise side, not the sunset side. It is the side to see the day that is coming, not to see the day that is gone." During this campaign, my opponent has spent much of the campaign talking about the day that is gone. I'm talking about the day that's coming. I see a day where prosperity reaches every corner of America. I see a day when every child can read and write. I see a day when we achieve the peace that we all long for our children and our grandchildren.

When I campaigned across your State 4 years ago, I made this pledge, that if elected, I would uphold the honor and the dignity of the office. With your help, with your hard work, I will do so for 4 more years.

God bless. Thank you all for coming. Thank you all.

NOTE: The President spoke at 11:50 a.m. at the Brown County Veterans Memorial Complex. In his remarks, he referred to John Gard, speaker, Wisconsin State Assembly; Robert Chicks, tribal council president, Stockbridge-Munsee Band of the Mohican Nation; Wayne LaPierre, Jr., executive vice president and chief executive officer, National Rifle Association; entertainer Lee Greenwood; and former President Saddam Hussein of Iraq.

Remarks in Minneapolis, Minnesota
October 30, 2004

The President. Thank you all for coming. We appreciate you coming. Thank you all. Thanks for coming. Laura and I are honored so many came to say hello. We, first, want to thank you for lifting our spirits. How good does it get—Arnold yesterday, Mike Tice today. I'm proud to be introduced by a leader and somebody who's getting results. Thanks for coming, Mike. Laura and I are thrilled you are here.

We are here to ask for your vote. We are here to ask for your help. It is close to voting time. That's the time when people in a free society do their obligations and go to the polls. We have a duty in this country to vote. I'm here to get your friends—I'm here to ask you to ask your friends and neighbors to do their duty. Get our fellow Republicans to the polls. Get wise independents to the polls—[*laughter*]—discerning Democrats like Mayor Randy Kelly from St. Paul, Minnesota, to the polls. I appreciate you, friend.

The Democrat mayor of St. Paul is not alone. There are a lot of Democrats who, just like you, want America to be a safer, stronger, and better place. When you get people headed to the polls, remind them, if they want a safer America, a stronger America, and a better America, put me and Dick Cheney back in office.

Perhaps the most important reason why people should reelect me is so that Laura is the First Lady for 4 more years.

I'm proud of my runningmate, Dick Cheney. I don't want to offend anybody who is follically challenged, but I fully recognize that the Vice President doesn't have the waviest hair in the race. [*Laughter*] The people of this great State will be pleased to know I didn't pick him because of his hairdo. I picked him because of his judgment, his experience. He is getting the job done for the American people.

I am proud of your Governor, Tim Pawlenty, and so are the people of Minnesota. I want to thank my friend and your United States Senator, Norm Coleman, for his leadership. I want to thank the Members of Congress who are here, Congressman John Kline, Congressman Jim Ramstad, Congressman Mark Kennedy, for their service.

I want to thank Pat Anderson. I want to thank all the candidates running for office. I want to thank my friend Rudy Boschwitz for being such a strong and loyal supporter. I want to thank Gary Cayo, the president of the Minnesota Fraternal Order of Police, for his support and the support of the Fraternal Order of Police all across our country. I want to thank Billy Dean.

Most of all, I want to thank you all. I want to thank the grassroots activists who are putting up the signs, making the phone calls, doing the hard work necessary to have such a big rally as this one. I want to thank you for what you have done and what you are going to do, which is to turn out that vote. No doubt in my mind, with your help, we will carry Minnesota and win a great victory in November. [*Applause*] Thank you all.

This election takes place in a time of great consequence. The person who sits in the Oval Office for the next 4 years will set the course on the war on terror and the direction of our economy. America needs strong, optimistic, determined leadership, and I'm ready for the job.

My 4 years as your President have confirmed some lessons and taught some new ones. I've learned to expect the unexpected, because war and emergency can arrive suddenly on a quiet morning. I've learned firsthand how hard it is to send young men and women into battle, even if it's the right cause. I've been grateful for the lessons I've learned from my parents: Respect every person; do your best; live every day to its fullest. I've been strengthened by my faith and humbled by its reminder that every life is part of a larger story.

I know how a President needs to lead. As Presidents from Lincoln to Roosevelt to Reagan so clearly demonstrated, a President must not shift with the wind. A President has to make the tough decisions and stand by them.

In the last 4 years, Americans have learned some things about me as well. Sometimes I'm a little too blunt. I get that from my mother. [*Laughter*] Sometimes I mangle the English language. I get that from my father. [*Laughter*] But all the time, whether you agree with me or not, you know where I stand and where I intend to lead this country.

Audience members. Four more years! Four more years! Four more years!

The President. You cannot say that about my opponent.

Audience members. Boo-o-o!

The President. Consistency is not his long suit. [*Laughter*] The people of this country will vote next Tuesday. I am confident they will vote for consistency, for conviction, and for principle. And with your help, we'll win in November the 2d.

This election comes down to five clear choices for America's families. The first clear choice is the most important because it concerns the security of your family. All progress on every other issue depends on the safety of our citizens. Americans go to the polls in a time of war and ongoing threats. The terrorists who killed thousands of innocent people are still dangerous and determined to strike. The outcome of this election will set the direction of the war against the terrorists. The most solemn duty of the American President is to protect the American people. If America shows uncertainty or weakness during these troubled times, the world will drift toward tragedy. This is not going to happen on my watch.

Since that terrible morning of September the 11th, 2001, we've fought the terrorists across the Earth, not for pride, not for power but because the lives of our citizens are at stake. Our strategy is clear—our strategy is clear. We've strengthened protections for the homeland. We're reforming and strengthening our intelligence capabilities. We're transforming our All-Volunteer Army. There will be no draft. We are determined. We are steadfast. We are resolute. We will stay on the offensive against the terrorists around the world so we do not have to face them here at home.

Because we led, the world is changing. Afghanistan is a free nation and an ally in the war on terror. Pakistan is capturing terrorist leaders. Saudi Arabia is making raids and arrests. Libya is dismantling its weapons programs. The army of a free Iraq is fighting for the freedom of its people. And more than three-quarters of Al Qaida's key members and associates have been brought to justice.

So long as I'm your President, I will use every asset at our disposal to protect the American people, and perhaps the strongest asset we have is our belief in liberty, our belief that liberty can transform societies. I want the youngsters here to understand what has taken place in a brief period of time.

It wasn't all that long ago in Afghanistan that young girls couldn't go to school because the country was run by the ideologues of hate called the Taliban. And if their mothers didn't toe the line, they were taken into the public squares and whipped and sometimes taken to a sports stadium and executed. Because this great Nation acted to defend ourselves, because we upheld the doctrine that said, "If you harbor a terrorist, you're equally as guilty as the terrorist," millions of citizens—millions of citizens—voted in a Presidential election in Afghanistan. And the first voter was a 19-year-old woman.

And America is better off as freedom spreads around the world. Iraq will have Presidential elections in January. Think how far that society has come from the days of torture chambers and mass graves and the brutal rule of a fierce tyrant. Freedom is on the march.

I believe everybody longs to be free. I believe deep in everybody's soul is the desire to live in a free society. I believe that not because freedom is America's gift to the world; freedom is the Almighty God's gift to each man and woman in this world.

A President must lead with consistency and strength. In a war, sometimes your tactics change but never your principles. And Americans have seen how I do my job. On good days, on bad days, when the polls are up or the polls are down, I am determined to protect the American people.

And I am the Commander in Chief of a great United States military. I want to thank those who wear our Nation's uniform who have joined us today. I want to thank the military families who are with us today, and I want to thank the veterans of the United States of America who've set such a great example. And I assure you and I assure our vets and our families and those men and women in uniform that you'll have the resources—the military will have the resources they need to complete their mission.

That's why I went to the United States Congress and asked for $87 billion of supplemental funding in September of 2003. That money was necessary. That money was important. We had troops in harm's way, and they needed the full support of the Government. And we received good bipartisan support, so strong that only 12 Senators voted against the funding——

Audience members. Boo-o-o!

The President. ——2 of whom were my opponent and his runningmate. But as you gather the vote, I want you to remind people of this fact. Four Members of the Senate—only 4 out of 100—voted to authorize force and voted against the support for our troops in combat. Two of those four were my opponent and his runningmate.

Audience members. Boo-o-o!

The President. Now, they asked him why he made the vote he did, and you might remember perhaps the most famous quote of the 2004 campaign when he said, "I actually did vote for the 87 billion, before I voted against it."

Audience members. Boo-o-o!

The President. I haven't spent a lot of time in the coffee shops in this great State, but I doubt I'm going to find hardly anybody who talks that way in Minnesota.

He's given several reasons why he made that vote, but perhaps the most revealing of all was when he said, "The whole thing is a complicated matter." [*Laughter*] My fellow Americans, there is nothing complicated about supporting our troops in combat.

The American people have been watching this election carefully, and they noticed my opponent's positions are kind of like the weather here in Minnesota. If you don't like it, wait a little bit, and it will change. [*Laughter*] He was for the war and against the war, for the war and against the war. But his record on national security has a far deeper problem than election-year flip-flopping. On the largest national security issues of our time, he has been consistently wrong.

When Ronald Reagan was confronting the Soviet Union at the height of the cold war, Senator Kerry said that President Reagan's policy of peace through strength was making America less safe.

Audience members. Boo-o-o!

The President. History has shown that Senator Kerry was wrong and President Ronald Reagan was right.

When former President Bush led a coalition against Saddam Hussein in 1991 because he had invaded Kuwait, Senator Kerry voted against the use of force to liberate Kuwait.

Audience members. Boo-o-o!

The President. History has shown that Senator Kerry was wrong and former President Bush was right.

In 1994, just one year after the first bombing in the World Trade Center, Senator Kerry proposed massive cuts in America's intelligence budget, so massive that even his Massachusetts colleague, Ted Kennedy, opposed them. History has shown that Senator Kerry was wrong and—we've got to be fair about it—Senator Kennedy was right.

During the last 20 years, in key moments of challenge and decision for America, my opponent has chosen the position of weakness and inaction. With that record, he stands in opposition not just to me but to the great tradition of the Democratic Party. The party of Franklin Roosevelt and Harry Truman and John Kennedy is rightly remembered for confidence and resolve in times of war and in hours of crisis. Senator Kerry has turned his back on "pay any price" and "bear any burden," and he's replaced those commitments with "wait and see" and "cut and run."

Many Democrats in this country do not recognize their party anymore, and today I want to speak to every one of them: If you believe that America should lead with strength and purpose and confidence in our ideals, I'd be honored to have your support, and I'm asking for your vote.

Audience members. Four more years! Four more years! Four more years!

The President. We have big differences about how to protect our country's families. I recall that moment in one of our debates when my opponent said that America must submit to a "global test" before we commit troops.

Audience members. Boo-o-o!

The President. As you can tell, that's kind of how I felt too. [*Laughter*] As far as I can tell, that means our country must get permission from foreign capitals before we act in our own defense. I'll work with our allies, and I'll work with our friends. I believe in building coalitions, and we have done just that. But I will never turn over America's national security decisions to leaders of other countries.

We have differences of opinion, clear differences of opinion about this war on terror. Recently, my opponent said that September the 11th didn't change him much at all. That's what he said.

Audience members. Boo-o-o!

The President. Well, September the 11th changed me. It changed my view of the world and how we must defend ourselves. I remember standing in the ruins of the Twin Towers on September the 14th, 2001. It's a day that will be forever etched in my memory, the sights and the sounds. I can remember those voices of the workers in hardhats yelling at me, "Whatever it takes." I remember looking in the eye of a fellow who grabbed me by the arm, and he said, "Do not let me down." Ever since that morning—ever since that day, I wake up every morning trying to better figure out how to protect America. I will never relent in defending this country, whatever it takes.

The second clear choice in this election concerns your family's budget. When I ran for President 4 years ago, I pledged to lower taxes for America's families, and I kept my word. We doubled the child credit to $1,000 per child to help the moms and dads in America. We reduced the marriage penalty. We believe the Tax Code ought to encourage marriage, not penalize marriage. We dropped the lowest bracket to 10 percent. We reduced taxes on everybody who pays taxes. And we're growing. This economy is getting stronger.

Remind your friends and neighbors as you round them up to go to the polls— [*laughter*]—what we have been through. Six months prior to my arrival in Washington, the stock market was in serious decline, and then we had a recession and corporate scandals. And the attacks of September the 11th cost us about a million jobs in the 3 months following that fateful day.

But our policies are working. We're on the path to growth. This economy is as strong as it's been in nearly 20 years. The homeownership rate is at an alltime high in America. More minority families own a home all across this country than anywhere at any time in our history. Minnesota farmers are making a living. The farm economy is strong in America. The entrepreneurial spirit is strong. Small businesses are flourishing all across America. We've added 1.9 million new jobs in the last 13 months. The national unemployment rate is 5.4 percent. And let me put that in perspective for you: It's lower than the average rate of the 1970s, the 1980s, and the 1990s. And the unemployment rate in Minnesota is 4.6 percent. We are strong, and we will get stronger.

My opponent has different plans for your budget. He's going to take a big chunk out of it.

Audience members. Boo-o-o!

The President. You know, he voted against the child tax credit. He voted against marriage penalty relief. He voted against lower taxes. If he'd have had his way, the average family in Minnesota would be paying $2,000 more per year in Federal taxes.

Audience members. Boo-o-o!

The President. Now, that probably doesn't seem like a lot to some of them in Washington, but I understand it's a lot for the families in this part of the world. It means a lot to people trying to raise their children. It means a lot to people struggling to put food on the table and meet their expenses.

He's been in the Senate 20 years; he has voted to raise taxes 98 times. That's five times for every year in the Senate. I would call that a leading indicator— [*laughter*]—a predictable pattern. [*Laughter*] If you put that in this context, he promised $2.2 trillion in new Federal spending. Now, that's trillion with a "T." That's a lot. Even for a Senator from Massachusetts, that's a lot. [*Laughter*] And so they asked him, "How are you going to pay for it?" And he said, "Well, we'll just tax the rich." You have heard that before.

First of all, most small businesses around Minnesota and around the country pay tax at the individual income-tax level. See, most small businesses are Subchapter S or sole proprietorships. And by the way, 70 percent of new jobs in America are created by small businesses. And so when you raise the top two brackets, you're taxing job creators. It makes no economic sense to tax the entities that are creating the new jobs in our country.

And secondly, he has promised 2.2 trillion, but raising the top two brackets only raises between 600 and 800 billion. That's what I would call a tax gap, the difference between what is promised and what's delivered. Given his record, I think you understand how he's going to fill that tax gap. Yes, he's going to tax you. But we're not going to let him; we will carry Minnesota and win next Tuesday.

The third clear choice in this election involves the quality of life for our Nation's families. A good education and quality health care are important to a successful life. As candidate, I pledged to challenge the soft bigotry of low expectations by reforming our public schools. And I kept my word. I proudly signed the No Child Left Behind Act to raise the standards. See, we believe every child can learn, and we expect every school to teach.

We're spending more money at the Federal level, and in return, we expect measurement. See, you cannot solve a problem until you diagnose the problem. And as a result of the law we put in place, we are now diagnosing and solving problems. Math and reading scores are up across America, and we are closing an achievement gap for minority students. And we will not go back to the days of low expectations and mediocrity in our schools.

We will continue to improve life for our families by making health care available and affordable. We will take care of the poor and the indigent by expanding community health centers. We have a duty to help people who cannot help themselves. And that's why we'll make sure our program for children of low-income families is fully subscribed, to make sure people get the health care and the help they need. But I also recognize that most of the uninsured in America work for small businesses. And to help small businesses better afford insurance, we must allow them to pool risk across jurisdictional boundaries so they can buy insurance at the same discounts that big companies are able to do. We will expand health savings accounts to help our small businesses and families.

And to make sure health care is available and affordable, we will do something about the junk lawsuits that are running up the cost of medicine and running too many doctors out of practice. We have a problem in this Nation. I have met too many ob-gyns that no longer practice because the premiums are too high. See, they can't afford to stay in practice. These lawsuits are driving them out of practice. I met too many patients, expectant moms who are traveling miles to find an ob-gyn, and they are deeply concerned about the quality of health care that they and their little one will receive. This is a national problem, and it requires a national solution. You cannot be pro-doctor and pro-patient and pro-personal-injury-trial-lawyer at the same time. You have to choose.

My opponent has made his choice. He voted 10 times against medical liability reform, and he put a personal-injury trial lawyer on the ticket.

Audience members. Boo-o-o!

The President. I've made my choice. I'm standing with the doctors of Minnesota. I'm standing with the patients of Minnesota. I'm standing with the families of Minnesota. I am for medical liability reform.

My opponent has a different view when it comes to health care. In one of the debates, I remember the questioner said, "Tell me about your health care plan." He looked square in the camera, and he said, "My health care plan, well, the Govern-ment doesn't have anything to do with it." I could barely contain myself. [*Laughter*]

The Government has got a lot to do with it. Eighty percent of the people, according to his plan, would be signed up by the Government. If you raise Medicaid and make it easier for people to get on Medicaid, it provides an incentive for small businesses to stop writing insurance because the Government will write the insurance. And when the Government writes the checks, the Government makes the rules. And when the Government makes the rules for your health care, the Government makes decisions for you and they make decisions for your doctors. The wrong prescription for American families is to federalize health care.

In all we do to improve health care for our families, we will make sure that the decisions are made by doctors and patients, not by officials in Washington, DC.

The fourth clear choice in this election involves your retirement. Our Nation has made a solemn commitment to America's seniors on Social Security and Medicare. When I ran for President 4 years ago, I promised to keep that commitment and improve Medicare by adding prescription drug coverage. I kept my word. Medicare needed to be modernized for our seniors. We would pay thousands of dollars for a heart surgery under Medicare but not a dime for the prescription drugs that could prevent the heart surgery from being needed in the first place. And that wasn't fair to our seniors. So I brought people together, and I proudly signed a Medicare reform bill that will make prescription drugs available for all our seniors beginning in 2006.

And we will keep the promise of Social Security for our seniors, and we will strengthen Social Security for years to come. I want you to tell your friends and neighbors about what took place in the 2000 campaign. You might remember those ads and the fliers when people said, "If George W. gets elected, the seniors will not get their checks." Well, tell them

George W. did get elected, and the seniors got their checks. And the seniors will continue to get their checks. And baby boomers like me and a couple others out there I'm looking at—[*laughter*]—will get their checks. The Social Security trust is in good shape for us.

But we need to worry about our children and our grandchildren. We need to worry about whether or not the Social Security system will be available when they need it. And that's why I believe younger workers ought to be allowed to take some of their own payroll taxes and set up a personal savings account, an account that will earn a better rate of return, an account they own, an account the Government can never take away.

My opponent takes a little different point of view on this. First, he said he'd protect Social Security, but he forgot to tell the American people he's voted eight times to tax Social Security benefits.

Audience members. Boo-o-o!

The President. See, he can run from his record, but we're not going to let him hide. And he has offered nothing to help the younger generation when it comes to strengthening Social Security. See, the job of a President is to confront problems, not to pass them on to future generations and future Presidents. I'm going to bring people together, and we will work to make sure the Social Security system is strong and viable for generations to come.

The fifth clear choice in this election involves the values that are crucial for our Nation. We stand for things. We stand for the appointment of Federal judges who know the difference between personal opinion and the strict interpretation of the law. We stand for marriage and family, which are the foundations of our society. I'll reach out to Americans of every belief and move this goodhearted Nation toward a culture of life. We believe in a culture of life. I proudly signed the ban on partial-birth abortion.

My opponent—Senator Kerry has had a different view on these issues. He voted against the ban on partial-birth abortion. He voted against the Defense of Marriage Act and, at one time in his campaign, actually said that the heart and soul of America can be found in Hollywood.

Audience members. Boo-o-o!

The President. The heart and soul of America is found in communities all across the great State of Minnesota.

All these choices make this one of the most important elections in our history. And the decision is in the best of hands. It is in the hands of the American people. In less than 72 hours, the American people will be voting, and the decision comes down to who do you trust.

Audience members. You!

The President. I stand—I offer leadership and results for a time of threat and challenge. I'm asking for people's votes. I'm asking for their trust. I'm asking for your help. I have a view of the future that is bright. I see clearly where I want to lead this country, and it is to a better day.

One of my favorite quotes was written by a fellow Texan named Tom Lea. He said, "Sarah and I live on the east side of the mountain. It is the sunrise side, not the sunset side. It is the side to see the day that is coming, not to see the day that is gone." During this campaign, my opponent has spent much of the time talking about the day that is gone. I'm talking about the day that's coming.

I see a great day coming for America. I see a day when prosperity reaches every corner of our country. I see a day where every child can read and write and add and subtract. And I see a day in which this world becomes more peaceful by spreading liberty, that we achieve the peace we all want for our children and for our grandchildren.

When I campaigned across your State 4 years ago, I made this pledge: If I got elected, I would uphold the honor and the dignity of the office to which I had been elected. With your help, with your hard work, I will do so for 4 more years.

God bless. Thank you all for coming.

NOTE: The President spoke at 2:17 p.m. at the Target Center. In his remarks, he referred to Gov. Arnold Schwarzenegger of California; Mike Tice, head coach, National Football League Minnesota Vikings; State Auditor Patricia Anderson of Minnesota; former Senator Rudy Boschwitz; entertainer Billy Dean; and former President Saddam Hussein of Iraq.

Remarks in Orlando, Florida
October 30, 2004

The President. Thank you all for coming. Laura and I really thank you for taking time out of your Saturday evening to come by and lift our spirits, and we're grateful for your presence. We're going to carry Florida with your help.

Perhaps the most important reason to put me back in office is so that Laura will be the First Lady for 4 more years.

I'm proud of my runningmate, Dick Cheney. Look, I readily concede he doesn't have the waviest hair in the race. People of Orlando will be pleased to know I didn't pick him up—pick him because of his hair. [*Laughter*] I picked him because of his judgment. I picked him because of his experience. He's getting the job done for the American people.

We are some kind of proud in my family of brother Jeb. We share the same campaign consultant: Mother. [*Laughter*] We're both listening to her. Also proud my brother Marvin Bush is with us today. Thank you for coming, big Marv.

I want to thank the Lieutenant Governor, Toni Jennings, Attorney General Charlie Crist, Congressman Ric Keller, Congressman Tom Feeney. I want to thank Rich Crotty. I want to thank my friend Mel Martinez. Put him in the Senate; he'll do a great job. I want to thank Mark Wills. I want to thank Shawn Michaels, professional wrestler. I was hoping to see him backstage—if I could ask him if it was real. [*Laughter*]

I want to thank all the grassroots activists who are here. I want to thank you for putting up the signs, making the phone calls. I know how much work went into putting this great rally together. I thank you for what you have done, and I want to thank you for what you're going to do as we're coming down the stretch run. I need your help. I need your work. We will carry Florida and win a great victory on November the 2d.

My 4 years as your President have confirmed some lessons and taught me some new ones. I have learned to expect the unexpected, because war and emergency can arrive suddenly on a quiet autumn morning. I've learned firsthand how hard it is to send young men and women into battle, even when the cause is right. I've been grateful for the lessons I've learned from our parents: Respect every person; do your best; live every day to its fullest. I have been strengthened by my faith and humbled by its reminder that every life is part of a larger story.

I know how a President needs to lead. As Presidents from Lincoln to Roosevelt to Reagan so clearly demonstrated, a President must not shift in the wind. A President has to make tough decisions and stand by them. The American President must not follow the path of the latest polls. The role of the President is to lead based on principle and conviction and conscience. Especially in a time of war, mixed signals only confuse our friends and embolden our enemies. Mixed signals are the wrong signals for an American President to send.

In the last 4 years, Americans have learned a few things about me as well. Sometimes I'm a little too blunt. I get that from my mother. Sometimes I mangle the English language. I get that from my dad. [*Laughter*] But all the time, whether you agree with me or not, you know where I stand and where I'm going to lead this Nation.

You can't—you cannot say that about my opponent. I think it's fair to say that consistency is not his long suit. Next Tuesday, the American people will vote for conviction and consistency. And with your help, we're going to win this election.

This election comes down to five choices for your family. The first clear choice is the most important because it concerns the security of your family. All progress on every other issue depends on the safety of our citizens. Americans will go to the polls Tuesday in a time of war and ongoing threats. The terrorists who killed thousands of innocent people are still dangerous, and they're determined to strike. The outcome of this election will set the direction of the war against terror. The most solemn duty of the American President is to protect the American people.

If America shows——

Audience members. Four more years! Four more years! Four more years!

The President. If America shows uncertainty or weakness in these troubling times, the world will drift toward tragedy. This is not going to happen on my watch.

Our strategy is clear. We've strengthened the protections for the homeland. We're reforming our intelligence capabilities. We are transforming our military. The All-Volunteer Army will remain an all-volunteer army. There will be no draft. We are relentless. We are steadfast. We are determined. We will fight the terrorists across the globe so we do not have to face them here at home.

Because we led, the world is changing. Afghanistan is a free nation and an ally in the war on terror. Pakistan is capturing terrorist leaders. Saudi Arabia is making raids and arrests. Libya is dismantling its weapons program. The army of a free Iraq is fighting for freedom. And more than three-quarters of Al Qaida's key members and associates have been brought to justice.

We will use every asset at our disposal to protect the American people. And one of the best assets we have is freedom. I believe in the power of liberty to transform society. I want the younger Americans here to realize what has happened in a brief period of time. Three-and-a-half years ago, young girls couldn't go to school in Afghanistan because the Taliban were so barbaric and backwards. And if their mothers didn't toe the ideological line of hatred, they were taken into the public square and whipped and sometimes to a sports stadium and executed. Because we acted in our own interest, because we upheld the doctrine that said, "If you harbor a terrorist, you're equally as guilty as the terrorist," millions of people voted in the Presidential election in Afghanistan. And the first voter was a 19-year-old woman.

Freedom is powerful. Iraq is still dangerous, but Iraq will be having elections in January. Think how far that country has come. It is in our interests, it is in our children's interests that we promote liberty and freedom around the world. I believe everybody yearns to be free. Freedom is not America's gift to the world; freedom is the Almighty God's gift to each man and woman in this world.

A President must lead with consistency and strength. In a war, sometimes your tactics change but never your principles. And you have seen how I do my job. On good days and on bad days, when the polls are up or the polls are down, I am determined to protect the American people. And I will always support the United States military. I want to thank those who wear our Nation's uniform who are here today. I want to thank the military families who are here today. And I want to thank the veterans who have set such a great example for those who wear the uniform.

We will support our troops in harm's way. That's why I went to the United States Congress in September of 2003 and asked for $87 billion of supplemental funding. This was necessary support. We had troops in Afghanistan and in Iraq. We received great support for that piece of legislation, so strong only 12 Members of the United States Senate opposed the funding for our troops in harm's way.

Audience members. Boo-o-o!

The President. Two of those twelve were my opponent and his runningmate. But I want to tell you another statistic.

Audience members. Boo-o-o!

The President. Let me tell you one more statistic. There were only four Members of the Senate who voted to authorize force and then did—voted against supporting our troops in harm's way—only four Members, two of whom were my opponent and his runningmate.

Audience members. Boo-o-o!

The President. So they asked him several times why he made the vote he made. One of those answers was perhaps the most famous quote of the 2004 campaign when he said, "I actually did vote for the 87 billion, right before I voted against it."

Audience members. Flip-flop! Flip-flop! Flip-flop!

The President. I have spent enough time in the great State of Florida to know not a people—not a lot of people talk that way here. [*Laughter*] He's given several explanations since, but I think the most revealing explanation of all about his vote against supporting our troops was when he said, "The whole thing was a complicated matter." There is nothing complicated about supporting our troops in combat.

Senator Kerry's record on national security has a far deeper problem than election-year flip-flopping. On the largest national security issues of our time, he has been consistently wrong. When Ronald Reagan was confronting the Soviet Union at the height of the cold war, Senator Kerry said that President Reagan's policy of peace through strength was making America less safe.

Audience members. Boo-o-o!

The President. Well, history has shown that Senator Kerry was wrong and President Ronald Reagan was right.

When former President Bush led a coalition against Saddam Hussein to get him out of Kuwait after he invaded Kuwait in 1991, Senator Kerry voted against the use of force to liberate Kuwait.

Audience members. Boo-o-o!

The President. History has shown that Senator Kerry was wrong and former President Bush was right.

In 1994, just one year after the first bombing of the World Trade Center, Senator Kerry proposed massive cuts in America's intelligence budget, so massive that his colleague from Massachusetts, Ted Kennedy, voted against it.

Audience members. Boo-o-o!

The President. Well, history has shown that Senator Kerry was wrong and—we've got to be fair about it—Senator Kennedy was right.

During the last 20 years, in key moments of challenge and decision for America, Senator Kerry has chosen the position of weakness and inaction. With that record, he stands in opposition not just to me but to the great tradition of the Democratic Party. The party of Franklin Roosevelt, of Harry Truman, of John Kennedy is rightly remembered for confidence and resolve in times of crisis and in times of conflict. Senator Kerry has turned his back on "pay any price" and "bear any burden." He has replaced those commitments with "wait and see" and "cut and run."

Many Democrats in this country do not recognize their party anymore. Today I want to speak to every Democrat: If you believe that America should lead with strength and purpose and confidence in our ideals, I would be honored to have your support, and I'm asking for your vote.

Audience members. Four more years! Four more years! Four more years!

The President. When you're out rounding up the vote, when you're getting people to go to the polls like I know you're going to do, remind them we have big differences as to how to best protect our country and our families. In one of our debates, my opponent said that America must pass a "global test" before we commit our troops.

Audience members. Boo-o-o!

The President. I know, you're probably thinking I made that up, but I was standing right there pretty close to him when he said it. [*Laughter*] I was just as startled as you are. As far as I can tell, it means our country must get permission from foreign capitals before we act. As President, I will work with our friends. I will strengthen our alliances. But I will never turn over national security decisions to leaders of other countries.

In a recent interview, my opponent said that September the 11th didn't change him much at all. Well, it changed me. It changed me a lot. It gave me—it caused me to think about how to protect America in a different way from the past. I stood in the ruins of the Twin Towers on September the 14th, 2001. It is a day I will never forget. I'll never forget the workers in hardhats yelling at me at the top of their lungs, "Whatever it takes." I will never forget the fellow who grabbed me by the arm. He looked me right in the eye, and he said, "Do not let me down." Ever since that day, I wake up every morning trying to figure out how to best protect the American people. I will never relent in the security of this country, whatever it takes.

The second clear choice in this election concerns your family's budget. When I ran for President 4 years ago, I pledged to lower taxes for the American families. I kept my word. We doubled the child credit to $1,000 per child, and that helps moms and dads. We reduced the marriage penalty. Our Tax Code ought to encourage marriage, not penalize marriage. We dropped the lowest bracket to 10 percent. We reduced income taxes for everybody who pays income tax. And our economic recovery plan is working.

Remember what we have been through. Six months prior to my arrival in Washington, the stock market was in serious decline. That foretold a recession. We had corporate scandals. And the attacks on America cost us about a million jobs in the 3 months after September the 11th.

But our economic policies are working. Our economy is growing at rates as fast as any in nearly 20 years. We've added 1.9 million new jobs in the last 13 months. The homeownership rate is at an alltime high in America. More minority families own a home than ever before in our Nation's history. Florida's farmers and ranchers are making a living. The entrepreneurial spirit is strong. The small-business sector of our economy is thriving and doing well. The national unemployment rate is 5.4 percent, and the unemployment rate in the great State of Florida is 4.5 percent. This economy is strong, and it is getting stronger.

My opponent has a different plan for your budget. He plans to take a big chunk out of it.

Audience members. Boo-o-o!

The President. He's been in the United States Senate for 20 years, and he's voted to raise taxes 98 times.

Audience members. Boo-o-o!

The President. That's five times for every year he's been in the Senate. I would call that a predictable pattern, a leading indicator. [*Laughter*] During the campaign, he's made some big promises too. He's promised $2.2 trillion of new spending. That is trillion with a "T." That's a lot. That's a lot even for a Senator from Massachusetts.

Audience members. Boo-o-o!

The President. So they asked him how he's going to pay for it. He said, well, he's just going to tax the rich. We've heard that before. There's a problem with that. If you run up the top two brackets like he says he's going to do, it raises between 600 and 800 billion dollars. That is far short of the 2.2 trillion. That's called a tax gap. Guess who usually gets to fill the tax gap?

Audience members. We do!

The President. You do. But we're not going to let him tax you; we're going to carry Florida and win next Tuesday.

The third choice in this election involves the quality of life for our Nation's families. A good education and quality health care are important to America's families. As a candidate, I pledged to challenge the soft bigotry of low expectations by reforming our public schools. I kept my word. I signed the No Child Left Behind Act and proudly so. It's a great piece of legislation. We increased Federal funding for our schools, particularly for the disadvantaged and special-ed kids, and that's important. But also what's important is to measure. We said, "In return for extra money, show us whether our children can read and write and add and subtract," because we believe every child can read and we believe every school must teach.

You cannot solve a problem unless you diagnose the problem. We're now diagnosing and solving problems all across America, particularly in States like Florida because of your good Governor. We're closing an achievement gap for minority students all across America, and we're not going to go back to the old days of low expectations and mediocrity.

We'll continue to work to make health care more accessible and affordable. We have a duty to take care of those who can't help themselves. That's why I'm such a strong believer in community health centers, places where the poor and the indigent can get good primary and preventative care. I believe and I know we must work with our Governors and mayors to make

sure that the program for children from low-income families is fully subscribed so our children can get good health care.

But I also understand that most of the uninsured work for small businesses. And we ought to allow small businesses to pool risk across jurisdictional boundaries so they can buy insurance at the same discounts that big companies are able to do. We'll expand health savings accounts to help our families and small businesses.

And to make sure health care is available and affordable for families all across this country, we will do something about the frivolous and junk lawsuits that are running good doctors out of practice and running up the cost of your health care. We have a national problem when it comes to litigation. I have met too many ob-gyns, some from the State of Florida, that have been run out of their practice because the lawsuits have caused their premiums to be too high. And I have met too many expectant moms that are deeply concerned about the quality of health care they're going to get for themselves and their child. You cannot be pro-doctor, pro-patient, and pro-personal-injury-trial-lawyer at the same time. I think you have to make a choice.

My opponent made his choice. He's voted against medical liability reform 10 times in the Senate, and he put a personal-injury trial lawyer on the ticket.

Audience members. Boo-o-o!

The President. I have made my choice. I'm standing with Florida's docs and Florida's patients and Florida's families. I'm for medical liability reform—now.

We have a difference of opinion when it comes to health care. In one of those debates, they asked my opponent about his health care plan, and he said, "The Government doesn't have anything to do with it." I could barely contain myself. [*Laughter*] The Government has got a lot to do with it. Eighty percent of the people would end up on a Government plan. If you make it easier for people to sign up for Medicaid, it is likely small businesses will stop writing insurance for their employees because the Government will. And that moves people from the private sector to the Government plans. And when the Government writes the checks, the Government makes the rules. And when the Government makes the rules for your health care, the Government starts making decisions for you and decisions for your doctors. Federalizing health care is the wrong prescription for America's families. In all we do to improve health care, we'll make sure the decisions are made by doctors and patients, not by officials in Washington, DC.

The fourth clear choice in this election involves your retirement. Our Nation has made a solemn commitment to America's seniors on Social Security and Medicare. When I ran for President 4 years ago, I promised to keep that commitment and to improve Medicare by adding prescription drug coverage. I kept my word. I told the Congress Medicare needed to be modernized. You know, Medicare would pay thousands of dollars for a heart—for heart surgery, but it wouldn't pay one dime for the prescription drugs that could prevent the heart surgery from being needed in the first place. That didn't make any sense. So I brought Republicans and Democrats together. We modernized Medicare. And beginning in 2006, all seniors will be able to get prescription drug coverage under Medicare.

We'll keep the promise of Social Security for our seniors, and we will strengthen Social Security for generations to come. Every election, politicians try to scare our seniors and say that they're not going to get their checks if somebody like me gets elected. They said that in 2000. I got elected, and the seniors got their checks. The seniors will always get their checks. Baby boomers like me and like some others I see out there—[*laughter*]—we'll get our checks.

But we need to worry about our children and our grandchildren. We need to worry about whether or not Social Security will be there when they need it. And that is

why I think younger workers ought to be allowed to take some of their own payroll taxes and set up a personal savings account, an account they call their own, an account the Government cannot take away.

My opponent and I take a different approach toward Social Security. He said he's going to protect Social Security, but he forgot to tell the people that he's voted eight times for higher taxes on Social Security benefits.

Audience members. Boo-o-o!

The President. He can run, but he cannot hide. And when it comes to the next generation, he's offered no reform. The job of the President is to confront problems, not to pass them on to future Presidents and future generations. In a new term, I will bring people together to strengthen Social Security for generations to come.

The fifth clear choice in this election is on the values that are important for our country. We stand for marriage and family, which are the foundations of this society. We stand for a culture of life in which every person matters and every being counts. I proudly signed the ban on partial-birth abortion. We stand for the appointment of Federal judges who know the difference between personal opinion and the strict interpretation of the law.

My opponent has a different point of view. He voted against the ban on partial-birth abortion.

Audience members. Boo-o-o!

The President. He voted against the Defense of Marriage Act.

Audience members. Boo-o-o!

The President. And at one time in his campaign, he said the heart and soul of America can be found in Hollywood.

Audience members. Boo-o-o!

The President. Most of our families don't look to Hollywood as a source of values. The heart and soul of America is found in communities like Orlando, Florida.

All these choices make this one of the most important elections in our history.

And the decision is in the best of hands. It is in the hands of the American people.

I've got a clear view of where I want to take this country. I clearly see a better tomorrow. One of my favorite quotes is by a fellow Texan named Tom Lea. He said, "Sarah and I live on the east side of the mountain. It is the sunrise side, not the sunset side. It is the side to see the day that is coming, not to see the day that is gone." In the course of this campaign, my opponent has spent much of his time talking about the day that is gone. I'm talking about the day that's coming.

I see a great day coming for America. I see a day where prosperity reaches every corner of our country. I see a day in which every child can read and write and add and subtract. And I see a day that after all the struggle, peace comes, a peace we want for our children and our grandchildren.

You know, when I campaigned across the State of Florida 4 years ago, I made this pledge, that if I got elected, I would uphold the honor and the dignity of the office. With your help, with your hard work, I will do so for 4 more years.

God bless. Thank you all for coming. Thank you all.

NOTE: The President spoke at 8 p.m. at Tinker Field. In his remarks, he referred to Gov. Jeb Bush, Lt. Gov. Toni Jennings, and State Attorney General Charlie Crist of Florida; Richard T. Crotty, chairman, Orange County, FL; Mel R. Martinez, senatorial candidate in Florida; and entertainer Mark Wills.

Remarks in Miami, Florida
October 31, 2004

The President. Thank you all for coming. We're honored you're here. Thank you all. Thank you for coming. Thank you for being here. Thanks for taking time out of your Sunday morning to come by and say hello. Laura and I are honored you're here. I'm here to ask for your help. You need to get your friends and neighbors to go to the polls. You're voting today; you're voting on Tuesday. Tell your friends and neighbors, in a free society, we have an obligation to vote. Tell them, if they want a safer America, a stronger America, and a better America *por todos,* to vote for me and Dick Cheney. *Con su apoyo, vamos a ganar.*

The most important reason—perhaps the most important reason to put me back in is so that Laura will be the First Lady for 4 more years.

Audience members. Laura! Laura! Laura!

The President. Que bella. Que magnifica.

I want to thank my Vice President, who's working hard. He does not have the waviest hair in this race. I don't want to offend some of you out there who are follically challenged—you'll be happy to hear I didn't pick him because of his hairdo. [*Laughter*] I picked him because of his experience. I picked him because of his judgment. He's getting the job done.

I want to thank my *hermanito.* What a great Governor he is. He loves Miami, and he loves the people of Miami. And I want to thank First Lady Columba Bush for being such a gracious first lady for Florida.

It's really important that when you get in that booth and get your friends to go to the booth to remember there's an important Senate race here in Florida. I'm going to say it as strongly as I can, Mel Martinez is the right man for Florida. And we love Kitty Martinez as well. She's a classy lady.

I want to thank the three Congressmen from this part of the world that are here, starting with the Congresswoman from this district, Ileana Ros-Lehtinen, *mi amiga. Y tambien los hermanos,* Diaz-Balart, Lincoln y Mario. Thank you all for your steadfast and strong support.

I appreciate Tom Gallagher being here. I want to thank Marco Rubio, who's here with us today.

Listen, there are a lot of Democrats supporting my candidacy. There may be some here. You know the Democrat Party left you; you didn't leave it. And I want to thank Miami Beach Mayor David Dermer, Democrats for Bush. Mr. Mayor, we are proud you're here. Thank you, sir. I want to thank all the other State and local officials.

I know that there are some members of the 1972 Miami Dolphins football team here. Thank you all for coming. You guys haven't aged a bit. [*Laughter*] Thanks for setting such a great example.

I want to thank the grassroots activists. I want to thank you all for putting up the signs. I want to thank you for making the phone calls. No doubt in my mind, we'll carry Florida again and win a great victory on Tuesday.

Audience members. Four more years! Four more years! Four more years!

The President. This election takes place in a time of great consequence. The person who sits in the Oval Office for the next 4 years will set the course of the war on terror and the direction of our economy. America will need strong, determined, optimistic leadership. I am ready for the work ahead.

My 4 years as your President has confirmed some lessons, and they've taught me some new ones. I've learned to expect the unexpected because horror can arrive suddenly on a quiet morning. I've learned firsthand how hard it is to send young men and women into battle, even if the cause is right. I'm grateful to the lessons I've learned from our parents: Respect for every person; do your best; live every day to its fullest. I've been strengthened by my faith and humbled by its reminder—and I've

been humbled by its reminder that every life is part of a larger story.

The President must lead with clarity and purpose. As Presidents from Lincoln to Roosevelt to Reagan so clearly demonstrated, a President must not shift in the wind. A President has to make the tough decisions and stand by them. The role of the President is not to follow the latest polls. The role of the President is to lead based upon principle and conviction and conscience, and that is how I will continue to lead this Nation.

During the last 4 years, I've learned that whatever your strengths are, you're going to need them. And whatever your shortcomings, the people will notice them. [*Laughter*] Sometimes I am a little too blunt. I get that from my mother. [*Laughter*] Sometimes I mangle the English language. [*Laughter*] I get that from my dad. [*Laughter*] But all the time, whether you agree with me or not, you know where I stand, what I believe.

And you can't say that about my opponent.

Audience members. Boo-o-o!

The President. It is fair to say that consistency is not his long suit. [*Laughter*] My opponent looks—I look at an issue, and I take a principled stand. My opponent looks at an issue and tries to take every side. [*Laughter*] The people of Florida know the difference, and Tuesday, Florida will vote for strong leadership based upon conviction and consistency and support the Bush-Cheney ticket.

This election comes down to some clear choices on vital issues facing every American family. The first clear choice concerns your budget. When I ran for President 4 years ago, I pledged to lower taxes for America's families. I kept my word. We doubled the child credit. We reduced the marriage penalty. We dropped the lowest bracket to 10 percent so our working families would have more money in their pocket. The plan is working. Real after-tax income—that's the money you've got to spend—is up about 10 percent since I took office.

Our economy has been through a lot. When you're out gathering up the vote, remind people what the economy has been through. Six months prior to my arrival in Washington, the stock market was in serious decline. Then we had a recession and corporate scandals, and the attacks on our country cost us about a million jobs in the 3 months after the attack, after September the 11th.

But we acted. I led. The tax relief is now leading our economy forward. It's working. America's economy is strong, and it's getting stronger. We added 1.9 million jobs in the last 13 months. The home-ownership rate in America is at an alltime high. More minority families own a home than ever before in our Nation's history. Our farmers are making a living. The entrepreneurial spirit is strong in America. The national unemployment rate is 5.4 percent. That's lower than the average rate of the 1970s, 1980s, and 1990s. And the unemployment rate in the great State of Florida is 4.5 percent. Our economic plans are working.

My opponent has got a plan.

Audience members. Boo-o-o!

The President. It involves the promises he makes and the money he intends to take. For the Senator from Massachusetts, he's voted to raise taxes 98 times.

Audience members. Boo-o-o!

The President. That's five times every year he's been in the Senate. I would call that a predictable pattern, a leading indicator. [*Laughter*] In this campaign he's also pledged to spend 2.2 trillion new dollars. That's a lot. That's trillion with a "T." [*Laughter*] That is even—that's a lot for a Senator from Massachusetts. I mean, it's—[*laughter*].

They asked him how he's going to pay for it, and he said he's just going to tax the rich. You've heard that before. By raising the top two brackets, you raise between 600 and 800 billion dollars. That's far short

of the 2.2 trillion. That's what we call a tax gap. And guess who gets to fill the tax gap?

Audience members. We do!

The President. Yes, you do. We're not going to let him tax you; we're going to carry Florida and win a victory.

The second clear choice in this election involves the quality of life for our Nation's families. I ran for President to challenge the soft bigotry of low expectations by reforming our schools. I kept my word. We passed education reforms to bring high standards to the classrooms, and reading and math scores are now on the rise. We're closing an achievement gap for minority students all across America. And we're not going to go back to the old days of low expectations and mediocrity.

We'll continue to improve life for our families by making health care more affordable and available. We'll expand health savings accounts so small businesses can cover their workers and more families are able to save tax-free with health care accounts they manage and call their own. We'll create association health plans so small businesses can join together and buy insurance at the same discounts that big companies can do. We'll help our families by expanding community health centers and making sure every eligible child is enrolled in our low-income health insurance programs.

And we will make sure health care is available and affordable by getting rid of these junk lawsuits that are running the docs out of practice. For the sake of quality health care, we need medical liability reform—now. My vision is for better and more affordable health care where decisions are made by doctors and patients, not by officials in Washington, DC.

My opponent has a different approach to these issues. He voted for education reform, but now he wants to weaken the accountability standards.

Audience members. Boo-o-o!

The President. And he's proposing a big-Government health care plan.

Audience members. Boo-o-o!

The President. I heard him in the debates—you probably did too—when he said, "The Government doesn't have anything to do with it." That's what he said about his plan. I could barely contain myself. [*Laughter*] The Government has got everything to do with it. And the wrong prescription for American families is to federalize health care in America.

And when it comes to these lawsuits, my opponent has voted against medical liability reform not once but 10 times. And he put a personal-injury trial lawyer on the ticket.

Audience members. Boo-o-o!

The President. He can run, but he cannot hide.

The third clear choice in this election involves your retirement. We made a solemn commitment to America's seniors on Social Security and Medicare. When I ran for President 4 years ago, I promised to keep that commitment and improve Medicare by adding prescription drug coverage. I kept my word. Seniors are already getting discounts on medicine with drug discount cards. Low-income seniors are getting direct help to pay for prescriptions. And beginning in 2006, all seniors will be able to get prescription drug coverage under Medicare.

My opponent has got a record on this issue. He voted against the Medicare bill that included prescription drug coverage. In this campaign, he's promised to repeal the bill, and then he promised to keep it. [*Laughter*]

Audience members. Flip-flop! Flip-flop! Flip-flop!

The President. It sounds familiar, doesn't it? He doesn't change positions only on national security issues. [*Laughter*] He also tries to scare seniors about their Social Security. But he forgets to mention that he is the one who voted eight times to raise taxes on Social Security benefits.

Audience members. Boo-o-o!

The President. He can run from that record——

Audience members. But he cannot hide!

The President. I've kept the promise of Social Security for our seniors. I will always keep the promise of Social Security for our seniors. But we need to worry about our children and our grandchildren when it comes to Social Security. We need to worry about whether the system will be there when they need it. That's why I believe younger workers ought to take some of their personal payroll taxes and set up a personal savings account, an account they call their own.

The fourth clear choice——

Audience members. Four more years! Four more years! Four more years!

The President. The fourth choice in this election is on the values that are so crucial to keeping our families strong. I stand for marriage and family, which are the foundations of our society. I stand for a culture of life in which every person matters and every being counts. I proudly signed the ban on partial-birth abortion. I stand for appointing judges who know the difference between personal opinion and the strict interpretation of the law.

On these issues, my opponent and I are miles apart. He voted against the ban on partial-birth abortion. He voted against the Defense of Marriage Act.

Audience members. Boo-o-o!

The President. He said there would be a litmus test when it came to appointing judges. There is a mainstream in American politics, and John Kerry sits on the far left bank. [*Laughter*] He can——

[*At this point, there was a disruption in the audience.*]

The President. Yes, he can run from being the most liberal Senator——

Audience members. Viva Bush! Viva Bush! Viva Bush!

The President. The final choice in this election is most important of all because it concerns the security of your family. All progress on every other issue depends on the safety of our citizens. The most solemn duty of the American President is to protect the American people. If America shows uncertainty or weakness during these troubled times, the world will drift toward tragedy. This is not going to happen on my watch.

Our strategy is clear. We've strengthened protections for the homeland. We're reforming and strengthening our intelligence capabilities. We're transforming the army. We will have no draft; the army will remain an all-volunteer army. We are staying on the offensive. We're chasing the terrorists around the globe. We will find them and bring them to justice so we do not have to face them here at home.

Pakistan was—we're making progress. Every day, we're making progress. Afghanistan is now an ally in the war on terror. Pakistan and Saudi are making raids and arrests. Libya is dismantling its weapons programs. An army of a free Iraq is fighting for freedom. And Al Qaida no longer controls Afghanistan. We shut down its camps. We are systematically destroying the Al Qaida network around the world. More than three-quarters of Al Qaida have been brought to justice, and the rest of them know we're on their trail.

My opponent has taken a different approach—except when he hadn't. [*Laughter*] Here again, consistency has not been his long suit. The Commander in Chief must be consistent in this dangerous world. Senator Kerry says that we're better off with Saddam Hussein out of power—except when he says that removing Saddam made us less safe.

Audience members. Boo-o-o!

The President. He said in our second debate that he always believed Saddam was a threat—except, a few questions later, when he insisted Saddam Hussein was not a threat.

Audience members. Boo-o-o!

The President. He says he was right when he voted to authorize the use of force against Saddam Hussein, but that I was wrong to use force against Saddam Hussein.

Audience members. Boo-o-o!

The President. The problem with Senator Kerry's record on national security are deeper than election-year flip-flops. For 20 years, on the largest national security issues of our time, he has been consistently wrong. During the cold war, Senator Kerry voted against crucial weapons systems and opposed President Ronald Reagan's policy of peace through strength. History——

Audience members. Boo-o-o!

The President. History has shown that Senator Kerry was wrong and President Ronald Reagan was right.

When former President Bush assembled an international coalition to drive Saddam Hussein from Kuwait, Senator Kerry voted against the use of force.

Audience members. Boo-o-o!

The President. History has shown that Senator Kerry was wrong and former President Bush was right.

Only a year after the first bombing of the World Trade Center, the Senator proposed massive cuts in America's intelligence budget, cuts so extreme that even his fellow Massachusetts colleague, Ted Kennedy, voted against the cuts.

Audience members. Boo-o-o!

The President. History has shown Senator Kerry was wrong—and let's be generous about this—Senator Kennedy was right. [*Laughter*]

Just one year ago, I went to the Congress and proposed $87 billion in funding to support our troops in combat. The Commander in Chief must support our troops in harm's way.

Audience members. U.S.A.! U.S.A.! U.S.A.!

The President. Prior to the vote, on national TV, Senator Kerry said it would be irresponsible to vote against the troops.

Audience member. [*Inaudible*] [*Laughter*]

The President. And then he did the irresponsible thing: He voted against the troops.

Audience members. Boo-o-o!

The President. And then he entered the flip-flop hall of fame—[*laughter*]—by saying, "I actually did vote for the 87 billion, right before I voted against it." [*Laughter*] He's given several explanation since then, but the most revealing—perhaps the most revealing is when he said, "The whole thing was a complicated matter." There's nothing complicated about supporting our troops in combat.

Audience members. U.S.A.! U.S.A.! U.S.A.!

The President. The differences on how we'll defend our families are significant. My opponent said in one of the debates that America must pass a "global test."

Audience members. Boo-o-o!

The President. I'm not making that up. I heard him. So did you. We'll work with our friends and allies, but I will never, ever turn over America's national security decisions to leaders of other countries.

Recently, my opponent said September the 11th "didn't change him much at all," end quote. Well, September the 11th changed me. My eyes are wide open to the realities of this world. I fully understand my duty to protect the American people. A few days after the attacks of September the 11th, I stood in the ruins of the Twin Towers. I will never forget the sights and sounds of that day, workers in hardhats yelling at me at the top of their lungs, "Whatever it takes." I remember the man grabbed me by the arm. He looked me square in the eye, and he said, "Do not let me down." Ever since that day— from that day forward, I've gotten up every morning thinking about how to better protect our country. I will never relent in defending America, whatever it takes.

We will use all the assets at our disposal to protect America. We will wage a relentless, comprehensive campaign to protect you. And one of the most powerful, powerful assets we have is freedom. We believe in the power of liberty to transform societies. Free nations do not breed resentments and export terror. Free nations become allies in the war on terror.

Think about what has happened in Afghanistan in a relatively brief period of time. It wasn't all that long ago that young girls couldn't go to school and their mothers were taken into the public square and whipped because the ideologues of hate, the Taliban, had such a dim view of the world. Because we acted in our self-interest, because we upheld the doctrine that said, "If you harbor a terrorist, you are equally as guilty as the terrorist," millions of people went to the polls in Afghanistan to vote for their President. The first voter was a 19-year-old woman.

Iraq is dangerous, but it's moving toward elections. There will be elections in January. Think about how far that country has come from the days of torture chambers and mass graves. Freedom is on the march, and America and the world are better for it.

And over the next 4 years, we will continue to press hard and ensure that the gift of freedom finally reaches the men and women of Cuba.

Audience members. Viva Bush! Viva Bush! Viva Bush!

The President. We will not rest—we will not rest. We will keep the pressure on until the Cuban people enjoy the same freedoms in Havana they receive here in America. I strongly believe the people of Cuba should be free from the tyrant. I believe that everybody yearns to be free. Freedom is not America's gift to the world; freedom is the Almighty God's gift to each man and woman in this world.

My fellow citizens, these are historic times, and a lot is at stake in this election. The future safety and prosperity of America are on the ballot. Ultimately, this election comes down to who can you trust.

Audience members. You!

The President. I offer a record of leadership and results in a time of challenge, and I ask for your vote.

If you believe that taxes should stay low so families can pay the bills and small businesses can expand and our economy can continue to create new jobs, I ask you, come stand with me.

If you believe in high standards for our public schools and parents and doctors—patients and doctors should be in charge of health care, I ask you, come stand with me.

If you believe that this Nation must honor the commitments of Medicare and strengthen Social Security for the next generation, I ask you, come stand with me.

If you believe that this Nation should honor family and marriage and make a place for the weak and vulnerable, I ask you, come stand with me.

If you believe America should fight the war on terror with all our might and lead with unwavering confidence in our ideals, I ask you, come stand with me.

If you are a Democrat who believes your great party has turned too far left in this year, I ask you, come stand with me.

If you are a minority citizen and you believe in free enterprise and good schools and the enduring values of family and faith, if you're tired of your vote being taken for granted, I ask you, come stand with me.

If you are a voter who believes that the President of the United States should say what he means and do what he says and keep his word, I ask you, come stand with me.

Audience members. Four more years! Four more years! Four more years!

The President. When I traveled your State 4 years ago, I made this pledge, that if I got elected, I would uphold the honor and the dignity of the office to which I had been elected. With your help—*con su apoyo*, I will do so for 4 more years.

Gracias. Vamos a ganar. Thank you all.

NOTE: The President spoke at 12:07 p.m. at the Coconut Grove Expo Center. In his remarks, he referred to Gov. Jeb Bush of Florida and his wife, Columba; Mel R. Martinez, senatorial candidate in Florida, and his wife, Kitty; Tom Gallagher, chief financial officer, Florida Department of Financial Services; Florida State Representative Marco Rubio; and President Fidel Castro Ruz of Cuba.

Remarks in Tampa, Florida
October 31, 2004

The President. Thank you all for coming. We really appreciate you coming out on a Sunday afternoon. I'm here to ask for your vote, and I'm here to ask for your help. Find your friends and neighbors and tell them we have a duty to vote, and get them going to the polls. Turn the Republicans out. Turn the independents out. Find discerning Democrats like my friend the former mayor of Tampa, who is a Bush supporter, Dick Greco, like Senator Zell Miller from Georgia. When you get them going to the polls, tell them, if they want a safer America, a stronger America, and a better America, to put me and Dick Cheney back in office.

Perhaps the most important reason why you should put me back in is so that Laura will be the First Lady for 4 more years.

Audience members. Laura! Laura! Laura!

The President. I'm proud of my runningmate, Dick Cheney. I readily concede he doesn't have the waviest hair in the race. [*Laughter*] You'll be happy to hear I didn't pick him because of his hairdo. I picked him because of his experience. I picked him because of his judgment. He's getting the job done for the American people.

I am proud of your Governor, my brother Jeb Bush. He is doing a fabulous job. We both share the same campaign consultant: Mother. [*Laughter*] My brother Marvin is with us too, and I want to thank Marv for coming. He's the good-looking one. [*Laughter*]

I'm proud to be introduced by General Norman Schwarzkopf, a great American and a great general. I want to thank his daughter, Jessica, for joining us today. I want to thank my friend Congressman Mike Bilirakis for being here today. I want to thank Congressman Adam Putnam for being here today. I want to thank the Lieutenant Governor and the attorney general for being with us today. I want to urge you, when you go to the polls, make sure you vote for Mel Martinez as the United States Senator. And I appreciate his wife, Kitty, joining us. I want to thank my friend Mayor Greco for joining us. I want to thank Mel Tillis for being here. Mel, I'm proud you're here. Tino Martinez—how good does that get? Thanks for coming, Tino.

I want to thank all the grassroots activists who are here, the people putting up the signs, the people making the phone calls. I want to thank you for what you have done. I want to thank you for what you're going to do over the next 48 hours. You're going to turn out the vote. We'll win Florida again and win a great victory in November.

This election takes place in a time of great consequence. The person who sits in the Oval Office for the next 4 years will set the course in the war on terror and the direction of our economy. This country needs strong, determined, optimistic leadership, and I'm ready for the job.

My 4 years as your President have confirmed some lessons and taught me some new ones. I have learned to expect the unexpected because horror can arrive quietly—quickly on a quiet morning. I've learned firsthand how hard it is to send young men and women into battle, even when the cause is right. I'm grateful for the lessons I've learned from my parents: Respect every person; do your best; live every day to its fullest. And I've been strengthened by my faith and humbled by its reminder that every life is part of a larger story.

The American President must lead with clarity and purpose. As Presidents from Lincoln to Roosevelt to Reagan so clearly demonstrated, a President must not shift with the wind. The President has to make tough decisions and stand by them. The role of a President is not to follow the path of the latest polls. The role of the President is to lead based on principle, conviction, and conscience.

During these 4 years, I've learned that whatever your strengths are, you're going to need them. And whatever your shortcomings are, the people will notice them. [*Laughter*] Sometimes I am a little too blunt. I get that from my mother. Sometimes I mangle the English language. I get that from my father. But all the time, whether you agree with me or not, you know where I stand, what I believe, and where I'm going to lead.

You can't say that about my opponent.

Audience members. Boo-o-o!

The President. It is fair to say that consistency is not his long suit. I look at an issue and take a principled stand. My opponent looks at an issue and tries to take every side. And the people of Florida know the difference. And Tuesday, Florida will vote for strong, consistent, convicted—conviction and new—and our leadership. Florida will go to the polls and make sure that Bush-Cheney has got 4 more years.

Audience members. Four more years! Four more years! Four more years!

The President. This election comes down to some clear choices on vital issues for American families. The first clear choice concerns your family budget. When I ran for President 4 years ago, I pledged to lower taxes for American families. I kept my word. We doubled the child credit. We reduced the marriage penalty. We dropped the lowest bracket to 10 percent so working families can have more money to spend. As a result of these policies, real after-tax income—that would be money in your pocket—is up by about 10 percent since I took office.

We've been through a lot. When you're out rounding up the vote, remind people that the stock market was in serious decline 6 months prior to my arrival. Then we had a recession and corporate scandals and the attack on our country that cost us a million jobs in 3 months.

But we acted. And because we acted, our economy is growing again. We're creating new jobs. Our economy is growing at rates as fast as any in nearly 20 years. We added 1.9 million new jobs in the last 13 months. Homeownership rate is at an alltime high. More minority families own a home than ever before in our history. The entrepreneurial spirit is strong in America. Small businesses are flourishing. The national unemployment rate is 5.4 percent. That's lower than the average rate of the 1970s, 1980s, and 1990s. And in Florida, the unemployment rate is 4.5 percent. This economy is strong, and it is getting stronger.

My opponent has an economic plan. It involves the promises he makes and the money he intends to take from you.

Audience members. Boo-o-o!

The President. He's got a record. He's got a record. He's voted to increase taxes 98 times in the 20 years he was in the Senate. That's five times every year he was in the Senate. That's a predictable pattern. That's a leading indicator. He's also promised $2.2 trillion in new Federal spending. That's trillion with a "T." That's a lot. That's a lot even for a Senator from Massachusetts.

They asked him how he's going to pay for it. He said, "Oh, don't worry, we'll just tax the rich." You have heard that before. The problem is, when you raise the top

two brackets, you only raise between 600 and 800 billion dollars. That is far short of the 2.2 trillion he has promised. That's a tax gap. Given his record, guess who's going to get to fill the tax gap? You are. We're not going to let him tax you; we're going to carry Florida and win on November the 2d.

Second clear choice involves the quality of life for our Nation's families. I ran for President to challenge the soft bigotry of low expectations by reforming our public schools. I have kept my word. We passed education reforms to bring high standards to our classrooms. Reading and math scores are on the rise. We're closing the achievement gap by helping our minority students. My vision for a new term is to build on these reforms and extend them still to our high schools so that no child is left behind in America.

We'll continue to improve life for our families by making health care more affordable and available. We will expand health savings accounts so more small businesses can cover their workers and more families are able to save tax-free for health care accounts they manage and call their own. We will expand association health plans to help small businesses. They should be allowed to join together to share risk so they can buy insurance at the same discounts big companies do. We will expand community health centers to help the poor and the indigent, and we'll make sure every eligible child is enrolled in our low-income health insurance program.

And to make sure health care is available and affordable, we will do something about the junk lawsuits that are running good doctors out of practice and running up the cost of health care. I am for medical liability reform—now. In all we do to reform health care, the decisions will be made by doctors and patients, not by officials in Washington, DC.

My opponent has a different approach. He voted for education reform but now wants to weaken the accountability standards. He has proposed a big-Government health care plan. You might remember one of our debates when he looked square in the camera and said—when they asked him about his health care plan, he said, "The Government doesn't have anything to do with it." I could barely contain myself. [*Laughter*] The Government has got a lot to do with it. Eighty percent of the people would be signed up to a Government program under his plan. Eight million Americans would lose their private health insurance and end up on a Government program. He's voted against medical liability reform 10 times. He put a personal-injury trial lawyer on the ticket.

Audience members. Boo-o-o!

The President. Federalizing health care is the wrong prescription for American families. He can run, but he cannot hide.

The third clear choice in this election involves your retirement. Our Nation has made a solemn commitment to America's seniors on Social Security and Medicare. When I ran for President 4 years ago, I promised to keep that commitment and improve Medicare by adding prescription drug coverage. I kept my word. Seniors are already getting discounts on medicine with drug discount cards. Low-income seniors are getting direct help to pay for prescription drugs. And beginning in 2006, all seniors will be able to get prescription drug coverage under Medicare.

My opponent has a record. He voted against the Medicare bill that included prescription drug coverage. Remind your friends and neighbors of that when they're headed to the polls. In this campaign, he promised to repeal the Medicare bill, and then he's promised to keep it. Sounds familiar, doesn't it?

Audience members. Flip-flop! Flip-flop! Flip-flop!

The President. He tries to scare seniors about their Social Security. But he forgot to mention he's the one who voted to tax Social Security benefits eight times.

Audience members. Boo-o-o!

The President. I have kept the promise of Social Security for our seniors, and I will always keep the promise of Social Security for our seniors.

But I also know the job of a President is to confront problems, not to pass them on to future Presidents and future generations. That's why in a new term, I'll work with members of both political parties to make sure the Social Security system is strengthened for a younger generation to come.

The fourth clear choice in this election is on the values that are crucial to keeping our families strong. I stand for marriage and family, which are the foundations of our society. I stand for a culture of life in which every person matters and every being counts. And I proudly signed the ban on partial-birth abortions. I stand for the appointment of Federal judges who know the difference between personal opinion and the strict interpretation of the law.

On these issues, my opponent and I are miles apart. He said he would only appoint judges who pass a liberal litmus test. He was part of the extreme minority who voted against the Defense of Marriage Act. He voted against the ban on partial-birth abortion. There is a mainstream in American politics, and John Kerry sits on the far left bank. He can run from that liberal record, but he cannot hide.

The final choice in this election is the most important of all because it concerns the security of your family. All progress on every other issue depends on the safety of our citizens. The most solemn duty of the American President is to protect the American people. If America shows uncertainty or weakness during these troubling times, the world will drift toward tragedy. This is not going to happen on my watch.

Our strategy is clear. We're strengthening our homeland. We're reforming and strengthening the intelligence capabilities. We will transform our military. There will be no draft. The All-Volunteer Army will remain an all-volunteer army. We are steadfast. We are determined. We are staying on the offensive so we do not have to face the terrorists here at home.

And we're making progress. Afghanistan is an ally in the war on terror. Pakistan and Saudi Arabia are making raids and arrests. Libya is dismantling its weapons program. The army of a free Iraq is fighting for freedom. Al Qaida no longer controls territory like it did in Afghanistan. We have shut down its camps. We are systematically destroying the Al Qaida network across the world. More than three-quarters of Al Qaida's key members and associates have been brought to justice. And the rest of them know we're on their trail.

My opponent has taken a different approach—except when he hadn't. [*Laughter*] Consistency is not his long suit, as I mentioned. Senator Kerry says we're better off with Saddam out of power—except when he said that removing Saddam made us less safe. He said in our second debate that he always believed Saddam was a threat—except, a few questions later, when he insisted Saddam Hussein was not a threat. He says he was right when he voted to authorize the use force against Saddam Hussein but I was wrong to use force against Saddam Hussein.

The problems with—the problem with my opponent's record on national security are deeper than election-year reversals. For 20 years, on the largest national security issues of our time, he has been consistently wrong. During the cold war, Senator Kerry voted against critical weapons systems and opposed President Reagan's policy of peace through strength. History has shown that Senator Kerry was wrong and President Ronald Reagan was right.

When President—when former President Bush assembled an international coalition led by General Norman Schwarzkopf to drive Saddam Hussein from Kuwait, Senator Kerry voted against the use of force to liberate Kuwait.

Audience members. Boo-o-o!

The President. History has shown that Senator Kerry was wrong and former President Bush was right.

One year after the first bombing of the World Trade Center, the Senator proposed massive cuts in America's intelligence. The cuts were so extreme that even his fellow Massachusetts Senator, Ted Kennedy, voted against them. History has shown that Senator Kerry was wrong and—let's be fair—Senator Kennedy was right.

I know there are some members of the military with us today, and I want to thank you for your dedication. I want to thank you for your service. I want to thank the military families who are with us today. And I want to thank the veterans who have joined us today. I want to thank our veterans for having set such a great example to those who wear our Nation's uniform. And I want to assure you like I've assured families all across our country, we will make sure our troops have that which they need to complete their missions.

That is why I went to the United States Congress last September—September of 2003—and asked for $87 billion in funding to support our troops in both Afghanistan and Iraq. On national TV, my opponent said it would be irresponsible to vote against the troops. And then he did the irresponsible thing and he voted against funding for our troops.

Audience members. Boo-o-o!

The President. And then he entered the flip-flop hall of fame by saying, quote, "I actually did vote for the 87 billion, right before I voted against it."

Audience members. Flip-flop! Flip-flop! Flip-flop!

The President. He's given several answers since then, but perhaps the most illustrative is when he said, "The whole thing is a complicated matter." My fellow Americans, there's nothing complicated about supporting our troops in combat.

We have a difference of opinion on how to protect our families. You might remember in one of the debates, my opponent said there must be a "global test" before we commit troops.

Audience members. Boo-o-o!

The President. I'm not making that up. I heard him loud and clear. As far as I can tell, that means America must submit to the will of others before we defend ourselves. Listen, I'll work to build alliances. I will strengthen our coalitions. But I will never turn over America's national security decisions to leaders of other countries.

My opponent was—recently said that September the 11th didn't change him much at all. Well, September the 11th changed me. It changed my outlook about what we need to do to protect the American people. I remember standing in the ruins of the Twin Towers on September the 14th, 2001. I remember the sights and sounds of that day. There were workers in hardhats yelling at me at the top of their lungs, "Whatever it takes." I remember the man who grabbed me by the arm. He looked me square in the eye, and he said, "Do not let me down." Ever since that day, I wake up every morning trying to better figure—figure out how to better protect the American people. I will never relent in defending our country, whatever it takes.

We will use all our assets to protect the American people. We will wage a comprehensive strategy to protect you. Perhaps the biggest asset we have of all is freedom. I believe in the power of liberty to transform nations. Free nations do not breed resentment and export terror. Free nations become allies in the war on terror.

Think about what's happening in Afghanistan in a relatively brief period of time. I want the youngsters to hear what life was like in that country 3½ years ago. Young girls couldn't go to school. And if their mothers didn't toe the line of the ideologues of hate, they were taken into the public square and whipped and sometimes killed in a sports stadium.

Because we acted in our self-defense, because we upheld a doctrine that I clearly laid out that said, "If you harbor a terrorist, you're equally as guilty as the terrorist," millions of citizens in Afghanistan voted in a Presidential election. And the first voter was a 19-year-old woman.

Iraq is dangerous. It's dangerous because Iraq is heading toward a free society. There will be Presidential elections in January. Think how far that country has come from the days of torture chambers and mass graves. Freedom is on the march, and America is more secure for it. I believe that everybody yearns to be free. Freedom is not America's gift to the world; freedom is the Almighty God's gift to each man and woman in this world.

These are historic times, and there is a lot at stake in this election. The future and safety—the future safety and prosperity of America are on the ballot. Ultimately, this election comes down to who do you trust—who do you trust to lead this Nation? I offer a record of leadership and results at a time of threat and challenge.

If you believe that taxes should stay low so families can pay their bills and small businesses can create new jobs, I ask you, come stand with me.

If you believe in high standards for our public schools, I ask you, come stand with me.

If you believe patients and doctors should be in charge of the health care system, I ask you, come stand with me.

If you believe that this Nation must honor the commitments of Medicare and strengthen Social Security for the generations to come, I ask you, come stand with me.

If you believe that this Nation should honor marriage and family and make a place for the weak and the vulnerable, I ask you to come stand with me.

If you believe America should fight the war on terror with all our might and lead with unwavering confidence in our ideals, I ask you to come stand with me.

If you are a Democrat who believes your party has turned too far to the left this year, I ask you to come stand with me.

If you're a minority citizen and you believe in free enterprise and good schools and the enduring values of faith and family, if you are tired of your vote being taken for granted, I ask you to come stand with me.

And if you are a voter who believes that the American President should say what he means and do what he says and keep his word, I ask you to come stand with me.

Four years ago, when I traveled your State, I made this pledge, that if I won the election, I would uphold the honor and the dignity of the office to which I had been elected. With your help, with your hard work, I will do so for 4 more years.

Thanks for coming. On to victory. Thank you all.

NOTE: The President spoke at 2:35 p.m. at Legends Field. In his remarks, he referred to Gov. Jeb Bush, Lt. Gov. Toni Jennings, and State Attorney General Charlie Crist of Florida; Mel R. Martinez, senatorial candidate in Florida, and his wife, Kitty; entertainer Mel Tillis; Tino Martinez, first baseman, Major League Baseball Tampa Bay Devil Rays; and former President Saddam Hussein of Iraq.

Remarks in Gainesville, Florida
October 31, 2004

The President. Thank you all. Thank you all for coming. So Jeb said, "Why don't we go to Gainesville? Maybe a couple hundred will show up and say hello." I said, "Well, I'm more than willing to go." I can't thank you all enough for coming. Thanks for taking time out of your Sunday afternoon. You're lifting our spirits, and we appreciate it.

I'm here to ask for your vote and your help. I'm here to ask you to take your friends and neighbors to the polls. Remind them we have a duty in our free country to vote. We have an obligation, in my judgment, to participate in our democratic system. Now, when you're lining up votes, of course look for our fellow Republicans and independents, but don't forget to get discerning Democrats to go to the polls, people like Senator Zell Miller from right north of here. And when you get them headed to the polls, remind them, if they want a safer America, a stronger America, and a better America, to put me and Dick Cheney back in office.

Perhaps the most important reason of all to put me back in is so that Laura is the First Lady for 4 more years.

Audience members. Laura! Laura! Laura!

The President. I'm proud of my runningmate, Dick Cheney. I don't want to offend anybody here who's follically challenged, but I readily concede my runningmate doesn't have the waviest hair in the race. [*Laughter*] But I suspect the people of north-central Florida are going to be pleased to know I didn't pick him because of his hairdo. I picked him because of his judgment. I picked him because of his experience. He's getting the job done for the American people.

I'm proud of brother Jeb. What a great Governor, and what a great brother. Jeb and I share the same campaign consultant: Mother. [*Laughter*] And my brother Marvin is with us too. I'm proud Marv is here. Thanks for coming, Marvin. I love my family, and I'm glad that—I'm a fortunate man to have such a great family.

Listen, I want to urge you, when you go to the polls, to vote for Mel Martinez for the next Senator of your State. I know him well. He'll make a great United States Senator for Florida. I want to thank Congressman Cliff Stearns for joining us today. He does a great job for the people of this part of the world. I want to thank all the other candidates, people running for office. I want to thank Carole Jean Jordan and all the grassroots activists who are here.

I want to thank the Bellamy Brothers for being here. I'm proud to call them friend. I'm glad they are here.

I want to thank you for what you have done. It takes a lot of work to turn out a crowd this big. I want to thank you for what you're going to do: Call your friends; call your neighbors; turn them out. We'll carry Florida again and win a great victory on Tuesday.

This election takes place in a time of great consequence. The person who sits in the Oval Office for the next 4 years will set the course of the war on terror and the direction of our economy. America will need strong, determined, optimistic leadership, and I am ready for the work ahead.

My 4 years as your President have confirmed some lessons and have taught me some new ones. I've learned to expect the unexpected, because war can arrive quietly on a quiet morning. I have learned firsthand how hard it is to send young men and women into battle, even when the cause is right. I am grateful for the lessons I've learned from my parents: Respect every person; do your best; live every day to its fullest. I have been strengthened by my faith and humbled by its reminder that every life is part of a larger story.

I've learned how crucial it is for the American President to lead with clarity and purpose. As Presidents from Lincoln to Roosevelt to Reagan so clearly demonstrated, a President must not shift with the wind. A President should make the tough decisions and stand by them. The role of a President is not to follow the path of the latest polls; the role of a President is to lead based on principle and conviction and conscience.

During these 4 years, I've learned that whatever your strengths are, you're going to need them, and whatever your shortcomings are, people will notice them. [*Laughter*] Sometimes I'm a little too blunt. I get that from my mother. Sometimes I mangle the English language. I get that from my father. [*Laughter*] But all the time, no matter whether you agree with me or not, you know where I stand, what I believe, and where I'm going to lead.

You cannot say that about my opponent.

Audience members. Boo-o-o!

The President. I think it is fair to say that consistency is not his strong suit. I look at an issue and take a principled stand. As we've learned in this campaign, my opponent looks at an issue and tries to take every side. The people of Florida know the difference. And on Tuesday, Florida will vote for strong leadership and send me and Dick Cheney back to Washington.

This election comes down to clear choices on five vital issues, issues facing every family in our country. The first clear choice concerns your family budget. When I ran for President 4 years ago, I pledged to lower taxes for our families. I kept my word. We doubled the child credit. We reduced the marriage penalty. We believe the code ought to encourage marriage, not penalize marriage. We dropped the lowest bracket to 10 percent. And as a result of these good policies, real after-tax income—the money in your pocket, the money you have available for spending—is up by about 10 percent since I took office.

And this economy of ours has been through a lot. The stock market was in serious decline 6 months prior to my arrival. Then we had a recession and corporate scandals and an attack on our country that cost us a million jobs in 3 months after September the 11th.

But we acted. And our policies are paying off. Our economy is growing at rates as fast as any in nearly 20 years. We've added 1.9 million jobs in the last 13 months. Homeownership rate is at an all-time high. More minority families own a home than ever before in our history. The entrepreneurial spirit is strong. Our small businesses are flourishing. Florida's farmers and ranchers are making a good living. The unemployment rate is 5.4 percent across this country. Let me put that in perspective for you: That's lower than the average rate of the 1970s, the 1980s, and the 1990s. The unemployment rate in the great State of Florida is 4.5 percent. This economy is strong, and it is getting stronger.

My opponent has an economic plan too. He voted to increase taxes 98 times.

Audience members. Boo-o-o!

The President. That's in 20 years. That's five times a year, nearly. I would call that a predictable pattern, a leading indicator. In this campaign, he's also promised $2.2 trillion of new spending. That is trillion with a "T." That's a lot even for a Senator from Massachusetts. [*Laughter*]

They asked him how he's going to pay for it. He threw out that same old, tired line, "We're going to tax the rich." By raising the top two brackets, you raise between 6 and 800 billion dollars. That's far short of the 2.2 trillion. There is a tax gap. And given his record, guess who he's going to ask to fill it? You. The good news is, we're not going to let him tax you; we will carry Florida and win on November the 2d.

The second clear choice in this election involves the quality of life for our Nation's families. I ran for President to challenge and end the soft bigotry of low expectations by reforming our schools. I kept my word. We passed education reforms to bring high standards to the classrooms of America. Math and reading scores are up. We're closing an achievement gap for minority students across this country. My vision for a new term is to build on these reforms and extend them to our high schools so that no child is left behind in America.

We will continue to improve our lives for our families by making health care more

available and affordable. We'll expand health savings accounts. We will allow small businesses to join together so they can buy insurance at the same discounts that big companies are able to do. We'll help our families in need. We'll help patients and doctors by getting rid of the frivolous and junk lawsuits that are running docs out of practice and running up your medicine. I'm standing with the families of Florida. I'm standing with the doctors of Florida. I am for medical liability reform—now. In all we do to improve the health care for our families, we will make sure the decisions are made by doctors and patients, not by officials in Washington, DC.

My opponent has a different approach. He voted for the education reform but now wants to weaken the accountability standards. He's proposing a big-Government health care plan. You might remember in the debate, they said, "Talk about your health care plan." He looked straight in the camera, and he said, "The Government doesn't have anything to do with it." I could barely contain myself. [*Laughter*] The Government has got a lot to do with it. Eighty percent of the people on his plan end up on a Government plan. He's voted against medical liability reform 10 times. He's put a personal-injury trial lawyer on the ticket.

Audience members. Boo-o-o!

The President. He can run from his record, but he cannot hide.

The third clear choice in this election involves your retirement. Our Nation has made a solemn commitment to America's seniors on Social Security and Medicare. When I ran for President 4 years ago, I promised to keep that commitment and improve Medicare by adding prescription drug coverage. I kept my word. Seniors are getting discounts on medicine with drug discount cards. Low-income seniors are getting help to pay for their prescription. And beginning in 2006, all seniors will be able to get prescription drug coverage through Medicare.

My opponent has a record on this issue. He voted against the Medicare bill that included prescription drug coverage. In this campaign, he said he promised to repeal the bill, and then shortly thereafter, he promised to keep it. That sounds familiar. He also tries to scare our seniors about their Social Security, but he conveniently forgets that he's the one that voted eight times for higher taxes on Social Security benefits. He can run, but he cannot hide.

I've kept the promise of Social Security for our seniors, and I will always keep the promise of Social Security for our seniors. But I understand we have a problem for the younger generation coming up. Baby boomers, like me and some others I see out there, are in pretty good shape when it comes to Social Security, but we need to worry about the younger folks. That's why I believe younger workers ought to be able to take some of their own payroll taxes and set up a personal savings account, a personal savings account they call their own. In a new term, I'll bring people together to strengthen Social Security for generations to come.

The fourth clear choice in this elections are on the values that are so crucial to keeping our families strong. I stand for marriage and family, which are the foundations of our society. I stand for a culture of life in which every person counts and every being matters. I proudly signed the ban on partial-birth abortion. I stand for the appointment of Federal judges who know the difference between personal opinion and the strict interpretation of the law.

On these issues, my opponent and I are miles apart. He said he would only appoint judges who pass his liberal litmus test. He was part of an extreme minority that voted against the Defense of Marriage Act, and he voted against the ban on partial-birth abortion.

Audience members. Boo-o-o!

The President. There is a mainstream in American politics, and John Kerry sits on the far left bank. He can run from his liberal record, but he cannot hide.

The final choice in this election is the most important one of all because it concerns the security of your family. All progress on every other issue depends on the safety of our citizens. The most solemn duty of the American President is to protect the American people. If America shows uncertainty or weakness during these troubled times, the world will drift toward tragedy. This is not going to happen on my watch.

Our strategy is clear. We are strengthening protections for the homeland. We are reforming and strengthening our intelligence capabilities. We are transforming the United States military. The All-Volunteer Army will remain an all-volunteer army. There will be no draft. We are determined. We are relentless. We will stay on the offensive. We are fighting the terrorists abroad so we do not have to face them here at home.

And we're succeeding. Afghanistan is an ally in the war on terror. Pakistan and Saudi Arabia are making raids and arrests. Libya is dismantling its weapons programs. The army of a free Iraq is fighting for freedom, and Al Qaida no longer controls territory like Afghanistan. They no longer have training camps there. We are systematically destroying the Al Qaida network across the world. More than three-quarters of Al Qaida's key members and associates have been brought to justice, and the rest of them know we are on their trail.

The leader must be consistent. The leader must not send mixed signals to the world. My opponent has taken a different approach. Senator Kerry says that we're better off with Saddam Hussein out of power, except when he says that removing Saddam made us less safe. He said in our second debate that he always believed Saddam was a threat, except a few questions later, when he insisted Saddam Hussein was not a threat. He said he was right when he voted to authorize the use of force against Saddam Hussein, but I was wrong to use force to remove Saddam Hussein.

Audience members. Boo-o-o!

The President. The problems of Senator Kerry's record on national security are deeper than election-year reversals. For 20 years, on the largest national security issues of our time, he has been consistently wrong. During the cold war, Senator Kerry voted against critical weapons systems and opposed Ronald Reagan's policy of peace through strength. History has shown that Senator Kerry was wrong and President Ronald Reagan was right.

When former President Bush assembled an international coalition to drive Saddam Hussein from Kuwait, Senator Kerry voted against the use of force to liberate Kuwait.

Audience members. Boo-o-o!

The President. History has shown that Senator Kerry was wrong and former President Bush was right.

One year after the bombing—the first bombing of the World Trade Center, the Senator proposed massive cuts in America's intelligence, so massive that even his fellow Massachusetts liberal, Ted Kennedy, would not support them. History has shown that Senator Kerry was wrong and—let's be fair about it—Senator Kennedy was right.

We will be relentless; we will be strong; we will be consistent in our security, in securing this country. And we've got a great United States military to help. I thank those who wear our Nation's uniform who are with us today. I thank the military families who are here with us today. And I thank the veterans who have set such a great example for those who wear the uniform. I assure you, we'll keep our commitment I made to the troops and their families and to our vets. We will make sure our troops have all the resources they need to complete their missions.

That is why I went to the Congress in September of 2003 and asked for $87 billion of supplemental funding. It was important funding. It was necessary funding. It was funding to support troops in harm's way in both Iraq and Afghanistan. And we received great bipartisan support for that funding, so strong only 12 Members of the United States Senate voted against it, 2 of whom were my opponent and his runningmate.

Audience members. Boo-o-o!

The President. Senator Kerry said on national TV prior to that vote that it would be irresponsible to vote against the troops. Then the polls began to change. And he did the irresponsible thing, and he voted against the troops. Then he entered the flip-flop hall of fame by saying, "I actually did vote for the 87 billion, right before I voted against it." He's given a lot of answers since then about that vote, but I think the most revealing of all is when he said, "The whole thing was a complicated matter." [*Laughter*] My fellow Americans, there's nothing complicated about supporting our troops in combat.

We have differences on how to best protect America's families. During one of the debates, my opponent said that America must pass a "global test" before we commit troops.

Audience members. Boo-o-o!

The President. Some of you probably think I'm making that up. I heard him. He was standing right there. You see, to me that means that we've got to get permission before we get troops. I'll work with our allies. I'll continue to build alliances. But I will never turn over America's national security decisions to leaders of other countries.

Audience members. Four more years! Four more years! Four more years!

The President. A couple of weeks ago, Senator Kerry said that September the 11th didn't change him much at all. September the 11th changed me. It changed my outlook about what we need to do to protect this country. A few days after that attack, I stood in the ruins of the Twin Towers, on September the 14th, 2001. It was a day I'll never forget. I'll never forget the sights and sounds. I will never forget the workers in hardhats who were yelling at me at the top of their lungs, "Whatever it takes." I'll never forget the person that grabbed me by the arm, and he looked me in the eye, and he said, "Do not let me down." Ever since that day, I wake up every morning trying to figure out how to better protect this country. I will never relent in the security of America, whatever it takes.

During the next 4 years——

Audience members. Four more years! Four more years! Four more years!

The President. During the next 4 years, we will use every asset at our disposal to wage a comprehensive strategy to defend you. And perhaps the strongest asset we have is freedom. I believe in the power of liberty to transform nations. Free nations do not breed resentments. Free nations do not export terror. Free nations become allies in the war on terror. And by spreading freedom, we'll achieve the peace we all want for our children and our grandchildren.

I want the younger folks here to think about what's happened in Afghanistan in just 3 years. Society there was grim under the reign of the Taliban. These people were ideologues of hate. Young girls couldn't go to school. If their mothers didn't toe the line, they'd get whipped in the public square and sometimes executed in a sports stadium. But because we acted to defend ourselves, because we upheld a doctrine that said, "If you harbor a terrorist, you're equally as guilty as the terrorist," millions of people in that country went to the polls to vote for President. And the first voter was a 19-year-old woman.

Iraq is still dangerous. It's a dangerous place because that country is headed toward a free society. There will be elections in January. Think how far that country has come from the days of torture chambers and mass graves. Freedom is on the march, and America and the world are better for it. I believe everybody yearns to be free. Freedom is not America's gift to the world;

freedom is the Almighty God's gift to each man and woman in this world.

These are historic times, and a lot is at stake in this election. The future safety and prosperity of America are on the ballot. Ultimately, though, this election comes down to who you can trust—who you can trust to keep your families secure, who you can trust to spread prosperity. I proudly offer a record of leadership and results at a time of threat and challenge.

If you believe that taxes should stay low so families can pay the bills and small businesses can create new jobs, I ask, come stand with me.

If you believe in high standards for our public schools, I ask you, come stand with me.

If you believe patients and doctors should be in charge of health care, I ask you, come stand with me.

If you believe that this Nation must honor the commitments of Medicare and strengthen Social Security for generations to come, I ask, come stand with me.

If you believe that this Nation should honor marriage and family and make a place for the weak and the vulnerable, I ask you, come stand with me.

If you believe America should fight the war on terror with all our might and lead with unwavering confidence in our ideals, I ask you to come stand with me.

If you are a Democrat who believes your party has turned too far to the left this year, I ask you to come stand with me.

If you are a minority citizen and you believe that free enterprise and good schools and enduring values of family and faith, and if you're tired of your vote being taken for granted, I ask you to come stand with me.

If you are a voter who believes that the President of the United States should say what he means and do what he says and keep his word, I ask you to come stand with me.

Four years ago, when I traveled your State asking for the vote, I made a pledge that if elected, I would uphold the honor and the dignity of the office. With your help, with your hard work, I will do so for 4 more years.

Thanks for coming. God bless. Thank you all.

NOTE: The President spoke at 4:25 p.m. at the University Air Center. In his remarks, he referred to Gov. Jeb Bush of Florida; Carole Jean Jordan, chairman, Republican Party of Florida; entertainers the Bellamy Brothers; and former President Saddam Hussein of Iraq.

Remarks in Cincinnati, Ohio
October 31, 2004

The President. Thank you all. Thank you all for coming. I am here to ask for your vote, and I am here to ask for your help. We have come to the great city of Cincinnati, Ohio, asking for you to turn your friends and neighbors out to the polls on Tuesday. With your help, we will carry Ohio again and win a great victory on Tuesday.

Perhaps the most important reason of all to put me back into office is so that Laura will be the First Lady for 4 more years.

I'm proud of my runningmate, Dick Cheney. I admit it, he does not have the waviest hair in the race. [*Laughter*] You all will be happy to know I didn't pick him because of his hairdo. I picked him because of his judgment, his experience. He's getting the job done for the American people.

I want to thank one of Cincinnati's great citizens, Johnny Bench, for having introduced me today. We can judge a person by the company he keeps, and I'm keeping good company up here on this stage. I'm proud you're here, Johnny. Thank you very much.

I'm proud to be here with some elected officials from the great State of Ohio. Governor Bob Taft and First Lady Hope Taft are with us. Thank you for coming. Senator Mike DeWine. Senator George Voinovich is out campaigning, but put him back into office for 6 more years.

I'm proud to be here with Senator Jim Bunning from Kentucky, and I hope the citizens of Kentucky put him back into office. And we love Mary as well.

Steve Chabot, the Congressman from this district, is with us. Congressman, thank you. My friend Congressman Rob Portman is with us tonight. Thank you for being here, Rob.

The Lieutenant Governor from Ohio, Jennette Bradley, is with us. State Treasurer Joe "Write in My Name" Deters is with us. I want to thank Betty Montgomery. I want to thank all the State and local officials. I want to thank Mike Sodrel, who is from the Indiana Ninth Congressional District. I strongly support Mike's bid for the United States Congress. And I strongly support the bid of Geoff Davis from Kentucky's Fourth Congressional District.

I want to thank my friend Anthony Munoz for being here today. I'm proud to call him friend. Marty Brennaman. I want to thank my friend Larry Gatlin and brother Rudy for joining us today. Yes. I want to thank the Wil Gravatt Band.

But most of all, I want to thank you all. I want to thank the people who have been putting up the signs and making the phone calls and doing all the hard work. You're turning out this vote on Tuesday.

This election takes place in a time of great consequence. The person who sits in the Oval Office for the next 4 years will set the course of the war on terror and the direction of our economy. America will need strong, determined, optimistic leadership, and I am ready to get the job done for 4 more years.

Audience members. Four more years! Four more years! Four more years!

The President. My 4 years as your President confirmed some lessons and taught some new ones. I've learned to expect the unexpected. I've learned firsthand how hard it is to send young men and women into battle. I am grateful for the lessons I have learned from my parents: Respect every person; do your best; live every day to its fullest. I've been strengthened by my faith and humbled by its reminder that every life is part of a larger story. I understand how crucial it is for the American President to lead with clarity and purpose. As Presidents from Lincoln to Roosevelt to Reagan so clearly demonstrated, a President must not shift with the wind. A President has to make tough decisions and stand by them.

The role of the President is not to follow the path of the latest polls. The role of a President is to lead based on principle and conviction and conscience. During these 4 years, I've learned that whatever your strengths are, you are going to need them, and whatever your shortcomings are, people will notice them. Sometimes I'm a little too blunt. I get that from my mother. [*Laughter*] Sometimes I mangle the English language. I get that from my dad. [*Laughter*] But all the time, whether you agree with me or not, you know where I stand, what I believe, and where I'm going to lead.

You cannot say that about my opponent.

Audience members. Boo-o-o!

The President. I think it's fair to say that consistency is not his strong suit. [*Laughter*] I look at an issue and take a principled stand. My opponent looks at an issue and tries to take every side. And the people of Ohio know the difference. And that's one of the reasons why on Tuesday we're going to carry your great State.

This election comes down to clear choices on five vital issues facing every American family. The first clear choice concerns your family's budget. When I ran for President 4 years ago, I pledged to lower taxes for American families. I kept my word. We doubled the child credit. We reduced the marriage penalty. We believe the Tax Code ought to encourage, not penalize marriage. We reduced taxes on everybody who pays taxes. As a result of these good policies, real after-tax income—the money in your pocket to spend on groceries or house payments or rent—is up 10 percent since I took office.

When you're out there convincing your friends and neighbors to vote, remind them what our economy has been through. Six months prior to my arrival in Washington, the stock market was in serious decline. And then we faced the recession and corporate scandals and an attack on our country that cost us a million jobs in just 3 months after the attack.

But we acted. Our economy is creating jobs and growing faster than any major economy in the world. We've added—homeownership rate is at an alltime high in America. More minorities own a home today than ever before in our Nation's history. The entrepreneurial spirit is strong. Small businesses are flourishing all across the State of Ohio. Ohio farmers are making a living. We added more than 1.9 million new jobs in the last 13 months. The national unemployment rate is 5.4 percent. That's lower than the average rate of the 1970s, the 1980s, and the 1990s.

I've traveled your State a lot. I know that in certain areas of this State, people are struggling. But we're making progress. Ohio added 5,500 new jobs last month. Your unemployment rate has gone from 6.3 to 6 percent in one month. This economy is strong, and it is getting stronger.

My opponent has an economic plan too. He voted to increase taxes 98 times in the 20 years he's been in the United States Senate.

Audience members. Boo-o-o!

The President. That's five times every year he's been in the Senate. I would call that a leading indicator—*[laughter]*—a predictable pattern. Couple that with the fact that he's promised $2.2 trillion in new Federal spending—that's trillion with a "T." That's a lot—*[laughter]*—even for a Senator from Massachusetts. *[Laughter]*

They asked him how he's going to pay for it. He said, "Oh, we'll just tax the rich." The problem is, is that by raising the top two brackets, one, you penalize the small-business sector of this country, and secondly, you only raise between 600 and 800 billion dollars. That's far short of the 2.2 trillion. That's what I would call a tax gap. Given his record, it's not hard to figure out who's going to fill that tax gap. You are. But the good news is, we're not going to let him tax you; we're going to win Ohio, Kentucky, and Indiana.

Audience members. Four more years! Four more years! Four more years!

The President. The second clear choice in this election involves the quality of life for our Nation's families. I ran for President to challenge the soft bigotry of low expectations by reforming our public schools. I kept my word. We passed education reforms to bring high standards to the classroom. Math and reading scores are now on the rise. We're closing the achievement gap for minority children all across this country. My vision for a new term is to build on these reforms and extend them to our high schools so that no child is left behind in America.

We'll continue to improve life for our families by making health care more affordable and available. We'll expand health savings accounts. We'll allow small businesses to join together and buy insurance at the same discounts that big companies are able to buy insurance for. We'll help our families in need by expanding community health centers.

And we will help Ohio families and patients and doctors by getting rid of the frivolous and junk lawsuits that make health care too expensive. In all we do to improve health care, we will make sure the medical decisions are made by doctors and patients, not by officials in Washington, DC.

As you can imagine, my opponent has a different approach. He voted for the education reform but now wants to weaken the accountability standards. He's proposing a big-Government health care plan. I don't know if you remember the debate when they said, "Tell us about your health care plan." And one of the things he said was, "The Government doesn't have anything to do with it." I could barely contain myself. *[Laughter]* The Government has got a lot to do with it. Eighty percent of the people would end up on the Government plan with his vision. And that is the wrong prescription for American families.

Now, we got a different point of view when it comes to our docs and patients. He voted against medical liability reform 10 times, and he put a personal-injury trial lawyer on the ticket.

Audience members. Boo-o-o!

The President. He can run, but he cannot hide.

The third clear choice in this election involves your retirement. Our Nation has made a solemn commitment to America's seniors on Social Security and Medicare. When I ran for President 4 years ago, I promised to keep that commitment and improve Medicare by adding prescription drug coverage. I kept my word. Seniors are already getting discounts on medicine with drug discount cards. Low-income seniors are getting direct help to pay for prescriptions. And beginning in 2006, all seniors will be able to get prescription drug coverage under Medicare.

My opponent has got a record on that. He voted against the Medicare bill that included prescription drugs. In the campaign, he's promised to repeal the bill, and then shortly thereafter, he promised to keep it. Sounds familiar. He tries to scare seniors about their Social Security. But he forgets to mention that he is the one who voted eight times to raise taxes on Social Security benefits.

Audience members. Boo-o-o!

The President. I have kept the promise of Social Security for our seniors. And I'll always keep the promise of Social Security for our seniors. And the Social Security trust is in pretty good shape for baby boomers like me and a couple of other folks I see out there.

But we need to worry about our children and our grandchildren when it comes to Social Security. We need to worry about whether or not the Social Security system will be there when they retire. And that is why I believe younger workers ought to be allowed to take some of their payroll taxes and put it in a personal savings account, an account that earns a better interest, an account they call their own.

The fourth clear choice in this election is on the values that are so crucial to keeping our families strong. I stand for marriage and family, which are the foundations of our society. I stand for a culture of life in which every person matters and every being counts. And I proudly signed the ban on partial-birth abortion. And I stand for the appointment of Federal judges who know the difference between personal opinion and the strict interpretation of the law.

On these issues, my opponent and I are miles apart. He said he would only appoint judges who pass a liberal litmus test. He was part of an extreme minority that voted against the Defense of Marriage Act. He voted against the ban on partial-birth abortion.

Audience members. Boo-o-o!

The President. There is a mainstream in American politics, and my opponent sits on the far left bank. [*Laughter*] He can run from his record, but he cannot hide.

The final choice in this election is the most important of all because it concerns the security of your family. All progress on every other issue depends on the safety of our citizens. The most solemn duty of

the American President is to protect the American people. If America shows uncertainty or weakness during these troubled times, this world will drift toward tragedy. This is not going to happen on my watch.

Since that terrible morning of September the 11th, 2001, we've fought the terrorists across the Earth, not for pride, not for power but because the lives of our citizens are at stake. Our strategy is clear. We've strengthened protections for the homeland. We're reforming and strengthening our intelligence services. We're transforming our military. There will be no draft. The All-Volunteer Army will remain an all-volunteer army. We are fighting the terrorists abroad so we do not have to face them here at home. We are determined. We are relentless. And we are succeeding.

Afghanistan is free and is an ally in the war on terror. Pakistan and Saudi Arabia are making raids and capturing terrorist leaders. Libya is dismantling its weapons programs. The army of a free Iraq is fighting for freedom. And Al Qaida no longer controls Afghanistan. We've shut down its camps. We are systematically destroying the Al Qaida network across the world. More than three-quarters of Al Qaida's known leaders and associates have been brought to justice. And the rest of them know we're on their trail.

And one of the reasons we're protecting America better than we have in the past is because we've got a great United States military. I'm proud to be the Commander in Chief of such a fine group of people. I want to thank the military families who have joined us today for your sacrifices. I want to thank the veterans who are here for having set such a great example to those who wear the uniform. And I assure you, we'll keep our commitment to our troops. We'll make sure they have that which they need to complete their missions.

That's why I went to the United States Congress in September of 2003 and asked for $87 billion of supplemental funding. That was vital funding. That was necessary funding. That was important funding. And we received great support. As a matter of fact, only 12 Members of the United States Senate voted against that funding, 2 of whom were my opponent and his runningmate.

Audience members. Boo-o-o!

The President. On national TV, Senator Kerry said it would be irresponsible to vote against the troops. And then when the vote came around, he did the irresponsible thing and voted against the troops.

Audience members. Boo-o-o!

The President. And then he entered the flip-flop hall of fame by saying this—[*laughter*]—"I actually did vote for the 87 billion, right before I voted against it."

Audience members. Flip-flop! Flip-flop! Flip-flop!

The President. He's given several explanations for that vote since, but perhaps the most revealing of all was when he said, "The whole thing was a complicated matter." My fellow Americans, there is nothing complicated about supporting our troops in combat.

Senator Kerry has a pattern of switching positions in this campaign. In the second debate, he said he always believed Saddam Hussein was a threat—except, a few questions later, when he insisted Saddam Hussein was not a threat. He said he was right when he voted to authorize the use of force against Saddam Hussein but that I was wrong to use force against Saddam Hussein.

Yet, the problems with Senator Kerry's record on national security are deeper than election-year reversals. For 20 years, on the largest national security issues of our time, he has been consistently wrong. During the cold war, Senator Kerry voted against critical weapon systems and opposed President Ronald Reagan's policy of peace through strength. History has shown that Senator Kerry was wrong and President Ronald Reagan was right.

When former President Bush assembled an international coalition to drive Saddam Hussein from Kuwait, Senator Kerry voted against the use of force to liberate that country.

Audience members. Boo-o-o!

The President. History has shown that Senator Kerry was wrong and former President Bush was right.

Only a year after the first bombing of the World Trade Center, the Senator proposed massive cuts in America's intelligence, cuts so extreme that his fellow Massachusetts Senator opposed them. History has shown that Senator Kerry was wrong—and we've got to be fair—Senator Kennedy was right. [*Laughter*]

We have big differences about how to protect you, about how to protect America's families. In one of the debates, Senator Kerry said we must be subject to a "global test" before we commit troops.

Audience members. Boo-o-o!

The President. I'm not making that up. [*Laughter*] He wasn't standing that far away from me when he said it. [*Laughter*] The best I can tell, my opponent's "global test" means that America must get permission from foreign capitals before taking action to defend our country.

Audience members. Boo-o-o!

The President. I'll build on our alliances. I will work with our friends and allies to protect ourselves and to protect freedom. But I will never submit America's national security decisions to leaders of other countries.

Senator Kerry the other day said that September the 11th didn't change him much. September the 11th changed my outlook. I remember standing in the ruins of the Twin Towers on September the 14th, 2001. It's a day I will never forget. There were workers in hardhats yelling at me at the top of their lungs, "Whatever it takes." I remember the first-responder who had just come out of the rubble who grabbed me by the arm, and he looked me square in the eye, and he said, "Don't let me down." Ever since that day, I wake up every morning trying to figure out how to better protect our country. I will never relent in defending America, whatever it takes.

Audience members. U.S.A.! U.S.A.! U.S.A.!

The President. We will continue to use all our Nation's assets to protect the American people. We will wage a comprehensive strategy to protect you. Perhaps the strongest asset we have is freedom. See, I believe in the power of liberty to transform societies. I believe free nations do not breed resentments and export terror. Free nations become allies in the war on terror. Freedom will help us keep the peace we all long for for our children.

Think about what's happened in the recent history of the world. It wasn't all that long ago that young girls couldn't go to school in Afghanistan because that country was run by the barbarians called the Taliban. And if their mothers didn't toe their line of ideological hatred, they would be whipped in the public square and sometimes executed in the sports stadium. But because we acted to defend ourselves, because we acted to uphold a doctrine which said, "If you harbor a terrorist, you're equally as guilty as the terrorist," millions of people went to the polls to vote for a President in Afghanistan. The first voter was a 19-year-old woman.

Iraq is a dangerous place today because Iraq is moving toward freedom. There will be elections in Iraq in January. And think how far that society has come from the days of torture chambers and mass graves. Freedom is on the march in this world, and America is more secure because of it. Much of our foreign policy is driven by my deep belief that everybody yearns to be free. See, freedom is not America's gift to the world; freedom is the Almighty God's gift to each man and woman in this world.

These are historic times, and a lot is at stake in this election. The future safety and prosperity of America are on the ballot. But ultimately, this election comes down to who can you trust—who can you trust to provide security for your family? Who can you trust to make sure this economy continues to grow?

If you believe that taxes should stay low so families can pay the bills and small businesses can create jobs, I ask, come stand with me.

If you believe in high standards for our public schools, I ask you to come stand with me.

If you believe that patients and doctors should be in charge of the health care, I ask you to come stand with me.

If you believe this Nation must honor the commitments of Medicare and strengthen Social Security for generations to come, I ask you, come stand with me.

If you believe this Nation should honor marriage and family and make a place for the weak and the vulnerable, I ask you to come stand with me.

If you believe that America should fight the war on terror with all our might and lead with unwavering confidence in our ideals, I ask you to come stand with me.

If you are a Democrat who believes your party has turned too far to the left this year, I ask you to come stand with me.

If you are a minority citizen and you believe in free enterprise and good schools and the enduring values of family and faith, and if you're tired of your vote being taken for granted, I ask you to come stand with me.

And if you are a voter who believes that the President of the United States should say what he means and do what he says and keep his word, I ask you to come stand with me.

In 2000, when I campaigned across the State of Ohio and Indiana and Kentucky, I made this pledge: I said if I got elected, I would uphold the honor and the dignity of the office to which I had been elected. With your help, with your hard work, I will do so for 4 more years.

God bless, and thanks for coming. Thank you all.

NOTE: The President spoke at 8:07 p.m. at the Great American Ball Park. In his remarks, he referred to pro baseball Hall of Famer Johnny Bench; Mary Bunning, wife of Senator Jim Bunning; Ohio State Treasurer Joseph T. Deters, write-in candidate for county prosecutor, Hamilton County, OH; Auditor of State Betty Montgomery of Ohio; pro football Hall of Famer Anthony Munoz; Marty Brennaman, broadcaster, Major League Baseball Cincinnati Reds; entertainers the Gatlin Brothers and the Wil Gravatt Band; and former President Saddam Hussein of Iraq.

Remarks in Wilmington, Ohio
November 1, 2004

The President. Thank you all for coming today. There's nothing like an early morning rally in the great State of Ohio. I can't think of a better place to kick off the last day of this campaign than with the good folks here in Ohio. I want to thank you for coming. Thank you for your support. With your help, we will carry this great State and win tomorrow.

I'm here to ask for your help. You get your friends and neighbors to go to the polls. Find our fellow Republicans, wise independents, and discerning Democrats, and tell them, if they want a safer America and a stronger America and a better America, to put me and Dick Cheney back in office.

Perhaps the most important reason why people ought to put me back in is so that Laura is the First Lady for 4 more years.

I'm proud of my runningmate, Dick Cheney. You know, he doesn't have the waviest hair in the race. [*Laughter*] You'll be pleased to hear I didn't pick him because of his hairdo. [*Laughter*] I picked him because he can get the job done. I picked him because of his experience. I picked him because of his judgment.

I'm proud to be traveling today with Curt Schilling. Everybody knows him as a great pitcher. I know him as a great husband, a great dad, and a man of great character. He's a champion on the field, and he's a champion off the field. And like me, he married well, and I'm proud that Shonda is with us today too. Thank you all for coming. Appreciate you being here.

I'm proud to be here with Michael DeWine and his wife, Fran, the Senator from the great State of Ohio. I'm asking you to make sure you vote for George Voinovich for United States Senator. I want to thank Congressman Mike Turner for being here and his wife, Lori.

I want to thank your Governor, Bob Taft, and your Lieutenant Governor, Jennette Bradley, for coming today. Thank you all for coming. I want to thank all the State and local officials.

I want to thank the entertainment, the Wil Gravatt Band and the Wilmington, East Clinton, Blanchester, and Clinton-Massie High School marching bands. I will try to keep my remarks short so you can make sure you study before class starts. [*Laughter*]

I'm here with a message for the people of Ohio. I know the economy of this State has been through a lot, but we are moving in the right direction. And to do so, we've got to keep your taxes low. And I want you to remind your friends and neighbors that my opponent will raise the taxes on Ohio's families and Ohio's small businesses.

Audience members. Boo-o-o!

The President. In a new term, I will put pro-growth—keep pro-growth, pro-small-business, pro-farmer policies in place. I will defend your deepest values, and I will work every day to make sure your families are safe. And you can count on me. I'm asking for your help, and there is no doubt in my mind, with your help, we will win Ohio again and win a great victory tomorrow.

The election takes place in a time of great consequence. The person who sits in the Oval Office for the next 4 years will set the course of the war on terror and the direction of our economy. America will need strong, determined, optimistic leadership, and I am ready for the job ahead.

The American President must lead with clarity and purpose. As Presidents from Lincoln to Roosevelt to Reagan so clearly demonstrated, a President must not shift with the wind. A President has to make the tough decisions and stand by them. The role of the President is not to follow the latest polls. The role of the President is to lead based on principle and conviction and conscience.

During these 4 years, I've learned that whatever your strengths are, you are going to need them, and whatever your shortcomings are, the people will notice them. Sometimes I am a little too blunt. I get that from my mother. [*Laughter*] Sometimes I mangle the English language. I get that from my father. [*Laughter*] But all the time, whether you agree with me or not, you know where I stand, what I believe, and what I intend to do.

This election comes down to five clear choices for America's families. The first clear choice concerns your family's budget. When I ran for President 4 years ago, I pledged to lower taxes for America's families. I have kept my word. We've doubled the child credit. We reduced the marriage penalty. We believe the Tax Code ought to encourage, not penalize marriage. We dropped the lowest tax bracket to 10 percent. We reduced taxes on everybody who pays taxes. And as a result of these good policies, our economy is growing at faster rates than any in nearly 20 years. Real after-tax income is up by 10 percent, and that's good for America's families. Home-ownership rate in America is at an alltime

high. More minority families own a home today than ever before in our Nation's history.

Ohio's farmers are making a living. The entrepreneurial spirit is strong in America. Small businesses are flourishing all across your State. We've added 1.9 million jobs—new jobs in the last 13 months. The unemployment rate across this country is 5.4 percent. That's lower than the average rate of the 1970s, the 1980s, and the 1990s.

There have been some tough times in Ohio, but last month alone, we added 5,500 jobs. The unemployment rate has dropped from 6.3 percent to 6 percent in this State. This economy is strong, and it is getting stronger.

My opponent has got an economic plan. He's been in the United States Senate for 20 years, and he's voted to raise taxes 98 times. That's five times every year in the Senate. That's what I would call a leading indicator, a predictable pattern. Plus, he's promised about $2.2 trillion in new Federal spending. That is trillion with a "T." That is a lot. That's a lot even for a Senator from Massachusetts.

So they said, "How are you going to pay for it?" He said, "Well, we'll just tax the rich." But that leaves a tax gap. See, you can only raise between 600 and 800 billion. That's far short of the 2.2 trillion he promised. Given his record, guess who's going to have to fill the tax gap? You are. But the good news is he's not going to tax you because we're going to carry Ohio and win tomorrow.

Audience members. Four more years! Four more years! Four more years!

The President. The second clear choice in this election involves the quality of life for our Nation's families. I ran for President to challenge the soft bigotry of low expectations by reforming our public schools. I kept my word. We passed education reforms, good, solid education reforms to bring high standards to our classrooms. Math and reading scores are now up in America. We're closing an achievement gap by helping our minority children. My vision for a new term is to build on these reforms, extend them to our high schools so no child is left behind in America.

We'll continue to improve life for our families by making health care more affordable and available. We'll expand health savings accounts. We'll allow small businesses to join together so they can buy insurance at the same discount that big companies are able to do.

We'll help our families in need. And we'll help our families and patients and doctors by getting rid of the frivolous and junk lawsuits that run up the cost of health care. This is an issue in this campaign. My opponent voted against medical liability reform not once, not twice, but 10 times. He put a personal-injury trial lawyer on the ticket.

Audience members. Boo-o-o!

The President. I'm standing with the families of Ohio. I'm standing with the docs of Ohio. I am for medical liability reform—now. In all we do to improve health care, we will make sure the decisions are made by doctors and patients, not by officials in Washington, DC.

My opponent has a different approach. He voted for education reform, and now he wants to weaken the accountability standards. He's proposing a big-Government health care plan. I remember that debate when he looked square in the camera when they asked him about his health care plan. He said, "The Government didn't have anything to do with it." I could barely contain myself. [*Laughter*] The Government has got a lot to do with it. Eighty percent of the people would end up on a Government program. The wrong prescription for American families is to federalize your health care.

The third clear choice in this election involves your retirement. Our Nation has made a solemn commitment to America's seniors on Social Security and Medicare.

When I ran for President 4 years ago, I promised to keep that commitment and improve Medicare by adding prescription drugs for our seniors. I have kept my word. Seniors are getting discounts on medicine with their drug discount cards, and beginning in 2006, all seniors will be able to get prescription drug coverage under Medicare.

When you're out gathering up the vote, remind people my opponent has got a record on this issue. He voted against the Medicare bill that included prescription drug coverage. He's trying to scare our seniors in this campaign. That's an old, tired practice. But as he does so, I want you to tell your friends and neighbors, he's the one that voted to tax Social Security benefits eight times. We'll keep the promise of Social Security for our seniors. We will always keep the promise of Social Security for our seniors.

But we need to worry about our children and our grandchildren when it comes to the Social Security system. Baby boomers like me are in fine shape when it comes to the Social Security trust. I see a couple of others out there too. [*Laughter*] But the job of a President is to confront problems, not to pass them on to future generations. And that's why I'll bring people together to make sure we strengthen the Social Security system for generations to come.

Fourth clear choice in this election is on the values that are crucial for our families. I stand for marriage and family, which are the foundations of our society. I stand for a culture of life in which every person matters and every being counts. I proudly signed the ban on partial-birth abortion. I stand for the appointment of Federal judges who know the difference between personal opinion and the strict interpretation of the law.

We have a difference of opinion on these issues. My opponent voted against the ban on partial-birth abortion. He voted against the Defense of Marriage Act. There is a mainstream in American politics, and Senator John Kerry sits on the far left bank. [*Laughter*] He can run from that liberal record, but he cannot hide.

The final choice in this election is the most important of all because it concerns the security of your family. All progress on every other issue depends on the safety of our citizens. The most solemn duty of the American President is to protect the American people. If this country of ours shows any uncertainty or weakness during these troubling times, the world will drift toward tragedy. This is not going to happen on my watch.

Audience members. Four more years! Four more years! Four more years!

The President. Our strategy is clear. We have strengthened the protections for our homeland. We are reforming and strengthening our intelligence capabilities. We are transforming the great United States military. There will be no draft. We will keep the All-Volunteer Army an all-volunteer army. We are relentless, and we are determined. We are staying on the offensive. We will chase the terrorists overseas so we do not have to face them here at home.

The 9/11 Commission report said America is safer but not yet safe. We're making progress. Afghanistan is an ally in the war on terror. Pakistan and Saudi Arabia are making raids and capturing terrorist leaders. Lybia is dismantling its weapons programs. The army of a free Iraq is fighting for freedom. Al Qaida no longer controls Afghanistan. We've shut down their camps. We are systematically destroying the Al Qaida network across the world. More than three-quarters of its key leaders and associates have been brought to justice, and the rest of them know we're on their trail.

And we are making progress because we have a great United States military. I want to thank those who wear the uniform who are here. I want to thank the military families who are here. And I want to thank the veterans who have set such a great example for those who wear the uniform.

And I want to assure you, we will keep our commitment that I have made to our troops and to their families.

That's why in September of 2003, I went to the United States Congress and asked for $87 billion of important supplemental funding. That's money that went to our troops in combat in Iraq and in Afghanistan. It was important, really important. My opponent, on national TV, said prior to that vote, "It would be irresponsible to vote against funding for the troops." And then he started to go down in the polls, and he voted against funding for our troops.

Audience members. Boo-o-o!

The President. And then he entered the flip-flop hall of fame by saying this: "I actually did vote for the 87 billion, right before I voted against it." I haven't spent a lot of time in the coffee shops around here, but I bet you a lot of people don't talk that way. [*Laughter*]

They kept pressing him. He's given a lot of explanations about the 87—voting against the 87 billion, but I think the most revealing of all was when he said, "The whole thing was a complicated matter." My fellow Americans, there is nothing complicated about supporting our troops in combat.

The problem with Senator Kerry's record on national security are deeper than election-year reversals. Twenty years—for 20 years, on the largest national security issues of the time, he has been consistently wrong. During the cold war, Senator Kerry was critical, was against President Ronald Reagan's policy of peace through strength. Well, history has shown that Senator Kerry was wrong and President Ronald Reagan was right.

When former President Bush assembled an international coalition to drive Saddam Hussein out of Kuwait, Senator Kerry voted against the use of force to liberate Kuwait. History has shown that Senator Kerry was wrong and former President Bush was right.

One year after the bombing of—the first bombing of the World Trade Center, the Senator proposed massive cuts in our intelligence budgets, so massive that his colleague from Massachusetts, Ted Kennedy, opposed them. Well, history has shown that Senator Kerry was wrong—and we've got to be fair about it—Senator Kennedy was right. [*Laughter*]

During our debates, it became clear we have a different attitude about how to protect American families. He said America must pass a "global test" before we commit force. I'm not making that up. I heard it, and so did you. As far as I can tell, a "global test" means that America must get permission to defend ourselves. I will build on our alliance. I will strengthen our relationships overseas, but I will never turn over America's national security decisions to leaders of other countries.

We have a different point of view about how to protect our families. My opponent said that September the 11th didn't change him much at all. Well, September the 11th changed me. It changed my outlook. Perhaps the best way to describe to you about how I feel is that experience I had at the Twin Towers on September the 14th, 2001, in the rubble. And I remember the workers in hardhats yelling at me at the top of their lungs, "Whatever it takes." I remember the person coming out of that rubble, and he grabbed me by arm. He looked me square in the eye, and he said, "Do not let me down." Ever since that day, I wake up every morning trying to figure out how to better protect our families and our country. I will never relent in defending America, whatever it takes.

Audience members. Four more years! Four more years! Four more years!

The President. We will use every asset at our disposal to protect you. We will wage a comprehensive strategy to defend our country. And perhaps the most powerful asset we have is freedom. I believe in the power of liberty to transform societies. I know that free nations do not breed resentments and export terror. Free nations become allies in the war on terror. Freedom will help us keep the peace we want for our children and our grandchildren.

I want the younger folks here to remember and think about what has taken place in a quick period of time. It wasn't all that long ago in Afghanistan that young girls could not go to school, and if their mothers didn't toe the line of the ideologues of hate that ran that country, they would be taken into the public square and whipped and sometimes shot in a sports stadium. But because we acted in our own self-defense, because we upheld a doctrine that said, "If you harbor a terrorist, you're equally as guilty as the terrorist," millions of people in Afghanistan voted for a President. And the first voter was a 19-year-old woman. Freedom can change societies for the better.

Iraq is dangerous. It is dangerous because that society is heading toward democracy. Think how far that society has come from the days of torture chambers and mass graves. There will be Presidential elections in January. I believe every soul desires to be free. Freedom is not America's gift to the world; freedom is the Almighty God's gift to each man and woman in this world.

These are historic times, and there is a lot at stake in this election. The future safety and prosperity of this country are on the ballot. Ultimately, though, this election comes down to who do you trust—who do you trust to make the tough decisions? Who do you trust to lead this country to a better tomorrow?

If you believe that taxes should stay low so families can pay your bills and small businesses create jobs, I ask you to come stand with me.

If you believe in high standards for our public schools, I ask you to come stand with me.

If you believe patients and doctors should be in charge of the health care, I ask you to come stand with me.

If you believe this Nation must honor the commitments of Medicare and strengthen Social Security for generations to come, I ask you to come stand with me.

If you believe that this Nation should honor marriage and family and make a place for the weak and the vulnerable, I ask you to come stand with me.

If you believe America should fight the war on terror with all our might and lead with unwavering confidence in our ideals, I ask you to come stand with me.

If you are a Democrat who believes your party has turned too far to the left this year, I ask you to come stand with me.

If you are a minority citizen and you believe in free enterprise and good schools and the enduring values of family and faith, and if you're tired of your vote being taken for granted, I ask you to come stand with me.

And if you're a voter who believes that the President of the United States should say what he means and does what he says and keeps his word, I ask you to come stand with me.

Audience members. Four more years! Four more years! Four more years!

The President. Four years ago when I traveled across Ohio, I made a pledge that if I were to be elected, I would uphold the honor and the dignity of the office to which I had been elected. With your help, with your hard work, I will do so for 4 more years.

On to victory. Thanks for coming. Thank you all.

NOTE: The President spoke at 7:22 a.m. at Airborne Airpark. In his remarks, he referred to Shonda Schilling, wife of Curt Schilling, pitcher, Major League Baseball Boston Red Sox; and former President Saddam Hussein of Iraq. He also referred to the National Commission on Terrorist Attacks Upon the United States (9/11 Commission).

Remarks to Reporters on Arrival in Pittsburgh, Pennsylvania
November 1, 2004

We're coming down the stretch, and I feel great. Thank you for asking. [*Laughter*] This is a seven-stop day, because I want to continue telling the people what I intend to do to protect them and how I intend to put policies in place to make sure America is a hopeful place. I'm looking forward to the day. I really am. I'm excited by the size of the crowds. I'm energized by the support that I have received across this country. It's an opportunity to thank people who have worked so hard on behalf of my candidacy and to tell them how grateful I am for all of the sacrifices they have made on behalf of their country. It's also a chance to remind them that when they work hard, that I'm confident we're going to win.

I want to thank you all for working so hard coming down the stretch. I know you're tired, but look at it this way: It's like that marathoner, Stretch [Richard Keil, Bloomberg News]; that finish line is in sight. And I just want to assure you, I've got the energy, the optimism, and the enthusiasm to cross the line.

But thank you all. We'll see you during the course of what's going to be a great day. Thanks.

NOTE: The President spoke at 9 a.m. at Pittsburgh International Airport. A tape was not available for verification of the content of these remarks.

Remarks in Burgettstown, Pennsylvania
November 1, 2004

The President. Thank you all. Thank you all for coming. Thanks for being here. I am so honored so many came out to say hello. I'm here to ask for your vote and ask for your help. It is close to voting time, and I'm out here to ask you to get our fellow Republicans and wise independents and discerning Democrats here in western Pennsylvania to do our duty and go to the polls tomorrow. And remind your friends and neighbors, if they want a safer America and a stronger America and a better America, to put me and Dick Cheney back into office.

Perhaps the most important reason to put me back in is so that Laura will be the First Lady for 4 more years. I regret that she's not here. We started——

Audience members. Aw-w-w!

The President. I understand. [*Laughter*] We were campaigning together yesterday.° She's off on her own for a while, which is wise use of her time. [*Laughter*] A lot of people have come to know her like I know her. She is a warm, compassionate, great First Lady.

I'm proud of my runningmate, Dick Cheney. I really don't intend to insult anybody who's follically challenged—[*laughter*]—but I readily concede that the Vice President does not have the waviest hair in the race. [*Laughter*] The people of western Pennsylvania will be pleased to know I didn't pick him because of his hairdo. [*Laughter*] I picked him because of his judgment and his experience. He's getting the job done.

I want to thank Curt and Shonda Schilling for taking time out of a busy life to come and endorse my candidacy for President. We all know him as a great baseball player. I know him as a great dad, a wonderful husband, a man of enormous character and value. I'm proud to have his

---

° White House correction.

support. And Santorum talks about Shonda lobbying the Congress; she's pretty effective about lobbying the President too. [*Laughter*] I want to thank them for their concern, their care, and their compassion. Thank you all for coming.

I want to thank my friend the Senator from Pennsylvania, Ricky Santorum. I wish Senator Arlen Specter all the best. When you put me in, put him in too. I appreciate Congressman Tim Murphy, his dedication and service in the United States Congress. I want to thank Congresswoman Melissa Hart for her service. I want to thank all the candidates who are here, those running statewide and those running locally. I want to thank my friend Lynn Swann for his friendship and leadership.

I want to thank Mark Wills and Daron Norwood for being here today. Both of them are fine singers.

I want to thank the Wingmen for Bush. They are a coalition of guys I served with. I am honored they're here. I appreciate your friendship. Thank you all for taking time to come.

Most of all, I want to thank the grassroots activists for being here. I want to thank you for putting up the signs. I want to thank you for making the phone calls. I want to thank you for what you have done and what you're going to do over the next 24 hours. By turning out the vote, by finding people who are concerned about the future of this country, we are going to carry Pennsylvania and win a great victory on Tuesday.

Tomorrow the people of this good State and the people of our Nation will be heading to the polls. And I'm excited about election day, and I'm optimistic about the future of this country. You know, one of my favorite sayings comes from a fellow Texan who said this: He said, "Sarah and I live on the east side of the mountain.

It is the sunrise side, not the sunset side. It is the side to see the day that is coming, not to see the day that is gone." During the course of this campaign, my opponent has spent a lot of time talking about the day that is gone. I'm talking about the day that's coming.

I see a great day coming for America. I see a day where prosperity reaches every corner of this country. I see a day where every child is able to read and write and add and subtract. I see a day in which this world becomes more peaceful so our children and our grandchildren can grow up in the peace we all want. I see a day that's better for every American. And tomorrow, the American people have a chance to bring that better day by voting for Bush-Cheney.

The American President must lead with clarity and purpose. The role of the President is not to follow the path of the latest polls. The President must lead based on principle and conviction and conscience.

During these 4 years, I've learned that whatever your strengths are, you're going to need them, and whatever your weaknesses are, people will notice them. Sometimes I'm a little too blunt. I get that from my mother. Sometimes I mangle the English language. [*Laughter*] I get that from my dad. [*Laughter*] But all the time, whether you agree with me or not, you know where I stand, what I believe, and where I'm going to lead.

This election——

Audience members. Four more years! Four more years! Four more years!

The President. This election comes down to clear choices on five vital issues facing our families. And the first clear choice concerns your family's budget. When I ran for President 4 years ago, I pledged to lower taxes for American families. And I kept my word. We doubled the child credit to help moms and dads. We reduced the marriage penalty. We believe the Tax Code ought to encourage, not penalize marriage. We lowered taxes on everybody who pays taxes.

As a result of these policies, our economy is growing at rates as fast as any in nearly 20 years. Real after-tax income—the money in your pocket—is up by 10 percent since I've been your President. Homeownership rate is an alltime high in America, and more minority families own a home today than ever before in our history.

Pennsylvania's farmers are making a living. The entrepreneurial spirit is strong. Small businesses are flourishing all across the State. We've added 1.9 million new jobs in the last 13 months. The national unemployment rate is 5.4 percent. Let me put that in perspective for you: That's lower than the average rate of the 1970s, the 1980s, and the 1990s. And the unemployment rate here in Pennsylvania is 5.3 percent. This economy is strong, and it is getting stronger.

People in western Pennsylvania need to hear this message. I know this State depends on a healthy steel and coal economy. And we will keep taxes low. We will insist on free and fair trade, and we will make those industries strong so the Pennsylvania recovery keeps on creating jobs for the Pennsylvania people.

My opponent has an economic plan.

Audience members. Boo-o-o!

The President. Let me remind you of his history. He's been in the United States Senate 20 years. He's voted to raise taxes 98 times.

Audience members. Boo-o-o!

The President. That's five times for every year he's been in the Senate. I would call that a predictable pattern, a leading indicator. [*Laughter*] And when you couple that with the fact that he's promised 2.2 trillion in new spending——

Audience members. Boo-o-o!

The President. ——you begin to get a sense of his economic plan. That's 2.2 trillion with a "T." That is a lot even for a Senator from Massachusetts. They asked him how he was going to pay for it. He said he'll tax the rich. You have heard that before. You can't raise enough money to pay for 2.2 trillion. There is a tax gap. There is a gap between what he has promised and what he can deliver, and given his record, guess who is going to get to fill that tax gap?

Audience member. We are!

The President. Hard-working people of western Pennsylvania. We are not going to let him tax you; we're going to carry Pennsylvania and win on November the 2d.

The second clear choice involves the quality of life for your families. I ran for President to challenge the soft bigotry of low expectations by reforming our public schools. And I have kept my word. We passed education reforms to bring high standards to our classrooms. Math and reading scores are now on the rise. We're closing the achievement gap by helping minority children. My vision for a new term is to build on these reforms and extend them to our high schools so that no child is left behind in America.

We'll continue to improve life for our families by making health care more affordable and available. We will expand health savings accounts. We will allow small businesses to join together so they can buy insurance at the same discount that big companies are able to do.

We will help our families in need, and we will do something about these junk lawsuits that are making it hard to find good doctors in Pennsylvania. We have a difference of opinion on these lawsuits. My opponent has voted against medical liability reform not once, twice, three times but 10 times as a Member of the United States Senate.

Audience members. Boo-o-o!

The President. He put a personal-injury trial lawyer on the ticket.

Audience members. Boo-o-o!

The President. I understand the problem you face here in Pennsylvania. I've talked to too many ob-gyns in this State that are having problems staying in practice. I've talked to too many expectant moms that are worried about their health care. I'm

standing with the doctors of Pennsylvania. I'm standing with the patients of Pennsylvania. I am for medical liability reform—now. In all we do to improve health care, we will make sure the decisions are made by doctors and patients, not by officials in Washington, DC.

My opponent takes a different approach. He voted for the education reforms but now wants to weaken the accountability standards.

Audience members. Boo-o-o!

The President. He's proposed a big-Government health care plan. I remember that debate when he looked square in the camera and he said the Government didn't have anything to do with it, when he was talking about his health care plan. I could barely contain myself. The Government has got a lot to do with it. Eighty percent of the people end up on a Government-run plan. The wrong prescription for American families is to federalize your health care. He can run from his record, but he cannot hide.

The third clear choice involves your retirement. Our Nation has made a solemn commitment to America's seniors on Social Security and Medicare. When I ran for President 4 years ago, I promised to keep that commitment and improve Medicare by adding prescription drug coverage. I have kept my word. Seniors are already getting discounts on medicine with drug discount cards. And beginning in 2006, all seniors will be able to get prescription drug coverage under Medicare.

My opponent has a record. He voted against the Medicare bill that included prescription drug coverage.

Audience members. Boo-o-o!

The President. And his campaign is trying to scare our seniors when it comes to Social Security. But he forgets to mention that he is the one who voted to increase taxes on Social Security benefits eight times.

Audience members. Boo-o-o!

The President. I have kept the promise of Social Security, and we will always keep the promise of Social Security for our seniors. And baby boomers like me and some others out there I see are in good shape when it comes to the Social Security trust.

But we need to to worry about our children and our grandchildren. That's why I believe younger workers ought to be able to take some of their payroll taxes and set up a personal savings account, an account they call their own. In a new term, I will bring people together to strengthen Social Security for generations to come.

The fourth clear choice in this election is on the values that are so crucial to keeping our families strong. I want the Democrats and Republicans, independents of western Pennsylvania to understand this: I stand for marriage and family, which are the foundation of our society. I stand for a culture of life in which every person matters and every being counts. I proudly signed the ban on partial-birth abortions. I stand for the appointment of Federal judges who know the difference between personal opinion and the strict interpretation of the law.

On issue after—on these issues, my opponent and I are miles apart. He voted against the ban on partial-birth abortion.

Audience members. Boo-o-o!

The President. He voted against the Defense of Marriage Act.

Audience members. Boo-o-o!

The President. There is a mainstream in American politics, and John Kerry sits on the far left bank. He can run from his record, but he cannot hide.

The final choice——

Audience members. Four more years! Four more years! Four more years!

The President. The final choice in this election is the most important of all because it concerns the security of your family. All progress in every other issue depends on the safety of our citizens. The most solemn duty of the American President is to protect the American people. If this country shows uncertainty or weakness during these troubled times, the world will drift toward tragedy. This is not going to happen on my watch.

Our strategy is clear. We are protecting our homeland. Tom Ridge, the former Governor of this great State, is doing a wonderful job. We're reforming and strengthening our intelligence capabilities. We are transforming our All-Volunteer Army. There will be no draft. We are determined. We are relentless. We are steadfast. We're staying on the offensive. We are fighting the terrorists abroad so we do not have to face them here at home.

We're succeeding. Afghanistan is free and an ally in the war on terror. Pakistan and Saudi Arabia are making raids and capturing terrorist leaders. Libya is dismantling its weapons program. The army of a free Iraq is fighting for freedom. Al Qaida no longer controls Afghanistan. We've shut down its camps there. We are systematically destroying the Al Qaida network.

We are making progress on protecting the American people because we've got a great military. We will keep it a great military. And I want to thank those who wear our Nation's uniform for your service. I want to thank the military families who are here for your sacrifice for our country. I want to thank the veterans who are here for having set such a great example to those who wear the uniform. And I assure you, we'll make sure our troops have that which they need to complete their missions.

That's why, in September of 2003, I went to the United States Congress and asked for $87 billion to support our troops in combat. It was a very important funding request. My opponent said on national TV that it would be irresponsible to vote against the funding for our troops. And then, because the political polls changed, he changed his position, and he did the irresponsible thing, and he voted against funding for our troops.

Audience members. Flip-flop! Flip-flop! Flip-flop!

The President. And then he entered the flip-flop hall of fame by saying this—upon his entry, here is what he said: "I actually did vote for the 87 billion, right before I voted against it."

Audience members. Boo-o-o!

The President. I doubt many people in western Pennsylvania talk that way. [*Laughter*] He's given a lot of explanations since that vote, but I think the most revealing is this. He said, "The whole thing was a complicated matter." [*Laughter*] My fellow citizens, there is nothing complicated about supporting our troops in combat.

Senator Kerry's record on national security has far deeper problems than election-year reversals. For 20 years, on the largest national security issues, he has been consistently wrong. During the cold war—I want the citizens of this—of western Pennsylvania to hear the truth here—during the cold war, Senator Kerry voted against critical weapons systems and opposed President Ronald Reagan's policy of peace through strength.

Audience members. Boo-o-o!

The President. History has shown that Senator Kerry was wrong and President Ronald Reagan was right.

When former President Bush assembled an international coalition to drive Saddam Hussein from Kuwait, Senator Kerry voted against the use of force to liberate Kuwait.

Audience members. Boo-o-o!

The President. History has shown that Senator Kerry was wrong and former President Bush was right.

One year after——

[*At this point, there was a disruption in the audience.*]

Audience members. Boo-o-o!

The President. One year after the first bombing of the World Trade Center, the Senator proposed massive cuts in America's intelligence budget, so massive——

[*The disruption in the audience continued.*]

Audience members. Boo-o-o!

The President. So massive that his colleague Ted Kennedy opposed them. Well, history has shown that Senator Kerry was wrong—and we got to be fair—Senator Kennedy was right. [*Laughter*]

We have a difference of opinion. And as you gather up the vote, remind people about this difference of opinion as to how to better secure our Nation's families——

[*The disruption in the audience continued.*]

The President. My opponent suggested America must pass a "global test" before we defend ourselves.

Audience members. Four more years! Four more years! Four more years!

The President. I will always work with our friends and allies, but I will never turn over America's national security decisions to leaders of other countries.

Senator Kerry says September the 11th didn't change him much at all. It changed me. It changed my outlook about how to better defend this country. I remember going to the ruins of the Twin Towers on September the 14th, 2001. It's a day I'll never forget. There were workers in hard-hats there yelling at me at the top of their lungs, "Whatever it takes." I remember the man who came out of the rubble, and he grabbed me by the arm. He looked me in the eye, and he said, "Do not let me down." Ever since that day, I get up every morning trying to figure out how to better protect our country. I will never relent in defending this country, whatever it takes.

Over the next 4 years, we will defend this country. We will use every asset at our disposal, and one of the most powerful assets we have is freedom. I believe in the power of liberty to transform societies.

I want the youngsters here to realize what has happened in a short period of time in Afghanistan. It wasn't all that long ago that young girls could not go to school, and their mothers were taken into the public squares and whipped and sometimes shot in a sports stadium, because the ideologues of hate, the Taliban, had such a dim view of the world.

Because we acted to defend ourselves, because we upheld the doctrine that said, "If you harbor a terrorist, you're equally as guilty as the terrorist," millions of citizens went to the polls to vote for their President. The first voter was a 19-year-old woman. Freedom is on the march. And free societies help us keep the peace we all want.

Iraq is still dangerous. That's because that country is headed toward democracy. There will be elections in Iraq in January. Think how far that country has come from the days of torture chambers and mass graves.

I believe every person wants to live in a free society. I believe mothers and dads want to raise their children in a free and peaceful world. I believe this not because freedom is America's gift to the world; freedom is the Almighty God's gift to each man and woman in this world.

Audience members. Four more years! Four more years! Four more years!

The President. We are living in historic times, and a lot is at stake in this election. The future safety and prosperity of America are on the ballot. The truth of the matter is, this election comes down to who do you trust—who do you trust to make this country secure? Who do you trust to offer leadership and results in a time of challenge to America?

If you believe that taxes should stay low so families can pay the bills and small businesses can expand and create jobs, I ask you to come stand with me.

If you believe in high standards for public schools, I ask you to come stand with me.

If you believe that patients and doctors should be in charge of health care, I ask you to come stand with me.

If you believe this Nation must honor the commitments of Medicare and strengthen Social Security for generations to come, I ask you to come stand with me.

If you believe that this Nation should honor marriage and family and make a place for the weak and the vulnerable, I ask you to come stand with me.

If you believe America should fight the war on terror with all our might and lead with unwavering confidence in our ideals, I ask you to come stand with me.

If you are a Democrat who believes your party has turned too far to the left this year, I ask you to come stand with me.

If you are a minority citizen and believe in free enterprise and good schools and the enduring values of family and faith, and if you are tired of your vote being taken for granted, I ask you to come stand with me.

And if you are a voter who believes that the President of the United States should say what he means and do what he says and keep his word, I ask you to come stand with me.

When I traveled your great State 4 years ago, I made a pledge that if elected, I would uphold the honor and the dignity of the office. With your help, with your hard work, I will do so for 4 more years.

Thanks for coming. Thank you all.

NOTE: The President spoke at 9:38 a.m. in the Post-Gazette Pavilion at Star Lake. In his remarks, he referred to Curt Schilling, pitcher, Major League Baseball Boston Red Sox, and his wife, Shonda; entertainers Mark Wills and Daron Norwood; Lynn C. Swann, chairman, President's Council on Physical Fitness and Sports; and former President Saddam Hussein of Iraq.

Remarks in Milwaukee, Wisconsin
November 1, 2004

The President. Thank you all. Thank you all for coming. Thank you all for coming. I want to thank all the cheese heads who are here. It's close to voting time, and I'm here to ask for your vote and your help. Get your friends and neighbors to go to the polls tomorrow. Get our fellow Republicans to go to the polls, wise independents, and discerning Democrats. And when you get them headed to the polls, remind them that if they want a safer America, a stronger America, and a better America, to put me and Dick Cheney back in office.

Perhaps the most important reason to put me back in is so that Laura will be First Lady for 4 more years. I am sorry that she's not here today.

Audience members. Aw-w-w!

The President. That's generally the reaction. [*Laughter*] She's campaigning. You've come to know her like I know her. She's warm. She's compassionate. She is a strong First Lady.

I'm proud of my runningmate, Dick Cheney. I readily concede that he does not have the waviest hair in the race. [*Laughter*] You'll be pleased I didn't pick him because of his hairdo. [*Laughter*] I picked him because of his experience, his judgment, and he's getting the job done for the American people.

I'm proud of my friend and your former Governor, Tommy Thompson. He's done a great job. He's done a fantastic job for the people. You trained him well. [*Laughter*] And I want to thank Sue Ann Thompson for her sacrifice and for letting—allowing Tommy to work so hard on behalf of the people of the United States.

I want to thank Congressman Paul Ryan and Janna; Congressman Jim Sensenbrenner and Cheryl; and Congressman Mark Green for such a great job in the United States Congress. I want to thank the statehouse people who are here. I want to thank the local government people who are here. Old Scott W. is with us. At least that's what I call him. The high sheriff is with us. Sheriff Clarke, thanks for coming.

I've been most impressed during my travels throughout Wisconsin to have met and talked with a man who will make a great United States Senator, Tim Michels. I wish Jerry Boyle all the best in his run for the Fourth Congressional District.

I want to thank Morgan Hamm for coming today. I appreciate him being here. He's been a great Olympic champ from the State of Wisconsin. I want to thank Keith Tozer and Tom Crean, great basketball coaches here in Milwaukee. I want to thank Brooks and Dunn for being here. I'm so honored they traveled. I can't thank both of the guys enough—and their band. I also want to thank our longtime friends the Oak Ridge Boys for being here. Thank you all.

I want to thank all the people who've worked so hard in this State over the last year to get ready for tomorrow. I understand people have been working hours, day after day. I want to thank you for making the phone calls and putting up the signs and preparing these fantastic bus trips we have taken all across your State. I want to thank you for what you have done. I want to thank you for what you're going to do. You're going to turn out a big vote, and we're going to carry Wisconsin.

Tomorrow the people of this good State go to the polls and vote, and I'm excited about the election day. I'm optimistic about this country and our future. I see a brighter day, a more hopeful America for every citizen.

One of my favorite sayings is by a fellow Texan named Tom Lea. Here is what he said. He said, "Sarah and I live on the east side of the mountain. It is the sunrise side, not the sunset side. It is the side to see the day that is coming, not to see the day that is gone." During this campaign, my opponent spent much of the time talking about the day that is gone. I'm talking about the day that's coming.

I see a great day coming for America, a day where prosperity reaches every corner of our country, a day where every child is able to read and write and add and subtract, a day in which this world of ours becomes more peaceful for our children and our grandchildren. Tomorrow the people of Wisconsin and America have a chance to bring that better day by voting for strong, competent, and principled leadership. I'm here asking for your vote.

The American President must lead with clarity and purpose. The role of the President is not to follow the path of the latest poll. The role of a President is to lead based on principle and conviction and conscience.

During these 4 years, I've learned that whatever your strengths are, you are going to need them; whatever your shortcomings are, the people will notice them. [*Laughter*] Sometimes I'm a little too blunt. I get that from my mother. [*Laughter*] Sometimes I mangle the English language. I get that from my father. [*Laughter*] But at all times, whether you agree with me or not, you know where I stand, what I believe, and where I'm going to lead this country.

This election comes down to five clear choices for our families. The first clear choice concerns your family's budget. When I ran for President 4 years ago, I pledged to lower taxes for America's families. I kept my word. We doubled the child credit to help moms and dads. We reduced the marriage penalty. We believe the Tax Code ought to encourage, not penalize, marriage. We reduced taxes on everybody who pays taxes.

And the result of our good policies is clear to all. Our economy is growing at rates as fast as any in nearly 20 years. We've added 1.9 million jobs in the last 13 months. The farmers of Wisconsin—the farm income in Wisconsin is up. The entrepreneurial spirit is strong in America. The small-business sector is alive and well. The homeownership rate is at an alltime high, and more minority families own a home today than ever before in our Nation's history. The national unemployment rate is 5.4 percent. Let me put that in perspective for you: That's lower than the average rate of the 1970s, the 1980s, and the 1990s. The unemployment rate in the great State of Wisconsin is 5 percent. This economy of ours is strong, and it is getting stronger.

And I have a message for the people of Wisconsin: To keep your economy growing, we will keep your taxes low. We will make sure the small-business sector remains vibrant, and we will make sure Wisconsin farmers continue to make a good living.

My opponent has got an economic plan as well.

Audience member. Tax everything! [*Laughter*]

The President. Let me remind you of his record. He voted 98 times to increase taxes. That's in 20 years in the Senate.

Audience members. Boo-o-o!

The President. That's five times a year. You might say it's a predictable pattern—[*laughter*]—a leading indicator. [*Laughter*] In this campaign, the Senator has pledged to raise taxes on the top two brackets. When you hear a politician say he's going to raise taxes, that's generally a promise they keep. [*Laughter*] He's proposing $2.2 trillion in new Federal spending. That's trillion with a "T."

Audience members. Boo-o-o!

The President. That is a lot. That's a lot even for a Senator from Massachusetts. And yet, by raising the top two brackets, he falls short of the 2.2 trillion. As a matter of fact, there is a significant tax gap. Given his record, guess who he's going to call upon to fill the tax gap? The middle class of our country. We're not going to let him tax you; we're going to carry Wisconsin tomorrow and win a victory on Tuesday.

The second clear choice in this election involves the quality of life for our Nation's families. I believe every child can learn, and I expect every school to teach. When I ran for President, I promised to challenge the soft bigotry of low expectations by reforming our schools. I kept my word. We passed education reforms to bring high standards to our classrooms. Math and reading scores are on the rise. We're closing the achievement gap by helping minority students. My vision for a new term is to build on these reforms and extend them to our high schools so that no child is left behind in America.

We will continue to improve life for our families by making health care more affordable and available. We'll expand health savings accounts. We'll allow small businesses to join together and buy insurance at the same discounts that big companies are able to do. We will help our families who need help. But we will also do something about the frivolous lawsuits that are running up the cost of your health care and running good doctors out of practice.

We have a difference of opinion on this big issue. My opponent has voted against medical liability reform not 1 time, not 2 times, but 10 times as a Member of the United States Senate.

Audience members. Boo-o-o!

The President. And he put a personal-injury trial lawyer on the ticket.

Audience members. Boo-o-o!

The President. I'm standing with Wisconsin's docs. I'm standing with Wisconsin's patients. I am standing with Wisconsin's families. I am for real medical liability reform—now. In all we do to improve health care, we will make sure the decisions are made by doctors and patients, not by officials in Washington, DC.

My opponent has got a different approach. You might remember in one of the debates when they asked him about his health care plan, he looked square in the camera and said, "The Government doesn't have anything to do with it." [*Laughter*]

I could barely contain myself. [*Laughter*] The Government has got a lot to do with it. Eighty percent of the people will end up on a Government plan under his vision. Federalizing health care for America's families is the wrong prescription.

The third clear choice in this election involves your retirement. Our Nation has made a solemn commitment to America's seniors on Social Security and Medicare. When I ran for President 4 years ago, I promised to keep that commitment and improve Medicare by adding prescription drug coverage. I worked with Tommy Thompson. We got the job done, and I kept my word. Seniors are getting discounts on medicine with drug discount cards. And beginning in 2006, all seniors will be able to get prescription drug coverage under Medicare.

My opponent has a record. He voted against the Medicare bill that included prescription drug coverage for our seniors. He's also trying to scare seniors about their Social Security. But he forgets to mention that he has voted eight times to raise taxes on Social Security benefits.

Audience members. Boo-o-o!

The President. He can run from his record, but he cannot hide.

I've kept the promise of Social Security for our seniors, and I will always keep the promise of Social Security for our seniors. And the Social Security trust is in pretty good shape for baby boomers like me and some others out there I see. [*Laughter*]

But we need to worry about our children and grandchildren when it comes to Social Security. The job of the President is to confront problems, not to pass them on to future generations and future Presidents. I believe younger workers ought to be allowed to take some of their payroll taxes and set it aside in a personal savings account, an account they call their own.

The fourth clear choice in this election is on the values that are crucial to keeping our families strong. I stand for marriage and family, which are the foundations of our society. I stand for a culture of life in which every person matters and every being counts. I proudly signed the ban on partial-birth abortion. I stand for the appointment of Federal judges who know the difference between personal opinion and the strict interpretation of the law.

On these issues my opponent and I are miles apart. He voted against the ban on partial-birth abortion.

Audience members. Boo-o-o!

The President. He voted against the Defense of Marriage Act, even though most Democrats supported it. There is a mainstream in American politics, and John Kerry sits on the far left bank. He can run from his liberal philosophy, but he cannot hide.

The final choice in this election is the most important one of all because it concerns the security of your family. All progress on every other issue depends on the safety of our citizens. The most solemn duty of the American President is to protect the American people. If this country shows uncertainty or weakness during these troubling times, this world of ours will drift toward tragedy. This is not going to happen on my watch.

Our strategy to protect America is clear. We strengthened protections for the homeland. We are reforming and strengthening our intelligence capabilities. We are transforming the All-Volunteer Army. There will be no draft. We are relentless. We are determined. We are staying on the offensive. We are fighting the terrorists abroad so we do not have to face them here at home.

We are succeeding. Afghanistan is free and an ally in the war on terror. Pakistan and Saudi Arabia are making arrests and capturing terrorist leaders. Libya is dismantling its weapons programs. The army of a free Iraq is beginning to defend its freedom. Al Qaida no longer controls Afghanistan. We have shut down its camps there. We are systematically destroying the Al Qaida network.

Audience members. Four more years! Four more years! Four more years!

The President. I am proud to be the Commander in Chief of such a great United States military. And we have a great military because of the character of the men and women who wear our Nation's uniform. I want to thank the military families who are here for your sacrifice and your courage. I want to thank the veterans who are here for having set such a great example for those who wear the uniform. And I want to assure our troops and our families that their loved ones will have all they need to complete their missions.

That's why I went to the United States Congress and asked for $87 billion of supplemental funding. This was necessary. This was important funding to support our troops. My opponent said that it would be irresponsible to vote against funding for our troops—until his poll numbers began to go down, and then he voted against funding for our troops.

Audience members. Boo-o-o!

The President. And then he entered the flip-flop hall of fame. And as he entered, he said this famous quote: "I actually did vote for the $87 billion, before I voted against it." He has has a lot of explanations about that vote since then, but I think the most revealing is this. He said, "The whole matter was a complicated matter." My fellow Americans, there is nothing complicated about supporting our troops in combat.

The problems with Senator Kerry's record on national security are deeper than election-year reversals. For 20 years, on the largest national security issues of our time, he has been consistently wrong. During the cold war, Senator Kerry voted against critical weapons systems and opposed President Ronald Reagan's policy of peace through strength. History has shown that Senator Kerry was wrong and President Ronald Reagan was right.

When former President Bush assembled an international coalition to drive Saddam Hussein from Kuwait, Senator Kerry voted against the use of force to liberate Kuwait.

History has shown that Senator Kerry was wrong and former President Bush was right.

Only a year after the first bombing of the World Trade Center, the Senator proposed massive cuts in America's intelligence, so extreme that even his colleague from Massachusetts, Ted Kennedy, opposed them. History has shown that Senator Kerry was wrong—and we must be fair—Senator Kennedy was right. [*Laughter*]

We have a clear difference of opinion on how to best defend America's families. My opponent has said that America must submit to a "global test" before we commit force.

Audience members. Boo-o-o!

The President. I'm not making that up. [*Laughter*] He was standing right about there when he said it. [*Laughter*] As far as I can tell, that means that America must get permission from foreign capitals. I will work on alliances. I will continue to strengthen our friendships around the world. But I will never, never turn over America's national security decisions to leaders of other countries.

Audience members. U.S.A.! U.S.A.! U.S.A.!

The President. We have a difference of opinion about the world in which we live. The Senator said that September the 11th did not change him much at all. September the 11th changed me. It changed my outlook about how—what we needed to do to defend this country. September the 14th, 2001, I stood in the ruins of the Twin Towers. I'll never forget the sights and sounds of that day. I will never forget the workers in the hardhats yelling at me at the top of their lungs, "Whatever it takes." I remember the man who grabbed me by the arm, and he looked me in the eye, and he said, "Do not let me down." From that day forward, I've gotten up every morning thinking about how to better protect America. I will never relent in defending this country, whatever it takes.

Over the next 4 years, we'll use every asset at our disposal to protect you. Perhaps the most powerful asset we have is freedom. I believe in the power of liberty to transform societies. I know that free nations do not breed resentments and export terror. Free nations become allies in the war on terror. Free nations will help us keep the peace we want for our children and our grandchildren.

I want you all to think, particularly the young here, to think about what has taken place in a brief period of time. In Afghanistan, young girls couldn't go to school, and their mothers were taken to the public squares and whipped and sometimes shot in a sports stadium, because of the ideology of hate of the Taliban. But because we acted to defend ourselves, because we acted to uphold a doctrine, which said, "If you harbor a terrorists, you're equally as guilty as the terrorist," millions of people voted in a Presidential election in Afghanistan. And the first voter was a 19-year old woman.

Freedom is powerful, and freedom can be threatening to the terrorists. And that's why Iraq is so dangerous. But we're headed toward free elections there. Think how far that society has come from the days of torture chambers and mass graves. See, I believe everybody deserves and wants to be free. I believe deep in everybody's soul is the desire to live in freedom. I believe moms and dads across this world want to raise their children in a free society. I believe this because I understand freedom is not America's gift to the world; I believe this because I know that freedom is the Almighty God's gift to each man and woman in this world.

My fellow citizens, these are historic times, and a lot is at stake in this election. The future safety and prosperity of America are on the ballot. Ultimately, this election comes down to, who do you trust? Who do you trust to defend the country?

Audience members. You!

The President. Who do you trust to extend prosperity?

If you believe that taxes should stay low so families can pay their bills and small businesses can create new jobs, I ask you to come stand with me.

If you believe in high standards for our public schools, I ask you to come stand with me.

If you believe that patients and doctors should be in charge of health care, I ask you to come stand with me.

If you believe this Nation must honor the commitments of Medicare and strengthen Social Security for generations to come, I ask you to come stand with me.

If you believe this Nation should honor marriage and family and make a place for the weak and the vulnerable, I ask you to come stand with me.

If you believe America should fight the war on terror with all our might and lead with unwavering confidence in our ideals, I ask you to come stand with me.

If you are a Democrat who believes your party has turned too far to the left this year, I ask you to come stand with me.

If you are a minority citizen and you believe in free enterprise and good schools and the enduring values of family and faith, and if you're tired of your vote being taken for granted, I ask you to come stand with me.

And if you are a voter who believes that the President of the United States should say what he means and do what he says and keep his word, I ask you to come stand with me.

Four years ago, when I traveled your great State asking for the vote, I made this pledge, that if elected, I would uphold the honor and the dignity of the office. With your help, with your hard work, I will do so for 4 more years.

Thanks for coming. God bless. Thank you all.

NOTE: The President spoke at 11:38 a.m. at the U.S. Cellular Arena. In his remarks, he referred to Sue Ann Thompson, wife of Secretary of Health and Human Services Tommy G. Thompson; Milwaukee County Executive Scott K. Walker; Milwaukee County Sheriff David A. Clarke, Jr.; Morgan Hamm, 2004 Olympic gold medalist, men's gymnastics; Keith Tozer, vice president of soccer operations and head coach, Major Indoor Soccer League Milwaukee Wave; Tom Crean, head coach, Marquette University men's basketball team; entertainers Brooks & Dunn and the Oak Ridge Boys; and former President Saddam Hussein of Iraq.

Remarks in Des Moines, Iowa
November 1, 2004

The President. Thank you all for coming. Thank you all. Senator, what I have learned is every day is a good day to be in Iowa. And I've really enjoyed campaigning in your State in 2000, now in 2004. And I'm here one more time to ask for your vote and ask for your help. I'm asking for you to go to your friends and neighbors and tell them we have a duty in our country to vote. Go to our fellow Republicans, wise independents, and discerning Democrats. And tell them, if they want a stronger America, a safer America, and a better America, to put me and Dick Cheney back in office.

Perhaps the most important reason why people should put me back in is so that Laura is the First Lady for 4 more years. I'm sorry she's not with me right now. She's working—[*laughter*]—thankfully, for me. [*Laughter*] She gives a lot of speeches, and when she speaks, the American people see a warm, compassionate, strong First Lady.

And I'm really proud of Barbara and Jenna. I want to thank them for joining up. I can't think of a better way to complete the last day of this campaign than to be campaigning with two girls I love. And guess who surprised me today? My sister, Dorothy, is with us. Thank you, Doro. I'm a lucky man. I've got a great family, and I love my family. I'm looking forward to working with them as we complete this campaign.

I've got a great Vice President too. I'm real proud of Dick Cheney. I don't want to offend anyone here who is follically challenged, but I readily concede the Vice President doesn't have the waviest hair in the race. But I know the people of Des Moines, Iowa, will be pleased to hear that I didn't pick him because of his hairdo. I picked him because of his judgment, and I picked him because of his experience. And he's getting the job done for the American people.

I can't tell you how proud I am to be able to work with your United States Senator Chuck Grassley. He's an accomplished, effective Senator for Iowa. He is really good at what he does. I know you're going to put him back into office. He is so good at what he does, I've got a job for him on the South Lawn of the White House—got a lot of grass. [*Laughter*] And we love Barbara Grassley too. Chuck's wife is a fine, fine woman.

I want to thank my friend Congressman Jim Nussle, the chairman of the Budget Committee in the House of Representatives, for coming today.

I want to thank the State auditor here. I want to thank the majority leader. I want to thank the Urbandale mayor. I want to thank all the State and local officials. I want to thank some candidates who are here. I want to thank Stan Thompson, who's running for the United States Congress. He's the right man for the job.

I want to thank all the grassroots activists who are here. I want to thank those of you who have been putting up the signs and making the phone calls. I want to thank you for all the work you've done over the past year to get ready for tomorrow. I want to thank Dave Roederer. I want to thank my friend Becky Beach.

I want to thank the—John Stone is with us. Thank you for coming, John. I'm proud you're here. How about Cael Sanderson, gold medalist—what a great ambassador for Iowa, a great ambassador for the United States.

I want to thank you for all you've done and what you're going to do over the next 24 hours. With your help, with your hard work, by turning out this vote, there is no doubt in my mind we will carry Iowa and win a great victory on Tuesday.

Tomorrow the people of this good State and the people of America go to the polls. I'm excited about Election Day. I'm looking forward to it, and I'm also optimistic about the future of this country. I see a brighter day and a more hopeful day. One of my favorite quotes was said by a fellow Texan named Tom Lea. He said, "Sarah and I live on the east side of the mountain. It is the sunrise side, not the sunset side. It's the side to see the day that is coming, not to see the day that is gone." During the course of this campaign, my opponent has spent much of it talking about the day that is gone. I'm talking about the day that's coming.

I see a day where prosperity reaches every corner of this country. I see a day where every child is able to read and write and add and subtract. I see a day in which this world becomes more peaceful, where we achieve the peace we want for our children and our grandchildren. Tomorrow the people of this country have a chance to bring that better day by voting for strong and principled and optimistic leadership by voting for Bush-Cheney.

The American President must lead with clarity and purpose. The role of the President is not to follow the path of the latest polls. The role of the President is to lead based upon principle and conviction and conscience. During these 4 years, I have learned that whatever your strengths are, you're going to need them, and whatever your shortcomings are, people will notice them. [*Laughter*] Sometimes I'm a little too blunt. I get that from my mother. [*Laughter*] Sometimes I mangle the English language. [*Laughter*] I get that from my father. [*Laughter*] But at all times, whether you agree with me or not, you know where I stand, what I believe, and where I intend to lead.

This election comes down to five clear choices for America's families. The first clear choice concerns your family's budget. When I ran for President 4 years ago, I pledged to lower taxes for American families. I have kept my word. We doubled the child credit to help moms and dads. We reduced the marriage penalty. We believe the Tax Code ought to encourage, not penalize marriage. We reduced the taxes on everybody who pays taxes.

As a result of these good policies, our economy is growing at rates as fast as any in nearly 20 years. Real after-tax income is up 10 percent since I've been the President. Homeownership in America is at an alltime high. More minority families own their home than ever before in our Nation's history. Small businesses are flourishing. We've added 1.9 million new jobs since September of 2003. The national unemployment rate is 5.4 percent. Let me put that in perspective for you: That's lower than the average rate of the 1970s, the 1980s, and the 1990s. Farm income in Iowa is up, and the unemployment rate in this State is 4.7 percent. This economy of ours is strong, and it is getting stronger.

I have a message for the people of Iowa. We're going to open up foreign markets for Iowa corn and other products. We'll promote renewables like ethanol and bio-diesel. We will keep this farm economy strong, and the people of Iowa can count on me to keep my word.

My opponent has an economic plan. I want you to remember he voted 98 times to increase taxes, in 20 years in the Senate. That is five times a year.

Audience members. Boo-o-o!

The President. That is a predictable pattern. [*Laughter*] That's a leading indicator. [*Laughter*] There's not enough to pay for all his promises. He's proposing $2.2 trillion, and he said he's only going to raise the top two brackets. See, that raises about 600, 800 billion, but that's far short of the 2.2 trillion he's promised. There is a tax gap. And given his past history, guess who is going to have to fill the tax gap?

Audience members. We are!

The President. The middle-income families of the America. The good news is, he's not going to be able to tax you; we're going to carry Iowa and win a great victory.

The second clear choice in this election involves the quality of life for our Nation's families. I believe every child can learn and every school must teach. I went to Washington to challenge the soft bigotry of low expectations and reform our public schools. I kept my word. We passed education reforms that bring high standards to the classrooms. Math and reading scores are now on the rise. We are closing the achievement gap by helping minority children. My vision for a new term is to build on these reforms and extend them to our high schools so no child is left behind in America.

We'll continue to improve life for our families by making health care more affordable and available. We'll expand health savings accounts. We'll allow small businesses to join together so they can buy insurance at the same discounts big companies are able to do. We'll help families in need, and we will do something about these junk lawsuits that are running up the cost of medicine and driving good docs—we're driving good docs out of practice.

My opponent and I disagree on this medical liability issue. I see it as a national problem that requires a national solution. He's voted against medical liability reform 10 times, and he put a personal-injury trial lawyer on the ticket.

Audience members. Boo-o-o!

The President. I'm standing with the doctors of Iowa. I'm standing with the patients of Iowa. I am for medical liability reform—now. In all we do to improve health care, we'll make sure the medical decisions are made by doctors and patients, not by officials in Washington, DC.

My opponent has a different approach. He voted for education reform but now wants to weaken the accountability standards. He's proposing a big-Government health care plan. You might remember one of the debates, when they asked him about his health care plan, he looked in the camera and said, "The Government doesn't have anything to do with it." I could barely contain myself. [*Laughter*] The Government has got a lot to do with it. Eighty percent of the people end up on a Government health care plan under his vision. And that is the wrong prescription for American families.

The third clear choice in this election involves your retirement. Our Nation has made a solemn commitment to America's seniors on Social Security and Medicare. When I ran for President 4 years ago, I promised to keep that commitment and improve Medicare by adding prescription drug coverage. With the help of Senator Grassley and with the help of Congressman Nussle, I kept my word. We have modernized Medicare for our seniors. And beginning in 2006, all seniors will be able to get prescription drug coverage under Medicare.

When you're out rounding up the votes here in Iowa, I want you to remember what that Medicare did for Iowa's rural hospitals. You might remember that issue about how the rural hospitals in this State were not being treated fairly. Because of the law I signed, because of the hard work of this

Senator and this Congressman, Iowa's hospitals are now being treated fairly under Medicare.

My opponent voted against that Medicare bill that helped Iowa's hospitals and provided prescription drug coverage for our seniors. He's also said that he's going to do something to protect Social Security, except what he forgot to tell you is that he voted eight times to raise taxes on Social Security benefits.

Audience members. Boo-o-o!

The President. He can run from that record, but he cannot hide.

I know they're trying to scare some seniors, this being election time, about Social Security. But I have kept the promise of Social Security for our seniors. I will always keep the promise of Social Security for our seniors. And the Social Security trust is in pretty good shape for baby boomers like me and some others out there I see. [*Laughter*]

But we need to worry about our children and our grandchildren. We need to worry about whether the Social Security system will be there for them when they retire. That's why I believe younger workers ought to be allowed to take some of their payroll taxes and set up a personal savings account, an account that earns a better rate of return than the trust, an account they call their own and the Government cannot take away.

The fourth clear choice in this election is on the values that are so crucial to keeping our families strong. I stand for marriage and family, which are the foundation of our society. I stand for a culture of life in which every person matters and every being counts. I was proud to sign the bill that banned partial-birth abortions. I stand for the appointment of Federal judges who know the difference between personal opinion and the strict interpretation of the law.

On these issues, my opponent and I are miles apart. He was part of an extreme minority that voted against the Defense of

Marriage Act and voted against the ban on partial-birth abortion.

Audience members. Boo-o-o!

The President. There is a mainstream in American politics, and John Kerry sits on the far left bank. He can run from that record, but he cannot hide.

The final choice in this election is the most important of all because it concerns the security of your family. All progress on every other issue depends on the safety of our citizens. The most solemn duty of the American President is to protect the American people. If this country shows weakness or uncertainty during these troubled times, the world will drift toward tragedy. This isn't going to happen on my watch.

Our strategy is clear. We've strengthened protections for the homeland. We are reforming and strengthening our intelligence gathering capabilities. We are transforming our military. There will be no draft. We'll keep the All-Volunteer Army an all-volunteer army. We are relentless. We are determined to protect this country. We're staying on the offensive. We will fight the terrorists abroad so we do not have to face them here at home.

We're succeeding. Afghanistan is an ally in the war on terror. Pakistan and Saudi Arabia are making raids and capturing terrorist leaders. Libya is dismantling its weapons programs. The army of a free Iraq is defending freedom. And Al Qaida no longer controls Afghanistan. We've shut down camps there, and we are systematically destroying the Al Qaida network across the world.

And we're able to do so because we have a great United States military, and I want to thank those who wear our Nation's uniform. I want to thank the loved ones of those who wear our Nation's uniform, and I want to thank the veterans who are here, who have set such a great example to those who wear our Nation's uniform. And I want to assure you, we will keep our commit-

ments to make sure our troops have all they need to complete their missions.

That is why I went to the Congress in September of 2003, and asked for $87 billion in supplemental funding. It was a very important request. At first, my opponent said, "It would be irresponsible to vote against the funding for the troops." Then his poll numbers began to decline, and he voted against the funding for our troops.

Audience members. Boo-o-o!

The President. And then he entered the flip-flop hall of fame. [*Laughter*] And as he entered, as he entered, he said this: "I actually did vote for the 87 billion, right before I voted against it." [*Laughter*] He's given several explanations on that vote since then, but I think the most revealing is when he said, "The whole thing is a complicated matter." [*Laughter*] My fellow Americans, there's nothing complicated about supporting our troops in combat.

It is important for our fellow citizens to know the facts. See, the problems with Senator Kerry's record on national security are deeper than election-year reversals. For 20 years, on the largest national security issues, he's been consistently wrong. During the cold war, Senator Kerry voted against critical weapons systems and opposed President Ronald Reagan's policy of peace through strength. History has shown that Senator Kerry was wrong and President Ronald Reagan was right.

When former President Bush assembled an international coalition to drive Saddam Hussein from Kuwait, Senator Kerry voted against the use of force to liberate Kuwait. History has shown that Senator Kerry was wrong and former President Bush was right.

Only a year after the first bombing of the World Trade Center, the Senator proposed massive cuts in America's intelligence, cuts so extreme that even his fellow Senator from Massachusetts, Ted Kennedy, would not support them. History has shown that Senator Kerry was wrong and—

we have got to be fair—Senator Kennedy was right. [*Laughter*]

We have differences of opinion as to how to protect the American people. My opponent believes that America must submit to what he calls a "global test."

Audience members. Boo-o-o!

The President. I'm not making that up. [*Laughter*] I heard him say it—[*laughter*]— in the debate. As far as I can tell, my opponent's "global test" means that America must get permission in order to defend ourselves. I will work with our allies, and I will strengthen our alliances, but I will never turn over America's national security decisions to leaders of other countries.

We have a difference of opinion as to better—how to better protect America. My opponent has said September the 11th didn't change him much at all. Well, it changed me. I'll never forget the day I stood in the ruins of the Twin Towers, September the 14th, 2001. There were workers in hardhats there yelling at me at the top of their lungs, "Whatever it takes." I remember the man who came out of the rubble, and he grabbed me by the arm, and he looked me in the eye, and he said, "Do not let me down." Ever since that day, I've gotten up every morning thinking about how to better protect our country. I will never relent in defending America, whatever it takes.

For the next 4 years, we'll use every asset at our disposal to protect the American people. The strongest asset we have is to spread freedom. Free nations do not breed resentments and export terror. Free nations become allies in the war on terror. Free nations will help us keep the peace that we want for our children and our grandchildren. I believe in the power of liberty to transform society.

Think about what's happened in a brief period of time in Afghanistan. It wasn't all that long ago that that country was the home base of Al Qaida, and young girls were not allowed to go to school because the Taliban were so backward and so dark

in their vision. And if their mothers did not toe the line, they were taken in the public square and whipped and sometimes shot in a sports stadium. But because we acted to protect ourselves, because we upheld a doctrine that I laid out for the world that "If you harbor at terrorist, you're equally as guilty as the terrorist," millions of people went to the polls to vote for the President of Afghanistan. And the first voter was a 19-year-old woman. Think about that. Freedom is a powerful force to transform society.

Iraq is dangerous. It is dangerous because democracy is advancing. But think of how far that country has come from the days of torture chambers and mass graves and the brutal reign of a tyrant who hated America. They will be having Presidential elections in January. Freedom is on the march, and we're more secure for it. I believe everybody yearns to be free.

I believe that moms and dads around the world want to raise their children in free societies. I understand freedom is not America's gift to the world, but I do understand freedom is the Almighty God's gift to each man and woman in this world.

My fellow citizens, these are historic times, and a lot is at stake in this election. The future safety and prosperity are on the ballot. Ultimately, though, this election comes down to, who do you trust? Who do you trust to protect you?

Audience members. You!

The President. Who do you trust to spread prosperity?

Audience members. You!

The President. If you believe that taxes should stay low so families can pay the bills and small businesses can create jobs, I ask you to come stand with me.

If you believe in high standards for our public schools, I ask you to come stand with me.

If you believe patients and doctors should be in charge of health care, I ask you to come stand with me.

If you believe this Nation must honor the commitment of Medicare and strengthen Social Security for generations to come, I ask you to stand with me.

If you believe that this Nation should honor marriage and family and make a place for the weak and the vulnerable, I ask you, come stand with me.

If you believe America should fight the war on terror with all our might and lead with unwavering confidence in our ideals, I ask you to come stand with me.

If you are a Democrat who believes your party has turned too far to the left this year, I ask you to come stand with me.

If you are a minority citizen and you believe in free enterprise and good schools and the enduring values of family and faith, and if you are tired of your vote being taken for granted, I ask you to come stand with me.

And if you are a voter who believes that the President of the United States should say what he means and do what he says and keep his word, I ask you to come stand with me.

Four years ago, when I traveled your great State asking for the vote, I made this pledge, that if elected, I would uphold the honor and the dignity of the office. With your help, with your hard work, we will carry Iowa, and I will do so for next 4 years.

Thank you all for coming. God bless.

NOTE: The President spoke at 2 p.m. at the Iowa State Fairgrounds. In his remarks, he referred to Auditor of State David A. Vaudt of Iowa; Chuck Gipp, majority leader, Iowa State House of Representatives; Mayor Brad Zaun of Urbandale, IA; Stan Thompson, candidate in Iowa's Third Congressional District; David Roederer, Iowa State chairman, and Becky Beach, Iowa State steering designee, Bush-Cheney '04, Inc.; entertainer John Stone; Cael Sanderson, 2004 Olympic gold medalist, freestyle wrestling; and former President Saddam Hussein of Iraq.

Remarks in Sioux City, Iowa
November 1, 2004

The President. Thank you all. Thank you all for coming. We are honored to be in Sioux land. Thanks for coming. It's good to be in a part of the world where the cowboy hats outnumber the ties. Senator Grassley is right. Laura and I feel right at home with folks like you all, and thanks for coming out to lift our spirits. We're coming down the stretch. I'm here to ask for your vote, I'm here to ask for your help.

I'd like you to get your friends and neighbors to go to the polls tomorrow. Turn out our fellow Republicans, wise independents, and discerning Democrats. And when you get them headed to the polls, remind them, if they want a safer America and a stronger America and a better America, to put me and Dick Cheney back in office.

Perhaps the most important reason of all that I should be reelected is so that Laura is the First Lady for 4 more years. And there's nothing better than coming down the stretch in a Presidential campaign with two women I love, our daughters Barbara and Jenna.

I'm proud of my runningmate, Dick Cheney. I don't want to offend anybody here who is follically challenged, but I readily concede that Vice President Cheney does not have the waviest hair in the race. [*Laughter*] But I'm confident that you'll appreciate the fact I didn't pick him because of his hairdo. I picked him because of his judgment. I picked him because of his experience.

I'm proud to call Chuck Grassley friend. I know you're proud to call him United States Senator. He's a really fine Senator, and we have done a lot of work together. I—it's important that he remain the chairman of the Finance Committee, and one way to make sure he remains the chairman of the Finance Committee is for the people of South Dakota to elect John Thune to the United States Senate. I know John Thune, and there's no doubt in my mind that he will make a great United States Senator for the people of South Dakota. I want to thank Congressman Steve King from the great State of Iowa for being here.

I want to thank Sioux City Mayor Dave Ferris for being here today. I know the mayor didn't ask me for any advice, but I'm going to give him some. Fill the potholes. [*Laughter*] Mr. Mayor, thank you for your service. Mr. Mayor, I appreciate it.

I want to thank the speaker of the house, Christopher Rants. I want to thank all the State and local officials. I want to thank my friend Ricky Skaggs for being here, and his band. But most of all, I want to thank you all. Thanks for coming. Thanks for what you have done and thanks for what you're going to do as we come down the stretch, putting up the signs and making the phone calls and turning out the votes. No doubt in my mind, we'll carry Iowa and win a great victory in November.

I am excited about this election, and I am optimistic about the future of our country. I see a brighter day and a more hopeful America. One of my favorite sayings comes from a fellow Texan named Tom Lea. He said, "Sarah and I live on the east side of the mountain. It is the sunrise side, not the sunset side. It is the side to see the day that is coming, not to see the day that is gone." During the course of this campaign, my opponent has spent much of the time talking about the day that is gone. I'm talking about the day that's coming.

I see a great day coming for America. I see a day where prosperity reaches every corner of our country. I see a day where every child is able to read and write and add and subtract. I see a day in which this world becomes more peaceful, where we achieve the peace we want for our children and our grandchildren. And tomorrow, the people of America have a chance to bring that better day by voting for strong, confident, optimistic leadership by voting for Bush-Cheney.

The American President must lead with clarity and purpose. The role of the President is not to follow the path of the latest polls. The role of the President is to lead based upon principle, conviction, and conscience.

During the last 4 years, I've learned that whatever your strengths are, you are going to need them, and whatever your shortcomings are, the people are going to notice them. [*Laughter*] Sometimes I'm a little too blunt. I get that from my mother. [*Laughter*] Sometimes I mangle the English language. I get that from my father. [*Laughter*] But all the time, no matter whether you agree with me or not, you know where I stand, what I believe, and where I'm going to lead this country.

This election comes down to five clear choices for America's families. The first clear choice concerns your family budget. When I ran for President 4 years ago, I pledged to lower taxes for American families, and I have kept my word. We doubled the child credit to help moms and dads all across America. We reduced the marriage penalty. We believe the Tax Code ought to encourage, not penalize marriage. We reduced taxes on everybody who pays taxes. And as a result of these good policies, our economy is growing as fast—at rates as any—as fast in nearly 20 years. Real after-tax income—that's money in your pocket—is up 10 percent since I have been the President. Our farmers and ranchers are making a good living all across America.

Homeownership rate is at an alltime high. More minority owns—more minority families own a house than ever before in our Nation's history. The entrepreneurial spirit is strong in America. Our small businesses all across the Nation are doing well. We've added 1.9 million new jobs in the last 13 months. The national unemployment rate is 5.4 percent. That's lower than the average rate of the 1970s, the 1980s, and the 1990s. In the great State of Iowa, the unemployment rate is 4.7 percent. This economy is strong, and it is getting stronger.

I've a message for the farmers and ranchers of Iowa and South Dakota and Nebraska. We will continue to open up foreign markets for your products. We'll promote renewables like ethanol and biodiesel. We will keep our farm economy strong, and you can count on me to keep my word.

My opponent has an economic plan. I want you to remember he has voted to increase taxes 98 times in 20 years as a United States Senator.

Audience members. Boo-o-o!

The President. That is five times a year. You might say that is a predictable pattern, a leading indicator. In this campaign the Senator has pledged to raise taxes on the top two brackets. But that's not enough to pay for his priorities. See, he's promised $2.2 trillion in new Federal spending. That is trillion with a "T." That's a lot even for a Senator from Massachusetts.

But raising those top two brackets, that penalizes your small-business owner, and at the same time, it doesn't even come close to paying for his promises. There's a tax gap. That's a gap between what he has promised and what he can deliver. And you know who usually fills that tax gap? Middle-class families do. We're not going to let him tax you; we're going to win on Tuesday.

The second clear choice in this election involves the quality of life for our Nation's families. I believe every child can learn and that every school must teach. I went to Washington to challenge the soft bigotry of low expectations and to reform our public schools. I have kept my word. We passed education reforms to bring high standards to the classrooms. Math and reading scores are on the rise. We're closing the achievement gap by helping minority students all across America. In a new term, we will build on these reforms, extend them to our high schools so that no child is left behind in America.

We'll continue to improve life for our families by making health care more affordable and available. We will expand health savings accounts. We will allow small businesses to join together so they can buy insurance at the same discounts available to big companies.

We will help families in need, and we will help our patients and doctors all across America by doing something about these junk lawsuits that are running up the cost of medicine. I have met too many ob-gyns across our country that are having to stop practicing medicine because these lawsuits are running up their premiums. And I have met too many expectant moms who are desperately concerned about their health and the health of their little one because they have to drive miles to find a doctor. We have a national problem when it comes to these frivolous lawsuits.

My opponent voted 10 times against medical liability reform, and he put a personal-injury trial lawyer on the ticket.

Audience members. Boo-o-o!

The President. I'm standing with the doctors of America. I'm standing with the patients of America. I am for real medical liability reform. In all we do to improve health care, we will make sure that the medical decisions are made by doctors and patients, not by officials in Washington, DC.

My opponent has got his ideas on health care. You might remember one of the debates when they asked him about his health care plan. He looked right in the camera, and he said, "The Government doesn't have anything to do with it." I could barely contain myself. [*Laughter*] The Government has got a lot to do with it. Eighty percent of the people end up on a Government plan under his vision. Federalizing health care is the wrong prescription for American families.

The third clear choice in this campaign involves your retirement. Our Nation has made a solemn commitment to our seniors on Social Security and Medicare. When I ran for President 4 years ago, I promised to keep that commitment and improve Medicare by adding prescription drug coverage. I have kept my word.

I remember campaigning in 2002 in Iowa with Senator Grassley. I remember all those newspaper editorials saying that Iowa hospitals, rural hospitals were being treated unfairly under Medicare. So I worked with the Senator. Now, Iowa's hospitals are being treated fairly under Medicare because of the work we have done. So are the rural hospitals in Nebraska and South Dakota. And beginning in 2006, all seniors will be able to get prescription drug coverage under Medicare.

My opponent has a record. He voted against the Medicare bill that included prescription drug coverage. He also tries to scare seniors about Social Security. But he forgets to tell you that he's the one who voted eight times to tax Social Security benefits. He can run from his record, but he cannot hide.

I have kept the promise for Social Security, and I will always keep the promise for Social Security for our seniors. And baby boomers like me and some other ones out there that I'm looking at are in pretty good shape when it comes to the Social Security trust.

But we need to worry about our children and our grandchildren when it comes to Social Security. We need to worry about whether or not the Social Security system will be there when they need it. And that is why I think younger workers ought to be allowed to take some of their own pay-

roll taxes and set up a personal savings account, an account that earns a better rate of return, an account they call their own.

The fourth clear choice in this election is on the values that are crucial to keeping our families strong. I stand for marriage and family, which are the foundations of our society. I stand for a culture of life in which every person matters and every being counts. And I proudly signed the ban on partial-birth abortion. I stand for the appointment of Federal judges who know the difference between personal opinion and the strict interpretation of the law.

On these issues, my opponent and I are miles apart. He was part of an extreme minority that voted against the Defense of Marriage Act, and he voted against the ban on partial-birth abortion.

Audience members. Boo-o-o!

The President. There is a mainstream in American politics, and Senator John Kerry sits on the far left bank. He ran run from his liberal record, but he cannot hide.

The final choice in this election is the most important of all because it concerns the security of your family. All progress on every other issue depends on the safety of our citizens. The most solemn duty of the American President is to protect the American people. If America shows uncertainty or weakness in these troubled times, the world will drift toward tragedy. This will not happen on my watch.

Our strategy is clear. We have strengthened the protections for our homeland. We are reforming and strengthening our intelligence capabilities. We are transforming our All-Volunteer Army. There will be no draft. We are relentless. We are steadfast. We are determined to protect the American people. We're staying on the offensive. We're fighting the terrorists abroad so we do not have to face them here at home.

We are succeeding. Afghanistan is an ally in the war on terror. Pakistan and Saudi Arabia are making arrests and capturing terrorist leaders. Libya is dismantling its weapons programs. The army of a free Iraq is defending freedom. Al Qaida no longer controls Afghanistan. We have shut down its camps. We are systematically destroying the Al Qaida network. More than three-quarters of Al Qaida's key members and associates have been brought to justice, and the rest of them know that we're on their trail.

One reason we're succeeding is because we have a great United States military. I want to thank those who are here who wear our Nation's uniform. I want to thank the military families who are with us today, and I want to thank all the veterans here who have set such a great example for our military.

Audience members. U.S.A.! U.S.A.! U.S.A.!

The President. I have made a commitment to our military and to the families of our military that our troops will have all that is necessary to complete their missions. That is why in September of 2003, I proposed $87 billion in funding for our troops in Iraq and Afghanistan. It was vital funding. Most of the people in Washington supported that funding. My opponent, on national TV, initially said, "It would be irresponsible to vote against the funding for the troops." And then his poll numbers went down, and he voted against the funding for our troops.

Audience members. Boo-o-o!

The President. And then he entered the flip-flop hall of fame. And he entered the flip-flop hall of fame by saying this: "I actually did vote for the $87 billion, right before I voted against it." [*Laughter*] I haven't spent much time in the coffee shops around here, but I feel pretty comfortable in predicting that not many people talk like that in Sioux land.

He's given several explanations of that vote since then. But perhaps the most revealing of all is when he said, "The whole thing is just a complicated matter." [*Laughter*] My fellow Americans, there is nothing complicated about supporting our troops in combat.

The problem with Senator Kerry's record on national security are deeper than election-year reversals. For 20 years, on the largest national security issues of our time, he has been consistently wrong. During the cold war, Senator Kerry voted against critical weapons systems and opposed President Ronald Reagan's policy of peace through strength. History has shown that Senator Kerry was wrong and President Ronald Reagan was right.

When former President Bush assembled an international coalition to drive Saddam Hussein from Kuwait, Senator Kerry voted against the use of force to liberate Kuwait. History has shown that Senator Kerry was wrong and former President Bush was right.

Only a year after the first bombing of the World Trade Center, the Senator proposed massive cuts in America's intelligence, cuts so extreme that even his fellow Massachusetts Senator, Ted Kennedy, would not support them. History has shown that Senator Kerry was wrong—and we have got to be fair about it—Senator Kennedy was right.

We have a difference of opinion as to how to protect America. My opponent says that America must submit to what he has called a "global test" before we take action to defend ourselves.

Audience members. Boo-o-o!

The President. I'm not making that up. [*Laughter*] I heard it during one of the debates. As far as I can tell, my opponent's "global test" means America must get permission to defend our country. I'll work with allies and I'll work with our friends, but I will never turn over America's national security decisions to leaders of other countries.

Senator Kerry said recently that September the 11th did not change him much at all. Well, it changed the way I look at the world. I'll never forget going to the ruins of the Twin Towers on September the 14th, 2001. There were workers in hardhats there yelling at me at the top of their lungs, "Whatever it takes." I remember the fellow coming out of the rubble, and he grabbed me by the arm, and he looked me in the eye, and he said, "Do not let me down." Ever since that day, I wake up every morning trying to figure out how to better protect the American people. I will never relent in defending America, whatever it takes.

Over the next 4 years, we'll use every asset at our disposal to protect the American people. And one of the most—one of the strongest assets we have is freedom. Free nations do not breed resentments and export terror. Free nations become allies in the war on terror. By spreading freedom, it helps us to achieve the peace we all want. I believe in the power of liberty to transform society.

Just think about what's happened in Afghanistan in just 3 short years. That country used to be the home base of Al Qaida and its training camps. Little girls were not allowed to go to school because of the barbaric vision of the Taliban. And if their mothers did not toe their line, their ideological line, they were taken into the public squares and whipped and sometimes shot in a sports stadium. Because we acted to protect our country, because we upheld the doctrine that I laid out that said, "If you harbor a terrorist, you're equally as guilty as the terrorist," millions of people went to the polls to vote for a President of Afghanistan. And the first voter was a 19-year-old woman.

It's an amazing story about the power of liberty to transform a society. Iraq is still very dangerous, and the reason it is, is because democracy is emerging, is because the society is becoming free and freedom scares these terrorists. They can't stand the thought of a free society in their midst. But think how far Iraq has come from the days of torture chambers and mass graves and the brutal reign of a barbaric tyrant.

I believe every soul in the world yearns to be free. I believe mothers and dads want to raise their children in a free world. I believe all these things not because freedom is America's gift to the world; I believe it because freedom is the Almighty God's gift to each man and woman in this world.

My fellow citizens, these are historic times, and a lot is at stake in this election. The future safety and prosperity of America are on the ballot. But ultimately, this election comes down to who can you trust—who can you trust to protect your family? Who can you trust to put plans in place to make sure prosperity spreads its wings?

If you believe that taxes should stay low so families can pay the bills and small businesses can create new jobs, I ask you to come stand with me.

If you believe in high standards for our public schools, I ask you, come stand with me.

If you believe patients and doctors should be in charge of health care, I ask you to come stand with me.

If you believe that this Nation must honor the commitments of Medicare and strengthen Social Security for generations to come, I ask you to come stand with me.

If you believe that this Nation should honor marriage and family and make a place for the weak and the vulnerable, I ask you to come stand with me.

If you believe America should fight the war on terror with all our might and lead with unwavering confidence in our ideals, I ask you to come stand with me.

If you are a Democrat who believes your party has turned too far to the left this year, I ask you to come stand with me.

If you are a minority citizen and you believe in free enterprise and good schools and the enduring values of family and faith, and if you are tired of your vote being taken for granted, I ask you to come stand with me.

And if you are a voter who believes that the President of the United States should say what he means and do what he says and keep his word, I ask you to come stand with me.

Audience members. Four more years! Four more years! Four more years!

The President. Four years ago, when I traveled throughout Sioux land asking for the vote, I made this pledge: If elected, I would uphold the honor and the dignity of the office. With your help, with your hard work, I will do so for 4 more years.

God bless and thanks for coming. Thank you all.

NOTE: The President spoke at 4:41 p.m. at the Tysons Event Center. In his remarks, he referred to Christopher Rants, speaker, Iowa State House of Representatives; entertainer Ricky Skaggs and his band, Kentucky Thunder; and former President Saddam Hussein of Iraq.

Letter to Congressional Leaders on Continuation of the National Emergency With Respect to Sudan
November 1, 2004

Dear Mr. Speaker: (*Dear Mr. President:*)

Section 202(d) of the National Emergencies Act (50 U.S.C. 1622(d)) provides for the automatic termination of a national emergency unless, prior to the anniversary date of its declaration, the President publishes in the *Federal Register* and transmits to the Congress a notice stating that the emergency is to continue in effect beyond the anniversary date. Consistent with this provision, I have sent the enclosed notice, stating that the Sudan emergency is to continue in effect beyond November 3, 2004, to the *Federal Register* for publication. The most recent notice continuing this emergency was published in the *Federal Register* on October 31, 2003 (68 *FR* 62211).

The crisis between the United States and Sudan constituted by the actions and policies of the Government of Sudan that led

to the declaration of a national emergency on November 3, 1997, has not been resolved. These actions and policies are hostile to U.S. interests and pose a continuing unusual and extraordinary threat to the national security and foreign policy of the United States. Therefore, I have determined that it is necessary to continue the national emergency declared with respect to Sudan and maintain in force the comprehensive sanctions against Sudan to respond to this threat.

Sincerely,

GEORGE W. BUSH

NOTE: Identical letters were sent to J. Dennis Hastert, Speaker of the House of Representatives, and Richard B. Cheney, President of the Senate. The notice is listed in Appendix D at the end of this volume.

Remarks in Albuquerque, New Mexico
November 1, 2004

The President. Thank you all. Thank you all for coming. We're coming down the stretch, and there's no better place to come than Albuquerque, New Mexico. We are

honored you've come out tonight. Thanks for being here. Laura and I are so thrilled that so many have come out to say hello. You're lifting our spirits.

And we are here to ask for your vote and to ask for your help. Tomorrow is voting day, and I'm asking you to get your friends and neighbors to go to the polls. Turn out our fellow Republicans, wise independents, and discerning Democrats. And tell them, if they want a safer America and a stronger America and a better America, to put me and Dick Cheney back in office.

Perhaps the most important reason to put me back in is so that Laura will be First Lady for 4 more years. And there's no better way to come down the stretch with two women I love, our twins, Barbara and Jenna.

I'm proud of my runningmate, Dick Cheney. I readily concede he does not have the waviest hair in the race. [*Laughter*] You all will be pleased I didn't pick him because of his hairdo. [*Laughter*] I picked him because of his experience. I picked him because of his judgment.

I'm really proud of your Senator, Pete Domenici. What a fantastic man. He's as good as they come in public service. He does a fabulous job for New Mexico, and like me, he married well when he married Nancy.

I'm also proud to know a fantastic Congresswoman in Heather Wilson. I want to thank Heather's husband, Jay, for joining us today. I can't tell you how important it is to send Heather Wilson back to the United States Congress.

It is such an honor to be here with Little Texas and Ricochet. Thank you all for playing. I want to thank my friend Bob Martinez of the New Mexico Fraternal Order of Police. I was so proud to get the endorsement of the FOP across this country. Thank you for coming, Bob.

I want to thank Allen and John and Ken and all the grassroots activists who are here. I want to thank you for putting up the signs. I want to thank you for making the phone calls. *Con su apoyo, vamos a ganar.* Tomorrow we're going to carry New Mexico.

Audience members. Viva Bush! Viva Bush! Viva Bush!

The President. Thank you. I feel so incredibly optimistic about the future of our country. I see a brighter and more hopeful day for every American. One of my favorite sayings comes from a fellow Texan named Tom Lea. He was from El Paso, right across the line, I might add. He said, "Sarah and I live on the east side of the mountain. It is the sunrise side, not the sunset side. It is the side to see the day that is coming, not to see the day that is gone." During the course of this campaign, my opponent has spent much of the time talking about the day that is gone. I'm talking about the day that's coming.

I see a great day coming for this country, a day where prosperity reaches every corner of America, a day when every child is able to read and write and add and subtract, a day in which this world becomes more free and so we're able to achieve the peace we want for our children and our grandchildren. Tomorrow the people of America have a chance to bring that better day by voting for strong, confident, optimistic leadership, by voting Bush-Cheney.

Audience members. We want Bush! We want Bush! We want Bush!

The President. The American President must lead with clarity and purpose. The role of a President is not to follow the path of the latest polls. The role of the President is to lead based upon principle and conviction and conscience. During these 4 years, I have learned that whatever your strengths are, you are going to need them; whatever your shortcomings are, the people are going to notice them. Sometimes, I am a little too blunt. I get that from my mother. Sometimes I mangle the English language. [*Laughter*] I get that from my dad. But all times, whether you agree with me or not, you know where I stand, what I believe.

This election comes down to five vital issues for our families. The first clear choice concerns your family's budget.

When I ran for President 4 years ago, I pledged to lower taxes for America's families. I kept my word. As a result of our good policies, our economy is growing at rates as fast as any in nearly 20 years. We've added 1.9 million new jobs in the last 13 months. Our farmers and our ranchers are making a living. The entrepreneurial spirit is strong in America. Small businesses are flourishing. Homeownership rates are at an alltime high. More minority families own a home than ever before in our Nation's history. The national unemployment rate is 5.4 percent, which is lower than the average rate of the 1970s, the 1980s, and the 1990s. And the unemployment rate in New Mexico is 5.3 percent. This economy is strong, and it is getting stronger.

My opponent has got plans for your family budget, and that's to take a big chunk out of it.

Audience members. Boo-o-o!

The President. He's been in the Senate for 20 years, and he's voted to raise taxes 98 times.

Audience members. Boo-o-o!

The President. That's nearly five times every year he's been in the Senate. I would call that a predictable pattern. I'd call that a leading indicator. And when you couple that with the fact that he's promised to raise $2.2 trillion—he said he's going to pay for it by raising the—by taxing the rich. You can't raise enough money by running up the top two brackets to pay for 2.2 trillion. You raise about 6 to 800 billion. That's way short of what he has promised. I would call that a tax gap. [*Laughter*] And given his record, guess who's going to have to fill that tax gap.

Audience members. We are!

The President. You are. The good news is, we're going to carry New Mexico tomorrow and win.

The second clear choice in this election involves the quality of life for our families. Every school must teach, and I believe every child can learn. I went to Washington to challenge the soft bigotry of low expecta-tions and reform our public schools. I kept my word. We're raising standards. We're raising standards. Math and reading scores are on the rise. We're closing the achievement gap by helping minority children. In a new term, we'll build on these reforms and extend them to our high schools so that no child is left behind in America.

We will work to make sure our families have got good health care by making health care more affordable and available. We'll expand health savings accounts. We'll allow small businesses to join together so they can buy insurance at the same discounts that big companies are able to do. We will help our families in need, and we will do something about these junk lawsuits that are running up the cost of health care and running good docs out of practice.

We have got a national problem when it comes to these lawsuits. I have met too many ob-gyns during the course of this campaign who have had to quit practice because their premiums are too high as a result of lawsuits. I have met too many expectant moms who are desperately worried about whether they're not going to get the health care they need. See, you can't be pro-doctor, pro-patient, and pro-personal-injury-trial-lawyer at the same time. My opponent veto—voted against medical liability reform 10 times, and he put a personal-injury trial lawyer on the ticket.

Audience members. Boo-o-o!

The President. I am standing with the patients of New Mexico and the doctors of New Mexico. I'm standing for medical liability reform—now.

My opponent's got an idea about health care. You might remember one of the debates when he said that the Government didn't have anything to do with his plan. I could barely contain myself. [*Laughter*] The Government has got a lot to do with it. Eight out of ten people end up on the Federal plan under his vision, and that is the wrong prescription for American families. In all we do to reform health care, we will make sure the decisions are made by doctors and patients, not by officials in Washington, DC.

The third clear choice in this election involves your retirement. We have made a solemn commitment to America's seniors on Social Security and Medicare. And when I ran for President 4 years ago, I promised to keep that commitment and improve Medicare by adding prescription drugs for our seniors, and I kept my word. Beginning in 2006, all seniors will be able to get prescription drug coverage under Medicare.

And I have kept the word on Social Security. I remember those campaigns when they said, "If George W. gets elected, you're not going to get your checks." Well, I got elected, and our seniors got their checks. And they will continue to get their checks.

But we need to do something about the youngsters. We need to do something about Social Security—reforming Social Security for our children and our grandchildren. That's why I'm for personal savings accounts. I believe younger workers ought to take some of their own payroll taxes and set up a personal savings account that will earn a better rate of return, a personal savings account they call their own, an account the Government cannot take away. The job of a President is to confront problems, not to pass them on to future generations and future Presidents. In a new term, I'll bring people together to make sure Social Security is sound and secure for generations to come.

The fourth clear choice in this election is on the values that are crucial to keeping our families strong. I stand for marriage and family, which are the foundations of our society. I stand for a culture of life in which every person matters and every being counts. I proudly signed the ban on partial-birth abortions. And I stand for the appointment of Federal judges who know the difference between personal opinion and the strict interpretation of the law.

My opponent has a different opinion. He was part of an extreme minority that voted against the Defense of Marriage Act that President Clinton signed into law. He voted against the ban on partial-birth abortion.

Audience members. Boo-o-o!

The President. There is a mainstream in American politics, and John Kerry sits on the far left bank. He can run from his liberal record, but he cannot hide.

The final choice in this election is the most important of all because it concerns the security of your family. All progress on every other issue depends on the safety of our citizens. The most solemn duty of the American President is to protect the American people. If our country shows any uncertainty or weakness in this decade, the world will drift toward tragedy. This is not going to happen on my watch.

Our strategy is clear. We have strengthened protections for the homeland. We're reforming and strengthening our intelligence capabilities. We are transforming our military. There will be no draft. The All-Volunteer Army will remain an all-volunteer army. We are resolute. We are determined. We are staying on the offensive. We are fighting the terrorists abroad so we do not have to face them here at home.

And we are succeeding. Afghanistan is an ally in the war on terror. Pakistan and Saudi Arabia are making raids and capturing terrorist leaders. Libya is dismantling its weapons programs. The army of a free Iraq is defending freedom. Al Qaida no longer has training camps in Afghanistan. We are systematically destroying the Al Qaida network across the world. More than three-quarters of Al Qaida's key members and associates have been brought to justice, and the rest of them know that we're on their trails.

And one reason we're succeeding is we've got a fantastic military, and I want to thank those who wear our Nation's uniform for your service. And I thank the military families who are here tonight, and thank you for your service to our country.

And I thank the veterans who are here, who have set such a great example for those who wear the uniform. And I want to assure you all, we'll keep our commitment I have made to our troops and their families they will have that which is necessary to complete their missions.

That's why I went to the United States Congress and asked for $87 billion in supplemental funding to support our troops in combat. It was an important piece of legislation, and we got widespread support. As a matter of fact, Senator Kerry, on national TV, at one time said, "It would be irresponsible to vote against the funding for our troops." And then his poll numbers went down, and he did the irresponsible thing. He voted against the funding.

Audience members. Boo-o-o!

The President. And then he entered the flip-flop hall of fame. And as he entered the hall of fame, he said this: "I actually did vote for the 87 billion, before I voted against it."

Audience members. Boo-o-o!

The President. I have spent a lot of time in New Mexico, and I've never heard a person talk that way. [*Laughter*] He's given a lot of reasons why he voted the way he did, but the most telling of all was when he said, "The whole thing was a complicated matter." [*Laughter*] There's nothing complicated about supporting our troops in combat.

We have a difference of opinion when it comes to protecting the homeland. My opponent believes that America must submit to what he calls a "global test" before we commit troops.

Audience members. Boo-o-o!

The President. I'm not making that up. [*Laughter*] He actually said that. I was standing pretty close to him when he did. [*Laughter*] As far as I can tell, that "global test" means that America must get permission before we defend ourselves. Listen, I'll work with our allies. I will strengthen our alliances. But I will never turn over America's national security decisions to leaders of other countries.

Recently, my opponent said that September the 11th did not change him much at all.

Audience members. Boo-o-o!

The President. September the 11th changed me, and it changed my outlook on how to defend this country. I will never forget standing in the ruins of the Twin Towers on September the 14th, 2001. There were workers in hardhats there yelling at me at the top of their lungs, "Whatever it takes." I remember the person that came out, had been in the rubble, and he grabbed me by the arm. He looked me in the eye, and he said, "Do not let me down." Ever since that day, I wake up every morning trying to figure out how to better protect our country. I will never relent in defending America, whatever it takes.

Audience members. U.S.A.! U.S.A.! U.S.A.!

The President. During the next 4 years, we'll wage a comprehensive strategy to defend our country, and we will use every asset at our disposal. And one of the most powerful assets we have is freedom. Free nations do not breed resentment. Free nations do not export terror. Free nations become allies in the war against terror. By spreading freedom, we help keep the peace. I believe in the power of liberty to transform societies.

I want the younger folks here to realize what has taken place in a brief period of time. Think about what's taken place in the last 3½ years of your life. Take Afghanistan. Afghanistan used to be the home base of Al Qaida, where they could train. Young girls could not go to school in that country because the Taliban were so backward and barbaric. And if their mothers did not toe their line of ideological hatred, they were taken into the public squares and whipped and sometimes executed in a sports stadium. But because we acted to defend ourselves, because we acted to uphold a doctrine that I declared which said, "If you harbor a terrorist, you are equally as guilty as the terrorist," millions of people in Afghanistan—because we upheld that doctrine, millions of people in Afghanistan voted in a Presidential election. And the first voter was a 19-year-old woman. Think about that. Freedom is on the march, and we're safer because of it.

Iraq is still dangerous. It is dangerous because that society is becoming more free and heading toward democracy. And think about how far that country has come since the days of a rule of a brutal tyrant who had torture chambers and mass graves, who used weapons of mass destruction on his own people. Freedom is on the march, and the world is better off for it.

I believe that everybody yearns to be free. I believe that mothers and dads want to raise their children in a free society. I believe all this not because freedom is America's gift to the world; freedom is the Almighty God's gift to each man and woman in this world.

These are historic times, and a lot is at stake in this election. The future safety and prosperity of America are on the ballot. The truth of the matter is this election ultimately comes down to who you can trust. Who can you trust to make this country secure? Who can you trust to make this society a more hopeful place?

If you believe that taxes should stay low so families can pay the bills and small businesses can continue to create jobs, I ask you to come stand with me. If you believe in high standards for public schools, I ask you to come stand with me. If you believe patients and doctors should be in charge of health care, I ask you, come stand with me. If you believe that this Nation must honor the commitments of Medicare and strengthen Social Security for generations to come, I ask you to come stand with me. If you believe that this Nation should honor marriage and family and make a place for the weak and the vulnerable, I

ask you to come stand with me. If you believe America should fight the war on terror with all our might and lead with unwavering confidence in our ideals, I ask you to come stand with me.

If you are a Democrat who believes your party has turned too far to the left this year, I ask you to come stand with me. If you are a minority citizen and you believe in free enterprise and good schools and the enduring values of family and faith, and if you are tired of your vote being taken for granted, I ask you to come stand with me. And if you are a voter who believes that the President of the United States should say what he means and does what he says—do what he says and keeps his word, I ask you to come stand with me.

Audience members. Four more years! Four more years! Four more years!

The President. When I traveled your great State 4 years ago, I made this pledge, that if I got elected, I would uphold the honor and the dignity of the office to which I had been elected. With your help, with your hard work, we're going to win tomorrow, and I will carry that honor and dignity for 4 more years.

God bless, and thank you for coming. Thank you all.

NOTE: The President spoke at 6:55 p.m. at the Journal Pavilion. In his remarks, he referred to Nancy Domenici, wife of Senator Pete V. Domenici; Jay Hone, husband of Representative Heather Wilson; Bob Martinez, State president, New Mexico Fraternal Order of Police; Col. Allen Weh, USMC (Ret.), chairman, New Mexico Republican Party; John Sanchez, southwest regional chairman, Bush-Cheney '04, Inc.; and Ken Zangara, New Mexico State chairman, Bush-Cheney '04, Inc., and chairman, Bernalillo County Republican Party.

Remarks in Dallas, Texas
November 1, 2004

The President. Thank you all. Thank you all for coming. I really appreciate you being here. It's great to be back where it all started. Tomorrow my fellow Texans are going to the polls to help us start the next 4 years.

Ten years ago when I first ran for Governor, I had my last campaign rally in Dallas, and we won. Tonight, after six other stops, I'm having my last campaign rally in Dallas, and we're going to win.

I appreciate all your help and all your hard work. And I've got a pretty good feeling that Texas is going to be a red State tomorrow. You're going to start a trend.

I want to thank all our friends who are here tonight. You know, we're blessed by having a lot of friends. I want to thank you from the bottom of my heart for all you have done for us for so many years and what you're going to do tomorrow and for the years ahead. With your help, this will be the beginning of a new term to make America a safer place, a stronger place, and a better place.

I've had a fantastic time traveling our country. I love to get out amongst the people. I love America. I love its citizens. I've been telling people what I intend to do for the next 4 years, but the most—probably the most important reason to put me back in is so that Laura will be the First Lady for 4 more years. She has put her SMU degree to good work.

And I want to thank Gerald Turner and the trustees of SMU and all the SMU students who are here today for coming out to say hello. I'll try to keep my speech short so you can get back and do your homework. [*Laughter*] Make sure you vote. Make sure you go to the polls.

One of the greatest things about this campaign is I've had a chance to campaign with Barbara and Jenna. I love them dearly.

They are fantastic young women. No, you can't have their phone number. [*Laughter*]

I'm proud of my nephew, George P. Bush, and his wife, Mandi. Thanks for coming.

I've got a great runningmate in Dick Cheney. He's done a great job as the Vice President. I'm looking forward to working with him for the next 4 years.

I want to thank my friend Pete Sessions for introducing Laura. It is really important that you send Pete Sessions back to the United States Congress.

I see a lot of friends from the statehouse days. I'm really proud that the Governor of the great State of Texas is with us, Rick Perry. Thanks for coming, Governor. And the Lieutenant Governor, David Dewhurst, is with us. Appreciate you coming. I want to thank all the other statehouse officials. I know the speaker of the house is with us, Speaker Tom Craddick and Nadine. They're from our old hometown of Midland.

I want to thank the really fine United States Senator from the State of Texas, Kay Bailey Hutchison, and the other Senator, who is also a really fine United States Senator, John Cornyn. I want to thank the Members of the Congress who are here, Ralph Hall and Jeb Hensarling, Kay Granger, and Michael Burgess. I'm proud you all are here.

Three candidates for the United States Congress who are here who I proudly support: Kenny Marchant, running for the 24th District; Louis Gohmert, running out of CD 1, Congressional District 1 in east Texas. I wish you all the best, Louis. And I'm looking forward to having a new Congressperson represent me in the Crawford area, and that person is going to be Arlene Wohlgemuth.

I want to thank Toby Keith for being here. It means a lot that he's here. It sounds like he ought to be running. [*Laughter*] I want to thank Tracy Byrd. I want to thank the SMU Mighty Mustang Band. Thanks for coming. I want to thank my friend Chuck Norris, who's here.

Most of all, thank you all for coming. It's been a fantastic day traveling around our country. There's no better place to end it than right here in big "D"—Dallas, Texas.

I understand this about the Presidency: The American President must lead with clarity and purpose. The role of the President is not to follow the path of the latest polls. The President must not change positions for the sake of political convenience. The President must lead based on principle and conviction and conscience.

During these 4 years, I have learned that whatever your strengths are, you're going to need them, and whatever your shortcomings are, people are going to notice them. [*Laughter*] Sometimes I'm a little too blunt. I get that from my mother. Sometimes I mangle the English language. [*Laughter*] I get that from my father. [*Laughter*] But all times, whether you agree with me or not, you know where I stand, what I believe, and where I'm going to lead.

I have been letting the people know what I intend to do for the next 4 years. I'm running to make sure this economy stays strong by keeping our taxes low and doing something about these lawsuits that are making it hard on our small-business owners. I'm running to make sure every child can learn and keep the high standards in our public schools so no child is left behind in America.

I'm running to make sure health care is available and affordable, and to reduce the cost of medicine and to keep good doctors in practice, we've got to get rid of these junk lawsuits that are running up the cost of medicine. In all we do to reform health care in Washington, we'll make sure the decisions are made by doctors and patients, not by officials in Washington, DC.

I believe the President's job is to confront problems, not to pass them on to future Presidents and future generations. We've got a problem with Social Security. Social Security is fine for those who are now on Social Security, and we'll always keep the promise to our seniors. Social Security is okay for baby boomers like me and like some others out there I see. But we need to worry about our children and our grandchildren when it comes to Social Security. I believe younger workers ought to be able to take some of their own payroll taxes and set up a personal savings account, an account they call their own.

Over the next 4 years, I'll continue to stand for the values that are important to our Nation. I stand for marriage and family, which are the foundations of our society. I stand for a culture of life in which every person matters and every being counts. And I stand for the appointment of Federal judges who know the difference between personal opinion and the strict interpretation of the law.

During the course of this campaign, after all the debates and all the speeches, it is clear there are big differences between me and my opponent. He's from Massachusetts, and I'm from Texas. He is a committed liberal, and I am a compassionate conservative. He's voted to cut our intelligence budget and major weapons systems. I am for a strong national defense. He has promised to raise taxes.

Audience members. Boo-o-o!

The President. And that is generally a promise most politicians keep. I'm for keeping your taxes low.

And we've got a big difference when it comes to protecting the American people. The most important job of the American President is to protect the American people. If America shows uncertainty or weakness during these troubling times, this world of ours will drift toward tragedy. This is not going to happen on my watch. We are steadfast. We are resolved. We will chase the terrorists around the world so we do not have to face them here at home.

There are big differences of opinion about how to protect America. During one of our debates, my opponent said that America must pass a "global test" before we commit troops.

Audience members. Boo-o-o!

The President. I'm not making that up. [*Laughter*] I heard him say it. [*Laughter*] He was standing right about there. As far as I can tell, that means this Nation of ours must go to other nations to seek permission before we secure our defense.

Audience members. Boo-o-o!

The President. In a new term, I will work with our allies and I will strengthen our alliances, but I will never turn over America's national security decisions to leaders of other countries.

Now, we have big differences. I have told the families of our military and those who wear the uniform they will have all they need. The military will have all it needs to complete their missions in Afghanistan and Iraq. That's why I went to the Congress and asked for $87 billion for supplemental funding in September of 2003. It was important funding. It was necessary funding for our troops. And we received great bipartisan support. As a matter of fact, my opponent first said that it would be irresponsible to vote against funding for the troops—until his poll numbers went down. [*Laughter*] And then he actually did the irresponsible thing and he voted against funding for our troops.

Audience members. Boo-o-o!

The President. And then he entered the flip-flop hall of fame. And as he entered that hall of fame, he said, "I actually did vote for the 87 billion, before I voted against it." [*Laughter*] I have spent hours in the coffee shops of Texas. I have never heard anybody in this great State talk that way.

He has given a lot of explanations about that vote since then, but I think the most revealing explanation was this. He said,

"The whole thing was a complicated matter." [*Laughter*] There's nothing complicated about supporting our troops in combat. [*Laughter*]

We have a difference of—we have a different understanding about this war on terror. My opponent says September the 11th didn't change him much at all.

Audience members. Boo-o-o!

The President. Well, September the 11th changed me, and it changed my outlook about how to protect you, about how to do my duty to protect the American people. I will never forget the day I went to the ruins of the Twin Towers. It was September the 14th, 2001. There were workers there in hardhats yelling at me at the top of their lungs, "Whatever it takes." I remember a man grabbed me by the arm, and he looked me in the eye, and he said, "Do not let me down." Ever since that day, I wake up every morning trying to figure out how to better protect our country. I will never relent in our Nation's defense, whatever it takes.

Audience members. U.S.A.! U.S.A.! U.S.A.!

The President. Fantastic way to win—way to end what has been a great campaign. These are historic times. There's a lot at stake in this election. The future safety and prosperity of America are on the ballot. The truth of the matter is, this election comes down to who do you trust? Who do you trust?

Audience member. You!

The President. The American people will trust the candidate who can see a better day, who can clearly see that you can't lead this Nation unless you know where you want to lead it. And I know exactly where I want to take this Nation for the next 4 years.

One of my favorite sayings comes from a fellow Texan, Tom Lea. He said, "Sarah and I live on the east side of the mountain. It is the sunrise side, not the sunset side. It is the side to see the day that is coming, not to see the day that is gone." During much of this campaign, my opponent has been talking about the day that is gone. I'm talking about the day that's coming. I'm talking about a better day for every American. I see a day where prosperity reaches every corner of our country, a day where every child is able to read and write. And I see a day, because we spread freedom, that this world becomes more peaceful, and we achieve the peace we want for our children and our grandchildren.

Now, I see a better day. And tomorrow the people of America have a chance to bring that better day to all of us by voting for strong, confident, optimistic leadership, by sending me and Dick Cheney back to Washington, DC.

Four years ago when I traveled our country asking for the vote, I made a pledge that if I was elected, I would uphold the honor and the dignity of the office.

Because of your friendship, because of the hard work of many people here, because of the votes tomorrow, I will continue to uphold the honor and the integrity of the Presidency for 4 more years.

Thank you for coming. God bless. On to victory. Thank you all.

NOTE: The President spoke at 10:57 p.m. in the Moody Coliseum at Southern Methodist University. In his remarks, he referred to R. Gerald Turner, president, Southern Methodist University; Gov. Rick Perry and Lt. Gov. David Dewhurst of Texas; Tom Craddick, speaker, Texas State House of Representatives, and his wife, Nadine; entertainers Toby Keith and Tracy Byrd; and actor Chuck Norris. The transcript released by the Office of the Press Secretary also included the remarks of the First Lady, who introduced the President.

Remarks on Election Day and an Exchange With Reporters in Crawford, Texas
November 2, 2004

The President. It's such a wonderful feeling to vote. This election is in the hands of the people, and I feel very comfortable about that. The people know where I stand. I've enjoyed this campaign. It's been a fantastic experience traveling our country, talking about what I believe and where I'm going to lead this country for 4 more years. You know, there's just something refreshing about giving it your all and then saying the people will make the right decision. And I believe I'm going to win.

Yes, Stretch [David Gregory, NBC News].

2004 Election

Q. Mr. President, I wonder why—why do you believe this election is this close?

The President. Well, first of all, it's been a lot of issues we've debated, big issues of war and peace and the economy. I've got a philosophy everybody understands. I've got a clear view about how to lead. But we'll see how it goes tonight. You know I'm not a very good prognosticator. You're the pundit. You're the person who makes all the forecasts. And we'll see what the people say. That's where we are. Now is the time for the people to express their will.

Yes, Scott [Scott Lindlaw, Associated Press].

Q. Mr. President, any butterflies?

The President. I don't. I know I've given it my all. I feel calm. I feel—I am confident that the people—in the judgment of the people. I'm one of these candidates, I feed off the enthusiasm of the people. Yesterday was an amazing day in my political life, did seven stops. The enthusiasm was contagious. I'm so grateful for the thousands of people who have been working on my behalf and who are praying for me and Laura. It was a great day yesterday, and the whole campaign was a fantastic experience. I'm very comfortable that I got my message out. The people know where I stand. The people know I know how to lead. The people know I have a vision for the future of this country. And we're going to go one stop in Ohio to tell the volunteers thanks for their work, and we'll go back and wait—await the outcome.

Q. Mr. President, what about all the passion in this country—I mean, you have generated so much passion both for you and against you. How do you account for that?

The President. Well, I take that as a compliment. It means I'm willing to take a stand. A lot of politicians take positions, but they don't take a stand. I take a stand, and I tell people what I believe and what I think. These are very troubling times, and I believe a President must lead by being resolute and firm and strong and clear. And the people know that. That's why I'm comfortable about this election. I've given it my all, and more importantly, I have clarified the differences between what I believe and what my opponent believes.

Any other questions besides Stretch? He seems to be dominating. [*Laughter*] Perhaps the rest of you are somewhat groggy. [*Laughter*]

Central Issue of 2004 Election

Q. Sir, what does it really come down for voters when they walk in the booth today? For American voters, what is the issue, what does it come down to?

The President. The issue is, who do you trust? This is a campaign of trust. Who do you trust to secure this country? Who do you trust to lead with firmness and steadfast resolution, protect the American people? Who do you trust to adhere to the values, the values that most people agree with? And who do you trust to keep this economy growing?

Q. And you trust the results will come out tonight?

The President. Absolutely. I trust the judgment of the American people. I love our democracy, and I have got great faith in the wisdom of the people of this country.

Big Stretch [Richard Keil, Bloomberg News].

Closure on the 2004 Election

Q. Does it feel to you like we'll know the results tonight? Or will it be a nailbiter like it was 4 years ago?

The President. Well, of course, these are the pundits—there are pundits and prognosticators like you all. You're doing a fabulous job of speculating what may happen. My hope, of course, is that this election ends tonight. I think it's very important for it to end tonight. The world watches our great democracy function. There would be nothing better for our system for the election to be conclusively over tonight so that—I think it's going to be—so I can go on and lead this country and bring people together, set an agenda, which will be to make sure America is secure, expand our prosperity, and move forward and bring Republicans and Democrats together.

Listen, we're off. I've enjoyed it. Thank you for your coverage.

Senator John F. Kerry

Q. Any words for Senator Kerry this morning?

The President. I wish him all the best. You know, he and I are in the exact same position. We've given it our all, and I'm—I'm sure he is happy, like I am, that the campaign has come to a conclusion. All I can tell you is I know that I've put my full amount of energy in this campaign, and I've enjoyed it. And I am enthused, and I have been uplifted by the spirit of the—of our supporters and by the prayers of our supporters.

Anyway, thank you all very much.

NOTE: The President spoke at 7:42 a.m. at the Crawford Fire Station. A tape was not available for verification of the content of these remarks.

Remarks to Campaign Volunteers and an Exchange With Reporters in Columbus, Ohio
November 2, 2004

The President. Thank you all for doing this. Listen, we've come to thank our volunteers here in Ohio. They represent thousands of people all across the country who are making the calls and turning out the vote. I have been uplifted by the fact that thousands of people are working on my behalf and the fact that thousands pray for me and Laura and our country.

One of the best ways to help send a signal about how appreciative I am is to come and thank people in person. Obviously, Ohio is an important State. It's a State that we intend to carry. I know we've got a lot of work to do. There's a lot of people, as you can tell, in this building, working hard in Columbus, and they're working hard all across the State of Ohio. So this is an exciting time. The polls will be closing in 5 or 6 hours—however long it is. [*Laughter*] And I'm confident we'll carry Ohio, and I'm confident we'll carry the Nation. And I look forward to leading this Nation for 4 more years. I'm running because I've got more to do, more to— more work to be done to keep this country secure, more work to be done to make sure prosperity reaches every corner of the land.

I want to thank all our supporters here in Ohio for their hard work.

Legal Issues

Q. Are you getting updates on legal wrangling out there on the plain?

The President. No, I really haven't. Call my lawyer. [*Laughter*]

Turnout for the 2004 Election

Q. Sir, does a big turnout help both sides, and should it?

The President. Listen, I am for a turnout as big as possible. I believe everybody should vote. We have a duty in this country to vote. I hope every citizen in Ohio and elsewhere does their duty. And I think it's—and I think we'll have a good turnout, and I will be grateful if there's a big turnout. I think it's good for our system.

Election Outcome

Q. Is it going to be a divided country, no matter what happens, if it's a close election?

The President. Oh, you know, I was asked that question by another one of the pundits earlier, trying to guess about the outcome of the election. You need to talk to the experts. I can just tell you what I've seen. I've seen enthusiasm, a willingness for people to put in extra hours of work. And we'll find out how it goes tonight. This election is in the best of hands: It's in the hands of the voters of Ohio and voters all around the country.

Q. Sir, you may think you're no pundit, but you've clearly paid pretty close attention. Give us a sense of how involved you are in tracking the numbers and voter turnout and——

The President. Well, David [David Gregory, NBC News], since I last talked to you, which was outside the voting booth in Crawford—[*laughter*]—which was a couple of hours ago, I've had a couple of cups of coffee. I spent some quality time with my wife. I am going to run this race out to its fullest. I will be able to—both of us will be able to say that we campaigned as hard as we possibly could. I have made the differences as clear as possible about why I think I am the best leader for the country for the next 4 years. You know, we'll find out tonight what the American people think, and I'm looking forward to it.

Thank you all.

NOTE: The President spoke at 11:42 a.m. at the Ohio Bush-Cheney '04 campaign headquarters. A tape was not available for verification of the content of these remarks.

Remarks in a Victory Celebration
November 3, 2004

Thank you all. Thank you all for coming. We had a long night and a great night. The voters turned out in record numbers and delivered an historic victory.

Earlier today, Senator Kerry called with his congratulations. We had a really good phone call. He was very gracious. Senator Kerry waged a spirited campaign, and he and his supporters can be proud of their efforts. Laura and I wish Senator Kerry and Teresa and their whole family all our best wishes.

America has spoken, and I'm humbled by the trust and the confidence of my fellow citizens. With that trust comes a duty to serve all Americans, and I will do my best to fulfill that duty every day as your President.

There are many people to thank, and my family comes first. Laura is the love of my life. [*Applause*] I'm glad you love her too. [*Laughter*] I want to thank our daughters, who joined their dad for his last campaign. I appreciate the hard work of my sister and my brothers. I especially want to thank my parents for their loving support.

I'm grateful to the Vice President and Lynne and their daughters, who have worked so hard and been such a vital part of our team. The Vice President serves America with wisdom and honor, and I'm proud to serve beside him.

I want to thank my superb campaign team. I want to thank you all for your hard work. I was impressed every day by how hard and how skillful our team was. I want to thank Marc, Chairman Marc Racicot, and the campaign manager, Ken Mehlman, and the architect, Karl Rove. I want to thank Ed Gillespie for leading our party so well.

I want to thank the thousands of our supporters across our country. I want to thank you for your hugs on the ropelines. I want to thank you for your prayers on the ropelines. I want to thank you for your kind words on the ropelines. I want to thank you for everything you did to make the calls and to put up the signs, to talk to your neighbors, and to get out the vote. And because you did the incredible work, we are celebrating today.

There's an old saying, "Do not pray for tasks equal to your powers. Pray for powers equal to your tasks." In 4 historic years, America has been given great tasks and faced them with strength and courage. Our people have restored the vigor of this economy and shown resolve and patience in a new kind of war. Our military has brought justice to the enemy and honor to America. Our Nation has defended itself and served the freedom of all mankind. I'm proud to lead such an amazing country, and I'm proud to lead it forward.

Because we have done the hard work, we are entering a season of hope. We'll continue our economic progress. We'll reform our outdated Tax Code. We'll strengthen the Social Security for the next generation. We'll make public schools all they can be. And we will uphold our deepest values of family and faith.

We will help the emerging democracies of Iraq and Afghanistan so they can grow in strength and defend their freedom. And then our service men and women will come home with the honor they have earned. With good allies at our side, we will fight this war on terror with every resource of our national power so our children can live in freedom and in peace.

Reaching these goals will require the broad support of Americans. So today I want to speak to every person who voted for my opponent: To make this Nation stronger and better, I will need your support and I will work to earn it. I will do all I can do to deserve your trust. A new term is a new opportunity to reach out to the whole Nation. We have one country, one Constitution, and one future that binds us. And when we come together and work together, there is no limit to the greatness of America.

Let me close with a word to the people of the State of Texas. We have known each other the longest, and you started me on this journey. On the open plains of Texas, I first learned the character of our country, sturdy and honest and as hopeful as the break of day. I will always be grateful to the good people of my State. And whatever the road that lies ahead, that road will take me home.

The campaign has ended, and the United States of America goes forward with confidence and faith. I see a great day coming for our country, and I am eager for the work ahead.

God bless you, and may God bless America.

NOTE: The President spoke at 3:08 p.m. at the Ronald Reagan Building and International Trade Center. In his remarks, he referred to Marc Racicot, campaign chairman, and Ken Mehlman, campaign manager, Bush-Cheney '04, Inc.; and Edward W. Gillespie, chairman, Republican National Committee. The Office of the Press Secretary also released a Spanish language transcript of these remarks.

Remarks Following a Cabinet Meeting
November 4, 2004

I just met with my Cabinet. I am proud of every person here. They've done a great job for the country. I reminded them that even though our election just ended, we've still got work to do. I talked about an agenda that we will complete and an agenda that we will take forward.

I made it clear to them I was glad the election was over and reminded them that we're here for a reason. And to a person, they understand that it's such an honor to serve America, it's a privilege to sit around

this table, and that we will all continue to do the people's business.

But anyway, I want to thank them all for their hard work. I am—when I told the people that I put together a fantastic group of men and women, I meant every word of that, and I want to thank them all for their service.

Thank you.

NOTE: The President spoke at 10:48 a.m. in the Cabinet Room at the White House. The

Office of the Press Secretary also released a Spanish language transcript of these remarks. A tape was not available for verification of the content of these remarks.

The President's News Conference
November 4, 2004

The President. Thank you all. Please be seated. Yesterday I pledged to reach out to the whole Nation, and today I'm proving that I'm willing to reach out to everybody by including the White House press corps. [*Laughter*]

This week the voters of America set the direction of our Nation for the next 4 years. I'm honored by the support of my fellow citizens, and I'm ready for the job.

We are fighting a continuing war on terror, and every American has a stake in the outcome of this war. Republicans, Democrats, and independents all love our country, and together we'll protect the American people. We will preserve—we will persevere until the enemy is defeated. We will stay strong and resolute. We have a duty, a solemn duty to protect the American people, and we will.

Every civilized country also has a stake in the outcome of this war. Whatever our past disagreements, we share a common enemy, and we have common duties to protect our peoples, to confront disease and hunger and poverty in troubled regions of the world. I'll continue to reach out to our friends and allies, our partners in the EU and NATO, to promote development and progress, to defeat the terrorists, and to encourage freedom and democracy as alternatives to tyranny and terror.

I also look forward to working with the present Congress and the new Congress that will arrive in January. I congratulate the men and women who have just been elected to the House and the Senate. I will join with old friends and new friends to make progress for all Americans.

Congress will return later this month to finish this current session. I urge Members to pass the appropriations bill that remain, showing spending discipline while focusing on our Nation's priorities. Our Government also needs the very best intelligence, especially in a time of war. So I urge the Congress to pass an effective intelligence reform bill that I can sign into law.

The new Congress that begins its work next year will have serious responsibilities and historic opportunities. To accelerate the momentum of this economy and to keep creating jobs, we must take practical measures to help our job creators, the entrepreneurs and the small-business owners. We must confront the frivolous lawsuits that are driving up the cost of health care and hurting doctors and patients. We must continue the work of education reform to bring high standards and accountability not just to our elementary and secondary schools but to our high schools as well.

We must reform our complicated and outdated Tax Code. We need to get rid of the needless paperwork that makes our economy—that is a drag on our economy, to make sure our economy is the most competitive in the world.

We must show our leadership by strengthening Social Security for our children and our grandchildren. This is more than a problem to be solved. It is an opportunity to help millions of our fellow citizens find security and independence that comes from owning something, from ownership.

In the election of 2004, large issues were set before our country. They were discussed every day on the campaign. With the campaign over, Americans are expecting a bipartisan effort and results. I'll reach out to everyone who shares our goals. And I'm eager to start the work ahead. I'm looking forward to serving this country for 4 more years.

I want to thank you all for your hard work in the campaign. I told you that the other day, and you probably thought I was just seeking votes. [*Laughter*] But now that you voted, I really meant it. I appreciate the hard work of the press corps. We all put in long hours, and you're away from your families for a long period of time. But the country is better off when we have a vigorous and free press covering our elections. And thanks for your work. Without overpandering, I'll answer a few questions. [*Laughter*]

Hunt [Terence Hunt, Associated Press].

Middle East/Iraq

Q. Mr. President, thank you. As you look at your second term, how much is the war in Iraq going to cost? Do you intend to send more troops or bring troops home? And in the Middle East, more broadly, do you agree with Tony Blair that revitalizing the Middle East peace process is the single most pressing political issue facing the world?

The President. Now that I've got the will of the people at my back, I'm going to start enforcing the one-question rule. That was three questions. [*Laughter*]

I'll start with Tony Blair's comments. I agree with him that the Middle East peace is a very important part of a peaceful world. I have been working on Middle Eastern peace ever since I've been the President. I've laid down some—a very hopeful strategy on—in June of 2002, and my hope is that we will make good progress. I think it's very important for our friends the Israelis to have a peaceful Palestinian state living on their border. And it's very important for the Palestinian people to have a peaceful, hopeful future. That's why I articulated a two-state vision in that Rose Garden speech. I meant it when I said it, and I mean it now.

What was the other part of your question?

Q. Iraq.

The President. Oh, Iraq, yes. Listen, we will work with the Allawi Government to achieve our objective, which is elections, on the path to stability, and we'll continue to train the troops. Our commanders will have that which they need to complete their missions.

And in terms of the cost, I—we'll work with OMB and the Defense Department to bring forth to Congress a realistic assessment of what the cost will be.

Supreme Court Nominations/The Cabinet

Q. Thank you, Mr. President. How will you go about bringing people together? Will you seek a consensus candidate for the Supreme Court if there's an opening? Will you bring some Democrats into your Cabinet?

The President. Again, he violated the one-question rule right off the bat. Obviously, you didn't listen to the will of the people. But first of all, there's no vacancy for the Supreme Court, and I will deal with a vacancy when there is one. And I told the people on the campaign trail that I'll pick somebody who knows the difference between personal opinion and the strict interpretation of the law. You might have heard that several times. I meant what I said. And if people are interested in knowing the kind of judges I'll pick, look at the record. I've sent up a lot of judges, well-qualified people who know the law, who represent a judicial temperament that I agree with, and who are qualified to hold the bench.

The second part of your two-part question?

Q. Any Democrats to your Cabinet, by any chance?

The President. I haven't made any decisions on the Cabinet yet.

Bipartisanship

Q. How else will you bring people together?

The President. We'll put out an agenda that everybody understands and work with people to achieve the agenda. Democrats want a free and peaceful world, and we'll—and right away, right after September the 11th we worked very closely together to secure our country. There is a common ground to be had when it comes to a foreign policy that says the most important objective is to protect the American people and spread freedom and democracy. There's common ground when it comes to making sure the intelligence services are able to provide good, actionable intelligence to protect our people. It's not a Republican issue. It's a Republican and Democrat issue. So I'm—plenty of places for us to work together.

All right, Gregory [David Gregory, NBC News].

War on Terror/Promoting Democracy

Q. Thank you, Mr. President. On foreign policy, more broadly, do you believe that America has an image problem in the world right now because of your efforts in response to the 9/11 attacks? And, as you talked down the stretch about building alliances, talk about what you'll do to build on those alliances and to deal with these image problems, particularly in the Islamic world.

The President. I appreciate that. Listen, I've made some very hard decisions, decisions to protect ourselves, decisions to spread peace and freedom. And I understand that in certain capitals and certain countries, those decisions were not popular.

You know, you said—you asked me to put that in the context of the response on September the 11th. The first response, of course, was chasing down the terror networks, which we will continue to do. And we've got great response around the world in order to do that. There's over 90 nations involved with sharing information, finding terrorists, and bringing them to justice. That is a broad coalition, and we'll continue to strengthen it.

I laid out a doctrine, David, that said, "If you harbor a terrorist, you're equally as guilty as the terrorists," and that doctrine was ignored by the Taliban, and we removed the Taliban. And I fully understand some people didn't agree with that decision. But I believe that when the American President speaks, he'd better mean what he says in order to keep the world peaceful. And I believe we have a solemn duty, whether or not people agree with it or not, to protect the American people. And the Taliban and their harboring of Al Qaida represented a direct threat to the American people.

And of course, then the Iraq issue is one that people disagreed with. And there's no need to rehash my case, but I did so, I made the decision I made, in order to protect our country, first and foremost. I will continue to do that as the President. But as I do so, I will reach out to others and explain why I make the decisions I make.

There is a certain attitude in the world, by some, that says that it's a waste of time to try to promote free societies in parts of the world. I've heard that criticism. Remember, I went to London to talk about our vision of spreading freedom throughout the greater Middle East. And I fully understand that that might rankle some and be viewed by some as folly. I just strongly disagree with those who do not see the wisdom of trying to promote free societies around the world.

If we are interested in protecting our country for the long term, the best way to do so is to promote freedom and democracy. And I simply do not agree with those who either say overtly or believe that certain societies cannot be free. It's just not a part of my thinking. And that's why during the course of the campaign, I was—I believe I was able to connect, at least with those who were there, in explaining my policy, when I talked about the free elections in Afghanistan.

There were—there was doubt about whether or not those elections would go forward. I'm not suggesting any of you here expressed skepticism, but there was. There was deep skepticism, and because there is a attitude among some that certain people may never be free—they just don't long to be free or incapable of running an election, and I disagree with that. And the Afghan people, by going to the polls in the millions, proved that this administration's faith in freedom to change people's habits is worthy. And that will be a central part of my foreign policy. And I've got work to do to explain to people about why that is a central part of our foreign policy. I've been doing that for 4 years.

But if you do not believe people can be free and can self-govern, then all of a sudden the two-state solution in the Middle East becomes a moot point, invalid. If you're willing to condemn a group of people to a system of government that hasn't worked, then you'll never be able to achieve the peace. You cannot lead this world and our country to a better tomorrow unless you see a better—unless you have a vision of a better tomorrow. And I've got one, based upon a great faith that people do want to be free and live in democracy.

John [John Roberts, CBS News], and then I'll get to Terry [Terry Moran, ABC News]. No followups today, Gregory.

Q. Thank you, sir.

The President. I can see one—yes.

Troop Levels in Iraq

Q. Would you like it? Now that the political volatility is off the issue because the election is over, I'd like to ask you about troop levels in Iraq in the next couple of months leading up to elections. The Pentagon already has a plan to extend tours of duty for some 6,500 U.S. troops. How many more will be needed to provide security in Iraq for elections, seeing as how the Iraqi troops that you're trying to train up are pretty slow coming on line?

The President. Yes, first of all, the—we are making good progress in training the Iraqi troops. There will be 125,000 of them trained by election time.

Secondly, I have yet to—I have not sat down with our Secretary of Defense talking about troop levels. I read some reports during the course of the campaign where some were speculating in the press corps about the number of troops needed to protect elections. That has not been brought to my attention yet. And so I would caution you that what you have either read about or reported was pure speculation thus far. These elections are important, and we will respond, John, to requests of our commanders on the ground. And I have yet to hear from our commanders on the ground that they need more troops.

Terry.

Religious Values

Q. Mr. President, your victory at the polls came about in part because of strong support from people of faith, in particular, Christian evangelicals and Pentecostals and others. And Senator Kerry drew some of his strongest support from those who do not attend religious services. What do you make of this religious divide, it seems, becoming a political divide in this country? And what do you say to those who are concerned about the role of a faith they do not share in public life and in your policies?

The President. Yes. My answer to people is, I will be your President regardless of your faith, and I don't expect you to agree with me necessarily on religion. As a matter of fact, no President should ever try to impose religion on our society. A great— the great tradition of America is one where people can worship the way they want to worship. And if they choose not to worship, they're just as patriotic as your neighbor. That is an essential part of why we are a great nation. And I am glad people of faith voted in this election. I'm glad—I appreciate all people who voted. I don't think you ought to read anything into the politics, the moment, about whether or not this Nation will become a divided nation over religion. I think the great thing that unites us is the fact you can worship freely if you choose, and if you—you don't have to worship. And if you're a Jew or a Christian or a Muslim, you're equally American. That is such a wonderful aspect of our society. And it is strong today, and it will be strong tomorrow.

Jim [Jim Angle, FOX News].

Social Security Reform

Q. Thank you, sir. Mr. President, you talked once again this morning about private accounts in Social Security. During the campaign, you were accused of planning to privatize the entire system. It has been something you've discussed for some time. You've lost some of the key Democratic proponents, such as Pat Moynihan and Bob Kerrey, in the Congress. How will you proceed now with one of the key problems, which is the transition cost—which some say is as much as $2 trillion—how will you proceed on that? And how soon?

The President. Well, first, I made Social Security an issue. For those of you who had to suffer through my speeches on a daily basis, for those of you who actually listened to my speeches on a daily basis, you might remember, every speech I talked about the duty of an American President to lead. And we have—we must lead on Social Security because the system is not going to be whole for our children and our grandchildren.

And so the answer to your second question is, we'll start on Social Security now. We'll start bringing together those in Congress who agree with my assessment that we need to work together. We've got a good blueprint, a good go-by. You mentioned Senator Moynihan. I had asked him prior to his passing to chair a committee of notable Americans to come up with some ideas on Social Security, and they did so. And it's a good place for Members of Congress to start.

The President must have the will to take on the issue not only in the campaign but now that I'm elected. And this will—reforming Social Security will be a priority of my administration. Obviously, if it were easy, it would have already been done. And this is going to be hard work to bring people together and to make—to convince the Congress to move forward, and there are going to be costs. But the cost of doing nothing is insignificant to—is much greater than the cost of reforming the system today. That was the case I made on the campaign trail, and I was earnest about getting something done. And as a matter of fact, I talked to members of my staff today, as we're beginning to plan to—the strategy to move agendas forward, about how to do this and do it effectively.

Q. If I could, Mr. President——

The President. Yes—no, no, you're violating the followup rule. It would hurt Gregory's feelings.

King [John King, Cable News Network]. It's a new——

Q. Mr. President, thank you.

Q. That's always one of my concerns.

The President. Hurting Gregory's feelings? He is a sensitive guy, well centered, though. [*Laughter*]

2004 Election Night/1992 Election

Q. I'm not going there. Mr. President, you were disappointed, even angry, 12 years ago when the voters denied your father a second term. I'm interested in your thoughts and the conversation with him yesterday as you were walking to the Oval Office, and also whether you feel more free to do any one thing in a second term that perhaps you were politically constrained from doing in a first.

The President. At 3:30 in the morning on—I guess it was the day after the election, he was sitting upstairs, and I finally said, "Go to bed." He was awaiting the outcome and was hopeful that we would go over and be able to talk to our supporters, and it just didn't happen that way.

So I asked him the next morning when he got up, I said, "Come by the Oval Office and visit." And he came by, and we had a good talk. He was heading down to Houston. And it was—there was some uncertainty about that morning as to when the election would actually end. And it wasn't clear at that point in time, so I never got to see him face to face to watch his, I guess, pride in his tired eyes as his son got a second term.

I did talk to him, and he was relieved. I told him to get a nap. I was worried about him staying up too late. But—so I haven't had a chance to really visit and embrace.

And you're right, '92 was a disappointment. But he taught me a really good lesson, that life moves on. And it's very important for those of us in the political arena, win or lose, to recognize that life is bigger than just politics, and that's one of the really good lessons he taught me.

Electoral Process/President's Agenda

Q. Do you feel more free, sir?

The President. Oh, in terms of feeling free, well, I don't think you'll let me be too free. There's accountability and there are constraints on the Presidency, as there should be in any system. I feel it is necessary to move an agenda that I told the American people I would move. There's something refreshing about coming off an election, even more refreshing since we all got some sleep last night, but there's—you go out and you make your case, and you tell the people, "This is what I intend to do." And after hundreds of speeches and three debates and interviews and the whole process, where you keep basically saying the same thing over and over again, that—when you win, there is a feeling that the people have spoken and embraced your point of view. And that's what I intend to tell the Congress, that I made it clear

what I intend to do as the President, now let's work to—and the people made it clear what they wanted—now let's work together.

And it's one of the wonderful—it's like earning capital. You asked, do I feel free. Let me put it to you this way: I earned capital in the campaign, political capital, and now I intend to spend it. It is my style. That's what happened in the—after the 2000 election, I earned some capital. I've earned capital in this election, and I'm going to spend it for what I told the people I'd spend it on, which is—you've heard the agenda: Social Security and tax reform, moving this economy forward, education, fighting and winning the war on terror. We have an obligation in this country to continue to work with nations to help alleve poverty and disease. We will continue to press forward on the HIV/AIDS initiative, the Millennium Challenge Account. We will continue to do our duty to help feed the hungry. And I'm looking forward to it. I really am.

It's been a fantastic experience campaigning the country. You've seen it from one perspective. I've seen it from another. I saw you standing there at the last, final rally in Texas, to my right over there. I was observing you observe, and you saw the energy. And there was just something uplifting about people showing up at 11 o'clock at night, expressing their support and their prayers and their friendship. It's a marvelous experience to campaign across the country.

Mike [Mike Allen, Washington Post].

The Cabinet

Q. Mr. President—thank you, Mr. President. Do you plan to reshape your Cabinet for the second term, or will any changes come at the instigation of individuals? And as part of the same question, may I ask you what you've learned about Cabinet government, what works, what doesn't work? And do you mind also addressing the same question about the White House staff? [*Laughter*]

The President. The post-election euphoria did not last very long here at the press conference. [*Laughter*]

Let me talk about the people that have worked with me. I had a Cabinet meeting today, and I thanked them for their service to the country and reminded them we've got a job to do and I expected them to do the job.

I have made no decisions on my Cabinet and/or White House staff. I am mindful that working in the White House is really—is exhausting work. The people who you try to get to leak to you spend hours away from their families, and it is—there is—the word "burnout" is oftentimes used in the—in Washington, and it's used for a reason, because people do burn out. And so obviously, in terms of those who are—who want to stay on and who I want to stay on, I've got to make sure that it's right for their families and that they're comfortable, because when they come to work here in the White House, I expect them to work as hard as they possibly can on behalf of the American people.

In the Cabinet, there will be some changes. I don't know who they will be. It's inevitable there will be changes. That happens in every administration. To a person, I am proud of the work they have done. And I fully understand we're about to head into the period of intense speculation as to who's going to stay and who's not going to stay, and I assured them that—today I warned them of the speculative period. It's a great Washington sport to be talking about who's going to leave and who their replacements may be and handicapping, you know, my way of thinking.

I'll just give you—but let me just help you out with the speculation right now. I haven't thought about it. I'm going to start thinking about it. I'm going to Camp David this afternoon with Laura, and I'll begin the process of thinking about the Cabinet and the White House staff. And we'll let you know at the appropriate time when decisions have been made. And so, nice try, Mike.

Yes, Ed [Ed Chen, Los Angeles Times], and then——

Q. What you learned——

The President. Learned and not learned about the Cabinet?

Q. What works, what doesn't.

The President. Yes, well, first I've learned that I put together a really good Cabinet. I'm very proud of the people that have served this Government, and they, to a man and a woman, worked their hearts out for the American people. And I've learned that you've got to continue to surround yourself with good people. This is a job that requires crisp decisionmaking, and therefore, in order for me to make decisions, I've got to have people who bring their point of view into the Oval Office and are willing to say it.

I always jest to people, the Oval Office is the kind of place where people stand outside—they're getting ready to come in and tell me what for, and they walk in and get overwhelmed in the atmosphere, and they say, "Man, you're looking pretty." And therefore, you need people to walk in on those days when you're not looking so good and saying, "You're not looking so good, Mr. President." And I've got—those are the kind of people that served our country.

We've had vigorous debates, which you all, during the last 4 years, took great delight in reporting, differences of opinion. But that's what you want if you're the Commander in Chief and a decisionmaker. You want people to walk in and say, "I don't agree with this," or "I do agree with that, and here's what my recommendation is." But the President also has to learn to decide. You take—you know, there's ample time for the debate to take place and then decide and make up your mind and lead. That's what the job's all about.

And so I have learned how important it is to be—to have a really fine group of people that think through issues and that are not intimidated by the process and who walk in and tell me what's on their mind.

Ed, and then Stevenson [Richard Stevenson, New York Times].

Small-Business Agenda

Q. Good morning. Sir, does it bother you that there's a perception out there that your administration has been one that favors big business and the wealthy individuals? And what can you do to overcome that, sir?

The President. Ed, 70 percent of the new jobs in America are created by small businesses. I understand that. And I have promoted during the course of the last 4 years one of the most aggressive pro-entrepreneur, small-business policies. Tax relief—you might remember—I don't know if you know this or not, but 90 percent of the businesses are sole proprietorships or Subchapter S corporations. [*Laughter*]

Q. We've heard it.

The President. Tax relief helped them. This is an administration that fully understands that the job creators are the entrepreneurs. And so in a new term, we will make sure the tax relief continues to be robust for our small businesses. We'll push legal reform and regulatory reform because I understand the engine of growth is through the small-business sector.

Stevenson.

Model for Bipartisanship

Q. Sir, given your commitment to reaching out across party lines and to all Americans, I wonder if you could expand on your definition of bipartisanship and whether it means simply picking off a few Democrats on a case-by-case basis to pass the bills you want to pass or whether you would commit to working regularly with the Democratic leadership on solutions that can win broad support across party lines?

The President. Do you remember the No Child Left Behind Act? I think that's the model I'd look at if I were you. It is a— I laid out an agenda for reforming our public schools. I worked with both Republicans and Democrats to get that bill passed. In a new term, we'll continue to make sure we do not weaken the accountability standards that are making a huge difference in people's lives, in these kids' lives. But that's the model I'd look at, if I were you.

And we'll—there's a certain practicality to life here in Washington. And that is, when you get a bill moving, it is important to get the votes, and if politics starts to get in the way of getting good legislation through, you know, that's just part of life here. But I'm also focused on results. I think of the Medicare bill. You might remember that old, stale debate. We finally got a bill moving. I was hoping that we'd get strong bipartisan support. Unfortunately, it was an election year, but we got the votes necessary to get the bill passed. And so we will—I will—my goal is to work on the ideal and to reach out and to continue to work and find common ground on issues.

On the other hand, I've been wisened to the ways of Washington. I watched what can happen during certain parts of the cycle, where politics gets in the way of good policy. And at that point in time, I'll continue to—you know, I'll try to get this done. I'll try to get our bills passed in a way, because results really do matter, as far as I'm concerned. I really didn't come here to hold the office just to say, "Gosh, it was fun to serve." I came here to get some things done, and we are doing it.

Yes, Big Stretch [Bill Sammon, Washington Times].

Yasser Arafat

Q. Thank you, Mr. President. I know you haven't had a chance to learn this, but it appears that Yasser Arafat has passed away.

The President. Really?

Q. And I was just wondering if I could get your initial reaction? And also your thoughts on, perhaps, working with a new generation of Palestinian leadership?

The President. I appreciate that. My first reaction is, God bless his soul. And my second reaction is, is that we will continue to work for a free Palestinian state that's at peace with Israel.

Yes.

Legislative Agenda

Q. Mr. President, as you look at your second-term domestic priorities, I wonder if you could talk a little bit about how you see the sequence of action on issues beyond Social Security—tax reform, education. And if you could expand a little bit for us on the principles that you want to underpin your tax reform proposal—do you want it to be revenue neutral? What kinds of things do you want to accomplish through that process?

The President. I appreciate that. I was anticipating this question, that, what is the first thing you're going to do? When it comes it legislation, it just doesn't work that way, particularly when you've laid out a comprehensive agenda. And part of that comprehensive agenda is tax simplification.

The—first of all, a principle would be revenue neutral. If I'm going to—if there was a need to raise taxes, I'd say, "Let's have a tax bill that raises taxes," as opposed to, "Let's simplify the Tax Code and sneak a tax increase on the people." It's just not my style. I don't believe we need to raise taxes. I've said that to the American people, and so the simplification would be the goal.

Now, secondly, that—obviously, that it rewards risk and doesn't—it doesn't have unnecessary penalties in it. But the main thing is that it would be viewed as fair, that it would be a fair system, that it wouldn't be complicated, that there's a kind of—that loopholes wouldn't be there for special interests, that the code itself be viewed and deemed as a very fair way to encourage people to invest and save and achieve certain fiscal objectives in our country as well.

One of the interesting debates will be, of course, in the course of simplification,

will there be incentives in the code—charitable giving, of course, and mortgage deductions are very important. As Governor of Texas, when I—sometime I think I was asked about simplification, I always noted how important it was for certain incentives to be built into the Tax Code, and that will be an interesting part of the debate.

Certain issues come quicker than others in the course of a legislative session, and that depends upon whether or not those issues have been debated. I think of, for example, of the legal issue—the legal reform issues. They have been—medical liability reform had been debated and got thwarted a couple of times in one body in particular on Capitol Hill. And so the groundwork has been laid for some legislation that I've been talking about. On an issue like tax reform it's going to—tax simplification—it's going to take a lot of legwork to get something ready for a legislative package. I fully understand that. And Social Security reform will require some additional legwork, although the Moynihan Commission has laid the groundwork for what I think is a very good place to start the debate.

The education issue is one that could move pretty quickly because there has been a lot of discussion about education. It's an issue that the Members are used to debating and discussing. And so I think—all issues are important. And the timing of issues as they reach it through committee and floor really depend upon whether or not some work has already been on those issues.

A couple more questions. Bob [Bob Deans, Cox Newspapers].

Fallujah/Freedom in Iraq

Q. Mr. President, American forces are gearing up for what appears to be a major offensive in Fallujah over the next several days. I'm wondering if you could tell us what the objective is, what the stakes are there for the United States, for the Iraqi people, and the Iraqi elections coming up in January?

The President. In order for Iraq to be a free country, those who are trying to stop the elections and stop a free society from emerging must be defeated. And so Prime Minister Allawi and his Government, which fully understands that, are working with our generals on the ground to do just that. We will work closely with the Government. It's their Government. It's their country. We're there at their invitation. And—but I think there's a recognition that some of these people have to—must be defeated, and so that's what they're thinking about. That's what you're—that's why you're hearing discussions about potential action in Fallujah.

Heidi [Heidi Pryzbyla, Bloomberg News].

Federal Deficit

Q. Thank you, sir. Many within your own party are unhappy over the deficit, and they say keeping down discretional spending alone won't help you reach your goal of halving the deficit in 5 years. What else do you plan to do to cut costs?

The President. Well, I would suggest they look at our budget that we've submitted to Congress, which does, in fact, get the deficit down—cut in half in 5 years and is a specific, line-by-line budget that we are required to submit and have done so.

The key to making sure that the deficit is reduced is for there to be, on the one hand, spending discipline, and I—as you noticed in my opening remarks, I talked about these appropriations bills that are beginning to move. And I thought I was pretty clear about the need for those bills to be fiscally responsible, and I meant it. And I look forward to talking to the leadership about making sure that the budget agreements we had are still the budget agreements, that just because we had an election, that they shouldn't feel comfortable changing our agreement. And I think they understand that.

Secondly, the other way to make sure that the deficit is—decreases is to grow the economy. As the economy grows, there will be more revenues coming into the Treasury. That's what you have seen recently. If you notice, there's been some write-downs of the budget deficit. In other words, the deficit is less than we thought because the revenues is exceeding projections. And the reason why the revenues is—the revenues are exceeding projections—"Sometimes I mangle the English language. I get that"—[*laughter*].

Q. Inside joke.

The President. Yes, very inside. [*Laughter*]

The revenues are exceeding projections, and as a result, the projected deficit is less. But my point there is, is that with good economic policy that encourages economic growth, the revenue streams begin to increase. And as the revenue streams increase, coupled with fiscal discipline, you'll see the deficit shrinking. And we're focused on that.

I do believe there ought to be budgetary reform in Washington, on the Hill, Capitol Hill. I think it's very important. I would like to see the President have a line-item veto again, one that passed constitutional muster. I think it would help the executive branch work with the legislative branch to make sure that we're able to maintain budget discipline.

I've talked to a lot of Members of Congress who are wondering whether or not we'll have the will to confront entitlements, to make sure that there is entitlement reform that helps us maintain fiscal discipline. And the answer is yes. That's why I took on the Social Security issue. I believe we have a duty to do so. I want to make sure that the Medicare reforms that we've put in place remain robust, to help us make sure Medicare is available for generations to come.

And so there is a—I've got quite an active agenda to help work with Congress to bring not only fiscal discipline, but to make sure that our progrowth policies are still in place.

Herman [Ken Herman, Austin American-Statesman]. I'm probably going to regret this. [*Laughter*]

Q. I don't know if you had a chance to check, but I can report you did eke out a victory in Texas the other day.

The President. Thank you, sir.

Bipartisanship

Q. Congratulations. I'm interested in getting back to Stevenson's question about unity. Clearly, you believe you have reached out and will continue to reach out. Do you believe the Democrats have made a sincere and sufficient effort to meet you somewhere halfway, and do you think now there's more reason for them to do that in light of the election results?

The President. I think that Democrats agree that we have an obligation to serve our country. I believe there will be good will, now that this election is over, to work together. I found that to be the case when I first arrived here in Washington, and working with the Democrats and fellow Republicans, we got a lot done. And it is with that spirit that I go into this coming session, and I will meet with both Republican and Democrat leaders, and I am—they'll see I'm genuine about working toward some of these important issues.

It's going to be—it's not easy. These—I readily concede I've laid out some very difficult issues for people to deal with. Reforming the Social Security system for generations to come is a difficult issue; otherwise, it would have already been done. But it is necessary to confront it. And I would hope to be able to work with Democrats to get this done. I'm not sure we can get it done without Democrat participation, because it is a big issue, and I will explain to them and I will show them Senator Moynihan's thinking as a way to begin the process. And I will remind everybody here that we have a duty to leave behind a better America and when we see a problem, to deal with it. And I think the—I think Democrats agree with that.

And so I'm optimistic. You covered me when I was the Governor of Texas. I told you that I was going to do that as a Governor. There was probably skepticism in your beady eyes there. [*Laughter*] But you might remember, we did—we were able to accomplish a lot by—and Washington is different from Austin, no question about it. Washington—one of the disappointments of being here in Washington is how bitter this town can become and how divisive. I'm not blaming one party or the other. It's just the reality of Washington, DC, sometimes exacerbated by you because it's great sport. It's really—it's entertaining for some. It also makes it difficult to govern at times.

But nevertheless, my commitment is there. I fully—am now more seasoned to Washington. I've cut my political eyeteeth, at least the ones I've recently grown here in Washington. And so I'm aware of what can happen in this town. But nevertheless, having said that, I am fully prepared to work with both Republican and Democrat leadership to advance an agenda that I think makes a big difference for the country.

Listen, thank you all. I look forward to working with you. I've got a question for you. How many of you are going to be here for a second term? Please raise your hand. [*Laughter*] Good. Gosh, we're going to have a lot of fun, then. Thank you all.

NOTE: The President's news conference began at 11:17 a.m. in Room 450 of the Dwight D. Eisenhower Executive Office Building. In his remarks, he referred to Prime Minister Tony Blair of the United Kingdom; and Prime Minister Ayad Allawi of the Iraqi Interim Government. As regards journalist Bill Sammon's question asking for the President's reaction to the death of Chairman Yasser Arafat of the Palestinian Authority, the reports of Chairman Arafat's death were inaccurate.

Statement on the Death of Shaykh Zayid bin Sultan Al Nuhayyan of the United Arab Emirates
November 4, 2004

The United States mourns the passing of a great friend of our country, Shaykh Zayid bin Sultan Al Nuhayyan of the United Arab Emirates. Shaykh Zayid was the founder and President of the UAE for more than 30 years, a pioneer, an elder statesman, and a close ally. He and his fellow rulers of the seven Emirates built their federation into a prosperous, tolerant, and well-governed state. I offer my condolences and those of the American people to the family of Shaykh Zayid and to the Government and people of the United Arab Emirates on their great loss.

Statement Congratulating President Hamid Karzai on His Election as President of Afghanistan
November 4, 2004

I congratulate President Karzai on his election victory. I commend the millions of Afghan men and women who voted in the first democratic election in their Nation's history. Through this simple act of voting, the Afghan people declared to the world their determination to move beyond a brutal legacy of oppression, terror, and fear to a future of hope, democracy, and freedom. The large turnout by Afghan women, who made up 40 percent of all voters, confirms that there is a vital role for women in the politics of a nation proud of its Islamic heritage. The election also makes clear that a free Afghanistan is a partner in the war on terror, a beacon of hope in a troubled region of the world, and an example to other countries working to realize the promise of freedom.

Letter to Congressional Leaders on Continuation of the Emergency Regarding Weapons of Mass Destruction
November 4, 2004

Dear Mr. Speaker: (*Dear Mr. President:*)

Section 202(d) of the National Emergencies Act (50 U.S.C. 1622(d)) provides for the automatic termination of a national emergency unless, prior to the anniversary date of its declaration, the President publishes in the *Federal Register* and transmits to the Congress a notice stating that the emergency is to continue in effect beyond the anniversary date. In accordance with this provision, I have sent to the *Federal Register* for publication the enclosed notice, stating that the emergency posed by the proliferation of weapons of mass destruction and their delivery systems declared by Executive Order 12938 on November 14, 1994, as amended, is to continue in effect beyond November 14, 2004. The most recent notice continuing this emergency was signed on October 29, 2003, and published in the *Federal Register* on October 31, 2003 (68 FR 62209).

Because the proliferation of weapons of mass destruction and the means of delivering them continues to pose an unusual and extraordinary threat to the national security, foreign policy, and economy of the United States, I have determined the national emergency previously declared must continue in effect beyond November 14, 2004.

Sincerely,

GEORGE W. BUSH

NOTE: Identical letters were sent to J. Dennis Hastert, Speaker of the House of Representatives, and Richard B. Cheney, President of the Senate. An original was not available for verification of the content of this letter. The notice is listed in Appendix D at the end of this volume.

Letter to Congressional Leaders Reporting on the Global Deployments of United States Combat-Equipped Armed Forces
November 4, 2004

Dear Mr. Speaker: (*Dear Mr. President:*)

I am providing this consolidated supplemental report, prepared by my Administration and consistent with the War Powers Resolution (Public Law 93–148), as part of my efforts to keep the Congress informed about deployments of U.S. combat-equipped armed forces around the world. This supplemental report covers operations in support of the global war on terrorism, Kosovo, and Bosnia and Herzegovina.

On March 21, 2003, consistent with the War Powers Resolution, I reported that I had directed U.S. Armed Forces, operating with other coalition forces, to commence combat operations on March 19, 2003, against Iraq. Thereafter, I included information regarding the deployment of U.S. forces in Iraq in reports on Iraq to the Congress under Public Laws 107–243 and 102–1, as amended. On July 2, 2004, I delegated to the Secretary of State the authority to make these detailed reports on Iraq, but I am including information about the deployment of U.S. forces in Iraq in this consolidated war powers report.

The Global War on Terrorism

Since September 24, 2001, I have reported, consistent with Public Law 107–40 and the War Powers Resolution, on the combat operations in Afghanistan against al-Qaida terrorists and their Taliban supporters, which began on October 7, 2001, and the deployment of various combat-equipped and combat-support forces to a number of locations in the Central, Pacific, and Southern Command areas of operation in support of those operations and of other operations in our global war on terrorism.

I will direct additional measures as necessary in the exercise of the U.S. right to self-defense and to protect U.S. citizens and interests. Such measures may include short-notice deployments of special operations and other forces for sensitive operations in various locations throughout the world. It is not possible to know at this time either the precise duration of combat operations or the precise scope and duration of the deployment of U.S. Armed Forces necessary to counter the terrorist threat to the United States.

United States Armed Forces, with the assistance of numerous coalition partners, continue to conduct the U.S. campaign to pursue al-Qaida terrorists and to eliminate support to al-Qaida. These operations have seriously degraded al-Qaida's training capabilities. United States Armed Forces, with the assistance of numerous coalition partners, ended the Taliban regime in Afghanistan and are actively pursuing and engaging al-Qaida and remnant Taliban fighters. United States forces also have supported the International Security Assistance Force in providing security in connection with the Afghan elections.

The United States continues to detain several hundred al-Qaida and Taliban fighters who are believed to pose a continuing threat to the United States and its interests. The combat-equipped and combat-support forces deployed to Naval Base, Guantanamo Bay, Cuba, in the U.S. Southern Command area of operations since January 2002, continue to conduct secure detention operations for enemy combatants at Guantanamo Bay.

The U.N. Security Council authorized a Multinational Force (MNF) in Iraq under unified command in U.N. Security Council Resolution 1511 of October 16, 2003, and reaffirmed its authorization in U.N. Security Council Resolution 1546 of June 8, 2004, noting the Iraqi Interim Government's request to retain the presence of the MNF. The mission of the MNF is to contribute to security and stability in Iraq, including by assisting in building the capability of Iraqi security forces and institutions, as the Iraqi people plan democratic elections and as reconstruction continues. The U.S. contribution to the MNF is more than 135,000 military personnel.

In furtherance of our efforts against terrorists who pose a continuing and imminent threat to the United States, our friends and allies, and our forces abroad, the United States continues to work with friends and allies in areas around the world. U.S. combat-equipped and combat-support forces are located in the Horn of Africa region, and the U.S. forces headquarters element in Djibouti provides command and control support as necessary for military operations against al-Qaida and other international terrorists in the Horn of Africa region, including Yemen. These forces also assist in enhancing counterterrorism capabilities in Kenya, Ethiopia, Yemen, Eritrea, and Djibouti. In addition, the United States continues to conduct maritime interception operations on the high seas in the areas of responsibility of all of the geographic combatant commanders. These maritime operations have the responsibility to stop the movement, arming, or financing of international terrorists.

NATO-Led Kosovo Force (KFOR)

As noted in previous reports regarding U.S. contributions in support of peacekeeping efforts in Kosovo, the U.N. Security Council authorized Member States to establish KFOR in U.N. Security Council Resolution 1244 of June 10, 1999. The mission of KFOR is to provide an international security presence in order to deter renewed hostilities; verify, and, if necessary, enforce the terms of the Military Technical Agreement between NATO and the Federal Republic of Yugoslavia (which is now Serbia and Montenegro); enforce the terms of the Undertaking on Demilitarization and Transformation of the former Kosovo Liberation Army; provide day-to-day operational direction to the Kosovo Protection Corps; and maintain a safe and secure environment to facilitate the work of the U.N. Interim Administration Mission in Kosovo (UNMIK).

Currently, there are 23 NATO nations contributing to KFOR. Eleven non-NATO contributing countries also participate by providing military personnel and other support personnel to KFOR. The U.S. contribution to KFOR in Kosovo is about 1,800 U.S. military personnel, or approximately 10 percent of KFOR's total strength of approximately 18,000 personnel. In addition, U.S. military personnel occasionally operate from Macedonia, Albania, and Greece in support of KFOR operations.

The U.S. forces have been assigned to a sector principally centered around Gnjilane in the eastern region of Kosovo.

For U.S. KFOR forces, as for KFOR generally, maintaining a safe and secure environment remains the primary military task. The KFOR operates under NATO command and control and rules of engagement. The KFOR coordinates with and supports UNMIK at most levels; provides a security presence in towns, villages, and the countryside; and organizes checkpoints and patrols in key areas to provide security, protect minorities, resolve disputes, and help instill in the community a feeling of confidence.

In accordance with U.N. Security Council Resolution 1244, the UNMIK continues to transfer additional competencies to the Kosovar Provisional Institutions of Self-Government, which includes the President, Prime Minister, multiple ministries, and the Kosovo Assembly. The UNMIK retains ultimate authority in some sensitive areas such as police, justice, and ethnic minority affairs.

NATO continues formally to review KFOR's mission at 6-month intervals. These reviews provide a basis for assessing current force levels, future requirements, force structure, force reductions, and the eventual withdrawal of KFOR. NATO has adopted the Joint Operations Area plan to regionalize and rationalize its force structure in the Balkans. The UNMIK international police and the Kosovo Police Service (KPS) have full responsibility for public safety and policing throughout Kosovo except in the area of Mitrovica, where the KFOR and UNMIK share this responsibility due to security concerns. The UNMIK international police and KPS also have begun to assume responsibility for guarding patrimonial sites and established border-crossing checkpoints. The KFOR often augments security in particularly sensitive areas or in response to particular threats.

NATO-Led Stabilization Force in Bosnia and Herzegovina (SFOR)

Regarding U.S. contributions in support of peacekeeping efforts in Bosnia and Herzegovina, the U.N. Security Council authorized, in U.N. Security Council Resolution 1551 of July 9, 2004, Member States to continue SFOR for an additional period of 6 months in anticipation of the conclusion of SFOR's operations, and the commencement of a European Union (EU) mission, including a military component, in Bosnia and Herzegovina by the end of 2004. The mission of SFOR is to provide a deterrent presence to help stabilize and consolidate the peace in Bosnia and Herzegovina, contribute to a secure environment, and perform key supporting tasks including support to the international civil presence in Bosnia and Herzegovina.

The U.S. force contribution to SFOR in Bosnia and Herzegovina is approximately 1,000 personnel. United States personnel comprise approximately 12 percent of the approximately 8,500 personnel assigned to SFOR. Currently, 20 NATO nations and 8 others provide military personnel or other support to SFOR. Most U.S. forces in Bosnia and Herzegovina are assigned to Multinational Task Force, North, headquartered near the city of Tuzla. United States forces continue to support SFOR efforts to apprehend persons indicted for war crimes and to conduct counterterrorism operations.

In June 2004 at the Istanbul Summit, NATO Heads of State and Government welcomed the offer of the EU to establish a new and separate mission in Bosnia, including a military component, and decided to establish a new NATO Headquarters in Sarajevo at the end of SFOR's operations. This NATO Headquarters, to which U.S. forces will be assigned, will have the principal task of providing advice on defense reform. The NATO headquarters also will undertake certain supporting operational tasks, including counterterrorism and supporting the International Criminal Tribunal for the Former Yugoslavia with regard to the detention of persons indicted for war crimes.

I have directed the participation of U.S. Armed Forces in all of these operations pursuant to my constitutional authority to conduct U.S. foreign relations and as Commander in Chief and Chief Executive. Officials of my Administration and I communicate regularly with the leadership and other Members of Congress with regard to these deployments, and we will continue to do so.

Sincerely,

GEORGE W. BUSH

NOTE: Identical letters were sent to J. Dennis Hastert, Speaker of the House of Representatives, and Ted Stevens, President pro tempore of the Senate.

The President's Radio Address
November 6, 2004

Good morning. This week, the voters of America set the direction of our Nation for the next 4 years. I am honored by the support of my fellow citizens. I commend Senator John Kerry for a spirited campaign.

Now the election is behind us, and our country is ready to move forward. Our Nation is fighting a continuing war on terror, and every American has a stake in the outcome. Republicans and Democrats and independents love our country, and together, we will protect the American people. We will persevere until the enemy is defeated and our Nation is safe from danger. Every civilized country also has a stake in the outcome of this war. Whatever our past disagreements, we share a common enemy and common duties to confront disease and hunger and poverty in troubled regions of our world.

I will continue reaching out to friends and allies, including our partners in NATO and the European Union, to promote development and progress, to defeat the terrorists, and to encourage freedom and democracy as the alternatives to tyranny and terror.

Here at home, we have serious responsibilities and historic opportunities. To accelerate the momentum of this economy and to keep creating jobs, we must take practical measures to help the small-business sector. We must confront the junk and frivolous lawsuits that are driving up the cost of health care and hurting doctors and patients. We must continue to work on education reform to bring high standards and accountability, not just to elementary schools but to the high schools as well. We must reform our complicated and outdated Tax Code to get rid of needless paperwork and make our economy more competitive in the world. And we must show our leadership by strengthening the Social Security system for our children and grandchildren. This is more than a problem to be solved; it is an opportunity to help millions of our fellow citizens find the security and independence of ownership.

Reaching these goals will require the broad support of Americans. To make this Nation stronger and better, I will need the support of Republicans and Democrats and independents, and I will work to earn it. I will do all I can do to deserve your trust.

A new term is a new opportunity to reach out to the whole Nation. We have one country, one Constitution, and one future that binds us. And when we come together and work together, there is no limit to the greatness of America.

In the election of 2004, large issues were set before the country and discussed every day of the campaign. Now Americans are expecting bipartisan effort and results. My administration will work with both parties in Congress to achieve those results and to meet the responsibility we share.

With the campaign over, the United States of America goes forward with confidence and faith. I see a great day coming for our country, and I'm eager for the work ahead.

Thank you for listening.

NOTE: The address was recorded at 10:15 a.m. on November 5 at Camp David, MD, for broadcast at 10:06 a.m. on November 6. The transcript was made available by the Office of the Press Secretary on November 5 but was embargoed for release until the broadcast. The Office of the Press Secretary also released a Spanish language transcript of this address.

Remarks Following a Visit With Wounded Troops at Walter Reed Army Medical Center
November 9, 2004

Listen, I've—Laura and I have just toured one of the wards upstairs. I am—every time I come to Walter Reed, I'm struck by the courage and bravery of our men and women who wear the uniform. It's such an honor to meet the troops who are wounded. And it's so uplifting to see their spirit, their drive to become rehabilitated, their love of their country, their support of the mission.

Laura and I spent time with the moms and dads and husbands and wives of those who are wounded, and I was struck by just the patriotic sense that they have and that—their strong support for their loved ones.

Every time I come to the hospital, one of the things I try to determine is to—whether or not our troops and their families are being treated with first-class care. It's very important for all of us involved in decisionmaking to know that a troop who had been injured in Iraq or Afghanistan is immediately brought to care. And to a person, they were very strong in their support and praise to how this hospital is run.

I want to thank the generals, the doctors, the nurses for running this hospital. I

mean—it's such a comforting sense for me to be able to tell a loved one, "Your person hurt, your loved one will get the best care possible."

And finally, we've got troops in harm's way in the Fallujah area right now, and our prayers are with the soldiers and their loved ones as they're doing the hard work necessary for a free Iraq to emerge. There are still terrorists there who are trying to stop the march of freedom. And at the request of the Allawi Government and alongside of Iraqi troops, coalition forces are now moving into Fallujah to bring to justice those who are willing to kill the innocent and those who are trying to terrorize the Iraqi people and our coalition, those who want to stop democracy. And they're not going to succeed.

And so we wish our troops all the best and Godspeed to them as well. Thank you all.

NOTE: The President spoke at 3:01 p.m. In his remarks, he referred to Prime Minister Ayad Allawi of the Iraqi Interim Government. A tape was not available for verification of the content of these remarks.

Statement on the Resignation of Donald L. Evans as Secretary of Commerce
November 9, 2004

Don Evans is one of my most trusted friends and advisers. He has been a valuable member of my economic team. Don has worked to advance economic security and prosperity for all Americans. He has worked steadfastly to make sure America continues to be the best place in the world to do business.

To encourage job creation here at home, Don has worked closely with me to reduce taxes, open markets for American goods and services, and promote a level playing field abroad.

Don shares my belief that the promise of America means our best days lie ahead. Together, we have worked to make that a reality.

I thank Don for his outstanding service to our Nation and wish him and Susie all the best as they return home to Texas.

NOTE: The Office of the Press Secretary also made available Secretary Evans's letter of resignation.

Statement on the Resignation of John Ashcroft as Attorney General
November 9, 2004

John Ashcroft has worked tirelessly to help make our country safer. During his 4 years at the Department of Justice, John has transformed the Department to make combating terrorism the top priority, including making sure our law enforcement officials have the tools they need to disrupt and prevent attacks. In doing so, he has made sure that the rights of Americans are respected and protected.

I applaud his efforts to prevent crime, vigorously enforce our civil rights laws, crack down on corporate wrongdoing, protect the rights of victims and those with disabilities, reduce crimes committed with guns, and stop human trafficking. I appreciate his work to fight Internet pornography. I am grateful for his advice on judicial nominations and his efforts to ensure that my judicial nominees receive fair hearings and timely votes.

John has served our Nation with honor, distinction, and integrity. I appreciate his service and wish him and Janet all the best.

NOTE: The Office of the Press Secretary also made available Attorney General Ashcroft's letter of resignation.

Letter to Congressional Leaders on Continuation of the National Emergency With Respect to Iran
November 9, 2004

Dear Mr. Speaker: (*Dear Mr. President:*)

Section 202(d) of the National Emergencies Act (50 U.S.C. 1622(d)) provides for the automatic termination of a national emergency unless, prior to the anniversary date of its declaration, the President publishes in the *Federal Register* and transmits to the Congress a notice stating that the emergency is to continue in effect beyond the anniversary date. Consistent with this provision, I have sent the enclosed notice, stating that the Iran emergency declared by Executive Order 12170 on November 14, 1979, is to continue in effect beyond November 14, 2004, to the *Federal Register* for publication. The most recent notice continuing this emergency was published

in the *Federal Register* on November 13, 2003 (68 *Fed. Reg.* 64489).

Our relations with Iran have not yet returned to normal, and the process of implementing the January 19, 1981, agreements with Iran is still underway. For these reasons, I have determined that it is necessary to continue the national emergency declared on November 14, 1979, with respect to Iran, beyond November 14, 2004.

Sincerely,

GEORGE W. BUSH

NOTE: Identical letters were sent to J. Dennis Hastert, Speaker of the House of Representatives, and Richard B. Cheney, President of the Senate. The notice is listed in Appendix D at the end of this volume.

Remarks Following Discussions With North Atlantic Treaty Organization Secretary General Jakob Gijsbert de Hoop Scheffer and an Exchange With Reporters
November 10, 2004

President Bush. It's my honor to welcome the Secretary General of NATO to the Oval Office. This is the first meeting I've had, since my reelection, with a leader from overseas. I'm proud you're the person, Secretary General, because, first of all, I've got a very close personal relationship. I've come to admire his leadership and his fortitude. And secondly, my Nation is committed to a strong and vibrant NATO.

NATO is playing a very constructive role in Afghanistan. Today we had a chance to revisit one of the great moments of modern history, when millions of people went to the polls to vote for a President in a country that had been ruled by the Taliban only

3 years ago, and we were rejoicing in the fact that the first voter was a 19-year-old woman. And NATO is playing a very active role in Afghanistan.

And NATO is playing a role in helping to train Iraqi citizens so that they can become the people that defend their country against those who are trying to stop freedom. And I want to thank you for that, Mr. Secretary General.

We talked about the need to make sure NATO is relevant, that NATO is constructed in a way that is not only effective but one that continues to foster free societies and democracy around the world.

And I thank you for your vision and your commitment. Welcome to the Oval Office.

Secretary General de Hoop Scheffer. Thank you very much. Well, thank you very much, Mr. President. The fact that I am sitting here now in the Oval Office as the first foreign visitor is the best proof, I think, for the full commitment of the United States of America and this President Bush to NATO. And that's of the utmost importance, because NATO is the unique transatlantic forum where everything we have, the big challenges of the world we are facing in the world today should be discussed, and NATO is the only organization which can deliver.

We delivered, as the President said, in Afghanistan. Less burkas and more ballot boxes, that's what it's all about. We are delivering in Kosovo. We are delivering by setting up a training implementation mission in Iraq. There is no second forum. There's no second organization in the world like NATO, where 26 democracies are defending values, democracy, respect for human rights, freedom of religion, and all those basic values which are at the heart of all these 26 societies.

And it gives me pleasure to have the full support—I knew that already, of course—to have the full support of President Bush for this endeavor. Of course, I think NATO has a very challenging agenda, and I'll make sure that we can deliver— NATO can deliver, that we can face all those challenges successfully.

Thank you so much, and it's a great pleasure to be here in the Oval Office once again.

President Bush. Welcome back.

We'll be glad to answer a couple of questions. Scott [Scott Lindlaw, Associated Press], why don't you start it off.

Future Cooperation With the Palestinian Authority

Q. Thanks, Mr. President. In June 2002, you urged the Palestinian people to replace Yasser Arafat with a leader, in your words,

"not compromised by terror." Arafat today is gravely ill. In fact, Palestinians have already selected his successor. Do you see a new opening for peace here?

President Bush. I do. There will be an opening for peace when leadership of the Palestinian people steps forward and says, "Help us build a democratic and free society." And when that happens—and I believe it's going to happen, because I believe all people desire to live in freedom—the United States of America will be more than willing to help build the institutions necessary for a free society to emerge, so that the Palestinians can have their own state. The vision is two states, a Palestinian state and Israel, living side by side in peace, and I think we've got a chance to do that. And I look forward to being involved in that process.

Adam [Adam Boulton, Sky News].

Secretary of State Powell

Q. Mr. President, today you met with your Secretary of State. Do you want him to stick around to lead your efforts to revive the Middle East peace talks?

President Bush. I'm proud of my Secretary of State. He's done a heck of a good job.

Heidi [Heidi Pryzbyla, Bloomberg News].

Troop Levels in Iraq

Q. Yes, sir. Can elections in Iraq be free and fair without the participation of Sunnis? And you've also said you'll give the commanders in Iraq what they need. Does this mean that you're open to substantially increasing the level of troops?

President Bush. That is a loaded question, and I don't blame you for asking it. The commanders on the ground will have that which they need, and they have yet to say, "We need a substantial number of troops." As a matter of fact, I met with the commanders on the ground today— General Casey, and he—a commander on the ground, General Casey, the commander on the ground. And he said that things are going well in Fallujah and they're making very good progress in securing that country.

But I haven't changed—the job of the Commander in Chief is to set the strategy and to set the direction of policy and say to those who are in charge of implementing the policy, "You'll have that which you need." And I have said that ever since we've begun operations in Iraq. I said it when we began operations in Afghanistan, and it's still true. And if the commanders were to bring forth a request, I would look at it—I would listen to it very seriously and implement the request. They have yet to do so.

Sunni Participation in Iraqi Elections

Q. Do you need Sunni participation to make the elections free and fair?

President Bush. Well, I'm confident when people realize that there's a chance to vote on a President, they will participate.

People want to be free. This is tough right now in Iraq because there are people that are willing to commit violent acts to stop elections. But as I reminded our citizens prior to the Afghanistan elections, there's a deep desire in every soul to vote and to be free and to participate in the Presidential elections, which is precisely what happened in Afghanistan in spite of the doubt of some and in spite of the violence that took place in Afghanistan prior to the vote. I believe that a lot of citizens in Iraq will want to vote for their leaders. And I believe that because I believe deep in everybody's soul is a desire to be free.

Thank you all.

NOTE: The President spoke at 2:52 p.m. in the Oval Office at the White House. In his remarks, he referred to Gen. George W. Casey, Jr., USA, commanding general, Multi-National Force—Iraq. A reporter referred to Chairman Yasser Arafat of the Palestinian Authority.

Remarks on the Nomination of Alberto R. Gonzales To Be Attorney General
November 10, 2004

Good afternoon. I'm pleased to announce my nomination of Judge Al Gonzales to be the Attorney General of the United States. This is the fifth time I have asked Judge Gonzales to serve his fellow citizens, and I am very grateful he keeps saying yes.

A decade ago, when I was elected Governor of Texas, I asked Al to be my general counsel. He went on to distinguished service as Texas's secretary of state and as a justice of the Texas Supreme Court.

Since I arrived in Washington 4 years ago, he has served with skill and integrity in the White House as Counsel to the President. I have counted on Al Gonzales to help select the best nominees for the

Federal courts, one of the President's most important responsibilities.

His sharp intellect and sound judgment have helped shape our policies in the war on terror, policies designed to protect the security of all Americans, while protecting the rights of all Americans. As the top legal official on the White House staff, he has led a superb team of lawyers and has upheld the highest standards of government ethics. My confidence in Al was high to begin with; it has only grown with time.

Over the past decade, I've also come to know the character of this man. He always gives me his frank opinion. He is a calm and steady voice in times of crisis. He has an unwavering principle, a respect for the law, and he and Becky are dear friends of Laura and my—of me, and I'm also very friendly with Graham and Gabriel Gonzales.

My newest Cabinet nominee grew up in a two-bedroom house in Texas with his parents and seven siblings. Al's mother and dad, Pablo and Maria, were migrant workers who never finished elementary school, but they worked hard to educate their children and to instill the values of reverence and integrity and personal responsibility. These good people lived to see their son, Al, study at Rice University and Harvard Law School. Maria still lives in Humble, Texas, in the house her husband built, and I can only imagine how proud she is today of her son, Al.

Serving as Attorney General is one of the most challenging duties in our Government. As the Nation's chief law enforcement officer, Al will continue our administration's great progress in fighting crime, in strengthening the FBI, in improving our domestic efforts in the war on terror. As a steward of civil rights laws, he will ensure that Americans are protected from discrimination so that each person has the opportunity to live the American Dream, as Al himself has done.

With the Senate's approval, Judge Gonzales will succeed another superb public servant, Attorney General John Ashcroft. Attorney General Ashcroft has served with excellence during a demanding time. In 4 years, he's reorganized the Department of Justice to meet the new threat of terrorism.

He's fairly and forcefully applied the PATRIOT Act and helped to dismantle terror cells inside the United States. During his watch, violent crime has dropped to a 30-year low and prosecutions of crimes committed with guns have reached an alltime high. Drug use amongst our students is down. Confidence in the financial markets has been restored because the Attorney General aggressively prosecuted corporate fraud. And thanks to John Ashcroft's leadership, America has stepped up its efforts to prosecute the cruel exploitation of children by Internet pornographers. The Nation is safer and more just today because John Ashcroft has served our country so well.

I'm committed to strong, principled leadership at the Department of Justice, and Judge Al Gonzales will be that kind of leader as America's 80th Attorney General. I urge the Senate to act promptly on this important nomination. I look forward to welcoming my great friend to the Cabinet. Congratulations.

NOTE: The President spoke at 3:40 p.m. in the Roosevelt Room at the White House. In his remarks, he referred to Rebecca Gonzales, wife of Attorney General-designate Alberto R. Gonzales. The transcript released by the Office of the Press Secretary also included the remarks of Attorney General-designate Gonzales. The Office of the Press Secretary also released a Spanish language transcript of these remarks.

Remarks at the Iftaar Dinner
November 10, 2004

Thank you all. Please be seated. Thank you. Thank you all for coming, and welcome to the White House, and *Ramadan Mubarak.* I'm honored to be with so many friends and distinguished guests.

As we gather during this holy month, America is stronger and more hopeful because of the generosity and compassion of our Muslim citizens. Our Nation is safer and more prosperous because we have a close relationship with our Islamic friends around the world. And tonight we honor the traditions of a great faith by hosting the Iftaar dinner here at the White House.

I want to acknowledge our Secretary of State, Colin Powell. I appreciate his great service. I want to thank our Secretary of Energy, Spence Abraham, who is with us today. I want to thank Dr. Elias Zerhouni for his great work at the National Institutes of Health. Thank you. I want to thank all the distinguished Ambassadors who are with us today.

I want to thank the American Muslim leaders who've joined us. I appreciate you coming from all around the country. I want to thank Imam Faizul Khan of the Islamic Center of Washington, who will lead the blessing tonight. And tonight we also remember the late Shaykh Zayid, the founder of the United Arab Emirates, who passed away last week. He was a wise leader, and America joins the people of the UAE in honoring his memory.

For Muslims in America and around the world, Ramadan is a special time of reflection, fasting, and charity. It is a time to think of the less fortunate and to share God's gifts with those in need. It is a time of spiritual growth and prayer, and the heartfelt prayers offered by Muslims across America are a blessing for our whole Nation.

Ramadan is also a time for togetherness and thanksgiving. And Muslims gather to break the fast, and there is so much to be thankful for. I know you're thankful for your families and communities, and we all pray for their safety and happiness in the year ahead. Here in America, Muslims also think of their brothers and sisters in distant lands where lives are being lifted up by liberty and by hope.

In Iraq, families are observing this holy month in a free society. After enduring decades of tyranny and fear, the Iraqi people are guiding their nation toward democracy. And this January, they will choose their leaders in a free election.

In Afghanistan, brave men and women have transformed a country, and they have inspired our world. Just over 3 years ago, the Taliban government controlled Afghanistan. They harbored terrorists and denied basic rights to millions of citizens. And today, the Taliban is gone from power; women have their freedom; girls go to school; and last month, the people of Afghanistan stood in long lines to cast their vote in a free election.

The elections in Afghanistan and Iraq will be counted as landmark events in the history of liberty. And America will always be proud of our efforts to bring liberty and hope to those nations. Freedom is not America's gift to the world; freedom is the Almighty God's gift to each man and woman in this world.

Over the next 4 years, we'll work to ensure that the gift of freedom reaches more men and women in the broader Middle East. By working with leaders in that region, we can advance reform and change in a vital part of the world. And as we do so, we'll build a better future for all mankind.

As we defend liberty and justice abroad, we must honor those values here at home. At our founding, America made a commitment to justice and tolerance, and we keep that commitment today. We reject ethnic and religious bigotry in every form. We strive for a welcoming society that honors the life and faith of every person. We will always protect the most basic human freedom, the freedom to worship the Almighty God without any fear.

In recent years, Americans of many faiths have come to learn more about our Muslim brothers and sisters. And the more we learn, the more we find that our commitments are broadly shared. As Americans, we all share a commitment to family, to protect and to love our children. We share a belief in God's justice and man's moral responsibility. We share the same hope for a future of peace. We have so much in common and so much to learn from one another.

Once again, I wish you a blessed Ramadan. I want to thank you for joining us at the White House for this Iftaar, and may God bless you all.

NOTE: The President spoke at 5:58 p.m. on the State Floor at the White House. In his remarks, he referred to Imam Faizul Khan, administrator, Islamic Society of the Washington Area.

Statement on the Death of Yasser Arafat
November 10, 2004

The death of Yasser Arafat is a significant moment in Palestinian history. We express our condolences to the Palestinian people. For the Palestinian people, we hope that the future will bring peace and the fulfillment of their aspirations for an independent, democratic Palestine that is at peace with its neighbors. During the period of transition that is ahead, we urge all in the region and throughout the world to join in helping make progress toward these goals and toward the ultimate goal of peace.

Remarks at a Veterans Day Ceremony in Arlington, Virginia
November 11, 2004

Thank you for that warm welcome. Laura and I are honored to be here today. Mr. Secretary, thank you for your kind introduction, and thank you for your strong leadership in making sure our veterans have got the very best care possible. Secretary Principi has done a fantastic job for the American veteran.

I thank the members of my Cabinet who have joined us today. I appreciate the Chiefs of Staff and other members of the United States military who have joined us. I want to thank all the veterans who are here today. I want to thank the representatives of veterans organizations. And I want to thank my fellow Americans.

Veterans Day is set aside to remember every man and woman who has taken up arms to defend our country. We honor every soldier, sailor, airman, marine, and coastguardsman who gave some of the best years of their lives to the service of the United States and stood ready to give life,

itself, on our behalf. Twenty-five million military veterans walk among us, and on this day, our Nation thanks them all.

These are the hidden heroes of a peaceful nation, our colleagues and friends, neighbors and family members who answered the call and returned to live in the land they defended.

Our veterans are drawn from several generations and many backgrounds. They're Americans who remember the swift conflict of the Persian Gulf war and a long cold war vigil, the heat of Vietnam and the bitter cold of Korea. They are veterans in their eighties who served under MacArthur and Eisenhower and saved the liberty of the world. And still with us in the year 2004 are a few dozen Americans who fought the Kaiser's army and celebrated the end of the Great War on this day in 1918. The last doughboys are all more than 100 years old. Our Nation will always be proud of their service.

Some of our veterans are young men and women with recent memories of battle in mountains and in deserts. In Afghanistan, these brave Americans helped sweep away a vicious tyranny allied with terror and prepared the way for a free people to elect its own leaders. In Iraq, our men and women fought a ruthless enemy of America, setting the people free from a tyrant who now sits in a prison cell.

All who have served in this cause are liberators in the best tradition of America. Their actions have made our Nation safer in a world full of new dangers. Their actions have also upheld the ideals of America's founding, which defines us still. Our Nation values freedom, not just for ourselves but for all. And because Americans are willing to serve and sacrifice for this cause, our Nation remains the greatest force for good among all the nations on the Earth.

Some of tomorrow's veterans are in combat in Iraq at this hour. They have a clear mission, to defeat the terrorists and aid the rise of a free government that can defend itself. They are performing that mission with skill and with honor. They are making us proud. They are winning.

Our men and women in the military have superb training and the best equipment and able commanders. And they have another great advantage: They have the example of American veterans who came before. From the very day George Washington took command, the uniform of the United States has always stood for courage and decency and shining hope in a world of darkness. And all who have worn that uniform have won the thanks of the American people.

Today we're thinking of our fellow Americans last seen on duty, whose fate is still undetermined. We will not rest until we have made the fullest possible accounting for every life.

Today we also recall the men and women who did not live to be called veterans, many of whom rest in these hills. Our veterans remember the faces and voices of fallen comrades. The families of the lost carry a burden of grief that time will lighten but never lift. Our whole Nation honors every patriot who placed duty and country before their own lives. They gave us every day that we live in freedom. The security of America depends on our active leadership in the world to oppose emerging threats and to spread freedom that leads to the peace we all want. And our leadership ultimately depends on the commitment and character of the Armed Forces.

America has needed these qualities in every generation, and every generation has stepped forward to provide them. What veterans have given our country is beyond our power to fully repay, yet today we recognize our debt to their honor. And on this national holiday, our hearts are filled with respect and gratitude for the veterans of the United States of America.

May God bless our veterans and their families, and may God continue to bless our great Nation. Thank you.

NOTE: The President spoke at 11:36 a.m. in the Amphitheater at Arlington National Cemetery. In his remarks, he referred to former President Saddam Hussein of Iraq. The Veterans Day proclamation of November 9 is listed in Appendix D at the end of this volume.

The President's News Conference With Prime Minister Tony Blair of the United Kingdom
November 12, 2004

President Bush. Thank you. Welcome. I'm pleased to welcome a statesman and a friend back to the White House. Prime Minister Blair is a visionary leader. I've come to know him as a man of unshakeable convictions. America's alliance with Great Britain has never been stronger, and we're working closely every day to spread that freedom that leads to peace.

Our two nations have shared in some of the most hopeful and positive achievements of our time. The people of Afghanistan have now chosen their President in a free election. The Taliban and the terrorists did everything they could to intimidate the long-suffering people of that country. Yet men and women lined up at the polls, some of them waiting for hours to have their first taste of democracy. The success of Afghanistan's election is a standing rebuke to cynicism and extremism and a testimony to the power of liberty and hope. The people of the United States and Great Britain can be proud of the role we have played in aiding the rise of a free nation and, in so doing, making our countries more secure.

Together we're serving the same cause in Iraq. Prime Minister Allawi authorized military operations to rid Fallujah of Saddam holdouts and foreign terrorists, and American and Iraqi forces have made substantial progress in the last several days. Our coalition is training Iraqi security forces who are performing bravely and taking increasing responsibility for their country's security. British, American, and other coalition forces are helping provide stability that is necessary for free elections. And U.N. officials are helping the Iraqi people prepare for those elections, to be held in January.

As those elections draw near, the desperation of the killers will grow, and the violence could escalate. The success of democracy in Iraq will be a crushing blow to the forces of terror, and the terrorists know it. The defeat of terror in Iraq will set that nation on a course to lasting freedom and will give hope to millions, and the Iraqi people know it.

The United States and Great Britain have shown our determination to help Iraqis achieve their liberty and to defend the security of the world. We'll continue to stand with our friends, and we will finish the job.

Prime Minister Blair and I also share a vision of a free, peaceful, a democratic broader Middle East. That vision must include a just and peaceful resolution of the Arab-Israeli conflict based on two democratic states, Israel and Palestine, living side by side in peace and security.

Our sympathies are with the Palestinian people as they begin a period of mourning. Yet the months ahead offer a new opportunity to make progress toward a lasting peace. Soon Palestinians will choose a new President. This is the first step in creating lasting democratic political institutions through which a free Palestinian people will elect local and national leaders.

We're committed to the success of these elections, and we stand ready to help. We look forward to working with a Palestinian leadership that is committed to fighting terror and committed to the cause of democratic reform. We'll mobilize the international community to help revive the Palestinian economy, to build up Palestinian security institutions to fight terror, to help the Palestinian government fight corruption, and to reform the Palestinian political system and build democratic institutions. We'll also work with Israeli and Palestinian leaders to complete the disengagement plan from Gaza and part of the West Bank.

These steps, if successful, will lay the foundation for progress in implementing the roadmap and then lead to final status negotiations.

We seek a democratic, independent, and viable state for the Palestinian people. We are committed to the security of Israel as a Jewish state. These objectives—two states living side by side in peace and security—can be reached by only one path, the path of democracy, reform, and the rule of law.

All that we hope to achieve together requires that America and Europe remain close partners. We are the pillars of the free world. We face the same threats and share the same belief in freedom and the rights of every individual. In my second term, I will work to deepen our transatlantic ties with the nations of Europe. I intend to visit Europe as soon as possible after my inauguration. My Government will continue to work through the NATO Alliance and with the European Union to strengthen cooperation between Europe and America.

America applauds the success of NATO and EU enlargement and welcomes the stability and prosperity that that enlargement brings. We must apply the combined strength and moral purpose of Europe and America to effectively fight terror and to overcome poverty and disease and despair, to advance human dignity, and to advance freedom.

In all that lies ahead in the defense of freedom, in the advance of democracy, and the spread of prosperity, America, the United Kingdom, and all of Europe must act together.

Mr. Prime Minister, welcome.

Prime Minister Blair. Thank you, Mr. President, and thank you for your gracious welcome to me here in the White House. And once again, many congratulations on your reelection.

There are three major issues that arise. The United States and the United Kingdom have stood together since September the 11th, 2001, in order to combat this new form of global terrorism that we face. And the three things that we can do most to make sure that we defeat this terrorism, apart from being ever vigilant on security, are, first of all, to bring democracy to Afghanistan, which we are doing, as the successful election of President Karzai shows. And that is quite magnificent tribute not just to the courage of the Afghan people but, actually, also to the power of democracy.

Secondly, we have to complete our mission in Iraq, make sure that Iraq is a stable and a democratic country. And I have no doubt at all that whatever the difficulties the terrorists and insurgents, supporters of Saddam Hussein may pose for us, that we will overcome those difficulties—ourselves, the multinational force, together with the Iraqi Government—and ensure that Iraq can be that democratic, stable state that the vast majority of Iraqis, I know, will want to see.

And the third thing is, as the President rightly said a moment or two ago, we meet at a crucial time where it is important that we revitalize and reinvigorate the search for a genuine, lasting, and just peace in the Middle East. I would like to repeat my condolences to the Palestinian people at this time.

As you will have seen, we have set out the steps that we believe are necessary to get into a process that will lead to the two-state solution that we want to see. And I think those steps are very clear. They are, first of all, making sure that we set out a clear vision—that clear vision was articulated by President Bush some time ago, repeated by him today—of a two-state solution, two democratic states living side by side together in peace.

The second thing is, we need to support those Palestinian elections. That is a chance for the first beginnings of democracy to take hold on the Palestinian side. So it's important that we support it.

Thirdly, however, if we want a viable Palestinian state, we need to make sure that the political, the economic, and the security infrastructure of that state is shaped and helped to come into being. We will mobilize international opinion and the international community in order to do that.

The fourth thing is that Prime Minister Sharon's plan for disengagement is important. I think we recognized that when we were here at the White House back in April of this year. That disengagement plan is now going forward. It's important that we support it, and then, on the basis of this, we are able, in accordance with the principles of the roadmap, to get back into final status negotiation, so that we have that two-state solution. And I think there is every possibility that we can do this, with the energy and the will and the recognition that in the end, it is only if the two states that we want to see living side by side are indeed democratic states where the rule of law and human rights are respected in each of them, that a just° peace could be secured.

I would also like to support very strongly what the President has just said about the transatlantic alliance. Again, I think there is a tremendous desire and willingness on the part of, certainly, our partners in the European Union to make sure that that alliance is strong. It's necessary for the security of the world. It's necessary for us to be able to tackle many of the problems that confront us.

I look forward to working with the President over these coming months in order to try and secure that progress that we have laid out for you today. And also, of course, we've had the opportunity to discuss the upcoming G–8 Presidency of the United Kingdom, and we intend to take those issues forward as well.

So, Mr. President, once again, many, many thanks.

President Bush. Sure.

° White House correction.

Prime Minister Blair. Thank you for your alliance and for your leadership at this time.

President Bush. Welcome, thanks.

Terry [Terence Hunt, Associated Press].

Situation in the Middle East

Q. Thank you, Mr. President. Thank you. With Yasser Arafat's death, what specific steps can Israel take to revive peace negotiations? And do you believe that Israel should implement a freeze on West Bank settlement expansion?

President Bush. I believe that the responsibility for peace is going to rest with the Palestinian people's desire to build a democracy and Israel's willingness to help them build a democracy. I know we have a responsibility as free nations to set forth a strategy that will help the Palestinian people head toward democracy. I don't think there will ever be lasting peace until there is a free, truly democratic society in the Palestinian territories that becomes a state. And therefore, the responsibility rests with both the Palestinian people and the leadership which emerges, with the Israelis to help that democracy grow, and with the free world to put the strategy in place that will help the democracy grow.

Prime Minister Blair. James.

Prospects for Middle East Peace

Q. James Blitz, Financial Times. Mr. President, can you say today that it is your firm intention that by the end of your second term in office, it is your goal that there should be two states, Israel and Palestine, living side by side?

President Bush. I think it is fair to say that I believe we've got a great chance to establish a Palestinian state, and I intend to use the next 4 years to spend the capital of the United States on such a state. I believe it is in the interests of the world that a truly free state develop. I know it is in the interests of the Palestinian people that they can live in a society where they can express their opinion freely, a society where they can educate their children without hate, a society in which they can realize their dreams if they happen to be an entrepreneur. I know it's in Israel's interest that a free state evolve on her border. There's no other way to have a lasting peace, in my judgment, unless we all work to help develop the institutions necessary for a state to emerge: civil society, based upon justice; free speech; free elections; the right for people to express themselves freely. The first step of that is going to be the election of a new President, and my fervent hope is that the new President embraces the notion of a democratic state.

I hate to put artificial timeframes on things. Unfortunately, I've got one on my existence as President. It's not artificial; it's actually real. And I'd like to see it done in 4 years. I think it is possible. I think it is possible.

I think it is impossible to think that the President of the United States or the Prime Minister of Great Britain can impose our vision. I think it's unrealistic to say, "Well, Bush wants it done, or Blair wants it done. Therefore, it will happen." But I think it is very possible that it can happen, because I believe people want to live in a free society, and our job is to help it happen.

Thank you. Steve [Steve Holland, Reuters].

President's Upcoming Visit to Europe

Q. Thank you, Mr. President. Prime Minister Blair wants a international conference on the Middle East. What has to happen before you would sign on to that? And will you name a U.S. envoy? And what would you like to accomplish on this Europe trip that you're planning?

President Bush. Let's see here. [*Laughter*] I'll start with the—accomplishing on the Europe trip. It is to remind people that the world is better off, America is better off, Europe is better off when we work together. And there's a lot we can accomplish working together. There's a lot we have accomplished working together.

We're working very closely to find Al Qaida and bring members of Al Qaida to justice. We've worked closely to free Afghanistan. We're working closely to interdict the flow of weapons of mass destruction. The Proliferation Security Initiative is based—the membership of which is a lot of members of the EU. I mean, there's a lot of things we're working together on. NATO expansion we worked together on. It was such a refreshing moment when the new leaders of—the leaders of the new countries in NATO walked in the room in the Czech Republic. It was a fantastic moment to see these proud members walk in and say, "We're now a member of the greatest alliance ever." And there's a lot we can continue to do.

First two questions?

Prospects for Middle East Peace

Q. Prime Minister Blair's idea about an international conference——

President Bush. Yes.

Q. ——and the sending of a U.S. envoy to the Middle East.

President Bush. Right. In the spirit of the last question, we'll do what it takes to get a peace. And the conference—what the Prime Minister and I discussed last night is, do not we have an obligation to develop a strategy? And the answer is, absolutely, we have an obligation. And one way to do that is to include the Quartet to bring nations together and say, "Here's what it takes to help the Palestinians develop a state that is truly free." And I'm all for conferences, just so long as the conferences produce something. And we had a long discussion about whether or not a conference could produce a viable strategy that we could then use as a go-by for our own obligations as well as the obligations of the Palestinians, for them to have their own state. And the answer is, if that conference will do that, you bet I'm a big supporter.

But one thing is for certain: We are going to develop a strategy, so that once the elections are over, we'll be able to say, "Here's how we will help you. If you want to be helped, here's what we're willing to do. If you choose not to be helped, if you decide you don't want a free, democratic society, there's nothing we can do. If you think you can have peace without democracy"—again, I think you'll find that—I can only speak for myself, that I will be extremely doubtful that it will ever happen. I've seen it work too many times—tried too many times.

Now, there's going to be people around who say, "The Palestinians can't develop a democracy. It's impossible for them to live in a free society." I strongly disagree with that. And so the whole premise of this strategy that we'll outline is all based toward that vision of a free and truly democratic society emerging.

See, what's going to happen is, when that happens, there will be great trust developed between Israel and the Palestinian people. Free societies are able—societies able to develop trust between each other, and there's clearly a lack of trust right now. And so, yes, I mean, we will do that what it takes to put a strategy in place and advance it and call upon other nations to develop—to work with us.

Prime Minister Blair. Yes, that's absolutely right. I mean, what we will do is anything that is necessary to make the strategy work. The important thing is that, first of all, there's got to be an agreement as to what a viable Palestinian state means. And what we're really saying this morning is that that viable state has to be a democratic state.

The second thing is, how do we get there? How do we enable the Palestinians to get there? We will do whatever it takes to help build support for that concept, to work through the details of it and make sure that it can actually be brought into being. But the bottom line has got to be that if you want to secure Israel and you want a viable Palestinian state, those are two states living side by side, and they are

democratic states living side by side. And we've got the chance over the next few months, with the election of a new Palestinian President, to put the first marker down on that.

Trevor.

Iran

Q. Trevor Cavanagh from The Sun. Mr. President, I know that Iran, as well as Iraq, has been a very significant part of the agenda for this week, and I'd like to ask you whether, in light of the nuclear ambitions of Iran, whether America would tolerate a nuclear Iran? And if the answer to that is no, would Britain, Mr. Prime Minister, stand as four-square behind America on this issue as it has done on Iraq?

President Bush. Let me make sure I understand your question. You're saying a—Iran with a nuclear weapon——

Q. Nuclear power.

President Bush. Nuclear power or nuclear weapon?

Q. Nuclear weapon.

President Bush. Okay. No, we don't want Iran to have a nuclear weapon, and we're working toward that end. And the truth of the matter is, the Prime Minister gets a lot of credit for working with France and Germany to convince the Iranians to get rid of the processes that would enable them to develop a nuclear weapon.

Prime Minister Blair. Absolutely. And there's an agreement in the international community to make sure that Iran comes into compliance with its international obligations. And we've been working with France and Germany but, obviously, with the United States and others too, to make sure that that happens.

President Bush. Let's see here. Cochran. John [John Cochran, ABC News].

Q. I'm totally shocked. [*Laughter*]

President Bush. That's why I called on you. [*Laughter*]

Democracy in the Middle East

Q. You know, you talk about democracy being so necessary. There are those who would say there is sometimes a harsh peace of a dictator. What if the Palestinian state comes up with somebody who is not a democrat but is willing to have peace with the Israelis? And let me transfer that to the Iraqis as well. What if the Iraqis come up with somebody who's not friendly to the United States, is not a democrat, but it's peaceful. Is this something you can live with?

President Bush. Well, first of all, if there's an election, the Iraqis will have come up with somebody who is duly elected. In other words, democracy will have spoken. And that person is going to have to listen to the people, not to the whims of a dictator, not to their own desires, personal desires. The great thing about democracy is you actually go out and ask the people for a vote, as you might have noticed recently. And the people get to decide, and they get to decide the course of their future. And so it's a contradiction in terms to say a dictator gets elected. The person who gets elected is chosen by the people. And so I don't—I'm not——

Q. You can be elected and be a tyrant.

President Bush. Well, you can be elected and then be a strong man, and then you get voted out, so long as you end up honoring democracy. But if you're true to democracy, you'll listen to the people, not to your own desires. If you're true to democracy, you'll do what the people want you to do. That's the difference between democracy and a tyrant.

And the Palestinians may decide to elect a real strong personality. But we'll hold their feet to the fire to make sure that democracy prevails, that there are free elections. And if they don't—the people of the Palestinian territory don't like the way this person is responding to their needs, they will vote him or her out.

And the reason why I'm so strong on democracy is, democracies don't go to war with each other. And the reason why is, the people of most societies don't like war, and they understand what war means. And one of these days, the people of the Palestinian—the Palestinians will realize that there is a bright future because freedom is taking hold—a future that enables their children to get educated, a future in which they can start their businesses, a future in which they're certain that the money that's going into the treasury of their government is being spent fairly, in a transparent way, a future in which corruption is not the norm, a future in which rule of law prevails. And that leads to a peaceful society.

I've got great faith in democracies to promote peace. And that's why I'm such a strong believer that the way forward in the Middle East, the broader Middle East, is to promote democracy.

I readily concede there are skeptics, people who say democracy is not possible in certain societies. But remember, that was said right after World War II with Japan. And today, one of the people that I work closest with is my friend Prime Minister Koizumi. And it's a—it's remarkable to me that we sit down at the same table, talking about keeping the peace in places like North Korea, and it really wasn't all that long ago in the march of history that we were enemies. The Prime Minister knows Koizumi. He's a good man. And he's an ally because democracy took hold in Japan. And yet there was a lot of skeptics. When you look at the writings right after World War II, a lot of people said, "You're wasting your time to try to promote democracy in Japan." There were some, I suspect maybe in Great Britain and I know in America, that were writing, "You're wasting your time to promote democracy in Germany," after World War II. And yet fortunately, people who preceded us had great faith in liberty to transform societies. And that's what we're talking about is taking place.

And it's hard, and it's difficult, particularly in a society like Iraq, because the terrorists understand the stakes of freedom. And they're willing to kill people in brutal fashion to stop it. And I believe we have a duty and an obligation to work to make sure democracy takes hold. It's a duty to our own country. It's a duty to generations of Americans and children of Great Britain to help secure the peace by promoting democratic societies.

Prime Minister Blair. First of all, I should say, Koizumi is a good man not just because I know him, but—[*laughter*]—although that helps a lot, I think. [*Laughter*]

But I think the President said something here that I really think is very, very important. In the politics—when I was first a member of Parliament and making my way up the greasy pole and all the rest of it, there was a view in foreign policy that you dealt with countries on the basis of whatever attitude they had towards you, but really, whatever they did within their own countries, that was up to them and didn't really make a difference to your long-term relationship. I think what we are learning today is that there is not stability of any true, long-term kind without democratic rights for free people to decide their government. Now, that doesn't mean to say we try and interfere with every state around the world, but it does mean that there's been a shift, and I think a shift quite dramatically, since 9/11 in the thinking that is informing our view of how we make progress.

That's why it wasn't enough to go into Afghanistan and root out Al Qaida or knock down the Taliban. We actually had to go there and say, "No, we must replace that with a democratic form of government," because, in the end, if we replace it simply with another dictator, then we'll get the same instability back. That's why in Iraq, we decided, when Saddam was removed, we didn't want another hard man coming in, another dictator.

Now, it's a struggle, because democracy is hard to bring into countries that have never had it before. But I've no doubt at all that the Iraqi people, given the chance—and indeed, you can see this in some of the local elections now down in the south of Iraq—given the chance, they'll want to elect their leaders. Why wouldn't they? I mean, why would they want a strong-arm leader who's going to have the secret police, no freedom of speech, no free press, no human rights, no proper law courts? The people want the freedom. What we recognized, I think, today, is that we're not going to have our security unless they get that freedom.

So when we come to the issue of Israel and Palestine, I think what we are saying is, we are going to work flat-out to deliver this. But people have to understand, we can't deliver something unless the people whom it affects actually want it to happen. And we don't believe there will be a viable future for a state of Palestine unless it's based on certain key democratic principles.

Now, I think that's a tremendous thing. And I also think that in the end—of course, you're right, people can vote for the people they'd like to vote for in elections, right? That's what democracy is about. I think we've got to have some faith, though, in the ability of ordinary people, decent people, to decide their own future. Because it's a curious thing, you look at all these Eastern European countries—Central, Eastern European countries in the European Union now, just democracies over the last 10 years—fierce election debates, changes of Government, often difficult circumstances when the Governments change. But you go to those countries and talk to the people there, and their sense of liberation and their sense of self-worth as a result of the freedom they have—that is the best testament to why it's sensible to have faith in democracy.

And sometimes when people say, "Well it's—you've got a Republican President and a progressive politician from across the water," but in my view, people from different sides of the political spectrum should be able to come together to argue that policy case, because democracy is something that should unite us, whatever political position we have.

David.

United Kingdom-United States Relations

Q. David Charter from The Times in London. Mr. President, first, the Prime Minister is sometimes, perhaps unfairly, characterized in Britain as your poodle. I was wondering if that's the way you may see your relationship? And perhaps, more seriously, do you feel for the——

Prime Minister Blair. Don't answer yes to that question. If you do, I would be— [*laughter*]—that would be difficult.

Q. Do you feel, for the strong support that Britain has given you over Iraq, that you have to pay back Britain for that support in some way?

President Bush. The Prime Minister made the decision he did because he wanted to do his duty to secure the people of Great Britain. That's why he made the decision—plenty capable of making his own mind. He's a strong, capable man. I admire him a lot. You know why? When he tells you something, he means it. You spend much time in politics, you'll know there's some people around this part of the—this kind of line of work where they tell you something, they don't mean it. When he says something, he means it. He's a big thinker. He's got a clear vision, and when times get tough, he doesn't wilt. When they—when the criticism starts to come his way—I suspect that might be happening on occasion—he stands what he believes in. That's the kind of person I like to deal with. He is a—I'm a lucky person—a lucky President, to be holding office at the same time this man holds the Prime Ministership.

These are troubled times. It's a tough world. What this world needs is steady, rock-solid leaders who stand on principle, and that's what the Prime Minister means to me.

Prime Minister Blair. I just want to add one thing, which is that, well, this concept of payback—we are—we're not fighting the war against terrorism because we are an ally of the United States. We are an ally of the United States because we believe in fighting this war against terrorism. We share the same objectives. We share the same values. And if we look back over our own history in the last half-century or more, we, both of us, in different ways, the United States and Britain, have a cause to be thankful for this alliance and this partnership. And I should we—I believe we should be thankful that it is as strong as it is today. And as long as I remain Prime Minister of our country, it will carry on being strong, not because that's in the interests of America, simply, or in the interests of the international community, but because I believe passionately it is in the interests of Britain.

President Bush. Good job. Thank you, sir.

Thank you all.

NOTE: The President's news conference began at 11:25 a.m. in the East Room at the White House. In his remarks, he referred to President Hamid Karzai of Afghanistan; Prime Minister Ayad Allawi of the Iraqi Interim Government; and Prime Minister Junichiro Koizumi of Japan. Prime Minister Blair referred to Prime Minister Ariel Sharon of Israel; and former President Saddam Hussein of Iraq.

Joint Statement Between the United States of America and the United Kingdom Concerning the Middle East Peace Process
November 12, 2004

The United States and the United Kingdom share a vision of freedom, peace, and democracy for the Broader Middle East. That vision must include a just and peaceful resolution of the Arab-Israeli conflict, based on two democratic states—Israel and Palestine—living side by side in peace and security. Now is the time to seize the opportunity of new circumstances in the region to redouble our efforts to achieve this goal. This will require a series of steps which we look forward to taking with our international partners and the parties.

First, we re-commit to the overarching two-state vision set out by President Bush in his statement of June 24, 2002 and repeated in the Roadmap.

Second, we will support the Palestinians as they choose a new President within the next sixty days and as they embark upon an electoral process that will lead to lasting democratic institutions.

Third, following that, the President and the Prime Minister have agreed to mobilize international support behind a plan to ensure that the Palestinians have the political, economic, and security infrastructure they need to create a viable state. There will be no lasting solution without a Palestinian state that is democratic and free, including free press, free speech, an open political process, and religious tolerance. Such a state will need a credible and unified security structure capable of providing security for the Palestinians and fighting terrorism. There must also be effective economic development and transparent financial structures which provide for the economic and social needs of the Palestinian people. The plan will be developed intensively over the coming period of time in concert with all the relevant partners.

Fourth, we endorse and support the disengagement plan of Prime Minister Sharon from Gaza and stipulated parts of the West Bank as part of this overall plan.

Fifth, these steps lay the basis for more rapid progress on the Roadmap as a reliable guide leading to final status negotiations.

NOTE: An original was not available for verification of the content of this joint statement.

The President's Radio Address
November 13, 2004

Good morning. Earlier this week, Prime Minister Allawi of Iraq authorized military operations to rid the city of Fallujah of Saddam holdouts and foreign terrorists. American marines and soldiers, alongside Iraqi security forces, are on the offensive against the killers who have been using Fallujah as a base of operations for terrorist attacks and who have held the local population in the grip of fear.

Fighting together, our forces have made significant progress in the last several days. They are taking back the city, clearing mosques of weapons and explosives stockpiled by insurgents, and restoring order for law-abiding citizens.

In the course of this operation, Iraqi troops have discovered new evidence of the enemy's brutality. An Iraqi general has described hostage slaughter houses, where terrorists have killed innocent victims and proudly recorded their barbaric crimes. The terrorists have shown once again the stakes of this struggle. They seek to spread fear and violence throughout Iraq, throughout the broader Middle East, and throughout the world, and they will fail. The terrorists will be defeated. Iraq will be free, and the world will be more secure. Our commitment to the success of democracy in Iraq is unshakable, and we will prevail.

Ultimately, Iraq must be able to defend itself, and Iraqi security forces are taking increasing responsibility for their country's security. As we see in Fallujah and as we saw in Najaf and elsewhere, Iraqi security forces are standing and fighting and risking their lives for the future of their nation. As terrorists have targeted these forces, still more brave Iraqis have come forward as volunteers. Today, nearly 115,000 trained and equipped Iraqi soldiers, police officers, and other security personnel are serving their country. The Iraqi Government is on track to meet its goal of fielding more than 200,000 security personnel by the end of next year.

In January, the Iraqi people will elect a transitional National Assembly, which will draft a new constitution to prepare the way for the election of a permanent Iraqi Government. The Iraqi people, like the people of Afghanistan before them, are embracing a democratic future even in the face of threats and intimidation. Throughout the country, Iraqi men and women are registering to vote; political parties are forming; candidates for office are stepping forward.

International support for the Iraqi election is essential, and that support continues to grow. Military forces from some 30 nations are working alongside Iraqi forces, helping to establish stability and security. A U.N. team is providing critical technical support to Iraq's independent electoral commission. Other diplomatic personnel are helping the Iraqi people prepare for those elections to be held on schedule in January.

As those elections draw near, the desperation of the killers will grow, and the violence could escalate. The success of democracy in Iraq would be a crushing blow to the forces of terror, and the terrorists know it. The defeat of terror in Iraq will set that nation on a course to lasting freedom and will give hope to millions, and the Iraqi people know it. And a free, democratic Iraq will inspire reformers throughout the Middle East and make America more secure.

The United States and our allies have shown our determination to help Iraqis achieve their liberty. We will continue to stand by our friends, and we will finish the job.

Thank you for listening.

NOTE: The address was recorded at 12:50 p.m. on November 12 in the Cabinet Room at the White House for broadcast at 10:06 a.m. on November 13. The transcript was made available by the Office of the Press Secretary on November 12 but was embargoed for release until the broadcast. In his remarks, the President referred to Prime Minister Ayad Allawi of the Iraqi Interim Government; and former President Saddam Hussein of Iraq. The Office of the Press Secretary also released a Spanish language transcript of this address.

Statement on the Resignation of Colin L. Powell as Secretary of State
November 15, 2004

Colin Powell is one of the great public servants of our time. He is a soldier, a diplomat, a civic leader, a statesman, and a great patriot. I value his friendship. He will be missed. On behalf of all Americans, I thank him for his many years of service, and I wish him and Alma all the best.

In his 4 years as Secretary of State, Colin forged new alliances that are helping America win the war on terror and reinvigorated old and honored friendships. He has helped to build two great coalitions that have liberated more than 50 million people in Afghanistan and Iraq from brutal dictators and which are now helping those nations emerge as successful democracies. He was a key architect of the Broader Middle East Initiative, which is helping to spread freedom and democracy in that region.

His diplomatic skills also helped to end regional conflicts and lower tensions on the Indian subcontinent. Through his advocacy, he focused the world's attention on the plight of the suffering in Sudan, Liberia, and Haiti. His role in resolving the EP–3 incident early in my administration showed the calm judgment and steady resolve he has brought to our foreign policy. Thousands of dedicated foreign policy professionals are grateful for his leadership in modernizing and strengthening the Department of State.

NOTE: The Office of the Press Secretary also made available Secretary Powell's letter of resignation.

Statement on the Resignation of Roderick R. Paige as Secretary of Education
November 15, 2004

Rod Paige has been at the forefront of fundamentally reforming and improving our Nation's public education system so that no child is left behind in America. His passion for taking on the status quo and fighting for reform underscores his strong commitment to our country's young people and his desire to give them a brighter future. Throughout his life, Rod has overcome great obstacles and achieved great success. He represents the best of America.

We have only begun the long-term transformation of education so that future generations can enjoy all of the promise and opportunity America has to offer. Thanks to the hard work of Rod Paige, we have a very strong start and are well on our way to fulfilling that promise.

I am thankful for Rod's leadership during this important time and am grateful for his friendship. I wish him all the best.

NOTE: The Office of the Press Secretary also made available Secretary Paige's letter of resignation.

Statement on the Resignation of Spencer Abraham as Secretary of Energy
November 15, 2004

Spence Abraham has been a valued member of the Cabinet and a strong and steady leader of the Department of Energy. He helped develop our National Energy Policy to reduce our country's reliance on foreign sources of energy and to provide reliable, affordable, and environmentally sound energy for America's future. He launched new technological research initiatives that will lead to the next generation of pollution-free automobiles and clean coal powerplants. In the war on terror, Spence Abraham played a pivotal role in keeping the most dangerous weapons out of the hands of the most dangerous people through his work on nuclear nonproliferation.

I am very grateful for Spence's service and thank him for his sacrifice and hard work for America. I wish him and Jane all the best.

NOTE: The Office of the Press Secretary also made available Secretary Abraham's letter of resignation.

Statement on the Resignation of Ann M. Veneman as Secretary of Agriculture
November 15, 2004

Ann Veneman has been a strong advocate for America's farm and ranch families. As Secretary of Agriculture, she has been a valuable member of my Cabinet, working to ensure that we promote economic opportunities for farmers and ranchers, ensure a safe and wholesome food supply, and sell American farm products all around the world.

I commend Ann for her efforts to enact and implement a responsible farm bill with strong conservation provisions. I greatly appreciate Ann's leadership in ensuring that we responded quickly and effectively to protect the American food supply following the discovery of BSE in the United States and following September 11th. She has helped ensure commonsense forest management and skillfully implemented the Healthy Forests Initiative. She has played a key role in opening markets and in ensuring a level playing field for America's farm products.

Ann has served our country with distinction and integrity. I appreciate her fine work and wish her well.

NOTE: The Office of the Press Secretary also made available Secretary Veneman's letter of resignation.

Statement on the Resignation of Edward W. Gillespie as Chairman of the Republican National Committee
November 15, 2004

Ed Gillespie has done an outstanding job as chairman of the Republican National Committee. He helped bring many new people to our cause by sharing our vision of a safer world and more hopeful America. His successful efforts in outreach, registration, and voter turnout will be an enduring legacy on which to build a long-lasting governing coalition.

Republicans now hold the Presidency, majorities in both Houses of Congress, and the majority of governorships and State legislatures. That's due to a lot of hard work by many people, and one of the most important contributions has been the personal commitment, creativity, and leadership of Ed Gillespie these past years.

I thank Ed for his exceptional service and friendship and wish him and Cathy all the best.

Remarks on the Nomination of Condoleezza Rice To Be Secretary of State and the Appointment of Stephen J. Hadley as National Security Adviser
November 16, 2004

The President. Good afternoon. I'm pleased to announce my nomination of Dr. Condoleezza Rice to be America's Secretary of State. Condi Rice is already known to all Americans and to much of the world.

During the last 4 years, I've relied on her counsel, benefited from her great experience, and appreciated her sound and steady judgment. And now I'm honored that she has agreed to serve in my Cabinet. The Secretary of State is America's face to the world. And in Dr. Rice, the world will see the strength, the grace, and the decency of our country.

Both Condi and I have been proud to serve with our friend Secretary of State Colin Powell. He has been one of the most effective and admired diplomats in America's history. Secretary Powell has helped to rally the world in a global war. He's helped to resolve dangerous regional conflicts. He's helped to confront the desperate challenges of hunger, poverty, and disease. He has been tireless and selfless and prin-

cipled, and our entire Nation is grateful for his lifetime of service.

I'm also grateful that Steve Hadley has agreed to become my new National Security Adviser. Steve served Presidents Nixon, Ford, and Bush before me, and he has done a superb job as Dr. Rice's deputy during these past 4 years. Steve is a man of wisdom and good judgment. He has earned my trust, and I look forward to his continued vital service on my national security team.

When confirmed by the Senate, Condoleezza Rice will take office at a critical time for our country. We're a nation at war. We're leading a large coalition against a determined enemy. We're putting in place new structures and institutions to confront outlaw regimes, to oppose proliferation of dangerous weapons and materials, and to break up terror networks.

The United States has undertaken a great calling of history to aid the forces of reform and freedom in the broader Middle East so that that region can grow in hope instead of growing in anger. We're pursuing a positive new direction to resolve the Arab-Israeli conflict, an approach that honors the peaceful aspirations of the Palestinian people through a democratic state and an approach that will ensure the security of our good friend Israel.

Meeting all of these objectives will require wise and skillful leadership at the Department of State, and Condi Rice is the right person for that challenge. She's a recognized expert in international affairs, a distinguished teacher and academic leader, and a public servant with years of White House experience. She displays a commitment to excellence in every aspect of her life, from shaping our strategy in the war on terror to coordinating national security policy across the Government to performing classical music on stage. Above all, Dr. Rice has a deep, abiding belief in the value and power of liberty, because she has seen freedom denied and freedom reborn.

As a girl in the segregated South, Dr. Rice saw the promise of America violated by racial discrimination and by the violence that comes from hate. But she was taught by her mother, Angelena, and her father, the Reverend John Rice, that human dignity is the gift of God and that the ideals of America would overcome oppression. That early wisdom has guided her through life, and that truth has guided our Nation to a better day.

I know that the Reverend and Mrs. Rice would be filled with pride to see the daughter they raised in Birmingham, Alabama, chosen for the office first held by Thomas Jefferson. Something tells me, however, they would not be surprised. [*Laughter*]

As many of you know, Condi's true ambition is beyond my power to grant. [*Laughter*] She would really like to be the commissioner of the National Football League. I'm glad she's put those plans on hold once again. The Nation needs her. I urge the Senate to promptly confirm Condoleezza Rice as America's 66th Secretary of State.

Congratulations.

[*At this point, Secretary-designate Rice made brief remarks.*]

The President. Good job. Thank you all.

NOTE: The President spoke at 12:33 p.m. in the Roosevelt Room at the White House. The transcript released by the Office of the Press Secretary also included the remarks of Secretary-designate Rice.

Remarks at the Thanksgiving Turkey Presentation Ceremony
November 17, 2004

Thank you all. Please be seated. Welcome. Welcome to a beautiful day here in the Rose Garden. I'm pleased to welcome Biscuits—[*laughter*]—the National Thanksgiving Turkey. Biscuits, welcome. [*Laughter*]

This is an election year, and Biscuits had to earn his spot at the White House. Over the past week, thousands of voters cast ballots on the White House web site. It was a close race. You might say it was neck and neck. [*Laughter*] When all the voters were in—all the votes were in, Biscuits and his runningmate, Gravy, prevailed over the ticket of Patience and Fortitude. [*Laughter*] The Vice President and I are here to congratulate Biscuits for a race well run.

It came down to a few battleground States. [*Laughter*] It was a tough contest, and it turned out some 527 organizations got involved—[*laughter*]—including Barnyard Animals for Truth. [*Laughter*] There was a scurrilous film that came out, "Fahrenheit 375 Degrees at 10 Minutes Per Pound." [*Laughter*] Now it's a time for healing.

This day took a lot of planning, and I want to thank all those who helped. I appreciate Secretary of Agriculture Ann Veneman. She has served our Nation with class and distinction. I'm going to miss having her in my Cabinet, and I wish her all the best.

Congressman, I'm honored you are here. Thanks for coming. I know that you're deeply concerned about the fate of this year's Thanksgiving turkey. You're a man of deep compassion.

I want to thank everyone here with the National Turkey Federation, especially John O'Carroll and Alice Johnson. Welcome.

I want to thank Kevin Foltz and his family for the fine job they did in raising Biscuits and Gravy on their farm in Mathias, West Virginia. They fed the turkeys American corn and American soybeans. And from the looks of it, he had a pretty healthy appetite. [*Laughter*] I'm also grateful to Kevin's children, Kolby, Kollin, and Korey, who helped to coach the turkeys to face the cameras on their big day here.

We've also got some special guests from the Immaculate Conception School. I'm glad you took this field trip to the White House. I'm grateful to your school and the parish for sharing some of your blessings during the holidays. This is the 40th year Immaculate Conception has provided food baskets to families in the Shaw neighborhood to make sure they have plenty to eat for their Thanksgiving dinner. For the sake of our feathered guests, I'm not going to elaborate on the contents of those baskets. [*Laughter*]

The Thanksgiving tradition dates back to our Nation's earliest days. We are a nation founded by men and women who deeply felt their dependence on God and always gave Him thanks and praise. As we prepare for Thanksgiving in 2004, we have much to be thankful for, our families, our friends, our beautiful country, and the freedom granted to each one of us by the Almighty.

During this holiday season, we think especially of our men and women of the Armed Forces, many of whom are spending Thanksgiving far from home. Last Thanksgiving, I had the privilege of meeting with our military serving in Baghdad area of Iraq. Those men and women, like all who wear our Nation's uniform, have volunteered to serve. Through their courage and skill and sacrifice, they are keeping our country safe and free. America is proud of our military. We're proud of our military families, and we give them our thanks every day of the year.

The National Thanksgiving Turkey will soon be on stage for all to see, but he's not going to end up on the table. I'm granting him a Presidential pardon. Not only will I grant the pardon to Biscuits; I will also grant one to Gravy as well. I wish them well as they begin their new life at Frying Pan Park in the great State of Virginia.

Laura and I and the Vice President wish every American a happy Thanksgiving. May God bless you all, and may God continue to bless our country.

NOTE: The President spoke at 10:15 a.m. in the Rose Garden at the White House. In his remarks, he referred to John O'Carroll, chairman, and Alice L. Johnson, president, National Turkey Federation. The Thanksgiving Day proclamation of November 23 is listed in Appendix D at the end of this volume.

Remarks on the Nomination of Margaret Spellings To Be Secretary of Education
November 17, 2004

The President. Thank you all. Please be seated. Good morning. I'm proud to announce my nomination of Margaret Spellings to be the Secretary of Education.

I've known Margaret Spellings for more than a decade. I have relied on her intellect and judgment throughout my career in public service. As Governor of Texas, I called on her to serve the children of our State as my chief education adviser, a job she carried out with conviction and great results.

When I was elected President, I asked her to serve as Assistant to the President for Domestic Policy. I've benefited from her knowledge and experience on many issues, from health care to immigration to job training. I'm now calling on this energetic reformer to serve the children of America by continuing our vital work of improving our Nation's public schools.

Margaret Spellings has a special passion for this cause. She believes that every child can learn and that every school can succeed. And she knows the stakes are too high to tolerate failure. She believes in high standards and improving the resources necessary—and providing the resources necessary to meet those standards. In Margaret Spellings, America's children, teachers, and parents will have a principled, determined ally in my Cabinet. She has my complete trust, and she will be an outstanding Secretary of Education.

With the Senate's approval, Margaret Spellings will continue the work of a fine educator and leader, Secretary Rod Paige. As Secretary of Education, this humble and decent man inspired his Department and implemented the most significant Federal education reform in a generation. Today, thanks to the No Child Left Behind Act, students of every background are making hopeful progress in reading and math. The Nation's schools are stronger because of Rod Paige's leadership. I'm grateful for his friendship. I'm grateful for his years of service.

We've made great progress in our schools, and there is more work to do. Margaret Spellings and I are determined to extend the high standards and accountability measures of the No Child Left Behind Act to all of America's public high schools. We must ensure that a high school diploma is a sign of real achievement, so that our young people have the tools to go to college and to fill the jobs of the 21st century. And in all our reforms, we will continue to stand behind our Nation's teachers, who work so hard for our children.

The issue of education is close to my heart. And on this vital issue, there is no one I trust more than Margaret Spellings. Two decades ago, as a young aide in the Texas State legislature, Margaret dedicated herself to strengthening public schools. She went on to help lead the Texas Association of School Boards, to advise two Governors on school reform, and to serve 4 years as my top domestic policy adviser right here in the White House. And now her talent and idealism have brought her to the highest education office in the land. Through it all, she has kept her good humor and her perspective on life. She is a devoted, loving mother to Mary and Grace, and Laura and I are proud to count her and Robert as good friends.

I urge the Senate to promptly confirm Margaret Spellings as America's eighth Secretary of Education. And I look forward to having her in my Cabinet.

Congratulations.

[*At this point, Secretary-designate Spellings made brief remarks.*]

The President. Good job.

NOTE: The President spoke at 11:07 a.m. in the Roosevelt Room at the White House. The transcript released by the Office of the Press Secretary also included the remarks of Secretary-designate Spellings.

Message to the Congress Transmitting the Japan-United States Social Security Agreement
November 17, 2004

To the Congress of the United States:

Pursuant to section 233(e)(1) of the Social Security Act, as amended by the Social Security Amendments of 1977 (Public Law 95–216, 42 U.S.C. 433(e)(1)), I transmit herewith the Agreement between the United States of America and Japan on Social Security, which consists of two separate instruments: a principal agreement and an administrative arrangement. The Agreement was signed at Washington on February 19, 2004.

The United States-Japan Agreement is similar in objective to the social security agreements already in force with Australia, Austria, Belgium, Canada, Chile, Finland, France, Germany, Greece, Ireland, Italy, Korea, Luxembourg, the Netherlands, Norway, Portugal, Spain, Sweden, Switzerland, and the United Kingdom. Such bilateral agreements provide for limited coordination between the United States and foreign social security systems to eliminate dual social security coverage and taxation, and to help prevent the lost benefit protection that can occur when workers divide their careers between two countries. The United States-Japan Agreement contains all provisions mandated by section 233 and other provisions which I deem appropriate to carry out the purposes of section 233, pursuant to section 233(c)(4).

I also transmit for the information of the Congress a report prepared by the Social Security Administration explaining the key points of the Agreement, along with a paragraph-by-paragraph explanation of the provisions of the principal agreement and the related administrative arrangement. Annexed to this report is the report required by section 233(e)(1) of the Social Security Act, a report on the effect of the Agreement on income and expenditures of the United States Social Security program and the number of individuals affected by the Agreement.

The Department of State and the Social Security Administration have recommended the Agreement and related documents to me.

I commend to the Congress the United States-Japan Social Security Agreement and related documents.

GEORGE W. BUSH

The White House,
November 17, 2004.

Message to the Congress Transmitting a Report on the Squirrel River in Alaska
November 17, 2004

To the Congress of the United States:

I transmit herewith the enclosed study, findings, and report for the Squirrel River in Alaska. The report and my recommendations are submitted pursuant to my authority under Article II, section 3, of the Constitution of the United States, and consistent with section 5(a) of the Wild and Scenic Rivers (WSR) Act, Public Law 90–542, as amended. The Squirrel River suitability study was authorized by Public Law 96–487 (Alaska National Interest Lands Conservation Act).

The study conducted by the Bureau of Land Management determined that all 100 miles of the river are nonsuitable for inclu-

sion in the National WSR System. Consistent with the study, I recommend that the Congress take no action to designate the river. The withdrawal provided by section 5(a) of the WSR Act would expire within 3 years of the date of this message (unless other action is taken by the Congress). Approximately 81,501 acres of State-selected lands would be opened to mineral entry although mineral potential has been assessed as very low and there are no past or active mining claims.

GEORGE W. BUSH

The White House,
November 17, 2004.

Remarks at the Dedication of the William J. Clinton Presidential Center and Park in Little Rock, Arkansas
November 18, 2004

President Clinton, Senator Clinton, President Carter and Mrs. Carter, President Bush and Mother—[*laughter*]—Governor and Mrs. Huckabee, distinguished guests, ladies and gentlemen: Laura and I are really pleased to be a part of this happy and historic occasion. On this day of dedication, we honor the man from Hope, Arkansas, who became the 42d President of the United States. Mr. President, congratulations.

This Presidential library chronicles a vivid era in American history for the benefit of future generations. It will contribute to the vitality of this fine city and to the great State of Arkansas. The collections here record the dedication and hard work of thousands who brought talent and idealism to public service. And at the center of that era, at the head of that administration was

an able and energetic American. President Bill Clinton led our country with optimism and a great affection for the American people, and that affection has been returned. He gave all to his job, and the Nation gave him two terms.

In the early 1990s, the American people saw a young, well-spoken, relatively unknown Governor rise to national prominence. Yet for decades here in Arkansas, the signs of destiny were clear. When young William entered a new school in the fourth grade, a classmate recalls, "He didn't mean to, but he just took the place over." [*Laughter*] When Governor Clinton declared his candidacy for President in this city, his close friends were not surprised in the least. They'd always known that Bill Clinton's moment in history would come.

Arkansas is a State that knows political skill when you see it. A fellow in Saline County was asked by his son why he liked Governor Clinton so much. He said, "Son, he'll look you in the eye. He'll shake your hand. He'll hold your baby. He'll pet your dog—all at the same time." [*Laughter*]

Over the years, Bill Clinton showed himself to be much more than a good politician. His home State elected him the Governor in the 1970s, the 1980s, and the 1990s because he was an innovator, a serious student of policy, and a man of great compassion. In the White House, the whole Nation witnessed his brilliance and his mastery of detail, his persuasive power, and his persistence. The President is not the kind to give up a fight. His staffers were known to say, "If Clinton were the *Titanic*, the iceberg would sink." [*Laughter*]

During his Presidency, Bill Clinton seized important opportunities on issues from welfare to free trade. He was a tireless champion of peace in the Middle East. He used American power in the Balkans to confront aggression and halt ethnic cleansing. And in all his actions and decisions, the American people sensed a deep empathy for the poor and the powerless. Shortly before leaving office, President Clinton said, "Christ admonished us that our lives will be judged by how we do unto the least of our neighbors." Throughout his career, Bill Clinton has done his best to live up to that standard, and Americans respect him for it.

At every stage of his remarkable life, President Clinton has made and kept countless friends, who share in the joy of this day. And three people in particular have the largest part in this remarkable story. One day more than 30 years ago, inside the Yale Law Library, a fellow student walked over to Bill Clinton and said, "If you're going to keep staring at me and I'm going to keep staring back, we ought to at least know each other's name. Mine's Hillary Rodham. What is yours?" [*Laugh-ter*] That was a good day for both of them and the beginning of a partnership unique in American history. So today we honor the former first lady of Arkansas, the former First Lady of America, the United States Senator from New York, Senator Hillary Rodham Clinton.

Perhaps the Clintons's greatest achievement is their daughter, who moved into the White House as a young girl and left as an accomplished young lady. It's not easy to be a teenager in the White House, but it's a lot easier when you have a loving mother and a loving father that Chelsea Clinton had.

This magnificent Presidential library and the American life it celebrates would not have been possible without the love and sacrifice of a special lady. Among his heroes, President Clinton always includes his mother, Virginia Kelley, "a working woman and a widow." Virginia was there when her son took the oath of office, and we know that she would be incredibly proud of this day.

The story that began in a little house on Hervey Street in Hope, Arkansas, is the kind of story that inspires people from every background, all over America. In this great Nation, it is always possible for a child to go as far as their talent and vision can take them. Visitors to this place will be reminded of the great promise of our country, and the dreams that came true in the life of our 42d President. The William J. Clinton Presidential Library is a gift to the future by a man who always believed in the future. And today we thank him for loving and serving America.

God bless.

NOTE: The President spoke at 12:20 p.m. In his remarks, he referred to Gov. Mike Huckabee of Arkansas and his wife, Janet.

Remarks at a Presidential Luncheon in Little Rock
November 18, 2004

Thank you all. Mr. President, thank you very much, sir. Senator Clinton and Chelsea, Mother and Dad—it works every time when I say "Mother," you know? [*Laughter*] President Zedillo and Prime Minister Peres and distinguished guests: Laura and I are really pleased to be with you this afternoon. Thanks for such gracious hospitality. It is our honor to join in dedicating this magnificent library. The tour was fantastic. The people of Arkansas are going to love having the library here. The people of America are going to love coming here. It's really well done.

I know many here today were involved in creating this impressive library. I want to thank you for contributing and helping. And I know many here who served in the administration that is chronicled here. All of you were drawn to the talent and the vision and the energy of President Bill Clinton.

Today we recognize the first person from Arkansas to serve as the Chief Executive of our country, the first in his party to win reelection since Franklin Roosevelt, and a leader who filled the White House with energy and with joy.

During 8 eventful years, Bill Clinton applied tremendous gifts to the service of this country and for the cause of peace, and we're grateful for his service. Americans trusted their future to a man who deeply believed in our future. And Americans continued to like the man that he so clearly liked.

One man's journey from Hope, Arkansas, to the White House, the story told in this library, is an American story. It's a story of talent recognized early and lifelong friendships and hard work that was rewarded. The boy who shook the hand of John F. Kennedy in the Rose Garden has shaken the hands of many young people and inspired them with his idealism. And this library will carry that message into the future.

Americans look to our former Presidents as elder statesmen. In the case of President Clinton, the elder statesman is about one month younger than I am. [*Laughter*] His public service came early, and his service to America has not ended. So on this special afternoon I ask you to join me in a toast: To the past and to the future of our Nation's 42d President.

God bless you.

NOTE: The President spoke at 2:20 p.m. in a pavilion at the William J. Clinton Presidential Center and Park. In his remarks, he referred to former President Ernesto Zedillo of Mexico; and former Foreign Minister Shimon Peres of Israel. A tape was not available for verification of the content of these remarks.

Letter to the Speaker of the House of Representatives Transmitting a Budget Amendment for the Low Income Home Energy Assistance Program
November 19, 2004

Dear Mr. Speaker:

I ask the Congress to consider the enclosed FY 2005 budget amendment for the Low Income Home Energy Assistance Program in the Department of Health and Human Services. I designate $300 million in requested contingency funding for this program as an emergency requirement.

The details of this proposal are set forth in the enclosed letter from the Director of the Office of Management and Budget.

Sincerely,

GEORGE W. BUSH

Remarks Following Discussions With President Hu Jintao of China in Santiago, Chile
November 20, 2004

President Bush. Mr. President, thank you for this very frank exchange. I told the President that I look forward to working with him over the next 4 years to continue our close work on keeping peace—peace on the Korean Peninsula and peace throughout the Pacific region—and to spread peace throughout the world. And I'm looking forward to working with him on those matters.

We also spent time talking about our economic relationships, about how we'll work over the next 4 years to continue to spread prosperity to both our people, to make sure the relationship is fair and equitable on both sides.

I invited President Hu to come and visit the United States as soon as he can, and he invited me to China. Neither of us committed because we don't have our schedules in front of us, but nonetheless, we did commit to make sure our relationship is healthy and strong.

Thank you, Mr. President.

President Hu. Friends from the press, I just had a talk with President Bush through which we covered many grounds. I first re-offered my congratulations to him on his reelection to the—Presidency of the United States. We together reviewed how much this relationship has come in the past 4 years. We expressed satisfaction over the positive programs made in a constructive and cooperative relationship between the two countries.

We agree that the second term of President Bush will be an important period for continued development of China-U.S. relations. We are also committed to stronger coordination and cooperation between the two countries on economic matters and in terrorism, as well as important international and regional issues.

We also exchanged views on the question of Taiwan. I expressed my high appreciation to President Bush's adherence to the one-China policy and the three communiques and to his opposition to Taiwan independence.

We also discussed the nuclear issue on the Korean Peninsula. Both sides expressed the hope that the issue can be solved peacefully through dialog.

I would like to thank President Bush for inviting me to visit the United States, and I have also invited him to visit China. Thank you, Mr. President.

President Bush. Thank you all.

NOTE: The President spoke at 9:18 a.m. at the Hyatt Regency Santiago. A tape was not available for verification of the content of these remarks.

Remarks Following Discussions With Prime Minister Junichiro Koizumi of Japan and an Exchange With Reporters in Santiago
November 20, 2004

President Bush. It was my honor to have spent some quality time with my friend the leader of our strong ally, Japan. I enjoyed visiting with the Prime Minister. He's a man of clear vision and inner strength.

We covered a wide range of subjects, including the North Korean Peninsula and Iraq. I also explained to him that my Nation is committed to a strong dollar, and I assured him that in my upcoming contacts in working with Congress, we'll work to reduce our short-term and long-term deficit. It was a great conversation.

Prime Minister Koizumi. I'm very happy to be able to see the President in person, the first time after his reelection. And we have shared a view that the U.S. had a great effect in terms of security and also in terms of the well-being of the world economy. And I completely agree with the view of the President that a strong dollar has good impact on the U.S. economy and is also important for the world economy.

And I was also gratified to know that President Bush has a strong intent for further strengthening the framework of cooperation, international cooperation, to cope with the issue of Iraq.

And we also agreed to continue to place importance on the six-party talks process concerning North Korea and that we would also continue to pursue a diplomatic solution to dismantle all their nuclear programs.

It was a very short meeting, but it was a meeting of great content; so I'm very happy about that.

President Bush. A couple of questions. AP lady [Jennifer Loven, Associated Press].

North Korea

Q. Yes, sir. Thank you. Can I ask you what level of flexibility you're willing to accept towards North Korea to try to bring them back to the table?

President Bush. What's very important is for the leader of North Korea to understand that the six-party talks are—will be the framework in which we continue to discuss the mutual goal we all have, which is to rid the Korean Peninsula of nuclear weapons, and that here, at this summit, I will not only speak with my friend the Prime Minister of Japan but also the President of South Korea, the President of China, and the President of Russia about making sure that our intention remains the same, that we work together to achieve the goal. And the leader of North Korea will hear a common voice.

Somebody from the Japanese press?

U.S. Forces in Japan

Q. Was there discussion concerning the realignment of U.S. force in Japan?

Prime Minister Koizumi. We had a very good discussion from the viewpoint of maintaining the deterrence capability of U.S. force in Japan and also of reducing the burden that the U.S. bases are posing on Japanese communities, including Okinawa. We had a good discussion from this kind of point of view. And we also agreed that we would have the relevant authorities, the foreign ministry and defense authorities, both countries—have them discuss this issue in more detail.

President Bush. David [David Morgan, Reuters].

Iran

Q. Mr. President, given the intelligence failures over weapons of mass destruction in Iraq, do you think the U.S. now faces a more skeptical world in—when it comes to the nuclear program in Iran?

President Bush. We appreciate the efforts of the Governments of France, Germany, and Great Britain to convince the Iranians to give up any nuclear ambitions they may have. And the reason why they're involved is because they do believe that Iran has got nuclear ambitions, as do we, as do many around the world. And it's very important for the Iranian Government to hear a—to hear that we are concerned about their desires, and we're concerned about reports that show that prior to a certain international meeting, they're willing to speed up processing of materials that could lead to a nuclear weapon. This is a very serious matter. The world knows it's a serious matter, and we're working together to solve this matter.

Iraqi Elections

Q. There will be elections—elections to be held in Iraq at the end of January next year, and I'd like to know if there were any discussions on what kind of efforts you will be making towards making this election a success?

Prime Minister Koizumi. Successful reconstruction and nation-building in Iraq is just not an important matter for Japan and the United States; it's an issue for the entire international community. And of course, there were some disagreements concerning the beginning of the use of force in that country in the international community, but the U.N. resolution providing for reconstruction efforts in Iraq was adopted by overwhelming consensus. And we have to make this effort into a success. And from that standpoint, Japan intends to continue to do as much as it can based on its own initiatives.

And I told Mr. President that we would like for him to leave it to us to decide what kind of assistance that we would be providing, and the President was agreeable to this.

President Bush. Thank you all.

NOTE: The President spoke at 10:05 a.m. at the Hyatt Regency Santiago. In his remarks, he referred to President Roh Moo-hyun of South Korea; President Hu Jintao of China; President Vladimir Putin of Russia; and Chairman Kim Chong-il of North Korea. A tape was not available for verification of the content of these remarks.

The President's Radio Address
November 20, 2004

Good morning. This weekend I am on my first trip outside the United States since the election, traveling to South America for the Asian-Pacific Economic Cooperation Summit. I am meeting with many allies and friends to strengthen our ties across the Pacific and discuss practical ways we can enhance prosperity, advance liberty, and improve our shared security.

America and the nations of Latin America and Asia share many vital interests. All Pacific nations benefit from free and fair trade, the foundation of this region's remarkable prosperity. The United States has completed free trade agreements with nations throughout Asia and the Americas, including Australia and Singapore, Chile, the five nations in Central America, and the Dominican Republic. We are also negotiating new agreements with Thailand, Panama, and the Andean nations of South America. America has opened our markets, and I will urge other countries to do the same.

Pacific nations also have a clear interest in spreading the benefits of liberty, democracy, and good government across this vital part of the world. From the recent history of the Asia-Pacific region, we know that freedom is indivisible. The economic liberty that builds prosperity also builds a demand for limited government and self rule. Modernization and progress eventually require freedom in all its forms. And the advance of freedom is good for all, because free societies are peaceful societies.

America and our friends are helping other countries lay the foundations of democracy by establishing independent courts, a free press, political parties, and trade unions, by instituting the rule of law, and by keeping up the fight against corruption.

America joined with other members of the Organization of American States to create the Inter-American Democratic Charter. This charter recognizes democracy as the fundamental right of all peoples in the Americas and pledges our governments to promoting and defending the institutions of liberty.

All Pacific nations must also keep up the fight against the forces of terror that threaten the success of our economies and the stability of the world. At last year's summit, APEC leaders started a major initiative to strengthen the security of ports and transportation networks, to defend our aircraft from the threat of portable missiles, and to end the flow of terrorist finances. This year, APEC leaders will work together to improve the security of our ships and ports. We will develop a new system to track and stop the travel of suspected terrorists using forged or stolen documents. And we launched new programs to support APEC

members that have the will to fight terror but need help in developing the means. Terrorism is a threat, not just to the West or to the wealthy but to every nation. And every nation must fight the murderers.

During my trip, I will also meet with President Lagos of Chile and President Uribe of Colombia to reaffirm our strong ties with those nations. Colombia is making progress in the fight against terrorists who traffic in illegal drugs, and America is standing with the Colombian Government to oppose the drug trade that destroys lives in our countries and threatens the stability of our hemisphere.

In my second term, I will continue to pursue a confident foreign policy agenda that will spread freedom and hope and make our Nation more secure. America seeks wider trade and broader freedom and greater security for the benefit of America, our partners, and all of the world.

Thank you for listening.

NOTE: The address was recorded at 8:35 a.m. on November 18 in the Cabinet Room at the White House for broadcast at 10:06 a.m. on November 20. The transcript was made available by the Office of the Press Secretary on November 19 but was embargoed for release until the broadcast. In his remarks, the President referred to President Ricardo Lagos of Chile; and President Alvaro Uribe of Colombia. The Office of the Press Secretary also released a Spanish language transcript of this address.

Remarks Following Discussions With Prime Minister Paul Martin of Canada in Santiago
November 20, 2004

President Bush. Listen, Mr. Prime Minister, thanks. We had a great discussion, and I am looking forward to coming to your great country in 2 weeks' time—in less than 2 weeks' time—looking forward

to continued discussions on important issues and looking forward to bringing the greetings of my great country to your great country.

Prime Minister Martin. Well, we're looking forward to having you. I think that it's—I think we've got a lot of—we have a lot of issues to discuss, in terms of North America and also in terms of the world. And I think we're going to have very good discussions, and Canadians are looking forward to having you.

President Bush. Thank you.

NOTE: The President spoke at 12:07 p.m. at the Hyatt Regency Santiago. A tape was not available for verification of the content of these remarks.

Remarks at the Closing Session of the Asia-Pacific Economic Cooperation Summit in Santiago
November 20, 2004

Thank you very much. *Sientese. Gracias.* Thank you for the warm welcome. It is such an honor to be in Chile. Who is ever responsible for the weather, thank you very much. Laura and I are delighted to be here. Chile is such a fabulous country. It's a great place to talk about entrepreneurship and the entrepreneurial spirit. It's a country which shows the world what is possible when you create the right conditions for economic vitality and economic growth. And we're so honored to be here.

I want to thank my friend Ricardo Lagos for organizing this summit. I appreciate the business leaders who are here. I thank you for your interest in working collaboratively with business leaders from around the world. And as a result of vision and hard work, we meet today on the eastern rim of an incredibly dynamic region.

In our lifetimes, we've seen the Asia-Pacific region grow in wealth and freedom beyond many—beyond that which many thought was possible. If you think back about 20 years ago, what people thought about the Asian-Pacific region, they couldn't imagine such prosperity and such wealth and such freedom. And that's what APEC is all about, as far as I'm concerned. And that's why it's an honor to be here at this summit with my fellow leaders.

Incredibly enough, APEC economies account for nearly half of all the world trade and half of the world's economic output. For somebody who is interested in prosperity for my own citizens, it's a good place to hang out, with that much trade, commerce. And I believe that this new century, with the right policies, can extend the prosperity even further. And that's what we're here to discuss.

I believe we must increase the flow of trade and capital. I know our societies must reward enterprise and open societies and open markets. I know we've got to reject the blocks and barriers that divide economies and people. And I believe, with the right policies, we can continue to grow.

I'm honored to be here today with a man who has served our country so well, a great United States Secretary of State, Colin Powell. Right after my speech, he's headed to the Middle East. That's a heck of a retirement, Mr. Secretary. [*Laughter*] I look forward to your report when you get back.

I want to thank the U.S. members of the APEC Business Advisory Council. I want to thank you for your hard work. I want to thank you for representing our country so well. I appreciate Gary Benanav and Mike Drucker—Mike Ducker and Robert Prieto for your hard work in organizing this summit and representing the business leaders who are here.

You know, what's interesting about our country is that for years, we were isolated from the world by two great oceans, and for a while we got a false sense of security as a result of that. We thought we were protected forever from trade policy or terrorist attacks because oceans protected us. What's interesting about today's world is that the oceans now connect us. It didn't take all that long in the march of history for that change to take place. And therefore, America must respect and value the friendships that we're able to make as a result of our transatlantic and transpacific ties. Right after I'm inaugurated, I'll go to Europe to renew our transatlantic ties, to remind the people of Europe how important my administration regards our vital Atlantic alliance.

And of course, our Nation is Pacific country as well. And that's why the APEC ° conferences are so important. Do you realize, the capital of our 50th State is nearly as close to Sydney and Manila as it is to Washington, DC? That's a Pacific Rim nation. More than 15 percent of Americans claim Hispanic or Asian-Pacific heritage. Our APEC partners account for nearly two-thirds of all American exports and imports. America's future is inseparable from our friends in the Pacific. And by working together and by continuing to foster reasonable progrowth economic policies, the fellowship of Pacific nations will continue to be strong. That's what I'm here to tell you.

There is a different attitude in the world about foreign policies, particularly if you happen to be an influential nation. In the past, many powerful nations preferred others to remain underdeveloped and therefore dependent. It was a cynical doctrine. And that doctrine is unsuited for our times. In this century, countries benefit from healthy, prosperous, confident partners. Weak and troubled nations export their ills—problems like economic instability and illegal immigration and crime and ter-

---

° White House correction.

rorism. America and others sitting around the table here at APEC understand that healthy and prosperous nations export and import goods and services that help to stabilize regions and add security to every nation. So we've got three clear goals to help spread prosperity and hope and to secure the peace.

We want to seek wider trade and broader freedom and greater security for the benefit of our partners and for the benefit of all. That's what I'm going to do over the next 4 years. The first goal is to lower barriers to trade and investment and to promote sound fiscal policies for all our governments. Free and fair trade combined with prudent fiscal discipline are the foundation of the region's remarkable prosperity, and I'm committed to staying on the path to progrowth—proeconomic growth—economic growth by progrowth policies. We're doing our part.

You know, we've overcome a lot in the U.S. economy. We faced a recession, coupled with terrorist attacks, which affected our capacity to grow. But we stimulated our economy by cutting taxes. And America is growing again, and people are working. And the question ahead is, how do we make sure we maintain growth?

We need legal reform in the United States. We got to make sure that those who risk capital are rewarded for taking risk and not subject to needless and frivolous lawsuits. We need regulatory reform in the United States. Our Tax Code is too complex. So I'm going to work with members of both political parties to simplify the Tax Code.

But I also understand there is concern about whether or not our Government is dedicated to dealing with our deficits, both short term and long term. I look forward to standing up in front of the Congress in my State of the Union and telling them why I submitted a budget that will help us deal with the short-term deficit of the United States, and I will do that. And I'll also work with Members of Congress to deal with the unfunded liabilities of our entitlement systems, so that we can say clearly to the world, the United States of America is committed to deficit reduction, both short term and long term.

Overall, the economy of this part of the world is expected to grow by nearly 5 percent this year. And that's good news, and the United States wanted to be a part of that growth. We can add to that progress by reducing trade barriers that I believe are an obstacle to economic growth everywhere, especially in the developing world. And so this Government and our country is strongly committed to the WTO's Doha round of negotiations. And my trade minister will be strongly committed to ensure the success of the WTO round. And we need your help in making sure that nations around the APEC table are focused on the benefits of global trade, that we put aside some differences that could prevent Doha from going forward.

We will continue to assist our Asia-Pacific partners in meeting their WTO obligations. We are encouraging Russia and Vietnam in their efforts to join the WTO. The history between our countries has changed dramatically between America and Vietnam and Russia. The tensions are no longer existing. Conflict is behind us, and we have a chance to work with those countries for the common good, and we will.

We're going to be aggressive about our bilateral trade agreements and our regional trade agreements. We've completed trade agreements with nations throughout Asia and the Americas, including Australia, Singapore, Chile, the five nations of Central America, and the Dominican Republic. We are working on new agreements with Thailand, Panama, the Andean nations of South America. We're moving ahead with the enterprise for the ASEAN initiative, which is lowering trade barriers and strengthening economic ties in Southeast Asia. We're committed to the Bogor goals, which call for free trade among developed nations of the Asian-Pacific region by 2010 and free

trade among all APEC economies by 2020. We seek free trade in the Americas, uniting the markets of all 34 free nations in the Western Hemisphere.

I think you can tell that I believe free trade is necessary for economic development, that free trade is essential to prosperity. But it is not sufficient, and we understand that. All governments in the region must make the difficult choices needed to stabilize economies and to keep public finances on foot. We have been impressed by the reform programs in Chile and Colombia and Uruguay that have spurred growth and investment in those countries and throughout the region.

My Nation and many others have acted to lift the crushing burden of debt that limits the growth of developing economies and holds millions of people in poverty, and we will continue to do so. We will continue working to relieve the current debt of those highly indebted poor countries that pursue sound fiscal policy. We will continue to encourage our large trading partners to adopt flexible market-based exchange rates for their currencies. Expanding prosperity has lifted millions in our region out of poverty, has bound our nations closer together, and has benefited all our people. And my administration will continue to promote pro-growth, pro-trade economic policies for the good of all.

Our second goal is to spread the benefits of freedom and democracy and good government across parts of the world. We've seen progress toward these goals in the recent history of the Asia-Pacific region. We've seen some interesting lessons of history as free markets take hold: The demand for limited government and self-rule builds. That's why it's important to promote free trade and open market policies.

In the long run, economic freedom and political liberty are indivisible, and the advance of freedom is good for all, as free societies are peaceful societies. My Government and many others are working with countries to lay the foundations for democracy by helping them institute the rule of law and independent courts and a free press and political parties and trade unions. We have joined with other members of the Organization of American States to create the Inter-American Democratic Charter. This charter recognizes democracy as a fundamental right of all peoples in the Americas and pledges our governments to promoting and defending the institutions and habits of liberty.

Because political liberty and economic freedom go hand in hand, America and many nations have changed the way we fight poverty, curb corruption, and provide aid. In 2002, we created the Monterrey Consensus, a bold approach that links new aid from developed nations to real reform in developing ones. We created the Millennium Challenge Account in America that says we'll increase aid and help to nations which are willing to fight corruption, which are willing to educate their people, which are willing to spend money on the health of their citizens, and nations which are willing to expand economic freedom. We owe that to the taxpayers of the United States, to promote the habits necessary for free societies to develop. And we believe every nation is capable of fighting corruption, is capable of putting good economic policies in place, is capable of educating their people and helping defeat the scourge of bad health care.

Developing nations have responded, and we appreciate that, but not nearly as much as the people who live in their countries. They've responded by fighting corruption, by building schools and hospitals, and passing new laws that reward enterprise from their people.

The United Nations also has an important role, and America has proposed a democracy fund to help countries lay the foundations of democracy and help set up voter precincts and polling places and support the work of election monitors.

The growth of free and hopeful societies depends on controlling the spread of deadly diseases, especially AIDS and tuberculosis and malaria. HIV/AIDS cases are growing in the Asian-Pacific region. It's an issue we just discussed with the leaders around the table. Last year more than 1 million new HIV infections occurred in Asia, one out of every five infections worldwide. My Nation is working to fight this disease through a $15 billion Emergency Plan for AIDS Relief—15 billion over 5 years, which helps—provides help for 100 nations around the world. Earlier this year, we expanded the focus of this effort by committing new resources to Asia.

As part of this effort, the United States is supporting the United Nations Global Fund, and other nations need to participate in that fund. It's not the United States global fund; it is the world global fund. And so I'm going to continue to urge nations here at this APEC Summit to contribute to that fund, to help defeat this pandemic that has swept across the continent of Africa and now threatens nations in Asia. It is the greatest—AIDS is the greatest health crisis of our time, and all nations must join in a united effort to turn the tide against this terrible disease.

The spread of liberty is our most powerful weapon in the fight against hatred and terror. And we've seen some amazing events take place in the history of liberty. Perhaps the most amazing of all took place in Afghanistan when millions of people showed up to vote for the President of that country some 3 years after that country had been ruled by the barbarians called the Taliban. And the most amazing moment of all in this march of democracy was the fact that the first voter was a 19-year-old woman. Freedom has taken place in parts of the world where people never dreamt freedom is possible, and as a result, the world is better for it.

Our third great goal is to help keep up the fight against the forces of terror that threaten the success of our economies and the stability of the world. Every nation represented here has a stake in this conflict. Terrorism is a threat not just to the West or to the wealthy but to all of us. And all of us must do everything we can to defeat the murderers.

We're determined to end the state sponsorship of terror. And my Nation is grateful to all that participated in the liberation of Afghanistan. We're determined to prevent the proliferation of deadly weapons and materials and to enforce the just demands of the world. And my Nation is grateful to the soldiers of those nations who've helped to deliver the Iraqi people from an outlaw dictator. We're determined to destroy terrorist networks wherever they operate, and the United States is grateful to every nation that is helping to seize terrorist assets and to track down their operatives and to disrupt their plans.

APEC nations are playing a crucial role in the war on terror, for which we are very grateful. We'll continue to work with nations that have the will to fight terror but need help in developing the means. We're sharing intelligence and increasing our cooperation in customs and law enforcement to stop terrorists before they can strike. We're moving forward on the initiatives of last year's summit in Bangkok to strengthen the security of our ports and transportation networks, to defend our aircraft from the threat of portable missiles, and to end the flow of terrorist finances.

America has joined with Singapore to found a new research institute, which opened this year, dedicated to stopping the spread of deadly diseases and combating the threat of bioterrorism. We're working to ensure that the shores of the Pacific remain peaceful. In Santiago, APEC leaders committed to signing by 2005 the additional protocol of the IAEA safeguards agreements, which requires nations to declare a broad range of nuclear activities and facilities and allows the International Atomic Energy Agency to inspect those facilities.

And I appreciate that cooperation and that commitment.

We also agreed to further strengthen our Nation's export controls and to develop a new system to track and stop the travel of suspected terrorists using forged or stolen documents. Through the Proliferation Security Initiative, many nations are also fighting the trade in deadly weapons. And over the past years we've had notable successes, most particularly the disruption of the A.Q. Khan network and its willingness and capacity to spread deadly technology to nations that would like to inflict harm on the—to inflict harm on nations like APEC members.

Five APEC members are working to convince North Korea to abandon its pursuit of nuclear weapons, and I can report to you today, having visited with the other nations involved in that collaborative effort, that the will is strong, that the effort is united, and the message is clear to Mr. Kim Chong-il: Get rid of your nuclear weapons programs.

In all our efforts, we'll maintain and strengthen the alliance among our nations that have served the peace so well. By making our countries safer, these steps will also create a more secure business environment and boost confidence in our economies. You know as well as I know that terrorist attacks affect the capacity of people to make a living. We discovered that firsthand in the United States of America when we lost nearly a million jobs in the 3 months after the September the 11th attacks. The people of Bali, Indonesia, know what I'm talking about when it comes to terrorist attacks. We have an obligation as nations to work together to stop terrorism.

And you in the private sector have an important role to play. The new inspection technologies that you create can shorten delays and reduce insurance costs and cut redtape. By working closely with customs officials of APEC governments to establish better procedures, you can make the delivery of goods and services more secure and more efficient.

These are great goals that I've just talked about: goals to advance our common prosperity, goals to spread freedom and dignity, and goals to strengthen our common security. And I have come here to Chile to tell my colleagues and friends, the United States of America is committed to achieving those goals for the next 4 years.

Thank you for your interest. Thank you for coming.

NOTE: The President spoke at 4:47 p.m. at the Casa Piedra. In his remarks, he referred to President Ricardo Lagos of Chile; Gary Benanav, Mike Ducker, and Robert Prieto, United States members, Asia-Pacific Economic Cooperation Business Advisory Council (ABAC); A.Q. Khan, former head of Pakistan's nuclear weapons program; and Chairman Kim Chong-il of North Korea.

Statement on Congressional Passage of the "Individuals With Disabilities Education Improvement Act of 2004"
November 20, 2004

Improving education for all of America's schoolchildren is one of my highest priorities, and an important part of this effort is improving education for students with disabilities. The "Individuals with Disabilities Education Improvement Act of 2004" will help children learn better by promoting accountability for results, enhancing parental involvement, using proven practices and materials, providing more flexibility, and reducing paperwork burdens for teachers, States, and local school districts.

Like all students, children with disabilities have the best chance to pursue America's great promise with a good education. My administration will continue to work to provide this opportunity to all Americans, who expect and deserve an outstanding education system.

This legislation shows that we can accomplish a great deal when we work together, and I commend the Congress for this bipartisan achievement. I look forward to signing it into law.

Statement on Congressional Action on Fiscal Year 2005 Omnibus Appropriations Legislation
November 20, 2004

I commend the Congress for reaching agreement on the Fiscal Year 2005 omnibus appropriations bill. This legislation is in keeping with my goal to further strengthen the economy by cutting the budget deficit in half over 5 years. With resources already provided to continue to fight the war on terror and to protect the homeland, we have held to the fiscally responsible limits

Congress and I agreed to and still adequately funded our domestic priorities like education, health care, and veterans' programs. This accomplishment would not have been possible without the excellent work of the leadership and Appropriations Committee chairmen of both the House and Senate. I look forward to signing a final bill into law.

Remarks Following Discussions With President Vicente Fox of Mexico in Santiago
November 21, 2004

President Bush. Listen, thank you very much for coming, Mr. President. It's great to see you.

We've just had a very frank and constructive discussion about important issues regarding our two countries. I was very pleased to hear from the President that the economy in Mexico is growing, in large part thanks to his strong leadership. And that is very good news for the United States and our workers, because we have so much trade with Mexico.

We spent a great deal of time talking about the immigration issue. I told President Fox that I had campaigned on this issue. I made it very clear my position that we need to make sure that where there's a willing worker and a willing employer, that that job ought to be filled legally in cases where Americans will not fill that job. I explained to the President that we share a mutual concern to make sure our border is secure. One way to make sure the border is secure is to have reasonable immigration policies. And finally, I assured him that we want people from Mexico treated with respect and dignity.

I look forward to working with my friend over the next couple of years to get a lot done for the benefit of both our countries.

President Fox. Thank you very much, Mr. President. This has been a very good opportunity to discuss the issues on our bilateral agenda. And I think that our friendship, our relationship is strong. It's a very optimistic one, and I think that we will continue to build on it to make this partnership even stronger.

And the first thing is that Mexico wants to fulfill its responsibility to make its economy grow, make it stronger, to have more jobs in Mexico. That is our first priority. And in order to do this, what we discussed today is that we are looking to the future. We're looking to the future in economic development with the United States and our bilateral relationship but also in the trilateral relationship with the region, in order to be able to grow, to generate more jobs, and generate more opportunity.

And we're going to be working on this purpose in order to further what we're trying to achieve in the area of social security, in order to be ever more efficient and competitive. And the other thing that we hope to do is to be able to meet later on in Washington, DC, and then finish off some of these issues we've been discussing, perhaps putting them in the shape of some form of agreement.

And as pointed out, this growth is leading to an increase in jobs, particularly in the border area, and this, in turn, generates more opportunities for our people.

And finally, I extended my congratulations to President Bush on his reelection. We both stated that we are very willing to continue to build on our relationship and to do even more in the 2 remaining years of the Fox administration and the next 4 years of the Bush administration.

President Bush. Gracias.

NOTE: The President spoke at 8:27 a.m. at the Hyatt Regency Santiago. A tape was not available for verification of the content of these remarks.

Statement on the Paris Club Agreement To Reduce Iraq's International Debt
November 21, 2004

I congratulate the Iraqi Interim Government and the Paris Club of creditor nations for today's agreement to reduce dramatically Iraq's international debt. The Iraqi people have an historic opportunity to build a free and democratic Iraq after more than two decades of political oppression and economic devastation under the brutal regime of Saddam Hussein. The Paris Club agreement represents a major international contribution to Iraq's continued political and economic reconstruction. I encourage non-Paris Club creditor nations to agree to comparable debt reduction for Iraq.

The Paris Club leadership deserves particular thanks for its efforts in making this agreement possible. I also commend Secretaries Powell and Snow and Special Presidential Envoy James Baker for their tireless efforts in working with creditor nations to reach this agreement.

The President's News Conference With President Ricardo Lagos of Chile in Santiago
November 21, 2004

President Lagos. My good friend President Bush, Laura, members of the President's delegation, members of my administration, authorities, friends: We're very pleased, for the third time this year, to meet with President Bush and to be able to continue in this way with a modern, mature relationship which our two countries have been able to achieve historically.

As I was telling you, you're not the first George Bush to come to La Moneda. His father was here when we worked in order to consolidate our democracy. But you're the first President to come here at the dawn of the 21st century. And as a consequence, we must use all our energies towards a future agenda, an agenda in which most of the time we will be in agreement; sometimes we won't. But that's life, and that's what a more mature and a richer agenda can do for you.

Our area of cooperation is extremely broad. We share essential values which make our ties stronger. We want democratic societies that are pluralistic, in which the capacity for enterprise will be an opportunity for many—open societies. As we've said over the past few days, economic growth and trade are incompatible with terrorism and incompatible with corruption. For that reason, the decisions we're making at this APEC meeting.

Today too we have reviewed the progress of the free trade agreement between Chile and the United States. After 9 months of enforcement, this agreement has led to major results. Our shipments to the United States have increased by 27 percent. The shipments from the United States to Chile have increased by 25 percent. And the free trade commissions of both countries continue working in order to be able to fulfill the obligations we still have outstanding and, at the same time, to accelerate the removal of tariffs.

Today, for us in Chile, 1,350 companies are sending to the United States over 1,350 products, which ties in directly with the

creation of jobs here in Chile. Trade, therefore, equals more and better jobs. More
and better jobs consolidate a democracy.

And we have other fields of cooperation.
And that's why we spoke about the English
language and how important it is to be
able to foster through our ministries the
learning of English. As a country, we wish
to be a bridge. We want to be a bridge
and a platform in the flows of international
trade and the flows in the Asia and Pacific
region.

We also spoke about Latin America. We
spoke about the importance that our commitment in Haiti has and the reasons why
we are present in that country and why
we need the cooperation of many to be
able to move Haiti forward. We want there
to be elections in Haiti, but this requires
the conditions for elections, so that there
is a possibility of good governance in the
long term. We've also pointed out that the
political reality shows itself in many areas
where they feel that progress is not reaching them. In the Americas, we need to
work within our governments so that
progress reaches those who need it most.
And we definitely believe that economic
progress and social progress are basic.

And the President was kind enough to
talk to us as well about issues of international peace. We have very closely followed the position of President Bush on
the situation in the Palestine and the
prospectives of consolidating a state there
with a democratically elected government
as a way for Palestinians and Israelis to
be able to live together in peace.

And, why not say this as well: We've
agreed in today's meeting on the need to
push forward the negotiations for the Doha
round in the WTO. There we need to lend
all our efforts for that international forum
to be able to reach rules for freer, fairer
trade and thus be able to cement the futures of our countries.

And so we have agreement on bilateral
issues, regional issues, and modestly speaking, multilateral issues. And that, therefore,

is the reason why we have so much ahead
of us. And for all of that, your visit here
today is a very welcome one, and we Chileans are happy to have you with us. You
are welcome, sir.

President Bush. Thank you, Mr. President. Thank you very much. Laura and I
are pleased to be here in Chile, and we
thank the President and Mrs. Duran and
the people of this fantastic country for the
wonderful hospitality.

I'm honored to stand with the President
of this great nation. I congratulate President Lagos on hosting the APEC Leaders'
Meeting and on helping to ensure its success. You did a really good job.

Chile is a remarkable country. Chileans
are a good-hearted people who treasure
their freedom. They're committed to democracy. The people of this country understand the importance of economic freedom.
Modern Chile insists on the rule of law
by ensuring the basic rights and freedoms
of its people. The prosperity and progress
that grow from this conviction is important.
It's important for Latin America, and it's
important for the rest of the world.

The United States and Chile are partners
in addressing the challenges and opportunities facing our hemisphere. President Lagos
and I agreed that the surest path to prosperity is through free and fair trade. Success of our free trade agreement is a model
for other countries. Exports have risen dramatically in both our countries, and both
the Chilean people and the people of the
United States have benefited. And through
the establishment of free trade in the
Americas, we are committed to a future
in which every free nation in the hemisphere can share in the benefits of open
markets and in the creation of new jobs.

The friendship between our two peoples
is deeper than the ties of commerce. The
United States and Chile also share a strong
commitment to human freedom. Today
President Lagos and I discussed ways to
strengthen democratic institutions throughout the Americas and around the world.

I appreciate his advice. I enjoy listening to his wisdom. Chile plays a leading role in the Community of Democracies, a caucus of democratic nations from every corner of the world whose representatives meet regularly to support the advance of freedom. Chile will host the next ministerial meeting of the Community, and we look forward to those discussions, which will examine ways to spread the benefits of liberty.

The President and I also reaffirmed our determination to fight terror, to bring drug trafficking to bear, to bring justice to those who pollute our youth, to bring greater security and stability to our hemisphere. Chile has been a leader in the efforts to strengthen security initiatives among the nations of the Americas, and I appreciate your leadership, Mr. President.

Your nation has expanded joint military exercises and security cooperation with key regional partners. Chile has sent 600 troops to support peacekeeping operations in Haiti, and we thank you for that strong contribution. Chilean soldiers have also made important contributions to peacekeeping efforts in Cyprus, in East Timor, and Bosnia. These are the actions of an ally of the United States, a good citizen of Latin America, and a friend of liberty.

Along with my fellow citizens, I look forward to a future of even stronger and closer relations between our two countries in the years ahead.

Thank you for your hospitality.

Trade Relations With China/U.S. Deficit

Q. President Bush, good afternoon. China has a very close rapprochement with Latin America, a lot of investment in this region. And in your second Presidency, are you going to do anything so you don't lose your influence in this region? And second, many business people are worried if you're going to be doing anything about the fiscal deficit in your country during your second term.

President Bush. First, China is a growing country. Today we heard from Hu Jintao about the phenomenal growth rates that he expects for his economy, and that's positive. I think it's helpful for there to be universal prosperity. China represents great opportunities for Chile and the United States. And we look forward to working with China. We've got a lot of trade with China, and we want to continue to have good trading relations with China.

We got a lot of trade in the hemisphere. We got a free trade agreement with Chile. NAFTA is a strong driver for prosperity in our own neighborhood, and we'll continue to advance free trade throughout this hemisphere. I, frankly, don't view trade—China's actions and the actions of the United States as zero sum. I view it as a positive development.

Secondly, at the meeting today people expressed concern about the value of the U.S. dollar, and I reiterated the fact that my Government has a strong dollar policy. And the best way to affect those who watch the dollar's value is to make a commitment to deal with our short-term and long-term deficits.

As far as our short-term deficit goes, I'll present a budget that continues us on the path to reducing our deficit in half over a 5-year period of time. We're in the fourth year of—first year of—we finished the first year of a 5-year period to reduce the deficit in half. Congress is working on the appropriations bill that meets those targets. I look forward to signing it when they come back and finally finish the package in early December.

A long-term deficit issue really relates to unfunded liabilities when it comes to Social Security and Medicare. In my recent campaign, I made it clear that I think it's very important for us to address those long-term unfunded liabilities. For example, in Social Security, I talked about the need for personal savings accounts for younger workers as a part of a solution. Frankly, the Chilean model serves as a good example for those that are going to be writing the law in the United States.

And so my commitment to the international world is that we'll deal with the short-term deficit and the long-term unfunded liabilities, so that people can then take a look at our dollar in terms of fiscal austerity in Washington.

Press Secretary Scott McClellan. The first question from the American press will come from Finlay Lewis of Copley News Service.

Temporary-Worker Program

Q. Thank you, Mr. President. Your administration recently received a letter from 21 or 22 Members of the House raising skeptical questions about your guest-worker program. Now, you met with President Fox earlier today, and I'm wondering how much—specifically how much political capital—that you're so proud of—you're going to spend on trying to overcome the built-in resistance to that plan. Specifically, what kind of steps are you proposing to take to sell it to the Congress?

President Bush. Finlay, I am proud of my political capital. That's what you get when you win an election, and in the course of that election, I talked about immigration reform. I think it's important for our country to recognize that people are coming to our country to do jobs that Americans won't do, and therefore, I think a program that recognizes the desire of some to come to America to work and the desire of some in America to employ them makes sense. It makes sense not only for our economy; it makes sense for border security. We'd much rather have security guards chasing down terrorists or drugrunners or drug smugglers than people coming to work. And so therefore, I think a guest-worker program is important, and I look forward to working with Congress on it.

I get letters all the time from people that are trying to steer me one way or the other when it comes to legislation. But I'm going to move forward. In the letter, I noticed that they said, "Well, this is because"—they're objecting to the program because it's an amnesty program. It's not an amnesty program. It's a worker program. It's a program that recognizes, however, that if somebody wants to become a citizen in the United States, they can get a line— in line with the people who have done so legally. I think it's necessary. I think it's an important piece of legislation. I look forward to working it. You asked me what my tactics are. I'm going to find supporters on the Hill and move it.

Iraq

Q. President Bush, good evening. Conservative calculations say that the Iraqi war has left many dead. This action has led to enormous protests all over the world. This week we saw them in Chile. You stated that you like to hear the wisdom of President Lagos. At any point did Chile say no to this invasion—Chile did say no to this invasion. Who was right and who was wrong? And how can we change this negative image of the White House that exists in large parts of the world right now?

President Bush. President Lagos didn't agree with my decision, and I respect that. He's still my friend.

Secondly, whether people agree with my decision or not, there are two things that they've got to agree with: One, the world is better off with Saddam Hussein not in power; and secondly, it is important to succeed in Iraq. It's important to develop a democracy there. I fully recognize some do not believe that a democracy can take hold in Iraq. I strongly disagree. I believe not only democracy can take hold in Iraq; I believe a democracy will take hold in Iraq.

I noticed today that the elections are on schedule for January* the 30th. Think how far that society has come from the days of mass grave and torture chambers to a

———————
* White House correction.

day in which they're going to be voting for a President. Prime Minister Allawi, the current leader of Iraq, is a strong, capable democrat. He believes in the possibilities of the people of Iraq, and he knows that a free society will unleash those possibilities.

And so the United States of America will stay the course, and we will complete the task. We will help Iraq develop a democracy, and the world will be better off for it. Free societies don't attack each other. Democracies listen to the aspirations of their people, not feed hatred and resentment and future terrorists. And what we're doing is the right thing in Iraq, and history will prove it right.

Press Secretary McClellan. Mark Silver from the Chicago Tribune.

Legislation To Restructure the Intelligence Community

Q. Thank you, Mr. President. With the intelligence reform bill apparently failing, how confident are you that Secretary Rumsfeld is not partly responsible for that? Is there something more you, personally, could have done? And what does this say about your ability to achieve your own legislative agenda in the next 2 years?

President Bush. I was disappointed that the bill didn't pass. I thought it was going to pass up until the last minute. So I look forward to going back to Washington to work with the interested parties to get it passed. I understand they're back into session to see if they can't get the bill passed, and I look forward to working with Members of the Senate and the House to get it passed.

It's very clear I wanted the bill passed. I talked to key Members of the House, as did my Vice President. And we'll continue working with them, and hopefully, we can get a bill done. I saw the Speaker today said that the matter wasn't complete; it wasn't over; it wasn't final—that we have a chance to get a bill. And therefore, when I get home, I'm looking forward to working it.

Thank you, sir.

President Lagos. Thank you.

NOTE: The President's news conference began at 8:10 p.m. at La Moneda. In his remarks, he referred to Luisa Duran de Lagos, wife of President Lagos; President Hu Jintao of China; former President Saddam Hussein of Iraq; and Prime Minister Ayad Allawi of the Iraqi Interim Government. A reporter referred to President Vicente Fox of Mexico. President Lagos spoke in Spanish, and his remarks were translated by an interpreter.

The President's News Conference With President Alvaro Uribe Velez of Colombia in Cartagena, Colombia
November 22, 2004

President Uribe. Mr. President, Mrs. Laura Bush, Lina Maria, members of the delegations of the U.S. and Colombia, friends from the media, citizens of the United States, and my fellow citizens of Colombia: Mr. President, Mrs. Bush, welcome to the historic city of Cartagena de Indias, an expression of this Colombia: full of possibilities, with many problems to re-solve, and with citizens who are happy, who are joyous, and who have not been made bitter by terrorism and the poverty that it has brought with it. Thank you, President Bush, and thank you, Mrs. Bush, for honoring us with your visit. We greatly appreciate the support of your Government and of the U.S. people.

While the Colombian people fight for democracy, terrorism has assassinated democratic fighters. While the Colombian people fight for growth, employment, and social justice, terrorism has halted our economy. It made poverty more acute and produced internal displacement and a stampede towards other countries. While the Colombian army destroys the antipersonnel landmines and gives the world the example of facing the terrorist threat by following the rule of law and respecting human rights, the terrorists have killed 600 Colombians over the last year, especially members of law enforcement forces. While the Colombian people love to live in peace and respect the ethical rule of not hurting your neighbor, terrorism only wreaks havoc and destruction.

The drugs that finance terrorism have sacrificed generations of Colombians, with thousands of young people who have been assassinated or put in jail, and their families are saddened. The drugs that finance terrorism threaten to destroy the Amazonian jungle. They already tried this by eliminating 1.7 million hectares of tropical forests in Colombia.

The support of the United States left behind speeches and has become an effective type of help. And we trust that the United States and President Bush will continue with that help until Colombia is free of the scourge of terrorism and drugs. We cannot stop this task halfway through. We will win, but we have not won yet. We have made progress, but the serpent is still alive.

President Bush, our success against terrorism will be the success of the people, of democracy, of the supremacy of law. Our success will be the guarantee for the happiness of our children and future generations. Our success will avoid contagion to other neighboring countries, and our success will be a reason for pride in the U.S. and Colombia for those who have suffered from the scourge of drugs.

The negotiation of a free trade agreement is a step in the process to unify the Americas, and we are sure that it will be an agreement reached with equity, offering opportunity for the agricultural sector, for small business, activities that we need to bolster in order to provide true alternatives of revindication for the poor and to foster the creativity of our social enterprises that are based on our capitalist society. The respect for intellectual property must be joined to the rights of researchers so that science can move forward and so that the people will have the right to have universal access to new medications and welfare.

We attach great importance to this visit, President Bush, just after your new victory and at the beginning of your second term. This is a new example of your friendship for Colombia and a clear indication of a renewed interest in Latin America. Latin America needs social cohesion, good governance, and trust in integration. The role of the United States in the multilateral institutions, in the IMF, your signals to the markets will be definitive so that this continent can build social justice. The role of the United States in the struggle against terrorism and in the respect for the tolerant debate of opposing ideas is definitive for good governance on the continent. The equity we need to guarantee in the free trade agreement is going to be a beacon to establish the necessary confidence for all the Americas to become integrated.

In this same spot your father stood, President George Bush, along with President Virgilio Barco, at a summit meeting against drugs. This historic city is pleased to show you its past and its promise for the future. Endowed by nature like other parts of Colombia, it is grateful for the generous help of the United States. This beautiful city, which is now adorned by your visit, wants you to take back to the people of the United States an invitation to come and visit. In order to do so and with your help, we have made a major effort, Mr. President, which translates into greater security.

We welcome you, President Bush, with gratitude and with friendship, in the midst of our emotional reflections of Abraham Lincoln and Simon Bolivar, both of them paradigms of a commitment to their peoples and the idea of authority and order to respect the law. In Gettysburg, President Lincoln made the democratic statement that establishes that the Government "of the people, by the people, and for the people must never perish from the face of this Earth." The message to the Ocana Convention by the Liberator, Bolivar, is for us a proposal that the strength of the state must guarantee the life of the weak and must guarantee the Government and the strength of institutions as a warranty of virtue and the permanence of our Nation.

Thank you very much, President Bush, for this wonderful visit. Thank you, Mrs. Bush.

President Bush. I appreciate those kind words. Laura and I are so honored to be here. We want to thank you and Mrs. Uribe for such warm hospitality, such gracious hospitality. I want to thank your Cabinet and thank the Colombian people as well.

I'm proud to be with my friend President Uribe. *El es mi amigo.* He's a strong—and he's courageous, like the nation he leads. He has been tireless in the fight against terror, and he's making progress on behalf of the people of Colombia. President Uribe and the Colombian people are dedicated to the triumph of democracy and the rule of law against the forces of violence. And the United States stands with you.

Our two nations share in the struggle against drugs. The drug traffickers who practice violence and intimidation in this country send their addictive and deadly products to the United States. Defeating them is vital to the safety of our peoples and to the stability of this hemisphere. President Uribe and I also share a basic

optimism. This war against narcoterrorism can and will be won, and Colombia is well on its way to that victory.

During the President's tenure in office, he's built an impressive record. Kidnapings in Colombia are significantly down. Terrorist attacks and homicides have declined. Cocaine seizures have risen dramatically. And since July of last year, dozens of leaders and financiers of the FARC narcoterrorist organization have been killed or captured. President Uribe has also reformed Colombia's judicial system and is aggressively fighting corruption.

My Nation will continue to help Colombia prevail in this vital struggle. Since the year 2000, when we began Plan Colombia, the United States has provided more than $3 billion in vital aid. We'll continue providing aid.

We've helped Colombia to strengthen this democracy, to combat drug production, to create a more transparent and effective judicial system, to increase the size and professionalism of its military and police forces, to protect human rights, and to reduce corruption. Mr. President, you and your Government have not let us down. Plan Colombia enjoys wide bipartisan support in my country, and next year I will ask our Congress to renew its support so that this courageous nation can win its war against narcoterrorists.

Full and final victory also requires the spread of prosperity and progress throughout this nation and throughout this region. President Uribe's economic reforms have created jobs and improved living standards. Investor confidence is up. Unemployment is down, and growth is strong.

Our two nations also share a strong commitment to advancing free and fair trade and economic growth throughout the Americas. We're working hard on a free trade agreement that will link the United States and Colombia, as well as other Andean nations of South America, in a wider economic partnership. As hope advances, violence and extremism will retreat. President Uribe has a vision for a better Colombia, a vision of peace and prosperity that he is pursuing with skill and energy. He is a fierce opponent of terror and drug trafficking. He's a defender of Colombia's democracy, and I'm proud to call him friend.

Gracias, Senor Presidente.

President Uribe. Thank you, President. Thank you very much.

Plan Colombia/Free Trade Agreement

Q. Mr. President, President Bush, good afternoon. How far are you willing to pursue the groups that you have labeled as terrorists in Colombia, including the self-defense groups? And how do you see the peace process that is being carried out here with the self-defense groups?

And President Uribe, what did President Bush actually say to you about helping Colombia and being a little more flexible with regard to the FTA, especially with the farmers in our country? Thank you.

President Bush. First, let me talk about the security situation and the President's strategy to defeat groups like the FARC. If I didn't think he had an effective strategy and the willingness to fight the FARC, I wouldn't be standing here in this great nation saying I'm going to work with Congress to continue the support. In other words, I believe in results. My administration is a results-oriented administration.

And so when I first met with the President in the Oval Office a couple of years ago, we talked about how to achieve results for the good of Colombia and for the good of our hemisphere. And he said he was going to do the following things, and he did. And so to answer your question, we will support him in this strategy, because it's working.

President Uribe. Thank you, President. Can I answer him first? The issue of the free trade agreement—we understand that the FTA has to be totally equitable. It has to be passed not just by the U.S.

Congress but also by Colombia's Congress and also by the public opinion of the U.S. and of Colombia.

President Bush has understood throughout this process in assisting Colombia how important it is for the legal farming business in Colombia to prosper so that we have opportunities for our farmers. We understand that it's very difficult to negotiate an agreement where everyone is working in good faith, but we will be able to get ahead for our people. And this will build more trust between our nations, and it will be a reason for prosperity, but also it will be a major step forward in uniting the Americas.

Iran

Q. The IAEA, Mr. President, has said that they apparently believe that Iran's claim they've suspended uranium enrichment is true. Are you skeptical at all of that, and if so, why?

President Bush. Well, let's say I hope it's true. And I think the definition of truth is the willingness for the Iranian regime to allow for verification. You know, they have said some things in the past, and it's very important for them to verify and earn the trust of those of us who are worried about them developing a nuclear weapon. And that's just not the United States; it's France and Great Britain and Germany and other nations around the world who understand the dangers of the Iranian Government having a nuclear weapon.

And so it looks like there is some progress, but to determine whether or not the progress is real, there must be verification. And we look forward to seeing that verification.

Plan Colombia

Q. President Bush has committed himself here broadly to extend Plan Colombia and to continue helping Colombia. I'd like to know how you're going to convince your Congress to continue helping us at a time that's so difficult with your own deficit after the war in Iraq, and how much assistance will there be? Is it going to be as much as the 3 billion that has been given over the last 4 years? [*Laughter*]

President Bush. Well, I thought I'd go to the Congress—look, here's what you've got to do with the Congress. You say, first of all, it's an important issue. And the issue is whether or not we're willing to stand with a friend to help defeat narcotrafficking. Most Members of Congress understand it is important to help Colombia defeat the narcotraffickers. And so the first question is whether or not there will be a consensus about the importance. I think there will be.

And secondly, do we want to continue spending money on the project that's important? And the answer to that question is, only if there are results. And there have been significant results. The number of acres under cultivation are down significantly. The number of arrests are up. The number of murders is down. In other words, this man's plan is working. And there is a focused strategy. How do we know? Because our Ambassador is working closely with the Government. Southern Command is working closely with the Government. We're very aware of not only the strategy but the will of this Government to implement the strategy.

And so, to answer your question, I'm very optimistic about continued funding. And I look forward to working with Congress to achieve a level that will make the plan effective.

Martin—Morgan [David Morgan, Reuters], I mean. Morgan. Martin, Morgan—what the heck.

President's Visit to Chile

Q. Thank you, Mr. President. Last night in Santiago, a dinner for 200 guests had to be scaled back dramatically after the Chileans objected to U.S. security plans that must have been in place for some time. And the night before that, you had to come to the rescue of your own security man. Why do you think there was such friction between the U.S. delegation and the Chilean delegation?

President Bush. This is a question? [*Laughter*] Look, we had a fabulous dinner last night. It was really wonderful to be in the presence of President Lagos and his Cabinet, and I thought the visit was a spectacular visit. And I appreciated the hospitality of our Chilean friends, just like I appreciate the hospitality of our Colombian friends.

You know, we're making good progress, thanks to strong leadership. The President said, "Thanks to America, things are going well." No, he's got it backwards. It's not thanks to America, things are going well; it's thanks to strong leadership that things are going well. It's thanks to a strategy that's working. It's thanks to a Cabinet that is dedicated to what's best for the interests of the Colombian people.

Thank you very much.

President Uribe. Thank you, Mr. President.

President Bush. I appreciate it.

President Uribe. Do you want to get in one more?

President Bush. That's plenty. No, thank you.

NOTE: The President's news conference began at 2:40 p.m. at the Escuela Naval de Cadetes "Almirante Padilla." In his remarks, he referred to Lina Maria Moreno de Uribe, wife of President Uribe; U.S. Ambassador to Colombia William Braucher Wood; and President Ricardo Lagos of Chile. He also referred to FARC, the Revolutionary Armed Forces of Colombia. President Uribe spoke in Spanish, and his remarks were translated by an interpreter.

Memorandum on Strengthening Central Intelligence Agency Capabilities
November 18, 2004

Memorandum for the Director of Central Intelligence

Subject: Strengthening Central Intelligence Agency Capabilities

The Final Report of the National Commission on Terrorist Attacks Upon the United States recommended:

> The Central Intelligence Agency (CIA) Director should emphasize (a) rebuilding the CIA's analytic capabilities; (b) transforming the clandestine service by building its human intelligence capabilities; (c) developing a stronger language program, with high standards and sufficient financial incentives; (d) renewing emphasis on recruiting diversity among operations officers so they can blend more easily in foreign cities; (e) ensuring a seamless relationship between human source collection and signals collection at the operational level; and (f) stressing a better balance between unilateral and liaison operations.

I approve and direct you to implement these recommendations, recognizing that significant progress has already been made in rebuilding the CIA's capabilities under the Strengthening Intelligence Initiative and the Director of Central Intelligence's (DCI) Strategic Direction, especially with respect to all-source analysis, clandestine operations, information sharing, and foreign languages.

Working within the framework established by the Strengthening Intelligence Initiative, I direct you to implement within the CIA measures to:

(1) Further strengthen the core capabilities of the CIA to meet the intelligence challenges presented by international terrorism, the proliferation of weapons of mass destruction (WMD), and other critical national security issues, including, but not limited to, its capabilities to:

(a) Perform all-source intelligence analysis that, among other qualities, routinely considers, and presents to national security policymakers, diverse views;

(b) Conduct clandestine collection operations involving human sources and technical methods unilaterally, with other elements of the Intelligence Community, and with foreign partners, and conduct covert action operations as directed by the President;

(c) Share information rapidly and proactively with other agencies of the United States Government, including specifically those responsible for national security and homeland security, while protecting the sources and methods of its collection from unauthorized disclosure, giving top priority to support of governmental actions to detect, prevent, preempt, and disrupt terrorist threats and attacks on the United States, its people, and its allies and interests around the globe; and

(d) Collect, process, analyze, and disseminate intelligence information using personnel proficient in foreign languages, and develop information technology tools to assist in effective processing and use of foreign language information.

(2) Ensure that the CIA processes, shares, and disseminates to the President, Vice President in the performance of Executive functions, and other appropriate officials in the executive branch, including the heads of departments and agencies with elements in the Intelligence Community, terrorism

information and other information relevant to national security and homeland security including as directed by Executive Order 13356 of August 27, 2004, entitled "Strengthening the Sharing of Terrorism Information to Protect Americans."

Building on levels attained under the DCI's Strategic Direction I, measures implemented in accordance with the foregoing shall include, but not be limited to, actions to:

(1) Strengthen CIA intelligence analysis capabilities substantially and promptly through actions to:

(a) Increase, as soon as feasible, the number of fully qualified, all-source analysts by 50 percent;

(b) Assign fully qualified, all-source analysts in a manner that strengthens CIA and Intelligence Community analytical capabilities focused on terrorism, proliferation of WMD, the Near East and South Asia, and other key strategic areas in Asia, while maintaining substantial analytical capabilities focused on other issues and regions;

(c) Increase investment in development of their analytic expertise, field experience, and training in advanced analytical methods, including for geospatial analysis; and

(d) Continue to acquire and develop tools that enable analysts to connect to counterparts inside and outside of government, increase the speed of the analytic workflow, and deal with the rapidly increasing volume of all-source information.

(2) Strengthen CIA human intelligence operations capabilities substantially and promptly through actions to:

(a) Increase, as soon as feasible, the number of fully qualified officers in the Directorate of Operations by 50 percent;

(b) Ensure that a majority of these officers are collectors drawn from diverse backgrounds with the skills, experience, and training needed for the effective conduct of human intelligence operations;

(c) Assign substantial numbers of these officers to collection missions reflecting the priorities established through the National Intelligence Priorities Framework; and

(d) Integrate effectively, as appropriate to particular collection activities, human intelligence collection capabilities and signals and other technical intelligence collection capabilities.

(3) Improve the foreign language capabilities of the CIA through actions to:

(a) Increase, as soon as feasible, the number of CIA officers tested and proficient in mission-critical languages by 50 percent; and

(b) Develop and employ information technology tools to assist in processing and use of information in foreign languages.

(4) Fully implement directives concerning information sharing, information technology, information privacy, and security including Executive Order 13354 of August 27, 2004, entitled "National Counterterrorism Center" and Executive Order 13356.

(5) Double, as soon as feasible, the number of officers who are engaged in research and development to find new ways to bring science to bear in the war on terrorism, countering the proliferation of WMD, and against new and emerging threats.

I direct you to submit to me within 90 days from the date of this memorandum, through the Assistant to the President for National Security Affairs and the Director of the Office of Management and Budget, a detailed budget and implementation plan, including performance measures, with timelines for achievement of specific, measurable goals. In addition to the capabilities enumerated above, this plan shall also include a description, with appropriate performance measures, of steps underway at the CIA to develop and implement new collection strategies against difficult targets, to integrate human and technical collection tools, to assure appropriate access by analysts to information on the sources of critical intelligence reporting, to expand relationships with experts outside of government and otherwise ensure diverse views are routinely reflected in finished intelligence products. A copy of this plan will be provided to the Commission on the Intelligence Capabilities of the United States Regarding Weapons of Mass Destruction, which will advise me on the adequacy of the plan, especially with respect to countering the threat posed by WMD. Beginning in June 2005, I direct you to report to me at least semi-annually, through the Assistant to the President for National Security Affairs and the Director of the Office of Management and Budget, on progress made implementing this memorandum.

This memorandum shall be implemented subject to the availability of appropriations and in a manner consistent with applicable law, including the Constitution and laws protecting the freedom and information privacy of Americans.

GEORGE W. BUSH

NOTE: This memorandum was released by the Office of the Press Secretary on November 23.

Memorandum on Further Strengthening Federal Bureau of Investigation Capabilities
November 18, 2004

Memorandum for the Attorney General

Subject: Further Strengthening Federal Bureau of Investigation Capabilities

The Final Report of the National Commission on Terrorist Attacks Upon the United States recommended:

> A specialized and integrated national security workforce should be established at the Federal Bureau of Investigation (FBI) consisting of agents, analysts, linguists, and surveillance specialists who are recruited, trained, rewarded, and retained to ensure the development of an institutional culture imbued with a deep expertise in intelligence and national security.

I approve and direct you to implement the recommendation, recognizing that significant progress has already been made in strengthening the FBI's capabilities, especially with respect to the FBI's intelligence organization, information sharing, personnel development, and recruiting.

To build upon this foundation, and to strengthen further the FBI's ability to prevent, preempt, and disrupt terrorist threats to and attacks against the United States, I direct you to implement within the FBI measures to:

(1) Continue to improve the FBI's ability to collect, process, analyze, and disseminate to appropriate officials in the executive branch, including appropriate officials within the Intelligence Community, information relevant to national security and homeland security;

(2) Ensure full and seamless coordination and cooperation between the FBI and all other elements of the Intelligence Community, including the Central Intelligence Agency, the Department of

Homeland Security, and the National Counterterrorism Center; and

(3) Ensure that the activities described in subparagraphs (1) and (2) of this paragraph are performed in a manner consistent with our national intelligence priorities and constitutional protections.

The measures directed in the preceding paragraph shall include, but not be limited to, measures to:

(1) Ensure that the Director of the FBI (Director), not later than 90 days from the date of this memorandum, allocates sufficient resources and authority to the new FBI Intelligence Directorate to perform its assigned mission. The Intelligence Directorate shall have responsibility for all components and functions of the FBI judged by the Attorney General, in consultation with the Director of Central Intelligence, to be necessary for the performance of its mission, including development of the intelligence cadre, field intelligence operations oversight, human source development and management, the FBI's collection against nationally determined intelligence requirements, information sharing and dissemination policy, language services, strategic analysis, and program and budget management;

(2) Within resources available to the Department, create within the FBI, not later than 90 days from the date of this memorandum, a specialized, integrated intelligence cadre (including special agents, analysts, linguists, and surveillance specialists), and implement a separate career track program permitting employees within the intelligence cadre to pursue their entire career, including promotion to the most senior positions in the FBI, within this cadre. This effort shall include the establishment, not later than 90 days from the date of this directive, of specific requirements for the

following: training; career development; certification, recruiting, hiring, and selection; integration of the cadre into the FBI's field intelligence groups and headquarters divisions; and senior-level field and headquarters management. These requirements shall be fully consistent with the standards defined in Executive Order 13355 of August 27, 2004, entitled "Strengthened Management of the Intelligence Community;"

(3) Recommend, as part of the Fiscal Year 2006 budget development process, the most appropriate methods for aligning the FBI's budget structure according to its four main programs: intelligence, counterterrorism and counterintelligence, criminal, and criminal justice services;

(4) Recommend, as part of the Fiscal Year 2006 budget development process, the appropriate funding levels for each program to ensure that the FBI is able to:

(a) Carry out its overriding priority to prevent, preempt, and disrupt terrorist threats to and attacks against our homeland, our people, our allies, and our interests around the globe;

(b) Collect, process, share, and disseminate, to the greatest extent permitted by applicable law, to the President, the Vice President in the performance of Executive functions, and other officials in the executive branch, all "terrorism information," as defined in Executive Order 13356 of August 27, 2004, entitled "Strengthening the Sharing of Terrorism Information to Protect Americans," and other information necessary to safeguard our people and advance our national security and homeland security interests; and

(c) Facilitate the above functions by increasing the availability of secure facilities to allow for the expanded use of secure systems for the storage and exchange of classified materials;

(5) Recommend, if necessary, not later than 60 days from the date of this memorandum, any amendments to statutes, executive orders, or presidential directives required to provide the personnel, procurement, information sharing, or other authorities necessary for the FBI to meet its national security responsibilities;

(6) Ensure that, in addition to creating a separate intelligence career track, the FBI creates an intelligence officer certification program and requires such certification for advancement to senior FBI operational management positions. This certification program shall include requirements for applicable skills, training courses, assignments to other intelligence, national security, or homeland security components of the executive branch, and shall be fully consistent with the standards defined in Executive Order 13355;

(7) Provide to me, not later than 90 days from the date of this memorandum through the Assistant to the President for National Security Affairs and the Assistant to the President for Homeland Security, a comprehensive plan with performance measures, including timelines for achievement of specific, measurable progress, in each of the following areas:

(a) Analysis (including standards for the recruitment, hiring, training, and performance of FBI analysts);

(b) Products (including product standards, standards for measuring the responsiveness of those products to nationally determined priorities, measures of the percentage of products written to the lowest possible classification level and the percentage transmitted and posted using secure systems, measures of the effectiveness of products in meeting the needs of State and local governments, as appropriate, and measures of customer satisfaction);

(c) Sources (including standards for asset validation, asset contributions to filling intelligence gaps, and new source development, with particular emphasis on human sources);

(d) Field intelligence operations (including standards for assessing staffing and infrastructure, intelligence production management processes, and the number of field intelligence group supervisors certified as Intelligence Officers); and

(e) Contribution of the FBI's intelligence products to the intelligence and national security information made available to the President, the Vice President in the performance of Executive functions, and other officials in the executive branch, including the degree to which each FBI Field Office is collecting against, and providing information responsive to, national requirements.

A copy of this plan will be provided to the Commission on the Intelligence Capabilities of the United States Regarding Weapons of Mass Destruction. The Commission will advise me on the adequacy of the plan, particularly with respect to any matters concerning countering the threat posed by weapons of mass destruction;

(8) Implement, not later than 90 days from the date of this memorandum, a program to ensure that the FBI's recruitment and training program for agents and analysts enhances the FBI's ability to target and attract individuals with educational and professional backgrounds in intelligence, international relations, language, technology, and relevant skills;

(9) Report to me, through the Assistant to the President for Homeland Security and the Director of the Office of Management and Budget, on the actions and investments necessary to ensure that the architecture supporting FBI information systems is consistent with broader information architecture, and with other initiatives as I direct to facilitate information sharing across Federal, State, and local government agencies, and the private sector; and

(10) Beginning in June 2005, I direct you to report to me at least semi-annually through the Assistant to the President for National Security Affairs, the Assistant to the President for Homeland Security, and the Director of the Office of Management and Budget on the progress made implementing this memorandum and other relevant milestones in development of the FBI's intelligence program, including milestones related to analysis and the analyst workforce, intelligence production, intelligence sources, intelligence certification, and FBI field intelligence operations.

This memorandum shall be implemented subject to the availability of appropriations and in a manner consistent with applicable law, including the Constitution and laws protecting the freedom and information privacy of Americans.

GEORGE W. BUSH

NOTE: This memorandum was released by the Office of the Press Secretary on November 23.

Memorandum on Review of Organizational Responsibility for the Conduct of Certain Operations
November 18, 2004

Memorandum for the Secretary of State, the Secretary of Defense, the Attorney General, the Director of Central Intelligence

Subject: Review of Organizational Responsibility for the Conduct of Certain Operations

The Final Report of the National Commission on Terrorist Attacks Upon the United States recommended:

Lead responsibility for directing and executing paramilitary operations, whether clandestine or covert, should shift to the Defense Department. There it should be consolidated with the capabilities for training, direction, and execution of such operations already being developed in the Special Operation Command.

The Secretary of Defense and the Director of Central Intelligence jointly shall review matters relating to this recommendation and submit to me within 90 days, through the Assistant to the President for National Security Affairs, their written advice on whether and to what extent implementation of the recommendation is in the interest of the United States and what changes to law, executive orders, other presidential guidance, or policies would be necessary to implement such advice. Their review should include, but not be limited to, consideration of similarities and differences in the missions, legal authorities, funding, and support infrastructures of the Department of Defense and the Central Intelligence Agency with respect to operations to which the recommendation refers. A copy of the report will be provided to the Commission on the Intelligence Capabilities of the United States Regarding Weapons of Mass Destruction. The Commission will advise me on the report, particularly with respect to any matters concerning countering the threat posed by weapons of mass destruction.

In the course of their review, they shall obtain as necessary legal advice from the Attorney General and advice concerning potential effects on U.S. foreign relations from the Secretary of State.

GEORGE W. BUSH

NOTE: This memorandum was released by the Office of the Press Secretary on November 23.

Exchange With Reporters in Crawford, Texas
November 26, 2004

The President. I just had a great Thanksgiving with our daughters and my mother and dad and my mother-in-law. It's good to be back in Texas. I wish the Crawford Pirates all the best in their State playoff football game tonight. I know you agree with me.

I'll take a couple of questions.

Iraq/Iran

Q. Thank you, Mr. President. If I could ask you about a couple news developments today. Seventeen political parties in Iraq demanded postponement of the January 30th elections for at least 6 months. I wonder about your reaction to that. And there's a tentative deal on Iran's nuclear weapons, but I wonder whether you think Iran should be trusted, given their history.

The President. First of all, I appreciate the nations of Great Britain and Germany and France who are working to try to convince Iran to honor their international treaty obligations. And the only good deal is one that's verifiable. And I look forward to talking to the leaders of those countries, if they can get Iran to agree to a deal, to make sure that it's verifiable. I know that the Prime Minister of Great Britain wants a verifiable deal because I've talked to him personally about it.

In terms of Iraq, the Iraq election commission has scheduled elections in January,

and I would hope they would go forward in January.

Ukraine

Q. Mr. President, what are the consequences if Ukraine does not comply with international pressure and demands on the elections? And do you think that President Putin overstepped his bounds?

The President. There's just a lot of allegations of vote fraud that placed their election—the validity of their elections in doubt. The international community is watching very carefully. People are paying very close attention to this, and hopefully it will be resolved in a way that brings credit and confidence to the Ukrainian Government.

Yes.

White House Press Pool

Q. Mr. President——

The President. Identify yourself, please.

Q. I'm with Bloomberg News. I'm Jay Newton-Small.

The President. Thank you, welcome.

Q. Thank you.

The President. Do you know Scott [Scott Lindlaw, Associated Press]? [*Laughter*]

Q. Very well.

Q. We ride in a lot of vans together.

The President. You might ask him why he didn't shave. But go ahead.

Pool members. Aw-w-w!

The President. Well, I was just curious. [*Laughter*]

Q. Don't ask me.

The President. It looks like it's contagious, as a matter of fact.

Q. Left the razor at home.

The President. Please, sorry to interrupt.

World Trade Organization Sanctions

Q. Today the World Trade Organization finalized or approved sanctions the European Union will have against the United States, $150 million worth of sanctions for the Byrd amendment. Do you have any comments on that?

The President. Well, we've worked hard to comply with the WTO. I think it's important that all nations comply with WTO rulings. I'll work with Congress to get into compliance. As you might remember, we worked on the FISC/ETI bill because of the WTO ruling. We expect the WTO, as well, to treat our trading partners as they treat us. And that's why, for example, I filed complaint on the Airbus situation. We believe that the subsidies for Airbus are unfair for U.S. companies such as Boeing.

Yes, Mark [Mark Knoller, CBS Radio], hi.

Appropriations Legislation

Q. Hi. Sir, you said you're going to sign the big omnibus appropriations bill, but are you bothered by all the examples of porkbarrel spending that are in that bill?

The President. Mark, it's—first, the bill conforms to the budget that I worked out with the Congress, and I appreciate that. In other words, the size of the bill is a number that we agreed to early on—earlier this year. And I appreciate that, because part of making sure we cut the deficit in half is to work together on the overall size of our spending bills.

Now, secondly, obviously there's going to be things in these big bills that I don't particularly care for, and that's why I've asked Congress to give me a line-item veto. And the only way a President can affect that which is inside the bill, other than vetoing the entire bill, is to be able to pick out parts of a bill and express displeasure about it through a line-item veto. I hope the Congress will give me a line-item veto.

Listen, it's great to see everybody.

Northern Ireland

Q. Anything on Northern Ireland?

The President. Well, I talked to—evidently the word's out that I made a phone call this morning, and I did so. And I was just trying to be a part of the process of getting both Ian Paisley's group—Dr. Paisley's group and Gerry Adams's group to the table to get a deal done.

Q. To get——

The President. To get a deal done; in other words, to close the agreement that they've been working on for quite a while. Hopefully it will help. Of course, the primary movers are Prime Minister Blair and Bertie Ahern of Ireland, who have been working very diligently on this. I appreciate their efforts, and anything I can do to help keep the process moving forward, I'm more than willing to do so.

Listen, I've got to go eat a burger. Thank you all.

NOTE: The exchange began at 12:30 p.m. at the Coffee Station. In his remarks, the President referred to Prime Minister Tony Blair of the United Kingdom; President Vladimir Putin of Russia; Ian Paisley, leader, Democratic Unionist Party of Northern Ireland; Gerry Adams, leader, Sinn Fein of Northern Ireland; and Prime Minister Bertie Ahern of Ireland. A tape was not available for verification of the content of this exchange.

The President's Radio Address
November 27, 2004

Good morning. As Americans gather to celebrate this week, we show our gratitude for the many blessings in our lives. We are grateful for our friends and families who fill our lives with purpose and love. We're grateful for our beautiful country and for the prosperity we enjoy. We're grateful for the chance to live, work, and worship in freedom. And in this Thanksgiving week, we offer thanks and praise to the provider of all these gifts, Almighty God.

We also recognize our duty to share our blessings with the least among us. Throughout the holiday season, schools, churches, synagogues, and other generous organizations gather food and clothing for their neighbors in need. Many young people give part of their holiday to volunteer at homeless shelters or food pantries. On Thanksgiving and on every day of the year, America is a more hopeful nation because of the volunteers who serve the weak and the vulnerable.

The Thanksgiving tradition of compassion and humility dates back to the earliest days of our society. And through the years, our deepest gratitude has often been inspired by the most difficult times. Almost four centuries ago, the pilgrims set aside time to thank God after suffering through a bitter winter. George Washington held Thanksgiving during a trying stay at Valley Forge. And President Lincoln revived the Thanksgiving tradition in the midst of a civil war.

The past year has brought many challenges to our Nation, and Americans have met every one with energy, optimism, and faith. After lifting our economy from a recession, manufacturers and entrepreneurs are creating jobs again. Volunteers from across the country came together to help hurricane victims rebuild. And when the children of Beslan, Russia, suffered a brutal terrorist attack, the world saw America's generous heart in an outpouring of compassion and relief.

The greatest challenges of our time have come to the men and women who protect our Nation. We're fortunate to have dedicated firefighters and police officers to keep our streets safe. We're grateful for the homeland security and intelligence personnel who spend long hours on faithful watch. And we give thanks to the men and women of our military who are serving with courage and skill and making our entire Nation proud.

Like generations before them, today's Armed Forces have liberated captive peoples and shown compassion for the suffering and delivered hope to the oppressed. In the past year, they have fought the terrorists abroad so that we do not have to face those enemies here at home. They've captured a brutal dictator, aided last month's historic election in Afghanistan, and helped set Iraq on the path to democracy.

Our progress in the war on terror has made our country safer, yet it has also brought new burdens to our military families. Many service men and women have endured long deployments and painful separations from home. Families have faced the challenge of raising children while praying for a loved one's safe return. America is grateful to all our military families, and the families mourning a terrible loss this Thanksgiving can know that America will honor their sacrifices forever.

As Commander in Chief, I've been honored to thank our troops at bases around the world, and I've been inspired by the efforts of private citizens to express their own gratitude. This month, I met Shauna Fleming, a 15-year-old from California who coordinated the mailing of a million thank you letters to military personnel. In October, I met Ken Porwoll, a World War II veteran who has devoted years of his retirement to volunteering at a VA medical center in Minneapolis. And we've seen the generosity of so many organizations like Give2theTroops, a group started in a basement by a mother and son that has sent thousands of care packages to troops in the field.

Thanksgiving reminds us that America's true strength is the compassion and decency of our people. I thank all those who volunteer this season, and Laura and I wish every American a happy and safe Thanksgiving weekend.

Thank you for listening.

NOTE: The address was recorded at approximately 7:15 a.m. on November 26 at the Bush Ranch in Crawford, TX, for broadcast at 10:06 a.m. on November 27. The transcript was made available by the Office of the Press Secretary on November 26 but was embargoed for release until the broadcast. The Office of the Press Secretary also released a Spanish language transcript of this address. The Thanksgiving Day proclamation of November 23 is listed in Appendix D at the end of this volume.

Remarks on the Nomination of Carlos M. Gutierrez To Be Secretary of Commerce
November 29, 2004

The President. Thank you all. I am proud to announce my nomination of Carlos Gutierrez to be America's next Secretary of Commerce. Carlos Gutierrez is one of America's most respected business leaders. He is a great American success story.

As CEO of the Kellogg Company, he has been an effective, visionary executive. He understands the world of business from the first rung on the ladder to the very top. He knows exactly what it takes to help American businesses grow and create jobs. I look forward to having his creativity and expertise in my Cabinet.

Carlos's family came to America from Cuba when he was a boy. He learned English from a bellhop in a Miami hotel and later became an American citizen. When his family eventually settled in Mexico City, Carlos took his first job for Kellogg as a truck driver, delivering Frosted Flakes to local stores. Ten years after he started, he was running the Mexican business, and 15 years after that, he was running the entire company. At every stage

of this remarkable story, Carlos motivated others with his energy and optimism and impressed others with his decency.

In his career, Carlos has been sustained by the values taught by his parents, Pedro and Olga, and by the love of his wife, Edi, and his children, Carlos, Erika, and Karina. I know Olga Gutierrez, who lives in Florida, is proud to see the boy she took from Cuba chosen to help strengthen the world's greatest and finest economy.

Carlos will carry on the work of a distinguished leader, Secretary Don Evans. During the past 4 years, our economy has overcome a recession, terrorist attack, corporate scandals, and the uncertainty that comes with war. In all these challenges, Don has been a strong and steady advocate for America's businesses and workers and entrepreneurs. Don has also been my friend for over three decades. I've counted on his wisdom and optimism and character at every step on my journey to the White House. Now Don's own journey leads him back to Texas, where we were young men together. Don is one of the finest people I have ever known. I will miss having him in Washington, and Laura and I wish him and Susie well.

When he's confirmed by the Senate, Carlos Gutierrez will take office at a time of historic opportunity for our changing economy. With Carlos's leadership, we'll help more Americans, especially minorities and women, to start and grow their own small business. We'll reduce the burden of junk lawsuits and regulations on our entrepreneurs. We'll reform our outdated Tax Code to eliminate needless paperwork and encourage savings, investment, and growth. We'll continue our commitment to free and fair trade. Carlos and I know that America's workers can compete with anybody in the world. And in all these policies, we will ensure that the American economy keeps creating jobs and remains dynamic and flexible far into the future.

In Carlos Gutierrez, the Department of Commerce will have an experienced man-

ager and an innovative leader. He will be a strong, principled voice for American business and an inspiration to millions of men and women who dream of a better life in our country. I ask the Senate to confirm this fine nominee as quickly as possible. I look forward to welcoming him into my Cabinet.

Congratulations.

[*At this point, Secretary-designate Gutierrez made brief remarks.*]

The President. Great job. Thank you. Congratulations.

NOTE: The President spoke at 11:10 a.m. in the Roosevelt Room at the White House. In his remarks, he referred to Susan Evans, wife of Secretary of Commerce Donald L. Evans. The transcript released by the Office of the Press Secretary also included the remarks of Secretary-designate Gutierrez. The Office of the Press Secretary also released a Spanish language transcript of these remarks.

Statement on the Resignation of Stephen Friedman as Director of the National Economic Council
November 29, 2004

Steve Friedman has been a trusted adviser and vital member of my economic team, working tirelessly to help make sure that America continues to be the best place in the world to do business.

Steve played a valuable role in enacting the Jobs and Growth Act of 2003 that helped move our economy from recession to the robust growth we are experiencing today. As a key member of my White House senior staff, Steve has led efforts to develop the policies that are strengthening our economy and helping to create jobs. Steve has done an excellent job of

coordinating the work of my economic team and has played a key role in developing the economic policies for my second-term agenda.

Steve is a good-hearted man who possesses great wisdom and a can-do attitude. I am grateful for his superb work and wish him and Barbara all the best as they fulfill their plan to return home to New York.

NOTE: The Office of the Press Secretary also made available Director Friedman's letter of resignation.

Memorandum on Improving Spectrum Management for the 21st Century
November 29, 2004

Memorandum for the Heads of Executive Departments and Agencies

Subject: Improving Spectrum Management for the 21st Century

In May 2003, I established the Spectrum Policy Initiative to promote the development and implementation of a U.S. spectrum management policy for the 21st century. This initiative will foster economic growth; promote our national and homeland security; maintain U.S. global leadership in communications technology; and satisfy other vital U.S. needs in areas such as public safety, scientific research, Federal transportation infrastructure, and law enforcement.

The existing legal and policy framework for spectrum management has not kept pace with the dramatic changes in technology and spectrum use. Under the existing framework, the Federal Government generally reviews every change in spectrum use. This process is often slow and inflexible and can discourage the introduction of new technologies. Some spectrum users, including Government agencies, have argued that the existing spectrum process is insufficiently responsive to the need to protect current critical uses.

As a result, I directed the Secretary of Commerce to prepare recommendations for improving spectrum management. The Secretary of Commerce then established a Federal Government Spectrum Task Force and initiated a series of public meetings to address improvements in policies affecting spectrum use by the Federal Government, State, and local governments, and the private sector. The recommendations resulting from these activities were included in a two-part series of reports released by the Secretary of Commerce in June 2004, under the title *Spectrum Policy for the 21st Century—The President's Spectrum Policy Initiative* (Reports).

Therefore, to the extent permitted by law and within existing appropriations, I hereby direct the heads of executive departments and agencies (agencies) to implement the recommendations in the Reports as follows:

Section 1. Office of Management and Budget.

Within 6 months of the date of this memorandum, the Office of Management and Budget (OMB) shall provide guidance to the agencies for improving capital planning and investment control procedures to better identify spectrum requirements and the costs of investments in spectrum-dependent programs and systems. Within 1 year of the date of this memorandum, agencies shall implement methods for improving capital planning and investment control procedures consistent with the OMB guidance, including making any modifications to agency capital planning procedures necessary to ensure greater consideration of more efficient and cost-effective spectrum use.

Section 2. Other Executive Departments and Agencies.

(a) Within 1 year of the date of this memorandum, the heads of agencies selected by the Secretary of Commerce shall provide agency-specific strategic spectrum plans (agency plans) to the Secretary of Commerce that include: (1) spectrum requirements, including bandwidth and frequency location for future technologies or services; (2) the planned uses of new technologies or expanded services requiring spectrum over a period of time agreed to by the selected agencies; and (3) suggested spectrum efficient approaches to meeting identified spectrum requirements. The heads of agencies shall update their agency plans biennially. In addition, the heads of agencies will implement a formal process to evaluate their proposed needs for spectrum. Such process shall include an analysis and assessment of the options available to obtain the associated communications services that are most spectrum-efficient and the effective alternatives available to meet the agency mission requirements. Heads of agencies shall provide their analysis and assessment to the National Telecommunications and Information Administration (NTIA) for review when seeking spectrum certification from the NTIA.

(b) Within 6 months of the date of this memorandum, the Secretary of Homeland Security, in coordination with the Secretary of Commerce and, as appropriate, the Chairman of the Federal Communications Commission, and considering the views of representatives from: (1) the public safety community, (2) State, local, tribal, and regional governments; and (3) the private sector, shall identify public safety spectrum needs.

(c) Within 1 year of the date of this memorandum, the Secretary of Homeland Security, in consultation with the Secretary of Commerce, the Director of the Office of Science and Technology Policy, the Director of the Office of Management and Budget, the Attorney General, the Secretaries of State, Defense, Transportation, Agriculture, and the Interior, the heads of other appropriate agencies, and, as appropriate, the Chairman of the Federal Communications Commission, shall develop a comprehensive plan, the Spectrum Needs Plan, to address issues related to communication spectrum used by the public safety community, as well as the continuity of Government operations. The Spectrum Needs Plan shall be submitted to the President through the Assistant to the President for Homeland Security, in coordination with the Assistant to the President for Economic Policy and other relevant components of the Executive Office of the President.

Section 3. Department of Commerce.

(a) Within 6 months after receiving the agency plans developed in section 2(a) of this memorandum, the Secretary of Commerce shall integrate the agency plans and Spectrum Needs Plan, based upon a Department of Commerce framework, into a Federal Strategic Spectrum Plan and shall assist in the formulation of a National Strategic Spectrum Plan. The Secretary of Commerce, in consultation with the Chairman of the Federal Communications Commission, as appropriate, shall update the National Strategic Spectrum Plan on a biennial basis thereafter.

(b) Within 1 year of the date of this memorandum, the Secretary of Commerce, in coordination with other relevant Federal agencies identified by the Secretary, shall develop a plan for identifying and implementing incentives that promote more efficient and effective use of the spectrum while protecting national and homeland security, critical infrastructure, and Government services.

(c) Within 6 months of the date of this memorandum, the Secretary of Commerce shall establish a plan for the implementation of all other recommendations included in the Reports. Not more than 1 year from the date of this memorandum, the Secretary of Commerce shall provide to the President a report describing the progress on implementing the recommendations in the Reports. The report shall include a section prepared by the Secretary of Homeland Security that describes the progress made with respect to public safety spectrum issues. This report shall be updated on an annual basis, until completion of the actions required by this memorandum. The heads of agencies shall provide the Secretary of Commerce and the Secretary of Homeland Security with any assistance or information required in the preparation of the annual report.

(d) The plans in sections 3(a)–(c) and the annual report developed in section 3(c) of this memorandum shall be submitted to the President through the Assistant to the

President for Economic Policy, in coordination with the Assistant to the President for National Security Affairs and other relevant components of the Executive Office of the President.

(e) As appropriate, the Secretary of Commerce and heads of other agencies shall consult with the Chairman of the Federal Communications Commission regarding the implementation of the recommendations in the Reports.

Section 4. General.

(a) Nothing in this memorandum shall be construed to impair or otherwise affect the functions of the Director of the Office of Management and Budget relating to budget, administrative, or legislative proposals.

(b) This memorandum is intended only to improve the internal management of the Federal Government and is not intended to, and does not, create any right or benefit, substantive or procedural, enforceable at law or in equity, by a party against the United States, its departments, agencies, entities, instrumentalities, its officers or employees, or any other person.

(c) This order shall be implemented in a manner consistent with existing statutes, treaties, Executive Agreements, and Executive Orders affecting the operation of any of the departments, agencies, or instrumentalities of the Federal Government.

GEORGE W. BUSH

NOTE: This memorandum was released by the Office of the Press Secretary on November 30.

Letter to Congressional Leaders Transmitting an Alternative Plan for the Locality Pay Increase for Civilian Federal Employees
November 29, 2004

Dear Mr. Speaker: (Dear Mr. President:)

I am transmitting an alternative plan for the locality pay increase payable to civilian Federal employees covered by the General Schedule (GS) and certain other pay systems in January 2005.

Under title 5, United States Code, civilian Federal employees covered by the GS and certain other pay systems would receive a two-part pay increase in January 2005: (1) a 2.5 percent across-the-board increase in scheduled rates of basic pay derived from Employment Cost Index data on changes in the wages and salaries of private industry workers, and (2) a locality pay increase based on Bureau of Labor Statistics' salary surveys of non-Federal employers in each locality pay area, which would average about 10.6 percent for eligible employees. Including increases for blue-collar and other workers, the total Federal employee pay increase would cost about 11.2 percent of payroll in calendar year 2005. For Federal employees covered by the GS locality pay system, the overall average pay increase would be about 13.1 percent, far higher than the 1.5 percent total pay increase I proposed in my Fiscal Year 2005 budget.

For the reasons described below, I have determined that it is appropriate to exercise my statutory alternative plan authority to limit the January 2005 GS locality pay increase.

A national emergency has existed since September 11, 2001, which now includes Operation Enduring Freedom (in Afghanistan) and Operation Iraqi Freedom. Full statutory civilian locality pay increases averaging 10.6 percent in 2005 would divert resources from and interfere with our Nation's ability to fight the war on terror, with respect to which a national emergency is in effect under the law. Such increases would cost about $9.8 billion in fiscal year 2005 alone and would build in later years.

Accordingly, I have determined that—

Under the authority of section 5304a of title 5, United States Code, the locality pay percentages authorized in 2004 shall remain in effect in 2005.

Finally, the law requires that I include in this report an assessment of the impact of my decision on the Government's ability to recruit and retain well-qualified employees. This decision will not materially affect our ability to continue to attract and retain a quality Federal workforce. To the contrary, since the Congress has not funded the cost of a pay raise in excess of the 1.5 percent increase I proposed, agencies would have to absorb the additional cost

and could have to freeze hiring in order to pay the higher rates. Moreover, GS quit rates are at an all-time low of 1.6 percent per year, well below the overall average quit rate in private enterprise. Should the need arise, the Government has many compensation tools, such as recruitment bonuses, retention allowances and special salary rates, to maintain the high quality workforce that serves our Nation so very well.

Sincerely,

GEORGE W. BUSH

NOTE: Identical letters were sent to J. Dennis Hastert, Speaker of the House of Representatives, and Richard B. Cheney, President of the Senate. This letter was released by the Office of the Press Secretary on November 30.

Letter to Congressional Leaders Transmitting an Executive Order Modifying the Scope of the National Emergency Declared in Earlier Executive Orders Relating to Iraq
November 29, 2004

Dear Mr. Speaker: (*Dear Mr. President:*)

Consistent with subsection 204(b) of the International Emergency Economic Powers Act, 50 U.S.C. 1703(b) (IEEPA), I hereby report that I have issued an Executive Order (the "order") in which I modify the scope of the national emergency declared in Executive Order 13303 of May 22, 2003, expanded in Executive Order 13315 of August 28, 2003, and further modified in Executive Order 13350 of July 29, 2004. I have determined that an additional threat exists with respect to which the national emergency was declared and expanded in those Executive Orders. I have also determined that steps taken in Executive Order 13303 to deal with the national emergency declared therein need to be revised in light of United Nations Security Council Resolutions 1483 of May 22, 2003, and 1546 of

June 8, 2004, respectively. I have enclosed a copy of the order.

In Executive Order 13303 of May 22, 2003, I found that the threat of attachment or other judicial process against the Development Fund for Iraq, Iraqi petroleum and petroleum products and interests therein, and proceeds, obligations, or any financial instruments of any nature whatsoever arising from or related to the sale or marketing thereof, and interests therein, obstructed the orderly reconstruction of Iraq, the restoration and maintenance of peace and security in the country, and the development of political, administrative, and economic institutions in Iraq. I determined that this situation constituted an unusual and extraordinary threat to the national security and foreign policy of the United States, and I declared a national emergency to deal with that threat.

Consistent with IEEPA, as amended, (50 U.S.C. 1701 *et seq.*), the National Emergencies Act (50 U.S.C. 1601 *et seq.*), section 5 of the United Nations Participation Act, as amended (22 U.S.C. 287c) (UNPA), and section 301 of title 3, United States Code, in Executive Order 13303 I ordered, *inter alia*, that unless licensed or otherwise authorized pursuant to that order, any attachment, judgment, decree, lien, execution, garnishment, or other judicial process is prohibited, and shall be deemed null and void, with respect to the following:

(a) the Development Fund for Iraq, and

(b) all Iraqi petroleum and petroleum products, and interests therein, and proceeds, obligations, or any other financial instruments of any nature whatsoever arising from or related to the sale or marketing thereof, and interests therein, in which any foreign country or a national thereof has any interest, that are in the United States, that hereafter come within the United States, or that are or hereafter come within the possession or control of United States persons.

Consistent with United Nations Security Council Resolutions 1483 and 1546, I have determined that the steps taken in Executive Order 13303 to deal with the emergency declared therein need to be revised so that such steps do not apply with respect to any final judgment arising out of a contractual obligation entered into by the Government of Iraq, including any agency or instrumentality thereof, after June 30, 2004, and so that, with respect to Iraqi petroleum and petroleum products and interests therein, such steps shall apply only until title passes to the initial purchaser.

The new order provides that protections granted by section 1 of Executive Order 13303, as well as the protections granted by this order to the property of the Central Bank of Iraq, do not apply with respect to any final judgment arising out of a contractual obligation entered into by the Government of Iraq, including any agency or instrumentality thereof, after June 30, 2004.

In addition, the order modifies section 1 of Executive Order 13303 to provide that the protections granted therein to all Iraqi petroleum and petroleum products, and interests therein, apply only until title passes to the initial purchaser.

Furthermore, I now find that the threat of attachment or other judicial process against the assets of the Central Bank of Iraq constitutes one of the obstacles to the orderly reconstruction of Iraq, the restoration and maintenance of peace and security in the country, and the development of political, administrative, and economic institutions in Iraq. I have determined that the scope of the national emergency declared in Executive Order 13303, as expanded by Executive Order 13315, and modified by Executive Order 13350, be further modified to address this threat.

Consequently, the order modifies the actions taken to address the national emergency declared in Executive Order 13303, as expanded by Executive Order 13315, and further modified in Executive Order 13350, by amending section 1 of Executive Order 13303 to extend the protections granted therein against any attachment, judgment, decree, lien, execution, garnishment, or other judicial process to any accounts, assets, investments, or any other property of any kind owned by, belonging to, or held by the Central Bank of Iraq, or held, maintained, or otherwise controlled by any financial institution of any kind in the name of, on behalf of, or otherwise for the Central Bank of Iraq.

I have delegated to the Secretary of the Treasury, in consultation with the Secretary of State, the authority to take such actions, including the promulgation of rules and regulations, to employ all powers granted to the President by IEEPA and the UNPA as may be necessary to carry out the purposes of this order. The Secretary of the

Treasury may redelegate any of these func- tions to other officers and agencies of the United States consistent with applicable law. I have directed all agencies of the United States Government to take all ap- propriate measures within their authority to carry out the provisions of this order.

Sincerely,

GEORGE W. BUSH

NOTE: Identical letters were sent to J. Den- nis Hastert, Speaker of the House of Rep- resentatives, and Richard B. Cheney, Presi- dent of the Senate. This letter was released by the Office of the Press Secretary on No- vember 30. An original was not available for verification of the content of this letter. The Executive order of November 29 is listed in Appendix D at the end of this volume.

The President's News Conference With Prime Minister Paul Martin of Canada in Ottawa, Canada
November 30, 2004

Prime Minister Martin. Good afternoon. The President and I had a very good dis- cussion during the past few hours, both one-on-one and with Cabinet members and officials at the table. The President and I have had a productive meeting.

In fact, we agreed to put forward an agenda in which our two nations will co- operate in a practical way towards common goals. From this work plan, a set of con- crete milestones will be established in the new year. Furthermore, while this is a bilat- eral effort between our two countries, it is trilateral in ambition, and we'll be invit- ing our Mexican partners to join us, obvi- ously, in this project.

This work plan is aimed at achieving practical results for the people of our coun- tries, enhanced security, greater prosperity, and improved quality of life. And it's about working together to advance democratic values and fundamental freedoms around the world.

To do this, we've identified specific pri- orities and will task individuals within our respective governments with the responsi- bility of making these files move. We will bring new energy and tangible goals to this old and deep friendship. The objective is lasting progress and benefits for people in both countries.

Here at home, we will collaborate further to ensure our shared border is closed to terror but open to the safe movement of people and goods, which is so integral to our economic success. We'll focus on en- suring that our businesses have the capacity to compete with entrenched and emerging global competitors. We'll work together to make sure that we apply smart regulation that raise standards in both countries, and reinforce our mutual efforts to protect the environment, to fight crime, to stop traffic in humans and illegal drugs, and enhance our ability to combat infectious disease.

Abroad, we will cooperate in our efforts to foster democracy and help find a path to peace in the Middle East, protect civilian populations from grave threats, and build and protect the democratic institutions that are so important to the ability of troubled states to recover and to thrive—to multilat- eral cooperation in the world, and we will be forceful advocates of free trade, whether that be in North America or in the early completion of the Doha round.

At all times, we'll be vigilant in coun- tering and combating terrorism and halting the proliferation of weapons of mass de- struction.

Now, given the wide variety of areas that have been encompassed in corresponding the need to ensure direction and focus, I've asked the Deputy Prime Minister and the Minister of Foreign Affairs to work with the relevant ministers to oversee the efforts that we have now laid out before us and to report to me directly on progress in all areas of this work plan no later than next June.

President Bush and I are well aware that the prosperity of our nations, our status as open societies, and the well-being of our democratic institutions are linked now to the integrity of our collective security. And the work plan will be an important step forward toward the mutual protection of our citizens, our values, and our way of life.

Mr. President.

President Bush. Thank you very much, Mr. Prime Minister. Laura and I are so pleased to be here in Canada. We thank you for your warm hospitality. Thank you for the meetings we've had. And I'm proud to be standing with the Prime Minister. He's a strong leader. He's a statesman who's helping to build a better world. I want to thank you for your leadership and friendship.

Canada and the United States share a history, a continent, and a border. We also share a commitment to freedom and a willingness to defend it in times of peril. The United States and Canada fought side by side in two World Wars, in Korea and the Persian Gulf, and throughout the cold war. Today, we're standing together against the forces of terror. Long-term success in this war requires more than military might. It requires the advance of liberty and hope as the great alternatives to hatred and violence.

All free nations appreciate Canada's leadership: leadership of the security and stabilization mission in Afghanistan; leadership which helped make possible the first free nationwide election in that country's history. Afghanistan is a world away from the nightmare of its recent past, Mr. Prime Minister. It is building a decent and demo-

cratic future, and I want to thank you for your help.

Once again, people in that part of the world have demonstrated the power of liberty to overcome great challenges. Your vision is clear on that, Mr. Prime Minister, and I can't thank you enough for that.

We're also standing with the brave people of Iraq, who are preparing for elections on January the 30th. Both of our nations have a vital interest in helping the Iraqi people secure their country and build a free and democratic society. I want to thank the Prime Minister's resolve and his support for this great cause. The Canadian Government has pledged more than 200 million U.S. in humanitarian aid and reconstruction assistance and have agreed to relieve more than 450 million U.S. dollars in Iraqi debt. A free and democratic Iraq is rising in the heart of the Middle East. The success of liberty there will be a decisive blow to the ideology of terror and a model to reformers and democrats throughout the region.

As we seek freedom for the Afghan and Iraqi people, America and Canada are working to further the spread of democracy in our own hemisphere. In Haiti, Canada was a leader along with the United States, France, Chile, and other nations in helping to restore order. Canadian police are standing watch in Haiti at this hour, and the Prime Minister just visited the country to further the cause of political reconciliation. I appreciate your briefing on your visit.

Prime Minister Martin and I share a vision of a free and democratic Western Hemisphere in which every nation upholds human dignity, and we will work together to realize that vision.

Prime Minister Martin and I also discussed the situation in Ukraine. I informed the Prime Minister that I talked this morning to President Kwasniewski of Poland. President Kwasniewski will again lead a delegation, which will include a representative of the European Union, to the Ukraine to encourage the parties to reject violence and to urge the parties to engage in dialog toward a political and legal solution to the current crisis. Our common goal is to see the will of the Ukranian people prevail. The Prime Minister and I want to thank President Kwasniewski for his efforts, and we wish him all the success.

We also discussed ways to strengthen the security partnership that for more than six decades has helped to keep this continent peaceful and secure. We talked about the future of NORAD and how that organization can best meet emerging threats and safeguard our continent against attack from ballistic missiles.

We talked about our common commitment to securing our border. Canadians and Americans benefit from the free movement of people and commerce across the world's longest unfortified border. Yet, we must work to ensure that our ports of entry are closed to terrorists and criminals and deadly weapons. Under the Smart Border Action Plan, our two nations have developed more secure travel documents, increased our intelligence sharing, improved the collection and dissemination of passenger and customs data, and adopted better rules for processing visas. Under the NEXUS program, we're expediting transit for trusted travelers at 11 border crossings.

We discussed the vital links of commerce and trade that unite the Canadian and American people. Today, total trade between our two nations stands at nearly $400 billion; 23 percent of America's exports come into your nation; more than 80 percent of Canada's exports go into my country. Trade is important. America and Canada seek for the world the same open markets that are essential to our own prosperity. We're committed to the success of the Doha development agenda. We will continue to work to reduce agricultural subsidies that distort trade.

Listen, the relationship between Canada and the United States is indispensable to peace and prosperity on the North American Continent. The United States is fortu-

nate to have a neighbor with whom we share so many ties of values and family and friendship. We look forward to even stronger relationships in the years to come.

Thank you for your hospitality.

Prime Minister Martin. I noticed, Mr. President, you seem to draw a larger crowd than I do. [*Laughter*]

President Bush. I don't know if that's good or bad. [*Laughter*] It all depends on who shows up, I guess.

Canada-U.S. Relations

Q. My question is for President Bush, and then, Prime Minister, if you would respond *en Francais, s'il vous plait?*

In the days after September 11th, thousands of Canadians went to Parliament Hill to demonstrate solidarity with the U.S. and, in fact, in cities across the country. Yet, public opinion polls and other evidence suggest that now, today, our peoples are, in fact, diverging, that, in fact, our peoples are drifting apart. Why do you think that is? And do you have any responsibility for it?

President Bush. You know, I haven't seen the polls you looked at, and we just had a poll in our country where people decided that the foreign policy of the Bush administration ought to be—stay in place for 4 more years. And it's a foreign policy that works with our neighbors. Trade between our countries has never been stronger, but it's a foreign policy that also understands that we've got an obligation to defend our security. I made some decisions, obviously, that some in Canada didn't agree with, like, for example, removing Saddam Hussein and enforcing the demands of the United Nations Security Council.

But the agenda that the Prime Minister and I talked about is one that—where most people should agree: that we'll work to fight disease and poverty on the continent of Africa, for example; that we'll work to make sure our hemisphere is—trades as freely as possible; that we'll work to make sure that the Afghan people continue to enjoy the fruits of a democratic and free society; and that it's important for Iraq to become a democratic society, and I think it will be.

Now, look, I fully understand there are some in my country, probably in your country and around the world, that do not believe that Iraq has the capacity of self-government, that they're willing to sign those people up for tyranny. That's not what I think, and that's not what a lot of Americans think. And they believe that democracy is possible in Iraq. That's a legitimate point to debate. But I'm the kind of fellow who does what I think is right and will continue to do what I think is right. I'll consult with our friends and neighbors, but if I think it's right to remove Saddam Hussein for the security of the United States, that's the course of action I'll take. And some people don't like that. I understand that, but that's the good thing about a democracy, people can express themselves freely.

I, frankly, felt like the reception we received on the way in from the airport was very warm and hospitable, and I want to thank the Canadian people who came out to wave—with all five fingers—for—[laughter]—for their hospitality. [Laughter]

Prime Minister Martin. I know what you mean, Mr. President. I mentioned to the press who was with us in Chile that I found that we—that Spanish and English and French are three different languages, but that sign language is universal. [Laughter]

There is no doubt that, when one examines the values that we share, they are, indeed, the same. When the President was talking about the Ukraine, we have the same ideas about Ukraine; the same goes for Africa.

Obviously, there are disagreements on various questions of foreign policy. There are disagreements in terms of commerce— softwood lumber. We discussed that question. In fact, we discussed BSE. It is quite normal among countries to have this kind of disagreement. But we have common shared values, shared ambitions, and we share optimism also. I think that that is what is fundamental.

Ukraine

Press Secretary Scott McClellan. Scott Lindlaw with the Associated Press.

Q. Mr. President, President Putin said today that the political crisis in the Ukraine must be solved without foreign pressure. I wonder if you took that as some sort of warning toward the United States and whether you think he's lived up to his own words.

President Bush. I haven't seen his comments so I'm hesitant to talk about something that I haven't seen—his quote. But I would tell you that, like I said in my opening statement, I appreciate the efforts of President Kwasniewski of Poland to lead a delegation into the country to help resolve the differences among the parties in a peaceful way. It's very important that violence not break out there, and it's important that the will of the people be heard.

I'm aware of what the Prime Minister of Canada said yesterday about foreign involvement, and he had a very strong statement to—for countries to make sure that the process is fair and open, and that's what we're dedicated to.

And I want to again thank the President of Poland, Kwasniewski, for taking the lead. I—as best I could, I tried to encourage him to continue to play a constructive and useful role. And hopefully, this issue will be solved quickly, and the will of the people will be known.

Prime Minister Martin. Well, I'll just simply pick up. What I said yesterday was that the essence of democracy is that elections be free and open and transparent and that they be elections in which people can have confidence. And if you can't have confidence in the elections, then obviously, that there's a major flaw in your—in their democracy. I also said that I absolutely agree that elections within Ukraine have got to be free from outside influence, and that includes Russia.

Mad Cow Disease/Trade Issues

Q. I'm going to ask my question in French, but it will be for the both of you, so Mr. President, if you could put the translation on. [*Laughter*]

President Bush. Maybe I don't want to know the question. [*Laughter*]

Q. Of course you do. The mad cow crisis has been going on for a year and a half. It has cost millions of dollars to our farmers, and now they are blocking slaughterhouses. Mr. President and you, Mr. Prime Minister, what are you doing to settle the question right now?

Prime Minister Martin. The question—what she said—I'll translate—was, don't you think Canada has a great Government? The—[*laughter*].

President Bush. Yes. [*Laughter*]

Prime Minister Martin. Did you understand the question?

President Bush. Well, yes, I did. I heard the question. Want me to start?

Prime Minister Martin. Sure.

President Bush. Look, the Prime Minister has expressed the—a great deal of frustration that the issue hasn't been resolved yet, and I can understand his level of frustration. There are a series of regulations that are required by U.S. law, and the latest step has been that the Agriculture Department sent over some proposed regulations to handle this issue to what's called the Office of Management and Budget. This is a part of my office. I have sent word over that they need to expedite that request as quickly as possible.

I fully understand the cattle business. I understand the pressures placed upon Canadian ranchers. I believe that, as quickly as possible, young cows ought to be allowed go across our border. I understand the integrated nature of the cattle business, and I hope we can get this issue solved as quickly as possible.

There's a bureaucracy involved, and I readily concede we've got one. I don't know if you've got bureaucracy here in Canada or not, but we've got one in America, and there are a series of rules that have to be met in order for us to be able to allow the trafficking of cows back and forth, particularly those 30 months and younger. So we're working as quickly as we can. And I understand the impact it's had on your industry here.

Prime Minister Martin. I'll just continue, obviously. We discussed a number of contentious issues concerning BSE. As the President has just said, I expressed our frustration. Having said this, last week the President announced a very important step, the reference to the American Agency. And we hope that after a reasonable amount of time—we hope it won't be too long—we hope to obtain a favorable decision.

At the same time, we also discussed the question of softwood lumber. And once again, we expressed our frustration, and we said that a better way will have to be found to solve our differences. The system in place at the present time does not correspond to the reality of exchanges between our two countries. We'll have to find a better way.

On BSE, I believe that the President took a significant step last week in making the reference to the OMB. And one very much hopes that the time delays which are set out can be cut short simply—as a result of the fact that this has been studied to death. And of course, what we're really looking for is a scientifically based answer, and I think that the science has clearly demonstrated that a decision should be taken and a favorable decision to Canada should be taken as quickly as possible.

We discussed other issues as well. Softwood lumber was another one in which we not only raised the issue but also said that there is something the matter with the dispute settlement mechanism that simply allows these kinds of things to go on and on. And we believe that, in fact, we've got to find a better way.

Iran

Press Secretary McClellan. Steve Holland with Reuters.

Q. Thanks, Mr. President. Are you prepared to take Iran to the Security Council over its nuclear program? And are you disappointed the IAEA did not take a harder line yesterday?

President Bush. The Iranians agreed to suspend but not terminate their nuclear weapons program. Our position is, is that they ought to terminate their nuclear weapons program. So I viewed yesterday's decision by the Iranians as a positive step, but it's certainly not a—it's certainly not the final step. And it's very important, for whatever they do, to make sure that the world is able to verify the decision they have made. And so we've obviously got more work to do.

Q. [*Inaudible*]

President Bush. Well, I'm—he said I sound skeptical. It's taken a long time to get to the stage where Iran is willing to suspend. Think about all the hours of negotiations that our friends the French, the Germans, and the Brits have used to get them to suspend a program. What we're interested in is them terminating a nuclear weapons program in a verifiable fashion, and we'll continue to work with our friends.

The Prime Minister and I have discussed this issue. We discussed it at the G–8 in Sea Island, Georgia, and we continue to discuss it. He's got a very clear vision of this as well, and I appreciate his understanding that the world will be better off if Iran does not have a nuclear weapon.

Prime Minister Martin. Whether it's Iran, whether it's North Korea, I think that the world came to a very important decision many, many years ago, in terms of nuclear proliferation. Canada certainly, given the fact of our natural resources, we could be a nuclear power, and there were wise heads at that time that prevailed. And I would

hope that that view would be held universally today by those countries.

Canada-U.S. Border

Q. My question is to President Bush. After September 11th, there were complaints that the Canada-U.S. border was too porous. Since then there have been many changes. But can you please expand on your vision of the border in the future? Does North America need a common security perimeter? And as an aside, how do you think Canada decriminalizing marijuana would affect the border? [*Laughter*]

President Bush. It will probably affect those who use marijuana a lot more than it will affect the border. But the—we've got an obligation to defend our respective countries, and I am impressed by the Prime Minister's commitment to work jointly to share intelligence and to share information so that we can prevent those who would do harm to either the United States or Canada from being able to do so. Now—which presents a challenge. And that is, how do we make sure those who are coming from the United States into Canada are known to both sides and/or vice-versa? And at the same time, how do we make sure that we expedite trade and commerce?

And I think we're making very good progress toward that end. We spent some time talking today about issues in Windsor and Detroit. Believe it or not, the Prime Minister had that on his mind. And the amount of equipment that has been added there is substantial. The management of lanes is productive. The Deputy Prime Minister talked about perhaps the need for an additional bridge, which he asked us to consider.

My point is, is that I believe it is possible to be able to deal with terrorist activity and illegal activity and, at the same time, have a robust commercial relationship. And a lot of it has to do with using technologies in an effective way, and we're making good progress. And obviously, there's more progress to be done, and I'm impressed by the Prime Minister's commitment to work in a very close fashion to deal with somebody who may be willing to do harm to either of our countries. And that really is the first step toward making sure we're secured.

Yes.

Marijuana

Q. [*Inaudible*]—the issue of marijuana——

President Bush. I don't have a comment on what you're doing internally about that.

Prime Minister Martin. I just like doing press conferences with you. You get all the questions. [*Laughter*]

Intelligence Reform Legislation

Press Secretary McClellan. John King with CNN.

President Bush. Yes, King. Why don't you ask the Prime Minister a question. You heard him——

Q. I was just about to apologize for disappointing the Prime Minister. [*Laughter*] Mr. President, I'd like you to answer critics back home who say that they think you're trying to have it both ways on this intelligence reform bill, that you say you want the legislation, but they don't see a sustained effort, both publicly or privately, to challenge the members of your own party who are blocking the bill, like, say, you have done without hesitation many times when it comes to Democrats blocking your judicial nominees.

President Bush. Yes. Well, I want a bill. Let's see if I can say it as plainly as I can—I am for the intelligence bill. I have spoken with Duncan Hunter, Representative Hunter, about the bill. I spoke with Representative Sensenbrenner about the bill. Vice President Cheney today is meeting with members of the 9/11 Commission about the bill. I am—I believe the bill is necessary and important and hope we can get it done next week and look forward to talking to Speaker Hastert and Leader Frist here before the week is out to express to them why I just told you in public I'm for the bill—again.

Thank you.

Prime Minister Martin. Thank you.

President Bush. Gregory [David Gregory, NBC News], the Prime Minister needs a translator. [*Laughter*]

NOTE: The President's news conference began at 2:13 p.m. at the Lester B. Pearson Building. In his remarks, he referred to President Aleksander Kwasniewski of Poland; former President Saddam Hussein of Iraq; and President Vladimir Putin of Russia. Prime Minister Martin referred to Deputy Prime Minister Anne McLellan and Minister of Foreign Affairs Pierre Pettigrew of Canada. A portion of the Prime Minister's remarks and some questions from the Canadian press were in French, and a translation was provided.

Statement on the Resignation of Tom Ridge as Secretary of Homeland Security
November 30, 2004

Tom Ridge has been a key member of my Cabinet, working to help make America safer and stronger. As the Nation's first Assistant to the President for Homeland Security and first Secretary of Homeland Security, he oversaw the most extensive reorga-nization of the Federal Government in 50 years. His efforts have resulted in safer skies, increased border and port security, and enhanced measures to safeguard our critical infrastructure and the American public. In the fight against terrorism, he has played a vital role in protecting the American people from a real and ongoing threat.

Tom has served America for decades, including as a decorated Army soldier, as a United States Congressman, and as Governor of Pennsylvania. He is a long-time friend, and I thank him for his leadership and dedicated service to our country.

America is safer and our Government is better able to protect our people because of his hard work. I wish him and Michele all the best.

NOTE: The Office of the Press Secretary also made available Secretary Ridge's letter of resignation.

Remarks at a Dinner Hosted by Prime Minister Paul Martin of Canada in Gatineau, Canada
November 30, 2004

Thank you all. Thank you very much. Thank you. Thank you all very much. Thank you. The Prime Minister just said, "It's good to be home." I'm here to tell you, it's good to be in Canada. I want to thank you for the warm reception, and I was pleased to see when I opened up the menu that we'll be eating Alberta beef.

Mr. Prime Minister, Madam First Lady, former Prime Ministers, distinguished leaders of Canada, distinguished guests, and ladies and gentlemen, Laura and I are really honored to be here in this great nation. Canada is an old friend. Canada is an honored ally of America.

On this magnificent museum's coat of arms is a motto: Many cultures in one country. In your nation and in mine, people of many cultures, races, and religions embrace a set of ideals that proclaim the liberty and equality of all. These principles are the source of great unity in our diverse lands, and they are the foundation of a close and warm friendship between our two nations.

Our common bond of values and mutual respect have created an alliance that is unsurpassed in strength and depth and potential. Ours is one of the largest trading relationships in the world. We depend on each other to secure the energy resources that help our economies expand. We work to-

gether to protect the land and waters of our beautiful continent. Most importantly, our nations work together to protect our people from harm.

For nearly 50 years, the military personnel of your nation and mine have worked together as a single unit at NORAD to monitor the air approaches to North America and to protect us from attack. On September the 11th, it was a Canadian general, holding the chair at NORAD, who gave the order to initiate our defenses. In an era of new threats, American and Canadian law enforcement and intelligence agencies are working more closely than ever before, and our peoples are more secure because of it.

We also share the mission of spreading the blessings of liberty around the world. In October of this year, millions of Afghans, including millions of women, voted peacefully to elect a leader of moderation. We're working together for stability and prosperity in Haiti and the Sudan. With Canada's generous contribution, the reconstruction of Iraq will help that nation become a peaceful democracy.

Our efforts in these troubled regions are driven by our faith, faith in the ability of liberty to unite different cultures, races, and religions and faith in the ability of liberty to lift up people, to offer an alternative to hate and violence, and to change the world for the better.

And so, Mr. Prime Minister, in admiration for all you've done to create a world governed by liberty and justice and friendship, I offer a toast to you, to the people of Canada, and to the friendship of our two peoples.

NOTE: The President spoke at 7:15 p.m. at the Canadian Museum of Civilization. In his remarks, he referred to Sheila Martin, wife of Prime Minister Martin; former Prime Ministers Jean Chretien and John Napier Turner of Canada; Lt. Gen. E.A. Findley, Canadian Forces, deputy commander, North American Aerospace Defense Command; and President Hamid Karzai of Afghanistan. The Canadian Museum of Civilization is located across the Ottawa River from Ottawa, Ontario. The transcript released by the Office of the Press Secretary also included the remarks of Prime Minister Martin.

Statement on Signing the Veterans Health Programs Improvement Act of 2004
November 30, 2004

Today, I have signed into law H.R. 3936, the "Veterans Health Programs Improvement Act of 2004." The Act is designed to strengthen the management and administration of health care facilities and programs for our Nation's veterans.

Section 414(e)(4)(D) of the Act requires the Secretary of Veterans Affairs (Secretary) to include, in a written notice of a mission change for any of several departmental medical facilities, an analysis of any alternatives to the mission change proposed by the Department of Veterans Affairs. The executive branch shall construe this provision in a manner consistent with the President's constitutional authority to supervise the unitary executive branch and to withhold information the disclosure of which could impair the deliberative processes of the Executive or the performance of the Executive's constitutional duties.

Section 501(c) of the Act purports to require the Secretary to submit to the Congress recommendations for changes in law in certain circumstances. The executive branch shall implement this provision in a manner consistent with the President's constitutional authority to supervise the unitary executive branch and to recommend for the consideration of the Congress such measures as the President judges necessary and expedient.

GEORGE W. BUSH

The White House,
November 30, 2004.

NOTE: H.R. 3936, approved November 30, was assigned Public Law No. 108–422. This statement was released by the Office of the Press Secretary on December 1. An original was not available for verification of the content of this statement.

Remarks in Halifax, Canada
December 1, 2004

Thank you very much. Please be seated. Thank you all very much. Thanks for the warm welcome. Mr. Prime Minister, thank you, and Mrs. Martin, for a fantastic dinner last night in Ottawa. We really loved it. My only regret today is that Laura is not with me. She is—went home to thank those who have been decorating the White House for the great Christmas season that's coming up. I married well. [*Laughter*]

I appreciate the Premiers who are here. Premier Hamm, thank you for your hospitality. Premier Lord, Premier Binns, and Premier Williams, I appreciate you all joining. I want to specifically mention the Premiers because, as an ex-Governor, I feel a special kinship to those who—[*laughter*]—run the Provinces here in Canada. But thank you for your service. Ambassador Cellucci, mayors, local officials, distinguished guests, ladies and gentlemen, I am honored to be with you today to reaffirm America's enduring ties to your country. I am really glad to be in Canada, and I'm really glad to be among friends. I appreciate the warm hospitality we've received.

In the past year, I've come to know your new Prime Minister. We've met in Mexico, in the United States, in Chile, and now in Canada. Paul Martin is a leader who is asserting Canada's good influence in the world. And as I prepare for a second term in office, I look forward to a successful working partnership between our two countries.

Paul and I share a great vision for the future, two prosperous, independent nations joined together by the return of NHL hockey. [*Laughter*] I told Paul that I really have only one regret about this visit to Canada. There's a prominent citizen who endorsed me in the 2000 election, and I wanted a chance to finally thank him for that endorsement. I was hoping to meet Jean Poutine. [*Laughter*]

I'm proud to stand in this historic place, which has welcomed home so many Canadians who defended liberty overseas and where so many new Canadians began their North American dream. I'm grateful for the hospitality shown by the people of this fine city who have been so very kind to Americans before.

Three years ago, Halifax and other towns and villages, from Newfoundland to Manitoba to the Northwest Territories to British Columbia, welcomed, as the Prime Minister mentioned, more than 33,000 passengers on diverted flights. For days after September the 11th, Canadians came to the aid of men and women and children who were worried and confused and had nowhere to sleep. You opened your homes and your churches to strangers. You brought food, you set up clinics, you arranged for calls to their loved ones, and you asked for nothing in return.

One American declared, "My heart is overwhelmed at the outpouring of Canadian compassion. How does a person say thank you to a nation?" Well, that's something a President can do. And so let me say directly to the Canadian people and to all of you here today who welcomed Americans, thank you for your kindness to America in an hour of need.

That emergency revealed the good and generous heart of this country and showed the true feelings of Canadians and Americans toward each other. The affection that appeared in an instant will always be there, and it runs deep. Beyond the words of politicians and the natural disagreements that nations will have, our two peoples are one family and always will be.

We're united in part by the daily contact of commerce, and both our nations are better off for it. In the 10 years since the North American Free Trade Agreement was enacted, trade between the United

States and Canada has nearly doubled. Twenty-three percent of America's exports go directly north, and more than 80 percent of Canadians' exports go to my country. With so much trade, there are bound to be some disagreements. I proudly ate some Alberta beef last night, and—[*laughter*]— I'm still standing. [*Laughter*] With determined efforts and relying on sound science and mutual good will, we can resolve issues. Take, for example, those PEI potatoes. [*Laughter*] Right, Mr. Premier? [*Laughter*]

Canada represents America's most vital trade relationship in the whole world, and we will do all that is necessary to keep that relationship strong.

Yet, our ties go deeper than trade. Our community of values reaches back centuries. Canada and the U.S. may have disagreed on the wisdom of separating from the Crown, but we've always agreed on the great principles of liberty derived from our common heritage. We believe in the dignity of every human life, and we believe in the right of every person to live in freedom. We believe in free markets, humanized by compassion and fairness. We believe a diverse society can also be united by principles of justice and equality. The values we hold have made us good neighbors for centuries, and they will keep us as strong allies and good friends for the centuries to come.

These shared convictions have also led our great democracies to accept a mission in the wider world. We know it is not possible to live in quiet isolation of our peaceful continent, hoping the problems and challenges of other nations will pass us by. We know there can be no security, no lasting peace in a world where proliferation and terrorism and genocide and extreme poverty go unopposed.

We know that our own interests are served by an international system that advances human rights and open societies and free trade and the rule of law and the hope that comes from self-government. Both Canada and the United States have accepted important global duties, and we will meet those responsibilities for our own benefit and for the good of mankind.

Canada's leadership is helping to build a better world. Over the past decade, Canadian troops have helped bring stability to Bosnia and Kosovo. Canada's willingness to send peacekeepers to Haiti saved thousands of lives and helped save Haiti's constitutional government. Canadian troops are serving bravely in Afghanistan at this hour. Other Canadians stand on guard for peace in the Middle East, in Cyprus, Sudan, and the Congo.

Just 2 weeks ago, NATO countries showed their esteem for your military by electing General Ray Henault as Chairman of NATO's Military Committee. This admiration for your armed forces goes way back and for good reason. It was said during World War I, "The Canadians never budge." America respects the skill and honor and the sacrifice of Canadians' armed—Canada's armed forces.

Our nations play independent roles in the world, yet our purposes are complementary. We have important work ahead. A new term in office is an important opportunity to reach out to our friends. I hope to foster a wide international consensus among three great goals. The first great commitment is to defend our security and spread freedom by building effective multinational and multilateral institutions and supporting effective multilateral action.

The tasks of the 21st century, from fighting proliferation to fighting the scourge of HIV/AIDS to fighting poverty and hunger, cannot be accomplished by a single nation alone. The United States and Canada participate together in more multilateral institutions than perhaps any two nations on Earth, from NATO in Europe to the OAS in the Western Hemisphere to APEC in the Pacific. Canada and the United States are working with a coalition of nations through the Proliferation Security Initiative to stop and seize shipments of weapons of mass destruction materials and delivery systems on land and at sea and in the air.

America always prefers to act with allies at our side, and we're grateful to Canada for working closely with us to confront the challenges of Iran and North Korea. Multilateral organizations can do great good in the world.

Yet, the success of multilateralism is measured not merely by following a process but by achieving results. The objective of the U.N. and other institutions must be collective security, not endless debate. For the sake of peace, when those bodies promise serious consequences, serious consequences must follow. America and Canada helped create the United Nations, and because we remain committed to that institution, we want it to be more than a League of Nations.

My country is determined to work as far as possible within the framework of international organizations, and we're hoping that other nations will work with us to make those institutions more relevant and more effective in meeting the unique threats of our time.

Our second commitment is to fight global terrorism with every action and resource the task requires. Canada has taken a series of critical steps to guard against the danger of terrorism. You created the Department of Public Safety and Emergency Preparedness. You've toughened your antiterror laws. You're upgrading your intelligence. I want to thank the Government for all those constructive and important decisions.

Our two countries are working together every day—every day—to keep our people safe. That is the most solemn duty I have and the most solemn duty the Prime Minister has. From the Smart Border accord to the Container Security Initiative to the joint command of NORAD, we are working together. I hope we'll also move forward on ballistic missile defense cooperation to protect the next generation of Canadians and Americans from the threats we know will arise.

The energetic defense of our nations is an important duty. Yet, defense alone is not a sufficient strategy. On September the 11th, the people of North America learned that two vast oceans and friendly neighbors cannot fully shield us from the dangers of the 21st century. There's only one way to deal with enemies who plot in secret and set out to murder the innocent and the unsuspecting: We must take the fight to them. We must be relentless and we must be steadfast in our duty to protect our people.

Both of the countries have learned this lesson. In the early days of World War II, when the United States was still wrestling with isolationism, Canadian forces were already engaging the enemies of freedom from the Atlantic—across the Atlantic. At the time, some Canadians argued that Canada had not been attacked and had no interest in fighting a distant war. Your Prime Minister, McKenzie King, gave this answer: "We cannot defend our country and save our homes and families by waiting for the enemy to attack us. To remain on the defensive is the surest way to bring the war to Canada. Of course, we should protect our coasts and strengthen our ports and cities against attack," but the Prime Minister went on to say, "we must also go out and meet the enemy before he reaches our shores. We must defeat him before he attacks us, before our cities are laid to waste." McKenzie King was correct then, and we must always remember the wisdom of his words today.

In the new era, the threat is different, but our duties are the same. Our enemies have declared their intentions, and so have we. Peaceful nations must keep the peace by going after the terrorists and disrupting their plans and cutting off their funding. We must hold the sponsors of terror equally responsible for terrorist acts. We must prevent outlaw regimes from gaining weapons of mass destruction and providing them to terrorists. We must stay at these efforts with patience and resolve until we prevail.

Our third great commitment is to enhance our own security by promoting freedom and hope and democracy in the broader Middle East. The United States and Canada and all free nations need to look ahead. If, 20 years from now, the Middle East is dominated by dictators and mullahs who build weapons of mass destruction and harbor terrorists, our children and our grandchildren will live in a nightmare world of danger. That must not happen.

By taking the side of reformers and democrats in the Middle East, we will gain allies in the war on terror and isolate the ideology of murder and help to defeat the despair and hopelessness that feeds terror. The world will become a much safer place as democracy advances.

For decades of tyranny and neglect in the broader Middle East, progress toward freedom will not come easily. I know that. Yet, it is cultural condescension to claim that some peoples or some cultures or some religions are destined to despotism and unsuited for self-government.

Today in the Middle East, the doubters and pessimists are being proven wrong. We're seeing movement toward elections and greater rights for women and open discussion of peaceful reform. I believe that people across the Middle East are weary of poverty and oppression and plead in silence for their liberty. I believe this is an historic moment in the broader Middle East, and we must seize this moment by standing with everyone who stands for liberty.

We're standing with the people of Afghanistan, a nation that has gone from a safe haven for terrorists to a steadfast ally in the war on terror in 3½ short years. Canada deployed more than 7,000 troops and much of your navy in support of Operation Enduring Freedom. This year, your country has led the International Security Assistance Force in Kabul. The coalition we share is doing honorable work, yet democracy is taking hold in that country because the Afghan people, like people every-

where, want to live in freedom. They registered by the millions to vote in October. They stood in long lines on election day. An Afghan widow brought all four of her daughters to vote alongside her. She said, "When you see women here lined up to vote, this is something profound. I never dreamed this day would come." But that woman's dream finally arrived, as it will one day across the Middle East. These are unprecedented, historic events that many said would never come, and Canadians can be proud of the part you have played in the advance of human liberty.

We must also stand with the brave people of Iraq, who are preparing for elections on January the 30th. Sometimes, even the closest of friends disagree. And 2 years ago, we disagreed about the best course of action in Iraq. Yet, as your Prime Minister made clear in Washington earlier this year, there is no disagreement at all with what has to be done in going forward. We must help the Iraqi people secure their country and build a free and democratic society. The Canadian Government has pledged more than $200 million in humanitarian aid and reconstruction assistance and agreed to relieve more than $450 million in Iraqi debt. That help is greatly appreciated.

There's more work to be done together. Both Canada and the United States and all free nations have a vital interest in the success of a free Iraq. The terrorists have made Iraq the central front in the war on terror because they know what is at stake. When a free and democratic society is established in Iraq, in the heart of the Middle East, it will be a decisive blow to their aspirations to dominate the region and its people. A free Iraq will be a standing rebuke to radicalism and a model to reformers from Damascus to Tehran.

In Fallujah and elsewhere, our coalition and Iraqi forces are on the offensive, and we are delivering a message: Freedom, not oppression, is the future of Iraq. Freedom is a precious right for every individual, regardless of the color of their skin or the religion they may hold. A long night of terror and tyranny in that region is ending, and a new day of freedom and hope and self-government is on the way.

And we will stand with the Palestinian and Israeli peoples and help end the destructive conflict between them. Prime Minister Martin has expressed the desire of his Government to take a broader role in the quest for peace and democracy, and America welcomes your involvement. It's a time of change and a time of hope in that region.

We seek justice and dignity and a viable independent and democratic state for the Palestinian people. We seek security and peace for the state of Israel, a state that Canada, like America, first recognized in 1948. These are worthy goals in themselves, and by reaching them, we will also remove an excuse for hatred and violence in the broader Middle East.

Achieving peace in the Holy Land is not just a matter of pressuring one side or the other on the shape of a border or the site of a settlement. This approach has been tried before, without success. As we negotiate the details of peace, we must look to the heart of the matter, which is the need for a Palestinian democracy. The Palestinian people deserve a peaceful government that truly serves their interests, and the Israeli people need a true partner in peace.

Our destination is clear, two states, Israel and Palestine, living side by side in peace and security. And that destination can be reached by only one path, the path of democracy and reform and the rule of law. If all parties will apply effort, if all nations who are concerned about this issue will apply good will, this conflict can end and peace can be achieved. And the time for that effort and the time for that good will is now.

The United States and Canada face common threats in our world, and we share common goals that can transform our world. We're bound by history and geography and trade and by our deepest convictions. With so much in common and so much at stake, we cannot be divided. I realize and many Americans realize that it's not always easy to sleep next to the elephant. [*Laughter*] Sometimes, our laws and our actions affect Canada every bit as much as they affect us, and we need to remember that. And when frustrations are vented, we must not take it personally. As a member of Canada's Parliament said in the 1960s, "The United States is our friend, whether we like it or not." [*Laughter*] When all is said and done, we are friends, and we like it.

Three years ago, when the American planes were diverted away from home, passengers knew they were safe and welcome the moment they saw the Maple Leaf flag. One of them later said of the Canadians he met, "They taught me the meaning of the word 'friend.' " For generations, the nation of Canada has defined the word "friend," and my country is grateful.

God has blessed America in many ways. God has blessed us because we have neighbors like you. And today I ask that God continues to bless the people of Canada.

Thank you.

NOTE: The President spoke at noon at Pier 21. In his remarks, he referred to Prime Minister Paul Martin of Canada and his wife, Sheila; Premier John Frederick Hamm of Nova Scotia, Canada; Premier Bernard Lord of New Brunswick, Canada; Premier Patrick G. Binns of Prince Edward Island, Canada; and Premier Danny Williams of Newfoundland, Canada.

Remarks Prior to Discussions With President Olusegun Obasanjo of Nigeria and an Exchange With Reporters
December 2, 2004

President Bush. Mr. President, welcome back. It is great to see you. I'm looking forward to working with you over the next years to strengthen our relationship, to work on a prosperous continent of Africa, to work with you on implementing our strategy to help defeat the pandemic of HIV/AIDS. I look forward to our discussion today.

I particularly want to thank the President for his contributions to the peacekeeping forces of the African Union. We have worked together on issues such as Liberia, Sudan, and other important parts of the continent of Africa. I look forward to a fruitful relationship, and I'm glad you're here. I want to welcome you, and thank you for coming, sir.

President Obasanjo. Thank you very much, sir. Mr. President, let me start by congratulating you once again. And let me express our appreciation for receiving me and my delegation so very early in your preparation for the second term. Of course, you are receiving me not only in my capacity as President of Nigeria but also in my capacity as the Chairman of AU, continuing that organization.

I'm looking forward to this meeting to consolidate what we have been able to do together, like you have rightly said, in the area of peace and security and conflict resolution in Africa, in the area of trade and resource flow for Africa, and in the area of fight against terrorism by making the world, particularly Africa, a more peaceful and a more conducive continent to live in, and of course in the area of security, stability, and availability of some of the essential resources for the development of the world, but the—[*inaudible*]—in the Gulf region of our continent. I'm looking forward to being able to work with you.

President Bush. It's good to see you again, sir.

Scott [Scott Lindlaw, Associated Press], a couple of questions.

Secretary-General Kofi Annan of the United Nations

Q. Thank you, Mr. President. Do you think questions of fraud in the U.N.'s Oil for Food Programme have hurt Kofi Annan, and do you think he should resign, as Senator Coleman has urged?

President Bush. Yesterday I spoke about the United Nations. I said the United States participates in multilateral organizations, and we expect those organizations to be effective. You know, when an organization says there's going to be serious consequences if something doesn't happen, it better mean what it says.

And on this issue, it's very important for the United Nations to understand that there ought to be a full and fair and open accounting of the Oil for Food Programme. In order for the taxpayers of the United States to feel comfortable about supporting the United Nations, there has to be an open accounting, and I look forward to that process going forward.

Q. Should he resign, sir?

President Bush. I look forward to the full disclosure of the facts, a good, honest appraisal of that which went on. And it's important for the integrity of the organization to have a full and open disclosure of all that took place with the Oil for Food Programme.

Yes, Steve [Steve Holland, Reuters].

Ukraine

Q. Sir, should there be a new election in Ukraine, and should it be free of Russian influence?

President Bush. Well, I think any election, if there is one, ought to be free from any foreign influence. These elections ought to be open and fair. I appreciate the progress that is being made. I particularly want to again thank my friend the President of Poland, the President of Lithuania, and the EU for its involvement in helping to resolve the Ukrainian election crisis.

The position of our Government is that the will of the people must be known and heard. And therefore, I will—we will continue to monitor and be involved in a process that encourages there to be a peaceful resolution of this issue. And you know, there are different options on the table, and we're watching very carefully what is taking place. But any election in any country must be—must reflect the will of the people and not that of any foreign government.

Yes, Gregory [David Gregory, NBC News].

Iraq

Q. Mr. President, you're sending more troops to Iraq now. This comes on the heels of reports that Iraqi security forces appear to be underperforming, appear to be unprepared for elections in January. If that's the case, what would be so bad about postponing elections if there's the potential that those elections may be seen as illegitimate?

President Bush. Well, first of all, the elections should not be postponed. It's time for the Iraqi citizens to go the polls, and that's why we are very firm on the January 30th date. Secondly, I have always said that I will listen to the requests of our commanders on the ground. And our commanders requested some troops delay their departure home and the expedition of other troops to help these elections go forward. And I honored their request.

And thirdly, we are working hard to train Iraqis. And we have got certain benchmarks in mind. And General Petraeus is in charge

of training the Iraqi troops, and the Iraqi ministers in charge of that are meeting the goals. And the idea, of course, and the strategy, of course, is have the Iraqis defend their own freedom. And we want to help them have their Presidential elections. And at some point in time, when Iraq is able to defend itself against the terrorists who are trying to destroy democracy—as I have said many times—our troops will come home with the honor they have earned.

It's time for those people to vote, and I am looking forward to it. It's one of those moments in history where a lot of people will be amazed that a society has been transformed so quickly from one of tyranny and torture and mass graves to one in which people are actually allowed to express themselves at the ballot.

Thank you all very much.

Q. Mr. President. Mr. President——

President Bush. Yes, sir.

U.S. Role in Africa

Q. As you march into the second term, what will Africa be looking forward to in terms of America's contribution to security, especially in the Gulf of Guinea?

President Bush. No, I appreciate that. First of all, Africa was a very important part of my first term. I have met with the President—four or five times?

President Obasanjo. Four or five——

President Bush. So many times, it's hard to count.

President Obasanjo. And at the G–8, I think about 10 times.

President Bush. Ten times. I have met with other leaders from the continent of Africa a lot. I have traveled to Africa. I have made the—fighting the pandemic of HIV/AIDS a central part of my administration. I helped work to extend AGOA on the full belief that economic trade and the benefits of trade far exceed the benefits of direct aid. I've worked on a Millennium Challenge Account to help encourage the habits of good governance. And I will continue that focus and attention on the continent of Africa. I think it is vital that the continent of Africa be a place of freedom and democracy and prosperity and hope where people can grow up and realize their dreams. It's a continent that has got vast potential, and the United States wants to help the people of Africa realize that potential.

Thank you all.

NOTE: The President spoke at 9:38 a.m. in the Oval Office at the White House. In his remarks, he referred to President Aleksander Kwasniewski of Poland; President Valdas Adamkus of Lithuania; and Lt. Gen. David H. Petraeus, USA, chief, Office of Security Transition—Iraq.

Remarks on the Nomination of Governor Mike Johanns To Be Secretary of Agriculture
December 2, 2004

The President. Thank you all. Good morning.

I am pleased to announce my nomination of Governor Mike Johanns to be the Secretary of Agriculture.

Gov. Johanns. Thank you, Mr. President.

The President. Governor Johanns is an experienced public service—servant from America's agricultural heartland. As the son of Iowa dairy farmers, he grew up close to the land. He will bring to this position a lifetime of involvement in agriculture and a long record of a faithful friend to America's farmers and ranchers. He will lead an important agency with the executive skill he has learned as mayor and as a two-term Governor of Nebraska.

I've known Mike for a number of years, going back to my own service as a Governor. I know firsthand his deep commitment to a strong farm economy. He's been a leader on drought relief in Nebraska and throughout the Midwest. He's a strong proponent of alternative energy sources such as ethanol and biodiesel. He's traveled the world to promote American farm exports.

Governor Johanns is a man of action and of complete integrity. He knows how to bring people together to achieve results. He has been a superb leader for the people of Nebraska, and I'm grateful that he's agreed to take on this important new responsibility in my Cabinet.

Gov. Johanns. Thank you, Mr. President.

The President. I'm grateful as well to Secretary of Agriculture Ann Veneman for leading the Department of Agriculture these past 4 years. Secretary Veneman has earned the trust of farmers and ranchers across America, and the whole Nation has benefited from her service. Ann played a central role in passing the 2002 farm bill, which has been critical to the success of our farmers.

She's kept our Nation's commitment to fighting hunger and is overseeing major improvements in school nutrition programs. Ann led our efforts to prevent the spread of mad cow disease and worked hard to secure the food supply against the threat of bioterrorism. And she has helped set in motion an incredibly important effort to maintain the health of our forests and protect the lives and property from devastating wildfires.

I chose Ann Veneman for her great expertise, her sound judgment, and her bipartisan spirit, and she has displayed those qualities every day of her tenure. Ann has also carried out her duties while facing serious illness, and for that she's earned my increased admiration and the respect of her fellow citizens. I'm proud to know her, and I thank her for serving our country.

The policies we've pursued over the last 4 years have revived America's economies and have helped our farmers and ranchers earn greater income and to sell record amounts of food and fiber abroad. In a new term, we'll continue policies that are pro-growth, pro-jobs, and pro-farmer. We'll keep working to open new markets to American grain and beef and cotton and corn. We'll enforce trade laws to make sure other countries play by the rules. We will expand conservation programs to help farmers and to protect our soil and water and wildlife.

We will stand behind family farmers by keeping taxes low and ensuring the Federal death tax is repealed permanently. And when confirmed by the Senate, Mike Johanns will lead a Department of 113,000 dedicated public servants and be a champion of the farmers and ranchers who feed America and the world beyond.

I am grateful to Mike and to Stephanie, his wife, for their willingness to come to Washington. I look forward to welcoming Mike to my Cabinet.

Congratulations. I appreciate you.

Gov. Johanns. Thank you very much.

The President. You bet, Mike.

[*At this point, Gov. Johanns made brief remarks.*]

The President. Good job.

Gov. Johanns. Thank you.

NOTE: The President spoke at 11:42 a.m. in the Roosevelt Room at the White House. The transcript released by the Office of the Press Secretary also included the remarks of Gov. Johanns.

Remarks on Lighting the National Christmas Tree
December 2, 2004

Thank you all very much. Tonight we begin a joyous season, and the city of Washington is never more beautiful than during the holidays. At Christmastime, we celebrate good tidings first announced 2,000 years ago and still a source of great joy in our world. Laura and I are always happy to join in the Pageant of Peace, and we thank you all for coming this evening.

I thank our special guests. I want to thank Santa for such good weather. [*Laughter*] I appreciate Peter, the chairman of the Pageant of Peace, and his wife, Nancy. I want to thank John Betchkal, the president of the Christmas Pageant of Peace. I want to thank the members of the board of the Christmas Pageant of Peace for your hard work in putting on this joyous festival. I want to thank Secretary of the Interior Gale Norton. I want to thank other members of my Cabinet who are here tonight. I appreciate the Members of Congress who are here.

I want to thank Fran Mainella, who is the Director of the Parks Service, and all the National Parks Service employees. I thank Dr. Schuller and all the entertainers. Thanks so very much for being here tonight.

The season of Advent is always the season of hope. We think of the patient hope of men and women across the centuries who listened to the words of the prophets and lived in joyful expectation. We think of the hope of Mary, who welcomed God's plan with great faith. We think of the hope of the wise men who set out on a long journey guided only by a slender promise traced in the stars. We are reminded of the hope that the grandest purposes of the Almighty can be found in the humblest places. And we embrace the hope that all the love and gifts that come to us in this life are the signs and symbols of even a greater love and gift that came on a holy night. The old carol speaks of a "thrill of hope, the weary world rejoices, for yonder breaks a new and glorious morn." And every year at this time we feel the thrill of hope as we wait on Christmas Day.

This Christmas, as loved ones come together, some in our military are separated from family by the call of duty a long way from home. We have service men and women celebrating the holidays at bases from Europe to East Asia and on many fronts in the war on terror. Especially for those deployed in Afghanistan and Iraq, the work is dangerous and the mission is urgent. American service men and women are bringing freedom to many and peace to future generations. Their sacrifices defend us all, and all Americans are grateful to them and to our military families.

Across our country, citizens are supporting our people in uniform with their prayers and many acts of kindness. Often the effort is led by children. In Chantilly, Virginia, Brownie Troop 5179, who are here tonight, by the way, collected donations of candy and sun screen, bug spray, and handmade cards to send to our soldiers overseas. They gathered more than 200 pounds of gifts and made sure the packages arrived on time for the holidays. I'm sure those thoughtful gifts were gladly received.

And I thank the Brownies for reminding the good people of our military how much they mean to America. And to show our appreciation to the Brownies of Chantilly, Virginia, and all those who volunteer in our blessed land, we have two representatives of the Troop to help Laura and me light our national Christmas tree.

And so, if Nichole and Clara will come forward, we will turn on the lights. Are you ready? Now will you join me in the countdown? Five, four, three, two, one.

NOTE: The President spoke at 5:56 p.m. on the Ellipse during the annual Christmas Pageant of Peace. In his remarks, he referred to John Betchkal, president, Christmas Pageant of Peace; Peter Nostrand, chairman, Christmas Pageant of Peace, and his wife, Nancy; Robert H. Schuller, minister, Reformed Church in America; and Nichole Mastracchio and Clara Pitts, members, Brownie Troop 5179, Chantilly, VA.

Remarks on the Nomination of Bernard B. Kerik To Be Secretary of Homeland Security
December 3, 2004

The President. Good morning. I'm proud to announce my nomination of Commissioner Bernard Kerik as the Secretary of Homeland Security.

Bernie Kerik is one of the most accomplished and effective leaders of law enforcement in America. In his career, he has served as an enlisted military police officer in Korea, a jail warden in New Jersey, a beat cop in Manhattan, New York City corrections commissioner, and as New York's 40th police commissioner, an office once held by Teddy Roosevelt. In every position, he has demonstrated a deep commitment to justice, a heart for the innocent, and a record of great success.

I'm grateful he's agreed to bring his lifetime of security experience and skill to one of the most important positions in the Federal Government. Bernie is a dedicated, innovative reformer who insists on getting results. As the head of New York City jails, he cut inmate violence by more than 90 percent. As Mayor Rudy Giuliani's police commissioner, he had great success in reducing crime in New York City. His broad, practical, hands-on experience makes Bernie superbly qualified to lead the Department of Homeland Security.

When confirmed by the Senate, Bernie Kerik will build on the historic accomplishments of Secretary Tom Ridge. As the Department's first leader, Tom oversaw the large reorganization—the largest reorganization of the Government in nearly a half-century. He met urgent challenges with patience and purpose, and because of his service, our country is safer.

Tom also carried out his duties with skill and honesty and decency. He's been my friend for more than 20 years. He is one of the great public servants of our generation. Tom Ridge has our Nation's gratitude; he's got my gratitude; and I wish he and Michele all the best.

My nominee to succeed Secretary Ridge has the background and the passion that are needed to protect our citizens. As police commissioner on September the 11th, 2001, Bernie Kerik arrived at the World Trade Center minutes after the first plane hit. He was there when the Twin Towers collapsed. He knew the faces of the rescuers who rushed toward danger. He attended the funeral of the officers who didn't come back. Bernie Kerik understands the duties that came to America on Sep-

tember the 11th. The resolve he felt that morning will guide him every day on his job. And every first-responder defending our homeland will have a faithful ally in Bernie Kerik.

As he prepares for new responsibility, Bernie Kerik has the love and support of his family, his wife, Hala; his children, Joseph, Celine, and Angelina and Lisa. He will always be inspired by his father and hero, Donald Kerik, Sr., and his caring stepmother, Clara. Bernard Kerik has devoted his life to protecting his fellow citizens, and his example has led many others to take up that calling. He loves his country. He has gained the trust and admiration of millions. I call on the Senate to promptly confirm his nomination as the Secretary of Homeland Security.

Thank you for serving, Bernie, and congratulations.

Secretary-designate Kerik. Mr. President, thank you.

The President. Yes, sir.

[*At this point, Secretary-designate Kerik made brief remarks.*]

The President. Good job. Thank you, sir.

NOTE: The President spoke at 9:54 a.m. in the Roosevelt Room at the White House. In his remarks, he referred to Rudolph W. Giuliani, former mayor of New York City; and Michele Ridge, wife of Homeland Security Secretary Tom Ridge. The transcript released by the Office of the Press Secretary also included the remarks of Secretary-designate Kerik.

Remarks on Signing the Individuals with Disabilities Education Improvement Act of 2004
December 3, 2004

Thanks for coming. Good morning. I'm proud to be standing up here with friends from both sides of the political aisle who worked together to reauthorize the Individuals with Disabilities Education Act. It's a really good piece of legislation. It took a lot of hard work, and it shows what is possible in our Nation's Capital.

I want to thank Mike Castle for being the sponsor of the bill. I appreciate your hard work, Mike. I also appreciate being here with Senator Ted Kennedy, who has been a long-time advocate for the IDEA legislation. I appreciate you bringing your sister. Welcome. I want to thank Senator Mike Enzi from Wyoming and Senator Pat Roberts from Kansas, Senator Sessions from Alabama, Senator Lamar Alexander from Tennessee, and Congressman Ric Keller for being here as well. Thanks for your good work and your stalwart support.

I appreciate Gene Hickok. Dr. Hickok here is the Deputy Secretary of the U.S. Department of Education. I want to thank Doug Huntt, who is the commissioner of the Ohio Rehabilitation Services Commission, for agreeing to serve on the President's Commission on Excellence in Special Education. I want to thank you for your work on that, Dr. Huntt.

I appreciate Kyle Stevenson being up here today. Kyle, thank you for coming. I first got to meet Kyle at the—[*laughter*]—White House tee-ball game. He's a pretty good player. Thanks for coming. Stephanie, I appreciate you being here. It's good to see you again. I want to thank Isabelle June Bailey for being here. Isabelle June, thank you for being here. We're so proud you're here. Thank you for joining us. [*Laughter*] She's up here with her mom, Carolyn, and her dad, and two brothers, Alex and Ben, are with us today as well. Thank you all for coming.

America's schools educate over 6 million children with disabilities. In the past, those students were too often just shuffled through the system with little expectation that they could make significant progress or succeed like their fellow classmates. Children with disabilities deserve high hopes, high expectations, and extra help.

In the bill I sign today, we're raising expectations for the students. We're giving schools and parents the tools they need to meet them. We're applying the reforms of the No Child Left Behind Act to the Individuals with Disabilities Education Improvement Act so schools are accountable for teaching every single child. All our students deserve excellent teachers, so this law ensures that students with disabilities will have special education teachers with the skills and training to teach special education and their subject area.

Some students with disabilities will need intensive, individualized help. So this law, for the first time, will support tutoring programs to help children in schools that need improvement. When schools are so busy trying to deal with unnecessary and costly lawsuits, they have less time to spend with students. So we're creating opportunities for parents and teachers to resolve problems early. We're making the system less litigious so it can focus on the children and their parents.

The people who care most about the students are, of course, the teachers and especially the parents, who know their needs and know their names. So we're giving more flexibility and control over the students' education to parents and teachers and principals. We'll make sure that parents and schools can change a student's educational program to better meet their needs, without having to attend unnecessary meetings or complete unnecessary paperwork. We trust the local folks to meet high standards for all our kids, and this bill gives them the freedom and flexibility to meet our goals.

All students in America can learn. That's what all of us up here believe. All of us understand we have an obligation to make sure no child is left behind in America. So I'm honored to sign the Individuals with Disabilities Education Improvement Act of 2004, and once again thank the Members for being here.

NOTE: The President spoke at 10:20 a.m. in Room 350 of the Dwight D. Eisenhower Executive Office Building. In his remarks, he referred to Eunice Kennedy Shriver, founder, Special Olympics. H.R. 1350, approved December 3, was assigned Public Law No. 108–446.

Statement on Signing the Individuals with Disabilities Education Improvement Act of 2004
December 3, 2004

Today, I have signed into law H.R. 1350, the "Individuals with Disabilities Education Improvement Act of 2004." The Act strengthens the ability of the Federal Government to assist States in the education of children with disabilities.

The executive branch shall construe provisions of the Act that require taking account of race, culture, gender, age, region, socioeconomics, ideology, secularity, and partisan politics, including sections 612, 616, 618, 637, 663, 664, and 681 of the Individuals with Disabilities Education Act, as enacted by section 101 of the Act, and section 177(b)(3) of the Education Sciences Reform Act of 2002, as enacted by section 201(a)(2) of the Act, in a manner consistent with the First Amendment and the requirement of the Due Process Clause of the Fifth Amendment to the Constitution to afford equal protection of the laws.

The executive branch shall construe section 615(e)(2)(G) of the Individuals with Disabilities Education Act, as enacted by section 101 of the Act, as establishing a duty for a State to follow the specified statutory exclusionary rule only when that duty is a condition of a Federal grant or contract accepted by or under the authority of that State, as is consistent with the principles governing Federal-State relations enunciated by the Supreme Court of the United States in *Printz* v. *United States*.

GEORGE W. BUSH

The White House,

December 3, 2004.

NOTE: H.R. 1350, approved December 3, was assigned Public Law No. 108–446.

Statement on the Resignation of Tommy G. Thompson as Secretary of Health and Human Services
December 3, 2004

I have known Tommy Thompson for many years—first when we served as Governors and then as my Secretary of Health and Human Services. He is a friend and a true public servant who worked every day to make Americans healthier and to help more Americans in need achieve the dream of independence and personal responsibility.

He worked to modernize and add prescription drug coverage to Medicare for the first time in the program's history. He focused on expanding services to seniors, people with disabilities, and low-income Americans. He led the effort to broaden the network of community health centers across our country and to advance the development and use of health information technology. Throughout his career as Governor and as Secretary of Health and Human Services, Tommy has led efforts to reform welfare laws and help more people transition from welfare to work.

Tommy has been a stalwart member of my homeland security team, especially through his contributions to our Nation's response to the threat of bioterrorism. And he has done a superb job in our compassionate mission of helping those here and abroad fight the scourge of the HIV/AIDS virus.

Tommy served as Governor of Wisconsin for 14 years and has served as Secretary of Health and Human Services for 4 years, and I appreciate his desire to tackle new challenges. I wish Tommy and Sue Ann all the best.

NOTE: The Office of the Press Secretary also made available Secretary Thompson's letter of resignation.

Statement on the Resignation of John C. Danforth as United States Ambassador to the United Nations
December 3, 2004

Jack Danforth has served with distinction as United States Ambassador to the United Nations. He represented our Nation ably and well during a time when we are waging a global war on terror. Because of his tireless efforts as Special Envoy to the Sudan, the world is closer than ever to seeing an end to the Sudanese North-South conflict. Throughout his life, including as a distinguished United States Senator and as Attorney General of Missouri, Jack Danforth has been a man of strong convictions and deep integrity who has made our country better and stronger. I understand his desire to return home to Missouri, and I thank Jack for his superb service and his friendship. I wish Sally and him all the best.

Remarks Following Discussions With President Pervez Musharraf of Pakistan and an Exchange With Reporters
December 4, 2004

President Bush. It's my honor to welcome a friend, a leader, President Musharraf of Pakistan. He is a person with whom I've worked very closely over the past 4 years, a person with whom I look forward to working closely over the next 4 years. And we had a really good discussion.

We discussed international politics. I assured President Musharraf that there is an opportunity at hand to work toward the development of a Palestinian state and peace in the Middle East. I told him that this will be a priority of my administration. The goal is two states living side by side in peace and security.

We spent time talking about our bilateral relations. We reviewed the relationship between India and Pakistan. He has showed great courage in that relationship, leading toward what we hope will be a peaceful solution of what has been a historically difficult problem.

We talked about our own bilateral relations. The President and I are absolutely committed to fighting off the terrorists who would destroy life in Pakistan or the United States or anywhere else. And I appreciate very much your clear vision of the need for people of good will and hope to prevail over those who are willing to inflict death in order to achieve an ideology that is—the predominance of an ideology that is just backward and dark in its view.

I—we talked about commerce between our countries. The President is very concerned about whether or not Pakistan goods are being treated equally, as fairly as other goods coming into the United States. I listened very carefully to what he had to say. He had some constructive ideas as to how to deal with that situation.

Having brought up his economy, however, I reminded him that he's doing quite a good job of making sure that the economy grows in Pakistan so that people have got a chance to realize their dreams. And I congratulate you on the good stewardship of the Pakistan economy.

All in all, our relationships are good; they're strong; and they will remain that way. And I'm honored you're here.

President Musharraf. Thank you. Thank you very much, Mr. President. I don't have much to add to what the President has already said. We had a very wholesome interaction. And all that I would like to say, that I've come here basically to congratulate the President very sincerely, with all my sincerity, for having won the elections. And he does me an honor by receiving me on a Saturday. [*Laughter*]

And therefore, the other issues that we discussed were incidental and all the important issues—the most important issue, a resolution of the Palestinian dispute, in the interest of peace in the whole world, and I would repeat whatever the President has already said: Enhancement of our bilateral relations, enhancement of our commercial ties with the United States.

I'm grateful for the extreme understanding that the President has shown towards the concerns of Pakistan.

Thank you.

President Bush. Welcome. Welcome.

We'll answer a question from the American side, and the Pakistani side, and the American side, and Pakistani side. And that will be it, in the spirit of Saturday morning meetings. And so the first person that will be asking the question will be Mr. Mark Knoller [CBS Radio].

Homeland Security

Q. Thank you. Mr. President, what do you make of the warning sounded yesterday by Tommy Thompson that the American food supply may be at risk to terrorist attack?

President Bush. Tommy was commenting on the fact that we're a large company—country, with all kinds of avenues where somebody can inflict harm. And we're doing everything we can to protect the American people. I picked a good man to head the Homeland Security Department in Bernie Kerik. I hope the Senate confirms him quickly so he can get to work. There's a lot of work to be done. We've made a lot of progress in protecting our country, and there's more work to be done. And this administration is committed to doing it.

Q. Mr. President——

President Bush. Do you want to call on somebody?

President Musharraf. I know that—I know that you're trying your best to address the issue of terrorism all over the world, and obviously, the most important part is to protect your own, the United States, from terrorism.

President Bush. Actually, I wasn't asking you necessarily to answer the question; I was asking you to call on somebody from the Pakistani press, I'm sorry. [*Laughter*] You don't have to answer every question they ask me. I would advise you not answering those questions. [*Laughter*]

Pakistan-U.S. Relations

Q. Mr. President, the public perception in Pakistan is that Pakistan is doing much more, deeper cooperation, and doing more favors to the United States than Pakistan is getting anything in return. What is your comment, and what is the room for Pak-U.S. relations during your next term?

President Bush. Well, first of all, I don't view relations as, one, that there's a scorecard that says, you know, "Well, if we all fight terror together, therefore, somebody owes somebody something." This is a world in which cooperation is essential, and mutual cooperation is really essential between Pakistan and the United States.

Obviously, there's ways to strengthen our bilateral relations. The President and I are constantly discussing ways to do so. After all, he is the strongest advocate for the Pakistan people I have ever met. His duty is to represent Pakistan, and so, therefore, we talk about ways to enhance trade. Trade between the United States and Pakistan is good. It can be better, and we discussed ways to enhance that.

But our cooperation has been very strong. But let me just say something. Friends don't sit there and have a scorecard that says, "Well, he did this," or "He did that, and therefore, somebody is—there's a deficit." Our relationship is much bigger than that. Our relationship is one where we work closely together for the common good of our own people and for the common good of the world.

Jennifer [Jennifer Loven, Associated Press].

President Musharraf's Role in the War on Terror

Q. Thank you, sir. You've talked repeatedly about how pleased you've been with President Musharraf's cooperation in the arrest of Al Qaida suspects. But are you not disappointed that his army has somewhat downgraded the search for Usama bin Laden?

President Bush. Quite the contrary. His army has been incredibly active and very brave in southern Waziristan, flushing out an enemy that had thought they had found safe haven. His army has suffered casualty, and for that, we want to thank their loved ones for the sacrifice that their family has made.

The President has been a determined leader to bring to justice not only people like Usama bin Laden but to bring to justice those who would inflict harm and pain on his own people. Remember, this is a man whose life had been threatened by and still is threatened by Al Qaida leadership. He's the person who survived two direct assassination attempts. And there is nobody more dedicated than—in the protection of his own people than President Musharraf.

And I am very pleased with his efforts and his focused efforts, and our discussions today were to determine how best we can help the President achieve his objective and—which is not only protect himself but protect his country.

Pakistan-U.S. Relations/Pakistan's Role in the Middle East Peace Process

Q. Mr. President, it's determined that you have a long vision, long-term vision between Pakistan and the United States. How would you define it, and how do you see it in the days to come?

President Bush. I think the long-term vision is one that is a relationship which is very mature in this sense: that there is a commercial relationship which is fair and balanced, mutually beneficial to both people; a defense relationship which is one in which there is close collaboration and complementary efforts based upon the true threats of the 21st century; and thirdly, there's a relationship in which I can call upon my friend to help deal with international issues such as the development of a Palestinian state, one in which the aspirations of the Palestinian people are met and listened to because democracy has taken hold.

One of the interesting lessons that the world can look at is Pakistan. You see, there are some in the world who do not believe that a Muslim society can self-govern. Some believe that the only solution for government in parts of the world is for there to be tyranny or despotism. I don't believe that. The Pakistan people have proven that those cynics are wrong. And where President Musharraf can help in world peace is to help remind people what is possible. And the solution in the Middle East is for there to be a world effort to help the Palestinians develop a state that is truly free, one that's got an independent judiciary, one that's got a civil society, one that's got the capacity to fight off the terrorists, one that allows for dissent, one in which people can vote. And President Musharraf can play a big role in helping achieve that objective.

None of us can convince the Palestinians to say—or make the Palestinians adhere to this point of view, but we can help convince them. And that's precisely what I intend to do. And as a Palestinian state evolves there will be much more confidence, and when that happens, peace is more likely to happen.

And I look forward to working with this world leader on that important issue.

Thank you all for taking time out of your weekend. I know it's been a disappointment for you to have to work on Saturday, but— [*laughter*]—the press. But nevertheless——

President Musharraf. Because of me. [*Laughter*]

President Bush. ——the President and I are thrilled you're here.

Thank you.

NOTE: The President spoke at 9:50 a.m. in the Oval Office at the White House. In his remarks, he referred to Usama bin Laden, leader of the Al Qaida terrorist organization.

The President's Radio Address
December 4, 2004

Good morning. Since the attacks of September the 11th, 2001, American military forces, intelligence officers, and law enforcement officials have defended our country with skill and honor and have taken the fight to terrorists abroad. Here at home, we have created the Department of Homeland Security, strengthened our defenses, and improved the collection and analysis of vital intelligence. Yet we must do more.

To protect America, our country needs the best possible intelligence. The recommendations of the 9/11 Commission chart a clear, sensible path toward needed reforms to our Government's intelligence capabilities. I strongly support most of those recommendations, and my administration is already implementing the vast majority of those that can be enacted without a vote of Congress. In August, I established the National Counterterrorism Center, where all the available intelligence on terrorist threats is brought together in one place. Just last month, I issued two directives instructing the FBI and CIA to hire new personnel and to press forward with the transformation of these agencies to meet the threats of our time.

But other key changes require new laws. For the past few months, I have been working with the Congress to produce an intelligence reform bill that will make America more secure. Congress made good progress toward a strong new law. Provisions have been included to strengthen our ability to arrest those who aid and train terrorists, to hold dangerous terrorists who are awaiting trial, and to prosecute those who seek to acquire weapons of mass destruction.

The most important provisions of any new bill must create a strong, focused new management structure for our intelligence services and break down the remaining walls that prevent the timely sharing of vital threat information among Federal agencies and with relevant State, local, and private sector personnel. Our intelligence efforts need a Director of National Intelligence who will oversee all of the foreign and domestic activities of the intelligence community. The legislation I support preserves the existing chain of command and leaves America's 15 intelligence agencies, organizations, and offices in their current Departments. Yet the Director of National Intelligence will oversee all of America's intelligence efforts to help ensure that our Government can find and stop terrorists before they strike. To be effective, this position must have full budget authority over our intelligence agencies. The many elements of our intelligence community must function seamlessly, with an overriding mission

to protect America from attack by terrorists or outlaw regimes.

I will continue to work with the Congress to reach an agreement on this intelligence bill. I urge Members of Congress to act next week so I can sign these needed reforms into law.

We have made great progress against the terrorists who seek to harm our Nation. We are safer, but we are not yet safe. The enemy is still plotting, and America must respond with urgency. We must do everything necessary to confront and defeat the terrorist threat, and that includes intelligence reform. By remaining focused and determined in these efforts, we will strengthen the safety of our citizens and defend our Nation from harm.

Thank you for listening.

NOTE: The address was recorded at 7:50 a.m. on December 3 in the Cabinet Room at the White House for broadcast at 10:06 a.m. on December 4. The transcript was made available by the Office of the Press Secretary on December 3 but was embargoed for release until the broadcast. In his remarks, the President referred to the National Commission on Terrorist Attacks Upon the United States (9/11 Commission). The Office of the Press Secretary also released a Spanish language transcript of this address.

Statement on Signing the Miscellaneous Trade and Technical Corrections Act of 2004
December 3, 2004

Today, I have signed into law H.R. 1047, the "Miscellaneous Trade and Technical Corrections Act of 2004." The Act modifies temporarily certain rates of duty under the Harmonized Tariff Schedule of the United States and makes other amendments to U.S. trade laws.

The executive branch shall construe section 1560(b) of the Act, relating to inter-

action between the Bureau of Customs and Border Protection of the Department of Homeland Security and the Government of Canada, in a manner consistent with the President's constitutional authority to conduct the Nation's foreign affairs and to supervise the unitary executive branch.

As is consistent with the Appointments Clause of the Constitution, the executive branch shall construe section 401(I) of the Tariff Act of 1930, as amended by subsection 1561(a) of the Act, not to authorize the exercise of significant U.S. Governmental authority by foreign law enforcement officers.

Section 629(e) of the Tariff Act of 1930, as enacted by section 1561(b) of the Act, provides that any foreign customs or agriculture inspection official stationed in the United States under section 629(e) may exercise such functions, perform such duties, and enjoy such privileges and immunities as U.S. officials may be authorized to perform or are afforded in that foreign country by treaty, agreement, or law. The executive branch shall construe section 629(e) to authorize the executive branch to allow the specified foreign government officials to perform functions of such foreign government inside the United States on the same basis as the specified U.S. Government officials may perform their U.S. Government functions in that foreign country and, as is consistent with the Appointments Clause of the Constitution, shall not construe the

provision to authorize the exercise of significant U.S. Governmental authority by foreign officials.

The executive branch shall construe the repeal, in section 1561(c) of the Act, of section 127 of the Treasury and General Government Appropriations Act, 2003, as contained in the Consolidated Appropriations Act, 2003 (Public Law 108–7), as repealing the amendments that were made to title 19 of the United States Code by section 127. Such a construction of section 1561(c) is consistent with the text and structure of amendments to title 19 made by section 1561.

GEORGE W. BUSH

The White House,
December 3, 2004.

NOTE: H.R. 1047, approved December 3, was assigned Public Law No. 108–429. This statement was released by the Office of the Press Secretary on December 6. An original was not available for verification of the content of this statement.

Remarks Following Discussions With President Ghazi al-Ujayl al-Yawr of the Iraqi Interim Government and an Exchange With Reporters
December 6, 2004

President Bush. Mr. President, welcome to the Oval Office. Last time we met was in Georgia, and now you're here in Washington, DC. I'm really honored you're here.

First, I want to thank you for your courage and your vision for a united and free Iraq. The President and I just had a great conversation about the future of Iraq. He can speak for himself, but I came away that I'm talking to a man who has got great confidence in the Iraqi people's capacity to self-govern and a great belief in the fact that it's going to happen.

We talked about a variety of issues. We talked about how the United States can

continue to stand with those who believe in democracy. We talked about the security situation. We talked about the election process. And I assured the President that my comments about the need to have elections was real and genuine. I believe it's necessary for the Iraqi people to vote on January the 30th because it provides an opportunity for people to participate in democracy. It'll send the clear message to the few people in Iraq that are trying to stop the march toward democracy that they cannot stop elections. It will give the Iraqi people a chance to become invested in the future of that vital country.

And the President can speak for himself on the subject, but he was very reassuring to me, as he was yesterday in his comments to the American people.

All in all, Mr. President, I am really proud you're here. I look forward to working with you.

President Yawr. Thank you.

President Bush. And I look forward to achieving the common objective, which is an Iraq that is free and peaceful.

President Yawr. Thank you very much, sir. I've been honored this morning to meet the President of the United States—after all, we in Iraq are in debt for the United States for—and the courageous leadership of President Bush of liberating Iraq from a dynasty, a villain. Right now we are faced with the armies of darkness who are—who have no objective but to undermine the political process and incite civil war in Iraq. But I want to assure the whole world that this will never, ever happen, that we in Iraq are committed to move along. After all these sacrifices, there is no way on Earth that we will let it go in vain.

This is very important. Victory is not only possible; it's a fact. We can see it. It's there. We are committed. We see that we have all the reasons to prevail. We see that our enemy is an enemy that has only a short time because they have no roots in the Iraqi society, they have no ideology that they can sell to Iraq or the whole world.

There is unfairness by calling them Sunni insurgents—these are not Sunni. These are a mix of people who have one thing in common, hatred to the Iraqi society and hatred to democracy, people who are trying to stop us from having our first elections. We in Iraq, the whole Iraqi society are willing to participate in elections. Nobody in Iraq wants to boycott the elections, except for some politicians—but I'm talking about the mass public of Iraq. They all are very anxious to go and cast their votes and practice, for the first time in 45 years, their right and duty of voting for whoever they feel confidence in.

This is very important. I just came here to tell the President of the United States and the American public that we in Iraq are very appreciative for all the sacrifices, that this is a job that we see has honor and even a duty that we have to make everybody free. In Iraq, these people are trying to kidnap people in streets and sell them from one gang to another. This is slavery, and shame on anybody who can condone to slavery. We are going to face them. We are determined. And God bless you, sir.

President Bush. Thank you very much. Good job.

President Yawr. Thank you.

President Bush. We'll answer a couple of questions in the spirit of democracy.

Attack on U.S. Consulate in Jeddah/ Upcoming Iraqi Elections

Q. Mr. President, who do you think was behind today's attacks in Saudi Arabia, and what do you think was their motive? And on Iraq, if I could ask a little bit more, how can Iraqis feel secure about going to the polls on January 30th when there is so much violence and bloodshed?

President Bush. First, on the incident in Saudi Arabia, I want to thank the Saudi Government for responding as quickly as they did. We send our heartfelt condolences to the Saudi National Guard that died in the defense of our consulate. I want to thank the marines who are doing their job so splendidly. We will find out more about who caused the attacks. As I understand it, several of the attackers died, but several were captured by the Saudi Government, and I'm confident they will share the information with us.

The attacks in Saudi Arabia remind us that the terrorists are still on the move. They're interested in affecting the will of free countries. They want us to leave Saudi Arabia. They want us to leave Iraq. They want us to grow timid and weary in the face of their willingness to kill randomly and kill innocent people. And that's why these elections in Iraq are very important.

You remember all the dire threats prior to the elections in Afghanistan. People said, "If you vote in Afghanistan, you'll be killed." But the desire of people to vote overwhelmed the capacity of the terrorists. And this is the same message we're getting here in Iraq, that people who are willing to blow up people by the use of car bombs will do anything they can to stop democracy. And there is a reason why, because a free society in Iraq will be a major defeat for the terrorists.

And I think that the capacity of these killers to stop an election would send a wrong signal to the world and send a wrong signal to the Iraqi people, themselves. And the President has said that people want to vote, and I believe they ought to have a chance to vote. And we'll do everything we can, working with the Iraqis, to make the election sites as secure as possible. That's why the commanders on the ground have asked for additional troops, to help with the election process, and I granted them that request, Mr. President. And our commanders, working with Ambassador Negroponte and the Iraqi security forces, believe they can do a lot to make these polling places secure. You can never guarantee 100-percent security.

But Iraqi people have a chance to say to the world, "We choose democracy over terrorism." And that's going to be defining moment in that country.

Are you Al Jazeera?

Democracy in the Middle East

Q. Al Arabiyya.

President Bush. I mean, Al Arabiyya. Welcome.

Q. Mr. President, I know that the democracy is your major concern in Iraq and in the Middle East. Despite all difficulties, security difficulties we see in Iraq, are you confident that this election will produce a true democracy in Iraq and then will help your project in the Middle East?

President Bush. Yes. I appreciate that question. I am confident that when peoples are allowed to vote and express their will, peaceful societies emerge. And I'm confident that the process that has been set up by the international community to allow the people of Iraq to express their will is a major step in democracy in the greater Middle East. I believe the Iraqi people have got the capacity and the desire to self-govern. And these elections will be a very important moment in the advance of democracy.

The American people must understand that democracy just doesn't happen overnight. It is a process. It is an evolution. After all, look at our own history. We had great principles enunciated in our Declarations of Independence and our Constitution, yet we had slavery for 100 years. It takes a while for democracy to take hold. And this is a major first step in a society which enables people to express their beliefs and their opinions.

I also believe that success in Iraq will breed success elsewhere. I believe it is very possible for there to be a Palestinian state with the institutions of democracy in place that will allow for leadership to emerge that listens to the demands of the Palestinian people. And when such a state takes place, it will make peace much more possible with the Israelis. And so in a second term, not only will I work with our Iraqi friends to help them achieve democracy that the President has just said is the overwhelming desire of most people, but I'll also spend time and efforts to help the Palestinian people grow their own state and own democracy so we can achieve peace.

Steve [Steve Holland, Reuters].

Intelligence Reform Legislation

Q. Senator Warner has raised some concerns about the chain of command issue in the intelligence reform bill. Is this bill going to have to wait until next year?

President Bush. I certainly hope the bill gets to my desk soon. I believe we have addressed the concerns of, by far, the majority of Members of both the House and the Senate. As we speak, we're working with the key Members to address concerns. I call upon the Congress to pass the intelligence bill. It is a good piece of legislation. It is a necessary piece of legislation. It's a piece of legislation that is important for the security of our country.

Thank you.

NOTE: The President spoke at 9:35 a.m. in the Oval Office at the White House. In his remarks, he referred to U.S. Ambassador to Iraq John D. Negroponte.

Remarks Following Discussions With King Abdullah II of Jordan
December 6, 2004

President Bush. Your Majesty, welcome back to the Oval Office. It is my honor to receive you here again. And every time you come, I enjoy our conversations, and I'm impressed by the progress that your good country is making.

Today we had a chance to talk about the Jordanian economy and the growth of the economy. And the amount of trade between our countries is growing, which is to the benefit of the Jordanian people as well as to the American people. And I appreciate your leadership.

We also talked about, of course, Iraq. I expressed my strong belief that the Iraqi elections must go forward on time. And I appreciate His Majesty listening to my beliefs. And I assured His Majesty that the United States and my Government will be involved with Middle Eastern peace and that I believe that two states living side by side in peace, a Palestinian state and an Israeli state, is necessary for there to be peace and that we have a moment, a window of opportunity, and I intend to work very closely with His Majesty to seize that moment for the good of the Palestinian people and for the good of the Israelis, so that we can achieve peace that I know is on your mind.

So welcome, sir. I'm really glad to have you back.

King Abdullah. Thank you. Thank you, Mr. President. We're delighted to be back here and to thank you, Mr. President, for, really, the outstanding support that you are giving our part of the world, and the President's dedication to bring hope and peace, hopefully, to Israelis and Palestinians. I know that you have been committed in the past 4 years in identifying a future for the Israelis and the Palestinians and the Israelis and the Arabs. And again, the President today brought home to me how important that is. And I'm very delighted with that strong stand that you've always taken for a better Middle East.

As you mentioned, sir, we talked about the future of Iraq, and we work very closely together to bring a transition in Iraq as quickly as possible and a future for the Iraqi people. And I tremendously appreciate the effort that you've given all of us and your vision for a better world for all of us in our part of the world.

Thank you.

President Bush. Thank you, sir. Welcome. Appreciate you. Thank you.

NOTE: The President spoke at 11:10 a.m. in the Oval Office at the White House.

Letter to Congressional Leaders on the "Intelligence Reform and Terrorism Prevention Act of 2004"
December 6, 2004

Dear Leaders and Conferees:

My most solemn duty is protecting the American people, and reforming and strengthening our Nation's intelligence capabilities will help ensure the safety of our country. I call on Congress to pass an intelligence reform bill this week. An overarching principle for these needed reforms has been to create a strong Director of National Intelligence with full budget authority while preserving the chain of command within departments and agencies. We are very close to a significant achievement that will better protect our country for generations to come, and now is the time to finish the job for the good of our national security. Therefore, I want to reiterate my views on some issues of concern to Members.

When I met with the Congressional Bipartisan Leadership at the White House on September 8, 2004, I stated that the country needed a strong Director of National Intelligence with full budget authority. At the same time, I have stated that we need a bill that respects the chain of command within departments and agencies, including the Department of Defense, so as to ensure that all of the war-fighters' needs will be met. As Commander-in-Chief, it is ultimately my responsibility to ensure that both of these goals are realized, and they are captured in the attached formulation.

Accordingly, in developing implementing guidelines and regulations for this bill, it is my intention to ensure that the principles of unity of command and authority are fully protected. It remains essential to preserve in the heads of the executive departments the unity of authority over and accountability for the performance of those departments. In particular, as we continue to prosecute the global war on terrorism, the integrity of the military chain of command and the principle of battlefield unity of command must continue to be respected and in no way abrogated. These guidelines will also honor my commitment to provide the Director of National Intelligence full and meaningful budget authority over the National Intelligence Program. This is critical to make certain that the intelligence community is more effectively managed. The guidelines will also help ensure that the Director of National Intelligence has enhanced management authorities, including the ability to oversee and integrate all the foreign and domestic activities of the intelligence community, to achieve the unity of purpose needed to win the global war on terrorism.

With regard to other provisions in the legislation, I want to congratulate the Conference for adopting important and time-sensitive law enforcement provisions that:

- Strengthen current laws to make certain we can arrest those aiding terrorists, including those who have received military-style training in terror camps.
- Increase our ability to target terrorism financing.
- Ensure that dangerous terrorists are lawfully detained while awaiting trial.
- Help prevent attacks by shoulder-fired anti-aircraft missiles, known as MANPADs, and weapons of mass destruction by mandating appropriate penalties.
- Provide authority to help stop "lone wolf" terrorists.
- Expand our jurisdiction to prosecute those who seek weapons of mass destruction.
- It is imperative that Congress act this week to guarantee these vital tools become part of our arsenal immediately.

I also believe the Conference took an important step in strengthening our immigration laws by, among other items, increasing the number of border patrol agents and detention beds. There were other measures proposed that were not incorporated into the bill. My positions on these provisions were detailed in a letter from the Office of Management and Budget to Conferees on October 17, 2004. However, these omissions from the final bill should not prevent the Congress from passing this historic legislation now. I look forward to working with the Congress early in the next session to address these other issues, including improving our asylum laws and standards for issuing driver's licenses.

I appreciate all the work done to date by this Congress and the September 11th

Commission. These are some of the most challenging, complicated, and important issues facing our government. The Leaders and Conferees deserve great credit for working together to protect the safety of the American people.

Sincerely,

GEORGE W. BUSH

NOTE: The letter made available by the Office of the Press Secretary also included an attachment listing guidelines to ensure the effective implementation within the executive branch of the authorities granted to the Director of National Intelligence. An original was not available for verification of the content of this letter. The letter referred to S. 2845.

Letter to Congressional Leaders Providing Notification of the Proposed Reimbursement of the District of Columbia for Costs of Public Safety Expenses
December 6, 2004

Dear Mr. Speaker: *(Dear Mr. President:)*

In accordance with title I of the District of Columbia Appropriations Act, 2005, Public Law 108–335, I am notifying the Congress of the proposed use of $10,288,548 provided in title I under the heading "Federal Payment for Emergency Planning and Security Costs in the District of Columbia." This will reimburse the District for the costs of public safety expenses related to security events and responses to terrorist threats.

The details of this action are set forth in the enclosed letter from the Director of the Office of Management and Budget.

Sincerely,

GEORGE W. BUSH

NOTE: Identical letters were sent to J. Dennis Hastert, Speaker of the House of Representatives, and Richard B. Cheney, President of the Senate. This letter was released by the Office of the Press Secretary on December 7.

Remarks at Camp Pendleton, California
December 7, 2004

Thank you all. Thank you for the warm welcome. It was getting a little quiet back at the White House—[*laughter*]—so I decided to drop in on the Devil Dogs. Thank you for coming out to say hello. I've been looking forward to this for quite a while. It's a pleasure to be with so many squared-away, gung-ho United States marines.

I'm here to thank you for serving our country in a time when we need you. In a season where Americans stop to count their blessings, I want you to know one of America's greatest blessings is the men and women who wear our Nation's uniform. And many of you are blessed by having a husband or wife or a son and daughter who stand with you during this time of sacrifice. Our Nation is blessed because of our military families. Your fellow citizens are proud of you, and so is your Commander in Chief.

I appreciate Secretary of the Navy Gordon England for joining us today. I want to thank Major General Tim Donovan for his leadership. I want to thank Brigadier General James Williams for being here as well. I want to thank all the State and local officials. I want to thank the military families. But most of all, I want to thank the United States Marine Corps.

Last month, marines across the world broke out their dress blues to celebrate the 229th birthday of the Corps. But the men and women of Camp Pendleton's 1st Marine Expeditionary Force marked the occasion a little differently, by fighting the enemies in Iraq. As one Pendleton marine near the frontlines put it, "This is what we, as marines, do. It is where the American people expect us to be." The marines of Camp Pendleton are serving our Nation with valor and integrity.

This is the home of the 1st Marine Division, one of America's oldest and most decorated units. In Korea, the marines of the 1st Division were surrounded at the Chosin Reservoir by 10 divisions of Chinese troops. When Colonel Chesty Puller heard the news, he said, "They've got us right where we want them. We can shoot in every direction now." He wasn't bluffing. The 1st Marine Division made it out, destroying seven enemy divisions and up-

holding the great tradition of the Corps. That courage, determination, and devotion to duty have made the United States Marines one of the most feared and respected fighting forces in the world. And in these dangerous times, when terrorists seek to harm our families and murder free citizens, Americans are thankful that the marines are on the frontline, taking the fight to the enemy.

Since I took office almost 4 years ago, I have visited our troops around the world, and one of my first stops as the Commander in Chief was right here in Camp Pendleton. It was in the summer of 2001. I told you that day, because you're marines, you would be asked to perform our Nation's most difficult and dangerous missions. Since that day, you have performed every mission with honor and with courage and with commitment.

In the war on terror, you have fought enemies' freedom—freedom's enemies from the caves and mountains of Afghanistan to the deserts and cities of Iraq. Marines of Camp Pendleton's 15th Marine Expeditionary Unit were the first conventional forces to fight in Operation Enduring Freedom. They deployed hundreds of miles into a landlocked country to help seize the Kandahar Airport, hunted down the Taliban and Al Qaida fighters, and helped to liberate more than 28 million people from one of the world's most brutal regimes.

If any of you were in that 15th Marine Expeditionary Unit, I want you to hear what's happening today. Today the Vice President of the United States and the Secretary of Defense are in Kabul for the inauguration of Afghanistan's first democratically elected President. Afghanistan has been transformed from a haven for terrorists to a steadfast ally in the war on terror, and the American people are safer because of your courage.

When America led a coalition to enforce the demands of the free world and to end the regime of Saddam Hussein, the marines of Camp Pendleton made us proud once again. When the appointed hour came, the 1st Marine Division rolled across the border, pressing more than 500 miles over the Iraqi desert in less than one month. Backed by the 1st Force Service Support Group and the 3d Marine Aircraft Wing, you helped liberate the Iraqi capital, pulled down the statues of the dictator, and pushed north to secure the homeland of Tikrit. You drove Saddam Hussein from his palace into a spider hole, and now he sits in an Iraqi prison awaiting justice. Because of your bravery, because of your skill, America and the world are a safer place.

In recent days, the 1st Marine Expeditionary Force has once again shown America's purpose and resolve, this time in Fallujah. Block by block, building by building, marines and soldiers and Iraqi security forces took that city back from the terrorists and the insurgents, and when the smoke is cleared, we saw once again the true nature of the enemy. We found blood-stained torture chambers where hostages had been executed. We found videos of beheadings and brutal terrorist attacks. We found travel documents of foreign terrorists and equipment of forging Iraqi passports to make the foreign fighters appear to be Iraqi insurgents. We found more than 600 improvised explosive devices, including an ice cream truck that had been loaded with bombs for a terrorist attack.

In the battle for Fallujah, the terrorists hid weapons in the cemetery. They hid ammunition in private homes. They hid bombs in mosques, but they could not hide from the United States Marines.

We have dealt the enemy a severe blow. The terrorist Zarqawi has lost his main sanctuary in Iraq. The Ba'athist insurgents have lost one of their main bases of operation. We seized tons of weapons and shut down terrorist bombmaking factories, killed more than 2,000 enemy fighters, and captured thousands more. The enemies of freedom in Iraq have been wounded, but they're not yet defeated. They'll keep on fighting, and so will the Marine Corps.

Next month, Iraqis will vote in free and democratic elections. As election day approaches, we can expect further violence from the terrorists. You see, the terrorists understand what is at stake. They know they have no future in a free Iraq, because free people never choose their own enslavement. They know democracy will give Iraqis a stake in the future of their country. When Iraqis choose their leaders in free elections, it will destroy the myth that the terrorists are fighting a foreign occupation and make clear that what the terrorists are really fighting is the will of the Iraqi people.

The success of democracy in Iraq will also inspire others across the Middle East to defend their own freedom and to expose the terrorists for what they are, violent extremists on the fringe of society with no agenda for the future except tyranny and death.

So the terrorists will do all they can to delay and disrupt free elections in Iraq, and they will fail. As Iraqi President al-Yawr said in the Oval Office yesterday, the Iraqi people are anxious to go and cast their votes and practice, for the first time in 45 years, their right and duty of voting. Free elections will proceed as planned.

The United States has a vital interest in the success of a free Iraq. A free Iraq will be a major victory in the war on terror. Free nations do not export terror. Free nations listen to the hopes and aspirations of their people. Free nations are peaceful nations. And a free Iraq will make America more secure and the world a peaceful place.

America and our coalition have a strategy in place to aid the rise of a stable democracy in Iraq. To help the Iraqi Government provide security during the election period, we will increase U.S. troop strength by about 12,000 personnel for a total of 150,000 troops. As the election approaches, coalition forces will continue hunting the terrorists and the insurgents. We'll help the people of Fallujah and other cities to rebuild and to move forward. We'll continue training Iraqi security forces so the Iraqi people can eventually take responsibility for their own security.

Some Iraqi units have performed better than others, as you know. Some Iraqis have been intimidated enough by the insurgents to leave the service to their country. But a great many are standing firm. In Fallujah, Iraqis fought alongside our soldiers and marines with valor and determination. One American soldier who saw them up close in combat said, "They really excelled, kicking in the doors, clearing the houses, running out into fire to pick up wounded marines." The Iraqi security forces made up about 20 percent of the forces in Fallujah. They're killing the terrorists, blocking the escape routes, and saving American lives. These brave Iraqis are fighting for their freedom, and we are proud to stand by their side.

Our coalition is determined to help them succeed. We're working to develop a corps of well-trained senior, mid-level Iraqi officers. After all, Iraqi soldiers want to be led by Iraqis. NATO trainers are already in Iraq, and the Alliance will soon develop a new training center for the Iraqi security forces and a military academy outside of Baghdad. We will help the Iraqi Government build a force that no longer needs coalition support so they can defend their own Nation. And then American soldiers and marines can come home with the honor they have earned.

Our success in Iraq will make America safer for us and for future generations. As one Marine sergeant put it, "I never want my children to experience what we saw in New York, at the Pentagon, and in Pennsylvania." He said, "If we can eliminate the threat on foreign soil, I would rather do it there than have it come home to us." That's why we're on the offensive today in Fallujah and Mosul, Ramadi and north Babil. We're getting after the terrorists. We're disrupting their plans. We're holding the state sponsors of terror equally responsible for terrorist acts. We're working to prevent outlaw regimes from gaining weapons of mass murder and providing them to terrorists. We'll stay at these efforts with patience and resolve, and we will prevail.

A time of war is a time for sacrifice, especially for our military families. Being left behind when a loved one goes to war is one of the hardest jobs in the military. It is especially hard during the holidays. Families here at Camp Pendleton endure long separation. Carrying these burdens, you serve our country. America is grateful for your service.

Our Nation also honors the men and women who've been injured in the line of duty. I met some of these Americans. This Saturday, I'll be going to Bethesda to meet more. Many face a hard road ahead. They've inspired their comrades with their strength of will. General Sattler recently visited with some of the wounded in the Fallujah campaign. One marine was pretty beat up, but when he saw the general, he lifted his hand and said, "Sir, I've still got my trigger finger. I can get back out there." That is the spirit of the Corps, and America will show the same sense of duty. We will provide the best possible medical care for every American servicemember wounded in action.

And some of you have lost comrades and family members in the war on terror. Words can only go so far in capturing the grief and sense of loss for the families of those who have died, but you can know this: They gave their lives for a cause that is just. And as in other generations, their sacrifice will have spared millions from the lives of tyranny and sorrow. America prays for the families of the fallen, and we stand with the families of the fallen, and their sacrifice will always be remembered.

In the last 4 years, I've seen and the world has seen the courage and the skill and the decency of the United States military. You are a great force for good in this world. The American people know it, and they are behind you. Your service and sacrifice has touched the hearts of our people and inspired millions to show their gratitude.

Last month, I met a 15-year-old from California named Shauna Fleming, who collected a million thank you letters for our military personnel. In Washington, DC, veterans—Vietnam vet Steve Cobb and his wife, Tanya, have been coming out regularly to Andrews Air Force Base to meet wounded servicemembers returning from Iraq and Afghanistan. Those two good folks welcome the troops home, and they offer whatever help they can provide. Steve earned four Purple Hearts and the Silver Star in Vietnam, but this is what he said. He said, "When I came home, there was nobody but demonstrators to meet our troops. I never wanted to see another generation of troops come home without being welcomed and appreciated."

In Massachusetts, a contractor named John Gonsalves says—heard about a soldier who had lost both legs in an RPG attack in Iraq. So he started Homes for Our Troops, a nonprofit dedicated to building and adapting homes for disabled veterans with special needs. John says, "The war on terror is something the American people should all be a part of, not just the people on the frontlines in Afghanistan and in Iraq." He says, "We have a responsibility to do more for our veterans who are out there fighting every day and putting their lives on the line."

Here at Camp Pendleton, a nurse named Karen Guenther saw the financial strain on the families of the injured sailors and marines. Many spent weeks, even months away from home, standing by their loved ones recovering at a military hospital. They struggle with the cost of food and lodging and travel and lost income. So she and other Marine spouses started the Injured Marine Semper Fi Fund to raise money for those struggling military families. Since its founding here 6 months ago, it has grown into a national organization that has

helped over 300 military families across the United States, with more than $400,000 in grants.

As a wife of a wounded marine recently put it, "There was no redtape. They just helped. Had it not been for the Injured Marine Semper Fi Fund, I would not have been able to pay my bills for the past 3 months or stay at my husband's bedside."

These examples represent the true strength of the country, the heart and souls of your fellow citizens, and they make America proud. Across our country, Americans are coming together to surround our deployed forces and wounded warriors with love and support. We should be doing more, so I want to speak to our fellow citizens who might be listening today. I urge every American to find some way to thank our military and to help out the military family down the street. The Department of Defense has set up a web site: americasupportsyou.mil. If you're interested in finding out how you can help, go to americasupportsyou.mil. You can go there to learn about efforts in your own community to say you support our troops. In this season of giving, let us stand with the men and women who stand up for America, our military.

Every man and woman who serves at Camp Pendleton and all who wear the Marine Corps uniform are part of a great history. The general mentioned, 63 years ago today, our Nation was attacked at Pearl Harbor. And soon, the United States Marines were storming beaches and engaging the enemy in distant lands. In places like Guadalcanal and Iwo Jima, our fathers and our grandfathers struggled and sacrificed to defend freedom. And today, in places like Fallujah and north Babil, this generation of marines is fighting to extend freedom.

Today's war on terror will not end with a ceremony, a surrender ceremony on a deck of a battleship. But it will end with victory. Just as we defeated the threats of fascism and imperial communism in the 20th century, we will defeat the threat of global terrorism. And we will help the people of liberated countries to rebuild and to secure a future of freedom and peace.

I have confidence in our country, and I have faith in our cause. There's still important work ahead, yet the outcome is assured. History moves toward freedom because the desire for freedom is written in every human heart. And the cause of freedom is in the best of hands. It's in the hands of people like the United States Marine Corps.

The United States Marines will fight, in the words of the Rifleman's Creed, "until victory is America's and there is no enemy."

May God bless you, and may God continue to bless the United States of America.

NOTE: The President spoke at 9:34 a.m. In his remarks, he referred to Maj. Gen. Timothy E. Donovan, USMC, commanding general, Marine Corps Base Camp Pendleton; Brig. Gen. James L. Williams, USMC, acting commanding general, I Marine Expeditionary Force, Marine Corps Base Camp Pendleton; President Hamid Karzai of Afghanistan; senior Al Qaida associate Abu Musab Al Zarqawi; President Ghazi al-Ujayl al-Yawr of the Iraqi Interim Government; and Lt. Gen. John F. Sattler, commanding general, I Marine Expeditionary Force, Camp Fallujah, Iraq. The Office of the Press Secretary also released a Spanish language transcript of these remarks.

Message on the Observance of Hanukkah 2004
December 7, 2004

I send greetings to all those celebrating Hanukkah, the festival of lights.

On the 25th day of Kislev on the Hebrew calendar, Jews around the world commemorate the rededication of the Temple in Jerusalem more than 2,000 years ago. During this time of darkness, the Temple had been seized, and Judaism had been outlawed. Judah Maccabee and his followers fought for three years for their freedom and successfully recaptured Jerusalem and the Temple. Jewish tradition teaches that the Maccabees found only one small bottle of oil to be used for temple rituals, but that oil lasted eight days and nights. The miracle of this enduring light, remembered through the lighting of the Menorah, continues to symbolize the triumph of faith over tyranny.

The bravery of the Maccabees has provided inspiration through the ages. We must remain steadfast and courageous as we seek to spread peace and freedom throughout the world. This holiday season, we give thanks to God, and we remember the brave men and women of our Armed Forces and their families. We also pray that all who live under oppression will see their day of freedom and that the light of faith will always shine through the darkness.

Laura joins me in wishing you a blessed and Happy Hanukkah.

GEORGE W. BUSH

NOTE: An original was not available for verification of the content of this message.

Message to the Senate Transmitting the 1995 Revision of the Radio Regulations, With Appendices
December 7, 2004

To the Senate of the United States:

With a view to receiving the advice and consent of the Senate to ratification, I transmit herewith the 1995 Revision of the Radio Regulations, with appendices, signed by the United States at Geneva on November 17, 1995 (the "1995 Revision"), together with declarations and reservations of the United States as contained in the Final Acts of the World Radiocommunication Conference (WRC–95). I transmit also, for the information of the Senate, the report of the Department of State concerning these revisions.

The 1995 Revision, which was adopted at WRC–95, constitutes a revision of the International Telecommunication Union (ITU) Radio Regulations, to which the United States is a party. It provides for the simplification of the Radio Regulations, the introduction of new global mobile-satellite services, and new regulatory provisions both for non-geostationary satellites operating in the same frequency bands as geostationary satellites and for other new space services that share spectrum with the space research and terrestrial services.

Subject to the U.S. declarations and reservations mentioned above, I believe the United States should become a party to the 1995 Revision, which will facilitate the development of mobile-satellite and non-geostationary satellite orbit communication services by U.S. Government and industry. It is my hope that the Senate will take early action on this matter and give its advice and consent to ratification.

GEORGE W. BUSH

The White House,
December 7, 2004.

NOTE: This message was released by the Office of the Press Secretary on December 8.

Statement on Congressional Passage of the "Intelligence Reform and Terrorism Prevention Act of 2004"
December 8, 2004

I commend the Congress for passing historic legislation that will better protect the American people and help defend against ongoing terrorist threats.

We already have taken numerous steps to improve our intelligence capabilities, and the "Intelligence Reform and Terrorism Prevention Act of 2004" further strengthens intelligence gathering and operations. The legislation includes important reforms, such as creating a strong Director of National Intelligence with full budget authority to integrate and manage the foreign and domestic activities of the intelligence community. In addition, the law will further enhance the National Counterterrorism Center, established earlier this year and tasked with ensuring a unified effort across the Government for counterterrorism activities. It will also preserve the chain of command in our Cabinet departments and agencies and the military by respecting the clear lines of authority within the executive branch.

We remain a nation at war, and intelligence is our first line of defense against the terrorists who seek to do us harm. I am pleased the measure also contains many critical law enforcement tools that I have called for that will help make America more secure. I look forward to signing this landmark piece of legislation into law.

NOTE: The statement referred to S. 2845.

Statement on the Resignation of Anthony J. Principi as Secretary of Veterans Affairs
December 8, 2004

As a valuable member of my Cabinet, Tony Principi has served as a tireless advocate for 25 million veterans. He has insisted on results, and he has gotten results. Under Tony's leadership, we have honored our veterans for their service and sacrifice by increasing and improving health care services, working to eliminate the waiting list for medical care, and cutting the disability claims backlog. I appreciate his efforts to improve access to health care for low-income veterans and those with service-related disabilities. As we fight the war on terror, Tony has played a vital role in helping to streamline the transition from military to civilian status for our newest veterans.

I thank Tony for serving our veterans and our country with integrity and dignity. He is a good man and a good friend. I am grateful to Tony, Liz, and the entire Principi family.

NOTE: The Office of the Press Secretary also made available Secretary Principi's letter of resignation.

Statement on Signing the Consolidated Appropriations Act, 2005
December 8, 2004

Today, I have signed into law H.R. 4818, the "Consolidated Appropriations Act, 2005" (CAA). The CAA, consisting of eleven Divisions, consolidates into a single Act several appropriations bills that the Congress normally passes separately each year to fund the operations of the Federal Government, and also several bills that are not normally part of an appropriations bill.

Many provisions of the CAA are inconsistent with the constitutional authority of the President to conduct foreign affairs, command the Armed Forces, protect sensitive information, supervise the unitary executive branch, make appointments, and make recommendations to the Congress. Many other provisions unconstitutionally condition execution of the laws by the executive branch upon approval by congressional committees.

The executive branch shall construe as advisory provisions of the CAA that purport to direct or burden the Executive's conduct of foreign relations or to limit the President's authority as Commander in Chief. Such provisions include: in the Commerce-Justice-State Appropriations Act, sections 406, 611, 609, 627, and the provision regarding voting in the United Nations Security Council under the heading "Contributions for International Peacekeeping Activities"; in the Foreign Operations Appropriations Act, sections 506, 514, 531, 547, 561,

562, 580, 585, 593, and the provisions entitled "Other Bilateral Economic Assistance, Economic Support Fund" and "Andean Counterdrug Initiative"; as well as in Division J ("Other Matters"), section 3(b)(3) of the 225th Anniversary of the American Revolution Commemoration Act.

The executive branch shall also construe the provisions of the CAA in a manner consistent with the President's authority to supervise the unitary executive branch, including the authority to direct which officers in the executive branch shall assist the President in faithfully executing the law. Such provisions include in the Transportation-Treasury Appropriations Act, sections 618 and 628, and language relating to review by the Office of Management and Budget (OMB) of executive branch orders, activities, regulations, transcripts, and testimony, particularly language relating to OMB review of certain matters in reports to be submitted to the Congress through the Secretary of the Army.

The executive branch shall construe provisions in the CAA that purport to mandate or regulate submission of information to the Congress, other entities outside the executive branch, or the public, in a manner consistent with the President's constitutional authority to withhold information that could impair foreign relations, national security, the deliberative processes of the Executive, or the performance of the Executive's constitutional duties. Such provisions include: in the Agriculture Appropriations Act, section 717; in the Commerce-Justice-State Appropriations Act, sections 407, 409, and provisions concerning a budget proposal under the heading "National Intellectual Property Law Enforcement Coordination Council"; in the Energy and Water Appropriations Act, sections 112, 113, and 503; in the Foreign Operations Appropriations Act, section 559; in the Labor-HHS-Education Appropriations Act, a provision under the heading "Department of Health and Human Services, Office of the Secretary"; in the Transportation-Treasury Appropriations Act, sections 522 and 618; in the VA-HUD Appropriations Act, section 210; and in Division J, section 16 of the L–1 Visa and H–1B Visa Reform Act.

The executive branch shall construe provisions of the CAA that purport to make consultation with the Congress a precondition to the execution of the law as calling for, but not mandating, such consultation, as is consistent with the Constitution's provisions concerning the separate powers of the Congress to legislate and the President to execute the laws. Such provisions include: in the Foreign Operations Appropriations Act, sections 509, 512, 543, 569, 588, and provisions under the heading "International Disaster and Famine Assistance," "Transition Initiatives," "Andean Counterdrug Initiative," and "Debt Restructuring"; and in the Interior and Related Agencies Appropriations Act, provisions under the heading "National Park Service, Historic Preservation Fund," and "Administrative Provisions, Smithsonian Institution."

The executive branch shall construe provisions that purport to require or regulate submission by executive branch officials of legislative recommendations to the Congress consistently with the President's constitutional authority to recommend to the Congress such measures as he judges necessary and expedient. Such provisions include: in the Agriculture Appropriations Act, section 721; in the Commerce-Justice-State Appropriations Act, sections 628 and 902; in the Interior and Related Agencies Appropriations Act, section 102; in the Transportation-Treasury Appropriations Act, section 404; in the VA-HUD Appropriations Act, section 215; and in Division K, section 152 of the Small Business Reauthorization and Manufacturing Assistance Act of 2004.

In section 601 of the Energy and Water Appropriations Act, section 2 of the amended Tennessee Valley Authority Act shall be construed consistently with the President's constitutional authority to make nominations and appoint officers. So that section 522 of the Transportation-Treasury Appropriations Act may be faithfully executed, the executive branch shall construe subsection (c), which provides that an agency privacy officer's signature on a report to the agency inspector general shall constitute verification by the officer "that the agency is only using information in identifiable form as detailed in the report" to mean that the signature constitutes verification to the best of the officer's knowledge after diligent inquiry.

The executive branch shall construe as calling solely for notification the provisions of the CAA that are inconsistent with the requirements of bicameral passage and presentment set forth in the Constitution, as construed by the Supreme Court of the United States in 1983 in *INS* v. *Chadha*. Such provisions include: in the Agriculture Appropriations Act, sections 705, 718, 736, and a provision under the heading "Food and Drug Administration, Salaries and Expenses"; in the Energy and Water Appropriations Act, section 303; in the Interior and Related Agencies Appropriations Act, sections 305, 313, 329, 332, 333, and provisions under the headings "United States Fish and Wildlife Service, Administrative Provisions," "National Park Service, Construction," "Department of the Interior, Departmental Management, Salaries and Expenses," "Natural Resource Damage Assessment and Restoration, Administrative Provisions," "Forest Service, Wildland Fire Management," "Administrative Provisions, Forest Service," "Indian Health Service, Indian Health Facilities," "Administrative Provisions, Indian Health Service," and "Administrative Provisions, Smithsonian Institution"; in the Labor-HHS-Education Appropriations Act, section 208 and a provision under the heading "Pension Benefit Guaranty Corporation"; in the Transportation-Treasury Appropriations Act, sections 201, 211, 212, 217, 218, 403, 510, 511, 614, 623, and 642, and provisions under the headings "Department of Transportation, Office of the Secretary, Salaries and Expenses," "Department of Transportation, Office of the Secretary, Working Capital Fund," "Federal Transit Administration, Administrative Expenses," "Department of the Treasury, Departmental Offices, Salaries and Expenses," "Internal Revenue Service, Business Systems Modernization," "Office of Administration, Salaries and Expenses," "High Intensity Drug Trafficking Areas Program," and "Real Property Activities, Federal Building Fund, Limitations on Availability of Revenue"; and in the VA-HUD Appropriations Act, section 111 and provisions under the headings "Department of Veterans Affairs, Departmental Administration, Construction, Minor Projects" and "National Aeronautics and Space Administration, Administrative Provisions."

As is consistent with the principle of statutory construction of giving effect to each of two statutes addressing the same subject whenever they can co-exist, the executive branch shall construe the provision in the Energy and Water Appropriations Act under the heading "National Nuclear Security Administration, Weapons Activities" concerning transfer of funds from the Department of Defense to constitute an "express authorization of Congress" to which section 8063 of the Department of Defense Appropriations Act, 2005 (Public Law 108–287) refers.

A number of provisions in the CAA purport to allocate funds for specified projects and amounts set forth in the joint explanatory statement of managers that accompanied the CAA; to make changes in statements of managers that accompanied various appropriations bills reported from conferences in the past; or to direct compliance with a report of one committee of one House of Congress. The executive branch shall construe these provisions in a manner consistent with the bicameral passage and presentment requirements of the Constitution for the making of a law. Such provisions include in the Foreign Operations Appropriations Act, section 595; in the Labor-HHS-Education Appropriations Act, provisions under the headings "Innovation and Improvement," "Rehabilitation Services and Disability Research," "Higher Education," and "Institute of Education Sciences"; in the Transportation-Treasury Appropriations Act, sections 125 and 173; and in the VA-HUD Appropriations Act, provisions under the headings "Community Development Fund" and "Department of Housing and Urban Development, Management and Administration, Salaries and Expenses."

Several provisions of CAA relate to race, ethnicity, or gender. The executive branch shall construe such provisions in a manner consistent with the requirements that the Federal Government afford equal protection of the laws under the Due Process Clause of the Fifth Amendment to the Constitution.

Section 12 of the Legislative Branch Appropriations Act authorizes overseas travel for members of the U.S. Capitol Police in support of travel by Senators. To ensure consistency with the President's constitutional authority to conduct the Nation's foreign affairs, the executive branch shall construe section 12 as authorizing travel for the limited purposes of advance, security, and protective functions in support of the official travel of Senators. The executive branch shall construe the term "intelligence gathering" in section 1007 of the Legislative Branch Appropriations Act, which relates to activities of the U.S. Capitol Police outside their geographic jurisdiction, as limited to collection of information for law enforcement and protective functions authorized by other laws relating to the U.S. Capitol Police, as any other construction would be inconsistent with the Constitution's vesting of the executive power in the President.

The executive branch shall construe section 638 of the Transportation-Treasury Appropriations Act, relating to assignment of executive branch employees to perform functions in the legislative branch, in a manner consistent with the President's constitutional authority to supervise the unitary executive branch and as Commander in Chief, and recognizing that the President cannot be compelled to give up the authority of his office as a condition of receiving the funds necessary to carrying out the duties of his office.

GEORGE W. BUSH

The White House,
December 8, 2004.

NOTE: H.R. 4818, approved December 8, was assigned Public Law No. 108–447.

Letter to Congressional Leaders Concurring on the Designation of Funds for the African Union Security Force and Construction of a Mail Irradiation Facility in Washington, DC
December 8, 2004

Dear Mr. Speaker: (*Dear Mr. President:*)

I hereby concur with the Congress in the designation of two provisions totaling $100 million provided in the Consolidated Appropriations Act, 2005 (H.R. 4818), as emergency requirements.

These funds are necessary to support the African Union security force in Darfur, as well as to construct a mail irradiation facility in Washington, D.C. Additional information is set forth in the attached letter from the Director of the Office of Management and Budget.

Sincerely,

GEORGE W. BUSH

NOTE: Identical letters were sent to J. Dennis Hastert, Speaker of the House of Representatives, and Richard B. Cheney, President of the Senate.

Remarks on the Nomination of R. James Nicholson To Be Secretary of Veterans Affairs
December 9, 2004

The President. Thank you all. Please be seated. Good morning. I'm pleased to announce my nomination of Ambassador Jim Nicholson to the—to be the Secretary of Veterans Affairs.

Jim Nicholson is a patriot, a man of deep conviction who has answered his country's call many times. As a young man from Iowa, raised in modest circumstances, he became a cadet at West Point in the late 1950s and went on to become an Army Ranger and paratrooper. As a Ranger, he fought in Vietnam, where he won multiple decorations for bravery in combat, including the Bronze Star and the Combat Infantry Badge. After 8 years on active duty, he joined the Army Reserves, where he served for 22 more years before retiring as a full colonel.

Throughout his career, Jim has shown the same honor, integrity, and commitment to service that defined his life as a military officer. He and his wife, Suzanne, have given back generously to their community and have been leaders in numerous volunteer causes in their home State of Colorado. He was a respected chairman of the Republican National Committee. And for the past 3 years, he has served as the United States Ambassador to the Vatican. Jim has worked with the Vatican to advance many vital foreign policy goals, including fighting poverty, hunger, AIDS, expanding religious liberty around the world, and ending the brutal practice of human trafficking.

I'm grateful to Jim for his superb work as our Ambassador, and I now have asked him to accept a new assignment, to serve his country and his fellow veterans.

As Secretary of Veterans Affairs, he will lead a department of more than 230,000 employees responsible for ensuring our Nation's—that our Nation's veterans receive the health care and other benefits our country has promised them. Twenty-five million Americans are military veterans who stepped forward to serve when the Nation needed them. The Nation owes them in return a VA that is dedicated to effective, prompt attention to their needs. That has been a commitment of my administration for the last 4 years, and it will remain a commitment for the next 4 years.

When confirmed by the Senate, Jim Nicholson will succeed Tony Principi, who has been a fine member of my Cabinet. Secretary Principi is a man who insists on results, and he has gotten results. Thanks to his leadership, veterans and their families have seen many improvements in VA services. They're receiving better care, and their claims are processed more quickly. Tony Principi has made it the Department's highest priority to assist veterans with service-related disabilities, low incomes, and other special needs. He's also launched a program to help homeless veterans find permanent housing. In all his work as Secretary of Veterans Affairs, Tony Principi has shown himself to be an outstanding executive, a friend to his fellow veterans, and a goodhearted man. I'm proud of his service, and I wish him and Liz all the very best.

Jim Nicholson will build on Tony Principi's achievements in continuing to modernize the VA, especially the VA health care system. Jim has the judgment and the character and the management expertise to do this job well.

I thank him for agreeing to serve. I also thank Suzanne and other members of their family. I want to thank their son Nick and his wife, Charlotte; daughter, Katie, and son-in-law, Bo. I hope the Senate will confirm Jim Nicholson very soon. I look forward to welcoming him to my Cabinet.

Congratulations.

[*At this point, Secretary-designate Nicholson made brief remarks.*]

The President. Good job, Jim. Thank you. Congratulations.

NOTE: The President spoke at 9:47 a.m. in the Roosevelt Room at the White House. The transcript released by the Office of the Press Secretary also included the remarks of Secretary-designate Nicholson.

Remarks Following a Meeting With Social Security Trustees and an Exchange With Reporters
December 9, 2004

The President. It's been my honor to welcome the Social Security trustees here to the Oval Office. We had a good discussion about the problems that face the Social Security system, and there is a recognition among the experts that we have a problem. And the problem is America is getting older and that there are fewer people to pay into the system to support a baby boomer generation which is about to retire.

Therefore, the question is, does this country have the will to address the problem? I think it must. I think we have a responsibility to solve problems before they become acute. And therefore, I want to thank the trustees for their understanding and their work. I want to thank them for their recognition that this country must deal with this issue now. I look forward to working with the Members of Congress to do just that.

I had a meeting earlier on this week with Members of the United States House and Senate to discuss the importance of the Social Security issue. I fully recognize it's going to require a bipartisan effort to address this issue. I have articulated principles in the course of my campaign that I think are important. And it's very important for our—those who have retired to recognize that nothing is going to change when it comes to Social Security. And it's very important for those who are near retirement to understand nothing will change.

But for the sake of our younger workers, for the sake of younger Americans, we must be willing to address this problem. And I think it's vital to consider allowing younger workers, on a voluntary basis, to set aside some of their own payroll tax in personal accounts as part of a comprehensive solution to dealing with the Social Security issue.

So I want to thank the trustees for their hard work. I want to thank you for your understanding of the issue. And I appreciate your willingness to go out and help explain to the American people that the time is now, the time is ready for us to solve this problem.

I'll answer two questions. Scott [Scott Lindlaw, Associated Press].

Equipment for U.S. Troops

Q. Thanks, Mr. President. Secretary Rumsfeld heard some complaints from soldiers yesterday who said, among other things, they've got inadequate armor as they head into Iraq. Do you know how widespread this problem is, and what are we doing about it?

The President. First, I appreciate the fact that the Secretary went and visited our troops and took questions from the troops. I had the honor of visiting with our troops at Camp Pendleton on Tuesday. It's such an uplifting experience to be able to speak directly to the troops. And I had the honor of meeting with the families of the fallen as well.

The concerns expressed are being addressed, and that is we expect our troops to have the best possible equipment. And if I were a soldier overseas wanting to defend my country, I'd want to ask the Secretary of Defense the same question, and that is, "Are we getting the best we can get us?" And they deserve the best. And I have told many families I met with, "We're doing everything we possibly can to protect your loved ones in a mission which is vital and important." And that mission is to spread freedom and peace. And I want to thank all the troops who will be spending their Christmas season overseas, away from their families, for their sacrifice, and I want to thank the families once again for the sacrifices they have made as well.

Steve [Steve Holland, Reuters].

Social Security Reform

Q. The transition to personal accounts may cost $2 trillion. Can the country afford to borrow that much?

The President. I think what's really important in the discussions is to understand the size of the problem. And that is we are faced with a present value of unfunded liabilities of about $11 trillion. What's important, Steve, is, before we begin any discussion, is to understand the scope of the problem. And that's why these trustees are vital in helping educate the American people and Congress as to the size of the problem. And I will not prejudge any solution. I think it's very important for the first step to be a common understanding of the size of the problem and then for Members of both parties, in both bodies, to come together, to come and listen to the options available.

We have got a member of what was called the Moynihan Commission with us. They studied this problem in detail. They made some suggestions about how to move forward in solving the problem. Much of my thinking has been colored by the work of the late Senator Moynihan and the other members of the Commission who took a lot of time to take a look at this problem and who came up with some creative suggestions.

And so I look forward to working with Congress to address this issue in a straightforward manner.

Thank you all.

Payroll Taxes

Q. Are you against any withholding tax increase to pay for the transition, sir? Are you against——

The President. We will not raise payroll taxes to solve this problem.

NOTE: The President spoke at 10:28 a.m. in the Oval Office at the White House. In his remarks, he referred to the President's Commission to Strengthen Social Security.

Remarks on Lighting the Hanukkah Menorah
December 9, 2004

Welcome, everybody, to the White House. Hanukkah is a festive holiday that celebrates a great victory for freedom. We remember the liberation of Jerusalem and a miracle witnessed in the holy temple 2,000 years ago. For 8 days the oil burned, and the light of freedom still burns in Jewish homes and synagogues everywhere.

We are honored to celebrate the miracle of Hanukkah in the White House this evening. We have a beautiful menorah from the Boca Raton Synagogue in Boca Raton, Florida. Laura and I are grateful to have it here, and we thank Rabbi Kenneth Brander for making that possible.

I also thank the gentlemen from Kol Zimra, who will help us say the blessings over the candles and bless all of us with their music. Welcome.

The Talmud teaches that the menorah lights should perform no function other than to proclaim the miracle of a just and loving God. Every generation since Judah Maccabee has looked on these candles and recalled the sacrifices that are made for freedom. And in every generation, these lights have warmed the hearts of those not yet free.

Today, many Americans are sacrificing to bring freedom and hope to the oppressed. In this holiday season, we pray for the safety of our troops, for the success of the mission, and for their speedy return home.

And tonight we have asked the three eldest children of one of our Jewish chaplains, Army Chaplain Shmuel Felzenberg, now on duty in Iraq, to do the honors of lighting the menorah. Will Menachem, Chaim, and Miriam Felzenberg are here to light the candles.

Thank you.

NOTE: The President spoke at 4:30 p.m. in the Bookseller's Area in the East Wing at the White House.

Remarks on the Nomination of Samuel W. Bodman To Be Secretary of Energy
December 10, 2004

The President. Thank you. Good morning. Today I am announcing my nomination of Sam Bodman as Secretary of Energy. I am pleased to welcome Sam's wife, Diane, and all his family members—I emphasize "all"—for coming today. Welcome to the White House.

Sam Bodman is an experienced executive who has served in my administration as Deputy Secretary of Commerce and Deputy Secretary of the Treasury. During his varied and distinguished career in the private sector, Sam has been a professor at MIT, president of an investment firm, the chairman and CEO of an industrial company with operations worldwide. In academics, in business, and in government, Sam Bodman has shown himself to be a problemsolver who knows how to set goals, and he knows how to reach them. He will bring to the Department of Energy a great talent for management and the precise thinking of an engineer. I thank him for agreeing to serve once again.

The Department of Energy has responsibilities that directly affect all Americans, from the security of nuclear facilities to reducing the risk of nuclear proliferation around the world to environmental cleanup to enhancing conservation and developing new sources of energy for the future. Every day, employees at the Department of Energy are working to protect the American people and to ensure that our country's homes and businesses have reliable, safe, and affordable supplies of energy.

During the last 4 years, the Department of Energy has been active and effective and has delivered important results for the American people. We've taken vital steps to upgrade the Nation's energy infrastructure. We have begun an ambitious research program to develop a viable hydrogen-powered automobile. We have strengthened cooperation between the United States and foreign governments to safeguard nuclear materials and to fight proliferation.

For these achievements and more, the Nation is grateful to Secretary Spencer Abraham. As a United States Senator and a Cabinet Secretary, Spence has shown himself to be a man of integrity and wisdom. He's a good man, a superior public servant, and a friend. And I thank Spence for leading his Department so ably, and I wish him and Jane all the best.

During the next 4 years, we will continue to enhance our economic security and our national security through sound energy policy. We will pursue more energy close to home, in our own country and in our own hemisphere, so that we're less dependent on energy from unstable parts of the world. We will continue improving pipelines and gas terminals and powerlines, so that energy flow is reliable. We will develop and deploy the latest technology to provide a new generation of cleaner and more efficient energy sources. We will promote strong conservation measures.

In all these steps, we will bring greater certainty of costs and supply, and that certainty is essential to economic growth and job creation. And we will continue to work closely with Congress to produce comprehensive legislation that moves America toward greater energy independence. I'm optimistic about the task ahead, and I know Sam Bodman is the right man to lead this important and vital agency. So I urge the Senate to confirm his nomination without delay.

Congratulations, Sam.

[*At this point, Secretary-designate Bodman made brief remarks.*]

NOTE: The President spoke at 9:44 a.m. in the Roosevelt Room at the White House. The transcript released by the Office of the Press Secretary also included the remarks of Secretary-designate Bodman.

Remarks at Fort Belvoir, Virginia
December 10, 2004

Listen, Laura and I are thrilled to be out here, and we want to thank you all for greeting us and thank you for giving us a chance to participate in this assembly line of compassion.

First, I want to thank Elaine Rogers, who is the president of the USO of metropolitan Washington. Ned Powell—I appreciate Ned for being here as well. It turns out that my grandfather Prescott S. Bush was the first president and CEO of USO, so it's only fitting that I'm coming—working in the assembly line. [*Laughter*] But I want to thank you for your leadership.

I want to thank Cheryl Hall. I want to thank Colonel T.W. Williams, the garrison commander of Ft. Belvoir. I want to thank Command Sergeant Major Andre Douglas. He reminded me that he and I spent Thanksgiving together last year in Baghdad.

So it's great to see you again, Command Sergeant Major. I want to thank Mary Jo Myers, the wife of my friend General Richard Myers, Chairman of the Joint Chiefs.

Most of all, I want to thank all the volunteers who are here. I want to thank your spirit.

So, Scott asked me what's—what are we doing? I said, "We're sending packages to our troops overseas, a package full of all different goodies, you know, a little gum, playing cards." But you can't ever thank the troops enough. This is one way of saying America appreciates your service to freedom and peace and our security. You can't put enough playing cards in there; you can't put enough sticks of gum.

But I hope our troops understand that with this package comes a lot of support and a lot of affection from not only a husband or a wife or a mom or a dad but, equally important, an average citizen who you never met, somebody who deeply appreciates your service, somebody who understands the mission, and somebody who stands solidly with you as you work to make the world a better place.

I know it's hard for our families—military families to be separated from a loved one during any time but, in particular, during the holiday season. And so we ask for God's blessings, not only on our troops who are overseas, but we ask for the Lord's blessings on our family members.

This is—this whole operation here is cranking out a lot of care packages. So far,

480,000 soldiers overseas have received a care package. And with it, as I said, is a message of good will and hope. We're—this is an historic time we live in. The world is changing. And as it changes, as the world becomes more free, America becomes more secure and the peace we all long for becomes more real.

And so during these holiday seasons, we thank our blessings, and one of the greatest blessings of all is the United States military and their families. Thank you for having us. I look forward to coming by to thank each of you.

Our intention here is not to stop progress but to encourage progress. [*Laughter*] Thanks for your hard work. If any of our fellow citizens are interested to know how you can help, there's a web page set up at the Defense Department and/or at the USA Freedom Corps for ways to help the USO or any other organization that supports our United States military.

God bless you all, and thanks for letting us come by.

NOTE: The President spoke at 2:08 p.m. in the USO warehouse. In his remarks, he referred to Edward A. Powell, Jr., president and chief executive officer, United Service Organizations, Inc.; and Cheryl Laaker Hall, director, Operation USO Care Package. The Office of the Press Secretary also released a Spanish language transcript of these remarks.

Statement on Signing the Veterans Benefits Improvement Act of 2004
December 10, 2004

Today, I have signed into law S. 2486, the "Veterans Benefits Improvement Act of 2004." The Act modifies and extends housing, education, and other benefits for the Nation's veterans.

Section 3677(d)(2)(B) of title 38, United States Code, as enacted by section 108 of the Act, purports to require the Secretary of Veterans Affairs to make a recommendation to the Congress on whether to continue a specified pilot project beyond its statutory expiration date, which would require enactment of legislation. Section 4332 of title 38, as amended by section 202 of the Act, purports to require officials in the executive branch to submit recommendations for legislative action in certain circumstances. The executive branch shall implement these provisions in a manner consistent with the President's constitutional authority to supervise the unitary executive branch and to recommend for the consideration of the Congress such measures as the President judges necessary and expedient.

GEORGE W. BUSH

The White House,
December 10, 2004.

NOTE: S. 2486, approved December 10, was assigned Public Law No. 108–454.

The President's Radio Address
December 11, 2004

Good morning. Social Security is one of the great moral achievements of American Government. For almost 70 years, it has kept millions of elderly citizens out of poverty and assured young Americans of a more secure future.

The Social Security system is essential, yet it faces a deepening long-term problem. While benefits for today's seniors are secure, the system is headed towards bankruptcy down the road. If we do not act soon, Social Security will not be there for our children and grandchildren.

So this week I met with the bipartisan leadership of Congress and asked them to join me in a great cause, preserving the essential promise of Social Security for future generations. We must begin by recognizing an essential fact, the current Social Security system was created for the needs of a different era. Back in 1935, most women did not work outside the home and the average life expectancy for American workers was less than 60 years. Today, more moms are working and most Americans are blessed with longer lives and longer retirements. The world has changed, and our Social Security system must change with it.

Today, Social Security is not a personal savings plan. There is no account where your money goes to earn interest. Benefits paid to today's retirees come directly from the taxes paid by today's workers. And each year there are more retirees taking money out of the system and not enough additional workers to support them.

In the 1950s, there were about 16 workers paying for every Social Security beneficiary. Today, there are about three. And eventually, there will only be two workers per beneficiary. These changes single a looming danger. In the year 2018, for the first time ever, Social Security will pay out more in benefits than the Government collects in payroll taxes. And once that line into the red has been crossed, the shortfalls will grow larger with each passing year. By the time today's workers in their mid twenties begin to retire, the system will be bankrupt, unless we act to save it.

A crisis in Social Security can be averted if we in Government take our responsibilities seriously and work together today. I came to Washington to solve problems, not to pass them on to future Presidents and future generations. I campaigned on a promise to reform and preserve Social Security, and I intend to keep that promise.

I have set forth several broad principles to guide our reforms. First, nothing will change for those who are receiving Social

Security and for those who are near retirement. Secondly, we must not increase payroll taxes, because higher taxes would slow economic growth. And we must tap into the power of compound interest, by giving younger workers the option to save some of their payroll taxes in a personal account, a nest egg they can call their own, which Government cannot take away.

Saving Social Security for future generations will not be easy. If it were easy, it would have already been done. There will be costs, yet the costs of continued inaction are unacceptable. And the longer we wait, the more difficult it will be to fix the system. Saving Social Security will require bipartisan cooperation and the courage of leaders in both parties. The American people voted for reform in 2004, and now they expect us to work together and deliver on our promises. I look forward to working with Members of Congress on this important issue. Together we will make certain that America meets its duty to our seniors and to our children and grandchildren.

Thank you for listening.

NOTE: The address was recorded at 7:50 a.m. on December 10 in the Cabinet Room at the White House for broadcast at 10:06 a.m. on December 11. The transcript was made available by the Office of the Press Secretary on December 10 but was embargoed for release until the broadcast. The Office of the Press Secretary also released a Spanish language transcript of this address.

Exchange With Reporters in Bethesda, Maryland
December 11, 2004

Visit With Wounded Troops/President's Health

Q. How are you feeling, Mr. President?

The President. I'm—first of all, incredibly impressed by the health care that our military receives. I have just come from visiting with some of the wounded and their families, and the service that the doctors and nurses provide here for our troops is superb. It is such an honor to see those who have been put themselves—who have been injured and are now fighting back and recovering and seeing their spirit and their strength. And it's an uplifting experience to come here.

I can say to the loved ones in the military that their sons and daughters and husbands and wives get the very best medical care there is, and I am grateful for that.

As far as my own physical goes, I'm still standing. I, obviously, have just gone through a campaign, because—let me say, I've obviously gone through a campaign where I probably ate too many doughnuts, if you get my drift. My New Year's resolution has become apparent after getting on the scales. And although I think the doc will put out a report that shows you that I'm physically fit and still able to get on the stress tests, I'm a little overweight. And therefore, I fully intend to lose some inches off my waistline and some pounds off my frame. But other than that, I'm feeling great.

Thank you all.

NOTE: The exchange began at 1:42 p.m. at the National Naval Medical Center. A tape was not available for verification of the content of this exchange.

Remarks on the Nomination of Michael O. Leavitt To Be Secretary of Health and Human Services
December 13, 2004

The President. Thank you. Good morning. I am pleased to announce the nomination of Michael O. Leavitt as the Secretary of Health and Human Services. Last year I welcomed Mike to my Cabinet as the Administrator of the Environmental Protection Agency. In that office, he has enforced high standards and a spirit of cooperation and with good common sense. He has upheld this administration's commitment to sustain improvements in the quality of the natural environment. He has managed the EPA with skill and with a focus on results. I've come to know Mike as a fine executive, as a man of great compassion. He is an ideal choice to lead one of the largest departments of the United States Government.

The Department of Health and Human Services touches the life of every person in this country. From the safety of our food and medicine to the Medicare program to preparing for any kind of health emergency, HHS has comprehensive responsibilities for the health of Americans. To meet those responsibilities, the Department needs many thousands of skilled professionals and a leader who is able to act on many fronts all at once.

For the last 4 years, HHS has served the American people extremely well under the energetic leadership of Tommy Thompson. Early in his tenure, our Nation went on a wartime footing and had to prepare for emergencies of a kind never seen before. Secretary Thompson led the effort to prepare the medical infrastructure for any terrorist challenge.

At the same time, he has presided over dramatic increases in medical research, adding to the promise of hopeful new cures. He's helped set in motion major improvements in Medicare, which will benefit seniors all across America. He has worked closely with State and local officials to ensure that public health programs function as effectively as possible. And throughout his career as Governor and as Secretary of Health and Human Services, Tommy Thompson has led efforts to reform welfare laws and to help more people transition from welfare to work. Tommy Thompson is a good friend who has given every day of the last 38 years to public service. As he and Sue Ann move on to new challenges, Tommy has my deep gratitude for a job well done.

My new nominee for HHS Secretary, like Tommy Thompson, served many years as a Governor. The people of Utah elected Mike Leavitt to three terms, and during his administration, Utah was named one of the best managed State governments in the country. Governor Leavitt was a leader in welfare reform, resource management, and environmental stewardship. He improved child welfare services in the State and made strides toward expanding access to health care for children. He made government services more accessible through the Internet, and he always insisted that the government remain accountable to the people it serves.

When confirmed by the Senate, Mike Leavitt will be charged with a broad agenda for the health and safety of the American people. In this new term, we will implement the first-ever prescription drug benefit for seniors under Medicare. We will expand Federal cooperation with faith-based groups that provide essential services, such as counseling and treatment for addictions. We will continue pursuing the great promise of medical research, always ensuring that the work is carried out with vigor and moral integrity. We will not relent in our efforts to protect the American people from disease and the use of disease as a weapon against us.

Mike Leavitt is the right leader to lead HHS in meeting all these vital commitments. I thank him for accepting this new responsibility. I also thank his wife, Jackie, and their son Westin for being with us today. I urge the Senate to confirm Governor Leavitt's nomination as soon as possible.

Congratulations.

[*At this point, Secretary-designate Leavitt made brief remarks.*]

The President. Good job.

NOTE: The President spoke at 10:38 a.m. in the Roosevelt Room at the White House. The transcript released by the Office of the Press Secretary also included the remarks of Secretary-designate Leavitt. The Office of the Press Secretary also released a Spanish language transcript of these remarks.

Remarks on Presenting the Presidential Medal of Freedom
December 14, 2004

The President. Good morning, and welcome to the White House. Laura and I are proud to have you all here today, especially our three honorees and their families and their friends.

The Presidential Medal of Freedom is our Nation's highest civil award, given to men and women of exceptional merit, integrity, and achievement. Today this honor goes to three men who have played pivotal roles in great events and whose efforts have made our country more secure and advanced the cause of human liberty.

George Tenet learned the value of hard work as a busboy in the 20th Century Diner, the family restaurant in Queens, New York. Between work and school and athletics, George always kept up with current events and world affairs, and that enthusiasm led him into public service.

In Washington, George immersed himself in the field of intelligence work. After a long career in the legislative and executive branches of Government, George was tapped by President Bill Clinton to run the Agency he loved. His challenges at the CIA were many. George acted quickly and aggressively to rebuild the Agency's capabilities. He made the recruitment of new talent a top priority. Applications to join the Agency have now soared to more than 138,000 per year. Under George's leadership, the number of yearly graduates from the Clandestine Service Training Program have increased nearly sixfold. And just about every CIA officer can tell you a story about Director Tenet's hands-on style of management. He was often seen in the hallways, chewing on an unlit cigar— [*laughter*]—or showing up at their cafeteria table and talking shop.

George and his wife, Stephanie, came to know the people of the CIA, and the people of the CIA came to know them as decent, caring people who love their country and love their family, especially their son, John Michael.

Early in his tenure as DCI, George Tenet was one of the first to recognize and address the growing threat to America from radical terrorist networks. Immediately after the attacks of September the 11th, George was ready with a plan to strike back at Al Qaida and to topple the Taliban. CIA officers were on the ground in Afghanistan within days. Seasoned American intelligence officers, armed with laptop computers, Afghan clothes, and a visionary plan, rode horseback with the fighters of the Northern Alliance, identified key targets for our military, and helped to free a nation.

Since those weeks, CIA officers have remained on the hunt for Al Qaida killers. More than three-quarters of Al Qaida key members and associates have been killed or detained, and the majority were stopped as a result of CIA efforts. CIA officers were also among the first to enter the battle in Iraq, alongside their colleagues in uniform. In these years of challenge for our country, the men and women of the CIA have been on the frontlines of an urgent cause, and the whole Nation owes them our gratitude.

George is rightly proud of the people of the Agency, and I have been proud to work with George. George has carried great authority without putting on airs, because he remembers his roots. There's still a lot of Queens in George Tenet. [*Laughter*] A colleague once said that "George has the intellect of a scholar and the demeanor of a longshoreman." [*Laughter*] His tireless efforts have brought justice to America's enemies and greater security to the American people. And today we honor a fine public servant and patriot in George John Tenet.

General Tommy Franks was raised in Midland, Texas. Nothing wrong with that. [*Laughter*] I didn't know him then, but Laura and he went to the same high school. In those days, some people in Midland wondered about Tommy's future. Sounds familiar. [*Laughter*] At a recent high school reunion, Tommy's old principal told the general, "You weren't the brightest bulb in the socket," to which the general replied, "Ain't this a great country?" [*Laughter*]

America rewards talent, intelligence, and hard work, and the career of Tommy Franks is living proof. Tommy dropped out of college after 2 years to enlist in the Army. He quickly rose to become an officer, graduating from Officer Candidate School with honors and beginning his ascent through the ranks. He went on to finish his degree and earn one more. And he made the best decision of his life when he asked a young lady named Cathy Carley to marry him.

Tommy Franks served in Germany and Korea, at the Pentagon, and at the Army War College. He served in the Persian Gulf war. He served in Vietnam, where he was wounded twice. Yet his greatest challenges and his greatest service came after the attacks on September the 11th.

As the commander of CENTCOM, Tommy Franks held responsibility for defending American interests in some of the most remote and difficult terrain in the world. It's a job that requires the toughness of a general, the foresight of a strategist, the tact of a diplomat, and the skill of a good manager. Tommy Franks led the forces that fought and won two wars in the defense of the world's security and helped liberate more than 50 million people from two of the worst tyrannies in the world.

In Afghanistan, America and our allies, with a historically small force and a brilliant strategy, defeated the Taliban in just a few short weeks. The general likes to say that "no plan ever survived the first contact with the enemy." But in Iraq, Tommy Franks' plan did. A force half the size of the force that won the Gulf war defeated Saddam Hussein's regime and reached Baghdad in less than a month, the fastest, longest armored advance in the history of America warfare.

Today, the people of Iraq and Afghanistan are building a secure and permanent democratic future. One of the highest distinctions of history is to be called a liberator, and Tommy Franks will always carry that title.

General, the American people thank you for your courage, your leadership, and your lifetime of service in the cause of freedom and security. To the lists of medals and honors and awards you have already earned, I am proud to add the Presidential Medal of Freedom.

Jerry Bremer is a diplomat, a philanthropist, a businessman, and a fashion pioneer. [*Laughter*] Everyone knows the Bremer look—coat, dress shirt and tie, and desert combat boots. [*Laughter*] Beyond the fashion statement, Jerry will be remembered for his superb work in laying the foundations of a new democracy in the Middle East.

Jerry Bremer's life of service began in 1966, when he joined the Foreign Service. He was a special assistant to six different Secretaries of State and rose to become America's Ambassador to the Netherlands. In 1986, President Ronald Reagan appointed Jerry Ambassador-at-Large for Counterterrorism. Eventually, Speaker Hastert named him Chairman of the National Commission on Terrorism, and I chose him to serve on my Homeland Security Advisory Council.

When America and our coalition needed a seasoned diplomat and a manager to help the people of Iraq emerge from decades of oppression, I knew where to turn. For 14 months, Jerry Bremer worked day and night, in difficult, dangerous conditions, to stabilize the country, to help its people rebuild, and to establish a political process that would lead to justice and liberty. The job was demanding, requiring personal courage, calmness under fire, and hundreds of decisions every day. Yet, Jerry not only rose to the challenge, he found time nearly every day to study the Arabic language.

Jerry Bremer earned the respect and admiration of Iraqis and helped to assemble an exceptional group of Iraqi leaders for the Governing Council. With his help, these leaders drafted the Transitional Administrative Law, which charted the country's political future and established a bill of rights. In the final days of hammering out consensus on this landmark law, Jerry sat through day-long meetings, sometimes without ever speaking. His silence was essential to reassure Iraqis that the new law was entirely their own. Yet his presence was essential to reassure Iraqis of our coalition's steadfast commitment to their future and their success. Every political benchmark that the Iraqis set for themselves and that Jerry helped them meet was achieved on time or ahead of schedule, including the transfer of sovereignty that ended his tenure.

Sometimes, Iraqi officials would express doubts that the day would ever come. Jerry would pick up a photo of his granddaughter and say, "This is your guarantee I'm leaving." [*Laughter*]

Jerry, I know your wife, Francie, and your children, Paul and Leila, and your granddaughter, Sophia, are really glad to have you back.

When Jerry Bremer greeted visitors at his office in Baghdad, he always began, "Welcome to free Iraq." Jerry, Iraq is free today, and you helped make it so. And a free Iraq will help make generations of Americans more secure. Our Nation will always be grateful to Ambassador Jerry Bremer and his good work.

These three men symbolize the nobility of public service, the good character of our country, and the good influence of America on the world.

Now it is my honor to present the Presidential Medal of Freedom, and I ask the military aide to read the citations.

[*At this point, Maj. Steven T. Fischer, USA, Army Military Aide to the President, read the citations, and the President presented the medals.*]

The President. Thank you all for coming. Laura and I now invite you for a reception here to honor our honorees.

Congratulations.

NOTE: The President spoke at 11:30 a.m. in the East Room at the White House.

Remarks Following a Meeting With Prime Minister Silvio Berlusconi of Italy and an Exchange With Reporters
December 15, 2004

President Bush. There will be two opening statements, and then we'll take two questions per side. Thank you for coming.

Silvio, it's great to welcome you back to our country. I think it's fitting that one of the first world leaders to have visited after our elections is my friend Silvio Berlusconi. He is a close personal friend. He is a friend of the United States of America.

I told the Prime Minister I look forward to working with him over the next 4 years to make the world a better place for all, that I've got work to do in Europe. He gave me some very good advice about my upcoming trip. But he always gives me good advice, and I'm proud to have his advice.

We talked about peace between Israel and the Palestinian Authority. I think there's a very good chance that we can achieve that peace. I look forward to working toward that end. The Prime Minister had good advice on that subject as well.

He expressed his concerns about the relationship between the dollar and the euro. I told him we're going to take this issue on seriously with the Congress. The best thing that we can do from the executive branch of Government in America is to work with Congress to deal with our deficits. One deficit is a short-term budget deficit. Another deficit is the unfunded liabilities that come with Social Security and some of the health programs for the elderly. I told the Prime Minister that Social Security reform will be at the top of my agenda. I campaigned on the issue. I look forward to working with Members of Congress to resolve this long-term, unfunded issue so that the world financiers can take comfort in the fact that this Government will address one part of the budget deficit. There's a trade deficit. That's easy to re-solve; people can buy more United States products if they're worried about the trade deficit.

But we've had a good visit. And I'm proud my friend is here.

And finally, we discussed our mutual desire to spread freedom and peace. I want to thank the Prime Minister for his understanding about the need for the free world to succeed in Afghanistan and Iraq. He's the kind of man, when he gives you his word, he keeps his word, which is the sign of an impressive, strong leader.

So thank you for coming.

Prime Minister Berlusconi. Thank you, Mr. President, for your kind words. Thank you for the friendship you showed to me, to my Government, and my country.

And my behavior and the behavior of my Government is based on the fact that we share the same values. We appreciate strongly the fact that America has taken on the responsibility of defending and spreading peace and democracy all over the world. And we appreciate the fact the United States do that with sacrifices and a lot of suffering. So we fully share the work carried out by the American administration. And the political agenda, the program which has been announced for the next 4 years, is something we fully agree on.

We share the same opinion as to the need of reforming the United Nations in order to make it an institution which will be able to tackle the problems affecting this century and the multilateralism which has to take into account results to be achieved and complete facts. We agree on the fact that we have to continue the fight and the war on terror together. And we agreed on the fact that it is now the appropriate time to solve the Middle East issue.

And in particular, I agree on the way in which we keep on and carry on our relationship. It's a very frank, direct, straightforward, and spontaneous way, full of truth. And I think this was the deepest reason why President Bush succeeded so much, especially vis-a-vis the Americans. It is not politics. There is no politics which makes people say things which people do not believe in or think. President Bush tells me and all of the others always what's in his mind. And it is very positive that "yes" means really "yes" to him and "no" means "no." And I want to reassure President Bush that we'll do any possible effort to strengthen the relationship between the United States of America and Europe. Because I agree with him: The West is only one.

President Bush. Welcome. Anybody representing AP here? Oh, you are, Terry [Terence Hunt, Associated Press]. Go ahead.

Upcoming Iraqi Elections

Q. Iraq's Defense Minister says that Iran and Syrian intelligence agents are supporting Al Zarqawi and that Iran is trying to sway the January 30 elections. Do you believe these charges are accurate, sir? And is there anything the United States can do besides simply telling Iran and Syria to refrain?

President Bush. We have made it very clear to the countries in the neighborhood, including the two you mentioned, that we expect there to be help in establishing a society in which people are able to elect their leaders and that we expect people to work with the Iraqi Interim Government to enforce border, to stop the flow of people and money that aim to help these terrorists. We've made that very clear, and we'll continue to make it clear.

We have made it clear that for the good of the area, that there ought to be a peaceful country where the different religions can come together under the TAL which has been passed, the go-by for what a new

constitution should look like. And we will continue to make it clear to both Syria and Iran that—as will other nations in our coalition, including our friend the Italians—that meddling in the internal affairs of Iraq is not in their interests.

You want to call on somebody from the Italian press?

[At this point, an interpreter translated President Bush's remarks into Italian.]

The President. I'll be more polite to the translator from now on. [*Laughter*] Want to call on somebody from the——

Currency Exchange Rates

Q. You said you've discussed the euro-dollar ratio, and therefore, you discussed your relations between the two economic blocs. Can you say something more in detail about what you talked about and if there is, in the future, the possibility of a better balance between the euro and the dollar in terms of the exchange rate?

The President. The policy of my Government is a strong dollar policy.

Interpreter. I'm sorry, sir. I didn't hear you. [*Laughter*]

The President. She might not agree with it. [*Laughter*] We believe that the markets should make the decision about the relationship between the dollar and the euro. Therefore, to the extent that the Federal Government is involved with strengthening—making the conditions such that a strong dollar will emerge, we'll do everything we can in the upcoming legislative session to send a signal to the markets that we'll deal with our deficits, which, hopefully, will cause people to want to buy dollars.

Independently, the Federal Reserve, under the leadership of Alan Greenspan, raised the interest rates yet again, a signal to the world markets that the Chairman is also aware of the relative currency valuations between the euro and the dollar.

I'm not that generous yet. We love April [April Ryan, American Urban Radio Networks], but there's a limited number of questions.

Holland [Steve Holland, Reuters].

Social Security Reform

Q. Sir, you're going to this conference today. Some Democrats call the private accounts in Social Security a risky scheme. What happens if people lose money on their investments? Does the Government bail them out?

President Bush. Look, Steve, this is the issue about addressing the long-term liability issue. This is the Social Security issue. Like many nations in Europe, there's an issue with Social Security systems. Baby boomers are getting ready to retire, and there's not enough workers to sustain that which—that which has been promised. And so the fundamental question I placed before the Congress is: We have a problem; let's work together to deal with it.

I believe there's a consensus beginning to grow, that members of both political parties understand now is the time to address this problem. I believe one way to help make sure the system meets the needs of a younger generation is to allow younger workers to take some of their own taxes and invest in a personal savings account—under certain conditions. The people in our country have heard this notion, so-called "risky scheme" adjectives in the 2000 campaign and the 2004 campaign. I took the message to them. They realize, like I realize, now is the time to deal with the problem. And I look forward to working with both members—members of both parties to solve this problem.

But let me just give you one—this is a chance now to kind of start laying the groundwork for future questions. The great desire for people in Congress is for me to negotiate with myself. You notice I said the great desire for Members of Congress, not members of the press. And therefore, I will continue to articulate principles that I think are important and reach out to members of both parties to fashion a plan that solves the problem.

Prime Minister Berlusconi. The problem of Social Security is common to all of the Western World. And this is, luckily, due to the fact that we live longer because of the better standard of living and because of the discoveries made by medicine. In Europe, all governments are dealing with reforming Social Security systems, but one thing is for sure, that it needs to be done. That is, we have to extend the working life of the people.

I'm one of the strongest believers in that, because at my age, I'm convinced that one—at my age, you can keep on working pretty well. [*Laughter*] And you can tap on the experience you've kind of piled up over your working life.

President Bush. You look like a baby boomer. [*Laughter*]

Prime Minister Berlusconi. I thank you very much. It's medicine as well—also credit medicine. [*Laughter*]

President Bush. Final question. Do you want to call on somebody?

Prime Minister Berlusconi. I want to say something. We have already reformed our Social Security system in Italy. And this is one of the 24 reforms through which we are modernizing our country. And I've just said to President Bush that at the end of its term, my Government will have completed many more reforms than all of the previous governments in the Italian Republic.

President Bush. Very good.

A final question from the Italian press?

Proposed Joint Italian-U.S. Helicopter Production

Q. Did you debate the possibility that the President of the United States will soon fly on Italian helicopters? [*Laughter*]

President Bush. No, I appreciate that——

Prime Minister Berlusconi. The Italian helicopters almost completely made, manufactured, in the United States.

President Bush. With U.S. parts. I've got the message, yes. [*Laughter*]

Prime Minister Berlusconi. I can only say that I've been flying these helicopters for 30 years, and I'm still here.

President Bush. And you never crashed. [*Laughter*] That's a good start. [*Laughter*]

The Prime Minister brought up the issue. I'm very familiar with it. As you know, we delayed a decision until later on in the spring. I'm very aware of the joint venture. I understand the nature of U.S.

jobs that will be created in this venture, and I assured him the venture will be treated fairly.

Thank you for coming. Happy holidays. Happy holidays.

NOTE: The President spoke at 11:57 a.m. in the Oval Office at the White House. A reporter referred to Defense Minister Hazim Qutran al-Khuzai al-Shalan of the Iraqi Interim Government; and senior Al Qaida associate Abu Musab Al Zarqawi. Prime Minister Berlusconi spoke in Italian, and his remarks were translated by an interpreter.

Remarks in a Panel Discussion on the High Cost of Lawsuit Abuse at the White House Conference on the Economy
December 15, 2004

The President. Listen, thank you all for coming. I've just come off a campaign— [*laughter*]—and spent a great deal of time talking with the American people about how to make sure America is the best place in the world to do business. And there was a lot of discussion in the course of the last couple of months about what's the best philosophy to make sure that jobs are created here, that the entrepreneurial environment is strong, that small businesses can flourish but, most importantly, that people find jobs close to home.

And one of the things that I talked about was making sure that the environment for risking capital was conducive for job creation. And I tried to say that as plainly as I could. And one issue that I talked about, to make sure that costs were reasonable and that the cost of capital was reasonable, was legal reform, that the cost of frivolous lawsuits, in some cases, make it prohibitively expensive for a small business to stay in business or for a doctor to practice medicine, in which case, it means the

health care costs of a job provider or job creator has escalated or is escalating.

I talked about the competitive advantage that we must have in America if we expect jobs to stay here. The cost of lawsuits, relative to countries that we compete against, are high. In other words, the cost of litigation in America makes it more difficult for us to compete with nations in Europe, for example.

And so I want to thank our panelists for coming today to help add some expertise to this notion that if we can achieve legal reform in America, it'll make it a better place for people to either start a business and/or find work.

Now, there's much more to a comprehensive economic expansion program than just legal reform, but a cornerstone of any good program is legal reform. And there's a practical aspect to our discussions today, because I want the people who get to decide whether we're having legal reform to hear from experts, and that would be Members of the House and Senate from both sides of the aisle. I am here to not only thank our panelists but to make it clear as I possibly can that I intend to take a legislative package to Congress which says we expect the House and the Senate to pass meaningful liability reform on asbestos, on class action, and medical liability.

I want to thank my good friend Don Evans, who has served so well as the Secretary of Commerce. As you know, he has made the decision to go back to the State of Texas. I'm glad my departure was delayed by 4 years. [*Laughter*]

Secretary of Commerce Donald L. Evans. So am I. [*Laughter*]

The President. But I do want to thank him for serving so admirably, and I want to thank you for hosting this event.

Secretary Evans. Mr. President, thank you so much. We have a very distinguished panel but a far-reaching panel. As you know, the issue of lawsuit abuse has many, many facets to it. And so I'm delighted that we have been able to assemble a number of people that look at it from an economist perspective, an academia perspective, a small-business perspective, a health care perspective, because there's many, many issues that relate to lawsuit abuse in this country.

I want to thank you, Mr. President, for your leadership on this particular matter, your attention you've given to it. And I'm one of the—only one of those out there has—that have seen your focus on it for over 10 years. I remember full well in 1993, when you were running for Governor of the State of Texas, it was one of the very top issues on your agenda. And after becoming Governor, you led and you made a difference in that State. And because of the difference you've made in tort reform in the State of Texas, the State of Texas economy is a stronger economy than it otherwise would have been. And you're bringing that same leadership here to Washington, DC, and the Federal Government, because certainly there's things we can do in Federal Government that will create a better environment for entrepreneurs and

small-business owners to create jobs and grow our economy, and it had to do with legal reform and lawsuit reform.

Mr. President, you mentioned that I have served here for some 4 years as Secretary of Commerce, and one of the things I must say: One, it was an honor to serve the American people, and it certainly has been under your leadership. But as I've traveled across America, the one thing that I hear time and time again among manufacturers as well as service companies is the burdens of lawsuits, the burdens of junk and frivolous lawsuits and how they continue to weaken our economy and make it harder for us to compete domestically and internationally and not easier for us to compete domestically and internationally.

And that's the one question we ought to always ask ourselves when we make decisions in this town. Does this make it harder for us to compete and create jobs in America domestically, or does it make it easier for us to compete? So everything we do should say it makes it easier to compete and create jobs. And what lawsuit abuse has done is it not only threatens our competitiveness and innovation in the world, but it also—it harms our health care system; it raises the cost of health care in this country; it stifles innovation, et cetera.

Last year, our Department went around the country, and we held roundtable discussions—some small- and medium-sized manufacturers all across America. And we heard this same message, with an incredible amount of passion and energy, not just from the manufacturers but also service companies as well, and that is how important it is to deal with lawsuit reform and deal with it now. Because it's going to impact the creation of jobs in this country for generations to come. It's not only about today's economy, but it's the economy for your children and your grandchildren. And it's time to deal with it now.

Mr. President, you referred to some of the cost of tort reform or tort costs in this country. It represents over 2 percent of our gross domestic product, over $250 billion in tort costs into our economy. That is a lot more than most of our—it in fact, it is more, as a percentage, as well as absolute terms, of those that we compete with around the world. The manufacturing sector bears a disproportionate share of that, about 4½ percent. And so when you think of the tort cost in manufacturing products in this country, then compare it with wages and salaries in the manufacturing sector— 17½ percent of the cost of labor and wages goes—is part of the cost, where only— where 4½ percent is tort claims. So you can see how tort costs are a very significant price, a cost in everything that we purchase in this country.

I was in Missouri this last year, and I had a chance to really see up close and personal how it was impacting the health care industry. I talked to a David Carpenter, who is the CEO of North Kansas City Hospital, and what he told me was that there had been 30 doctors that had moved from Missouri to Kansas because Kansas had, indeed, passed tort reform and had put some caps in place. So you see it happening all across America, where doctors are moving around and trying to find a more friendly environment.

Lawsuit abuse is just simply piling up cost on the backs of not just companies but the American people. I like to call it a tort tax. If you take the total cost of tort claims and judgments in our country and divide it by the number of people in the country, it's a tort tax of about $809 per capita. So in everything that we purchase, everything that we buy, in there someplace is a tort tax or a tort cost. And so it's going to continue to drive up the cost of automobiles, groceries that we purchase, work boots that we purchase, whatever it is we purchase. It's going to continue to drive up those costs if we don't do something about it, and it's also going to continue to stifle innovation and the entrepreneurial spirit.

And what we ought to be doing is figuring out ways to lower risk and increase rewards, and that's exactly the opposite of what a junk and frivolous lawsuit does in a society. What they do is they increase risk and lower results so—and lower rewards.

So for us to continue to be the most competitive economy in the world, the most innovative economy in the world, this is an issue that we must deal with—and we must deal with it now.

Again, I'm delighted to have this outstanding panel here to discuss this subject, important subject and issue, and I would like to begin by calling on Professor George Priest, who is the professor of Yale University, holds a John M. Olin Professor of Law chair there. George will take us through some of the modern expansion of tort liability in America and discuss some of the reform possibilities that we ought to be considering.

Professor.

George Priest. Thank you, Mr. Secretary. Let me give you a little history about the expansion of liability. This problem of lawsuit abuse and the problem of excessive litigation is really pretty much a modern problem. Prior to the 1960s, tort law was really a backwater. It was dominated by principles of corrective justice; litigation was minuscule. But ideas began to change, and there came to be a conception that developed that tort law could be turned into an instrument of public policy according to which tort judgments, damage judgments, could be used to internalize costs, the harms the people had suffered, to persons and to the companies that had caused them.

And so the idea was, by internalizing these costs, there would be incentives created to make products safer, to make other services safer, and also to provide a form of insurance for individuals that had suffered some type of harm.

The other advantage, or the thought that there was an advantage, was that this could be done universally. That is, safety regulation, direct safety regulation by agencies, applies only in a very few number of industries. Using tort law as a regulatory mechanism, on the other hand, could be applied to all activities in a society, and so it could become universal. And based upon this conception, courts began to expand liability. They began first in the products liability field but then it expanded to other areas more generally.

Now, I believe that this conception, this idea of internalizing costs, has had some beneficial features, has had some beneficial effects. That is, I think that it did enhance safety and reduce harm over some range. But the problem that has arisen—and it really is a problem that arose several decades ago—is that there are limits to the extent to which tort law and litigation can be effective in increasing safety and reducing harms. But the problem is that this conception of internalizing costs doesn't recognize those limits, and so even though those limits have been exceeded, courts have continued to expand liability in area after area. And when liability is expanded beyond the point where it can really effectively encourage greater safety, where—beyond the point where these harms can practicably be reduced, there are two forms of harmful societal effects that result.

The first is—and it's the one you were talking about, Mr. Secretary—that the cost of litigation has to be passed on in the prices of products and services. Exactly as you say, it's a tax. And it's a tax that every citizen has and every consumer has to pay on every product and service that they buy. Just to give an example—and you mentioned this too—in today's litigation environment, auto manufacturers are basically absolutely liable any time there's a serious accident. They will always be sued, and they will always have to settle the case in some way. And what does that mean? That means that auto prices have to increase. That litigation has no effect on safety. It has no effect on the redesign of auto-

mobiles. We have an Agency, NHTSA, that is charged with monitoring auto safety. The litigation has no effect whatsoever. It simply adds to the costs. And adding to the costs hurts most severely the low-income in the society, because they're the least able to pay these costs and they're the ones that get the least return. Even if they do litigate, the damages they receive are lower than those of other citizens.

Now, in other industries, however, the results are even worse. That is, in some industries, liability has extended—has been extended to such an extent that the affected parties begin to make investments that are unproductive, that are not necessary, in order to try and shield themselves from liability. The medical industry is a good example. Defensive medicine is, in essence, counterproductive, and it's an investment that's made to try and ward off litigation for no useful purpose.

And the consequences of this whole— of the regime that we've created here is a legal system in which litigation is available with respect to every activity of the society. And worse, I think—and Phil Howard will talk about this too—we have been developing a culture in this society, in this country in which it's believed that any conceivable social problem can be solved by litigation. And so we have litigation trying to deal with every conceivable social issue.

Now, what can be done about it? Well, I think the most fundamental reforms have to come from the courts. It's the courts that created this problem, and it has to come from the courts in redefining liability rules. But what that means is it's extremely important to appoint or elect judges who are committed to tort reform. Now, what can—but there are other things that could be done, and there are some things that could be done at the congressional level, and I think the three reforms that the President mentioned are important reforms.

We need class action reform. The rules that were developed—and they were developed in the 1960s—with the thought of controlling class actions are quaint today, and there are many courtrooms in which there are no controls on class actions whatsoever. Now, the "Class Action Fairness Act" takes a step. What it does is push these class actions into the Federal courts where there is going to be some more control. With all respect, it's not a solution. It's going to help. It's a step that I think is a small step, but it's important. It's an important step.

I think Federal reform in particular industries, such as in the medical industry, a reform of medical malpractice, is important too, and it's a promising reform because all of us need doctors and all of us know that we have to control health costs. And all of us know too and can see easily what the harmful effects of expanding liability against needed medical services is. So medical malpractice reform is important as well.

Third—and you mentioned this, Mr. President, and I agree entirely—Congress can attempt to do something about asbestos litigation. Asbestos litigation is an extraordinary phenomenon. I've been studying it the last couple of years. It's just extraordinary. Everybody knows that there are hundreds of thousands of cases that have been filed and that there are millions more that are going to be filed. But I think few know exactly what kinds of cases these are. And let me just give you one example, and it's illustrative of what this problem is.

A short time ago in California, a man recovered 4.5 million against an asbestos—a company that had used asbestos. And the only exposure this man could document, the only time he had ever been exposed to asbestos, was one day when he was the child when his mother and grandfather took him to their church, whose ceiling was being remodeled. That was the entire exposure. One day of asbestos, and he recovers 4.5 million. This asbestos litigation is a vast system of redistribution within the society. And indeed, by the standards of that case, every American is a victim of asbestos. But

I certainly would say this: It is not a sign of a healthy society when every citizen can qualify as a litigant and file suit.

So I think there is an important need for legislation in many different areas to deal with this problem of excessive litigation. These reforms are—the three reforms that the President has talked about are going to be helpful. I think, again, they are small steps, but they're steps in the right direction, and they're steps that it's important to take and that every American should support.

Thank you.

The President. Nice job.

Secretary Evans. Yes, excellent job. Professor, thank you very much, for laying that out.

Speaking about asbestos, our next panelist is somebody who is personally being impacted by asbestos litigation, as are his 18 employees and the families that they're responsible for. And so, Mike, an entrepreneur from Monroe, Louisiana, who runs a company there—why don't you give us your perspective of asbestos litigation as it relates to your personal situation and company.

Mike Carter. Well, I have a business back in Monroe, Louisiana, Monroe Rubber and Gasket. And hopefully, I can be a small voice—or a big voice—for a lot of companies across the country that probably are in the same condition I am.

Probably about 3 years ago, I started receiving lawsuits for asbestos, and today I guess I've been inundated probably with about upwards of 100 now. And we're a small company. We can't legally fight these battles, and what's happened is, over time, some of these are being settled out of court. We've got an insurance carrier that, back at that time, carried our insurance and helped us litigate some of this stuff over time. But the problem is, is this is going to end very soon. We've got about a million dollar cap. And if we have to get involved in a suit in court and we get a verdict handed to us, it's a matter of us locking our doors.

But these things have been coming to us and coming to us, these lawsuits, as it is today. I've been to Washington on a couple of occasions, talking to our Senators from the State. We tried to get something passed within the State and failed to do that. But that's not stopping the lawsuits. We're neither a manufacturer nor an end user. All we've ever done and the thing we're guilty of is buying what we thought over the years was a safe product and re-selling it to an end user customer who asked for the product by name. And now, because all of the bigger corporations and the manufacturers have either gone bankrupt or filed—or gone out of business, now they're going to that next tier of companies, which is people like us, and they're pulling us into this trap.

And we can't afford to fight this. The last couple of times I've been to Washington, I pleaded with the people I thought could get something done, and I told them this may be the last time I'm here. I don't know how long this will go on. I've got probably seven or eight court dockets this next year, and if I have to go to these—that's not to say I'll ever be back again. And hopefully, this is going to be an opportunity for me, like I say, to be just a voice for the small business across America, and then hopefully, we can get something done this year.

It's just—it's unfortunate that I've had to spend hundreds of hours of my time away from the business trying to fight this stuff, trying to get somebody to listen and to make a difference with what we're doing. All we're trying to do is run an honest business, and we've done that for so many years, and it's just a shame that something like this can take all that away from you. And after we're gone, there's really nobody out there to hear you anymore.

And it's just becoming increasingly difficult to do business. And as we go out now and try to buy products from other companies, they tend to see our name on the—I guess the Bradstreet—Dun & Bradstreet, as having all these suits against us. They don't want to open us any lines of credit. We've reduced the amount of employees. We're just not rehiring, is what we're not doing. We've had probably five or six more at one point; we've got about 17 now. And we're trying to grow our business into other States. We can't do that because we just don't know what direction this is going to turn, and we don't want to get more in the pot now than we have. So it's affecting us in a way that we're not able to grow any more. We just—it's just a continuous fight, and we can't do anything. They just keep coming; the lawsuits keep coming.

And we're getting suits from people—the ones we're getting them from are end users, the mills, the chemical plants, the paper industry, that worked in those particular plants back years ago. And these trial lawyers, they'll come, and they'll set up a little hub and have these people come in—and do the advertising prior to them getting there—have them come in, run a quick test on them. If they show anything in their lungs—which any of us could have something on our lung, be it from smoking, be it from pollution, whatever it is—but they all of a sudden qualify to be in the suit.

And as this stuff continues to grow like this, it's—they will couple one or two sick people with 10 or 15 nonsick people and run them through the courts. And you know, in the South, we're known to have very sympathetic juries. And don't get me wrong, I'm very—extremely sympathetic to those individuals that are sick, and I think they need to be taken care of. But the problem is, 90 percent of the people filing suits today are nonsick individuals. They've just been exposed. And I think everybody in this room has been exposed to asbestos if you've ever walked through a school hallway or you've ever been anywhere. I mean, it's just the way it is. But to allow this to happen, those 90 percent of the people, nonsick that are getting this money right now, over the 10 percent of the people are not getting it, and they're the ones that deserve it.

But then again, I think those people should be responsible—that created this. And we, as just an honest-ran business, have not created this problem. And the gaskets and the things I've sold to these plants—we've had people come in and actually gauge us cutting the gasket out of the sheet, and there's no harmful asbestos dust or nothing in the air. But because during that timeframe we had asbestos beside our name, they're coming after us.

Secretary Evans. Mike, thank you very much. I appreciate your story.

The President. Let me make a comment on that. First of all, justice ought to be fair. And those who have hurt ought to have their day in—those who have been hurt ought to have their day in court. But a judicial system run amok is one that makes it really hard for small businesses to stay in business. And I appreciate you sharing your story with us. It's a—frankly, a painful tale to listen to because—what makes it even more painful, there's a lot of people like you.

Most new jobs in America are created by small-business owners. And when you hear a small-business owner talking like that, and he says we got a problem we'd better address now before it's too late— thank you for sharing it with us.

Mr. Carter. Thank you.

Secretary Evans. Yes, it's painful not only for you but the 18 employees and their families that you're responsible for. And we hear your story.

Here's a man that's responsible for about 350,000 employees. And Bob Nardelli of Home Depot, why don't you give everyone kind of your insight as to the lawsuit abuse, the impact on your employees as well as on your company.

Robert L. Nardelli. Well, thanks. First of all, Mr. President, thank you for this opportunity—Secretary Evans—to participate on what I think is probably the most important panel on the high cost of lawsuit abuse in the overall economic conference that, Mr. President, you've called together, the next couple of days.

I think what all of us in this room probably share—I think one of the things that we really want to try to make clear, and I'm going to reinforce in some of my comments what we've already heard—is that we're really not asking to be resolved— or absolved of our responsibility. All we're asking for is fairness, Mr. President, just as you said.

Lawsuit abuse is not a talking point anymore. I think it's a sore point for all of us and one that has to be addressed. Let me just put it in perspective, Mr. Secretary. Our customers, our 350,000 associates, as you've mentioned, and our supplier base, our shareholders of the company that I run and the company I love, are really being hurt every day. They're being hurt every day by a legal system, quite honestly, that's abusive. It's abusive to small businesses and big businesses alike.

I think there's excessive and unreasonable awards each and every day, that our taxpayers are paying more, Americans are being denied, Mr. Secretary, as you said, the essentials of goods and services and, perhaps most importantly, good paying jobs, wages, slowing investment growth, which is really dampening the entrepreneurial spirit of our country.

Let me give you an example. I like to think facts are friendly. The U.S. tort system basically costs every American about $2,400 a year, based on a recent survey that we looked at. Let me put that in Home Depot terms. That would allow every family to buy a kitchen and a complete home of appliances, refrigerators, washers, dryers, range, microwaves, et cetera.

So when I look at this issue, I basically see about three pressure points that I want to talk about today. First, it's the hijacking in broad daylight that the tort system calls the class action lawsuit. The second is the seemingly endless story of excessive awards in asbestos litigation. We just heard Mike talk about that. And third, it is the excessive awards in medical liability suits. Quite honestly, it won't be long before we see a line item on every doctor's bill that's handed out in this country for litigation.

I think what all three of these have in common, unfortunately, is that there's a fair and reasonable solution in hand just waiting for implementation. That's what makes it so maddening, I think, to all of us.

Let me expand. The class-action dilemma is probably a good place to start; it—since it's a trial bar who really reaps the reward. How many of you in this room have received a check for $1.18 in recognition for your participation in a class action suit that you didn't even know you were part of? And what really happens is the millions of dollars go to the lawyers. So is justice really being served, is the question. In fact, I think only 20 cents of each dollar actually goes to the claimants for real economic damages and lost wages and medical expense.

So what you have today is business on one side, and you've got the trial lawyers on the other side. And you have the worst combination of all: You've got deep pockets colliding with shallow principles. [*Laughter*]

Let me make another point, if I can, on this magnet court system. There's a place like Madison County, Illinois, and I think a lot of us know of that. There's been a 5000 percent increase, 5000 percent increase in the number of class action filings since 1998. You know, the issue at hand may have nothing to do with anybody in that county or that community, but the fact is, it hasn't stopped 49 other States from filing into that county.

So we really have, you know, quite honestly, I like to use the term, it's a "speed trap" for American civil litigation. I think that's kind of what we would classify it. So if we move, I think, as George said,

our class actions into the Federal courts, with standard rules from coast to coast, we have a chance at getting things a little more fair, a little closer to fairness. And people who have been hurt will certainly have the ability to get damages and get recovery, but in a much more fair environment, less abusive environment.

So if we continue to leave these issues, as I see it, of national importance to the whims of the greedy, Mr. President, instead of the needy, we're going to continue to have a huge price in this country to pay for abusive litigation.

Let me kind of close out and make a few final comments. That's why I think that this "Class Action Reform Act" is so important to be passed. I think it's great that we've had a lot of bipartisan support. I think what we need is some bipartisan action, Mr. President, as you said in your opening comments. Also, I would take this asbestos litigation—and we would classify it as the gift that just keeps on giving to trial lawyers, 30 years and no end in sight. According to RAND Institute, 70 billion has been spent on asbestos litigation, 200,000 claims have been filed against 8,400 companies since 2002. So we see that continuing to grow.

The "asbestos war," if you will, seems to be waged on—67 American companies have been put into bankruptcy. Now, here's the way I kind of like to look at that, is, while the lawyers are attacking corporate America, it's corporate Americans that are suffering. That's the issue. And we've had 60,000 corporate American jobs eliminated as a result of that.

So let me just conclude, Mr. President, and I really think that something has to be done. There's no better person to do that than you, in this term, in your second term. And we're tickled to death that your exodus was postponed for 4 years, let me say that. [*Laughter*] A great deal has been said about this issue, but I think the time is now. I think the emotion is high, and I'm here, Mr. President, to join you in leading the charge for relief from what I'll call trial lawyer tax.

Thank you for the opportunity.

The President. Good job.

Secretary Evans. Thank you, Bob. Bob, thank you very much. I think you're right. And when you talk about lawyers being on one side and business being on the other, and it's the families that are paying the price, the hard-working Americans. They're the ones caught in the middle. They don't always see it because they don't see the line item. Maybe it's on a medical bill. Maybe it ought to be on a lawnmower someday. What's the additional cost of a lawnmower because of tort costs.

Hilda, thank you so much for being here. Hilda Bankston. She's got a wonderful story to—it's a heartbreaking story to tell, but it's certainly a very moving story about the drugstore that she and her husband built in Fayette, Mississippi.

Hilda Bankston. Yes, sir. Thank you for the opportunity, Mr. Secretary.

My name is Hilda Bankston. I live in Fayette, Mississippi. I came to the United States from Guatemala in 1958. I met my husband, Navy Seaman 1st Class Mitchell Bankston while I was in the Marine Corps. When we got married, we fulfilled our lifetime dream of buying and operating a pharmacy. We worked hard, and my husband built a solid reputation as a caring and honest pharmacist in Fayette.

But one day, lawyers who were looking for—to strike it rich in Jefferson County, shook our world and dreams to their foundation. Bankston Drugstore was named as a defendant in a national mass action lawsuit, putting Jefferson County against two of the biggest manufacturers' drug companies, the manufacturers of Fen-Phen, FDA drug approved for weight loss. Though Mississippi does not allow for class action lawsuits, it does allow for consolidation of lawsuits in mass action.

Since ours was the only drugstore in Jefferson County and had filled prescriptions for Fen-Phen, the plaintiffs' lawyers could keep the case in a place already known for its lawsuit-friendly environment. Overnight, our life's work had gone from serving the public's health to becoming a means to an end for trial lawyers to cash in on money-making class action lawsuits.

Three weeks after being named in the first lawsuit, my husband of 35 years, who was 58 years old and in good health, died of a massive heart attack. Since then, we have been named in more than 100 mass actions against national pharmaceutical companies over a variety of different drugs.

I had to sell the pharmacy, but I still spend countless hours retrieving records for plaintiffs' lawyers and getting dragged into court again and again to testify. Attorneys handling these claims compare their actions to winning the lottery.

The lawsuit frenzy has hurt my family, my community, and the State of Mississippi. The county's reputation has driven liability insurance rates through the roof, and businesses no longer locate there for fear of litigation. No small business should have to endure the nightmare I have experienced. I'm not a lawyer, but I know something is wrong with our legal system when innocent bystanders are abused in the way I was. Please, pass action to reform legislation to help fix our lawsuit system before more small-business owners and their families will get hurt.

Thank you, Mr. President. Thank you, Mr. Secretary.

Secretary Evans. Thank you, Hilda, very, very much.

Philip Howard, partner with Covington & Burling, author of the book "The Death of Common Sense"—Philip will provide an overview of the medical liability explosion in our economy.

Philip K. Howard. Thank you, Mr. Secretary, and I really appreciate the open-mindedness of you and the President in allowing a practicing lawyer to join your panel. [*Laughter*]

We forget sometimes why law is the foundation of freedom, and it is because it's supposed to be reliable and people can count on it in their daily lives. They make some choices in a free country to move forward with their lives, whether it's to make investments or deal with others or volunteer on the playgrounds or in Little League. Law is supposed to be there to affirmatively defend reasonable conduct.

The law in this country is no longer reliable, and the cost of it, I submit, is far greater than anything any of you have talked about today.

And so, let's go to medical liability. We have heard, and you are going to hear again how horrible it is when our best trained professionals, physicians, get driven out of business. One out of seven obstetricians in this country are no longer practicing obstetrics. One out of four people in Pennsylvania last year had to change their doctors because they either quit or moved out of the State. That's because of the direct cost of litigation in this country. But that's only the beginning. The cost of health care is out of control. We can't even talk about containing the cost, but who's going to not order an MRI that somebody demands if you might get sued for $10 million for doing it.

This group, Common Good, that I founded a couple of years ago hired Harris Poll to survey all the doctors. Four out of five said that they admitted to ordering tests that they didn't think were needed. It is now part of the practice to waste money. We can't afford that. We've got 45 million people who don't have insurance. We have—and more every day because small businesses can't afford it. You can't contain costs, you can't provide health care for everybody until you have a solid foundation of justice that people can count on.

Quality—all of the quality experts have joined our coalition because their studies show them that the quality of health care in this country has suffered, and it has suffered because doctors and nurses no longer feel comfortable speaking up. They're afraid they may be taking responsibility.

So, you get—and at the same hospital where you get miracle cures, you'll have some mistake in a prescription, where somebody gets 500 milligrams instead of 5 milligrams. Studies are all—tragedies occur because people are afraid to speak up because they don't trust the system of justice. It's defended on the basis that it holds bad doctors accountable. Well, in fact, it does just the opposite. The current system of law—and it's true with unreliable law, generally—favors whoever is in the wrong.

And so if you're a doctor—if there's a doctor who is no good—and every hospital has this story—you try to fire them. What do they do? They hire a lawyer. They sue, or they threaten to sue. And the typical result is that they're allowed to keep practicing because people don't want to go through the 5 years of litigation for it to happen.

So what is needed here is far more than just—what is needed is to restore reliability. We need the rule of law back again. And I subscribe to everything that George—my friend George Priest said over there and the other panelists as well. We need to look at this not as a problem of just of business or just of doctors; we need to look at it as a problem for the whole society and what it means to live under the rule of law in a free country.

Thank you.

The President. Good job.

Secretary Evans. Thank you. Excellent job, Howard.

Barb Coen, Andy Kazar, both of Generations Women's Health Care out of Norton, Ohio. We certainly appreciate you being here to talk about your story. Barb and Andy will explain how medical liability crisis has caused, one, Barb to quit delivering babies, and the other, Andy, to lose her doctor.

Barb.

Barbara L. Coen. Thank you, Mr. President and Mr. Secretary, for the opportunity to be here today. I appreciate the fact,

Mr. President, you've kept your promise to help physicians take better care of patients by getting rid of the medical liability problem that we have in this country.

I am an obstetrician-gynecologist who can longer call herself an obstetrician. Three years ago, my partner, Dr. Susan Clark, and I started a small practice called Generations Women's Health Care in Norton, Ohio. We had the help of Barberton Citizen's Hospital for 2 years. At the end of 2 years, we were to be independent from the hospital and be operating on our own. At that time, we decided to look for medical liability insurance and were stunned to find that our premiums were going from $60,000 for our current space malpractice to $118,000 for claims-made liability.

At that time, we had 110 pregnant women in the practice and had 3 weeks to tell them they they had to find a new physician. Anyone who has ever had a baby understands the relationship between the obstetrician and that patient is so special. They're trusting you with their most precious possession, the life of that child. And it was awful to call those patients and tell them we couldn't take care of them. I got notes saying, "I promise I won't sue you. Please deliver my baby." It was absolutely heartbreaking. Some people were due the next week. It's an awful system that needs to be reformed.

The things that bother me the most about the medical liability system in this country right now is the Trial Lawyers Association will come out and tell you that medical liability is only 1 to 2 percent of health care costs every year. Well, when health care costs are $1.2 trillion, I think if you told anybody in this room, "Your salary next year is going to only be 1 to 2 percent of the national health care cost," it would be a substantial raise, wouldn't it? I mean, I think we'd all be pretty excited to be getting that.

The other thing that bothers me is 80 percent of frivolous—of lawsuits against physicians get thrown out. What if I was

only right 20 percent of the time? What if that was the standard I was held to? I see 30 patients a day. What if I only got it right on six of them? What's going to happen to the other 24? I think we need to hold these people to a higher standard, the same standard that physicians are held to. And I appreciate the fact that you're all working on reforming the system.

Thank you.

Secretary Evans. Thank you, Barb. Thank you very much. Nice job. Andy?

Aundria D. Kazar. My name is Andy, and thank you, sir, first of all, for having us here and letting us tell our stories. I appreciate it. I'm, as you can't tell, 32 weeks pregnant, and am also the practice manager for Drs. Susan Clark and Barbara Coen. When the decision was made at the end of August of '03 to no longer do obstetrics because looking at it, you know, financially it wasn't feasible, it was like, "Oh, that's okay, I can still see them." They've delivered my other two children, and I think anyone here knows the relationship that you have with your physician— you tell them stuff that you don't tell anyone.

And so with Barb and Sue doing my other two deliveries, it was like, "Oh, we're not going to have any more kids. I'll get through this, no big deal." Well, May, we're having another child. And it came to an issue of now who am I going to have, because the women that I trust more than anything else in the world, who have entrusted in me to run their practice and pay their bills and hire the employees and deal with patients—I can't go back to them for my most important thing that's going to happen to my husband and I.

So we decided that we needed to go find someone else, obviously, since they can't deliver me, even if I sign a piece of paper. We made a choice to see a midwife. And we have a wonderful midwife that we're seeing, but we were informed on Friday that the physician that backs her may not be continuing to practice.

So now, again, at 32 weeks pregnant, we are now on the look for another provider of service. And I don't feel that anyone should have to go through this. I mean, I know most of the physicians in town because of working in medicine for so long. I don't know how the normal, average person who doesn't can go and say, "Okay, how do I pick this doctor?" You know, "Oh gosh, are they going to be here in 6 months?" They're leaving—the physicians are leaving in mass exodus out of Ohio, because it's not cost-effective to run a practice there. And something needs to be done. And I'm asking you, please.

Secretary Evans. Andy, thank you.

The President. It's not the first time she's asked. Can I make a couple—I'm the President.

Secretary Evans. Oh, hold on just a minute. [*Laughter*]

The President. I met these two ladies before in Ohio. Philip said that one in seven doctors are leaving. In certain States, the number is much higher than that, and in certain specialties, the numbers are much higher than that. And just a couple of observations.

When I came to Washington, I thought that medical liability reform was a State issue. I was a Governor and a person who said, "We can do it better at the States than the Federal Government." It turns out, so far the States who have had medical liability reform have done it better than the Federal Government because we haven't done anything yet at the Federal level. Nevertheless, I looked at the impact of the defensive practice of medicine, at the unnecessary tests that doctors prescribe in order to make a defense when they get sued—not if they get sued but when. The odds are they'll be sued, and it costs the Federal budget about 27 billion a year.

And so when you cite the statistics from the trial lawyers, what they don't talk about is the defensive practice of medicine as a cost to society. There is a direct cost to the taxpayers. It's a quantifiable number.

It's a lot at 27 billion a year. And so I decided it's a national issue that requires a national solution.

You know, there's a lot of rhetoric when it comes to medical liability reform about accessibility and affordability of health care. It's a nice mantra. We all should be for accessibility and affordability. And so should Members of the United States Senate who have blocked medical liability reform to date, because these lawsuits are driving really fine, competent people out of the practice of medicine—like Barb— which makes medicine less accessible.

And then you heard not only the cost to our budget but the cost to an individual doctor to practice medicine is passed on to patients, which makes medicine less affordable. We need medical liability reform. This is a vital issue for the quality of life of thousands of people in our country. And I want to thank these two women for joining us again. I met them first in Canton, Ohio. They were just as articulate there as they are here, and their case is, unfortunately, one that's being repeated in many States around this Nation.

And so I told you then and I'm going to tell you again: This is a priority issue for not only me but for a lot of people in the Senate. I say the Senate—it will pass the House. It is being blocked by a few in the United States Senate, and the trial bar has made this the number one issue for them. But it's, as I think you mentioned, Hilda, the notion of a lottery— we cannot have the legal system to be a legal lottery. We want the legal system to be fair and balanced so people can get good health care, so small businesses can afford to stay in business, so we don't hear these horrible stories about someone drug through this class action meatgrinder that has caused her and her—to go out of business.

And so I want to thank you for all coming. I am passionate on the subject because I want America to be the best place in the world for people to find work or to raise their family or to get good health care. And I can assure you all that I intend to make this a priority issue as I stand before Congress, when I give the State of the Union, and as I talk to leaders of the Congress about what I think ought to be done in the upcoming legislative session.

Secretary Evans. Do you want to say anything else? [*Laughter*]

Thank you, Mr. President. You know, I'm also glad that this issue is going to be right at the center of every kitchen table all across America, because it's those Americans that are getting impacted by this in such a serious and harmful way, and they need to be sending the message to Washington, how they also want something done about it.

Well, we've got a few moments here for a couple of questions. Professor, let me come at you, if you don't mind, just for a minute. Can you share with us an example of how plaintiff attorneys are using leverage to threaten companies with settlements? And in addition to that, I notice where you have taught in the past—capitalism, insurance policy, tort law, product liability, but you've added a new course called "economic development." Are we starting to put this together finally in America, how this litigious society that we are in is having a dramatic impact on economic development in our country and job creation in our country?

Mr. Priest. Oh, I think it does have a dramatic impact on economic development in this country. What my course does is look cross-culturally, across countries to see how—to see what the determinants of development are. But I think there is no doubt that it's our litigation system that's dragging our country behind and keeping it from developing even faster.

Now, on your question about tactics that lawyers use, can you give me 2 or 3 hours—[*laughter*]—I could answer that. Actually, the class action is one of the most powerful tactics that trial attorneys use. You know, for all of the class actions that are filed, there are very few that are ever litigated. There are some litigated in the discrimination field, but of mass tort class actions, they're never litigated. They're not even anticipating litigating them when they file them. It's simply such a bludgeon that it's known that if the class is certified, which is a kind of legal technicality that doesn't—purportedly doesn't look at the merits of the case, then the companies that are sued have to settle, because, as Mike has pointed out, they have to settle the case, because otherwise the company's going to go down the drain because of the stakes involved in the case.

So there's this ideal of a class action of representing a wide set of consumers repairing wrongs at a small level over a wide number—it doesn't work that way. It's almost entirely a bludgeon as it's currently being employed by the trial lawyers.

The President. Let me ask you something.

Mr. Priest. Sure.

The President. You said that the pending legislation—I think you referred to it as a "small" step or a "better" step? There was an adjective which, frankly, wasn't a "huge" step. [*Laughter*]

Mr. Priest. It's not a huge step, no, no, no.

The President. All right. Well, let me ask you something: What should Congress do? I mean, for example, in the class action—the bill, as I understand it, takes it from the States—makes it more difficult to keep it in the State court and moves it to the Federal courts, reflecting the interstate nature of the lawsuits, which therefore make it more difficult to achieve these—help me out here.

Mr. Priest. Well, what it does is take it out of the bailiwick of the Madison Counties and the Jefferson, Mississippis, that—where local judges who have close ties with plaintiff attorneys—I don't want to use the word "conspire," but they have a mutually symbiotic relationship—[*laughter*]—in letting these class actions go forward.

The President. Got that part.

Mr. Priest. So it will help to send the case to an Article III judge, who—in the Federal courts that operates differently. But that's not going to solve the problem.

The President. Right. And so you said—help us with some solutions. Here's your chance.

Mr. Priest. The most important solution in class actions—but it's going to take more than the Congress; the courts are going to have to go along with this too—is to have—before certification—to have the courts evaluate whether there's any merit to the class action or not.

The President. Got you.

Mr. Priest. I mean, the problem—even class actions that are certified at the Federal level can operate as bludgeons against the defendants who face them. Now, it's harder to get it certified at the Federal level, and that's the benefit, the step that would be taken by the class action legislation that is currently on the table. But it's only a step. It's not going to solve the entire problem.

And what really has to be done is to get the—what you call junk litigation, the frivolous litigation, the litigation where there's really no merit to the underlying litigation and it wouldn't succeed if it were litigated, but it's too dangerous for the defendant to find that out and to gamble on whether—gamble the entire company on whether its lawyers or the opponent's lawyers are going to be more successful before the judge.

Secretary Evans. Phil, do you want to jump in here?

Mr. Howard. Yes, I do. I mean, judges in America today don't have the idea that part of their job is to actually draw the boundaries of what's a reasonable or excessive claim or what's a frivolous claim or not. People bring a claim, and they act like referees. I was debating the McDon-

ald's hot coffee judge—on Oprah, actually. [*Laughter*] It was really fun. But during a break he said, "You know, your theories are fine, but who am I to judge?" [*Laughter*]

And there's this idea out there that justice is kind of an open season. Well, it's not. The rule of law requires deliberate choices. This is a valid claim; this isn't. This is an excessive claim; this isn't. No one is making those judgments today, and the people who are the victims are all Americans. Every day when they're in the classroom, when they're going through their jobs and they're not saying what they think, or they're not taking the kids out on field trips because they're scared—they're scared because they don't trust the system of justice because the judges aren't doing their job.

Secretary Evans. We just have a few moments left, and I want to come over here to Mike and talk about jobs for just a minute, because you really represent the backbone of the American economy. You're a small business. They generate 70 percent of the new jobs in America. Give us a feel of how this is impacting your ability to create jobs or hire more employees. Can you give us any sense of that?

Mr. Carter. Well, it's impacting us directly because we're not able to grow our business like we would like to grow it. We can't man our business like we would like to man it. And as far as trying to grow into another sector, into another State possibly, and have a business—you don't know if you're setting yourself up for the fall. I mean, it scares you to try to grow anything. And when you get to a point like that, it's tough when you feel like you want to be aggressive, and you've got to just kind of hold back and pull the reins and sit there and wait to see how this stuff is going to unravel. It's just created—and there are so many companies across the United States in the same position that I'm in, but we've just not had anybody hear us yet. And it's just a great opportunity,

Mr. President, to be here and be able to tell you this, and Mr. Secretary as well——

The President. Thanks.

Mr. Carter. ——to get this voice out. And hopefully this year or sometime in the near future, something can be done on this, and get this straightened out to where we can go on and do what we do best, and that's run our businesses and grow our companies. And until that happens, we've got to kind of hold back and wait and see what happens with this because if we end up in one court with one verdict, like I say, we're upwards of 100 different lawsuits right now, and we just got pulled into a class action as well. And we just don't know——

The President. Let me ask George something here.

You've studied the legal systems of different countries compared to the United States?

Mr. Priest. Yes.

The President. Give people a sense for the difference.

Mr. Priest. Oh, well, it's entirely different. Most legal—there's no legal system like the United States. There is no legal system that has anywhere near the magnitude of litigation measured in any terms, per capita, according to gross national product. No, no, no, we're by far the most litigious society that there has ever been.

In Europe, for example, one of our great and growing competitors, litigation is nothing like this. Decisions are made chiefly by judges. They don't have juries, which is a difference. And I'm not saying we ought to get rid of juries. But it is a much more controlled and defined legal system. The numbers of lawsuits are miniscule compared to the United States. And what's happening, of course, is—I mean the Europeans know; the Europeans aren't fools— they're coming to the United States and trying to sue in the United States courts for losses that they have suffered there. And some of our courts are entertaining these lawsuits.

And it's not just the Europeans. We're having lawsuits brought in the United States from citizens all over the world because, again, in terms of litigation, if you're a plaintiff, this is the land of opportunity. [*Laughter*] That isn't what our country has been about, of course.

Secretary Evans. It's really an industry, yes.

The President. I think it's important for people to understand that, particularly people who are going to be deciding the fate of these bills, that we live in a global economy, that we either have a disadvantage or advantage based upon our regulatory system, legal system, capital system. And this is an area, clearly, where we have a disadvantage relative to competitors.

Mr. Priest. Can I add one thing?

The President. Yes.

Mr. Priest. With regard to each of the three reforms that you've talked about, Mr. President, those aspects of the legal system don't exist in Europe or any other place in the developed world. There are no class actions in Europe, England, anywhere. There are—there's no malpractice liability to the extent we have it here against doctors. Typically, there's no lawsuits at all against doctors because they're a different—it's a different form of system. And, third, there's no asbestos litigation. Again, the only asbestos litigation of any magnitude in the world is here in the United States.

Secretary Evans. Let me ask you about Canada, which happens to be our number one trading partner. How would you stack up——

Mr. Priest. Canada—well, Canada is a good—it's a good case, actually. Canada comes from an English legal environment. The jury system doesn't exist over a very wide range. There are some juries, not very many, as in England. There are different sets of procedural rules, such as the loser pays. If you file a lawsuit and you lose the case, then you've got to pay cost to the other side. And so there has been nothing like the litigation explosion that we've seen here over the last three decades in Canada—nothing like it.

Now, Canada is starting to change a little, and they're starting to entertain different forms of justice much like they see in the United States, and that's not to the benefit of Canada, and it's not to the benefit of Canadian growth. But their way—in terms of this litigation explosion, they're not—it's not close. It's not close.

Secretary Evans. Bob, one last statement.

Mr. Nardelli. Let me just make two points if I can. I think this whole issue about corporate America, outsourcing America, that isn't the case at all. And it's not even foreign countries winning jobs. This is about lawyers pushing jobs out of this country. And Mr. President, you said this continuum from supplier to redistribution, I mean, it's just added cost. Everybody has to pile on.

And I—to Mike's point, let me just say, in America today, where corporations would normally reach out and help these corporate Americans who, through no fault of their own, are losing jobs, because this continuum of responsibility or liability, acquisitions aren't being made. People aren't reaching out, because the minute you make one of these acquisitions, you take on that full responsibility. So it's really stagnating entrepreneurship and capital investment.

Secretary Evans. Bob, how does it impact your decision as to where you're going to locate your next plant and the American workers that you would therefore hire?

Mr. Nardelli. Well, we do a pretty rigorous job of identifying family formation per capita—for family income and so forth, Mr. Secretary. So we pretty much have to go where the customers are, in spite of these, what I'll call "swampland" jurisdictional areas. We'll still put a store in there because we're trying to serve our customers. It's a market-customer-back approach. But I would tell you that the cost, all the way up the supply chain, of everything that's been talked about here today just keeps piling on. And while we keep fighting to bring value to our customers, I think they become disadvantaged in this—just to take an example, of $2,400. You know, their standards of living are impacted because of this.

Secretary Evans. Thank you very much. Well, I just thank all of you—audience, everybody else—for coming. I think it gave us a chance to zero in on probably one of the central issues as it relates to economic growth and job creation in this country, not only in the near term but for generations to come. We appreciate all this insight very, very much. And believe me, we're going to work as hard as we can to make sure that Congress understands your message, your thoughts, and we get meaningful tort reform passed in this upcoming session.

Thank you all very much. Appreciate it.

NOTE: The discussion began at 1:32 p.m. at the Ronald Reagan Building and International Trade Center.

Remarks in a Panel Discussion on Financial Challenges for Today and Tomorrow at the White House Conference on the Economy
December 16, 2004

The President. Thank you all. Yes, Joshua. Thank you all for coming. Last night I had the honor of attending a reception for those who have participated in these series of panels, and I had a chance to thank them. I said something I think is true, which is, citizens can actually affect policy in Washington. In other words, I think people who end up writing laws listen to the voices of the people who—and can be affected by citizen participation. So I want to thank you all for doing this.

We're talking about significant issues over the course of these couple of days. We'll talk about an important issue today, which is how do we keep the economy growing, how do we deal with deficits. And I want to thank you all for sharing your wisdom about how to do so.

One thing is for certain: In all we do, we've got to make sure the economy grows. One of the reasons why we have a deficit is because the economy stopped growing. And as you can tell from the previous 4 years, I strongly believe that the role of Government is to create an environment that encourages capital flows and job creation through wise fiscal policy. And as a result of the tax relief we passed, the economy is growing. And one of the things that I know we need to do is to make sure there's certainty in the Tax Code, not only simplification of the Tax Code but certainty in the Tax Code. So I'll be talking to Congress about—that we need to make sure there is permanency in the tax relief we passed so people can plan.

If the deficit is an issue—which it is—therefore, it's going to require some tough choices on the spending side. In other words, the strategy is going to be to grow the economy through reasonable tax policy but to make sure the deficit is dealt with by being wise about how we spend money. That's where Josh comes in. He's the—as the Director of the OMB, he gets to help us decide where the tough choices will be made. I look forward to working with Congress on fiscal restraint, and it's not going to be easy. It turns out appropriators take their titles seriously. [*Laughter*]

Our job is to work with them, which we will, to bring some fiscal restraint—continue to bring fiscal restraint—after all, non-defense discretionary spending—non-

defense, non-homeland discretionary spending has declined from 15 percent in 2001 to less than 1 percent in the appropriations bill I just signed, which is good progress. What I'm saying is we're going to submit a tough budget, and I look forward to working with Congress on the tough budget.

Secondly, I fully recognize and this administration recognizes there—we have a deficit when it comes to entitlement programs, unfunded liabilities. And I want to thank the experts and the folks here who understand that. The first issue is to explain to Congress and the American people the size of the problem—and I suspect Congressman Penny will do that as well as Dr. Roper—and the problems in both Social Security and Medicare.

The issues of baby boomers like us retiring, relative to the number of payers into the system, should say to Congress and the American people, "We have a problem." And the fundamental question that faces Government, are we willing to confront the problem now or pass it on to future Congresses and future generations. I made a declaration to the American people that now is the time to confront Social Security. And so I am looking forward to working with Members of both Chambers and both parties to confront this issue today before it becomes more acute.

And by doing so, we will send a message not only to the American people that we're here for the right reason, but we'll send a message to the financial markets that we recognize we have an issue with both short-term deficits and the long-term deficits of unfunded liabilities to the entitlement programs.

And I want to thank the panelists here for helping to create awareness, which is the first step toward solving a problem. The first step in Washington, if you're interested in helping, is to convince people that there is a problem that needs to be addressed. And once we have achieved that objective, then there will be an interesting dialog about how to solve the problem.

I've got some principles that I've laid out. And first, on Social Security, it's very important for seniors to understand nothing will change. In other words, nobody is going to take away your check. You'll receive that which has been promised. Secondly, I do not believe we ought to be raising payroll taxes to achieve the objective of a sound Social Security system. Thirdly, I believe younger workers ought to be able to take some of their own payroll taxes and set them up in a personal savings account, which will earn a better rate of return, encourage ownership and savings, and provide a new way of, let me just say, reforming, modernizing the system to reflect what many workers are already experiencing in America, the capacity to manage your own asset base that Government cannot take away.

So with those principles in mind, I'm openminded—[*laughter*]—with the Members of Congress. [*Laughter*]

Anyway, thank you all for coming. I'm looking forward to the discussion.

Office of Management and Budget Director Joshua B. Bolten. Mr. President, thank you. Thank you for convening us. It warms my budget heart—[*laughter*]—that you've taken the time to come and talk about fiscal responsibility, which is so important, especially at this time. We've come through some tough years, Mr. President, during your tenure.

As you entered office, the economy was entering recession. We had the attacks of 9/11. We've had the war on terror. We've had corporate scandals that undermined confidence in the business community. All of those together took a great toll on our economy and especially on our budget situation, as you mentioned. And we've started to turn it around. The economy is well out of recession. It's growing strongly, as I think our panelists will talk about. And as a result of that, we are seeing a dramatically improving budget situation.

We originally projected our 2004 deficit to be about 4.5 percent of GDP, and when we got the final numbers just a few weeks ago it was down to 3.6 percent of GDP, a dramatic improvement. Now, that's still too large, but it's headed in the right direction. You mentioned, Mr. President, the 2005 spending bills that you just signed last week. I think those have to be regarded as a fiscal success, because you called on the Congress almost a year ago to pass those spending bills with growth of less than 4 percent overall and especially to keep the non-national-security-related portion of that spending below 1 percent, and they delivered. And that's the bill that you signed just last week. We're working now, Mr. President, as you know, on the 2006 budget. And I'm hopeful that we will keep that momentum of spending restraint going.

What I think we will be able to show, when we present your budget about 6 or 7 weeks from now, is that we are ahead of pace to meet your goal of cutting the deficit in half over the next 5 years. And I think that's very important. And I think our panelists will talk a little bit about why that is.

So let's step back a little bit from the Budget Director's preoccupations and talk more broadly about the economy. Our first panelist is Jim Glassman, who is senior U.S. economist at J.P. Morgan Chase. He's a frequent commentator in the financial press, I think well known in the financial community.

And Jim, let me open it with you and ask you to talk about how the budget situation is related to the economy overall, because that's really what people care about.

James Glassman. All right. Thanks, Josh. Thanks, President Bush, for inviting us here to participate in this discussion. It's a privilege.

The Federal budget is tied very closely to the fortunes of the economy. When the economy is down, revenues are down. When the economy comes back, revenues come back. In the last several years, we've seen that link very closely: The economy slowed down; revenues dried up; the budget deficit widened. It's happened many times before. And in Wall Street, Wall Street understands this link between the economy and the budget, and that's why—we anticipate that these circumstances are going to be temporary, and that's why long-term interest rates today are at the lowest level in our lifetime, even though we have a budget deficit that's widened. And in fact, now, with the economy on the mend, the revenues are coming back, and the budget deficit appears to us to be turning the corner. So I think the prospects are looking quite good for the budgets going in the next several years.

Now, to me, the link between the economy and the budget tells you there's an important message here, and that is: Policies that enhance our growth potential are just as important for our long-run fiscal health as are policies to reform Social Security and health care reform. We know how to do this, because over the last several decades we've been reforming our economy, deregulating many businesses, breaking down the barriers to trade. And it's no surprise that countries all around the world are embracing free market principles. Free markets is the formula that has built the U.S. economy to be the economic powerhouse that it is.

Now, I realize the last several years have been challenging for a lot of folks, and it's hard for folks to step back and appreciate the amazing things that are going on in the U.S. economy when they're struggling with this, with the current circumstances. But I have to tell you, what we are watching around the U.S. economy is quite extraordinary, and I would like to highlight two things in particular that are important features of what's going on in the U.S. economy, because it tells us—that basic message is, it tells us that we're on the right paths, and number two, it tells us how we might build on the policies that are helping to encourage growth.

The first important observation: Productivity. Productivity in the U.S. economy is growing almost 3 times as fast as the experts anticipated several years ago, a decade ago. Now, we know why that's happening: Economic reform has strengthened competition; the competition has unleashed innovation; that innovation is driving down the cost of technology; and businesses are investing in tools that allow us to do our jobs more efficiently. Why that's important? Because most of us believe that what's driving this productivity is information technology.

Now, in my mind, when we're at an extraordinary moment like this with rapid changes in technology, it opens up a lot of frontiers. Who is it that brings that technology and creates growth? Who is it that drives the economy? It's small businesses. That's where the dynamic part of the economy is. And so policies that focus on making the business environment user-friendly for small businesses, like the tax reform, are an important element of building on this productivity performance that's going on and building on the information technology.

Second important aspect of what's going on in the U.S. economy—everybody knows we faced an incredible number of shocks in the last several years. These shocks, which, by the way, destroyed almost half of the stock's market value in a short period of time, for a moment, were potentially as devastating as the shocks that triggered the Great Depression. And yet, the experts tell us the recession we just suffered in the last several years was the mildest recession in modern times. That tells you something about the resilience of the U.S. economy. It tells you that we have a very flexible economy to absorb these kinds of shocks. And I personally think that this is the result of a lot of the reforms that we've been putting in place in the last several decades. It has made us much more resilient.

I find this an even more incredible event because when you think about it, we had very little help around the world. The U.S. economy was carrying most of the load during this time. Japan, the number two economy, was trapped by deflation. Many of our new partners in East Asia have linked to the U.S. economy, and they're depending on their linkage with the U.S. economy to bring—in hopes of a better future. The European region has been very slow-growing. They've been consumed by their own problems. So, frankly, we've been in a very delicate place in the last several years; the U.S. economy was the main engine that was driving this. And yet, we had this incredible performance. I think it's quite important.

Now, when you ask economists to think about the future, where we're likely to go, it's very natural—the natural tendency is to believe that we're going to be slowing down eventually. And we can give you all kinds of reasons why this is going to happen, demographics, productivity slows down. My guess is we would have told you this story 10 years ago, 20 years ago, 100 years ago.

And I think what's quite incredible—I'm, frankly, somewhat skeptical of this vision that we all have, because, if you think about it, we've been growing 3.5 percent to 4 percent per year since the Civil War. If we can match that performance in the next 50 years—and I don't see why that's so hard to do, given the kinds of things we are discovering about our economy and the kinds of benefits we see from all this reform—then I think the fiscal challenge that we see in our mind's eye will be a lot less daunting than is commonly understood.

So, of course, I don't want to say that growth can solve all our problems. It won't. There clearly are challenges on the fiscal side, and it's important that we strengthen the link between personal effort and reward. And that's why it's right this forum should be focusing on Social Security reform and health care reform.

Thank you.

The President. May I say something?

Director Bolten. Mr. President. [*Laughter*]

The President. Thank you. [*Laughter*] Who says my Cabinet does everything I tell them to? [*Laughter*]

You know, it's interesting, you talked about the Great Depression, and if I might toot our horn a little bit, one of my predecessors raised taxes and implemented protectionist policies in the face of an economic downturn, and as a result, there was 10 years of depression. We chose a different path, given a recession. We cut taxes and worked to open up markets. And as you said, the recession was one of the shallowest.

And the reason I bring that up is that wise fiscal policy is vital in order to keep confidence in our markets and economic vitality growing. And that's one of the subjects we'll be talking to Congress about, which is wise fiscal policy. And that is the direct connection between the budget and spending and confidence by people who are willing to risk capital and therefore provide monies necessary to grow our job base.

Director Bolten. Mr. President, let's talk a little bit about how investors see those issues that you and Jim Glassman have just been talking about. Liz Ann Sonders is chief investment strategist to Charles Schwab & Company. She's a regular contributor to TV and print media on the market issues that investors care about.

And Liz Ann, let me just open it to you and ask you, how do investors see those broad macroeconomic issues that Jim was just talking about?

Liz Ann Sonders. Thanks, Josh. Thanks, Mr. President. I do spend a lot of time out on the road talking to individual investors. And I will say that the deficit issue is probably, if not the number one, certainly in the top three questions I get. I think there is a terrific amount of misunderstanding, though, about the nature of deficits, how you get there, how do you get out of a deficit situation, the cause and effect aspects of it, and I'll talk about that in a moment.

And we know that higher deficits are a burden on future taxpayers, but I think what, in particular, the market would like to see is the process by which we go about fixing this problem. And I think the markets are less concerned about the number itself and don't have some grand vision of an immediate surplus but the process by which we solve that problem.

There's a lot of ways to do that. It is all about choice. And certainly, there's one theory that the only way to solve it is to raise taxes. I don't happen to be in that camp, and I would absolutely agree with Jim and certainly with this administration that the policies absolutely have to be progrowth.

And I think the other benefit that we have right now—and Marty Feldstein talked about this yesterday—the difference between the Waco Summit and this conference today as representing a very strong economy right now versus a couple of years ago. And what that allows you to do is have this much stronger platform from which you can make a sometimes tougher decision. And I think that's a very important set of circumstances right now. I would agree with Jim, also, at the bond markets' perception of this, the fact that long-term interest rates are low, so we have at least have that camp of investors telling you that maybe the risks aren't quite high as some of the pessimists might suggest.

Forecasting is also difficult. I know your administration suggested that going beyond 5 years is a tough task, and it is. The market, however, builds itself on making forecasts for the future and oftentimes will develop a consensus about something. And I will say that I think the consensus is one maybe of a little bit—maybe not pessimism but not a lot of optimism from a budget deficit perspective. So, I think the opportunity comes with showing some effort. And you can really turn the psychology

of the market very, very quickly under a circumstance where maybe market participants are actually pleasantly surprised by the turn of events.

Typically, when you look back in history and you look at processes by which we've improved a deficit situation, those that have been accompanied by better economic growth have typically been those where the focus has been on spending restraint, entitlement reform. Those times where we have improved the deficit but it's been in conjunction with weaker economic growth are typically those periods where tax increases have been the process by which we have gotten there.

And I also think that many investors misunderstand the relationship between deficits and interest rates, and there is a theory building now that higher deficits automatically mean higher interest rates. Well, case in point, it's just the most recent experience, but we can even go back to the late nineties—the reason why we went from deficit to surplus was because the economy was so strong. Because the economy was strong, the Federal Reserve was raising interest rates. The reason why we went into deficit was because the economy got weak, which is the reason why the Federal Reserve had to lower interest rates. So you have to understand, again, the cause and effect here.

The path of least resistance, of course, is to make everybody happy, but something has to give. You've all talked about this, the "no free lunch" idea. But I'm just a strong believer that entitlement reform and long-term priorities take precedence right now over short-term fixes, certainly if it required tax increases. And I think that—Mr. President, you talked about having political capital—I'll go back to this idea that we now have economic capital that allows us to not disregard the short-term fixes for the deficit here but really take this opportunity for long-term structural reform.

I'm a big believer in personal accounts, empowering investors. My firm, built by "the Man," Chuck Schwab, is all about empowering individual investors. And I think these long-term adjustments that need to be made, which is really a part of this whole conference, are so important right now. And I think that's absolutely what the market wants to see.

Thanks.

The President. Good job. You're not suggesting that economic forecasts are as reliable as exit polling, are you? [*Laughter*]

Ms. Sonders. I'm not going there. [*Laughter*]

Director Bolten. Mr. President, I'm going to move on. [*Laughter*] I'm glad that Liz Ann raised the distinction, as you did in your opening remarks, between our short-term picture and our long-term picture. Our short-term picture is, indeed, looking a lot better. I think we'll be able to show a very clear path toward your goal of cutting the deficit in half over the next 5 years. But the long-term picture is very challenging.

We're very honored to have with us Tim Penny, who is a professor and co-director of the Hubert Humphrey Institute of Public Affairs. He's also a former Democratic Congressman and an expert on a lot of the long-term issues we're talking about.

And Congressman, let me turn it over to you and ask you to talk a little bit about what are these entitlement programs, and why are they important for our long-term budget picture.

Representative Tim Penny. Well, I think—thanks, Josh, and Mr. President. I think the first thing to note is that the long-term picture is rather bleak, that the status quo is unsustainable. And when you talk about the difference between discretionary and entitlement spending, that tells the story.

Discretionary spending, as you referenced earlier, is the part of the budget that we control annually. It comes out of the general fund. It's education. It's agriculture. It's defense. It's a whole lot of

stuff that we think about as the Government.

But the entitlement programs are those that are on automatic pilot. They're spelled out in law, and the checks go out year in and year out, based on the definitions in law. So if you're a veteran, you're entitled to certain health care benefits under this system. If you're a farmer and you grow certain crops, you're entitled to subsidies. There are some that are means-tested, in terms—we give them to you only if you need them, and that's where our welfare programs and much of our Medicaid spending comes into play. And then there are the non-means-tested entitlement programs, and among those are Medicare for the senior citizens and Social Security for senior citizens. So, they're age-based programs.

And those entitlement programs are the biggest chunk of the Federal budget. I think it's constructive to look back over history. In 1964, all of these entitlement programs plus interest on the debt, which is also a payment we can't avoid, consumed about 33 percent of the Federal budget. By 1984, shortly after I arrived in Congress, they consumed 57 percent of the Federal budget, and today, they consume 61 percent of the Federal budget.

Now, let's look forward a few decades and see where we're going to be with entitlement spending. By the year 2040, just three—well, actually four of these sort of mandatory programs are going to eat up every dime, income taxes, payroll taxes, all other revenues that we collect for the Federal Government. Medicaid, Medicare, Social Security, and interest on the debt will eat up everything. There won't be a dollar left in the budget for anything else by the year 2040. That tells you the long-term picture, and it is bleak. So something has to give. Doing nothing is not an option.

Let's look at Social Security alone. And this is something that my colleague, Mr. Parsons, will speak to in a few minutes. There are huge unfunded liabilities here.

We haven't honestly saved the current Social Security trust fund. Even though extra payroll tax dollars are coming in each year, they're not honestly being set aside for this program. Just by the year 2040, there's about $5 trillion of unfunded liability in that program. Now, we've got to come up with the money somehow to replace those promised dollars, and it's no easy task. And I know that a million, a billion, a trillion sort of gets lost on the average listener, so I always like to explain that if you're looking at a trillion dollars, just imagine spending a dollar every second, and it would take you 32,000 years to spend a trillion dollars. So even in Washington, that's big money. [*Laughter*] Or as we say in farm country, it's not chicken feed. [*Laughter*]

So the other way you can look at this is, your Social Security statement comes in the mail every year, and it gives you some sense of your promised benefits in the Social Security system. But on page two of this statement, there's an interesting asterisk. And the asterisk says, "By about the year 2040, we're not going to be able to pay you all of the benefits that we're promising you. We're going to be about 25 percent short of what we need to pay those benefits." So, what does that mean we would have to do if we wait until the last minute to fix this program? We'd either have to cut benefits dramatically, or we'd have to impose the equivalent of a 50 percent payroll tax increase on workers to get the money into the system to honor the promised benefits.

So huge benefits cuts or a huge tax increase—I don't think that's where we want to go, especially since 80 percent of Americans now pay more in payroll taxes than income taxes. I don't think that's a solution that they're going to applaud. But frankly, it is the kind of solution we're left with if we wait too long to fix the mess. We waited too long 20 years ago. When I first arrived in Congress in 1983, we had a Social Security shortfall. We were borrowing

money out of the Medicare fund to pay monthly Social Security checks. So what did we do, because we were already in a crisis? We cut benefits by delaying cost-of-living adjustments. We cut benefits by raising the retirement age, first to 67 and—66 and ultimately to 67, and we increased payroll taxes significantly during the 1980s. And so we basically said to future workers, based on that legislation in 1983, "You're going to pay more and get less."

I mean, to me, that's the problem with waiting until the last minute to fix this, is that you give people a worse deal. So my view on this is that, for the long term, we can't wait until the crisis hits to address the issue. We have to look at these challenges now and give the next generation a better deal. And if we plan ahead and plan appropriately, we can do that.

So we need to act before it's too late. And then I think we send all the right signals, and we do a better deal for younger workers than sort of the same old, "cut benefits, raise taxes," a solution that's been imposed in the past.

The President. I appreciate that. I think the issue has shifted. I think there are more people now who believe they'll never see a check than people who are worried that they'll have their check taken away. And I think it's important for Congress to understand that. And my attitude is exactly like Congressman's, and that is is that now is the time to deal with it. And it's going to be very important that we reassure our seniors who depend upon Social Security that nothing will change as—and that's been part of the political problem. And any time anybody mentioned the word Social Security, the next thing that followed was, "Yes, he's saying that because he's going to take away your check." And really what we're talking about is the new generation. I appreciate you pointing that out, Tim.

Representative Penny. If I can just add this one point, if we had saved these surpluses honestly, in personal accounts over the last 20 years, we'd be well on the way to fixing this problem by now. And so we may be a little late in getting this done, but it's still important to move in that direction.

The President. Thank you.

Director Bolten. Somebody who's been directly involved in and a leader in trying to formulate a solution for the Social Security problem is Dick Parsons, who is CEO and chairman of Time Warner. And he was Chairman of the President's Commission on Social Security, cochair with the late Senator Patrick Moynihan, whom I know we all miss at this time.

Mr. Parsons, we're grateful that you're here, and I wonder if you would follow on Congressman Penny's remarks and talk a little more specifically about your Commission's work, what problems you saw, what solutions you saw.

Richard D. Parsons. Thank you, Josh, Mr. President. The President said earlier that we have to recognize that we have a problem with Social Security. I think everybody does. And I don't know that they share the urgency that Tim just spoke to and the President just spoke to or really understand the nature of the problem. So, let me take a step back and talk about—approach it from a slightly different angle, talk about what is the problem with the Social Security system, which was created in 1935 as what they call a pay-as-you-go system.

Now, most people here know that, but it was amazing to me, when we had our Social Security Commission, we went all around the country, we had a number of public hearings, and the people would come and say, "Well, what are they doing with my money?" Well, what most people didn't know is they were taking your money that you pay in every day or every week when you get a paycheck, and within a very short period of time it's going out the other door to pay benefits, pay-as-you-go: Money comes in; it goes out to pay benefits.

Now, that system was created at a time when for every person who is eligible to participate—retirees, let's call them—there were 40 people in the workforce. There were 40 people working to support one. It was also created at a time when the average life expectancy for males was such that the average man would not live to see the day that he could qualify for Social Security. So, you would pay in, and the system was built in part—this is not cynical; it's just fact—on the notion that half the people who paid in would never get anything out because they would be dead.

So, where are we today? Today, there are three people in the workforce for everybody who's eligible for Social Security. Today life expectancy is expanded anywhere from 5 to 7 years, depending on gender, since the time the system was created, so that the great majority of the people who participate will live to see benefits. The fastest growing part of our population is 85 and up. So, we have a totally different set of circumstances that we're dealing with. And it's only going to get worse in the sense of—or more distant from the way—the situation that existed when the system was created. By the year 2020, you'll have two people in the workforce for every person eligible to receive benefits. And life expectancies will be even greater then.

So the whole factual basis that underlies this pay-as-you-go system has changed. And what's happened is—Tim mentioned that we have huge underfunded shortfalls in the system. If you—they usually do this on an actuarial basis out 75 years. If you look out 75 years and say, "How much does the system promise it will pay," and you look out 75 years and say, "Under the existing tax scheme, how much money are we going to be able to have to pay it," in current dollars, in actual dollars, it's about an $11 trillion to $12 trillion shortfall over 75 years. If you roll that back into the current dollars and you say, "What would it take today to close that," it's about $4 trillion. So that's the problem.

The problem is, we've promised more than the revenues that we have or that we can look to, to pay. So what's the solution? The traditional solutions are, as Tim just indicated, either we increase the taxes so you get more revenues in or you decrease the benefits so you get less money out. The problem with that is it's a Band-Aid. And given these demographic shifts that we're talking about and that we see, it simply can't last. You might be able to put one more Bandaid on the wound and patch us over for another 5 or 6 years.

But for example, some people say, "Why don't you just lift the wage cap?" Only the first $90,000, as of the beginning of the year, is subject to Social Security taxes. Well, even if you eliminated the wage cap, that only buys you 4, 5, 6 more years, and then you're back in the same problem. We have to face up to the fact that the country is in a different place than it was when this system was created. And the fix needs to be structural. It needs to be fundamental. We need to change the architecture of Social Security.

And what I mean by that is we gradually have to move from a system that is based on a pay-as-you-go basis when you had 40 people in the workforce for every one not, to a system that is on a fund-as-you-go basis, where people can begin to start to fund and put away the money that they will look to in their later years for their support and sustenance.

Now, this is not unprecedented. This is exactly what's happened in the business world. Every corporation in America, mine included, has been engaged over the last 20, 25 years in a migration from pay-as-you-go kind of pension arrangements to funded arrangements. Now, nobody has gotten there—very few have gotten there—probably Charles Schwab has gotten there, in terms of fully funded arrangements right now—but putting the money away now to pay liabilities in the future. This is what private accounts is all about. And that's why the Commission came down recom-

mending, in all of the options that we put forward, private accounts. It's the beginning of shifting from complete pay-as-you-go to starting to fund some of our future liabilities now.

And that's—at the end of the day, while the Government is, in law and in sort of a forced social reality, a different entity than the business community, economically, it's not. Economically, it's going to have to step up to the same reality that business had to step up to, that we can't continue a system that puts a huge burden on future generations that they're not going to be able to meet. We're going to have to start saving and funding our responsibility to ourselves on a current basis.

And that's why we made private accounts as a beginning step—this is not privatization of Social Security. What it really is, is—and again, this isn't unprecedented; this is what business has done—it's beginning to have a hybrid system where you have a floor, a base, below which no one can go that is funded on what they call a "defined benefit" basis—that you will get this money, this minimum amount of money, no matter what. But then you have an ability above that to enhance that on a defined contribution basis—i.e., you put money away now, invest it wisely, and it will come back to you and give you an even better standard of living in a future time.

So that's essentially the nature of the problem and why we thought that it was time for structural, architectural change to Social Security, not just tinkering. You can't—you know, tinkering can't work anymore. The demographics—this was Pat Moynihan's point. He would say, "Demography is your destiny. We just can't do what we've done in the past any longer. We've got to do something different." And this was an idea that made sense.

Director Bolten. Mr. President, you mentioned that for current seniors, this is not a debate for them, that those at or near retirement, this discussion that's going on now should not affect what they've been promised and what they can expect to get. It's the next generations that this is debate—that this debate is about and who should be concerned about it. You mentioned, Mr. President, that a lot of the next generation doesn't think that there will be benefits there for them.

Sandi Jaques is somebody, obviously, from that younger generation. She's a single mom from West Des Moines, Iowa, and she's active in a group called Women for Social Security Choice. And Sandi, let me ask you to speak for the—speak for regular folks and younger regular folks—[laughter]—and tell us why you got involved in this organization, why are you active on Social Security issues.

Sandra Jaques. Sure, Josh. Well, I think the President stated it the best when he said most people in my generation believe that we're more likely to never get a benefit than to have our check taken away from us. I guess it would be nice to get to the point where we had a check, and then we're worried about it being taken away.

So I guess I'm here because I want to make sure that we do get to the point where my generation retires and we do have Social Security around and intact for us. But more importantly, as you mentioned, I have a daughter at home. Her name is Wynter. She's 10 years old, and I want to make sure that she has Social Security when she retires as well.

And I believe that the only way to really get to that point is with personal retirement accounts. They're really the only way to update or modernize Social Security in a real way without tinkering it, as Mr. Parsons talked about and as Congressman Penny did when they were in Congress, because then you only resort to a tax increase or benefit cuts. With personal retirement accounts, you have money in an account, and that money is allowed to grow, and it's that growth that actually will help to fix Social Security for future generations.

Without that, if we wait, we will have to resort to raising payroll taxes or cutting benefits like they did in the eighties. To speak to raising payroll taxes on a personal level, I can't afford a payroll tax increase. In fact, I think I definitely pay more than enough right now, and that's another reason why I support Social Security reform. I am not one of these young people that is willing to give up on that money I'm already paying into the system. I want to see the system fixed so that I can get that money back when I retire.

And as Tim mentioned, by 2040—I actually retire in 2044 unless the retirement age is raised again—but in 2044, we're already at the point if we do nothing, I will get 25 percent less than what I should get under the current system right now. So, that is why this issue is very, very important to me.

But I also want to talk about current seniors right now. My grandma is already retired. My dad actually plans to retire next year and my mom a couple years after that. It's very important to me to make sure that their benefits remain intact for them. They—it's too late for them to invest in a personal retirement account. But because of that we need to make sure that we guarantee their benefits through their retirement, because it's something that they've been relying on. And it's, I think, our duty to make sure that we make sure that happens.

But at the same time, I also think it's the country's duty to make sure that we fix Social Security now so that it's around for when future generations retire because personal accounts are really the only way to give us retirement security in the future for me and, more importantly, my daughter. Because if I am faced with a 25 percent benefit cut when I retire, they may be looking at raising payroll taxes on my daughter and younger generations at that time. So really, that's why this is very important to me, Josh.

The President. You know, one of the interesting visions of personal savings accounts is that Sandi will be able to pass her account on to Wynter as part of Wynter's capacity to retire as well. It is a novel concept, clearly different from the current system where you don't pass anything on.

Ms. Jaques. That's a great point. That's also very important to me because if you do get to the point where you're raising payroll taxes or cutting benefits to make Social Security solvent at that time, you still don't own your benefits. With a personal account, you own the money that's in that account. And I'm sure Wynter will be hoping that I have a very modest retirement so that there is some left for her— [*laughter*]—when I die. But that's a very important aspect as well.

The President. One of the things on personal accounts that listeners must understand is that you cannot take—if a personal account, in fact, exists, you can't take it to the racetrack and hope to really increase the returns. [*Laughter*] It's not there for the lottery.

In other words, there will be reasonable guidelines that already exist in other thrift programs that will enable people to have choice about where they invest their own money, but they're not going to be able to do it in a frivolous fashion, which will mean two things. One, it's more likely there will be a rate of return higher than that which is in the Social Security trust and, secondly, more likely to be actual money available when you retire.

Director Bolten. Mr. President, we've been focused on—principally so far on the retirement security of today's and future seniors. It's also very important that seniors have some security about their health care situation. And so we're privileged to have with us Dr. Bill Roper, who is dean of the School of Medicine at the University of North Carolina in Chapel Hill. And he's also head of the UNC health care system. Dr. Roper also served in a previous Bush administration as—among other things, as the head of the Medicare system. So he knows a lot about this stuff. And let me just ask Dr. Roper to bring us out of the retirement system and into the health care system and tell us what are the challenges we face there and what do they mean for our budget situation.

William Roper. Thanks, Josh. And thank you, Mr. President. I think that is my role on this panel, is to say: Remember health care; remember Medicare. Surely, the focus on Social Security is important, but there's this other large and, indeed, faster growing entitlement program called Medicare. Just a few numbers to make the point: This year, the Medicare program is one-eighth of the entire Federal budget. Ten years from now, that's projected to be one-fifth of the Federal budget. And by 20 years from now, Medicare will be larger than Social Security, so it will be the largest Federal entitlement under current growth rates.

Another point: This year, 2004, the trust fund that our payroll taxes go into that pays for hospital and related benefits in Medicare—more money is going out of that trust fund to pay for current needs right now for seniors and others in the Medicare program than payroll taxes are going into it. So the balance in the trust fund is beginning to go down, and it's projected to be entirely exhausted, under current spending patterns, by the year 2019.

All of that is driven by changing demographics. We're aging as a society, and we have a more expensive health care system. Now, a lot of times we in the health policy community beat up on ourselves, saying that's a terrible thing that we're devoting so much to health care. I think it's important to point out that health care is something that we value tremendously as a society. The ability to spend so much on health care is part of our being a very healthy economy and a society that says we want to invest in our health, especially the health of seniors.

And many good things result from health care. A very careful study a few years ago by some economists showed that if you look carefully and count the costs and count the benefits, that technology—technological advances in health care are worth the cost. The benefits far outweigh the costs. And so we ought to continue to feel good about that, especially those investments in prevention that end up paying rich dividends down the line.

Projections about how much we're going to spend in Medicare is more difficult than the projections for Social Security. Everybody who is going to be a senior citizen 50 years from now has already been born, so we know how to project Social Security numbers. But we don't know what medical advances are going to occur, what new technologies, new treatments, new drugs, whatever, are going to be there. We don't know how much they're going to cost. Some will surely save money; some will cost more. The benefits there are substantial. But the simple point is, the growth rate for Medicare is unsustainable. We just can't devote the entire Federal budget to health care.

So the question becomes, how do we constrain that growth? What do we do about it? And broadly speaking, we face two options. One is to do what Medicare has done over the last several decades. And I was there in the eighties and the nineties, and we put in place what are called administered price systems, which is the Government deciding how much to pay hospitals and how much to pay doctors and running those systems so that we try to restrain the rate of growth to the extent possible.

The alternative, which many people, myself included, and you, sir, are advocating is a much greater reliance on individuals and empowering them to make choices, helping them see the value of investing in preventive behavior, better health for themselves long-term, providing information on who are the quality health care providers so that people can make choices about

where to go for themselves, and moving us towards a time when we will see head-to-head competition between alternatives to Medicare and the traditional Medicare program. The Medicare Modernization Act of last year took us important steps in that direction. But we have much more to do.

In general, we need to see that the philosophy of private accounts applies to Medicare, just as we've been talking about Social Security. So we need to move towards more choices for individuals, more competition in market forces and health care, and more organized, integrated care, especially for people with chronic illnesses, because they're the ones who end up costing so much. If we can intervene early with preventive techniques, as I said, we can lower that rate of growth in spending and end up with a program that we value just as much as the one that we value today, but doesn't cost as much.

The President. Thanks for mentioning the Medicare bill. One of the reasons I was strongly for it was because it did begin to interject a sense of choice for seniors into the marketplace. And secondly, it recognized that medicine has changed. And when you have a kind of a static system where Government makes the decisions, it's hard sometimes to get bureaucracies to adjust to the reality. And the reason why I believe the prescription drug benefit was a vital component of a new and modern Medicare system was so that we could prevent hospital stays, for example, by the judicious use of prescription drugs. And Medicare—I've said this a hundred times around the country—Medicare would pay for hospitalization for a heart attack but wouldn't pay for the prescription drugs the could prevent the heart attack from occurring in the first place, which didn't seem like a very cost-effective way to try to provide good health care.

And the reforms in the modernization program that we've got there has begun, I think, to address the inadequacies of Medicare as a result of decisions being made at the Federal level. But you're right, we've got more to do.

Dr. Roper. A lot more to do, but it's a step in the right direction.

The President. Thank you.

Director Bolten. Mr. President, I want to bring our economists back in now, because we've heard about some daunting challenges in the Social Security system, in the health care system—and let me ask Liz Ann first, what are markets and investors looking to the Federal Government to do at this point?

Ms. Sonders. Let me stay on Social Security reform for a minute. NBC/Wall Street Journal just had an interesting poll out this morning that was reported showing about 50 percent of the surveyed population was not for private accounts. What I found more interesting was a little bit later in the report, there were more questions asked than just that, and there was another more general question asked about, if these same folks had the opportunity to put more money in the stock market, would they? And 80 percent said yes.

So I think this goes back to this idea of a lot of misunderstanding, I think. One of the problems that we're dealing with now is because many in the Wall Street community very much believe in private accounts, there's this natural assumption that it must only be because Wall Street is going to be a huge beneficiary of these private accounts. And certainly what I think makes the most sense and the person for whom I work, Chuck Schwab, thinks makes most sense, is that you are very controlled. As you said, Mr. President, a thrift savings plan kind of program where your options are very limited; it's very index in nature. The fees are structured to be so minimal that in fact even the studies have shown that under any set of proposals Wall Street probably doesn't make any money on this for another 7 or 8 years. So I think there is this natural assumption that if Wall Street is for it, it must mean that they are going to be big financial beneficiaries of it.

I just think, again, it goes back to what I know you're a big supporter of, which is the democratization of the markets for individuals, putting more control in people's hands. And I think this, much like 401(k)s did as we moved from a benefit part of the non-Social Security retirement to more of a contribution style—it's really been one of the reasons why net worth has gone up. And I think Sandy made some wonderful points about the power that that puts in your own hands. And the fact that you can actually pass it on to future generations makes all the sense in the world to me.

Director Bolten. Liz Ann has focused on those personal accounts in particular. Let me ask Dick Parsons to say a little more in detail about what your Commission concluded about personal accounts and what's the right way to do this kind of thing.

Mr. Parsons. Fair enough. The point I was making earlier is that we've got to migrate from an unfunded plan, right, that assumes there are always going to be enough people in the workforce to take care of those who are not, to a funded plan where folks who are out of the workforce have had a chance, over the course of their working lives, to take care of themselves.

Now, that can be done one of two ways. The Government could do it. In other words, the Government could hang on to the money and actually save it instead of spend it, or you could give people the power to do it on their own behalf. And after—we went around the country, we talked to literally scores of people representing scores and scores and scores more. And clearly, I think, the sense of our fellow Americans and our sense as a Commission was, the better of those two choices is to begin to let people fund their own programs so that they, A, had a sense of ownership, of wealth creation. The object ought to be, at the end of the day, to put everybody in America in a place where, while the Government is the place of last resort when everything goes wrong, there are fewer and fewer of them because more and more of us can take care of ourselves, right? So that's the objective; that's the direction the Commission felt that this migration to a funded world should go.

Now, there are lots of examples of how you can do that. Sure, the President just said you don't want to say to everybody, "Well you just—you can hang on to 2 or 3 percent of your money and just put it in your pocket, do what you want with it." There's some people who would go to the track. People aren't ready for that just yet. But there are lots of examples of ways in which this can be done cost effectively. The Federal Thrift Savings Plan which the President referred to and which Liz Ann just talked about is a great example. That is a program that exists for people who work for the Federal Government now, who have this right. And it's been run for a number of years. Its results are superior, particularly compared to the returns you would get leaving that money with the Government. And the beneficiaries of that are the people who participate in that plan.

So we think that there ought to be, at least initially, limitations on how much discretion you have in terms of investing the funds and creating some kind of trust arrangement where there are people who are investment professionals who help structure and manage the costs of the initial options. But clearly, people ought to be able to start to save on their own behalf to create wealth for themselves so that they have that wealth to look to in their later years, as opposed to a Government promise only, which at some point in time is going to have to come up empty because you won't have a big enough revenue base to draw from to satisfy the problems.

Director Bolten. Congressman Penny, the—one of the critiques I've heard about taking some of the steps that Dick Parsons is talking about is that, look, this isn't a problem for decades to come. It may be a problem by the time Sandi retires but certainly not a problem now. Why do we have to wrestle with this tough political issue now? How do you answer that?

Representative Penny. You can pay me now or pay me later. Wasn't there a commercial on TV once where—and the purpose of the commercial was to say that you can spend a little bit now and fix this thing permanently, or you can just pay me forever. It's sort of like a credit card where you can pay it off now and be done with it, or you can pay the minimum payment forever. And that's sort of the choice we're facing here.

And if we choose not to address Social Security reform now and we let this thing drag along until we do get to a point of crisis, then we're going to be cutting and pasting and cutting and pasting, year after year after year, well into the future. It's going to unsettle the markets, because they're going to look at a fiscal house that is not in order. So that's the reason it's important to address this now.

I gave an example during my initial remarks about what did happen when we waited until the crisis was already upon us. We've now got a window of opportunity to address this issue, and I think we ought to take it.

And I do want to just add one point about polling data, because depending upon how you word the question, you get widely disparate responses. But I've seen polling data that indicates that for younger people like Sandi, support for Social Security reform that includes personal accounts is about 80 percent.

The President. That's right.

Representative Penny. So it's huge. And frankly, the support for personal accounts as part of the solution—and it has to be part of a package. And that's what we tried to address in the Commissions: How do you put this all together in order to make it work for the long term, in order to prefund as much of this as we can while retaining a basic safety net under the traditional system. It has got to be a package.

But when you talk about reform that includes personal accounts, it's strongly favored by everyone that currently is ineligible to join the AARP. [*Laughter*]

And it seems to me this is really who we're talking about, because, as you've said, we're not talking about any changes in the near term. People who are eligible to join the AARP today are going to be protected under the traditional system. But we ought to, on a voluntary basis, give people working today the option of pre-funding part of their retirement and then owning that retirement in a way that the Government can't take it away from them.

Director Bolten. Tim, the other thing I've heard—and I'm going to ask Jim Glassman to come in here—the other thing I've heard is, "Well, maybe you do have to deal with the problem now because it just gets harder to deal with it later. But we can deal with this Social Security problem, and in fact, we can deal with most of our fiscal problems by raising taxes." How do you react to that as an economist? And how do you think markets would react to that kind of solution?

Mr. Glassman. Well, I think markets would worry about that. Because markets would worry about what does that do to growth incentives and investment incentives and savings incentives? And I think, in the markets, we're interested in—we know it's a structural problem and we know that if you come up with structural changes and structural reforms, we're going to be much more impressed by that, because we don't need promises to cut this and that. What we need is to see that the reform that's taking place will be changing behavior and will be bringing market discipline into the process. And I think people would be pretty disappointed if the only solution you could think of was raising taxes.

The President. Why do markets matter to the person out there looking for work?

Mr. Glassman. You know, the markets are a barometer of this—this is where we, collectively, think about the future. And the

markets are a taste test of what people, collectively, think is going to be happening in the future. So it's—for one thing, it's a barometer of what we think of your policies. And for another thing, it affects us when we go to take out a mortgage loan. Interest rates go up, because we don't like what's happening, or we're worried about a policy that's not going to be fixing the problem, then we homeowners pay a price.

Director Bolten. Sandi, what—there has been talk about personal accounts here, and you've been around Iowa, I guess, campaigning for them. Tell me a little more specifically what it is that attracts you about them, what you would do with it, and whether you have any concerns about the safety of that, of making an investment in a personal account rather than letting the Government keep your money.

Ms. Jaques. Well, Tim already mentioned earlier, by the time I retire I should expect a 25 percent reduction in what I should expect to get. So I have a hard time thinking that I could do worse in a personal account than I could with the current system. So I guess I'm not worried at all about the security of my investments in a personal account. Because, as others have mentioned, the choices would be limited. I'm not going to be able to invest the money at the racetrack or invest it—you know, open up the paper and pick one stock and cross my fingers and hope that it does well. I will be given limited options for how to invest that in very diversified funds. So I'm not worried one bit that I would do better in a personal account than I would do under the current Social Security program because of the demographic changes that will take place before I retire.

But on a more broader sense, why personal accounts are important to me—it's very important to me because I think they're the only way to give me security in my retirement and my daughter's retirement without raising payroll taxes. I can look at paying the same percentage in payroll taxes until I retire but have a bigger account when I retire, because of the growth that will take place over the next 40 years that I work. I have 40 more years to work before I retire.

And if you raise payroll taxes, you're just going to be asking me to pay more but give me less when I retire. But with a personal account, I can pay the same amount in payroll taxes and use a portion of that to go to—into my personal account, so I can pay the same and get back more. Now, paying the same and getting back more when I retire—I don't know why anyone else is considering any other option than that because I can't think of a better deal than that.

Director Bolten. Dick Parsons.

Mr. Parsons. Yes, just—the other thing that I think people need to consider when Tim talks about a window of time to operate is, the statistics we saw in the Commission say by about the year 2020, you're going to have about two people working for every person retired. But that's still two to one. And where I come from, that's a majority. And you've got to ask yourself, are those two going to let the Congress tax them sort of into oblivion to pay for the one that's not in the workforce. I don't think so.

I think the limit—there is a limit to how much you can tax, which means that either benefits will have to come down—that's inevitable, and people who have been promised something and who believe that they're entitled to something and who've planned on getting it aren't going to get it—or essentially, you sort of monetize it that you just issue more money to pay those promises. But by doing that, a dollar buys 50 cents of what it used to buy, so that we're on a collision or a train wreck course. And Tim is 100 percent right when he says that the time to start to deal with that—you can't fix this problem with no pain, without making some sacrifices. But the time to start making those sacrifices is now, so that they're manageable, so that the markets can have confidence that we're on a course that

is going to avoid the train wreck. Because if we wait until later, it will be a huge train wreck for our whole economy.

Director Bolten. Mr. President, we're reaching the end of our time, and I'm going to do the smart thing and give you the last word. [*Laughter*]

The President. Thank you, Ambassador. [*Laughter*]

I love the idea of people being able to own something. You know, one of the most hopeful statistics in America is the fact that more and more people are owning their own home. It is a—it's just—I met a lot of people on the campaign trail that said, "I just bought my first home." And there's just such joy in their voice, that they were able to say, "This is my home."

I love the fact that more and more people are starting their own business. I think one of the unique things about America is that the entrepreneurial spirit is so strong that people are willing to take risks. People from all walks of life, all income levels are willing to take risks to start their own company. And it's a fantastic experience to meet people who say, "My business is doing well. I'm trying to do the best I can with my business."

And I like the idea of people being able to say, "I'm in charge of my own health care." In other words, "If I make a wise decision about how I live, I end up with more money in my pocket when it comes to a health care savings account." I particularly like the idea of a Social Security system that recognizes the importance and value of ownership. People who own something have a stake in the future of their country, and they have a vital interest in the policies of their Government.

And so I want to thank the panelists who are here for helping to illuminate the need to fix problems but, at the same time, recognizing the inherent optimism about promoting an ownership society in America. And I want to appreciate you helping advance this issue—these issues, so that when we begin the session after the new year, these will be foremost and forefront issues for the Congress to consider. Now is the time to solve problems and not pass them on. This is my message today. It'll be my message to Members of the United States Congress. We have come to Washington to serve, to solve problems and do the hard work so that when it's all said and done, they'll look back and say, well done, you did your job.

Thank you all for coming.

NOTE: The discussion began at 9:32 a.m. at the Ronald Reagan Building and International Trade Center. In her remarks, Ms. Sonders referred to Martin Feldstein, professor, Harvard University.

Remarks at the Closing of the White House Conference on the Economy
December 16, 2004

The President. Thank you all very much. Go ahead and sit down. First, thank you all for participating in this important series of seminars and speeches. I really thank you for sharing your time during what is a busy season. I particularly want to thank those who served on our panels for speaking clearly and helping people understand some of the issues that face our country. You know, it may be just that the panel on tax and regulatory burden could become the beloved holiday tradition here in Washington. [*Laughter*]

I really appreciate the different backgrounds of the people who spoke. We had your entrepreneur. We had your academic. We had your corporate leader. We just had plain old citizens show up. And I really want to thank you. The panels I participated in I thought were great.

It seems like to me there's some common themes that came through the discussions. First, our economy has come through a lot, and it's growing. I think people realize that, and that's positive. And there's a reason why people say it's growing, besides me, and that's because the facts say it's growing. I mean, we're growing at a pretty healthy rate of 4 percent over the last year. New jobs are being added. The manufacturing sector appears to be stronger. After all, they added 86,000 new jobs since January. Housing ownership and housing starts are still very robust and strong. Interest rates and mortgage rates are low. And there's the ingredients for growth available.

And what I also heard was that the good news shouldn't make us complacent. And I'm certainly not. The—one, I understand there's some areas of our country which are still struggling. I saw that firsthand during this past 90 days of active travel. There are some challenges as well that we heard about that we better get after and address now, before it's too late. And I intend to work with Members of the Congress and members here in this audience in the beginning of a new term to address the problems.

And here's how I see some of the problems. One, we need to update our Tax Code. It needs to be easier to understand and more simple. We need to make sure our health care system meets the needs of tomorrow. It's got to be flexible in its application. Consumers have got to have more say in the market. We need to reform our legal systems so the people, on the one hand, can get justice; on the other hand, the justice system doesn't affect the flows of capital.

Members of both parties are going to have to get together to work on this. This is not one of these series of issues that

require a—one-half of the body to participate. These issues are big enough for all
of us to need to work together. These are
compelling national issues that require a
national response.

I will work hard as the President to get
rid of zero-sum politics in Washington that
says, "Old George does fine if this passes,
and my party doesn't." We've got to get
rid of that. It's got to be that we all take
risk and share risk and share in the rewards, so that this notion about one party
benefits over the other if we happen to
do something positive for our Nation no
longer is the pervasive psychology here in
Washington, DC.

And I will remind people here in Washington that now is the time to confront
problems. It's so much easier, in politics
and in policy, to pass big problems on to
future generations. That's an easy pass. But
I didn't come up here to Washington—
and I know a lot of people in my Cabinet
didn't agree to serve—to pass problems on.
I like to confront problems. I like to work
with people so that we can say we left
behind a better America after it's all said
and done. And I don't have that much time
here in Washington, so I'm going to—so
I'm ready to work. And I want to thank
you all for helping us highlight the issues
that we have to work on.

I want to thank the members of my Cabinet. I'm so pleased to be working on these
problems with a fine Secretary of Treasury,
John Snow. You still have a Ph.D., right?
[*Laughter*] In spite of that, I'm confident
we can get a lot done here in Washington.
[*Laughter*]

I want to thank my friend Donnie Evans,
who's served so admirably here in 4 years.
I'm going to miss him when he goes back
to Texas. I appreciate Elaine Chao's service
as the Secretary of Labor, and I'm pleased
she'll be with this administration to work
on these issues. Joshua Bolten, member of
my Cabinet, head of the OMB—thanks for
being here, Josh. Thanks for your good
work. And finally, the Director of my Na-

tional Economic Council, Steve Friedman,
has done a fabulous job. He has decided
to go back into the private sector, for which
I am a little hostile. [*Laughter*] But I appreciate your service, friend. Good job.

One of the tests of leadership at all levels
of government is to confront problems before they become a crisis. And we've heard
about some of the problems. Let me refresh your memories about the problems
we have discussed. First, we've heard a lot
about the growing burden of lawsuits. We
have a litigious society, and it is a problem
that is clear and a problem that we will
confront.

According to a recent study, frivolous litigation has helped drive the total cost of
America's tort system to more than $230
billion a year. That's a lot of lawsuits. The
figure is more than twice the amount
Americans spent on automobiles in 2002.
A study published this summer showed that
tort liability costs for many small businesses
run at about $150,000 a year. That is a
significant burden for a small business to
bear. We believe, and many of you have—
believe that that money can be better
spent, that it's possible to have a justice
system that is fair and balanced, that if
you have a claim, you should be able to
go to an uncluttered court to have your
claim adjudicated.

Tort costs in America are far higher than
any other major industrialized nation. That
is bad news for America. It means that
other nations are able to have a judicial
system that is fair and balanced, and we're
not. It puts us at a competitive disadvantage. And in a world that is more closely
knit, America and American workers cannot
afford to be at a competitive disadvantage.

And lawsuits can just plain ruin somebody's life. Donnie headed a seminar yesterday, and I happened to be there, and
we heard the story of Hilda Bankston. I
think Hilda is probably still here. There
you go. First of all, Hilda was born in Nicaragua—*verdad*?

Hilda Bankston. Guatemala.

The President. Guatemala—see, I wasn't paying very close attention. [*Laughter*] Maybe I'll get the rest of the story right here. [*Laughter*] It's okay to correct the President, just not in front of all the TV cameras. [*Laughter*]

She and her husband, Mitchell, owned a drugstore in Fayette, Mississippi. I've never been to Fayette. I suspect it's one of those classic town squares in a southern city where the pharmacist is an integral part of the community. People come and go; people probably like to hang out and dig the latest gossip and all that—talked about the high school football team. The store got swept up in massive litigation just because it dispensed prescriptions—certain prescriptions. Small pharmacy, main square, Fayette, Mississippi, and a class action lawsuit sucks them into the legal system. She sold the pharmacy 5 years ago. She has spent countless hours being drug into the court system.

Here's what she said. She said, "My husband and I lived the American Dream until we were caught up in what has become an American legal nightmare." She went on to say, "I'm not a lawyer, but to me, something is wrong with our legal system when innocent bystanders are little more than pawns for lawyers seeking to strike it rich."

All Hilda asked for is a fair system, and the system right now isn't fair in this case. And we've got to do something about it. We've got to do something about it to make sure we're competitive. We've got to do something about it to make sure that there's not excessive costs, and we've got to do something about it to make sure people like Hilda don't get hurt by a system that was designed to protect people, not hurt people.

The people in Congress must know that excess litigation is not only a drag on our economy, but it is a constant source of fear and uncertainty—creates fear and uncertainty for people in the business community. To keep the economy growing strong in the future, we have got to lift the burden and reform our legal systems. The Nation needs class action lawsuit reform. The Nation needs to have asbestos legal reform. And this Nation needs medical liability reform. I'm looking forward to working with Congress to get legal reform done quickly in the upcoming legislative session.

We also heard about the rising cost of health care, which restricts access for our families and it makes it harder for employers to cover their workers. This problem is clear, and it will be confronted.

More than half of the uninsured Americans work for small businesses. Small-business owners know their employers well, and the ones I've talked to understand they have an obligation and a duty to help take care of them. But there's some times they're just not able to do so, particularly in the society in which we live today. After all, health care premiums have risen by 83 percent per employee over the last decade.

I just mentioned medical liability reform. There is no doubt in my mind, by passing real, substantive medical liability reform, it will help control the rising costs of health care. I believe small businesses should be allowed to join together to pool risk so they can negotiate for health care contracts just like big companies are able to do. And I'm pleased to report that we're—health savings accounts are beginning to work their way through our markets. After all, I just signed up for one 2 days ago. When it makes it to my level, you know it's going to be widespread these days. [*Laughter*] HSAs are making a difference.

Chris Krupinski owns an art and design studio in Fairfax. I talked to her last night. She's pretty enthusiastic about HSAs. If you didn't hear her talk, you should have. First of all, she is a—she went to insurance agent after insurance agent after insurance agent trying to find something she could afford, and eventually, she was paying $900 a month for insurance for she and her family. Then she heard about health savings accounts, innovative ways for people to cover catastrophic care for their family, at the same time manage the cashflow needs— their own cashflow needs so they can provide primary care as well. Now she pays $340 a month for a high-deductible plan, and she puts $290 a month into her HSA— puts her own money in, money that will earn interest tax-free, money she can take out tax-free, money that's her own money, and she's saving money for her family at the same time. In other words, this innovative plan enables her to control her own destiny when it comes to health care and, at the same time, provides her comfort in knowing that if there is a catastrophe, the health insurance will cover it for she and her family. She's paying less overall. She chooses her own doctor. She saves her own money, and she makes the health care decisions.

Fast-rising medical costs are a drag on this economy, and so there are some things we need to do together: One is expand health savings accounts; two, promote association health care plans—Congress needs to allow small businesses to pool risk; three, pass medical liability reform; four, continue to expand information technology throughout the health care system; five, move generic drugs faster to the market. In all we do, in all we do to reform health care, we've got to make sure the decisions are made by doctors and patients, not by bureaucrats in our Nation's Capital.

A lot of talk in this conference about the Tax Code and Federal regulations and the fact that regulations and the Tax Code cost billions of dollars a year. In the campaign, in the course of the campaign, I said to people, "The Tax Code is a complicated mess." Most people understood what I was talking about. Americans spend about 6 billion hours a year in filling out their tax returns, or at least trying to fill them out. [*Laughter*] The short form takes more than 11 hours to prepare. That's about the same amount of time it took to fill out the long form 10 years ago.

In the last 4 years, we passed major tax relief, and some of it is getting ready to expire. Take, for example, the death tax. It's getting ready to—the relief is getting ready to expire. In other words, the tax— death tax in 2011 is going to come back into being. Frankly, it's going to make estate planning awfully interesting in the year 2010. [*Laughter*] I want you to know that the death tax takes up more than 300 pages of laws and regulations in the current Tax Code. By getting rid of the death tax forever, we have simplified the code by 300 pages.

And not only that, I think it's good public policy. And so does Craig Lang. I met him before. He's a dairy farmer from Brooklyn, Iowa. His family farm has been in the family since 1860. That's when his great-great-grandfather arrived in Iowa. I wonder if he arrived from Brooklyn, New York. That would have been interesting, wouldn't it? [*Laughter*] Kind of the life goes full cycle thing. Anyway, Craig wants his children, of course, to inherit the farm. When we talk about the family farm, one way to make sure the family farm remains a family farm is that family members run the farm after the current generation moves on. He now, in order to deal with the death tax, which I hope expires forever, is now working with a lawyer, a CPA, and an insurance agent, just so he can structure things correctly to keep the farm in his own family.

Here's what he said. He said, "We pay property taxes. We pay income taxes, and we pay sales taxes every year. It's simply not fair to be taxed again for creating wealth." I think Craig has got a lot of dairy farmer wisdom. [*Laughter*] I believe, in order to keep this economy growing, in order to send the right message to people who are willing to risk capital, all the tax relief we passed must be made permanent. And that includes the repeal of the death tax.

But I also understand that in order to deal with budget deficits, which we discussed the morning—this morning, we need to be tough when it comes to Federal spending. I look forward to working with Josh. Josh's job is to develop a budget that meets priorities and shows fiscal restraint. We believe it's possible to do so. As a matter of fact, we not only believe it's possible; we believe it is necessary to do so. It is important for our fellow citizens to know we're willing to prioritize. It's important for the markets to see that we've got enough discipline in Washington, DC, to make hard decisions with the people's money.

I look forward to finishing our budget deliberations inside the White House. Upon completion, Josh will be sharing the news with the Members of Congress and the public. You will see fiscal discipline exercised inside the Oval Office this coming budget cycle.

We understand the effects of paperwork on our administration. Again, Josh is in charge of making sure that this administration culls out, as best as possible, unnecessary regulation.

I used to tease people when I was campaigning. We'd have these small-business forums—I see one of our participants over here—and I would say that I know you fill out paperwork, but what I don't know is whether anybody ever reads it in Washington. [*Laughter*] So one thing for certain is we've got to make sure that the paperwork which is never read is eliminated to the best extent possible, so our small businesses, in particular, and big businesses are able to focus their energies and their time and their capital on job creation.

I'm going to appoint a citizens panel to study the Tax Code and recommend simplification proposals. Secretary Snow will be charged with that effort. The members of the panel will, of course, include tax experts. It will also have people who aren't experts—well, they're experts; they'll be experts in paying tax. [*Laughter*] The idea is to take a look at what's possible, what is necessary, and work with Congress to get something done to simplify the Tax

Code. Now is the time to take on this important task.

In the conference, we heard much about the problems in the education system, which is not fully preparing our citizens for the jobs of the future. There is no doubt in my mind that if we expect to remain competitive in the world, we must educate every child.

Here is a startling statistic: Most new jobs in America are filled by people with at least 2 years of college. That's startling. What makes it even more startling is the fact that only one in four of our students gets there. That's a learning gap that must be closed. Twenty-five of the thirty fastest growing jobs in America require an education beyond high school. The median salary for someone with college experience is 69 percent greater than for someone who never attended college. That's a pretty good selling point, to say to somebody, "We want you to go to college."

Kay Haycock described the challenge—Kati Haycock described the challenge this way here at this forum. She said, "There are a huge number of American kids who are doing all the things they're supposed to do in high school and don't come close to having the skills and knowledge they need to succeed."

We started to change the system here in Washington with the No Child Left Behind Act. I understand that it's created some consternation. And it's created consternation because, in return for increased Federal spending, we finally started asking the question, "Can you read and write and add and subtract?" It's never seemed to me—for some, that's called an unfunded mandate. To me, that's called a necessary mandate, to make sure our children can learn.

All people who understand the importance of accountability are people who need to meet a bottom line, are people who are held accountable for signing up more accounts. Accountability is, in my judgment, crucial to making sure no child is left behind. How can you determine whether or not the curriculum—the reading curriculum you are using is working if you don't measure? How do you know whether or not the teacher training is working if you cannot measure to determine whether or not the pupils of a particular teacher are able to meet certain standards? How do you know how your school is doing relative to the school next door to you? How do you know how your State is doing relative to the State next door to you? How do you know how your children are doing relative to the world? You don't, unless you measure.

Secondly, measuring allows you to correct problems early. And so what we have done here in Washington, DC, is we have said, "In return for extra Federal money, we are going to insist that you measure." Notice I didn't say there would be a Federal test. That removes accountability away from those who are responsible for educating. It says, "You develop a test. You develop accountability standards". We'll norm it around the country in a reasonable way without undermining local authority, but we want to know. We want to know. And where there's success, we'll help you heap praise upon those who deserve success. But where there's failure, we will collectively blow the whistle so that we start getting it right.

There is nothing worse than a school system—and I—you know, I was a Governor at one time, and I remember excuse-laden school systems. And I remember people going, "Oh, my goodness, all of a sudden we're graduating children who can't read." And so we decided to do something about it, and that is get it done early, before it's too late. The No Child Left Behind Act is going to make a significant difference so long as Congress doesn't try to water it down.

And now we need to bring high standards and accountability to our high schools. And we've got to make sure our job train-

ing programs are working, that the job training programs actually train people for the jobs that exist, which means consolidation and flexibility.

I'm a big believer in the community college system in America. I think community colleges can help us address the needs and fill the achievement gap. I know community colleges are market-oriented places of higher education. They're affordable. They're accessible, and they're able to adjust to the demands of the local economy.

Some of the most hopeful moments I've had as President have gone into communities and have seen the curriculum of a community college that has been adjusted to the demands of the local employer base, so that if jobs were lost, for example, in the North Carolina textile industry, there was an active, viable, vibrant community college system able to train workers to become nurses in the health care industry that was creating enormous amounts of jobs. The community college system and higher education, itself, must become— every young person must access our community college system and be prepared to do so—or higher education, in order for our economy to remain competitive as we head into the 21st century.

Social Security reform, entitlement reform is an important topic we discussed today. You know, there's a—we talk about the deficit, and there is a short-term deficit here in Washington, which we're going to close in half over a 5-year period of time. But there is a long-term deficit as well. And that long-term deficit really is the unfunded liabilities of the entitlement programs which make up roughly two-thirds of the United States budget.

One of the things that we heard today from experts was that the Social Security system is safe today but is in serious danger as we head down the road of the 21st century. And this problem has got to be confronted now. And we heard from people that know what they're talking about on this stage this morning, saying that it is a far easier problem to manage today than it will be if we continue postponing solutions.

In 1950, there were 16 workers paying for every beneficiary. Today, there are about three, and when the younger workers retire, there will be only two workers per beneficiary. That should be a warning signal for those of us who are charged with having to confront problems and not pass them on to future Congresses or future generations. The system becomes untenable within a relatively quick period of time. The Social Security system is in the black today but in the long term has $10.4 trillion in unfunded liability. That's trillion with a "T." That means that a 20-year-old worker today is being promised retirement benefits that are 30 percent higher than the system can pay. By the year 2018, Social Security will pay out more in benefits than the Government collects in payroll taxes. And once that line into red has been crossed, the shortfalls will grow larger with each passing year. We have a problem.

Now, some will say, "Well, that's 2018. I'm not going to be around." But I don't think that's what a good public servant thinks—should think. I think somebody who is charged with responsibly representing the people must look at the data that I just described and say, "Now is the time to work together to confront the problem." I understand how Government works. Congressman Penny was talking about the last time we dealt with the Social Security issue in a real earnest way was when there was a crisis.

A lot of Government, if the truth be known, is crisis-oriented management. You know, we wait and wait and wait, and then the crisis is upon us and everybody demands a solution. The problem with that when it comes to a modernization of Social Security is, is that the longer we wait, the more expensive the solution becomes. And so one of my jobs, one of my charges is to explain to Congress as clearly as I can, the crisis is now. You may not feel it. Your constituents may not be overwhelming you with letters demanding a fix now, but the crisis is now. And so why don't we work together to do so. I will also assure Members of Congress that this is an issue on which I campaigned, and I'm still standing. In other words, it's a—[*applause*].

If anybody is interested in the politics of Social Security, here's my view. First of all, what has made Social Security a difficult issue to discuss is that many times when you discuss it, a flier would follow your discussion telling certain people in our society, generally those who have been on Social Security, that they're not going to get their check. I mean, that is fairly typical politics in the past. It really has been. And so people were afraid to address the issue, and I can understand why. If you talk about reforming Social Security, modernizing Social Security, you would get clobbered politically for it.

But that dynamic began to shift recently—recently being, I think the 2000 election. President Clinton, after the '96 election, had a lot of very important panels on the subject. He began to lay the groundwork for substantive, real change. He felt comfortable discussing it. I felt comfortable campaigning on it in two elections. I'll tell you why: Because once you assure the seniors that nothing will change, you're really speaking to people that don't believe they're going to get a check at all, and that is the younger generation coming up. And therefore, the dynamic has shifted. And therefore, there's millions of people wondering whether or not the Government has the courage to do something to make sure a younger generation will have a viable retirement system available when they retire. And that's how I see the issue.

I did talk about some principles during the course of the campaign: One was, nothing will change if you're retired or near retirement; two, I do not believe we should raise payroll taxes to try to fix the system; three, I do believe younger workers ought to be allowed to take some of their own money, some of their own payroll taxes, and, on a voluntary basis, set up a personal savings account, an account that will earn, an account that they manage, an account that earns a better rate of return than the current—that their money earns inside the current Social Security trust, an account that they can pass on from one generation to the next—in other words, it's your asset—and an account the Government can't take away.

I am—one of my strong beliefs is that all public policy, to the extent possible, ought to encourage ownership in America. I believe in owning things. I think it will be healthy for our system for people to own and manage their own retirement account. It will cause them to have a vital stake in public policy. People will ask more questions about fiscal responsibility than ever before. People will want to watch carefully decisions made by Government at all levels if they have a vital stake in watching their portfolio grow.

I will also say again, like we said this morning, that people are not going to be allowed to take their own money for their retirement account and take it to Vegas to shoot dice. [*Laughter*] This is going to be a managed account, similar to the Thrift Savings Plans that we Federal employees have available to us now.

These challenges I've just discussed are important challenges. They are big agenda items, but they should be. I mean, why think little when it comes to making sure America is still the center of excellence in the world? Great economies do not get weak all at once. They're kind of eaten away, you know, year by year, by challenges that people just refuse to meet. Slowly but surely, an economy, a great economy, can be eroded to the point of mediocrity. This Nation must never settle for mediocrity. This Nation must always, always strive for the best and leave behind a better America for our children and our grandchildren.

And so we've got to confront the problems I just talked about, and I want to thank you all for coming to highlight the problems. I assure you that I understand that success in dealing with these problems will require strong cooperation in Washington, that I have a responsibility to reach out to members of both political parties, and I will meet that responsibility. I look forward to working with you all to help make clear that not only are the problems existing but there's reasonable solutions to solve them.

In all we do, we've got to make sure that the American economy is flexible. One of the reasons why we're a great place in the world for people to do business and realize their dreams is because we have a flexible economy. We've got to make sure that we're always a competitive economy, we're willing to accept competition and take competition on. I happen to believe competition makes this a better world rather than a worse world. We've always got to stay on the leading edge of innovation. There's always got to be a proper role between Government and the economy. The role of Government is not to create wealth. The role of Government is to create an environment in which the entrepreneurial spirit is strong and vibrant.

And as I said this morning, when we meet these challenges, we can say to ourselves and perhaps other generations will eventually say about us, "Well done. You did the job you're supposed to do."

Thank you for helping us do our job. God bless. Thank you all.

NOTE: The President spoke at 1:27 p.m. at the Ronald Reagan Building and International Trade Center. In his remarks, he referred to Kati Haycock, director, Education Trust, Washington, DC; and former U.S. Representative Timothy J. Penny, senior fellow, Hubert H. Humphrey Institute of Public Affairs, University of Minnesota. The Office of the Press Secretary also released a Spanish language transcript of these remarks.

Remarks on Signing the Intelligence Reform and Terrorism Prevention Act of 2004
December 17, 2004

Good morning. In a few minutes, I will sign into law the most dramatic reform of our Nation's intelligence capabilities since President Harry S. Truman signed the National Security Act of 1947.

Under this new law, our vast intelligence enterprise will become more unified, coordinated, and effective. It will enable us to better do our duty, which is to protect the American people.

I want to thank the Members of Congress who have worked hard on this legislation. I particularly want to thank the leader of the Senate, Bill Frist, Speaker of the House Denny Hastert, and their counterparts in both bodies. I appreciate Senator Susan Collins from Maine and Senator Joe Lieberman from Connecticut for steering this legislation through the United States Senate. I appreciate Congressman Pete Hoekstra and Congresswoman Jane Harman for their leadership on this important issue as well. Welcome.

I want to thank all the Members of Congress who have joined us today for your good work on this legislation. I appreciate the members of my administration who helped, and that would be Director Porter Goss, Director Bob Mueller, Condi Rice, and Fran Townsend. I particularly want to thank the 9/11 Commission, ably led by Tom Kean and Lee Hamilton. I want to thank the Commission members who are here as well.

I pay my respects and offer our gratitude to the family members of the victims of September the 11th. Thank you for working hard on this issue. Thank you for remembering your loved one.

Nearly six decades ago, our Nation and our allies faced a new—the new world of the cold war and the dangers of a new enemy. To defend the free world from an armed empire bent on conquest, visionary leaders created new institutions such as the NATO Alliance. The NATO Alliance was begun by treaty in this very room. President Truman also implemented a sweeping reorganization of the Federal Government. He established the Department of Defense, the Central Intelligence Agency, and the National Security Council.

America, in this new century, again faces new threats. Instead of massed armies, we face stateless networks. We face killers who hide in our own cities. We must confront deadly technologies. To inflict great harm on our country, America's enemies need to be only right once. Our intelligence and law enforcement professionals in our Government must be right every single time. Our Government is adapting to confront and defeat these threats. We're staying on the offensive against the enemy. We'll take the fight to the terrorists abroad so we do not have to face them here at home.

And here at home, we're strengthening our homeland defenses. We created the Department of Homeland Security. We have made the prevention of terror attacks the highest priority of the Department of Justice and the FBI. We'll continue to work with Congress to make sure they've got the resources necessary to do their jobs. We established the National Counterterrorism Center, where all the available intelligence on terrorist threats is brought together in one place and where joint action against the terrorists is planned.

We have strengthened the security of our Nation's borders and ports of entry and transportation systems. The bill I sign today continues the essential reorganization of our Government. Those charged with protecting America must have the best possible intelligence information, and that information must be closely integrated to form the clearest possible picture of the threats to our country.

A key lesson of September the 11th, 2001, is that America's intelligence agencies must work together as a single, unified enterprise. The Intelligence Reform and Terrorism Prevention Act of 2004 creates the position of Director of National Intelligence, or DNI, to be appointed by the President with the consent of the Senate.

The Director will lead a unified intelligence community and will serve as the principle adviser to the President on intelligence matters. The DNI will have the authority to order the collection of new intelligence to ensure the sharing of information among agencies and to establish common standards for the intelligence community's personnel. It will be the DNI's responsibility to determine the annual budgets for all national intelligence agencies and offices and to direct how these funds are spent. These authorities, vested in a single official who reports directly to me, will make all our intelligence efforts better coordinated, more efficient, and more effective.

The Director of the CIA will report to the DNI. The CIA will retain its core of responsibilities for collecting human intelligence, analyzing intelligence from all sources, and supporting American interests abroad at the direction of the President.

The new law will preserve the existing chain of command and leave all our intelligence agencies, organizations, and offices in their current Departments. Our military commanders will continue to have quick access to the intelligence they need to achieve victory on the battlefield. And the law supports our efforts to ensure greater information sharing among Federal Departments and Agencies and also with appropriate State and local authorities.

The many reforms in this act have a single goal, to ensure that the people in Government responsible for defending America have the best possible information to make the best possible decisions. The men and women of our intelligence community give America their very best every day, and in return, we owe them our full support. As we continue to reform and strengthen the intelligence community, we will do all that is necessary to defend its people and the Nation we serve.

I'm now pleased and honored to sign into law the Intelligence Reform and Terrorism Prevention Act of 2004.

NOTE: The President spoke at 9:59 a.m. at the Andrew W. Mellon Auditorium. In his remarks, he referred to the National Commission on Terrorist Attacks Upon the United States (9/11 Commission). S. 2845, approved December 17, was assigned Public Law No. 108–458. The Office of the Press Secretary also released a Spanish language transcript of these remarks.

Statement on Signing the Intelligence Reform and Terrorism Prevention Act of 2004
December 17, 2004

Today, I have signed into law S. 2845, the "Intelligence Reform and Terrorism Prevention Act of 2004" (the "Act"). The Act strengthens the intelligence and counterterrorism capabilities of the United States, including by appropriate implementation of the recommendations in the Report of the National Commission on Terrorist Attacks Upon the United States, often called the 9/11 Commission.

Many provisions of the Act deal with the conduct of United States intelligence activities and the defense of the Nation, which are two of the most important functions of the Presidency. The executive branch shall construe the Act, including amendments made by the Act, in a manner consistent with the constitutional authority of the President to conduct the Nation's foreign relations, as Commander in Chief of the Armed Forces, and to supervise the unitary executive branch, which encompass the authority to conduct intelligence operations.

The executive branch shall construe provisions in the Act that mandate submission of information to the Congress, entities within or outside the executive branch, or the public, in a manner consistent with the President's constitutional authority to supervise the unitary executive branch and to withhold information that could impair foreign relations, national security, the deliberative processes of the Executive, or the performance of the Executive's constitutional duties. Such provisions include sections 1022, 1061, 3001(f)(4), 5201, 5403(e), and 8403, and sections 101A(f) and 102A(c)(7) of the National Security Act of 1947 as amended by sections 1011 and 1031, section 703(b), 704, and 706(f) of the Public Interest Declassification Act of 2000 as amended by section 1102, section 601 of the Foreign Intelligence Surveillance Act of 1978 as amended by section 6002, section 207 of the Afghan Freedom Support Act of 2002 as amended by section 7104, section 112(b) of title 1, United States Code, as amended by section 7120, and section 878 of the Homeland Security Act as amended by section 7407.

To the extent that provisions of the Act purport to require or regulate submission by executive branch officials of legislative recommendations to the Congress, the executive branch shall construe such provisions in a manner consistent with the President's constitutional authority to supervise the unitary executive branch and to submit for congressional consideration such measures as the President judges necessary and expedient. Such provisions include sections 1094, 1095, 4012(b), 4019, 5201, 6303,

6403, 7119, 7208, 7213, 7502, 7802, 7803, and 8403(c), section 119B(g) of the National Security Act of 1947 as amended by section 1023, and section 44925 of title 49, United States Code, as amended by section 4013. To the extent that provisions of the Act, including section 3001(g) and section 102A(e) of the National Security Act of 1947 as amended by section 1011, purport to require consultation with the Congress as a condition to execution of the law, the executive branch shall construe such provision as calling for, but not mandating, such consultation.

Several provisions of the Act, including Title III and section 7601, purport to regulate access to classified national security information. The Supreme Court of the United States has stated that the President's authority to classify and control access to information bearing on national security flows from the Constitution and does not depend upon a legislative grant of authority. The executive branch shall construe such provisions in a manner consistent with the Constitution's commitment to the President of the executive power, the power to conduct the Nation's foreign affairs, and the authority as Commander in Chief.

The executive branch shall construe as advisory provisions of the Act that purport to regulate the means by which the President obtains recommendations or information from subordinates in the executive branch, as is consistent with the constitutional commitment to the President of authority to supervise the unitary executive branch and to require the opinions of principal officers of executive departments. Such provisions include sections 103A(a), 103B(d), 106, 119(h), and 101A of the National Security Act of 1947, as amended by sections 1011, 1014, 1021, and 1031 of the Act.

The executive branch shall construe as advisory provisions of the Act that purport to require the conduct of negotiations with a foreign government or otherwise direct or burden the President's conduct of foreign relations, including sections 4026, 4072(c)(2), 5301 to the extent it involves foreign diplomats and other foreign officials, 7116, 7204, 7210, 7217, 7303(c), and 7703, and sections 104(d) and 206(d)(1) of the Afghanistan Freedom Support Act as amended by section 7104. Further, the executive branch shall construe section 6(j)(5) of the Export Administration Act of 1979 as amended by section 7102(c) of the Act, to identify a non-exclusive factor for the Secretary of State to consider in his discretion in making determinations under subsection 6(j), as is consistent with the use of the non-exclusive term "include" in the provision and the congressional decision reflected in the text of the statute to afford the President substantial latitude in implementation of the provision.

The executive branch shall construe provisions of the Act that relate to race, ethnicity, or gender in a manner consistent with the requirement that the Federal Government afford equal protection of the laws under the Due Process Clause of the Fifth Amendment to the Constitution.

GEORGE W. BUSH

The White House,
December 17, 2004.

NOTE: S. 2845, approved December 17, was assigned Public Law No. 108–458. An original was not available for verification of the content of this statement.

Letter to Congressional Leaders Transmitting the "U.S. Ocean Action Plan"
December 17, 2004

Dear Mr. Speaker: (Dear Mr. President:)
Consistent with section 4 of the Oceans Act of 2000 (Public Law 106–256; 33 U.S.C. 857–19), I transmit herewith the "U.S. Ocean Action Plan," a report and statement of proposals prepared by the Council on Environmental Quality in response to the Commission on Ocean Policy's final recommendations.

Sincerely,

GEORGE W. BUSH

NOTE: Identical letters were sent to J. Dennis Hastert, Speaker of the House of Representatives, and Richard B. Cheney, President of the Senate.

The President's Radio Address
December 18, 2004

Good morning. This week my administration hosted an important conference on America's economic future. We heard from businessowners, workers, economists, and many other Americans who are seeing hopeful signs throughout our country. Our economy has come through a lot these past 4 years, and now our people are benefiting from solid economic growth, steady gains in new jobs, record homeownership, and rising family incomes.

We also discussed some of the fundamental challenges facing our economy,

from junk lawsuits and burdensome regulation to the complicated Tax Code to the
need for vital reforms in education, health
care, and entitlements. I will work with
members of both political parties to confront these problems so we can keep our
economy flexible, innovative, and competitive, and so America remains the best place
in the world to do business.

Excessive litigation is one of the biggest
obstacles to economic growth. The tort system now costs America's economy more
than $230 billion a year, and no other
country faces a greater burden from junk
lawsuits. Our litigious society deters job
creation and consumes billions of dollars
that could be better spent on investment
and expansion. Frivolous lawsuits put
American workers at a competitive disadvantage in the global economy and have
a devastating impact on the medical community. When Congress convenes next
year, the House and Senate need to pass
sound reforms on our medical liability,
class-action, and asbestos litigation systems.

Another challenge in our economy is the
rising cost of health care. More than a half
of all uninsured Americans are small-business employees and their families. And
while many businessowners want to provide
health care for their workers, they just can't
afford the high cost. To help more Americans get care, we need to expand tax-free
health savings accounts, which are already
making a difference for small businesses
and families. We should encourage health
information technology that minimizes error
and controls costs. And Congress must
allow small firms to join together and buy
health insurance at the same discounts big
companies get.

To grow their businesses and create jobs,
small-business owners also need relief from
excessive taxes and regulation. The tax relief we passed has been critical to our economic recovery, and Congress needs to
make that tax relief permanent. We also
need to reform our complicated Tax Code
to encourage investment and growth and

reduce headache for taxpayers. And to promote innovation in hiring, we must lift the
burden of needless Federal regulation on
hard-working entrepreneurs.

As our businesses create advanced, high-
paying jobs, we must ensure that workers
have the education and skills to fill those
jobs. We've made a good start with the
No Child Left Behind Act, which is already
helping students make progress in the early
grades. Now we need to bring high standards and accountability to high schools and
make sure job-training programs prepare
workers for the innovative jobs of the 21st
century.

To help our young people, we must also
fix the long-term problems in the Social
Security system. Workers in their mid-
twenties today will find Social Security
bankrupt when they retire, unless we act
to save it. As we reform and strengthen
the system, we will deliver all the benefits
owed to current and near retirees. We must
not increase payroll taxes, and we must tap
into the power of markets and compound
interest by giving younger workers the option of saving some of their payroll taxes
in a personal investment account, a nest
egg they can call their own, which the government can never take away.

The week's conference provided a good
opportunity to discuss our economic challenges with Americans from many backgrounds and to set the issues clearly before
Congress. I'm open to good ideas from
Democrats and Republicans. I will work
with any who shares our goal of strengthening the economy. But I will not ignore
these challenges and leave them to another
day. We have a duty to the American people to act on these issues, and we will get
results.

Thank you for listening.

NOTE: The address was recorded at 7:44 a.m.
on December 17 in the Cabinet Room at the
White House for broadcast at 10:06 a.m. on
December 18. The transcript was made available by the Office of the Press Secretary on

December 17 but was embargoed for release until the broadcast. The Office of the Press Secretary also released a Spanish language transcript of this address.

The President's News Conference
December 20, 2004

The President. Good morning, and happy holidays to you all. I thought I'd come and answer some of your questions. Before I do so, I've got a statement I'd like to make.

We're nearing the end of a year where— of substantial progress at home and here— and abroad. In 2004, the United States grew in prosperity, enhanced our security, and served the cause of freedom and peace. Our duties continue in the new year. I'm optimistic about achieving results. America's economy is on solid footing, growth is strong, and the Nation's entrepreneurs have generated more than 2 million jobs in this year alone.

There's more we must do to keep this economy flexible, innovative, and competitive in the world. In a time of change, we must reform systems that were created to meet the needs of another era. Soon I will appoint a citizens panel to recommend ways we can transform the outdated Tax Code. I'll work with the new Congress to make health care more accessible and affordable, to reform the legal system, to raise standards of achievement in public schools, especially our high schools, and to fix the Social Security system for our children and our grandchildren.

Early in the year, I will also submit a budget that fits the times. We will provide every tool and resource for our military. We'll protect the homeland, and we'll meet other priorities of the Government. My budget will maintain strict discipline in the spending of tax dollars and keep our commitment to cutting the deficit in half over 5 years.

All of these goals require the energy and dedication of members of both political parties. Working in a spirit of bipartisanship, we will build the foundation of a stronger, more prosperous country. We'll meet our obligations to future generations as we do so.

Our duties to future generations include a sustained effort to protect our country against new dangers. Last week I signed legislation that continues the essential reorganization of our Government by improving the Nation's intelligence operations. Because we acted, our vast intelligence enterprise will be more unified, coordinated, and effective than ever before, and the American people will be more secure as a result.

Our country is also safer because of the historic changes that have come around the world in places like Afghanistan. This year brought the first Presidential election in the 5,000-year history of that country. And the Government of President Hamid Karzai is a steadfast ally in the war on terror. President Karzai and the Afghan people can be certain of America's continued friendship and America's support as they build a secure and hopeful democracy.

In Iraq, a people that endured decades of oppression are also preparing to choose their own leaders. Next month, Iraqis will go to the polls and express their will in free elections. Preparations are underway for an energetic campaign, and the participation is wide and varied. More than 80 parties and coalitions have been formed, and more than 7,000 candidates have registered for the elections. When Iraqis vote on January the 30th, they will elect 275 members to a transitional National Assembly as well as local legislatures throughout the country.

The new National Assembly will be responsible for drafting a constitution for a free Iraq. By next October, the constitution will be submitted to the people for ratification. If it is approved, then, by December, the voters of Iraq will elect a fully democratic constitutional government. My point is, the elections in January are just the beginning of a process, and it's important for the American people to understand that.

As the Iraqi people take these important steps on the path to democracy, the enemies of freedom know exactly what is at stake. They know that a democratic Iraq will be a decisive blow to their ambitions, because free people will never choose to live in tyranny. And so the terrorists will attempt to delay the elections, to intimidate people in their country, to disrupt the democratic process in any way they can. No one can predict every turn in the months ahead, and I certainly don't expect the process to be trouble-free. Yet, I am confident of the result. I'm confident the terrorists will fail, the elections will go forward, and Iraq will be a democracy that reflects the values and traditions of its people.

America and our coalition have a strategy in place to aid the rise of a stable democracy in Iraq. To help the Iraqi Government provide security during the election period, we will increase U.S. troop strength. Coalition forces will continue hunting the terrorists and the insurgents. We will continue training Iraqi security forces so the Iraqi people can eventually take responsibility for their own security.

We have a vital interest in the success of a free Iraq. You see, free societies do not export terror. Free governments respect the aspirations of their citizens and serve their hopes for a better life. Free nations are peaceful nations. And free nations in the heart of the Middle East will show what is possible to others who want to live in a free society.

In Iraq and elsewhere, we've asked a great deal of the men and women of our Armed Forces. Especially during this holiday season, those on duty far from home will be in our thoughts and our prayers. Our people in uniform and our military families are making many sacrifices for our country. They have the gratitude of our whole country.

Now I will be glad to answer some questions. Hunt [Terence Hunt, Associated Press].

Russia-U.S. Relations

Q. Thank you, Mr. President. A month ago in Chile, you asked Vladimir Putin to explain why he has taken actions widely seen as a move away from democracy. What do you think Mr. Putin's intentions are, and do you think that Russia's behavior has chilled relations with the United States?

The President. As you know, Vladimir Putin and I have got a good personal relationship, starting with our meeting in Slovenia. I intend to keep it that way. It's important for Russia and the United States to have the kind of relationship where, if we disagree with decisions, we can do so in a friendly and positive way.

When Vladimir made the decision, for example, on the—whether to elect Governors or appoint Governors, I issued a statement that said in a free society, in a society based upon Western values, we believe in the proper balance of power. I think he took that on and absorbed that in the spirit in which it was offered, the spirit of two people who've grown to appreciate each other and respect each other. I'll continue to work with him in a new term. Obviously, we have some disagreements. He probably has disagreements over some of the decisions I've made. Clearly, one such decision was in Iraq.

But this is a vital and important relationship, and it's a relationship where it's complicated—it's complex, rather than complicated. It's complex because we have joint efforts when it comes to sharing intelligence to fight terrorism. We've got work to do to secure nuclear materials. I look forward to working with the Russians to continue to expand cooperation. I think one of the things we need to do is to give the Russians equal access to our sites, our nuclear storage sites, to see what works and what doesn't work, to build confidence between our two Governments.

Obviously, there's a lot of trade that's taking place between Russia and the West and the United States. And that trade relationship is an important relationship. I told Vladimir that we would work in a new term for—to see if Russia could then be admitted to the WTO. I think that would be a positive step for relations between our two countries. And I'll continue to express my belief that balanced government, the sharing of power amongst government will lead to a—will lead to stability in Russia. And the relationship is an important relationship, and I would call the relationship a good relationship.

Defense Secretary Rumsfeld

Q. Thank you, Mr. President. Several Republican lawmakers recently have criticized Secretary Rumsfeld. What does he need to do to rebuild their trust?

The President. Well, first of all, when I asked the Secretary to stay on as Secretary of Defense, I was very pleased when he said yes. And I asked him to stay on because I understand the nature of the job of the Secretary of Defense, and I believe he's doing a really fine job.

The Secretary of Defense is a complex job. It's complex in times of peace, and it's complex even more so in times of war. And the Secretary has managed this Department during two major battles in the war on terror, Afghanistan and Iraq. And at the same time, he's working to transform our military so it functions better, it's lighter, it's ready to strike on a moment's notice—in other words, that the force structure meets the demands we face in the 21st century.

Not only is he working to transform the nature of the forces, we're working to

transform where our forces are based. As you know, we have recently worked with the South Korean Government, for example, to replace manpower with equipment, to keep the Peninsula secure and the Far East secure but, at the same time, recognizing we have a different series of threats. And he's done a fine job, and I look forward to continuing to work with him.

And I know the Secretary understands the Hill. He's been around in Washington a long period of time, and he will continue to reach out to Members of the Hill, explaining the decisions he's made. And I believe that in a new term, Members of the Senate and the House will recognize what a good job he's doing.

Let's see here. Let's go to the TV personalities. [*Laughter*] Let's start with you, Cochran [John Cochran, ABC News]. David [David Gregory, NBC News], prepare yourself.

Kerik Nomination/Vetting Process/Director of National Intelligence

Q. Any lessons you have learned, sir, from the failed nomination of Bernard Kerik? As you look forward now to pick a new Director of the Homeland Security Department and also as you pick a Director of National Intelligence, any lessons learned in terms of vetting and particularly with the DNI? What sort of qualities are you going to be looking for in that man or that woman that you choose?

The President. Well, first, let me say that I was disappointed that the nomination of Bernard Kerik didn't go forward. In retrospect, he made the right decision to pull his name down. He made the decision. There was a—when the process gets going, our counsel asks a lot of questions and a prospective nominee listens to the questions and answers them and takes a look at what we feel is necessary to be cleared before the FBI check and before the hearings take place on the Hill, and Bernard Kerik, after answering questions and thinking about the questions, decided to pull his name down. I think he would have done a fine job as the Secretary of Homeland Security, and I appreciate his service to our country.

We've vetted a lot of people in this administration. We vetted people in the first. We're vetting people in the second term, and I've got great confidence in our vetting process. And so the lessons learned is, continue to vet and ask good questions and get these candidates, the prospective nominees, to understand what we expect a candidate will face during a background check—FBI background check as well as congressional hearings.

Now, in terms of the NDI—DNI, I'm going to find someone that knows something about intelligence, and capable and honest and ready to do the job. And I will let you know at the appropriate time when I find such a person.

Gregory.

Training Iraqi Forces/Polls

Q. Mr. President, thank you. A year ago we were in this room, almost to the day, and you were heralding the capture of Saddam Hussein and announcing the end of Ba'athists' tyranny in Iraq. A year later, the chairman of the Armed Services Committee in the Senate said, after returning from Iraq, that—talking about Iraqi troops—the raw material is lacking in the willpower and commitment after they receive military training. At the same time, here at home a higher percentage of Americans is less confident of a successful conclusion in Iraq, 48 percent less confident to 41 percent. What's going wrong?

The President. Well, first let me talk about the Iraqi troops. The ultimate success in Iraq is for the Iraqis to secure their country. I recognize that; the American people recognize that. That's the strategy. The strategy is to work to provide security for a political process to go forward. The strategy is to help rebuild Iraq. And the strategy is to train Iraqis so they can fight off the thugs and the killers and the terror-

ists who want to destroy the progress of a free society.

Now, I would call the results mixed in terms of standing up Iraqi units who are willing to fight. There have been some cases where when the heat got on, they left the battlefield. That's unacceptable. Iraq will never secure itself if they have troops that when the heat gets on, they leave the battlefield. I fully understand that. On the other hand, there were some really fine units in Fallujah, for example, in Najaf, that did their duty. And so the—our military trainers, our military leaders have analyzed what worked and what didn't work. And I met with General Abizaid and General Casey in the White House last week. And I think it was before the—I think it was Thursday morning, if I'm not mistaken—I was going to say before the interminable press conference—I mean press party. Anyway. [*Laughter*]

Here's what—first of all, recruiting is strong. The place where the generals told me that we need to do better is to make sure that there is a command structure that connects the soldier to the strategy in a better way, I guess is the best way to describe it. In other words, they've got some generals in place and they've got foot soldiers in place, but the whole command structure necessary to have a viable military is not in place. And so they're going to spend a lot of time and effort on achieving that objective. And so the American people are taking a look at Iraq and wondering whether the Iraqis are eventually able— going to be able to fight off these bombers and killers. And our objective is to give them the tools and the training necessary to do so.

Q. What about that percentage, though, 48 to 41? More Americans losing confidence——

The President. You know, polls change, Dave. Polls go up. Polls go down. I can understand why people—they're looking on your TV screen and seeing indiscriminate bombing where thousands of innocent—or hundreds of innocent Iraqis are getting killed, and they're saying whether or not we're able to achieve the objective. What they don't see are the small businesses starting; 15 of the 18 provinces are relatively stable, where progress is being made; life is better now than it was under Saddam Hussein. And so there is—there are very hopeful signs.

But no question about it, the bombers are having an effect. You know, these people are targeting innocent Iraqis. They're trying to shake the will of the Iraqi people and, frankly, trying to shake the will of the American people. And car bombs that destroy young children or car bombs that indiscriminately bomb in religious sites are effective propaganda tools. But we must meet the objective, which is to help the Iraqis defend themselves and at the same time have a political process to go forward. It's in our long-term interests that we succeed, and I'm confident we will.

I saw an interesting comment today by somebody, I think in the Karbala area or Najaf area, who said, "Look, what they're trying to do"—"they" being the terrorists—"are trying to create sectarian violence." He said, "They're not going to intimidate us from voting. People want to vote. People want to live in a free society." And our job in these tough times is to work and complete our strategy.

Yes, John [John King, Cable News Network], and then John [John Roberts, CBS News].

Q. Mr. President, thank you.

The President. I had to work my way through all the mass medias.

Syria and Iran

Q. You mentioned that meeting with General Abizaid and General Casey. One of their complaints now and a complaint we have heard dating back more than a year ago, even to when combat was underway in Iraq, is what some called meddling, interference from Syria and Iran, people coming across the border, people going

back across the border, sometimes money. Now they say meddling in the political process. What specifically is the problem now, in your view? And there are some who watch this and see a series of complaints from the administration, but they say, "Will there ever be consequences?"

The President. Well, the—yes, I spent some time talking to our generals about whether or not there are former Saddam loyalists in Syria, for example, funneling money to the insurgents. And my attitude is, if there's any question that they're there, we ought to be working with the Syrian Government to prevent them from either sending money and/or support of any kind. We have sent messages to the Syrians in the past, and we will continue to do so. We have tools at our disposal, a variety of tools, ranging from diplomatic tools to economic pressure. Nothing is taken off the table. And when I said the other day that I expect these countries to honor the political process in Iraq without meddling, I meant it. And, hopefully, those governments heard what I said.

John.

Second-Term Agenda/Social Security Reform

Q. Thank you, Mr. President. You've made Social Security reform the top of your domestic agenda for a second term. You've been talking extensively about the benefits of private accounts. But by most estimations, private accounts may leave something for young workers at the end but wouldn't do much to solve the overall financial problem with Social Security. And I'm just wondering, as you're promoting these private accounts, why aren't you talking about some of the tough measures that may have to be taken to preserve the solvency of Social Security, such as increasing the retirement age, cutting benefits, or means testing for Social Security?

The President. Yes, I appreciate that question. First of all, let me put the Social Security issue in proper perspective. It is a very important issue, but it's not the only issue, very important issue we'll be dealing with. I expect the Congress to bring forth meaningful tort reform. I want the legal system reformed in such a way that we are competitive in the world. I'll be talking about the budget, of course. There is a lot of concern in the financial markets about our deficits, short-term and long-term deficits. The long-term deficit, of course, is caused by some of the entitlement programs, the unfunded liabilities inherent in our entitlement programs. I will continue to push on an education agenda. There's no doubt in my mind that the No Child Left Behind Act is meaningful, real, reform that is having real results. And I look forward to strengthening No Child Left Behind. Immigration reform is a very important agenda item as we move forward.

But Social Security as well is a big item. And I campaigned on it, as you're painfully aware, since you had to suffer through many of my speeches. I didn't duck the issue like others have done have in the past. I said this is a vital issue, and we need to work together to solve it. Now, the temptation is going to be, by well-meaning people such as yourself, John, and others here, as we run up to the issue, to get me to negotiate with myself in public, to say, you know, "What's this mean, Mr. President? What's that mean?" I'm not going to do that.

I don't get to write the law. I will propose a solution at the appropriate time, but the law will be written in the Halls of Congress. And I will negotiate with them, with the Members of Congress, and they will want me to start playing my hand: "Will you accept this? Will you not accept that? Why don't you do this hard thing? Why don't you do that?" I fully recognize this is going to be a decision that requires difficult choices, John. Inherent in your question is, do I recognize that? You bet I do. Otherwise, it would have been done.

And so I am—I just want to try to condition you. I'm not doing a very good job,

because the other day in the Oval when the press pool came in, I was asked about this, a series of question on—a question on Social Security with these different aspects to it. And I said, "I'm not going to negotiate with myself," and I will negotiate at the appropriate time with the law writers. And so thank you for trying.

The principles I laid out in the course of the campaign and the principles we laid out at the recent economic summit are still the principles I believe in. And that is, nothing will change for those near our Social Security; payroll—I believe you were the one who asked me about the payroll tax, if I'm not mistaken—will not go up.

And I know there's a big definition about what that means. Well, again, I will repeat, don't bother to ask me. Or you can ask me. I shouldn't—I can't tell you what to ask. It's not the holiday spirit. [*Laughter*] It is all part of trying to get me to set the parameters apart from the Congress, which is not a good way to get substantive reform done.

As to personal accounts, it is, in my judgment, essential to make the system viable in the out years to allow younger workers to earn an interest rate more significant than that which is being earned with their own money now inside the Social Security trust. But the first step in this process is for Members of Congress to realize we have a problem.

And so for a while, I think it's important for me to continue to work with members of both parties to explain the problem. Because if people don't think there's a problem, we can talk about this issue until we're blue in the face, and nothing will get done. And there is a problem. There's a problem because now it requires three workers per retiree to keep Social Security promises. In 2040, it will require two workers per employee to meet the promises. And when the system was set up and designed, I think it was, like, 15 or more workers per employee. That is a problem. The system goes into the red. In other words, there's more money going out than coming in, in 2018. There is an unfunded liability of $11 trillion. And I understand how this works. Many times, legislative bodies will not react unless the crisis is apparent, crisis is upon them. I believe that crisis is.

And so for a period of time, we're going to have to explain to Members of Congress, the crisis is here. It's a lot less painful to act now than if we wait.

Q. Can I ask a followup?

The President. No. [*Laughter*] Otherwise, it will make everybody else jealous, and I don't want that to happen.

Angle [Jim Angle, FOX News].

Personal Retirement Accounts

Q. Thank you, sir. Mr. President, on that point, there is already a lot of opposition to the idea of personal accounts, some of it fairly entrenched among the Democrats. I wonder what your strategy is to try to convince them to your view? And specifically, they say that personal accounts would destroy Social Security. You argue that it would help save the system. Can you explain how?

The President. I will try to explain how without negotiating with myself. It's a very tricky way to get me to play my cards. I understand that. I think what you—people ought to do is to go look at the Moynihan Commission report. The other day, in the discussions at the economic summit, we discussed the role of a personal account, in other words, what—how a personal account would work. And that is, the people could set aside a negotiated amount of their own money in an account that would be managed by that person, but under serious guidelines. As I said, you can't use the money to go to the lottery or take it to the track. There would be—it's like the— some of the guidelines that some of the Thrift Savings Plans right here in the Federal Government.

And the younger worker would gain a rate of return which would be more substantial than the rate of return of the money now being earned in the Social Security trust. And over time, that rate of return would enable that person to be— have an account that would make up for the deficiencies in the current system. In other words, the current system can't sustain that which has been promised to the workers. That's what's important for people to understand, and the higher rate of return on the negotiated amount of money set aside would enable that worker to more likely get that which was promised.

Now, the benefits, as far as I'm concerned, of the personal savings account, is, one, it encourages an ownership society. One of the philosophies of this government is, if you own something, it is—it makes the country a better—if more people own something, the country is better off. You have a stake in the future of the country if you own something. Secondly, it's capital available for—when people save, it provides capital for entrepreneurial growth and entrepreneurial expansion, which is positive. In other words, it enhances savings. And thirdly, it means that people can take their own assets, their own retirement assets, and pass them on, if they so choose, to their family members, for example. That's positive. That's a step.

The Social Security system was designed in a—obviously, in an era that is long gone, and it has worked in many ways. It's now in a precarious position, and the question is whether or not our society has got the will necessary to adjust from a defined benefit plan to a defined contribution plan. And I believe the will will be there, but I'm under no illusions. It's going to take hard work. It's going to take hard work to convince a lot of people, some of whom would rather not deal with the issue—why deal with the issue unless there is a crisis?—and some of whom have got preconceived notions about the benefits of what may be possible.

Okay, let's get away from the media. Yes, Carl [Carl Cannon, National Journal], thank you. I accused Carl of trying to look like Johnny Damon. [*Laughter*]

Timetable for Iraq/Training Iraqi Forces

Q. Mr. President, it's—140,000 Americans are spending this Christmas in Iraq, as you know, some of them their second Christmas there. Now, you outlined your vision for Iraq, both in your statement and in response to David Gregory. My question is, how long do you think it will take that vision to be realized, and how long will those troops be there?

The President. No, it's a very legitimate question, Carl. And I get asked that by family members I meet with, and people say, "How long do you think it will take?" And my answer is, you know, we would like to achieve our objective as quickly as possible. It is our commander—again—I can—the best people that reflect the answer to that question are people like Abizaid and Casey, who are right there on the ground. And they are optimistic and positive about the gains we're making.

Again, I repeat, we're under no illusions that this Iraqi force is not ready to fight. They're—in toto, there are units that are, and that they believe they'll have a command structure stood up pretty quickly, that the training is intense, that the recruitment is good, the equipping of troops is taking place. So they're optimistic that as soon as possible it can be achieved. But it's—I'm also wise enough not to give you a specific moment in time because, sure enough, if we don't achieve it, I'll spend the next press conference I have with you answering why we didn't achieve this specific moment.

Sanger [David Sanger, New York Times].

North Korea/Iran

Q. Thank you, Mr. President. You spent a good deal of time before the Iraq war, some in this room, explaining to us why the combination of Saddam Hussein as a dictator and the weapons that you thought at the time he had assembled made a case for regime change. In the case of North Korea and Iran, you have not declared yourself on the question of regime change, though North Korea, your intelligence agencies believe, may have added six or seven nuclear weapons in the past 2 years. And Iran seems to have a covert program, or at least your government believes it does. Where do you stand on regime change? And how would it be accomplished?

The President. I'll tell you where I stand, David. I stand on the—continuing the six-party talks with North Korea to convince Kim Chong-il to give up his weapons systems. As you might remember, our countries tried a strategy of bilateral relationships in hopes that we can convince Kim Chong-il. It didn't work. As a matter of fact, when we thought we had in good faith agreed to an agreement—I mean, agreed to a plan that would work, he, himself, was enriching uranium, or saw to it that the uranium was enriched. In other words, he broke the agreement.

I think it's an important lesson for this administration to learn and that the best way to convince him to disarm is to get others to weigh in as well—the Iranian situation as well. We're relying upon others, because we've sanctioned ourselves out of influence with Iran, to send a message that we expect them to—in other words, we don't have much leverage with the Iranians right now, and we expect them to listen to those voices, and we're a part of the universal acclaim.

I believe that—and so, therefore, we're dealing—this is how we're dealing with the issue. And it's much different between the situation in Iraq and Iran because of this. Diplomacy had failed for 13 years in Iraq. As you might remember—and I'm sure you do—all the U.N. resolutions that were passed out of the United Nations, totally ignored by Saddam Hussein.

And so diplomacy must be the first choice and always the first choice of an administration trying to solve an issue of, in this case, nuclear armament. And we'll continue to press on diplomacy.

Now, in terms of my vision for the future of the world, I believe everybody ought to be free. I believe the world is more peaceful as liberty takes hold. Free societies don't fight each other. And so we'll work to continue to send a message to reformers around the world that America stands strong in our belief that freedom is universal, and that we hope at some point in time, everybody is free.

Yes.

Federal Spending/Budget Process

Q. Thank you, Mr. President. You talked earlier about the importance of spending discipline in the Federal budget, but you went your entire first term without vetoing a single spending bill, even though you had a lot of tough talk on that issue in your first term. And I'm wondering, this time around, what are you going to do to convince Congress you really are serious about cutting Federal spending? Will you veto spending bills this time?

The President. Here's what happened. I submitted a budget, and Congress hit our number, which is a tribute to Senator Hastert and—I mean, Senator Frist and Speaker Hastert's leadership. In other words, we worked together. We came up with a budget, like we're doing now. We went through the process of asking our agencies, "Can you live with this," and, "If you don't like it, counter-propose."

And then we came up with a budget that we thought was necessary, and we took it to the leadership, and they accepted the budget. And they passed bills that met our budget targets. And so how could you veto a series of appropriations bills if the Congress has done what you've asked them to do?

Now, I think the President ought to have a line-item veto, because within the appropriations bills there may be some differences of opinion on how the money is being spent. But overall, they have done

a superb job of working with the White House to meet the budget numbers we submitted, and so the appropriations bill I just signed was one that conformed with the budget agreement we had with the United States Congress. And I really do appreciate the leadership not only of Speaker Hastert and Senator Frist but also the budget committee chairman. I talked to Senator Gregg this morning, as a matter of fact, who's running—he'll be heading the budget committee in the United States Senate.

And we're working very closely with Members of Congress as we develop the budget. And it's going to be a tough budget, no question about it, and it's a budget that I think will send the right signal to the financial markets and to those concerned about our short-term deficits. As well, we've got to deal with the long-term deficit issues. That's the issue that John Roberts talked about, which is the unfunded liabilities when it comes to some of the entitlement programs.

Ed [Ed Chen, Los Angeles Times].

Social Security Reform

Q. Good morning, Mr. President. I'd like to ask you, on Social Security, you said that you don't like to come to the table with—having negotiated with yourself. Yet, you have ruled out tax cuts and no cuts in benefits for the retired and the near-retired. I wonder how you square that statement. And also, what do you—in your mind, what is near-retired?

The President. Yes, well, that's going to fall in the negotiating with myself category. But look, it was very important for me in the course of the campaign, and it's going to be very important for all of us who feel like we have a problem that needs to be fixed, to assure Americans who are on Social Security that nothing will change.

Part of the problem, politically, with this issue in the past, Ed, as you know, is the minute you bring up Social Security reform, people go running around the country saying, "Really what he says is he's going to take away your check," or, "That which you have become dependent upon will no longer be available for you to live on." And so, therefore, part of setting the stage or laying the groundwork for there to be a successful reform effort is assuring our seniors that they just don't have to worry about anything. When they hear the debate that is taking place on the floor of the Congress, they just need to know that the check they're getting won't change, that promises will be met, that, you know, if there is to be an increase in their check, they'll get their check. In other words, the formula that has enabled them to the—to a certain extent—the formula they're relying on won't change, let me put it that way. I was trying to be really brilliant.

Now, what was the other part of your question?

Q. If I could just follow up. Why——
The President. Is this a followup or part of the question?

Q. You asked, though. [*Laughter*]
The President. Okay, yes, you're right. [*Laughter*]

Medicare Reform

Q. Why did you choose to take on Social Security and not Medicare, which some people believe is a worse problem?
The President. Well, I appreciate that, Ed, but we did take on Medicare. And it was the Medicare reform bill that really began to change Medicare as we knew it. In other words, it introduced market forces for the first time. It provided a prescription drug coverage for our seniors, which I believe will be cost effective. I recognize some of the actuaries haven't come to that conclusion yet. But the logic is irrefutable, it seems like to me, that if the Government is willing to pay $100,000 for heart surgery but not a dime for the prescription drug that would prevent the heart surgery from happening in the first place, aren't we saving money when we provide the money

necessary to prevent the surgery from being needed in the first place? I think we are. That's one of the differences of opinion that I had with the actuaries.

I readily concede I'm out of my lane. I'm not pretending to be an actuary. But I know that we made progress in modernizing the Medicare system. And there's more work to be done, no question about it. But as you know, it's a 3-year phase-in on Medicare—or 2-year phase-in from now. And in 2006, the prescription drug coverage will become available for our seniors. And I look forward to working with Members of Congress to make sure the Medicare system is solvent in the long run.

Let's have somebody new. Mike [Mike Allen, Washington Post], you want to—no, you're not new. [*Laughter*] That is a cheap shot. Go ahead—that is generous.

Immigration Reform

Q. Thank you. [*Laughter*] Yes, Mr. President——
The President. Yes, Mike, welcome.

Q. ——since early in your first term you've talked about immigration reform, but yet, people in your own party on the Hill seem opposed to this idea. And you've gotten opposition even on the other side. Do you plan to expend some of your political capital this time to see this through?
The President. Yes, I appreciate that—well, first of all, welcome. I'd like to welcome all the new faces—some prettier than others, I might add. [*Laughter*]

Yes, I intend to work with Members of Congress to get something done. I think this is an issue that will make it easier for us to enforce our borders. And I believe it's an issue that is—that will show the—if when we get it right, the compassionate heart of American people. And no question, it's a tough issue, just like some of the other issues we're taking on. But my job is to confront tough issues and to ask Congress to work together to confront tough issues.

Now let me talk about the immigration issue. First, we want our Border Patrol agents chasing crooks and thieves and drugrunners and terrorists, not good-hearted people who are coming here to work. And therefore, it makes sense to allow the good-hearted people who are coming here to do jobs that Americans won't do a legal way to do so. And providing that legal avenue, it takes the pressure off the border.

Now, we need to make sure the border is modern, and we need to upgrade our Border Patrol. But if we expect the Border Patrol to be able to enforce a long border, particularly in the south—and the north, for that matter—we ought to have a system that recognizes people are coming here to do jobs that Americans will not do. And there ought to be a legal way for them to do so. To me, that is—and not only that, but once the person is here, if he or she feels like he or she needs to go back to see her family, to the country of origin, they should be able to do so within a prescribed—in other words, and the card, the permit would last for a prescribed period of time. It's a compassionate way to treat people who come to our country. It recognizes the reality of the world in which we live. There are some people—there are some jobs in America that Americans won't do and others are willing to do.

Now, one of the important aspects of my vision is that this is not automatic citizenship. The American people must understand that, that if somebody who is here working wants to be a citizen, they can get in line like those who have been here legally and have been working to become a citizen in a legal manner.

And this is a very important issue, and it's a—and I look forward to working with Members of Congress. I fully understand the politics of immigration reform. I was the Governor of Texas, right there on the frontlines of border politics. I know what it means to have mothers and fathers come to my State and across the border of my State to work. Family values do not stop at the Rio Grande River, is what I used to tell the people of my State. People are coming to put food on the table; they're doing jobs Americans will not do.

And to me, it makes sense for us to recognize that reality and to help those who are needing to enforce our borders; legalize the process of people doing jobs Americans won't do; take the pressure off of employers so they're not having to rely upon false IDs; cut out the "coyotes" who are the smugglers of these people, putting them in the back of tractor trailers in the middle of August in Texas, allowing people to suffocate in the back of the trucks; stop the process of people feeling like they've got to walk miles across desert in Arizona and Texas in order just to feed their family, and they find them dead out there. I mean, this is a system that can be much better.

And I'm passionate on it because the nature of this country is one that is good-hearted and compassionate. Our people are compassionate. The system we have today is not a compassionate system. It's not working. And as a result, the country is less secure than it could be with a rational system.

Yes, sir. Let us take it overseas, across the pond.

Usama bin Laden/Guantanamo Bay Detainees

Q. Thank you very much, Mr. President. I wonder whether I could ask you two central questions about the war on terrorism. The first one is, do you have a sense of where Usama bin Laden is and why the trail on him seems to have gone cold? And secondly, how concerned are you by the reports of torture, to use your word, the interminable delays to justice, for the detainees held in Guantanamo and how much that damages America's reputation as a nation which stands for liberty and justice internationally?

The President. Right, thank you. If I had to guess, I would guess that Usama bin Laden is in a remote region on the Afghan-

Pakistan border. But I don't have to guess at the damage we have done to his organization. Many of his senior operators have been killed or detained. Pakistan Government has been aggressive in pursuit of Al Qaida targets in Waziristan.

And I appreciate the work of President Musharraf. He came the other day, on a Saturday morning, to the White House, and it was an opportunity to thank him once again for some of the bold steps he's taken. And Al Qaida is dangerous, no question about it. But we've got a good strategy, and it's a strategy that requires cooperation with other nations, and the cooperation has been great when it comes to sharing intelligence and cutting off finances and arresting people or killing people. We'll stay on the hunt.

In terms of the second part of your— oh, the damage. Look, we are a nation of laws and to the extent that people say, "Well, America is no longer a nation of laws," that does hurt our reputation. But I think it's an unfair criticism. As you might remember, our courts have made a ruling. They looked at the jurisdiction, the right of people in Guantanamo to have habeas review, and so we're now complying with the court's decisions. We want to fully vet the court decision, because I believe I have the right to set up military tribunals. And so the law is working to determine what Presidential powers are available and what's not available. We're reviewing the status of the people in Guantanamo on a regular basis. I think 200 and some-odd have been released. But you've got to understand the dilemma we're in. These are people that got scooped up off a battlefield, attempting to kill U.S. troops. I want to make sure, before they're released, that they don't come back to kill again.

I think it's important to let the world know that we fully understand our obligations in a society that honors rule of law to do that. But I also have an obligation to protect the American people, to make sure we understand the nature of the peo-

ple that we hold, whether or not there's possible intelligence we can gather from them that we could then use to protect us. So we'll continue to work the issue hard.

Let's see here, yes, Hutch [Ron Hutcheson, Knight Ridder]. Go ahead and yell it out, Hutch.

Defense Secretary Rumsfeld

Q. Going for another new face, huh?

The President. Yes. [*Laughter*]

Q. I'd like to go back to Secretary Rumsfeld——

The President. It's not a pretty face. [*Laughter*]

Q. Thank you. [*Laughter*] You talked about the big picture elements of the Secretary's job, but did you find it offensive that he didn't take the time to personally sign condolence letters to the families of troops killed in Iraq? And if so, why is that an offense that you're willing to overlook?

The President. Listen, I know how—I know Secretary Rumsfeld's heart. I know how much he cares for the troops. He and his wife go out to Walter Reed and Bethesda all the time to provide comfort and solace. I have seen the anguish in his— or heard the anguish in his voice and seen his eyes when we talk about the danger in Iraq and the fact that youngsters are over there in harm's way. And he is—he's a good, decent man. He's a caring fellow. Sometimes, perhaps, his demeanor is rough and gruff, but beneath that rough and gruff, no-nonsense demeanor is a good human being who cares deeply about the military and deeply about the grief that war causes.

Deans [Bob Deans, Cox Newspapers].

Situation in the Middle East

Q. Mr. President, I want to kick forward to the elections in Gaza in a few weeks if I could, please. As you know, Presidents back to Carter have searched for a solution to the Palestinian-Israeli conflict. Your dad worked hard for it. Your predecessor said once it was like going to the dentist without getting your gums numbed. I'm wondering what great——

The President. Guy had a way with words. [*Laughter*]

Q. I'm wondering, sir, what lesson you draw, though, from their efforts, how you think the war in Iraq may, at this point, have improved prospects for a Mideast peace, and whether you think you might sit in that diplomatic dental chair yourself this year?

The President. I've been in the diplomatic dental chair for 4 years. This is an issue we talk about a lot, but it became apparent to me that peace would never happen so long as the interlocutor in the peace process was not really dedicated to peace or dedicated to a state.

I was at—look, I gave the speech June 24, 2002, in the Rose Garden that laid out the vision about how to achieve—at least from my point of view, how to achieve a peaceful solution and something that I hope happens. But I'm realistic about how to achieve peace, and it starts with my understanding that there will never be peace until a true democratic state emerges in the Palestinian territory. And I'm hopeful right now because the Palestinians will begin to have elections, have—will have elections, which is the beginning of the process toward the development of a state. It is not the sign that democracy has arrived. It is the beginning of a process.

And we look forward to working with Israel to uphold her obligations to enable a Palestinian state to emerge. But we've got a good chance to get it done. And I just want the people—and I know the world is wondering whether or not this is just empty rhetoric or does—do I really believe that now is the time to move the process forward. And the answer is, now is the time to move the process forward. But we cannot shortcut the process by saying, you know, "Well, the Palestinians can't

self-govern. They're not suitable for a democracy."

I subscribe to this theory, that the only way to achieve peace is for there to be democracies living side by side. Democracies don't fight each other. And the last system didn't work, which was the hope that a Palestinian Authority, run by a singular head who on some days would say, "We're for peace," and some days would say, "Now is the time to attack," hope that everything would be fine. It just didn't work.

So I look forward to working with the world, the new Secretary of State, to work with the Palestinians to develop the structures necessary for a democracy to emerge. And I appreciate the fact that Prime Minister Tony Blair is willing to help that process by holding a conference with Palestinians that will help develop the state. And if the free world focuses on helping the Palestinians develop a state and there is leadership willing to accept the help, it's possible to achieve peace. And there are responsibilities for all parties. The Palestinians have responsibilities. The Israelis have responsibilities. The Americans have responsibilities. The EU has responsibilities. But we all have got to keep the big vision in mind in order to achieve the objective.

Listen, thank you all very much. I wish everybody—truly wish everybody a happy holidays. For those of you coming to Crawford, I look forward to not seeing you down there. [*Laughter*]

Thank you all.

Football

Q. Are you going to the Rose Bowl?

The President. No, I won't be going to the Rose Bowl. I'll be watching the Rose Bowl.

And by the way, in case you're not following high school football in Texas—atta boy, Jackson [David Jackson, Dallas Morning News]—the Crawford Pirates are the State 2A, Division II champs. And we look forward—don't we—to wave the championship banner above the Crawford High School.

All right, happy holidays.

NOTE: The President's news conference began at 10:32 a.m. in Room 450 of the Dwight D. Eisenhower Executive Office Building. In his remarks, he referred to President Hamid Karzai of Afghanistan; President Vladimir Putin of Russia; former President Saddam Hussein of Iraq; Gen. John P. Abizaid, USA, combatant commander, U.S. Central Command; Gen. George W. Casey, Jr., USA, commanding general, Multi-National Force—Iraq; professional baseball player Johnny Damon; Chairman Kim Chong-il of North Korea; Usama bin Laden, leader of the Al Qaida terrorist organization; President Pervez Musharraf of Pakistan; Joyce Rumsfeld, wife of Secretary of Defense Donald H. Rumsfeld; and Prime Minister Tony Blair of the United Kingdom. He also referred to the President's Commission to Strengthen Social Security (Moynihan Commission). The Office of the Press Secretary also released a Spanish language transcript of this news conference.

Remarks Following a Visit With Wounded Troops at Walter Reed Army Medical Center
December 21, 2004

Laura and I have just come from a remarkable place called the Fisher House, a facility where wounded soldiers and their families are provided comfort during their trials. And we just want to thank the people who have supported the Fisher House, thank the folks here at Walter Reed for providing such incredibly good health care.

Today we had a rocket attack that took a lot of lives. Any time of the year it's a time of sorrow and sadness when we lose a loss of life. This time of year is particularly sorrowful for the families as we head into the Christmas season. We pray for them. We send our heartfelt condolences to the loved ones who suffer today. Just want them to know that the mission is a vital mission for peace. The idea of a democracy taking hold in what was a place of tyranny and hatred and destruction is such a hopeful moment in the history of the world.

And I want to thank the soldiers who are there and thank those who have sacrificed and the families who are worried about them during this Christmas season for their sacrifices. This is a very important and vital mission. I'm confident democracy will prevail in Iraq. I know a free Iraq will lead to a more peaceful world. So we ask for God's blessings on all who are involved in that vital mission.

Thank you very much. Have a good holiday.

NOTE: The President spoke at 3:07 p.m.

Statement on Signing the Specialty Crops Competitiveness Act of 2004
December 21, 2004

Today, I have signed into law H.R. 3242, the "Specialty Crops Competitiveness Act of 2004" (the "Act"). The Act is designed to increase the competitiveness of fruits, vegetables, tree nuts, dried fruits, and nursery crops grown in the United States.

Section 1408A of the National Agricultural Research, Extension, and Teaching Policy Act of 1977, as amended by section 303 of the Act, purports to require the Secretary of Agriculture to take into consideration certain advisory board-approved findings and recommendations in preparing the Secretary's annual departmental budget proposal to the President and to disclose to the Congress how the Secretary addressed each such recommendation. The executive branch shall construe section 1408A in a manner consistent with the President's constitutional authority to supervise the unitary executive branch, to re-quire the opinions of principal officers of the executive departments, to recommend for the consideration of the Congress such measures as the President shall judge necessary and expedient, and to withhold information the disclosure of which could impair the deliberative processes of the Executive or the performance of the Executive's constitutional duties.

GEORGE W. BUSH

The White House,
December 21, 2004.

NOTE: H.R. 3242, approved December 21, was assigned Public Law No. 108–465.

Letter to Congressional Leaders Transmitting a Report on Implementation of Debt Reduction Authority
December 21, 2004

Dear Mr. Speaker: (Dear Mr. President:)
Consistent with section 1321 of the Foreign Relations Authorization Act, Fiscal Year 2003 (Public Law 107–228), I transmit herewith a report prepared by my Administration on implementation of the debt reduction authority conferred by Title XIII, Subtitle B of Public Law 107–228.

Sincerely,

GEORGE W. BUSH

NOTE: Identical letters were sent to J. Dennis Hastert, Speaker of the House of Representatives, and Richard B. Cheney, President of the Senate.

Statement on Signing the Intelligence Authorization Act for Fiscal Year 2005
December 23, 2004

Today, I have signed into law H.R. 4548, the "Intelligence Authorization Act for Fiscal Year 2005." The Act authorizes appropriations to fund United States intelligence activities, including activities essential to success in the war on terror.

The executive branch shall construe provisions in the Act, including sections 105, 107, and 305, that mandate submission of information to the Congress, in a manner consistent with the President's constitutional authority to supervise the unitary executive branch and to withhold information that could impair foreign relations, national security, the deliberative processes of the

Executive, or the performance of the Executive's constitutional duties.

Section 502 of the Act purports to place restrictions on use of the U.S. Armed Forces and other personnel in certain operations. The executive branch shall construe the restrictions in that section as advisory in nature, so that the provisions are consistent with the President's constitutional authority as Commander in Chief, including for the conduct of intelligence operations, and to supervise the unitary executive branch.

To the extent that provisions of the Act, such as sections 614 and 615, purport to require or regulate submission by executive branch officials of legislative recommendations to the Congress, the executive branch shall construe such provisions in a manner consistent with the President's constitutional authority to supervise the unitary executive branch and to submit for congressional consideration such measures as the President judges necessary and expedient.

Section 105 of the Act incorporates by reference certain requirements set forth in the joint explanatory statement of the House-Senate committee of conference or in a classified annex. The executive branch continues to discourage the practice of enacting secret laws and encourages instead appropriate non-binding uses of classified schedules of authorizations, classified annexes to committee reports, and joint statements of managers that accompany the final legislation.

GEORGE W. BUSH

The White House,
December 23, 2004.

NOTE: H.R. 4548, approved December 23, was assigned Public Law No. 108–487.

Statement on Signing Communications Legislation
December 23, 2004

Today, I have signed into law H.R. 5419, a bill consisting of three titles. Title I is the "ENHANCE 911 Act of 2004," which strengthens the ability of Americans to use the 911 telephone number to seek emergency assistance. Title II is the "Commercial Spectrum Enhancement Act," which facilitates the spectrum relocation of Federal entities so that certain spectrum can be reallocated to commercial users. Title III is the "Universal Service Antideficiency Temporary Suspension Act," which makes the Antideficiency Act temporarily inapplicable to certain collections, receipts, expenditures and obligations relating to universal communications service.

Section 104 amends section 158(a)(2) of the National Telecommunications and Information Administration Organization Act to call for executive branch officials to submit to congressional committees funding profiles for a specified 5-year program. The executive branch shall construe the provision in a manner consistent with the constitutional authority of the President to recommend for the consideration of the Congress such measures, including proposals for appropriations, as he judges necessary and expedient.

Sections 202 and 204 enact sections 113(g)(5) and 118(d) of the National Telecommunications and Information Administration Organization Act, which purport to condition the execution of a law upon notification to congressional committees coupled with either approval by the committees or the absence of disapproval by the committees within a specified time. The executive branch shall construe the provisions to legally require only notification to the committees, as any other construction would be inconsistent with the principles enunciated by the Supreme Court of the United States in *INS v. Chadha.* The Secretary of Commerce will continue as a matter of comity to work with the committees on matters addressed by these provisions.

As is consistent with the principle of statutory construction of giving effect to each of two statutes addressing the same subject whenever they can co-exist, the executive branch shall construe section 302 of the Act in a manner consistent with section 254 of the Communications Act of 1934, which provides the Federal Communica-

tions Commission with the authority to maintain funding caps for Universal Service Fund programs.

GEORGE W. BUSH

The White House,
December 23, 2004.

NOTE: H.R. 5419, approved December 23, including Title I, the ENHANCE 911 Act of 2004, Title II, the Commercial Spectrum Enhancement Act, and Title III, the Universal Service Antideficiency Temporary Suspension Act was assigned Public Law No. 108–494.

Statement on Signing the Comprehensive Peace in Sudan Act of 2004
December 23, 2004

Today, I have signed into law S. 2781, the "Comprehensive Peace in Sudan Act of 2004" (the "Act"). The Act is intended to help resolve conflict, reduce human suffering, and encourage freedom and democracy.

Section 6 of the Act includes provisions that, if construed as mandatory, would impermissibly interfere with the President's exercise of his constitutional authorities to conduct the Nation's foreign affairs, participate in international negotiations, and supervise the unitary executive branch. Section 6(a), for example, appears to require the President to implement the measures set forth in section 6(b)(2) of the earlier Sudan Peace Act (Public Law 107–245), which purports to direct or burden the conduct of negotiations by the executive branch with foreign governments, international financial institutions, and the United Nations Security Council. When necessary to avoid such unconstitutional interference, the executive branch shall construe the provisions of section 6 as advisory.

The executive branch shall construe provisions in the Act that mandate submission

of information to the Congress, or the public, in a manner consistent with the President's constitutional authority to supervise the unitary executive branch and to withhold information that could impair foreign relations, national security, the deliberative processes of the Executive, or the performance of the Executive's constitutional duties. Such provisions include sections 8 and 12 of the Sudan Peace Act as amended by section 5 of the Act.

Provisions of the Act define a particular entity as the "Government of Sudan" for purposes of implementing the Act and section 12 of the Sudan Peace Act (Public Law 107–245). The executive branch shall construe the provisions in a manner consistent with the President's constitutional authority for the United States to recognize foreign states and to determine what constitutes the governments of such foreign states.

GEORGE W. BUSH

The White House,
December 23, 2004.

NOTE: S. 2781, approved December 23, was assigned Public Law No. 108–497.

Message on the Observance of Christmas 2004
December 23, 2004

For 2,000 years, Christmas has proclaimed a message of hope: the patient hope of men and women across centuries who listened to the words of prophets and lived in joyful expectation; the hope of Mary, who welcomed God's plan with great faith; and the hope of wise men, who set out on a long journey guided only by a slender promise traced in the stars. Christmas reminds us that the grandest purposes of God can be found in the humblest places. And it gives us hope that all the love and gifts that come to us in this life are the signs and symbols of an even greater love and gift that came on a holy night.

The Christmas season fills our hearts with gratitude for the many blessings in our lives. With those blessings comes a responsibility to reach out to others. Many of our fellow Americans still suffer from the effects of illness or poverty. Others fight cruel addictions, cope with division in their families, or grieve the loss of a loved one. Christmastime reminds each of us that we have a duty to love our neighbor just as we would like to be loved ourselves. By volunteering our time and talents where they are needed most, we help heal the sick, comfort those who suffer, and bring hope to those who despair.

During the holidays, we also keep in our thoughts and prayers the men and women of our Armed Forces—especially those far from home, separated from family and friends by the call of duty. In Afghanistan, Iraq, and elsewhere, these courageous Americans are fighting the enemies of freedom and protecting our country from danger. By bringing liberty to the oppressed, our troops are defending the freedom and security of us all. They and their families are making many sacrifices for our Nation, and all Americans are deeply grateful.

Laura joins me in wishing all Americans a Merry Christmas.

GEORGE W. BUSH

NOTE: An original was not available for verification of the content of this message.

Message on the Observance of Kwanzaa 2004
December 23, 2004

I send greetings to those observing Kwanzaa.

During Kwanzaa, millions of African Americans and people of African descent gather to celebrate their heritage and ancestry. Kwanzaa celebrations provide an opportunity to focus on the importance of family, community, and history, and to reflect on the Nguzo Saba or seven principles of African culture. These principles emphasize unity, self-determination, collective work and responsibility, cooperative economics, purpose, creativity, and faith.

Kwanzaa strengthens the ties that bind communities across America and around the world and reflects the great promise and diversity of America.

Laura joins me in sending our best wishes for a joyous Kwanzaa.

GEORGE W. BUSH

NOTE: An original was not available for verification of the content of this message.

The President's Radio Address
December 25, 2004

Good morning. On this Christmas Day, as families across the Nation gather in our homes to celebrate, Laura and I extend to all Americans our best wishes for the holidays. We hope this Christmas is a time of joy and peace for each of you, and we hope it offers you a chance for rest and reflection as you look forward to the new year ahead.

The Christmas season fills our hearts with gratitude for the many blessings in our lives, and with those blessings comes a responsibility to reach out to others. Many of our fellow Americans still suffer from the effects of illness or poverty. Others fight cruel addictions or cope with division in their families or grieve the loss of a loved one.

Christmastime reminds each of us that we have a duty to our fellow citizens, that we are called to love our neighbor just as we would like to be loved ourselves. By volunteering our time and talents where they are needed most, we help heal the sick, comfort those who suffer, and bring hope to those who despair, one heart and one soul at a time.

During the holidays, we also keep in our thoughts and prayers the men and women of our Armed Forces, especially those far from home, separated from family and friends by the call of duty. In Afghanistan, Iraq, and elsewhere, these skilled and courageous Americans are fighting the enemies of freedom and protecting our country from danger. By bringing liberty to the oppressed, our troops are helping to win the war on terror, and they are defending the freedom and security of us all. They and their families are making many sacrifices for our Nation, and for that, all Americans are deeply grateful.

The times we live in have brought many challenges to our country. And in such times, the story of Christmas brings special comfort and confidence. For 2,000 years, Christmas has proclaimed a message of hope, the patient hope of men and women across centuries who listened to the words of prophets and lived in joyful expectation, the hope of Mary who welcomed God's plan with great faith, and the hope of Wise Men who set out on a long journey, guided only by a promise traced in the stars.

Christmas reminds us that the grandest purposes of God can be found in the humblest places, and it gives us hope that all the love and gifts that come to us in this life are the signs and symbols of an even greater love and gift that came on a holy night.

Thank you for listening, and Merry Christmas.

NOTE: The address was recorded at 7:50 a.m. on December 23 at Camp David, MD, for broadcast at 10:06 a.m. on December 25. The transcript was made available by the Office of the Press Secretary on December 23 but was embargoed for release until the broadcast. The Office of the Press Secretary also released a Spanish language transcript of this address.

Remarks on the Earthquake and Tsunamis in the Indian Ocean and an Exchange With Reporters in Crawford, Texas
December 29, 2004

The President. Good morning. Laura and I and the American people are shocked and we are saddened by the terrible loss of life from the recent earthquake and the tsunamis in the Indian Ocean. Our prayers go out to the people who have lost so much to this series of disasters. Our hearts are also with the Americans who have lost loved ones in this tragedy. Our Embassies are working with host governments to locate American citizens who are still missing and to assist those who have been injured or displaced.

This morning I spoke with the leaders of India, Sri Lanka, Thailand, and Indonesia. I expressed my condolences and our country's condolences. I told them of our support. I praised their steadfast leadership during these difficult time. We're grateful to the American and international organizations that are working courageously to save lives and to provide assistance, and I assured those leaders this is only the beginning of our help.

We are committed to helping the affected countries in the difficult weeks and months that lie ahead. We pledged an initial $35 million in relief assistance. We have deployed disaster experts to the region. All leaders expressed their appreciation for the hard work of our Ambassadors and their embassy staffs to help the countries in need. As well we're dispatching a Marine expeditionary unit, the aircraft carrier *Abraham Lincoln*, and the maritime preposition squadron from Guam to the area to help with relief efforts.

Secretary Powell is working hard. He has spoken with his counterparts in Japan, India, Australia, as well as other nations who are helping with the response, in order to begin building an international coalition for immediate humanitarian relief and long-term recovery and reconstruction efforts.

Based on these discussions, we've established a regional core group with India, Japan, and Australia to help coordinate relief efforts. I'm confident more nations will join this core group in short order. Under Secretary of State Marc Grossman will lead a U.S. task force to work with these partners to help coordinate interagency response in our own Government and to encourage other nations to participate in the relief efforts.

These past few days have brought loss and grief to the world that is beyond our comprehension. The United States will continue to stand with the affected governments as they care for the victims. We will stand with them as they start to rebuild their communities. And together the world will cope with their loss; we will prevail over this destruction.

Let me answer some questions. Deb [Deb Riechmann, Associated Press].

Iraqi Elections

Q. Mr. President, more than 50 people died yesterday alone in the Sunni Triangle area. And with the Sunnis backing out of the election, how concerned are you that the world and the Iraqis will view this election as credible?

The President. Well, you said "with the Sunnis backing out"; you mean a Sunni party has backed out, yes. I talked to President Yawr yesterday, who happens to be a Sunni, who on the one hand expressed concern about the security situation in Mosul and on the other hand reminded me that most people in Iraq, Sunni or Shi'a, want to vote. And so the task at hand is to provide as much security as possible for the election officials as well as for the people inside cities like Mosul, to encourage them to express their will.

Now, Usama bin Laden issued a statement, as you know, which made the stakes of this pretty clear to me. His vision of the world is where people don't participate in democracy. His vision of the world is where people kill innocent lives in order to affect their behavior and affect their way of living. His vision of the world is one in which there is no freedom of expression, freedom of religion, and/or freedom of conscience. And that vision stands in stark contrast to the vision of, by far, the vast majority of Iraqis and leaders like Prime Minister Allawi and President Yawr, whose vision includes the freedom of expression, the freedom of the right to vote.

And so the stakes are clear in this upcoming election. It's the difference between the ability for individuals to express themselves and the willingness of an individual to try and impose his dark vision on the world, on the people of Iraq and elsewhere. And it's very important that these elections proceed.

We just got off a conference call with our acting—not "acting"—Ambassador Negroponte is not in Baghdad, but Ambassador Jeffrey, his number two man, as well as General Casey, talking about how best to provide the security necessary for people to feel comfortable in voting.

Yes, ma'am.

United Nations/International Disaster Assistance

Q. Mr. President, were you offended by the suggestion that rich nations have been stingy in the aid over the tsunami? And is this a sign of another rift with the U.N.?

The President. Well, I felt like the person who made that statement was very misguided and ill-informed. The—take, for example, in the year 2004, our Government provided $2.4 billion in food, in cash, in humanitarian relief to cover the disasters for last year. That's $2.4 billion. That's 40 percent of all the relief aid given in the world last year, was provided by the United

States Government. No, we're a very generous, kindhearted nation.

You know, the—what you're beginning to see is a typical response from America. First of all, we provide immediate cash relief, to the tune of about $35 million. ° And then there will be an assessment of the damage, so that the relief is—the next tranche of relief will be spent wisely. That's what's happening now. I just got off the phone with the President of Sri Lanka. She asked for help to assess the damage. In other words, not only did they want immediate help, but they wanted help to assess damage so that we can better direct resources. And so our Government is fully prepared to continue to provide assistance and help.

It takes money, by the way, to move a expeditionary force into the region. In other words, we're diverting assets, which is part of our overall aid package. We'll continue to provide assets. Plus, the American people will be very generous, themselves. I mean, the 2.4 billion was public money—of course, provided by the taxpayers—but there's also a lot of individual giving in America. In this case, I think it's very important for Americans who want to give to provide cash to organizations that will be able to focus resources and assets to meet specific needs. In other words, a lot of times Americans, in their desire to help, will send blankets or clothes. That may be necessary, but to me it makes more sense to send cash to organizations that could then use that cash to make sure we match resources with specific needs on the ground. There are many NGOs now involved that understand what is specifically needed to meet the needs of these countries.

This has been a terrible disaster. I mean, it's just beyond our comprehension to think about how many lives have been lost. I know that our fellow citizens are particularly troubled to learn that many of the

---

° White House correction.

deaths were young children, and we grieve for their families, their moms and dads who are just, you know, heartsick during this—during these times.

Yes, Holly [Holly Rosenkrantz, Bloomberg News].

Debt Moratorium for Somalia and Indonesia

Q. Sir, Schroeder this morning said that the Paris Club nations should put a moratorium on the debt of Somalia and Indonesia. Is that something that people think the U.S. and other Paris Club nations should do, put a moratorium on these countries' debt?

The President. Well, we'll look at all requests. Right now we're assessing the short-term needs. We are—there are two issues that are involved, obviously, in these disasters: One, what can we do immediately to help; and then, what needs to happen in the long term to help these countries rebuild? And we're still at the stage of immediate help. But slowly but surely, the size of the problem will become known, particularly when it comes to rebuilding infrastructure and community, to help these affected parts of the world get back up on their feet.

Tsunami Early Warning Systems

Q. Mr. President, are you confident that the U.S. west coast residents, Hawaiian residents, Alaska residents, are well enough protected with early warning systems for possible tsunamis affecting this country in coastal waters?

The President. No, I appreciate that question. It's a—I think that part of the long-term strategy in how to deal with natural disaster is to make sure we have— "we," the world, has a proper tsunami warning system. As a matter of fact, the President of Sri Lanka also mentioned that to me. She said that one of the things that she and the Prime Minister of India have discussed—I'm not sure if they discussed it, but they're both thinking the same way,

let me put it to you that way—is the development of a proper warning system. And I think it's going to be very—I can't answer your question specifically, do we have enough of a warning system for the west coast. I am going to—I am now asking that to our agencies in Government, to let us know. I mean, that's a very legitimate question. Clearly, there wasn't a proper warning system in place for that part of the world, and it seems like to me it makes sense for the world to come together to develop a warning system that will help all nations.

Q. And seeing that as we have, does it concern you that we may not have that mechanism in place? Or is this something we can use through our civil defense air raid siren system?

The President. Yes, I just have to look into it. That's a very legitimate question. I am on the—I presume that we are in pretty good shape. I think our location in the world is such that we may be less vulnerable than other parts, but I am not a geologist, as you know. But I think it's a very legitimate question.

I've so far focused on the international approach towards tsunami warning systems, and it seems like to me it's a—it makes sense for governments to come together and figure out how best to provide a warning system that will help all nations be prepared for such a disaster. Obviously, such a warning system was not in place.

Yes, Richard [Richard Benedetto, USA Today].

Armored Humvees for U.S. Troops

Q. Mr. President, there continues to be criticism of the speed with which American troops are being armed in Iraq. Are you satisfied with the way the——

The President. In which the Iraqi troops are being armed?

Q. No, the U.S. troops.

The President. Oh, I beg your pardon.

Q. Are you satisfied with the pace with which the U.S. troops are being armed in Iraq?

The President. Are you talking about the armored vehicle issue, for example?

Q. That and others.

The President. Well, I have looked at the statistics on that, and we have stepped up the production of armored Humvees significantly. And the other issue is the re-armament of existing—of vehicles that are now in theater, vehicles that require a different armament structure than that which they initially were manufactured with. And I am told that those vehicles will be armed up by mid-summer of 2005. And what I know is, is that the Defense Department is working expeditiously with private contractors and with our military to get these vehicles armed up.

Well, listen, thank you all for coming by. I'm sorry to disrupt your day, but I felt like it was important to talk about what is going to be one of the major natural disasters in world history. And it's important for the world to know that our Government is focused and will continue to respond to help those who suffer.

Thank you.

New Year's Eve

Q. Any plans for New Year's Eve?

The President. Early to bed.

Q. New Year's resolutions?

The President. I'll let you know. Already gave you a hint on one, which is my waistline. I'm trying to set an example.

Thank you all.

NOTE: The President spoke at 8:38 a.m. at the Bush Ranch. In his remarks, he referred to President Ghazi al-Ujayl al-Yawr and Prime Minister Ayad Allawi of the Iraqi Interim Government; Usama bin Laden, leader of the Al Qaida terrorist organization; U.S. Ambassador to Iraq John D. Negroponte; Deputy Chief of Mission James Franklin Jeffrey, U.S. Embassy Baghdad, Iraq; Gen. George W. Casey, Jr. USA, commanding general, Multi-National Force—Iraq; President Chandrika Bandaranaike Kumaratunga of Sri Lanka; and Prime Minister Manmohan Singh of India. A reporter referred to Chancellor Gerhard Schroeder of Germany. A portion of these remarks could not be verified because the tape was incomplete. The related proclamation of January 1, 2005, honoring the memory of the victims of the Indian Ocean earthquake and tsunamis, was published in the *Federal Register* at 70 FR 1157.

Statement on the Indian Ocean Earthquake and Tsunamis
December 30, 2004

All Americans are shocked and saddened by the tragic loss of life and the destruction around the Indian Ocean. In this hour of critical need, America is joining with other nations and international organizations to do everything possible to provide assistance and relief to the victims and their families.

Already cargo aircraft, support personnel, naval units, and aid shipments have been dispatched. To coordinate this massive relief effort, firsthand assessments are needed by individuals on the ground. On Sunday, January 2, I will send a delegation of experts to the affected areas to meet with regional leaders and international organizations to assess what additional aid can be provided by the United States. The delegation will be led by Secretary of State Colin Powell and Governor Jeb Bush, who has extensive experience in the State of Florida with relief, rehabilitation, and reconstruction efforts following natural disasters. I look forward to receiving the delegation's assessment of the relief efforts so that our Government can best help those in need.

NOTE: The related proclamation of January 1, 2005, was published in the *Federal Register* at 70 FR 1157.

Statement on the Indian Ocean Earthquake and Tsunamis
December 31, 2004

The disaster around the Indian Ocean continues to grow both in size and scope. I have been monitoring closely the developments and our recovery and relief effort underway. I also look forward to the detailed report of the official delegation led by Secretary Powell and Governor Jeb Bush that will travel to the region very soon.

The United States has already provided an initial, substantial effort through existing emergency response resources, the formation of the core group, and military assets. To help coordinate the massive relief effort, disaster response officials are on the ground, and we have established a Support Center in Thailand that is manned and operational. More than 20 patrol and cargo aircraft have been made available to assess the disaster and deliver relief supplies. Many of those aircraft are on the scene. We have dispatched the aircraft carrier *Abraham Lincoln*, the maritime prepositioning squadron from Guam, and an amphibious ship carrying a Marine Expeditionary Unit. They will soon be in position to support relief efforts to include the generation of clean water. We are leading an international coalition to help with immediate humanitarian relief, rehabilitation, and long-term reconstruction efforts. India, Japan, and Australia have pledged to help us coordinate these relief efforts, and I am confident many more nations will join this core group in short order. Reports of strong charitable donations are also very encouraging and reflect the true generosity and compassion of the American people.

Initial findings of American assessment teams on the ground indicate that the need for financial and other assistance will steadily increase in the days and weeks ahead. Because of this information and based on the recommendation of Secretary Powell and Administrator Natsios, I am today committing $350 million to fund the U.S. portion of the relief effort. Our contributions will continue to be revised as the full effects of this terrible tragedy become clearer.

Our thoughts and prayers are with all those affected by this epic disaster.

NOTE: The related proclamation of January 1, 2005, was published in the *Federal Register* at 70 FR 1157.

Message on the Observance of New Year's Day, 2005
December 31, 2004

As we begin the New Year, our prayers go out to the people who have lost so much to the recent series of disasters in the Indian Ocean region. The past few days have brought loss and grief to the world that is beyond our comprehension. America will continue to stand with the affected governments to bring aid to those in need. Together the world will cope with the loss and prevail over this destruction.

In the United States, we go forward in the New Year with confidence and faith in the future.

Over the past year, Americans have shown resolve and patience in the war on terror. Our military men and women have brought justice to the enemy and honor to our country. Because of their bravery, over 50 million people in Iraq and Afghanistan are now free. At home, Americans have restored the vigor of our economy and answered the call to serve neighbors in need.

In the year ahead, we will persevere in the ongoing war on terror to make our Nation safer and stronger. We will continue to confront disease, hunger, and poverty at home and abroad. We will build on our economic progress and strengthen Social Security for the next generation so that all our citizens can realize the promise of America. And we will continue to improve our public schools and uphold our deepest values of faith, family, and service.

We are grateful to the men and women of our Armed Forces who serve and sacrifice to defend our liberty. These heroes and their families have the thanks and respect of our entire Nation. We pray for their safety and for peace and understanding throughout the world.

Laura joins me in sending our best wishes for a Happy New Year. May God bless you, and may God continue to bless America.

GEORGE W. BUSH

NOTE: An original was not available for verification of the content of this message.

Appendix A—Digest of Other White House Announcements

The following list includes the President's public schedule and other items of general interest announced by the Office of the Press Secretary and not included elsewhere in this book.

October 1

In the morning, in Miami, FL, the President had an intelligence briefing. Later, he traveled to Allentown, PA, where, upon arrival, he met with USA Freedom Corps volunteer Cheryl Hornung.

In the afternoon, the President traveled to Manchester, NH, where, upon arrival, he met with USA Freedom Corps volunteer Paul Freeman. Later, at the McIntyre Ski Area in Manchester, he participated in a Victory 2004 rally.

Later in the afternoon, the President returned to Washington, DC.

The President announced his intention to nominate Ronald Rosenfeld to be a Director on the Board of Directors of the Federal Housing Finance Board.

The President announced his intention to nominate Michael Butler to be a member of the Board of Trustees of the Morris K. Udall Scholarship and Excellence in National Environmental Policy Foundation.

The President announced his intention to appoint Robin Cook, Charles L. Glazer, and Peter S. Watson to be members of the Board of Trustees of the Woodrow Wilson International Center for Scholars.

The President announced his intention to appoint David Wayne Anderson, Cynthia R. Church, and Soyna E. Medina as members of the Board of Trustees of the American Folklife Center.

The President announced his intention to appoint the following individuals as members of the Commission on the Abraham Lincoln Study Abroad Fellowship Program:

John K. Andrews, Jr.;
Jim Edgar;
Lynette Boggs McDonald; and
Lyn Bracewell Phillips.

The President announced his intention to appoint Scott Wallace (Chairman), C. Martin Harris, and William W. Stead as members of the Commission on Systemic Interoperability.

October 2

In the morning, the President had an intelligence briefing. Later, he traveled to Columbus, OH, where, upon arrival, he met with USA Freedom Corps volunteer Karen Kindron. He then began a bus tour.

Later in the morning, the President traveled to Mansfield, OH.

In the afternoon, the President traveled to Cuyahoga Falls, OH. While en route aboard the bus, he met with leaders of the Fraternal Order of Police.

Later in the afternoon, the President returned to Washington, DC, arriving in the evening.

The White House announced that on October 1 the President declared a major disaster in New York and ordered Federal aid to supplement State and local recovery efforts in the area struck by severe storms and flooding on August 29–September 16.

The White House announced that on October 1 the President declared a major disaster in New York and ordered Federal aid to supplement State and local recovery efforts in the area struck by Tropical Depression Ivan on September 16–24.

The White House announced that on October 1 the President declared a major disaster in New Jersey and ordered Federal aid to supplement State and local recovery efforts in the area struck by Tropical Depression Ivan beginning on September 18 and continuing.

October 3

During the day, the President participated in a debate preparation session.

October 4

In the morning, the President had a telephone conversation with Prime Minister Silvio Berlusconi of Italy to congratulate him on the birth of his second grandson, to extend birthday greetings, and to discuss the September 28 release of two Italian hostages held in Iraq. He then had an intelligence briefing.

Later in the morning, the President traveled to Des Moines, IA, where, upon arrival, he met with USA Freedom Corps volunteer Tony Salem.

In the afternoon, the President traveled to Clive, IA. Later, he returned to Washington, DC.

October 5

In the morning, the President had an intelligence briefing.

In the evening, in the Residence, the President watched the Vice Presidential debate. Later, he had a telephone conversation with Vice President Dick Cheney to discuss the debate.

October 6

In the morning, the President had an intelligence briefing. Later, he traveled to Wilkes-Barre, PA, where, upon arrival, he met with USA Freedom Corps volunteers Blake, Mona, and Katherine Schomas.

Later in the morning, the President traveled to Detroit, MI, where, upon arrival in the afternoon, he met with USA Freedom Corps volunteer Robert Eastman. He then traveled to Farmington Hills, MI.

Later in the afternoon, the President returned to Washington, DC, arriving in the evening.

October 7

In the morning, the President had an intelligence briefing. He then had a telephone conversation with President Hu Jintao of China to discuss China-U.S. relations, the situation in North Korea, economic issues, and China-Taiwan relations.

Later in the morning, in the Oval Office, the President met with Finance Minister Adil Abd al-Mahdi of the Iraqi Interim Government.

In the afternoon, the President traveled to Wausau, WI, where, upon arrival, he met with USA Freedom Corps volunteer Dolores Milbeck. Later, he traveled to St. Louis, MO, where, upon arrival, he met with USA Freedom Corps volunteer Fred Ruhrwien.

The President made additional disaster assistance available to Florida by authorizing an increase in the level of Federal funding for Public Assistance projects undertaken as a result of

Tropical Storm Bonnie and Hurricane Charley and Hurricanes Frances, Ivan, and Jeanne.

The President declared a major disaster in South Carolina and ordered Federal aid to supplement State and local recovery efforts in the area struck by Tropical Storm Frances beginning on September 6 and continuing.

The President declared a major disaster in Minnesota and ordered Federal aid to supplement State and local recovery efforts in the area struck by severe storms and flooding beginning on September 14 and continuing.

The President declared a major disaster in the U.S. Virgin Islands and ordered Federal aid to supplement Territory and local recovery efforts in the area struck by Tropical Storm Jeanne on September 14–17.

The President declared a major disaster in Tennessee and ordered Federal aid to supplement State and local recovery efforts in the area struck by severe storms and flooding on September 16–20.

October 8

In the morning, the President had a telephone conversation with President-elect Susilo Bambang Yudhoyono of Indonesia to congratulate him on his October 4 election victory. He then had an intelligence briefing.

The President announced his intention to nominate Frederick William Hatfield to be a Commissioner of the Commodity Futures Trading Commission.

The President announced his intention to nominate Harold Damelin to be Inspector General of the Department of the Treasury.

The President announced his intention to nominate Edward L. Flippen to be Inspector General of the Corporation for National and Community Service.

The President announced his intention to nominate Brian David Miller to be Inspector General of the General Services Administration.

The President announced his intention to appoint Gen. Richard B. Myers, USAF, as a Governor on the Board of Governors of the American National Red Cross.

The President announced his intention to nominate Jorge A. Plasencia to be a member of the Advisory Board for Cuba Broadcasting.

The President announced his intention to nominate Carolyn L. Gallagher and Louis J. Giuliano to be Governors on the Board of Governors of the U.S. Postal Service.

The President announced his intention to appoint A. Wilson Greene and Katina P. Strauch as members of the National Museum and Library Services Board.

October 9

In the morning, the President had an intelligence briefing. Later, he and Mrs. Bush traveled to Waterloo, IA, where, upon arrival, he met with USA Freedom Corps volunteer Jim Glaza.

In the afternoon, the President and Mrs. Bush traveled to Chanhassen, MN, where, upon arrival, he met with USA Freedom Corps volunteer Ken Porwoll. Later, they traveled to the Bush Ranch in Crawford, TX.

October 10

In the evening, the President participated in a debate preparation session.

October 11

In the morning, the President had an intelligence briefing. Later, he traveled to Hobbs, NM, where, upon arrival, he met with USA Freedom Corps volunteer Jamie Gaston.

Later in the morning, the President traveled to Denver, CO, arriving in the afternoon. Upon arrival, he met with USA Freedom Corps volunteer Ashley Stieb.

Later in the afternoon, the President traveled to Morrison, CO. Later, he returned to Denver, CO. While en route, he participated in a debate preparation session.

October 12

In the morning, the President had an intelligence briefing. Later, he traveled to Colorado Springs, CO, where, upon arrival, he met with USA Freedom Corps volunteers Bob Carlone and Joe Henjum.

Later in the morning, the President traveled to Paradise Valley, AZ, arriving in the afternoon. Upon arrival, he met with USA Freedom Corps volunteer Marcelo Chan.

Later in the afternoon, the President traveled to Phoenix, AZ.

Also in the afternoon, the President participated in debate preparation sessions.

In the evening, the President participated in a debate preparation session. Later, he and Mrs. Bush, who joined the President earlier in the day, had dinner with Senator John McCain of Arizona and his wife, Cindy.

October 13

In the morning, the President had an intelligence briefing.

In the evening, the President and Mrs. Bush traveled to Tempe, AZ. Later, they returned to Phoenix, AZ.

October 14

In the morning, the President had an intelligence briefing. Later, he and Mrs. Bush traveled to Las Vegas, NV, where, upon arrival, he met with USA Freedom Corps volunteer Dick Cancellier.

• In the afternoon, the President and Mrs. Bush traveled to Reno, NV, where, upon arrival, he met with USA Freedom Corps volunteer Frank Schnorbus.

Later in the afternoon, the President and Mrs. Bush traveled to Central Point, OR, arriving in the evening. Upon arrival, he met with USA Freedom Corps volunteer Lois Rodger.

Later in the evening, the President and Mrs. Bush traveled to Jacksonville, OR.

October 15

In the afternoon, the President and Mrs. Bush traveled to Cedar Rapids, IA. While en route aboard Air Force One, he had an intelligence briefing. Upon arrival in Cedar Rapids, he met with USA Freedom Corps volunteer Linda Peterson.

Later in the afternoon, the President and Mrs. Bush traveled to Oshkosh, WI, where, upon arrival, he met with USA Freedom Corps volunteer Jeff Kemp.

In the evening, the President and Mrs. Bush returned to Washington, DC.

The President announced his intention to designate Darrell Irions and Dee J. Kelly, Jr., as members of the Board of Governors on the United Service Organizations, Inc.

The President announced his intention to designate William A. Moorman as Acting Assistant Secretary of Veterans Affairs for Management.

October 16

In the morning, the President had an intelligence briefing. Later, he and Mrs. Bush traveled to Sunrise, FL.

Later in the morning, the President and Mrs. Bush traveled to West Palm Beach, FL, arriving in the afternoon. Later, they traveled to Daytona Beach, FL.

Later in the afternoon, the President and Mrs. Bush returned to Washington, DC, arriving in the evening.

October 18

In the morning, the President had an intelligence briefing.

In the afternoon, the President traveled to Marlton, NJ, where, upon arrival, he met with USA Freedom Corps volunteer Jeff Jacobs.

Later in the afternoon, the President traveled to Boca Raton, FL, where, upon arrival in the evening, he met USA Freedom Corps volunteer Cathy Scheppke. He then attended a Victory 2004 dinner at a private residence.

Later in the evening, the President traveled to St. Pete Beach, FL.

The President declared a major disaster in Virginia and ordered Federal aid to supplement Commonwealth and local recovery efforts in the area struck by severe storms and flooding from the remnants of Hurricane Jeanne beginning on September 27 and continuing.

October 19

In the morning, the President had an intelligence briefing. He then traveled to St. Petersburg, FL. Later, he traveled to New Port Richey, FL.

In the afternoon, the President traveled to The Villages, FL. Later, he returned to Washington, DC, arriving in the evening.

October 20

In the morning, the President had an intelligence briefing. Later, he traveled to Mason City, IA, where, upon arrival, he met with USA Freedom Corps volunteer Matthew Meyer.

Later in the morning, the President traveled to Rochester, MN, where, upon arrival, he met with USA Freedom Corps volunteer Sister Chabanel Hayunga.

In the afternoon, the President traveled to Eau Claire, WI, where, upon arrival, he met with USA Freedom Corps volunteer Mick Jay Krueger.

Later in the afternoon, the President returned to Washington, DC, arriving in the evening.

October 21

In the morning, the President had an intelligence briefing. Then, in the Roosevelt Room, he participated in the signing ceremony for S. 2634, the Garrett Lee Smith Memorial Act. Later, in the Map Room, he participated in interviews with the Hispanic television networks Univision and Telemundo for later broadcast.

In the afternoon, the President traveled to Downingtown, PA, where, upon arrival in the afternoon, he met with USA Freedom Corps volunteer Charlotte Huber. Later, at St. Joseph's Roman Catholic Church, he met with Justin Cardinal Rigali, Archbishop of Philadelphia, PA.

Later in the afternoon, the President traveled to Hershey, PA. Later, he returned to Washington, DC, arriving in the evening.

October 22

In the morning, the President had an intelligence briefing. Later, he traveled to Wilkes-Barre, PA, where, upon arrival, he met with USA Freedom Corps volunteer Dolly Yunkunis.

Later in the morning, the President traveled to Canton, OH, where, upon arrival in the afternoon, he met with USA Freedom Corps volunteer Dan Yeric.

Later in the afternoon, the President traveled to St. Petersburg, FL, where, upon arrival in the evening, he met with USA Freedom Corps volunteer Chip Collins. He then attended a Victory 2004 dinner at a private residence. Later, he traveled to St. Pete Beach.

October 23

In the morning, the President had an intelligence briefing. He and Mrs. Bush then traveled to Fort Myers, FL. Later, they traveled to Lakeland, FL.

In the afternoon, the President and Mrs. Bush traveled to Melbourne, FL. Later, they traveled to Jacksonville, FL, where, upon arrival, he met with USA Freedom Corps volunteer Elwood Thalheimer.

In the evening, the President and Mrs. Bush traveled to the Bush Ranch in Crawford, TX.

October 24

In the afternoon, the President and Mrs. Bush traveled to Alamogordo, NM, where, upon arrival, he met with USA Freedom Corps volunteer Nicole Cox.

Later in the afternoon, the President and Mrs. Bush returned to the Bush Ranch in Crawford, TX, arriving in the evening.

October 25

In the morning, the President and Mrs. Bush traveled to Greeley, CO. While en route aboard Air Force One, he had an intelligence briefing.

Later in the morning, the President and Mrs. Bush traveled to Council Bluffs, IA, where, upon arrival in the afternoon, he met with USA Freedom Corps volunteer Donna Campbell. Later in the afternoon, the President and Mrs. Bush traveled to Davenport, IA, where, upon arrival, he met with USA Freedom Corps volunteer Tom Ryan.

In the evening, the President and Mrs. Bush traveled to La Crosse, WI.

October 26

In the morning, the President had an intelligence briefing. He and Mrs. Bush then began a bus tour by traveling to Onalaska, WI. Later, they traveled to Richland Center, WI.

In the afternoon, the President and Mrs. Bush traveled to Cuba City, WI. Later, they traveled to Dubuque, IA, concluding their bus tour.

Later in the afternoon, the President and Mrs. Bush returned to Washington, DC, arriving in the evening.

October 27

In the morning, the President had an intelligence briefing. He then participated in an interview with Jim Gray of the ESPN television channel for later broadcast.

Later in the morning, the President and Mrs. Bush traveled to Lititz, PA, where, upon arrival, he met with USA Freedom Corps volunteer Connie Rutt.

In the afternoon, the President and Mrs. Bush traveled to Vienna, OH, where, upon arrival, he met with USA Freedom Corps volunteer Bill Carney. Later, they traveled to Findlay, OH, where, upon arrival, he met with USA Freedom Corps volunteer Tom Joseph.

Later in the afternoon, the President and Mrs. Bush traveled to Pontiac, MI, where, upon arrival in the evening, he met with USA Freedom

Corps volunteer Mia Zimmerman. Upon arrival at the Superdome, they met with African American leaders.

Later in the evening, the President and Mrs. Bush traveled to Rochester, MI.

October 28

In the morning, the President had an intelligence briefing. He then had telephone conversations with John W. Henry, principal owner, Larry Lucchino, president and chief executive officer, and Curt Schilling, pitcher, Boston Red Sox, to congratulate them on winning the Major League Baseball World Series.

Later in the morning, the President traveled to Saginaw, MI. Later, he traveled to Dayton, OH. While en route aboard Air Force One, he participated in an interview with Judy Keen of USA Today. Upon arrival in Dayton, he met with USA Freedom Corps volunteer Carol McClure.

In the afternoon, the President traveled to Westlake, OH, where, upon arrival, he met with USA Freedom Corps volunteer Amy Poklar.

Later in the afternoon, the President traveled to Yardley, PA, where, upon arrival in the evening, he met with USA Freedom Corps volunteer Joe Morrison. Later, he returned to Washington, DC.

October 29

In the morning, the President had an intelligence briefing. Later, he and Mrs. Bush traveled to Manchester, NH, where, upon arrival, he met with USA Freedom Corps volunteer Joannie Barrett.

In the afternoon, the President and Mrs. Bush traveled to Portsmouth, NH. Later, they traveled to Toledo, OH, where, upon arrival, he met with USA Freedom Corps volunteer Norm Thal.

In the evening, the President and Mrs. Bush traveled to Columbus, OH, where, upon arrival, he met with USA Freedom Corps volunteer Peggy Valentino.

October 30

In the morning, the President had an intelligence briefing. He and Mrs. Bush then traveled to Grand Rapids, MI. While en route, aboard Air Force One, he participated in three separate interviews with Ohio network affiliate television stations. Upon arrival in Grand Rapids, he met with USA Freedom Corps volunteer Judy Hunt.

Later in the morning, the President and Mrs. Bush traveled to Green Bay, WI, where, upon arrival, he met with USA Freedom Corps volunteer Lila Cody. They then traveled to Ashwaubenon, WI.

In the afternoon, the President and Mrs. Bush traveled to Minneapolis, MN, where, upon arrival, he met with USA Freedom Corps volunteer Maya Babu.

Later in the afternoon, the President and Mrs. Bush traveled to Orlando, FL, arriving in the evening. Upon arrival, he met with USA Freedom Corps volunteer Malee Austin.

October 31

In the morning, the President had an intelligence briefing. Later, he participated in an interview with Tom Brokaw of NBC News. He and Mrs. Bush then traveled to Miami, FL, where, upon arrival, he met with USA Freedom Corps volunteer Eric Vaz.

In the afternoon, the President and Mrs. Bush traveled to Tampa, FL, where, upon arrival, he met with USA Freedom Corps volunteer Mildred Brisker. They then traveled to Gainesville, FL, where, upon arrival, he met with USA Freedom Corps volunteer Dr. Larry Smith.

Later in the afternoon, the President and Mrs. Bush traveled to Cincinnati, OH, where, upon arrival in the evening, he met with USA Freedom Corps volunteer Sue Stuempel.

November 1

In the morning, the President had an intelligence briefing. He and Mrs. Bush then traveled to Wilmington, OH.

Later in the morning, the President traveled to Pittsburgh, PA, where, upon arrival, he met with USA Freedom Corps volunteer Joan Roth. He then traveled to Burgettstown, PA. Later, he traveled to Milwaukee, WI, where, upon arrival, he met with USA Freedom Corps volunteer Cory Helland.

In the afternoon, the President traveled to Des Moines, IA, where, upon arrival, he met with USA Freedom Corps volunteer Brittany Overstreet. Later, he traveled to Sioux City, IA, where, upon arrival, he met with USA Freedom Corps volunteer Terri Ross.

Later in the afternoon, the President and Mrs. Bush, who joined him in Iowa, traveled to Albu-

querque, NM, where, upon arrival in the evening, he met with USA Freedom Corps volunteer Jade Wright.

Later in the evening, the President and Mrs. Bush traveled to Dallas, TX, where, upon arrival, he met with USA Freedom Corps volunteer Tish Aldridge. Later, they traveled to the Bush Ranch in Crawford, TX.

November 2

In the morning, the President and Mrs. Bush went to the Crawford Fire Station to vote. Later, they traveled to Columbus, OH.

In the afternoon, the President and Mrs. Bush returned to Washington, DC, where, upon arrival on the South Lawn, they were greeted by White House staff.

During the day, the President monitored election results.

November 3

In the morning, in the Oval Office, the President had separate telephone conversations with Representative Richard Burr, David Vitter, and Mel R. Martinez to congratulate them on their election victories in the North Carolina, Louisiana, and Florida Senate races, respectively.

Later in the morning, in the Oval Office, the President had intelligence and FBI briefings. He then had separate telephone conversations with former Representative John Thune, Representative Jim DeMint, Senator Jim Bunning, and former Representative Tom Coburn to congratulate them on their election victories in the South Dakota, South Carolina, Kentucky, and Oklahoma Senate races, respectively.

Later in the morning, in the Oval Office, the President received a telephone call from Democratic Presidential candidate John F. Kerry in which Senator Kerry conceded the November 2 election. During the call, the President expressed his appreciation for Senator Kerry's efforts in the campaign.

November 4

In the morning, the President had a telephone conversation with President Khalifa bin Zayid Al Nuhayyan of the United Arab Emirates to express his condolences on the death of his father, former President Shaykh Zayid bin Sultan Al Nuhayyan. He then had a telephone conversation with President Hamid Karzai of Afghanistan to congratulate him on his October 9 election victory.

Later in the morning, the President had separate telephone conversations with Prime Minister Ariel Sharon of Israel, Prime Minister Ayad Allawi of the Iraqi Interim Government, President Aleksander Kwasniewski of Poland, President Vladimir Putin of Russia, and Prime Minister Silvio Berlusconi of Italy, all of whom congratulated the President on his reelection victory. He then had an intelligence briefing.

In the afternoon, on the State Floor, the President met with campaign staff to thank them for their efforts during the campaign. He then traveled to Camp David, MD.

The President announced the November 3 recess appointments of Carolyn L. Gallagher and Louis J. Giuliano as Governors on the Board of Governors of the U.S. Postal Service.

November 5

In the morning, the President had an intelligence briefing.

During the day, the President had a video conference with the National Security Council to discuss the situation in Fallujah, Iraq.

November 6

In the morning, the President had an intelligence briefing.

The White House announced that the President will welcome Prime Minister Tony Blair of the United Kingdom to the White House for discussions on November 11–12.

November 7

In the afternoon, the President and Mrs. Bush returned to Washington, DC.

November 8

In the morning, the President had an intelligence briefing. Later, in the Oval Office, he met with Secretary of Defense Donald H. Rumsfeld. He also had a telephone conversation with Prime Minister Junichiro Koizumi of Japan to discuss the situation in North Korea.

November 9

In the morning, the President had an intelligence briefing.

The White House announced that the President will meet with North Atlantic Treaty Organization Secretary General Jakob "Jaap" Gijsbert de Hoop Scheffer at the White House on November 10.

The White House announced that the President will attend the 12th Asia-Pacific Economic Cooperation (APEC) Leaders' Meeting in Santiago, Chile, on November 20–21 and later will participate in an official visit with President Ricardo Lagos of Chile.

November 10

In the morning, the President had separate telephone conversations with President Gloria Macapagal-Arroyo of the Philippines, Prime Minister Lee Hsien Loong of Singapore, Prime Minister Pedro Santana Lopes of Portugal, and King Abdullah II of Jordan, all of whom congratulated the President on his reelection victory.

Later in the morning, the President had an intelligence briefing and met with the National Security Council. He then met with Secretary of State Colin L. Powell.

During the day, the President met with Senator John McCain of Arizona to discuss legislative priorities.

November 11

In the morning, the President had an intelligence briefing. Later, on the State Floor, he hosted a reception for veterans, leaders of veterans organizations, and Medal of Honor recipients.

Later in the morning, the President and Mrs. Bush traveled to Arlington, VA, where they participated in a wreath-laying ceremony at the Tomb of the Unknowns in Arlington National Cemetery.

In the afternoon, the President and Mrs. Bush returned to Washington, DC.

During the day, the President had separate telephone conversations with President Jorge Batlle Ibanez of Uruguay, Prime Minister Ferenc Gyurcsany of Hungary, European Commission President Jose Manuel Durao Barroso, Prime Minister Kjell Magne Bondevik of Norway, and President Ahmet Necdet Sezer of Turkey, all of whom congratulated the President on his reelection victory.

In the evening, in the Residence, the President had dinner with Prime Minister Tony Blair of the United Kingdom.

November 12

In the morning, the President had an intelligence briefing and met with the National Security Council. Later, in the Oval Office, he met with Prime Minister Tony Blair of the United Kingdom.

In the afternoon, in the Old Family Dining Room, the President had a working lunch with Prime Minister Blair. Later, on the State Floor, the President met with members of the Republican National Committee and the Victory Committee to thank them for their efforts during the campaign.

During the day, the President had separate telephone conversations with President Vaclav Klaus of the Czech Republic, President Valdas Adamkus of Lithuania, and President Paul Kagame of Rwanda, all of whom congratulated the President on his reelection victory.

The White House announced that the President will travel to Cartagena, Colombia, to meet with President Alvaro Uribe of Colombia on November 22.

The White House announced that the President and Mrs. Bush will host King Juan Carlos I and Queen Sofia of Spain for a private luncheon in Crawford, TX, on November 24.

November 13

In the morning, the President had an intelligence briefing.

November 15

In the morning, the President had an intelligence briefing and met with the National Security Council.

In the afternoon, in the State Dining Room, the President hosted a lunch for newly elected Members of the House of Representatives. Later, in the Oval Office, he met with Senate Majority Leader Bill Frist and Speaker of the House of Representatives J. Dennis Hastert to discuss legislative priorities.

The President announced his intention to nominate Jonathan Steven Adelstein to be a Commissioner of the Federal Communications Commission.

The President announced his intention to nominate Harold Jennings Creel, Jr., to be a Commissioner of the Federal Maritime Commission.

The President announced his intention to nominate Patricia Cushwa to be a member of the U.S. Parole Commission.

The President announced his intention to nominate Michael V. Dunn to be a Commissioner of the Commodity Futures Trading Commission.

The President announced his intention to nominate Tony Hammond to be a Commissioner of the Postal Rate Commission.

The President announced his intention to nominate Albert Henry Konetzni, Jr., to be a member of the Nuclear Regulatory Commission.

The President announced his intention to nominate Dallas Tonsager to be a member of the Farm Credit Administration Board.

The President announced his intention to nominate Raymond Thomas Wagner, Jr., to be a member of the Internal Revenue Service Oversight Board.

The President announced his intention to nominate Jay T. Snyder to be a member of the U.S. Advisory Commission on Public Diplomacy.

The President announced his intention to nominate Ernest J. Wilson III to be a member of the Board of Directors of the Corporation for Public Broadcasting.

The President announced his intention to nominate Sharon Tucker to be a member of the Board of Trustees of the Harry S. Truman Scholarship Foundation.

The President announced his intention to nominate Laurie Stenberg Nichols, Edward Alton Parrish, and Charles P. Ruch to be members of the Board of Trustees of the Barry Goldwater Scholarship and Excellence in Education Foundation.

The President announced his intention to nominate Jacob Joseph Lew and Mimi Mager to be members of the Board of Directors of the Corporation for National and Community Service.

The President announced his intention to nominate D. Jeffrey Hirschberg and Kenneth Y. Tomlinson (Chairman) to be members of the Broadcasting Board of Governors.

The President announced his intention to appoint John Salamone as a member of the Board of Trustees of the Christopher Columbus Fellowship Foundation.

November 16

In the morning, the President had separate telephone conversations with President Umar Hasan Ahmad al-Bashir of Sudan and Dr. John Garang de Mabior, Chairman of the Sudan People's Liberation Movement, to discuss the peace process in Sudan. He then had an intelligence briefing.

The White House announced that the President will visit Ottawa, Canada, from November 30 to December 1 to meet with Prime Minister Paul Martin of Canada.

The President announced his intention to appoint Stephen J. Hadley as Assistant to the President for National Security Affairs.

The President declared a major disaster in Delaware and ordered Federal aid to supplement State and local recovery efforts in the area struck by severe storms, tornadoes, and flooding from the remnants of Hurricane Jeanne on September 28 to October 2.

The President declared a major disaster in Alaska and ordered Federal aid to supplement State and local recovery efforts in the area struck by a severe winter storm, tidal surges, and flooding on October 18–20.

November 17

In the morning, in his private dining room, the President had a breakfast meeting with congressional leaders to discuss legislative priorities. At the meeting, he congratulated Senator Harry Reid of Nevada on his selection as new Senate minority leader. He then had an intelligence briefing.

Later in the morning, in the Oval Office, the President participated in a photo opportunity with Shauna Fleming, founder, A Million Thanks.

In the afternoon, in the Roosevelt Room, the President met with members of the Commission on the Intelligence Capabilities of the United States Regarding Weapons of Mass Destruction, who updated him on the Commission's progress.

Later in the afternoon, in the Oval Office, the President and Mrs. Bush presented the National Medal of Arts awards and the National Humanities Medal awards.

The President announced the following recipients of the National Medal of Arts for 2004:

Ray Bradbury;
Carlisle Floyd;
Frederick "Rick" Hart;
Anthony Hecht;
John Ruthven;
Vincent Scully;
Twyla Tharp; and
the Andrew W. Mellon Foundation.

The President announced the following recipients of the National Humanities Medal for 2004:

Marva Collins;

Gertrude Himmelfarb;
Hilton Kramer;
Madeleine L'Engle;
Harvey Mansfield;
John Searle;
Shelby Steele; and
the U.S. Capitol Historical Society.

The President announced his intention to appoint Harriet Miers as Counsel to the President.

November 18

In the morning, the President had an intelligence briefing. Later, he and Mrs. Bush traveled to Little Rock, AR.

In the afternoon, the President and Mrs. Bush traveled to the Bush Ranch in Crawford, TX.

November 19

In the morning, the President had an intelligence briefing. Later, he and Mrs. Bush traveled to Santiago, Chile, arriving in the evening.

Later in the evening, the President had a telephone conversation with Representative F. James Sensenbrenner, Jr., to discuss intelligence reform legislation.

The President announced that the following individuals will serve as the leadership of the 2005 Presidential Inaugural Committee:

Jeanne L. Phillips, chairman;
Greg Jenkins, executive director;
Bill and Kathy DeWitt, cochairs;
Brad Freeman, cochair; and
Mercer and Gabrielle Reynolds, cochairs.

The President announced that the following individuals will serve as members of the 2005 Presidential Inaugural Finance Committee:

Nancy and Rich Kinder;
Dawn and Al Hoffman;
Dawn and Roland Arnall;
Marcy and Bruce Benson;
Sue Ellen and Joe Canizaro;
Germaine and Jim Culbertson;
Marilyn and Sam Fox;
Martha and Dwight Schar; and
Patty and Roger Williams.

November 20

In the morning, the President had an intelligence briefing. Later, at the Hyatt Regency Santiago, he had separate meetings with President Hu Jintao of China, Prime Minister Junichiro Koizumi of Japan, President Roh Moohyun of South Korea, President Susilo Bambang

Yudhoyono of Indonesia, and Prime Minister Paul Martin of Canada.

In the afternoon, also at the Hyatt Regency Santiago, the President had a working lunch with President Vladimir Putin of Russia. Later, at the Espacio Riesco Convention Center, he attended the Asia-Pacific Economic Cooperation (APEC) Leaders' Meeting.

In the evening, at the Estacion Mapocho Cultural Center, the President and Mrs. Bush attended the APEC leaders' official dinner and a cultural presentation.

November 21

In the morning, at the Hyatt Regency Santiago, the President met with President Vicente Fox of Mexico. Then, at La Moneda Presidential Palace, he had separate brief meetings with Prime Minister Lee Hsien Loong of Singapore and President Alejandro Toledo of Peru. Later, also at La Moneda, he participated in a photo opportunity with APEC leaders and then attended the APEC Leaders' Meeting.

In the afternoon, at the Hyatt Regency Santiago, the President greeted U.S. Embassy staff and their families.

In the evening, at La Moneda Presidential Palace, the President met with President Ricardo Lagos of Chile. Later, he and Mrs. Bush had dinner with President Lagos and his wife, Luisa Duran de Lagos.

November 22

In the morning, the President had an intelligence briefing. Later, he and Mrs. Bush traveled to Cartagena, Colombia.

In the afternoon, at Casa de Huespedes, the President and Mrs. Bush participated in an arrival ceremony with President Alvaro Uribe of Colombia and his wife, Lina Maria Moreno de Uribe.

Later in the afternoon, also at Casa de Huespedes, the President had a meeting and a working lunch with President Uribe. He then participated in a photo opportunity with Major League Baseball players Edgar Renteria and Orlando Cabrera and youth from Colombian baseball camps.

Later in the afternoon, the President and Mrs. Bush traveled to the Bush Ranch in Crawford, TX, arriving in the evening.

November 23

In the morning, the President had intelligence, national security, and FBI briefings. Later, he met with the National Security Council by video teleconference.

November 24

In the morning, the President had an intelligence briefing.

In the afternoon, the President and Mrs. Bush welcomed King Juan Carlos I and Queen Sofia of Spain to the Bush Ranch for a private luncheon.

The White House announced that the President will welcome King Hamad bin Isa Al Khalifa of Bahrain to Washington, DC, for a working visit on November 29.

The White House announced that the President will welcome President Olusegun Obasanjo of Nigeria, current Chairman of the African Union, to the White House on December 2.

November 25

In the morning, the President had an intelligence briefing.

During the day, the President had several telephone conversations with members of the U.S. Armed Forces.

November 26

In the morning, the President had an intelligence briefing.

November 27

In the morning, the President had an intelligence briefing.

November 28

In the morning, the President and Mrs. Bush returned to Washington, DC, arriving in the afternoon.

November 29

In the morning, the President had an intelligence briefing.

In the afternoon, in the Oval Office, the President met with King Hamad bin Isa Al Khalifa of Bahrain.

The White House announced that the President will welcome President Pervez Musharraf of Pakistan to the White House on December 4.

The White House announced that the President will welcome President Abdoulaye Wade of Senegal to the White House on December 6.

The President announced his intention to nominate Carlos M. Gutierrez to be Secretary of Commerce.

November 30

In the morning, the President had an intelligence briefing. Later, he and Mrs. Bush traveled to Ottawa, Canada, where, upon arrival at Ottawa MacDonald-Cartier International Airport, they met Governor General Adrienne Clarkson of Canada.

Later in the morning, the President and Mrs. Bush went to Parliament Hill, where they met Prime Minister Paul Martin of Canada and his wife, Sheila. Later, they signed a guest book and met with Parliament officials. The President then met with Prime Minister Martin.

In the afternoon, in the Lester B. Pearson Building, the President had a working lunch with Prime Minister Martin. Later, he and Mrs. Bush traveled to Gatineau, Canada, where they participated in a tour of the National Archives Preservation Centre.

Later in the afternoon, the President and Mrs. Bush returned to Ottawa. Then, in the Government Conference Centre, the President met with leader of the Official Opposition, Stephen Harper. Later, in the Main Hall, he and Mrs. Bush, who joined him after his meeting with Mr. Harper, greeted Embassy staff.

In the evening, the President and Mrs. Bush went to the Canadian Museum of Civilization in Gatineau, where, in the Grand Hall, they participated in an official dinner hosted by Prime Minister and Mrs. Martin.

Later in the evening, the President and Mrs. Bush returned to Ottawa.

December 1

In the morning, the President traveled to Halifax, Canada. While en route aboard Air Force One, he had an intelligence briefing.

In the afternoon, the President returned to Washington, DC. Later, in the Oval Office, he met with 2004 Nobel Laureates Linda Buck, Finn Kydland, Edward Prescott, Frank Wilczek, David Gross, and Richard Axel.

In the evening, on the State Floor, the President hosted a holiday reception.

The White House announced that the President will meet with King Abdullah II of Jordan at the White House on December 6.

December 2

In the morning, the President had an intelligence briefing. Later, in Room 450 of the Dwight D. Eisenhower Executive Office Building, he made remarks to the American Legislative Exchange Council.

In the afternoon, the President had separate telephone conversations with Senate Majority Leader Bill Frist and Speaker of the House of Representatives J. Dennis Hastert to discuss legislative priorities.

In the evening, on the State Floor, the President hosted a holiday reception.

The President announced his intention to nominate Gov. Mike Johanns of Nebraska to be Secretary of Agriculture.

The President announced his designation of the following individuals as members of the Presidential delegation to the inauguration of President Hamid Karzai of Afghanistan:

Vice President Dick Cheney (head of delegation);
Lynne Cheney;
Donald H. Rumsfeld;
Zalmay Khalilzad;
Christina B. Rocca; and
Karen Hughes.

December 3

In the morning, the President had an intelligence briefing.

In the afternoon, in Room 350 of the Dwight D. Eisenhower Executive Office Building, the President participated in a signing ceremony for the Internet Tax Nondiscrimination Act.

In the evening, on the State Floor, the President hosted a holiday reception.

The White House announced that the President will welcome President Ghazi al-Ujayl al-Yawr of the Iraqi Interim Government to the White House on December 6.

The President announced his intention to nominate Bernard B. Kerik to be Secretary of Homeland Security.

The President announced his intention to nominate James William Carr, George M. Dennison, and Andrew J. McKenna, Jr., to be members of the National Security Education Board.

The President announced his intention to appoint Rebecca F. Denlinger, Gregory A. Peters, and Bruce Rohde as members of the National Infrastructure Advisory Council.

The President announced his intention to appoint Randall L. Stephenson as a member of the President's National Security Telecommunications Advisory Committee.

The President announced his intention to nominate Harry Robinson, Jr., to be a member of the Museum and Library Services Board.

December 4

In the morning, the President had an intelligence briefing.

In the afternoon, the President traveled to Philadelphia, PA, to attend the Army-Navy football game at Lincoln Financial Field. Before the game, he met with both teams in their locker rooms and participated in the opening coin toss. He watched the first half of the game from Army's side of the field and the second half from Navy's.

In the evening, the President returned to Washington, DC.

December 5

In the evening, the President and Mrs. Bush attended the Kennedy Center Honors ceremony at the John F. Kennedy Center for the Performing Arts.

December 6

In the morning, the President had an intelligence briefing.

In the afternoon, in the Oval Office, the President met with President Abdoulaye Wade of Senegal. Later, on the State Floor, he and Mrs. Bush participated in the Children's Christmas Reception and Program.

Later in the afternoon, in the Cabinet Room, the President met with bipartisan Members of Congress to discuss Social Security.

The President announced his intention to appoint Kenneth Marcus as Staff Director of the U.S. Commission on Civil Rights, with the concurrence of a majority of the Commission.

The President announced his appointment of Gerald A. Reynolds and Ashley L. Taylor as members of the U.S. Commission on Civil Rights.

The President announced his designation of Gerald A. Reynolds and Abigail Thernstrom as Chairperson and Vice Chairperson, respectively, of the U.S. Commission on Civil Rights, with the concurrence of a majority of the Commission.

December 7

In the morning, the President traveled to Miramar, CA. While en route aboard Air Force One, he had an intelligence briefing. Upon arrival, he met with Kathryn Ostapuk, whom he presented with the President's Volunteer Service Award.

Later in the morning, the President traveled to Camp Pendleton, CA, where he presented the Presidential Unit Citation to the Combined Joint Special Operations Task Force SOUTH/Task Force K–BAR. Later, he had lunch with military personnel.

In the afternoon, the President returned to Washington, DC, arriving in the evening.

December 8

In the morning, the President had an intelligence briefing and met with the National Security Council.

In the evening, on the State Floor, the President participated in separate holiday receptions with members of the Presidential Protective Detail and staff members of the White House and the Executive Office of the President.

December 9

In the morning, the President had an intelligence briefing. Later, he had telephone conversations with President Aleksander Kwasniewski of Poland and President Valdas Adamkus of Lithuania to discuss the situation in Ukraine.

In the afternoon, in an Oval Office ceremony, the President received diplomatic credentials from Ambassadors Federico Humbert de Arias of Panama, Francisco Tomas Duenas Leiva of Costa Rica, Jehangir Karamat of Pakistan, Mahamoud Adam Bechir of Chad, John Bruton of the European Commission, and Maris Riekstins of Latvia.

Later in the afternoon, in Room 476 of the Dwight D. Eisenhower Executive Office Building, the President met with rabbis and Jewish community leaders. Later, on the State Floor, he and Mrs. Bush participated in a holiday reception.

The White House announced that the President will travel to Europe in February 2005 for meetings with European leaders, beginning his consultations in Brussels, Belgium, on February 22, meeting with allied heads of state and Government at NATO. The President will also meet with the EU Presidency, the European

Council, and the European Commission President.

The President announced his intention to nominate Jim Nicholson to be Secretary of Veterans Affairs.

December 10

In the morning, the President had an intelligence briefing. Later, in the Residence, he participated in an interview with People magazine.

In the afternoon, in the Roosevelt Room, the President dropped by a meeting of the National Security Council and participants of the U.S.-Russia Volunteer Initiative.

Later in the afternoon, the President and Mrs. Bush traveled to Fort Belvoir, VA. Later, they returned to Washington, DC.

The White House announced that the President will host Prime Minister Silvio Berlusconi of Italy for a meeting and lunch on December 15.

The President announced his intention to nominate Samuel W. Bodman to be Secretary of Energy.

The President announced his intention to appoint the following individuals as members of the President's Committee on the National Medal of Science:

Bruce N. Ames;
Randolph W. Bromery;
Winfred M. Phillips; and
Jean'ne Marie Shreeve (Chairperson).

The President announced his intention to appoint the following individuals as members of the Helping to Enhance the Livelihood of People (HELP) Around the Globe Commission:

Carol Craigle Adelman;
Mary K. Bush;
Glenn Estess;
C. Boyden Gray (Chairman);
Carla Hills; and
Walter H. Kansteiner.

December 11

In the morning, the President had an intelligence briefing. Later, he traveled to the National Naval Medical Center in Bethesda, MD, where he had his annual physical examination and visited injured U.S. military personnel.

In the afternoon, the President returned to Washington, DC.

December 12

In the afternoon, the President and Mrs. Bush went to the National Building Museum where they participated in the taping of the annual "Christmas in Washington" concert for later television broadcast.

In the evening, the President and Mrs. Bush returned to the White House. Later, on the State Floor, they hosted a holiday reception.

December 13

In the morning, the President had an intelligence briefing.

The President announced his intention to nominate Michael O. Leavitt to be Secretary of Health and Human Services.

December 14

In the morning, the President had an intelligence briefing.

In the afternoon, at Blair House, the President and Mrs. Bush hosted a holiday reception for members of the diplomatic corps.

In the evening, on the State Floor, the President hosted a holiday reception.

The President announced the recess appointment of Ronald Rosenfeld as a director of the Board of Directors of the the the Federal Housing Finance Board, and his designation as Chairman of the Federal Housing Finance Board.

December 15

In the morning, the President had a telephone conversation with President-elect Traian Basescu of Romania to congratulate him on his December 12 election victory. He then had an intelligence briefing.

Later in the morning, in the Oval Office, the President met with Members of Congress and some of their constituents, who presented the President with gifts.

In the afternoon, in the Residence, the President had lunch with Prime Minister Silvio Berlusconi of Italy.

In the evening, in Room 350 of the Dwight D. Eisenhower Executive Office Building, the President participated in a holiday reception for moderators and panelists from the ongoing White House Conference on the Economy.

Later in the evening, on the State Floor, the President hosted a holiday reception.

December 16

In the morning, the President had an intelligence briefing.

In the evening, the President and Mrs. Bush hosted in a holiday reception for members of the press.

December 17

In the morning, the President had an intelligence briefing.

Later in the morning, in the Oval Office, the President received an update on the report of the U.S. Commission on Ocean Policy. He then signed Executive Order 13366—Committee on Ocean Policy.

The President announced his intention to appoint Bobby R. Burchfield as a member of the Antitrust Modernization Commission.

The President made additional disaster assistance available to West Virginia, which was impacted by severe storms, flooding, and landslides on September 16–27.

December 18

In the morning, the President had an intelligence briefing.

December 20

In the morning, the President had an intelligence briefing.

December 21

In the morning, the President had a telephone conversation with Prime Minister Recep Tayyip Erdogan of Turkey to discuss the European Union's decision to begin accession talks with Turkey on October 3, 2005, the situation in Iraq, and other issues. He then had an intelligence briefing.

Later in the morning, in the Oval Office, he met with Office of National Drug Control Policy Director John P. Walters, who presented him with the results of the 2004 Monitoring the Future survey.

In the afternoon, in the Oval Office, the President met with Kweisi Mfume, outgoing president and chief executive officer, National Association for the Advancement of Colored People.

Later in the afternoon, the President and Mrs. Bush traveled to Camp David, MD.

The White House announced that the President will travel to Germany and the Slovak Republic following his meetings on February 22,

2005, with NATO and European Union leaders in Brussels, Belgium. Chancellor Gerhard Schroeder of Germany will host the President in Germany on February 23. In addition to a bilateral program in the Slovak Republic on February 24, the President will meet with President Vladimir Putin of Russia.

December 22

In the morning, the President had an intelligence briefing.

December 23

In the morning, the President had an intelligence briefing.

December 24

In the morning, the President had an intelligence briefing.

During the day, the President had telephone conversations with members of the U.S. Armed Forces. He also had a telephone conversation with King Juan Carlos I of Spain to exchange best wishes and holiday greetings.

December 25

In the morning, the President had an intelligence briefing.

December 26

In the morning, the President and Mrs. Bush traveled to the Bush Ranch in Crawford, TX.

December 27

In the morning, the President had an intelligence briefing and a briefing on the December 26 earthquake and tsunamis in the Indian Ocean. He also had a telephone conversation with Secretary of State Colin L. Powell to discuss the earthquake and tsunamis in the Indian Ocean and the elections in Ukraine.

The White House announced that the President sent letters of condolence to the leaders of Bangladesh, Thailand, Sri Lanka, Indonesia, India, Maldives, and Malaysia, which were affected by the December 26 earthquake and tsunamis in the Indian Ocean.

December 28

In the morning, the President had an intelligence briefing and a briefing on the December 26 earthquake and tsunamis in the Indian Ocean.

December 29

In the morning, the President had an intelligence briefing.

December 30

In the morning, the President had separate telephone conversations with President Susilo Bambang Yudhoyono of Indonesia; Prime Minister Thaksin Chinnawat of Thailand; President Chandrika Bandaranaike Kumaratunga of Sri Lanka; and Prime Minister Manmohan Singh of India to express his condolences and pledge support following the December 26 earthquake and tsunamis in the Indian Ocean. He then had an intelligence briefing.

December 31

In the morning, the President had an intelligence briefing.

Appendix B—Nominations Submitted to the Senate

The following list does not include promotions of members of the Uniformed Services, nominations to the Service Academies, or nominations of Foreign Service officers.

Submitted October 5

Michael Butler,
of Tennessee, to be a member of the Board of Trustees of the Morris K. Udall Scholarship and Excellence in National Environmental Policy Foundation for a term expiring October 6, 2008, vice Eric D. Eberhard, term expired.

Ronald Rosenfeld,
of Oklahoma, to be a Director of the Federal Housing Finance Board for the remainder of the term expiring February 27, 2009, vice John Thomas Korsmo, resigned.

Submitted October 7

Harold Damelin,
of Virginia, to be Inspector General, Department of the Treasury, vice Jeffrey Rush, Jr., resigned.

Edward L. Flippen,
of Virginia, to be Inspector General, Corporation for National and Community Service, vice J. Russell George.

Frederick William Hatfield,
of California, to be a Commissioner of the Commodity Futures Trading Commission for the term expiring April 13, 2008, vice Thomas J. Erickson, term expired.

Brian David Miller,
of Virginia, to be Inspector General, General Services Administration, vice Daniel R. Levinson.

Jorge A. Plasencia,
of Florida, to be a member of the Advisory Board for Cuba Broadcasting for a term expiring October 27, 2006, vice Joseph Francis Glennon, term expired.

Withdrawn October 7

James B. Cunningham,
of Pennsylvania, a career member of the Senior Foreign Service, class of Career Minister, to be Representative of the United States of America to the Vienna office of the United Nations, with the rank of Ambassador, and to be Representative of the United States of America to the International Atomic Energy Agency, with the rank of Ambassador, which were sent to the Senate on April 8, 2004.

Submitted October 8

Carolyn L. Gallagher,
of Texas, to be a Governor of the U.S. Postal Service for the remainder of the term expiring December 8, 2005, vice Erensta Ballard, resigned.

Louis J. Giuliano,
of New York, to be a Governor of the U.S. Postal Service for a term expiring December 8, 2009, vice Albert Casey.

Submitted November 16

Jonathan Steven Adelstein,
of South Dakota, to be a member of the Federal Communications Commission for a term expiring June 30, 2008 (reappointment).

Harold Jennings Creel, Jr.,
of South Carolina, to be a Federal Maritime Commissioner for the term expiring June 30, 2009 (reappointment).

Patricia Cushwa,
of Maryland, to be a Commissioner of the U.S. Parole Commission for a term of 6 years, vice Janie L. Jeffers.

Michael V. Dunn,
of Iowa, to be a Commissioner of the Commodity Futures Trading Commission for the remainder of the term expiring June 19, 2006, vice James E. Newsome, resigned.

Carolyn L. Gallagher,
of Texas, to be a Governor of the U.S. Postal Service for the remainder of the term expiring December 8, 2005, vice Erensta Ballard, resigned, to which position she was appointed during the last recess of the Senate.

Louis J. Giuliano,
of New York, to be a Governor of the U.S. Postal Service for a term expiring December 8, 2009, vice Albert Casey, to which position he was appointed during the last recess of the Senate.

Alberto R. Gonzales,
of Texas, to be Attorney General, vice John Ashcroft, resigned.

Tony Hammond,
of Virginia, to be a Commissioner of the Postal Rate Commission for a term expiring October 14, 2010 (reappointment).

D. Jeffrey Hirschberg,
of Wisconsin, to be a member of the Broadcasting Board of Governors for a term expiring August 13, 2007 (reappointment).

Albert Henry Konetzni, Jr.,
of New York, to be a member of the Nuclear Regulatory Commission for a term expiring June 30, 2009, vice Richard A. Meserve, resigned.

Jacob Joseph Lew,
of New York, to be a member of the Board of Directors of the Corporation for National and Community Service for a term expiring October 6, 2008, vice Arthur J. Naparstek, term expired.

Mimi Mager,
of the District of Columbia, to be a member of the Board of Directors of the Corporation for National and Community Service for a term expiring December 27, 2007, vice Mark D. Gearan, term expired.

Laurie Stenberg Nichols,
of South Dakota, to be a member of the Board of Trustees of the Barry Goldwater Scholarship and Excellence in Education Foundation for a term expiring March 3, 2010, vice Donna Dearman Smith, term expired.

Edward Alton Parrish,
of Virginia, to be a member of the Board of Trustees of the Barry Goldwater Scholarship and Excellence in Education Foundation for a term expiring April 17, 2008, vice Hans Mark, resigned.

Charles P. Ruch,
of South Dakota, to be a member of the Board of Trustees of the Barry Goldwater Scholarship and Excellence in Education Foundation for a term expiring August 11, 2010, vice Niranjan Shamalbhai Shah, term expired.

Jay T. Snyder,
of New York, to be a member of the U.S. Advisory Commission on Public Diplomacy for a term expiring July 1, 2007 (reappointment).

Kenneth Y. Tomlinson,
of Virginia, to be a member of the Broadcasting Board of Governors for a term expiring August 13, 2007 (reappointment).

Kenneth Y. Tomlinson,
of Virginia, to be Chairman of the Broadcasting Board of Governors (reappointment).

Dallas Tonsager,
of South Dakota, to be a member of the Farm Credit Administration Board, Farm Credit Administration for a term expiring May 21, 2010, vice Michael M. Reyna, term expired.

Sharon Tucker,
of Georgia, to be a member of the Board of Trustees of the Harry S. Truman Scholarship Foundation for a term expiring December 10, 2005, vice E. Gordon Gee, term expired.

Raymond Thomas Wagner, Jr.,
of Missouri, to be a member of the Internal Revenue Service Oversight Board for a term expiring September 14, 2009 (reappointment).

Ernest J. Wilson III,
of Maryland, to be a member of the Board of Directors of the Corporation for Public Broadcasting for a term expiring January 31, 2010 (reappointment).

Jennifer M. Anderson,
of the District of Columbia, to be an Associate Judge of the Superior Court of the District of Columbia for the term of 15 years, vice Steffen W. Graae, retired.

A. Noel Anketell Kramer,
of the District of Columbia, to be an Associate Judge of the District of Columbia Court of Appeals for the term of 15 years, vice John Montague Steadman, retired.

Withdrawn November 16

Ann C. Rosenthal,
of Iowa, to be a member of the Board of Directors of the National Institute of Building Sciences for a term expiring September 7, 2003, vice Steve M. Hays, term expired, and for a term expiring September 7, 2006 (reappointment), which were sent to the Senate on June 12, 2003.

Lawrence T. Di Rita,
of Michigan, to be an Assistant Secretary of Defense, vice Victoria Clarke, which was sent to the Senate on November 21, 2003.

Submitted November 17

A. Wilson Greene,
of Virginia, to be a member of the National Museum and Library Services Board for a term expiring December 6, 2009 (reappointment).

Katina P. Strauch,
of South Carolina, to be a member of the National Museum and Library Services Board for a term expiring December 6, 2009, vice Elizabeth J. Pruet, term expiring.

Submitted December 7

James William Carr,
of Arkansas, to be a member of the National Security Education Board for a term of 4 years, vice Manuel Trinidad Pacheco, term expired.

George M. Dennison,
of Montana, to be a member of the National Security Education Board for a term of 4 years, vice Bruce Sundlun, term expired.

Andrew J. McKenna, Jr.,
of Illinois, to be a member of the National Security Education Board for a term of 4 years, vice Robert N. Shamansky, term expired.

Harry Robinson, Jr.,
of Texas, to be a member of the National Museum Services Board for a term expiring December 6, 2008 (reappointment).

Appendix C—Checklist of White House Press Releases

The following list contains releases of the Office of the Press Secretary which are not included in this book.

Released October 1

Transcript of a press gaggle by Press Secretary Scott McClellan

Statement by the Press Secretary announcing that on September 30 the President signed H.R. 5149, H.R. 5183, and H.J. Res. 107

Released October 2

Statement by the Press Secretary on disaster assistance to New York, signed October 1

Statement by the Press Secretary on disaster assistance to New York, signed October 1

Statement by the Press Secretary on disaster assistance to New Jersey, signed October 1

Released October 4

Transcript of a press gaggle by Press Secretary Scott McClellan

Statement by the Press Secretary announcing that the President signed H.R. 1308

Statement by the Press Secretary conveying the President's congratulations to Susilo Bambang Yudhoyono on his victory in the Republic of Indonesia's Presidential election

Fact sheet: President Bush Signs Tax Relief Bill Benefiting Millions of American Families

Released October 5

Statement by the Press Secretary announcing that the President signed H.R. 265, H.R. 1521, H.R. 1616, H.R. 1648, H.R. 1658, H.R. 1732, H.R. 2696, H.R. 3209, H.R. 3249, H.R. 3389, H.R. 3768, and S.J. Res. 41

Fact sheet: Providing Needed Relief to Hurricane Ravaged Areas

Released October 6

Transcript of a press gaggle by Press Secretary Scott McClellan

Statement by the Press Secretary announcing that the President signed H.R. 4654

Released October 7

Statement by the Press Secretary on disaster assistance to Florida

Statement by the Press Secretary on disaster assistance to South Carolina

Statement by the Press Secretary on disaster assistance to Minnesota

Statement by the Press Secretary on disaster assistance to the U.S. Virgin Islands

Statement by the Press Secretary on disaster assistance to Tennessee

Released October 8

Transcript of a press gaggle by Press Secretary Scott McClellan

Fact sheet: Elections in Afghanistan

Released October 12

Transcript of a press gaggle by Press Secretary Scott McClellan

Released October 13

Transcript of a press gaggle by White House Communications Director Dan Bartlett

Statement by the Press Secretary announcing that the President signed H.R. 4837 and S. 1778

Statement by the Press Secretary on the appointment of Meghan L. O'Sullivan as Special Assistant to the President and Senior Director for Strategic Planning and Southwest Asia at the National Security Council

Statement by the Press Secretary on the appointment of Reuben Jeffery III as Special Assistant to the President and Senior Director for International Economic Affairs at the National Security Council

Statement by the Press Secretary on the appointment of Robert L. Wilkie as Special Assistant to the President and Senior Director for

Legislative Affairs at the National Security Council

Released October 14

Transcript of a press gaggle by Press Secretary Scott McClellan

Fact sheet: Fulfilling the President's Commitment to Hurricane Victims

Released October 15

Transcript of a press gaggle by Press Secretary Scott McClellan

Released October 16

Statement by the Deputy Press Secretary announcing that the President signed S. 2292

Released October 17

Statement by the Press Secretary announcing that the President signed H.R. 982, H.R. 2408, H.R. 2771, H.R. 4115, H.R. 4259, and H.R. 5105

Released October 18

Transcript of a press gaggle by Press Secretary Scott McClellan

Statement by the Press Secretary on action to support the deployment of the expanded African Union mission in Sudan

Statement by the Press Secretary congratulating King Norodom Sihamoni on assuming Cambodia's throne

Statement by the Press Secretary announcing that the President signed H.R. 4011, H.R. 4567, H.R. 4850, S. 551, S. 1421, S. 1537, S. 1663, S. 1687, S. 1814, S. 2052, S. 2180, S. 2319, S. 2363, and S. 2508

Statement by the Press Secretary on disaster assistance to Virginia

Fact sheet: Providing the Resources Necessary To Protect America

Released October 20

Transcript of a press gaggle by Press Secretary Scott McClellan

Statement by the Press Secretary announcing that the President signed H.R. 854 and S. 2895

Released October 21

Transcript of a press gaggle by Press Secretary Scott McClellan

Statement by the Press Secretary: Humanitarian Assistance for the People of Darfur

Statement by the Press Secretary: President Signs the North Korean Human Rights Act

Statement by the Press Secretary announcing that the President signed H.R. 5122, S. 33, S. 1791, S. 2178, S. 2415, S. 2511, S. 2634, S. 2742

Released October 22

Transcript of press gaggles by Press Secretary Scott McClellan

Statement by the Press Secretary announcing that the President signed H.R. 4520

Statement by the Press Secretary announcing that the President signed S. 2195

Released October 25

Transcript of a press gaggle by Press Secretary Scott McClellan

Statement by the Press Secretary announcing that the President signed H.R. 1533, H.R. 2608, H.R. 2714, H.R. 2828, H.R. 3858, H.R. 4175, H.R. 4278, H.R. 4555, H.R. 5185, S. 524, S. 1368, S. 2864, S. 2883, and S. 2896

Released October 27

Transcript of a press gaggle by Press Secretary Scott McClellan

Statement by the Press Secretary announcing that the President signed S. 1134 and S. 1721

Released October 28

Transcript of a press gaggle by Press Secretary Scott McClellan

Released October 29

Transcript of press gaggles by Press Secretary Scott McClellan

Statement by the Press Secretary on resolution of the dispute investigated by Presidential Emergency Board No. 238

Statement by the Press Secretary announcing that on October 28 the President signed H.R. 4200

Released October 30

Statement by the Press Secretary announcing that the President signed H.R. 712, H.R. 867, H.R. 2010, H.R. 2023, H.R. 2400, H.R. 2984, H.R. 3056, H.R. 3217, H.R. 3391, H.R. 3478, H.R. 3479, H.R. 3706, H.R. 3797, H.R. 3819, H.R. 4046, H.R. 4066, H.R. 4306, H.R. 4381, H.R. 4471, H.R. 4481, H.R. 4556, H.R. 4579, H.R. 4618, H.R. 4632, H.R. 4731, H.R. 4827, H.R. 4917, H.R. 5027, H.R. 5039, H.R. 5051, H.R. 5107, H.R. 5131, H.R. 5133, H.R. 5147, H.R. 5186, H.R. 5294, H.J. Res. 57, S. 129, S. 144, S. 643, and S. 1194

Released November 3

Transcript of a press gaggle by Press Secretary Scott McClellan

Released November 5

Statement by the Press Secretary on the President's conversation with Prime Minister Jan Peter Balkenende of the Netherlands, in his capacity as President of the European Council

Released November 6

Statement by the Press Secretary on the upcoming visit of Prime Minister Tony Blair of the United Kingdom

Released November 8

Transcript of a press briefing by Press Secretary Scott McClellan

Released November 9

Transcript of a press briefing by Press Secretary Scott McClellan

Statement by the Press Secretary on the selection of Millennium Challenge Account-eligible countries for FY 2005

Statement by the Press Secretary on the upcoming visit of NATO Secretary General Jakob "Jaap" Gijsbert de Hoop Scheffer

Statement by the Press Secretary on the President's upcoming visit to Santiago, Chile, to attend the 12th Asia-Pacific Economic Cooperation (APEC) Leaders' Meeting and later participate in an official visit with President Ricardo Lagos of Chile

Released November 10

Transcript of a press briefing by Press Secretary Scott McClellan

Released November 11

Fact sheet: Honoring the Courage of America's Veterans

Released November 12

Statement by the Press Secretary on the President's upcoming visit to Cartagena, Colombia, to meet with President Alvaro Uribe

Statement by the Press Secretary on the upcoming visit of King Juan Carlos I and Queen Sofia of Spain to Crawford, TX

Released November 13

Statement by Dr. Jonathan Reiner, Director of the Cardiac Catheterization Laboratory at George Washington University Hospital, on the Vice President's medical evaluation

Released November 15

Transcript of a press briefing by Press Secretary Scott McClellan

Released November 16

Transcript of a press briefing by Press Secretary Scott McClellan

Statement by the Press Secretary on the President's upcoming visit to Ottawa, Canada

Statement by the Press Secretary on disaster assistance to Delaware

Statement by the Press Secretary on disaster assistance to Alaska

Released November 17

Transcript of a press briefing by Press Secretary Scott McClellan

Statement by the Press Secretary expressing sympathy to the family of Margaret Hassan

Announcement of the National Medal of Arts and National Humanities Medal recipients

Released November 18

Transcript of a press gaggle by Press Secretary Scott McClellan

Statement by the Press Secretary on the election process in Ukraine

Released November 19

Statement by the Press Secretary announcing that the President signed S. 2986

Released November 21

Statement by the Press Secretary announcing that the President signed H.J. Res. 114

Fact sheet: U.S. Actions at the APEC Leaders' Meeting: Ensuring Security, Promoting Prosperity

Fact sheet: U.S. Actions at the APEC Leaders' Meeting: Expanding Trade and Fighting Corruption

Fact sheet: APEC Leaders Commit To Fight Corruption and Ensure Transparency

Released November 23

Transcript of a press gaggle by Deputy Press Secretary Claire Buchan

Statement by the Deputy Press Secretary on indications of fraud committed in the Ukrainian Presidential election

Released November 24

Statement by the Deputy Press Secretary on the upcoming visit of King Hamad bin Isa Al Khalifa of Bahrain

Statement by the Deputy Press Secretary on the upcoming visit of Nigerian President and current Chairman of the African Union Olusegun Obasanjo

Released November 29

Transcript of a press briefing by Press Secretary Scott McClellan

Statement by the Press Secretary on the upcoming visit of President Pervez Musharraf of Pakistan

Statement by the Press Secretary on the upcoming visit of President Abdoulaye Wade of Senegal

Released November 30

Transcript of a press gaggle by Press Secretary Scott McClellan

Statement by the Press Secretary announcing that the President signed H.R. 1113, H.R. 1284, H.R. 1417, H.R. 1446, H.R. 1964, H.R. 3936, H.R. 4516, H.R. 4593, H.R. 4794, H.R. 5163, H.R. 5213, and H.R. 5245

Joint Communique: Common Security, Common Prosperity: A New Partnership in North America

Released December 1

Transcript of a press gaggle by Press Secretary Scott McClellan

Statement by the Press Secretary on the upcoming visit of King Abdullah II of Jordan

Released December 2

Transcript of a press briefing by Press Secretary Scott McClellan

Statement by the Press Secretary on continued U.S. support for Nobel Peace Prize winner Aung San Suu Kyi and the Burmese people

Statement by the Press Secretary announcing that the President will award the Presidential Medal of Freedom to L. Paul Bremer III, Tommy R. Franks, and George J. Tenet

Released December 3

Transcript of a press briefing by Press Secretary Scott McClellan

Statement by the Press Secretary on the upcoming visit of President Ghazi al-Ujayl al-Yawr of the Iraqi Interim Government

Statement by the Press Secretary announcing that the President signed H.R. 1047, H.R. 1630, H.R. 2912, H.J. Res. 110, H.J. Res. 111, H.J. Res. 115, S. 150, S. 434, S. 1146, S. 1241, S. 1727, S. 2042, S. 2214, S. 2302, S. 2484, S. 2693, S. 2640, and S. 2965

Released December 6

Transcript of a press briefing by Press Secretary Scott McClellan

Released December 7

Transcript of a press gaggle by Deputy Press Secretary Trent Duffy

Released December 8

Transcript of a press briefing by Press Secretary Scott McClellan

Statement by the Press Secretary announcing that the President signed H.R. 4818 and S. 2618

Released December 9

Transcript of a press briefing by Press Secretary Scott McClellan

Statement by the Press Secretary announcing the President's upcoming visit to Europe

Released December 10

Transcript of a press briefing by Press Secretary Scott McClellan

Statement by the Press Secretary on the upcoming visit of Prime Minister Silvio Berlusconi of Italy

Statement by the Press Secretary announcing that the President signed H.R. 2655, H.R. 4302, S. 437, S. 1466, S. 2192, S. 2486, S. 2873, and S. 3014

Statement by the Press Secretary on Bernard B. Kerik's withdrawing his name from consideration for Secretary of Homeland Security

Announcement: Securing Our Economic Future: White House Conference on the Economy, December 15–16, 2004

Released December 13

Transcript of a press briefing by Press Secretary Scott McClellan

Released December 14

Transcript of a press briefing by Press Secretary Scott McClellan

Released December 15

Fact sheet: Securing Our Economic Future: The White House Conference on the Economy

Released December 16

Transcript of a press briefing by Press Secretary Scott McClellan

Released December 17

Transcript of a press briefing by Press Secretary Scott McClellan

Transcript of a telephone press briefing by Council of Economic Advisers Chairman N. Gregory Mankiw on the administration's forecast for 2005

Transcript of a press briefing by White House Council on Environmental Quality Chairman James Connaughton on the U.S. Oceans Action Plan

Statement by the Press Secretary announcing that the President signed H.R. 4012

Statement by the Press Secretary on additional disaster assistance to West Virginia

Released December 21

Transcript of a press briefing by Press Secretary Scott McClellan

Statement by the Press Secretary announcing the President's upcoming visit to Germany and the Slovak Republic

Statement by the Press Secretary announcing that the President signed H.R. 480, H.R. 2119, H.R. 2523, H.R. 3124, H.R. 3147, H.R. 3204, H.R. 3242, H.R. 3734, H.R. 3884, H.R. 4232, H.R. 4324, H.R. 4620, H.R. 4807, H.R. 4829, H.R. 4847, H.R. 4968, H.R. 5360, H.R. 5364, H.R. 5365, H.R. 5370, and H.J. Res. 102

Released December 22

Statement by the Press Secretary announcing 36 countries which continue to be eligible for economic and trade benefits under the African Growth and Opportunity Act

Released December 23

Statement by the Press Secretary announcing the President's intent to renominate 20 judicial nominees when the Senate reconvenes

Statement by the Press Secretary announcing that the President signed H.R. 530, H.R. 2457, H.R. 2619, H.R. 3632, H.R. 3785, H.R. 3818, H.R. 4027, H.R. 4116, H.R. 4548, H.R. 4569, H.R. 4657, H.R. 5204, H.R. 5363, H.R. 5382, H.R. 5394, H.R. 5419, S. 1301, S. 2657, S. 2781, and S. 2856

Released December 24

Announcement: List of President Bush's Christmas Eve Telephone Calls to Members of the Armed Forces

Released December 26

Statement by the Deputy Press Secretary: Earthquake and Tidal Waves in the Bay of Bengal

Released December 27

Transcript of a press gaggle by Deputy Press Secretary Trent Duffy

Released December 28

Transcript of a press gaggle by Deputy Press Secretary Trent Duffy

Released December 30

Transcript of a press gaggle by Deputy Press
Secretary Trent Duffy

Appendix D—Presidential Documents Published in the Federal Register

This appendix lists Presidential documents released by the Office of the Press Secretary and published in the Federal Register. The texts of the documents are printed in the Federal Register (F.R.) at the citations listed below. The documents are also printed in title 3 of the Code of Federal Regulations and in the Weekly Compilation of Presidential Documents.

PROCLAMATIONS

PROCLAMATIONS—Continued

OTHER PRESIDENTIAL DOCUMENTS—Continued

OTHER PRESIDENTIAL DOCUMENTS—Continued

Subject Index

Name Index

Dean, Howard—2396, 2549, 2557, 2564, 2584, 2590, 2598, 2619, 2744, 2786, 2794, 2801

Degenhart, Sarah—2416

Delpesce, Vernon—2352

DeMint, Jim—3152

Denlinger, Rebecca F.—3157

Dennison, George M.—3157, 3165

Dent, Charles W.—2309

Dermer, David—2872

Deters, Joseph T.—2889

DeVos, Elisabeth D.—2379, 2777, 2784, 2842

Dewhurst, David—2930

DeWine, Frances—2770, 2792

DeWine, Mike—2323, 2331, 2344, 2654, 2770, 2792, 2797, 2799, 2828, 2835, 2889, 2895

DeWitt, Katharine Cramer—3155

DeWitt, William O., Jr.—3155

Di Rita, Lawrence T.—3165

Diaz-Balart, Lincoln—2872

Diaz-Balart, Mario—2872

Dieter, Gwynneth A.E.—2459

DiMarco, Nicholas—2344

Dockery, Paula—2673

Dole, Bob—2799

Domenici, Nancy—2925

Domenici, Pete V.—2446, 2693, 2925

Donovan, Timothy E.—3052

Douglas, Andre—3066

Downer, Alexander—3141

Ducker, Michael—2987

Duelfer, Charles A.—2386, 2402, 2418, 2429, 2434, 2449, 2457, 2463, 2472, 2648

Duenas, Tomas—3158

Dunn, Michael V.—3154, 3163

Dunn, Ronnie—2907

Duran de Lagos, Luisa—2995, 3156

Durao Barroso, Jose Manuel—3153

Eastman, Robert—3148

Eckhoff, Jon—2613, 2614

Edgar, Jim—3147

Edwards, John—2311, 2326, 2334, 2342, 2347, 2350, 2356, 2365, 2374, 2381, 2408, 2433–2435, 2439, 2441, 2447, 2450, 2452, 2454, 2457, 2462, 2464, 2470, 2473, 2510, 2512, 2516, 2518, 2519, 2523, 2525, 2530, 2532, 2537, 2540, 2546, 2549, 2554, 2556, 2561, 2564, 2583, 2590, 2595, 2597, 2603, 2606, 2611, 2619, 2623, 2629, 2641, 2644, 2651, 2667, 2669, 2674, 2676, 2681, 2683, 2688, 2690, 2694, 2696, 2717, 2724, 2727, 2733, 2740, 2744, 2746, 2752, 2756, 2759, 2763, 2766, 2771, 2775, 2778, 2781, 2788, 2795, 2803, 2808, 2811, 2823, 2825, 2829, 2832,

Edwards, John—Continued
2837, 2840, 2844, 2847, 2853, 2856, 2860, 2863, 2867, 2869, 2874, 2880, 2885, 2887, 2891, 2893, 2897, 2903, 2909, 2915, 2920, 2926

Egeland, Jan—3142

Ehlers, Vernon J.—2842

Emmons, Matt—2467

England, Gordon R.—3052

Ensign, John—2507, 2513

Enzi, Michael B.—3039

Erdogan, Recep Tayyip—3160

Estess, Glenn E., Sr.—3159

Evans, Donald L.—2955, 3012, 3078, 3081, 3083, 3085–3092, 3110

Evans, Hank—2361–2363

Evans, Sam—2807

Evans, Susan Marinis—2955, 3013

Fannin, Lisa—2476

Fannin, P. Robert—2476

Farley, Daniel—2402

Feeney, Tom—2632, 2865

Feller, Bob—2799

Felzenberg, Chaim—3065

Felzenberg, Menachem—3065

Felzenberg, Miriam—3065

Felzenberg, Shmuel—3065

Ferris, Dave—2919

Findley, Eric A. "Rick"—3026

Fitzpatrick, Mike—2807

Flake, Cheryl—2476

Flake, Jeff—2476

Fleming, Shauna—3011, 3055, 3155

Flippen, Edward L.—3148, 3163

Floyd, Carlisle—3155

Foley, Mark—2551, 2666

Foltz, Kevin—2977

Foltz, Kolby—2977

Foltz, Kollin—2977

Foltz, Korey—2977

Ford, Elizabeth A. "Betty"—2842

Ford, Gerald R., Jr.—2842, 2975

Fowler, Rob—2413

Fox, Marilyn—2423, 3155

Fox, Sam—2423, 3155

Fox, Vicente—2993, 3156

France, Bill, Jr.—2559

Franks, Cathy—2459, 3072

Franks, Josephine—2476

Franks, Tommy R.—2401, 2459, 2704, 2711, 2714, 2727, 2743, 2750, 2757, 2764, 2772, 2779, 2799, 2805, 2837, 3072, 3073

Franks, Trent—2476

Document Categories List